The South American herpetofauna : its origin, evolution, and dispersal

William Edward Duellman, Symposium on the South American Herpetofauna (1977 : Lawrence, Kan.), Society for the Study of Amphibians and Reptiles, Herpetologists League

Nabu Public Domain Reprints:

You are holding a reproduction of an original work published before 1923 that is in the public domain in the United States of America, and possibly other countries. You may freely copy and distribute this work as no entity (individual or corporate) has a copyright on the body of the work. This book may contain prior copyright references, and library stamps (as most of these works were scanned from library copies). These have been scanned and retained as part of the historical artifact.

This book may have occasional imperfections such as missing or blurred pages, poor pictures, errant marks, etc. that were either part of the original artifact, or were introduced by the scanning process. We believe this work is culturally important, and despite the imperfections, have elected to bring it back into print as part of our continuing commitment to the preservation of printed works worldwide. We appreciate your understanding of the imperfections in the preservation process, and hope you enjoy this valuable book.

THE SOUTH AMERICAN HERPETOFAUNA: ITS ORIGIN, EVOLUTION, AND DISPERSAL

WILLIAM E. DUELLMAN

EDITOR

Museum of Natural History

and

Department of Systematics and Ecology
The University of Kansas
Lawrence, Kansas 66045, USA

MONOGRAPH
OF THE
MUSEUM OF NATURAL HISTORY,
THE UNIVERSITY OF KANSAS
NUMBER 7
1979

MONOGRAPH OF THE MUSEUM OF NATURAL HISTORY,
THE UNIVERSITY OF KANSAS
Number 7, pages 1–485, 172 figures in text

Issued December 28 1979

© 1979 by The Museum of Natural History, The University of Kansas, Lawrence, Kansas

All rights reserved No part of this book may be reproduced in any form or by any means without permission in writing from the publisher

ISBN Number 0-89338-008-3

Cover design by Linda Trueb

PRINTED BY
UNIVERSITY OF KANSAS PRINTING SERVICE
LAWRENCE, KANSAS, USA

*Dedicated
to the memories of
three herpetologists who
contributed so much to our knowledge of
the South American herpetofauna*

Roberto Donoso-Barros (1922–1975)
Bertha Lutz (1894–1976)
James A Peters (1922–1972)

PREFACE

This volume is the result of a symposium of the same title held on 11–13 August 1977 in conjunction with the joint annual meetings of the Herpetologists' League and the Society for the Study of Amphibians and Reptiles at Lawrence, Kansas. I originally conceived the idea for such a symposium in August 1975 while returning from a 15-month sojourn in South America. My interactions with many South American biologists during that trip had convinced me that the time was appropriate for a thorough discussion of ideas and presentation of our existing knowledge of the South American herpetofauna. The initial response from colleagues was heartening, so during the following year the symposium was organized. Unfortunately, owing to various circumstances not all subjects were covered; obvious omissions in this volume are chapters on the South American-North American herpetofaunal relationships and the herpetofaunas of the Brasilian Highlands, the Atacama Desert, and the caatinga and campos cerrados of Brasil.

This volume is organized in much the same way as was the symposium, except that my introductory chapter provides an overview of the South American herpetofauna. Chapter 2 deals with the fossil record of amphibians and reptiles in South America, and Chapters 3 and 4 are concerned with the relationships of the South American herpetofauna with those of Africa and Australia. The Quaternary biogeography of the continent is the subject of Chapters 5–7. Treatments of regional herpetofaunas are found in Chapters 8–15, and the

Participants in the Symposium on the South American Herpetofauna held in Lawrence, Kansas, 11–13 August 1977. Front row (left to right): Alberto Veloso M., Beryl B. Simpson, Jaime E. Péfaur, Ana Maria Báez, José M. Cei. Second row: Lars Brundin, Thomas E. Lovejoy, Donn E. Rosen, Jürgen Haffer, Thomas H. Fritts, Ramón Formas, Raymond F. Laurent. Back row: William E. Duellman, James R. Dixon, Marinus S. Hoogmoed, John D. Lynch, W. Ronald Heyer, Michael J. Tyler, José M. Gallardo.

final chapter is devoted to the conservation of the herpetofauna

I am grateful to the contributors to this volume for their scholarly efforts and for their patience and understanding while it was being produced. For their participation in the symposium, I thank the contributors and Lars Brundin, Thomas H Fritts, W Ronald Heyer, Jaime E Péfaur, Donn E Rosen, and Alberto Veloso M. Their enthusiastic participation contributed a high level of scholarly interaction, as well as much good cheer.

During the editing of this volume I called upon many colleagues to review manuscripts. The quality of the papers included herein benefited from reviews by Avelino Barrio, Lars Brundin, Richard Estes, Thomas H Fritts, Steven Gorzula, W Ronald Heyer, Philip S Humphrey, Jean Lescure, Alan E Leviton, John D Lynch, Larry D Martin, Braulio Orejas-Miranda, Jaime E Péfaur, Alan H Savitzky, Beryl B Simpson, Linda Trueb, T van der Hammen, Alberto Veloso M and Richard G Zweifel. The drawings for many of the papers were executed by Debra K Bennett, Staff Illustrator of the Museum of Natural History at The University of Kansas. Jaime E Péfaur translated many of the summaries and edited the Spanish of others. Linda Trueb's competent editorial review of the manuscripts is evident in their consistency and style. Rose Etta Kurtz retyped many pages of manuscript, and Rebecca A Pyles painstakingly worked on the index. To all of these persons I owe a debt of gratitude for their endeavors in behalf of this volume.

Throughout the early phases of development and organization of the symposium, as well as during the production of this volume, Philip S Humphrey, Director of the Museum of Natural History, has provided advice, encouragement and support. Ronald K Calgaard, Vice Chancellor for Academic Affairs, and George R Waggoner, Associate Vice Chancellor for International Programs, The University of Kansas gave enthusiastic support for the symposium. Richard F Treece of the Bureau of Conferences and Institutes coordinated the logistics of the meetings. Without their interest and aid the symposium and this volume would not have been possible.

Financial support for bringing together the participants in the symposium was generously provided by the National Science Foundation (DEB 76-16767), the World Wildlife Fund (WWF-US-71) and the Office of Academic Affairs, The University of Kansas. Support for the preparation of the index was provided by a grant from the General Research Fund of The University of Kansas.

William E Duellman
Lawrence, Kansas
September 6, 1979

CONTENTS

1. The South American Herpetofauna: A Panoramic View
   William E. Duellman 1

2. The South American Herpetofauna: An Evaluation of the Fossil Record
   Ana María Báez and Zulma B. de Gasparini 29

3. Herpetofaunal Relationships Between Africa and South America
   Raymond F. Laurent 55

4. Herpetofaunal Relations of South America with Australia
   Michael J. Tyler 73

5. Quaternary Biogeography of Tropical Lowland South America
   Jürgen Haffer 107

6. Late Cenozoic Environmental Changes in Temperate Argentina
   Ana María Báez and Gustavo Juan Scillato Yané 141

7. Quaternary Biogeography of the High Montane Regions of South America
   Beryl B. Simpson 157

8. The Amphibians of the Lowland Tropical Forests
   John D. Lynch 189

9. Origin and Distribution of Reptiles in Lowland Tropical Rainforests of South America
   James R. Dixon 217

10. The Herpetofauna of the Guianan Region
    Marinus S. Hoogmoed 241

11. Origin and Distribution of the Herpetofauna of the Dry Lowland Regions of Northern South America
    Carlos Rivero-Blanco and James R. Dixon 281

12. Composición, Distribución y Origen de la Herpetofauna Chaqueña
    José M. Gallardo 299

13. The Patagonian Herpetofauna
    José M. Cei 309

14. La Herpetofauna de los Bosques Temperados de Sudamerica
    J. Ramón Formas 341

15. The Herpetofauna of the Andes: Patterns of Distribution, Origin, Differentiation and Present Communities
    William E. Duellman 371

16. Refugia, Refuges and Minimum Critical Size: Problems in the Conservation of the Neotropical Herpetofauna
    Thomas E. Lovejoy 461

Subject Index 465

Taxonomic Index 470

1. The South American Herpetofauna: A Panoramic View

William E. Duellman

*Museum of Natural History and
Department of Systematics and Ecology
The University of Kansas
Lawrence, Kansas 66045
USA*

A vast array of dinosaurs still inhabited the earth, ratite birds watched curiously as furry mammals experimented with new ways of reproduction, and varieties of anurans and squamates set out on diverse evolutionary courses while turtles continued their conservative approach to a changing world. They witnessed the breakup of the earth as Gondwanaland was split by the magma, giving birth to a new ocean and somewhat later the fracture of the land again to create a large island continent—South America—destined to drift in a northwestward arc for nearly fifty million years before establishing a narrow connection with a neighbor of long ago and far away—North America.

During that long period of isolation of South America, some of the archaic groups of plants and animals became extinct, some dwindled in numbers leaving only a few scattered relicts, and others prospered and gave rise to new and diverse kinds in the face of changing environments for the island was not static. Tectonic events and climatic changes shaped the landscapes in an ever-changing scene. Great areas of the land were inundated by epeiric seas, the southern end of the continent cooled and desiccated as world zonation of climates was established, the rise of a gigantic mountain chain interrupted the winds and modified the climates and gave birth to thousands of small streams that coalesced in their descents to the lowlands and formed huge rivers, and finally, cooling brought glaciation and fluctuations in climate and sea level that brought about changes in the drainages and the biota. Late in this scenario man entered South America and began preying upon the animals, clearing land, cultivating plants, and building temples.

So it was when Columbus "discovered" South America on his third voyage in 1498, when Ferdinand Magellan arrived in 1520, and at the beginning of the conquest of the New World by Francisco Pizarro in 1532. For nearly two centuries the decimation of the native human populace (by the sword, the Bible and disease) was second in importance only to the frenetic search for El Dorado—the real and fabled materialistic riches of South America. With the exception of pitifully few men, no attention was given to the natural riches of the continent. But in the 18th Century European naturalists began exploring South America, as related so eloquently by von Hagen (1948 xiii)

> For it was the explorer-naturalists who opened South America. It was these knowledge thirsting men who, because they were deemed harmless, were permitted entry behind the Green Curtain when others were not. It was the naturalists who methodically and systematically pushed aside the frontiers of South America and dug it from its oblivion. With an enthusiasm that bridged every barrier, they climbed the Andes, they swept down the dark mysterious rivers, they trekked across the deserts and struggled through the Laocoon entanglements of its fire-fly spangled jungles. They dispelled legends, they uncovered facts, they rediscovered rubber, studied quinine and the coca leaf. They measured the earth's surface, they crawled into the jungle and collected plants, they studied the animals, they measured the tides. It was the naturalists who opened South America.

Early collections reaching Europe formed substantial natural history cabinets, and some of these were illustrated and described, the most ambitious undertaking was that by Albertus Seba, who in the 1730's published his classic "Thesaurus" in four volumes. The illustrations in Seba's work and specimens that reached Upsala formed the basis for names of South American species by Linnaeus in 1758. In the 19th Century, some of the world's most famous naturalists worked in South America—Charles Marie de La Condamine, Alexander von Humboldt, Alfred R. Wallace, Henry W. Bates, Richard Spruce, and of course Charles Darwin. These men made extensive natural history collections, but these included few, if any, amphibians and reptiles. Plants, insects, and birds were the chief goals of most of the collectors.

Five European naturalists made important contributions to the early knowledge of the South American herpetofauna in the early 1800's through their collections and their writings—Maximilian A. P. zu Wied-Neuwied, Alcide D. D'Orbigny, Johann B. von Spix, Marcos X. Jiménez de la Espada, and Johann J. Tschudi. Some of the collections made by those men, plus many small collections that reached European museums provided the basis for countless papers on South American amphibians and reptiles by Albert Gunther, Wilhelm Peters, Oskar Boettger, Franz Steindachner and the most prolific of European herpetologists—George Boulenger. During the latter part of the 19th Century, South American specimens reached the United States; most of these were reported on by Edward D. Cope.

By the beginning of the present century several centers of biological research had been established in South America. Early pioneers in herpetological research included Julio Koslowsky in Argentina, R. A. Philippi in Chile, and Alipio de Miranda-Ribeiro and Adolfo Lutz in Brasil. By the mid-20th Century investigations on the South American herpetofauna flourished. But as research on amphibians and reptiles broadens to include studies on the ecology, life history, and behavior, the need still remains for descriptive morphology and systematics. Ever increasing human disturbance of natural environments, especially the rainforests, eliminates forever many components of the biota before they become known to science.

COMPOSITION OF THE HERPETOFAUNA

The complex history and diverse topography and climate of South America have produced an extraordinarily rich and diverse herpetofauna. Currently more than 2,200 species are recognized in more than 300 genera in 37 families (Tables 1.1–1.2). These numbers are bound to increase with future discoveries. The rate of discovery of new species in South America is astonishing. As examples, of the 313 species of hylid frogs now known from South America, 100 have been named in the last two decades (1960–present). Peters and Donoso-Barros (1970) listed 71 species of *Anolis* and 14 additional species have been named. Likewise, many new species of frogs, especially *Centrolenella*, *Colostethus*, and *Eleutherodactylus*, and of salamanders (*Bolitoglossa*) are being discovered and named yearly.

A far higher percentage of the living amphibians of the world than of the reptiles inhabits South America. In this respect amphibians are more like birds, whereas reptiles are more like mammals (Table 1.3).

Review of the Families

In this brief review, each family is discussed with respect to its origin (Table 1.4), temporal and geographic distribution in South America (Table 1.5, Fig. 1.1), and differentiation and dispersal in South America. Marine reptiles are not included.

Plethodontidae.—Known from Pliocene and Pleistocene deposits in North America, the family is highly differentiated there (23 genera, about 200 species). Two genera that are most speciose in Central America (*Bolitoglossa* and *Oedipina*) also occur in South America. There, *Oedipina* (2 species) occurs only in the Chocó, whereas *Bolitoglossa* (24 species) inhabits the Chocó, Amazonia, and the northern Andes. Plethodontid salamanders entered South America from Central America after the closure of the Panamanian Portal (Wake, 1966).

TABLE 1.1—Taxonomic Composition of the South American Herpetofauna (° =endemic to South America)

Family	Genera Total	Genera Endemic	Species Total	Species Endemic
Amphibia				
Plethodontidae	2	—	24	21
Pipidae	1	—	5	4
Leptodactylidae	41	37	411	396
Bufonidae	7	4	95	88
Brachycephalidae°	2	2	2	2
Rhinodermatidae°	1	1	2	2
Dendrobatidae	3	—	75	69
Pseudidae°	2	2	4	4
Hylidae	22	15	313	285
Centrolenidae	2	1	57	52
Ranidae	1	—	1	—
Microhylidae	16	13	31	28
Rhinatrematidae°	2	2	10	10
Typhlonectidae°	4	4	18	18
Caeciliidae	9	6	47	44
Reptilia				
Pelomedusidae	1	—	7	7
Chelidae	7	7	15	15
Kinosternidae	1	—	3	2
Chelydridae	1	—	1	1
Emydidae	2	—	5	2
Testudinidae	1	—	5	4
Gekkonidae	16	7	64	56
Iguanidae	27	20	240	220
Teiidae	38	28	151	140
Scincidae	1	—	8	7
Anguidae	2	1	8	7
Amphisbaenidae	6	5	45	44
Anomalepidae	4	1	17	16
Leptotyphlopidae	1	—	34	32
Typhlopidae	1	—	3	3
Boidae	5	2	10	6
Aniliidae	1	1	1	1
Tropidophiidae	2	—	4	3
Colubridae	77	39	409	357
Micrundae	2	1	32	27
Viperidae	3	—	46	39
Crocodylidae	4	2	7	5

TABLE 1.3 - Comparison of Numbers of Species of Tetrapod Vertebrates in South America with World Fauna

Class	Total	South American	Percentage South American
Amphibians	3,307	1,095	33
Reptiles	5,954	1,115	19
Birds	8,656[a]	2,780[b]	32
Mammals	4,060[c]	810[d]	20[e]

[a] Brodkorb (1972)
[b] Meyer de Schauensee (1964)
[c] Anderson and Jones (1967)
[d] Hershkovitz (1972)
[e] The figure 810 includes Central America and the West Indies, so the total number and percentage for South America will be lower

Leiopelmatidae—With living representatives only in North America (*Ascaphus*) and New Zealand (*Leiopelma*), this family is represented in South America only by the fossils of *Vieraella* and *Notobatrachus* from the Jurassic of Patagonia (Estes and Reig, 1973)

Pipidae—At present restricted to sub-Saharan Africa and tropical America, pipids have an extensive fossil record in Gondwanaland—Early Cretaceous of Israel, Upper Cretaceous-Miocene of southern Africa, and Late Cretaceous-Eocene of South America (Estes, 1975) Early Cenozoic fossils from South America are representatives of the living African genus *Xenopus* One South American genus, *Pipa*, contains five species in the tropical lowlands (three genera recognized by some authors) *Pipa parva* enters eastern Panamá

Leptodactylidae—This is the most diverse and speciose anuran family in South America, where it is known back as far as the late Paleo-

TABLE 1.2—Summary of the Taxonomic Composition of the South American Herpetofauna

Ordinal group	Families Total	Families Endemic	Genera Total	Genera Endemic	Species Total	Species Endemic
Salamanders	1	—	2	—	24	21
Anurans	11	3	98	75	996	930
Caecilians	3	2	15	12	75	72
TOTAL AMPHIBIANS	15	5	115	87	1,095	1,023
Turtles	6	—	13	7	36	31
Lizards	5	—	84	56	471	430
Amphisbaenians	1	—	6	5	45	44
Snakes	9	—	96	44	556	484
Crocodilians	1	—	4	2	7	5
TOTAL REPTILES	22	—	203	114	1,115	994
TOTAL	37	5	318	201	2,210	2,017

cene (Báez and Gasparini, this volume) Although the family is unquestionably of Gondwanan origin, the relationships of the leptodactylids are not clear. Lynch (1971) recognized the South American and Australian frogs plus the South African *Heleophryne* as one family, the Leptodactylidae, but he (1973) separated the Old World genera into the Myobatrachidae. This arrangement was followed generally by Savage (1973), Duellman (1975), Heyer (1975), and Heyer and Liem (1976), but not by Tyler (this volume). Heyer (1975) suggested that leptodactylids might have evolved from leiopelmatids; this idea was elaborated upon by Lynch (1978).

Within South America, the primitive Telmatobiinae are primarily distributed in temperate regions—the tribe Telmatobiini in Patagonia, austral forests, and the high Andes. More advanced telmatobiines are in temperate and tropical regions—Odontophrynini in the Chaco, southeastern Brasil, and nonforested regions in eastern Brasil, Grypiscini on the Brasilian Shield, Eleutherodactylini most diverse in northwestern South America but also occurring on the Brasilian and Guianan shields and in Amazonia, and also speciose in Middle America and the West Indies. The diversity of eleutherodactyline genera and the differentiation of *Eleutherodactylus* in Middle America are indicative of immigration of eleutherodactylines into Central America prior to the establishment of the isthmian link in the late Pliocene (Savage, 1973; Lynch, 1976). The Ceratophryinae are widespread in Chacoan, Amazonian, and Guianan lowlands. The Elosiinae are restricted to the Brasilian Shield. The Leptodactylinae are widespread in tropical and subtropical lowlands, with a primitive genus (*Pleurodema*) also inhabiting Patagonia, austral forests, and the Andes (Duellman and Veloso, 1977). *Physalaemus*, *Pleurodema*, and *Leptodactylus* have entered Central America, and the latter also is in the West Indies.

Bufonidae.—The earliest fossil bufonids are from the Paleocene of Brasil (Estes and Reig, 1973), followed by the Oligocene *Neoprocoela*, which is a member of the Eurasian *Bufo calamita* group, according to Tihen (1962) and Báez and Gasparini (this volume) but referred to the telmatobiine leptodactylids by Lynch (1971). By the Miocene *Bufo* was present in South America, North America, Europe, and Africa (Tihen, 1972). The absence of bufonids from the Australo-Papuan Region (except for the introduced *Bufo marinus*) combined with the fossil history of the group, strongly suggests a western Gondwanaland origin of the family (Blair, 1972; Savage,

TABLE 1.4.—Postulated Geographic Origins of Families of Amphibians and Reptiles Inhabiting South America
(NA = North America, SA = South America, † = Extinct in South America)

Pangaea	Laurasia	Gondwanaland	Uncertain
Leiopelmatidae†	Plethodontidae (NA)	Pipidae	Testudinidae
Boidae	Kinosternidae (NA)	Leptodactylidae	Gekkonidae
	Chelydridae (NA)	Bufonidae	Scincidae
	Emydidae	Brachycephalidae (SA)	Amphisbaenidae
	Trionychidae†	Rhinodermatidae (SA)	Typhlopidae
	Anguidae	Pseudidae (SA)	Leptotyphlopidae
	Anniellidae	Hylidae	Colubridae
	Viperidae	Centrolenidae (SA)	Crocodylidae
		Ranidae	
		Microhylidae	
		Rhinatrematidae (SA)	
		Typhlonectidae (SA)	
		Caeciliidae	
		Pelomedusidae	
		Chelidae	
		Meiolaniidae†	
		Iguanidae (SA)	
		Teiidae (SA)	
		Anomalepidae (SA)	
		Tropidophiidae (SA)	
		Micruridae (SA)	

TABLE 1.5—Distribution of Herpetofaunal Family Groups in Major Eco-physiographic Regions in South America

Family group	Chocó	Caribbean-Orinoco	Amazonia	Guiana Shield	Atlantic Forest	Brasilian Shield	Chaco	Pampas-Patagonia	Austral Forest	Atacama Desert	Andes	Central America
Amphibia												
Plethodontidae	+	−	+	−	−	−	−	−	−	−	+	+
Pipidae	−	+	+	+	−	+	−	−	−	−	−	+
Ceratophryinae	+	+	+	+	+	−	+	+	−	−	−	−
Telmatobiinae	+	+	+	+	+	+	+	+	+	−	+	+
Elosiinae	−	−	−	−	+	+	−	−	−	−	−	−
Leptodactylinae	+	+	+	+	+	+	+	+	+	−	+	+
Bufonidae	+	+	+	+	+	+	+	+	+	+	+	+
Brachycephalidae	−	−	−	−	+	−	−	−	−	−	−	−
Rhinodermatidae	−	−	−	−	−	−	−	−	+	−	−	−
Dendrobatidae	+	+	+	+	+	−	−	−	−	−	+	+
Pseudidae	−	+	+	+	−	−	+	−	−	−	−	−
Phyllomedusinae	+	+	+	+	+	+	+	−	−	−	+	+
Hemiphractinae	+	−	+	−	−	−	−	−	−	−	+	+
Amphignathodontinae	+	−	+	−	+	+	−	−	−	−	+	+
Hylinae	+	+	+	+	+	+	+	−	−	−	+	+
Centrolenidae	+	−	+	+	+	+	−	−	−	−	+	+
Ranidae	+	+	+	+	−	−	−	−	−	−	−	+
Microhylidae	+	+	+	+	+	+	+	+	−	−	+	+
Rhinatrematidae	+	+	+	+	−	−	−	−	−	−	+	−
Typhlonectidae	−	+	+	+	−	−	−	+	−	−	−	−
Caeciliidae	+	+	+	+	+	+	−	−	−	−	+	+
Reptilia												
Pelomedusidae	−	+	+	+	−	−	−	−	−	−	−	−
Chelidae	−	+	+	+	+	+	−	−	−	−	−	−
Kinosternidae	+	+	+	+	+	+	+	−	−	−	−	+
Chelydridae	+	−	−	−	−	−	−	−	−	−	−	−
Emydidae	+	−	−	+	−	−	+	−	−	−	−	+
Testudinidae	+	+	+	+	+	+	+	+	−	+	−	+
Gekkoninae	+	+	+	+	+	+	+	+	−	+	+	+
Sphaerodactylinae	+	+	+	+	−	−	−	−	−	−	+	+
Iguaninae	+	+	+	+	+	+	−	−	−	−	−	+
Basiliscinae	+	+	−	−	−	−	−	−	−	−	+	+
Anolinae	+	+	+	+	+	+	−	−	−	−	+	+
Tropidurinae	−	+	+	+	+	+	+	+	+	+	+	−
Teiidae	+	+	+	+	+	+	+	+	−	+	+	+
Scincidae	+	+	+	+	+	+	+	−	−	−	−	+
Anguidae	+	−	+	+	+	+	+	−	−	−	−	+
Amphisbaenidae	+	+	+	+	+	+	+	+	−	−	+	+
Anomalepidae	+	+	+	+	+	+	−	−	−	−	+	+
Leptotyphlopidae	+	+	+	+	+	+	+	+	−	+	+	+
Typhlopidae	+	−	+	+	+	+	−	−	−	−	−	+
Boidae	+	+	+	+	+	+	+	−	−	−	+	+
Aniliidae	−	−	+	+	−	−	−	−	−	−	−	−
Tropidophiidae	+	−	−	−	+	−	−	−	−	−	+	−
Xenodontinae	+	+	+	+	+	+	+	+	+	+	+	+
Colubrinae	+	+	+	+	+	+	−	−	−	−	+	+
Micruridae	+	+	+	+	+	+	+	+	−	+	+	+
Crotalinae	+	+	+	+	+	+	+	+	−	+	+	+
Crocodylidae	+	+	+	+	+	+	+	−	−	−	−	+

1973, Laurent, this volume). *Bufo* and six other genera occur in South America, and *Bufo* and seven other genera occur in Africa (principally tropical western Africa), but *Bufo* and five other genera inhabit southeastern Asia and adjacent islands. One genus (*Crepidophryne*) is endemic to Central America, and *Bufo* is widespread in the Holarctic Region. Differing views have been expressed on the dispersal of *Bufo* (Blair, 1972; Savage, 1973; Duellman, this volume; Laurent, this volume).

Bufo occurs throughout South America, but only members of the *Bufo spinulosus* group are present in Patagonia, the austral forests, and the high Andes (Cei, 1968, 1972). *Rhamphophryne* and *Atelopus* are primarily northern Andean, *Dendrophryniscus* is in Amazonia and the Brasilian Shield, *Melanophryniscus* in the Chaco and adjacent areas, and *Oreophrynella* in the Guiana Highlands (Trueb, 1971; McDiarmid, 1971).

Brachycephalidae.—Unknown in the fossil record, the two small frogs comprising this family are restricted to humid coastal lowlands of southeastern Brasil (Izecksohn, 1971). Although superficially resembling a specialized bufonid, brachycephalids lack Bidder's Organs (McDiarmid, 1971), an uniquely derived character in the Bufonidae (Lynch, 1973). The phylogenetic position of this endemic South American family is not clear, but presumably it arose from a leptodactylid-primitive bufonid stock.

Rhinodermatidae.—Known from two species restricted to austral forests (Formas, et al., 1975), *Rhinoderma* is considered to be most closely related to the bufonids by Lynch (1971, 1973) and must be considered as of temperate South American origin.

Dendrobatidae.—Lacking a fossil record but composed of three Recent genera, the dendrobatids are especially speciose in the northern Andes, Choco, and western Amazonia, but also occur in eastern Amazonia and on the Guianan and Brasilian shields. Lynch (1971) demonstrated that the dendrobatids are derived from the elosiine leptodactylids and thus are of South American origin. Species of all three genera occur in lower Central America, presumably having arrived there after the closure of the Panamanian Portal in the late Pliocene.

Pseudidae.—An autochthonous South American family containing two genera and four species (Gallardo, 1961) and widely distributed in tropical and subtropical cis-Andean lowlands, these aquatic frogs have been considered as relatives of the leptodactylids (Savage and Carvalho, 1953) or hylids (Lynch, 1973).

Hylidae.—Although Estes and Reig (1973) mentioned the existence of Paleocene hylid material from Brasil, these specimens have not yet been described. The mid-Miocene *Australobatrachus* from Australia has been referred to the Hylidae by Tyler (1974), a presumed hylid is known from the Oligocene of North America (Holman, 1968), and *Hyla* is known from the Miocene of Europe (Noble, 1928). By far the greatest diversity of hylids is in South America (22 genera, 313 species), as compared with Middle America (15 genera, 129 species; Duellman, 1970). Six *Hyla*, plus two endemic genera (*Osteopilus* and *Calyptahyla*) inhabit the West Indies (Trueb and Tyler, 1974). The Holarctic hylid fauna is depauperate, but in the Australo-Papuan Region 118 species are known in the genera *Litoria* and *Nyctimystes* (Duellman, 1977; Tyler and Davies, 1978), and nine more if *Cyclorana* is included in the family (Tyler, et al., 1978; Tyler, this volume). Like the leptodactylids, the Australian hylids are of questionable relationship with the South American hylids. Savage (1973) resurrected the family name Pelodryadidae for the Australo-Papuan "hylids" and considered them to be derived independently from the Neotropical hylids. Tyler (this volume) emphasized the lack of evidence for such an arrangement. In Australia, *Cyclorana* seems to be intermediate between the Australian "leptodactylids" and "hylids" and may prove to establish a phylogenetic link between the two families on that continent. No such intermediates are

FIG. 1.1. Major eco-physiographic regions of South America. Temperate regions: Austral forests (AF), Patagonia (PA). Tropical evergreen forests: Amazonia (AM), Choco (CH), Atlantic coast (AC). Tropical and subtropical nonforests: Caribbean coastal desert (CD), Llanos (LL), Savannas (black), Caatinga (CA), Cerrados (CE), Gran Chaco (GC), Pampas (PA), Monte (MO), Espinal (LS), Matorral (MA), Atacama Desert (AD). Mountains (stippled): Andes (A), Guiana Highlands (G), Brasilian Highlands (B).

Regiones ecofisiográficas mayores de Sudamérica

known in South America, and even the monophyly of the Neotropical hylids has been questioned. Maxson (1976) provided immunological evidence that the phyllomedusines were not closely related to the other hylids.

Within South America, the phyllomedusine hylids are widespread in Amazonia, Atlantic forests, and the Guianan and Brasilian shields. *Phyllomedusa* is primarily South American with only two species (one endemic) in Central America, the Central American *Agalychnis* is represented by three species in the Chocó and one endemic species in western Amazonia. The hemiphractines are restricted to northwestern South America with one species entering Central America (Trueb, 1974). The amphignathodontines are most speciose in northwestern South America (two species enter Central America), but with three genera on the Brasilian Shield and one in the Guiana Highlands. Among the hylines, all of the South American genera are endemic to the continent, except one species of *Phrynohyas* and several species groups of *Hyla* that enter Central America. Two species of the Middle American *Smilisca* enter South America.

Assuming that at least the Neotropical hylids arose in South America, some stocks must have entered Central America by waif dispersal prior to the closure of the Panamanian Portal in the late Pliocene. These stocks were the ancestors of the several genera and species groups of *Hyla* endemic to Middle America. After the closure of the portal several groups dispersed northward into Central America (*Phyllomedusa, Hemiphractus, Gastrotheca, Phrynohyas, Hyla albomarginata, H. boans, H. bogotensis, H. leucophyllata,* and *H. rubra* groups) and representatives of two Middle American genera (*Agalychnis* and *Smilisca*) dispersed into South America.

Centrolenidae —No fossils are known. Two genera and 46 species inhabit cloud forests in the Andes, whereas a few species occur on the Guianan and Brasilian shields and in Amazonia, the Chocó, and Central America (Duellman, 1977). Obviously of South American origin with Late Cenozoic dispersal into Central America, the relationships of the centrolenids usually are thought to be with the hylids, but no convincing evidence is available.

Ranidae —Although no fossils are known before those in the Oligocene of North America (Holman 1968), the center of origin and dispersal of ranids quite clearly is in Africa (Savage, 1973), and presumably occurred after the rift of South America and Africa in the Cretaceous. The single South American ranid, *Rana palmipes* is widespread in Central America and must have entered South America after the establishment of the isthmian link. The species is widespread in the tropical lowlands of South America.

Microhylidae —This large and diverse family presents one of the most controversial issues in anuran phylogeny and classification. Although the family is clearly of Gondwanan origin, the present interpretations of phylogeny and biogeography are in conflict at times. Savage (1973) based his biogeography of the microhylids on Starrett's (1973) interpretation of anuran phylogeny as demonstrated by larvae. Zweifel (1972), Lynch (1973), Sokol (1975), and Tyler (this volume) provided compelling arguments based on diverse morphological, developmental, and biogeographic evidence against the Starrett and Savage model.

All South American microhylids belong to the subfamily Microhylinae, which is shared with North America, tropical southeastern Asia, and the Malayan Archipelago. It is most logical biogeographically and phylogenetically that the Neotropical microhylids evolved in isolation in South America and that a stock that subsequently gave rise to the North American *Gastrophryne* and *Hypopachus* managed to enter Central America from the south during mid-Cenozoic times, microhylines are known from the Miocene of Florida (Holman, 1967). The 16 genera of South American microhylids occur throughout the tropical and subtropical lowlands with the greatest diversity in the southern part of their range, particularly on the Brasilian Shield. Three genera (3 species) entered Central America after the connection of the continents.

The monotypic *Geobatrachus* in the Sierra Nevada de Santa Marta in northern Colombia tentatively was referred to the Microhylidae by Lynch (1971), but Duellman (1975) showed that this small frog has a combination of characters that precludes its assignment to any family as presently defined *Geobatrachus* has not been included in the numerical account of the microhylids

Rhinatrematidae—Lacking fossils and endemic to South America, these primitive caecilians are a sister group of the ichthyophiids (Nussbaum, 1977), a family restricted to India, tropical southeastern Asia, Malayan Archipelago, and the Philippines. Both South American genera occur on the Guianan Shield and one (*Epicrionops*) has four species on the forested slopes of the northern Andes.

Typhlonectidae—The specialized aquatic caecilians are autochthonous to South America, where they are distributed discontinuously in the Caribbean and Amazonian lowlands and in the Paraná Basin.

Caeciliidae—The presence of a single fossil from the Paleocene of Brasil (Estes and Wake, 1972), possibly referable to this family, signifies a long history of caecilians in South America, where nine genera and 46 species now occur in the humid lowland tropics and forested slopes of the northern Andes. Four genera inhabit Middle America, the endemism there in *Dermophis* and *Gymnopis* indicates that a caecilian stock entered Central America prior to the establishment of the isthmian link, whereas the other two (*Caecilia* and *Oscaecilia*) are both widespread in South America and evidently dispersed into Central America after the closure of the Panamanian Portal. The presence of caeciliids in tropical Africa (6 genera), India (3 genera), and the Seychelles Islands (3 genera), as well as in South America, is indicative of a widespread Gondwanan distribution prior to the Late Cretaceous.

Pelomedusidae—The classical, present Gondwanaland distribution pattern of pelomedusid turtles is complicated by their occurrence in Cretaceous deposits in Europe and North America and in the Eocene of Asia. However, the family has an extensive fossil record beginning in the Cretaceous in both South America and Africa (Wood, 1970). The single South American genus, *Podocnemis*, is widely distributed in the cis-Andean tropical lowlands.

Chelidae—Considered to be a derivative of the Pelomedusidae (Gaffney, 1975, 1977), the chelids are known as fossils only from Australia (early Tertiary to Pleistocene) and South America (Eocene to Pleistocene). The seven genera endemic to South America are widely distributed in the cis-Andean tropics, mostly in Amazonia.

Kinosternidae—Known as far back as the Oligocene in North America, the great majority of kinosternids (4 genera 19 species) occur in North America and northern Central America. Only three species of *Kinosternon* occur in lower Central America, one of these also is widespread in cis-Andean South America, and two vicariant species occur in the Chocó. The kinosternids obviously are a postportal entrant into South America from the north.

Chelydridae—The snapping turtles have an extensive fossil record throughout the Cenozoic in North America, where two genera are extant. One species of *Chelydra* inhabits lower Central America, and one occurs in the Chocó in South America. *Chelydra* obviously is a recent immigrant into South America.

Emydidae—This family has an extensive fossil record in the Holarctic Region and today is distributed mainly in North America and the Oriental Region. The genus *Chrysemys* (=*Pseudemys*) is speciose in North America and in the West Indies, occurs in Central America (same species in northern South America), and is represented by another species in the Paraná Basin. Two species of the Central American *Rhinoclemys* occur in the Chocó, and *Rhinoclemys* is known from the Pleistocene of Ecuador. Possibly an early *Chrysemys* stock waifed to South America, but *Rhinoclemys* and *Chrysemys scripta* certainly entered the continent from the north subsequent to the establishment of the isthmian link.

Meiolaniidae—This extinct family known from South America (Late Cretaceous to early Eocene) and Australia (Miocene to Pleistocene) seems to antedate the testudinids. Their fossil record suggests a Gondwanan history similar to that of the chelids.

Testudinidae—This family is cosmopolitan except in the Australo-Papuan Region, and possibly had its initial radiation in Laurasia (Cracraft, 1974). The genus *Geochelone* occurs today in South America, Africa, India, southeastern Asia, and on the Galápagos Islands; it is known from the late Oligocene through the Pleistocene in South America where it presently occurs throughout cis-Andean lowlands southward to northern Patagonia. Auffenberg (1971) suggested that the South American stock probably entered the continent from the north in the Oligocene; this implies waif dispersal.

Trionychidae.—Although presently widespread in sub-Saharan Africa and in the Oriental Region, trionychids have an extensive fossil history in the Holarctic Region, where *Trionyx* occurs today in North America. Wood and Patterson (1973) reported a trionychid from the late Pliocene of Venezuela; probably this was a waif, because no other fossil or Recent trionychids are known south of northeastern México.

Gekkonidae.—Although the gekkonids were considered to be of uncertain geographic origin by Cracraft (1974), reevaluation of Kluge's (1967) phylogenetic scheme of the family suggests that the gekkonids are early Gondwanan. The primitive eublepharines occur in Africa, southern Asia, and North America. The diplodactylines are dominant in Australia and have dispersed onto islands in the southwest Pacific. Sphaerodactylines are restricted to tropical America. The gekkonines are pantropical, being most diverse in the Indian, Oriental, and Ethiopian regions but also with many representatives in Australia and on Pacific islands. Of the 11 genera of gekkonines in South America, only eight are endemic to the American tropics, if the Old World species presently assigned to *Phyllodactylus* are not considered to be congeneric, as suggested by Dixon and Anderson (1973). Except for the speciose *Phyllodactylus* in dry habitats in western and northern South America (also Middle America, West Indies, and Galápagos Islands), most of the endemic genera are represented by only one or two species and all live in eastern South America save for the monotypic *Thecadactylus* in western Amazonia, the Chocó, Guianan Shield, Central America, and Lesser Antilles. The only genus with more than two species is *Homonota* (8 species) in temperate cis-Andean areas; the related *Garthia* with two species occurs in the southern Atacaman Region. The other gekkonines in South America (*Gymnodactylus*—3 species, *Hemidactylus*—5, and *Lygodactylus*—2) are most speciose in Africa.[1] In fact, all but one of the species of *Hemidactylus* in America are widespread in Africa and elsewhere.

The presence of gekkonids in the Paleocene of Brasil (Estes 1970) suggests that gekkonines may have been present in South America prior to the separation of Africa and South America in the Cretaceous (Bons and Pasteur 1977). Trans-Atlantic waifing could explain the presence in South America of African genera, such as *Gymnodactylus* and *Hemidactylus*, but some of the latter most likely were transported by man.

Of the five genera of sphaerodactyline geckos in South America two (*Coleodactylus* and *Pseudogonatodes*) are endemic to forested cis-Andean regions in northern South America. *Gonatodes* is widespread in tropical lowlands, and one species has dispersed northward into Central America and the West Indies. *Lepidoblepharis* occurs in northwestern South America and has two species in Panamá. *Sphaerodactylus* is most speciose in the West Indies but with a few species in Central America, two of which extend into South America.

Iguanidae.—This large and diverse family is first known in the fossil record from the Upper Cretaceous of Brasil (Estes and Price, 1973) and is diverse in the late Paleocene of Brasil (Estes 1970). The earliest North American fossils are from the Eocene. Evidently an early iguanid stock reached North America prior to the separation of the continents or waifed between the two. Informally, the iguanids are divided into five major groups (Etheridge, 1964, 1967). The sceloporines differentiated in North America and were paralleled by an extensive radiation of tropidurines in temperate South America. The iguanines and basiliscines are primarily Middle American with genera of the former endemic to the Galápagos Islands (*Amblyrhynchus* and *Conolophus*) and the West Indies (*Cyclura*), one species of *Iguana* and three of *Basiliscus*

---
[1] Smith et al (1977) recognized the South American *Lygodactylus* as the sole representatives of the genus *Vanzoia* but Kluge (pers comm) informed me that the South American species are perfectly good examples of *Lygodactylus*

have entered northern South America. The anolines are widely distributed in the tropics of South America, Middle America, and the West Indies. Obviously waif dispersal between South America and the emerging Antilles and Central America during the Tertiary accounted for some of the patterns of distribution, many of which have been masked by more recent dispersal after the closure of the Panamanian Portal. It certainly seems safe to assume that the origin of tropidurines and some anolines was in South America.

The presence of two genera of iguanids on Madagascar has been interpreted as evidence for the former occurrence of the family in Africa with subsequent extinction there (perhaps owing to competition with agamids and chamaeleontids). The similarity of caudal structure of the Madagascaran iguanids to the tropidurines (Etheridge, 1967) and the presence of iguanids in the Cretaceous of South America do not contradict that hypothesis. The iguanine *Brachylophus*, endemic to islands in the southwest Pacific, apparently is an example of long-distance rafting via the Trans-Pacific Current (Cogger, 1974).

Teiidae.—Although presumed teiids are known from the Late Cretaceous in North America, those do not seem to be ancestral to living North American teiids, whereas late Paleocene teiids of South American resemble extant Neotropical genera (Estes, 1970). All living teiid genera occur in South America, where they are widespread throughout the continent, except for Patagonia and the austral forests. Five genera have representatives in the West Indies, and 10 genera extend into Central America. With the exception of *Cnemidophorus*, which is widespread and speciose in North America, all other teiids probably arrived in Central America after the formation of the isthmian link.

Scincidae.—Although skinks are known from the Paleocene of Brasil and the Late Cretaceous of North America (Estes, 1976), only four genera presently occur in the Americas; this is only a small fraction of the family containing at least 80 genera and more than 1,000 species (Greer, 1970). Occurring throughout South America, except for the Andes and cool temperate regions, are eight species of *Mabuya*, a genus containing about 75 additional species in Africa, Madagascar, southern Asia, and the Pacific islands, plus an additional two species in Central America and the Antilles. Tihen (1964) suggested an Eurasian origin of the North American skinks (*Eumeces* and *Scincella*), but an African origin of the South American *Mabuya* seems to be reasonable.

Anguidae.—Presently distributed primarily in North America, western Eurasia and southeastern Asia, the anguids have an extensive fossil history dating from the Late Cretaceous in North America (Meszoely, 1970). Two genera occur in South America. *Diploglossus* is speciose in Central America and the West Indies, and one of the South American species is shared with Central America. The endemic South American *Ophiodes* (4 species) in the south-central part of the continent apparently evolved from an anguid stock that entered South America from the north in the Cenozoic.

Amphisbaenidae.—Numerous fossil amphisbaenians are known from the Paleocene to Miocene in North America, Eocene to Pliocene of Europe, and Oligocene of Mongolia. With the exception of *Bipes* and the Palearctic *Blanus*, the amphisbaenids (sensu Berman, 1973) are Neotropical and African—10 genera in Africa (one ranging into Europe) and six in South America (plus one endemic to Cuba). The generic and specific differentiation in Africa (10 genera, 52 species) and South America (6 genera, 45 species), and the possible presence of *Amphisbaena* in both Africa and South America (Gans, 1967), plus 10 species endemic to the West Indies and one South American species extending into Central America, are suggestive of an African-South American amphisbaenid interchange. However, the place of origin of the amphisbaenids still remains problematic.

Anomalepidae.—Unknown as fossils, 17 of the 20 species and all four genera of anomalepids occur in South America. One species each of *Anomalepis*, *Helminthophis* and *Liotyphlops* occurs in Central America and another species of *Liotyphlops* ranges from Costa Rica into northern South America. On the basis of present distributions, the anomalepids seem to be a South American group that only recently invaded Central America

In South America the family is widespread in trans-Andean and cis-Andean tropical lowlands

Leptotyphlopidae —The single genus in this family containing about 64 species is widespread in tropical and subtropical South America, Middle America, southwestern United States Africa, and southwestern Asia No fossils are known On the basis of present distribution it is reasonable to suggest that the leptotyphlopids had a western Gondwanaland origin and subsequently spread northward into Central and North America and independently into Asia

Typhlopidae —These fossorial snakes are known from two genera (*Typhlina*, 33 species in Australia, New Guinea, Solomon and Fiji islands) and *Typhlops* (about 114 species throughout tropical and subtropical parts of the world, except Australia) Only three species occur in South America, another five are in Central America, and 16 occur in the West Indies Thus, with respect to the total differentiation of the family, the Neotropics are poor in typhlopids The only fossils (Eocene-Miocene of Europe) are of no help in interpreting the paleobiogeography of the group In the absence of any evidence for the occurrence of typhlopids in North America, a western Gondwanaland origin for the Neotropical stocks might be suggested

Boidae —Represented by an extensive, world-wide fossil record from the Upper Cretaceous through the Eocene (only Pleistocene in Australia), the boids seem to have been the dominant snakes throughout the world in the Early Cenozoic Evidently they had dispersed widely before the breakup of Pangaea The Early Cenozoic South American boid *Madtsoia* also is known from the Late Cretaceous of Madagascar, and a related boid, *Wonambi*, is known from the Pleistocene of Australia (Tyler, this volume) In some respects the distribution of these fossils parallels that of living boines—eight genera in the Neotropics, two in Madagascar, one in New Guinea and islands in the southwest Pacific Presently the family is widespread in tropical South America and especially diverse in Amazonia

Aniliidae —These problematic fossorial snakes have a long history in northern continents, dating from the Middle Cretaceous in North America and the Eocene of Europe A Late Cretaceous snake, *Dinilysia* from Patagonia, is considered to be related to aniliids (Rage, 1977), and true aniliids were reported from the Eocene of Brasil by Báez and Gasparini (this volume), who support Cracraft's (1974) contention that aniliids are of Laurasian origin Nonetheless, entry into South America possibly was by way of Africa The one living South American aniliid is widespread in cis-Andean tropical lowlands

Tropidophiidae —Structurally, the tropidophiids are intermediate between the boids and colubroid snakes *Tropidophis* has three widely dispersed species in South America (northern Andes and southeastern Brasil) and 12 species in the West Indies *Trachyboa* and *Ungaliophis* occur in the Chocó and Central America The tropidophiids are considered to be of South American origin with subsequent northward dispersal

Colubridae —The poor fossil record and taxonomic chaos of the colubrids (*sensu lato*) permit only the most general comments to be made about this immense and important family My use of subfamilial designations follows that of Dowling (1975) but eliminates some apparent misapplications not especially germane to the Neotropical colubrids A brief summary of the colubrid snakes follows

1 Xenodontinae 93 genera, about 570 species Sixty genera occur in South America, 22 of these are shared with Central America Seven genera are endemic to the West Indies 13 are restricted to North America (north of the Isthmus of Tehuantepec in southern México), and 13 are Middle American Included in this group of rear-fanged genera are fossorial, terrestrial aquatic, and arboreal snakes Most arboreal xenodontines are nocturnal, and few (*Alsophis, Dromicus, Leimadophis, Lygophis*) are diurnal racer-like snakes Most xenodontines feed on frogs, lizards, or other snakes

2 Lycodontinae 79 genera, about 285 species These rear-fanged snakes are distributed primarily in the African and Oriental regions and peripherally in northern Australia and the Palearctic Region

3 Colubrinae 74 genera, about 440 species Widespread in the Holarctic Region, some genera occur in the Ethiopian and Ori-

ental regions, and two genera reach Australia. Thirty-two genera occur in the New World; of these, 12 are in South America, but only one of those (*Drymoluber*) does not occur in Central America. Most of the colubrines in South America (*Chironius, Dendrophidion, Drymarchon, Drymobius, Drymoluber, Leptophis, Masticophis, Mastigodryas, Spilotes*) are diurnal racer-like snakes that are terrestrial or arboreal.

4. Natricinae. 34 genera, about 170 species (excluding from the Natricinae the Old World snakes more appropriately referred to Acrochordidae and Homalopsinae). The natricines are widely distributed in the Holarctic and Oriental regions, with a few representatives in Africa and one in northern Australia. Nine genera of natricines occur in North America, with *Thamnophis* extending to Costa Rica.

Even if these subfamilial groups are monophyletic the historical biogeography of the colubrids still remains shrouded. It is evident from the distributions of the subfamilies that centers of dispersal (and perhaps of origin) can be ascertained, but ancestors cannot. Apparently the xenodontines evolved in South America and the lycodontines in the African-Indian-Asian Arc and had corresponding parallel radiations in the New World and Old World, respectively. Colubrines and natricines probably are Holarctic in origin. If these truly are the centers of origin and dispersal, it is possible to make some reasonable generalizations about the South American colubrid fauna.

1. Although colubrids are known from the Eocene (Rage, 1975a,b), they became dominant in the upper Miocene (Holman, 1976), when they first appear in South America (Báez and Gasparini, this volume).
2. Xenodontines evolved in South America, where they are the dominant snakes today and the only colubrids in the southern part of the continent.
3. Some xenodontine snakes were present in Middle America in the Cenozoic, these differentiated, and some of them dispersed as far as northeastern North America.
4. Colubrine stocks in North America invaded Central America, and some of them may have waifed to South America before the closure of the Panamanian Portal in the late Pliocene.
5. With the closure of the Panamanian Portal in the late Pliocene there was an interchange of South American xenodontines northwards and Middle American colubrines and xenodontines southward.
6. Natricines never have extended farther south than Central America.
7. The West Indian colubrid fauna is composed of xenodontines derived either from Central or South America (some widespread colubrine species are recent immigrants into the Lesser Antilles).

Micruridae.—Formerly associated with the Elapidae, micrurids have been shown to be an independently derived group from *Elapomorphus-Apostolepis* xenodontines in South America (Savitzky, 1978). An upper Miocene fossil from Nebraska (Holman, 1977), together with the presence of *Micruroides* and numerous species of *Micrurus* in Central America, is suggestive of dispersal of micrurids into Central America in the Cenozoic with additional interchange after the closure of the Panamanian Portal. *Micrurus* has 27 endemic species in South America and ranges throughout the lowlands and moderate elevations south to northern Patagonia; the monotypic *Leptomicrurus* is restricted to Amazonia.

Viperidae.—Although the vipers are primarily an Old World group, which apparently originated in the Palearctic Region (Marx and Rabb, 1965), one lineage—the crotaline vipers—may have evolved in the Oriental Region and dispersed via Beringia to North America (Burger, 1971). The earliest North American fossil crotalines are of Miocene age (Holman, 1977). The presence of the presumably primitive crotaline *Lachesis muta* in northwestern South America and lower Central America suggests that the crotaline vipers entered South America after the establishment of the isthmian link. On the other hand, the presence of many species of *Bothrops* throughout South America as far south as Patagonia, as well as many different species in Middle America, is suggestive of an earlier dispersal into South America. *Bothrops* is known as a fossil in South America only from the Pleistocene of Bolivia. The presence of *Bothrops* in the West Indies attests to their abilities of over-water dispersal. *Crotalus* certainly is a post-Pliocene immigrant into South America, where it has spread throughout non-forested tropical areas.

Crocodylidae—Present distributions and fossil records indicate that the alligatorines and *Crocodylus* entered South America from the north (Sill 1968, Báez and Gasparini this volume), although Paleocene crocodylines in South America are suggestive of possible African derivation. Likewise, the presence of gavial-like crocodilians in South American deposits (Báez and Gasparini, this volume) implicates at least the early crocodilians in a Gondwanan distribution. Possibly the crocodilians presently living in South America were derived from North American stocks, whereas the ancient Gondwanan crocodilians are extinct in South America. Obviously, entry of crocodilians into South America from the north prior to the formation of the isthmian link was facilitated by their abilities at traversing open water. Only *Caiman* is widespread throughout the tropical lowlands of South America, *Crocodylus* is restricted to the northern part of the continent (one species endemic to the llanos). The other two genera (*Melanosuchus* and *Paleosuchus*) are in western Amazonia.

EXTRA-CONTINENTAL RELATIONSHIPS

Elsewhere in this volume detailed comparisons of the origins of the African and Australian herpetofaunas with respect to that of South America have been made by Laurent and Tyler, respectively. In this section I compare the compositions and taxonomic diversities of those three faunas. Furthermore I provide a discussion of the herpetofaunal relationships between South America and North America and between South America and the West Indies.

Herpetofaunas of Gondwanan Continents

South America contains 37 living families of amphibians and reptiles, Africa 26, and Australia 17. Among the amphibians only three families are shared by the three continents—Leptodactylidae (only one genus with three species in Africa), Ranidae (only one species each in South America and Australia), and Microhylidae (only two genera with seven species in Australia). Two additional families are shared by South America and Africa (Pipidae and Bufonidae) and one (Hylidae) by South America and Australia. Among the nonmarine reptiles, six families are common to the three continents—Crocodylidae, Gekkonidae, Scincidae (only one genus with eight species in South America), Typhlopidae, Boidae, Colubridae (only four genera with six species in Australia). Five additional families are shared by Africa and South America (Pelomedusidae, Testudinidae, Amphisbaenidae, Leptotyphlopidae and Viperidae). Three other families are shared by Africa and Australia (Agamidae, Varanidae, Elapidae), whereas only one other (Chelidae) is shared by South America and Australia. Faunal resemblance factors (Duellman, 1966) at the family level are highest between Africa and Australia (0.56), followed by Africa and South America (0.54) and Australia and South America (0.40). South America has five endemic families of amphibians plus two others that have dispersed only to lower Central America, but no endemic families of reptiles. Africa has one endemic family of lizards (Cordylidae), one of caecilians (Scolecomorphidae) and one of frogs that has dispersed to Madagascar and the Seychelles Islands (Hyperoliidae). Australia has no endemic families, but the Pygopodidae is shared only with New Guinea.

Examination of the amount of taxonomic diversity in anurans and lizards on each continent reveals that the South American anuran fauna is much more diverse than that on the other continents but that Africa has the most species of lizards.* Analyses of diversity in-

---

*Data for Australia were gathered primarily from Cogger (1975), for African lizards chiefly from Mertens (1963-1966), Wermuth (1965, 1967, 1968) and Creer (1970, 1974), for African frogs and South American frogs and lizards from my personal compilations. Owing to the absence of modern comprehensive works on African snakes, a complete computational analysis of snakes was not attempted. South America has 9 families, 96 genera, and 556 species of snakes, compared with 4 families, 36 genera, and 104 species of nonmarine snakes in Australia. The species/area values for snakes are 31.2 for South America and 13.5 for Australia.

cluded the differentiation of genera and species on each continent and the numbers of species per unit area (Table 1 6).

The taxonomic diversity among South American frogs is extremely high in two families—Leptodactylidae and Hylidae; these contain 64 percent of the genera and 73 percent of the species of South American frogs. These same two families are the dominant components of the Australian amphibian fauna, accounting for 88 percent of the genera and 95 percent of the species. The dominant African families are Bufonidae and Ranidae, together accounting for 44 percent of the genera and 73 percent of the species.

In South America the dominant families of lizards are the Iguanidae and Teiidae (combined, 77% of genera, 83% of species). In Australia the Scincidae alone accounts for 37 percent of the genera and 54 percent of the species, whereas the Gekkonidae and Agamidae are secondary (combined 48% of the genera, 32% of species). Gekkonids and scincids are the most diverse African families (60% of genera, 56% of species) followed by cordylids and lacertids (35% of genera, 28% of species).

The presence or absence of families on the three continents relates primarily to historical factors, whereas the diversity within families may be dependent upon the amount of time that the family has occupied the continent or perhaps also the size of the area. Furthermore, ecological factors may be extremely important in the evolutionary diversity of a family provided that the family has been established on the continent for a sufficient period of time. There is no easy or objective way to measure habitat diversity within and between the three continents.

One method is to compare the sizes of the continents with respect to taxonomic diversity. Africa is by far the largest of the continents (30,264,000 km²) followed by South America (17,793,000 km²) and Australia (7,687,000 km²). Analyses of numbers of species per unit area show that South America has an excessive number of frogs and Australia an excessive number of lizards, all other values are negative (Table 1 6).

Lizards usually are most diverse and numerous in xeric areas, and the vast majority of Australia is xeric. Likewise most of Africa is arid, and this is reflected in the large number of lizards (506 species) on that continent.

TABLE 1 6—Taxonomic Diversity of Anurans and Lizards on Gondwanan Continents

	South America	Africa	Australia
Anurans			
Families	11	7	4
Genera	98	63	26
Species	996	355	155
Genera/Family	8 9	9 0	6 5
Species/Genus	10 2	5 6	6 0
Species/Family	90 5	50 7	38 8
Species/million km²	56 0	11 7	20 1
Deviation from expected	+26 7	−17 6	−9 2
Lizards			
Families	5	7	5
Genera	84	78	54
Species	471	506	364
Genera/Family	16 8	11 1	10 8
Species/Genus	5 6	6 5	6 7
Species/Family	94 2	72 3	72 8
Species/million km²	26 5	16 7	47 3
Deviation from expected	−3 7	−13 5	+17 1

However, proportional to size, Africa has fewer species of lizards than either Australia or South America. The comparatively few lizards in Africa might be related to the vast areas of extreme deserts (Sahara and Kalahari), which although inhabited by some specialized lizards are not species rich. Another factor might be the presence of herds of large mammals on the plains (Janzen, 1976). Furthermore, Pianka (1971) and Pianka and Huey (1971) suggested that lower species diversity of lizards in the Kalahari Desert as compared with central Australian deserts may be a result of the comparatively richer avian fauna in the Kalahari.

Frogs are most diverse in humid tropical forests. By comparison with the South American forests, the lowland tropical forests in Africa and Australia are much smaller; the Congo Basin has about 2,000,000 km² of rainforest, whereas the Amazon Basin has 4 500,000 km² (Richards, 1973). Furthermore, the South American lowland tropical rainforests are in three distinctly separate units—Amazonian, trans-Andean, and Atlantic coastal, each harboring 203, 111, and 168 endemic species of amphibians, respectively (Lynch, this volume). Quaternary climatic-vegetational changes in west African rainforests (Moreau, 1963, 1969) apparently resulted in the elimination of proportionately more of the lowland tropical forests there than in South America (Haffer, 1974). Montane rainforests (cloud forests) are much more extensive in South America than in Australia, and especially in Africa. In South America these forests support rich, localized anuran faunas.

The comparative herpetofaunal diversity in the three Gondwanan continents first is the result of historical components that were either present on the continents when they were formed or emigrated there after the continents became discrete units. However, the taxonomic diversity is primarily a factor of habitat diversity. In comparison with the other continents, South America offers a much more diverse landscape, climate, and vegetation. The cool temperate rainforests, Patagonian steppes, and high Andean punas and páramos stand in marked contrast to the pampas, llanos, caatinga, and Atacama Desert, which in turn harbor distinctly different biotas than do the lowland and montane rainforests.

Herpetofaunal Comparisons of North and South America

It has been nearly half a century since Dunn's (1931) then classic essay on the herpetofauna of the Americas. Dunn's approach was based entirely on Matthew's (1915) hypothesis of northern origin and southward dispersal of mammalian orders. Savage (1966) provided a well-documented account of the distribution patterns of amphibians and reptiles in Central America and emphasized the degree of differentiation and endemism in that fauna by recognizing a Mesoamerican herpetofauna distinct from the Nearctic and Neotropical faunas. Although the patterns delineated by Savage are realistic, the interpretation of the origins and times of dispersal can now be modified by new paleontological and geomorphological information.

Of primary importance to a biogeographical analysis of the Central-South American region is the history of the connection of the two major continental masses. According to Dietz and Holden (1970), after the initial breakup of Pangaea in the Early Jurassic (≈ 180 m y b p) there was no direct land connection between North America and South America until the Late Tertiary, although the positions of the two continents converged beginning in the mid-Cretaceous. An island arc, the proto-Antilles, existed between nuclear Central America and South America in the Cretaceous and Early Tertiary (Holden and Dietz, 1972; Malfait and Dinkelman, 1972); this arc moved eastward, relative to the westward drift of the American continents, through the Tertiary and formed the present Lesser Antilles. The region of lower Central America (Costa Rica and Panamá), or the isthmian link, formed as a volcanic archipelago in the Oligocene; additional land emerged, and the archipelago coalesced with nuclear Central America 10–12 m y b p and finally with South America about 5.7 m y b p.

During the late Mesozoic (180–90 m y b p) South America had direct land connections with Africa (Grant, 1971; Reyment and Tait, 1972; Larson and Ladd, 1973) and with Australia via Antarctica until the Eocene or Oligocene (≈ 50 m y b p) (McGowran, 1973; Veevers and McElhinny, 1976). Throughout the Cenozoic until the late Pliocene (5.7 m y b p) there was no land connection with North and Central America. Thus, for about 45 million years South America was isolated from other continents. However, the island arc (proto-Antilles) in the Late Cretaceous and Early Tertiary and the Central American Archipelago in the Middle to Late Tertiary provided opportunities for limited faunal exchange between the continents.

Fossil evidence (albeit scanty or nonexistent for some groups) and present patterns of distribution and speciation provide a basis for analysis of the herpetofaunal interchange between Central America and South America (see preceding review of families and Savage, 1966). Examination of the family groups of amphibians and reptiles that have entered into the exchange (Table 1.7) shows two modes of entry. The first is by means of dispersal across one of two archipelagos—the early proto-Antillean island arc or the later Central American Archipelago. The second is by direct dispersal after the establishment of the isthmian link.

My analysis shows no amphibians entering South America from the north via the archipelago but five amphibian family groups dispersing northward via the island route. Pre-

TABLE 1 7—Postulated Herpetofaunal Exchange Between South America and Central America

Family group	Across Panamanian Portal		Via Isthmian Link	
	N→S	S→N	N→S	S→N
Plethodontidae	—	—	+	—
Pipidae	—	—	—	+
Eleutherodactylini	—	+	+?	+
Leptodactylinae	—	—	—	+
Bufonidae	—	—	+	+
Dendrobatidae	—	—	—	+
Phyllomedusinae	—	+	+	+
Hemiphractinae	—	—	—	+
Amphignathodontinae	—	—	—	+
Hylinae	—	+	+	+
Centrolenidae	—	—	—	+
Ranidae	—	—	+	—
Microhylidae	—	+	—	+
Caeciliidae	—	+	+	+
Kinosternidae	—	—	+	—
Chelydridae	—	—	+	—
Testudinidae	+	—	—	—
Gekkoninae	—	—	—	+
Sphaerodactylinae	—	+	+	+
Iguanidae (primitive)	—	+	—	—
Iguaninae	+	—	+	—
Basiliscinae	—	—	+	—
Anolines	—	+	+	+
Teiidae	—	+	+	+
Scincidae	—	—	—	+
Anguidae	+	—	+	—
Amphisbaenidae	—	—	—	+
Anomalepidae	—	—	—	+
Leptotyphlopidae	—	+	—	—
Typhlopidae	—	+	—	—
Tropidophiidae	—	—	—	+
Xenodontinae	—	+	+	+
Colubrinae	+?	—	+	+?
Micrurinae	—	+?	+?	+
Crotalinae	+?	—	+	+?
Crocodylidae	+	—	+	+

sumably all of these (Eleutherodactylini, Phyllomedusinae, Hylinae, Microhylidae, Caeciliidae) dispersed northward via the Central American Archipelago, which emerged in the Oligocene However, the Hylinae may have dispersed earlier via the proto-Antilles, for hylne frogs are known from the Oligocene in North America, have had an extensive radiation in North America and nuclear Central America, and have dispersed into Eurasia (presumably via Beringia) Also it is possible that a proto-pipid frog entered North America via the proto-Antillean arc, this frog could be the ancestor of the Rhinophrynidae now restricted to México and nuclear Central America but known from the Paleocene-Oligocene of North America

Reptilian dispersal via the islands apparently was much more extensive than that of the amphibians Probable dispersers via the proto-Antillean island arc are primitive iguanid lizards (south to north) and anguid lizards (north to south) Dispersal via the Middle to Late Tertiary Central American Archipelago included testudinids, iguanines, crocodylids and perhaps some colubrines and crotalines (all north to south) and gekkonines, anolines, teiids, leptotyphlopids, typhlopids, xenodontines, and perhaps sphaerodactylines and micrurids (all south to north) The iguanine dispersal is postulated for the migration of an *Amblyrhynchus-Conolophus* stock to the Galápagos Islands from the South American mainland, but possibly this stock waifed directly from Central America (Avery and Tanner, 1971) Colubrine southward dispersal probably was late in the history of the archipelago, if indeed these snakes did enter South America prior to the isthmian link The evolution of the alpha and beta groups of *Anolis* north and south of the isthmus bespeaks the separation of the two groups on the two land masses (Etheridge, 1959, Savage, 1966) Possibly crocodilians and gekkonines also dispersed via the proto-Antillean island arc

Overland dispersal after the establishment of the isthmian link involved more northward than southward dispersal by amphibians, but it did permit entry into South America for the first time of plethodontid salamanders (2 genera) and ranid frogs (1 species), all widespread taxa in Central America Other groups moving southward were some phyllomedusine and perhaps some eleutherodactyline frogs that were part of the Mesoamerican fauna evolved from South American stocks that earlier had invaded Central America Also, a member of the *Bufo valliceps* group (*B coniferus*) invaded South America The northern infusion of South American taxa includes some groups that have speciated (S) and/or dispersed widely (D) in Central America— *Eleutherodactylus* (SD), *Leptodactylus* (SD), *Physalaemus* (D), *Bufo marinus* (D), *Hyla ebraccata* (D) and *microcephala* (SD) groups and *Centrolenella* (SD) Most of the other South American amphibians have dispersed only into lower Central America and have not speciated there—*Pipa* (eastern Panamá), *Pleurodema*, *Bufo typhonius*, *Elachistocleis Relictivomer*, *Caecilia* and *Oscaecilia* (central Panamá), *Hemiphractus* and *Gastrotheca* (western Panamá), *Glossostoma* (Costa Rica), and *Bufo haematiticus* (Nicaragua). The South American *Phyllomedusa buckleyi* group has a species endemic to lower Central America (Duellman, 1970). All three genera of South American dendrobatids occur in lower Central America; each has undergone some speciation (Savage, 1968). The *Atelopus varius* group has invaded Central America (to Costa Rica) and has undergone a bewildering diversification (Savage, 1972).

Late Tertiary and Quaternary overland dispersal amongst reptiles also was extensive. Southward dispersal brought chelydrid and kinosternid turtles, basiliscine lizards, and possibly colubrine and crotaline snakes into South America for the first time, whereas simultaneously the first *Mabuya*, *Amphisbaena*, and anomalepid and tropidophiid snakes reached Central America. Mesoamerican groups originally derived from South American stocks (beta anoles, *Cnemidophorus*, and many xenodontine snakes) dispersed into South America. Many South American taxa (*Thecadactylus*, alpha anoles, *Ameiva*, microteiids and xenodontine and micrurid snakes) moved northward.

The herpetofauna of eastern Panamá contains many genera that are chiefly South American—*Pipa*, *Rhamphophryne*, *Hemiphractus*, *Gastrotheca*, *Elachistocleis*, *Caecilia*, *Geochelone*, *Lepidoblepharis*, *Enyalioides*, *Echinosaura*, *Amphisbaena*, *Corallus*, *Trachyboa*, *Atractus*, *Diaphorolepis*, and *Pseudoboa*. The herpetofauna of the Chocoan lowlands of northwestern South America contains many species that are familiar to the herpetologist working in lower Central America, whereas the fauna in the Amazon Basin is greatly different (at least at the species level), compare data given by Savage (1966) with those presented by Lynch (this volume) and Dixon (this volume).

Herpetofauna of the West Indies

Although the West Indies are peripheral to a discussion of the South American herpetofauna, it is germane to this essay to ascertain the herpetofaunal relationships of the two regions inasmuch as many genera and some species are common to the two. The history of the Caribbean Plate and the tectonic movements in the Antillean-Caribbean region have not been resolved, but Rosen (1975) summarized (and extended) the existing geological data and proposed a plausible vicariance model of Caribbean biogeography.

Excluding introduced taxa, the herpetofauna of the West Indies (not including Trinidad, Tobago, Bonaire, Aruba, and Curaçao) consists of 505 species in 57 genera (Schwartz and Thomas 1975), 476 of the species and 18 of the genera are endemic to the West Indies. Schwartz (1978) gave a brief description of the herpetogeography of the West Indies.

Twenty-two genera of reptiles are primarily mainland taxa having one or two species extending into the West Indies. Fifteen of these are South American taxa that extend into the Lesser Antilles—*Phyllodactylus* (also Greater Antilles) *Thecadactylus*, *Iguana*, *Bachia*, *Cnemidophorus*, *Gymnophthalmus*, *Kentropyx*, *Mabuya* (also Greater Antilles), *Boa*, *Corallus*, *Chironius*, *Clelia*, *Mastigodryas*, *Pseudoboa*, and *Bothrops*. Five are Central American taxa that extend into the Greater Antilles—*Gonatodes*, *Tretanorhinus*, and *Ctenosaura*, *Boa*, and *Coniophanes* only reaching Isla San Andres and/or Isla Providencia. Three are North American taxa that reach Cuba—*Natrix fasciata*, *Kinosternon bauri*, and *Crocodylus acutus*, the latter also has invaded the Lesser Antilles from South America and there is an endemic species of *Crocodylus* on Cuba. The geckos *Tarentola* and *Hemidactylus* may have arrived by waifing from any one of many sources, although the other species of *Tarentola* are circum-Mediterranean. Two of the *Leptodactylus* and one each of *Eleutherodactylus* and *Hyla* are mainland species. The five west Indian *Chrysemys* probably stem from an invasion from North America.

Among the endemic or taxonomically rich genera in the West Indies, the hylid genera (*Calyptahyla*, *Osteopilus*, and *Hyla*) were studied by Trueb and Tyler (1974), who inferred five invasions of the Greater Antilles by separate hylid stocks, probably from South America by rafting; however, it is possible that the stocks for some of these were on the proto-Antilles and drifted part of the way to their present positions. The same might be true for the monotypic Cuban eleutherodactyline *Sminthillus* and some of the West Indian stocks of *Eleutherodactylus*. Lynch (1971) suggested that most of the West Indian *Eleutherodactylus*, plus *Sminthillus* and the Mexican *Syrrhophus* and *Tomodactylus* possibly represented one eleutherodactyline lineage and that the *Eleutherodactylus inoptatus* group of Hispaniola and the mainland *Eleutherodactylus* formed another lineage. If these suppositions are correct, minimally two eleutherodactyline invasions of the West Indies are required. The nine Greater Antillean *Bufo* seem to be related (Schwartz, 1972), but their affinities with mainland taxa have yet to be determined.

Amongst the lizards, the dominant genus is *Anolis*, represented by two groups of species (alpha and beta, fide Etheridge, 1959), plus two endemic genera (*Chamaeleolis* and *Chamaelinorops* in Cuba and Hispaniola respectively). The alpha anoles inhabit the Greater and Lesser Antilles and are widespread in South America, whereas the beta anoles occur in Central and South America and the Greater Antilles. Williams (1969 and in Trueb and Tyler, 1974) required minimally two invasions of the Greater Antilles by *Anolis* and two for the endemic genera. *Cyclura* is related to *Ctenosaura* of Middle America (Avery and Tanner, 1971), the ancestral stock of *Cyclura* presumably arrived in the Greater Antilles from Central America. This also probably is true for the ancestral xantusiid stock that gave rise to *Cricosaura* endemic to Cuba (Savage 1963) and that of *Diploglossus* represented by some Central American and many West Indian species. Possibly an earlier or separate invasion was responsible for the endemic Hispaniolan anguid *Wetmorena*. Two of the speciose Antillean genera seem to be of South American origin—*Ameiva* and *Leiocephalus*. Etheridge (1966) showed *Leiocephalus* to be a tropidurine related to *Liolaemus* (restricted to temperate South America). *Sphaerodactylus*, with 56 species in the West Indies, may have evolved there from an early sphaerodactyline invasion; if so, the few mainland species (Central America and Chocó) are the result of dispersal of stocks back to the mainland.

All of the colubrid snakes (save the North American *Natrix fasciata*) in the West Indies are xenodontines. Maglio (1970) demonstrated relationships of the seven endemic genera and *Alsophis* with diverse mainland xenodontines and concluded that four separate xenodontine invasions of the West Indies from either Central or South America were necessary in the evolution of the West Indian xenodontines. Presumably the tropidophiid stock that gave rise to the 12 species of *Tropidophis* in the Greater Antilles and the Bahamas came from South America, perhaps via Central America.

Too little is known about the relationships of the Antillean *Aristelliger*, amphisbaenids, *Leptotyphlops*, and *Typhlops* to speculate on their origins except that it is unlikely that they invaded from North America.

CONTINENTAL PATTERNS OF DISTRIBUTION

It is becoming increasingly evident that the patterns of climate and vegetation have changed drastically in South America since the beginning of the Cretaceous. Axelrod (1972) argued convincingly that the interior of the large African American continent was arid prior to the birth of the South Atlantic Ocean, which brought maritime and mesic climates to western Africa and eastern South America for the first time. Some elements of the arid-adapted west Gondwanan flora survived in South America (and Africa) (Solbrig, 1976, Sarmiento, 1976), while much of the continent was mesic. Subsequent to the Eocene, temperate South America gradually became cooler and drier (Axelrod and Bailey, 1969, Wolfe, 1971, Báez and Scillato Yané, this volume). The uplift of the Andes beginning in the Miocene drastically modified wind patterns and resulted in great changes in climate and vegetation (Simpson, this volume), and the formerly widespread Tertiary-Chaco Paleoflora (Solbrig, 1976) became fragmented on the Pacific slopes as the climatic effects of the developing Humboldt Current resulted in desiccation of the land in the Late Tertiary (Jeannel, 1967) Pleistocene climatic fluctuation effected the entire continent with cool and warm periods in the south (Báez and Scillato Yané this volume), humid and dry periods in the lowland tropics (Haffer, this volume) and extensive glaciation in the Andes (Simpson this volume).

Although the fossil record of the herpetofauna in South America is still fragmentary, sufficient material exists, especially when placed with the better data from mammals and the paleofloras to give a faint impression of past distributions especially in the southern part of the continent (Báez and Gasparini, this volume) It is evident that there has been a northward retreat of the tropical biota especially those types requiring mesic environments Conceivably much of the present and adapted temperate herpetofauna has evolved rather recently in response to increasingly xeric conditions, as postulated for xeric floras by Axelrod (1967) Thus, the archaic frogs in the austral forests are relicts, like the forests themselves (Vuilleumier, 1968, Lynch, 1971)

The fossil record is especially secretive about the presently large and diverse herpetofauna of the tropical forests Presumably most of this fauna evolved at the generic level by the mid Tertiary, or at least by the Pliocene Endemic Andean groups apparently evolved with the uplift of the Andes and probably are not older than the Pliocene Speciation in many lowland tropical groups (Haffer, 1974 this volume) and Andean groups (Simpson, 1975, this volume, Duellman, this volume) seems to have occurred in the Pleistocene

Thus we are faced with contrasting pictures—presumed recent speciation and apparently rapid evolutionary rates in the lowland tropics and in the Andes, as well as in some temperate groups adapted to xeric conditions, versus the survival of many old taxa in habitat refugia in the austral forests and also in the ancient Brasilian and Guianan highlands (Hoogmoed, this volume)

Various contributors to this volume have analyzed distributions within certain regions (e g, Patagonia) or biotopes (e g, lowland tropical rainforests) here I attempt to provide a broad synthesis of patterns in the entire continent Data for many groups and/or regions are inadequate for a detailed analysis, instead I present a general picture of the diverse distribution patterns and give examples of each

Temperate Herpetofaunas

Austral Forests —The cool moist forests of southern Chile and adjacent Argentina represent an unique biotope in South America, characterized by a highly endemic herpetofauna composed mostly of primitive leptodactylid frogs (*Alsodes, Batrachyla, Caudiverbera Eupsophus Hylorina, Telmatobufo*) mostly restricted to forests south of 37°S Lat (Fig 1 2A) The distributions of all of the species are mapped by Formas (this volume) The herpetofauna of the austral forests mostly is relictual and presumably consists (at least in amphibians) of remnants of groups that were widespread in temperate South America in the Early Tertiary With few minor exceptions (*Bufo spinulosus, Tachymenis peruviana*) none of the species extends beyond the present limits of the region, but some species of *Liolaemus* and *Pleurodema* have congeners in adjacent regions The Atacama Desert to the north and the Patagonian steppe to the east are effective barriers to the dispersal of groups inhabiting the austral forests

Patagonian Steppe —The cool dry steppes of southern Argentina interdigitate in the north with the monte (Cei, this volume) The Patagonian herpetofauna contains some ancient relicts (telmatobine leptodactylid frogs and some tropidurine iguanid lizards) but also many species of *Liolaemus* that have differentiated in the Pleistocene (Cei, this volume) Some Patagonian groups have relatives in the adjacent monte and the pampas, or in the austral forests, but the major latitudinal expansion has been northward in the Andes best exemplified by *Liolaemus* (Fig 1 2B)

Tropical and Subtropical Herpetofaunas

Herein distinction is made between two primary biotopes, as follow 1) Forests—tropical evergreen forests, including rainforest and cloud forest, and 2) Nonforests—the deciduous scrub or thorn forests, and savannas, grasslands and deserts Although each of these categories, especially the latter, contains diverse vegetation formations they seem to have reality with respect to major patterns of distribution of the herpetofauna

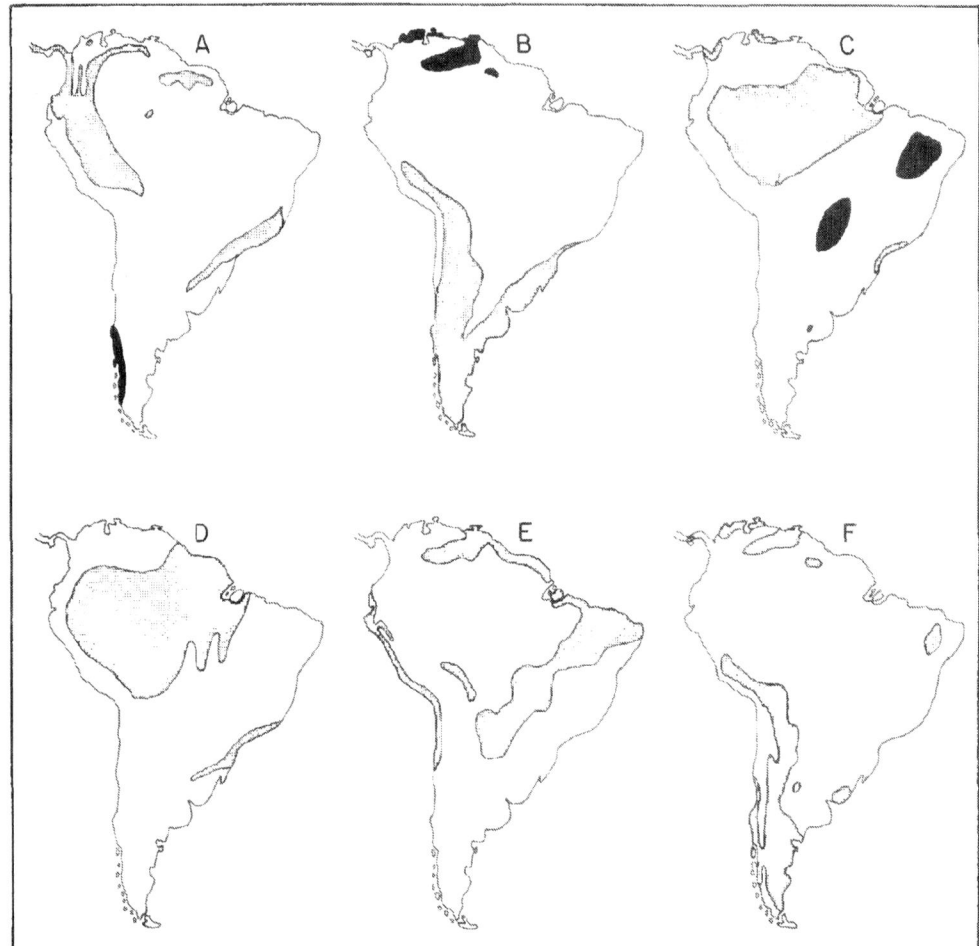

Fig. 1:2. Distribution patterns of the South American herpetofauna: A. *Batrachyla* in austral forests (black); *Centrolenella* principally in cloud forests but also entering lowland tropical rainforest (stippled). B. *Liolaemus*, an austral group entering adjacent subtropical areas and extending northward in the Andes (stippled); *Pleurodema brachyops*, widespread in nonforests in northern South America (black). C. *Hyla parviceps* group with vicariant species in lowland rainforests; three species are in the Amazon Basin and one each in the other areas (stippled); *Phyllopezus* with disjunct populations in nonforested areas of the caatinga, cerrados, and pampas (black) (after Vanzolini, 1974). D. *Osteocephalus* with species on Andean and Guianan slopes and others in lowland rainforests. E. *Tropidurus* with species inhabiting diverse nonforested environments throughout tropical South America and the Galápagos Islands. F. *Pleurodema*, a temperate South American genus with vicariant species in the Andes and in nonforested environments to Panamá.

Patrones de distribución de la herpetofauna sudamericana. A. *Batrachyla en los bosques australes* (negro); *Centrolenella principalmente en bosques neblinos pero también entra las tierras bajas de la selva lluviosa tropical* (punteado). B. *Liolaemus, un grupo austral entra los áreas subtropicales adyacentes y se extende hacia el norte en los Andes* (punteado); *Pleurodema brachyops diseminado en ambientes no forestales en el norte de Sudamérica* (negro). C. *Hyla parviceps con especies vicarias en las tierras bajas del bosque lluvioso, tres especies en la Amazonia y una especie en cada una de los otros áreas* (punteado); *Phyllopezus poblaciones disjuntas en áreas sin bosque de caatinga, cerrado y pampas* (según Vanzolini, 1974) (negro). D. *Osteocephalus con especies en las laderas andinas y guianense y otras especies en las tierras bajas del bosque pluvial.* E. *Tropidurus con especies habitando diversos ambientes no forestales através de Sudamérica tropical y las Islas Galápagos.* F. *Pleurodema, un género de la región templada de Sudamérica con especies vicarias en los Andes y en ambientes no forestales hasta Panamá.*

Forests—The vast Amazonian rainforests and the smaller areas of rainforest in the Chocó and along the southeastern coast of Brasil contain the richest herpetofaunas in South America (Lynch, this volume; Dixon, this volume). Especially diverse in these forests are dendrobatid and hylid frogs, anoline and teiid lizards, and xenodontine colubrid snakes. The herpetofaunas of the montane rainforests or cloud forests in the Andes, Guiana Highlands and the Brasilian Highlands are primarily altitudinal extensions of the lowland groups (Hoogmoed this volume; Duellman this volume). However, in the montane forests, certain groups are either endemic or far more diverse than in the lowlands—frogs of the families Centrolenidae (Fig 1 2A), Dendrobatidae (*Colostethus*), and Leptodactylidae (*Eleutherodactylus*) and salamanders of the genus *Bolitoglossa* (Andes only).

Distribution patterns are highly variable (see Duellman, 1978 Fig 197, for examples of Amazonian distributions). A few widespread species, such as *Boa constrictor* inhabit all of the lowland forests, but these species usually also inhabit intervening nonforest areas. More commonly, vicariant species occur in the different areas of rainforest (Fig 1 2C). Widespread and speciose genera, such as *Eleutherodactylus Hyla* and *Anolis*, are found throughout the lowland and montane forests, but usually there are distinct combinations of species at different elevations as shown for *Eleutherodactylus* by Lynch and Duellman (1979). These patterns are more readily discernible in smaller genera such as *Osteocephalus* (3 Amazonian species, 1 Guianan, 2 Andean, and 1 coastal Brasilian, Fig 1 2D) or *Enyalioides* (2 Amazonian species, 2 Chocoan, and 3 Andean).

The differentiation of populations in Quaternary forest refugia (Haffer, 1969 1974) has been postulated for lizards (Vanzolini and Williams, 1970), frogs (Duellman, 1972; Heyer, 1973; Duellman and Crump, 1974) and snakes (Dixon, this volume).

Nonforests—The tropical and subtropical nonforested biotopes are more extensive, diverse and fragmented than the forests. In northern South America are the coastal deserts, savannas, and the extensive llanos, south and east of the Amazon Basin are the dry areas of northeastern Brasil (Caatinga), the interior savannas (cerrados) and the Gran Chaco. Subtropical, cis-Andean, nonforests include the pampas espinal and monte in Argentina; west of the Andes are the matorral and the Atacama Desert (Fig 1 1).

Distributions of many species of plants and animals indicate that various combinations of these nonforest environments were continuous with one another in the not-too-distant past. Pleistocene climatic fluctuations resulted in drier periods (interglacials) that allowed for expansion of the nonforests (Haffer, 1974; Vanzolini 1976). Gallardo (1969, 1971, this volume) emphasized the faunal relationships among the chaco, pampas and monte, and Vanzolini (1968, 1974, 1976) demonstrated distribution patterns in the cerrados and caatinga. The herpetofaunal relationships among the coastal deserts, llanos and savannas of northeastern South America are analyzed by Rivero-Blanco and Dixon (this volume) and Hoogmoed (this volume).

The trans-Andean area consists of a narrow coastal strip and Andean slopes to 2000–3000 m 1–37°S Lat. The dry upper Marañón Valley and associated valleys in the Huancabamba Depression are separated from the trans-Andean arid zone by passes at less than 3000 m. The coastal deserts and matorral have a small, but largely endemic, herpetofauna including three endemic genera of lizards—*Garthia* (2 species), *Callopistes* (2) and *Dicrodon* (3). The dominant groups are two genera of lizards, *Tropidurus* (Dixon and Wright, 1975), and *Phyllodactylus* (Dixon and Huey, 1970), both of which have representatives in the dry valleys east of the Andes and on the Galápagos Islands. For much of the length of the coastal desert in northern Chile and southern Perú, the entire herpetofauna is composed of solely two species of *Tropidurus* and one of *Phyllodactylus*.

The Humboldt Current sweeps the coast of Chile and Perú and swings westward past the Galápagos Islands, 600 km off the coast of Ecuador. This current has been important in rafting stocks of Atacaman reptiles—*Tropidurus, Phyllodactylus, Alsophis* (=*Dromicus*)—to the Galápagos.

Several patterns of distribution are evident in the nonforested regions. Some species such as *Pleurodema brachyops* and *Phimophis guianensis* are widespread in the northern regions (Fig. 1.2B), whereas others are restricted to the coastal deserts or llanos. Some ceratophryine frogs, some snakes, and several lizards have series of populations, subspecies or species distributed from the caatinga southwestward in the cerrados to the chaco or even into the monte or pampas (Fig. 1.2C). Such open habitats obviously were continuous, or nearly so, in the past so as to permit the dispersal of such nonforest taxa as *Tropidurus*, *Cnemidophorus* and *Bufo granulosus* (Webb, 1978). Some of the taxa in the Atacama Desert are not represented east of the Andes, except in the upper Marañón Valley, but *Phyllodactylus* also is diverse in northern South America, Middle America, and the West Indies. *Tropidurus* is widely distributed in tropical nonforested environments on both sides of the Andes (Fig. 1.2E). At least one temperate group (*Pleurodema*) has dispersed northward in nonforests to northern South America (Duellman and Veloso, 1977) (Fig. 1.2F).

Montane Herpetofaunas

The three major highland regions of South America—the ancient Guianan and Brasilian highlands and the young Andes—have little in common herpetologically. With few exceptions, there are no isolated sister groups at high elevations that do not have relatives at low elevations. Hylid frogs of the genera *Cryptobatrachus* (northern Andes) and *Stefania* (Guiana Highlands) and teiid lizards *Euspondylus* in the same regions, are primary examples. Hylid frogs of the genera *Gastrotheca* and *Flectonotus* occur in the Andes and in the Brasilian Highlands, but some of these species occur at low to moderate elevations, even though at present none lives in the intervening lowlands. The herpetofaunas of the highland regions seem to have been derived independently from the adjacent lowlands. In the case of the Andes, the fauna is composed of a southern assemblage derived from Patagonia and a northern assemblage derived from the tropical lowlands (Duellman this volume).

FUTURE OF THE HERPETOFAUNA

I have attempted to interpret the past and to describe the present; now I provide a prognosis for the study of the South American herpetofauna. South America has the richest herpetofauna of any continent, but the fauna is still poorly known taxonomically. Our knowledge of systematic and ecological relationships is even less. Human devastation of vast areas of forest that a few years ago were unexplored is eliminating forever important, and in many cases unknown, aspects of the biota. Although biologists have had some influence on the control of this exploitation there is little hope that we can preserve all that we may wish to save. Thus, we are faced with two courses of action—salvage collecting and preservation of diverse natural preserves.

Random collecting of the biota, even in reasonably well known areas, commonly results in new information on distributions, taxonomy, or life histories. However, collecting efforts need to be intensified and planned to sample biota before they are destroyed. In the case of amphibians and reptiles, efforts must be made to obtain not only series of well-preserved specimens but also tissues for karyological and biochemical studies, colored photographs, tape recordings of calls (of frogs), life history data and extensive notes on habitats and behavior. We cannot necessarily expect that a visit to the same region five or ten years hence, or even next year, will permit the collection of these data. The collection of these kinds of materials and data must be encouraged and supported at every level internationally. The impending biological crisis has no national boundaries; responsible and effective collectors should be encouraged to make adequate collections throughout the continent. Systematic collections under responsible direction of trained biologists will be one of the most important biological resources of the future; materials in these collections made available internationally to qualified investigators will be the basis for not only systematic studies but much evolutionary synthesis.

The establishment of large natural reserves in areas of high species richness and endemism can preserve large segments of the herpetofauna. However, such reserves should not be established strictly for conservation purposes. It is in these reserves that biologists can undertake long-range studies of communities, population dynamics, behavior, and life history. The resulting kinds of information complement those obtained from salvage collecting and contribute substantially to our total understanding of the biota.

Actions of these kinds are necessary now; a few years hence will be too late for some of the regions and their herpetofaunas. Without such actions the papers assembled in this volume will not be the preliminary assessments as intended, but instead they might be the last word on the South American herpetofauna.

ACKNOWLEDGMENTS

In the preparation of this paper I have drawn freely on the manuscripts submitted by other contributors to this volume. I am indebted to Richard Etheridge and John D. Lynch for some of the data and to Juan Manuel Renjifo for translating the summary. An earlier draft of the manuscript benefited from critical review by John D. Lynch, Gregory K. Pregill, Linda Trueb, and Margaret Davies, whose austral invectives in the pits decidedly influenced the effectiveness of my writing.

RESUMEN

La herpetofauna sudamericana se compone de 1,095 especies de anfibios distribuidos en 115 géneros y 15 familias, 1,115 especies de reptiles en 203 géneros y 22 familias (excluyendo los taxa marinos). De los 318 géneros y 2,210 especies, 201 géneros y 2,017 especies son endémicas de este continente. Entre las familias de reptiles, no encontramos ninguna endémica en sudamerica, en cambio existen cinco familias endémicas de anfibios.

Durante 45–50 millones de años la fauna sudamericana evolucionó aislada del resto de los continentes formaban Gondwanalandia, solo hasta la relativamente reciente conexión (5.7 millones de años) con Norte América por la vía del Istmo de Panamá. Antes del establecimiento de la conexión terrestre, un archipielago proveo las veces de filtro entre Norte y Sur América, el cual fue cruzado en ambas direcciones por algunos grupos. El mayor intercambio entre las dos faunas se llevo a cabo una vez fue establecida la conexion entre los dos continentes. Seis familias de anfibios y 15 de reptiles son compartidas por Norte y Sur América. Además cuatro familias de anfibios y cuatro familias de reptiles sudamericanas también se encuentran en Centro América.

Gran parte de la herpetofauna Antillana se compone de grupos neotropicales, algunos de los cuales invadieron las islas especialmente las islas menores de las Antillas provenientes de Sudamerica; otros grupos invadieron las islas desde Centro América.

De las 37 familias sudamericanas, tres de anfibios y seis de reptiles son compartidas con Africa y Australia. Un total de cinco familias de anfibios son compartidas con Africa y cuatro familias con Australia. Entre las familias de reptiles, 11 son comunes con Africa y siete con Australia. De este modo, las relaciones a nivel de familias entre las herpetofaunas son mayores entre Sudamérica y Africa que entre Sudamérica y Australia. La mayor semejanza existe entre Australia y Africa. Comparado con los otros continentes que formaban Gondwanalandia, Sudamérica tiene un número desproporcionadamente alto de anuros y Australia de saurios.

La presencia o ausencia de las familias en los tres continentes se debe principalmente a factores históricos, mientras que la diversidad dentro de las familias depende del tiempo que estas hayan estado en el continente, el tamaño del área de este y su diversidad ecológica.

En Sudamerica la herpetofauna evolucionó respondiendo a los cambios de las condiciones climáticas durante el Cenozóico, aparentemente muchas de las especies que existen actualmente evolucionaron en el Quaternario. Las herpetofaunas de las regiones templadas incluyen aquellas encontradas en los bosques australes y las estepas patagónicas. Los bosques están restringidos a zonas aisladas, mientras que las estepas se han dispersado hasta el monte subtropical adyacente y hacia el norte en los Andes.

Las herpetofaunas tropicales y subtropicales incluyen aquellas asociadas con bosques tropicales siempre verdes y bosques montañosos y agregaciones asociadas con ambientes sin bosques grandes—pampas, monte, espinal, chaco, matorral cerrado, caatinga, sabanas, llanos y desiertos. Cada una de estas regiones tiene su fauna característica. Las herpetofaunas de las tierras altas en los Andes, en Guiana y en Brasil tienen poco en común, aparentemente cada una se derivó independientemente de las faunas encontradas en las tierras bajas adyacentes.

Con el fin de adquirir material para estudios en el futuro y conservar agregaciones de la herpetofauna sudamericana antes de que la destrucción causada por el hombre elimine aún más la biota es necesario hacer extensas y bien documentadas colecciones de la herpetofauna a lo largo del continente así como establecer grandes reservas naturales en áreas ricas en especies y endemismos donde estudios biológicos de la fauna puedan ser llevados a cabo en el futuro.

LITERATURE CITED

Anderson, S., Jones, J. K., Jr. 1967. Recent mammals of the world. A synopsis of families. Ronald Press, New York, 453 p.

Auffenberg, W. 1971. A new fossil tortoise, with remarks on the origin of South American testudines. Copeia 1971(1):106-117.

Avery, D. F., Tanner, W. W. 1971. Evolution of the iguanine lizards (Sauria, Iguanidae) as determined by osteological and myological characters. Brigham Young Univ. Sci. Bull. Biol. Ser. 12(3):1-79.

Axelrod, D. I. 1967. Drought, diastrophism, and quantum evolution. Evolution 21:201-209.

Axelrod, D. I. 1972. Edaphic aridity as a factor in angiosperm evolution. Amer. Nat. 106:311-320.

Axelrod, D. I., Bailey, H. P. 1969. Paleotemperature analysis of Tertiary floras. Paleogeogr. Paleoclimatol. Paleoecol. 6:163-195.

Berman, D. S. 1973. *Spathorhynchus fossorium*, a middle Eocene amphisbaenian (Reptilia) from Wyoming. Copeia 1973(4):704-721.

Blair, W. F. 1972. Summary, pp. 329-343 in Blair, W. F. (ed.) Evolution in the genus *Bufo*. Univ. Texas Press, Austin, 459 p.

Bons, J., Pasteur, G. 1977. Solution histologique a un probleme de taxonomie herpetologique interessant les rapports paleobiologiques de l'Amerique du Sud et de l'Afrique. Acad. Sci. Paris, Ser. D 284:2547-2550.

Brodkorb, P. 1971. Origin and evolution of birds, pp. 20-55 in Farner, D. S., King, J. R. (eds.) Avian biology, 1. Academic Press, New York, 586 p.

Burger, W. L. 1971. Genera of pitvipers (Serpentes Crotalidae). PhD Dissert. Univ. Kansas 186 p.

Cei, J. M. 1968. Remarks on the geographical distribution and phyletic trends of South American toads. Pearce-Sellards Ser. Texas Mem. Mus. (13):1-20.

Cei, J. M. 1972. *Bufo* of South America, pp. 82-92 in Blair, W. F. (ed.) Evolution in the genus *Bufo*. Univ. Texas Press, Austin, 459 p.

Cogger, H. G. 1974. Voyage of the banded iguana. Australian Nat. Hist. 18:144-149.

Cogger, H. G. 1975. Reptiles and amphibians of Australia. Reed, Sydney, 584 p.

Cracraft, J. 1973. Continental drift, paleoclimatology, and evolution and biogeography of birds. J. Zool. 179:455-545.

Cracraft, J. 1974. Continental drift and vertebrate distribution. Ann. Rev. Ecol. Syst. 5:215-261.

Dietz, R. S., Holden, J. C. 1970. Reconstruction of Pangaea. Breakup and dispersion of continents, Permian to present. J. Geophys. Res. 75:4939-4956.

Dixon, J. R., Anderson, S. C. 1973. A new species and genus of gecko (Sauria, Gekkonidae) from Iran and Iraq. Bull. South California Acad. Sci. 72:155-160.

Dixon, J. R., Huey, R. B. 1970. Systematics of the lizards of the gekkonid genus *Phyllodactylus* of mainland South America. Nat. Hist. Mus. Los Angeles Cty. Contrib. Sci. (192):1-78.

Dixon, J. R., Wright, J. W. 1975. A review of the lizards of the iguanid genus *Tropidurus* in Peru. Ibid (271):1-39.

Dowling, H. G. 1975. A provisional classification of snakes. 1974 Yearbook Herpetology. Herpetol. Inter. Search Syst., New York, pp. 167-170.

Duellman, W. E. 1966. The Central American herpetofauna. An ecological perspective. Copeia 1966(4):700-719.

Duellman, W. E. 1970. The hylid frogs of Middle America. Univ. Kansas Mus. Nat. Hist. Monogr. (1):1-753.

Duellman, W. E. 1972. South American frogs of the *Hyla rostrata* group (Amphibia, Anura, Hylidae). Zool. Meded. Rijks Mus. Nat. Hist. Leiden 47:177-192.

Duellman, W. E. 1975. On the classification of frogs. Univ. Kansas Mus. Nat. Hist. Occas. Pap. (42):1-14.

Duellman, W. E. 1977. Liste der rezenten Amphibien und Reptilien. Hylidae, Centrolenidae, Pseudidae. Das Tierreich (95):1-225.

Duellman, W. E., Crump, M. L. 1974. Speciation in frogs of the *Hyla parviceps* group in the upper Amazon Basin. Univ. Kansas Mus. Nat. Hist. Occas. Pap. (23):1-40.

Duellman, W. E., Veloso, M. A. 1977. The phylogeny of *Pleurodema* (Anura, Leptodactylidae). A biogeographic model. Ibid (64):1-46.

Dunn, E. R. 1931. The herpetological fauna of the Americas. Copeia 1931(3):106-119.

ESTES, R. 1970. Origin of the Recent North American lower vertebrate fauna. An inquiry into the fossil record. Forma Functio 3: 139–163.

ESTES, R. 1975. Fossil *Xenopus* from the Paleocene of South America and the zoogeography of pipid frogs. Herpetologica 31: 263–278.

ESTES, R. 1976. Middle Paleocene lower vertebrates from the Tongue Formation, southeastern Montana. J. Paleontol. 50: 500–520.

ESTES, R., PRICE, L. I. 1973. Iguanid lizard from the Upper Cretaceous of Brasil. Science 180: 744–751.

ESTES R., REIG, O. A. 1973. The early fossil record of frogs. A review of the evidence, pp. 11–63 in VIAL, J. L. (ed.) Evolutionary biology of the anurans. Contemporary research on major problems. Univ. Missouri Press, Columbia, 470 p.

ESTES R., WAKE, M. 1972. The first fossil record of caecilian amphibians. Nature 239: 228–231.

ETHERIDGE, R. 1959. The relationships of the anoles (Reptilia Sauria Iguanidae). An interpretation based on skeletal morphology. PhD Dissert. Univ. Michigan, 236 p.

ETHERIDGE, R. 1964. The skeletal morphology and systematic relationships of sceloporine lizards. Copeia 1964(4): 610–631.

ETHERIDGE, R. 1966. The systematic relationships of West Indian and South American lizards referred to the iguanid genus *Leiocephalus*. Ibid. 1966(1): 79–91.

ETHERIDGE, R. 1967. Lizard caudal vertebrae. Ibid. 1967(4): 699–721.

FORMAS, R., PUGIN, F., JORQUERA, B. 1975. La identidad del batracio chileno *Hemmectes rufus* Philippi, 1902. Physis 34: 147–157.

GAFFNEY, E. S. 1975. A phylogeny and classification of the higher categories of turtles. Bull. Amer. Mus. Nat. Hist. 155: 387–436.

GAFFNEY, E. S. 1977. The side-necked turtle family Chelidae. A theory of relationships using shared derived characters. Amer. Mus. Novit. (2620): 1–28.

GALLARDO, J. M. 1961. On the species of Pseudidae. Bull. Mus. Comp. Zool. Harvard Univ. 125: 108–134.

GALLARDO, J. M. 1969. Las especies de saurios (Reptilia) de la Provincia de Santa Fe, Argentina, y consideraciones sobre su ecología y zoogeografía. Neotropica 15: 73–81.

GALLARDO, J. M. 1971. Composición faunística de los saurios de la Provincia de La Pampa, Republica Argentina. Ibid. 17: 44–48.

GANS, C. 1967. A check list of Recent amphisbaenians (Amphisbaenia Reptilia). Bull. Amer. Mus. Nat. Hist. 135: 61–105.

GRANT, N. K. 1971. South Atlantic, Benue Trough, and Gulf of Guinea Cretaceous triple junction. Geol. Soc. Amer. Bull. 82: 2295–2298.

GREER, A. E. 1970. A subfamilial classification of scincid lizards. Bull. Mus. Comp. Zool. Harvard Univ. 139: 151–183.

GREER, A. E. 1974. The generic relationships of the scincid lizard genus *Leiolopisma* and its relatives. Australian J. Zool. Suppl. Ser. (31): 1–67.

HAFFER, J. 1969. Speciation in Amazonian forest birds. Science 165: 131–137.

HAFFER, J. 1974. Avian speciation in tropical South America. Publ. Nuttall Ornith. Club (14): 1–390.

HAGEN, V. W. VON. 1948. The green world of the naturalists. Greenberg, New York, 392 p.

HERSHKOVITZ, P. 1972. The Recent mammals of the Neotropical Region. A zoogeographic and ecological review, pp. 311–431 in KEAST, A., ERK, F. C., GLASS, B. (eds.) Evolution, mammals, and southern continents. State Univ. New York Press, Albany, 543 p.

HEYER, W. R. 1973. Systematics of the marmoratus group of the frog genus *Leptodactylus*. Nat. Hist. Mus. Los Angeles Cty. Contr. Sci. (251): 1–50.

HEYER, W. R. 1975. A preliminary analysis of the intergeneric relationships of the frog family Leptodactylidae. Smithsonian Contrib. Zool. (199): 1–55.

HEYER, W. R., LIEM, D. S. 1976. Analysis of the intergeneric relationships of the Australian frog family Myobatrachidae. Ibid. (233): 1–29.

HOLDEN, J. C., DIETZ R. S. 1972. Galapagos core, NazCoPac triple junction and Carnegie/Cocos ridges. Nature 235: 266–269.

HOLMAN, J. A. 1967. Additional Miocene anurans from Florida. Q. J. Florida Acad. Sci. 30: 121–140.

HOLMAN, J. A. 1968. Lower Oligocene amphibians from Saskatchewan. Ibid. 31: 273–289.

HOLMAN, J. A. 1976. Snakes from the Rosebud Formation (Middle Miocene) of South Dakota. Herpetologica 32: 41–48.

HOLMAN, J. A. 1977. Upper Miocene snakes (Reptilia, Serpentes) from southeastern Nebraska. J. Herpetol. 11: 323–335.

IZECKSOHN, L. 1971. Novo genero e nova especie de Brachycephalidae do Estado do Rio de Janeiro Brasil (Amphibia, Anura). Bol. Mus. Nac. Rio de Janeiro, Zool. (280): 1–12.

JANZEN, D. H. 1976. The depression of reptile biomass by large herbivores. Amer. Nat. 110: 371–400.

JEANNEL, R. 1967. Biogéographie de l'Amerique australe, pp. 401–460 in DELAMERE DEBOUTTEVILLE, C., RAPOPORT, E. (eds.) Biologie de l'Amerique australe, 3. C.N.R.S. Groupe Francais Argiles C. R. Reun. Etud., Paris, 831 p.

KEAST, A. 1972. Continental drift and the evolution of the biota on southern continents, pp. 23–87 in KEAST, A., ERK, F. C., GLASS, B. (eds.) Evolution, mammals, and southern continents. State Univ. New York Press, Albany, 543 p.

KLUGE, A. C. 1967. Higher taxonomic categories of gekkonid lizards and their evolution. Bull. Amer. Mus. Nat. Hist. (135): 1–60.

LARSON R. L., LADD, J. W. 1973. Evidence for the opening of the South Atlantic in the Early Cretaceous. Nature 246: 209–212.

LYNCH, J. D. 1971. Evolutionary relationships, osteology and zoogeography of leptodactyloid frogs. Univ. Kansas Mus. Nat. Hist. Misc. Publ. (53): 1-238.

LYNCH, J. D. 1973. The transition from archaic to advanced frogs, pp. 133-182 in VIAL, J. L. (ed.). Evolutionary biology of the anurans: Contemporary research on major problems. Univ. Missouri Press, Columbia. 470 p.

LYNCH, J. D. 1976. The species groups of the South American frogs of the genus *Eleutherodactylus* (Leptodactylidae). Univ. Kansas Mus. Nat. Hist. Occas. Pap. (61): 1-24.

LYNCH, J. D. 1978. A re-assessment of the telmatobiine frogs of Patagonia. Ibid. (72): 1-57.

LYNCH, J. D., DUELLMAN, W. E. 1979. The *Eleutherodactylus* of the Amazonian slopes of the Ecuadorian Andes (Anura: Leptodactylidae). Univ. Kansas Mus. Nat. Hist. Misc. Publ. (in press).

MALFAIT, B. T., DINKELMAN, M. G. 1972. Circum-Caribbean tectonic and igneous activity and the evolution of the Caribbean Plate. Geol. Soc. Amer. Bull. 82: 251-272.

MAGLIO, V. J. 1970. West Indian xenodontine colubrid snakes: Their probable origin, phylogeny, and zoogeography. Bull. Mus. Comp. Zool. Harvard Univ. (141): 1-53.

MARX, H., RABB, G. B. 1965. Relationships and zoogeography of the viperine snakes (Family Viperidae). Fieldiana Zool. 44: 161-206.

MATTHEW, W. D. 1915. Climate and evolution. Ann. New York Acad. Sci. 24: 171-318.

MAXSON, L. R. 1976. The phylogenetic status of phyllomedusine frogs (Hylidae) as evidenced from immunological studies of their serum albumins. Experientia 32: 1149-1150.

McDIARMID, R. W. 1971. Comparative morphology and evolution of frogs of the Neotropical genera *Atelopus*, *Dendrophryniscus*, *Melanophryniscus*, and *Oreophrynella*. Nat. Hist. Mus. Los Angeles Cty. Sci. Bull. (12): 1-66.

McGOWRAN, B. 1973. Rifting and drift of Australia and the migration of animals. Science 180: 759-761.

MERTENS, R. 1963. Liste der rezenten Amphibien und Reptilien: Helodermatidae, Varanidae, Lanthanotidae. Das Tierreich (79): 1-26.

MERTENS, R. 1966. Liste der rezenten Amphibien und Reptilien: Chamaeleonidae. Ibid. (83): 1-37.

MLSZOELY, C. 1970. North American fossil anguid lizards. Bull. Mus. Comp. Zool. Harvard Univ. 139: 87-149.

MEYER DE SCHAUENSEE, R. 1964. The birds of Colombia. Livingston Publ. Co., Narberth, Pa., 427 p.

MOREAU, R. E. 1963. Vicissitudes of the African biomes in the late Pleistocene. Proc. Zool. Soc. London 141: 395-421.

MOREAU, R. E. 1969. Climatic changes and distribution of forest vertebrates in West Africa. J. Zool. 158: 39-61.

NOBLE, G. K. 1928. Two new fossil Amphibia of zoogeographic importance from the Miocene of Europe. Amer. Mus. Novit. (303): 1-13.

NUSSBAUM, R. A. 1977. Rhinatrematidae: A new family of caecilians (Amphibia: Gymnophiona). Occas. Pap. Mus. Zool. Univ. Michigan (682): 1-30.

PATTERSON, B., PASCUAL, R. 1968. The fossil mammal fauna of South America. Q. Rev. Biol. 43: 409-451.

PETERS, J. A., DONOSO-BARROS, R. 1970. Catalogue of the Neotropical Squamata. Part II. Lizards and amphisbaenians. U.S. Natl. Mus. Bull. (297): 1-293.

PIANKA, E. R. 1971. Lizard species diversity in the Kalahari Desert. Ecology 52: 1024-1029.

PIANKA, E. R., HUEY, R. B. 1971. Bird species diversity in the Kalahari and the Australian deserts. Koedoe 14: 123-130.

RAGE, J.-C. 1973 (1974). Les serpents des Phosphorites du Quercy. Paleovert 6: 273-303.

RAGE, J.-C. 1975b. Un caenophidien primitif (Reptilia: Serpentes) dans l'Eocène inférieur. C. R. Somm. Seances Soc. Geol. France 1975: 46-47.

RAGE, J.-C. 1977. La position phylétique de *Dinilysia patagonica*, serpent du Crétacé supérieur. C. R. Acad. Sci. Paris, Ser. D 284: 1765-1768.

RAVEN, P. H., AXELROD, D. I. 1974. Angiosperm biogeography and past continental movements. Ann. Missouri Bot. Gard. 61: 539-673.

REYMENT, R. A., TAIT, E. A. 1972. Biostratigraphic dating of the early history of the South Atlantic Ocean. Philos. Trans. Roy. Soc. London 264: 55-95.

RICHARDS, P. W. 1973. The tropical rain forest. Sci. Amer. 229: 58-67.

ROSEN, D. E. 1975. A vicariance model of Caribbean biogeography. Syst. Zool. 24: 431-464.

SARMIENTO, G. 1976. Evolution of arid vegetation in tropical America, pp. 65-99 in GOODALL, D. W. (ed.). Evolution of desert biota. Univ. Texas Press, Austin, 250 p.

SAVAGE, J. M. 1963. Studies on the lizard family Xantusiidae IV. The genera. Nat. Hist. Mus. Los Angeles Cty. Contrib. Sci. (71): 1-38.

SAVAGE, J. M. 1966. The origins and history of the Central American herpetofauna. Copeia 1966(4): 719-766.

SAVAGE, J. M. 1968. The dendrobatid frogs of Central America. Ibid. 1968(4): 745-776.

SAVAGE, J. M. 1972. The harlequin frogs, genus *Atelopus* of Costa Rica and western Panama. Herpetologica 28: 77-94.

SAVAGE, J. M. 1973. The geographic distribution of frogs: Patterns and predictions, pp. 351-445 in VIAL, J. L. (ed.). Evolutionary biology of the anurans: Contemporary research on major problems. Univ. Missouri Press, Columbia. 470 p.

SAVAGE, J. M. 1974. The isthmian link and the evolution of Neotropical mammals. Nat. Hist. Mus. Los Angeles Cty. Contrib. Sci. (260): 1-51.

SAVAGE, J. M., CARVALHO, A. I. DE. 1953. The family position of Neotropical frogs currently referred to the genus *Pseudis*. Zoologica 38:193–200.

SAVITZKY, A. H. 1978. The origin of the New World proteroglyphous snakes and its bearing on the study of venom delivery in snakes. PhD Dissert. Univ. Kansas, 387 p.

SCHWARTZ, A. 1972. The native toads (Anura, Bufonidae) of Hispaniola. J. Herpetol. 6:217–231.

SCHWARTZ, A. 1978. Some aspects of the herpetogeography of the West Indies, pp. 31–51 in GILL, F. B. (ed.), Zoogeography in the Caribbean. Acad. Nat. Sci. Philadelphia Spec. Publ. (13) 1–128.

SCHWARTZ, A., THOMAS, R. 1975. A check-list of West Indian amphibians and reptiles. Carnegie Mus. Nat. Hist. Spec. Publ. (1) 1–216.

SILL, W. D. 1968. The zoogeography of the crocodilians. Copeia 1968(1):76–88.

SIMPSON, B. B. 1975. Pleistocene changes in the flora of the high tropical Andes. Paleobiology 1:273–294.

SMITH, H. M., MARTIN, R. L., SWAIN, T. A. 1977. A new genus and two new species of South American geckos (Reptilia, Lacertilia). Pap. Avulsos Zool. (Sao Paulo) 30:195–213.

SOKOL, O. M. 1975. The phylogeny of anuran larvae. A new look. Copeia 1975(1):1–23.

SOLBRIG, O. T. 1976. The origin and floristic affinities of the South American desert and semi-desert regions, pp. 7–49 in GOODALL, D. W. (ed.), Evolution of desert biota. Univ. Texas Press, Austin, 250 p.

STARRETT, P. H. 1973. Evolutionary patterns in larval morphology, pp. 251–271 in VIAL, J. L. (ed.), Evolutionary biology of the anurans. Contemporary research on major problems. Univ. Missouri Press, Columbia, 470 p.

TIHEN, J. A. 1962. A review of New World fossil bufonids. Amer. Midl. Nat. 68:1–50.

TIHEN, J. A. 1964. Tertiary changes in the herpetofaunas of temperate North America. Senckenbergiana Biol. 45:265–279.

TIHEN, J. A. 1972. The fossil record, pp. 8–13 in BLAIR, W. F. (ed.), Evolution in the genus *Bufo*. Univ. Texas Press, Austin, 459 p.

TRUEB, L. 1971. Phylogenetic relationships of certain Neotropical toads with the description of a new genus (Anura, Bufonidae). Nat. Hist. Mus. Los Angeles Cty. Contrib. Sci. (216) 1–40.

TRUEB, L. 1974. Systematic relationships of Neotropical horned frogs, genus *Hemiphractus* (Anura, Hylidae). Univ. Kansas Mus. Nat. Hist. Occas. Pap. (29) 1–60.

TRUEB, L., TYLER, M. J. 1974. Systematics and evolution of the Greater Antillean hylid frogs. Ibid (24) 1–60.

TYLER, M. J. 1974. First fossil frogs from Australia. Nature 248:711–712.

TYLER, M. J., DAVIES, M. 1978. Species groups within the Australopapuan hylid frog genus *Litoria* Tschudi. Australian J. Zool. Suppl. 63:1–47.

TYLER, M. J., DAVIES, M., KING, M. 1978. The Australian frog *Chiroleptes dahlii* Boulenger: Its systematic position, morphology, chromosomes and distribution. Trans. Roy. Soc. South Australia 102:17–23.

VANZOLINI, P. E. 1968. Geography of the South American Gekkonidae (Sauria). Arq. Zool. (Sao Paulo) 17:85–112.

VANZOLINI, P. E. 1974. Ecological and geographical distribution of lizards in Pernambuco, northeastern Brasil (Sauria). Pap. Avulsos Zool. (Sao Paulo) 28:61–90.

VANZOLINI, P. E. 1976. On the lizards of a cerrado-caatinga contact: Evolutionary and zoogeographical implications (Sauria). Ibid 29:111–119.

VANZOLINI, P. E., WILLIAMS, E. E. 1970. South American anoles: The geographic differentiation and evolution of the *Anolis chrysolepis* species group (Sauria, Iguanidae). Arq. Zool. (Sao Paulo) 19:1–298.

VEEVERS, J. J., McELHINNY, M. W. 1976. The separation of Australia from other continents. Earth Sci. Rev. 12:139–159.

VUILLEUMIER, F. 1968. Origin of frogs of Patagonian forests. Nature 219:87–89.

WAKE, D. B. 1966. Comparative osteology and evolution of the lungless salamanders, family Plethodontidae. Mem. South California Acad. Sci. (4) 1–111.

WEBB, S. D. 1978. A history of savanna vertebrates in the New World. Part II. South America and the great interchange. Ann. Rev. Ecol. Syst. 9:393–436.

WERMUTH, H. 1965. Liste der rezenten Amphibien und Reptilien. Gekkonidae, Pygopodidae, Xantusiidae. Das Tierreich (80) 1–246.

WERMUTH, H. 1967. Liste der rezenten Amphibien und Reptilien. Agamidae. Ibid (86) 1–127.

WERMUTH, H. 1968. Liste der rezenten Amphibien und Reptilien. Cordylidae. Ibid (87) 1–30.

WILLIAMS, E. E. 1969. The ecology of colonization as seen in the zoogeography of anoline lizards on small islands. Q. Rev. Biol. 44:345–389.

WOLFE, J. A. 1971. Tertiary climatic fluctuations and methods of analysis of Tertiary floras. Palaeogeogr. Palaeoclimatol. Palaeoecol. 9:27–57.

WOOD, R. C. 1971. The fossil Pelomedusidae (Testudines, Pleurodira) of Africa. PhD Dissert. Harvard Univ., 345 p.

WOOD, R. C., PATTERSON, B. 1973. A fossil trionychid turtle from South America. Breviora (415) 1–10.

ZWEIFEL, R. G. 1972. Results of the Archbold Expeditions. No. 97. A revision of the subfamily Asterophryinae, family Microhylidae. Bull. Amer. Mus. Nat. Hist. 148:411–546.

2. The South American Herpetofauna: An Evaluation of the Fossil Record

Ana María Báez

*Departamento de Geología
Facultad de Ciencias Exactas y Naturales
Universidad de Buenos Aires
Buenos Aires, Argentina*

Zulma B. de Gasparini

*Facultad de Ciencias Naturales y Museo
Universidad Nacional de La Plata
La Plata, Argentina*

The presence of fossil remains of amphibians and reptiles related to living taxa in South America has been documented since the last century. Nevertheless, examination of this literature reveals that in many cases the names are only mentioned and the material has not been studied; in many other cases it is evident that a revision is badly needed.

Partial reviews concerning several South American countries have been carried out (Argentina: Pascual, 1970, Pascual and Odreman Rivas, 1971, Gasparini and Baez, 1975; Brasil: Paula Couto, 1970; Colombia: Hoffstetter, 1970a; Ecuador: Hoffstetter, 1970b; Peru: Hoffstetter, 1970c; Uruguay: Mones, 1972, 1975). Also, Báez and Gasparini (1977) critically examined the Cenozoic record of amphibians and reptiles in that continent and analyzed distributional shifts, relating them to the Cenozoic environmental changes that occurred as a result of different geological events.

In this paper, the available paleontological data are summarized in an attempt to evaluate the information that the fossil record can provide about the historical development of these groups in South America. The taxonomic assignment and the geographic and stratigraphic references are sometimes doubtful, questionable referrals are not considered. Some recent finds are currently under study and identification of genera and species is not yet available, thus only an analysis at the family level is possible at present. The main areas that have yielded fossil amphibians and reptiles referable to modern groups are shown in figures 2.4-7. A checklist of the material recorded there and the corresponding literature references appear in Appendix 2.1.

Inspection of the fossil record reveals that many families comprising the present South American herpetofauna have a considerable antiquity in that continent. Their presence, and even that of some recent genera, extends back to the late Mesozoic and early Tertiary (Figs. 2.1-3). Thus, it is essential to consider the past changes in the geographical position of South America and its connections with other continents, especially from the Middle Mesozoic onward, for those changes must have affected distribution patterns.

According to recent paleomagnetic data (Vilas and Valencio, 1978a), South America was part of Gondwanaland, which may have existed up to the Late Jurassic. It was still joined to Africa during the Early Cretaceous (Reyment and Tait, 1972; Douglas, Moullade and Nairn, 1973; Vilas and Valencio, 1978), while faunal relations with Antarctica-Australia seem to have been possible up to the Early Tertiary (Raven and Axelrod, 1975). There is no clear evidence that a direct land connection between North and South America existed from the Jurassic to the end of the Tertiary (Malfait and Dinkelman, 1972; McKenna, 1973). Nevertheless, a discontinuous pathway along a chain of volcanic islands could have been established at different times (Haffer, 1970; Malfait and Dinkelman, 1972). There is no agreement concerning the time of final reconnection between both Americas. Some evidence indicates that the Isthmus of Panama was established during

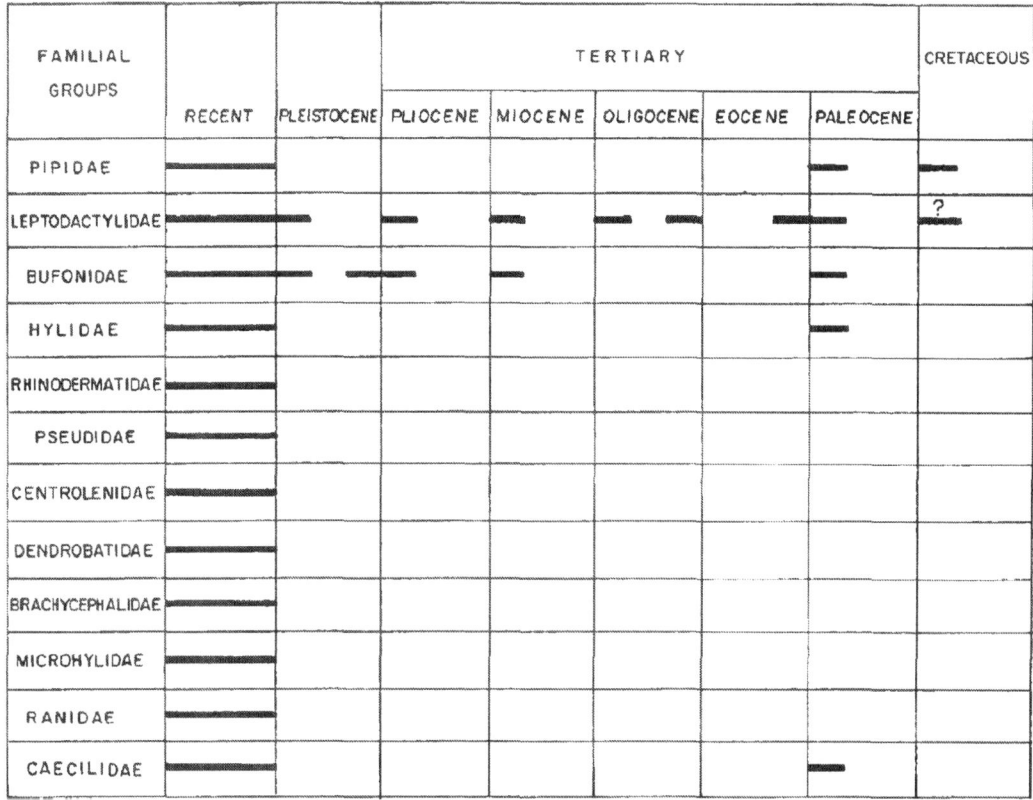

Fig. 2:1. Chronological range (Cretaceous-Recent) of Anura and Gymnophiona in South America. Distribución cronológica (Cretácico-Reciente) de Anura y Gymnophiona en América del Sur.

the late Pliocene–early Pleistocene (Patterson and Pascual, 1968); others favor its earlier existence (Emiliani et al., 1972; Savage, 1974). Thus, it is implied that biogeographical relationships with Africa and Australia may have been close until the end of the Mesozoic, whereas those with North America became more important by the Late Tertiary.

Available paleomagnetic data suggest that the latitudinal position of South America did not alter significantly since the latest Paleozoic, although displacements of about 5°, at most, may have existed in some areas because of the different orientation of the continent (Vilas and Valencio, 1978, 1979). Thus, these changes are disregarded here because they are insufficient to account for the different distributions of many groups in the past as evidenced by the fossil record.

The dispersal history of amphibians and reptiles also has been very closely related to past climates. In South America climatic-ecologic conditions were more equable during at least the Cretaceous and early Tertiary. Various kinds of evidence indicate that a warm and humid climate prevailed then at high latitudes (Pascual and Odreman Rivas, 1971; Archangelsky and Romero, 1974; Petriella and Archangelsky, 1975). Throughout the Cenozoic, geologic events of different magnitude provoked physiographic, and consequently, climatic and floristic changes. Although these changes restricted the dispersal of some groups, they multiplied the available environments and thereby promoted the appearance of new adaptive types.

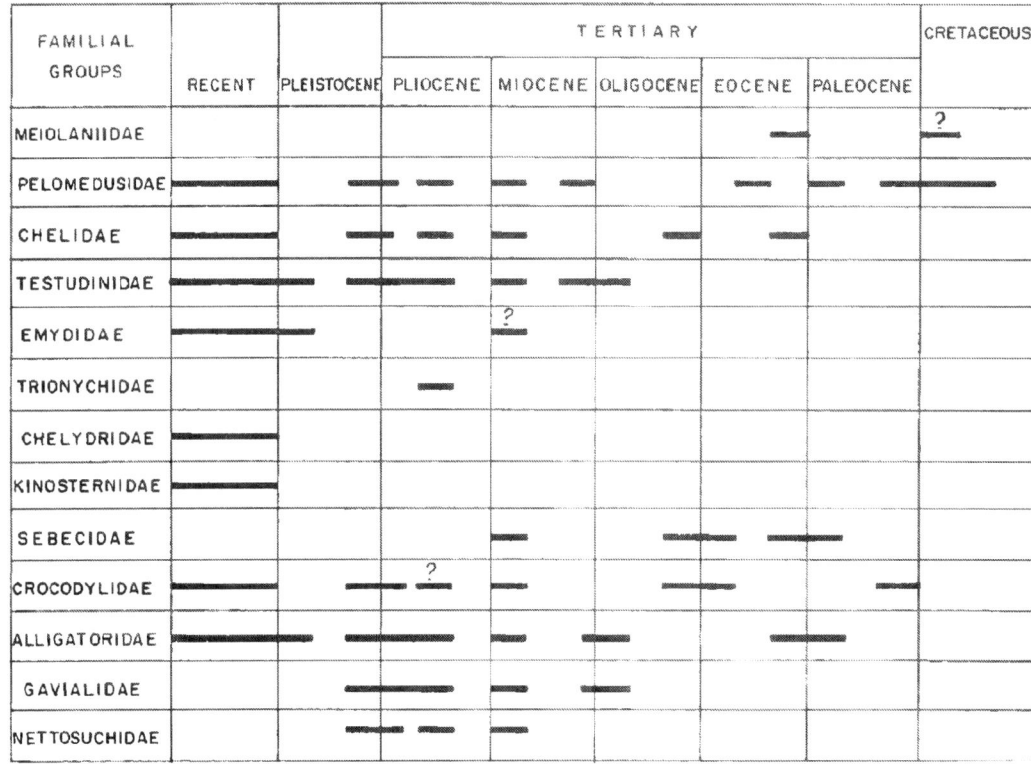

Fig. 2:2. Chronological range (Cretaceous-Recent) of Testudines and Crocodilia in South America. Family groups without Cenozoic records have not been included.

Distribución cronológica (Cretácico-Reciente) de Testudines y Crocodilia en América del Sur. Las familias sin registros cenozoicos no han sido incluidas.

THE FOSSIL RECORD OF MODERN GROUPS OF AMPHIBIANS AND REPTILES IN SOUTH AMERICA

The oldest known fossils referable to family groups that comprise the present South American herpetofauna appear in that continent in Cretaceous deposits. The presence of pipid frogs, iguanid lizards and pelomedusid turtles in the Late Cretaceous is documented by the fossil record. Pelomedusid turtles were quite diversified and widely distributed at that time (Fig. 2:4). It is noteworthy that the extant pelomedusid genus *Podocnemis* was present then. Leptodactylid frogs perhaps also are present in Cretaceous horizons.

The earliest Cenozoic records of amphibians and reptiles come almost exclusively from southern South America—Patagonia and southeastern Brasil (Fig. 2:5). The early and late Paleocene Patagonian localities have yielded remains of turtles (only pelomedusids can be ascertained definitely), eusuchian crocodilians (including crocodylids) and boid snakes. Most of this material is very fragmentary, but these records are quite interesting from a paleoclimatic point of view, for they indicate humid subtropical conditions at latitudes of about 45°S. On the other hand, the rich and diversified assemblage of late Paleocene age of Itaboraí, Brasil, provides more comprehensive information about the family groups that were inhabiting South America at that time. However, most of this material has yet to be studied.

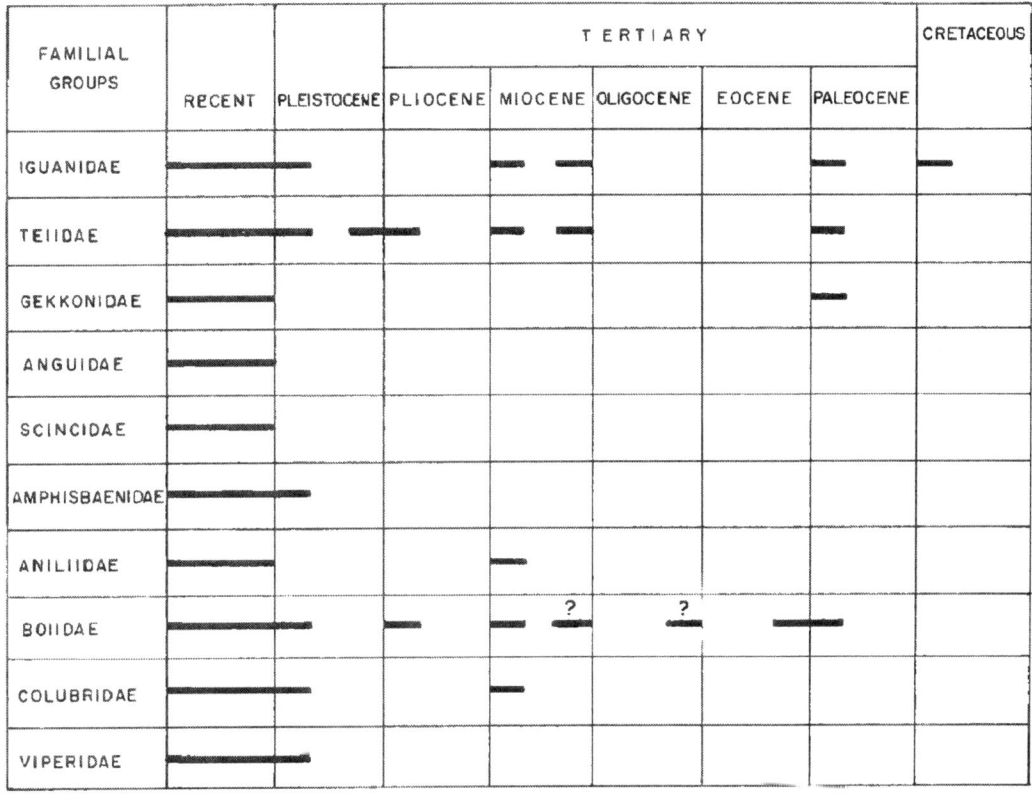

Fig. 2:3. Chronological range (Cretaceous-Recent) of Squamata, exclusive of scolecophidian snakes, in South America.
Distribución cronológica (Cretácica-Reciente) de Squamata, excluyendo serpientes scolecofidias, en América del Sur.

In the known Paleocene sites, fourteen families have been recorded, all of them (except the extinct sebecid crocodilians) are represented in the present-day fauna of South America. They include the Caeciliidae, Pipidae, Leptodactylidae, Bufonidae, Hylidae, Pelomedusidae, Crocodylidae, Alligatoridae, Iguanidae, Teiidae, Gekkonidae, Aniliidae, and Boidae. Among these families we can recognize elements that are of diverse historical backgrounds, and that joined the fauna of present-day South America at different times and developed *in situ*.

Presently-known Eocene faunas also were found mainly in the southern part of the continent (Fig. 2:5). Sebecid and alligatorid crocodilians are still recorded at latitudes of about 46°S, thereby indicating that at least warm temperate conditions persisted there. Noteworthy is the appearance of chelid turtles, whose extinct and living representatives have been found only in Australia and South America. The Eocene remains have been referred to the extant genus *Hydromedusa*, which now extends as far south as 36°S. The living leptodactylid genus *Caudiverbera* is known from Eocene deposits of Patagonia, where it was associated with crocodilian remains.

The earliest known Cenozoic records of amphibians and reptiles in northernmost South America come mainly from Oligocene sites, especially several localities in the upper and middle Magdalena River Valley, Colombia (Fig. 2:6). These assemblages are characterized by the abundance of mesosuchian

(Sebecidae) and eusuchian (Alligatoridae, Crocodylidae, Gavialidae) crocodilians, which is explained by the presence there of an extensive lowland with local swamps and lakes (Van Houten and Travis, 1968) All of the families recorded from those horizons also are represented in older deposits of more southern latitudes, except gavialid crocodilians, whose affinities are still uncertain

Oligocene localities in central Patagonia (Fig 2 6) have yielded remains of the extant lepodactylid genera *Eupsophus* and *Caudiverbera*, whose presence there was made possible by the prevalence of more mesic conditions at that time The oldest known testudinid turtle in South America a species of the genus *Geochelone* related to the living *C chilensis* (Auffenberg 1971), is recorded in the upper Oligocene of Patagonia

Very rich, late Miocene faunas are known from the upper Magdalena River Valley, Colombia, where the general environmental conditions of Oligocene times did not change significantly, although important tectonic events took place in the Miocene (Irving, 1971) Most of the families present there have previous records in the continent, the majority being represented by extant genera or species *Bufo marinus, Podocnemis expansa, Tupinambis* cf *T teguixin, Dracaena, Eunectes, Caiman* Also a turtle, *Geochelone hesterna*, closely related to the living *G carbonaria* and *G denticulata* (Auffenberg 1971) was recorded The appearance of two families Colubridae and Nettosuchidae, in the fossil record is noteworthy The latter are endemic eusuchian crocodilians seemingly restricted to tropical regions from Miocene to Plio-Pleistocene times

The southernmost records of Cenozoic amphibians or reptiles on the continent come from early to middle Miocene deposits of southern Patagonia (Fig 2 6) Iguanids, teiids and other lizards, turtles and snakes have been found there, but all of this material has yet to be restudied The post-Miocene history of the Patagonian herpetofauna is not documented in the fossil record The increasing aridity that developed there as a consequence of the Andean tectonic movements and the continuous uplift of that area throughout the late Cenozoic made the preservation of remains unlikely

Numerous crocodilian fossils, all referable to the suborder Eusuchia (Alligatoridae, Gavialidae, Nettosuchidae and probably Crocodylidae) are recorded in the upper Pliocene of northern Venezuela (Fig 2 7) The gigantic size exhibited by many members of these taxa and the appearance of the extant alligatorid, *Melanosuchus* is noteworthy The possible presence of trionychid turtles there should be noted This group is not represented in the present fauna of South America, and may have reached the continent from the north

In Pliocene times the Río Paraná constituted, as it does today, an important pathway for the southward migration of elements of the subtropical biota This explains the record of alligatorid and gavialid crocodilians in Pliocene deposits near the city of Paraná, Argentina (Fig 2 7) Among them, *Caiman latirostris* and possibly *Rhamphostomopsis* were already represented in the late Miocene faunas of Colombia

Numerous remains of amphibians and reptiles have been reported from horizons of late Pliocene age in Monte Hermoso, Argentina (Fig 2 7) The presence there of the living teiid genus *Callopistes* is especially significant considering its present range, which is on the arid Pacific lowlands of Perú and Chile

The relatively few Pleistocene sites that have yielded amphibians or reptiles are important because they document the past presence of families that currently inhabit South America, and that have not been recorded in older deposits Among these families are emydids, viperids, and amphisbaenids The Pleistocene records also suggest that significant environmental changes occurred at that time, because the distribution of some taxa is inconsistent with the present distribution of their habitats For example, the Pleistocene faunules from Talara, northwestern Perú (Lemon and Churcher, 1961, Hoffstetter, 1970c) and from the Santa Elena Peninsula, southwestern Ecuador (see Appendix 2 1), indicate that more mesic environments prevailed in those areas in the near past

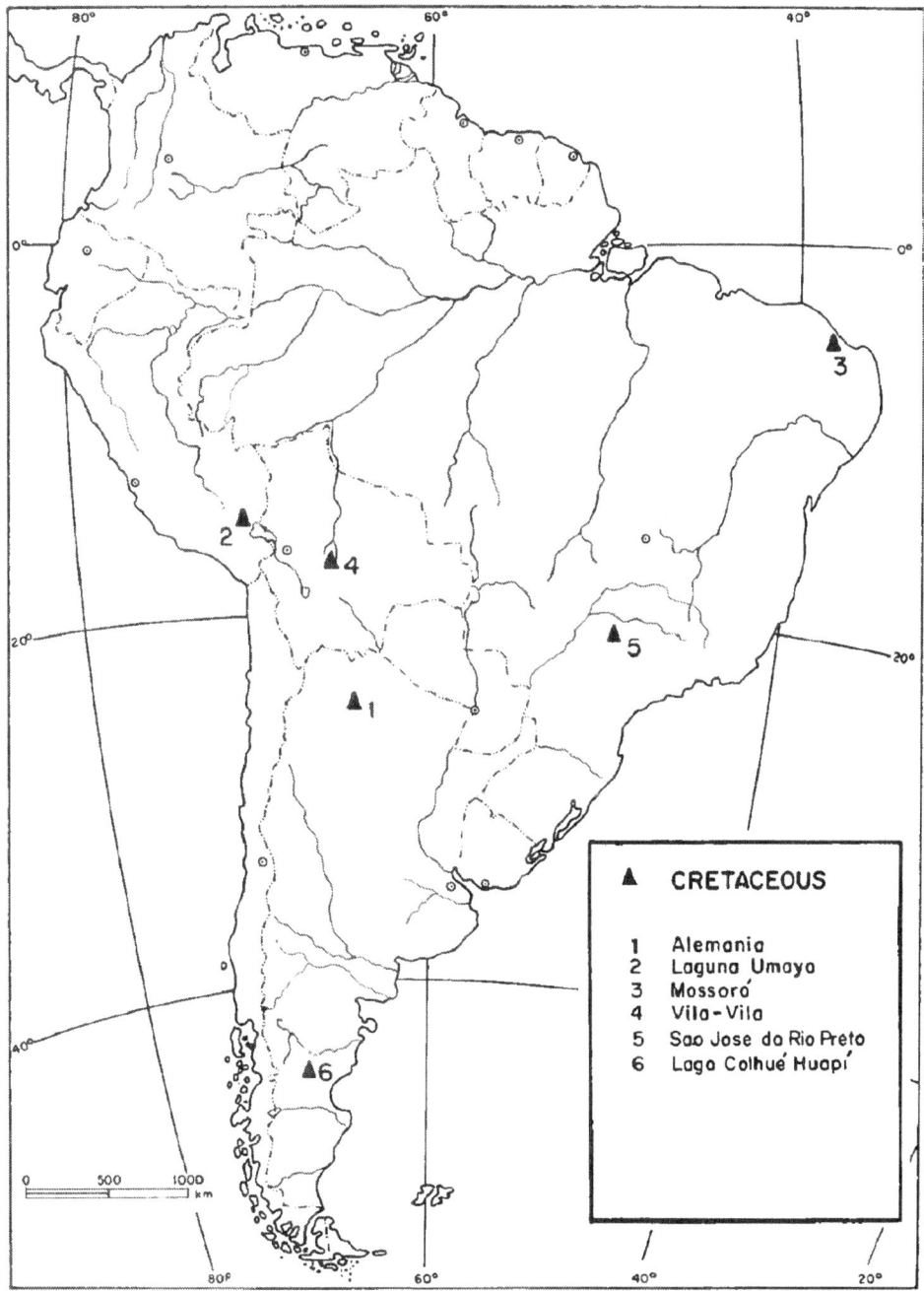

Fig. 2:4. Major areas in South America that have yielded Cretaceous amphibians and/or reptiles of modern groups.
Principales áreas en América del Sur que han brindado anfibios y/o reptiles cretácicos de grupos modernos.

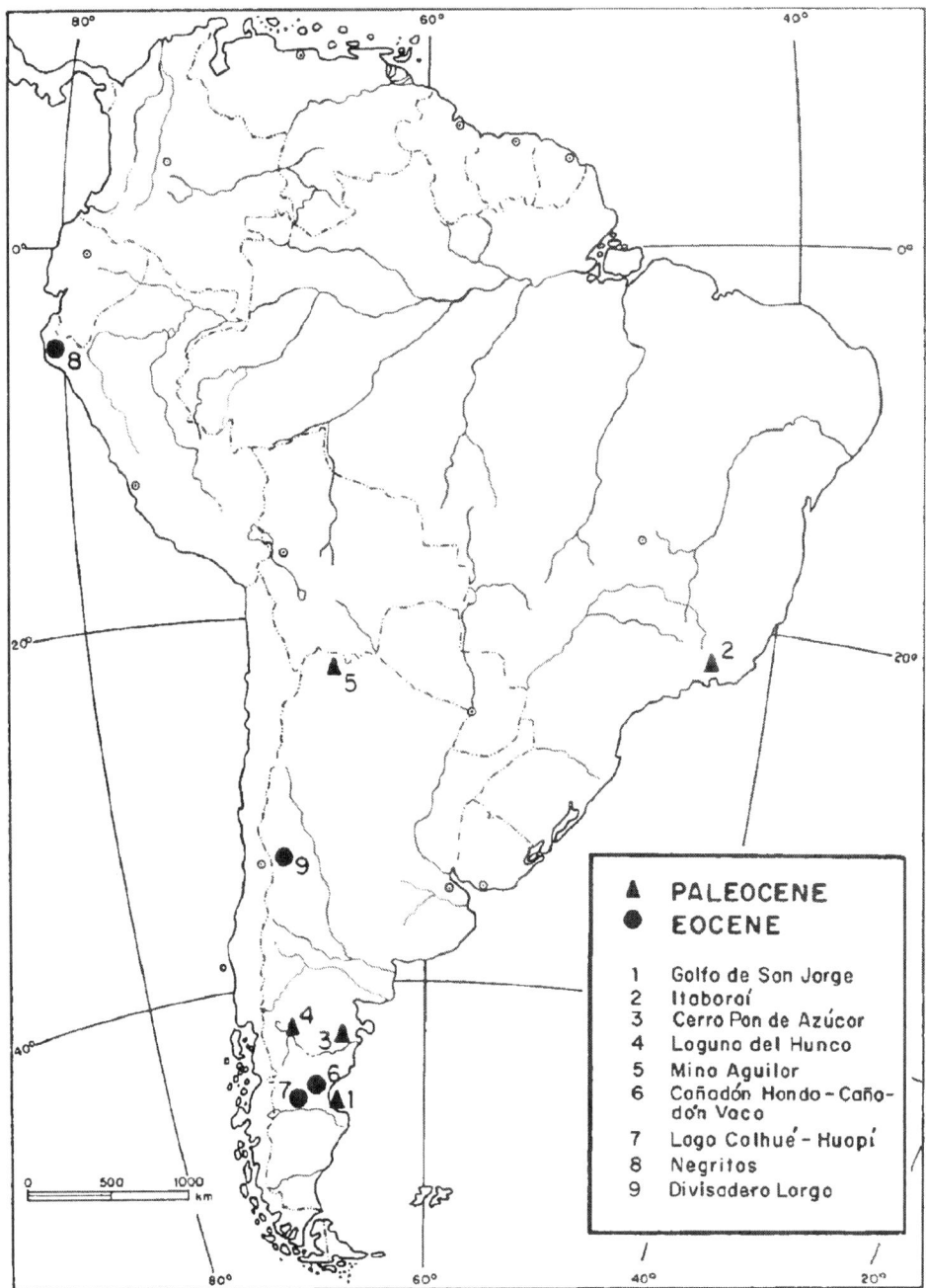

Fig. 2:5. Major areas in South America that have yielded amphibians and/or reptiles of Paleocene and Eocene age.

Principales áreas en América del Sur que han brindado anfibios y/o reptiles de edad paleocena y eocena.

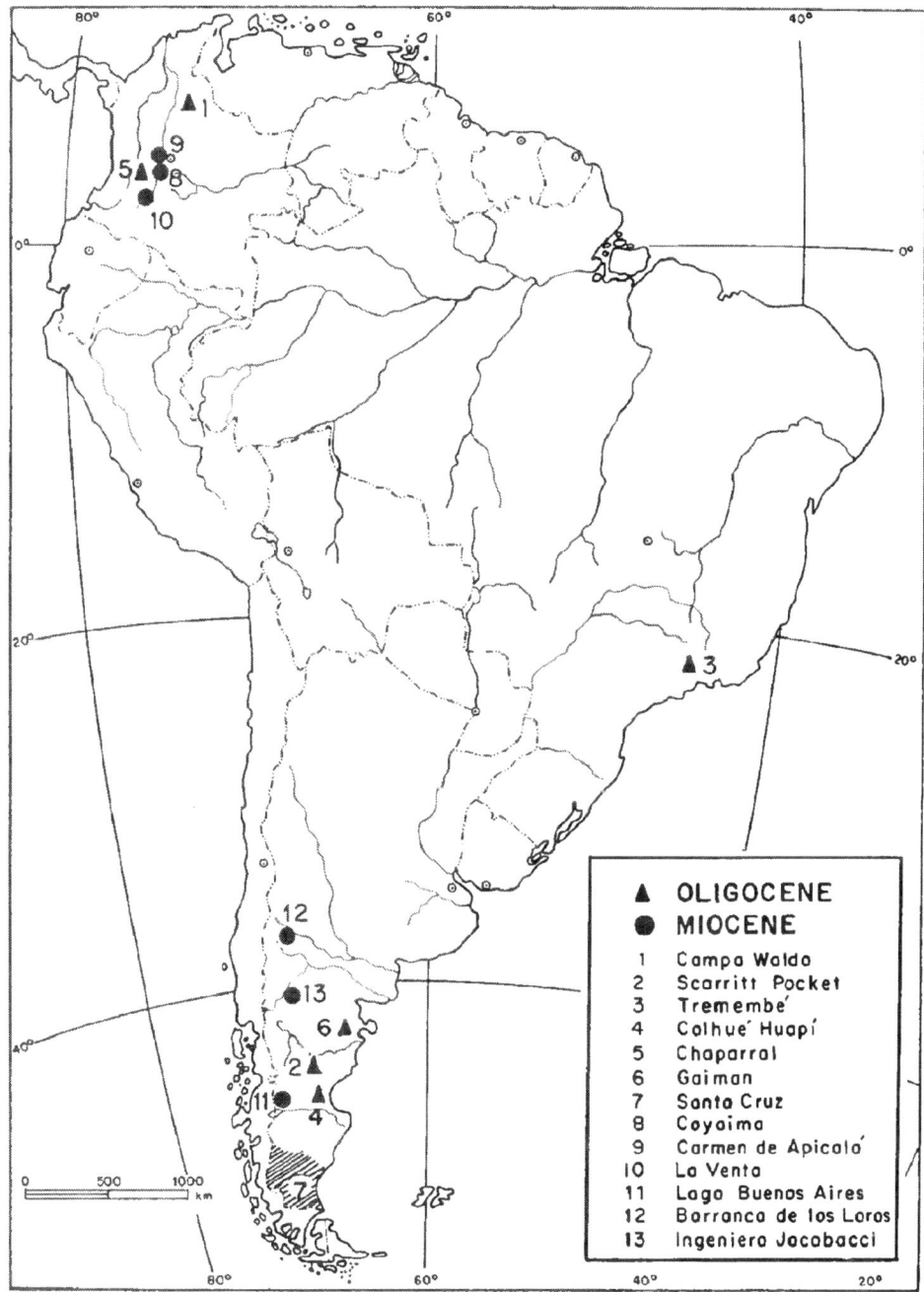

Fig. 2:6. Major areas in South America that have yielded amphibians and/or reptiles of Oligocene and Miocene age.
Principales áreas en América del Sur que han brindado anfibios y/o reptiles de edad oligocena y miocena.

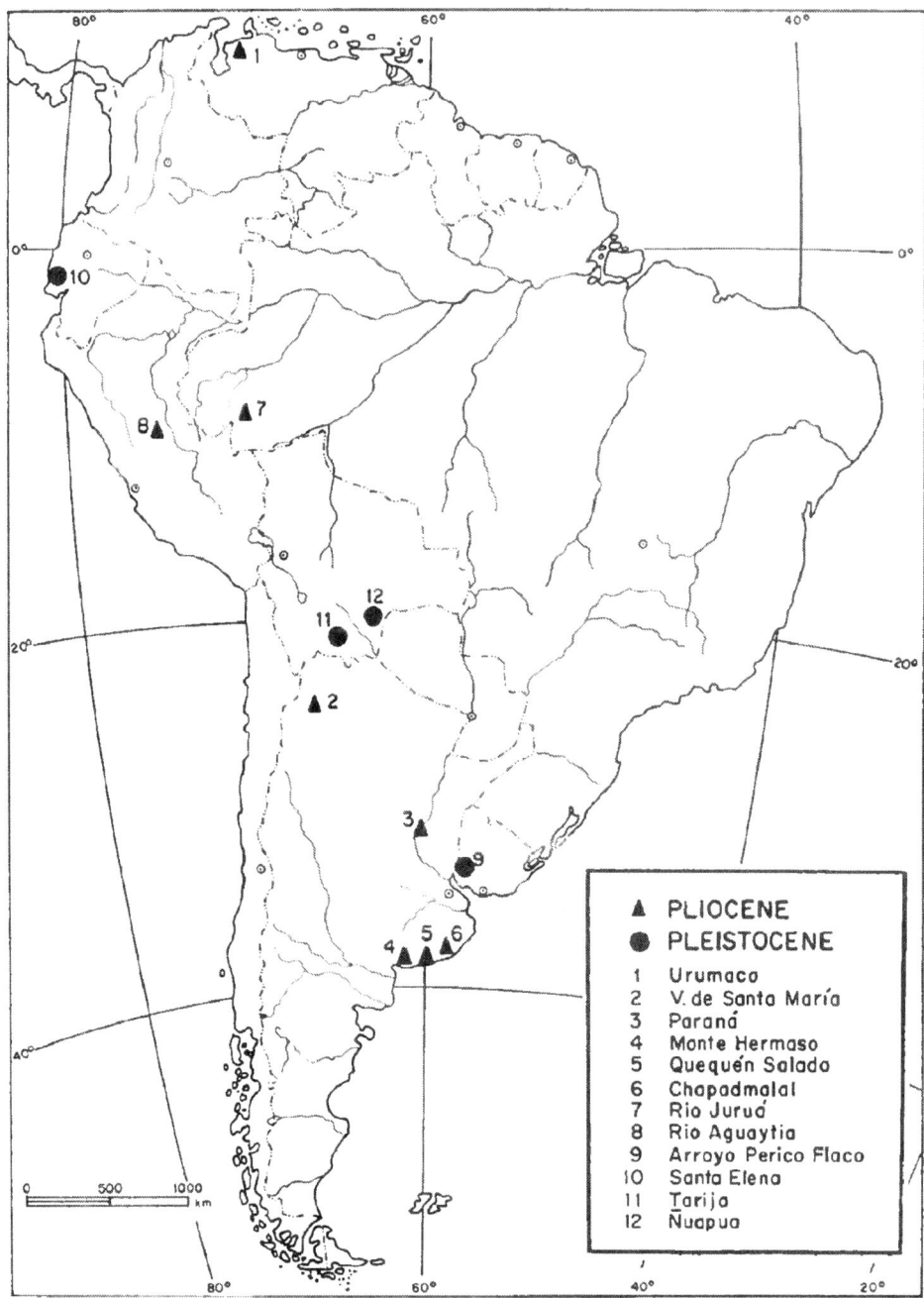

FIG. 2;7. Major areas in South America that have yielded amphibians and/or reptiles of Pliocene and Pleistocene age.
Principales áreas en América del Sur que han brindado anfibios y/o reptiles de edad pliocena y pleistocena.

AMPHIBIANS

The fossil record of modern amphibian groups in South America is largely restricted to anurans. The only known caecilian fossil is from the late Paleocene of Brasil; this record implies that caecilians are old components of the South American herpetofauna. No salamander fossils are known from South America.

The considerable diversity of anuran groups already present by the early Tertiary in South America is noteworthy. Furthermore, their phylogenetic relationships and the fact that some of them were represented by taxa similar to extant South American genera or species indicate that they have had a long history there. However, many families that comprise the present anuran fauna are unknown as fossils.

The aquatic frogs of the family Pipidae now live in South America and Africa; they constitute an ancient, independent lineage. The earliest pipids are from the Early Cretaceous of Israel (Nevo, 1968) but their origin probably extends back into the Jurassic. Unquestionable pipids occur in the Cretaceous and Tertiary of both Africa and South America; this strongly suggests that pipids were components of the Gondwanan fauna. Furthermore, remains referable to the African genus Xenopus have been recorded from both continents (Ahl, 1926, Vergnaud-Grazzini 1966, Brom et al., 1974, Estes, 1975a,b, Baez, 1976). The fossil record indicates that different phyletic lines of pipids have existed in South America. The oldest known example there is *Saltenia ibanezi* from the Late Cretaceous of northwestern Argentina. Members of the extant genus *Xenopus* have been recorded in the late Paleocene of Brasil and Argentina. No fossil taxa directly ancestral to the living Neotropical Pipinae are known.

The Leptodactylidae are another ancient component of the South American fauna. The oldest known remains unquestionably referable to the family come from late Paleocene deposits in Brasil; undescribed taxa close to living genera and perhaps even an extant genus are present there (Estes and Reig, 1973). This group probably is represented in the Late Cretaceous of Perú (Sigé, 1968), but that record has not been confirmed. Other early presumed records outside of South America have been discarded or questioned (Hecht 1963, Estes, 1964, 1969 Reig 1968, Lynch, 1971, Savage, 1973). Available evidence indicates that the Leptodactylidae in its restricted sense (Lynch 1973) may have differentiated in South America from a stock associated with temperate forests (Lynch, 1971, Savage, 1973, Heyer 1975). The proposed relationships to leiopelmatids (Heyer, 1975) are significant in that the latter inhabited Patagonia by Jurassic times (Estes and Reig 1973). Leptodactylids must have dispersed northward early in their history. Widespread occurrence of subhumid environments in middle latitudes in the Late Jurassic and Early Cretaceous might have been influential in the development of xeric-adapted types of leptodactylids (Baez and Gasparini, 1977). Telmatobiine leptodactylids, which represent an ancient radiation, are recorded in the Tertiary of Patagonia. The extant genus *Caudiverbera* appears in early Eocene, early and late Oligocene, and late Miocene deposits. By the early Oligocene two other genera were present—the living *Eupsophus* and the extinct *Neoprocoela*; the assignment of *Neoprocoela* to this family has been discussed by Tihen (1962, 1972) and Lynch (1971). These records furnish evidence of their former wider distribution east of the Andes, and therefore reflect the mesic climate that prevailed in those now arid regions (Gasparini and Báez, 1975). Ceratophryine leptodactylids, which some authors give familial status, are first recorded in the late Miocene of northern Patagonia but they must have originated much earlier. The basic adaptation of this group to an arid environment (Heyer, 1975) could account for the paucity of paleontological evidence for its early evolution because few fossil-bearing horizons representing those environments are known, particularly in the Late Mesozoic and Early Tertiary. Remains referable to the extant genus *Ceratophrys* (specific allocation undetermined) are known from the late Pliocene and middle Pleistocene of Argentina (Baez and Gasparini, 1977). The living *C. ornata* probably is represented in the late Pliocene of Argentina (Reig 1958) and late Pleistocene of Bolivia, and *C. aurita* is known from the latest Pleistocene in Brasil (Lynch, 1971). Records of other leptodactylids are limited to the living genus *Leptodactylus* from Pleistocene deposits.

The earliest known record of the cosmopolitan bufonid toads (absent from Australia and Madagascar) is from the late Paleocene of Brasil. Although this material has not yet been described the presence of members of living species groups of *Bufo* has been recognized (Estes and Reig 1973). This supports the proposal that bufonids are ancient components of the South American fauna and that they could have had a southern origin (Lynch, 1971; Reig 1972; Savage, 1973). No unquestionable bufonids are known in North America prior to the early Miocene (Tihen, 1972). Moreover, assignment of specimens of Early Tertiary age from Europe to the Bufonidae is highly doubtful; remains referable to the genus *Bufo* are unknown there before the middle Miocene (Tihen, 1972). Different evidence suggests that South America is the most likely area of origin of *Bufo* (Blair, 1972). Although sparse, the fossil record indicates that considerable diversification within that genus took place in South America at least since the Early Tertiary. Members of the *marinus* group of *Bufo* have been reported as far back as the late Miocene, although an earlier differentiation of that group seems likely. Tihen (1972) and Estes and Reig (1973) considered *Neoprocoela* to be a member of the *Bufo calamita* group, which is now confined to the Old World (also see Gallardo, 1962).

The Hylidae is poorly represented in the fossil record. The earliest remains referred to this family are from the late Paleocene of Brasil, but the material is still undescribed (Estes and Reig, 1973). This testifies to the early presence of hylid frogs in South America, and is consistent with the high degree of differentiation that they attained there during the time of isolation, as well as their possible origin on that continent (Savage, 1973). The now widespread genus *Hyla* has been recorded from the early Oligocene of Canada (Holman, 1968) and the early Miocene of Florida in the United States (Tihen, 1964). The paleontological data add little information to the biogeographical history of hylids.

Frogs are ancient members of South American fauna. Pipids, leptodactylids, bufonids and hylids are old components and are the only frog families represented in the South American fossil record. Other groups such as rhinodermatids and dendrobatids, differentiated on that continent probably during the Tertiary. On the other hand, ranids are late immigrants from the north.

REPTILES

Pelomedusid turtles presently inhabit South America, Africa and Madagascar, but they were more widely distributed in Late Mesozoic and Early Tertiary times (Romer, 1966; Gaffney and Zangerl 1968; Wood 1970, 1976b; Jimenez Fuentes, 1971, 1975; Gaffney 1975). The earliest-known pelomedusids are from Early Cretaceous deposits in Africa (Broin et al, 1974), and remains of Late Cretaceous age have been reported from South America, North America, Africa, and Europe. The greater proximity of continents at that time (Smith, Briden and Drewry, 1973), coupled with the presumed marine habits of some of these turtles (Wood, 1972, 1976b) could have favored such wide distribution. The majority of the South American fossil pelomedusids that have been described are referred to the genus *Podocnemis*, which is still present in South America and Madagascar. The presence of that genus in South America extends back to the Late Cretaceous, at which time the genus was represented by a species, *P. elegans* noted as being "strikingly modern in aspect" (Wood 1971:275).[1] Numerous fossil remains have been assigned to *Podocnemis*, but there is no general agreement concerning the validity of species (Wood and Gamero, 1971; Báez and Gasparini, 1977). By the late Miocene the extant *P. expansa* was already in existence. Remains referable to the genus *Podocnemis* are cited outside of South America from Africa and western Europe. Pelomedusids referable to other genera have been described from the

---

[1] Dr. F. de Broin (pers. comm.) considers that *Podocnemis elegans* may belong to the extinct pelomedusid genus *Roxochelys*, related to *Podocnemis*.

Cenozoic of South America. A species of the genus *Taphrosphys* occurs in the Eocene of coastal Peru. That genus, which includes marine forms, is also recorded from the Cretaceous of North America and Paleocene of Africa (Wood 1975). The gigantic Pliocene *Stupendemys geographicus* exhibits many unusual characteristics, and its affinities are still not clear (Wood, 1976b).

The freshwater turtles of the family Chelidae occur today in South America, Australia and New Guinea. The geographical location of fossils assigned to this group indicates that they could have had an essentially similar former range because the only known unquestionable records come from the early Eocene of southern Argentina, middle Tertiary of Australia, and Oligocene or Miocene of Tasmania (Warren, 1969). That evidence suggests an area of dispersal that included also Antarctica and that the past relations between South American and Antarctica-Australia (McGowran 1973, Dalziel et al., 1973, Sclater and Fisher, 1974) could account for the present range. A species of the extant South American genus *Hydromedusa* is the oldest member (Eocene) of the family recorded so far (Wood and Moody, 1976). Two extinct species of the now monotypic genus *Chelus* have been described—*C. colombianus* from the late Miocene of Colombia and *C. lewisi* from the Pliocene of Venezuela (Wood, 1976a). Neither of these seem to have been directly ancestral to the living species, thereby indicating that different lineages evolved within the genus (Wood 1976a).

Testudinid turtles are represented in South America by the genus *Geochelone*, with a world-wide distribution in the Early Tertiary. Fossils having similarities with an extant Asiatic species have been recorded from Eocene deposits in North America and Africa, and also from the early Oligocene of North America, Asia and Western Europe (Auffenberg 1974). The earliest representative of the genus *Geochelone* in South America is *G. gringorum* from the late Oligocene of Patagonia (Simpson 1942). Auffenberg (1971) suggested that the ancestors of the South American species comprising the distinctive subgenus *Chelonoides*, probably entered that continent from the north during the Oligocene or even earlier. It is noteworthy that even though chelonians are known since the Late Cretaceous, no testudinids have been reported before the late Oligocene, whereas their presence is documented frequently since the late Miocene. Assuming an entrance from the north this partially could result from the fact that most known early Tertiary reptile-bearing sites are in the southern part of the continent. However, an arrival earlier than late Eocene times seems improbable. *Geochelone gringorum* is closely related and may be ancestral to the living *G. chilensis*, which became adapted to drier conditions (Auffenberg, 1971). Increasingly xeric environments developed in western mid-latitudes east of the Andes since the Pleistocene (Báez and Scillato Yané this volume). The related Pliocene *G. gallardoi* has been recorded in areas where a marked dry season presumably existed. *Geochelone hesterna* from the late Miocene of Colombia is thought to be ancestral to the extant species *G. carbonaria* and *G. denticulata* that now live in the northern part of the continent (Auffenberg 1971).

Although emydid turtles now occur in South America their presence there during the Tertiary is still uncertain. The existence of remains referable to the Emydidae among the material collected from late Miocene deposits in Colombia was mentioned by Medem (1966, 1968), but the record has not been substantiated. The extant genus *Geoemyda* is known from the late Pleistocene of Ecuador.

No fossil records of the Chelydridae and Kinosternidae are known in South America. Trionychids, old members of the North American faunas, are not present today in South America. Their presence in northern Venezuela in the late Pliocene could have resulted from waif dispersal but their colonization was not successful (Wood and Patterson 1973).

In the Late Cretaceous and Early Tertiary a peculiar group of land turtles of uncertain affinities, the Meiolaniidae, was also part of the herpetofauna of southern South America. They also have been recorded in Australia where they survived until Pleistocene times.

In summary, pelomedusids are ancient components of the chelonian faunas of South

America, being continuously represented since the Late Mesozoic. *Podocnemis*, the only living genus in South America, is known since the Late Cretaceous; it has undergone considerable speciation. Chelids also are old members of the fauna, even though no occurrence prior to the early Eocene is known. No land turtles are known from the Late Mesozoic and Early Tertiary besides meiolaniids. Their ecological role was assumed later by the testudinid *Geochelone*, which entered the continent probably in Eocene–Oligocene times.

The fossil record of the lizard family Iguanidae in South America is fragmentary, a situation that contrasts with its significance in the present Neotropical herpetofauna. Although the former presence of this group in Asia and Europe has been discarded (Hoffstetter, 1962; Estes, 1970), fossils referable to this family have been recorded in North America, but none antedates the early Eocene (Estes and Price, 1973). The earliest record of an iguanid is from the Upper Cretaceous of Brasil, and the family is represented by at least five species in the late Paleocene fauna from Itaboraí, Brasil, thereby indicating an early radiation in South America (Estes, 1970). Presently-known data are consistent with the suggested Gondwanan origin of iguanids (Cracraft, 1973). The group could have entered North America from the south by waif dispersal, becoming quite diversified by Miocene times (Robinson and Van Devender, 1973). By the Miocene, iguanids attained a wide distribution in South America, but little is known of the taxa present at that time (Baez and Gasparini, 1977). Extant representatives of the family are recorded from late Pleistocene deposits. *Iguana* in coastal Ecuador (Hoffstetter, 1970b) and *Leiosaurus bellii* in central-western Argentina (Van Devender, 1977).

The evolution of teiids took place primarily in South America, where they are most diverse and widely distributed today. In the Late Cretaceous teiids were present in North America (Estes, 1964, 1969), although these early records do not seem to be of direct significance in the establishment of the Recent teiids there (Estes, 1970). On the other hand, fossil remains referable to the Teiidae and resembling primitive living South American taxa have been recorded from the late Paleocene of Brasil (Estes, 1970). Their absence in the Cretaceous is not surprising because continental Middle and Late Mesozoic faunas are still poorly known in South America. Practically all later teiid fossils (Miocene–Pleistocene) have been referred to the extant South American genera *Tupinambis*, *Dracaena*, *Callopistes*, and *Dicrodon*, although differences in distributions are evident when compared with their present ranges (Baez and Gasparini, 1977).

Very few fossil records of the other lizard families now inhabiting South America are known from that continent. However gekkonids occur in the upper Paleocene of Brasil. Although this is the earliest known record of the family, the origin of gekkonids could extend back to the Late Mesozoic, upon consideration of their relationships with some Jurassic European and Asiatic taxa (Hoffstetter, 1964; Kluge, 1967). Living South American representatives might have been derived from different sources; the strong African affinities of sphaerodactylines (Kluge, 1967) could be interpreted as resulting from the past connections of those continents (Estes, 1970). The presence of scincids in South America was extended back to the Paleocene (Estes, 1976). These lizards are seemingly already represented in the Late Cretaceous North American faunas (Estes, 1976).

Even though the fossil record of lizards in South America is extremely poor, it is evident that iguanids and teiids, both well represented there today, were characteristic components of the Cenozoic herpetofaunas of that continent, where they underwent considerable diversification. Those groups, and also gekkonids, seem to comprise an ancient faunal element. The presence of anguids in South America has not yet been documented by the fossil record. They are present in North America since the Late Cretaceous and seem to have had an essentially northern dispersal (Hoffstetter, 1962; Estes, 1964; Meszoely, 1970).

Snake remains have been recorded in South America from the Late Cretaceous through the Pleistocene. With a few exceptions, no good descriptions are available, and much of the material has been assigned only to families. At least in the Early Tertiary the ophidian fauna was comprised mostly of boids. They were represented by the large snakes of the genus *Madtsoia*, of the extinct subfamily Madtsoiinae which were recorded from the late Paleocene and early Eocene of Patagonia. Species of that genus also are known from the Late Cretaceous of Madagascar (Hoffstetter 1961) and of Niger (Broin et al., 1974), a distribution that suggests their derivation from a Gondwanan stock. Remains assigned to the Boidae have been cited from the late Paleocene of Brasil and late Pleistocene of Bolivia. The living South American genus *Eunectes* occurs in late Miocene deposits of Colombia. Boids probably were also represented in the early–middle Miocene of southern Patagonia and the Pliocene of Parana Argentina, but those records have not been substantiated (Gasparini and Báez 1975, Báez and Gasparini 1977).

Anilids, now restricted to the Oriental and Neotropical regions, were represented in the Early Tertiary faunas of South America. A snake of controversial phylogenetic position, *Dinilysia patagonica* was recorded from the Late Cretaceous of central-western Argentina (Smith Woodward, 1901, Huene, 1929). Its affinities to modern anilids were pointed out by Estes, Frazzetta and Williams (1970) but it was retained in the monotypic family Dinilysiidae. However, *Dinilysia* was considered to be closer to boids, although not ancestral to them, by Rage (1977). True anilids are present in the late Paleocene of Brasil, but the material has not yet been described. The late Miocene *Colombophis portai* from Colombia more closely resembles the extant Asiatic *Cylindrophis* than *Anilius*, now living in South America (Hoffstetter, 1967b, Hoffstetter and Rage, 1977). The earliest known record of anilids is from the Middle-Late Cretaceous of Canada (Fox, 1975), their presence in North America is documented from that time through the Early Tertiary (Estes, 1976). The group also occurs in Eocene deposits of Europe (Hoffstetter, 1962 Rage, 1974). Reinterpretation of relationships of *Dinilysia* and the known fossil record of anilids seems to be more consistent with the postulated Laurasian origin of that group (Cracraft 1973). The evidence, however, is still meager.

The earliest known colubrid snake in South America is from late Miocene deposits in Colombia, other fossil colubrids in South America are from the late Pleistocene. True colubrids appear in the late Eocene of Europe (Rage, 1974). In North America their presence has been documented since the early Miocene (Holman, 1976b), they become dominant elements of snake faunas by the late Miocene (Holman, 1976a). Thus, an entry in South America from the north during the Miocene was suggested (Hoffstetter, 1967b, Hoffstetter and Rage, 1977). However, it is noteworthy that the relationship of some Miocene colubrids from the United States to living Central or South American forms could indicate that they were derived from a more southern source (Tihen, 1964).

Fossil viperids, which were referred to the Crotalinae are known in South America only from late Pleistocene deposits in Bolivia. They could be late immigrants from the north (Reig, 1962 Báez and Gasparini, 1977), although their arrival in South America should have preceded that record. In the early Miocene, typical viperids appear in Europe (Hoffstetter 1962). Viperid remains, tentatively assigned to the Crotalinae, were reported from the middle Miocene of North America (Holman, 1976c). All evidence indicates, as in the case of colubrids, that the early history of this group is still largely unknown.

The fossil record of snakes in South America is not only meager but remains practically unstudied. At least during the Early Tertiary henophidians predominated, although lineages different from those evolving in the northern continents seem to have been present there. Available paleontological data do not give much information concerning the origin of cenophidians in the South American continent. Scolecophidians are not yet recorded.

The Crocodylidae in South America now are restricted to the northern part of the continent. However, among the early Paleocene taxa assigned to that group, *Necrosuchus ionensis* Simpson, 1937, inhabited southern Argentina. The affinities of this crocodilian have not been clearly established. Crocodylids appear in the fossil record in Cretaceous deposits of comparable age in North America Africa and Asia (Sill, 1968) Thus, it is doubtful if the ancestors of *Necrosuchus* came from North America, at this time is is impossible to determine their area of origin From the Oligocene onward, crocodylids are recorded north of the Amazonian Basin with a latitudinal distribution similar to the present one No fossil *Crocodylus* is known from South America, except for a doubtful record from the Pliocene of Maranhão, coastal Brasil (Maury, 1923) Available evidence suggests that the living representatives of that genus are late immigrants from the north The relationships of the peculiar crocodylid, *Charactosuchus fieldsi* Langston, 1965 from the late Miocene of Colombia are still unknown

Alligatorid crocodilians are distributed more widely than crocodylids in South America The earliest known representatives in that continent occur in the late Paleocene of Brasil and they probably also are present in deposits of that age from southern Argentina In both cases, the material has not been studied yet The validity of the Paleocene *"Notocaiman stromeri"* from Patagonia, proposed as an ancestor of *Caiman*, has been discarded (Gasparini and Báez, 1975) The presence of alligatorids in North America extends back to the Cretaceous, and a center of origin there was suggested by Sill (1968) Nevertheless, available data are inconclusive The Eocene *Eocaiman cavernensis* is the oldest member of the family described from South America Langston (1965) pointed out its modern aspect and suggested that it could have been ancestral to *Caiman*, *Melanosuchus*, and perhaps also to the peculiar *Balanerodus* Kahn (1955) did not rule out the possibility that it could be referred to the extant genus *Caiman* This indicates that taxa closely related to living South American representatives of this family were already present on that continent by the Early Tertiary In the late Miocene of Colombia an extant genus and probably also a species (*Caiman latirostris*) are known (Gasparini and Báez 1975) The recent *Caiman yacare* is known from the Pliocene of Argentina and *Melanosuchus* from the Pliocene of Venezuela

Today, gavialids are restricted to the Ganges Basin, India, but they may have inhabited South America in the Tertiary It is still controversial if the South American longirostrine crocodilians are true gavialids or constitute a different lineage (Langston, 1965, Gasparini, 1968, Sill, 1968 1970, Hoffstetter 1970a, Hecht and Malone, 1972, Báez and Gasparini 1977) The oldest gavialids are known from Eocene deposits in Egypt (Hecht and Malone, 1972) The Asiatic and South American forms could have originated from an African stock, their dispersal would have been facilitated by their capacity to swim in marine waters In South America the first gavialids appear in deposits of late Oligocene-early Miocene age from the northern part of the continent, they became extinct by the Plio-Pleistocene The referral of South American forms to the genus *Gavialis* is doubtful, because they are different from the Asiatic members of that genus

The extinct Nettosuchidae is an endemic group from mesic tropical environments of the northern and central part of the continent from the late Miocene to the earliest Pleistocene

Crocodilians of the more primitive and extinct suborder Mesosuchia are known in South America during a large part of the Tertiary These forms belong to the family Sebecidae (Sebecosuchia, Gasparini, 1972) and are known from the Paleocene through the Miocene They were peculiar, mostly terrestrial crocodiles, and inhabitants of the tropical forests (Langston, 1965, Molnar, 1969, 1977, Neill, 1971, Gasparini, 1972) Sebecids seem to have had a long history on the continent, where they probably originated from baurosuchids

The great diversity of Cenozoic crocodilian faunas in South America is noteworthy Species referable to five families (Sebecidae, Crocodylidae, Alligatoridae, Gavialidae Nettosuchidae) have lived there, but only two of those groups (Crocodylidae, Alligatoridae) are present now Available evidence suggests that the differentiation of sebecids and nettosuchids occurred in South America The most conspicuous groups were the Sebecidae and Alligatoridae, the latter being represented throughout the Cenozoic and the most important crocodilian family there today On the other hand, the fossil record of crocodylids is comparatively poor, it seems likely that they never were important components of the South American herpetofauna. The living representatives of this family are not related to the earliest forms recorded from early Tertiary deposits in the southern part of the continent.

DISCUSSION

This review of the fossil record of amphibians and reptiles of South America discloses how poor that record actually is and how many questions concerning the history of the groups still remain unanswered. The available paleontological data are insufficient to provide a comprehensive picture of the evolutionary, faunal, and distributional changes that occurred in South America. It is pertinent to emphasize here that practically no special techniques for fossil collecting have been applied; for the most part, the discovery of amphibians and reptiles has been haphazard. Comparison of local faunas is difficult, for in many cases little weight can be given to the differences in composition of known assemblages; thus, evolutionary and zoogeographic interpretations are still tentative.

The records of certain groups, such as turtles and crocodilians, greatly outnumber those of other groups which could be partially the result of the fact that most known sites that have yielded amphibian or reptile remains represent lowland and aquatic habitats. This could also explain the absence of other groups associated with different ecological conditions. In general, little is known about the herpetofaunas that inhabited the northern and central part of the continent, not only in the cratonic areas but also in the intercratonic basins. These regions have a considerable significance from the zoogeographic point of view in that they have been considered areas of origin of diverse groups.

The oldest known remains referable to modern groups of amphibians and reptiles occurring in South America are from the Late Cretaceous deposits, except for the record of leiopelmatid frogs (*Vieraella* and *Notobatrachus*) in the Jurassic of Patagonia. The next important sample is the late Paleocene records from Itaboraí, Brasil, the earliest assemblage which offers a broad picture of the groups already comprising the fauna of the continent. According to available data from that sample, little similarity to the North American assemblages of comparable age are evident (Estes, 1976; Báez and Gasparini, 1977). Basically, the family groups recorded from the known Paleocene and Eocene sites evolved in isolation in South America and comprise the present fauna. Some of them such as leptodactylids, bufonids, pelomedusids, chelids, teiids, alligatorids, were already represented by forms related to their living representatives on that continent. It is evident that the early history in South America of many of those groups extends back well into the Mesozoic. Unfortunately, Mesozoic records are very scarce, and the earliest known Tertiary samples (except that from Itaboraí, Brasil) are badly preserved and not diverse (Gasparini and Báez, 1975). Of the additional family groups recorded from Oligocene and Miocene deposits, testudinids and perhaps emydids could have arrived from the north by overwater transport at different times. The known late Cenozoic records provide little information concerning the faunal interchange between the Americas when the isthmian link was established.

Different lines of evidence indicate that in the Early Tertiary a humid and warm temperate climate prevailed at high latitudes in South America as well as in North America (Dawson, et al., 1976). In the southernmost part of South America, the known assemblages of that age are archaic, being comprised of extinct groups that do not now exist in the area. Tectonic events throughout the Cenozoic altered the physiographic conditions and the subsequent climatic and floristic changes affected the composition of the local faunas. The modification of the Patagonian herpetofauna from the early Eocene onward clearly illustrates this point. The subtropical elements, such as crocodilians, disappeared from that region. Furthermore, the gradual desiccation of climate related to the Andean uplift presumably resulted in the confinement of taxa adapted to humid and aquatic environments to the more mesic western areas. The change of the biota in the region of the present upper Magdalena Valley, Colombia, in relation to the uplift of the Eastern Cordillera and increasing aridity (Howe, 1974) is another example. Many components of the rich late Miocene La Venta fauna, living on the broad flood plains that prevailed there are absent from that now semiarid area (Fields 1959).

Many fundamental aspects in the history of the South American herpetofauna have yet to be elucidated. The amount of paleontological information that has accumulated in recent years enables us to expect that future studies will clarify these problems.

ACKNOWLEDGMENTS

For their valuable comments and provision of data, we are indebted to Drs France de Broin, Richard Estes, J Alan Holman, Bryan Patterson and Roger Wood. Special thanks are extended to Dr William E Duellman, who kindly revised and corrected the manuscript.

RESUMEN

En este trabajo se sintetiza la información disponible sobre el registro fósil de los grupos que integran la actual herpetofauna de América del Sur, en un intento de valorar el aporte que el mismo brinda al conocimiento del desarrollo histórico de dichos grupos en ese continente. En tal sentido, se han tomado en cuenta no solo los registros sudamericanos sino también aquellos otros directamente relacionados y provenientes de otras partes del mundo. Para integrar los resultados en un contexto coherente se consideró muy especialmente la disposición y relación de América del Sur con respecto a otras masas continentales a partir del Mesozoico medio. También se tomaron en cuenta los principales eventos geológicos acaecidos desde fines del Cretácico a la actualidad en dicho continente, valorando su incidencia en los cambios fisiográficos los que, evidentemente, actuaron sobre la composición y distribución de la herpetofauna.

La mención de anfibios y reptiles cenozoicos en América del Sur es relativamente frecuente, sin embargo muchas de las asignaciones taxonómicas como las referencias geográficas y cronoestratigráficas son dudosas. Ello conjuntamente con el hecho de que la mayoría de los hallazgos son aislados, sin formar parte de asociaciones representativas, hace que las conclusiones resulten aún tentativas. En general los datos disponibles permiten un análisis a nivel familiar.

El examen del registro señala la notable antigüedad en América del Sur, de muchas de las familias de anfibios y reptiles que viven en ese continente. Todas las familias registradas en el Terciario temprano son integrantes de la herpetofauna actual sudamericana, excepto las tortugas meiolánidas y los cocodrilos sebécidos, ambos extinguidos. Es evidente que esas familias tienen distinto abolengo habiéndose integrado o diferenciado in situ alocrónicamente, desde fines del Cretácico al menos. De acuerdo a las evidencias paleontológicas la antigüedad en América del Sur de los pípidos, iguánidos pelomedúsidos, meiolánidos, muy probablemente los quélidos y posiblemente los leptodactílidos se remonta al Mesozoico tardío. De estas familias, los pípidos, meiolánidos y quélidos son de origen gondwánico. La diferenciación de los sebécidos y leptodactílidos, en sentido estricto habría tenido lugar en América del Sur. Los datos paleontológicos son aún insuficientes para dilucidar el origen de otras familias ya presentes en el Terciario temprano. En el Terciario medio y tardío se constata la presencia de familias no registradas en sedimentos más viejos. Algunos de esos grupos pudieron haber arribado a América del Sur por medios de dispersión accidental en diferentes momentos durante su aislamiento. Tal sería el caso de los testudínidos, trioníquidos gaviálidos, crocodílidos directamente relacionados a las formas actuales y tal vez los emídidos. Los cocodrilos nettosúquidos, actualmente extinguidos, se diferenciaron in situ. De la confrontación con la herpetofauna actual se desprende que numerosas familias no están presentes en el registro. Algunas de ellas tales como los ránidos, ánguidos, chelídridos y tal vez kinostérnidos podrían ser invasores tardíos, llegados a través del Istmo de Panamá. Otras por el grado de endemismo y relaciones filogenéticas serían más antiguas integrantes de la fauna de este continente, no obstante no habérselas registrado fósiles hasta el momento. Tal es el caso, por ejemplo, de dendrobátidos y rinodermátidos.

La localización geográfica de los depósitos portadores de anfibios y reptiles ha sido también tomada en consideración. Resulta evidente que, con pocas excepciones, es escasa o nula la información disponible sobre las faunas de anfibios y reptiles que habitaron la parte norte del continente, tanto en las áreas cratónicas como en las cuencas intercratónicas. Estas regiones revisten especial interés por cuanto se ha señalado su importancia como áreas de origen de diversos grupos. Recién a partir del Oligoceno se conocen registros de los grupos considerados en el extremo más septentrional, fundamentalmente en Colombia y Venezuela. En cambio, en la parte sur del continente, en la Patagonia extrandina, varias han sido las localidades donde depósitos del Terciario temprano brindaron restos de anfibios y reptiles. Según diversas evidencias, en ese tiempo las condiciones ambientales fueron más benignas que las actuales en esa región, por lo que la herpetofauna fósil que allí se registra es muy distinta de la que habita esa área en nuestros días.

El registro fósil es aún inadecuado para brindar un panorama integral de los cambios ocurridos en la composición de las diversas faunas regionales en consonancia con las modificaciones ambientales, del mismo modo limita el conocimiento de la evolución intrafamiliar a través del tiempo. La búsqueda sistemática y la aplicación de técnicas adecuadas permitirán sin duda, un mayor aporte de la paleontología al conocimiento de la historia de la herpetofauna sudamericana.

LITERATURE CITED

AHL, E. 1926. Anura, Aglossa, pp. 141-142 in KAISER, I., BEETZ, W. (eds.) Die Diamantenwüste Sudwest Afrikas 2. D. Reimer, Berlin, 535 p.

AMBROSETTI, J. 1890. Observaciones sobre los reptiles fósiles oligocenos de los terrenos terciarios antiguos del Paraná. Bol. Acad. Nac. Cien. Cordoba 10:489-499.

AMEGHINO, F. 1893. Sobre la presencia de vertebrados de aspecto mesozoico en la formación Santacruceña de Patagonia austral. Rev. Jardín Zool. Buenos Aires 1:75-84.

AMEGHINO, F. 1899. Sinopsis geologico paleontologica. Suplemento. La Plata, Folio 13 p.

ANTUNES, M. T. 1975. Iberosuchus, crocodile sebecosuchien nouveau, de l'Eocene iberique au Nord de la Chaîne Centrales et l'origine du Canyon de Nazaré. Comun. Serv. Geol. Portugal 59:285-330.

ARCHANGELSKY, S., ROMERO, F. 1974. Los registros más antiguos del polen de Nothofagus (Fagaceae) de Patagonia (Argentina y Chile). Bol. Soc. Bot. Mexico 33:13-30.

ARID, F., VIZOTTO, L. 1966. Um quelonio fóssil de São José do Rio Prêto. Rev. Cien. Cultura 18:422-428.

AUFFENBERG, W. 1971. A new fossil tortoise, with remarks on the origin of South American testudines. Copeia 1971(1):106-117.

AUFFENBERG, W. 1974. Checklist of fossil land tortoises (Testudinidae). Bull. Florida State Mus. Biol. Ser. 18:121-251.

BÁEZ, A. M. 1975. Los anuros de la Formación Las Curtiembres (Cretácico superior), provincia de Salta, República Argentina. Evolución de la familia Pipidae (Amphibia, Anura) en relación a la historia paleogeográfica. Tesis Doctoral Univ. Buenos Aires, 141 p.

BÁEZ, A. M. 1976. El significado paleogeográfico y paleoecológico de los pípidos (Amphibia, Anura) fósiles de América del Sur. VI Congr. Argent. Geol., Bahía Blanca, 1975, 1:333-340.

BÁEZ, A. M. 1977. Sobre Teracophrys Ameghino, nomina nuda (Anura Leptodactylidae) de la Formación Colhué-Huapi (Oligoceno superior), Provincia del Chubut, República Argentina. Rev. Asoc. Geol. Argentina 32:145-151.

BÁEZ, A. M., GASPARINI, Z. B. DE 1977. Orígenes y evolución de los anfibios y reptiles del Cenozoico de América del Sur. Acta Geol. Lilloana 14:140-232.

BLAIR, W. F. 1972. Summary, pp. 329-343 in BLAIR W. F. (ed.) Evolution in the genus Bufo. Univ. Texas Press, Austin, 459 p.

BRAVARD, A. 1858. Monografía de los terrenos marinos terciarios del Paraná. Diario Oficial de Gobierno "El Nacional Argentino". (Not seen)

BROIN, F. DE 1971. Une espèce nouvelle de tortue pleurodire (?Roxochelys vilavilensis n.sp.) dans le Cretacé superieur de Bolivie. Bull. Soc. Geol. France (7)13:445-452.

BROIN, F. DE, BUFFETAUT, E., KOENIGUER, J. C., RAGE, J. C., RUSSELL, D., TAQUET, P., VERGNAUD-GRAZZINI, C. WENZ, S. 1974. La faune de vertébrés continentaux du gisement d'In Beceten (Sénonien du Niger). C. R. Acad. Sci. Paris, Ser. D 279:169-172.

BURMEISTER, H. 1883. Monografía de los terrenos marinos terciarios del Paraná. An. Mus. Publ. Buenos Aires 3: 45–94.

BURMEISTER, H. 1885. Examen crítico de los mamíferos y reptiles fósiles denominados por don Augusto Bravard. Ibid. 3: 95–174.

CASAMIQUELA, R. 1958. Un anuro gigante del Mioceno de Patagonia. Rev. Asoc. Geol. Argentina 13: 171–183.

CASAMIQUELA, R. 1960. Datos preliminares sobre un pipoideo fósil de la Patagonia. Actas y Trabajos 1 Congr. Sudamer. Zool., La Plata 1959, 4: 17–21.

CASAMIQUELA, R. 1963. Sobre un par de anuros del Mioceno de Río Negro (Patagonia) Wawelia gerholdi n. gen. et sp. (Ceratophrydidae) y Gigantobatrachus parodii (Leptodactylidae). Ameghiniana 3: 141–162.

CASAMIQUELA, R. 1967. Sobre un nuevo Bufo fósil de la Provincia de Buenos Aires (Argentina). Ibid. 5: 161–168.

CATTOI, N., FREIBERG, M. 1958. Una nueva especie de 'Podocnemis' del Cretáceo argentino. Physis 21 (60): 58–66.

CEI, J. 1972. Bufo of South America, pp. 82–90 in BLAIR, W. F. (ed.) Evolution in the genus Bufo. Univ. Texas Press, Austin, 459 p.

CHANI, J. 1976. Relaciones de un nuevo Teiidae (Lacertilia) fósil del Plioceno superior Callopistes bicuspidatus n. sp. Inst. Miguel Lillo, Univ. Nac. Tucumán, Publ. Especial, pp. 133–153.

CRACRAFT, J. 1973. Vertebrate evolution and biogeography in the Old World tropics pp. 373–393 in TARLING, D., RUNCORN, S. (eds.) Implications of continental drift to the earth sciences, Vol. 1. Academic Press, New York, 622 p.

DALZIEL, I., KLIGFIELD, R., LOWRIE, W., OPDYKE, N. D. 1973. Palaeomagnetic data from the southernmost Andes and the Antarctandes. Ibid. 87–101.

DAWSON, M., WEST, R., LANGSTON, W., HUTCHISON, J. 1976. Palaeogene terrestrial vertebrates northernmost occurrence, Ellesmere Island, Canada. Science 192: 781–782.

DOUGLAS, R., MOULLADE, M., NAIRN, A. 1973. Causes and consequences of drift in the South Atlantic, pp. 513–534 in TARLING, D., RUNCORN, S. (eds.) Implications of continental drift to the earth sciences, Vol. 1. Academic Press, New York, 622 p.

EMILIANI, C., GAERTNER, S., LIDZ, B. 1972. Neogene sedimentation on the Blake Plateau and the emergence of the Central American Isthmus. Palaeogeogr., Palaeoclimatol., Palaeoecol., 11: 1–10.

ESTES, R. 1961. Miocene lizards from Colombia, South America. Breviora (143): 1–11.

ESTES, R. 1964. Fossil vertebrates from the late Cretaceous Lance Formation eastern Wyoming. Univ. Calif. Publ. Geol. Sci. 49: 1–180.

ESTES, R. 1969. Relationships of two Cretaceous lizards (Sauria, Teiidae). Breviora (317): 1–8.

ESTES, R. 1970. Origin of the Recent North American lower vertebrate fauna. An inquiry into the fossil record. Forma Functio 3: 139–163.

ESTES, R. 1975a. Xenopus from the Palaeocene of Brazil and its zoogeographic importance. Nature 254: 48–50.

ESTES, R. 1975b. Fossil Xenopus from the Palaeocene of South America and the zoogeography of pipid frogs. Herpetologica 31: 263–278.

ESTES, R. 1976. Middle Paleocene lower vertebrates from the Tongue Formation, southeastern Montana. J. Paleontol. 50: 500–520.

ESTES, R., FRAZZETTA, T., WILLIAMS, E. 1970. Studies on the fossil snake Dinilysia patagonica Woodward. Part 1. Cranial morphology. Bull. Mus. Comp. Zool. Harvard Univ. 140: 25–74.

ESTES, R., PRICE, LL. 1973. Iguanid lizard from the upper Cretaceous of Brazil. Science 180: 748–751.

ESTES, R., REIG, O. 1973. The early fossil record of frogs. A review of the evidence pp. 11–63 in VIAL, J. L. (ed.) Evolutionary biology of the anurans. Contemporary research on major problems. Univ. Missouri Press, Columbia, 470 p.

ESTES, R., WAKE, M. 1972. The first fossil record of caecilian amphibians. Nature 239: 228–231.

ESTES, R., WASSERSUG, R. 1963. A Miocene toad from Colombia, South America. Breviora (193): 1–13.

FIELDS, R. 1959. Geology of the La Venta badlands, Colombia, South America. Univ. Calif. Publ. Geol. Sci. 23: 403–444.

FOX, R. 1975. Fossil snakes from the Upper Milk River Formation (Upper Cretaceous), Alberta. Canad. J. Earth Sci. 12: 1557–1563.

GAFFNEY, E. 1975. A revision of the side-necked turtle Taphrosphys sulcatus (Leidy) from the Cretaceous of New Jersey. Amer. Mus. Novit. (2571): 1–24.

GAFFNEY, E., ZANGERL, R. 1968. A revision of the chelonian genus Bothremys (Pleurodira, Pelomedusidae). Fieldiana Geol. 16: 193–239.

GALLARDO, J. M. 1962. A propósito de Bufo variegatus (Günther), sapo del bosque húmedo Antartándico, y las otras especies de Bufo neotropicales. Physis 23 (64): 93–102.

GASPARINI, Z. B. DE. 1968. Nuevos restos de Rhamphostomopsis neogaeus (Burm.) Rusconi 1933 (Reptilia, Crocodilia) del Mesopotamiense (Ploceno medio-superior) de Argentina. Ameghiniana 5: 299–311.

GASPARINI, Z. B. DE. 1972. Los Sebecosuchia (Crocodilia) del territorio argentino. Consideraciones sobre su "status" taxonómico. Ibid. 9: 23–34.

GASPARINI, Z. B. DE. 1973. Revisión de los Crocodilia (Reptilia) fósiles del territorio argentino. Su evolución, sus relaciones filogenéticas, su clasificación y sus implicancias estratigráficas. Tesis Doctoral, Univ. Nac. La Plata, 169 p.

GASPARINI, Z. B. DE, BÁEZ, A. M. 1975. Aportes al conocimiento de la herpetofauna terciaria de la Argentina. Actas I Congr. Argent. Paleontol. Bioestr., Tucumán 1974, 2: 377–415.

HAFFER, J. 1970. Geologic-climatic history and zoogeographic significance of the Uraba Region in northwestern Colombia. Caldasia 10:603–636.

HECHT, M. 1963. A reevaluation of the early history of the frogs. Part II. Syst. Zool. 12:20–35.

HECHT, M., MALONE, B. 1972. On the early history of the gavialid crocodilians. Herpetologica 28:281–284.

HEYER, W. R. 1975. A preliminary analysis of the intergeneric relationships of the frog family Leptodactylidae. Smithsonian Contr. Zool. (199):1–55.

HOFFSTETTER, R. 1959. Un dentaire de *Madtsoia* (Serpent géant du Paléocene de Patagonie). Bull. Mus. Natl. Hist. Nat. Zool. Paris, (2) 31:379–386.

HOFFSTETTER, R. 1961. Nouveaux restes d'un serpent Boide (*Madtsoia madagascariensis* nov. sp.) dans le Cretacé inferieur de Madagascar. Ibid. (2) 33:152–160.

HOFFSTETTER, R. 1962. Revue des recents acquisitions concernant l'histoire et la systématique des Squamates, pp. 243–279 *in* Problemes actuels de Paléontologie (Evolution des Vertébrés). Colloq. Int. CNRS Paris 104:474 p.

HOFFSTETTER, R. 1963. La faune Pleistocene de Tarija (Bolivie). Note préliminaire. Bull. Mus. Natl. Hist. Nat. Zool., Paris (2) 35:195–203.

HOFFSTETTER, R. 1964. Les Sauria du Jurassique superieur et specialment les Gekkota de Baviere et de Mandchourie. Senckenbergiana Biol. 45:281–324.

HOFFSTETTER, R. 1967a. Remarques sur les dates d'implantation des differents groupes de serpents terrestres en Amérique du Sud. Comp. Rend. Somm. Soc. Géol. France 1967:93–94.

HOFFSTETTER, R. 1967b. Observations additionelles sur les serpents du Miocene de Colombie et rectification concernant la date d'arrivee des colubridés en Amerique du Sud. Ibid. 1967:209–210 32:419–426.

HOFFSTETTER, R. 1968. Ñuapua, un gisement de vertebres pleistocenes dans le Chaco Bolivien. Bull. Mus. Natl. Hist. Nat. Zool., Paris (2) 40:823–836.

HOFFSTETTER, R. 1970a. Vertebrados cenozoicos de Colombia. Actas IV Congr. Latinoamer. Zool., Caracas 1968, 2:931–954.

HOFFSTETTER, R. 1970b. Vertebrados cenozoicos de Ecuador. Ibid. 2:955–970.

HOFFSTETTER, R. 1970c. Vertebrados cenozoicos y mamiferos cretacicos del Peru. Ibid. 2:971–984.

HOFFSTETTER, R., RAGE, J. C. 1977. Le gisement de vertebres miocenes de La Venta (Colombie) et sa faune de Serpents. Ann. Paleontol. (Vertebres) 63:161–190.

HOLMAN, J. 1968. Lower Oligocene amphibians from Saskatchewan. Q. J. Florida Acad. Sci. 31:273–289.

HOLMAN, J. 1976a. Snakes from the Rosebud Formation (Middle-Miocene) of South Dakota. Herpetologica 32:41–48.

HOLMAN, J. 1976b. A boid and a colubrid snake from the Harrison Formation (Lower Miocene, Arikareean) of Sioux County, Nebraska. Ibid. 32:387–389.

HOLMAN, J. 1976c. Snakes of the Split Rock Formation (Middle Miocene), Central Wyoming. Ibid. 32:419–426.

HOWE, M. 1974. Nonmarine Neiva Formation (Pliocene?) Upper Magdalena Valley Colombia regional tectonism. Geol. Soc. Amer. Bull. 85:1031–1042.

HUENE, F. VON. 1929. Los saurisquios y ornitisquios del Cretáceo argentino. An. Mus. La Plata 3:1–196.

IRVING, E. M. 1971. La evolucion estructural de los Andes mas septentrionales de Colombia. Inst. Nac. Invest. Geol. Min. Colombia, Bol. Geol. 19:1–90.

JIMENEZ FUENTES, E. 1971. Los reptiles fósiles del Valle del Duero. *Podocnemis carbajosai* nov. sp. del Eoceno de Salamanca. Estud. Geol. (Madrid) 27:85–93.

JIMENEZ FUENTES, E. 1975. *Duerochelys arribasi*, nov. gen., nov. sp., Pelomedusidae du Ludien du Bassin du Duero (Espagne). Bull. Géol. Soc. France (7) 17:410–415.

KALIN, J. 1955. Crocodilia, pp. 695–781 *in* PIVETEAU, J. (ed.) Traité de Paleontologie, Masson et Cie., Paris 5:1–1113.

KLUGE, A. 1967. Higher taxonomic categories of gekkonid lizards and their evolution. Bull. Amer. Mus. Nat. Hist. 135:1–59.

LANGSTON, W. 1965. Fossil crocodilians from Colombia and the Cenozoic history of the Crocodilia in South America. Univ. Calif. Publ. Geol. Sci. 52:1–157.

LANGSTON, W. 1966. *Mourasuchus* Price, *Nettosuchus* Langston, and the family Nettosuchidae (Rept. Crocodilia). Copeia 1966(4):882–885.

LEMON, R., CHURCHER, C. 1961. Pleistocene geology and paleontology of the Talara region, Northwest Peru. Amer. J. Sci., 259:410–429.

LYNCH, J. 1971. Evolutionary relationships, osteology and zoogeography of leptodactyloid frogs. Univ. Kansas Mus. Nat. Hist. Misc. Publ. (53):1–238.

LYNCH, J. 1973. The transition from archaic to advanced frogs, pp. 133–182 *in* VIAL, J. L. (ed.) Evolutionary biology of the anurans. Contemporary research on major problems. Univ. Missouri Press, Columbia, 470 p.

MALFAIT, B., DINKELMAN, M. 1972. Circum-Caribbean tectonic and igneous activity and the evolution of the Caribbean Plate. Geol. Soc. Amer. Bull. 83:251–272.

MAURY, C. 1924. Fosseis terciarios do Brasil com descripção de novas formas cretaceas. Serv. Geol. Min. Brasil, Monogr. 4:1–711.

McGOWRAN, G. 1973. Rifting and drift of Australia and the migration of mammals. Science, 180:759–761.

McKenna, M 1973 Sweepstakes, filters, corridors, Noah's arks and beached Viking funeral ships in paleogeography, pp 295–308 in Tarling, D, Runcorn, S (ed) Implication of continental drift to the earth sciences Vol 1 Academic Press, New York, 622 p

Medem, F 1966 Contribuciones al conocimiento sobre la ecología y distribución geográfica de *Phrynops (Batrachemys) dahli*, (Testudinata, Pleurodira, Chelydae) Caldasia 9 467–489

Medem, F 1968 Desarrollo de la herpetología en Colombia Rev Acad Colombiana Cien Exactas, Fís Nat 13 149–200

Medina, C 1976 Crocodilians from the Late Tertiary of Northwestern Venezuela *Melanosuchus fisheri* sp nov Breviora (438) 1–14

Meszoely, C 1970 North America fossil anguid lizards Bull Mus Comp Zool Harvard Univ 139 87–149

Molnar, R 1969 Jaw musculature and jaw mechanics of the Eocene crocodilian *Sebecus icaeorhinus* M A Thesis Univ Texas, Austin, 89 p

Molnar, R 1977 Crocodile with laterally compressed snout First find in Australia Science, 197 62–64

Mones, A 1972 Lista de los vertebrados fósiles del Uruguay I Chondrichthyes, Osteichthyes, Reptilia, Aves Comun Paleontol Mus Hist Nat Montevideo 1 23–36

Mones, A 1975 Notas paleontológicas uruguayas, III Vertebrados fósiles nuevos o poco conocidos (Chondrichthyes, Osteichthyes, Amphibia, Mammalia) Ameghiniana 12 313–349

Mook, C 1921 *Brachygnathosuchus braziliensis*, a new fossil crocodilian from Brazil Bull Amer Mus Nat Hist 44 43–50

Mook, C 1941 A new fossil crocodilian from Colombia Proc U S Natl Mus 91 55–58

Neill, W 1971 The last of the ruling reptiles Alligators, Crocodiles and their kin Columbia University Press New York 486 p

Nevo, E 1968 Pipid frogs from the Early Cretaceous of Israel and pipid evolution Bull Mus Comp Zool Harvard Univ 136 255–318

Parodi Bustos, R, Figueroa Caprini, M, Kracliewich, J, Del Corro, G 1960 Noticia preliminar acerca del yacimiento de anuros extinguidos de Puente Morales (Depto de Guachipas, Prov de Salta) Rev Fac Cienc Nat Salta Univ Nac Tucuman 1 5–25

Pascual, R 1970 Evolución de comunidades, cambios faunísticos e integraciones biocenóticas de los vertebrados cenozoicos de Argentina Actas IV Congr Latinoamer Zool, Caracas 1968, 2 991–1089

Pascual, R, Odreman Rivas, O 1971 Evolución de las comunidades de los vertebrados del Terciario argentino Los aspectos paleozoogeográficos y paleoclimáticos relacionados Ameghiniana 8 372–412

Patterson, B, Pascual, R 1968 The fossil mammal fauna of South America Q Rev Biol, 43 409–451

Paula Couto, C de 1970 Evolução de comunidades, modificações faunísticas e integrações biocenóticas dos vertebrados cenozoicos do Brasil Actas IV Congr Latinoamer Zool Caracas 1968, 2 907–930

Petriella, B, Archangelsky, S 1975 Vegetación y ambiente en el Paleoceno de Chubut Actas I Congr Argent Paleontol Bioestr, Tucuman, 1974, 2 257–270

Price, Ll 1953 Os quelônios de Formação Bauru, Cretáceo terrestre do Brasil meridional Dept Nac Prod Min Div Geol Min, Rio de Janeiro 147 1–34

Price, Ll 1954 Um quelônio pleurodiro no Calcário da Serie Apodi Cretáceo do Estado do Rio Grande do Norte Dept Nac Prod Min Div Geol Min, Notas Prelim Estud, Rio de Janeiro 85 1–12

Price, Ll 1964 Sobre o crânio de um grande crocodilídeo extinto do Alto no Juruá, Estado de Acre An Acad Brasil Cien 36 59–66

Rage, J-C 1974 Les serpents des Phosphorites du Quercy, Palaeovert, 6 274–303

Rage, J-C 1975 Un serpent du Paléocène du Niger Etude préliminaire sur l origine des caenophidiens (Reptilia, Serpentes) C R Acad Sci Paris, Ser D 281 515–518

Rage, J-C 1977 La position phylétique de *Dinilysia patagonica*, serpent du Cretace superieur Ibid 284 1765–1768

Raven, P, Axelrod, D 1975 History of the flora and fauna of Latin America Amer Sci 63 420–429

Reig, O 1958 Notas para una actualización del conocimiento de la fauna de la Formación Chapadmalal Acta Geol Lilloana, Tucuman 2 255–283

Reig, O 1959 Primeros datos descriptivos sobre los anuros del eocretácico de la provincia de Salta, República Argentina Ameghiniana 1 1–8

Reig O 1962 Las integraciones cenogenéticas en el desarrollo de la fauna de vertebrados de América del Sur Ibid 2 131–140

Reig, O 1968 Peuplement en vertebres tetrapodes de l Amérique du Sud, pp 215–260 in Delamare Deboutteville, C, Rapoport, E (eds) Biologie de l Amerique australe C N R S Groupe Francais Argiles, C R Reun Ldud 4 1–472

Reig, O 1972 *Macrogenioglottus* and the South American bufonid toads pp 14–36, in Blair, W F (ed) Evolution in the genus *Bufo* Univ Texas Press, Austin, 457 p

Reyment, R, Tait, E 1972 Biostratigraphical dating of the early history of the South Atlantic Ocean Phil Trans Roy Soc London, B Biol Sci 264 55–95

Robinson, M, Van Devender, T 1973 Miocene lizards from Wyoming and Nebraska Copeia 1973 698–704

Romer, A 1966 Vertebrate Paleontology 3-d ed Univ Chicago Press, Chicago, 468 p

Rovereto, C 1914 Los estratos araucanos y sus fósiles An Mus Nac Hist Nat Buenos Aires 25 1–247

Royo y Gómez, J 1945-46 Los vertebrados del Terciario continental colombiano Rev Acad Colombiana Cien Exactas Fis Nat 6 496-512

Rusconi, C 1933 Observaciones críticas sobre reptiles terciarios de Paraná (Alligatoridae) Rev Univ Nac Cordoba 20 57-106

Rusconi, C 1935 Observaciones sobre los gaviales fósiles argentinos An Soc Cient Argentina 119 203-214

Rusconi, C 1946 Ave y reptil oligoceno de Mendoza Bol Paleontol Buenos Aires 21 1-3

Savage, J 1973 The geographic distribution of frogs Patterns and predictions, pp 351-445 in Vial, J L (ed) Evolutionary biology of the anurans Contemporary research on major problems Univ Missouri Press, Columbia, 470 p

Savage, J 1974 The isthmian link and the evolution of Neotropical mammals Nat Hist Mus Los Angeles Cty Contrib Sci (260) 1-51

Schaeffer, B 1949 Anurans from the Early Tertiary of Patagonia Bull Amer Mus Nat Hist 93 41-68

Sclater, J, Fisher, R 1974 Evolution of the East Central Indian Ocean, with emphasis on the tectonic setting of the Ninetyeast Ridge Geol Soc Amer Bull 85 683-702

Segura, P 1944 Estudio de la primera especie de tortuga fósil de Costa Rica con algunas generalidades sobre el orden Testudines Fac Farm Guatemala, 6 9-29 (Not seen)

Sigé, B 1968 Dents du micromammifères et fragments de coquilles d oeufs de dinosauriens dans la faune de vertébres du Crétacé supérieur de Laguna Umayo (Andes peruviennes) C R Acad Sci, Paris, Ser D 267 1495-1498

Sill, W 1968 The zoogeography of the crocodiles Copeia 1968(1) 76-88

Sill, W 1970 Nota preliminar sobre un nuevo gavial del Plioceno de Venezuela y una discusión de los gaviales sudamericanos Ameghiniana 7 151-159

Simpson, G 1933a A new fossil snake from the Notostylops Beds of Patagonia Bull Amer Mus Nat Hist 67 1-22

Simpson, G 1933b A new crocodilian from the Notostylops Beds of Patagonia Amer Mus Novit (623) 1-9

Simpson, G 1935 Early and middle Tertiary geology of the Gaiman region, Chubut, Argentina Ibid 775 1-29

Simpson, G 1937a New reptiles from the Eocene of South America Ibid 927 1-3

Simpson, G 1937b An ancient eusuchian crocodile from Patagonia Ibid 965 1-20

Simpson, G 1938 *Crossochelys*, Eocene horned turtle from Patagonia Bull Amer Mus Nat Hist 74 221-254

Simpson, G 1942 A Miocene tortoise from Patagonia Amer Mus Novit (1209) 1-6

Simpson, G, Minoprio, L, Patterson, B 1962 The mammalian fauna of the Divisadero Largo Formation, Mendoza, Argentina Bull Mus Comp Zool Harvard Univ 127 239-293

Smith, A, Briden, J, Drewry, G 1973 Phanerozoic world maps, pp 1-42 in Hughes, N (ed) Organisms and continents through time Spec Pap Palaeontol (Paleo Assoc London) 12 1-334

Smith Woodward, A 1901 On some extinct reptiles from Patagonia of the genera *Miolania*, *Dinilysia* and *Genyodectes* Proc Zool Soc London, 1901 169-184

Staesche, K von 1937 *Podocnemis brasiliensis* n sp aus der Oberen Kreide Brasiliens Neues Jahrb Mineral Geol Palaeontol Abh Abt A 77 291-309 Reprod by Minist Agricult, Div Geol Min, Brasil, Bol 114 (1944)

Stirton, R 1953 Vertebrate paleontology and continental stratigraphy in Colombia Geol Soc Amer Bull 64 603-622

Suarez, J 1969 Um quelônio da formação Bauru Dept Geograf, Fac Filos Cién Letras, Pres Prudente 2 35-54

Tihen, J 1962 New world fossil bufonids Amer Midl Nat 68 1-50

Tihen, J 1964 Tertiary changes in the herpetofaunas of temperate North America Senckenbergiana Biol 45 265-279

Tihen, J 1972 The fossil record, pp 8-13 in Blair, W F (ed) Evolution in the genus *Bufo* Univ Texas Press, Austin, 457 p

Van Denveder, T 1977 Observations on the Argentine iguanid lizard *Leiosaurus belli* Duméril and Bibron (Reptilia, Lacertilia, Iguanidae) J Herpetol 11 238-241

Van Houten, F, Travis, R 1968 Cenozoic deposits of the Upper Magdalena Valley, Colombia Bull Amer Soc Petrol Geol 52 675-702

Vergnaud-Grazzini, C 1966 Les amphibiens du Miocène de Beni-Mellal Notes Serv Geol Maroc 27 (198) 43-69

Vergnaud-Grazzini, C 1968 Amphibiens pleistocenes de Bolivie Bull Soc Geol France, (7) 10 688-695

Vilas, J, Valencio, D 1978 Paleomagnetism of the South American and African rocks and the age of the South Atlantic Rev Brasil Geociencias 18 3-10

Vilas, J, Valencio, D 1979 Paleomagnetism of South American rocks and the Gondwana Continent Seminar on Past configuration of Gondwana and geological correlation through time IV Internat Gondwana Symp, Calcutta 1977 (in press)

Warren, J 1969 Chelid turtles from the mid-Tertiary of Tasmania J Paleontol 43 179-182

Wieland, G 1923 A new Parana Pleurodira Amer J Sci 5 1-14

Williams, E 1950 *Testudo cubensis* and the evolution of Western Hemisphere tortoises Bull Amer Mus Nat Hist 95 1-36

Williams, E 1956 *Podocnemis bassleri*, a new species of pelomedusid turtle from the late Tertiary of Peru Amer Mus Novit (1782) 1-10

Wood, R 1970 A review of the fossil Pelomedusidae (Testudines, Pleurodira) of Asia Breviora (357) 1-23

Wood, R 1971 The fossil Pelomedusidae (Testudines, Pleurodira) of Africa PhD Dissert Harvard Univ, 345 p

Wood, R 1972 A fossil pelomedusid turtle from Puerto Rico Breviora (392) 1-13

Wood, R 1975 Redescription of "Bantuchelys" congolensis, a fossil pelomedusid turtle from the Paleocene of Africa Rev Zool Bot Africaines 89 127-144

Wood, R 1976a Two new species of Chelus (Testudines, Pleurodira) from the Late Tertiary of northern South America Breviora (435) 1-26

Wood, R 1976b Stupendemys geographicus, the world's largest turtle Ibid (436) 1-31

Wood, R, Gamero, M de 1971 Podocnemis venezuelensis a new fossil pelomedusid (Testudines Pleurodira) from the Pliocene of Venezuela and a review of the history of Podocnemis in South America Ibid (376) 1-23

Wood R Moody, R 1976 Unique arrangement of carapace bones in the South American chelid turtle Hydromedusa maximiliani (Mikan) J Zool 59 69-78

Wood, R, Patterson, B 1973 A fossil trionychid turtle from South America Breviora (415) 1-10

Zangerl, R 1947 Redescription of Taphrosphys olssoni a fossil turtle from Peru Fieldiana Geol 10 29-40

APPENDIX

Appendix 2 1 —The fossil amphibians and reptiles recorded from the areas shown in figures 4-7 and their corresponding bibliographic references are listed below, the numbers correspond to those on the maps (Figs 4-7) The areas have been designated by conspicuous geographic names Taxonomic entities not recognized in recent studies are excluded

CRETACEOUS

1 Alemania, Provincia de Salta Argentina (Late Cretaceous)
ANURA Pipidae *Saltenia ibanezi* Reig, 1959 (Reig 1959 Parodi Bustos et al 1960, Báez 1975)

2 Laguna Umayo Departamento de Puno, Peru (Late Cretaceous)
ANURA Leptodactylidae ? (Sigé, 1968)
CROCODILIA (Sigé, 1968)

3 Mossoró Estado do Rio Grande do Norte, Brasil (Late Cretaceous)
TESTUDINES Pelomedusidae *Apodichelys lucianoi* Price, 1954

4 Vila-Vila, Departamento de Cochabamba, Bolivia (Late Cretaceous)
TESTUDINES Pelomedusidae ? *Roxochelys vilavilensis* Broin, 1971

5 São Jose do Rio Preto, Estado de São Paulo Brasil (Late Cretaceous)
TESTUDINES Pelomedusidae *Podocnemis brasiliensis* Staesche, 1937² (Price, 1953 And and Vizotto, 1966, Broin, 1971), *Roxochelys wanderleyi* Price, 1953, *Podocnemis elegans* Suarez, 1969² Pieropolis, Estado de Minas Gerais, Brasil (Late Cretaceous)
SQUAMATA Sauria Iguanidae *Pristiguana brasiliensis* Estes and Price, 1973

6 Northwest of Lago Colhue-Huapi, Provincia del Chubut, Argentina (Late Cretaceous ?)
TESTUDINES Meiolaniidae *Niolamia patagonica* Ameghino, 1899 (Smith Woodward, 1901, Simpson, 1938)

PALEOCENE-EOCENE

1 Golfo de San Jorge, Provincia del Chubut, Argentina (early Paleocene)
TESTUDINES (Gasparini and Báez, 1975, Báez and Gasparini 1977)
CROCODILIA Crocodylidae *Necrosuchus ionensis* Simpson, 1937 (Gasparini and Baez, 1975)

2 Itaboraí, Estado de Rio de Janeiro, Brasil (late Paleocene)
ANURA Pipidae *Xenopus romeri* Estes, 1975 (Estes, 1975a b) Leptodactylidae (Estes, 1970), Bufonidae (Estes, 1970), Hylidae (Estes, 1970)
GYMNOPHIONA Caeciliidae *Apodops pricei* Estes and Wake, 1972
TESTUDINES Pelomedusidae *Podocnemis* sp (Paula Couto, 1970)
SQUAMATA Sauria Iguanidae (Estes, 1970) Teiidae (Estes 1970 Paula Couto, 1970), Gekkonidae (Estes, 1970) Serpentes Boidae (Estes, 1970, Paula Couto, 1970), Aniliidae (Estes, 1970, Hoffstetter and Rage, 1977)
CROCODILIA Sebecidae *Sebecus* sp (Paula Couto, 1970), Alligatoridae (Paula Couto, 1970)

---

² F de Broin (pers comm) considers the assignment of *P brasiliensis* and *P elegans* to the genus *Podocnemis* to be questionable

3 Cerro Pan de Azucar, Provincia del Chubut, Argentina (late Paleocene)
TESTUDINES (Simpson, 1935)
SQUAMATA Serpentes Boidae *Madtsoia* cf *M bai* Simpson 1933 (Simpson, 1935, Hoffstetter, 1959)
CROCODILIA (Simpson, 1935)

4 Laguna del Hunco, Provincia del Chubut, Argentina (late Paleocene)
ANURA Pipidae *Xenopus pascuali* (Casamiquela, 1960) (Estes 1975b, Casparini and Baez, 1975, Baez, 1976)
TESTUDINES Pleurodira (Gasparini and Báez, 1975)

5 Mina Aguilar, Provincia de Jujuy, Argentina (late Paleocene–early Eocene)
TESTUDINES (Gasparini and Báez, 1975)
CROCODILIA (Gasparini and Baez, 1975)
Quebrada de Humahuaca, Provincia de Jujuy, Argentina (late Paleocene–early Eocene)
TESTUDINES Pelomedusidae *Podocnemis argentinensis* Cattoi and Freiberg, 1958 (Gasparini and Baez, 1975, Báez and Gasparini, 1977)

6 Cañadon Hondo, near Paso Niemann, Provincia del Chubut, Argentina (early Eocene)
ANURA Leptodactylidae *Caudiverbera casamayorensis* (Schaeffer, 1949) (Lynch, 1971)
TESTUDINES Meiolaniidae *Crossochelys corniger* Simpson 1937 (Simpson 1937a 1938) Chelidae *Hydromedusa* sp (Wood and Moody, 1976)
CROCODILIA Sebecidae *Sebecus icaeorhinus* Simpson, 1937

7 Lago Colhue-Huapí, Provincia del Chubut, Argentina (early Eocene)
CROCODILIA Alligatoridae *Eocaiman cavernensis* Simpson, 1933b

8 Negritos, Departamento de Piura, Perú (middle Eocene)
TESTUDINES Pelomedusidae *Taphrosphys olssoni* (Schmidt) (Zangerl, 1947, Gaffney, 1975)

9 Divisadero Largo, Provincia de Mendoza, Argentina (late Eocene)
TESTUDINES (Simpson et al, 1962)
SQUAMATA Serpentes (Simpson et al, 1962)
CROCODILIA Sebecidae ? *Ilchunaia parca* Rusconi, 1946 (Gasparini 1972)

OLIGOCENE–MIOCENE

1 Campo Waldo, Departamento de Santander, Colombia (Oligocene)[a]
CROCODILIA Sebecidae *Sebecus* sp (Langston, 1965), Crocodylidae (Langston 1965)
TESTUDINES (Stirton, 1953)

2 Scarrit Pocket, Provincia del Chubut, Argentina (early Oligocene)
ANURA Leptodactylidae *Caudiverbera caudiverbera* (Linnaeus) (Schaeffer 1949, Lynch, 1971), *Eupsophus* sp (Schaeffer 1949), *Neoprocoela edentatus* (Schaeffer, 1949)

3 Tremembe, Estado de São Paulo, Brasil (early Oligocene)
TESTUDINES Chelidae (Wood and Patterson, 1973)

4 South of Lago Colhue-Huapi, Provincia del Chubut, Argentina (late Oligocene)
ANURA Leptodactylidae *Caudiverbera* sp (Schaeffer, 1949 Báez, 1977)

5 Chaparral, Departamento de Tolima, Colombia (late Oligocene–early Miocene)
CROCODILIA Alligatoridae *Balanerodus logimus* Langston 1965, Gavialidae (Langston, 1965)

6 Gaiman, Provincia del Chubut, Argentina (late Oligocene)
TESTUDINES Testudinidae *Geochelone gringorum* (Simpson 1942) (Williams 1950, Auffenberg 1971, de la Fuente, pers comm)

7 Southern Provincia de Santa Cruz, Argentina (early–middle Miocene)
SQUAMATA Sauria Iguanidae (Ameghino, 1899 Gasparini and Báez, 1975, Baez and Gasparini, 1977) Teiidae *Diasemosaurus occidentalis* Ameghino, 1893 (Gasparini and Baez, 1975), Serpentes (Ameghino 1899)

8 Coyaima, Departamento de Tolima, Colombia (late Miocene)
TESTUDINES Chelidae *Chelus colombianus* Wood, 1976a
SQUAMATA Sauria Teiidae cf *Tupinambis* (Estes, 1961)
CROCODILIA Sebecidae *Sebecus* sp (Langston, 1965), Alligatoridae (Langston, 1965), Crocodylidae (Langston, 1965), Gavialidae ? *Gavialis colombianus* Langston 1965

9 Carmen de Apicala, Departamento de Tolima, Colombia (late Miocene)
TESTUDINES Pelomedusidae (Royo y Gomez, 1945-1946, Stirton (1953), Chelidae *Chelus colombianus* Wood, 1976a
CROCODILIA Alligatoridae *Eocaiman* sp (Langston, 1965), *Caiman neivensis* Mook, 1941 (Langston, 1965)

---

[a] The Tertiary amphibian and reptile bearing deposits of Colombia are assigned chronologically according to Van Houten and Travis (1968) and Irving (1971) in an earlier paper the authors (1977) followed Stirton (1953)

10 Quebrada La Venta, Villavieja, Departamento de Huila, Colombia (late Miocene)
    ANURA   Bufonidae *Bufo marinus* Linnaeus (Estes and Wassersug, 1963)
    TESTUDINES Pelomedusidae *Podocnemis expansa* (Schweigger, 1912) (Medem, 1966, 1968), Chelidae *Chelus colombianus* Wood, 1976a Testudinidae *Geochelone (Chelonoides) hesterna* Auffenberg, 1971, Emydidae (Medem, 1968)
    SQUAMATA Sauria Iguanidae (Estes, 1961), Teiidae *Tupinambis* cf *T. teguixin* (Estes 1961) *Dracaena colombiana* Estes, 1961, Serpentes Aniliidae *Colombophis portai* Hoffstetter and Rage, 1977, Boidae *Lunectes strtoni* Hoffstetter and Rage, 1977, Colubridae (Hoffstetter 1967b, Hoffstetter and Rage 1977)
    CROCODILIA Sebecidae *Sebecus huilensis* Langston 1965 *Sebecus* sp (Langston, 1965), Alligatoridae *Eocaiman* sp (Langston, 1965), *Caiman venensis* Mook, 1941 (Langston, 1965), *Caiman* cf *C. latirostris* (Daudin, 1802) (Langston, 1965, Baez and Gasparini, 1977), Crocodylidae *Charactosuchus fieldsi* Langston, 1965, Nettosuchidae *Mourasuchus atopus* Langston, 1965 (Langston, 1966), Gavialidae cf *Rhamphostomopsis* (Langston 1965)
11 North of Lago Buenos Aires, Provincia de Santa Cruz, Argentina (late Miocene)
    ANURA   Leptodactylidae *Caudiverbera caudiverbera* Linnaeus (Casamiquela, 1958, Lynch, 1971)
12 Barranca de los Loros, Provincia de Río Negro, Argentina (late Miocene)
    ANURA   Leptodactylidae *Caudiverbera caudiverbera* Linnaeus (Casamiquela, 1963, Lynch, 1971)
13 Ingeniero Jacobacci, Provincia de Río Negro, Argentina (late Miocene)
    ANURA   Leptodactylidae *Wawelia gerholdi* Casamiquela, 1963

PLIOCENE-PLEISTOCENE

1 Urumaco, Estado de Falcón, Venezuela (middle Pliocene)
   TESTUDINES Pelomedusidae *Stupendemys geographicus* Wood, 1976b, Chelidae *Chelus lewisi* Wood, 1976a, Trionychidae (Wood and Patterson, 1973), Testudinidae (Wood and Patterson, 1973)
   CROCODILIA Alligatoridae *Melanosuchus fisheri* Medina, 1976, Crocodylidae ? *Gryposuchus* sp (Patterson, pers comm), Gavialidae *Ikanogavialis gameroi* Sill 1970, Nettosuchia *Mourasuchus amazonensis* Price, 1964 (Patterson, pers comm)
2 Valle de Santa María, Provincia de Catamarca Argentina (middle Pliocene)
   TESTUDINES Testudinidae *Geochelone gallardoi* (Rovereto, 1914) (Auffenberg, 1974)
3 Paraná, Provincia de Entre Ríos, Argentina (middle-late ? Pliocene)
   TESTUDINES Testudinidae *Geochelone* sp (Gasparini and Baez, 1975), Chelidae (Wieland, 1923)
   SQUAMATA Sauria Teiidae (Ambrosetti, 1890, Gasparini and Baez, 1975, Baez and Gasparini, 1977), Serpentes Boidae (Bravard 1858 Burmeister, 1883, 1885)
   CROCODILIA Alligatoridae *Caiman latirostris* (Daudin, 1802) (Gasparini and Baez, 1975), *C. australis* (Burmeister, 1885), cf *C. yacare* (Daudin, 1802) (Gasparini and Báez, 1975), *C.* sp (Gasparini and Báez 1975, Baez and Gasparini, 1977), Gavialidae *Rhamphostomopsis neogaeus* (Burmeister, 1885) (Rusconi 1933, 1935, Gasparini, 1968)
4 Monte Hermoso Provincia de Buenos Aires, Argentina (late Pliocene)
   ANURA   Leptodactylidae *Ceratophrys prisca* Ameghino, 1899 (Rovereto, 1914), Bufonidae (Gasparini and Baez, 1975)
   TESTUDINES Testudinidae *Geochelone gallardoi* (Rovereto, 1914) (Auffenberg, 1974)
   SQUAMATA Sauria Teiidae *Tupinambis* sp (Rovereto 1914), *Callopistes bicuspidatus* Chani, 1976
5 Río Quequén Salado, Provincia de Buenos Aires, Argentina (late Pliocene)
   ANURA   Bufonidae *Bufo pisanoi* Casamiquela, 1967
6 Chapadmalal, Provincia de Buenos Aires Argentina (late Pliocene)
   ANURA   Bufonidae *Bufo pisanoi* Casamiquela, 1967, Leptodactylidae *Ceratophrys* sp (Reig, 1958)
7 Río Juruá Estado do Acre, Brasil (Plio-Pleistocene)
   TESTUDINES Pelomedusidae *Podocnemis* sp (Paula Couto, 1970), Chelidae *Chelus* sp (Paula Couto, 1970), Testudinidae *Geochelone* sp (Paula Couto, 1970)
   SQUAMATA Serpentes (Paula Couto, 1970)
   CROCODILIA Alligatoridae *Brachygnatosuchus brasiliensis* Mook, 1921, *Purussaurus* sp (Paula Couto, 1970), Crocodylidae ? *Gryposuchus* (Paula Couto, 1970), Gavialidae ? *Gavialis* (Paula Couto, 1970, Baez and Gasparini, 1977), Nettosuchidae *Mourasuchus* sp (Paula Couto, 1970), *Mourasuchus amazonensis* Price, 1964
8 Río Aguaytía, West of Río Ucayali, Peru (Pliocene ?, Pleistocene ?)
   TESTUDINES Pelomedusidae *Podocnemis bassleri* Williams, 1956
9 Arroyo Penco Flaco, branch of Río Negro, Departamento de Soriano, Uruguay (Pleistocene)
   ANURA   Leptodactylidae *Leptodactylus* sp (Mones 1975)

10 Peninsula de Santa Elena, Provincia de Guayas, Ecuador (late Pleistocene)
   TESTUDINES Testudinidae *Geochelone* sp (Hoffstetter, 1970b) Emydidae *Geoemyda* (=*Callopsis*) sp (Hoffstetter, 1970b)
   SQUAMATA Sauria Iguanidae *Iguana* (Hoffstetter 1970b), Teiidae *Dicrodon* (Hoffstetter, 1970b)
   CROCODILIA Alligatoridae (Hoffstetter, 1970b)
11 Tarija, Departamento de Tarija, Bolivia (late Pleistocene)
   ANURA Leptodactylidae *Ceratophrys* sp (Vergnaud-Grazzini, 1968), Bufonidae *Bufo* cf *B marinus horribilis* Weigmann (Vergnaud-Grazzini, 1968)
   SQUAMATA Sauria Teiidae *Tupinambis teguixin* (Hoffstetter, 1963)
12 Ñuapua, near Carandaiti, Bolivia—Horizon 1 (middle Pleistocene)
   TESTUDINES Testudinidae *Geochelone* sp (Hoffstetter, 1968)
   Ñuapua near Carandaiti, Bolivia—Horizon 2 (late Pleistocene)
   ANURA Leptodactylidae *Leptodactylus* cf *L ocellatus* (Linnaeus) (Vergnaud-Grazzini 1968), *Ceratophrys* cf *C ornata* (Bell) (Vergnaud-Grazzini, 1968), Bufonidae *Bufo* cf *B paraenemis* (Vergnaud-Grizzini 1968)
   SQUAMATA Sauria Teiidae *Tupinambis teguixin* (Linnaeus) (Hoffstetter, 1968), Serpentes Boidae (Hoffstetter, 1968), Colubridae (Hoffstetter, 1968), Viperidae (Crotalinae) (Hoffstetter, 1968)
   AMPHISBAENIA Amphisbaenidae *Leposternon* ? (Hoffstetter, 1968)

3. Herpetofaunal Relationships Between Africa and South America

Raymond F. Laurent[*]

Investigador Titular
Fundación Miguel Lillo
Miguel Lillo 205
4000 Tucumán, Argentina

At the height of the Matthewsian theory of continental biogeography (Matthew, 1915; Darlington, 1957), the very title of this paper would have been almost preposterous, at least in the influential herpetological centers of North America dominated by Noble (1931), Dunn (1923, 1931), and Schmidt (1946). The dissident voices of Jeannel (1942), Du Toit (1937) and others were stifled as inconsequential. Africa and South America were supposed to have had no relationships whatever for a very long time. Indeed the differences between the Ethiopian and Neotropical herpetofaunas are striking and seem to support the idea of independent histories. Most dominant groups are represented in Africa and South America by pairs of adaptive equivalents or vicarious groups in Simpson's (1965) sense (Table 3.1).

Faunal similarities between Africa and South America have been explained by extinctions in the Holarctic Region. In some cases the fossil record seems to bear out this explanation (e.g., turtles of the family Pelomedusidae). When such paleontological evidence was lacking, it often was implied. Dunn (1931) emphasized that it would not be sane reasoning to postulate a trans-Atlantic land bridge just because no fossils were known from the northern continents. When Dunn made his statement the fossil record was much poorer than it is now. Presently, some credence can be given to negative evidence, namely the lack of fossils, in North America and Europe of groups that elsewhere have extensive fossil records (e.g. turtles and crocodilians).

New evidence definitely points to the union of Africa and South America into a single continent from at least the Late Carboniferous until the Cretaceous. Then a graben formed a narrow gulf north and south of a residual bridge between northeastern Brasil and Nigeria. During the last half of the Turonian the continents were split with the birth of the South Atlantic Ocean, which initially was quite narrow. This scenario was described by Reyment (1975) and is supported by convincing geological evidence—paleomagnetism (Creer, 1973), fit of the continents (Dietz and Holden, 1970), sea floor spreading (Heirtzler, 1968, Francheteau, 1973), and plate tectonics with the fitting of cratons and rocks (Hurley, 1968; Dietz and Holden, 1970; Douglas et al., 1973). The stratigraphic concordances are especially striking (Reyment and Tait, 1972), as well as the structure of the coastal basins with their immense amounts of fresh water sediments (Martin 1968), which suggest a graben phase like that of the African Rift Valleys. The salt deposits in Angola, Gabon and Brasil are reminiscent of later phases like that of Lake Turkana or the Red Sea (Reyment, 1975).

Paleontological data are still more convincing (Báez and Gasparini, this volume). The amphi-Atlantic distribution of the mesosaurians of the early Permian (Romer, 1966) is strong evidence for a Gondwanan land mass (Colbert, 1973). The early Triassic of Argentina has revealed a *Cynognathus* fauna almost identical to that of the upper Beaufort beds of South Africa (Bonaparte, 1967). Two

TABLE 3.1—Family Groups of Amphibians and Reptiles that have Trans-Atlantic Counterparts

South America	Africa
Leptodactylidae	Ranidae (*sensu* Liem, 1970)
Hylidae	Hyperoliidae (*sensu* Liem, 1970)
Iguanidae	Agamidae + Chamaeleontidae
Teiidae	Lacertidae
Boinae	Pythoninae
Crotalinae	Viperinae

[*] Investigator Principal del CONICET

groups of mammals provide evidence that the Atlantic was not the wide ocean of today in the Eocene and Oligocene. Primates and caviomorph rodents, conspicuously lacking in the early South American mammalian fauna, nevertheless entered the continent long before the Late Cenozoic invasion via Panama. Classically, it was assumed that they entered South America by island-hopping from North America (Wood, 1950, Simpson, 1965, Patterson and Pascual, 1968). However, another hypothesis assuming an African origin and a trans-Atlantic migration has been maintained by Lavocat (1974) and Hoffstetter (1972, 1977). Krommelbein (1971) showed that the fossil, fresh water ostracods from the coastal basins of Reconçavo, Sergipe, Brasil, and of Gabon are almost identical. Two different ammonite faunas (one in the Potiguar Basin in northern Brasil and another in the Sergipe-Alagoas Basin) existed until the lower Turonian. Then the African-Brasilian isthmus disappeared, and the two faunas mingled (Beurlen, 1961, Reyment, 1958, 1970). These data provide evidence for the birth of the Atlantic Ocean and the separation of Africa and South America in the middle Turonian, about 90–95 m y b p.

This establishes a firm basis on which to proceed to determine which groups existed in both continents before their separation and which emigrated from one to the other before or after their separation. The Hennigian systematists and biogeographers (Brundin, 1966, Croizat, 1964, Nelson, 1973, Croizat et al., 1974) have insisted on the necessity of vicariance events in determining generalized tracts in reconstructing biogeographic histories. Their conclusions are in general agreement with plate tectonics, mainly because their work has been based on these premises rather than because they emphasize vicariance at the expense of geocenters and dispersal (Appendix 3.1). Their approach is applicable to the study of relationships between the African and South American faunas. There was an old African-Brasilian (Inabresian, *fide* Jeannel, 1942) fauna, and there also are vicariant groups.

SUMMARY OF DISTRIBUTION PATTERNS

The first step in a biogeographic analysis must be a summary of distribution patterns or generalized tracts" (Croizat, 1964). These patterns are listed below:

1. *Gondwanan or West Gondwanan groups* —Geotrypetes-Apodops, Pipidae, Pelomedusidae, Amphisbaenidae, Typhlopidae, Leptotyphlopidae
2. *South American groups that invaded Africa before the separation of the continents* —Bufonidae, Iguanidae (extinct in Africa but surviving in Madagascar)
3. *Presumed Indian groups that invaded South America via Africa before the separation of the continents* —Microhylidae
4. *African groups that invaded South America after the separation of the continents* —Gavialidae (?), Gekkoninae, Scincidae, Amphisbaenidae (?), Colubrinae (?)
5. *Holarctic groups that invaded Africa and South America from the north* — Testudinidae, Crocodylidae, Colubrinae (?)
6. *African groups that recently invaded South America by a northern route* — Ranidae
7. *Neotropical groups absent from Africa* —Rhinatrematidae, Dermophiinae,[1] Caeciliidae, Typhlonectidae, Bolitoglossini, Leptodactylidae,- Hylidae,[3] Centrolenidae, Pseudidae, Dendrobatidae, Sphaerodactylinae, Iguanidae, Teiidae, Anguidae, Boini, Xenodontinae, Micrurinae, Crotalinae

---

[1] The reasons for splitting the Caeciliidae and recognizing the Herpelinae are given by Laurent (in press).

[2] The African Heleophryninae are considered to be members of the Myobatrachidae by Lynch (1973).

[3] The Hylidae, as well as other groups, like Discoglossidae, Pelobatidae, Salamandridae and Anguidae are present in northern Africa. That part of Africa belongs to the Palaearctica Region and is not considered to be relevant here, although the past existence of some of its fauna in the Ethiopian Region cannot be ruled out entirely.

8. *African and Old World groups absent from South America*—Scolecomorphidae, Herpelinae, Heleophryninae, Hyperoliidae, Agamidae, Chamaeleontidae, Lacertidae, Cordylidae, Varanidae, Pythoninae, Lycodontinae, Dasypeltinae, Elapidae, Viperinae

9. *Groups that apparently once lived in Africa but are now extinct there*—Iguanidae

10. *Groups that presumably were pan-Gondwanan in the Jurassic*—Leiopelmatidae

Two patterns are more prevalent than others—groups present in South America but not in Africa, and present in Africa but not in South America. A third pattern involves groups that are present in both continents.

RELATIONSHIPS OF PATTERNS TO CONTINENTAL HISTORIES

Amphibians

Caecilians—The distribution of caecilians indicates that they are a typical Gondwanan group. Estes and Wake (1972) described the only known fossil caecilian, *Apodops*, from the Paleocene of southeastern Brasil. The fossil tends to confirm a Gondwanan distribution, especially because *Apodops* resembles the African *Geotrypetes* and may be closely related to it.

Possibly *Geotrypetes* is more archaic than either of the primitive families Rhinatrematidae and Ichthyophiidae. It is said to have a free, dentate ectopterygoid, a bone generally lost and always edentulous in other caecilians. Furthermore, it has two pairs of openings in the skull (temporal and interpterygoidal). According to the Lissamphibian hypothesis, such vacuities should be primitive and their disappearance a secondary adaptation to fossorial habits.[1]

---

[1] This seems more likely than the theory of Carroll and Currie (1975), who related the Gymnophiona to microsaurians, because the loss of so many cranial bones is more easily visualized as the result of fenestration than an effect of further solidification of an already continuously roofed skull.

Geotrypetes has as many chromosomes as the ichthyophids, which also include the Indian *Uraeotyphlus* (Nussbaum, pers. comm.). Also, caecilians, like other lissamphibians, demonstrate a negative correlation between chromosome number and the number of derived character states (Laurent, in press). Thus, *Apodops* might belong to an African-Brasilian group of primitive caecilians, from which the African and Neotropical caecilians descended. By this reasoning, the other caecilians are actually different in South America and Africa. The South American Rhinatrematidae is more primitive than the Ichthyophidae (Nussbaum, 1977). The aquatic South American Typhlonectidae and the fossorial African Scolecomorphidae are specialized groups apparently derived from old stocks. The remaining genera have been placed in the Caeciliidae. The specialized *Caecilia* and *Oscaecilia* should be separated from the bulk of the family (Laurent, in press). The other genera can be divided into an Old World subfamily Herpelinae with splenial teeth (except in the specialized *Boulengerula*) and a New World subfamily Dermophiinae without splenial teeth (except in *Gymnophis*, therefore deemed primitive) (Laurent, in press). These subfamilies are most likely sister groups.

Salamanders—All South American salamanders are members of the Plethodontidae and obvious immigrants from Central America (Wake 1966). However, I must stress a recent discovery, as interesting as it is unexpected, of a salamander in Senonian (Upper Cretaceous) beds of Niger (de Broin et al, 1975). The genus and even the family have not been determined. The age is not fixed precisely, because the Senonian is a long period following the Turonian (85 m y b p) and lasting until the end of the Mesozoic (Maastrichian, about 65 m y b p). Salamanders have been considered as exclusively Holarctic. Therefore, their presence in equatorial Africa, perhaps quite soon after the formation of the Atlantic Ocean, indicates the possibility of an older salamander fauna in Africa and perhaps in South America.

Archaeobatrachians—The only living archaeobatrachians in South America are the pipids, which apparently are an early specialized derivative from Jurassic frogs. The pipids have a typical west Gondwanan distribution and are now common to Africa and South America. They are known from both continents by a number of Mesozoic and Cenozoic fossils, beginning with the Early Cretaceous of Israel (Nevo, 1968). It has been argued that the pipids might have lived in the northern continents and subsequently migrated independently into South America and Africa. However, the family is conspicuously absent in the fossil record in the north, it is replaced there by the ecologically similar palaeobatrachids, now extinct, but apparently common from the Jurassic to the Pliocene.[6] Estes (1975a) reported a fossil of *Xenopus* from the Paleocene of Brasil and referred the Eocene *Shelania* from Patagonia to the same genus. Therefore, there is little reason to doubt the Inabresian[d] origin of the family. Estes (1975b) synthesized the phylogeny of the pipids. Of the two lower Cretaceous genera from Israel, *Cordicephalus* seems to be ancestral to *Xenopus*, whereas *Thoraciliacus* seems to be an early specialized derivative of the primitive stem of the family. No other fossil is known from the Cretaceous before the separation of Africa and South America. In the Late Cretaceous (Senonian, 80–85 m y b p) there is *Saltenia* in northwestern Argentina and *Xenopus* and other pipids similar to *Pipa* or *Hymenochirus* in western Africa. *Eoxenopoides* from southwestern Africa (about the limit of the Mesozoic and Cretaceous, 65 m y b p) is a specialized derivative of *Xenopus*. All more recent fossils are referred to *Xenopus*—two in South America [Paleocene (±60 m y b p) of southeastern Brasil (Estes, 1975a) and Eocene (±50 m y b p) of Patagonia (Casamiquela, 1961)] and two in Africa [Miocene (±20 m y b p) of southwestern Africa (Ahl, 1926) and of Morocco (Vergnaud-Grazzini, 1966)] *Xenopus* presently is speciose in Africa, where the specialized *Hymenochirus* and *Pseudhymenochirus* occur in forests. *Xenopus* is extinct in South America, but perhaps through a *Saltenia*-like stock it gave rise to the modern South American pipids, now restricted to forested regions of northern and eastern South America (Estes, 1975b).

Other archaeobatrachians have lived in South America (Báez and Gasparini, this volume). *Vieraella* (Lower Jurassic) and *Notobatrachus* (Upper Jurassic) were placed in the Leiopelmatidae by Estes and Reig (1973), who suggested that the leiopelmatids radiated during the Jurassic in Gondwanaland and that *Ascaphus* is a remnant of a northward migration at the end of the Mesozoic. *Leiopelma* survived in New Zealand, where it is the only frog. Discovery of fossil leiopelmatids in other parts of Gondwanaland, especially Africa, is expected.

Neobatrachians.—Estes and Reig (1973) and Laurent (in press) believed that the neobatrachians are a Gondwanan group. Possibly the neobatrachians were derived from the southern Discoglossoidea (Leiopelmatidae) through a grade exemplified by the Australian family Myobatrachidae, which perhaps formerly had a pan-Gondwanan range.

Among the neobatrachians, only the Bufonidae, Microhylidae and Ranidae are present on both Africa and South America. Of these, the ranids are represented in South America only by *Rana palmipes*, a Central American species of recent entry. According to Noble (1931), the bufonids and microhylids originated in the Holarctic and subsequently invaded the southern continents. Blair (1972b) suggested that *Bufo* originated in South America. Estes and Reig (1973) reported *Bufo* from the Paleocene of Brasil, whereas no other bufonid fossils are known before the Miocene or Oligocene (Hecht, 1963). The fossil record and the rich Neotropical radiation of bufonids (9 genera, more than 120 species) support Blair's conclusions.

From a South American center of origin, three avenues of bufonid dispersal are conceivable—1) through Antarctica and Australia, 2) through Africa, and 3) through North America. The first obviously is out of the

---

[6] According to some workers (e g, Estes and Reig 1973), the Palaeobatrachidae is related to the Pipidae, but Vergnaud-Grazzini and Hoffstetter (1972) believed that the similarities are the result of convergence. However Estes (1975b) argued convincingly that they are in the same superfamily.

[d] The term "Inabresia" was coined by Jeannel (1942) for the African-Brasilian continent.

question because the Australian region is devoid of bufonids The last was suggested by Blair (1972b) Laurent (1972, 1975) did not reject dispersal through North America but proposed that bufonids also dispersed through Africa Laurent was influenced by Estes (1970, pers comm) insistence that no bufonid entered North America before the Miocene There is further evidence in favor of an African dispersal route 1) The South American bufonid radiation is the largest (Trueb, 1971, McDiarmid, 1971, Cei, 1972) and the African is next with seven genera and about 50 species (Tihen, 1960 Tandy and Keith, 1972) followed by Eurasia with only six genera and about 40 species and finally North America with one genus and some 20 species 2) Few bufonids have retained an omosternum, a plesiomorphic character for the family These include the *Bufo haematiticus* group in northern South America, the African genus *Nectophrynoides*, and possibly *Werneria* in west Africa [7] 3) Relationships between the Neotropical and African bufonids is supported by the high degree of genetic compatibility between the South American *Bufo arenarum* and the African *B regularis* (Blair, 1972a), by the striking similarity of peculiar species like the African *B superciliaris* and the Neotropical *B blombergi* (Blair, 1972b), and by serological affinities (Cei, 1977) Such evidence induced Laurent (in press) to emphasize the African route rather than the North American one A dispersal following the described route need not exclude a Miocene invasion of North America from South America but the African dispersal was much earlier (± 90 m y b p versus ± 25 m y b p) and therefore much more important to the evolutionary biogeography of the family

The systematic position of the Microhylidae is the most controversial matter in the taxonomy of frogs Boulenger (1882) considered them (as the Engystomatidae) to be related to the Ranidae, because of their firmi-sternal pectoral girdle Noble (1931) supported Boulenger Orton (1957) emphasized the apparent primitiveness of the microhylid tadpoles which are similar in many respects to those of pipids Orton believed that it was unlikely that such an adaptive complex of features as the larval mouth in most anurans would be lost, therefore, she thought that the microhylids were related to the pipids and represented an early radiation among frogs This contention was resisted by several herpetologists beginning with Griffiths (1963) The traditionalists include Griffiths and Carvalho (1965), Tihen (1965), and Kluge and Farris (1969) The "Ortonists" include Hecht (1963), Inger (1967), and Starrett (1973), who based her opinion on a detailed study of tadpoles Savage (1973) enthusiastically based a new zoogeographic scheme on the apparent strengths of Starrett's conclusions, and even included Australia in the original Gondwanan realm of the family (see Tyler, this volume, for contrary zoogeographic arguments) Lynch (1973) showed that such an evolutionary scheme of the microhylids required the independent acquisition of no less than 13 characters present in the ranids In a detailed study of tadpole structure, Sokol (1975) demonstrated that the microhylids had lost the larval papillae, denticles and horny beaks [8] Therefore, the microhylids are related to the ranoids

Microhylids have a semirelictual distribution, intermediate between the scattered patterns of some old families, such as the Discoglossidae and Pelobatidae, and the compact patterns of the more modern, still radiating groups like the Ranidae and Bufonidae Therefore, the microhylids must be older than the ranids This idea is supported by the presence of 28 chromosomes in the microhylid *Kaloula*, the number is not the result of secondary fusions and therefore is a plesiomorphic feature similar to the karyotype of *Discoglossus* The presence of a variety of microhylids in South America also supports the

---

[7] Andersson (1903) mentioned the presence of a vestigial omosternum in his description of *Stenoglossa*, a synonym of *Werneria*, but Amiet (1976) said that the omosternum is absent in the genus Nonetheless the species of *Werneria* resemble toads of the *Bufo haematiticus* group

[8] Blommers-Schlosser (1975) confirmed Sokol's conclusions by discovering that in the Scaphiophryninae, the most primitive subfamily of microhylids, the tadpoles have papillae and a slightly sinistral spiracle (median in other subfamilies)

antiquity of the family, the ranids barely enter South America

Assuming that the microhylids evolved, like the ranoids, in the eastern part of Gondwanaland, their radiation was around the Indian Ocean (tropical Asia, East Indies, and Madagascar) The most primitive subfamilies (Scaphiophryninae and Dyscophinae) live in Madagascar and tropical Asia The eastern groups in New Guinea (Sphenophryninae and Asterophryinae) are not relevant here, but the other subfamilies are—Brevicipinae, Hoplophryninae[9] and Phrynomerinae in Africa, Cophylinae in Madagascar, and Microhylinae in Asia and America

We can dismiss as improbable an Holarctic origin of the family for the primitive subfamilies live in the tropics Thus, only Madagascar and the Gondwanan part of Asia are likely centers of origin of the microhylids Both are possible, for during its northward drift India apparently was connected at times with Madagascar by garlands of islands (McKenzie and Sclater, 1973), some of which continue to exist as the Seychelles, Amirante, Mascarene, Maldive and Laccadive Islands (Appendix 3 2) Later, contacts were with Malaysia and Indochina through the Nicobar and Andaman islands, allowing the Indian fauna to invade eastern Asia, Indonesia and even the East Indies The African invasion likely passed through the Mozambique Channel and its islands (e g Comores) The African groups of microhylids are now highly differentiated

The American microhylines are a problem According to the Matthewsian theory, the microhylines originated in tropical Asia, invaded the eastern Palaearctic Region, and passed into North America by the Bering isthmus and into South America by island-hopping well before the Pliocene There are serious objections to this hypothesis In Asia, as well as in America, the primitive genera having a complete pectoral girdle are in the tropics, these are *Kalophrynus*, *Chaperina*, *Melanobatrachus* and *Gastrophrynoides* in Asia and *Otophryne* and *Dermatonotus* in South America The genera living in temperate Asia (*Microhyla*) and North America (*Gastrophryne*) have reduced pectoral girdles Carvalho (1954) Nelson (1966), Nelson and Cuellar (1968) questioned the affinities between the Asiatic and American microhylines There is a possible trans-Gondwanan pathway from India to Madagascar to Africa to South America that is marked by a series of genera having complete pectoral girdles—*Kalophrynus* (tropical Asia), *Melanobatrachus* (India), Scaphiophryninae and *Dyscophus* (Madagascar), Brevicipinae and *Parhoplophryne* (Africa) and *Otophryne* and *Dermatonotus* (South America) If such a dispersal took place, it might have occurred before or slightly after the birth of the Atlantic Ocean

Chromosome numbers support this hypothesis (Morescalchi, 1973, Bogart and Nelson, 1976, Bogart et al, 1976) In Asia, *Kaloula* has 28 chromosomes, which equals the relatively primitive number of *Discoglossus*, other Asian genera (*Uperodon Ramanella Microhyla*) are known to have 26 chromosomes In Africa there are 26 in *Phrynomerus* and 24 in *Breviceps* In America there are 26 chromosomes in the primitive genera *Otophryne* and *Glossostoma*, 24 in *Chiasmocleis* and 22 in seven genera, including the widespread *Gastrophryne* and *Elachistocleis*

Considering now only those families that are present on one side of the Atlantic, we see some striking parallelisms South American leptodactylids, rhinodermatids and dendrobatids are paralleled by the terrestrial ranids and hyperolids in Africa, the hylids and centrolenids in South America are paralleled by the arboreal ranids (*Chiromantis*) and hyperolids in Africa Moreover, some peculiar adaptations in one continent have counterparts in the other—the aquatic South American pseudids (coexisting with pipids) versus African pipids, the rheophilous South American telmatobiines versus African heleophrynines, atelopine bufonids and brachycephalids in South America versus *Didynamipus* in Africa In some cases the resemblances are striking For example, compare *Physalaemus biligonigerus* in South America with *Tomopterna delalandii* (and congeners) in Africa, compare the South American *Leptodactylus*

---

[9] *Melanobatrachus* is included in the Microhylinae (Savage, 1973, Laurent, in press)

fuscus with African species of *Ptychadena*, and the *Hyla leucophyllata* group in South America with species of *Afrixalus* On the other hand, some adaptations are unique to one continent Africa has nothing like the marsupial tree frogs (Amphignathodontinae), South America has no frog emulating the sexual dichromatism of the tribe Hyperolini (for other examples, see Laurent, 1973)

Reptiles

Chelonians —The Pelomedusidae is a classical case of an amphi-Atlantic distribution, which has been explained by Matthewsians as an Holarctic origin and southward migrations Others have explained the distribution by the fragmentation of a primitively Gondwanan range The alternatives are not clear, for there are northern fossils Some very old turtles from Germany generally classified in other suborders are really pleurodires (de Broin, pers comm) These are the Triassic *Proterochersis* (Proganochelydia) and the Jurassic *Platychelys* (Amphichelydia) [10] Quite an array of other northern genera are known from Upper Cretaceous to Oligocene beds belonging to the shores of the young Atlantic Ocean According to de Broin (pers comm) the marine coastal Bothremydidae is a sister family of the Pelomedusidae The oldest pelomedusid fossil is *Platycheloides* from the Lower Cretaceous of Africa Thus, the family was in existence before the birth of the Atlantic Ocean Later, the exclusively African pelomedusines (not known before Oligocene) were separated from the Podocnemiinae, which flourished in South America, Africa, Europe (*Neochelys*, Eocene-Oligocene), and even India (*Schweboemys*, Pliocene), and survived in Africa until the Pleistocene, in South America and in Madagascar (*Erymnochelys*)

The Cryptodira, rather common in Laurasia in Jurassic and Cretaceous times, are present in Africa and South America, they seem to be rather recent immigrants into South America—Oligocene for *Geochelone* (Simpson, 1942), Miocene for Emydidae (Medem, 1968), a short Pliocene apparition for the Trionychidae in Venezuela (Wood and Patterson, 1973) Only the Testudinidae and Trionychidae became established in Africa, where they are known since the Miocene (Romer, 1966)

Crocodilians —The living crocodilians do not show significant similarities between South America and Africa The Crocodylidae is present in both continents but relatively unimportant in South America, the Alligatoridae, absent from Africa, radiated impressively in South America However, before the formation of the Atlantic Ocean in the Cretaceous, the crocodilian fauna, composed exclusively of mesosuchians, was much the same in South America and Africa Thus, the African Libycosuchidae were small, blunt-snouted crocodiles, very similar to the South American Notosuchidae (Sill, 1968, Buffetaut, 1976) [11] The gigantic, long-snouted pholidosaurid genus *Sarcosuchus* was common to Brasil and west Africa (Buffetaut pers comm) After the severance of the last remnants of a bridge, the faunas gradually became different Although the mesosuchians were dominant over the eusuchians until well into the Cenozoic in the scattered Gondwanan continents, they became subordinate to them in Laurasia (Buffetaut, pers comm) The Dyrosauridae (Upper Cretaceous and Early Cenozoic mesosuchians), extremely long-snouted, gavial-like creatures, although essentially African, also lived at the end of the Cretaceous on the west side of the still trench-like Atlantic, but this can be ascribed to their littoral habits (Buffetaut, 1976) Other gavial-like crocodilians, now extinct, were part of the Neotropical eusuchian radiation in the Tertiary Sill (1968) considered them as Gavialidae, but possibly they are another case of parallel evolution (Báez and Gasparini, this volume) If they are true gavialids, their dispersal through a

---

[10] Gaffney (1975) specifically removed *Proterochersis* from the Proganochelydia, because they have a fused pelvis like the pleurodires, he explicitly included *Platychelys* in the Pleurodira

[11] Steel (1973) suggested that the groups might have evolved in parallel, but Buffetaut (1976) and Sill (1968) recognized two families while admitting that they probably have a common ancestor Nopsca (1928) recognized them as subfamilies, but Mook (1936), von Huene (1956) and Romer (1956, 1966) did not even make that distinction

still narrow ocean in the Eocene seems to be the only explanation of their distribution, for the family is first known in the Eocene (Hecht and Malone 1972) of Africa

Lizards—Only the Gekkonidae and Iguanidae are involved in the Afro-American separation Other families of lizards seem to be parallel radiations after the separation—Agamidae and Chamaeleontidae similar to the Iguanidae Lacertidae, Cordylidae and Scincidae emulating the Teiidae and some terrestrial iguanids, the Varanidae copied by large teiids, like *Tupinambis* Also there is the ecological similarity between the numerous "microteiids" and the lygosomine skinks (Laurent, 1973)

Although some archaic lizards were present in the Triassic, these apparently have little in common with Jurassic ones, which belong to the modern infraorders (Robinson, 1967, Hoffstetter, 1955 1967) Some of the modern families were present in the Cretaceous Thus when Africa and South America drifted apart, several recent families were already in existence The iguanid, *Pristiguana* (Estes and Price, 1973), from the Cretaceous of Brasil has some characters of the Teiidae Chromosome morphology is similar in iguanids and teiids (Gorman, 1970)

The Gekkonidae may be the oldest family of modern lizards It existed in Brasil in the Paleocene (Estes, 1970) The Jurassic Ardeosauridae presumably is ancestral to the gekkonids and so similar to them (Hoffstetter, 1964) that in a cladistic system they could be included in the gekkonids Therefore the presence of gekkonids in western Gondwanaland before the formation of the Atlantic graben is realistic

The relict and disjunct distribution of the Eublepharinae is best explained by a northern origin On the other hand, the Sphaerodactylinae is likely to be a strictly Neotropical derivative of a Gondwanan stock Most of the South American Gekkoninae seem to have come from Africa by waif dispersal after the formation of the Atlantic Ocean This is fairly certain and recent for the species common to both continents, such as *Hemidactylus brooki* and *H mabouia* (Kluge, 1969) and hardly less obvious for *Tarentola* (Kluge, 1967, Vanzolini, 1968) This dispersal was easier when the Atlantic Ocean was narrower Other gekkonine stocks (e g , *Briba* and *Bogertia*) may have entered South America in the Late Cretaceous or Early Cenozoic Possibly some (e g , *Homonota*) immigrated into South America before the separation of the continents Bons and Pasteur (1977) suggested an early immigration for the two Neotropical species assigned to the African genus *Lygodactylus*

Estes and Price (1973) believed that the Iguanidae originated in South America when it was still united to Africa and invaded Africa where they became extinct, and Madagascar, where they survived Alternatively, they could have originated in Africa, where the related agamids and chamaeleontids supplanted them If the Iguanidae and Teiidae have a common ancestor, the presence of teiids in North America in the Cretaceous, contrasting to the absence of iguanids there (Estes 1970), is puzzling and cannot be explained with our present data

The past existence of iguanids in Africa is hardly questionable, for they are still living in Madagascar Is their extinction in Africa the result of competition with agamids? Not likely, because the African agamids are not diverse and therefore unlikely to out-compete the diversified iguanids Also, it is unlikely that the chameleons out-competed the iguanids, except for possibly some arboreal types, for the chameleons are a highly specialized group of lizards Furthermore, the agamids are probably relatively recent immigrants into Africa from Eurasia Rafting of iguanids and teiids from South America to Africa is not possible now because of the direction of the ocean currents, but 50–80 m y b p such an event was more likely In the reverse direction, the feasibility of a successful crossing has been proved by *Hemidactylus* (Kluge, 1969), but no cases are documented for agamids, chamaeleontids, lacertids, or cordylids

If, as indicated by Estes and Price (1973), iguanids and teiids are respectively the roots of the Iguania and Scincomorpha radiations, an eastern invasion of "eoteiids" is suggested Estes (pers comm) sees the teiids as an essentially Neotropical radiation with a lacertoid derivation through northern Gondwanaland. The Scincidae have relationships between the southern Atlantic continents, but the few South American species of *Mabuya* probably came from Africa long after the separation of the continents.

Amphisbaenians.—The worm-lizards have a typical western Gondwanaland distribution. They are an old group, and their existence in the Inabresian continents is likely. Fossils are known from North America (Eocene to Pleistocene) and belong to several extinct genera, as well as to the extant *Rhineura* and *Leposternon*, now surviving only in South America (Romer, 1966). The extinct *Omoiotyphlops* is from the Eocene-Pliocene of Europe (Romer 1966, Hoffstetter, 1962). Therefore the range of the amphisbaenids underwent a contraction similar to that of many tropical groups that lived in Europe and North America.[12]

Snakes.—Among the primitive scolecophidians the Leptotyphlopidae has about the same range as the amphisbaenians and presumably the same history. The Typhlopidae has a pantropical range, which can be deemed pan-Gondwanan until there is contrary evidence.

The Boidae also is considered to be a Gondwanan group, nonetheless, the present distribution is the result of complex migrations. Primitive fossil genera have been found in southern continents—*Laparrentophis* in the Lower Cretaceous of northern Africa, *Dinilysia* in Patagonia (Upper Cretaceous), and *Madtsoia* in South America, Africa, and Madagascar (Upper Cretaceous to Paleocene).

Presently the surviving boids in South America and Africa are not closely related. The Neotropical tribe Boini may be descended *in situ* from archaic South American boids, but the African Erycinae and Pythoninae probably came from elsewhere. Hoffstetter and Rage (1972) believed that the Erycinae, which may have originated in North America from a South American boine stock, was present in North America in the Paleocene or earlier and in Europe in the Eocene. Another lineage (Rage, 1977), using the Bering pathway, entered Africa in the lower Miocene. Rage (pers. comm.) contemplates three possible origins for the Pythoninae—Africa or Australasia, both of which he considers to be doubtful, and Asia, a choice also favored by Underwood (1976, pers. comm.). Thus, boids supposedly migrated from North America to Asia via the Bering land bridge. A fourth possibility is the Indian raft (see Appendix 3.2), which may explain why boids flourish in Australasia and how they later came to Africa from Asia, presumably in Miocene times.[13]

The least understood of all groups is the vast array of higher snakes, the caenophidians or Colubroidea. Until recently, the fossil record of caenophidians was exclusively Holarctic and only back to the Miocene. New data show that caenophidians existed in Europe in the lower Eocene and the Colubridae (*sensu lato*) is known from the middle Oligocene.[14] Rage (1975) described *Nigerophis* from the Paleocene of Africa; this genus seems to be intermediate between the caenophidians and the Palaeophidae. Such a systematic position suggests an aquatic origin of modern snakes and makes their paleogeographic history even more difficult to interpret. Rabb and Marx (1973) suggested that the group perhaps had a tropicopolitan distribution before the Gondwanan fragmentation, but Rage (1976) disagreed. The scarcity and primitiveness of the few colubroids from the early Cenozoic support Rage rather than Rabb and Marx.

The problem is compounded by the taxonomic uncertainty that prevails within the Colubridae (*sensu lato*). Most attempts to clarify the systematics have resulted in 1) recognition of small groups that can be separated from the bulk of the genera, or 2) partition of larger groups that are highly controversial (Dunn, 1928; Bogert, 1940; Bourgeois 1968, Underwood 1967, Dowling, 1975, Smith et al., 1977). Dowling's (1975) classification

---

[12] The Oligocene fossils, *Changlosaurus* and *Crythiosaurus*, from Mongolia are not amphisbaenians (Gans, pers. comm.).

[13] Rage (pers. comm.) still prefers the Bering route, but he does not reject the Indian hypothesis.

[14] A record from the upper Eocene (Rage, 1974) is doubtful (Rage, pers. comm.).

is beautifully simple, resulting in geographically discrete groups, namely New World Xenodontinae (following Dunn's scheme) and Old World Lycodontinae. This concept is in agreement with the probable belated birth and radiation of the family as suggested by the fossil record. Thus, parallel radiations into terrestrial, aquatic and fossorial groups took place in South America and Africa.

On the other hand, Underwood's (1967) revolutionary classification, which was severely criticized by others (namely, Dowling 1975, Hoffstetter, 1968, Smith et al, 1977), implied trans-Atlantic relationships. The similarities between the fossorial African *Calamelaps* and the South American *Atractus*, the aquatic *Limnophis* (or *Hydraethiops*) with *Helicops*, or the terrestrial *Lycophidion* and *Oxyrhopus* simply may be the result of convergence. Of course, this is the most likely hypothesis, but rafting should not be dismissed off handedly.

Three adaptive types of arboreal colubrids correspond to three groups distinguished by Bourgeois (1968), as follows: 1) large-headed snakes with vertical pupils and slender necks (Boiginae), 2) streamlined but rather robust green snakes with round pupils (Philothamninae), 3) very slender snakes with round or horizontal pupils, commonly with pointed heads and venom (Dispholidinae). The similarities between the Neotropical *Leptodeira* and the African *Boiga-Dipsadoboa-Crotaphopeltis* group are probably only convergence but on the basis of Bourgeois (1968) criteria the Neotropical *Oxybelis* can be grouped with the African *Thelotornis*, in spite of its round pupil.[15] Likewise, genera such as *Leptophis* and *Chironius* in South America would belong to the African Philothamninae.

Because of the relatively recent development of the colubrids, it is unlikely that any groups had an Inabresian distribution. Trans-Atlantic rafting may have occurred, but probably only in one direction (Africa to South America). Hoffstetter (1972) convincingly argued that hystricomorph rodents and monkeys entered South America across the Atlantic Ocean. The reverse migration has never been advocated, except in the beginning of the Atlantic era, when the sea was very narrow. Now the ocean currents are favorable for westward rafting in the tropics. If this situation prevailed for a long time, it may explain why the Neotropical fauna is so obviously richer than the Ethiopian fauna. South America might have received a sizable faunistic contribution from Africa without giving anything in exchange, at least for the last 50 million years.

Savitzky (1978) provided evidence that the micrurines are a derivative of Neotropical rear-fanged colubrids such as *Elapomorphus*, rather than relatives of the Old World cobras. This removes a zoogeographic problem. Thus, Africa contributed no venomous snakes to South America for the Crotalinae are absent in Africa. The Viperidae appears in the fossil record in the lower Miocene in northern continents. Its general range suggests an open radiation without insular or peninsular traps. A Laurasian origin is likely, as clearly deductible from the study of *Azemiops* by Liem et al (1971).

CONCLUSIONS

Present geological knowledge indicates that Africa and South America were united and formed a single continent from at least Carboniferous times, during most of the Mesozoic until the Turonian in the Cretaceous. The final split of the continents and the birth of the Atlantic Ocean occurred 90-95 m y b p. Fossil evidence shows the existence of a common fauna before the Turonian—mesosaurians of the Permian, the *Cynognathus* fauna of the Triassic, and mesosuchian crocodiles of the Jurassic and Cretaceous. Both pre-Atlantic and post-Atlantic distributions are hypothesized for groups of amphibians and reptiles (Figs 3 1).

Leiopelmatid frogs existed in the Jurassic in South America, and pipid frogs and pelomedusid turtles existed in Africa in the Early Cretaceous. The continents were united then, so it is reasonable to assume that leiopelmatids also lived in Africa, and that pipids and pelomedusids were present in South America be-

---

[15] For osteological reasons, Bourgeois (1968) put *Rhamnophis* and *Thrasops* in the Dispholidinae, notwithstanding their round pupils

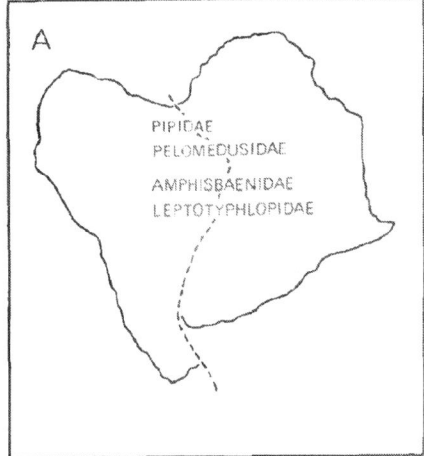
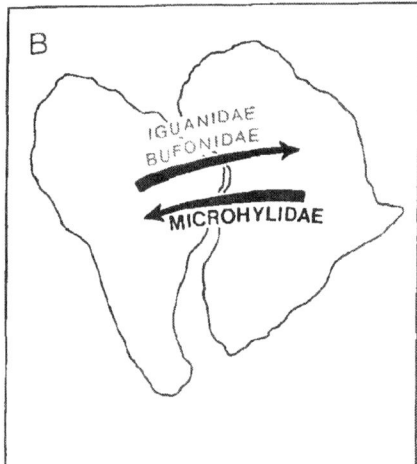
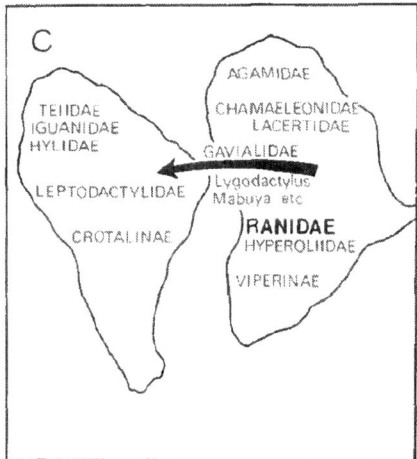

fore the birth of the Atlantic Ocean. In Late Cretaceous beds of South America, there are doubtful leptodactylids and iguanids. In the Paleocene beds of Brasil there are caecilians, leptodactylids, hylids and bufonids. In Africa there are only an unidentified salamander in the Senonian and a primitive colubroid in the Paleocene.

In some groups (bufonids and iguanids) the characteristics of the fossils and the present range of the group and its inferred phylogeny are suggestive of a pre-Atlantic western Gondwanan range. In other cases, similar conclusions can be assumed on distributional data alone without the benefit of pertinent paleontological data. Amphi-Atlantic ranges of the gekkonids, amphisbaenians, leptoptyphlopids and typhlopids are examples. The myobatrachid frogs have a doubtful fossil in Cretaceous beds of India. Their presence in western Gondwanaland in Early Cretaceous times is assumed. My hypothesis is that, according to vicariance principles, a myobatrachid stock could have become leptodactylids in western Gondwanaland (South America), ranoids in mid-western Gondwanaland (Africa), microhyloids in mid-eastern Gondwanaland (Madagascar, India), and pelodryadids in eastern Gondwanaland (Australia). The microhylids are supposed to have radiated early enough to spread to Africa and South America just before or after the separation of the continents.

The other families generally are quite different in Africa and South America, suggesting a post-Atlantic radiation. The Neotropical leptodactylids, alligatorids, iguanids, podocnemine turtles (which must have crossed Africa to reach Madagascar), teiids, anguids,

---

FIG. 3.1. A. Pre-Atlantic Gondwanan distributions—groups present in South America and Africa before the separation. B. Last pre-Atlantic faunistic exchanges—groups that migrated from one continent to the other just before the separation or perhaps soon afterwards. C. Post-Atlantic distributions and later one-way dispersals.

A. *Distribuciones gondwanense preatlánticas—grupos presentes en Sudamérica y Africa largo tiempo antes de la división*. B. *Ultimo intercambio faunístico preatlántico—grupos que migraron de un continente al otro, justo antes de la división o, tal vez, pronto después de ella*. C. *Distribuciones postatlánticas y después dispersión "waif" unidireccional*.

boids, xenodontine colubrids, micrurines and crotalines are paralleled, respectively, by Ethiopian ranoids, crocodylids, agamids chamaeleontids pelomedusines, lacertids, cordylids, scincids pythonines lycodontine colubrids, elapids and viperines

Some measure of competitive exclusion cannot be ruled out completely, although definite misgivings have been expressed about the universality of Gause's principle (Fryer and Iles 1972) The expansion of three important Neotropical families outside of South America suggests the presence of rival groups is indeed an obstacle The bufonids have no obvious competitors and are nearly cosmopolitan The hylids invaded the entire Holarctic Region where no other tree frogs exist, but failed to spread into the Old World tropics, where other groups of tree frogs occur The leptodactylids, which met ranids when they were barely out of their Neotropical stronghold, barely encroached upon southern North America Such an effect must be considerably magnified in colonization by rafting, because the indigenous populations have an overwhelming advantage in numbers Colonizers can succeed only if they enter an empty ecological niche or if they are superior to the indigenous species

ACKNOWLEDGMENTS

I am grateful to William E Duellman for his critical comments and to the Consejo Nacional de Investigaciones Científicas y Técnicas of Argentina and the Fundación Miguel Lillo, which authorized this work J am also indebted to various colleagues for valuable help and information—F de Broin, E Buffetaut, R Estes C Gans J C Rage, A Savitzky, and G Underwood

RESUMEN

El contraste evidente entre las faunas herpetológicas sudamericana y africana parece a primera vista apoyar las teorías zoogeográficas de Matthew (1915) y Darlington (1957) Los grupos dominantes son completamente distintos aunque en general ecológicamente similares y a menudo relacionados Dermophiinae al oeste del Océano y Herpelinae al este, y así en seguida, Leptodactylidae y Ranoidea terrestres Hylidae y Ranoidea arborícolas, Iguanidae y Agamidae (con Chamaeleontidae) Teiidae y Lacertidae, Podocneminae y Pelomedusinae, Alligatoridae y Crocodylidae, Boinae y Pythoninae, Xenodontinae y Lycodontinae

Sin embargo, la tectónica de las placas y otros progresos recientes de la geología comprobaron sin dejar lugar a duda que África y Sud América estaban unidas en un solo continente hasta el Turoniano es decir hasta hace más o menos 90 millones de años

Rastros de la comunidad faunística de esta época remota persistieron en antiguos grupos que no dominan la escena, como los Gimnofionos, Pipidae, Pelomedusidae, Gekkonidae, Amphisbaenidae, Leptotyphlopidae y Typhlopidae Pero aun en estos ejemplos, la divergencia debida a su evolución por separado durante cerca de 100 millones de años es generalmente obvia

Hay también familias que aparentemente después de haber nacido en una región occidental u oriental del Continente de Gondwana invadieron el resto poco antes de su fragmentación o tal vez poco después, ya que travesías de mares estrechos como son océanos recién nacidos no presentan dificultades mayores Así, aparentemente los Bufonidae, Iguanidae, quizás los Teiidae nacidos en Sudamérica invadieron África, los primeros para seguir en conquista del mundo, los lagartos para evolucionar en otros grupos y/o estar desplazados por ellos últimamente (Agamidae y Chamaeleontidae, Lacertidae, Cordylidae y Scincidae)

Los Microhylidae, que el autor considera como un antiguo grupo de Neobatracios de origen Indico-Malgache hicieron, al parecer, el viaje inverso, ya que la selva amazónica alberga géneros bastante primitivos, como *Otophryne*

Aun más tarde hay pruebas de que la travesía del Atlántico no fue imposible, ya que la invasión de América por Gekkonidae de los géneros *Hemidactylus* (Kluge, 1969) y *Tarentola* se hizo a fines del Cenozoico Por consiguiente se puede suponer que tales migraciones ocurrieron durante todo el Cenozoico, con frecuencia decreciente, por supuesto, a medida que los continentes se alejaban. La direccion de los corrientes favorece claramente las travesías de Este a Oeste de manera que America del Sur cesó temprano de enriquecer la fauna africana, mientras que al contrario Africa mandó probablemente emisarios bastante numerosos a Sudamérica, no solamente salamanquesas sino también escincidos del genero *Mabuya* y, tal vez varios grupos de culebras arborícolas. Es interesante notar que los anfibios no tuvieron exito en este tipo de aventura, porque, en general no aguantan bien el agua salada y, tal vez la competencia de los Anfibios sudamericanos no permitía lo que se llamó el acceso ecológico en su continente.

LITERATURE CITED

AHL, E 1926 Anura Aglossa Xenopodidae, pp 141-142 in KAISER, B (ed) Die Diamantenwuste Sudwest Afrikas 2 D Reimer, Berlin

AMIET, J L 1976 Observations anatomiques et biologiques sur le genre *Wernera* Poche, 1903 (Amphibiens, Anoures, Fam *Bufonidae*) Rev Zool Africaine 90 33-45

ANDERSSON, L C 1903 Neue Batrachier aus Kamerun von den Herren Dr Y Sjostedt und Dr S Junger gesammelt Verh Zool Bot Ges Wien 53 141-145

BLURIEN, K 1961 Die palaogeographische Entwicklung des sudatlantischen Ozeans Nova Acta Leopoldina 24 1-36

BLAIR, W F 1972a Evidence from hybridization, pp 196-232 in BLAIR, W F (ed) Evolution in the genus *Bufo* Univ Texas Press, Austin, 459 p

BLAIR, W F 1972b Summary, pp 329-343 in BLAIR, W F (ed) Evolution in the genus *Bufo* Ibid

BLOMMERS-SCHLOSSER, R M A 1975 Observations on the larval development of some Malagasy frogs with notes on their ecology and biology (Anura Dyscophinae, Scaphiophryninae and Cophylinae) Beaufortia 21 7-25

BOGART J P, NELSON, C E 1976 Evolutionary implications from karyotypic analysis of frogs of the families Microhylidae and Rhinophrynidae Herpetologica 32 199-208

BOGART, J P, PYBURN W F, NELSON, C E 1976 The karyotype of *Otophryne robusta* (Anura Microhylidae) Ibid 32 208-210

BOGERT, C M 1940 Herpetological results of the Vernay Angola Expedition, with notes on African reptiles in other collections Part 1 Snakes, including an arrangement of African Colubridae Bull Amer Mus Nat Hist 77 1-107

BONAPARTE, J F 1967 New vertebrate evidence for a southern transatlantic connection during the lower and the middle Triassic Palaeontol 10 554-63

BONS, J PASTEUR G 1977 Solution histologique à un probleme de taxinomie herpetologique interessant les rapports paleobiologiques de l'Amerique de Sud et de l'Afrique C R Acad Sci Paris, Ser D 284 2547-50

BOULENGER, G A 1882 Catalogue of the Batrachia Salientia S Ecaudata in the collection of the British Museum London, 503 p

BOURGEOIS M 1968 Contribution à la morphologie comparee du crâne des ophidiens de l'Afrique Centrale Publ Univ Off Congo Lubumbashi 18 1-293

BROIN F DE, BUFFETAUT E, KOENIGUER, J C, RAGE, J C, RUSSELL, D, TAQUET, P, VERGNAUD-GRAZZINI, C, WENZ, S 1975 La faune de vertebres continentaux du gisement d In Beceten (Senonien du Niger) C R Acad Sci Paris, Ser D 279 469-472

BRUNDIN, L 1966 Transantarctic relationships and their significance K Sven Vetenskapsakad Handl (4)11(1) 1-472

BUFFETAUT, E 1976 Sur la repartition géographique hors d'Afrique des Dyrosaundae, Crocodiliens Mesosuchiens du Cretace terminal et du Paleogene C R Acad Sci Paris, Ser D 283 487-90

CARROLL, R L, CURRIE, P J 1975 Microsaurs as possible apodan ancestors J Zool 57 229-247

CARVALHO, A L de 1954 A preliminary synopsis of the genera of American microhylid frogs Occas Pap Mus Zool Univ Mich (555) 1-19

CASAMIQUELA, R 1961 Un pipoideo fosil de Patagonia Rev Mus La Plata, Secc Paleontol 4 71-123

CEI J M 1972 *Bufo* of South America, pp 82-90 in BLAIR, W F (ed) Evolution in the genus *Bufo* Univ Texas Press, Austin, 459 p

CEI, J M 1977 Serological relationships of the Patagonian toad *Bufo variegatus* (Gunther) Bull Serol Mus 52 2

COLBERT, E H 1973 Continental drift and the distribution of fossil reptiles, pp 395-412 in TARLING, D H, RUNCORN, S K (eds) Implications of continental drift in the earth sciences, Vol I Academic Press, New York, 622 p

CREER, K M 1973 On the arrangement of the landmasses and the configuration of the geomagnetic field during the phanerozoic, pp 47-76 in TARLING, D H, RUNCORN, S K (eds) Implications of continental drift in the earth sciences Ibid

CROIZAT, L 1964 Space, time, form The biological synthesis Published by author, Caracas, 881 p

CROIZAT, L, NELSON, G, ROSEN, D E 1974 Centers of origin and related concepts Syst Zool 23 265-287

DARLINGTON, P J, JR 1957 Zoogeography the geographical distribution of animals John Wiley and Sons, New York, 675 p

DIETZ, R S, HOLDEN, J C 1970 The break-up of Pangaea Sci Amer 223 30-41

DOUGLAS, R G, MOULLADE, M, NAIRN, A E M 1973 Causes and consequences of drift in South Atlantic pp 517–537 *in* TARLING, D H, RUNCORN, S K (eds) Implications of continental drift in the earth sciences Vol 1 Academic Press, New York, 622 p

DOWLING, H G 1975 A provisional classification of snakes 1974 Yearbook Herpetology Herpetol Infor Search Syst New York pp 167–170

DUELLMAN, W E 1978 The biology of an equatorial herpetofauna in Amazonian Ecuador Univ Kansas Mus Nat Hist, Misc Publ (65) 1–352

DUNN, E R 1923 The geographical distribution of the Amphibians Amer Nat 57 129–136

DUNN, E R 1928 A tentative key and arrangement of the American genera of Colubridae Bull Antivenin Inst Amer 2 18–24

DUNN, E R 1931 The herpetological faunas of the Americas Copeia 1931(3) 106–119

DU TOIT, A 1937 Our wandering continents Oliver and Boyd, Edinburgh 366 p

ESTES, R 1970 Origin of the North American lower vertebrate fauna An inquiry into the fossil record Forma Functio 3 139–163

ESTES, R 1975a African frog *Xenopus* (Pipidae) from the Palaeocene of Brasil and its zoogeographic importance Nature 254 48–50

ESTES, R 1975b Fossil *Xenopus* from the Palaeocene of South America and the zoogeography of pipid frogs Herpetologica 31 263–278

ESTES, R, PRICE, L I 1973 Iguanid lizard from the upper Cretaceous of Brasil Science 180 748–751

ESTES, R, REIG, O 1973 The early fossil record of frogs A review of the evidence pp 11–63 *in* VIAL, J L (ed) Evolutionary biology of the anurans Contemporary research on major problems Univ Missouri Press, Columbia 470 p

ESTES, R WAKE M 1972 The first fossil record of caecilian amphibians Nature 239 228–231

FRANCHETEAU, J 1973 Plate tectonic model of the opening of the Atlantic ocean south of the Azores pp 197–202 *in* TARLING, D H, RUNCORN, S K (eds) Implications of continental drift in the earth sciences Vol 1 Academic Press, New York, 622 p

FRYER, C, ILES, T D 1972 The cichlid fishes of the great lakes of Africa T F H Publ, Neptune City, N J, 641 p

GAFFNEY, E S 1975 A phylogeny and classification of the higher categories of turtles Bull Amer Mus Nat Hist 155 391–436

GORMAN, G C 1970 Chromosomes and the systematics of the family Teiidae (Sauria Reptilia) Copeia 1970(2) 230–245

GRIFFITHS, I 1963 The phylogeny of the Salientia Biol Rev 38 241–292

GRIFFITHS, I, CARVALHO, A L DE 1965 On the validity of employing larval characters as major phyletic indices in Amphibia Salientia Rev Brasileira Biol 25 113–121

HECHT, M 1963 A reevaluation of the early history of the frogs Part II Syst Zool 12 20–35

HECHT, M MALONE, B 1972 On the early history of the gavialid crocodilians Herpetologica 28 281–284

HEIRTZLER, J R 1968 Sea-floor spreading Sci Amer 219 60–70

HOFFSTETTER, R 1955 Squamates de type moderne, pp 606–662 *in* PIVETEAU J (ed) Traite de Paléontologie, Paris 1113 p

HOFFSTETTER, R 1962 Revue des récentes acquisitions concernant l'histoire et la systématique des squamates Colloq Int C N R S Paris 104, 474 p

HOFFSTETTER, R 1964 Les Sauria du Jurassique supérieur et spécialment les Gekkota de Bavière et de Mandchourie Senckenbergiana Biol 45 281–324

HOFFSTETTER, R 1967 Coup d'oeil sur les Sauriens (= Lacertiliens) des Couches de Purbeck (Jurassique supérieur d'Angleterre) Colloq Int C N R S Paris 163 349–71

HOFFSTETTER, R 1968 [Review of] A contribution to the classification of snakes by G Underwood Copeia 1968(1) 201–213

HOFFSTETTER, R 1972 Relationships, origin and history of the ceboid monkeys and caviomorph rodents A modern reinterpretation Evol Biol 6 323–348

HOFFSTETTER, R 1977 Primates Filogenia e historia biogeografica Stud Geol Univ Salamanca 13 211–253

HOFFSTETTER, R, RAGE, J-C 1972 Les Erycinae fossiles de France (Serpentes, Boidae) Compréhension et histoire de la sous-famille Ann Paleontol Vertebr 58 81–124

HUENE, F VON 1956 Paläontologie und Phylogenie der niederen Tetrapoden Fischer, Jena, 761 p

HURLEY, P M 1968 The confirmation of continental drift Sci Amer 218 52–64

INGER, R F 1967 The development of a phylogeny of frogs Evolution 21 369–383

JEANNEL, R 1942 La genèse des faunes terrestres Presses Univ France, Paris, 514 p

KLUGE, A G 1967 Higher taxonomic categories of gekkonid lizards and their evolution Bull Amer Mus Nat Hist 135 1–59

KLUGE, A G 1969 The evolution and geographical origin of the New World *Hemidactylus mabouia-brooki* complex (Gekkonidae, Sauria) Misc Publ Mus Zool Univ Michigan (138) 1–78

KLUGE, A G, FARRIS, S J 1969 Quantitative phyletics and the evolution of the anurans Syst Zool 18 1–32

KROMMELBEIN, K 1971 Non-marine Cretaceous ostracodes and their importance for the hypothesis of Gondwanaland Proc 2nd IUGS Gondwana Symp South Africa pp 617–619

LAURENT, R F 1972 La distribution des amphibiens et les translations continentales 17th Inter Cong Zool, Monaco, 1 1–16

LAURENT, R F 1973 A parallel survey of equatorial amphibians and reptiles in Africa and South America pp 259–266 *in* MEGGERS B J, AYENSU E S, DUCKWORTH W D (eds) Tropical forest ecosystems in Africa and South America Smithsonian Inst Press, Washington, D C, 350 p

LAURENT, R F 1975 La distribution des amphibiens et les translations continentales Mem Mus Natl Hist Nat Paris Ser A Zool 88 176–191

LAURENT, R F In press Systématique et distribution geographique (des Amphibiens) in GRASSE P P (ed) Traité de Zoologie 14, fasc 2 Amphibiens

LAUGHTON, A S, SCLATER, J G, MCKENZIE, D P 1973 The structure and evolution of the Indian ocean, pp 203–212 in TARLING D H, RUNCORN, S K (eds) Implications of continental drift in the earth sciences Vol 1 Academic Press New York, 622 p

LAVOCAT, R 1974 What is an hystricomorph rodent? Symp Zool Soc London 34 7–20

LIEM, K F, MARX, H, RABB, G B 1971 The viperid snake Azemiops Its comparative cephalic anatomy and phylogenetic position in relation to Viperinae and Crotalinae Fieldiana Zool 59 65–126

LIEM, S S 1970 The morphology, systematics and evolution of the Old World tree frogs (Rhacophoridae and Hyperoliidae) Fieldiana, Zool 57 1-145

LYNCH J D 1973 The transition from archaic to advanced frogs, pp 133–182 in VIAL, J L (ed) Evolutionary biology of the anurans Contemporary research on major problems Univ Missouri Press, Columbia, 470 p

MARTIN, H 1968 A critical review of the evidence for a former direct connection of South America with Africa, pp 25–53 in FITTKAU, E J, ILLIES, J, KLINGE, H, SCHWABE, G H, SIOLI, H (eds) Biogeography and ecology in South America W Junk, The Hague, 946 p

MATTHEW, W D 1915 Climate and evolution Ann New York Acad Sci 24 171–318

McDIARMID, R W 1971 Comparative morphology and evolution of frogs of the Neotropical genera Atelopus, Dendrophryniscus, Melanophryniscus and Oreophrynella Nat Hist Mus Los Angeles Cty Sci Bull (12) 1–66

McKENNA, M C 1973 Sweepstakes, filters, corridors, Noah's arks and beached Viking funeral ships in palaeogeography, pp 295–308 in TARLING, D H, RUNCORN, S K (eds) Implications of continental drift in the earth sciences Vol 1 Academic Press, New York 622 p

McKENZIE, D P, SCLATER, J G 1973 The evolution of the Indian Ocean Sci Amer 228 62–72

MEDEM, F 1968 Desarrollo de la herpetologia en Colombia Rev Acad Colombiana Cien Exactas Fis Nat. 13 149–200

MOOK, C C 1934 The evolution and classification of the Crocodilia J Geol 42 295–304

MORESCALCHI, A 1973 Amphibia, pp 233–318 in CHIARLLLI, A B, CAPANNA, E (eds) Cytotaxonomy and vertebrate evolution Academic Press, New York, 783 p

NELSON, C E 1966 The evolution of frogs of the family Microhylidae PhD Dissert Univ Texas, Diss Abst 27, 3719 B

NELSON, C E, CUELLAR, H S 1968 Anatomical comparison of tadpoles of the genera Hypopachus and Gastrophryne (Microhylidae) Copeia 1968 (2) 423–424

NELSON, G 1973 Comments on Leon Croizat's biogeography Syst Zool 22 312–320

NEVO, E 1968 Pipid frogs from the Early Cretaceous of Israel and pipid evolution Bull Mus Comp Zool Harvard Univ 136 255–318

NOBLE, G K 1931 The biology of the Amphibia McGraw-Hill Book Co, New York, 577 p

NOPSCA, F 1928 The genera of Reptiles Paleobiol 1 163–188

NUSSBAUM R A 1977 Rhinatrematidae A new family of Caecilians (Amphibia Gymnophiona) Occas Pap Mus Zool Univ Mich (682) 1–30

ORTON, G L 1957 The bearing of larval evolution on some problems in frog classification Syst Zool 6 79–86

PATTERSON, B, PASCUAL R 1968 The fossil mammal fauna of South America Q Rev Biol 43 409–451

RABB, G B, MARX, H 1973 Major ecological and geographic patterns in the evolution of colubroid snakes Evolution 27 69–83

RAGE, J -C 1974 Les Serpents des phosphorites du Quercy Palaeovert 6 274–303

RAGE, J -C 1975 Un serpent du Paleocene du Niger Etude preliminaire sur l'origine des caenophidiens (Reptilia, Serpentes) C R Acad Sci Paris, Ser D 281 515–18

RAGE, J -C 1976 Paleontologie, phylogenie et paleobiogeographie des serpents PhD Dissert Univ Paris

RAGE, J -C 1977 L'origine des Colubroides et des Acrochordoides (Reptilia, Serpentes) C R Acad Sci Paris, Ser D 286 595–597

REYMENT, R A 1958 Factors in the distribution of fossil cephalopods Stockholm Contrib Geol 1 91–184

REYMENT, R A 1970 Vertically imbedded cephalopods shells Some factors in the distribution of fossil cephalopods Palaeogeogr Palaeoclimatol Palaeoecol 7 103–111

REYMENT, R A 1975 Paléontologie évolutive et nouvelle tectonique Mem Mus Natl Hist Nat Paris Ser A Zool 88 8–18

REYMENT, R A, TAIT, E A 1972 Biostratigraphical dating of the early history of the South Atlantic Ocean Phil Trans Roy Soc London, B Biol Sci 264 55–95

ROBINSON, P 1967 The evolution of the Lacertilia Colloq Int C N R S, Paris 163 395–407

ROMER, A S 1956 Osteology of the reptiles Univ Chicago Press, Chicago, 772 p

ROMER, A S 1966 Vertebrate Paleontology 3rd ed Univ Chicago Press, Chicago 468 p

SAVAGE, J M 1973 The geographic distribution of frogs Patterns and predictions, pp 351–445 in VIAL J L (ed) Evolutionary biology of the anurans Contemporary research on major problems Univ Missouri Press, 470 p

SAVITZKY, A H 1978 The origin of the New World proteroglyphous snakes and its bearing on the study of venom delivery in snakes PhD Dissert Univ Kansas, 367 p

SCHMIDT, K P 1946 On the zoogeography of the Holarctic Region Copeia 1946 (3) 144–152

SILL W D 1968 The zoogeography of the Crocodilia Copeia 1968(1) 76–88

SIMPSON, G G 1942 A Miocene tortoise from Patagonia Amer Mus Novit (1209) 1–6

SIMPSON, G G 1965 The geography of evolution Chilton, Philadelphia, 249 p

SMITH, H M, SMITH, R B, SAWIN, H L 1977 A summary of snake classification (Reptilia, Serpentes) J Herpetol 11 115–121

SOKAL, R R, CROVELLO, T J 1970 The biological species concept A critical evaluation Amer Nat 104 127–153

SOKOL, O M 1975 The phylogeny of anuran larvae A new look Copeia 1975(1) 1–24

STARRETT, P H 1973 Evolutionary patterns in larval morphology, pp 251–271 in VIAL, J L (ed) Evolutionary biology of the anurans Contemporary research on major problems Univ Missouri Press, Columbia, 470 p

STEEL, R 1973 Crocodylia Handbuch der Paläoherpetologie 16 1–116

TANDY, M, KEITH, R 1972 Bufo of Africa, pp 119–170 in BLAIR, W F (ed) Evolution in the genus Bufo Univ Texas Press, Austin, 459 p

TIHEN J A 1960 Two new genera of African bufonids with remarks on the phylogeny of related genera Copeia 1960 (3) 225–233

TIHEN, J A 1965 Evolutionary trends in frogs Amer Zool 5 309–318

TRUEB, L 1971 Phylogenetic relationships of certain Neotropical toads with the description of a new genus (Anura Bufonidae) Nat Hist Mus Los Angeles Cty Contr Sci (216) 1–40

UNDERWOOD, G 1967 A contribution to the classification of snakes Brit Mus (Nat Hist), London, 179 p

UNDERWOOD, G 1976 A systematic analysis of boid snakes pp 151–175 in BELLAIRS, A, COX, C B (eds) Morphology and Biology of Reptiles Linnean Soc London Symp Series 3, 290 p

VANZOLINI, P E 1968 Geography of the South American Gekkonidae (Sauria) Arq Zool (São Paulo) 17 85–111

VERGNAUD-GRAZZINI, C 1966 Les amphibiens du Miocene de Beni-Mellal Notes Serv Geol Maroc 27 43–69

VERGNAUD-GRAZZINI, C HOFFSTETTER, R 1972 Presence de Palaeobatrachidae (Anura) dans des gisements tertiaires français Caractensation, distribution et affinites de la famille Palaeovert 5 157–177

WAKE, D 1966 Comparative osteology and evolution of the lungless salamanders family Plethodontidae Mem South Calif Acad Sci (4) 1–111

WOOD A E 1950 Porcupines, paleogeography and parallelism Evolution 4 87–98

WOOD, R, PATTERSON, B 1973 A fossil trionychid turtle from South America Breviora (415) 1–10

APPENDICES

APPENDIX 3 1—Vicariance, dispersal and centers of origin

According to the Hennigian and cladistic theories, the concepts of dispersal and centers of origin, cherished by so many zoologists from Darwin to Darlington, Simpson and Mayr, are useless (Croizat et al, 1974), whereas the concept of vicariance is the master key to biogeographic problems Perhaps it is true that the importance of vicariance has been overlooked in the zoogeographic conjectures of the past decades, but surely not to the extent implied by these authors The model of allopatric speciation, one of the main tenets of the synthetic evolutionary theory, is the very basis of the vicariance concept But this does not necessitate the rejection of other causes of biotic distributions Dispersal occurs, for there is more than one species at almost every locality (more than 80 species of frogs at Santa Cecilia, Ecuador, as noted by Duellman, 1978) Croizat and his coworkers admit that distributions are not static but fail to allow that dispersal is as important as vicariance Furthermore they belittle the concept of the genocenter under the pretext that a species may have a huge array of disjunct populations over an entire continent Such enormous genetic pools are not especially productive evolutionarily They impose a great deal of inertia to the spreading of genetic changes On the contrary, innovative processes, such as genetic drift, genetic revolution, quantum and tachytelic evolution, occur in small, transitory and local populations Nevertheless, it is futile to seek genocenters when adequate data are lacking It might be said for genocenters, as Sokal and Crovello (1970) did for the biological species concept that the concept is not operational However, this does not preclude the existence of centers of origin, even if we are unable to discover their location, exactly as the non-operationality of the biological species concept does not eliminate the fact that the cessation of gene exchange between two populations is such a momentous event in evolution that it is inconceivable to ignore it, even if we are unable to pinpoint its occurrence

APPENDIX 3 2—The Indian raft

It is now generally believed that India drifted away from Antarctica, Madagascar and Africa sometime at the end of the Mesozoic and travelled northwards through the Indian Ocean to collide with Laurasia in the Miocene The dating of the separation is still doubtful—about 100 m y b p from Antarctica and maybe the Paleocene (60 m y b p) from Madagascar Little attention has been given to the impact of the Indian fauna on the evolutionary zoogeography in the Tertiary This is an unfortunate omission, not justified by lack of evidence The Eocene *Indobatrachus* seems to belong to the Myobatrachidae, and the primitive snake family Uropeltidae survives in southern India and Sri Lanka The rationale for my hypothesis is as follows

1. India broke from Madagascar and Africa during the late Cretaceous or early Tertiary
2. As a large island it rafted away from Madagascar northwards along the Mascarene Ridge, leaving behind the Seychelles, Amirante and finally the Laccadive and Maldive islands (Laughton et al, 1973, McKenzie and Sclater 1973)
3. The Indian fauna evolved in isolation for about 50 million years, evolution was enhanced by the changing climates
4. Some faunistic exchanges remained with Madagascar and Africa through the intervening islands, like the Seychelles, and possibly others that have since disappeared
5. These small islands provided opportunities for genetic drift and quantum and tachytelic evolution favoring major adaptive shifts (e g, Microhylidae, Savage 1973)
6. Perhaps other exchanges took place in front of and/or on the eastern side when the Indian Noah's Ark (McKenna, 1973) drew near Laurasia, gliding along the Ninety-east Ridge and finally along the Nicobar and the Andaman islands
7. The fate of much of the Indian fauna must have been extinction
8. Some elements escaped early to Madagascar and Africa and proved successful in their expansion (e g Microhylidae)
9. Other elements escaped later in northern, northeastern and eastern directions (e g, other Microhylidae and perhaps Agamidae, Varanidae, Pythoninı, Elapidae)

Four groups of reptiles (Agamidae Varanidae, Pythoninı, Elapidae) have patterns of distribution that can be explained by an Indian differentiation Each has a strong Indo-Malaysian component, another strong Australasian component, and a weak African component as if there had been a late invasion of Africa from Asia

Subsequent to writing this account, I have been informed by R Hoffstetter that recent data show that the Indian Subcontinent collided with Laurasia not later than the Eocene

4. Herpetofaunal Relationships of South America With Australia

Michael J. Tyler

*Department of Zoology
University of Adelaide
Adelaide, South Australia 5001
Australia*

In reviewing the extent of South American herpetofaunal relationships with Australia, while simultaneously considering South American-African relationships (Laurent, this volume), it is helpful to recognize that vast differences have existed in the opportunity for faunal exchange. South America and Africa may be regarded as lovers who experienced and exploited a large zone of contact and had considerable opportunity for interchange and exchange across it. In contrast, the South American-Australian relationship suffered from being in the form of an arranged engagement of longer duration. The couple never so much as touched one another at any time. The only contact was via a related intermediary named Aunt Arctica, whose presence between them effectively prevented a comparable degree of intimacy, and who is now outwardly cool and distinctly secretive about revealing what took place between them.

The benefit of employing such an analogy lies in emphasizing the fact that Australia and South America have always been physically separated. This separation always has been extensive, because the intervening Antarctica is a vast continent with a surface area of 1,165,500,000 km², comparable in size to South America north of the Tropic of Capricorn, and considerably greater than Australia (7,700,000 km²). A North to South traverse of Antarctica involves a distance of approximately 4,000 km.

When Antarctica was an integral component of Gondwanaland, the herpetofaunal elements shared at any one time by South America and Australia also would have occurred on Antarctica. Certainly a topography, climate, and vegetation equable to the maintenance of reptiles and amphibians had to exist on Antarctica, and at least some of the modern families could just as well have originated there as on the adjacent landmasses. Thus any realistic concept of intercontinental exchange avoids reference to "journeys" along "routes," and only visualizes the expansion and retraction of populations. Cartoons in an otherwise serious paper by Rich (1975) on the origins of the Australian nonpasserine avifauna, illustrate the errors to which some investigational philosophies may have succumbed.

The study of intercontinental herpetofaunal relationships faces problems of variation of systematic interpretation of taxa, and these materially influence the degree of faunal similarity. For example, if the numerically dominant Australian terrestrial and arboreal frogs are regarded as members of the Leptodactylidae and Hylidae, respectively, all anuran families found in Australia are shared with South America. Superficially at least, the anuran relationship appears likely to prove a close one. However, if the names Myobatrachidae and Pelodryadidae are employed for these same groups, it is difficult to avoid a bias towards a quite different interpretation. In fact it would appear that, for the purposes of intercontinental comparisons, there is a mystique surrounding a family name that does not extend to other nomenclature.

Over the past few years there have been substantial contributions to the study of plate tectonics, continental drift, palaeoclimate and the past flora and fauna of Australia. Many of these papers are highly relevant to the interpretation of evolutionary opportunities and the nature of the diversification of the herpetofauna. Here I have attempted to bring together the most recent literature as a general background before examining the evidence to

Fig 4 1 Australia, New Guinea and adjacent landmasses
Australia, Nueva Guinea y tierras adyacentes

establish the origins of the modern, non-marine Australian herpetofauna, and its affinities to the herpetofauna of South America A map of Australia and associated landmasses is shown in figure 4 1

PALAEOENVIRONMENTAL CONSIDERATIONS

Onset of drifting —Previously there has been considerable variation in estimates of the onset of the northwards drift of Australia away from east Antarctica, ranging from a low of 43 m y b p (Jardine and McKenzie, 1972) to a high of 180–100 m y b p (Fooden, 1972, Savage 1973) However, it is now placed at 55–52 m y b p, with most authors favoring 53 m y b p (McGowran, 1973, Sclater et al, 1974, Coleman and Packham, 1976, Veevers and McElhinny, 1976) McGowran's studies of the Antarctic-Australian suture led him to suggest that, despite the onset of drift, there was no substantial barrier to the passage of land animals prior to the early Eocene (49 m y b p)

Climatic, floral and faunal changes —Because *Nothofagus* forests now occur in some temperate areas, such as southeast Australia including Tasmania, and in New Zealand it has been possible to deduce that *Nothofagus* is associated classically with temperate climatic conditions (Axelrod, 1975) Thus, with evidence of *Nothofagus* occurring in the Eocene at several localities in southern Australia, the inference might be drawn that, at the time of the separation of Australia from East Antarctica the southern Australian fauna was probably cool-temperate Certainly this assumption would be valid for *N fusca* and *N menziesi*, which now exist in Australia New Zealand, Chile and Argentina However, the important species is *N brassi*, which now exists in New Guinea and New Caledonia and clearly is a subtropical species Formerly, its distribution was far more extensive, being known in Australia and New Zealand from the Early Cretaceous to the mid-Pliocene, in West Antarctica from the early Palaeocene to the mid-Eocene and from Chile and Argentina from the Early Cretaceous to the late Oligocene (Schlinger, 1974)

Further evidence of the southern Australian climate being subtropical has been established by Lange (1976) from his study of microfossil epiphyllous germlings, and by Christophel and Blackburn (1978) from their assessment of the Eocene South Australian Maslin Bay flora The geomorphological evidence of widespread subtropical conditions are summarized by Bowler (1976)

Central Australia is another portion of the continent whose palaeoclimatic conditions have been misinterpreted. Axelrod (1960) envisaged deterioration throughout the Cenozoic leading to arid to semiarid conditions by the Miocene There is now evidence that central Australia bore large, permanent lakes in the Miocene Lungfishes, teleosts, turtles, crocodiles, lizards, and frogs shared the site with a vast diversity of marsupials and birds The surrounding vegetation was dense, ranging from rainforests to extensive areas of grassland Gallery forests extended along the watercourses, and the presence of *Nothofagus* and *Podocarpus* are interpreted to be evidence of high rainfall There was southern communication with the sea at some stage (Callen and Tedford, 1976) The records of crocodiles and turtles at former freshwater sites in central Australia are particularly numerous (see also Newsome and Rochow, 1964) However, these represent the most conspicuous and most readily recognized reptile fossils, the search for smaller material has only just begun

At some stage, the area between central Australia and the north coast also was moist This is demonstrated by the cabbage palms, *Livistona mariae*, now restricted to a colony of 3,000 at Finke River in central Australia Their nearest relatives lie 1,000 km away in the northwest of the continent (Latz 1975) Palaeontological and geomorphological evidence demonstrate that central Australia provided numerous niches for mesic animals until the end of the Pleistocene (Wopfner and Twidale, 1967, Mabbut, 1967, Twidale 1972) Certainly deserts have featured in Australia for a long period and have had an essential role in lizard speciation (Pianka, 1972) It has been suggested that in the Quaternary much of the now moist extreme southwest of the continent was arid (Glassford and Killigrew, 1976) However the extent of Australia affected by aridity appears to have been exaggerated

The minimal morphological differentiation of the central Australian hylid frog fauna is wholly consistent with aridity being a late Pleistocene feature Thus the species *Litoria caerulea* and *L rubella* are relicts of a much richer fauna, surviving because of tolerance of adults or larvae to high temperature or possibly for some other reason. But for the contrary evidence of Glassford and Killigrew (1976), it is possible that Australia has not been any more arid than it is today and, to judge from the nature and abundance of vegetation cover now stabilizing sand dunes in some areas, a trend towards climatic amelioration has already begun. However, the Pleistocene record is of minimal relevance to this review.

THE NATURE OF THE AUSTRALIAN-ORIENTAL COLLISION

Modern New Guinea is composed of three distinct and roughly longitudinally arranged portions. The southern portion and the intervening Arafura Sea originally represented the leading edge of the Australian continental plate. The central cordillera is predominantly a much younger feature; uplift commenced in the Miocene. Finally there is a row of isolated mountain ranges on the north coast, each of which is composed of older volcanic rocks.

The history of the evolution of New Guinea, and of the area to the east and west is extremely complex. Similarly only the broadest of principles of the nature of the collision of the plates has yet been established. The following contributions provide a brief spectrum of opinions and are a source of many other references: Thompson (1967), Falvey and Taylor (1974), Coleman (1975), Denham (1975), Mackenzie (1975), Taylor (1975), Tilbury (1975) and Coleman and Packham (1976). Only recently attempts have been made to reconstruct the nature of the plate collision. Mackenzie (1975) suggested that mountain ranges now on the north coast of New Guinea represent an arc of islands that persisted through to the Miocene, and became accreted during the collision of the plate margins (Fig. 4:2). Coleman and Packham (1976:204) favored this concept: "For the moment, we accept the likelihood that north coastal New Guinea is a piece of crust, probably an arc segment, in collision with Australia-New Guinea." New Britain, to the east of New Guinea, therefore represents an island of the same arc, but which did not come directly into contact with New Guinea.

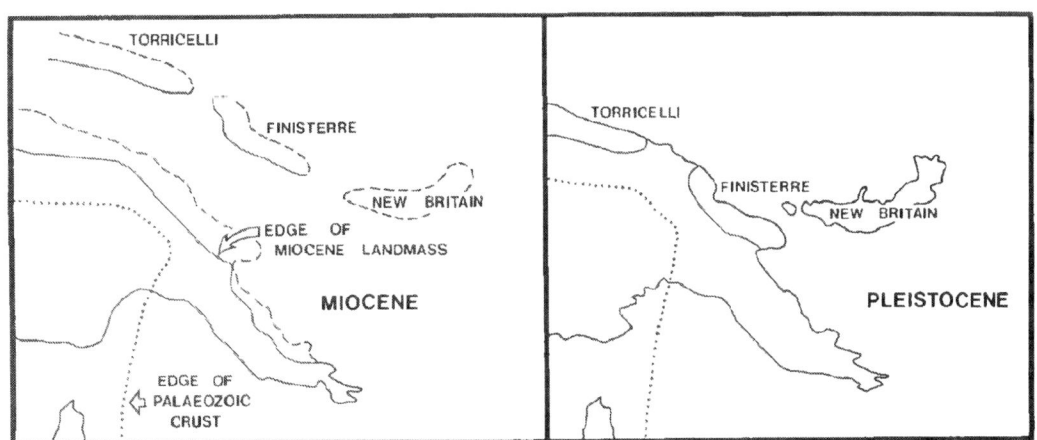

Fig. 4:2. Reconstruction of the collision of eastern New Guinea with islands in the mid-Miocene. The left figure represents the early Miocene prior to collision, with the landmass approaching a chain of islands. The right figure shows two of the islands (now known as the Torricelli Mountains and the Finnisterre block) accreted into New Guinea, thereby becoming part of the northern New Guinea coastline. (After McKenzie, 1975.)

Reconstrucción de la colisión del este de Nueva Guinea con islas en el Mioceno medio. La figura de la izquierda representa el Mioceno inferior previo a la colisión, con la masa de tierra alcanzando una cadena de islas. La figura de la derecha muestra dos de las islas (conocidos como Montañas Torricelli y el Bloque Finnisterre) adheridas a Nueva Guinea, llegando a formar parte de la costa del norte de Nueva Guinea. (De McKenzie, 1975.)

HERPETOFAUNAL ORIGINS

In very broad terms, the ancestral stocks of the South American and Australian faunas were derived from two distinct centers. For South America there was an initial Gondwanan source, reinforced following the drifting of Africa, followed by a later North American infusion. For Australia there was similarly an initial Gondwanan source followed by an Oriental one.

A basic problem is to determine for each continent which taxa are of Gondwanan ancestry. The recent literature includes several assessments (Keast, 1971, 1973; Cracraft, 1973, 1974, 1975; Savage, 1973). For Australia the distinction between the Gondwanan element and the more recent Oriental one should be distinguishable on the basis of morphological divergence and by the nature of geographic distribution. This is because the Australian-Oriental collision occurred in the mid-Miocene, so that animals in Australia of Oriental origin should have distinct affinities and comparable geographic distributions with animals in the Oriental Region. Conversely, such relationships should be lacking among the Gondwanan component and there should be minimal geographic distribution outside the Australian continent. Thus I propose to establish the constituents of the Gondwanan element of the Australian fauna primarily by a process of identifying, and so eliminating the Oriental element.

On an historic and biogeographic basis the Oriental element of the Australian herpetofauna will fit into one of two categories, as follows: 1) Animals that occurred within the northern chain prior to the mid-Miocene collision with Australia. All of these would have entered that area from the west. They could range from the Philippine Islands to Fiji. To be recognizable as pre-collision components, they should be more abundant on islands east of New Guinea than in New Guinea itself. 2) Animals that have dispersed from west to east following the accretion of the chain within northern New Guinea. Such animals are likely to show a progressive west to east reduction in diversity and to be poorly represented on the islands east of New Guinea.

It is worth contemplating that some of the deficiencies of Wallace's Line and of other attempts to delineate the Oriental and Australian faunas exist because in reality there are three components. Hence to the recognized Australian and post-collision Oriental colonizers, biogeographers have failed to recognize the existence of the additional pre-collision Oriental unit.

ORIENTAL ELEMENTS

Ranidae

The overall distribution of the Ranidae in the Australian Region is wholly consistent with the concept of entry from the adjacent Oriental Region to the west. What is less satisfactorily explained is the existence of two endemic species of *Platymantis* in Fiji far to the east, whereas none occurs in Australia. In terms of diversity and abundance of ranid species, New Guinea is equally anomalous to the extent that this component of its fauna is depauperate when compared with those of smaller islands to the west and to the east. Thus there are 20 ranids in the Philippine Islands, 10 on New Guinea, but 24 on the Solomon Islands. Those anomalies are highlighted by the study of the genus *Platymantis*, including species previously referred to *Cornufer* (Fig. 4.3). Viewing such a distribution pattern has led to the assumption that the distribution of *Platymantis* in New Guinea is relictual (Zweifel 1969).

In support of a concept that *Platymantis* was formerly far more widely distributed in New Guinea than it is today, there is evidence of close phylogenetic relationships existing between species that are geographically isolated from one another. An example is *P. batantae* of Batanta adjacent to the Vogelkop Peninsula of Irian Jaya (West New Guinea), which Zweifel (1969) considered most closely related to *P. gilliardi* and *P. mimicus* of New Britain about 2000 km distant. *Platymantis punctata* of northern New Guinea and *P. myersi* of Bougainville, Solomon Islands, with which it has affinities, are separated by a similar distance. Inger (1954:355) evidently drew comparable conclusions when he suggested that the closest relations of *P. meyeri* of the Philippine Islands " . . . are not with other

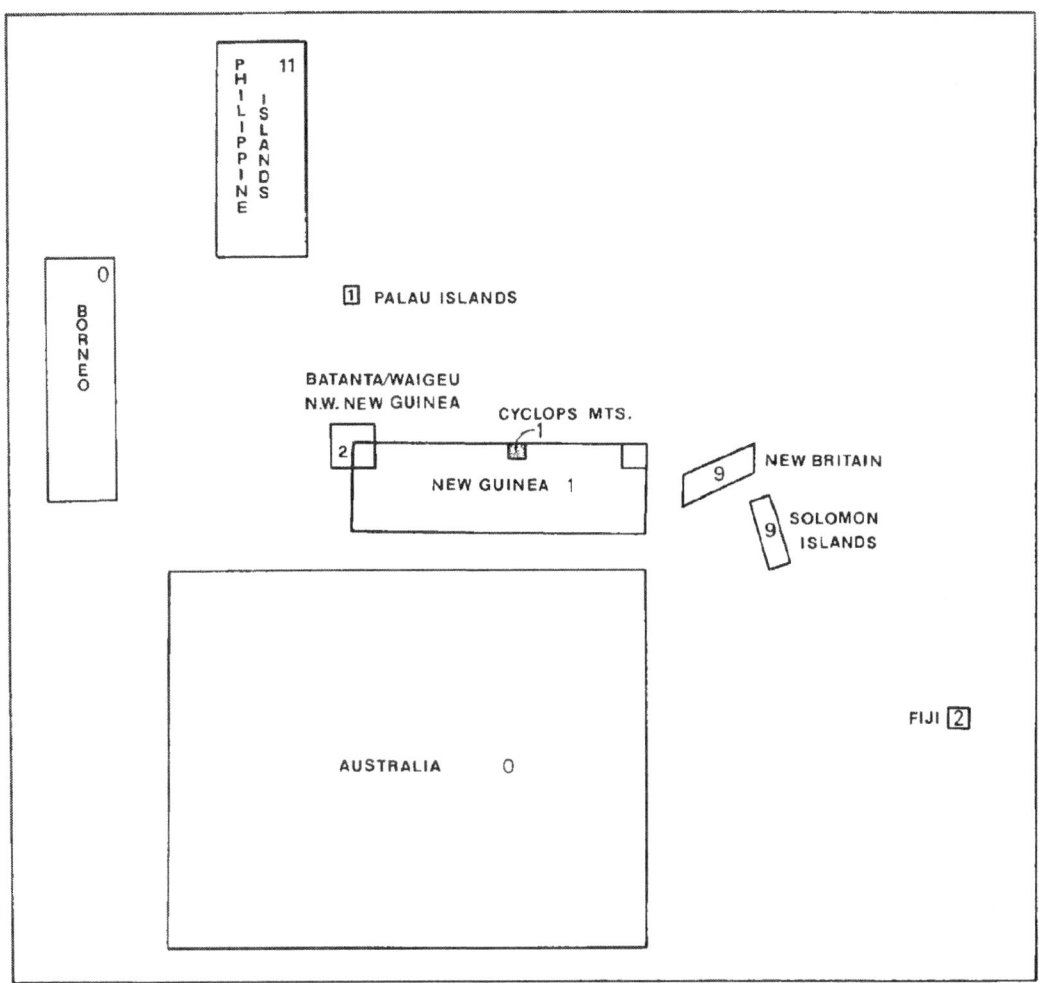

Fig. 4:3. Modern distribution and numbers of species of frogs of the genus *Platymantis* (Ranidae).
Distribución actual y números de especies de batracios del género Platymantis *(Ranidae)*.

Philippine *Cornufer [Platymantis]* but instead seem to be with non-Philippine species." Brown and Alcala (1970) proceeded a step further and declared that the distribution of *Platymantis* within the Philippines is relictual, thereby accounting for the predominance of the genus in the north of that group of islands. An interpretation of *Platymantis* as relicts is most readily made if the relevant landmasses are visualized as being static and the animal populations conveniently mobile. An alternative interpretation is one in which it is possible to contemplate mobile landmasses and relatively static insular populations.

Clearly, there are several major centers of ranoid evolution in different parts of the world; the Philippine Islands with seven genera and 29 species is one of them. The adjacent and larger land mass of Sabah (Borneo) to the southwest has fewer. *Platymantis* probably evolved within the Philippines in the Late Tertiary and subsequently dispersed southeastwards into New Britain, the Solomon Islands and Fiji by rafting. Presumably this would require marine equatorial currents following patterns essentially similar to those today. The primary radiation is from the Philippines to New Britain and the Solomon

Islands (Fig 4 4) The direction of secondary radiations is a reflection of demonstrable phylogenetic affinities of the extant species New Britain evidently was a major source of colonizing species, leading to the occurrence of *P batantae* on Batanta and *P punctata* on Waigeo Island off the Vogelkop Peninsula *P cheesmanae* on the Cyclops Mountains, and possibly *P papuensis* on the Finisterre Mountains (subsequently extending throughout northern New Guinea)

When the Australian continental mass collided with the Oriental island chain, it therefore acquired four species (or stocks) of *Platymantis* (Fig 4 4) Three of them (*batantae, cheesmanae* and *punctata*) have remained almost entirely within the original confines of the islands on the north coast and have not spread appreciably in New Guinea The fourth (*papuensis*) has extended as far as the south coast in the extreme west of New Guinea This species ranges to New Britain and the Solomon Islands but it is known to inhabit the intertidal zone and is well suited to dispersal by land and by sea (Tyler, 1976a) Nevertheless with the time scale available, its dispersal in New Guinea remains modest (Fig 4 5) Perhaps this implies the existence of an Australopapuan competitor and hence an ecological, rather than a physical, barrier to dispersal

The source of the stock that gave rise to the two endemic species on Fiji is uncertain The intervening and florally rich New Hebrides lacks *Platymantis* or any other endemic species of frogs The Australian hylid *Litoria aurea* has been introduced there recently possibly from New Caledonia, where it was introduced at the turn of the century (Tyler, 1976a, 1979) The striking success of the New Hebrides introduction tends to eliminate any possibility of extinction as an explanation for the absence of frogs there

Rana represents a more recent ranid arrival The number of species on the various landmasses north of Australia exhibits a progressive reduction from west to east in accord with an Oriental origin (Fig 4 6)

Microhylidae

Microhylids occur in South and North America, Africa, Madagascar, Asia including Indonesia and the Philippines New Guinea and northern Australia The Australopapuan unit is the most prolific with 13 genera and 102 species (Zweifel, 1972, Menzies and Tyler, 1977) compared with 16 genera but only 32 species in South America (Walker, 1973, Walker and Duellman, 1974, Nelson, 1975)

Parker (1934) was the last contributor to treat this family in its entirety Subsequent contributions have tended to examine single geographic components and the overall phylogenetic relationships of the diverse genera remain obscure Cracraft (1973) and Bogart and Nelson (1976) outlined the principal issues, of which contention has centered on interpretation of the origin of the family, and particularly its relationship to the Ranidae

In reality, the wide variety of opinions that have been offered on the origin of this family reflects the extreme morphological complexity of the constituent members and the absence of a satisfactory, modern synthesis This is demonstrated particularly well by the varying subfamilial classifications that have been proposed

Within the context of South American-Australian faunal studies, the contributions of Savage (1973) must be considered in detail Savage's conclusions differed quite strikingly from those of Parker (1934) Whereas the latter recognized two subfamilies occurring within and confined to the Australopapuan area (Asterophryinae and Sphenophryninae), Savage recognized only one to which the name Asterophryinae was applied Savage (1973 355) considered that the only distinction between the Asterophryinae and the Sphenophryninae was that " the former usually have an amphicoelous vertebra just anterior to the sacrum and the other presacral vertebrae procoelous (diplasiocoelous), while the latter have all presacral vertebrae procoelous" Savage reinforced his argument of the inherently trivial nature of such a distinction, by pointing out that although *Genyophryne* has uniformly procoelous vertebrae, it had been referred to the amphicoelous Asterophryinae by Parker (1934)

Savage wrote without the benefit of access to a contemporary study by Zweifel (1971), who reexamined the diagnostic characteristics of both subfamilies in general and of *Genyo-*

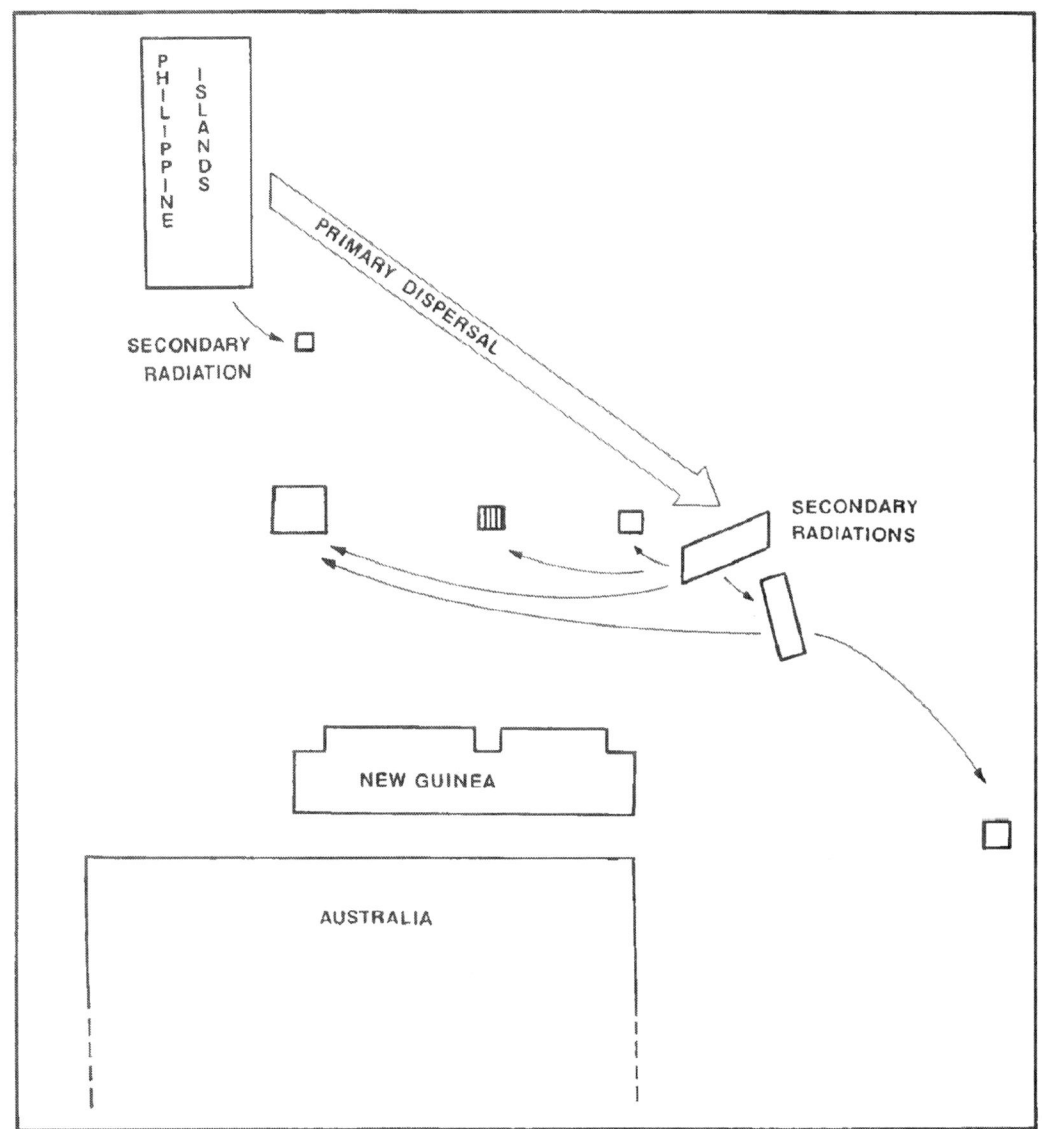

Fig. 4:4. Dispersal routes and the distribution of *Platymantis* by the early Miocene. The row of squares in the center of the figure represents the original Oriental island arc system. (From left to right: stippled = Batanta + Waigeo Island; hatched = Torricelli Mountains; open = Finnisterre Range.) When New Guinea collided with these islands, the latter occupied the indentations shown on the north coast of New Guinea, leading to the situation shown in figure 3.

Rutas de dispersión y la distribución de Platymantis *en el Mioceno inferior. La fila de cuadrados en el centro de la figura representa la sistema original de islas Orientales. (De izquierda a derecha: punteado = Batanta + Isla Waigeo; achurado = Montañas Torricelli; blanco = Cerros Finnisterre.) Cuando Nueva Guinea chocó con estas islas, la última ocupada las irregularidades mostrados en la costa norte de Nueva Guinea, conduciéndo a la situación mostrada en la figura 3.*

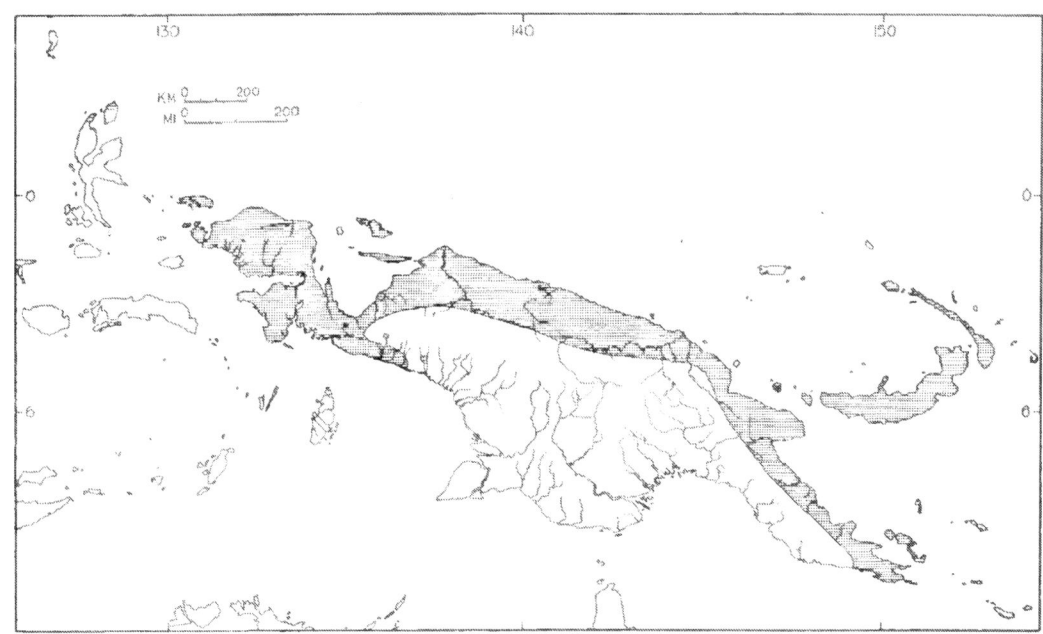

Fig. 4:5. Distribution of *Platymantis papuensis* on New Guinea and adjacent islands. Populations on islands east of the mainland may represent an undescribed species (R. G. Zweifel, pers. comm.).
Distribución de Platymantis papuensis *en Nueva Guinea y islas adyacentes. Las poblaciones de las islas al este del continente pudieran ser una especie no descrita (R. G. Zweifel, pers. com.).*

phryne in particular. Zweifel (1971) concluded that, despite certain equivocal features, *Genyophryne* was properly considered a member of the Sphenophryninae, and he proceeded to redefine the Asterophryninae and Sphenophryninae on the basis of distinctions of maxillae, dentaries, vertebral column and tongue. My studies of superficial mandibular musculature (Tyler, 1974a) provide additional data supporting such a recognition of two subfamilial units (Table 4:1).

A further action by Savage (1973) of considerable impact was that of including within the Asterophryninae (*sensu lato*) *Calluella*, an Asian genus uniquely associated by Parker (1934) with the Malagasy Dyscophinae.

TABLE 4:1.—Diagnostic Characters of Australopapuan Microhylid Frogs.
(Data from Zweifel, 1971, and Tyler, 1974a)

Character	Asterophryninae	Sphenophryninae
Maxillae	Often overlapping premaxillae, and usually in contact	Not overlapping premaxillae Never in contact medially
Dentaries	In contact anteriorly (except in *Hylophorbus*)	Not in contact
Vertebral column	Diplasiocoelous	Procoelous
Tongue	Subcircular, entirely adherent, often with a median furrow and posterior pouch	Oval, half-free behind, lacking median furrow and posterior pouch
Interhyoideus muscle	Anteriorly underlies intermandibularis (except in *Hylophorbus*)	Does not underly intermandibularis

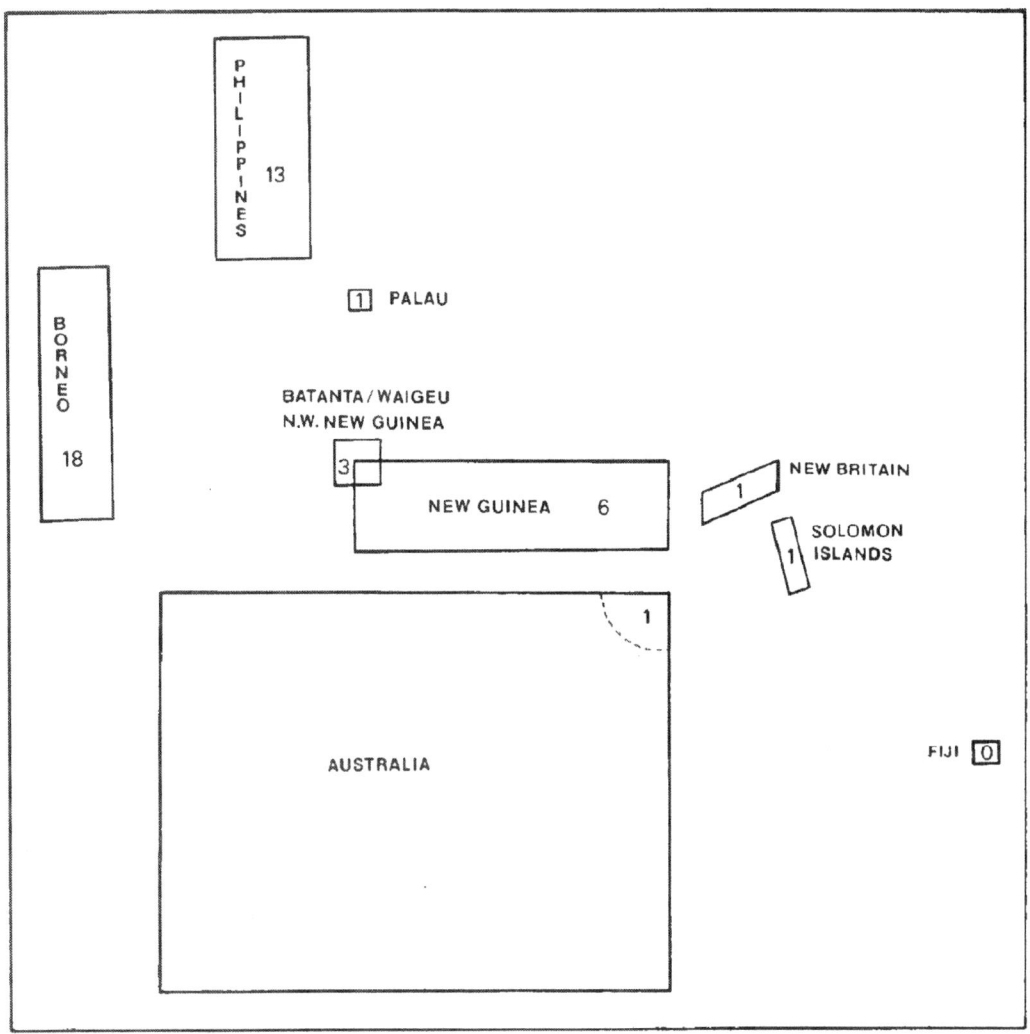

Fig. 4:6. Distribution and numbers of species of *Rana* in Australia and the adjacent Oriental Region and Pacific area.
Distribución y números de especies de Rana *en Australia y la adyacente Región Oriental y areas del Pacífico.*

Unquestionably, the former union provided a biogeographic disjunction that was difficult to interpret. Nevertheless, to associate *Calluella* with the Asterophryinae introduces new anomalies of even greater magnitude. This is because the Asterophryinae and Sphenophryinae are composed exclusively of frogs exhibiting direct development. The inclusion of *Calluella* among the Australopapuan species introduces species with a free-living larval stage. The magnitude of this introduction can only be appreciated when the considerable diversity of scansorial, terrestrial, semi-aquatic and fossorial frogs is seen to be united by sharing uniformly similar ontogenies. To accommodate *Calluella* in the Asterophryinae (*sensu lato*) also has a profound biogeographic impact, extending the range of the subfamily from the Australian Region to as far as western China. Evidence contradicting this step can be obtained from biogeographic and from morphological sources, but it involves resurrecting and modifying concepts refuted by Savage.

Few authors have contemplated the possibility of microhylids being widely distributed in Gondwanaland in the Cretaceous. Admittedly, the concept of the entry of the family into Australia from Indonesia antedated acceptance of continental drift and sea-floor spreading. However such an entry has been supported by many authors, of which Laurent (1975) is the most recent. Savage (1973) proposed the interesting hypothesis that the Microhylidae was present in the tropical portions of each of the southern land masses prior to the fragmentation of Gondwanaland. He further put forward an ingenious account of a turbulent climatic history for Australia, so as to account for the family's present abundance in New Guinea (13 genera, 95 species) and almost total absence from Australia (2 genera, 7 species). Savage's hypothesis demands considerable mobility for the Australopapuan populations. In particular there is the need for extinction of the Australian component, followed by diversification in New Guinea and the subsequent recolonization of Australia by immigrants from New Guinea.

The distribution of the Microhylids in Australia, New Guinea and the adjacent portion of the Oriental Region is shown in figure 4.7. The frogs are predominantly montane. Interpretation of the origin of the Australopapuan microhylids must accommodate three important facts. 1) The highly adapted montane microhylids of New Guinea are unlikely to be any older than the orogeny of the mountains that they inhabit. 2) The geographically most widely distributed genera (*Cophixalus*, *Oreophryne*, and *Sphenophryne*) all have representatives at low altitudes. 3) Microhylids do not occur in any part of southern Australia [therefore excluding geographic areas affected by the aridity that Savage (1973) believed to have caused their demise].

Whereas Savage visualized the Australopapuan microhylids as a Gondwanan element and thus a group whose origins involved a direct ancestry to South American frogs, I subscribe to the more orthodox opinion of an Oriental ancestry for the Papuan stock. This view can be supported on historical, biogeographic, and morphological grounds. Provided with the evidence of the nature of the collision of the Australian continental plate with the pre-existing chain of Oriental islands an Oriental origin seems highly likely for the Australopapuan stock. Thus, *Cophixalus*, *Oreophryne*, and *Sphenophryne* were probably established within the chain at the time of the collision. The absence of these genera in the Solomon Islands and islands farther south, and the presence in New Britain of only a single species each of *Oreophryne* and *Sphenophryne* (Tyler, 1967) indicate that microhylids passed eastwards after the colonization of the same areas by ranids. It follows that the ancestry of the Papuan microhylid fauna must be far less complicated than an examination of the diverse modern genera would indicate. The important criterion for their success appears to have been the inherent ability to colonize the New Guinean montane environments that evolved during the rapid elevation immediately after the collision.

Cophixalus, *Oreophryne*, *Sphenophryne*, and in fact all Australopapuan microhylids exhibit direct development. In this regard they differ from all Oriental microhylids. Direct development has enormous selective advantage in situations where there is a shortage of suitable aquatic breeding sites. The first step in its evolution is probably acquisition of macrolecithal eggs without altering the metabolic demands of the embryo. The potential for delayed emergence from the vitelline membranes would result. In terms of the anatomical structure of the tadpole, it follows that any deferment of the onset of larval life is most likely to permit economy in the elaboration of the vast digestive system. This results from the existence of increased food reserves, and of decreased demands upon the use of the larval digestive apparatus.

There are several Oriental microhylids that exhibit trends towards delayed emergence. Inger (1966) provided ecological notes of species in which enlarged and unpigmented ova have been found. In the genus *Kalophrynus* the eggs of some species are pigmented, whereas in others such as *K. pleurostigma* they are unpigmented, and the larvae

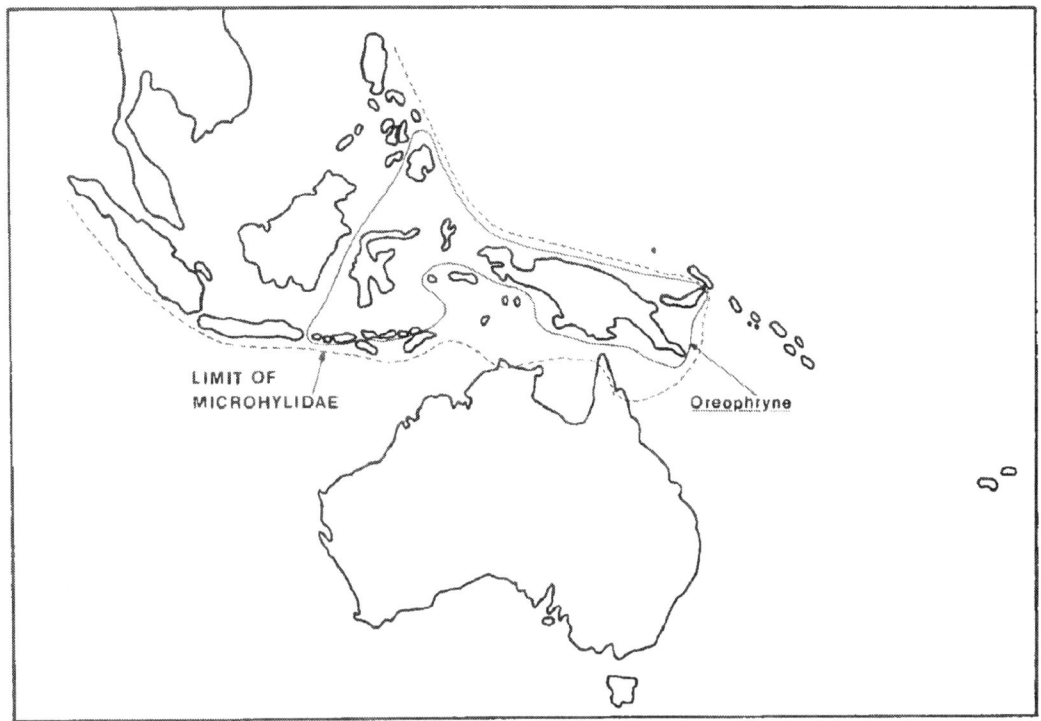

Fig. 4:7. The Australian and adjacent Oriental and Pacific areas showing the distribution of the Microhylidae (broken line) and the range of the most widely distributed Australopapuan genus, *Oreophryne* (continuous line).

Distribución de Microhylidae (linea entrecortada) y el rango del más extendido de todos los géneros australopapua, Oreophryne *(linea continua) en Australia y las areas Oriental y Pacifico adyacentes.*

have poorly developed intestines: ". . . only two loops visible ventrally and appears to be full of yolk." (Inger, 1966:135).

The origin of the Asterophryinae from sphenophrynine ancestors has been considered previously. Zweifel (1972:431) observed that of the asterophryine genera *Hylophorbus* ". . . differs from *Cophixalus* of the Sphenophryninae only in having the tongue less free, and in having a diplasiocoelous rather than procoelous vertebral column. Therefore it may be that the Asterophryinae sprang from stock much like the present-day *Cophixalus*." Tyler (1974a) similarly concluded that the superficial mandibular musculature of *Hylophorbus* is comparable to the uniform condition of *Cophixalus* and other sphenophrynines, and that the various conditions in the Asterophryinae can be derived from the generalized sphenophrynine muscle pattern.

The superficial mandibular musculature of South and North American microhylids exhibits a progressive trend of elongation of a single pair of slender, supplementary elements of the intermandibularis muscle (Emerson, 1976). In many respects these structures resemble those found in Papuan sphenophrynines, but the interhyoideus muscle is more closely involved in the vocal sac, and the structure of the vocal sac is distinctive. It forms an involuted pouch dorsal to the intermandibularis in at least some of the South American taxa, but there is no such trend in sphenophrynines, and in the asterophryines the interhyoideus forms a single sheet lying ventral to the intermandibularis (Fig. 4:8). Variation in microhylid muscle architecture on each of the major continents is shown in figure 4:9; the nature of the diversity is indicative of complex separate radiations.

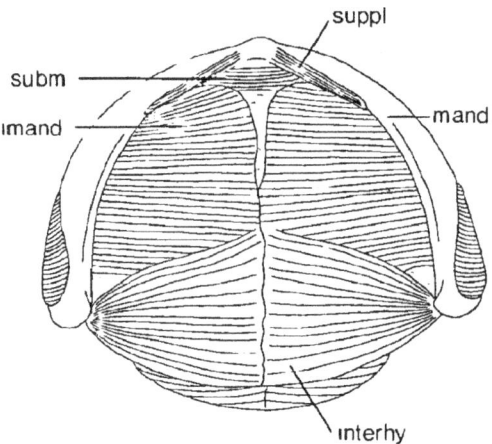

FIG 4 8 Superficial mandibular musculature of the Papuan microhylid frog *Phrynomantis stictogaster*, ventral view with skin removed Interhy = interhyoideus, imand = intermandibularis, mand = mandible, subm = submentalis, suppl = supplementary element of intermandibularis

Musculatura mandibular superficial del batracio microhylido Phrynomantis stictogaster, visto desde la cara ventral con la piel removida

Recently, our knowledge of microhylid karyotypes has been extended to many additional species, particularly by the contributions of Bogart and Nelson (1976) and Blommers-Schlosser (1976) It is generally accepted that a diploid karyotype of 26 is primitive for several families, including the microhylids This number is retained in the three Papuan and 13 Madagascan species studied, but is of variable occurrence elsewhere (Table 4 2)

Varanidae

The varanid lizards constitute a group of small to large animals that are more diversified in Australia than elsewhere The modern distribution of the family (and sole genus, *Varanus*) forms a broad arc from Africa to Australia, King and King (1975) supported an Asian origin Formerly, varanids were distributed far more extensively, extending farther north and occupying Mongolia through to Europe and to North America (McDowell and Bogert, 1954, Hoffstetter, 1961) The 19 Australian species of *Varanus* are placed in two groups—1) small species lacking lateral compression of the tail and often referred to the subgenus *Odatria*, and 2) the large, typical monitors

Hecht (1975) reviewed the fairly extensive history of the Varanidae noting that the Late Cretaceous, Paleocene and Eocene records from North America, Europe, and Mongolia, combined with the absence of the family in South America are indicative of a Laurasian origin The fossil record in Australia suggests that varanids may have entered Australia on two occasions The giant *Megalania prisca* of southeastern Australia is known only from Pleistocene deposits Although McDowell and Bogert (1954) synonymized *Megalania* with *Varanus*, Hecht (1975) redescribed and redefined the fossil genus and provided adequate evidence to merit its recognition Thus, it is possible that *Megalania* and *Varanus* represent separate invasions of Australia *Megalania prisca* is the largest lizard known (total length up to 8 m and an estimated weight up to 600 kg) Fossil *Varanus* have been reported from the Miocene by Stirton, Tedford, and Miller (1961), from the Pliocene by Archer and Wade (1976), and from the Pleistocene by Smith (1976) and Molnar (1978) Thus *Megalania* and *Varanus* were contemporaneous

The success of the carnivorous and carrion-consuming varanids in Australia was attributed by Storr (1964) to the absence of eutherian carnivores Hecht (1975) suggested that *Megalania* represented the carnivore of the Australian megafauna preying upon some of the large herbivorous marsupials that were so abundant in the Pleistocene

Within South America the teid genus *Tupinambis* is the only lizard approaching the niche filled by *Varanus* in Australia, *Tupinambis* is omnivorous

Scincidae

Throughout the world there are over 800 species of skinks unevenly distributed among four subfamilies The widespread distribution of the family and varying interpretations of its systematics and phylogeny are biogeographically undesirable attributes The major systematic treatments are those of Mittleman (1952) and Greer (1970), I have adopted Greer's scheme

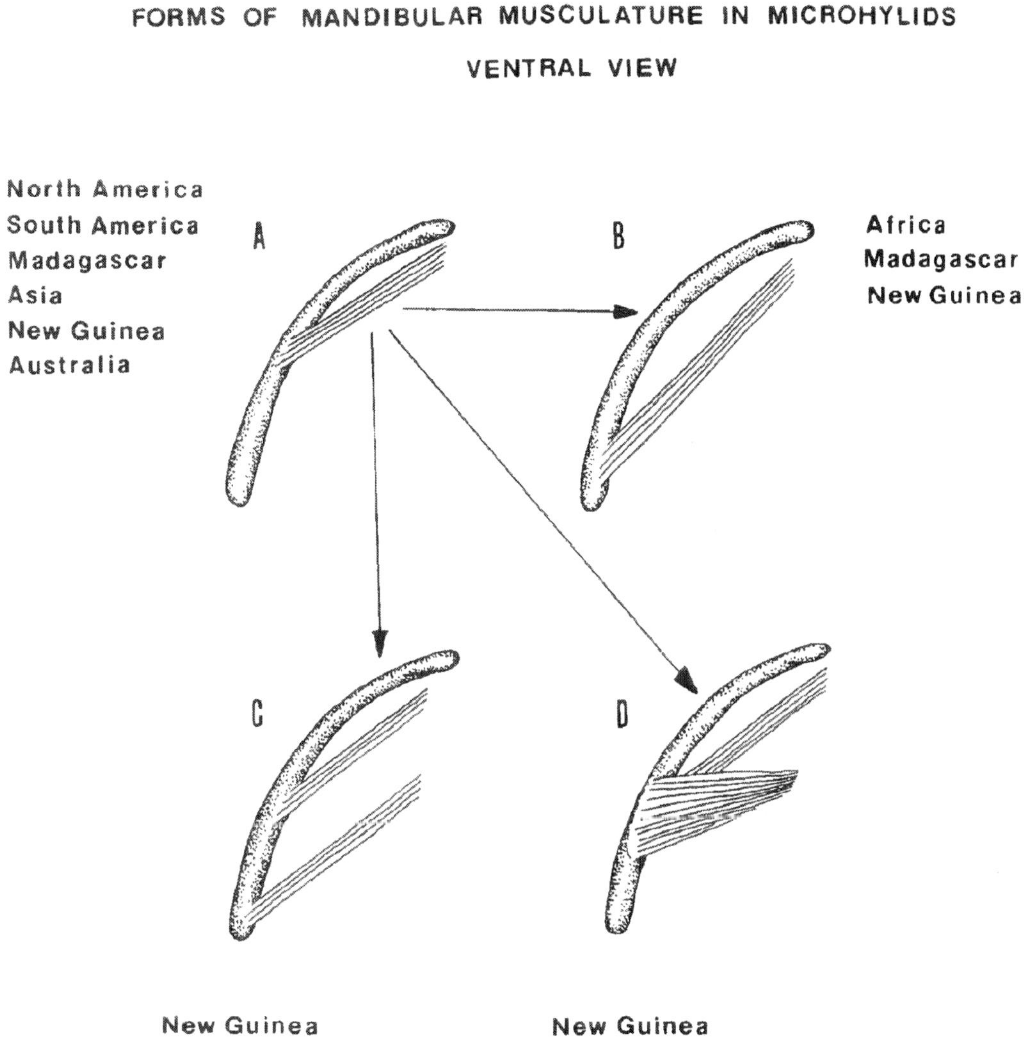

FORMS OF MANDIBULAR MUSCULATURE IN MICROHYLIDS
VENTRAL VIEW

North America
South America
Madagascar
Asia
New Guinea
Australia

A

B

Africa
Madagascar
New Guinea

C

D

New Guinea

New Guinea

Fig. 4:9. Schematic representation of the orientation of supplementary muscle elements in microhylid frogs. In each figure the muscle slip is shown on a single mandible and is viewed from the ventral surface. The simplest form of this muscle is a slip at the apex of the mandibles as in figure 8. This migrates posteriorly along the mandible as shown in A and B, or partially migrates and then divides into two slips of various forms (C and D).

Representación esquemática de la orientación de los elementos del músculo suplementario en batrachios microhylidos. En cada figura la porción muscular se muestra en una sola mandíbula, y se lo ve desde la cara ventral. La forma más simple de este músculo es como una porción en la punta de las mandíbulas como en la figura 8. Esto migra posteriormente a lo largo de la mandíbula como se muestra en A y B, o migra parcialmente y se divide en dos porciones de varias formas (C y D).

Greer considered the Scincinae to be the most primitive group within a distribution that is predominantly Laurasian but also occupies the entire African continent and Madagascar as well. *Eumeces* has a remarkably disjunct distribution, with isolates ranging from North Africa to India, China to Vietnam, and Middle to North America. Disjunctions

TABLE 12.—Microhylid Karyotypes

Continent	Genus	Species	2n	Authority
North America	Gastrophryne	2	22	Morescalchi 1968b, Bogart & Nelson 1976
	Hypopachus	2	22	Leon 1970, Bogart & Nelson 1976
South America	Arcovomer	1	22	Bogart & Nelson 1976
	Dermatonotus	1	22	Rabello 1970, Beçak et al 1970
	Llachistocleis	1	22	Bogart & Nelson 1976
	Glossostoma	1	26	Bogart & Nelson 1976
	Hemiptophryne	1	22	Bogart & Nelson 1976
	Otophryne	1	26	Bogart Pyburn & Nelson 1976
	Stereocyclops	1	22	Bogart & Nelson 1976
Asia	Kaloula	2	24, 28	Morescalchi 1968a, 1968b, Bogart & Nelson 1976, Sato 1936
	Microhyla	1	26	Bai 1956
	Ramanella	1	26	Bai 1956
	Uperodon	1	26	Natarjan 1953
Africa	Breviceps	1	24	Bogart & Nelson 1976, Morescalchi 1968a, 1968b
	Phrynomerus	1	26	Morescalchi 1968a, 1968b, Bogart & Nelson 1976
Madagascar	Anodontohyla	2	26	Blommers 1971, Blommers-Schlosser 1976
	Dyscophus	4	26	Blommers 1971, Blommers-Schlosser 1976
	Mantipus	1	26	Blommers 1971, Blommers-Schlosser 1976
	Platyhyla	1	26	Blommers 1971, Blommers-Schlosser 1976
	Platypelis	2	26	Blommers 1971, Blommers-Schlosser 1976
	Paracophyla	1	26	Blommers 1971, Blommers-Schlosser 1976
	Plethodontohyla	2	26	Blommers 1971, Blommers-Schlosser 1976
New Guinea	Cophixalus	2	26	Cole & Zweifel 1971
	Phrynomantis*	1	26	Cole & Zweifel 1971

* Identified as *Asterophrys sp* by Cole and Zweifel, this individual was subsequently referred to *Phrynomantis stictogaster* by Zweifel (1972, p 501)

in at least some other components of the Scincidae are explained most readily in terms of independent origins from the *Eumeces* stock

The Acontinae and Feylininae are confined to southern, central, and western Africa and are regarded as independent derivatives of the Scincinae, whereas the Lygosominae are found throughout Australia, in all but the extreme south of South America, Middle America, southern North America, in most of Africa, and the entire Oriental Region

Greer (pers comm) considers that the present distribution and radiation of the Scincidae can be explained without reference to continental drift Greer (1970 178) considered the lygosomines " are clearly derived from scincines and are morphologically the most advanced skinks " Thus, within Australia the problem of interpretation of the vast degree of diversification is the time available for that radiation and diversification However, skinks evidently are adept at dispersal over sea water and the timing of their arrival in Australia remains unknown No pre-Pleistocene fossils are known from the Australian Region which is scarcely surprising, considering the state of the fossil record

Agamidae

The absence of agamids from South America and their present, virtually continuous range from Africa to Australia are highly indicative of the Oriental origin of the Australian component of the family The relatively poor representation of the family in New Guinea reflects the ecological differences between New Guinea and Australia The highly successful radiation of agamids in Australia is not unique to agamids, and probably reflects the wide variety of niches open to the early colonizers Archer and Wade (1976) reported a small undetermined species similar to *Amphibolurus* from the Pliocene

Carettochelyidae and Trionychidae

The carettochelyid turtles have an unusual distribution pattern but, as yet, there is no evidence of their former presence in South America. Known from the Eocene of North America and the late Miocene to Present of New Guinea (Glaessner, 1942), the sole living representative *Carettochelys insculpta* was first reported from rivers of northern Australia by Cogger (1970), and since has been shown by Schodde, Mason, and Wolfe (1972) to be distributed quite widely in the Northern Territory. This species evidently has a high tolerance to salt water. Carettochelyids represent a relict family, but it is not necessarily one of any great antiquity within the region. They probably represent the first trionychoid invasion that was followed by *Pelochelys bibroni*, which did not extend beyond New Guinea. Both species probably entered the Australian Region in the Miocene. A trionychid has been found in the middle Pliocene of Venezuela (Wood and Patterson, 1973).

Elapidae

Within Australia and New Guinea the elapid fauna is exceptionally diverse. Authors vary in the number of species and genera that they recognize, but Cogger (1975) recognized 26 genera and 65 species in Australia. Such numbers and diversity would seem to require a great evolutionary time span. This seems to conflict with the existence of endemism within the Solomon Islands (*Salomonelaps* and *Loveridgelaps*) and even as far as Fiji (*Ogmodon*) (McDowell, 1970). Moreover, elapids extend in a slightly disjunct arc through to Africa, an Oriental origin seems likely for many of them. Whether this applies to all components of the Australian elapid fauna will have to await completion of the splendid work commenced by McDowell (1967, 1970).

The elapid fossil record currently is confined to a species of *Pseudonaja* differing from *P. nuchalis* from the Pleistocene deposits at Naracoorte South Australia, by Smith (1975) and Pliocene vertebrae from northern Queensland tentatively referred to the Elapidae by Archer and Wade (1976).

Colubridae

The colubrids occur mainly in the northern and eastern portions of the Australian continent. Some of the genera, such as *Stegonotus*, range through Australia and New Guinea into the Oriental Region. The phylogenetic affinities of *Stegonotus* appear to be with the Oriental *Dinodon* (McDowell 1972). An Oriental route of entry for the colubrids as a whole seems to be unquestionable.

Acrochordidae and Uropeltidae

Two acrochordids occur in New Guinea, in Australia they are restricted to the extreme north of the continent. These aquatic species are either both referred to *Acrochordus*, or one to that genus and the other to *Chersydrus*. Each species is distributed extensively in Indonesia and farther west, and they represent a recent Oriental invasion. The uropeltid genus *Cylindrophis* can be included within the fauna of the Australian Region because it reaches the Aru Islands between Australia and New Guinea (McDowell, 1975). In other respects, it is an exclusively Oriental genus, and it has certainly entered the Australian Region very recently.

Typhlopidae

Typhlopids occur on almost all continents. *Typhlops* has a range almost equivalent to the entire family, extending throughout Asia to New Guinea. The Australian species now are referred to the genus *Typhlina*, which resembles *Typhlops* in external features, but differs substantially in the nature of the male genitalia (Guibé, 1948; Robb, 1966). Cogger (1975) listed 22 species of *Typhlina* in Australia, and McDowell (1974) listed 11 from New Guinea and the Solomon Islands. *Typhlina* extends as far south as Fiji. The nature of the distribution pattern indicates an Oriental origin for the Australian component but the date of its entry is uncertain. Its distribution in the southwest Pacific is extensive and it may be well disposed to sea dispersal.

Boidae

The Boidae is described by Cracraft

(1973 384) as " an excellent example of Gondwanan dispersal" However for Australia the boids may have had a rather checkered history The distribution of *Python* in an almost continuous arc from Africa to Australia provides further evidence of origin outside Australia There has been a fairly pronounced successful radiation within Australia, attributed by Storr (1964) to the absence of the Felidae McDowell (1975) recognized three groups among the Australian Pythoninae distinguished by the presence or absence of labial scale pits and prehensile adaptations to the structure of the tail The first of these contains *Liasis*, and the second *Python*, *Morelia* and *Chondropython* McDowell considered the latter two genera to be only weakly defined and maintained that a good case could be made for referring them all to *Python* Such is the state of herpetological exploration in Australia that a giant new species of *Python* was discovered in the Northern Territory in 1975 (Gow, 1977) However, the third group containing *Aspidites* was defined more satisfactorily by possessing several features not exhibited by other genera The Boinae is represented in New Guinea by two species of *Candoia*

Smith (1976) upset the concept of all of the Australian boids being completely attributable to radiation from a northern entry of a *Python* ancestor From the Naracoorte Caves in the southeast of South Australia, she described the fossil genus and species *Wonambi naracoortensis* She considered *Wonambi* to be related most closely to *Madtsoia bai* (Palaeocene-Eocene of Patagonia) and *M madagascariensis* (Cretaceous of Madagascar) The Naracoorte Caves provide an exceptionally rich fossil fauna and although of only late Pleistocene age, many forms of vertebrates recovered from them are now extinct

Wonambi naracoortensis was described from a series of vertebrae, Smith estimated that they were derived from a snake with a body length of approximately 5 m A fragment of left maxilla associated with the vertebrae bore teeth approximately 7 mm in length It differs from extant Australian boids in lacking accessory processes beneath the prezygapophyses in possessing weak subcentral ridges and paracotylar foramina, and in exhibiting a slight posterior slope to the neural spine

If *Wonambi* is correctly associated with the Boidae, Australia may have been colonized by the family twice—an initial entry antedating the drift of Australia from Antarctica, and a second entry, presumably in the Miocene If so when *Python* first appeared in the north of the continent, *Wonambi* or its ancestors inhabited at least the southeastern part

The only other fossil record of Australian boids is the report by Archer and Wade (1976) of three vertebrae of a very large species in the lower Pliocene Allingham Formation in north Queensland These authors do not associate it with a modern species, but noted (op cit 385) that it is " morphologically very similar to modern species of *Morelia*"

GONDWANAN ELEMENTS

As demonstrated here, the Gondwanan elements are predominantly anuran The fossil record is only just being assembled, and it is best dealt with here rather than within the individual families

Australian Fossil Frog Record

Until recently there were no known fossils of frogs in the Australian Region Tyler (1974a) reported the discovery of an isolated left ilium amongst a rich vertebrate assemblage taken at Lake Palankarinna, north of Lake Eyre, in the northern part of South Australia Subsequently, this ilium became the holotype of the new genus and species *Australobatrachus ilius*, tentatively referred to the Hylidae (Tyler, 1976) More recently, 19 more ilia have been found in sediments from Lake Palankarinna (Tyler, unpublished) These include a number of additional specimens of *A ilius*, several specimens of an undescribed species of the leptodactylid *Limnodynastes* and also a *Litoria* species closely related to, and possibly representing *L caerulea* The age of the Lake Palankarinna fauna is uncertain but is considered to be most likely mid-Miocene Thus the age coincides with the collision of the Australopapuan and Oriental plates

A rich Pleistocene fauna, including 166 frog ilia of extant species, has been taken at two cave sites at Naracoorte in the lower southeast of South Australia (Tyler, 1977). The fossils include *Litoria ewingi*, *Limnodynastes* cf. *dumerili*, *L. tasmaniensis*, *Ranidella signifera*, and *Geocrinia* cf. *laevis*, all of which occur in that area today. Unfortunately, as yet there are no known frog fossils of an age predating the Australopapuan-Oriental collision. However, it is noteworthy that *Limnodynastes* and *Litoria* were established in the Miocene at Lake Palankarinna.

Hylidae

Until about 1970 the confamilial status of the hylids of Australia and New Guinea ("Australopapuan") with those of South America had not been disputed, and in fact *Hyla* was applied quite uniformly to Australopapuan and Neotropical species (creating numerous problems of homonymy but apparently not of biogeography). The disjunct nature of the distribution of *Hyla* (*sensu lato*) was the principal area of interest long before the homogeneity of the genus (and later of the family) was really questioned. Within the framework of a concept of static continents, Parker (1929) suggested that the Hylidae might be of North American origin, radiating from there in several different directions, of which South America and Australia were the ultimate destinations of two. The major gap between the depauperate Oriental *Hyla* and the relatively numerous Australian species remained a serious obstacle to adequate explanations of dispersal although Darlington (1957) suggested that the arboreal rhacophorids have displaced and now replace the hylids in that intermediate area.

The first suggestion of a direct association between South American and Australian hylid species was made by Beaufort (1951), who visualized an Antarctic land bridge as a route for entry to Australia from South America. During the past decade fresh interpretations of the phylogeny and systematics of the hylids of Australia and South America have far exceeded the comparative faunal studies desirable to support some of the conclusions reached.

Tyler (1971) studied a suite of characters associated with the superficial mandibular musculature, and the vocal sac that it contains, in representatives of numerous families and including almost all known hylid genera. He noted that anatomical divergence occurred principally in association with taxonomic units recognized as genera. He demonstrated that the Australopapuan *Hyla* constituted a single morph distinguishable from species from other parts of the world. Consequently he proposed the resurrection of *Litoria* Tschudi to accommodate the Australopapuan species and further considered *Litoria* and *Nyctimystes* to be a unique, monophyletic group.

Cracraft (1973) reported the above findings without variation, but in 1974 suggested only that the distinction of Asiatic and Australopapuan species had been demonstrated and he introduced the topic of Australopapuan-South American hylid affinities as though it were a new proposal. Savage (1973) acknowledged some of my data in press as evidence refuting the confamilial status of the two groups of frogs, and accordingly resurrected the family name Pelodryadidae Gunther to accommodate them.

Bagnara (1974) published rather conflicting data. From his discovery of the occurrence of rhodomelanochrome in the skin of Neotropical phyllomedusines and some, but not all, Australian hylids, he made two radical proposals. These were 1) that the Australian species of *Litoria* exhibiting rhodomelanochrome are more closely related phylogenetically to South American phyllomedusines than to sympatric congeners, and suggested therefore 2) that *Litoria* was a highly heterogeneous assemblage. More recently, Bagnara (1976) reiterated the common origin of the phyllomedusine-*Litoria* component more forcefully.

Laurent (1975) envisaged a totally different origin for the Australopapuan species, suggesting independent origin *in situ* from a formerly world-wide leptodactylid ancestor, which he visualized as the ancestral stock of several families on different continents. Contemplating a wholly autochthonous origin he employed the name Nyctimystinae for the Australopapuan fauna.

In an attempt to stabilize the classification

of these and other frogs, Duellman (1975) offered a number of solutions to controversial issues. Among his actions he continued to include Australopapuan species in the Hylidae.

In order to crystalize the current controversy and to aid the transcontinental study of the Hylidae, it is necessary to restate or clarify the following issues: 1) the phylogenetic relationships of the Indonesian hylids (those on the periphery of the Australian population and geographically closest to the Oriental species), 2) whether the Australopapuan species genuinely constitute a monophyletic group, 3) the phylogenetic relationships of the Australian species, and 4) the phylogenetic relationships of the Australian and South American hylid faunal units.

The Indonesian hylid fauna.—The northwestern geographic limit of *Litoria* occurs in the Indonesian islands of Timor and the Lesser Sunda Islands of Sumba, Savu and Alor. This latter assemblage represents the eastern end of an archipelago forming an intimate link to the Malaysian Peninsula far to the northwest. Therefore, the *Litoria* fauna of the Timor-Lesser Sunda group is of importance to any contemplation of entry of hylids into Australia from the northwest.

The only species (*L. everetti*) occurring in the relevant area is a member of the *L. peroni* group represented elsewhere in the Australopapuan area by five described species—*peroni*, *everetti*, *amboinensis*, *rothi* and *darlingtoni*. The total geographic range of this species group is exceptionally extensive (Tyler and Davies, 1978a). It appears that the group evolved in Australia or New Guinea and is now radiating in several directions and extending its range. Thus, it is confirmed that the phylogenetic affinities of *L. everetti* are with other Australopapuan species and not with the southernmost Oriental hylid (*Hyla chinensis*).

Monophyletic or polyphyletic origins.—Insofar as the Australopapuan fauna is concerned, the issue is whether the frogs referred to the Hylidae are a monophyletic group. Ecologically, at least, they are incredibly diverse, filling a spectrum of niches occupied on other continents by different families. A superficial examination of the diversity of structure may render the casual observer critical of Australopapuan hylid systematics. Nevertheless the magnitude of diversity need be no indication of polyphyly. Tyler (1971) proposed the concept of monophyletic origin on the basis of his studies of superficial mandibular musculature and vocal sac structure. Subsequent karyotypic data assembled by Stephenson and Stephenson (1970), Woodruff (1972) Morescalchi and Ingram (1974), and Menzies and Tippett (1976) have in no way caused this concept to change. All of the hylids karyotyped to date have $2n = 26$, except *L. infrafrenata* ($2n = 24$), and in that instance a model for derivation from $2n = 26$ has been proposed (Menzies and Tippett, 1976).

Phylogenetic relationships of Australian species.—Tyler and Davies (1978a) examined the morphology, osteology, myology, distribution, and biology of 92 of the 94 species of *Litoria* currently recognized. They found that these species can be associated in no less than 37 species groups. Insofar as all geographic areas occupied by *Hyla* are concerned this total of groups is not exceptionally high. In reality the number of species per species group is remarkably similar in several geographic areas (Table 4.3). Although more concerned with the initial step of establishing phenetic groupings, Tyler and Davies demonstrated that Australian hylids occupy an incredible gamut of niches.

Tyler (1970, 1972a) suggested that there exists a close phylogenetic relationship between Australian hylids and leptodactylids. The core of this suggestion related to the leptodactylid genus *Cyclorana*. That genus as then constituted comprised a group of squat-bodied and also some elongate species. Lynch (1971) regarded them an integral component of the Australian leptodactylid fauna. Tyler (1971, 1972a) studied superficial mandibular musculature in all Australian leptodactylids and his conclusions differed from those of Lynch only in his appraisal of *Cyclorana* in which he noted distinct hylid affinities. Tyler (1970) suggested that the similarities of the Australian hylids and leptodactylids implied the existence of a single common ancestor

TABLE 4 3—Relationship Between Number of Species and Number of Species Groups of Selected Hylid Genera on Different Continents

Geographic area	Genus	No of species	No of groups	Species/Group
Australia	Litoria	46	22	2 09 1
New Guinea	Litoria	51	24	2 12 1
Australia & New Guinea°	Litoria	94	37	2 54 1
Middle America°°	Hyla	73	28	2 61 1
North America°°	Hyla	12	4	3 00 1

° Includes a component common to Australia and New Guinea
°° Data from Duellman (1970)

Robinson and Tyler (1973) examined the relative predominance of the catecholamines epinephrine and norepinephrine (dopamine was not detected) in the adrenal glands of various Australian hylids and leptodactylids, including *Cyclorana* They found that epinephrine was the predominant transmitter in all hylids examined and that norepinephrine was predominant in all leptodactylids, except *Cyclorana* In the absence of any biochemical convergence associated with ecological convergence, they regarded catecholamine selection as an exceptionally conservative feature

The major issues to be explored are, as follow 1) Do the Australopapuan hylids exhibit a close phylogenetic relationship with any of the sympatric leptodactylids, or 2) is there a closer relationship with South American hylids or leptodactylids? Hence it is conceivable that Australopapuan hylids and South American hylids enjoy a reasonably close relationship, or that the Australopapuan hylids are independently derived from a South American leptodactylid stock, and that resemblance only reflects convergence

Before exploring the nature of the resemblance of hylids from each of the continents, it is worthwhile discussing here the novel proposition introduced by Bagnara and Ferris (1975) on the basis of the significance of the presence of rhodomelanochrome in some but not all *Litoria* (see p 90) Maxson (1976) rejected this conclusion on the basis of immunological data and Tyler and Davies (1978b) reexamined the phylogenetic relationships of the same species studied by Bagnara and Ferris, together with additional species Employing features of adult myology, osteology, larval structure, and reproductive biology, as well as pigment, their findings conflict with those of Bagnara and Ferris They found that Australian congeners are genuinely more closely related with one another than some *Litoria* are with phyllomedusines Their findings also tend to reinforce further the recognition of the phyllomedusinae as a subfamilial unit Some of the biochemical features employed by Bagnara as indicators of close phylogenetic relationships tend to be particularly subject to convergence, and Guttman (1973) outlined the problems that arise when the relationships of higher taxa are based on such characters

Phylogenetic relationships of Australian and South American hylids —Numerically at the level of species, genera, and families, South America is clearly the most major center in the world of evolution of modern taxa of anurans There is no reason to suppose that the Hylidae evolved in Australia and migrated to South America, but the obvious reverse option raises a number of most interesting questions When some South American hylid frogs are placed directly beside Australian frogs and compared one with another, the confamilial association is stretched to the limit South America simply does not possess frogs that resemble the *Litoria aurea*, *L caerulea* and *L freycineti* groups Similarly, there are numerous dominant components of the South American fauna that do not have counterparts in Australia

Irrespective of the magnitude of divergence between South American and Australian species the fact remains that all possess intercalary structures and so are referred to the family Hylidae On a continental basis the species are indeed different Savage (1973), using Tyler's (1971) data, considered the distinction adequate to merit family status, and so termed the Australopapuan unit "Pelodryadidae" I too recognize the morphological distinction and the monophyletic origin of the Australopapuan unit, but I find only adequate grounds for an intrinsic division within the current concept of the Hylidae. Therefore, I favor recognition of a subfamily to accommodate *Litoria Nyctimystes* and (as indicated in later discussion) *Cyclorana*. Because all family group names are of equal status for the purposes of nomenclatural priority, Pelodryadinae (derived from Pelodryadidae Gunther, 1858) takes priority over Nyctimystinae Laurent, 1975.

It is worth noting that when Maxson and Wilson (1975) implemented Savage's concept of the Pelodryadidae because of results of estimated mean albumin-immunological distances between continental populations, they overestimated the continental divergence time. Their immunological distance of 100 units equates with 60 million years, so that the existence of 100 immunological units between any two taxa involves acceptance of 60 million years isolation between the populations. Their calculation of an immunological distance of approximately 129 units between the relevant Australian and South American populations can be interpreted in two ways, but may well be excessive. The physical separation of Australia from Antarctica is now established at 52–55 m y b p. This total compares with 77 m y b p calculated by immunological techniques. If the latter is the period of isolation of the stocks, ecological or physical barriers on the Antarctic land mass are called for to explain the separation of populations prior to rifting.

Wallace, Maxson and Wilson (1971) found greater immunological distances existing between South American and the adjacent North American species, than between North American and the geographically distant single Australian species examined. Maxson (1978) demonstrated a high degree of compatability between North American and European *Hyla*. Maxson and Wilson (1971) noted that where discrepancies exist between organismal resemblance and albumin resemblance, it is to be attributed to differential rates of organismal evolution. As an example they cited *Acris*, which exhibits albumin and haemoglobin affinities to North American *Hyla*, and yet is strikingly different from such species in anatomy, gross structure, biology and ecology. Duellman (1970: 647) accepted such evidence with considerably less tolerance: "Despite the divergent nature of *Acris* with respect to other hylids, and the superficial similarity of *Acris* to ranids, the inescapable fact remains that *Acris* has procoelous vertebrae, an arciferal pectoral girdle, intercalary cartilages and claw-shaped terminal phalanges—a combination of characters that seemingly inextricably ally the genus with the hylids."

It is equally reasonable to suggest that organismal evolution is unlikely to be constrained along any linear path of morphological divergence as assessed by human observers. Hence, systematists have a quandry that is of their own making, and while the Hylidae remains defined as it is now, the Pelodryadinae remains an integral component of it.

Cyclorana is a problematic genus. By virtue of the fossorial habit of most of its species and the absence of intercalary structures it formerly has been accommodated in the Leptodactylidae (Parker, 1940, Lynch, 1971). More recent evidence has demonstrated similarities between *Cyclorana* and pelodryadine hylids in myology (Tyler, 1972a), adrenal catecholamines (Robinson and Tyler, 1973), in larval structure and biology (Watson and Martin, 1973), and in cranial osteology (Fig 4.10). A closer examination of the morphology of *Cyclorana* species resulted in the discovery of intercalary structures in *C. inermis*, *C. alboguttatus*, and *C. dahlii*, and led to these species being referred to the hylid genus *Litoria* by Straughan (1969), Tyler (1974b) and Tyler Davies and King (1978) respectively.[1]

In consequence of these actions and of the resurrection of one species and the description of five new species (Tyler and Martin, 1975, 1977), *Cyclorana* now is composed exclusively of robust fossorial frogs lacking intercalary structures but retaining a closer affinity to hylid than to leptodactylid frogs. Awareness of this presumably led Heyer and Liem (1976) to omit *Cyclorana* from their

---
[1] The customary term "intercalary cartilages" is not used because these structures are bony in 46 of 71 Australopapuan hylid species studied (Tyler and Davies, 1978a). Ossification bears no correlation with finger length habits or geographic distribution. However, all large or moderately large arboreal species retain a cartilaginous state.

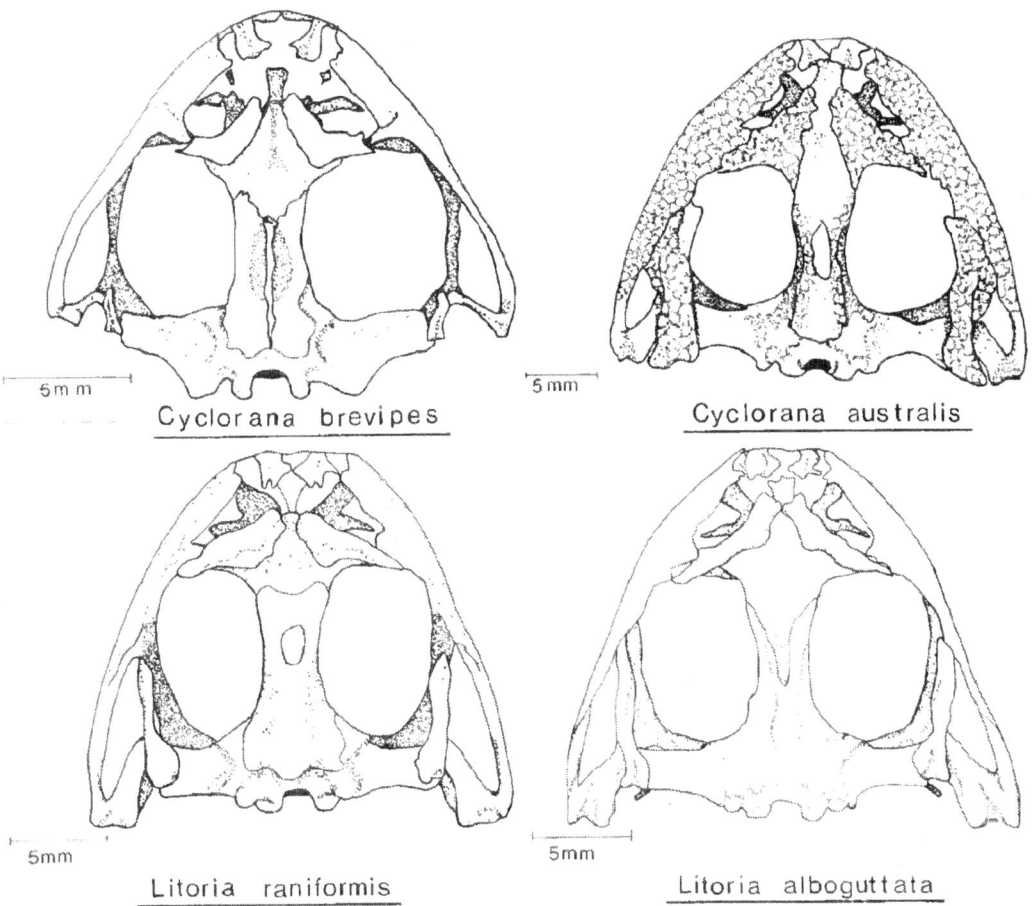

Fig. 4:10. Skulls of certain species of *Cyclorana* and *Litoria*.
Cráneos de ciertas especies de Cyclorana y Litoria.

phylogenetic analysis of the Australopapuan leptodactylidae (Myobatrachidae).

Because all hylids exhibit axillary amplexus and Australian leptodactylids (except *Mixophyes*) inguinal, it follows that the embrace of *Cyclorana* should be of relevance in determining its phylogenetic relationships. I have observed amplexus in four species of *Cyclorana*. Initially the grasp is high in a circumcervical position, as though the male intends to strangle his mate. However the grasp slides posteriorly to an inguinal position.

Within the Hylidae, *Cyclorana* appears to be related most closely to the *Litoria aurea* species group, which now includes two species previously referred to *Cyclorana*. This group may prove to be the sister group of *Cyclorana* and merit elevation to distinct generic identity.

Leptodactylidae (Myobatrachidae)

It is valid to describe the current state of nomenclature and phylogeny of Australian leptodactylid frogs as distinctly unstable. Even to refer to them here as Leptodactylidae rather than Myobatrachidae is in total opposition to the sincere efforts of many workers. I do so now because I seek a reevaluation of the steps that led to the nomenclatural change, and because I suspect that the examination of South American-Australian relationships is best served by nomenclatural conservatism

Parker's (1940) review of Australasian species brought a considerable degree of stability to the nomenclature of many Australian genera. Parker recognized two subfamilies—Cycloraninae (which he erected) and the Myobatrachinae. Lynch (1971) provided a splendid historical account of the classification of the Leptodactylidae, and in so doing, placed Parker's contribution in an historical perspective. Following the publication of Parker's monograph, A. R. Main and his colleagues undertook the first detailed biological, herpetofaunal studies. The result of their work (and of that of their students) was the description of numerous new species. Nevertheless, the genera recognized and sustained by Parker were in no way challenged. Certainly *Neobatrachus* was resurrected from the synonymy of *Heleioporus* by Main, Lee, and Littlejohn (1958), but in over 25 years only one new genus was erected—*Taudactylus* by Straughan and Lee (1966). At that time it was tempting to assume that Australia's leptodactylid fauna was already reasonably well established. However, as late as 1960, only 59 of the currently recognized total of 79 species had been discovered. (*Cyclorana* has been excluded from these totals.) Close examination of some of the numerically large genera then recognized (e.g., *Crinia*) indicated an unsuspected heterogeneity. In fact, because most *Crinia* were small species, the genus had in reality become a repository for a great variety of frogs only sharing small stature. It followed that closer examination led to the erection of some new genera and the resurrection of others (Tyler, 1972b; Blake, 1973).

Collection of *Rheobatrachus silus* by Liem (1973) represented one of the most extraordinary herpetological discoveries of this century. In its gross morphology as an aquatic frog with profuse dermal mucous glands, fully webbed toes, long pointed fingers and incredible aquatic maneuverability, the resemblance to pipids such as *Xenopus* and particularly to the South American leptodactylid *Telmatobius*, is extremely striking. *Rheobatrachus silus* was found to be even more noteworthy when Corben, Ingram, and Tyler (1974) reported that the female broods the larvae within her stomach.

Subsequently a robust-bodied, fossorial frog was found living in coastal sandhills in a remote and arid part of Western Australia. Named *Arenophryne rotunda* by Tyler (1976c), this genus has affinities with both *Myobatrachus* and *Pseudophryne*. More recently, another new and as yet undescribed genus (Tyler et al., 1979) was discovered in the northern portion of Western Australia and the Northern Territory. This form produces a foam nest, has tadpoles with suctorial mouths and elongate tails, and the adult exhibits enormous tympana.

The subdivision of existing genera initiated by Tyler (1972b) and Blake (1973) took a further, and more radical, step with actions of Heyer and Liem (1976) who described three more new genera to accommodate known species—*Paracrinia* for *Crinia haswelli*, *Australocrinia* to accommodate two southeastern species referred to *Ranidella* by Blake (1973), and *Kankanophryne* for *Pseudophryne occidentalis*. They also resurrected *Platyplectron* without defining it or naming the constituent species.

Unfortunately the data on which this study by Heyer and Liem is based are, as yet, unpublished, being available only in a paper by Liem cited as "in press." Thus, it is simply not possible to comprehend or assess several of the decisions reached by these authors and I am unable to recognize the genera in the following discussion.

In attempting to provide a brief resumé of the case for the familial and subfamilial status of the Australian frogs, I must at the outset put forth the evidence that has been provided for family distinction. Lynch (1973) and Savage (1973) well may be considered the prime initiators of the concept of the Myobatrachidae as a family unit distinct from the Leptodactylidae. In their respective views of the classification of the Anura they, and other authors, differed in many respects, and Duellman (1975) attempted to synthesize the various expressed opinions and produce a classification that constituted a compromise. Duellman recognized the distinctness of the Myobatrachidae, but his brief diagnoses did not include a single nongeographic feature by which the majority of species of one family could be distinguished from those of the other I draw attention to this fact not in an attempt to score a point, but solely to highlight the fact that the case for considering the Myobatrachidae a separate family still needs to be substantiated

Duellman (1975) was able to accommodate *Rheobatrachus* within the Myobatrachidae arguing that neither the suite of primitive morphological character states, nor the bizarre reproductive mode should exclude it Lynch (1971) employed a graphic technique enabling him to compare the relative primitiveness of a large number of nonarchaic frogs If *Rheobatrachus* is added to Lynch's frog groups and the 13 nonreproductive characters are scored, *Rheobatrachus* has a total score of 0 It is the bizarre reproductive state that produces a positive sum I wholly support Heyer and Liem's (1976) action of placing *Rheobatrachus* in a separate subfamily, the Rheobatrachinae Therefore, within the Australian Region there is an enormous diversity of animals in terms of the nature of character states, and a crucial question is whether the disjunction between the Australian and South American subfamilies is best reflected by regarding them as members of different families Intrasubfamilial variation is more extensive among the Australian subfamilies than in any other comparable units on other continents, and it is this variation that renders their definition so difficult (Lynch, 1973 170–171)

The South African *Heleophryne* forms the Heleophryninae, which Lynch placed in the Myobatrachidae It would be extremely interesting to test this assignment by means of the comparison of serum albumins employing the techniques for frogs of Wallace, Maxson, and Wilson (1971) Because the African continent separated from Gondwanaland between the mid Jurassic and mid-Cretaceous (100–155 m y b p), but South America from Gondwanaland in the Cenozoic (25–45 m y b p), the absence of myobatrachids from South America is curious indeed Morescalchi (1973) and Morescalchi and Ingram (1974) noted that *Cyclorana alboguttatus* (now *Litoria alboguttata*) is karyologically less differentiated than many Australian leptodactylid genera and approaches some primitive leptodactylids from other geographical areas (*Heleophryne*, the Ceratophryinae, many Telmatobiinae, all with $2n = 26$)

On gross morphological grounds, the resemblance between some Australian and South American genera is striking If the South American *Batrachyla* should be found tomorrow in the cool temperate forests of the southern section of the Australian Great Dividing Range, it would be compared with *Kyarranus* and *Philoria* found to be highly similar, and attract little comment

Lynch (1973) pointed out that there were several systematic options in any cladistic study of the leptodactyloid frogs, and he maintained that separating the Limnodynastinae ("Cycloraninae" of Lynch without *Cyclorana*), Heleophryninae, and Myobatrachinae from the Leptodactylidae, reduced the gradation of characters within the latter family The knowledge of each of these units remains incomplete, and other more radical options are still open For example, on biogeographic grounds, frogs associated with heleophrynines or myobatrachines should occur among the cool temperate Austral fauna of South America Alternatively, other data might reinforce the existing myobatrachine-telmatobiine links, or the degree of distinction between the Myobatrachinae and the Limnodynastinae, thereby meriting independent family status for each of the latter For the present there seems to be a good case for including the Australian species in the Leptodactylidae while the other avenues are being explored

Gekkonidae

In recent years the status of the higher taxa of gekkonid lizards has attracted considerable attention Underwood (1954) recognized three families—Eublepharidae, Sphaerodactylidae, and Gekkonidae, with two subfamilies (Gekkoninae and Diplodactylinae) Kluge (1967) recognized only one family (the Gekkonidae) containing each of the other four units as subfamilies Some of Kluge's concepts of the origins, dispersal, and evolutionary relationship of these subfamilies have been variously criticized by Maderson

(1972), Moffat (1973), and Russell (1976) Kluge's (1967) interpretation was made with the assumption that continental drift was neither tenable as an hypothesis, nor germane to the resolution of the study. This led to conclusions that must be reexamined within the context of continental drift as an acceptable hypothesis. For example, there is his assumption that the Australian Diplodactylinae evolved from a primitive southeast Asian gekkonid stock during the Late Mesozoic. However, for that entire era, Australia lay far to the south and was still united to western Antarctica, the rift and long northwards drift towards southeast Asia only commenced in the early Cenozoic. Therefore, as Cracraft (1975) pointed out, the prospect of a successful overwater dispersal of geckos from Asia to Australia in the Mesozoic is remote indeed.

In addition to hosting the pantropical gekkoninae, the endemic subfamilies of South America and Australia probably exhibit similar historical patterns of gekkonid evolution. Certainly a significant feature of the disjunctly distributed eublepharines is their absence from South America, Madagascar and Australia. Such a distribution is explained most readily by adopting Kluge's concept of an African or Asian site of origin. The general consensus of opinion is that the sphaerodactylines of South America and the diplodactylines of Australia evolved within their present geographic ranges. The diplodactylines extended to New Caledonia, the Loyalty Islands, and New Zealand evolving in New Zealand to form an ovoviviparous group. Arrival of the diplodactylines in New Zealand has been suggested to be a Miocene event, but if the subfamily existed in Australia in the Cenozoic it could have entered New Zealand via the Lord Howe Rise.

Many of the gekkonines are remarkably well suited to transoceanic dispersal. *Phyllodactylus* has an incredible geographic range occurring in the Americas, Africa, Madagascar, Australia, New Caledonia, New Zealand, and the Galapagos Islands. However, Dixon and Anderson (1973) indicated that *Phyllodactylus* may be heterogeneous, species in the Eastern Hemisphere should be separated generically from *Phyllodactylus*. A number of gekkonines are dispersed by man. Recent karyotypic studies in Australia have demonstrated within well-established gekkonine and diplodactyline species the existence of numerous biological species, none of which has yet been accorded formal taxonomic status (King, 1973, 1975, 1977, King and Rofe, 1976). For example, King (1977) recognized five discretely distributed and chromosomally distinct populations within what is now termed *Diplodactylus vittatus*. When all of these new taxa are named, it is clear that the Australian gekkonid fauna will be vast numerically.

Chelidae

Presently, the pleurodire chelonians are restricted to South America, Africa, Australia and New Guinea. Of the constituent families now extant the Chelidae occurs in the Neotropical and Australian Regions, whereas the Pelomedusidae occurs in Africa, Madagascar and South America. In terms of diversity and radiation, the South American genera and species have been more labile, and study of the extant Australian members suggests an exceptionally conservative history. In a phylogenetic study, Gaffney (1977) envisaged the Australian genus *Pseudemydura* as possibly the sister group of all other Australian and South American genera.

At present, there are four recognizable genera of extant Australian chelids—*Chelodina*, *Elseya*, *Emydura* and *Pseudemydura*. Fossil records are becoming quite numerous, but the majority of them are based upon totally disarticulated shell fragments lacking sufficient detail to provide adequate diagnostic characters for generic determinations.

The first report of fossil chelids from Australia is that of Lydekker (1889) who reported fragments of *Chelodina* and *Emydura* from various localities. De Vis (1894) proposed *Trionyx australiensis* for a substantial quantity of fragments (probably chelid) taken at Darling Downs, and then (1897) described one new genus and four new species from the same or adjacent localities. These specimens are in urgent need of review. Records of Pleistocene chelids from Queensland reported by Longman (1929) are fragmentary and lack diagnostic characters (Warren, 1969).

Evidence of the conservative nature of the

chelid fauna was provided by Warren (1969) who reported *Emydura* sp. aff. *macquari* from siltstones in Tasmania. Reported to be of Oligocene-Miocene age they are now considered somewhat older and of Early Tertiary age (J. W. Warren, pers. comm.). Chelids are no longer extant in Tasmania, and *E. macquari* is now confined to the Murray-Darling drainage system of the southeastern Australian mainland. With the discovery of freshwater turtle remains from Tasmania and also from various Miocene to Pleistocene deposits on the mainland (Callen and Tedford, 1976; Archer and Wade, 1976), it is likely that previously chelids have occupied almost all of the Australian continent and New Guinea as well. Contraction of their ranges is probably a Pleistocene phenomenon.

The intercontinental relationships of chelids is, superficially at least, extremely close (e.g., *Elseya* and *Platemys*). However, the Lower Cretaceous *Chelycarapookus arcuatus* Warren (1975) (Chelycarapookidae) (previously identified erroneously as *Emydura macquari* by Chapman, 1919) needs to be examined. Unfortunately, with the posterior portion of the plastron of that fossil missing, whether the pelvic girdle was attached or not remains unknown, so that even the infra-order position of the family is uncertain. Warren (1975) noted that in *Chelycarapookus* neurals probably were present between all costals, and suggested tentatively that with loss of the neurals, Australian chelids could have been derived from a chelycarapookid ancestor. However Rhodin and Mittermeier (1977), apparently without sighting the description of *Chelycarapookus*, reported that neurals occur regularly in one species of Australian chelid and irregularly in several other species. Gaffney's (1975) study of the phylogeny and classification of turtles almost exclusively relied upon cranial characters, and, in common with most Australian chelid remains, the head and neck of *Chelycarapookus* remain unknown.

Crocodiles

The crocodiles include two quite distinct components differing in their ancestry and are probably of separate Gondwanan and Oriental origins. The extant species of *Crocodylus* are clearly of Oriental origin or derived from an Oriental stock, and are confined to the north of the Region—*C. porosus* of southeastern Asia, New Guinea and Australia, *C. novaeguineae* of New Guinea and *C. johnsoni* of Australia.

The fossil fauna is substantial both in quantity and diversity, and a number of highly significant finds has been reported recently. Molnar (1977) described from Chillagoe in North Queensland an incomplete skull, with a high and laterally compressed snout and probably ziphodont dentition. The subsequent discovery of Pleistocene *Palorchestes* cf. *P. azael* at the same site was interpreted as evidence of a Pleistocene age for the ziphodont (Molnar, 1978), and indicated that ziphodonts had survived in Australia long after their extinction elsewhere in the world.

Hecht and Archer (1977) reported two forms of ziphodonts from the Pleistocene of South Australia and southeast Queensland, respectively. The former is reported to compare favorably with the type of the sebecosuchian *Sebecus icaeorhinus* from the Eocene of Patagonia. The authors suggested that the assumed sebechosuchian *Planocrania datangensis* from the Early Tertiary of China is in reality probably an eusuchian, so that origin of the Sebecosuchia is clearly from Gondwanaland.

AUTOCHTHONOUS ELEMENT

Pygopodidae

The legless, fossorial lizard family Pygopodidae is the only reptilian family restricted to the Australian Region. Kluge (1974) recognized eight genera and 30 species of pygopodids. Kluge's (1976) analysis of phylogenetic relationships within the family led to the recognition of only six genera. Following the work of Underwood (1957), there has been general acceptance that the pygopodid-gekkonid relationship is extremely close, and it follows that the most likely origin for the pygopodids is within Australia directly from a gekkonid stock.

Many pygopodid species are restricted

either to the southwest or to the southeast of the continent, a distribution pattern common to numerous vertebrates and attributed to speciation in the Pleistocene, associated with the glacial-interglacial climatic oscillations. Thus, the implication of the existence of such distribution patterns is that speciation of these same populations is not of any great antiquity. Somewhat in conflict is the total absence of pygopodids from the southern island of Tasmania and the presence of only a single species on Kangaroo Island. If these indicate that pygopodids occupied the adjacent mainland only after isolation of these islands from the mainland (8,000–10,000 y.b.p.), the southern speciation pattern evidently is more complex.

Western Pacific Island Faunas and Oceanic Dispersal

Although South America now is separated from Australia by the vast expanses of the Pacific Ocean, the nature of the major oceanic surface currents provides a mechanism for westward dispersal of animals by rafting from South America in the direction of Australia.

The west coast of South America is swept by the north flowing Humboldt Current which meets the transpacific southern equatorial current at mid-latitudes. The latter current travels westward and eventually disperses around all of the islands of the Pacific south of the Equator.

Thirty years ago Thor Heyerdahl's raft Kon-Tiki demonstrated the transport potential of the southern equatorial current by travelling from Perú to the Tuamotu Archipelago in French Polynesia south of the Marquesas Islands. Had his vessel been driven two or three degrees northwards, he would have passed between the Marquesas and the Tuamotu Archipelago, and continued much farther west on a longer journey terminating in Western Samoa, Fiji or Tonga. This longer journey is probably the route of the ancestral stocks of the iguanids of Fiji and Tonga—*Brachylophus fasciatus* and *B. brevicephalus*, respectively. South American derivates are not evident elsewhere and the remaining elements of the herpetofauna of the islands in the west and southwest Pacific area are representative of two other sources—1) overwater dispersal principally from the north and northeast, and 2) land communication with Australia via the exposed Lord Howe Rise.

Fiji and New Zealand are the most southerly of the large landmasses in the Pacific and merit specific mention.

Fiji.—In addition to the iguanid *Brachylophus* (discussed by Cogger, 1974), Gorham (1965) stated that an additional 14 lizards occur on Fiji. These are gekkonids and scincids, but only one possibly is endemic. The presence of two boids, one elapid (endemic), and one typhlopid so far southeast tends to support the hypothesis that these are all of Oriental source and not Gondwanan elements. As noted previously, the two endemic ranids on Fiji (*Platymantis vitiensis* and *P. vitianus*) were derived from the same source route. In the case of the ranids, the absence of frogs from the intermediate potential stepping stones of New Hebrides and New Caledonia remains an apparently inexplicable anomaly. Additional references dealing with the Fijian herpetofauna are Barbour (1923), Brown and Myers (1949), and Gorham (1968).

New Zealand.—The most well known component of the New Zealand herpetofauna is the rhynchocephalian reptile, the Tuatara *Sphenodon punctatus*. This relic was probably quite widely distributed elsewhere in the Mesozoic, as evidenced by the extensive fossil record of rhynchocephalians at that time. The remaining terrestrial reptiles are 35 species of lizards (almost all are endemic) of the families Gekkonidae and Scincidae. The geckos include three endemic genera that are unique among gekkonids in being ovoviviparous, whereas the endemic skinks are members of genera widely distributed outside New Zealand.

In their recent survey of New Zealand vertebrates, Bull and Whittaker (1975) accepted Kluge's (1967) interpretations of the origin of the gekkonids resulting in their statement (op. cit. 239) "The geckos form part of the Malayo-Pacific element of the New Zealand fauna and probably entered New Zealand in the Miocene when the climate was warmer and the land more extensive than now." They further visualized fairly extensive oceanic dispersal by rafting from New Caledoma or directly from Australia. A totally different interpretation would result by considering the connection between New Zealand and the Lord Howe Rise and the exceptionally close proximity of the Lord Howe Rise to Australia in Early Cenozoic (Griffiths and Varne, 1972).

If geckos really arrived in New Zealand no earlier than the Miocene, they have been evolving rapidly ever since along a unique path. Therefore, acceptance of an Early Cenozoic entry avoids any concept of an explosive radiation, and provides an adequate time span for speciation *in situ* along novel lines. Kluge's (1967) hypothesis of gekkonid evolution and dispersal did not accommodate continental drift. Accordingly, it is not surprising that his interpretations of the source of the faunal ancestors is at variance with one incorporating this phenomenon.

The endemic frog fauna of New Zealand is even more bizarre than the reptile fauna and is represented by three species of *Leiopelma*. Whether *Leiopelma* and *Ascaphus* of North America should be placed in a single family (Ascaphidae), or whether *Leiopelma* should constitute the Leiopelmatidae remains a matter of debate. However, there is no argument to the concept that these genera represent relics of a fauna that was widely distributed. Estes and Reig (1973) referred *Vieraella* and *Notobatrachus* of the Early and Late Jurassic of Patagonia to the Ascaphidae.

Until recently *Leiopelma hamiltoni* was known only from a small heap of stones occupying one quarter of a hectare on the South Island. Now it is known from an additional fifteen hectares on the small Maud Island off the coast (Bull and Whitaker, 1975). *Leiopelma archeyi* and *L. hochstetteri* are distributed somewhat more widely on the North Island, but Bull and Whitaker (op. cit. 235) stated that in the recent past ("... probably within the last 1,000 years ...") *Leiopelma* was far more widespread, being known from five sites where it no longer occurs today. They described subfossil material as being about twice the size of the extant species, but otherwise similar in skeletal features. Thus, the animals involved would have been as much as 100 mm in length. Either the morphological change to existing species was effected in a millenium or the subfossils represent extinct species; in either case it seems to be unprofitable to speculate about the characteristics of their immediate postdrift ancestors.

Within the context of discussion of southwest Pacific biological origins, the concepts of Nur and Ben-Avraham (1977) on a lost Pacific continent (formerly lying close to the east coast of Australia) must be considered. Nevertheless the present study of the anurans has not required such a landmass to explain their origins.

CONCLUSIONS

When the amphibian and reptile families now found in Australia are examined, one by one, to determine whether their affinities lie with South American or with Oriental stocks, it rapidly becomes apparent that Oriental sources predominate, and that Australian-South American links are few indeed. At the commencement of drifting in the Eocene, the Australian herpetofauna included the following families shared with South America:

Gekkonidae (Diplodactylinae) —The nature of the extensive radiation within Australia may well support the concept that the Gekkonidae was the only lizard family present in Australia.

Boidae (? Madtsoinae) —The presence of this family hinges upon the Pleistocene *Wonambi* whose phylogenetic affinities are with snakes outside the Oriental Region. Extant genera certainly arrived in the Miocene.

Chelidae —A Gondwanan component probably of considerable antiquity. Within Australia, fossils extending to the Early Tertiary represent modern species. The origin of the family is uncertain, but the Lower Cretaceous *Chelycarapookus arcuatus*, for which Warren (1975) erected the Chelycarapookidae exhibits postcranial features that render it a potential chelid ancestor.

Crocodylidae —The first fossils of a sebecosuchian crocodile fauna have just been discovered.

Hylidae —Previous concepts of South American and Australian tree frogs representing a single family do not as yet appear to have been refuted.

Leptodactylidae—Irrespective of the final assessment of the familial disposition of the Australian genera and species, the South American affinities of the Australian members are indisputable

These six families represent the elements of the Australian herpetofauna destined to persist through to the Holocene. It follows that by modern standards the total herpetofauna was incredibly depauperate and lacked many significant elements. Pygopodids evolved in Australia probably during the period of isolation

The serious deficiencies were remedied from the Miocene onwards as Australia and the eastern outliers of the Oriental Region approached one another on their collision course. The commencement of colonization by families such as the Scincidae probably antedated the mid Miocene. Others such as the Typhlopidae, Carettochelyidae, Microhylidae, Varanidae, and Crocodylidae probably were acquired at the time of the collision, while the Ranidae entered then and again in a subsequent wave. In broad terms, the Oriental influence upon Australia probably was more significant than the North American influence upon South America, because South America had a more diverse and better established herpetofauna before the time of contact

ACKNOWLEDGMENTS

For the invitation to participate in the symposium "The South American Herpetofauna" and for the funding making this possible, I am greatly indebted to The University of Kansas, and particularly to the convenor, William E Duellman

Many of the ideas and assessment proposed in this paper arose from or were stimulated by discussions or correspondence with many of my colleagues. For this great help I gratefully acknowledge the contributions of Bob Lange, John M Legler, Brian McGowan, Allen E Greer, Rowley Twidale and George R Zug

Margaret Davies prepared figures 4 1 and 4 10, whereas figures 4 3-4 7 and 4 9 are the work of Debra Bennett. The manuscript was typed by Mrs J Russell-Price. I am also indebted to Richard G Zweifel for permission to reproduce the map of New Guinea upon which figure 4 5 was prepared

RESUMEN

Las oportunidades para un intercambio herpetofaunístico gondwánico entre Sud América y Australia fueron muchos menores que aquellos entre Sud América y África, debido a la expansión de la Antártica Al comienzo de la separación de Australia de Sud América (53 m a a p) el continental sureno Australiano era subtropical Condiciones húmedas con una diversidad de anfibios y reptiles ocupaban el centro de Australia hasta el Pleistoceno superior cuando un incremento de la aridez eliminó muchos sitios acuáticos

De todos los posibles modos de establecer cuales segmentos de la herpetofauna australiana eran compartidas con Sud América como resultado de un intercambio gondwánico, se ha seleccionado determinar que familias que están hoy presentes en Australia y Nueva Guinea, fueron adquiridas cuando Australia colidió con la Región Oriental en el Mioceno medio. Un análisis de tal evento demuestra que un grupo de islas adheridas a lo que es la actual costa norte de Nueva Guinea Por ende si éstas islas estaban pobladas con anfibios y reptiles algunos, al menos, debieron haberse integrado a la herpetofauna australopapua a través de esta vía

Se propone un modelo que involucra la dispersión de algunos géneros a través de las Islas Orientales desde las Filipinas a Fiji en el Mioceno (el género de batracios ranidos *Platymantis*) La colisión de tierras agregó este rana a la fauna de Nueva Guinea y los actuales extremos de diversidad al Oeste y al Este de Nueva Guinea reflejan la edad de especiación. En contraste otros géneros arribaron desde el Oeste después de la colisión, resultando en una progresiva reducción del número de especies desde el Oeste al Este

Entonces los patrones de distribución geográfica de los elementos Orientales en Australia varían de acuerdo con la fecha de entrada relativa a la colisión de Australia. Sin embargo, el tópico más importante es las relación de los anfibios y reptiles de Australia que aquellos de la Región Oriental adyacente. Bajo esta criterio, las Ranidae, Microhylidae, Varanidae, ? Scincidae, Agamidae, Carettochelyidae, Trionychidae, Elapidae, Colubridae, Acrochordidae, Uropeltidae, Typhlopidae, y Boidae entraron a la región geográfica australiana después del Mioceno medio. Los Boidae son únicos por tener un genuino componente gondwánico (si *Wonambi* del Pleistoceno se relaciona con *Madtsoia*), y otro Oriental.

Correspondientemente, la herpetofauna gondwánica de Australia no poseía la gran mayoría de los elementos de esa fauna. Un buen ejemplo está dado por la presencia de los Hylidae y Leptodactylidae (y por la mantención del uso de estos nombres familiares para los animales modernos de Australia). Aparte de estos existían sólo los Chelidae y los geckos diplodactylinos, de los cuals los Pygopodidae probablemente evolucionaron como los únicos representantes australianos.

Una deriva pasiva permitió a los largartos iguánidos viajar largas distancias desde la costa oeste de Sud América a Fiji y a Tonga. A pesar de que la dirección de las corrientes transpacíficas (Este a Oeste) favorece ls dispersión desde Sud América a Australia más que la dirección opuesta, los inmigrantes sudamericanos han alcanzado las islas del Pacífico Sur, pero aún no han filtrado has alcanzar las costas del continente australiano.

LITERATURE CITED

ARCHER, M., WADE, M. 1976. Results of the Ray E. Lemley Expeditions, Part 1. The Allingham Formation and a new Pliocene vertebrate fauna from northern Queensland. Mem Queensland Mus 17(3) 379-397

AXELROD, D. I. 1960. The evolution of flowering plants, pp 227-305 *in* TAX, S. (ed.) Evolution after Darwin 1, Univ Chicago Press, Chicago, 629 p

AXELROD, D. I. 1975. Plate tectonics and problems of angiosperm history. Mem Mus Natl Hist Nat, Paris Sec C 88 72-86

BAGNARA, J. T., FERRIS, W. 1975. The presence of phyllomedusine melanosomes and pigments in Australian hylids. Copeia 1975(3) 592-595

BAGNARA, J. T. 1976. Color change, pp 1-52 *in* LOFTS, B. (ed.) Physiology of the Amphibia Vol III, Academic Press, New York, 597 p

BAI, A. R. K. 1956. Analysis of chromosomes in two genera of Microhylidae (Amphibia Anura). Proc Natl Inst Sci India, Part B 22 1-5

BARBOUR, T. 1923. The frogs of the Fiji Islands. Proc Acad Nat Sci Philadelphia 75 111-115

BEAUFORT, L. F. DE. 1951. Zoogeography of the land and inland waters. Sidgwick and Jackson, London, 208 p

BECAK, M. L., DENARO, I., BECAK, W. 1970. Polyploidy and mechanisms of karyotypic diversification in Amphibia. Cytogenetics 9 225-238

BLAKE, A. J. D. 1973. Taxonomy and relationships of myobatrachine frogs (Leptodactylidae). A numerical approach. Australian J Zool 21 119-149

BLOMMERS, R. 1971. Karyotype de *Anodontohyla montana* Angel (Anura, Microhylidae) de massif de l'Andringitra (Madagascar). Terre Mal 10 261-265

BLOMMERS-SCHLOSSER, R. M. A. 1976. Chromosomal analysis of twelve species of Microhylidae (Anura) from Madagascar. Genetica 46 199-210

BOGART, J. P., NELSON, C. E. 1976. Evolutionary implications from karyotypic analysis of the families Microhylidae and Rhinophrynidae. Herpetologica 32 199-208

BOGART, J. P., PYBURN, W. NELSON, C. E. 1976. The karyotype of *Otophryne robusta* (Anura Microhylidae). Ibid 32 208-210

BOWLER, J. M. 1976. Aridity in Australia. Age, origins and expression in aeolian landforms and sediments. Earth-Sci Rev 12 279-310

BROWN, W. C., ALCALA, A. C. 1970. The zoogeography of the herpetofauna of the Philippine Islands, a fringing archipelago. Proc California Acad Sci 38(6) 105-130

BROWN, W. C., MYERS, G. S. 1949. A new frog of the genus *Cornufer* from the Solomon Islands, with notes on the endemic nature of the Fijian frog fauna. Amer Mus Novit (1418) 1-10

BULL, P. C., WHITAKER, A. H. 1975. The amphibians, reptiles birds and mammals, pp 231-276 *in* KUSCHEL, G. (ed.) Biogeography and ecology in New Zealand. W. Junk, The Hague, 689 p

CALLEN, R. A., TEDFORD, R. H. 1976. New late Cainozoic rock units and depositional environments, Lake Frome area, South Australia. Trans Roy Soc South Australia 100 125-168

CHAPMAN, F. 1919. On a fossil tortoise in ironstone from Carapook near Casterton. Proc Roy Soc Victoria 32 (new ser) (1) 11-13

CHRISTOPHEL, D. C., BLACKBURN, D. I. 1978. Tertiary megafossil flora of Maslin Bay, South Australia. A preliminary report. Alcheringa 2 311-319

COGGER, H. G. 1970. First record of the pitted-shelled turtle *Carettochelys insculpta* from Australia. Search 1 41

COGGER, H. G. 1974. Voyage of the banded iguana. Australian Nat Hist 18 144-149

COGGER, H. G. 1975. Reptiles and amphibians of Australia. Reed, Sydney, 584 p

COLL, C. J., ZWEIFEL, R. G. 1971. Chromosomes of a New Guinean microhylid frog, *Cophixalus riparius* Zweifel. Herpetol Rev 3 15-16

COLEMAN, P J 1975 The Solomons as a non-arc Bull Australian Soc Explor Geophys, 6(2–3) 60–61

COLEMAN, P J, PACKHAM, G H 1976 The Melanesian borderlands and India-Pacific plates' boundary Earth-Sci Rev 12 197–233

CORBEN, C J, INGRAM, G J, TYLER, M J 1974 Gastric brooding Unique form of parental care in an Australian frog Science 186 946–947

CRACRAFT, J 1973 Vertebrate evolution and biogeography in the Old World tropics Implications of continental drift and palaeoclimatology pp 373–393 in TARLING, D H, RUNCORN S K (eds) Implications of continental drift to the earth sciences Vol 1 Academic Press, London 622 p

CRACRAFT, J 1974 Continental drift and vertebrate distribution Ann Rev Ecol Syst 5 215–261

CRACRAFT, J 1975 Mesozoic dispersal of terrestrial faunas around the southern end of the world Mem Mus Natl Hist Nat Paris, Ser A 88 29–54

DARLINGTON, P J 1957 Zoogeography The geographical distribution of animals Wiley, New York, 675 p

DENHAM, D 1975 Distribution of underthrust lithospheric slabs and focal mechanisms—Papua New Guinea and Solomon Islands Region Bull Australian Soc Explor Geophys 6(2–3) 78–79

DE VIS, C W 1894 The lesser chelonians of the Nototherian drifts Proc Roy Soc Queensland 10 123–127

DE VIS C W 1897 The extinct fresh-water turtles of Queensland Ann Queensland Mus 3 3–7

DIXON, J R, ANDERSON, S C 1973 A new species and genus of gecko (Sauria Gekkonidae) from Iran and Iraq Bull South California Acad Sci 72 155–160

DUELLMAN, W E 1970 The hylid frogs of Middle America Univ Kansas Mus Nat Hist Monogr (1) 1–753

DUELLMAN W E 1975 On the classification of frogs Univ Kansas Mus Nat Hist Occas Pap (42) 1–14

EMERSON, S B 1976 A preliminary report on the superficial throat musculature of the Microhylidae and its possible role in tongue action Copeia 1976 (3) 546–551

ESTES, R, REIG, O A 1973 The early fossil record of frogs A review of the evidence, pp 11–63 in VIAL, J L (ed) Evolutionary biology of the anurans Contemporary research on major problems Univ Missouri Press, Columbia, 470 p

FALVEY, D A, TAYLOR L W H 1974 Queensland Plateau and Coral Sea Basin Structure and time—stratigraphic patterns Bull Australian Soc Explor Geophys 5(4) 123–126

FOODEN, J 1972 Breakup of Pangaea and isolation of relict mammals in Australia, South America and Madagascar Science 175 894–898

GAFFNEY, E S 1975 A phylogeny and classification of the higher categories of turtles Bull Amer Mus Nat Hist 155 387–436

GAFFNEY, E S 1977 The side necked turtle family Chelidae A theory of relationships using shared derived characters Amer Mus Novit (2620) 1–28

GLAESSNER, M F 1942 The occurrence of the New Guinea turtle (Carettochelys) in the Miocene of Papua Rec Australian Mus 21 106–109

GLASSFORD, D K, KILLIGREW, L P 1976 Evidence for Quaternary westward extension of the Australian desert into south-western Australia Search 7 394–396

GORHAM, S W 1965 Fiji frogs (with synopses of the genera Cornufer and Platymantis) Zool Beitr 11 381–435

GORHAM, S W 1968 Fiji frogs Life history data from field work Ibid 11 427–446

COX, C F 1977 A new species of Python from Arnhem Land Aust Zool 19 133–139

GREER, A E 1970 A subfamilial classification of scincid lizards Bull Mus Comp Zool Harvard Univ 139 151–184

GRIFFITHS J R, BARNE, R 1972 Evolution of the Tasman Sea, Macquarie Ridge and Alpine Fault Nature (Phys Sci) 235 83–86

GUIBE, J 1948 Contribution a l'etude de l'appareil génital des typhlopides (Ophidiens) Bull Soc Zool France 73 224–228

GUTTMAN, S I 1973 Biochemical techniques and problems in anuran evolution, pp 183–203 in VIAL J L (ed) Evolutionary biology of the anurans Contemporary research on major problems Univ Missouri Press, Columbia, 470 p

HECHT, M K 1975 The morphology and relationships of the largest known terrestrial lizard Megalania prisca Owen from the Pleistocene of Australia Proc Roy Soc Victoria (new ser) 87(2) 239–250

HECHT, M K, ARCHER, M 1977 Presence of xiphodont crocodilians in the Tertiary and Pleistocene of Australia Alcheringa 10 383–385

HEYER, W R LIEM, D S 1976 Analysis of the intergeneric relationships of the Australian frog family Myobatrachidae Smithsonian Contn Zool 233 1–29

HOFFSTETTER, R 1961 Nouveaux restes d'un serpent boide (Madtsoia madagascariensis nov sp) dans la Cretace superieur de Madagascar Bull Mus Natl Hist Nat Zool Paris (2) 33 152–160

INGER R F 1954 Systematics and zoogeography of Philippine amphibia Fieldiana Zool 33(1) 181–531

INGER, R F 1966 The systematics and zoogeography of the amphibia of Borneo Ibid 52 1–402

JARDINE, N, MCKENZIE, D 1972 Continental drift and the dispersal and evolution of organisms Nature 231(5332) 20–24

KEAST, A 1971 Continental drift and the evolution of the biota on southern continents Q Rev Biol 46 335–378

KEAST, A 1973 Contemporary biotas and the separation sequence of the southern continents, pp 309–343 in TARLING, D H, RUNCORN, S K (eds) Implications of continental drift to the earth sciences Vol 1 Academic Press, London, 622 p

KING, M. 1973. Chromosomes of two Australian lizards of the families Scincidae and Gekkonidae. Cytologia 38: 205–210.

KING, M. 1975. Chromosomal studies on Australian lizards. Ph.D. Dissert. Univ. Adelaide, 150 p.

KING, M. 1977. Chromosomal and morphometric variation in the Gekko *Diplodactylus vittatus* Gray. Australian J. Zool. 25: 43–57.

KING, M., KING, D. 1975. Chromosomal variation in the lizard genus *Varanus* (Reptilia). Australian J. Biol. Sci. 28: 89–108.

KING, M., ROFE, R. 1976. Karyotypic variation in the Australian Gecko *Phyllodactylus marmoratus* (Gray) (Gekkonidae Reptilia). Chromosoma 54: 75–87.

KLUGE, A. G. 1967. Higher taxonomic categories of gekkonid lizards and their evolution. Bull. Amer. Mus. Nat. Hist. 135: 1–60.

KLUGE, A. G. 1974. A taxonomic revision of the lizard family Pygopodidae. Misc. Publ. Mus. Zool. Univ. Michigan (147): 1–221.

KLUGE, A. G. 1976. Phylogenetic relationships in the lizard family Pygopodidae. An evaluation of theory, methods and data. Ibid. (152): 1–72.

LANGE, R. I. 1976. Fossil epiphyllous "Germlings" their living equivalents and their palaeohabitat indicator value. Neues Jahrb. Geol. Palaeontol. Abh. 151: 142–165.

LATZ, P. K. 1975. Notes on the relict palm *Livistona mariae* F. Muell. in central Australia. Trans. Roy. Soc. South Australia 99: 189–195.

LAURENT, R. F. 1975. La distribution des amphibiens et les translations continentales. Mem. Mus. Natl. Hist. Nat., Paris 88: 176–191.

LEON, P. E. 1970. Report of the chromosome numbers of some Costa Rican anurans. Rev. Biol. Trop. 17: 119–124.

LIEM, D. S. 1973. A new genus of frog of the family Leptodactylidae from SE Queensland, Australia. Mem. Queensland Mus. 16: 159–170.

LONGMAN, N. A. 1929. Palaeontological notes. Specimens from a well at Brigalow. Ibid. 9: 247–252.

LYDEKKER, R. L. 1889. Catalogue of fossil amphibians and reptiles in the British Museum (Natural History) Part 3. British Museum, London, 254 p.

LYNCH, J. D. 1971. Evolutionary relationships, osteology and zoogeography of leptodactyloid frogs. Univ. Kansas Mus. Nat. Hist. Misc. Publ. (53): 1–238.

LYNCH, J. D. 1973. The transition from archaic to advanced frogs pp. 133–182 in VIAL J. L. (ed.) Evolutionary biology of the anurans. Contemporary research on major problems. Univ. Missouri Press, Columbia 470 p.

MABBUTT, J. A. 1967. Denudation chronology in Central Australia. Structure, climate and landform inheritance in the Alice Springs area, pp. 144–181 in JENNINGS, J. N., MABBUTT, J. A. (eds.) Landform studies from Australia and New Guinea. Australian Natl. Univ. Press, Canberra, 434 p.

MACKENZIE, D. E. 1975. Volcanic and plate tectonic evolution of central Papua and New Guinea. Bull. Australian Soc. Explor. Geophys. 6(2–3): 65–67.

MADERSON, P. F. A. 1972. The structure and evolution of holocrine glands in sphaerodactyline and eublepharine gekkonid lizards. Copeia 1973 (3): 559–571.

MAIN, A. R., LEE, A. K., LITTLEJOHN, M. J. 1958. Evolution in three genera of Australian frogs. Evolution 12: 224–233.

MAXSON, L. R. 1976. The phylogenetic status of phyllomedusine frogs (Hylidae) as evidenced from immunological studies of their serum albumins. Experientia 32: 1149–1150.

MAXSON, L. R., WILSON, A. C. 1975. Albumin evolution and organismal evolution in tree frogs (Hylidae). Syst. Zool. 24: 1–15.

McDOWELL, S. B. 1967. *Aspidomorphus*, a genus of New Guinea snakes of the family Elapidae, with notes on related genera. J. Zool. 151: 497–543.

McDOWELL, S. B. 1970. On the status and relationships of the Solomon Island elapid snakes. Ibid. 161: 145–190.

McDOWELL, S. R. 1972. The species of *Stegonotus* (Serpentes, Colubridae) in Papua New Guinea. Zool. Meded. Rijks Mus. Nat. Hist. Leiden 47: 6–26.

McDOWELL, S. B. 1974. A catalogue of the snakes of New Guinea and the Solomons, with special reference to those in the Bernice P. Bishop Museum. Part 1, Scolecophidia. J. Herpetol. 8: 1–57.

McDOWELL, S. B. 1975. A catalogue of the snakes of New Guinea and the Solomons, with special reference to those in the Bernice P. Bishop Museum. Part II Anilioidea and Pythoninae. Ibid. 9: 1–79.

McDOWELL, S. B., BOGERT, C. M. 1954. The systematic position of *Lanthanotus* and the affinities of the anguimorphan lizards. Bull. Amer. Mus. Nat. Hist. 105: 1–142.

McGOWRAN, B. 1973. Rifting and drift of Australia and the migration of mammals. Science 180: 759–761.

MENZIES, J. I., TIPPETT, J. 1976. Chromosome numbers of Papuan hylid frogs and the karyotype of *Litoria infrafrenata* (Amphibia, Anura, Hylidae). J. Herpetol. 10: 167–173.

MENZIES, J. I., TYLER M. J. 1977. The systematics and adaptations of some Papuan microhylid frogs which live underground. J. Zool. 183: 431–464.

MITTLEMAN, M. B. 1952. A generic synopsis of the lizards of the subfamily lygosominae. Smithsonian Misc. Collect. 117: 1–35.

MOFFAT, L. 1973. The concept of primitiveness and its bearing on the phylogenetic classification of the Gekkota. Proc. Linn. Soc. New South Wales 97: 275–301.

MOLNAR, R. E. 1977. Crocodile with laterally compressed snout. First find in Australia. Science 197: 62–64.

MOLNAR, R. E. 1978. Age of the Chillagoe crocodile. Search 9(4): 156–158.

MORESCALCHI, A 1968a Initial cytotaxonomic data on certain families of amphibious Anura (Diplasiocoela, after Noble, T C) Experientia 24 280-283

MORESCALCHI, A 1968b Hypothesis on the phylogeny of the Salientia, based on karyological data Ibid 24 964-966

MORESCALCHI, A 1973 Amphibia, pp 233-248 in CHIARELLI, A B, CAPANNA, E (eds) Cytotaxonomy and vertebrate evolution Academic Press, London, 783 p

MORESCALCHI, A, INGRAM, G J 1974 New chromosome numbers in Australian Leptodactylidae (Amphibia, Salientia) Experientia 30 1134-1135

NATARJAN, R 1953 A note on the chromosomes of *Cacopus systoma* Proc 40th Indian Sci Congress, Lucknow pp 180-181

NELSON, C E 1975 Another new miniature 4-toed South American microhylid frog (Genus *Syncope*) J Herpetol 9 81-84

NEWSOME A E, ROCHOW, K A 1964 Vertebrate fossils from Tertiary sediments in central Australia Australian J Sci 26 252

NUR, A, BEN-AVRAHAM, Z 1977 Lost Pacifica continent Nature 270 41-45

PARKER, H W 1929 Two fossil frogs from the Lower Miocene of Europe Ann Mag Nat Hist (10) 4 (21) 270-281

PARKER, H W 1934 A monograph of the frogs of the family Microhylidae British Museum (Natural History) London, 208 p

PARKER, H W 1940 The Australasian frogs of the family Leptodactylidae Novit Zool 42 1-106

PIANKA, E R 1972 Zoogeography and speciation of Australian desert lizards An ecological perspective Copeia 1972 (1) 127-144

RABELLO M N 1970 Chromosomal studies in Brazilian anurans Caryologia 23 45-59

RHODIN, A G J, MITTERMEIER, R A 1977 Neural bones in chelid turtles from Australia and New Guinea Copeia 1977 (2) 370-372

RICH P V 1975 Antarctic dispersal routes, wandering continents, and the origin of Australia's non-passeriform avifauna Mem Natl Mus Victoria (36) 63-125

ROBB, J 1966 The structure and possible function of the cloacal pouches of male Australian typhlopids Australian J Zool 14 27-30

ROBINSON, R L, TYLER, M J 1972 The catecholamine content of the adrenal glands of frogs as an index of phylogenetic relationships Comp Gen Pharmacol 3 167-170

RUSSELL, A P 1976 Some comments concerning interrelationships amongst gekkonine geckos, pp 217-244 in BELLAIRS, A D'A, COX, B (eds) Morphology and biology of reptiles Linn Soc Symp (Ser 3), 290 p

SAVAGE J M 1973 The geographic distribution of frogs Patterns and predictions, pp 351-445 in VIAL J L (ed) Evolutionary biology of the anurans Contemporary research on major problems Univ Missouri Press Columbia, 470 p

SCHLINGER, F J 1974 Continental drift, *Nothofagus*, and some ecologically associated insects Ann Rev Entomol 19 323-343

SCHODDE, R, MASON, I, WOLFE, T O 1972 Further records of the pitted-shelled turtle (*Carettochelys insculpta*) from Australia Trans Roy Soc South Australia 96 115-117

SCLATER, J G, VON DER BORCH, C, VEEVERS, J J, HEKINIAN, R, THOMPSON, R W, PIMM, A C, MCGOWRAN, B, GARTNER, S, JOHNSON, D A 1974 Regional synthesis of the deep sea drilling results from leg 22 in the eastern Indian Ocean, pp 815-831 in VON DER BORCH C SCLATER, J G, VEEVERS, J J Initial reports of the Deep Sea Drilling Project 22, 890 p

SMITH, M J 1975 The vertebrae of four Australian elapid snakes Trans Roy Soc South Australia 99 71-84

SMITH M J 1976 Small fossil vertebrates from Victoria Cave, Naracoorte, South Australia IV Reptiles Ibid 100 39-51

STEPHENSON, E M, STEPHENSON, N G 1970 Karyotypes of two Australian hylid frogs Chromosoma 30 38-50

STIRTON, R A, TEDFORD, R H, MILLER, A H 1961 Cenozoic stratigraphy and vertebrate paleontology of the Tirari Desert, South Australia Geogr Rev 62 40-70

STORR, G M 1964 Some aspects of the geography of Australian reptiles Senckenbergiana Biol 45 577-589

STRAUGHAN J R 1969 *Hyla inermis* (Peters), a species hitherto erroneously referred to the leptodactylid genus *Cyclorana* (Anura, Hylidae/Leptodactylidae) Zool Meded Rijks Mus Nat Hist Leiden 43 207-212

STRAUGHAN, J R LEE, A K 1966 A new genus and species of leptodactylid frog from Queensland Proc Roy Soc Queensland 77 63-66

TAYLOR I W H 1975 Deposition and tectonic patterns in the western Coral Sea Bull Australian Soc Explor Geophys 6 33-35

TILBURY, L A 1975 Lineations in the Bismarck Sea Ibid 6 72

TWIDALE, C R 1972 Evolution of sand dunes in the Simpson Desert Central Australia Trans Instit British Geogr (56) 77-109

TYLER, M J 1967 Microhylid frogs of New Britain Trans Roy Soc South Australia 91 187-190

TYLER, M J 1970 Patterns of distribution and the origins of the Papuan hylid frog fauna Search 1 246-247

TYLER, M J 1971 The phylogenetic significance of vocal sac structure in hylid frogs Univ Kansas Mus Nat Hist Occas Pap (19) 319-360

TYLER, M J 1972a Superficial mandibular musculature, vocal sacs and the phylogeny of Australo-Papuan leptodactylid frogs Rec South Australian Mus 16 1-20

TYLER, M J 1972b A new genus for the Australian leptodactylid frog *Crinia darlingtoni* Zool Meded Rijks Mus Nat Hist Leiden 47 193-201

Tyler, M J 1974a Superficial mandibular musculature and vocal sac structure in the Anura M Sc Thesis, Univ Adelaide, 134 p

Tyler, M J 1974b First frog fossils from Australia Nature 248 (5450) 711-712

Tyler, M J 1974c The systematic position and geographic distribution of the Australian frog *Chiroleptes alboguttatus* Gunther Proc Roy Soc Queensland 85 27-32

Tyler, M J 1976a Frogs William Collins, Sydney 236 p

Tyler, M J 1976b Comparative osteology of the pelvic girdle of Australian frogs and description of a new fossil genus Trans Roy Soc South Australia 101 3-14

Tyler, M J 1976c A new genus and two new species of leptodactylid frogs from Western Australia Rec Western Australian Mus 4 45-52

Tyler, M J 1977 Pleistocene frogs from caves at Naracoorte South Australia Trans Roy Soc South Australia 101 85-89

Tyler, M J 1979 The introduction and current distribution in the New Hebrides of the Australian hylid frog *Litoria aurea* Copeia (In press)

Tyler, M J, Davies, M 1978a Species groups within the Australopapuan hylid frog genus *Litoria* Tschudi Australian J Zool Suppl 63 1-47

Tyler, M J, Davies, M 1978b Phylogenetic relationships of Australian hyline and Neotropical phyllomedusine frogs of the family Hylidae Herpetologica 34 219-224

Tyler, M J, Davies, M, King, M 1978 The Australian frog *Chiroleptes dahlii* Boulenger Its systematic position, morphology, chromosomes and distribution Trans Roy Soc South Australia 102 17-23

Tyler, M J, Martin, A A 1975 Australian leptodactylid frogs of the *Cyclorana australis* complex Ibid 99 93-99

Tyler, M J, Martin, A A 1977 Taxonomic studies of some Australian leptodactylid frogs of the genus *Cyclorana* Steindachner Rec South Australian Mus 17 261-276

Tyler, M J, Roberts, J D 1973 Noteworthy range extensions for some South Australian frogs South Australian Nat 99 113-117

Tyler, M J, Martin, A A, Davies, M 1979 Biology and systematics of a new limnodynastine genus (Anura Leptodactylidae) from northwestern Australia Australian J Zool 27(1) 135-150

Underwood, C L 1954 On the classification and evolution of geckos Proc Zool Soc London 124 469-492

Underwood, G L 1957 On lizards of the family Pygopodidae A contribution to the morphology and phylogeny of the Squamata J Morphol 100 207-268

Veevers, J J, McElhinny, M W 1976 The separation of Australia from other continents Earth-Sci Rev 12 139-159

Walker, C F 1973 A new genus and species of microhylid frog from Ecuador Univ Kansas Mus Nat Hist Occas Pap (20) 1-7

Walker C F, Duellman, W E 1974 Description of a new species of microhylid frog, *Chiasmocleis*, from Ecuador Ibid (26) 1-6

Wallace, D G, Maxson, L R, Wilson, A C 1971 Albumin evolution in frogs A test of the evolutionary clock hypothesis Proc Natl Acad Sci USA 68 3127 3129

Warren, J W 1969 Chelid turtles from the mid-tertiary of Tasmania J Palentol 43 179-182

Warren, J W 1975 A fossil chelonian of probably Lower Cretaceous age from Victoria, Australia Mem Natl Mus Victoria 29 23-28

Watson, G F, Martin, A A 1973 Life history, larval morphology and relationships of Australian leptodactylid frogs Trans Roy Soc South Australia 97 33-45

Wood R, Patterson, B 1973 A fossil trionychid turtle from South America Breviora 415 1-10

Woodruff, D S 1972 Australian anuran chromosome numbers Herpetol Rev 4 208

Wopfner, H, Twidale C R 1967 Geomorphological history of the Lake Eyre Basin, pp 119-143 in Jennings, J N, Mabbutt, J A (eds) Landform studies from Australia and New Guinea Australian National Univ Press, Canberra 434 p

Zweifel, R C 1969 Frogs of the genus *Platymantis* (Ranidae) in New Guinea, with the description of a new species Amer Mus Novit (2374) 1-19

Zweifel, R G 1971 Results of the Archbold Expeditions No 96 Relationships and distribution of *Genyophryne thomsoni*, a microhylid frog of New Guinea Ibid (2469) 1-13

Zweifel, R G 1972 Results of the Archbold Expeditions No 97 A revision of the frogs of the subfamily Asterophryinae Family Microhylidae Bull Amer Mus Nat Hist 148 411-546

5. Quaternary Biogeography of Tropical Lowland South America

Jurgen Haffer

Tommesweg # 60
4300 Essen-1
West Germany

Research into the Quaternary biogeography of the Neotropical Region has been intensified during recent years as biologists became increasingly aware of the fact that Pleistocene climatic-vegetational fluctuations caused vast changes in the distribution of forest and nonforest biotas. Comparatively restricted populations of previously widely distributed plants and animals were isolated in remnant habitats during adverse climatic periods and differentiated at a varying rate depending upon the size of the restricted population (i.e., the size of the "refuge" area), the degree of isolation, and the varying "plasticity" of systematic groups following the model of geographic speciation (Mayr, 1942, 1963). The interpretation of Quaternary forest and savanna fragmentation provides biologists with a mechanism to explain extensive recent speciation in the South American lowlands, the occurrence of widely disjunct populations of related taxa and other biogeographical phenomena that could not be accounted for in the absence of natural barriers to interbreeding and dispersal (Meggers, 1977). The studies recently completed in the fields of Neotropical ornithology, herpetology, entomology, and botany yield comparable results and, hopefully, will stimulate further investigations needed to test the model of Quaternary differentiation proposed. Probably only few Neotropical plants and animals have survived from the Late Tertiary until the present time without evolutionary change—a notion popular among biologists only one or two decades ago. It is held that speciation events leading to extensive differentiation of faunas and floras during the Tertiary continued into the Quaternary possibly at a somewhat accelerated pace because of rapid environmental changes.

In this review I characterize, in a brief introductory section, the climate and vegetation of tropical lowland South America and their Quaternary history as far as it is known today. The main portion of this paper is a detailed discussion of recent research into the Quaternary biogeography of various groups of South American animals and plants. The results of these studies concern biologists interested in the historical aspects of tropical biotas and should prove useful for comparative purposes to students of the Neotropical herpetofauna in particular.

CLIMATE AND VEGETATION

The climate of the lowlands of tropical South America varies from wet, humid, or moist, especially near mountain ranges and in the equatorial Amazon region, to dry or even arid in northeastern Brasil and along the Caribbean coast of northern Venezuela and Colombia. The northern tradewind belt moves southward into northern South America during the northern winter causing a pronounced dry season. Alternating wet and dry seasons occur over most of tropical South America, even to some extent in portions of the lower Amazon Valley. The dry seasons are least pronounced and the annual rainfall correspondingly high in the upper Amazon Valley, near the Atlantic coast of northeastern and southeastern tropical South America as well as in the vicinity of the Andes especially in the Pacific Chocó region of western Colombia, and along the Caribbean slope of the Middle American mountains.

Tall evergreen forests grow in areas of high rainfall (Fig 5 1) and grade through semi-evergreen and deciduous forests into thorn forest and scrub as the annual rainfall decreases and the influence of a prolonged dry season increases. Variations are caused by local conditions of soil and topography. Characteristic plant associations of the nonforest regions of interior Brasil are the cerrado, a typical woodland savanna, and the caatinga, an open thorn woodland rich in cacti. Extensive grass savannas are found in the north and south of the Amazon forest in areas where flooding lasts several months each year and alternates with a severe dry season (eastern Colombian and central Venezuelan llanos, the savannas of eastern Bolivia and the varzea campos of the lower Amazon Valley). Extensive discussions of the climate and vegetation of South America have been published by Schweidtfeger (1976), Hueck (1966), and Hueck and Seibert (1972); see also the recent literature review by Haffer (1974).

The vast Amazonian forest covers some 6,000,000 km^2 of central South American lowlands from the Andes to the Atlantic coast including the upper Orinoco region of southern Venezuela and the Guianas to the northeast of the Solimões-Amazon basin itself. Rivers bordered by characteristic vegetation zones of varying width and isolated savanna enclaves interrupt the immense and superficially uniform forests. Interspersed savannas are concentrated in a transverse zone of reduced annual precipitation extending from southern Venezuela across the lower Amazon River into northeastern Brasil, others occur between the upper Madeira and Purús rivers (Fig. 5.1). Extensive forests in Amazonia grow on infertile leached soils of the terra firme in areas where Tertiary strata and "basement" rocks of the Guianan and Brasilian shields form the subsoil. Only rather small areas of Amazonia are underlain by fertile soil, especially along major river valleys and in the Andean foreland. Erosive material from the Andes is transported eastward into the Amazonian lowlands and forms soils that are considerably richer in nutrients than the soils of the adjacent terra firme between large river courses (Fittkau, 1969, 1974). This simplified scheme is currently being modified through detailed interpretation of radar images, field controls, and extensive mapping in Amazonia (Hammond, 1977).

CLIMATIC-VEGETATIONAL HISTORY OF THE NEOTROPICAL LOWLAND REGION DURING THE QUATERNARY

Humid tropical vegetation, perhaps somewhat drier in midlatitudes, covered most of the exposed land area of South America during early Tertiary time (Wolfe, 1971; Solbrig 1976). Forests slowly retreated northward in the Patagonian region during the second half of the Tertiary when the Andes were gradually uplifted and the climate became cooler and drier, possibly in response to periodic polar glaciations which began during the Miocene. The glacial phases gained momentum with time until, during the Quaternary, vast polar glaciers repeatedly advanced toward lower latitudes and extensive montane glaciers covered the higher slopes of tropical mountains. Extensive continental shelf areas were emergent during the glacial periods of lowered world sea level and were submerged during interglacial phases. Interglacial seas even encroached over low lying coastal plains, such as northern Colombia, and covered a huge portion of the Amazon Valley.

Although temperatures in the tropical lowlands remained "tropical" during glacial periods ($\approx$3°C lower than today), alternating humid and arid climatic phases of the Quaternary caused vast changes in the distribution of forest and nonforest vegetation. Forests broke into isolated remnants during cool dry periods (glacial phases) and expanded and coalesced during warm, humid phases (interglacial periods). Conversely, nonforest vegetation expanded during glacials and retreated during interglacial phases. Geoscience data are insufficient so far to map the changing distribution of forest and nonforest vegetation during the various climatic periods and, in particular, to locate accurately areas of remnant forests during arid phases which served as "refugia" for animal populations. From the location of current rainfall maxima and the topographic relief (which was already in existence during most of the Pleistocene) one would tentatively conclude that several areas along the northern slopes and foreland of the mountains in the interior Guianas, along the eastern slopes and foreland of the Andes, as well as along the northern margin of the Brasilian tableland remained humid and for-

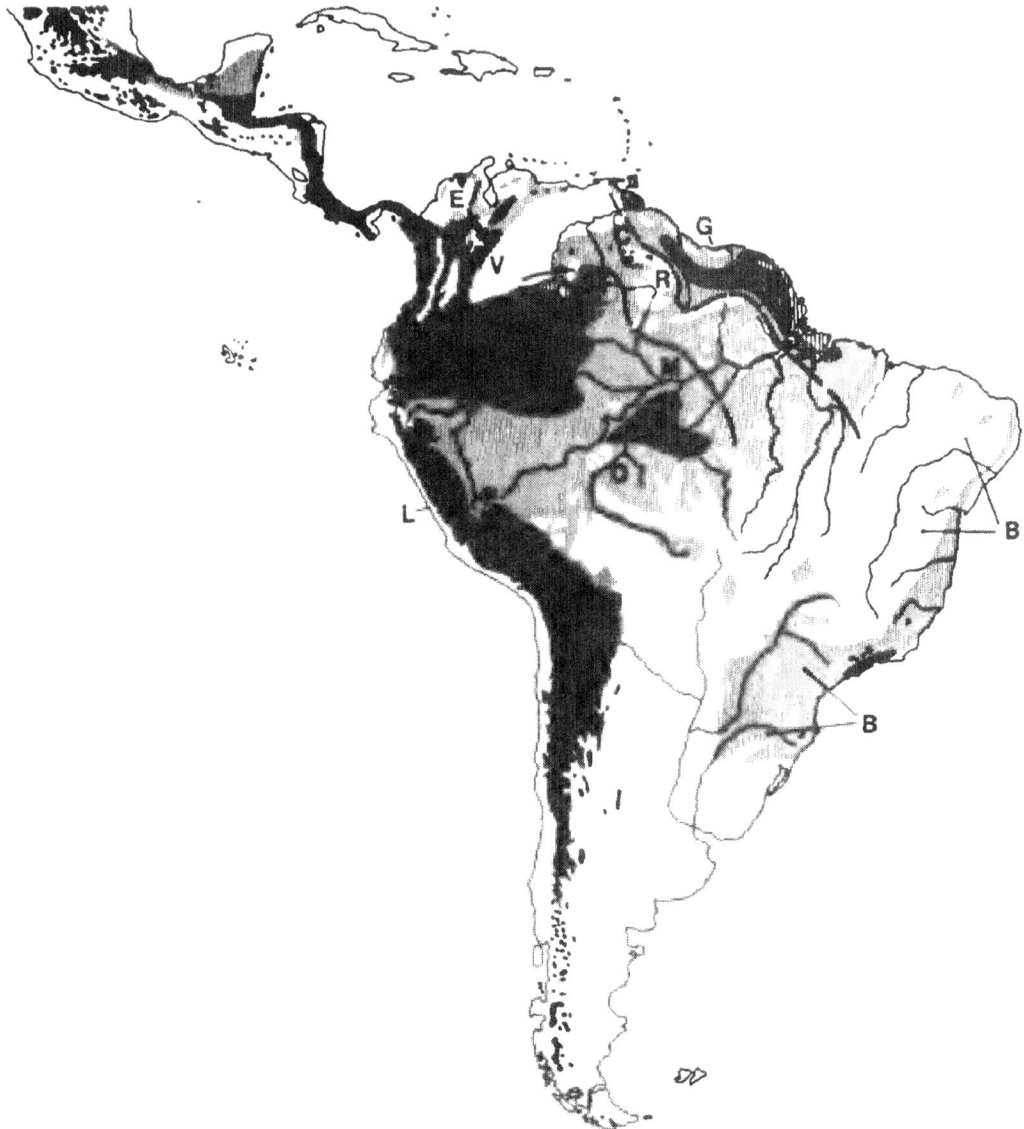

Fig. 5:1. Distribution of humid tropical lowland forest and location of rainfall centers in Middle and South America. Explanations: Shaded = humid forest, often semideciduous around savanna regions. Hatched vertically = areas receiving over 2500 mm of rain per year. Solid = Andean cordilleras and Middle American mountains of more than 2000 m elevation. Heavy dashed lines delimit the dry transverse zone of lower Amazonia characterized by numerous isolated savanna enclaves. Letters designate areas of paleoecological research. (See text for details.)

Distribución de selva húmeda y posición de centros de lluvia en las tierras bajas tropicales de Centro y Sud América. Explicaciones: Matizado = selva húmeda; frecuentemente selva semidecidua alrededor de regiones de savanas. Rayado vertical = áreas recibiendo más que 2500 mm de lluvia anuales. Negro = Cordilleras andinas y montañas de Centro América con alturas mayores que 2000 m. Líneas rayadas anchas delimitan la zona seca transversal de Amazonía baja caracterizada por numerosas savanas aisladas. Las letras indican las áreas de investigaciones paleoecológicas. (Ver el texto para detalles.)

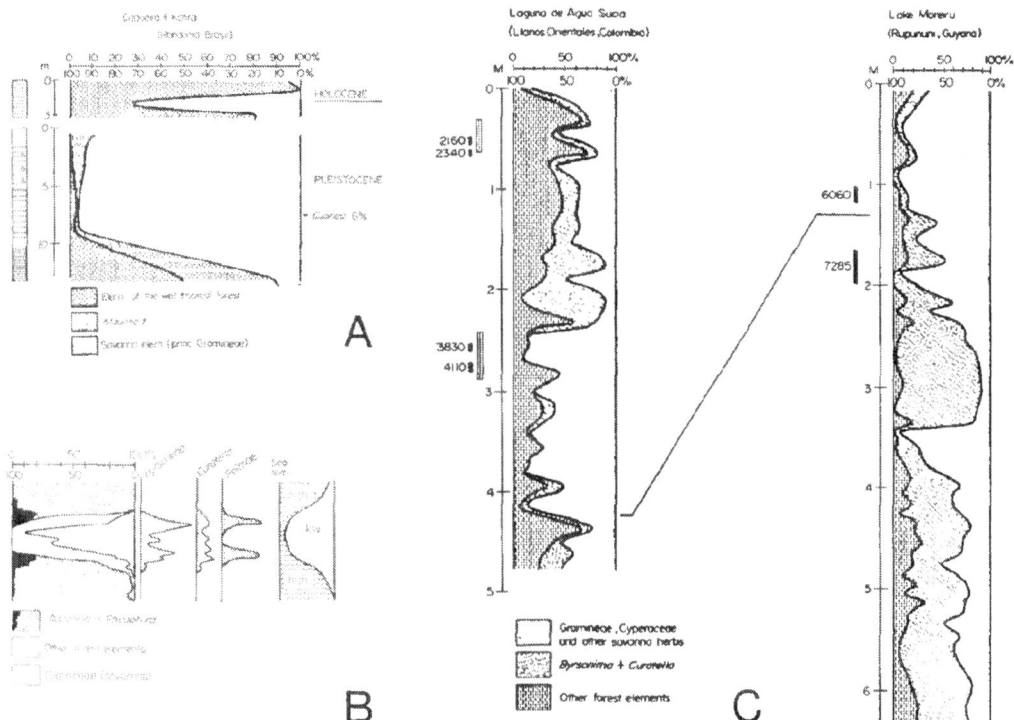

FIG. 5.2. Pollen diagrams from central and northern South America (after van der Hammen, 1974). Explanations: A. Pollen diagram from Capoeira and Katira, Rondônia, Brasil. B. Scheme of the succession of vegetation types (as reflected in the pollen diagram) during an interglacial-glacial-interglacial cycle in the present coastal plain of Guyana-Surinam. C. Pollen diagrams of the late Pleistocene and Holocene from areas at present covered with savanna vegetation (Llanos Orientales, Colombia; Rupununi, Guyana). Four-digit numbers indicate years before present.

Diagramas palinológicos de la parte central y septentrional de Sudamérica (según van der Hammen, 1974). Explicaciones: A. *Diagrama palinológico de Capoeira y Katira, Rondônia, Brasil.* B. *Esquema de sucesión de la vegetación (según diagramas palinológicos) durante un ciclo interglacial-glacial-interglacial en la planicie costanera de Guyana-Surinam.* C. *Diagramas palinológicos del Pleistoceno tardío y Holoceno de regiones hoy cubiertas por savanas (Llanos orientales de Colombia; Rupununi, Guyana).*

ested during dry climatic periods forming isolated "forest refugia."

During Quaternary periods of raised sea level (interglacials), extensive areas of the central and upper Amazonian lowlands were converted into shallow inland lakes. Sioli (1957) and Irion (1976) discussed certain aspects of the history of river sedimentation and erosion as related to sea level fluctuations.

The evidence for the above generalizations about Pleistocene climatic-vegetational fluctuations in tropical lowland South America is derived from palynological, geomorphological, geological, and climatological studies conducted in widely scattered parts of tropical South America (see earlier reviews by Sombroek, 1966; Haffer, 1969, 1974; Vanzolini and Williams, 1970; Fittkau, 1974; van der Hammen, 1974; Garner, 1974, 1975; Raven and Axelrod, 1974; Brown, 1977a,b).

Palynological data (Figs. 5:2–3).—The pollen contents of bore hole samples from Katira Creek, 120 km southeast of Porto Velho (Rondônia, upper Rio Madeira, Brasil; O of Fig. 5:1), indicate that in this rainforest region the forest was temporarily replaced by open savanna vegetation, presumably during a late Quaternary period of drought (van der Hammen, 1972, 1974; Absy and van der Hammen, 1976). Pollen profiles from lake deposits

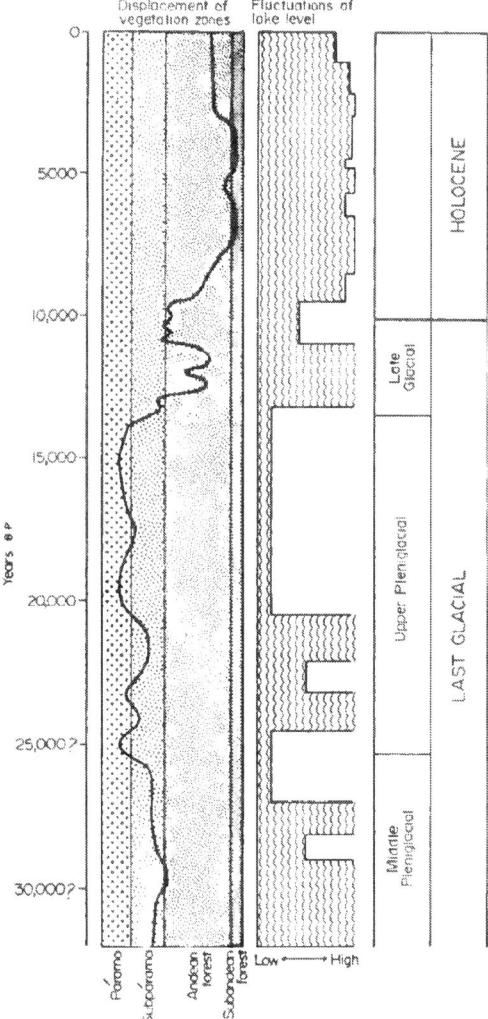

Fig. 5:3. Displacement of vegetation zones and fluctuations of lake level, Laguna de Fúquene, Eastern Andes, Colombia during the late Pleistocene and Holocene (after van der Hammen, 1974).

Desplazamiento de zonas de vegetación y fluctuaciones del nivel de agua, Laguna de Fúquene, Cordillera Oriental, Colombia, durante el Pleistoceno tardío y Holoceno (según van der Hammen, 1974).

in the grasslands of eastern Colombia (V of Fig. 5:1) and interior Guyana (R of Fig. 5:1) demonstrate that a dry forest, or closed savanna woodland, preceded the open savannas found in these regions today (Wijmstra and van der Hammen, 1966). Pollen diagrams from the coastal lowlands of Guyana and Surinam show a considerable extension of savannas during glacial periods of lowered sea level.

The extensive palynological work by van der Hammen and his associates in the Andes of Colombia permits the tracing of the development of montane vegetation in this area during the Pliocene upheaval of the northern Andes and analyzing the Pleistocene movements of vegetation belts (van der Hammen et al., 1973; van Geel and van der Hammen, 1973). An interesting discovery is the fact that the climate in the Colombian Andes was very dry during the peak of the last glaciation (21,000–13,000 y.b.p.). This agrees with earlier findings by geomorphologists working in the Neotropical lowlands, who concluded that the major dry and humid phases of the Pleistocene probably correlate with glacial and interglacial periods, respectively (Bigarella and Andrade, 1965). Other dry phases are marked on the Fúquene diagram from Colombia (Fig. 5:3) and occurred earlier than the long arid peak and also later (9,500–11,000 y.b.p., "El Abra"). Pollen studies of Quaternary sediments are urgently needed from many tropical lowland areas. Their results will be important in determining regional variations in the extent of vegetational fluctuations and in locating areas of continued forest growth ("refugia") during arid climatic periods.

Geomorphological data (Fig. 5:4).—Different surface land forms develop under dry as compared to humid climates and, when preserved after climatic change, permit interpretations of the recent climatic history of a given region. For example, many erosional features observed in portions of Amazonia today could not have originated under the present forest cover. During dry climatic phases, mechanical erosion of the largely unforested surface of a given region was accentuated, leading to the deposition of extensive gravel beds in valleys and on coastal plains, where they continue onto the continental shelf that was partially land during glacial periods. The gravel plains were dissected during humid interglacial periods, but a thick vegetation cover protected the surface from mechanical erosion, which then was mainly chemical.

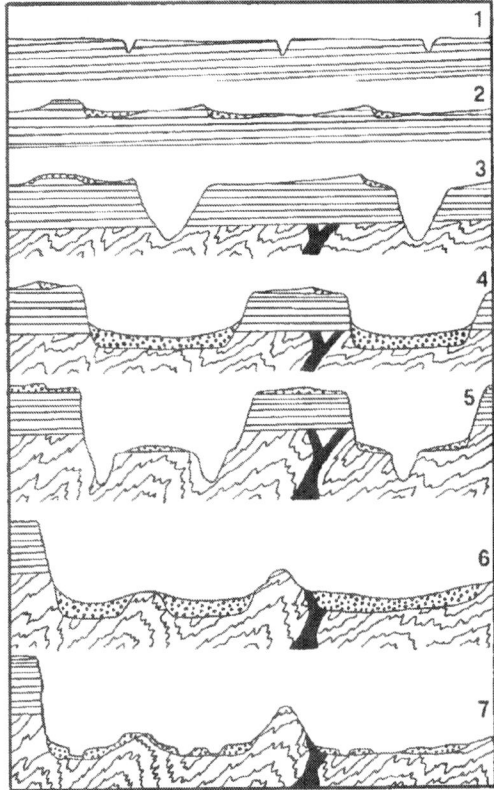

Fig. 5:4. Schematic cross section profiles of the sequence of geomorphic development in the Río Caroní area, southern Venezuela (after Garner, 1966). Explanations: Humid climatic periods (1,3,5,7) characterized by fluvial incision alternate with arid periods (2,4,6) when extensive aggradation occurred.

Perfiles esquemáticos demostrando el desarollo geomorfológico de la región del Río Caroní, Venezuela meridional (según Garner, 1966). Explicaciones: Períodos húmedos (1,3,5,7), caracterizados por incisión de ríos, alternados con períodos áridos (2,4,6) cuando ocurrió agradación extensiva.

Extensive geomorphological observations indicate an alternation of humid and arid climatic periods in northern, eastern, and central Brasil (B of Fig. 5:1) during the Quaternary (Tricart, 1959; Bigarella and de Andrade, 1965; Bigarella, 1971; Fairbridge, 1976; Fränzle, 1976). The last severe arid phase occurred in Brasil during the interval 4,000 and 2,500 y.b.p. and may have caused a separation of the upper and lower Amazon forests along the dry transverse zone from southern Venezuela to northeastern Brasil. Forests reexpanded during the following humid period, which extends to the present time, and led to the isolation of the presently remaining savanna enclaves within the Amazon forest.

Side-scanning radar images obtained through aerial surveys reveal geomorphological features in forested areas where frequent cloud cover had prevented air photography. Interpretation of surface land forms based on radar mosaics holds promise for a comparatively rapid geomorphological mapping of vast areas, especially in Amazonia, thereby permitting regional differences in the climatic history of extensive forest regions to be recognized. Initial results of radar interpretation and ground checks have been published by Tricart (1974, 1975) and Journaux (1975), who worked in lower Amazonia. Tricart surveyed the Santarém region and noted intensive dissection of the surface that had occurred under nonforest vegetation, probably during part of the marine regression corresponding to the last glacial period. The area later was covered with forests upon the return of a humid climate during the postglacial Flandrian transgression. Journaux (1975) also concluded that a major and relatively long semi-arid phase had preceded the present humid period. During the last 13,000 years, the forest has reoccupied savanna regions to the north and south of the lower Río Amazonas. By contrast, savannas apparently advanced at the expense of forests in one study area near the border of Brasil and Surinam (Tirios region) during postglacial time. Further observations on the climatic history of Amazonia based on geomorphological studies have been published by Bremer (1973), Eden (1974), Klammer (1975), Zonneveld (1975), and Mousinho (1971). The last author worked in the Manáus region of central Amazonia (M of Fig. 5:1) and found evidence in the Upper Quaternary strata indicating alternating dry and humid climatic phases, which probably correlate with the last glacial and postglacial periods, respectively.

The landscape development in southern Venezuela (Río Caroní drainage system; C of Fig. 5:1), as well as along parts of the western and eastern slopes of the Peruvian

Andes (L and P of Fig 5 1), during the Quaternary has been interpreted by Garner (1959, 1966, 1968) on the basis of a sequence of alternating humid and dry periods The Caroni region in southern Venezuela was unforested repeatedly when severe planation and aggradation occurred (Fig 5 4) Forests have returned to this area comparatively recently Lateritic crusts, stone lines, dissected gravel deposits, settled dunes, or the morphology of the landscape of parts of central and northern Brazil indicated to Barbosa (1958), Ab'Saber (1957, 1967), Cole (1960) and Klammer (1963 299, 305) that the present humid climate was preceded by a more arid climatic phase Sauma (1974) obtained corresponding results in coastal Ecuador

An interpretive map of South America by Ab'Saber (1977) depicts the distribution of major vegetation types during the dry climatic phase of the last glacial period (18,000–13,000 y b p) as reconstructed by the author from primarily geomorphological data (e g, pediments fluvial terraces, stone lines, paleosols, iron crusts) gathered over 20 years The lowland tropical forests are shown to be restricted to a number of isolated areas that agree in size and location to refugia proposed by several biogeographers as discussed below

Geological data—The occurrence of arkosic sands (30-60% felspars) of Late Wisconsin age in the shelf sediments off northeastern South America led Damuth & Faubridge (1970) to postulate that the climate of tropical lowland South America during the last glacial phase was much drier than today Millman et al (1975) and Irion (1976) challenged this conclusion and suggested the possibility of an Andean or central Amazonian origin of the arkosic sands, which would diminish their paleoclimatic significance Further data and interpretations of Quaternary continental shelf deposits in tropical latitudes will be of interest Studies of sea-bottom cores taken in the Caribbean Sea and of foraminiferal assemblages and eolian biogenic detritus indicate aridity during temperature minima (Bonatti and Gartner, 1973, Prell, 1973, Parmenter and Folger 1974).

Irion and Absy (1978) studied lake sediments from the central Amazon Valley (Manaus region) that were deposited during the last glacial stage and in postglacial time The authors did not identify indications of periodic influence of dry savanna climate in these sediment cores Possibly, fairly humid conditions and broad gallery forests persisted along the Amazon River and its tributaries during (late) Pleistocene dry climatic phases Irion and Absy (1978) further felt that the surface land forms in central Amazonia do not favor an interpretation of repeated climatic reversals in that area during the Quaternary Hopefully, sedimentological and palynological material will soon become available from the terra firme regions between large Amazonian rivers These regions are more critical for testing the theory of Pleistocene vegetational fluctuations in Amazonia than the broad river valleys where probably more or less extensive gallery forests remained during dry climatic periods

Climatological data—Regional variation of annual rainfall in central South America is mainly determined by the surface relief which had originated at least in Late Tertiary time, although some uplifting of the Andes and the Guianan and Brasilian shields probably did occur later during the Quaternary Precipitation is increased near the Atlantic coast, on exposed slopes of the Guianan mountains, and near the Andes By contrast the total rainfall decreases on the leeward side of mountains and in a zone across lower Amazonia Even though climatic patterns during Pleistocene glacial and interglacial periods probably differed considerably from the present situation, it appears reasonable to assume that during arid phases the forests in Amazonia disappeared first from areas that presently receive the least amount of rain per year and, conversely, survived longest in areas of heavy rainfall Cool dry periods occurred 20,000–13 000 y b p, 11,000–9 500 y b p, and 3,500–2,800 y b p (van Geel and van der Hammen, 1973, Vanzolini and Williams, 1970, Heine, 1974) The last two periods probably did not cause so much forest fragmentation as the earlier one, which coincided with the last glacial period Zonneveld (1968) discussed the climatic changes in northern South America

Paleontological data—Rich fossil deposits

at a number of localities in several South American countries, especially in Argentina, southeastern Brasil, and Ecuador, indicate the existence of a peculiar Neotropical mammal fauna in forest and nonforest habitats during the Tertiary and Quaternary periods (Patterson and Pascual, 1968, Paula Couto, 1975) This fauna had evolved in geographic isolation during the Mesozoic and Tertiary from an ancestral mammal fauna of western Gondwanaland (Fittkau, 1969, Fooden, 1972) and came in direct contact with the North American mammal fauna in the Pliocene, when the Central American isthmus was closed (review by Savage, 1974, Webb, 1978) Pleistocene bird remains are known from northwestern Perú and western Ecuador (Campbell, 1976, 1979) The famous fossil deposits in the limestone caverns at Lagôa Santa, Minas Gerais (Brasil) may be only subrecent in age

Despite the outstanding general scientific significance of the South American fossil faunas, their contribution toward elucidating biogeographical events in the tropical lowlands during the Quaternary is still limited The notable extinction of mammals in South America during the late Pleistocene, mainly of the larger, more specialized herbivores and their predators, has been attributed to climatic-vegetational changes, to hunting pressure by prehistoric man or to both (Martin and Wright, 1967, Axelrod, 1967) Hershkovitz (1969 27) stated that " postglacial decrease in humidity, aggravated by drastic seasonal fluctuations, might well have been the more important factor in the extermination of larger Middle and South American mammals" However, the problem remains unsolved and the discussion of late Pleistocene extinctions continues (MacNeish, 1976, Grayson, 1977, Webb, 1978)

QUATERNARY BIOGEOGRAPHY OF TROPICAL LOWLAND SOUTH AMERICA

Several biogeographical theories have been proposed to explain the origin of present-day distribution patterns in South American animals and plants and to rationalize the history of faunal differentiation at the species and subspecies level in the Neotropical lowlands These theories concern the problem of the origin of the large diversity of life in the Neotropics and mainly refer to the question of which processes led to the separation of small populations in the vast tropical lowlands Spatial isolation was known since the studies of Charles Darwin, Moritz Wagner and Ernst Mayr (1942, 1963) as the prerequisite of geographic (allopatric) speciation [1] Agents causing the isolation of daughter populations from a previously more widespread parent population in tropical South America are thought to be 1) paleogeographic changes in the distribution of land and sea, 2) the development of the system of broad Amazonian rivers, or 3) vegetational fluctuations under the changing climate of the past These three theories are discussed in some detail below

Constancy theory —No major speciation or subspeciation occurred in the tropical lowlands during the Quaternary, when equable environmental conditions were fairly constant and continued unchanged from the Tertiary into Recent times (or, at least, climatic changes were of minor importance) Extant Neotropical species and subspecies, as well as their distribution patterns, are thought to have originated during the Tertiary when populations were repeatedly isolated and reconnected owing to paleogeographic changes in the distribution of land and sea caused by epeirogenic and orogenic events (e g, uplift of the shield areas and the Andes, respectively, or foundering of forelands off the present coast lines) Tertiary species presumably survived relatively unchanged until today, although some impoverishment of the fauna may have occurred This theory was generally accepted during early parts of this century and among recent authors, by Croizat (1958, 1976) for the Neotropical fauna, Emsley (1965) for butterflies, and Hershkovitz (1969) for certain mammals This interpretation may also be called the "Tertiary island theory" According to this theory, differences

---

[1] A number of other theories attempt an explanation of the maintenance (as opposed to the origin) of high tropical species diversity and emphasize niche reduction through ecological specialization under an equable climate, increased competition, or the great age of tropical habitats and their stability through time

between the forest faunas to the west and east of the Andes presumably originated from the uplift of the Andes, which split a pre-existing, widespread lowland fauna into a trans-Andean and a cis-Andean (Amazonian) portion (Chapman 1917 89, Croizat, 1976 766).

It appears certain that the isolation of large populations owing to Tertiary paleogeographic and also climatic-vegetational changes did play a major role in establishing basic distributional and evolutionary patterns of the Neotropical fauna and flora at higher taxonomic levels of families and genera However, the data on Pleistocene fossils and on environmental fluctuations, reviewed above, indicate conspicuous changes in the composition and distribution of the Neotropical biotas during the Quaternary period, probably leading to extensive evolutionary changes at the species and subspecies levels in many groups after the close of the Tertiary This, of course, does not exclude the possibility of members of less plastic groups in the present fauna, especially among invertebrates, having survived relatively unchanged since Tertiary times Because the Andes arose in the form of strings of growing islands from a marine geosynchnal basin, there was no pre-Andean continuous and widespread lowland fauna occupying what was later to become the Andes and their forelands Moreover, the separation of trans- and cis-Andean lowlands and their faunas was not complete, thus frequent exchanges of these faunas through the Caribbean lowlands of northern Colombia north of the Andes were possible during the Quaternary

River theory —This theory is an attempt to explain the differentiation in the rich Amazonian biota Uniform and widespread populations are assumed to have been divided into two or more subpopulations and effectively isolated by the developing network of large Amazonian rivers during the Early Quaternary period The isolated subpopulations deviated to the level of subspecies and species on opposite river banks This theory has been invoked on different occasions to explain certain situations but has never been proposed formally or quantitatively tested Field naturalists observed repeatedly that the Amazon or one of its tributaries separate for some distance the ranges of numerous subspecies of allied species of animals [Wallace, 1853, Bates 1864 (for various groups of animals), Sclater and Salvin 1867 Hellmayr, 1910, 1912, Snethlage, 1913 Mayr, 1942 228, and Sick, 1967 (for birds), Hershkovitz 1968, 1969 (for monkeys)] However, many of these species circumvent large streams or, in the case of subspecies, hybridize in the headwater regions where the narrowing rivers cease to be barriers to dispersal (Haffer, 1969, 1974 1978) The distribution of numerous other species is unaffected by Amazonian rivers The river theory also leaves unexplained how a forest of the size, or nearly the size, of the present Amazon forest could have existed without major rivers The development of the great forest and of its large rivers probably was one interrelated process The forest cannot be envisioned without the rivers and vice versa

Partial flooding of the Amazon Valley during interglacial periods and shifting river courses in this region indeed may have isolated some local animal populations on temporary islands, where they may have differentiated as subspecies or even species (Willis, 1969 393) The same applies to islands on the continental shelves of South America, which were connected with the mainland during glacial periods of lowered world sea level and isolated during interglacial periods (Muller, 1970, Vanzolini, 1973 Reboucas-Spieker, 1974)

Refuge theory —Forest and nonforest biomes alternately broke into isolated blocks and expanded and coalesced under the changing humid to arid climatic conditions of the Quaternary period According to this theory, plant and animal populations isolated in the restricted forest and nonforest refugia during adverse climatic phases either became extinct, survived without much change or, more often, differentiated to the level of subspecies or species before they came into secondary contact with previously conspecific populations of other refugia during a following favorable expansive phase. If a population reached sexual and ecological isolation from its neighboring allies, it could disperse widely in the now continuous habitat before its extensive range was fragmented during the next adverse climatic phase Rivers in Amazonia probably were not a causal factor of speciation (except perhaps in a few cases) but merely limited or modified the dispersal of populations from the forest refugia

This theory proposes that the intensive earlier processes of faunal differentiation during the Tertiary continued into the Quaternary. The theory was based initially on analyses of distribution and speciation patterns in several groups of Neotropical birds (Haffer, 1967, 1969, 1970, 1974, 1975), reptiles (Vanzolini, 1970, 1973, Vanzolini and Williams, 1970), and vertebrates in general (Muller, 1972, 1973).[2] Subsequently, it has been corroborated by the results of studies on Amazonian *Drosophila* flies (Spassky et al., 1971, Winge, 1973) butterflies (Brown et al., 1974, Brown, 1976, 1977a,b), and trees (Prance, 1973). The theory is essentially the refuge model developed to explain faunal differentiation during the Pleistocene in northern latitudes (Stresemann, 1919, Reinig, 1937, 1938a,b). This model was applied later to Australia (Keast, 1959, 1961) Africa (Carcasson, 1964, Moreau, 1966, Kingdon, 1971) and finally to the Neotropics.

As to the chronology of the speciation process, recent authors agree that species may evolve under favorable conditions in geologically short periods of time [i.e., during the time span of Pleistocene climatic phases or even shorter periods (Selander, 1971, Vanzolini, 1970, 1973)]. Brodkorb (1971 46 ff) stated in a paleornithological review "The Quaternary was a period of almost constant change. The living species of birds arose at various times during the Pleistocene epoch.

Postglacial evolution has been mainly at the subspecific level. The evidence continues to amass that all living species of birds arose during the Quaternary scarcely more than 13 [living species of birds] have been reported, tenuously, from the Tertiary. It was formerly held that neospecies originated in the Pliocene or even earlier, but little evidence exists to support this theory. Pending critical re-evaluation, all Pliocene reports of neospecies should be disregarded.' Similarly, Ballmann (1977) concluded that most of the extant avian species originated during the Pleistocene. Vuilleumier (1975 480) summarized the current consensus stating that " the distribution patterns of taxa at the species or genus levels, especially the diversity gradients observed at present, are only remotely related to Tertiary dispersal, but are instead the result of Pleistocene events much Pleistocene speciation has taken place in the tropics "

An analysis of forest and nonforest refugia could be based on criteria derived from the following evidence 1) Direct evidence from fossil records and from studies in various other geoscience fields, such as palynology, pedology, and geomorphology. As shown above, the sparse data presently available do permit several general conclusions to be drawn regarding vegetational fluctuations in tropical lowland South America. However, it is still inadequate to map in detail the changing distribution of forest and nonforest vegetation through time or to delineate accurately forest refugia of varying sizes that must have existed during arid climatic phases 2) Indirect evidence based on an historic interpretation of biogeographical data concerning the present flora and fauna. Because the forest and nonforest refugia are geological-paleontological rather than biological phenomena, conclusions based on such indirect evidence alone should be formulated cautiously 3) Combination of direct and indirect evidence derived from the available paleoecological and fossil data as well as from extant faunas and floras. Given the present state of knowledge this method appears to be the most promising today. It is reviewed in the following section in some detail, for the results so far obtained readily explain many biogeographic phenomena observed in the Neotropical Region

The authors who advocated the Tertiary island theory, the Quaternary river theory, and the Quaternary refuge theory determined, as a first step, general patterns of vicariance in the continental biotas (i.e., the patterns of allopatric differentiation of species and subspecies, including phenomena of secondary contact between vicariant populations). The

---

[2] Several earlier authors briefly suggested in general terms climatic-vegetational fluctuations as a cause of Pleistocene faunal differentiation without discussing details (Fox 1949, Turner, 1965, Muller, 1968), see also the review by Vuilleumier (1971)

cited authors then studied the causes of the vicariance patterns and identified geographic-geological or vegetational changes that led to the repeated appearance and disappearance of barrier zones. This procedure of historic-biogeographical analysis agrees with a recent recommendation by Croizat, Nelson, and Rosen (1974:269) and earlier authors. As far as the Neotropical lowland fauna is concerned, most of the above biogeographers probably also would agree with Croizat et al. (1974:269) who emphasized the zoogeographical and historical importance of " . . . a continuing temporal sequence of vicariant events, and . . . subsequent dispersal modifying earlier vicariant patterns." The underlying causes of allopatric differentiation in the Neotropical lowlands during the Quaternary probably were processes of alternating fragmentation and coalescence of vegetation zones [i.e., "small-scale" vicariance events as compared to major vicariance events caused by changes of geography in connection with regional uplift/subsidence and continental drift during earlier geological periods (Tertiary, Cretaceous, etc.)]. Climatic-vegetational fluctuations probably caused allopatric speciation on a world-wide scale through much of the earth's Mesozoic and Cenozoic history, although such fluctuations were more accentuated during the rapid climatic changes of the Quaternary. A correlation of several aspects of geographical differentiation presently observed in the Neotropical lowland fauna with the known geographic-paleoclimatological changes of the recent geological past appears to be the most parsimonious interpretation. Among the proposed theories, only that of Quaternary forest contraction and expansion explains satisfactorily the recurrent distribution patterns in different groups of Amazonian animals and plants, such as the clustering of contact zones in central Amazonia over portions of the Guianan and Brasilian shields and the overlapping (congruent) ranges of localized species in the upper Amazonian lowlands, which were covered by shallow seas during most of the Tertiary.

Additional biogeographic data on tropical South American animals and plants, as well as detailed comparative geological studies, are needed to evaluate the varying proportions of species and subspecies that merely survived in the forest and nonforest refugia, differentiated in the refugia or became extinct in the refugia. The construction and comparison of cladograms for the geological units (islands, refugia) and groups of organisms of a given region as suggested by Platnick and Nelson (1978) and Rosen (1978) may eventually facilitate such an analysis.

In order to avoid misunderstanding, several terms used in the following discussion are defined below.

Distribution center. Area inhabited by most or all members of a group of localized species and/or subspecies with similar ecologic preferences; area of high endemism. A purely descriptive term. Synonyms are core area of distribution, core area of endemism.[3] Mapped by superimposing the ranges of species in the group considered and drawing contour lines of equal numbers of species in the group.

Center of evolution. Area with high endemism in species and subspecies surrounded by and separated from other centers by variously extensive belts where contact zones of closely related parapatric species and hybridizing subspecies are clustered. This term refers to biological phenomena and is interpretive, especially if the contact zones are believed to be secondary, that is, having originated from populations expanding their ranges and establishing contact with previously isolated neighboring populations. In this case the term "center of dispersal" also is used and, if differentiation is considered to be synonymous with evolution, the term "center of differentiation" may be applied (Miller, 1941; Behle, 1963). These are mapped as a combination of distribution centers and contact zones or by contour lines, which illustrate varying hybrid levels of populations around centers of evolution.

Refuge. A restricted area within the center of evolution (center of dispersal) where the habitat in question presumably remained

---

[3] The terms "nuclear area" (Kernareal, Arealkern) or "equiformal area" have been used by earlier authors who developed the center concept in the Palearctic region (Hultén 1937, Reinig 1937, 1938a,b, 1950; de Lattin, 1957; see review by Udvardy, 1969).

more or less constant during adverse climatic periods thus serving as a refuge for animal and plant populations. This is an interpretive nonbiological term referring to climatological, pedological, palynological and other geoscience phenomena. The term "refuge" is somewhat inappropriate as animals and plants did not actively seek shelter in the refuge. Rather, remnant populations remained in the remnant habitats of varying size where they did or did not survive under fairly constant ecological conditions.

A Method of Historic-Biogeographical Analysis

In order to trace the history of differentiation of a given species, information is required on 1) patterns of its geographic variability, 2) patterns of its abundance in space and time, and 3) details on its ecologic requirements and range limits. The latter may be determined through hybridization, ecological competition or by climatic-edaphic factors. Therefore, systematic and ecological field work on a large number of species is a prerequisite to any biogeographical analysis. Initially sufficient data are available for representatives of only a few groups of Neotropical animals, such as certain birds, reptiles and insects, and several groups of plants.

Given this information, two zoogeographical phenomena related to the concept of allopatric speciation and the available geoscience data are combined in the proposed method to establish patterns of vicariance in South America and to suggest tentatively the location of restricted refugia in tropical lowland South America where animals and plants survived adverse climatic-vegetational phases of the Quaternary (Fig. 5.5).

Step 1: Mapping of secondary contact zones.—Populations of related taxa which met in the recent geologic past after a period of isolation either hybridized or excluded each other geographically without hybridization or they overlapped their ranges depending upon the stage they had reached in the speciation process (Mayr, 1942, 1963). The zones of secondary contact between hybridizing subspecies and parapatric species often are clustered in fairly restricted areas or belts indicating that entire faunas met there and partly fused in the past. Such suture zones (Remington, 1968) point out the former existence of major ecological barriers, although the barriers themselves have long since disappeared. In several cases horizontal shifts of the contact zones may have occurred after contact was established. For this reason, conclusions about the presumed location of former barrier zones should be based on several or many contact zones so as to minimize potential errors involved. (Steps 1 and 2 are independent of each other and may be reversed.)

Step 2: Mapping of distribution centers.— Geographically restricted species (independent species or allospecies of superspecies) frequently inhabit similar portions of an extensive and superficially uniform habitat such as the Amazon forest and form localized species clusters. In order to map these clusters of species we superimpose their more or less congruent ranges and trace contour lines of equal numbers of species in the group. Following this procedure, centers of distribution become apparent where all or most member species coexist. In this way, peaks of species numbers or areas of maximal overlap of breeding ranges in a group of species are emphasized and ill-defined range boundaries are de-emphasized. The number of sympatric species in each group as mapped by contour lines decreases at varying rates away from the center. However, the total number of bird species present between the mapped centers is more or less compensated for by species from a neighboring cluster and by species with extensive ranges in Amazonia (Haffer, 1978). We may envision two alternative interpretations of the diversity gradients around Neotropical core areas of distribution. 1) An historical interpretation. The dispersal distance of the species from a central area of survival/origin decreases away from the center mostly due to increasing competition with species spreading from other centers. 2) An ecological interpretation. For the species of each group, ecological conditions are more favorable in the central portion of the group area than toward the periphery, or the habitat quality might change (e.g. forests approaching a savanna region), or rivers or mountains act as differential barriers.

Step 3: Comparison of the location of

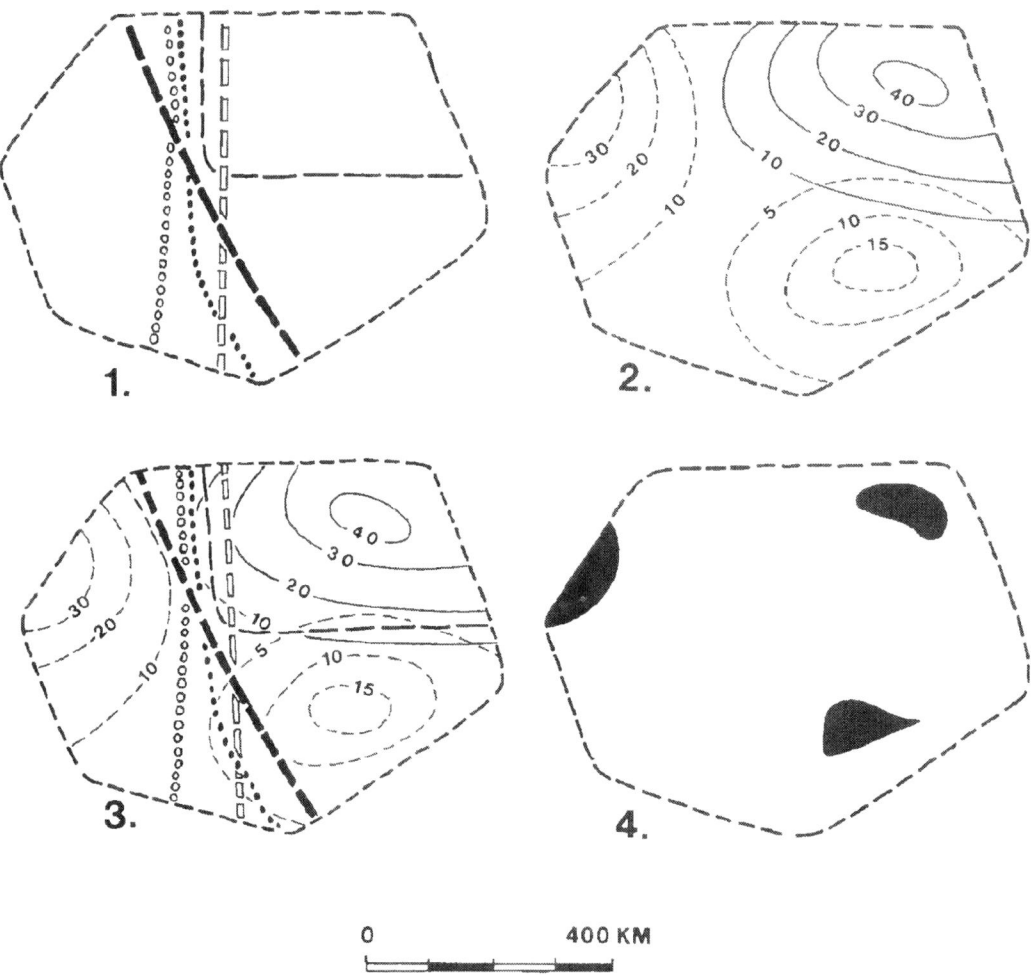

FIG. 5:5. Reconstruction of Quaternary refugia in an extensive and fairly uniform forest or nonforest habitat (dashed outline). Schematic representation. Explanations: 1. Mapping of secondary contact zones of allied parapatric species and hybridizing subspecies. Contact zones often cluster in certain regions forming faunal suture zones. 2. Mapping of distribution centers formed by fairly localized species and subspecies clusters (contours indicate numbers of sympatric species and subspecies in the groups considered). 3. Comparison of location of suture zones and distribution centers. 4. Mapping of refugia related to the dispersal centers taking into consideration all available data on relief, climate, geomorphology and palynology related to the areas under consideration.

Reconstrucción de refugios cuaternarios en medio de un extenso ambiente y más o menos uniforme (selva o savana; delimitada por un margen rayado). Explicaciones: 1. Mapeo de zonas de contacto secundario entre especies parapátricas y subespecies con hibridación. Zonas de contacto frecuentemente se encuentran en ciertas áreas formando así zonas de sutura. 2. Mapeo de centros de distribución formadas por grupos de espécies y subespécies localizadas (líneas de contorno indican el número de especies y subespecies simpátricas en los grupos de organismos bajo consideración). 3. Comparación de la posición de zonas de sutura y de los centros de distribución. 4. Mapeo de refugios relacionados a los centros de dispersión teniendo en cuenta todos los datos disponibles sobre el relieve, clima, geomorfología, y palinología de la región.

contact zones and distribution centers.—Often clusters of secondary contact zones fall between core areas, thereby supporting the interpretation that the distribution centers functioned as centers of dispersal in the past. This interpretation is particularly applicable in the case of hybridizing subspecies and parapatric species that characterize neighboring centers and meet in the intervening area where other contact zones of more wide ranging forms are clustered as well. Because the contact zones and centers often involve different species, full complementarity between them cannot be expected. Thus, there are many contact zones between forms whose present ranges comprise more than one distribution center. This is schematically indicated in the diagram (Fig. 5:5, no. 3), where several forms occupying the entire eastern portion of the habitat with a northern and a southern center meet western forms along contact zones that are not restricted to the area between the centers.

If biogeographical analyses are based exclusively on the population structure of several widespread and geographically variable species, a patchwork of subspecies ranges separated by more or less extensive hybrid zones exists. Superimposition of the various species maps may show that the ranges of pure subspecific populations with uniform character expression and the location of separating hybrid belts more or less coincide in the different species (Fig. 5:6). Contour lines illustrate varying hybrid levels of populations around the centers. Analyses also may be based on the population structure of a single species, and distribution maps of several individual characters may be prepared (e.g., Vanzolini and Williams, 1970, for the lizard *Anolis chrysolepis*). The character maps may then be superimposed and contoured in a similar manner as those of subspecies. Coinciding areas of uniform characters with low variability often cluster in core areas that are separated by zones of high character variability coinciding with hybrid belts between subspecies ranges.

Step 4: Mapping of the refugia related to the dispersal centers.—Ideally, this can be accomplished using geoscience data exclusively. Having established on the basis of zoogeographical data that a given distribution

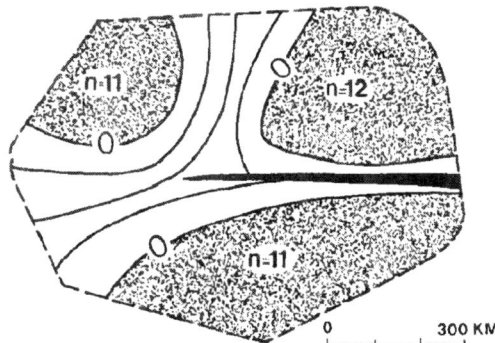

Fig. 5:6. Schematic representation of centers of subspecies endemism (stippled) in an extensive and fairly uniform habitat (dashed outline). Explanations: Superimposed ranges of "pure" subspecies populations and separating hybrid belts in different species often cluster in certain areas. Number of differentiated forms of various species superimposed is indicated (n = 11 or 12). Average hybrid level of combined species populations is mapped by contour lines (0 = "pure"). A barrier to gene-flow (broad river or mountain range) is schematically shown as a black bar; the populations on either side of the barrier are mostly pure, as limited gene-flow takes place between subspecies of only a few species whose ranges have been superimposed.

Diagrama esquemático de centros de endemismo subespecífico (punteado) dentro de un hábitat relativamente extenso y uniforme (delimitado por una línea entrecortada). Explicaciones: Rangos superimpuestos de poblaciones de subespecies "puras" y los cinturones de hibridización en varias espécies muchas veces se juntan en determinadas regiones. El número de formas diferenciadas de las especies superpuestas está indicado (n = 11 ó 12). El nivel promedio de hibridización en las poblaciones de especies combinadas está mapeado por líneas de contorno (0 = "puro"). Una barrera para el flujo genético (un gran río ó una montaña) está indicada esquematicamente por una faja negra. La mayoría de las poblaciones en ambos lados de la barrera son "puras"; un flujo genético restringuido ocurre solamente entre unas pocas poblaciones separadas.

center probably was a center of dispersal in the past, we proceed to postulate the approximate location, size and shape of the corresponding refuge area of forest or nonforest vegetation within the central portion of the center, taking into consideration all available geoscience data from the region, however deficient these data may be. Medium elevation areas with high rainfall near the base of mountains or plateau regions are prime candidates for forest refugia whose postulated extent during the maximum of the arid climatic period remains highly speculative. The model assumes that the species and subspecies characterizing a given center were confined to the postulated refuge prior to dispersal and prior to establishing secondary contact with other forms spreading from distant centers. Obviously, the former existence and changing size of the refugia ultimately can be traced only through detailed palynological, pedological, and geomorphological studies rather than through zoogeographical analyses. After all, the refugia are geological-paleoclimatological, not biological, phenomena. However, as long as only scattered geoscience data are available, zoogeographical analyses as outlined above will help our understanding of biotic differentiation in lowland tropical South America during the Quaternary. In general, the locations of distribution centers of the Amazonian forest biota correlate well with the locations of forest refugia tentatively derived from rainfall, relief and geoscience data alone (p. 108), thus strengthening an historical interpretation of the biogeographical core areas (Simpson and Haffer, 1978; Brown and Ab'Saber, 1979).

Endler (1977) suggested that parapatric speciation occurs frequently in nature and that the hybrid zones in Amazonia might actually be zones of primary intergradation caused by strong environmental gradients. However the geoscience data reviewed above (but not discussed by Endler) favor the interpretation of allopatric rather than parapatric speciation for the many hybridizing and non-hybridizing populations of plants and animals in contact. The Amazonian forest refugia are geological-paleoclimatical not biological phenomena.

Biogeographical Studies on the Forest Fauna and Flora

Some of the major regional conclusions regarding the Quaternary differentiation and dispersal of Neotropical biotas are summarized, as follows: 1) Extensive speciation took place in many groups of Neotropical animals and plants that were repeatedly isolated in refugia and later expanded their ranges during favorable expansive phases. 2) During humid climatic periods, extensive forests probably permitted a direct connection of the Amazonian fauna and flora with those of the Atlantic forest in eastern Brasil across the central Brasilian Plateau and along the coastal region of northeastern Brasil, where scattered forests are still preserved on isolated mountains (Muller, 1973; Haffer, 1974; Brown, 1976, 1977b). 3) The cis-Andean and trans-Andean forest biotas probably were connected repeatedly both north of the Andes in the Caribbean lowlands of northern Colombia and through the north Peruvian Andes from the upper Marañón Valley via the low Porculla Pass so as to reach the forested Pacific lowlands of Colombia from the south (Chapman, 1926; Haffer, 1967, 1975; Muller, 1973). 4) The relations between the Middle and South American nonforest bird faunas are less pronounced than those of the forest faunas of these two areas (Mayr, 1964). 5) There are numerous conspecific populations inhabiting the nonforest regions of northern South America and central Brasil, respectively, being separated by the entire width of the Amazon forest. Because their dispersal under present climatic-vegetational conditions is highly unlikely, a rather recent direct communication of nonforest faunas across Amazonia during one or more arid climatic periods seems probable. This theory also explains the close relationship of the fauna and flora of the Amazonian savanna enclaves with those of the nonforest regions to the north and south of Amazonia (Hueck, 1966; Haffer, 1969; Muller, 1973).

The authors of the studies reviewed below are aware of the tentative nature of the results obtained and of the suggestions made. Moreover the nascent theory of ecological refugia during the Quaternary, like any theory, cannot be proven but only disproven by the results of additional studies on the paleoclimatology, vegetational history, and zoogeography of South America. I wish to emphasize with Meggers (1977) that the efforts by biologists and archeologists at present are not more than a search for correlations and patterns useful as guides for investigation. The strikingly similar results as to the basic patterns of differentiation in various unrelated groups of Neotropical animals tend to support the refuge theory and justify continued research into this field of enquiry. Biogeographers working on the Neotropical fauna proposed for the lowlands of Middle and South America a total of 40 areas that are assumed to have served as refugia for the forest fauna at various times during the Quaternary. These areas are listed and briefly described in Appendix 5:1.

Birds.—Numerous secondary contact zones of avian species and subspecies pairs are clustered in north-central Amazonia—in southern Venezuela and in the Rio Negro region of northern Brasil (Fig. 5:7), where Guianan forms from the east established contact with western forms that had spread from upper Amazonia (Haffer, 1969, 1974). These contact zones represent range limits either of hybridizing subspecies or of non-hybridizing competing species; the ranges were mapped in conjunction with studies of patterns of geographic variation in several groups of Amazon forest birds. South of the Rio Amazonas, contact zones are scattered over a more extensive area, where we may distinguish an upper Amazonian and a south-central Amazonian suture zone. A distributional analysis of the Amazonian forest avifauna (Haffer, 1978) indicated the existence of six core areas of distribution (Fig. 5:7) or localized species clusters, each of them composed of 10 to 50 species. The six clusters together are characterized by a total of around 150 species or about 25 percent of the Amazon forest bird fauna. Most of the remaining forest birds (75%) are more widely distributed, their ranges comprising two or more distribution centers. There are conspicuous clusters of lower and upper Amazon forest birds, as well as smaller groups of northern and southern Amazon forest birds, in addition to those species that inhabit even larger areas of Amazonia and beyond (see Haffer, 1978, for more details). A number of other species have an irregular, spotty distribution or are known from only a single locality. The mapped contact zones in Amazonia (Fig. 5:7) are mostly located between distributional core areas which probably functioned as centers of dispersal. The complementarity of contact zones and distribution centers is less well developed in central Amazonia, where a number of birds spreading from the species-rich

Fig. 5:7. Location of secondary contact zones (above) and of distribution centers in the Amazon forest avifauna (below). Explanations: Secondary contact zones (dashed) are concentrated in north-central Amazonia (a), upper Amazonia (b), and south-central Amazonia (c). A continuous line delimits the Amazon forest (above). Fairly localized species clusters (each composed of 10 to 50 species) form the distribution centers A to F (below). Adapted from Haffer, 1974, Fig. 9.13 and Haffer, 1978. Additional clusters of endemic species characterize the Atlantic forests of southeastern Brasil and the trans-Andean forests of northwestern South America.

Posición de zonas de contacto secundario (arriba) y de centros de distribución en la avifauna de la selva amazónica (abajo). Explicaciones: Zonas de contacto secundario (líneas rayadas) se encuentran en la Amazonía norcentral (a), en la alta Amazonía (b) y en la Amazonía surcentral (c). Una línea continua delimita la selva amazónica (arriba). Grupos de especies bastante localizadas forman los centros de distribución (A–F; abajo) cada uno de ellos formado por 10 a 50 especies. Adaptado de Haffer, 1974, Fig. 9.13 y Haffer, 1978. Otros grupos de especies endémicas caracterizan la selva atlántica de Brasil meridional y la selva transandina de Sudamérica noroccidental.

upper and lower Amazonian centers are in contact within the area of the "weak" Imerí and Rondônia centers (characterized by comparatively few species).

Based on geoscience data, Quaternary forest refugia in Amazonia probably were located near the windward base of hilly ranges and mountains, such as the northern margin of the Brasilian Plateau, the eastern base of the Andes and the northern base of the mountains in the interior Guianas. These areas correlate well with the location of the zoogeographically defined distribution centers which, therefore, are assumed to indicate the approximate location of Quaternary forest refugia. Additional refugia for the avifauna (Fig. 5.8) based on similar geological and zoogeographical criteria have been proposed for the Atlantic forest of southeastern Brasil (Muller, 1973; Jackson, 1978) and for the trans-Andean forest region in western Colombia and in Middle America (Haffer, 1967, 1969, 1974, 1975). A recent study of a complex Neotropical avian genus on the basis of the refuge concept is Fitzpatrick's (1976) analysis of the *Todirostrum* flycatcher group, also see the recent review by Dorst (1976).

Lizards and frogs.—Analysing the population structure and character variation in the Amazonian *Anolis chrysolepis* group, Vanzolini and Williams (1970) and Vanzolini (1970, 1973) arrived at conclusions regarding the history of faunal differentiation during the Quaternary that are strikingly similar to those reached by Haffer (1969, 1974). Several extensive areas of uniform character expression (core areas) in *Anolis chrysolepis* are separated by regions where complex character variation suggests hybridization or introgression along zones of secondary contact. Vanzolini and Williams (1970) interpreted this situation as being the result of secondary intergradation of populations that had differentiated in geographic isolation, and they assumed changes in the distribution of forest in Amazonia during the course of climatic fluctuations. These authors reconstructed several forest refugia around the periphery of Amazonia (Fig. 5.8), most of which coincide closely with those proposed by Haffer (1969, 1974) for birds. Additional forest refugia probably determined the differentiation of Neotropical forest reptiles and will be identified when other species are studied in detail. Muller (1972, 1973) using mostly herpetological and ornithological data described several broad centers of dispersal but did not suggest specific refugia. A comparison shows that the boundaries of Muller's centers rarely coincide with those of avifaunal core areas but fall in the peripheral gradient of decreasing species numbers or coincide with river barriers. Muller (1973) did not state the criteria he used to delimit the various broad centers which on his maps are frequently separated only by narrow corridors.

In recent years, several herpetologists accepted the notion of a Pleistocene origin of numerous species and subspecies of Neotropical frogs, lizards and snakes in forest refugia: Duellman (1972, 1978), Heyer (1973), Duellman and Crump (1974), and Silverstone (1975, 1976) for certain Amazonian and trans-Andean frogs, Gallardo (1965, 1972) and Lynch (this volume) for the South American amphibian fauna generally, Dixon (this volume) for Amazonian reptiles, Echternacht (1973) for Middle American lizards (*Ameiva*), Hoogmoed (1973; this volume) for the herpetofauna of the Guianas, Jackson (1978) for two genera of eastern Brasilian iguanid lizards and C. W. Myers (1973, 1974) for two genera of snakes. Dixon (this volume) and Lynch (this volume) mapped clusters of endemic reptile and amphibian species in upper and lower Amazonia. These centers of distribution more or less coincide with similar centers established for the forest avifauna. At this stage, a more quantitative treatment of available distributional data would be desirable, such as the derivation of herpetological distribution centers by means of contoured diversity maps of localized species clusters and a comparison of the location of secondary contact zones with that of dispersal centers and postulated refugia.

Insects.—The distribution and population structure of two groups of Neotropical insects are relatively well known and permit initial biogeographic analyses—1) Certain *Drosophila* flies that have been collected and analysed extensively in the course of genetic investigations and 2) butterflies of the genus *Heliconius*. Spassky et al. (1971) summarized the distribution of several semispecies and closely related species of *Drosophila*. These authors and Winge (1973) concluded that the various forms may have originated in for-

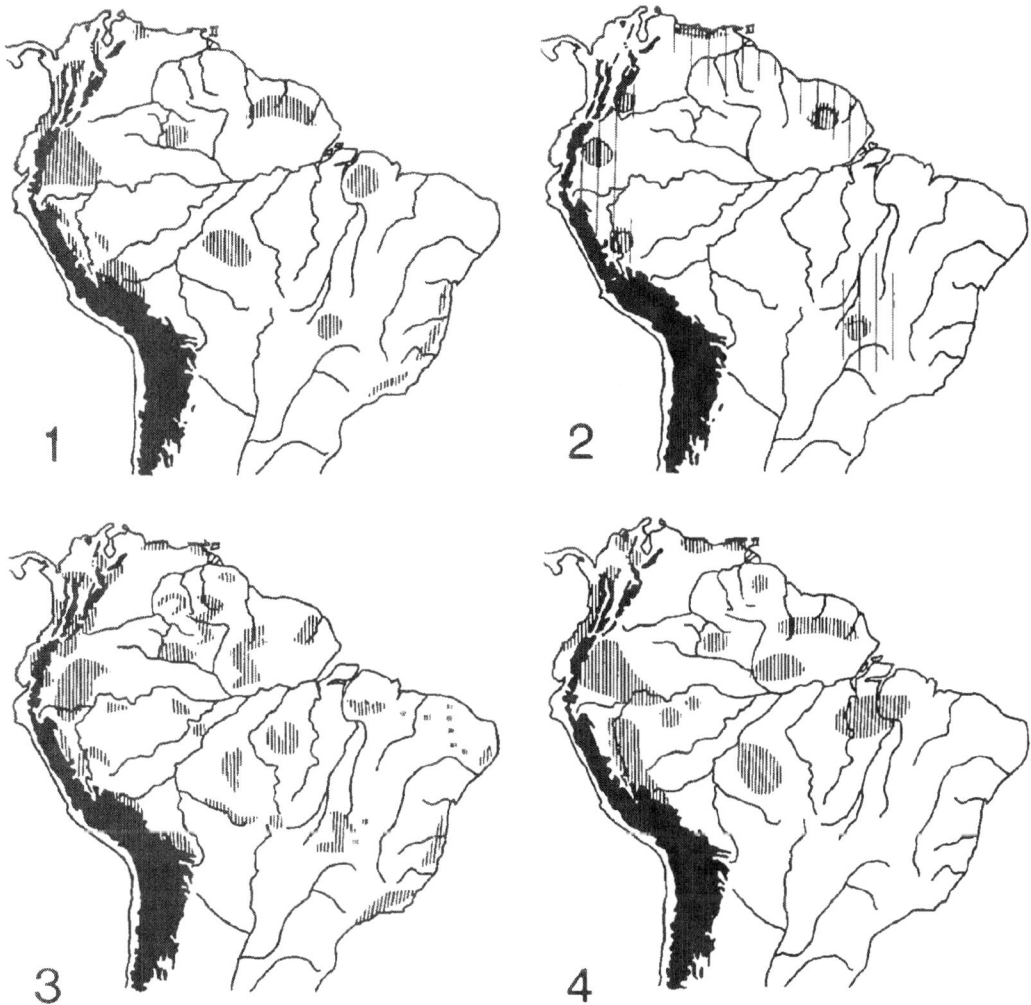

Fig. 5:8. Location of presumed Quaternary forest refugia (hatched) in tropical lowland South America. Explanations: 1. Reconstruction based on the distribution patterns of Neotropical birds (Haffer, 1967, 1969, 1974). 2. Reconstruction based on the population structure of Amazonian lizards (*Anolis chrysolepis* group, Vanzolini and Williams, 1970, Vanzolini, 1970; wide hatches indicate core areas). 3. Reconstruction based on the distribution patterns of subspecies and species of *Heliconius* butterflies (Brown et al., 1974, Brown 1977a,b). 4. Reconstruction based on the distribution patterns of four families of Amazonian trees (Prance, 1973).

Posición de presuntos refugios cuaternarios de selva húmeda (rayado) en las tierras bajas tropicales de Sudamérica. Explicaciones: 1. Reconstrucción basada en los patrones de distribución de aves neotropicales (Haffer, 1967, 1969, 1974). 2. Reconstrucción basada en la estructura de poblaciones de lagartos amazónicos (grupo de Anolis chrysolepis, Vanzolini y Williams, 1970, Vanzolini, 1970; líneas verticales indican áreas nucleares). 3. Reconstrucción basada en la distribución de subespecies y especies de mariposas del género Heliconius (Brown et al., 1974, Brown, 1977a,b). 4. Reconstrucción basada en la distribución de cuatro familias de árboles amazónicos (Prance, 1973).

est refugia as proposed for the evolution of birds and reptiles. The colorful *Heliconius* butterflies inhabit the entire humid Neotropical Region. They are famous for their complicated Muellerian mimicry rings comprising many races that are strikingly different phenotypically. Rich material of these butterflies in private and public collections permits fairly detailed analyses. On the basis of genetic and distributional studies of several species of *Heliconius*, Turner (1965, 1971) felt that climatic-vegetational fluctuations of the Pleistocene might explain the origin of secondary range overlap of related forms and repeated speciation, which led to the complex pattern of diverse, related and mimicking species in this genus. Additional detailed biogeographical studies of the genus *Heliconius* and other groups involved in mimicry rings by Brown et al (1974), Brown (1976, 1977a,b), Turner (1976a,b, 1977) and Sheppard et al (1978) have greatly extended this initial analysis (Fig 5.9) see also the work by Blandin (1977) and Descimon (1977). Conclusions are based on a revision of 162 species of Heliconiini and Ithomiinae, family Nymphalidae, representing a total of 905 geographically differentiated forms. Brown (unpubl.) analysed the distribution and differentiation of other groups of Neotropical butterflies (*Morpho*, *Phycoides*, Callicorini, *Anaea Parides*) and obtained results that are similar to those on the species of *Heliconius*. A number of very different subspecies occupy forest areas of varying size and are connected by zones of hybridization of varying widths. The method of analysis was as follows. By comparing the location of hybrid zones and the ranges of differentiated forms (subspecies) in the various species, these entomologists derived centers of endemism (based on 8 to 50 local differentiated forms of the species analysed). However, Brown (1977a,b) did not explain details of delimitation of the centers of endemism, i.e. which criteria he used to determine the widely varying width of the areas separating the centers. Considering geomorphological, palynological and climatological data Brown et al (1974) and Brown (1976, 1977a,b) continued their analysis by postulating the location and shape of forest refugia in the central portion of the centers of evolution. The majority of the 40 forest refugia in Middle and South America reconstructed from data on *Heliconius* species (Fig 5.8) coincide with refugia postulated for other groups. In several instances discrepancies exist as may be expected. Brown (pers comm) currently is preparing more detailed contour maps defining core areas on the basis of superimposed species maps, which illustrate by contour lines the hybrid levels of local butterfly populations (Brown and Ab'Saber 1979).

Plants.—D R Simpson (1972) supported the refuge theory, in particular for the forest region of eastern Peru, on evidence of genera of Rubiaceae. Parallels between the distribution of certain Neotropical palms and birds also exist (Moore, 1973). On the basis of a phytogeographic study of several genera of Amazon forest trees in the families Chrysobalanaceae, Dichapetalaceae, and Caryocaraceae, Prance (1973) also supported the theory of plant speciation in Quaternary forest refugia of tropical South America (see also Foreie 1976). In each of the tree genera studied, there are several areas of repeated endemism coinciding with the refuges proposed (Figs 5.8, 5.10). Hopefully, a quantitative derivation of the postulated refugia on the basis of contoured plant species diversity maps and, if available, the location of contact zones will be published when phytogeographical data on additional groups of Amazon plants become available.

The distribution patterns of two other groups of Amazon trees—members of the Leguminosae and Memecyleae—do not clearly support the interpretation of speciation in restricted refugia yet they do not negate the possibility (Langenheim et al 1973, Morley, 1975). The ranges of most of these plants are quite extensive and, as pointed out by the authors cited above, expansion from refugia may have obscured refuge boundaries. However, four species of *Mourin* occupy restricted ranges in northeastern Amazonia, this correlates with refugia proposed by Prance (1973). Nevertheless Morley (1975) felt that

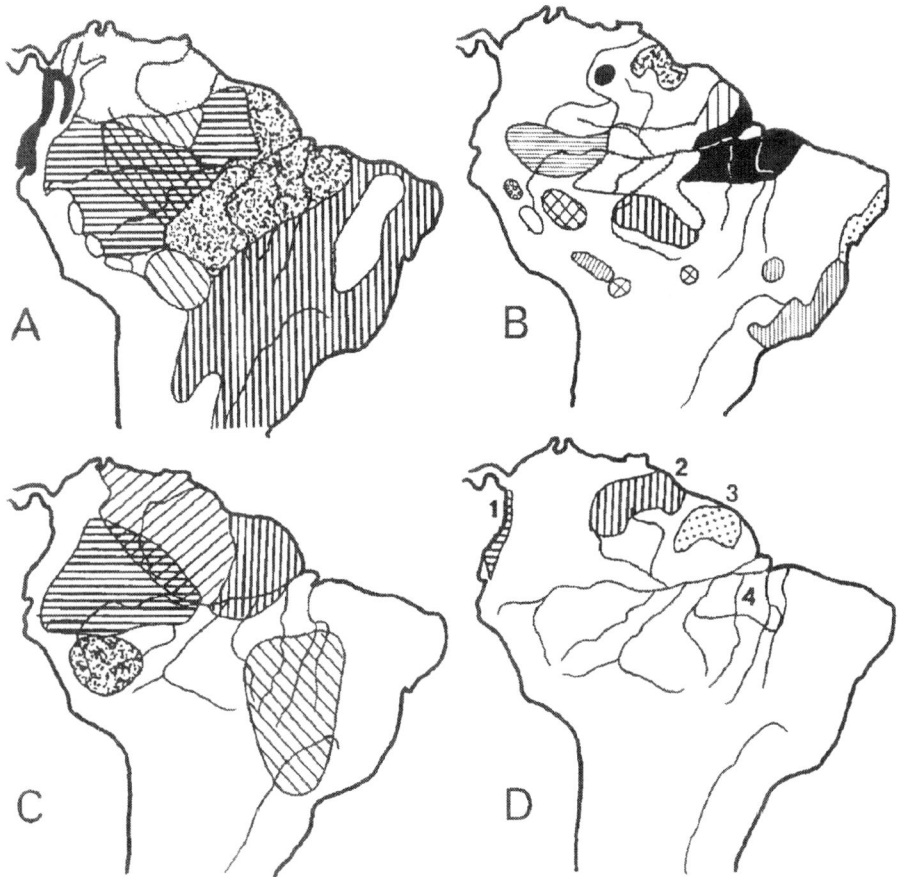

Fig. 5:9. Distribution patterns of certain butterflies (A,B), lizards (C), and frogs (D) in tropical lowland South America. Explanations: A. Distribution of geographical races of *Heliconius erato* shown by different patterns. Hybrid zones are omitted. Overlap of shading indicates variable populations (after Brown et al., 1974). B. Distribution of geographical races of *Hypothyris ninonia* shown by different symbols; distribution in Amazonia is probably continuous (after Brown, 1977b). C. *Anolis chrysolepis*, females; summary of geographic differentiation, number of scales across snout (after Vanzolini and Williams, 1970, map 6, p. 166). D. Distribution of several poison-arrow (or poison-dart) frogs of the genus *Dendrobates*: *D. histrionicus* (1), *D. leucomelas* (2), *D. tinctorius* (3), *D. galactonotus* (4) (after Silverstone, 1975).

Distribución de ciertas mariposas (A,B), lagartos (C) y anuros (D) en las tierras bajas de Sudamérica. Explicaciones: A. Distribución de subespecies de Heliconius erato; *zonas de hibridización fueron omitidas. Símbolos superpuestos indican poblaciones variables (según Brown et al., 1974). B. Distribución de subespecies de* Hypothyris ninonia; *áreas en la Amazonia son probablemente continuas (según Brown, 1977b). C.* Anolis chrysolepis, *hembras; número de escamas a través de las narinas (según Vanzolini y Williams, 1970, mapa 6, p. 166). D. Distribución de varios anuros del género* Dendrobates: *D.* histrionicus *(1), D.* leucomelas *(2), D.* tinctorius *(3), D.* galactonotus *(4) (según Silverstone, 1975).*

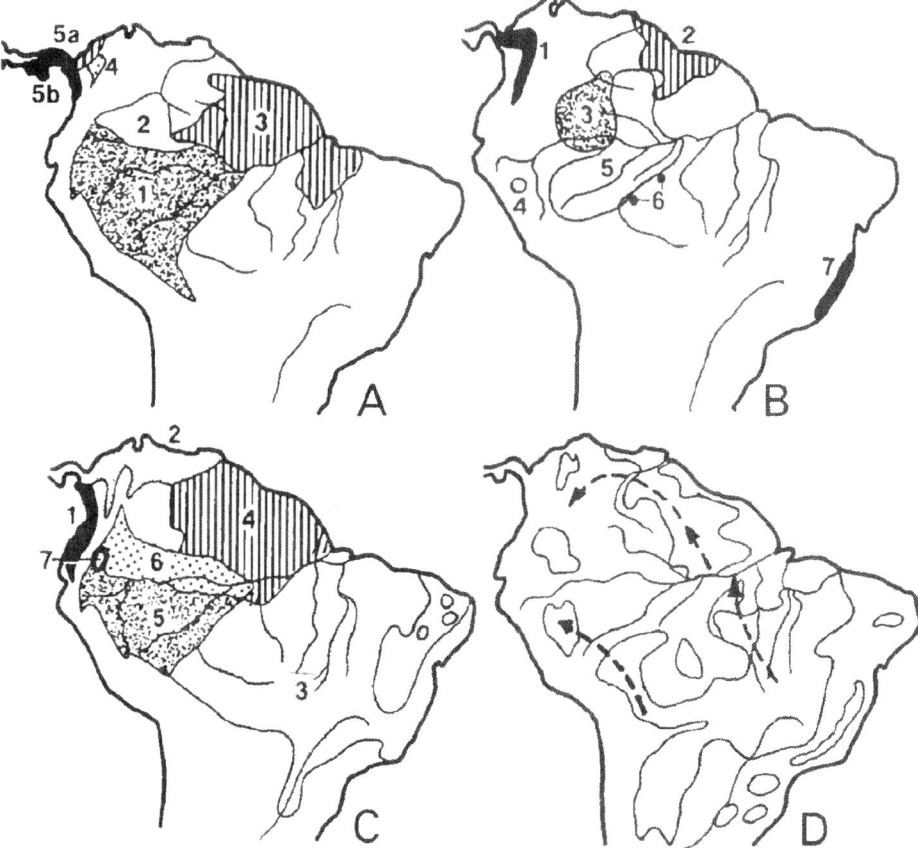

Fig. 5:10. Distribution of certain Neotropical monkeys (A), plants (B), birds (C), and of the Ge-Pano-Carib ancestral language stock among Indian tribes (D). Explanations: A. Distribution of tamarins, genus *Saguinus*: *Saguinus* sp. (1), *S. inustus* (2), *S. midas* (3), *S. leucopus* (4), *S. o. oedipus* (5a), *S. o. geoffroyi* (5b) (after Hershkovitz, 1969). B. Distribution of various species of *Caryocar*: *C. amygdaliferum* (1), *C. nuciferum* (2), *C. gracile* (3), *C. amygdaliforme* (4), *C. pallidum* (5), *C. dentatum* (6), *C. edule* (7) (after Prance, 1973). C. Distribution of the Green Jacamars, *Galbula galbula* superspecies: *G. ruficauda melanogenia* (1), also widespread in Middle America *G. r. ruficauda* (2), *G. r. rufoviridis* (3), *G. galbula* (4), *G. cyanescens* (5), *G. tombacea* (6), *G. pastazae* (7) (after Haffer, 1974). D. Distribution of the Ge-Pano-Carib linguistic stock (shaded) and suggested dispersal routes of the nonforest fauna from central Brasil into and across Amazonia (after Meggers, 1977).

Distribución de ciertos monos neotropicales (A), plantas (B), aves (C) y del grupo lingüístico ancestral Ge-Pano-Carib entre tribus de indios (D). Explicaciones: A. Distribución de monos del género Saguinus: Saguinus *sp. (1), S. inustus (2), S. midas (3), S. leucopus (4), S. o. oedipus (5a), S. o. geoffroyi (5b) (según Hershkovitz, 1969). B. Distribución de varias especies de* Caryocar: *C. amygdahferum (1), C. nuciferum (2), C. gracile (3), C. amygdaliforme (4), C. pallidum (5), C. dentatum (6), C. edule (7) (según Prance, 1973). C. Distribución de los jacamares verdes,* Galbula galbula *superespecie: G. ruficauda melanogenia (1), G. r. ruficauda (2), G. r. rufoviridis (3), G. galbula (4), G. cyanescens (5), G. tombacea (6), G. pastazae (7) (según Haffer, 1974). D. Distribución del grupo lingüístico ancestral Ge-Pano-Carib (matizado) y presumidas rutas de dispersión de fauna savanófila desde Brasil central a través la Amazonía (según Meggers, 1977).*

the distribution of the species he studied can be largely accounted for on the basis of present conditions ("although with some difficulty") Clearly numerous additional groups of Neotropical plants must be studied in order to gather the basic data needed for a critical appraisal of the refuge theory from a botanical point of view

Mammals—The patterns of distribution of several groups of Neotropical forest mammals and their differentiation at the subspecies and species level (Hershkovitz 1968, 1969, 1972, 1978, Avila-Pires, 1974) appear to be similar to patterns observed in birds and insects Therefore, I suggest for these examples of mammals an historic interpretation of differentiation on the basis of Quaternary climatic-vegetational fluctuations This would seem to offer a fairly straight-forward explanation of speciation in cases like that of the tamarin monkeys (*Saguinus*) (Fig 5 10) Several species of tamarins coexist in upper Amazonia The only lower Amazonian species (*S midas*) may have originated in the Guiana refuge and later established secondary contact with the upper Amazonian species in the upper Rio Negro region (*S "inustus"*) and also crossed the lower Rio Amazonas southward Another example is the several species of Capuchin monkeys (*Cebus albifrons* superspecies) The trans-Andean *Cebus capucinus*, the upper Amazonian *C albifrons* and the Guianan *C griseus* divide the Neotropical forests among themselves without geographical overlap in the manner of many avian superspecies Kinzey and Gentry (1979) recently interpreted the distributional history of the Amazonian titi monkeys *Callicebus moloch* and *C torquatus* on the basis of Pleistocene forest refugia

A number of contact zones between related mammals are clustered in northwestern Colombia near the junction of the Panamanian isthmus with the South American mainland and could have been established when sea level fell in postglacial time and/or when forests reoccupied this region after a postglacial or late Pleistocene period of drought— the tapirs *Tapirus bairdii/T terrestris*, the spider monkeys *Ateles fusciceps/A geoffroyi*, the howler monkeys *Alouatta villosa/A seniculus*, the tamarins *Saguinus o geoffroyi/S o oedipus* A critical appraisal of the differentiation patterns in these and other groups of Neotropical mammals in the light of the refuge theory is needed Hershkovitz (1969, 1972) and Moynihan (1976) did not attach major importance to the refuge theory (but see the remarks by Avila-Pires, 1974 178 and Kinzey and Gentry, 1979) In the case of African forest mammals Kingdon (1971 67) stated with confidence that past climatic changes, repeatedly isolating and then reuniting the forest areas of Africa have been a major mechanism in the speciation of forest mammals Monkeys, duikers, squirrels and other rodents show morphological differences that frequently coincide with the forest refuges"

Prehistoric man—In an interesting application of the biogeographical model of diversification to cultural distributions in tropical lowland South America Meggers (1977 292) stated that ' some of the characteristics observed by biologists can be discerned, among them heterogeneity, disjunct distributions, and widespread dispersals " Prehistoric man probably arrived in South America during the late Pleistocene (MacNeish, 1976) and witnessed several climatic reversals Therefore, certain cultural adaptations and dispersal patterns may be explained on the basis of vegetational fluctuations The present distribution of the Ge-Pano-Carib ancestral language stock (Fig 5 10) correlates closely with the routes postulated for the intrusion of nonforest fauna into and across Amazonia from open habitats in central Brasil (Meggers, 1977)

Fish—No detailed studies of the pattern of geographic differentiation in the aquatic vertebrate and invertebrate faunas of tropical lowland South America are available However, it appears that the strong climatic-vegetational changes and sea level fluctuations of the Quaternary had numerous effects on the aquatic fauna of Neotropical rivers, as indicated by the comment of Lowe-McConnell (1975 261)

> In the rivers of South America the adaptive radiations of the characoids and various catfish groups are as remarkable as those of the cichlids in the African Great Lakes Differentiation has proceeded much further in these groups, certain families or subfamilies now

having particular feeding habits (approaching the condition in marine fishes) The semi-isolated conditions in tributary streams, varzea, oxbow and marginal lakes, would appear to offer ideal conditions for allopatric speciation. Oscillations in river levels, due to factors ranging in scale from sudden local downpours of rain to long-term climatic cycles, and geomorphological changes leading to river captures, give abundant opportunities for species evolved in semi-isolated communities to come together. Species from many areas then accumulate, as the overall extinction rate appears to be low.

Certain distributional aspects of the Neotropical freshwater fish fauna have been discussed by Gery (1969) and Muller and Weimer (1976).

Distribution Patterns of Nonforest Birds

The refuge theory is also applicable to an interpretation of the latest differentiation in Neotropical nonforest biotas. However, fewer studies have been performed on the nonforest fauna compared to the recent work on forest animals and plants reviewed above. The most diverse Neotropical nonforest faunas are those of the chaco, cerrado, and caatinga regions, which form a broad diagonal belt across central South America of the llanos grass plains and coastal scrub of northern South America and the fauna of the dry Pacific slope of Middle America. Each of these faunas has many endemic elements of its own, attesting to the prolonged independent history of these vegetation zones (Sick 1965, 1966, Muller, 1973). On the other hand, the following examples taken from the nonforest avifauna seem to support the notion of vegetational changes in the recent geological past permitting contact of populations that are widely isolated under present climatic conditions (Fig 5.11). There are a number of birds that enter Amazonian savanna enclaves from the north or from the south. In other cases, conspecific populations or closely related allospecies are separated by the entire width or length of the Amazon forest. In these and many similar cases it is difficult to imagine that long-distance dispersal could have led to establishment of the isolated populations. Rather, the assumption of more or less continuously connected nonforest habitat across Amazonia during dry climatic phases of the Quaternary permitting the expansion of nonforest faunas appears to be more realistic. In this connection detailed studies of the biota presently inhabiting isolated nonforest enclaves (savanna islands) within the Amazon forest region would be particularly interesting (e.g. Brown and Benson, 1977). Short (1975) reviewed the chaco avifauna of northern Argentina and Bolivia and mapped secondary contact zones and other zones of avian interaction (Fig 5.11) also emphasizing fairly recent vegetational changes and their influence on avifaunal distribution.

DISCUSSION

The refuge theory may serve as a framework for future studies on the Quaternary zoogeography of Middle and South America and lead to the accumulation of additional data required to test the concepts reviewed above. I discuss below several general aspects of the refugia and their effect on the differentiation of isolated populations.

Location of forest refugia during successive arid phases.—Surface relief probably was a major factor in determining, through local rainfall maxima and favorable soil conditions, the location of extensive remnants of humid forests during dry climatic periods (Haffer, 1969 Vanzolini, 1970, 1973). Therefore, the major postulated Amazonian refugia are located near the base of the Andes, near mountain ranges of northeastern Amazonia, and near the northern margin of the central Brasilian Plateau. Because the present surface relief probably originated in late Tertiary time and was approximately the same as today during the Quaternary favorable areas probably served repeatedly as forest refugia during successive arid periods, thus enhancing the differentiation of certain populations that were isolated repeatedly in the same refuge ("resonance effect," Vanzolini 1973). However, owing to probable differences of climatic conditions during the various arid phases, many refugia probably did not occupy exactly correlative locations during successive periods of forest retreat, especially those Amazonian refugia unrelated to positive relief. Details must remain speculative.

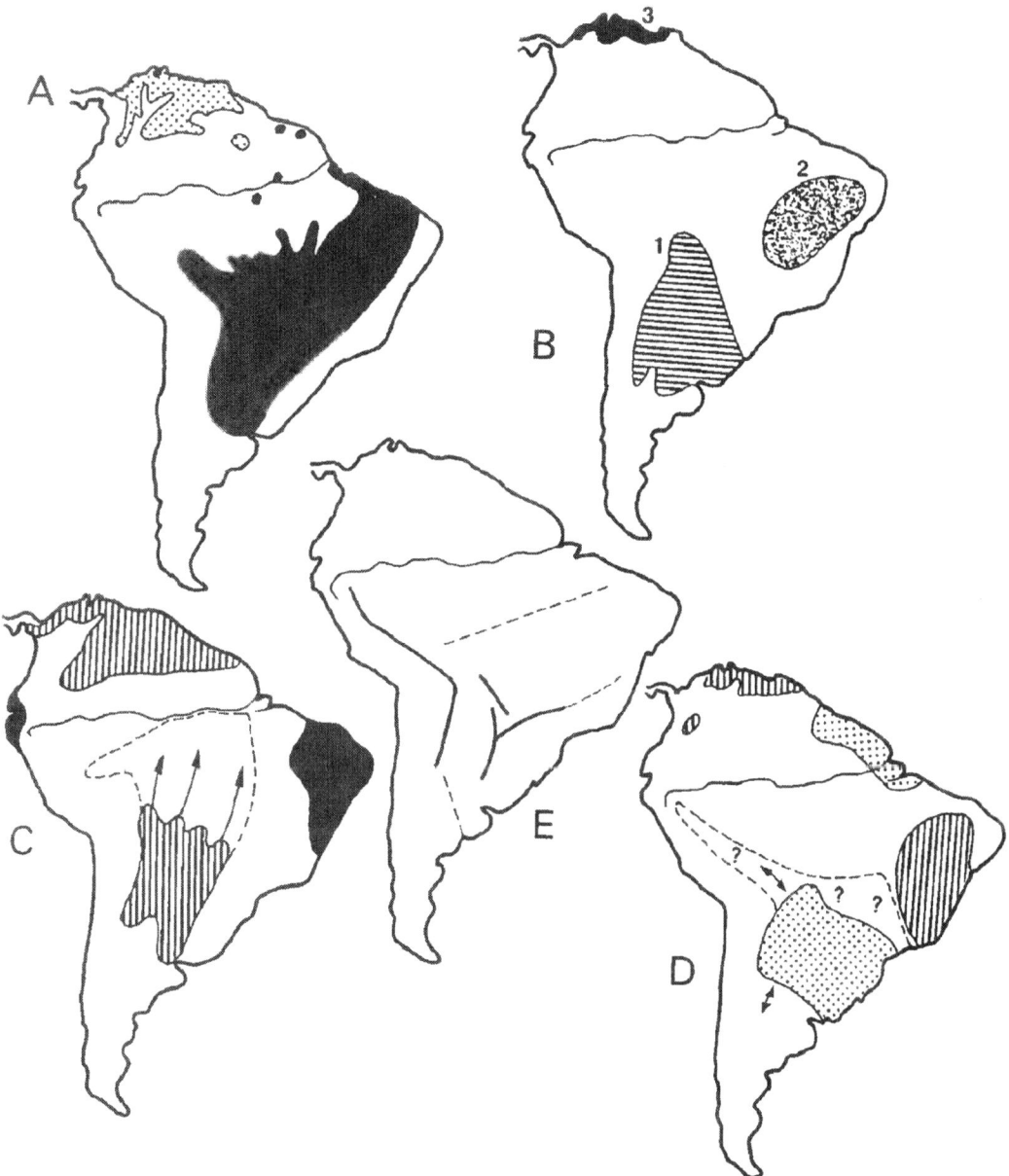

Fig. 5:11. Distribution of certain nonforest birds in tropical lowland South America (after Short, 1975). Explanations: A. Ranges of the wren *Campylorhynchus griseus* (stippled) and the white woodpecker *Melanerpes candidus* (solid). Note isolated populations on Amazonian savanna enclaves; *C. griseus* has another isolated population in southwestern México. B. Disjunct ranges of Picazuro Pigeon (*Columba picazuro*; 1, 2) and its allospecies *C. corensis* (3). C. Ranges of *Fluvicola pica* (hatched) and *F. nengeta* (solid); southern race of *F. pica* is partly migratory as indicated by arrows and dashed line. D. Range of Red-crested Finch (*Coryphospingus cucullatus*, stippled) and its allospecies *C. pileatus* (hatched). E. Narrow range disjunc-

Comparison of Neotropical forest refugia —As illustrated in figure 5.8, only a few large refugia have been proposed for vertebrates, compared to more numerous and many smaller refugia proposed for insects and plants. These differences may reflect either different periods of isolation or, more probably, different survival ability of insects, plants, birds, and mammals in refugia of varying size.

Differentiation of refuge populations — Geographic-ecological isolation of animal populations in the refugia probably had at least two effects through which genetic-morphological differentiation was initiated 1) Interruption of gene-flow permitted local adaptations and chance deviations to develop in short periods of time (Mayr, 1942, 1963), the amount of differentiation depending upon the degree of geographic isolation the size of the refuge population, and the "plasticity" of the various systematic groups 2) If gene-flow normally is unimportant in maintaining genetic cohesion within species such as Amazonian butterflies (Ehrlich & Gilbert, 1973, Turner, 1976a,b), geographic isolation may cause evolution through other effects Turner (1977) suggested disorderly extinction of species in the refugia as probably responsible for rapid deviation of refuge populations in mimetic butterflies. The species composition of the floras and faunas in the refugia probably came to differ through disorderly extinction even though the distribution of species in the original continuous forest may have been comparatively uniform. Turner (1977 110–115) concluded

> The effects of extinction on the ecosystem are likely to be far-reaching. Even if no butterfly species became extinct in any refuge, other extinctions in the fauna and flora would produce long lasting changes in the abundance of butterfly species. Thus a formerly rare distasteful species might become very common in a refuge, and hence the best protected. There would then be a strong tendency for other distasteful species to change their patterns to mimic the common one. Hence disorderly extinction will cause each refuge to differ in the commonest and best protected butterfly pattern this would be ample cause for the divergence of the races of *Heliconius*, as they converged to different patterns in different refuges

Thus adaptation to a changing biotic environment is in itself a sufficient cause of race formation other causes such as founder effect and adaptation to the physical environment do not have to act in order that races should be formed

Rate of evolution —The present consensus is that few vertebrate species date back to the Pliocene most neospecies having developed since the beginning of the Pleistocene 1.8 of 2 million years ago (see p 117) Increased knowledge on the absolute age and the regionally varying effect of climatic cycles will permit speculations on the rate of Quaternary speciation in particular groups of animals. Models will be constructed that assign periods of species or subspecies differentiation to particular phases of forest or savanna fragmentation. Thus Vanzolini and Ab'Saber (1968) related the dispersal and differentiation of two species of *Liolaemus*, southeastern Brasilian lizards to dated climatic-vegetational shifts. However, Muller and Steinger (1977) contested their conclusions on the basis of studies of the systematics of these lizards. Turner (1976) discussed fairly recent speciation and subspeciation in certain *Heliconius* butterflies in relation to late and postglacial arid climatic phases

---

tions, zones of hybridization, and other zones of avian interaction involving Chacoan birds, black lines indicate location of zones involving 5 to 12 situations and dashed lines indicate location of zones involving 3 to 4 situations

Distribución de ciertas aves sabanófilas en las tierras bajas tropicales de Sudamerica (segun Short, 1975) Explicaciones A Áreas de distribucion del cucarachero Campylorhynchus griseus *(punteado) y del carpintero blanco* Melanerpes candidus *(negro) Notese las poblaciones de estas especies aisladas en las sabanas de la selva amazónica,* C griseus *tambien se encuentra en el sudoeste de México* B Áreas disyunctas de las palomas Columba picazuro *(1,2) y de su alloespecie* C corensis *(3)* C Areas de distribucion de Fluvicola pica *(rayadas) y de* F nengeta *(negras), la raza meridional de* F pica *es parcialmente migratoria lo que está indicado por flechas y una linea rayada* D Areas de distribución de Coryphospingus cucullatus *(punteadas) y de su alloespecie* C pileatus *(rayadas)* E Disyunciones estrechas zonas de hibridización y otras zonas de interacción de aves de la region chaqueña. Lineas continuas indican la posicion de zonas que se refieren a 5–12 parejas avianas, lineas entrecortadas de zonas que se refieren a 3–4 parejas avianas

Such correlations will remain speculative, although the order of magnitude of the rate of differentiation may become apparent in well documented groups

Forest refugia and forest reserves —Large forest areas are destroyed in South America annually for agricultural purposes Less humid and accessible forests have suffered more than humid sections in remote regions The development plan for the Brasilian portion of Amazonia includes an extensive road building program that threatens the integrity of the largest remaining tropical forest region of the world (Goodland and Irwin, 1975, Prance and Elias, 1977) Most South American countries have established forest reserves in the hope of ensuring the preservation of the protected habitat Proposals have been made in Perú, Venezuela, Guyana and Brasil to base forest preservation policies on the concept of Pleistocene forest refugia and to adjust the location, size and outline of specific forest reserves to proposed refugia and to recent results of applied biogeography (Wetterberg et al, 1976, for Brazil, see also Wilson and Willis, 1975, Diamond 1976, Lovejoy, this volume) It would also be of interest to preserve the biota in certain selected inter-refugial areas where extensive hybridization of refuge populations along zones of secondary contact takes place Such areas would be " incomparable natural laboratories for the study of biological diversity and ecological genetics " (Brown, 1977a 157)

Quaternary history of the Neotropical and Ethiopian lowland faunas compared —Climatic-vegetational fluctuations during the Quaternary have affected tropical Africa to a similar degree or possibly more than the lowlands of tropical South America (Moreau 1963, 1966, Carcasson, 1964, Livingstone, 1975) Moreau (1966 161) stated " the redistribution of Kalahari sand over most of the present Congo forest area, towards the end of the mid-Pleistocene indicates that the forest must have been vastly reduced and pushed into edges and corners, presumably with concurrent extinctions The resultant isolations of surviving populations would have been conducive to speciation, and of course highly effective if it continued long enough " There may have been available no more than three large forest refugia for the entire western and central African lowland forest fauna (besides remnant eastern African forests), because large portions of tropical Africa above 500 m elevation have been uninhabitable for the tropical fauna during cold periods These few African forest refugia contrast with many more refugia or groups of refugia postulated for the Neotropical lowland region The greater richness of the Neotropical forest fauna may result from repeated speciation in a larger number of Quaternary forest refugia, which were smaller and scattered over a much more extensive tropical lowland region than in Africa (Vanzolini, 1973, Haffer, 1974)

Final suggestions —In concluding this review, I list several suggestions for the continuation of studies in the historical biogeography of the Neotropical lowland biotas The results of such studies will be helpful in evaluating various aspects of the refuge theory discussed above

1. Analyze range limits of localized species and the contact zones of parapatric species in uniform habitats
2. Analyze the population structure and geographical patterns of phenotypic variation in widespread species leading to meaningful application of the subspecies concept (compare comments in this regard by Myers and Daly, 1976 200, with respect to herpetological studies)
3. Analyze abundance patterns of species in space and time
4. Quantify distribution centers (dispersal centers) by constructing contour maps of species diversity and of hybrid levels of populations in secondary contact around and between the centers
5. Describe details of the delimitation of a refuge within a core area of evolution, i e, the biogeographical and/or geological criteria used
6. Study presently operating factors that might explain certain distribution patterns (e g patchy occurrence of species in a continuous habitat because of ecological competition, occurrence of certain species on habitat islands due to long distance dispersal)

7. Study nonforest faunas which have been somewhat neglected in recent years compared to forest faunas and analyze the relationship of forest and nonforest faunas (e.g., Sick, 1966, Vanzolini 1974).
8. Study the processes of differentiation that operated in the ecological refuge islands and evaluate the significance and if possible the amount of faunal extinction during adverse climatic-vegetational periods.

ACKNOWLEDGMENTS

The following persons kindly advised on recent publications concerning the subject matter of this article or obtained copies of publications unavailable to me while I was stationed in Tehran, Iran, during 1973–1977 J J Bigarella, K S Brown, Jr, H Descimon E J Fittkau H F Garner H Klinge, B J Meggers P Muller C W Myers, R A Paynter, G T Prance, P Raven, B B Simpson, R Tuck, J R G Turner, and P E Vanzolini Keith Brown, Jr (Campinas, Brasil) and Beryl Simpson (Austin, Texas) read this manuscript and made valuable suggestions for certain changes I gratefully acknowledge their advice

RESUMEN

Fluctuaciones del clima y de la vegetación durante el cuaternario causaron vastos cambios en la distribución de la selva y de los ambientes no-forestales en América del Sur Poblaciones relativamente pequeñas de plantas y animales probablemente fueron aisladas y se diferenciaron en remanentes (refugios) de antiguos ambientes durante períodos de clima adverso Estas poblaciones muchas veces alcanzaron el nivel de nueva subespecie o especie antes de establecer contacto secundario con poblaciones de otros refugios durante períodos expansivos bajo un clima favorable Numerosas especies probablemente se extinguieron durante las fluctuaciones pleistocénicas de la vegetación Posiblemente sólo unas pocas especies del Terciario tardío sobrevivieron en los refugios pleistocénicos sin apreciable cambio evolucionario

Un metodo propuesto para el análisis histórico-biogeográfico y la reconstrucción de antiguos refugios recomienda, primero, mapear la posición de zonas de contacto secundario de especies parapátricas y de subespecies que hibridizan Estas zonas muchas veces se encuentran mas o menos superpuestas en ciertas regiones Estas 'zonas de sutura' indican la posición de antiguas barreras, aún cuando las barreras ecológicas mismas desaparecieron hace mucho tiempo Segundo, se identifica a grupos de especies y subespecies características con areas de distribución mas o menos restrictas y congruentes, se superpone estas áreas de distribución y se delinea el número de especies, lo que lleva uno a la identificación de centros de distribución Tercero, se compara la posición de estos centros de distribución con la de las "zonas de sutura" Las últimas puedan encontrarse entre los centros propuestos, en esta manera permitiendo la interpretación de los centros de distribución como centros de dispersión Los refúgios estan reconstruidos basados solamente en datos geocientíficos, o en la parte central de los centros zoogeográficos teniendo en cuenta todos los datos geocientíficos disponibles (palinológicos, geomorfológicos, etc) de la región

Resultados de estudios biogeográficos recientes sobre aves, ciertas mariposas, lagartos y plantas de las selvas neotropicales apoyan la teoría de refugios Un total de 40 refugios forestales fueron propuestos para Centro y Sud América existiendo mas refugios para insectos que para mamíferos Esta diferencia posiblemente refleja distintas aptitudes para sobrevivir y/o capacidades de modificación de estos organismos en refugios de distintos tamaños Fluctuaciones de vegetación durante el cuaternario probablemente determinaron también la evolución de los animales de ambientes no-forestales sudamericanos Se necesita pruebas directas adicionales para determinar la posición de los refugios de selva y savana durante el cuaternario basadas en datos geomorfológicos, pedológicos y palinológicos

LITERATURE CITED

AB'SABER, A N 1957 Conhecimentos sobre as flutuações climáticas do Quaternario no Brasil Bol Soc Brasil Geol 6 41–48 [Reprinted in Noticia Geomorfologica 1 24–30, 1958]

AB'SABER A N 1967 Problemas geomorfologicos da Amazonia brasileira pp 35–67 in LENT H (ed) Atas Simposio Biota Amazônica, Vol 1 (Geociencias), 484 p

AB'SABER, A N 1977 Espaços ocupados pela expansão dos climas secos na America do Sul por ocasião dos periodos glaciais quaternarios Paleoclimas 3 1–19

ABSY, M L, VAN DER HAMMEN, T 1976 Some palaeoecological data from Rondônia southern part of the Amazon Basin Acta Amazônica 6 293–299

AVILA-PIRES, F D DE 1974 Caracterização zoogeografica da Provincia Amazônica II—A familia Callithricidae e a zoogeografia Amazônica Anais Acad Brasil Cienc 46 159–181

AXELROD, D I 1967 Quaternary extinctions of large mammals Univ California Publ Sci 72 1–42

BAUMANN, P 1977 Neuere Erkenntnisse uber die zeitliche Entstehung der rezenten Vogelarten Mitt Bayer Staatssamml Palaeontol Hist Geol 17 169–175

BARBOSA, A 1958 Geomorfologia do Territorio do Rio Branco Not Geomorfol (Sao Paulo) 1(1) 16–18

BATES, H W 1864 The Naturalist on the River Amazons John Murray, London, 406 p

BEHLE, H W 1963 Avifaunistic analysis of the Great Basin region of North America Proc XIII Int Ornith Congr pp 1168–1181

BIGARELLA, J J 1965 Subsidios para o estudo das variações de nivel oceânico no quaternario brasileiro An Acad Brasil 37(suppl) 263–278

BIGARELLA, J J 1971 Variações climaticas no quaternario superior do Brasil e sua datação radiometrica pelo metodo de carbono 14 Inst Geogr (Sao Paulo), Paleoclimas 1 1–22

BIGARELLA, J J, ANDRADE, G O DE 1965 Contribution to the study of the Brazilian Quaternary Geol Soc Amer, Spec Pap 84 433–451

BLANDIN, P 1977 La distribution géographique des Brassolinae (Lepidoptera—Nymphalidae) Faits et problemes, pp 161–218 in DESCIMON H (ed) Biogéographie et Evolution en Amerique tropicale Publ Lab Zool Ecole Normale Sup, 9 1–344

BONATTI, E GARTNER, S 1973 Caribbean climate during Pleistocene ice ages Nature 244 563–565

BREMER H 1973 Der Formungsmechanismus im tropischen Regenwald Amazoniens Z Geomorphol, Suppl 17 195–222

BRODKORB, P 1971 Origin and evolution of birds, pp 19–55 in FARNER, D S, KING, J R (eds) Avian Biology Vol 1 Academic Press, New York, 586 p

BROWN, K S, JR 1976 Geographical patterns of evolution in Neotropical Lepidoptera Systematics and derivation of known and new Heliconini (Nymphalidae Nymphalinae) J Entomol B (London) 44 201–242

BROWN K S, JR 1977a Geographical patterns of evolution in Neotropical forest Lepidoptera (Nymphalidae Ithomiinae—Heliconini) pp 118–160 in DESCIMON, H (ed) Biogéographie et Evolution en Amerique tropicale Publ Labor Zool Ecole Normale Sup 9 1–344

BROWN, K S, JR 1977b Centros de evolução refugios quaternarios, e conservação de patrimonios geneticos na região neotropical Padrões de diferenciação em Ithomiinae (Lepidoptera Nymphalidae) Acta Amazonica 7 75–137

BROWN, K S, JR, AB SABER A N 1979 Ice-age forest refugia and evolution in the Neotropics Correlation of paleoclimatological, geomorphological and pedological data with modern biological endemism Inst Geogr (Sao Paulo), Paleoclimas 5 30 p

BROWN K S JR, BENSON, W W 1977 Evolution in modern Amazonian non-forest islands Heliconius hermathena Biotropica 9 95–117

BROWN, K S, JR, SHEPPARD, P M, TURNER J R G 1974 Quaternary refugia in tropical America Evidence from race formation in Heliconius butterflies Proc Roy Soc London B, 187 369–378

CAMPBELL, K E, JR 1976 The late Pleistocene avifauna of La Carolina southwestern Ecuador Smithsonian Contrib Paleobiol 27 155–168

CAMPBELL, K L, JR 1979 The Pleistocene avifauna of the Talara tar seeps, northwestern Peru Royal Ontario Mus Life Sci Contrib (in press)

CARCASSON, R H 1964 A preliminary survey of the zoogeography of African butterflies East African Wildl J 2 122–157

CHAPMAN, F M 1917 The distribution of bird-life in Colombia A contribution to a biological survey of South America Bull Amer Mus Nat Hist 36 1–729

CHAPMAN, F M 1926 The distribution of bird life in Ecuador a contribution to the study of the origin of Andean bird life Ibid 55 1–784

COLE, M M 1960 Cerrado, caatinga and pantanal The distribution and origin of the savanna vegetation of Brasil Geogr J 126 166–179

CROIZAT, L 1958 Panbiogeography, 1 (The New World) Published by author, Caracas, Venezuela, 1058 p

CROIZAT L 1976 Biogeografia analitica y sintetica ("Panbiogeografia") de las Americas Biblioteca Acad Cien Fis, Mat Nat, Caracas, 15–16 1–890

CROIZAT, L NELSON C ROSEN, D F 1974 Centers of origin and related concepts Syst Zool 23 265–287

DAMUTH J E FAIRBRIDGE, R W 1970 Equatorial Atlantic deep-sea arkosic sands and ice age aridity in tropical South America Geol Soc Amer Bull 81 189–206

DESCIMON, H. 1977. Biogéographie, mimetisme et speciation dans le genre *Agrias* Doubleday (Lep., Nymphalidae, Charaxinae), pp 307-344 in DESCIMON, H. (ed) Biogéographie et Evolution en Amérique Tropicale. Publ Labor Zool Ecole Norm Sup 9 1-344

DIAMOND, J M 1976 Relaxation and differential extinction on land-bridge islands Applications to natural preserves Proc 16th Int Ornith Congr pp 616-628

DORST, J 1976 Historical factors influencing the richness and diversity of the South American avifauna Proc 16th Int Ornith Congr pp 17-35

DUELLMAN, W E 1972 South American frogs of the *Hyla rostrata* group (Amphibia, Anura, Hylidae) Zool Meded Rijks Mus Nat Hist Leiden 47(14) 177-192

DUELLMAN, W E 1978 The biology of an equatorial herpetofauna in Amazonian Ecuador Univ Kansas Mus Nat Hist Misc Publ (65) 1-352

DUELLMAN, W E, CRUMP, M L 1974 Speciation in frogs of the *Hyla parviceps* group in the upper Amazon Basin Univ Kansas Mus Nat Hist Occas Pap (23) 1-40

ECHTERNACHT, A C 1971 Middle American lizards of the genus *Ameiva* (Teiidae) with emphasis on geographic variation Univ Kansas Mus Nat Hist Misc Publ (55) 1-86

EDEN, M J 1974 Palaeoclimatic influences and the development of savanna in southern Venezuela J Biogeogr 1 95-109

EHRLICH, P R, GILBERT, L E 1973 Population structure and dynamics of the tropical butterfly *Heliconius ethilla* Biotropica 5 69-82

EMSLEY, M G 1965 Speciation in *Heliconius* (Lep, Nymphalidae) Morphology and geographic distribution Zoologica 50 191-254

ENDLER, J A 1977 Geographic variation, speciation and clines Monogr Popul Biol 10, Princeton Univ Press, Princeton, N J, 247 p

FAIRBRIDGE, R W 1976 Shellfish-eating Preceramic Indians in coastal Brazil Science 191 353-359

FITTKAU, E J 1969 The fauna of South America, pp 624-658 in FITTKAU, E J, ILLIES, J, KLINGE, H, SCHWABE, G H, SIOLI, H (eds) Biogeography and ecology in South America Vol 2 Junk, The Hague, 946 p

FITTKAU, E J 1974 Zur okologischen Gliederung Amazoniens. I Die erdgeschichtliche Entwicklung Amazoniens Amazoniana 5 77-134

FITZPATRICK, J W 1976 Systematics and biogeography of the Tyrannid genus *Todirostrum* and related genera (Aves) Bull Mus Comp Zool Harvard Univ 147 435-463

FOODEN, J 1972 Breakup of Pangaea and isolation of relict mammals in Australia South America and Madagascar Science 175 894-898

FORERO, E 1976 A revision of the American species of *Rourea* subgenus *Rourea* (Connaraceae) Mem New York Bot Garden 26 1-119

FOX, R M 1949 The evolution and systematics of the Ithomiidae (Lepidoptera) bull Univ Pittsburgh 45 36-47

FRANZLE, O 1976 Die Schwankungen des pleistozanen Hygroklimas in Sudost-Brasilien und Sudost-Afrika Biogeographica 7 143-162

GALLARDO, J M 1965 The species *Bufo granulosus* Spix (Salientia Bufonidae) and its geographic variation Bull Mus Comp Zool Harvard Univ 134 107-138

GALLARDO, J M 1972 Origen de las faunas sudamericanas de amfibios Comun Mus Argentino Cienc Nat "Bernardino Rivadavia" Inst Nac Invest Cien Nat Zool 4 17-32

GARNER, H F 1959 Stratigraphic-sedimentary significance of contemporary climate and relief in four regions of the Andes mountains Geol Soc Amer Bull 70 1327-1368

GARNER, H F 1966 Derangement of the Rio Caroni, Venezuela Rev Geomorphol Dynamique 2 53-80

GARNER, H F 1968 Tropical weathering and relief in FAIRBRIDGE, R W (ed) Encyclopedia of Geomorphology Vol 3 Reinhold Book Corp, New York, 1295 p

GARNER, H F 1974 The origin of landscapes Oxford Univ Press London, 734 p

GARNER, H F 1975 Rain forests, deserts and evolution An Acad Brasil Ciênc 47 127-133 (Suplemento)

GERY, J 1969 The freshwater fishes of South America, pp 828-848 in FITTKAU, E J, ILLIES, H KLINGE, H, SCHWABE, G H, SIOLI, H (eds) Biogeography and ecology in South America Vol 2, Junk, The Hague, 946 p

GOODLAND, R J A, IRWIN, H S 1975 Amazon jungle Green hell or red desert? An ecological discussion of the highway construction program in the Amazon basin Elsevier, New York, 156 p

GRAYSON, D K 1977 Pleistocene avifaunas and the overkill hypothesis Science 195 691-693

HAFFER, J 1967 Speciation in Colombian forest birds west of the Andes Amer Mus Novit (2294) 1-57

HAFFER, J 1969 Speciation in Amazonian forest birds Science 165 131-137

HAFFER, J 1970 Art-Entstehung bei einigen Waldvogeln Amazoniens J Ornith 111 285-331

HAFFER, J 1974 Avian speciation in tropical South America With a systematic survey of the toucans (Ramphastidae) and jacamars (Galbulidae) Publ Nuttall Ornithol Club, Cambridge (14) 1-390

HAFFER, J 1975 Avifauna of northwestern Colombia, South America Bonn Zool Monogr (7) 1-182

HAFFER, J 1978 Distribution of Amazon forest birds Bonn Zool Beitr 29 38-78

HAMMOND, A L 1977 Remote sensing I Landsat takes hold in South America II Brazil explores its Amazon wilderness Science 196 511-515

HEINE, K 1974 Bemerkungen zu neueren chronostratigraphischen Daten zum Verhaltnis glazialer und pluvialer Klimabedingungen Erdkunde 28 303-312

HELLMAYR, C E 1910 The birds of the Rio Madeira Novit Zool. 17 257-428.

HELLMAYR, C E 1912 Zoologische Ergebnisse einer Reise in das Mundungsgebiet des Amazonas II Vogel Abh Bayer Akad Wiss Math-Phys Kl 26(2) 1-142

HERSHKOVITZ, P 1968 Metachromism or the principle of evolutionary change in mammalian tegumentary colors Evolution 22 556-575

HERSHKOVITZ, P 1969 The Recent mammals of the Neotropical Region A zoogeographic and ecological review Q Rev Biol 44 1-70

HERSHKOVITZ, P 1972 The Recent mammals of the Neotropical region A zoogeographic and ecological review, pp 311-432 in KEAST, A, ERK, F C, CLASS, B (eds) Evolution, mammals, and southern continents State Univ New York Press, Albany, 543 p

HERSHKOVITZ, P 1978 Living New World monkeys (Platyrrhini) Vol 1 Univ Chicago Press, Chicago, 1117 p

HEYER, W R 1973 Systematics of the marmoratus group of the frog genus *Leptodactylus* (Amphibia, Leptodactylidae) Nat Hist Mus Los Angeles Cty Contrib Sci (251) 1-50

HOOGMOED, M S 1973 Notes on the herpetofauna of Surinam, IV The lizards and amphisbaenians of Surinam Biogeographica 4 Junk, The Hague, 419 p

HUECK, K 1966 Die Wälder Südamerikas Fischer, Stuttgart (Portuguese translation by H REICHARDT As Florestas da America do Sul, Sao Paulo 1972), 422 p

HUECK, K, SEIBERT, P 1972 Vegetationskarte von Sudamerika Fischer Stuttgart

HULTEN, E 1937 Outline of the history of arctic and boreal biota during the Quaternary period Thule, Stockholm, 168 p

IRION, G 1976 Die Entwicklung des zentral- und oberamazonischen Tieflands im Spat-Pleistozan und im Holozan Amazoniana 6 67-79

IRION, G, ABSY, M L 1978 Paleoclimate in central Amazonia is reflected by Quaternary sediments Tenth Int Congr Sedimentology, Jerusalem 1 331-332 (Abstract)

JACKSON, J F 1978 Differentiation in the genera *Enyalius* and *Strobilurus* (Iguanidae) Implications for Pleistocene climatic changes in eastern Brazil Arq de Zool Sao Paulo 30(1) 79 p

JOURNAUX, A 1975 Recherches geomorphologiques en Amazonie brésilienne Bull Cent Geomorph Caen 20 1-67

KEAST, A 1959 Vertebrate speciation in Australia Some comparisons between birds marsupials, and reptiles, pp 380-407 in LEEPER, G W (ed) Evolution of living organisms Melbourne Univ Press, p

KEAST, A 1961 Bird speciation on the Australian continent Bull Mus Comp Zool Harvard Univ 123 305-495

KINZEY, W G, GENTRY, A H 1979 Habitat utilization in two species of *Callicebus*, pp 89-100 in SUSSMAN, R (ed) Primate ecology—Problem-oriented field studies Wiley & Sons, New York (in press)

KINGDON, J 1971 East African mammals An atlas of evolution in Africa, Vol 1 Academic Press, London, 446 p

KLAMMER, G 1963 Zur Morphologie der Trummererze des Eisenquarzitmassivs von Urucum in Mato Grosso, Brasilien Z Geomorphol N F 7 289-307

KLAMMER, G 1971 Uber plio-pleistozane Terrassen im unteren Amazonasgebiet Ibid 15 62-106

KLAMMER, G 1975 Beobachtungen an Hangen im tropischen Regenwald des unteren Amazonas Ibid 19 273-296

LANGENHEIM, J H, LEE Y T, MARTIN, S S 1973 An evolutionary and ecological perspective of Amazonian Hylaea species of *Hymenaea* (Leguminosae Caesalpinioideae) Acta Amazônica 3 5-38

LATTIN, G DE 1957 Die Ausbreitungszentren der holarktischen Landtierwelt Verh Dtsch Zool Ges pp 380-410

LIVINGSTON, D A 1975 Late Quaternary climatic change in Africa Ann Rev Ecol Syst 6 249-280

LOWE-MCCONNELL, R H 1975 Fish Communities in tropical freshwaters Their distribution, ecology and evolution Longman, London, 377 p

MACNEISH, R S 1976 Early man in the New World Amer Sci 64 316-327

MARTIN, P S, WRIGHT, H E (eds) 1967 Pleistocene extinctions The search for a cause Yale Univ Press, New Haven, 453 p

MAYR, E 1942 Systematics and the origin of species Columbia Univ Press, New York (Dover Reprint, 1964), 334 p

MAYR E 1963 Animal species and evolution Harvard Univ Press, Cambridge, 797 p

MAYR E 1964 Inferences concerning the Tertiary American bird faunas Proc Natl Acad Sci 51 280-288

MEGGERS B J 1975 Application of the biological model of diversification to cultural distributions in tropical lowland South America Biotropica 7 141-161

MEGGERS, B J 1977 Vegetational fluctuation and prehistoric cultural adaptation in Amazonia Some tentative correlations World Archeol 8 257-303

MILLER, A H 1941 A review of centers of differentiation for birds in the western Great Basin region Condor 43 257-267

MILLIMAN, J D, SUMMERHAYES, C P, BARRETTO, H T 1975 Quaternary sedimentation on the Amazon continental margin A model Geol Soc Amer Bull 86 610-614

MOORE, H E, JR 1973 Palms in the tropical forest ecosystems of Africa and South America, pp 63-88 in MEGGERS, B J, AYENSU, E S, DUCKWORTH W D (eds) Tropical forest ecosystems in Africa and South America A comparative review Smithsonian Inst Press, Washington 350 p

MOREAU, R E 1963 Vicissitudes of the African biomes in the late Pleistocene Proc Zool Soc London 141 395-421

MOREAU, R E 1966 The Bird Faunas of Africa and its islands Academic Press, New York, 424 p

MORLEY, T 1975 The South American distribution of the Memecyleae (Melastomataceae) in relation to the Guiana area and to the question of forest refuges in Amazonia Phytologia 31 279–296

MOUSINHO, M R 1971 Upper Quaternary process changes of the middle Amazon area Geol Soc Amer Bull 82 1073–1078

MOYNIHAN, M 1976 The New World Primates Adaptive radiation and the evolution of social behavior, languages, and intelligence Princeton Univ Press, Princeton, N J , 363 p

MULLER, P 1968 Die Herpetofauna der Insel von São Sebastião (Brasilien) Saarbrucker Zeitung, Saarbrucken, 68 p

MULLER, P 1970 Vertebratenfaunen brasilianischer Inseln als Indikatoren fur glaziale und postglaziale Vegetationsfluktuationen Abhandl Dtsch Zool Ges Wurzburg 1969 97–107

MULLER, P 1972 Centres of dispersal and evolution in the Neotropical Region Studies on the Neotropical Fauna 7 173–185

MULLER, P 1973 The dispersal centres of terrestrial vertebrates in the Neotropical Realm Junk The Hague, 244 p

MULLER, P , WEIMER, G 1976 Bemerkungen zu den Verbreitungszentren der sudamerikanischen Callichthyiden und Cichliden Amazoniana 6 105–121

MULLER P , STEINICKE, F 1977 Chorologie und Differzierungsgeschwindigkeit brasilianischer Liolaemus-Arten (Sauria, Iguanidae) Verhandl Ges Ökologie, Kiel, pp 429–440

MYERS, C W 1973 A new genus for Andean snakes related to Lygophis boursieri and a new species (Colubridae) Amer Mus Novit (2522) 1–37

MYERS, C W 1974 The systematics of Rhadinaea (Colubridae), a genus of New World snakes Bull Amer Mus Nat Hist 153 1–262

MYERS, C W , DALY, J W 1976 Preliminary evaluation of skin toxins and vocalizations in taxonomic and evolutionary studies of poison-dart frogs (Dendrobatidae) Ibid 157 173–262

PARMENTER, C , FOLGER, D W 1974 Eolian biogenic detritus in deep sea sediments A possible index of equatorial ice age aridity Science 185 695–698

PATTERSON, B , PASCUAL, R 1968 The fossil mammal fauna of South America Q Rev Biol 43 409–451

PAULA COUTO, C DE 1975 Mamíferos fósseis do Quaternario do sudeste brasileiro Int Symp on the Quaternary, southern Brazil (July 1975), Spec Contrib , Bol Paranaense de Geociencias 33 89–132

PLATNICK, N J NELSON, G 1978 A method of analysis for historical biogeography Syst Zool 27 1–16

PRANCE, G T 1973 Phytogeographic support for the theory of Pleistocene forest refuges in the Amazon basin, based on evidence from distribution patterns in Caryocaraceae Chrysobalanaceae, Dichapetalaceae and Lecythidaceae Acta Amazônica 3 5–28

PRANCE, G T , ELIAS, T S (eds) 1977 Extinction is forever Threatened and endangered species of plants in the Americas and their significance in ecosystems today and in the future New York Botanical Garden, 437 p

PRELL, W 1973 Evidence for Sargasso Sea-like conditions in the Colombia Basin Caribbean Sea, during glacial periods Geol Soc Amer Abstr Progr 1973 Meetings, Dallas p 771

RAVEN, P H , AXELROD, D I 1974 Angiosperm biogeography and past continental movements Ann Missouri Bot Garden 61 539–673

RAVEN, P H , AXELROD, D I 1975 History of the flora and fauna of Latin America Amer Sci 63 420–329

REBOUÇAS-SPIEKER, R 1974 Distribution and differentiation of animals along the coast and in continental islands of the State of São Paulo, Brasil 2 Lizards of the genus Mabuya (Sauria, Scincidae) Pap Avul Zool Sao Paulo 28 197–240

REINIG W F 1937 Die Holarktis Ein Beitrag zur diluvialen and alluvialen Geschichte der zirkumpolaren Faunen- und Florengebiete Fischer, Jena, 124 p

REINIG, W F 1938a Elimination und Selektion Eine Untersuchung uber Merkmalsprogressionen bei Tieren und Pflanzen auf genetisch- und historisch-chorologischer Grundlage Fischer, Jena, 146 p

REINIG, W F 1938b On the history of Holarctic floral and faunal habitats in the Quaternary period Res Prog 4 67–72

REINIG W F 1950 Chorologische Voraussetzungen fur die Analyse von Formenkreisen, pp 346–378 in JORDANS, A VON, PEUS, F (eds) Syllegomena Biologica, Festschrift Otto Kleinschmidt Ziemsen, Wittenberg 472 p

REMINGTON, C L 1968 Suture-zones of hybrid interaction between recently joined biotas, pp 321–428 in DOBZHANSKY, I (ed) Evolutionary Biology Vol 2 Appleton-Century-Crofts, New York, 458 p

ROSEN, D E 1978 Vicariant patterns and historical explanation in biogeography Syst Zool 27 159–188

SARMA, A V N 1974 Holocene paleoecology of south coastal Ecuador Proc Amer Philos Soc 118 (1) 93–134

SAVAGE, J M 1974 The Isthmian link and the evolution of Neotropical mammals Nat Hist Mus Los Angeles Cty Contr Sci (260) 1–51

SCHWERDTFEGER, W (ed) 1976 Climates of Central and South America World survey of climatology Vol 12 Elsevier, Amsterdam, 532 p

Sclater, P. L., Salvin, O. 1867. List of birds collected by Mr. Wallace on the lower Amazons and Rio Negro. Proc. Zool. Soc. London 1867: 566–596.

Sellander, R. K. 1971. Systematics and speciation in birds, pp. 57–147 in Farner, D. S., King, J. R. (eds.). Avian Biology Vol. 1. Academic Press, New York. 586 p.

Sheppard, P. M., Turner, J. R. G., Brown, K. S., Jr., Benson, W. W. 1978. Genetics and the evolution of Mullerian mimicry in *Heliconius* butterflies. Phil. Trans. Roy. Soc. London (in press).

Short, L. L. 1975. A zoogeographic analysis of the South American Chaco avifauna. Bull. Amer. Mus. Nat. Hist. 154: 163–352.

Sick, H. 1965. A fauna do cerrado. Arq. Zool. (Sao Paulo) 12: 71–93.

Sick, H. 1966. As aves do cerrado como fauna arborícola. An. Acad. Brasil. Cienc. 38: 355–363.

Sick, H. 1967. Rios e enchentes na Amazonia como obstaculo para a avifauna, pp. 495–520 in Lent, H. (ed.). Atas do Simposio sobre a Biota Amazônica Vol. 5 (Zool.). Conselho Nacional de Pesquisas, Rio de Janeiro. 603 p.

Silverstone, P. A. 1975. A revision of the poison-arrow frogs of the genus *Dendrobates* Wagler. Nat. Hist. Mus. Los Angeles Cty. Sci. Bull. (21) 1–55.

Silverstone, P. A. 1976. A revision of the poison-arrow frogs of the genus *Phyllobates* Bibron in Sagra (family Dendrobatidae). Ibid. (27) 1–53.

Simpson, B. B., Haffer, J. 1978. Speciation patterns in the Amazonian forest biota. Ann. Rev. Ecol. Syst. 9: 497–518.

Simpson, D. R. 1972. Especiacion en las plantas lenosas de la Amazonia peruana relacionada a las fluctuaciones climaticas durante el Pleistoceno. Resumenes del 1 Congr. Latinoamericano de Botan., Mexico.

Sioli, H. 1957. Sedimentation im Amazonasgebiet. Geol. Rundschau 45: 608–633.

Snethlage, L. 1913. Uber die Verbreitung der Vogelarten in Unteramazonien. J. Ornithol. 61: 169–539.

Solbrig, O. T. 1976. The origin and floristic affinities of the South American temperate desert and semidesert regions, pp. 7–49 in Goodall, D. W. (ed.). Evolution of Desert Biota. Univ. Texas Press, Austin. 250 p.

Sombroek, W. G. 1966. Amazon soils. Wageningen, 303 p.

Spassky, B., Richmond, R. C., Perez-Salas, S., Pavlovsky, O., Mourão, C. A., Hunter, A. S., Hoenigsberg, H., Dobzhansky, T., Ayala, F. J. 1971. Geography of the sibling species related to *Drosophila willistoni*, and of the semispecies of the *Drosophila paulistorum* complex. Evolution 25: 129–143.

Stresemann, E. 1919. Uber die europäischen Gimpel. Beitr. Zoogeogr. Paläarkt. Region 1: 25–56.

Tricart, J. 1959. Divisão morfoclimatica do Brasil Atlantico Central. Biol. Paulista Geogr. 31: 3–44.

Tricart, J. 1974. Existence de periodes seches au Quaternaire en Amazonie et dans les regions voisines. Rev. Géomorph. Dynamique 4: 145–158.

Tricart, J. 1975. Influence des oscillations climatiques recentes sur le modele en Amazonie Orientale (Region de Santarem) d'apres les images radar lateral. Z. Geomorphol. N.F. 19: 140–163.

Turner, J. R. C. 1965. Evolution of complex polymorphism and mimicry in distasteful South American butterflies. Proc. XII Intern. Congr. Entomol. London (1964) 267.

Turner, J. R. C. 1971. Studies of Mullerian mimicry and its evolution in Burnet moths and heliconid butterflies, pp. 224–260 in Creed, R. (ed.). Ecological genetics and evolution. Blackwell Scient. Publ. Co. Oxford. 391 p.

Turner, J. R. G. 1976a. Muellerian mimicry. Classical beanbag evolution and the role of ecological islands in adaptive race formation, pp. 185–218 in Karlin, S., Nevo, E. (eds.). Population genetics and ecology. Academic Press, New York, 832 p.

Turner, J. R. G. 1976b. Adaptive radiation and convergence in subdivisions of the butterfly genus *Heliconius* (Lepidoptera Nymphalidae). J. Zool. 58: 297–308.

Turner, J. R. G. 1977. Forest refuges as ecological islands. Disorderly extinction and the adaptive radiation of muellerian mimics, pp. 98–117 in Descimon, H. (ed.). Biogeographie et Evolution en Amérique Tropicale. Publ. Labor. Zool. Ecole Normale Sup. 9: 1–344.

Udvardy, M. D. F. 1969. Dynamic Zoogeography. Reinhold, New York. 445 p.

van der Hammen, T. 1972. Changes in vegetation and climate in the Amazon basin and surrounding areas during the Pleistocene. Geol. Mijnbouw 51: 641–643.

van der Hammen, T. 1974. The Pleistocene changes of vegetation and climate in tropical South America. J. Biogeogr. 1: 3–26.

van der Hammen, T., Werner, J. H., van Dommelen, H. 1973. Palynological record of the upheaval of the northern Andes. A study of the Pliocene and Lower Quaternary of the Colombian Eastern Cordillera and the early evolution of its high-Andean biota. Rev. Palaeobot. Palynol. 16: 1–122.

van Geel, B., van der Hammen, T. 1973. Upper Quaternary vegetational and climatic sequence of the Fuquene area (Eastern Cordillera Colombia). Palaeogeogr. Palaeoclimatol. Palaeoecol. 14: 9–92.

Vanzolini, P. E. 1970. Zoologia sistematica geografica e origem das especies. Inst. Geogr., Univ. São Paulo, Teses Monogr. 3: 1–56.

Vanzolini, P. E. 1973. Paleoclimates, relief and species multiplication in equatorial forests, pp. 255–258 in Meggers, B. J., Ayensu, E. S., Duckworth, W. D. (eds.). Tropical forest ecosystems in Africa and South America. A comparative review. Smithsonian Inst. Press, Washington. 350 p.

VANZOLINI, P E 1974 Ecological and geographical distribution of lizards in Pernambuco northeastern Brazil (Sauria) Pap Avul Zool (São Paulo) 28 61–90

VANZOLINI, P E, AB SABER, A N 1968 Divergence rate in South American lizards of the genus *Liolaemus* (Sauria Iguanidae) Ibid 21 205–208

VANZOLINI, P E, WILLIAMS, E E 1970 South American anoles The geographic differentiation and evolution of the *Anolis chrysolepis* species group (Sauria Iguanidae) Arq Zool (São Paulo) 19 1–298

VUILLEUMIER, B S 1971 Pleistocene changes in the fauna and flora of South America Science 173 771–780

VUILLEUMIER, F 1975 Zoogeography, pp 421–496 in FARNER, D S, KING, J R (eds) Avian biology Vol 5 Academic Press New York, 586 p

WALLACE, A R 1853 A Narrative of travels on the Amazon and Rio Negro Reeve and Co, London Dover reprint (1972) of Ed 2, 1889, 363 p

WEBB, S D 1978 A history of savanna vertebrates in the New World Part II South America and the great interchange Ann Rev Ecol Syst 9 393–426

WETTERBERG, G B, JORGE PADUA, M T, CASTRO C S DE 1976 Uma análise de prioridades em conservação da natureza na Amazonia Seria Técnica, 8 Ministerio de Agricultura Inst Brasil Desenvolvimento Florestal, Brasilia, 62 p

WIJMSTRA, T A, VAN DER HAMMEN, T 1966 Palynological data on the history of tropical savannas in northern South America Leidse Geol Meded 38 71–83

WILLIS, E O 1969 On the behavior of five species of *Rhegmatorhina*, ant-following antbirds of the Amazon basin Wilson Bull 81 363–395

WILSON, E O, WILLIS, E O 1975 Applied biogeography, pp 522–534 in CODY, M L, DIAMOND, J M (eds) Ecology and evolution of communities Harvard Univ Press, Cambridge, 545 p

WINGE, H 1973 Races of *Drosophila willistoni* sibling species Probable origin in Quaternary forest refuges of South America Genetics 74 (suppl) 297–298

WOLF, J A 1971 Tertiary climatic fluctuations and methods of analysis of Tertiary floras Palaeogeogr Palaeoclimatol Palaeoecol 9 27–57

ZONNEVELD, J S 1968 Quaternary climatic changes in the Caribbean and N South America Eiszeitalter Ggw 19 203–208

ZONNEVELD, J S 1975 Some problems of tropical geomorphology Z Geomorphol N F 19 377–392

APPENDIX

APPENDIX 5 1—Postulated Quaternary Forest Refugia in the Neotropical Region

In the following list brief descriptions are given of 40 Quaternary forest refugia in the Neotropical Region postulated by several authors during the last ten years (Haffer, Vanzolini Muller, Prance, Brown Sheppard Turner see compilation and table in Brown, 1976 228–235, 1977a,b) These refugia probably were viable during one or another adverse climatic period or even repeatedly during the Quaternary Their locations are illustrated in figure 5 8

Middle American Refugia

1 Guatemala refuge Caribbean slope and foreland
2 Caribbean Costa Rica Caribbean slope and foreland
3 Chiriquí refuge Pacific slopes of southeastern Costa Rica and southwestern Panama
4 Darién refuge Mountains of eastern Panama

Peri-Andean Refugia

5 Nechi refuge Northern base of Colombian cordilleras
6 Chocó refuge Western slope and foreland of Cordillera Occidental of Colombia
7 Chimborazo refuge Western base and foreland of Cordillera Occidental in Ecuador (about 1° north to 2° south)
8 Cauca refuge Upper Rio Cauca Valley in south-central Colombia
9 Magdalena refuge lower eastern slopes of Central Cordillera of Colombia
10 Catatumbo refuge eastern base of Sierra de Perijá in northwestern Venezuela and northeastern Colombia (westernmost Maracaibo basin)
11 Rancho Grande refuge Coastal Venezuelan mountains
12 Sucre/Trinidad refuge Paria Peninsula and mountains of Trinidad
13 Apure refuge Eastern lowlands adjacent to junction of Venezuelan Merida mountains with Eastern Cordillera of Colombia
14 Villavicencio refuge Eastern base of Eastern Colombian Cordillera from Villavicencio south to behind Serrania de la Macarena
15 Putumayo refuge Upper rios Caqueta and Putumayo in Mocoa region and north into extreme upper Magdalena Valley southeastern Colombia
16 Abitigua refuge Upper rios Napo and Pastaza, above Puyo and Macas regions in eastern Ecuador
17 Napo refuge Lowlands of northern Peru and eastern Ecuador crossed by rios Caquetá, Putumayo, Napo and lower Pastaza, often combined with previous two refugia
18 Marañon refuge Southeast and east slopes of Andes in extreme south Ecuador and north Peru, above junction of Rio Santiago with Rio Marañon
19 Huallaga refuge Middle and upper Huallaga Valley from Moyobamba to above Tingo Maria, central Peru
20 Ucayali refuge Lower Andean slopes of Rio Pachitea Valley
21 Chanchamayo refuge Upper Perene and Apurimac Rivers, in broad high-elevation valleys

22 Inamban refuge Eastern base and foreland of Andes in extreme southeastern Perú, tributaries of upper Río Madre de Dios
23 Yungas refuge Yungas of La Paz south to area north of Cochabamba (Bolivia), extending to lowland forests northwest of Santa Cruz
24 Guipore refuge South slopes of the Sierra dos Parecís, southwestern Brasil

Guiana Shield Refugia

25 Imataca refuge Slopes of Sierra de Imataca south of Orinoco delta
26 Roraima refuge Slopes of Pacaraima and Parima Mountains and Roraima Mountains from Mt Auyantepui to the east
27 Ventuari refuge Slopes encircling Rio Ventuari southern Venezuela
28 Imeri refuge Slopes and forelands of Sierra Imeri, extreme northwestern Brasil and southern Venezuela
29 Guiana refuge Southern Surinam and southeastern Guyana, possibly also comprising forests northwest of Manaus, northern Brasil
30 Oyapock refuge Eastern, forested part of Tumuc-Humac Mountains on the border of Cayenne (French Guiana) and Amapá, Brasil

Amazon Basin Refugia

31 Belem refuge Lowlands southeast of Belem to western and southern Maranhão Brasil
32 Tapajos refuge Low hills in southwestern Para, Brasil from Itaituba on the Rio Tapajós south to the Serra do Cachimbo
33 Rondônia refuge Hill region between Rio Jiparana and upper Rio Roosevelt, Rondonia, Brasil
34 Madeira refuge Lowlands between Rios Madeira and lower Purus, north of Humaitá, Brasil
35 Tefe refuge Lowlands between the lower Purús and Juruá rivers, south of Tefé (=Ega), Brasil
36 Loreto refuge Lowlands east and west of the middle Rio Javary, Brasil/Peru border

Brasilian Shield Refugia

37 Araguaia refuge Forests from Jatu, Goias, Brasil north along ridges to central Goias
38 Pernambuco refuge Atlantic slope of hill country in Pernambuco and Alagoas northeastern Brasil
39 Bahia refuge Hills near base of mountains facing Atlantic Ocean from Bahia south to northern Espírito Santo, Brasil
40 Rio de Janeiro refuge Foothills and mountain slopes of Serra dos Orgãos, Serra da Bocaina, Serra de Itatiaia, and Serra da Cantareira

Jackson (1978) reconstructed and named several refugia in eastern Brasil on the basis of climatic data and his study of the geographical differentiation of a group of forest lizards (genus *Enyalius*)

Forest Remnants

Remnant forests exist under present climatic conditions on isolated mountains in generally dry northeastern Brasil (e g, Serra de Ibiapabá, Serrania de Batunte) and in central Brasil forming minirefugia

Islands

A Sierra Nevada de Santa Marta Montane island in northern Colombia Endemic elements inhabit moderate to high elevations Tropical species of forest along seaward and southeastern sides are mostly undifferentiated, related to Nechi forms
B Tobago Island near Trinidad
C Eastern Marajó Scrubby forest at the eastern tip of Marajo Island in the mouth of the Amazon harbors a number of differentiated forms of butterflies
D Tapará Isolated ridges in the Amazon opposite the mouth of the Rio Tapajos (Santarem)

6. Late Cenozoic Environmental Changes in Temperate Argentina

Ana María Báez
*Departamento de Geología
Facultad de Ciencias Exactas y Naturales
Universidad de Buenos Aires
Buenos Aires, Argentina*

Gustavo Juan Scillato Yané
*Facultad de Ciencias Naturales y Museo
Universidad Nacional de La Plata
La Plata, Argentina*

Present temperate South America lies mainly south of the Tropic of Capricorn (23°27'S) According to the Koppen climatic classification, based on both temperature and rainfall temperate climates are found in a large area including most of Paraguay, parts of Bolivia Brasil and Argentina, and Uruguay, as well as in a region along the Pacific coast south of 38°S (Eidt 1969) Nevertheless, we also have taken into consideration Patagonia and a strip of land lying in the rain shadow east of the Andes, where arid climates now prevail (Eidt, 1969) Their inclusion is justified because the geological events that provoked the development of increasing xeric conditions in Patagonia and the sub-Andean area also delineated the physical features and the basic climatic distribution that presently exists in the other regions here considered

From the climatic point of view an east-west change from the more humid eastern regions to the dry regions close to the Andes overlaps a latitudinal change between the warm north and the cool temperate south Thus, within the extensive area under consideration, several major regions can be recognized besides the Andean one Those in the Argentinian territory, to which we will refer principally are Mesopotamia Chaco Pampean Plain Sud Andean Region, and Patagonia (Fig 6 1)

Mesopotamia is distinctly defined geographically by the Río Paraná and the Río Uruguay Extensive lowlands, the Chaco-Pampean Plains, extend to the west of Mesopotamia At the western border of the plains are the easternmost slopes of the Sub-Andean Ranges (in the north) and the faulted blocks of the Pampean Ranges (in the south) West of these is the Sud-Andean Region, which extends west to the foot of the Andes The most southern region is Patagonia with its northern limit coinciding approximately with the Río Colorado

In this paper we discuss the different lines of evidence concerning the environmental changes that occurred in those regions since late Miocene times It is pertinent to point out here that particularly in this part of South America neither the majority of the lithostratigraphical units of the Cenozoic nor the chronostratigraphical ones (especially Stages) have been established formally The latter are the base upon which the corresponding chronological intervals (Ages), or geochronological units, are differentiated according to the American Code of Stratigraphical Nomenclature On the other hand, the faunistic content, fundamentally mammals, of the non-marine deposits has been comparatively well studied The results of these studies have permitted the establishment of a sequence of Provincial or Land-Mammal Ages, based on the characteristics of the mammal assemblages Tentatively, these Ages have been referred to the world-wide accepted Epochs (Simpson, 1940 Pascual et al, 1965) The stratigraphy and chronology of the continental Cenozoic, not only in the region considered here but in South America as a whole, are based mainly on the sequence of mamma-

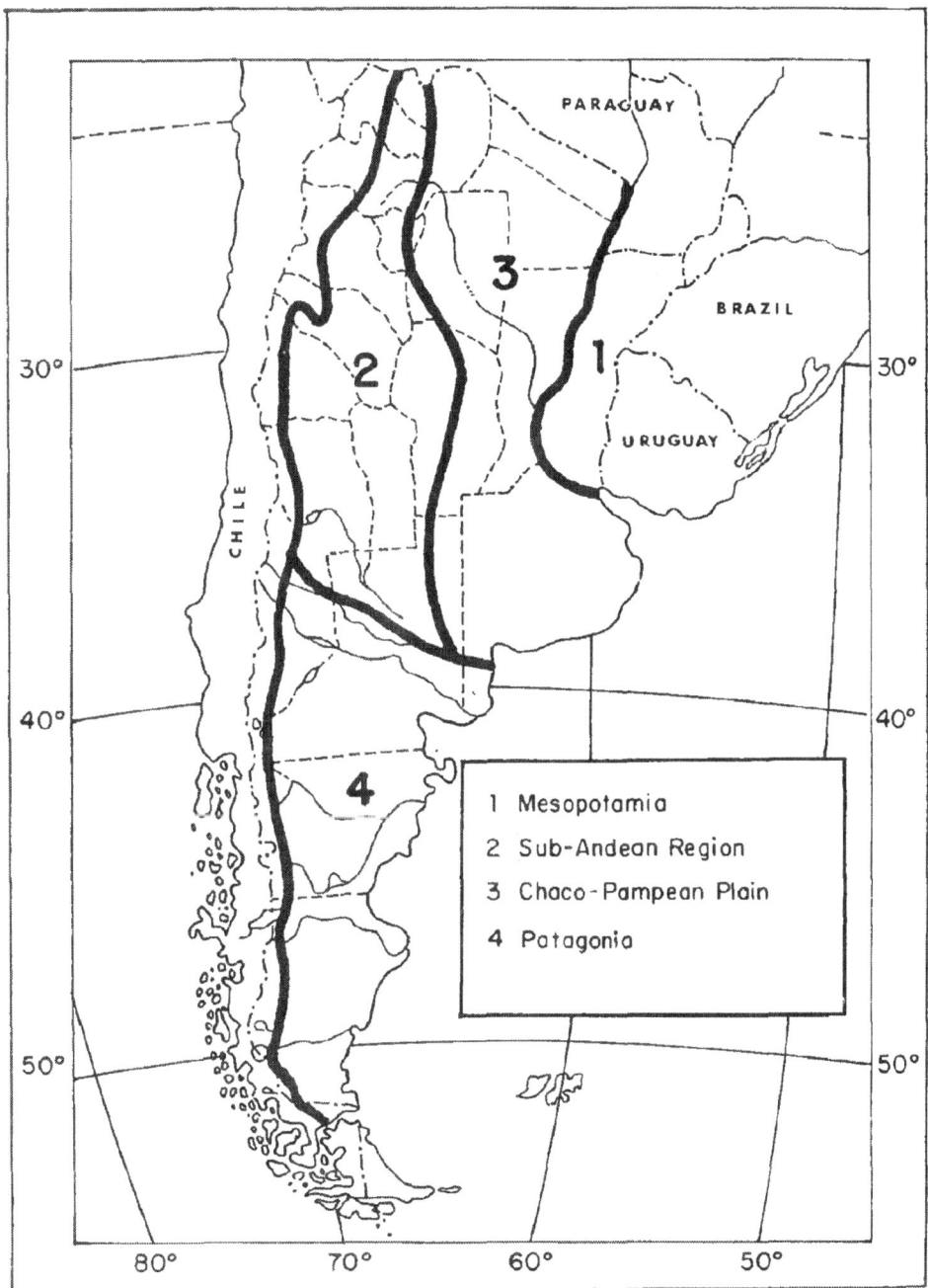

Fig. 6:1. Regions in the Argentinian territory considered in the text.
Regiones del territorio argentino consideradas en el texto.

lian faunas. The Provincial Ages assigned to the Pliocene and Pleistocene Epochs as well as the principal lithostratigraphical units referred to them are shown in figures 6.2–3. No reliable radiometric dates of the latter ages are available.

The chronology used in this paper is the one usually applied by South American paleontologists. Thus, the Miocene–Pliocene boundary is placed 10–12 m.y.b.p. However, recent studies in the European type areas indicate that this boundary should be placed about 5.5 m.y.b.p. This formal change implies the reference of the Chasicoan and Huayquerian Ages to the Miocene.

GENERAL CONDITIONS DURING THE MIOCENE

An understanding of the environmental changes that occurred during the late Cenozoic in temperate South America must take into consideration the conditions existing in geologically earlier times. To be more precise, the late Cenozoic changes are the culmination of processes that began in the late Miocene.

Early and middle Miocene (Santacruzian Age) sedimentary rocks are exposed in southern Patagonia, where they extend to the austral end of the continent. A milder and more equable climate at that time should have permitted the presence of a biota in latitudes up to 50°S which has extant relatives living mainly in subtropical forested areas. That is the case, for instance, of ceboid monkeys, echimyid rodents, myrmecophagid and megatherioid edentates, among the latter are the Megalonychidae and Nothotheriinae which are closely related to living tree sloths (Pascual, 1970; Pascual and Odreman Rivas 1971). Nevertheless, since the early Tertiary in Patagonia the herbivorous mammals show increasing dental adaptations indicating the spread of grasslands (Pascual and Odreman Rivas, 1971; Patterson and Pascual 1972).

In the late Miocene (Friasian Age) sedimentation predominantly occurred in piedmont areas of the northern Patagonian Andes, as well as in northern Patagonia. A pronounced uplift at that time is indicated by the abundance of psephitic material coming from the neighboring Andes (Pascual and Odreman Rivas 1971). This is consistent with other evidence based on radiometric studies indicating an increase in Andean tectonics from the late Miocene onwards (Rutland, Guest and Crastley, 1965). As a consequence of those movements, the Patagonian Andes reached sufficient elevations so as to act as a barrier to the moisture-laden Pacific winds. This had a profound ecological effect in the development of increasing xeric conditions in Patagonia and the subsequent impoverishment of the biota. Many savanna-woodland adapted animals retreated northwards while others, perhaps more eurythermal ones, survived in the more humid western area or west of the Andes (Gasparini and Báez, 1975; Báez and Gasparini, 1977). Paleobotanical data also show this pattern (Menendez, 1971: 364). Possibly there was a marked lowering of mean temperatures, especially in the southernmost region. Berggren and Van Couvering (1974) suggested that an extensive ice sheet was present in western Antarctica from 7 to 10 m.y.b.p. (early Pliocene according to the chronology used in this paper). Thus, temperatures might have been significantly cooler than in earlier times.

A progressive climatic deterioration in Patagonia, at least since the Miocene, is indicated by palynological data from deep-sea cores from the southwestern Atlantic Ocean (Groot et al, 1967). The Miocene assemblages have a high percentage of arboreal pollen and the appearance of a few xerophytic elements (such as *Ephedra*) which are absent in Eocene assemblages and abundant in the Pleistocene ones.

The "Parmense Sea" constituted a conspicuous geographic feature in late Miocene times. This Atlantic transgression extended over most of the Chaco-Pampean region and western Mesopotamia, from northeastern Patagonia to southern Paraguay (Camacho 1967).

PERIOD	EPOCH		LAND MAMMAL AGES OR PROVINCIAL AGES	LITHOSTRATIGRAPHICAL UNITS			
				N PATAGONIA	PAMPEAN PLAIN	MESOPOTAMIA	SUBANDEAN REGION
TERTIARY	PLIOCENE	LATE	MONTEHERMOSAN	?	CHAPADMALAL FM. / MONTE HERMOSO FM.	?	?
		MIDDLE	HUAYQUERIAN	"RIONEGRENSE"	EPECUEN FM.	"MESOPOTAMIENSE"	"ARAUCANENSE"
		EARLY	CHASICOAN	?	ARROYO CHASICO FM.	?	?

FIG. 6:2. Pliocene South American Provincial Ages and main referable mammal-bearing lithostratigraphical units in the regions under study.
Edades Provinciales pliocénicas sudamericanas y principales unidades litoestratigráficas mamalíferas referibles en las regiones estudiadas.

CLIMATE-ECOLOGICAL CONDITIONS FROM PLIOCENE TO HOLOCENE TIMES

It should be stressed that the fossiliferous nonmarine deposits of early Paleocene to late Miocene age are well represented in Patagonia, whereas Pliocene and Pleistocene units are exposed principally to the north of Patagonia. By the late Miocene, a continuous regional uplift began in Patagonia; this uplift gradually created the present physiographic features at the same time that the Pampean Plain probably came into prominence.

The Plio-Pleistocene and Pleistocene-Holocene Boundaries

On a world-wide basis no significant stratigraphic or faunal discontinuity exists between the Pliocene and Pleistocene, as they are defined at present; thus a distinction between a Tertiary and Quaternary periods is invalid and rather artificial (Flint, 1965; Hays and Berggren, 1971; Berggren and van Couvering, 1974). As is discussed below, in the region under consideration the available data suggest that the climatic-ecological changes from Pliocene to Pleistocene times have not been drastic, especially in the Pampean Plain, where sequences of that age are known. This poses the problem of the recognition of the Plio-Pleistocene boundary (Pascual and Fidalgo, 1972). Nevertheless, the study of the mammalian faunas has provided a criterion for placing the boundary at the time of an event of great zoogeographic importance—the establishment of a direct land connection between North and South America, which allowed a faunal interchange. The appearance

PERIOD	EPOCH	LAND MAMMAL AGES OR PROVINCIAL AGES	LITHOSTRATIGRAPHICAL UNITS	
			PAMPEAN PLAIN	
			ATLANTIC COAST	NE BUENOS AIRES PROVINCE
QUATERNARY	PLEISTOCENE LATE	LUJANIAN	LOBERIA FM. SANTA ISABEL FM. ARROYO SECO FM.	LUJAN FM. BUENOS AIRES FM.
	PLEISTOCENE MIDDLE	ENSENADAN	MIRAMAR FM.	ENSENADA FM.
	PLEISTOCENE EARLY	UQUIAN	VOROHUE FM. BARRANCAS DE LOS LOBOS FM.	? "PRE-ENSENADENSE" PUELCHES FM.

Fig. 6:3. Pleistocene South American Provincial Ages and main referable mammal-bearing lithostratigraphical units in the regions under study.
Edades Provinciales pleistocénicas sudamericanas y principales unidades litoestratigráficas mamalíferas referibles en las regiones estudiadas.

of Nearctic mammals in the South American fossil record is the basis for correlation between the Land-Mammal Ages of both continents. Immigrants of known South American ancestry (megalonychid and mylodontid edentates) are first recorded in North America in the Hemphillian Mammal Age (middle Pliocene) (Hirschfeld and Webb, 1968). In South America, mammals of Nearctic origin (procyonid carnivores) appear in deposits corresponding to the Huayuerian Age, which mainly for that reason has been tentatively referred to the middle Pliocene (Pascual et al., 1965). A greater number of northern immigrants (cricetine rodents, a skunk and a peccary) are recorded in the Montehermosan (Reig, 1952) and many more in the Uquian. Many taxa of South American origin occur in Blancan-early Irvingtonian deposits in North America; thus, the Uquian has been grossly correlated with those faunal ages (Webb, 1976). According to this and the radiometric dates established for western North America, the Plio-Pleistocene boundary could be placed in the early Uquian (Marshall and Pascual, 1979).

The recognition of the Holocene as a distinct epoch has been criticized by some workers, who consider the Holocene to be only an interglacial interval within the Pleistocene. The massive extinction of the megafauna is the paleontological criterion used to place the Pleistocene-Holocene boundary. This extinction is verified at the end of the Lujanian Age in South America and in late Rancholabrean Age in North America (Martin, 1975), thereby providing some possible correlation of both ages (Pascual et al., 1965).

Nevertheless, a few elements of the megafauna survived into Holocene times. For example the ground-sloth *Mylodon* is known from deposits younger than 5394 ± 55 y b p in southern Chile (Saxon, 1976).

Glaciations

Very often the concept of the Quaternary has been equated with the Ice Age and the base of the Pleistocene considered synchronous with the onset of glaciation. But, in fact, climatic deterioration began to accelerate about 10 million years ago (early Pliocene) (Berggren and Van Couvering, 1974). Different lines of evidence indicate the occurrence of glaciation in polar and mountainous areas of both hemispheres at least since Pliocene times (Curry, 1966; Hays and Opdyke, 1967; Fleck et al., 1972; Mercer and Sander, 1975), but this does not imply the synchronous presence of lowland ice sheets in temperate regions.

The four classic Pleistocene glaciations of Europe (Gunz, Mindel, Riss, Wurm) traditionally have been correlated to those of North America (Nebraskan, Kansan, Illinoian, Wisconsin), but the problem is complex and has been oversimplified. Recent evidence has led to a complete revision of that scheme, and accurate intercontinental correlation of glacial events is still under debate (Berggren and Van Couvering, 1974). Widely differing opinions have been expressed concerning the number of major glacial episodes as well as the extension of glaciated areas in southern South America.

Four postulated major glaciations (Vallimanca, Colorado, Diamante, Atuel) on the Argentinian side of the Andes have been correlated with the classic four glaciations in the Northern Hemisphere by Groeber (1952, 1954). He contended that during the first two assumed glacial events, which were ascribed to the "Eoquaternary," extensive ice sheets covered the Andean region and Patagonia. In northern Patagonia glaciers were supposed to have reached the Atlantic Ocean south of Río Colorado. The other two glaciations were referred to the "Neoquaternary" and were restricted mainly to the Andean region. The existence of local centers of glaciation in Patagonia and the advance of a postulated "great Somuncurá glacier" extending to the sea during the youngest glaciations also have been suggested by Auer (1956, 1958, 1960, 1974).

Such schemes have been mostly discarded for recent investigations have demonstrated that much of the evidence of glacial action upon which those hypothesis were based are the result of different geomorphological processes (Polanski, 1963, 1965; Methol 1967; Fidalgo and Riggi 1970; Fidalgo, 1973). There is now general agreement that east of the Patagonian Andes glaciation extended for a relatively short distance reaching the present Atlantic coast only south of about 52°S (Antevs, 1929; Caldenius 1932; Flint and Fidalgo, 1963, 1968). On the other hand westward flowing glaciers reached the Pacific Ocean as far north as 43°S (Mercer 1976). The glaciated areas progressively decreased northwards, where they were confined mainly to mountainous areas even during full glacial times (Groeber, 1936; Frenguelli, 1957b).

Generally, three or four glaciations have been recognized on the eastern side of the Patagonian Andes although the interpretation of those glacial events has differed. They have been considered either as minor episodes roughly equivalent to the Wurm-Wisconsin and perhaps also to an older event (Caldenius, 1932; Flint and Fidalgo, 1963, 1968) or as different major glaciations (Feruglio, 1949; Auer, 1956, 1960, 1970). Moraine belts in the Chilean lake district have been attributed to three major glaciations (Laugenie, 1971; Mercer, 1972, 1976), the last was named the Llanquihue Glaciation by Heusser (1974). Recently, glacial deposits in southwestern Patagonia (about 50°S) have been dated between 1.2 and probably 1.0 m y b p, thus, they correspond to an early Pleistocene glaciation (Mercer and Sander, 1975). The available data permit reliable intercontinental comparison of only the most recent glacial fluctuations.

Environmental Changes from Pliocene to Holocene Times

It is premature to attempt a detailed account of the climatic and environmental changes in temperate South America from

Pliocene to Holocene times and their influence on biogeographic patterns. Many important factors and much of the evidence for the evaluation of past climates have been studied inadequately and interpretations frequently are contradictory. Therefore, only an account of major events and general trends is possible.

Few palynological, micropaleontological or isotopic dating studies have been carried out in this part of South America. Mainly, we have considered evidence provided by fossil mammals, especially distributional shifts of taxa whose ecological requirements are known, because the fossil record of other groups is very fragmentary. Closer attention to the stratigraphy of deposits in which fossils are collected and more accurate data on correlations and ages of assemblages are necessary in order to reconstruct the climatic fluctuations of such a short interval of the earth's history.

In many parts of the world mammalian faunas have furnished interesting clues to possible late Cenozoic climatic fluctuations, and the inferences based on them have been supported by other kinds of evidence. Thus, a basic chronological framework of the climatic record has been established. It is noteworthy that in southern South America Pleistocene mammals have only been recorded quite far from the glaciated area. No taxa indicative of extreme conditions have been recognized. Although in Pleistocene times glaciations were mainly restricted to the mountainous areas, temperature and moisture changes during glacial and interglacial intervals probably caused important shifting of the biotas of the nonmountainous regions. In order to provide a better understanding of the Late Cenozoic environmental changes, each region is considered separately.

Patagonia.—By the late Miocene, the development of increasingly xeric conditions had begun in this region. Nevertheless, in northern Patagonia, especially in the area of influence of the pre-Colorado and pre-Negro rivers, a warmer and more humid climate than that of today seems to have persisted during early and middle Pliocene. This is suggested by the record of a megalonychid edentate of the subfamily Orthotherinnae, which also could indicate a woody environment (Scillato Yané, Ulıana and Pascual, 1976). According to sedimentological and geomorphological data provided by Andreis (1965) and Volkheimer (1971) by the late Pliocene the climate at those latitudes had changed to drier and colder conditions.

Although the general trend in this region has been towards a drier climate as a result of the Andean uplift, some evidence suggests more humid conditions during certain phases of the Pleistocene. Few mammalian faunas of that age are known, but at least those tentatively referred to the upper Pleistocene (Ameghino 1902, 1906 Parodi 1930) support the presence of open environments.

The occurrence of paleargids andisols, a group of soils of Pleistocene age, in southern Patagonia testifies to the existence of a period of more humid conditions than at the present. Paleosoils from the tablelands of central and northern Patagonia are being studied by J. A. Ferrer (pers. comm.).

Prevalence of dry conditions in eastern Patagonia during Quaternary times is suggested by palynological analysis of sea cores from the Argentine Basin in the southwestern Atlantic Ocean (Groot and Groot, 1964, 1966). A cyclic alternation of two types of pollen zones occurs with depth. Those indicative of more pronounced arid environments (high percentage of Chenopodiaceae pollen) were considered to represent "glacial stages." Furthermore, certain features suggest eustatic lowering of sea level an inference also supported by the study of diatoms (Groot et al., 1967). More humidity could account for the relative increase of the arboreal pollen in the samples attributed to the "interglacial stages." This agrees with the climatic interpretation of the palynology of interglacial peat beds in northwestern Patagonia and Tierra del Fuego (Auer, 1958, 1970).

Humid glacial ages and relatively warm and dry interglacial ages in the Andean region of Argentina and central and southern Chile were proposed in accordance with a pollen diagram and the fluctuations of the carbonate content of a deep-sea core from the southeastern Pacific Ocean (Groot and Groot, 1966). However, palynological spectra of stratigraphic sections in the southern Chilean lake district reflect more complex climatic changes since the last interglacial as well as drier conditions during the Llanquihue Glaciation (Heusser, 1974).

Evidently, eustatic descent of sea level caused the emersion of much of the present continental shelf, thus eastern Patagonia supporting a steppe vegetation became larger. The probable connection of the Malvinas Islands to the mainland could explain the presence there of terrestrial species with relatives on the continent, for example the canid, *Dusycion australis* (Auer, 1958: 223–224). The sub-Antarctic forests, which now extend along the eastern slopes of the Andes as far north as about 36° (Fernández, 1976), could have descended to lower altitudes in glacial times (Vuilleumier, 1971).

Sub-Andean Region.—The rich mammalian faunas recorded in the Pliocene of this region have a marked subtropical character, thereby suggesting different environmental conditions from those existing at present. It is worth mentioning the occurrence of giant erethizontid and echimyid rodents, as well as anteaters (Rovereto, 1914), both myrmecophagids and cyclopodids (Hirschfeld, 1976), in areas where their living relatives are not found. Also dasypodids closely related to the living tropical and subtropical *Euphractus* were recorded by Scillato Yané (1975). Fossil trunks occur in Pliocene horizons but most of them have not been identified (Bodenbender, 1924, Frenguelli, 1937, Menéndez, 1962, Ramos, 1970). Those assigned to the leguminosid genus *Acacioxylon* exhibit growth rings that indicate wide seasonal differences of rainfall (Menéndez, 1962, 1971). These data suggest that environments similar to those of the present Western Chacoan district (*sensu* Cabrera 1971) could have existed in the Subandean Region. At that time, many of the mountain ranges that comprise the eastern border of this region were not so high as today and consequently did not constitute an effective barrier to the humid Atlantic winds. Thus some Chacoan species could have ranged farther west than they do now. The prevalence of semiarid to arid climates in intermontane basins in the northern areas is indicated by a variety of geological data (Bossi, 1969, Ramos 1970, Caminos, 1972, Gordillo and Lencinas, 1972).

The regions along the eastern side of the Andes, then lower and warmer than today, constituted an important pathway for migration between the subtropical regions and the more temperate southern Pampean Plain. Moreover, similar ecological conditions to the present phytogeographic Chacoan Province (*sensu* Cabrera, 1971), with open xerophytic woodland apparently existed in the southwestern part of Provincia de Buenos Aires. Upper Pliocene elements recorded from there, such as cariamid birds (Tonni, 1974), myrmecophagid anteaters (Kraglievich, 1934), and the anuran *Bufo paracnemis* (Gasparini and Báez, 1975) now are absent in that area.

The Sub-Andean Region was affected by important tectonic events during, and subsequent to, the Plio-Pleistocene. These had considerable physiographic and climatic consequences. The increasing rain-shadow effect accentuated the desiccation of climate. A fauna referred to the earliest Pleistocene in the northernmost part of the region has elements indicative of relatively humid conditions such as a beaver (Kraglievich, 1934). By that time a dry regime prevailed in the southern areas (Polanski, 1963). The few known later faunas denote a significant impoverishment in contrast to those of the Pliocene. Some mammals there at present are the cavid *Microcavia*, the mustelid *Lyncodon*, and the dasypodid *Chaetophractus vellerosus*.

Faunal connections with the southwestern Pampean Plain and Patagonia were enhanced by the development of an arid regime. The dry periods that affected the former area permitted a more eastern distribution of the xeric-adapted biota from the western regions. Similar expansion to the east of the semi-arid vegetation of the Monte during Pleistocene dry phases was suggested by Solbrig (1976).

Mesopotamia.—Pliocene vertebrates of this region are almost exclusively known from cliffs along the Río Paraná. Most of the remains of continental vertebrates have been found in sandstones and conglomerates that constitute the so-called "Mesopotamiense." They overlie typical marine deposits of the Atlantic transgression, the "Paranense Sea" which extended over a great part of the Chaco-Pampean Plain during the late Miocene (Frenguelli, 1920; Rossi de García, 1966). Within the "Mesopotamiense" there is an evident alternation of sediments corresponding to different environments but most are fluvio-deltaic sediments.

Fossil remains are indicative of humid subtropical conditions (Pascual and Odreman Rivas, 1971; Gasparini and Báez, 1975; Báez and Gasparini, 1977). Presumably the gallery forests along the river favored the southward extension of the tropical biota (Pascual and Odreman Rivas, 1971). A southward extension of tropical flora (Cabrera, 1971) and fauna (Ringuelet, 1955, 1961) is evident today, but the southward penetration probably was greater in Pliocene times, when the climate was warmer. There is an abundance of fossil tree trunks, turtles, large crocodiles, megalonychid and pampatheriine edentates, and dinomyid rodents in the Pliocene deposits. There is an absence of chinchillid and octodontid rodents and hegetotheriid and mesotheriid notoungulates which are characteristic of open environments.

The composition of these assemblages is quite different from those of about the same age in the Sub-Andean and Pampean regions. These differences reveal that these areas had distinct ecological and biogeographical features.

Pleistocene deposits are widely distributed in Mesopotamia, but in most cases neither their stratigraphy nor their paleontological content has been studied adequately; therefore, their chronological assignment is still uncertain. Even so the presence of certain taxa is quite interesting from the paleoenvironmental point of view. The record of the cavid rodent *Dolichotis* in the middle Pleistocene of northwestern Mesopotamia (Álvarez, 1974) indicates that at certain times the climate was drier than at present; drier conditions also are indicated by sedimentological data (Álvarez, 1974). At present *Dolichotis* is restricted to the Patagonian, Sub-Andean and southwestern Pampean regions.

Chaco-Pampean Plain.—This region started to acquire its present features after the regression of the late Miocene Paranense Sea" (Pascual and Odreman Rivas, 1971, 1973). Pliocene and Pleistocene stratigraphic sequences and their paleontological content are best known in the Provincia de Buenos Aires; therefore, our analysis will deal principally with that portion of the Chaco-Pampean Plain.

The available studies of successive faunas and sediments of Pliocene and Pleistocene age have not yet furnished evidence of drastic changes. In general there was an overall cooling trend from the more warm temperate conditions of the early Pliocene to the more moderate present ones with colder periods probably occurring during the Pleistocene. Concerning precipitation, at present the region has a permanently humid climate, with a change to drier conditions and some predominantly dry months in the western part. This regime seems to have prevailed during most of the Pliocene and Pleistocene but an increase of xeric conditions, especially during certain intervals, is evident (see below). Since this region came into existence, the dominant vegetation type has been grass steppe. However, the climatic fluctuations just mentioned would have favored greater eastward expansion of xerophytic forest, which presently borders the Pampean Plain to the west and north.

Echimyid rodents, now living in tropical and subtropical regions, are recorded from this area in the Pliocene and lower Pleistocene. Also in early Pliocene times (Chasicoan Age) megalonychid and nothrotheriine tree sloths were abundant there, but they are inconspicuous in later ages (Scillato Yané, 1977, 1979). These groups of rodents and edentates are found frequently in Miocene deposits of southern Patagonia; the northward shift of their southern limit of distribution reflects the climatic deterioration in the south. The occurrence of large dasypodids, closely related to the tropical and subtropical living *Euphractus*, in the Pliocene and of procyonids in the middle and upper Pliocene and lower Pleistocene is also significant. According to these and other faunal evidence, it can be postulated that throughout the Pliocene and early Pleistocene (Uquian Age) the climate was warmer than today, followed by a gradual cooling. This agrees with the more pronounced deterioration of climatic conditions in Patagonia after early Pleistocene time, as indicated by palynological data (Groot and Groot, 1966).

The evidence points to a desiccation of climate during the Pliocene. The abundance of sloths in the Chasicoan fauna suggests a humid regime (Scillato Yané, 1977, 1979) but contrasts with their absence in the Huayquerian. The presence of some sub-Andean elements in deposits assigned to the latter age also could be indicative of drier conditions at that time (Bondesio et al., 1979). By the late Pliocene, at least in the southwestern part of the Provincia de Buenos Aires, a regime characterized by seasonal differences in rainfall seems to have prevailed. An environment similar to that of the present Chacoan phytogeographic province, with open xerophytic woodlands has been inferred there from the composition of the fossil fauna (Tonni, 1974, Báez and Gasparini, 1977).

The stratigraphical units of early Pleistocene to Recent age, especially in the coastal area and in the northeastern part of the Provincia de Buenos Aires exhibit an alternation of subaqueous (fluvial, lacustrine paludal) and aeolian deposits (Kraghevich 1952 1953, Frenguelli, 1957a). These alternations of continental deposits of different origins have been associated with fluctuating climatic conditions, but there is no agreement as to what climatic condition, especially temperature, corresponds to each of the lithological changes. The existence of alternating humid and arid cycles during the late Pleistocene and Holocene also is indicated by geomorphological data (Tricart, 1973).

Intercalated marine and brackish-water levels occur discontinuously in different areas and have been correlated with the above mentioned continental subaqueous deposits which probably indicate humid conditions (Frenguelli, 1957a, Tricart, 1973). If the marine levels are interpreted as resulting from eustatic sea level rise, the correlation of the humid phases with the interglacial stages follows (Tricart, 1973). Accordingly, cold and arid or semiarid climates seem to have alternated with warm and humid ones. Preliminary palynological analysis of some samples from the Argentine shelf off the mouth of the Río de la Plata also suggests more pronounced aridity during the glacial stages (Groot et al., 1967 208).

The latest Pleistocene is represented in this area by the lower section of the Lobería Formation (Fig 6 3), where the last representatives of the megafauna still occur. Sedimentological characteristics (sand dunes and loess) and geomorphological evidence (Tricart, 1973) indicate extremely arid conditions at that time. This dry phase must have disturbed the equilibrium of the biota in that reduction of grazing land affected primarily the large herbivores, thus contributing to the extinction of the local megafauna.

The alternation of arid and humid climates can be explained by the changes in the distribution of ocean currents and wind systems over the South American continent during glacial and interglacial stages (Damuth and Fairbridge, 1970). During glacial phases the Chaco-Pampean Plain was under the influence of the dry southwesterly winds that acted as the depositional agent for the loess.

Even though the fossil record is rich, the available paleozoological data do not provide clear support to the environmental fluctuations during the Pleistocene and Holocene, for much of the material is not accurately assigned to stratigraphic levels. Furthermore, formational units have a long time range, during which climatic fluctuations took place. This probably explains the records of taxa that are indicative of opposing climatic conditions from a single locality and formation. Nevertheless, significant distributional shifts in the biota can be attributed to Pleistocene environmental changes. Drier conditions in the Pampean Plain are indicated by the occurrence of characteristic elements of the present Sub-Andean and Patagonian regions, such as the mustelid *Lyncodon* and the cavids *Dolichotis* and *Microcavia*, in Pleistocene deposits. *Dolichotis* also occurs in sediments of the same age in southern Uruguay (Calcaterra, 1972). On the other hand, more equable climatic conditions would have allowed procyonids and the dasypodid *Euphractus* to live on the Pampean Plain.

Other regions of temperate South America.—Available data from other areas within temperate South America do not permit us to outline a sequence of the climatic and environmental changes that occurred during the late Cenozoic. On the other hand, many geomorphological, sedimentological and phytogeographic studies have provided evidence of Quaternary fluctuations.

In the states of São Paulo, Paraná and Rio Grande do Sul in southeastern Brasil numerous mammalian remains have been recorded from Pleistocene continental units that tentatively have been referred to the Lujanian Age (late Pleistocene) of Argentina (Paula Couto, 1975). The mammalian fauna is predominantly one of savanna taxa and has Pampean affinities, especially the assemblage from Rio Grande do Sul. Some taxa could be indicative of different conditions than those existing at present; wild llamas of the genus *Palaeolama* are recorded from low altitudes thus suggesting a colder climate for the region. Paula Couto (1975) related the eastward shift of their range to a wider extension of the glaciated areas in the Andean region and adjacent plateaus where their close relatives are restricted today. Also, a former wider expansion towards the east of the "Andean forests" has been postulated to account for the presence of some Andean plant genera in the *Araucaria* forests of southeastern Brasil (Klein, 1975).

Sedimentological and geomorphological studies provide evidence for climatic changes and fluctuations during the Quaternary in southern Brasil. Distinct epochs of pedimentation, during which xeric conditions prevailed, have been established. These periods seem to be related to times of lowered sea level and thus are correlated with Pleistocene glacial phases (Bigarella, 1964). The evidence points to an alternation of semiarid and humid episodes during glacial and interglacial times respectively, with smaller climatic fluctuations within both the xeric and humid phases (Bigarella, 1964; Ab'Saber, 1977). These cyclic changes are also documented by phytogeographic data, although the chronology is far from clear (Klein, 1975).

CONCLUSIONS

The general trend of climatic change since the Pliocene has been towards a colder and drier regime, but this trend evidently has not been uniform and many fluctuations took place. Rain-shadow effects produced by the rising mountains constituted an important factor leading to the change of environmental conditions. Even though our knowledge of past climates in temperate South America is incomplete, the main environmental changes during the Late Cenozoic can be broadly outlined, as follows:

1. Development of an increasingly arid and cold regime began by late Miocene in Patagonia. Many forest-savanna inhabitants retreated north and west. In northern Patagonia warmer and more humid conditions persisted during early to middle Pliocene. In Quaternary times a dry and cold climate prevailed, especially in the eastern areas although there is evidence of more humid phases during the Pleistocene.

2. During Pliocene times the regions situated to the north of Patagonia had at least a warm-temperate climate. Many elements of the subtropical fauna reached a more southern distribution than they do today.

3. Plio-Pleistocene tectonic events accentuated the differentiation of the sub-Andean region, which formerly had connections in its northern part with the Chacoan region. Subsequent to that time an essentially dry regime was established there.

4. During the Pleistocene, glaciations extended over the Andean region and reached the present Atlantic coast only south of 52°S. In the northwestern ranges of Argentina glaciers were restricted to the highest elevations and upper portions of fluvial valleys.

5. In the middle and late Pleistocene and Holocene, the climate fluctuated in the Pampean Plain, especially the humidity. Dry phases favored geographic extension of xeric-adapted species, to the east and north. Also they may have caused the isolation or migration of more mesic types.

6. Evidence of important Quaternary climatic fluctuations in southeastern Brasil has been provided mainly by sedimentological, geomorphological, paleontological and phytogeographical studies. An alternation between warm and humid and relatively cold and dry periods, with minor fluctuations within those phases, has been proposed.

ACKNOWLEDGMENTS

We thank Mrs M Guiomar Vucetich, Drs Rosendo Pascual, Francisco Fidalgo, Eduardo Tonni, Geol José A Ferrer (Museo de La Plata), Dr Edgardo Romero (Facultad de Ciéncias Exactas y Naturales, Buenos Aires) y Prof Guillermo del Corro (Museo Argentino de Ciencias Naturales, Buenos Aires) for their valuable comments Special thanks are extended to Dr Víctor Ramos (Servicio Nacional Minero Geológico, Buenos Aires), who critically read the manuscript and provided useful information

RESUMEN

La actual zona templada de América del Sur incluye (de acuerdo con la clasificación climática de Koppen) Uruguay, la mayor parte de Paraguay, partes de Bolivia, Brasil y Argentina, así como una porción territorial a lo largo de la costa pacífica al sur de los 38°S Para los fines del presente estudio se han considerado también la región subandina y Patagonia, donde actualmente prevalecen climas áridos Esto se debe a que su historia paleoambiental se halla íntimamente ligada a la de los aludidos ámbitos actualmente templados

La mayor parte de las evidencias disponibles indicadoras de cambios ambientales, especialmente durante el Terciario tardío, se refieren al territorio argentino, en el que pueden considerarse cuatro regiones principales 1) Patagonia, 2) Área Subandina, 3) Mesopotamia, y 4) Llanura Chaco-Pampeana

Una adecuada comprensión de los cambios climático-ambientales acaecidos en Sudamérica templada durante el Cenozoico tardío requiere inevitablemente, la consideración de los tiempos geológicos anteriores Los datos disponibles indican un pronunciado deterioro de las condiciones que, aún hacia el Mioceno medio a tardío, eran mucho más benignas y uniformes que las actuales

Cabe señalar que en esta parte de América del Sur la mayoría de las unidades litoestratigráficas y cronoestratigráficas del Cenozoico continental no han sido formalmente establecidas De hecho, ha sido el reconocimiento de "Edades mastozoológicas" (tentativamente referidas a las Epocas de la escala geocronológica mundial) lo que ha provisto, para toda Sudamérica el principal criterio de correlación

Estudios de diversa índole (litológicos, geomorfológicos, paleontológicos fitogeográficos) han suministrado información que permite esbozar un relato de la evolución ambiental en las regiones consideradas

Hasta el Mioceno medio a tardío las condiciones prevalecientes en Patagonia fueron mucho más cálidas y húmedas que las hoy allí vigentes, así lo indica el registro de numerosos vertebrados cuyos parientes actuales viven en áreas intertropicales, parcialmente boscosas o selváticas A partir del Mioceno tardío se produjo un notable desecamiento (motivado por la circunstancia de que los Andes australes alcanzaron ya una altura suficiente como para actuar como efectiva barrera a los vientos húmedos del Pacífico) y una más progresiva atemperación (en parte coincidente con un parcial englazamiento de Antártida occidental) Estos cambios determinaron la retracción hacia el norte y oeste de muchos elementos de la biota

La consideración en particular del Cenozoico tardío nos remite, principalmente, al problema de los límites entre las Epocas implicadas (Plioceno Pleistoceno y Holoceno) El límite plio-pleistocénico no ha sido aún claramente determinado en Sudamérica, tentativamente se lo ubica hacia el Uquiense temprano (Blanquense tardío de USA) Tal incertidumbre responde tanto a la ausencia de un criterio unánime a nivel mundial en esta materia como a las dificultades implícitas en correlacionar las Edades locales sudamericanas con las de otros continentes El límite pleisto-holocénico coincide aproximadamente con el fin de la Edad Lujanense, señalado por una extinción masiva de la megafauna

El estudio de los eventos glaciales—cuya importancia fundamental en la evolución climática del Cenozoico tardío es universalmente reconocida—se halla aún en Sudamérica en una etapa preliminar No existe acuerdo en cuanto al número y extensión de las glaciaciones, pero puede desde ya desecharse el esquema simplista que establece una exacta correspondencia con las cuatro clásicamente reconocidas en el Pleistoceno del Hemisferio Norte. En el SO de Patagonia fueron recientemente reconocidos varios episodios glaciales que datan del Plioceno tardío y Pleistoceno temprano. Mucho mejor documentada está la glaciación suprapleistocénica groseramente correlacionada con Würm-Wisconsin del Hemisferio Norte, pero debe remarcarse que afectó especialmente a la región andina, y que sólo al sur de los 52°S los glaciares alcanzaron la actual costa atlántica.

La evolución ambiental durante el Cenozoico tardío en las cuatro áreas del territorio argentino mencionadas precedentemente puede sintetizarse así:

Patagonia—Con excepción de la región más septentrional, el clima fue frío y semiárido a árido durante la mayor parte del Plioceno. Estas condiciones parecen haberse acentuado durante el Cuaternario, si bien ciertas evidencias sugieren algunos lapsos más húmedos. Los datos disponibles no indican un extenso englazamiento.

Area Subandina—Durante el Plioceno el registro paleomastozoológico incluye numerosos taxa típicamente intertropicales, que indican condiciones parcialmente boscosas y cálidas, posiblemente algo más húmedas que las actuales, de tal modo, esta área (continua entonces con la chaqueña hacia el norte) obró como una "vía de conexión" del SO de la llanura pampeana con ámbitos francamente subtropicales. No obstante, como consecuencia de los Movimientos Andinos, existían ya cuencas intermontanas en la parte septentrional donde pudieron prevalecer condiciones más áridas. Los eventos tectónicos del Plioceno tardío-Pleistoceno temprano acentuaron notablemente el bloqueo a los vientos húmedos del NE, con la consecuente desecación progresiva del clima en toda esta región.

Mesopotamia—Durante el Plioceno las condiciones fueron aún más cálidas y húmedas que las hoy vigentes. El área influenciada por el río pre-Paraná obró ya entonces como una importantísima "vía de conexión" entre la llanura bonaerense y ámbitos biogeográficos más septentrionales. En el transcurso del Cuaternario siguieron prevaleciendo condiciones cálidas y húmedas, pero muy probablemente algunos lapsos más secos hicieron sentir su influencia tanto en esta región como en territorio uruguayo.

Llanura Chaco-Pampeana—Casi toda la documentación disponible se refiere a la mitad austral de esta área (Pampasia). Los estudios de las sucesivas "faunas" y sedimentitas pliocénicas y pleistocénicas no han revelado la ocurrencia de cambios drásticos. No obstante, a partir del Plioceno temprano tuvo lugar una progresiva atemperación. Desde el Pleistoceno medio hasta el Holoceno es factible reconocer varias fluctuaciones climáticas: lapsos relativamente cálidos y húmedos (con frecuente depositación fluvio-lacustre) alternaron con otros relativamente fríos y secos (en los que predominó ampliamente la sedimentación de "limos loessoides," o aún de verdaderos loess). Un análisis preliminar del contenido paleomastozoológico de las respectivas unidades estratigráficas avala, en general, esta interpretación. Es muy importante señalar que los lapsos presumiblemente cálidos y húmedos parecen coincidir con ingresiones marinas, en tanto que los fríos y secos corresponden a regresiones. Estos ascensos y descensos del nivel marino podrían ser de origen eustático.

En lo que atañe a otras áreas fuera del territorio argentino, no existe información suficiente sobre el Terciario tardío. En cambio, hay claras evidencias de fluctuaciones climáticas cíclicas especialmente para el Cuaternario del sudeste de Brasil. De acuerdo a datos de diversa índole, lapsos cálidos y húmedos alternaron con otros relativamente fríos y secos.

LITERATURE CITED

Ab Saber, A. N. 1977. Espaços ocupados pelo expansão dos climas secos na America do Sul, por ocasião dos periodos glaciales quaternarios. Paleoclimas 3:1-19.

Alvarez, B. B. 1974. Los mamíferos fósiles del Cuaternario de arroyo Toropi, Corrientes (Argentina). Ameghiniana 11(3):295-311.

Ameghino, F. 1902. L'age des formations sedimentaires de Patagonie. An. Soc. Cient. Argentina 54(6):283-312.

Ameghino, F. 1906. Les formations sedimentaires du Crétacé superieur et du Tertiaire de Patagonie. An. Mus. Nac. Hist. Nat. Buenos Aires (3a)8:1-568.

Andreis, R. 1965. Petrografía y paleocorrientes de la Formación Río Negro (Tramo General Conesa-Boca del Río Negro). Rev. Mus. La Plata, Secc. Geol. 5(36):245-310.

Antevs, E. 1929. Maps of the Pleistocene glaciations. Geol. Soc. America Bull. 40:631-720.

Auer, V. 1956. The Pleistocene of Fuego-Patagonia. Part I. The Ice and Interglacial Ages. Ann. Acad. Sci. Fennicae Ser. A3 45:1-226.

Auer, V. 1958. The Pleistocene of Fuego-Patagonia. Part II. The history of the Flora and Vegetation. Ibid., 50:1-239.

Auer, V. 1960. The Quaternary history of Fuego-Patagonia. Proc. Roy. Soc. London, Ser. B152:507-516.

Auer, V. 1970. The Pleistocene of Fuego-Patagonia. Part V. Quaternary Problems of Southern South America. Ann. Acad. Sci. Fennicae Ser. A3 100:1-194.

Auer, V. 1974. The isorhythmicity subsequent to the Fuego-Patagonia and Fenoscandian ocean level transgressions and regressions of the latest glaciation. Ibid. 115:1-88.

Báez, A. M., Gasparini, Z. B. de 1977. Orígenes y evolución de los anfibios y reptiles del Cenozoico de América del Sur. Acta Geol. Lilloana 14:140-232.

Berggren, W. A., Van Couvering, J. A. 1974. The Late Neogene. Palaeogeogr. Palaeoclimatol., Palaeoecol. 16:1-216.

Bigarella, J. J. 1964. Variações climáticas no Quaternário e suas implicações no revestimento florístico do Paraná. Bol. Paranaense Geogr. Curitiba 10-15.

Bodenbender, G. 1924. El calchaqueño y los Estratos de la Puna de Penck. Bol. Acad. Nac. Cien. Córdoba 26:405-468.

Bondesio, P., Laza, J. H., Scillato Yané, G., Tonni, E., Vucetich, M. G. 1979. Estado actual del conocimiento de los vertebrados de la Formación Arroyo Chasico (Edad Chasiquense, Plioceno Temprano) de la Provincia de Buenos Aires, República Argentina. Act. II Congr. Argentino Paleontol. y Bioestr. I Congr. Latinoamer. Paleontol. (in press).

Bossi, G. E. 1969. Geología y Estratigrafía del sector sur del valle de Choromoro. Parte I. Lecto. Acta Geol. Lilloana 10:17-64.

Cabrera, A. L. 1971. Fitogeografía de la República Argentina. Bol. Soc. Argentina Bot. 14(1-2):1-42.

Calcaterra, A. 1972. Dos roedores fósiles nuevos para Uruguay y confirmación de otro. Com. Paleontol. Mus. Hist. Nat. Montevideo 1:11-21.

Caldenius, C. 1932. Las glaciaciones cuaternarias en la Patagonia y Tierra del Fuego. Publ. (Buenos Aires) Dir. Nac. Min. y Geol. 95:1-150.

Camacho, H. H. 1967. Las transgresiones del Cretácico Superior y Terciario de la Argentina. Rev. Asoc. Geol. Argentina 22:253-280.

Caminos, R. 1972. Sierras Pampeanas de Tucumán, Catamarca, La Rioja y San Juan, pp. 41-79 in Leanza, A. L. (ed.) Geología Regional Argentina. Acad. Nac. Cienc. Córdoba, 869 p.

Curry, R. P. 1966. Glaciation about 3,000,000 years ago in the Sierra Nevada. Science 154:770-771.

Damuth, J. E., Fairbridge, R. W. 1970. Equatorial Atlantic deep-sea arkosic sands and Ice-Age aridity in tropical South America. Geol. Soc. Amer. Bull. 81:189-206.

Eidt, R. C. 1969. The climatology of South America, pp. 54-81 in Fittkau, E. J., Illies, J., Klinge, H., Schwabe, G., Sioli, H. (eds.) Biogeography and ecology in South America Vol. 1, Junk, The Hague 447 p.

Fernández, J. 1976. El límite boreal de los bosques andino-patagónicos. Bol. Soc. Argentina Bot. 17:307-314.

Feruglio, E. 1949. Descripción geológica de la Patagonia. Dir. Gral. Yac. Petrol. Fiscales, Buenos Aires 2:1-349.

Fidalgo, F. 1973. Consideraciones sobre los bajos situados al Norte de la provincia de Santa Cruz. Act. V Congr. Geol. Argentino 5:123-137.

Fidalgo, F., Riggi, J. C. 1970. Consideraciones geomórficas y sedimentológicas sobre los Rodados Patagónicos. Rev. Asoc. Geol. Argentina 25:130-443.

Fleck, R. J., Mercer, J. H., Nairn, A. E. M., Peterson, D. N. 1972. Chronology of Late Pliocene and Early Pleistocene glacial and magnetic events in Southern Argentina. Earth Planet Sci. Lett., 16:15-22.

Flint, R. F. 1965. The Plio-Pleistocene boundary, pp. 497-533 in International Studies on the Quaternary. Geol. Soc. Amer. Spec. Pap. 84.

Flint, R. F., Fidalgo, F. 1963. Geología glacial de la zona de borde entre los paralelos 39°10' y 41°20' de latitud sur en la Cordillera de los Andes (Argentina). Bol. Dir. Nac. Geol. Min. (Buenos Aires) 93:1-35.

Flint, R. F., Fidalgo, F. 1968. Drift glacial al Este de los Andes entre Bariloche y Esquel. Min. Ec. y Trab. Secret. Est. Energ. y Min., Inst. Nac. Geol. Min., Argentina, Bol. 119:1-19.

Frenguelli, J. 1920. Contribución al conocimiento de la geología de Entre Ríos. Bol. Acad. Nac. Cienc. Córdoba 24:55-256.

Frenguelli, J. 1937. Investigaciones geológicas en la zona salteña del Valle de Santa María. Inst. Mus. Univ. Nac. La Plata Obra Cincuentenario 2:215-572.

Frenguelli, J. 1957a. Neozoico, pp. 1-115 in Geografía de la República Argentina, Soc. Arg. Est. Geogr. GAEA 2:216 p.

Frenguelli, J. 1957b. El glaciarismo cuaternario, pp. 117-218 in Geografía de la República Argentina. Ibid. 2, 216 p.

Gasparini, Z. B. de, Báez, A. M. 1975. Aportes al conocimiento de la herpetofauna terciaria de la Argentina. Act. I Congr. Argentino Paleontol. Bioestr. 2:377-415.

GORDILLO, C., LENCINAS, A. 1972 Sierras Pampeanas de Cordoba y San Luis pp 1–39 in LLANZA, A. F. (ed) Geologia Regional Argentina Acad Nac Cienc Cordoba 869 p

GROEBER, P 1936 Oscilaciones de clima en la Argentina desde el Plioceno Holmbergia 1 71–84

GROEBER, P 1952 Glacial, Tardio y Postglacial en Patagonia Rev Mus Municipal Cienc Nat Tradicional de Mar del Plata 1 79–103

GROEBER, P 1954 Duración de las glaciaciones cuartarias en America del Sud y discusion de las condiciones Astronomico-climáticas conducentes a englazamiento Ibid 1 111–159

GROOT, J J, GROOT, C R 1964 Quaternary stratigraphy of sediments of Argentine Basin A palynological investigation Trans New York Acad Sci 26 881–886

GROOT, J J, GROOT, C R 1966 Pollen spectra from deep-sea sediments as indicators of climatic changes in Southern South America Mar Geol 4 525–537

GROOT, J J, GROOT, C R, EWING M, BURCKLE, L, CONOLLY, J R 1967 Spores, pollen diatoms and provenance of the Argentine Basin sediments, Prog Oceanogr 4 179–217

HAYS, J D, OPDYKE, N D 1967 Antarctic Radiolaria magnetic reversals and climatic change Science 158 1001–1011

HAYS, J D, BERGGREN, W A 1971 Quaternary boundaries and correlations pp 669–691 in FUNNEL, B M, RIEDEL, W R (eds) Micropaleontology of the Oceans Cambridge Univ Press, Cambridge, 828 p

HEUSSER, C J 1974 Vegetation and climate of the Southern Chilean Lake district during and since the last Interglaciation Quat Res (New York) 4 290–315

HIRSCHFELD, S E 1976 A new fossil anteater (Edentata, Mammalia) from Colombia, S A and evolution of the Vermilingua J Paleontol 50 419–432

HIRSCHFELD, S E, WEBB, S D 1968 Plio-pleistocene megalonychid sloths of North America Bull Florida State Mus, Biol Sci 12 213–296

KLEIN, R M 1975 Southern Brazilian phytogeographic features and the probable influence of upper Quaternary climatic changes in the floristic distribution pp 67–88 in BIGARELLA, J J, BECKER, R D (eds) Internat Symp Quaternary Bol Paranaense Geocien, Curitiba 33, 370 p

KRAGLIEVICH, J L 1952 El perfil geologico de Chapadmalal y Miramar, Provincia de Buenos Aires Rev Mus Municipal Cienc Nat Tradicional de Mar del Plata 1 8–37

KRAGLIEVICH, J L 1953 La llanura bonaerense a traves de un perfil geologico Rev Mundo Atómico (Buenos Aires) Año 4, 14 88–95, 99

KRAGLIEVICH, L 1934 La antiguedad pliocena de las faunas de Monte Hermoso y Chapadmalal, deducidas de su comparacion con las que le precedieron y sucedieron Imprenta El Siglo Ilustrado," Montevideo, 1–136

LAUGENIE, C 1971 Elementos de la cronologia glaciar en los Andes Chilenos meridionales Cuad Geogr Sur 1 7–20

MARSHALL, L G, PASCUAL, R 1979 Una preliminar escala temporal radiometrica de las Edades-mamifero del Cenozoico medio y tardio sudamericano Obra Centenario Museo La Plata (in press)

MARTIN, P S 1975 Palaeolithic players on the American stage Man's impact on the late Pleistocene megafauna pp 669–700 in IVES, J D, BARRY, R G (eds) Arctic and Alpine Environments Methuen & Co Ltd, 999 p

MENENDEZ, C A 1962 Leño petrificado de una leguminosa del Terciario de Tropunco, Provincia de Tucuman Ameghiniana, 2 121–126

MENENDEZ, C A 1971 Floras terciarias de la Argentina Ibid 8 357–368

MERCER, J H 1972 Chilean glacial chronology 20,000–11,000 C-14 years ago Some global comparisons Science 176 1118–1120

MERCER, J H 1976 The last glaciation in Chile A radiocarbon-dated chronology Act I Corgr Geol Chileno 1 D55–68

MERCER, J H, SANDER W 1975 Pliocene and early Pleistocene glaciations in southern Argentina, and the origin of the Patagonian gravel VI Congr Geol Argentino Resumenes 20

METHOL, E J 1967 Rasgos geomorfologicos de la Meseta de Somuncura Rio Negro Consideraciones acerca de los origenes de los pequeños bajos sin salida Rev Asoc Geol Argentina 22 295–311

PARODI, L 1930 Sobre nuevos restos de mamiferos de la fauna pampeana en Patagonia Physis 10 (35) 21–34

PASCUAL R 1970 Evolucion de comunidades, cambios faunisticos e integraciones biocenoticas de los vertebrados cenozoicos de Argentina Act IV Congr Latinomer Zool 2 991–1088

PASCUAL, R, FIDALGO, F 1972 The problem of the Plio-Pleistocene Boundary in Argentine (South America) Coll Pap Int Colloq on the Problem "The Boundary between Neogene and Quaternary (Moscow) 2 205–262

PASCUAL R, ORTEGA HINOJOSA, E J, GONDAR, D, TONNI, E 1965 Las Edades del Cenozoico mamalifero de la Argentina, con especial atencion a aquellas del territorio bonaerense An Com Inv Cient Prov Buenos Aires 6 165–193

PASCUAL, R ODREMAN RIVAS, O 1971 Evolucion de las comunidades de los vertebrados del Terciario argentino Los aspectos paleozoogeograficos y paleoclimaticos relacionados Ameghiniana 8 372–412

PASCUAL, R ODREMAN RIVAS, O E 1973 Las unidades estratigraficas del Terciario portadoras de mamiferos Su distribucion y sus relaciones con los acontecimientos distroficos Act V Congr Geol Argentino 3 293–338

PATTERSON, B PASCUAL, R 1968 The fossil mammal fauna of South America Q Rev Biol 43 409–451

Patterson, B., Pascual, R. 1972. The Fossil Mammal Fauna of South America, pp. 247–309 in Keast, A., Erk, F., Glass, B. (eds.) Evolution, Mammals and Southern Continents. State Univ. New York Press, Albany, 543 p.

Paulo Couto, C. de. 1975. Mamiferos fosseis do Quaternario do Sudeste Brasileiro, pp. 89–132 in Bigarella, J. J., Becken, R. D. (eds.) Internat. Symp. Quat. Bol. Paranaense Geocien. Curitiba 33, 370 p.

Polanski, J. 1963. Estratigrafia Neotectónica y Geomorfologia del Pleistoceno Pedemontano entre los rios Diamante y Mendoza (Provincia de Mendoza). Rev. Asoc. Geol. Argentina 17: 127–349.

Polanski, J. 1965. The maximum glaciation in the Argentine Cordillera, pp. 453–472 in Wright, H. E. Jr., Frey, D. (eds.) International Studies on the Quaternary. Geol. Soc. America Spec. Pap. 84.

Ramos, V. 1970. Estratigrafia y estructura del Terciario en la Sierra de los Colorados (Provincia de La Rioja, República Argentina). Rev. Asoc. Geol. Argentina 25: 358–382.

Reig, O. A. 1952. Sobre la presencia de mustelidos mefitinos en la Formación Chapadmalal. Rev. Mus. Municipal de Cienc. Nat. Tradicional Mar del Plata 1: 45–51.

Ringuelet, R. 1955. Panorama zoogeográfico de la provincia de Buenos Aires. Notas Mus. La Plata 18 (Zool. 156): 1–15.

Ringuelet, R. 1961. Rasgos fundamentales de la zoogeografia de la Argentina. Physis 22: 151–170.

Rossi de Garcia, E. 1966. Contribución al conocimiento de los Ostracodos de la Argentina. I — Formación Entre Rios de Victoria Provincia de Entre Rios. Rev. Asoc. Geol. Argentina 21: 194–208.

Rovereto, C. 1914. Los estratos araucanos y sus fosiles. An. Mus. Nac. Hist. Nat. Buenos Aires 25: 1–250.

Rutland, R. W. R., Guest, J. E., Crastley, R. L. 1965. Isotopic ages and Andean uplift. Nature 208 (5001): 677–678.

Saxon, E. C. 1976. La prehistoria de Fuego-Patagonia colonizacion de un habitat marginal. An. Inst. Patagonia 7: 63–73.

Scillato Yané, G. J. 1975. Nuevo genero de Dasypodidae (Edentata, Xenarthra) del Plioceno de Catamarca (Argentina). Algunas consideraciones filogeneticas y zoogeograficas sobre los Euphractini. Act. 1 Congr. Argentino Paleontol. y Bioestr. 2: 449–461.

Scillato Yané, G. J. 1977. Nuevo Megalonychidae (Edentata, Tardigrada) de Edad Chasiquense (Plioceno temprano) del sur de la Provincia de Buenos Aires (Argentina). Su importancia filogenetica, biostratigráfica y paleobiogeográfica. Rev. Asoc. Cienc. Nat. Litoral (Santo Tomé, Santa Fe, Argentina) 8: 45–54.

Scillato Yané, G. J. 1979. Nuevo Nothrotheriinae (Edentata, Tardigrada) de Edad Chasiquense (Plioceno temprano) del sur de la Provincia de Buenos Aires, Republica Argentina. Su importancia bioestratigráfica, filogenética y paleobiogeográfica. Act. VII Congr. Geol. Argentino (in press).

Scillato Yané, G. J., Uliana, M. A., Pascual, R. 1976. Un Megalonychidae (Edentata, Pilosa) del Plioceno de la Provincia de Rio Negro (Argentina). Su importancia bioestratigráfica y paleobiogeográfica. Act. VI Congr. Geol. Argentino 1: 579–591.

Simpson, G. G. 1940. Review of the Mammal-bearing Tertiary of South America. Proc. Amer. Phil. Soc. 83: 649–709.

Solbrig, O. T. 1976. The origin and floristic affinities of the South American temperate desert and semidesert regions, pp. 65–99 in Goodall, D. W. (ed.) Evolution of the desert biota. Univ. Texas Press, Austin, 250 p.

Tonni, E. 1974. Un nuevo canamido (Aves, Gruiformes) del Plioceno Superior de la Provincia de Buenos Aires. Ameghiniana 11: 366–372.

Tricart, J. L. F. 1973. Geomorfologia de la Pampa deprimida. Base para los estudios edafologicos y agronomicos. Secr. Est. Agric. y Ganad. de la Nacion, Inst. Nac. Tecnol. Agrop., Colección Cient., 12, Imprenta 'CONI,' Buenos Aires, 202 p.

Volkheimer, W. 1971. Aspectos paleoclimáticos del Terciario argentino. Rev. Mus. Arg. Cienc. Nat. 'B. Rivadavia," Paleontol. 1: 243–262.

Vuilleumier, B. S. 1971. Pleistocene changes in the fauna and flora of South America. Science 173: 771–780.

Webb, S. D. 1976. Mammalian faunal dynamics of the great American interchange. Paleobiology 2: 220–234.

7. Quaternary Biogeography of the High Montane Regions of South America

Beryl B Simpson[1]

*Department of Botany
Smithsonian Institution
Washington, D C 20560
USA*

From 11°N to 55°S, the South American Andes span 66 degrees of latitude a distance of over 8000 km (Fig 7 1) At their widest point they are about 500 km broad Such an enormous land mass extending across one hemisphere and projecting into the other, must necessarily exhibit great diversity Elsewhere in South America, significantly high mountains are found only in southeastern Brasil and along the southern edge of the Guiana Shield (Fig 7 1) but the area of these mountains above 2000 m elevation is very small In several previous papers (Vuilleumier, 1971, Simpson, 1973 1975), I discussed Pleistocene events in the Andes, but within the last few years several studies have added to the knowledge of Andean Tertiary and Quaternary history In this review of the Quaternary history of the high montane regions of South America, I first review the current information about the formation of the Andean Cordillera and the other montane regions A background knowledge of the historical geology of the regions is necessary because their differing ages have an important bearing on the composition and diversity of the floras and faunas that were affected by Quaternary climatic changes After outlining the historical geology, I briefly describe the modern climate and vegetation of these regions and then turn to a discussion of Pleistocene biogeographical events

GEOLOGICAL HISTORY OF THE MONTANE REGIONS

The Andes

As mentioned by numerous authors (e g, Simpson, 1975), the "Andes" actually consist of a complex array of mountains that can be partitioned in several ways for purposes of discussion It is meaningful to discriminate units of the Andes by partitioning the Cordillera into geomorphological units as done by Harrington (1956) Ganssei (1973) and Simpson (1975) (Fig 7 2) Although in this treatment mountains often are referred to by the country in which they occur, the use of the country is merely for convenience as to locality the units being discussed are the geomorphological units or their parts in the regions mentioned A different and somewhat more detailed subdivision of the Cordillera into "tectonic segments" was proposed by Sillitoe (1974), Ganssei (1973) and others The boundaries of the major tectonic segments correspond with the boundaries of the geomorphological units (Fig 7 2)

Perhaps the single most important aspect of the geological history of all the Andean units is their recency of uplift (see Simpson 1975, Fig 2) Although there is some discrepancy in the exact timing of final uplift, the last major upheaval of almost all units was at the end of the Tertiary or within the Quaternary The final uplift of the Sierra Nevada de Santa Marta, the most northerly part of the Cordillera, has been dated toward the end of the Pleistocene (Ganssei, 1955) although the use of late moraines as evidence can be questioned Recent studies (van der Hammen, 1974, van der Hammen et al, 1973) have continued to document that the high elevation zones (above 2000 m) of the eastern Andes of Colombia were produced during the middle and later part of the Pliocene Garner (1975) questioned the evidence for late uplift of the northern mountain ranges The absence of traces of glacia-

---
[1] Present address Department of Botany, University of Texas, Austin, Texas 78712, USA

tions before the last part of the Pleistocene, used as evidence for late uplift (Herd and Naeser, 1974), can not be considered as conclusive evidence, because earlier moraines can be easily eliminated. Few studies extending to the beginning of the Pleistocene

have been made, but careful examination of one important long pollen core (Fig 7 3) clearly shows that plants characteristic of high elevations were absent in the Colombian Andes until the beginning of the Pleistocene (van der Hammen et al, 1973) Limited studies have been made in the Cordillera Occidental of Colombia but the available evidence seems to suggest that they were initially uplifted later than the ranges to the east (Shagam, 1975) and that they reached their present elevations after the end of the Tertiary (Burgl, 1961 Haffer, 1970a Herd and Naeser, 1974) In Venezuela, geological investigations of the Mérida Andes (Shagam 1975) show several early orogenies with the last initiated in the Oligocene and continuing to the present Significantly high elevations were achieved only relatively late in the Pleistocene (Schubert, 1974a)

The portions of the eastern and western Cordilleras extending through Ecuador have received little attention in recent years, but a summary of previous studies in this region (Sauer, 1971) indicated three stages of final uplift, the last of which occurred during the Pleistocene This last uplift was postulated to have accounted for all elevations above 2000 m (Sauer, 1965, diagram 7) The youthfulness of the high volcanic peaks in Ecuador is attested to, in part, by still active Volcán Cotopaxi

Earlier investigations of both the Eastern and Western Cordillera through Perú and Bolivia (Steinmann, 1930, Dollfus, 1959/1960 Ahlfeld, 1970) indicated Phocene-Pleistocene final uplifts of about 1000 to 3000 m More recently the orogenic history of the Andes has been interpreted in relation to plate tectonics (James, 1971, 1973 Gansser, 1973) James, in his interpretation of the uplift of the Bolivian Andes (1971) envisioned an im-

---

FIG 7 1 Distribution of high elevation areas in South America Areas above 2000 m are shaded on the western side of the continent For the southeastern Brasilian Highlands and the Guiana Tablelands areas above 1000 are indicated Inserts give climate diagrams showing mean monthly temperature and precipitation regimes at several high elevation stations The changes in annual dispersion of rainfall and yearly patterns of temperature from north to south along the Andes as well as the aridity of the western part of the central Andes are evident In the inset diagrams, mean monthly values of both temperature and precipitation are connected Areas shaded with vertical bars indicate times of excess precipitation, stippled areas are times of moisture deficit The left hand, vertical axis is calibrated in units of 10°C, the right hand vertical axis is calibrated in units of 20 mm of precipitation The horizontal axis indicates the month of the year (reversed in different hemispheres) Shaded areas along the base of the diagram show the months from which freezing temperatures have been recorded For each of the stations with an inset the following are given name, latitude, longitude, altitude, number of years from which data were recorded mean annual temperature and mean annual precipitation for this period A Bogotá, Colombia, 4°38′ N × 74°05′ W, 2556 m 94 years, 13 2°C, 940 9 mm B Riobamba, Ecuador 00°22 S × 78°34 W, 3058 m, 8 years, 11 5°C, 1361 mm C Cajamarca, Perú, 07°08 S × 78°28′W, 2621 m 9 years, 14°C, 716 mm D Cuzco, Peru 13°33 S × 71°59′W, 3312 m 17 years 12 5°C, 750 mm L Arequipa Perú 16°19 S × 71°33′W, 2525 m, 37 years, 13 8°C, 104 mm F El Alto (airport, La Paz), Bolivia, 16°30 S × 68°12 W 4105 m 28 years 7 5°C 564 mm G Oruro, Bolivia, 17°58 S × 67°07 W, 3708 m, 10 years, 7 5°C 282 mm H La Quiaca, Argentina 22°06 S × 65°36 W, 3459 m, 8 years, 9 5°C 322 mm I Cristo Redentor, Argentina, 32°50 S × 70°5′W 3829 m 27 years, −1 7°C, 354 mm J Itatiaia Brasil 22°20 S × 44°43 W, 2200 m, 20 years, 12 9°C, 2417 mm Data for Figure insets A–I from Schwerdtfeger (1976) and inset J from Brade (1956) Climate data for a complete year are not available from the Guiana Highlands

Distribución de las regiones de altura de Sudamérica La el lado oeste del continente las areas por encima de los 2000 m están sombreadas Para la region sudeste brasileño y los tablazos de la Guayana se indican las areas mayores de 1000 m Las inclusiones representan diagramas climaticos, que muestran la temperatura media mensual y los regimenes de precipitación, para varias estaciones de altura Los cambios en la dispersión anual de la lluvia y los patrones anuales de temperatura del norte a sur a lo largo de los Andes asi como la aridez del lado oeste de los Andes Centrales son evidentes En los diagramas, los valores medios mensuales de la temperatura y precipitación estan conectados Areas achuradas indican tiempo con exceso de precipitación, areas punteadas son tiempos con déficit de humedad La eje vertical izquierdo esta calibrado en unidades de 10°C, el derecho esta calibrado en unidades de 20 mm de precipitacion El eje horizontal indica los meses del año (inversos en diferentes hemisferios) La linea oscura en la base de los diagramas representa a los meses con registros de temperaturas de congelacion A cada estacion representada por una letra, le corresponde su nombre, latitud longitud, elevacion, número de años con registros, temperatura media anual y precipitación anual Información para las inclusiones A–I proviene de Schwerdtfeger (1976), para J de Brade (1956) Datos climaticos de un año completo no estan disponible para las Alturas Guayanenses

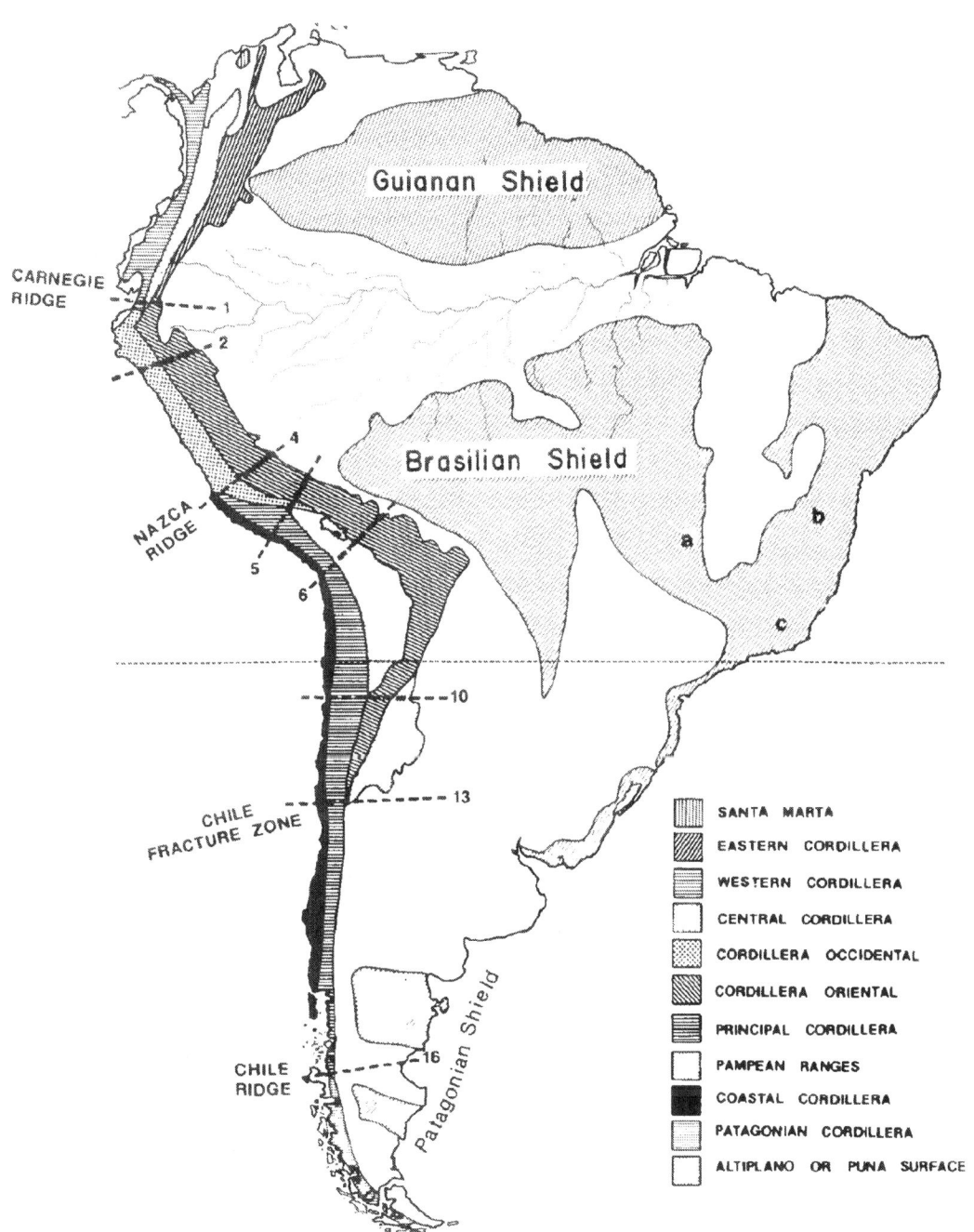

tial Cretaceous collision between the Nazca and the South American plates (Fig 7 2) leading to the original outline of most of the Cordillera He dated the final "crunch" and major upheaval as occurring at the end of the Tertiary During this last period, the Altiplano was postulated to have been raised to its present elevation of 3000 and 4500 m Although James' (1971) study was directed particularly at the Bolivian/Peruvian Andes, his conclusions probably extend to the majority of the Andean Cordillera, because the contact between the Nazca and South American plates extends from Ecuador to southern Chile Gansser (1973) also discussed the Andean orogenies in terms of plate tectonics, but he included the areas of the Andes where the South American Plate is in contact with other plates (Fig 7 2) and stressed the recent evidence that initial movements caused by contact of the plates were very early, probably Mesozoic, in some areas

In northwestern Argentina, the Pampean Ranges (Fig 7 2) were raised (Simpson and Vervoorst, 1977) after final Quaternary uplift of the Principal Cordillera to the west (Turner, 1972, Yngoven, 1972) Paralleling the Principal Cordillera from about latitude 14°S to about 44°S is the Coastal Cordillera (Fig 7 2), which apparently was uplifted somewhat earlier than most of the Andes (Okada 1971) Recent evidence (Cobbing et al, 1977 Dalmayrac et al, 1977) indicates that two small sections of this cordillera, one in Perú and one in Chile, are of Precambrian age Cobbing et al (1977) suggested that the Arequipa Massif in Perú is a rifted portion of the old South American shield areas Plio-Pleistocene movements were primarily involved in altering preexisting structure (Dessanti, 1972)

Dott et al (1977) indicated that the uplift of the Patagonian Cordillera of southern Chile was later than 77 to 81 million years ago and that most orogenic movements were completed by the Miocene

The Mountains of Southeastern Brasil

In southeastern Brasil, the Serra do Mar, Serra da Mantiqueira, and associated ranges were formed by the arching and fracturing

---

Fig 7 2 Schematic drawing of the major geomorphological units of the Andean Cordillera (redrawn from Simpson 1975) and the principal shields of the South American continent (from Putzer 1968) The tectonic segments are drawn from Sillitoe (1974) and Gansser (1973) Numbers to the left of the dotted lines refer to boundaries of tectonic segments (transverse faults that segment the descending lithosphere) as numbered in Sillitoe (1974) Missing numbers were assigned to segments omitted here Numbers included the following 1 Amotape Zone, the northern limit of the Central Andes 2 Huancabamba deflection, locality of the change in direction of the Andes from NW to NNE 4 Pisco or Abancay deflection, a proposed division of the Central Andes, a sharp step marks the beginning of the Coastal Cordillera 5 Northern limit of the Altiplano-Puno block 6 A change in strike of the Andes from N to NW and the narrowing of the Eastern Cordillera (the Ichilo Fault or the Arica Elbow line) 10 The southern edge of the Puno block 13 Boundary of the Norte Chico and Central Chilean regions, the northern limit of the Central Valley and the southern edge of the Precordillera and Sierra de Cordoba in Argentina 16 Southern limit of the Cordillera Principal In Southeastern Brasil letters refer to tectonic belts (from de Almeida, 1966) Dashed line is the Tropic of Capricorn

Dibujo esquemático de las unidades geomorfológicas mayores de la Cordillera de los Andes (redibujado de Simpson 1975) y de los principales escudos del continente Sudamericano (de Putzer 1968) Los segmentos tectonicos están dibujados de Sillitoe (1974) y Gansser (1973) Los numeros indican las fronteras de los segmentos tectonicos 1 Zona de Amotape, el limite norte de los Andes Centrales 2 Desviacion de Huancabamba, localidad del cambio de direccion de los Andes de NO a NNE 4 Desviacion de Pisco o Abancay, una division de la Cordillera Central propuesta, un marcado paso señala el comienzo de la Cordillera de la Costa 5 Limite norte del bloque Altiplano-Puno 6 Cambio direccional de los Andes de N a NO y el estrechamiento de la Cordillera Oriental (la falla de Ichilo o la linea de Codo de Arica) 10 Margen sureño del bloque del Puno 13 Separación del Norte Chico y Region Central en Chile, limite norte del Valle Central y borde sur de la Precordillera y la Sierra de Cordoba en Argentina 16 Limite sur de la Cordillera Principal En el sudeste del Brasil las letras indican cordones tectonicos (de de Almeida, 1966) La linea entrecortada señala al Tropico de Capricornio

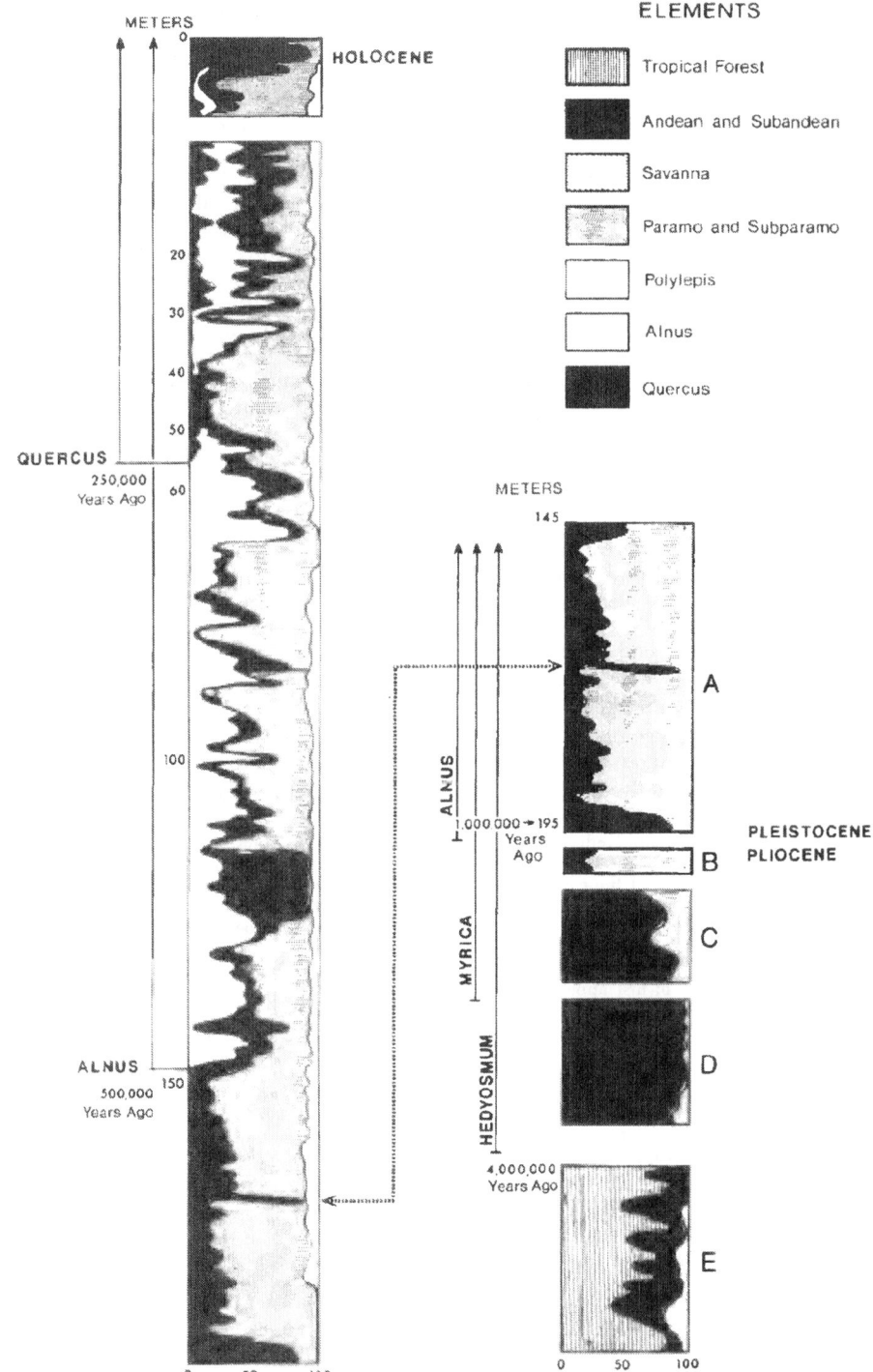

of the ancient Brasilian Shield along northeast-southwest lines. Rubidium-Strontium (Rb/Sr) age determinations of rock samples from several areas in southeastern Brasil have yielded dates that range in age from 500 to 2,000+ million years (de Almeida et al. 1973). Thus, although differing somewhat in age, all of these basement rocks are essentially Precambrian in age, and the Brasilian platform must have consolidated following an Precambrian orogenic cycle, possibly about 1,800 million years ago. More restricted orogenies apparently occurred between 900 and 1,300 million years ago. A final Precambrian orogeny that affected 40 per cent of the shield area (de Almeida et al., 1973) has been dated at about 450 to 700 million years ago.

Because most of the Brasilian Shield above 1200 m is covered with Cretaceous sediments, uplift to appreciable elevations must have occurred primarily during the Cenozoic. De Freitas (1951) concluded that three periods of epeirogenic movements account for the uplift to 1200 m or higher. The first of these probably occurred at the end of the Cretaceous and the last two in the Tertiary. The third may have extended into the Quaternary. It was during these last three phases of uplift that the Serras do Mar, Mantiqueira, Espinhaço and Borborema were fully formed.

The Guiana Highlands

Like the mountains of southeastern Brasil, the basement of the Guiana Highlands, or Tepuis, appears to be very old. For many years, the age of the rock formations comprising these abrupt table mountains emerging from the Guiana Shield was disputed. Most South American geologists tended to favor an interpretation of very ancient initial uplift (e.g., Oliveira and Leonardos, 1943) but some geologists such as Gansser (1954) concluded that they were first raised more recently perhaps in the Cretaceous. Part of the difficulty in interpreting the history of these mountains was the lack of fossils or geological stratigraphic sequences that could be correlated with those of known ages elsewhere on the continent. Since 1960, rock samples from a portion of the highlands in Guyana have been Rb/Sr dated as between 1,500 to 2,000 million years of age (Snelling, 1963). In southern Venezuela, Rb/Sr dates from several localities indicate rock ages of 1,700 to 2,100 million years (Hurley and Rand, 1973). The modern interpretation of the geological history of the Guiana Highlands (Léxico Estrat. Venezuela, 1970) is of a Precambrian basement about 3,000 to 3,100 million years old that was initially uplifted about 2,000 to 2,100 million years ago. Subsequent uplifts apparently occurred in the

FIG. 7.3. Pollen core diagrams (redrawn from van der Hammen, 1974, Figs. 3 and 5) from the high plain of Bogotá, Colombia. The base of the right hand core has been dated as older than 4 million years (Pliocene). The uppermost (separated) part of the core on the left is from Fuquene, Colombia. High elevation (subparamo) elements first appear in the uppermost Pliocene. Appreciable amounts of pollen (indicating species that are abundant) of páramo plants are found only at the beginning of the Pleistocene. In the diagrams, percentage of the total pollen recovered from a piece of a core that is represented by plants of a given vegetation type is recorded from left to right. Zero percent (absence) is on the left, and 100 percent would fill the box. The diagram also shows the times of first appearance in this area of the North American tree genera, *Alnus* and *Quercus* which migrated into South America after the closure of the Panama Portal. During the Pleistocene, interglacials are indicated by increases in the percentage of the total pollen that belongs to Andean forest genera. In glacial times, pollen of páramo plants dominate. Increases in the amounts of *Polylepis* indicate cool but quite moist conditions. The dotted arrow shows the corresponding portions of two cores taken from the high plain. On the right core, letters are designations of disjunct core segments.

Diagramas de cortes palinológicos (redibujados de van der Hammen, 1974, Figs. 3 y 5) de la Meseta de Bogotá Colombia. La base del corte de la derecha tiene una edad mayor que 4 millones de años (Plioceno). La parte alta del corte de la izquierda es de Fequene, Colombia. Elementos de altura (subpáramo) aparecen recien en el Plioceno tardío. Considerables cantidades de polen (indicadores de las especies mas abundantes) de plantas del paramo se encuentran sólo al comienzo del Pleistoceno. En los diagramas, el porcentaje del total de polen esta registrado en la base de izquierda a derecha, cero por ciento (ausencia) estaría a la izquierda, mientras que un 100 por ciento llenaría el diagrama. El diagrama también muestra los tiempos de la primera aparicion de los géneros de arboles norteamericanos *Alnus* y *Quercus* los cuales migraron a Sudamérica luego de establecida la comunicación en el Istmo de Panamá. Durante el Pleistoceno los interglaciales estan indicados por incrementos en el porcentaje del total de polen perteneciente a los géneros forestales andinos. En tiempos glaciales, el polen de plantas del páramo domina. Los incrementos en la cantidad de *Polylepis* indica condiciones frías pero húmedas. La flecha entrecortada muestra las porciones correspondientes de los cortes tomados en la sabana. En el corte de la derecha, las letras representan segmentos de cortes disjuntos.

Mesozoic, the Paleocene, and again later in the Tertiary. The recent history has been one of intense erosion and minor eustatic changes.

Summary

This cursory analysis of the geological history of the high mountains of South America has pointed out that there are two very distinct sets of montane areas. All of the Andean Cordillera, extending the length of the western edge of the continent is very young, in fact, it was raised above sea level only after the end of the Cretaceous, and elevations above 2000 m were achieved only within the last 2 to 5 million years. The faunas and floras of these high elevations could not have migrated into high elevation habitats nor begun to differentiate until the later Pliocene or Pleistocene. Quaternary climatic changes did not for the most part, modify a preexisting biota but were part of the actual story of the initiation and development of the high Andean flora and fauna. For the mountains of southeastern Brasil and the Guiana Highlands, which are composed of Precambrian/Cambrian rocks and which were progressively uplifted throughout the Mesozoic and Cenozoic, the Pleistocene was merely the latest stage of a long developmental history. Prior to the Pleistocene, there was a well-developed and established biota on which the climatic changes of the Quaternary had the combined effects of augmentation, decimation and modification.

MODERN CLIMATE

The Andean Cordillera flanking the western coast of South America, is strongly influenced by its proximity to the Pacific Ocean. The highlands of southeastern Brasil, 10° to 20° longitude farther east, come under the influence of Atlantic Ocean pressure systems. In contrast to both, the Guiana Highlands, far from any ocean, exhibit continental climatic patterns. When all of the high montane areas of South America are considered, they encompass most of the climatic patterns present across the continent. Moreover, because of their elevations, they have added complexities due to orographic effects. A brief description of the major climatic regimes provides a background against which Pleistocene climatic changes can be assessed. This outline consists of climate diagrams (Fig 7.1) and brief descriptions of the major temperature and precipitation regimes. A much more complete description of South American climates and references to local meteorological data can be found in Schweidtfeger (1976). Trewartha (1961) still provides one of the most lucid accounts of the more complex climates.

Tropical Andes

Most of the Colombian Andes and the Merida Range of Venezuela lies within the Equatorial Trough (zone over which the Intertropical Convergence Zone travels during the course of a year) and receives rainfall during two periods each year. The time of the heaviest precipitation is October to November, a second maximum occurs in April and May (Fig 7.1A). Throughout this area, precipitation is greatest at intermediate elevations (500–1500 m) and decreases with elevation. Both the Caribbean and the Pacific slopes receive about 1500 to 2000 mm of rainfall annually. The very high precipitation (up to 14,000 mm per year) on the Pacific coastal lowlands decreases inland and with elevation. The Cordillera Central of Colombia has slightly higher amounts of annual rainfall (up to 2600 mm per year) than the eastern or western Cordilleras. The major inter-Andean valleys of Colombia (Cauca and Magdelena) are dry at low elevations but their slopes receive as much as 1000 to 3000 mm of rain (respectively) a year (Johnson, 1976). The depth of these valleys and the aridity of their floors have acted as barriers to east-west migrations of montane forest and páramo elements throughout the Pleistocene (Fig 7.4).

At high elevations (>3500 m), the mean monthly temperatures are very constant over the course of a year. However, within one day temperatures at high elevations within the tropics (Fig 7 5) can exhibit a range equal to that displayed over the course of a year in temperate lowland areas. Maximum and minimum daily temperatures can differ by more than 20°C with the lowest nocturnal values below freezing.

The pattern of bimodal rainfall and constant mean monthly temperatures is found along the eastern slopes of the Andes from Colombia and Venezuela to southern Ecuador (Fig 7 IA,B). Beginning in south-central Ecuador, the bimodal pattern shifts to one of unimodality. At high elevations and along the western slopes, a pronounced dry season from April to August, develops (Fig 7 IC-II). Along the eastern slopes, total rainfall remains above 900 mm, although it is more or less concentrated into one season. Thus, as one goes south along the Andes, there is a change in the dispersion pattern in the rainfall, a reduction in the total precipitation, and an increasing difference in the amount of moisture that falls on the eastern and western slopes. The discrepancy between the two sides of the Andes reaches its maximum across the southern Altiplano (Fig 7 JE,F). On the western slopes of southern Perú and northern Chile, the climate is extremely arid and produces a barren desert. At the same latitude on the eastern slopes of southern Bolivia, enough precipitation falls to support upper montane cloud forest. The severe aridity of the western slopes is caused by a combination of several factors—1) the presence of a cold upwelling along the coast, 2) the flow of a cold oceanic current parallel to the coast, 3) the production of a rainshadow by the Eastern Cordillera, and 4) the strong Pacific anticyclone that lies off the coast of Perú. During some years the Pacific anticyclone, the force of the Humboldt current and the amount of upwelling are lessened. At such times, the Intertropical Convergence Zone extends farther south than in normal years, thereby resulting in relatively heavy rains on the coast and coastal mountains. The sporadic occurrence of this phenomenon, known as "El Niño," has led some researchers to postulate that a similar climatic pattern was prevalent during glacial periods (see section on Theories of Glacial Climatology).

Temperate Andes

As one goes south of the Tropic of Capricorn, major changes in climate are evident. Along the Pacific coast the Pacific anticyclone splits and the westerlies begin to exert an influence. Rainfall remains sparse between the latitudes of 27° and 31°S, but 90 percent of the moisture falls in the winter. At latitudes south of 31°S total precipitation increases as the summer months also begin to receive rainfall. At the latitude of Valdivia (40°S), the annual rainfall is as high as 3000 mm (5000 mm on the coast). The amount of summer precipitation increases to western Tierra del Fuego although the total amount per year is somewhat less than slightly farther north. In the southernmost regions, total precipitation decreases, but it falls almost constantly during the year, with 24 to 28 days of each month receiving some form of precipitation (Miller, 1976).

On the eastern side of the Andes south of the tropic (actually south of 29°S), the Andean slopes become dry. The moisture-laden winds of the tropical Atlantic reach only to about 29°S. In addition, the eastern slopes are the rain shadow flank of the Andes and are too far inland to receive any oceanic influences. As in the case of the western slopes at about the same latitude, rainfall becomes briefly bimodal and then shifts to a pattern of predominantly winter rainfall near the Río Colorado and Río Negro (37°S) (Prohaska 1976). Precipitation increases southward. South of 37°S, the Andean slopes intercept sufficient moisture to support deciduous beech forest.

From 27°S to the southern tip of the continent, the variation in the annual march of temperature becomes more and more pronounced, and yearly effects overshadow any diurnal temperature differences. In southern areas of the continent, the growing season is restricted to a few months of the year.

Eastern Tropical Mountains

Along the coast of southeastern Brasil, 70 to 80 percent of the rain falls between November and April with July and August being the driest part of the year. Total precipitation

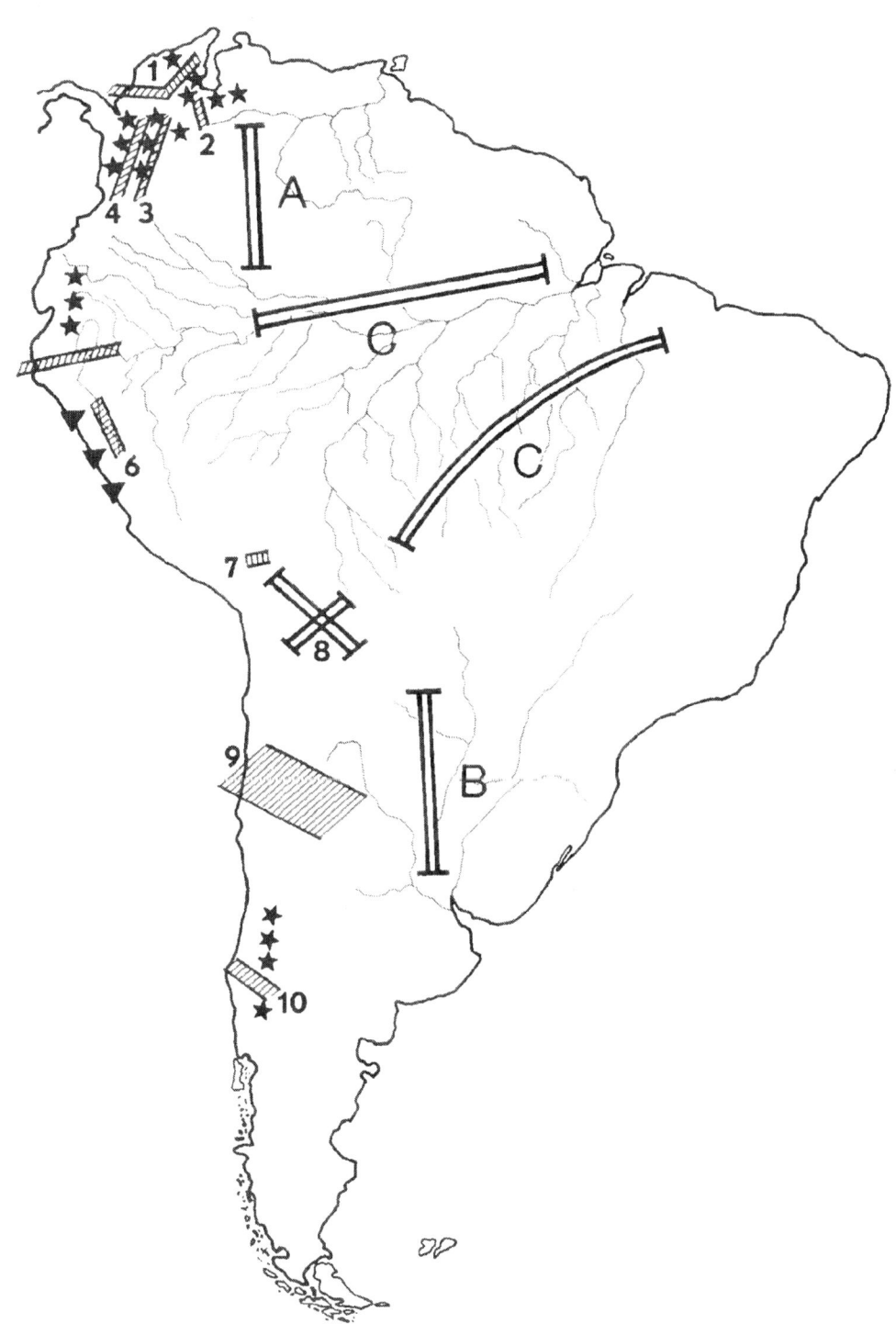

is quite high (2000 mm) and is thought to be attributable to the buildup of the subtropical anticyclone over the "hump" of Brasil (Trewartha, 1961) At elevations above 2200 m on Itatiaia mean monthly temperature differences during a year are between 15°C and 27°C Minimum temperatures of −6°C have been recorded Annual rainfall at this elevation exceeds 2400 mm (Brade, 1956, Fig 7 1J) Highlands farther inland from the coast are influenced primarily by the flow of unstable equatorial air that annually moves across central Brasil Here, rainfall is lower than along the coast, and

FIG 7 4 Barriers to population expansions of high elevation taxa during either glacial or interglacial periods 1 Lowland area of northeastern Colombia separating Sierra Nevada from the Eastern Cordillera of Colombia 2 Low arid area separating the Eastern Cordillera of Colombia and the Mérida Andes of Venezuela 3 Rio Magdalena Valley separating the Cordillera Oriental from the Cordillera Central of Colombia 4 Rio Cauca Valley separating the cordilleras Occidental and Central of Colombia 5 Northern Perú low area In all of the cases of barriers 1–5, east-west or north-south dispersal of high elevation elements is now prevented by areas of unsuitable low elevation habitat During glacial periods, the effects of these barriers would have been less severe 6 Upper Marañon Valley, an arid valley that was a glacial and interglacial barrier preventing east west exchange of elements, probably more effective in interglacial than in glacial times 7 Eastern side of Lake Titicaca where glacial ice flowed into the lake and prevented north-south biotic exchange This area is not a barrier at the present time 8 Glacial barriers for arid elements formed by lakes and bogs across the surface of the Altiplano during cold periods 9 Zone of continuous aridity across the cordillera which has served as a barrier to north-south migration during glacial and interglacial times 10 Rio Bio-Bio A modern and glacial barrier to north-south dispersal because of the climatic change at this latitude, the presence of the river itself and the glacial ice which followed the course of the river Asterisks indicate habitats isolated on mountain peaks during interglacial periods (paramos in the north and alpine habitats in the south) During glacial times, these habitats expanded, facilitating exchange The letter A refers to the area of lowland rainforest and llanos separating the Andes from the Guiana Highlands and preventing east-west colonization In glacial times, stepping stones of subtropical habitat may have been present in this region Letter B indicates thorn scrub (monte/chaco) separating the Andes from the highlands of southeastern Brasil A modern barrier presumably of narrower extent in glacial times Letter C designates the Amazon lowlands which separate the Guiana and the southeastern Brasil highlands An effective filter zone in both glacial and interglacial times but with stepping stones possible in glacial periods formed on the low tablelands of central Brasil The triangles indicate arid barriers between relict woodlands on the western slopes of the Peruvian Andes In humid periods, presumably during glacial times, these arid areas received sufficient moisture to allow continuous forest growth

Barreras para la expansión de las poblaciones de biota de altura durante los periodos glaciales o interglaciales 1 Area de tierras bajas del noreste de Colombia separando la Sierra Nevada de la Cordillera Oriental de Colombia 2 Area árida y baja separando la Cordillera Oriental de Colombia y los Andes de Mérida de Venezuela 3 Valle del Rio Magdalena separando la Cordillera Oriental de la Cordillera Central de Colombia 4 Valle del Rio Cauca separando las cordilleras Occidental y Central de Colombia 5 Areas bajas del norte del Perú En todos los casos de las barreras 1–5, la dispersión este-oeste o norte-sur de los elementos de alturas esta prevenido por areas de poca elevación Durante los periodos glaciales, los efectos de estas barreras habrian sido menos severos 6 Valle del Alto Marañon, un valle arido en cual durante la epoca glacial e interglacial fue barrera la cual evito el intercambio de elementos de este-oeste, probablemente la mas efectiva de las dos fue la epoca interglacial 7 Lado oriental del Lago Titicaca donde el hielo glacial fluyo y previno el intercambio biotico del norte a sur Esta area no es una barrera al tiempo presente 8 Barreras glaciales para elementos aridos formados por lagos y pantanos en el Altiplano durante periodos frios 9 Zona de aridez continua a lo largo de la cordillera que ha servido de barrera a la migracion norte sur durante los tiempos glaciales e interglaciales 10 Rio Bio-Bio, una barrera moderna y glacial para la dispersión norte-sur a causa del cambio climatico a esta latitud, la presencia del rio mismo y del hielo glacial que siguio el curso del rio Los asteriscos indican ambientes aislados sobre los topes de montañas durante los periodos interglaciales (páramos en el norte y ambientes alpinos en el sur) Durante el tiempo glacial estos ambientes se expandieron facilitando el intercambio La letra A refiere a las áreas de selva pluvial de tierras bajas y de llanos separando los Andes de las Alturas Cuayanesas y previniendo la colonizacion este oeste En tiempos glaciales, rutas de migraciones entrecortadas de ambientes subtropicales pueden haber estado presente en esta region La letra B indica un matorral espinoso (monte/chaco) separando los Andes de las alturas del sudeste del Brasil Una barrera moderna, probablemente de extension menor en tiempos glaciales La letra C designa las tierras bajas amazonicas que separan la Guayana y las alturas del sudeste brasileño Un filtro efectivo en los tiempos glaciales e interglaciales pero con rutas de migraciones entrecortadas posiblemente en periodos glaciales formadas en las mesetas bajas del Brasil central Los triangulos indican las barreras aridas entre selvas relictuales sobre las laderas occidentales de los Andes peruanos En periodos humedos, probablemente durante los periodos glaciales, estas areas humedas reciban suficiente humedad como para permitir el crecimiento forestal continuo

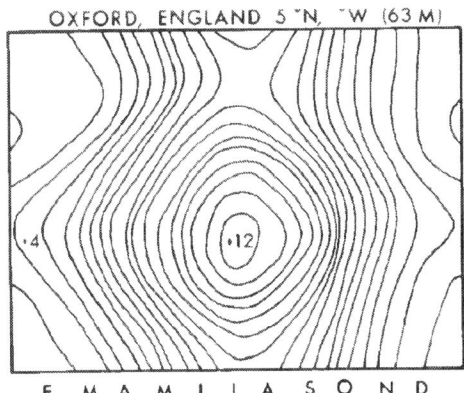

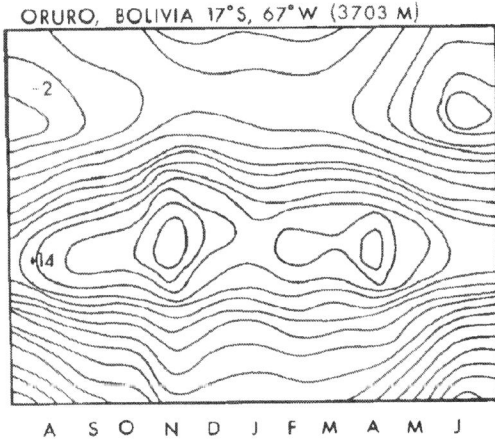

Fig. 7:5. Comparison of diurnal and annual temperature regimes in a lowland temperate and high elevation tropical area using thermoisopleths. In these diagrams, hourly mean temperatures are recorded (vertical axis) throughout the year (horizontal axis) and similar values are connected with lines. These diagrams have been somewhat simplified to make the patterns more apparent. The total temperature range of the two localities is about equal, 16°C, but at Oxford, England, the greatest temperature differences occur between summer and winter. At Oruro, Bolivia, the greatest differences between mean maximum and mean minimum temperatures occur within one day (during the summer). Upper figure from Troll, 1965, Fig. 1; lower figure from Troll, 1959, Fig. 4.

Comparación de regímenes de temperaturas diurnas y anuales en tierras bajas templadas y en tierras altas tropicales usando termoisoyetas. En estos diagramas las temperaturas medias por hora están registradas (eje vertical) a través del año (eje horizontal) y los valores similares están conectados por líneas. Los dibujos han sido simplificados para destacar más los patrones. El rango total de temperatura es casi

the majority falls in spring and summer (September–March) with the fall and winter (April–August) being the drier seasons. The tropical precipitation pattern is combined with a more temperate pattern of temperature at high elevations inland.

Interior Tropical Mountains

On the summits of the Guiana Highlands, rainfall is higher than on the surrounding lowlands. The eastern group of these tablelands receives about 2000 to 2500 mm per year and the western portion about 3300 to 3500 mm. At elevations above 1000 m, rain falls almost continuously throughout the year with slight reductions in March and September (Maguire, 1970; Snow, 1976). Because this area is so far removed from any oceanic influences, it is probable that the moisture has been derived, in part, from reevaporation or from evapotransporation of precipitation that previously fell as rain over the Amazon Basin (Snow, 1976). Temperatures are cool throughout the year, often dipping to 5°C at night (Maguire, 1970).

MODERN VEGETATION OF THE HIGH ELEVATION MOUNTAINS OF SOUTH AMERICA

In order better to understand how Pleistocene changes in the climate might have affected the vegetation of the highlands of South America, it is necessary to have some idea of the modern dominant vegetation types in the Andes and the eastern mountain ranges. In general, I confine my remarks to the vegetation above 2000 m. Naturally, such a condensed account must be rather general and somewhat superficial. The principal objective is to present an idea of where major breaks, both altitudinal and latitudinal, occur in the vegetation. In some cases, only a few characteristic plant genera are mentioned; in others, species are given. In the latter there

igual—16°C—en ambas localidades pero en Oxford, Inglaterra, las más grandes diferencias se dan entre verano e invierno. En Oruro, Bolivia, las mayores diferencias entre la media de las máximas y la media de las mínimas suceden en un día (durante el verano). La figura superior está tomada de la figura 1 de Troll, 1965; la figura inferior de la figura 4 de Troll, 1959.

are often changes in species of characteristic genera at key biogeographical points. In each case, a description of the physiognomy of the vegetation is given so as to present a visual aspect of the habitats. More detailed treatments can be found in Hueck (1966), Hueck and Seibert (1972) and Cabrera and Willink (1973). Because so much detail is lost in maps of large scale, I have not attempted to include a vegetation map. Hueck and Seibert (1972) produced the most comprehensive continent-wide vegetation map.

The Eastern Andes from Colombia and Venezuela to Northern Argentina

All of the eastern slopes of the Andes not hidden in valleys or obscured by a higher, more easterly ranges, are covered by upper montane forests. In some descriptions of the vegetation (Cabrera and Willink, 1973) this entire region is described simply as "humid montane forest" or "ceja." Yet, changes in the dominant taxa, if not in the physiognomy, do occur. In general, throughout the span (10°N–27°S), there is tall, humid, evergreen upper montane forest up to about 3500 m. Above the forest is a band of humid low scrub dominated by members of the Ericaceae (*Gaultheria*), Escalloniaceae (*Escallonia*), and Melastomataceae (*Micoma*). This scrub, composed of shrubs about 0.5 to 2 m tall, gives way to various supraforest vegetation types, described below, as one proceeds north to south. Although the upper montane forest is dominated throughout its length by members of the genera *Podocarpus* (Podocarpaceae), *Weinmannia* (Cunoniaceae), *Drimys* (Winteraceae) and various members of the Guttiferae such as *Clusia*, notable breaks do occur, and smaller, cohesive units can be distinguished. The first, in Colombia and Venezuela (10°N–1°N) spans altitudes of 2400 to 3800 m and locally ascends to 4200 m. The species of *Weinmannia* that dominate in Venezuela are *W. jahnii* and *W. microphylla*, along with *Podocarpus oleifolius*, *P. montanus*, and *P. rospigliosii*. Species of *Oreopanax* (Araliaceae), *Ilex* (Aquifoliaceae), and *Brunellia* (Brunelliaceae) are commonly mixed with other characteristic elements. From northern Ecuador to central Bolivia (1°N–16°S), the montane forest has an upper limit at a somewhat lower elevation, usually only to 3600 m, and can be considered the true "ceja." The dominant *Podocarpus* is *P. nubigenus* and the predominant *Weinmannia*, *W. fagaroides* Oreopanax, Alnus (Juglandaceae) and *Clusia* (Guttiferae) are also very common. South of Santa Cruz, Bolivia, and continuing into northern Argentina (16°S–27°S) there is a noticeable difference in the vegetation. At lower elevations, *Podocarpus* (*P. parleteoren*), *Eugenia* (Myrtaceae) and *Weinmannia* remain common along with *Ilex*. However at higher elevations, the forest becomes a semideciduous woodland with *Juglans* (*J. australis*, Juglandaceae), *Polylepis australis* (Rosaceae) and *Sambucus* (*S. peruviana*, Caprifoliaceae), mixed with the evergreen trees and *Alnus jorullensis*. The abrupt southern termination of the eastern montane forest coincides with a major climatic break that drastically reduces the rainfall on the eastern slopes (Fig. 7.1).

The High Elevation Habitats of Colombia, Venezuela and Parts of Ecuador and Perú

Above tree line (3500–4700 m) in the northern Andes, a low, humid, herbaceous vegetation covers the high elevation areas known as páramo (Cuatrecasas, 1968). Scattered through this zone are characteristic 'rosette' plants, primarily of the genus *Espeletia* (Compositae). Most of the vegetation is about 0.5 to 1 m tall with the rosette frailejónes (*Espeletia*) emergent and up to 7 m tall. In areas of suitable microhabitat, open woodlands of *Polylepis* (*P. sericea* and *P. cocuyensis*) occur. The dominant groups of plants are grasses (particularly *Calamagrostis* and *Swallenochloa*) and Compositae (*Espeletia*, *Diplostephium*, *Gynoxys*, *Loricaria*, *Aster*, *Baccharis*, *Senecio*). Several common genera such as *Lupinus* (Leguminosae), *Geranium* (Geraniaceae), and *Hypericum* (Hypericaceae) are familiar to temperate botanists. In wet páramos, the ground is often spongy with accumulated sphagnum and plant debris, and the landscape is usually shrouded in mist, if not drizzle. Analyses of the vegetation have shown that the dominant elements have not been derived by point by point vertical differentiation of the upper montane flora (Simpson, 1975). Rather, the differentiation of the flora has primarily been horizontal within the paramo zone, although several of the characteristic genera were originally derived from Neotropical stocks that grew at lower elevations. Many genera and species are restricted to one or two páramos (e.g., *Espeletia, Dipholostephium,* and *Loricaria*) or have undergone immense radiations within this regions. Other elements belong to genera common in high elevations throughout the Andes (*Senecio, Baccharis, Festuca, Mutisia, Polylepis*) or to those which migrated from North or Central America after the closing of the Panamanian portal (*Lupinus*).

The High Elevations of Ecuador and Perú and Easternmost Bolivia

There has been argument for years as to whether the area of Ecuador and Perú with low, humid, herbaceous vegetation dominated by grasses and Compositae should or should not be called páramo, but several authors (Cuatrecasas, 1968), consider the páramo zone to extend from Costa Rica to Perú. The most conspicuous difference between the areas south of northern Ecuador and those to the north is the absence of *Espeletia* to the south. Weberbauer (1945) tended to call humid high elevation areas in Perú "jalca." However, in Ecuador the term 'páramo' often is used as the common name for supraforest grasslands. Many of the same grass genera found in Colombia are dominant there, and the typical high elevation Ranunculaceae, Gentianaceae, Geraniaceae, legumes and Compositae are common.

Beginning in southwestern Ecuador and increasing in breadth across Bolivia to Argentina (4 or 5°S–27°S) the supraforest vegetation becomes (sporadically) drier and usually is called "puna." As in the case of the páramo, grasses and members of the Compositae dominate the vegetation. However, the most abundant grasses here are *Poa* (*P. humilis*), *Stipa* (*S. ichu*) and *Festuca*. The puna extends from elevations of about 3400 m to 4400 m or even higher. Dominant Compositae are *Werneria, Chuquiraga, Baccharis, Senecio* and *Lepidophyllum*. The aspect of the vegetation is more coarse than that of the páramo. Grasses tend to be clumped, shrubs have many xerophytic characteristics. Tightly compacted mat plants, such as *Azorella* (Umbelliferae), *Pycnophyllum* (Caryophyllaceae) and *Werneria* (Compositae), are common. Along the eastern side of Altiplano, the vegetation is often termed "wet puna" (Troll 1959), because it is more lush than that in the west. In the western portions, cacti, often ground-hugging, and various Bromeliaceae (*Puya, Tillandsia*) are locally abundant. Trees (*Polylepis*) are found in humid microsites up to elevations of 5200 m, but individuals are widely spaced, small, and very gnarled with reduced leaves.

The southwestern altiplano of Bolivia and adjacent regions of northern Argentina and Chile, are exceedingly dry (see Modern Climate) even grasses are sparse. The dominant plants are scattered Compositae (*Parastephia, Lepidophyllum* and *Nordophyllum*). Shrubs (1–1.5 m tall) of these genera, spaced up to 6 m apart, grow with small twisted shrubs of *Adesmia horrida* (Leguminosae). Cacti are sometimes found, and in southern Perú bromeliads are locally dominant. In intermontane valleys at lower elevations (3400 m–1000 m) in southern Bolivia and Argentina, columnar cacti (*Trichocereus terscheckii, T. pascana*) and scrubby trees and shrubs (*Prosopis ferox, Zuccagnia,* Leguminosae, *Gochnatia* and *Baccharis,* Compositae) are common. This semiarid scrub vegetation becomes dominant (with different species of *Prosopis*) along the eastern slopes of the Argentine Andes south of the ceja forest (27°S) until the latitude (36°S) where the deciduous *Nothofagus* forest begins to appear.

The West Slopes of the Andes of Colombia

Because of peculiar climatic events (Trewartha, 1961), the westernmost slopes of the Colombia Andes (extending into northern Ecuador) are covered by extremely humid montane forest, which extends narrowly inland and to about 1500 m elevation. Dominant elements include Annonaceae, Leguminosae, Moraceae, and palms. Above this zone there is upper montane forest merging into an ericaceous zone and, finally, páramo similar to that found on the other northern ranges.

The Western Slopes of the Andes from Ecuador to Central Chile

Along the west coast from south-central Ecuador to northern Chile (2°S–21°S) the vegetation becomes increasingly xerophytic and sparse. In southern Ecuador into Perú to about the latitude of Lima (12°S), the western slopes are covered with thorn scrub and cacti. Legumes such as *Prosopis* and *Acacia*, Bromeliaceae (*Puya*), Cactaceae (*Trichocereus*) and Compositae such as *Proustia*, *Franseria* and *Diplostephium* are dominant (Weberbauer, 1945; Tosi, 1960). This scrub extends to and merges with the dry puna at elevations of about 3000 m. In southern Perú, the vegetation becomes more and more sparse until, west of Arequipa only scattered bromeliads and a few cacti are visible. In northern Chile, vegetation of any prominence is virtually absent. When the infrequent rains occur, ephemerals appear, but such periods of flowering can be decades apart.

Once the latitude of about 21° to 27°S is reached vegetation reappears along the slopes and southward becomes increasingly dense. At first, thorn scrub appears, primarily around areas where streams descend from the mountains. This scrub extends elevationally from 300 m to about 3000 m and merges with the southern extension of the puna. The height of the vegetation is about 2 to 3 m and is quite open until it merges into the true evergreen material below. The dominant genera include *Adesmia*, *Acacia* and *Prosopis* (Leguminosae), Cactaceae (*Trichocereus*, *Eulychnia*) and Bromeliaceae (*Puya*).

South of 36°, the deciduous southern beech forests begin along the Pacific slopes with the appearance of *Nothofagus obliqua* and *N. procera* (Hueck, 1966). These same two taxa are the most common *Nothofagus* on the Argentine side of the Andes. Southward between 38 and 40°S, the forest becomes more lush. At the latitude of Valdivia (40°S) the species of *Nothofagus* (predominantly *N. betuloides* and *N. dombeyi*) are evergreen and the association is consequently called the evergreen rainforest or the Valdivian Forest. In addition to the evergreen species of *Nothofagus betuloides* and *Podocarpus* again becomes a dominant element (*P. nubigenus*) as well as *Drimys winteri*. Conifers such as *Fitzroya cupressoides* and *Araucaria* become conspicuous. Along with these stately trees are laurels including *Laurelia* and *Myrceugenella* (Myrtaceae). The forest becomes diminished in species and lower in stature as the Andes descend and the climate becomes harsher from 40°S to the tip of Tierra del Fuego. The beeches, *Nothofagus pumilio* and *N. antarctica* although reduced in size, continue to Tierra del Fuego.

The High Southern Andes

In the southernmost Andes (26°S to about 51°S) the area above tree line and below the level of the glaciers is covered by humid meadows similar in aspect to those of the Alps. As would be expected rosette herbs are abundant, especially members of the Compositae (*Perezia*, *Leucheria* and *Nassauvia*). Genera of families typical of the north temperate zone are common—*Ranunculus* (Ranunculaceae), *Cardamine* (Cruciferae), *Epilobium* (Onagraceae), *Primula* (Primulaceae), *Pinguicula* (Lentibulariaceae). In contrast to the páramos, these plants are covered by snow for much of the year and flower and fruit during late southern spring and summer (January to March).

The Highlands of Southern Brasil

In the extreme southern part of Brasil the highlands (600–1800 m) are covered with an open woodland with scattered trees of genera common in the Andes—*Araucaria* (*A. angustifolia*), *Podocarpus* (*P. lamberti*), *Drimys* (*D. brasiliensis*) and *Ilex* (*I. paraguariensis*). Grasses and various perennial herbs form the understory. Farther north along the extreme coastal area of southeastern Brasil, at elevations of 200 to 1800 m, is a band of evergreen humid forest dominated in the northern part by characteristic tropical legumes trees such as *Caesalpinia echinata*, *Apuleia ferra*, *Piptadenia peregrina*, *Parkia pendula*, *Machaerium* and *Cecropia* (Urticaceae), *Tecoma* (Bignoniaceae), *Geonoma*, and other palms (*Euterpe*, *Cocus*). In the more southern sector *Eugenia* (Myrtaceae), *Roupala*

(Proteaceae), *Tibouchina* and *Miconia* (Melastomataceae), various members of the Malpighiaceae, Cunoniaceae (*Weinmannia*) and numerous Compositae are dominant. On the uplands of the mountains (>1800 m) grasses dominate, especially Bambusoideae (*Chusquea penifolia* and *Cortaderia modesta*). Numerous shrubs, among them species of *Escallonia* and Compositae (e.g., *Senecio*) are common. There is much endemism but some herbaceous elements, such as *Perezia*, *Dasyphyllum* and *Trichocline* (Compositae) are shared with the Andes. The strange members of the Vochysiaceae and Velloziaceae, often cited as characteristic, are usually found at lower elevations and belong, properly speaking, to the Cerrado vegetation ("*campos rupestres*").

The Guiana Highlands

The Guiana Highlands are the least biologically explored of any of the South American montane regions. By 1970, over 2,000 plant species had been described from the few explored tepuis. Maguire (1970) estimated that at least 4,000 taxa eventually would be found. In contrast to the other regions described, endemism here is extremely high—perhaps as much as half of the flora. Certain families such as the Rapateaceae are almost confined to this area and have many genera with species restricted to the various mountain tops. Among the other families with especially large numbers of endemic genera and species are the Melastomaceae and the Myrtaceae.

Many primitive and endemic Compositae also are found in this region. Most of these *Stenopadus*, *Glossarion*, *Neblina*, *Chimantea*, *Quelchia*, *Achropogon* and *Duidea* belong to the tribe Mutisieae and are considered by some (Carlquist 1957, 1974) to be among the most primitive members of the family. The relationships of the flora of these highlands are obscure, because of the high percentage of endemic genera and families. There are few taxa closely related to groups found in the high Andes and only slightly more show floristic similarities with elements in the surrounding lowlands and mountains of southeastern Brasil (Brade, 1956, Maguire, 1970, Carlquist, 1974).

QUATERNARY OF THE HIGH MONTANE AREAS OF SOUTH AMERICA

Within the last few years, several studies have supplied new data that have altered or refined previous conclusions about the number, extent, and duration of glacial periods in South America and the moisture regimes during cold or warm periods. The most significant data come from the Colombian Andes and from the lake region of southern South America. In these and in a few additional areas, modern dating techniques combined with careful geological studies have contributed to the modification of many earlier ideas and to the resolution of some old problems.

As one might expect from the discussion of the climate and vegetation of the different mountainous areas throughout the continent, their Pleistocene histories differed considerably depending on elevation, latitude, longitude and exposure. In the most general terms, we can say that within the Pleistocene, and during times of world-wide sea-level lowering (glacial periods), cooler conditions existed with or without, an absolute increase in moisture. In times of high world-wide sea levels (interglacials), there was a warming of climate sometimes accompanied by increased precipitation.

The Northern Andes

As a result of 20 years of careful palynological and geological work of van der Hammen and his colleagues a firmly dated and fairly complete sequence of changes over the last 4 million years is available for the Eastern Andes of Colombia (van der Hammen 1974, and references therein). The sequences shown in a representative pollen core (Fig 7.3) indicate several things. First, high elevation, cool-climate-adapted taxa appear only at the very end of the Pliocene. The earliest of these elements includes *Myrica* sp (Myricaceae). As the plain around Bogota, from which these cores were made, became progressively uplifted (van der Hammen 1974, van der Hammen et al 1973), more and more plant taxa characteristic of high elevations appeared in the fossil record [e.g., *Lycopodium* (Lycopodiaceae), *Gunnera* (Haloragidaceae), *Geranium* (Geraniaceae), *Gentiana* (Gentianaceae) and *Lysipomia* (Campanulaceae)]. Later (Fig. 7.3), woody elements from North America such as *Alnus* (Betulaceae at >500,000 years b.p.) and still later *Quercus* (Fagaceae at >250,000 years b.p.) appeared. The arrival of these montane forest trees indicates the southward migration of Northern Hemisphere stocks after the closing of the Panamanian Portal at the end of the Pliocene (ca. 5.7 million years ago, Raven and Axelrod, 1974). A characteristic element of the high Andes that appears at more than 600,000 years b.p. is the genus *Polylepis*. This genus, a wind-pollinated member of the Rosaceae, had a complex history in Colombia that has been useful in interpreting changes in the climatic regime, because the northern species of this genus are restricted to cool and moist habitats (Fig. 7.3). By the end of the Pleistocene, the present flora had been established with 1) a mixture of species derived from North American genera that migrated southward (*Berberis*, Berberidaceae, *Draba* Cruciferae, *Hypericum*, Hypericaceae, *Gentiana*, Gentianaceae, *Bartsia*, Scrophulariaceae, *Valeriana* Valerianaceae), 2) south temperate taxa that migrated northward along the Andes as the increasing elevations provided progressively cool habitats (*Muehlenbergia* Gramineae, *Acaena*, Rosaceae, *Azorella*, Umbelliferae), and 3) a large number of endemic species derived by speciation within the high elevation zone from original Neotropical stocks (*Puya*, Bromeliaceae, *Rhizocephalum*, Campanulaceae, and *Espeletia*, *Diplostephium*, *Loricaria*, Compositae, see Simpson, 1975). As an analysis by Simpson (1975) and discussions by van der Hammen (1974) have indicated, this complex flora was produced, in large part, by Quaternary climatic changes. Although moraines do not provide evidence for glaciation in the region of the Sabana de Bogotá before the penultimate glaciation about 250,000 years b.p. van der Hammen (1974) interpreted the presence of cold-adapted species in the pollen cores at earlier dates as evidence of glaciations elsewhere. The ultimate glaciation began about 130,000 years b.p. The pollen-core composition at this time indicates initial cool and wet conditions followed by cold dry climates (Fig. 7.3). Woodlands of *Polylepis* covered the area about 30,000 years b.p., when conditions were cold and not excessively dry. The driest period seems to have been about 20,000 years b.p. At that time, traces of *Polylepis* disappeared altogether. During the very cold dry periods, vegetation zones were lowered about 1200 to 1500 m, and the temperatures probably were about 6 to 7°C cooler than at present. Following this last major glaciation there were minor advances and retreats, a notable advance occurred about 14,000 years b.p. Since that time, the climate has been cool and moist.

During glacial periods, when vegetation zones were lowered (and at the same time undoubtedly compressed elevationally), migrations of high elevation elements from one peak or range to another were facilitated. However, as indicated in Fig. 7.4 most of such migrations were north-south rather than east-west, because of the orientation of the cordilleras and the barrier effects of the deep inter-Andean valleys produced by the Magdalena, Cauca and Atrato rivers (Fig. 7.4). Differentiation of elements or distribution patterns that show the effects of these barriers can be seen in *Polylepis* (Simpson, in press) and numerous other plant genera (Simpson, 1975).

In Venezuela and in the Sierra Nevada de Santa Marta of Colombia, evidence has established with certainty the existence of only two glacial episodes assumed to be coincident with the last two major advances elsewhere (Shagam, 1975). Only late stratigraphic sequences have been analysed palynologically from Venezuela (Labouriau and Schubert, 1977), but geological evidence from moraines located in the Mérida Andes at Sierra de Santo Domingo (8°48′N, 70°48′W, Schubert, 1974a), Pico Bolívar (8°30′N, 71°00′W Schubert, 1974a), and Páramo La Culata (8°45′N 70°60′W, Schubert, 1974b) provide documentation for only the last major glacial advance. This means that there have been at least two periods of facilitated migration into these high elevation habitats and that these periods would have occurred during the final production (uplift) of these habitats. It should be noted in this context that the plant species diversity of the Mérida

Andes is lower than that of the Colombian Andes. It is possible that there were fewer opportunities for speciation *in situ* (fewer times of effective glaciation) than in the Colombian Andes.

Sauer's (1971) summary of the research on Ecuadorian Quaternary history indicated three glacial periods, the last of which reduced snow line 1500 to 2000 m. According to his reconstructions (Sauer, 1971, Fig 7.8), the Ecuadorian Andes were being continuously uplifted throughout the Pleistocene, and the first glacial advance had only minor effects because of the lack of appreciable land above 2000 m. By the time of the last glaciation the mountains had reached their present elevation. Despite the differing intensities felt from the three glaciations in Ecuador, Sauer (1971) correlated them with the Mindel, Riss and Wurm glaciations of Europe. During the last glaciation at least southward and northward (and probably to some extent across the central valley) migrations of high elevation taxa occurred in cooler and/or more humid periods. Because the high elevation areas of Ecuador are now in the form of relatively isolated peaks (Fig 7.4), many taxa exhibit differentiation from mountain to mountain. The restriction of taxa to mountains of certain regions can be seen in *Polylepis* (Simpson, in press), numerous other plant genera such as *Niphogeton* and *Arracacia* (Umbelliferae), *Llerasia* and *Mutisia* (Compositae) (see Simpson, 1975), and in some avian groups such as the *Atlapetes schistaceous* superspecies (Paynter, 1972).

In Perú where more stratigraphic work has been done, researchers (Hastenrath, 1967, Clapperton, 1972, Dollfus, 1976, and Nogami 1972), have interpreted levels of moraines as phases of the last or last two world-wide glacial advances (see below), although Steinmann (1930), postulated that there were at least three (one very ancient) glaciations in Perú. In any event, moraines show that snow line was lowered about 1000 to 1500 m in the east and 500 to 1000 m in the west (the drier slope of the Andes) several times during the Quaternary. In a north-south direction across Perú, the snow line depression was fairly constant despite the present decreasing annual precipitation southward (Hastenrath, 1967). Mercer and Palacios (1977) dated times of ice advance during the last glaciation in the Cordillera Vilcanota. The major advance ended between 28,000 and 14,000 years b.p. but minor advances occurred at about 11,500 and between 600 and 300 years b.p.

There is still much dispute about the amounts of precipitation received in Perú during glacial periods. Nevertheless, with the exception of Nogami (1972), most authors have come to the conclusion that there was an increase in total moisture received on the western slopes of the Peruvian and adjacent Chilean Andes at some time during the various glacial cycles. One or more periods of precipitation increase were postulated by Garner (1959) and Dollfus (1976) and accepted by Gansser (1973). Mercer and Palacios (1977) were unable to come to conclusions about ice age wetness. Possible moisture increases on the western montane flanks as outlined by Simpson (1975), would have allowed southward expansion of upper montane forest down the Pacific facing slopes (Fig 7.4). The present occurrence of relic patches of upper montane forest in sheltered, humid canyons along the western Andes prompted Koepcke (1961) to postulate that glacial periods had been accompanied by increases in precipitation in this region. Anthropological finds now indicate that rivers flowing from the Andes to the Pacific carried much more water at earlier times in the Pleistocene than at present and were able to support human settlements (Gansser, 1973).

In eastern Perú which normally receives a plentiful supply of rain, the depression of snow line and the increases in moisture would have been relatively less pronounced. It is doubtful that even the arid phases experienced by the Eastern Cordillera as envisioned by Garner (1959, Fig 8) would have altered the habitat sufficiently so as to have created a north-south migratory corridor for arid or semi-arid elements. However, during periods of increased precipitation on the highest portions of the Cordillera, it is likely that there was an exchange of mesophytic taxa from east to west across the nudos of the Peruvian Andes (Koepcke 1961, Fig 2). These nudos are east-west extensions of the Cordilleras Oriental and Occidental that form "bridges" across low inter-Andean regions. The most pronounced nudos occur slightly north of Lima (the Nudo de Pasco connecting the Cordillera Blanca and Negra with the Cordillera Oriental) and at about 15°S (Nudo de Vilcanota, connecting the Cordilleras Occidental Oriental and Auzangate). A common distribution pattern for plant taxa that indicates such a migratory route is the presence of populations in mesophytic habitats on the western slopes near Lima and then, disjunctly, across the Andes on the eastern slopes in or around the Urubamba Valley (Simpson, 1975).

Data from the entire puna surface is primarily geological, although several of the lakes on the Altiplano eventually may prove to be reliable sources of continuous pollen cores. The careful work of Kessler (1963) and the earlier work of Troll (1927), provide a basis for interpretations about the changing regimes and fluctuating snow lines of the Quaternary. Their findings indicate that during 'climax' phases of the last glaciation (and perhaps earlier) lake systems covered much of the Altiplano (Simpson, 1975, Fig 20) and that snow line was lowered 700 m below its present level on mountains flanking the plain. Vegetational changes on the nonflooded portions of the Altiplano during such periods may have been similar to those recorded near Lago Junín in central Perú (cited in Dollfus, 1976), namely, the production of bogs, perhaps seasonal bogs, dominated by members of the Cyperaceae and Juncaceae. Under such conditions, elements of the arid-scrub associations would have been restricted to higher, west-facing slopes of the Andes. The distributional ranges of xerophytic members of genera such as *Lepidophyllum*, *Mutisia*, *Perezia*, *Baccharis* *Senecio* (all Compositae) and other genera, such as *Cremolobus* (Cruciferae), would have been severely fragmented (see maps of present distributions of some of these taxa in Simpson, 1975 Fig 7.4). In contrast to these taxa, elements such as species of *Polylepis*, which are now restricted to river valleys and/or cloud belt areas, would have expanded their ranges. However, in the case of *Polylepis*, the exceedingly restricted modern distribution pattern is a result of both the present localized patchy nature of suitable microhabitats and drastic cutting by man. In the southern part of the Altiplano near Tarija fossil remains of *Megatherium*, *Scelidontherium*, *Macrauchenia*, and *Equus* (Ahlteld and Branisva, 1960) indicate the presence of grasslands in glacial times. This region is now covered by desert scrub vegetation.

In addition to humidity changes, studies of moraines on the mountains to the east of Lake Titicaca indicate at least four significant advances of ice some of which extended into the lake itself. Unfortunately, no correlations of these advances have been made with advances elsewhere and it is uncertain whether they represent stages in a late glaciation or independent major glacial advances.

Northwestern Argentina and the northern part of Chile differed in their Pleistocene history just as they now differ in their climate and vegetation. In this area of northern Argentina, both the vegetation of the puna and the ceja forests reach their southernmost limit. As in the case of the entire upper montane forest from Colombia to this latitude, Pleistocene climatic changes probably had little disruptive effect on the continuity of the band of forest. A more significant change that occurred during the Quaternary would have been the southward spread of many North American forest taxa that entered South America after the closing of the Panamanian Portal. Important genera such as *Alnus*, *Juglans*, and *Quercus* merged with native tropical and subtropical taxa such as *Drimys* and *Podocarpus* as they spread south. Alders and walnuts are now among the most characteristic trees of the upper forests in northern Argentina. Although the addition of these trees would not have altered the physiognomy of the forest the fact that they became dominants and increased the amount of deciduousness would have had a pronounced effect on the insects and other animals formerly associated with the montane forests.

In the inter-Andean valleys of northern Argentina, conditions were quite different. An analysis of many of the internally drained basins, such as the Bolsón de Pipanaco (27°S), indicates that at least once in the Pleistocene, presumably during glacial periods, some were covered by lakes (Simpson and Verhoorst, 1977) In addition, many of the higher peaks of the region such as the Nevados del Aconquija and the Sierra de Ambato were glaciated, with permanent snow lines reaching 500 m lower than any modern vestiges of ice The combination of the formation of these lakes and the increase in permanent snow indicates that cold periods at the latitude of the tropic were accompanied by increases in precipitation If conditions were appreciably wetter as well as colder, the monte vegetation now found in these valleys would have been eliminated or, at least, greatly restricted The arid-scrub monte associations presumably persisted farther south on the east side of the Andes and/or in parts of the modern Chaco The depauperate nature of the faunas now found in these isolated northern inter-Andean valleys has been attributed, in part, to the slow recolonization of the isolated pockets following Quaternary periods of decimation (Marcs 1976)

On the western side of the Andes between latitudes 18° and 27°S there is evidence of slight glaciation in the Chilean Provinces of Tarapacá and Antofagasta Most of the evidence of Pleistocene glaciations has been eroded away by modern weathering processes However, those moraines that remain indicate that on the Payachata Volcanos (18°10'S), glaciations reached to 4500 m Ice is now found only at elevations over 5500 m On Volcán Sajama as well, ice lobes may have reached as low as 4500 m and on Yarıcova 20°S down to 4000 m (Paskoff, 1977) Near the Salar de Huasco on the western edge of the Altiplano, Tricart (cited in Paskoff, 1977) found evidence of two, an older and a younger, glaciations, both of which left moraines at about 4200 m Although most glacial advances in this area remain undated, Tricart correlated these with times of high shorelines (presumably equivalent to lower sea levels) and hence glacial periods on a world-wide scale

Lakes were formed during cold periods in Tarapacá near the Peruvian border, as indicated by cold-water-adapted diatoms found fossilized in dry lake basins The Central Valley in the northern part of Antofagasta also was covered by a lake (Paskoff, 1977)

Farther to the south in Chile between 27° and 30°S, there is a poor record of Pleistocene conditions, although there are remnants of alluvial terraces in Copiapó (Paskoff 1977) Still farther to the south (30°–33°S) evidence of pronounced Quaternary events begin to appear This area, as indicated above, now is subject to pronounced changes resulting from latitudinal movements of the nearby atmospheric pressure system During the Pleistocene these movements must have been altered in some fashion All of the areas above 4000 m in this area were glaciated with ice extending to 2100 m elevation at 30°S, 2800 m at 33°S, 1700 m at 33°30'S (Maipo Valley), and to 1200 m at 34°S in the lower Central Valley (Paskoff 1977) This substantial increase in the amount of ice formation indicates both a significant glacial depression in ambient temperature and an increase in total moisture received during the year Terraces on the Pacific shore caused by increased precipitation have been shown to correspond in time to periods of eustatic sea-level changes dated as glacial The combined effect of cooler and wetter conditions in the region would have led to an environment amenable to growth of southern beech forests (Simpson, 1973, Fig 7 6) Remnants of the *Nothofagus* forest which was pushed to the north and capable of surviving in this area during glacial periods, can now be seen in small areas such as Fray Jorge (30°30'S), where woodlands with *Drimys*, *Myrceugenia*, *Gunnera*, and *Escallonia*, still persist Recently there has been discussion as to whether or not these woodlands are Pleistocene or pre-Quaternary relicts (Kummerow, et al, 1961) Geological data (Buot, 1970) and paleontological evidence (Hoffstetter and Paskoff, 1966) support an hypothesis of a Pleistocene age for these woodlands Consequently the last time(s) forests reached these areas would have been during cold, wet phases of the Pleistocene

In the centralmost portion of Chile at about the latitude of Santiago (33°S) and southward (to 39°S), evidence of glaciation is abundant Alpine glaciers extended down to elevations of 2800 m at Portillo and to 1600 m at Guardia Vieja (Paskoff, 1977) In the valley of the Río Bío-Bío, a low area of

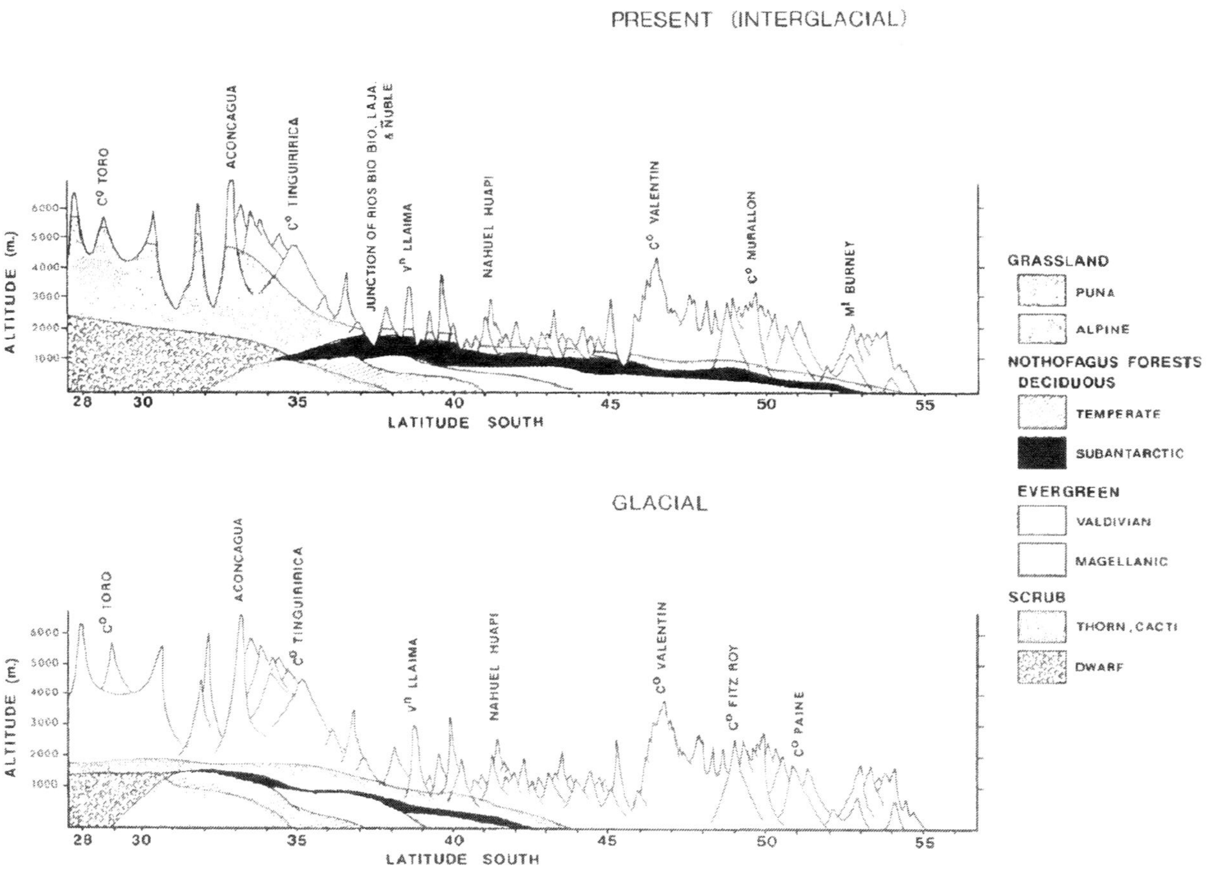

FIG. 7:6. Vegetation zones along the western slopes of the Chilean Cordillera (redrawn from Simpson, 1973) showing the lowering of the permanent snow line (white), the compression of vegetation zones, the continuity of the alpine zone and the northward extension of the beech forests in glacial times. The upper figure indicates modern snow line and the present distribution of the vegetation along the Pacific facing slopes.

Zonas de vegetación a lo largo de la vertiente occidental de la Cordillera Chilena (redibujada de Simpson, 1973) donde se muestra la disminución de la línea de las nieves permanentes, la compactación de las zonas vegetacionales, la continuidad de la zona alpina y la extensión hacia el norte de las selvas de robles en tiempos glaciales. La figura inferior muestra la línea de las nieves en la actualidad y la actual distribución de la vegetación en la vertiente Pacífica.

the Cordillera (Simpson, 1973), an ice tongue apparently reached as low as 1100 to 1200 m (Fig 7 6) Although so postulated by Bruggen (1950), there has been no recent evidence in this part of Chile to support an hypothesis of an ancient glaciation Paskoff (1977) accepted the evidence for only two, relatively recent, major advances in this region Fossil remains of cool-habitat-adapted vertebrates (*Mastodon, Mylodon, Equus*) have been associated with the last of these advances (Casamiquela 1969-1970, in Paskoff, 1977) Traces of these large vertebrates disappeared after 11 000 years b p

In the southern lake region there is firm documentation for four glaciations Between latitudes 39°–40°S, ice reached out from the Andes on several occasions westward to the base of the Coastal Cordillera The last two of these advances have been named the Rio Negro and El Salto, respectively The latter corresponds to the Llanquihue Glaciation of Heusser (1974) The earlier advances have neither been named nor dated

South of 40°, the Pleistocene geology is simplified Ice from the Andes flowed westward and downward into the Pacific, virtually eliminating all of the biota on the western slopes (Fig 7 6) However, the flora and fauna of the southern forest and bog associations persisted, because the climatic conditions allowed it to expand toward the Equator north of the sheet of ice (Figs 7 6-7, see also Vuilleumier, 1971 Fig 2, for a more detailed map of the extent of glacial ice)

For biogeographers interested in Quaternary biotic changes, one area in southern Chile has long remained controversial—the Island of Chiloé Many authors have postulated that the island was free of glacial ice and served as a refugium for southern elements at times of glacial maxima Others have claimed that the island was covered by ice and could have served no such function Recent geological and palynological investigations by Heusser and Flint (1977) settled the debate The northern part of the island was, indeed, covered by glacial ice during parts of three independent advances The first advance has not been dated, but the last two have been radiocarbon dated as having occurred at 57,000 and 43,000 years b p Palynological studies from cores showed that the coldest period was during the earliest advance and that grasses and Compositae become dominant during all of the glacial stages Several taxa now present, including some species of *Nothofagus* and *Podocarpus*, disappeared from the island However during the middle advance, other taxa, such as *Podocarpus andinus,* now found only in the Andes at elevations of 1200 to 1800 m, were present Other high latitude herbaceous species, such as *Lycopodium fuegiana* and *Diapetes muscosa* (Thymelaeaceae), were found in fossil associations with *Podocarpus andinus* Thus, it is possible that parts of Chiloe did harbor in glacial periods plant (and animal) taxa that are normally characteristic of higher elevations and latitudes

On the eastern side of the Andes, a wealth of new data has been gathered and summarized by Mercer (1976) about Pleistocene conditions of the lake region between 39° and 50°S With the exception of the Sabana de Bogota in Colombia, this area now has the most complete and well-dated Quaternary sequence of any region of South America Mercer and his colleagues have dated the oldest glacial advance with geological remains (49°28'S) at 3 5 million years The glacial advance which left the most extensive remains occurred 1 2 million years ago Subsequent to this, several smaller advances, culminating at about 13,000 years b p, took place The most extensive of this last series was about 56,000 years b p In his analysis, Mercer (1976) concluded that the Patagonian gravel hypothesized by Auer (1970) to have been deposited by a piedmont glacier, is in fact, a composite mixture of glacial outwash deposited over a time span dating from the mid-Phocene

Correlation of the Argentine glacial sequences with those of the Northern Hemisphere is still uncertain, but three advances during the Recent period (4 600–4 200 years b p , 2 700–2 000 years b p, and ca 1250 AD) coincide with advances of glacial ice elsewhere in the world (Mercer 1976)

Mercer's work does not include palynological investigations but some conclusions

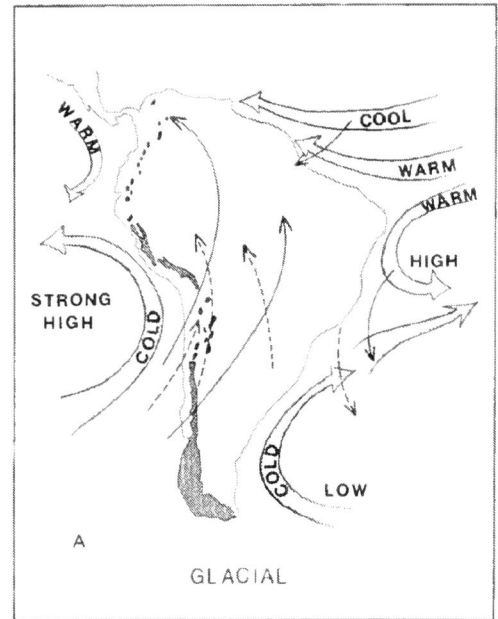 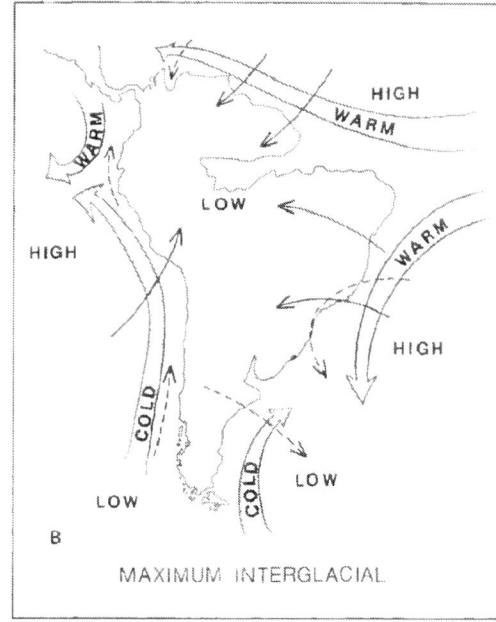

Fig. 7:7. Climatology of a maximum glacial (A) and interglacial (B) cycle following Fairbridge (1972) showing the proposed ocean current, pressure systems and wind direction changes. Continental outlines and the extent of glacial ice were drawn from Vuilleumier (1971). It is assumed in this model that during glacial periods, the intensities of the Atlantic and Pacific anticyclones (high pressure systems) and the force of the Humboldt Current were increased. The Amazon Basin was drier than at present because the influx of humid air from the northeast was prevented. Dotted arrows are January wind directions, solid lines are wind directions in July.

Climatología de un periodo glacial máximo (A) y de un interglacial (B) siguiendo a Fairbridge (1972). Se muestran las corrientes oceánicas propuestas, los sistemas de presión, y los cambios de dirección de los vientos. Los límites continentales y la extensión de los hielos glaciales fueron tomados de Vuilleumier (1971). Se asume en este modelo que durante los periodos glaciales, las intensidades de los anticiclones (sistemas de alto presión) del Atlántico y del Pacífico, y la fuerza de la corriente de Humboldt se incrementaron. La cuenca amazónica fue más seca que a lo presente debido a la ausencia de los vientos húmedos desde el noreste. Las flechas entrecortadas indican dirección del viento en Enero; las flechas continuas, la dirección de los vientos en Julio.

about the effects of the long series of glacial advances on the biota of southeastern South America can be drawn. First, the biota obviously has been subjected to periods of intense cold interspersed with periods as warm as, or warmer than, the present, since the middle of the Pliocene. Such fluctuations, as previously outlined by Simpson (1973), would have caused the high elevation biota of the region to migrate northward and/or downward several times. For elements in habitats above tree line, a succession of downward and outward migrations followed by retreat upward would have led to rapid differentiation of populations that were reduced in size and restricted in distribution during interglacial periods (Fig. 7:6). Forest elements, in contrast, would have been shifted in distribution, but their ranges would not have been subjected to fragmentation either during glacial or interglacial periods.

The investigations of Mercer (1976) also confirm the glacial limit at the base of the Andes on the eastern flanks as first established by Caldenius (1932). This limit of glacial ice provides a guide to the eastern limit of the southern beech forests during glacial periods. The tableland of Patagonia would have been neither a solid sheet of ice nor a broad expanse of forest. Rather, it probably was a boggy moorland periodically subjected to flooding and deposition of rubble during glacial periods. For further discussion of Quaternary climates in Patagonia, see Báez and Scillato Yane (this volume).

Eastern Highlands

In Eastern South America, there is poor documentation for events during the Quaternary and some debate as to the effects of various climatic changes. In the Serra do Mar, Bigarella and Mousinho (1966) described a series of terraces that they ascribed to changes in humidity during the Pleistocene. When an arid climatic cycle occurred, valleys were filled with debris (from short-lived stream flow) and sudden but sporadic showers produced slope retreat at the base of mountains leading to the formation of pediments. In succeeding humid phases these pediments were partially degraded (because of continuous washing by rainfall) and the debris in the valleys were partially swept and scoured away. A series of such climatic changes led to the superposition of eroded pediments and stream-bed patterns that these authors correlated with times of low sea level or glacial periods. However, as Beurlen (1970) has cautioned, beach levels *per se* are not necessarily an accurate indication of glacial advances. Other corroborative evidence of temporal correlations is needed. This evidence is provided, in part, by pollen sequences found elsewhere in South America that indicate dry phases were coincident (in tropical areas) with glacial advances in the Andes (van der Hammen, 1974).

At higher elevations, in the Serra da Mantiqueira, there are geomorphological remains that have led some authors (cited in Beurlen, 1970) to postulate the formation of a permanent glacier on Itatiaia during glacial times. Such formations include the presence of huge scattered boulders and U-shaped valleys (Ebert, 1960). However, there are no actual moraines. It is possible, in opposition to the conclusion of Ebert, that the boulders and the U-shaped valleys were products of mud flows and solifluction rather than glacial ice. Moreover, the presumed elevation of the Itatiaia glaciation was 2100 to 2500 m, an elevation lower than any Andean glaciation at similar latitudes. Odeman (cited in Beurlen, 1970) argued that the cooling on this isolated mountain could not have been sufficient to have caused ice formations at this low elevation. Consequently, the presence or absence of an alpine glacier on Itatiaia during Pleistocene glacial periods still remains uncertain.

There is no doubt, however, that the highest parts of Itatiaia, the rest of the Serra da Mantiqueira, and other highlands in southeastern Brasil were subjected to periods of cold and (at least) increased aridity relative to that of the present. In terms of the biota, the periods of cold would have led to a depression of vegetation zones accompanied by an increase in the superficial extent of the vegetation zones of the upper elevations. This increase in superficial distribution would have promoted migration to, and exchange of elements with, neighboring mountains (Fig 7.4). Several authors (Brade, 1956; Smith, 1962; Muller, 1968; Klein, 1975) have pointed out the relationships of components of the biota of the southeastern highlands with the biotas of the Andes and the lowland south temperate regions. Many genera such as *Araucaria*, *Podocarpus*, which show connections with the Andes, are remnants of ancient, widely distributed temperate forests (i.e., Early Tertiary) but many of the herbaceous genera, such as *Azara* (Flacourtiaceae), *Boopis* (Calyceraceae), *Escallonia* (Escalloniaceae), which are now found disjunctly in the highlands of southeastern Brasil may have spread to this region during cool periods of the Pleistocene. Other plant genera that are more widely distributed in high elevation and/or temperate regions of South America and also occur disjunctly in the highlands of southeastern Brasil (e.g. *Jamesonia*, *Gynograma* Polypodiaceae, *Anemone*, *Clematis*, *Ranunculus*, Ranunculaceae, *Berberis*, Berberidaceae, and *Lepichina*, Labiatae) also may have reached these mountains during cold periods.

In the Guiana Highlands virtually no Pleistocene geological studies have been conducted. All of the presumed reconstructions of Quaternary climatology have been made from inferences derived from data from other areas. Such data from the Andes to the west, the southeastern Brasilian Highlands to the south and the Caribbean to the north (Bonatti and Gartner, 1973) leave little choice but to assume that the Pantepui tablelands were cooler in times of glacial advance elsewhere in the tropics of South America and that vegetation zones of the upper elevations were lowered similarly to those elsewhere. As in the case of the páramos and the campos of the Brasilian highlands, a lowering of the upper elevation vegetation zones on these tablelands would have slightly increased their areal distribution and produced patches of subtropical forest on low mountains that are now covered by tropical forest. These changes in vegetation patterns would have fostered exchange among the tepuis and increased exchange of some elements with the Andes (Mayr and Phelps, 1967; Haffer, 1970b). Cook (1974), in a study of the origin of the avifauna of these highlands, pointed out that there is little correlation between the areal extent of the modern upper elevation zones, or the complexity of the vegetation of the various tepuis, and the number of breeding bird taxa found on each. This lack of correlation implies that there is not an equilibrium as would be expected following the predictions of the model of island biogeography (MacArthur and Wilson, 1967). Cook interpreted the lack of an equilibrium as an indication of the recent arrival of the avifauna. Mayr and Phelps (1967) also pointed out that the majority of the avian taxa on these highlands is derived from Andean, and hence young, stocks. Presumably, during glacial periods many successful colonizers from the Andes reached the Guiana Highlands and replaced an original, ancient avifauna. Nevertheless, it is interesting that there is little floristic connection between the tepuis and the Andes, despite the evidence from avian relationships. In contrast to the relatively low level of endemicity in the avifauna (10–30%), over 50 percent of the flora is estimated to be endemic. Moreover, the relationships of the flora of the Guiana Highlands, albeit distant, are primarily with the highlands of southeastern Brasil or even Africa rather than with the Andes. In view of the presumed recency of the avifauna and its successful migration eastward during the Pleistocene, it is puzzling that the flora has remained so distinct and remotely related to the flora of either the Andes or the surrounding lowlands.

THEORIES OF GLACIAL CLIMATOLOGY

Before extensive studies in the Southern Hemisphere had been made, many authors (e.g., Budel, 1951) assumed that Pleistocene climatic changes in both hemispheres involved simply an equatorial shift and latitudinal compression of the earth's climatic belts. The net effect of such shifts would have been to push high latitude climatic zones toward the Equator and to reduce the latitudinal extent of the mid-latitude semi-arid zones. This model of Quaternary climatology was based on European data and incorporated the apparent synchrony of cold and wet periods. It is now clear that in many regions portions of glacial cycles (often the coldest part) were arid rather than wet (Hammond, 1976). In South America investigations have shown that the Quaternary climatic picture was particularly confusing because the continent spans two hemispheres and is dominated by exceedingly high mountain ranges. A further impediment to an elucidation of the Pleistocene climates across the entire continent has been the lack of precise temporal correlations for what appear to be actual discrepancies in temperature-moisture relationships. Several hypotheses, not necessarily conflicting, have been proposed to explain the different climatic regimes in various parts of the continent.

Some authors (e.g., Nogami, 1972) have suggested that there was no major change at any time in the Pleistocene in the atmospheric circulation pattern over western South America. On the basis of observations that the snow line in the Andes during glacial advances was parallel to that now found, Nogami (1972) concluded that the "apparent" increase in moisture was only a reduction in evaporation caused by lower temperatures. However, most authors disagree, favoring instead changes in the force and/or location of the various high pressure systems that affect the South American climate. Fairbridge (1972) divided, for purposes of glacial climatology, cycles of climatic change (considered to be periods of 100,000 years) into four sub stages—the kataglacial with a cold wet climate, the periglacial with a very cold very dry climate, the anaglacial or initial interglacial phase with a cool dry climate changing to mild and wet conditions and the true interglacial with conditions similar to those of the present. As this complex scheme indicates, times of glacial advance would involve both arid and humid periods. Fairbridge (1972) attributed the older associations of glacial periods and "pluvials" to interpretations made on data from anaglacial or kataglacial phases of the cycle. Fairbridge further proposed that the aridity of the full glacial phase in the low latitudes of southern continents was caused by ocean-surface cooling and the buildup of semi-stable high pressure areas near tropical continents (Fig 7.7). In South America, semi-stable highs would have been located off the north coast of the Guianas, in the Atlantic Ocean off the tip of Brasil and off the coast of Perú (Fig 7.7).

Although the model proposed by Fairbridge (1972) explains the climates that have been proposed for eastern tropical South America, it does not account well for the complexities exhibited in the western tropical Andes nor for conditions found at high latitudes. Garner (1959) argued that Pleistocene glacial advances on the eastern and western slopes of the Peruvian Andes had been out of phase (Fig 7.8) and suggested that times of expansion of glacial ice on the Eastern Cordillera were synchronous with those in Antarctica (i.e., in phase with glacial advances in most areas of the world). He hypothesized that during such periods, the southern oceans and the Humboldt Current (originating in southern waters) would have become increasingly cold as the glacial cycle progressed causing a general cooling of the atmosphere in South America. The resulting general temperature depression would have led to the accumulation of ice (reduced melting) in areas where moisture was plentiful, such as over the Eastern Cordillera. He further proposed that the Western Cordillera would have experienced increased aridity. During the interglacial cycles in the Antarctic region, the southern oceans and the Humboldt Current would have become comparatively warm, and glaciers would have retreated in Antarctica and on the Eastern Cordillera. Garner (1959) proposed that at this time there was increased precipitation on the Western Cordillera and the expansion of glaciers there (Fig 7.8). Garner's hypothesis, while taking into account the complexities of the Andes and the apparent nonsynchrony of glacial advances on the two sides of the Peruvian Andes, appears to conflict with data from the Brasilian lowlands (Haffer, 1974) that there was aridity, rather than increased humidity, during full glacial phases. The Eastern Cordillera is under the same climatic influences that affect the Amazon Basin. Nevertheless it is possible that the height of the Andes was sufficient to cause increased precipitation at high elevations when the air from the southeast that picked up moisture and caused aridity in the lowlands reached them (see also Fairbridge, 1972).

In the most recent discussion of Andean Pleistocene climatology Dollfus (1976) stated that the climatic conditions on the two sides of the Equator differed during glacial maxima. North of the Equator cold periods were associated with dry conditions during periglacial phases, as proposed by Fairbridge (1972); south of the Equator, periglacial phases were cold and wet. Dollfus postulated that during major glacial advances, the equatorial high pressure system off western South America weakened and the onshore winds were reduced in force. The strength of the Humboldt Current was correspondingly reduced and the northern Andes of Perú received increased moisture in the form of showers. This hypothesis conflicts with that of Garner (1959). One point emphasized by Dollfus is that local conditions would have altered major climatic patterns and led to anomalies during Pleistocene glacial periods. The aridity of the Altiplano, which he dated as glacial, would have been a result of such local phenomena. He based this conclusion on the fact that under present conditions, the Altiplano is driest when the Amazon Basin receives abnormally high amounts of rainfall. It is evident that Dollfus hypothesis conflicts with the findings that during glacial periods the Amazon Basin was dry, not wet, and with the studies of

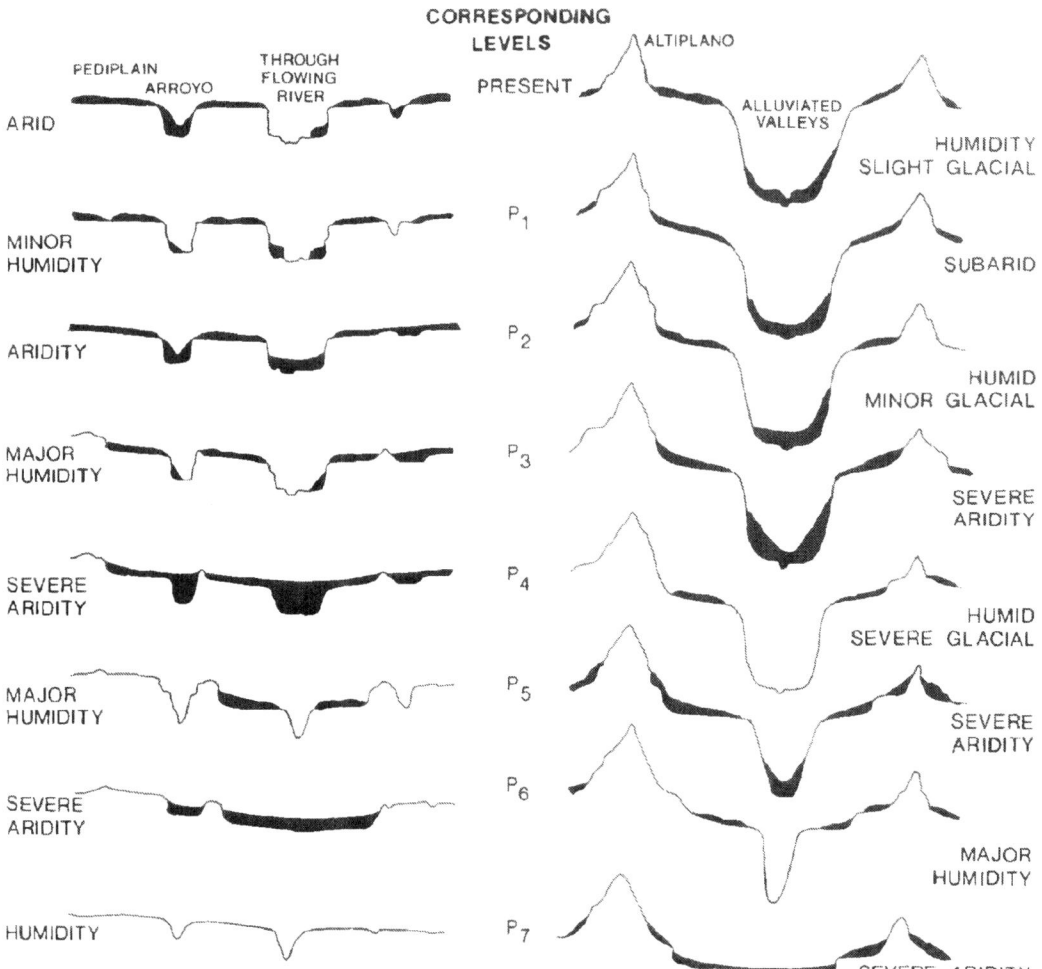

Fig. 7:8. Geomorphological sequences indicating Pleistocene climatic changes on the eastern and western slopes of the Peruvian Andes after Garner (1956). The eastern sequence is from the Urubamba Valley, Cordillera Oriental, Perú and the western sequence from southern Perú in the Cordillera Occidental west of Arequipa. Shading indicates aggradation accumulated during times of aridity. In humid periods, strongly flowing rivers and streams incise the rubble previously deposited in stream beds. Numbers are assigned to level of the same presumed age. Non-synchrony of arid and humid phases on the two cordilleras is indicated by the divergent geomorphological processes at the same level.

Secuencias geomorfológicas indicando los cambios climáticos del Pleistoceno en las vertientes oriental y occidental de los Andes peruanos de acuerdo a Garner (1956). La secuencia oriental corresponde al Valle de Urubamba, Cordillera Oriental, Perú, y la secuencia oeste corresponde al sur del Peru, en la Cordillera Occidental al oeste de Arequipa. El sombreado indica deposiciones acumuladas durante los tiempos de aridez. En períodos húmedos, fuertes flujos fluviales y de arroyos carcomieron la cama de piedra previamente depositada en la corriente. Los números corresponden a niveles de una misma presupuesta edad. La ausencia de sincronicidad de las fases húmedas y áridas en las dos cordilleras está indicada por los procesos geomorfológicos divergentes al mismo nivel.

Kessler (1963) that showed increased precipitation and lake formation across the Altiplano during glacial periods.

Obviously there is still disagreement about the time of Pleistocene humid phases during or after glacial cycles throughout South America. Nevertheless, the various theories about Pleistocene climatology show the importance of taking local factors into account and the dangers of overgeneralization from data derived from a limited area. As emphasized by Beurlen (1970) more palynological data and absolute datings are necessary before a truly meaningful and comprehensive picture of South American Quaternary climatology can be drawn.

ACKNOWLEDGMENTS

Thanks are due J. Haffer and J. L. Neff for their helpful suggestions on the manuscript and to A. Tangerini and S. Yankowski for the excution of the drawings.

RESUMEN

Las regiones altas (sobre 2000 m) de Sudamérica ocurren principalmente en la parte oeste del continente donde la Cordillera de los Andes corre paralela a la costa por más de 8000 km. Otras regiones altas con elevaciones por sobre los 1000 m se encuentran en el sudeste del Brasil y a lo largo de la frontera venezolana-guayanesa-brasilera. Los áreas por encima de los 2000 m en estas dos regiones, sin embargo, son bastante pequeñas. Las regiones montañosas del sudeste brasileño son conocidas colectivamente como las Alturas Brasileñas del Sudeste, y aquellos del norte como Alturas Guayanesas.

Geologicamente, el sistema andino completo es muy joven teniendo casi todas sus porciones bajo el nivel del mar hasta al final del Cretáceo. Aún cuando hay diferencias en detalles cronológicos, la mayoría de sus unidades geológicas esperimentaron pulsos de levantamiento a través del Terciario y del Cuaternario. La mayoría de las unidades emergieron al final del Cretáceo o al comienzo del Eoceno, esperimentaron un levantamiento mayor en el Mioceno y estuvieron sujetos a un levantemiento final e importante al tiempo del Plio-pleistoceno. Por el contrario, las Alturas Brasileñas del Sudeste y las Alturas Guayanesas han sido masas de tierras continentales desde tiempos pre-Cámbricos. Elevaciones hasta 1000 m o más probablemente ocurrieron desde el Cretáceo. Sin embargo como una consecuencia de las diferencias temporales para guarecer plantas y animales, las alturas del Este tienen una biota mas antigua y endémica que la de los altos Andes. Esto es porque todos aquellos plantas y animales que viven por sobre 2000–3000 m de elevación en los Andes han sufrido inmigración, colonización, y diferenciación sólo desde el término del Terciario. Los eventos climáticos y geológicos del Cuaternario fueron, entonces, una parte integral de la formación de esta biota. En las alturas del Este los elementos del Cuaternario constituyeron meramente una etapa mas de una larga historia evolutiva.

Dada la extensión latitudinale de la Cordillera de los Andes, clima y vegetación difieren grandemente de norte a sur. Del mismo modo, los efectos de los eventos climáticos del Cuaternario fueron diferentes de acuerdo a la posición latitudinal. En general, las temperaturas disminuyeron a través de la Cordillera en forma sincrónica con las expansiones mundiales de los hielos glaciales (denominados aquí períodos glaciales.) A lo largo de los Andes, la línea de las nieves también bajó. En algunas áreas, como en los Andes del norte, porciones de los ciclos glaciales parecen haber sido más secos que lo que ellos son hoy en día. En otros áreas como en el Altiplano y en las regiones templadas del sur, las condiciones glaciales parecen haber sido más húmedas que al presente. El numero de ciclos de expansión de los hielos glaciales a lo largo de la Cordillera varía desde un episodio tardío en algunos recientemente elevados picos en el extremo norte, hasta al menos cuatro en la región sureña chileno-argentina y donde el primero de los cuales ocurrió en el Plioceno.

En las Alturas Brasileñas del Sudeste la ocurrencia de una glaciacion no ha sido provada ciertamente aún cuando restos geomorfológicos sugieren períodos de extremo frío. Datos geomorfológicos adicionales implican ciclos fríos sincrónicos con períodos de aridez. Evidencias inferidas desde áreas contiguas sugieren que las Alturas Guayanesas fueron también más frías durante los períodos glaciales y probablemente experimentaron condiciones más secas durante partes de estos ciclos que aquellas presentas hoy.

Los afectos de los ciclos glaciales sobre la biota variaron consecuentemente en las distintas regiones montañosas. En áreas como los Andes del norte donde los picos emergentes contienen expansiones aisladas de páramos y los Andes del sur donde picos disjuntos están cubiertos con ambientes alpinos, los cambios climáticos glaciales permitieron expansiones de los rangos de elementos de altura y facilitaron la dispersión. Reducción del tamaño poblacional, aislamiento, y diferenciación ocurrieron primariamente durante los períodos interglaciales. Para los elementos de la puna, especialmente aquellos del Altiplano, la presencia de hielos glaciales y la formación de lagos glaciales causaron restricciones y aislamiento de poblaciones. En estos organismos expansiones de rango y reunificación de poblaciones que parecen haber sufrido sólo una diferenciación debil y expansiones recientes han producido los complejos patrónes biológicos de sobremontaje secundario e hibridización.

En el sudeste del Brasil y en las Alturas Guayanesas, los períodos glaciales fueron sin duda oportunidades en que los ambientes de altura se expandieron y, consecuentemente, durante las cuales las migraciones dentro de los sistemas montañosos se facilitaron. En el caso de las montañas del sudeste brasileño, una inmigración desde los altos Andes y/o desde los áreas temperados de altas latitudes también ocurrió durante los ciclos glaciales. Aún cuando la migración de aves desde los Andes a las Alturas Guayanesas pudiera haber sido similarmente promovida durante los períodos fríos, un análisis de la flora de esta región demuestra que pocas, si algunas, plantas colonizaron hacia el este durante el Pleistoceno.

Varias teorías han sido elaboradas para explicar los diversos regímenes de humedad/temperatura durante las diversas fases del Pleistoceno en diferentes partes del continente. Algunas de estas teorías explican todos los cambios climáticos en términos de una depresión de temperatura solamente. Otros proponen varios cambios en la ubicacion de los sistemas de presión atmosférica. Sin embargo, ninguna de estas hipótesis explica completamente todo el panorama continental. Se necesita más trabajos palinológicos y geomorfológicos combinados con determinaciones de edades más precisos para ofrecer una visión completa de los cambios climáticos del Cuaternario.

LITERATURE CITED

Ahlfeld, F. 1970. Zur Tektonic des Andinen Bolivien. Geol. Rundsch. 59:1124–1140.

Ahlfeld, F., Branisa, L. 1960. Geologia de Bolivia. Bosco, La Paz. 245 p.

Almeida, F. F. M. de, Amaral, G., Cordani, U. G., Kawashita, K. 1973. The Precambrian evolution of the South American cratonic margin south of the Amazon River, pp. 411–446 in Nairn, A. E. M., Stehli, F. G. (eds.) The Ocean Basins and Margins. Vol. 1. The South Atlantic. Plenum, New York. 584 p.

Auer, V. 1970. The Pleistocene of Fuego Patagonia Part V. Quaternary problems of southern South America. Ann. Acad. Sci. Fenn. Ser. A3 100:1–195.

Beurlen, K. 1970. Geologie von Brazilien. Gebruder Borntraeger, Berlin, 144 p. [Vol 9 of Beitrage zur regionalen Geologie der Erde, H. J. Martini (ed.)]

Bigarella, J. J., Mousinho, M. R. 1966. Slope development in southeastern and southern Brazil. Z. Geomorphol. 10:150–160.

Birot, P. 1970. Esquisse comparative des differents types de modele en roches cristallines dans la zone temperee chaude de l'Amerique du Sud. Rev. Geogr. Phys. Geol. Dynam. 4:299–312.

Bonatti, F., Gartner, S. Jr. 1973. Caribbean climate during the Pleistocene ice ages. Science 244:563–565.

Brade, A. C. 1956. A flora do Parque Nacional de Itatiaia. Bol. Parque Nac. Itatiaia, Brazil. Rio de Janeiro 5:1–92.

Bruggen, J. 1950. Fundamentos de la Geologia de Chile. Inst. Geogr. Militar, Santiago, Chile, 374 p.

Budel, J. 1951. Die Klimazonen des Eiszeitalters. Eiszeitalter 1:16–26.

Burgl, H. 1961. Historia geologica de Colombia. Rev. Acad. Colombiana Cien. Exactas Fis. Nat. 11:137–191.

Cabrera, A. I., Willink, A. 1973. Biogeografia de America Latina. General Secretariat of the Organization of the American States, Washington, DC. Monografia 13 Ser Biologia, 120 p.

Caldenius, C. C. 1932. Las glaciaciones Cuaternamas en la Patagonia y Tierra del Fuego. Geogr Annaler 14 1-164

CARLQUIST, S 1957 Anatomy of Guayana Mutisieae Mem N Y Bot Gard 9 441-476

CARLQUIST, S 1974 Island Biology. Columbia Univ Press, N Y, 660 p

CLAPPERTON, C M 1972 The Pleistocene moraine stages of west-central Perú. J Glaciol 11 255-263

COBBING, E J, OZARD, J M, SNELLING, N J 1977 Reconnaissance geochronology of the crystalline basement rocks of the Coastal Cordillera of Perú Geol Soc Amer Bull 88 241-246

COOK, R L 1974 Origin of the highland avifauna of southern Venezuela. Syst Zool 23 257-264

CUATRECASAS, J 1968 Paramo vegetation and its life forms, pp 163-186 in TROLL, C (ed) Geoecology of the mountainous regions of the tropical Americas Colloq Geog, Geogr Inst Univ Bonn 9 1-223

DALMAYRAC, B, LANCLOLOT, J R, LAYRELOUP, A 1977 Two-billion-year granulites in the Late Precambrian metamorphic basement along the southern Peruvian coast Science 198 49-51

DESSANTI, R N 1972 Andes Patagonicos septentrionales, pp 655-687 in LEANZA, A F (ed) Geologia regional Argentina Acad Nac Cien Cordoba, 869 p

DOLLFUS, O 1959/1960 Presentation de la structure des Andes centrales peruviennes Trav Inst Francais Etud Andines 8 53-64

DOLLFUS, O 1976 Les changements climatiques Holocenes dans les hautes Andes tropicales Bull Assoc Geogr Franc 433 95-103

DOTT, R H, JR, WINN, R D, JR, DEWIT, M J, BRUHN, R L 1977 Tectonic and sedimentary significance of Cretaceous Tekenika Beds of Tierra del Fuego Nature 266 620-622

EBERT, H 1960 Novas observações sobre a glaciação Pleistocenica na Serra do Itatiaia An Acad Bras Cienc 32 51-73

FAIRBRIDGE, R W 1972 Climatology of a glacial cycle Quat Res (N Y) 2 283-302

FREITAS, R O DE 1951 Ensaio sobre a tectonica moderna do Brazil Univ Sao Paulo Fac Filos Cienc Let Bol Geol 130 1-120

GANSSER, A 1954 The Guiana Shield (S America) Eclogae Geol Helv 47 77-112

GANSSER, A 1955 Ein Beitrage zur Geologie and Petrographie der Sierra Nevada de Santa Marta (Kolumbien Sudamerika) Schweiz Mineral Petrogr Mitt 35 209-279

GANSSER, A 1973 Facts and theories on the Andes J Geol Soc London 129 93-131

GARNER, H F 1959 Stratigraphic-sedimentary significance of contemporary climate and relief in four regions of the Andes mountains Geol Soc Amer Bull 70 1327-1368

GARNER, H F 1975 Radiometric evidence for pre-Wisconsin glaciation in the northern Andes Comment Geology 3 230-231

HAFFER, J 1970a Geologic-climatic history and zoogeographic significance of the Uraba region in northwestern Colombia Caldasia 10 603-636

HAFFER, J 1970b Entstehung and Ausbreitung nord-Andiner Bergvogel Zool Jahrb Abt Syst Oekol Geogr Tiere 97 301-337

HAFFER, J 1974 Avian speciation in tropical South America Publ Nuttall Ornithological Club Cambridge, Mass 14 390 p

HAMMOND, A L 1976 Paleoclimate Ice age earth was cool and dry Science 191 455

HARRINGTON, H J 1956 Main morphostructural regions of South America, pp xii-xviii in JENKS, W F (ed) Handbook of South American Geology Geol Soc Amer Mem 65, 378 p

HASTENRATH, S L 1967 Observations on the snow line in the Peruvian Andes J Glaciol 6 541-550

HERD D G, NAESER, C W 1974 Radiometric evidence for pre-Wisconsin glaciation in the northern Andes Geology 2 603-604

HEUSSER, C J 1974 Vegetation and climate of the southern Chilean Lake District during and since the last interglaciation Quat Res (N Y) 4 290-315

HEUSSER C J, FLINT, R F 1977 Quaternary glaciations and environments of northern Isla Chiloe, Chile Geology 5 305-308

HOFFSTETTER R, PASKOFF, R 1966 Presence des genres Macrauchenia et Hippidon dans la faune Pleistocene du Chili Bull Mus Natl Hist Nat Zool Paris (2)38 476-490

HUECK K 1966 Die Wälder Sudamerikas Gustav Fischer Verlag Stuttgart, 422 p

HUECK K, SEIBERT P 1972 Vegetationskarte von Sudamerika Mapa de la Vegetacion de America del Sur Ibid 69 pp

HURLEY P M, RAND, J R 1973 Outline of Precambrian chronology in lands bordering the South Atlantic exclusive of Brazil pp 391-410 in NAIRN, A F M, STEHLI, F C (eds) The ocean basins and margins 1 The South Atlantic, Plenum Press, N Y 583 p

JAMES D E 1971 Plate tectonic model for the evolution of the central Andes Geol Soc Amer Bull 82 3325-3346

JAMES D E 1973 The evolution of the Andes Sci Amer 229(2) 60-70

JOHNSON A M 1976 The Climate of Perú, Bolivia and Leuado, pp 174-218 in SCHWERTLGER, W (ed) Climates of Central and South America Elsevier, N Y, 532 p [Vol 12 of World Survey of Climatology H E Landsberg, ed in Chief]

KESSLER, A 1963 Uber Klima und Wasserhaushalt des Altiplano (Bolivien, Peru) während des Hochstandes der letzen Vereissung Erdkunde 17 165-173

KLEIN, R M 1975 Southern Brazilian phytogeographic features and the probable influence of Upper Quaternary climatic change in the floristic distributions, pp 67-88 in BIGARELLA, J J, BECKER, R D (eds) Internat Symp on the Quaternary (Southern Brazil July 1975) Bol Parana Geociene 33

KOLPCKE H-W 1961 Synokologische Studien an

der Westseite der peruanischen Anden. Bonn. Geogr Abhandl 29 1–320.

KUMMEROW, J, MATTE V, SCHLEGEL, I 1961 Zum problem der Nebelwalder and der zentral-chilenischen Kuste. Ber Dtsch Bot Ges 74 135–145.

LABOURIAU, M S L, SCHUBERT C 1977 Glacial and palynological studies in the Venezuelan Andes and late Quaternary instability. IV Symp Int Geol Tropical Panama 7–11 March 1977 p 103 [Abstract].

LEXICO ESTRATIGRAFICO DE VENEZUELA (ed. 2) 1970 Bol Geol Publ Especial 1 Minist Minas Hidrocarburos. Dir Geol 758 p.

MACARTHUR, R H, WILSON, L O 1967 Theory of Island Biogeography. Princeton Univ Press, Princeton, N J, 203 p.

MAGUIRE, B 1970 On the flora of the Guayana Highland. Biotropica 2 85–100.

MARES, M A 1976 Convergent evolution of desert rodents: Multivariate analysis and zoogeographic implications. Paleobiology 2 39–63.

MAYR, E, PHELPS, W H, JR 1967 The origin of the bird fauna of the south Venezuelan highlands. Bull Amer Mus Nat Hist 136 269–328.

MERCER, J H 1976 Glacial history of southernmost South America. Quat Res (N Y) 6 125–166.

MERCER, J H, PALACIOS, M O 1977 Radiocarbon dating of the last glaciation in Peru. Geology 5 600–604.

MILLER, A 1976 The climate of Chile pp 113–146 in SCHWERDTFEGER, W (ed) Climates of Central and South America. Elsevier, N Y, 532 p [Vol 12 of World Survey of Climatology, H E Landsberg ed in Chief].

MULLER, P 1968 Die Herpetofauna der Insel von São Sebastião (Brasilien). Saarbrucker Zeitung Verlag 68 p.

NOGAMI, M 1972 The snowline and climate during the last glacial period in the Andes mountains. Quat Res (Tokyo) 11 71–81.

OKADA, A 1971 On the neotectonics of the Atacama fault zone region—Preliminary notes on late Cenozoic faulting and geomorphic development of the Coast Range of northern Chile. Bull Dep Geogr Univ Tokyo 3 47–65.

OLIVEIRA, A I DE, LEONARDOS, O H 1943 Geologia do Brazil. Min Agricultura, Rio de Janeiro, 813 p.

PASKOFF, R P 1977 Quaternary of Chile: The state of research. Quat Res (N Y) 8 2–31.

PAYNTER, R A JR 1972 Biology and evolution of the Atlapetes schistaceus species group (Aves Emberizinae). Bull Mus Comp Zool Harvard Univ 143 297–320.

PROHASKA, J 1976 The climate of Argentina, Paraguay and Uruguay, pp 13–112 in SCHWERDTFEGER, W (ed) Climates of Central and South America. Elsevier, N Y, 532 p. [Vol 12 of World Survey of Climatology, H E Landsberg, ed in Chief].

PUTZER, H 1968 Uberblick uber die geologische Entwicklung Sudamerikas, pp 1–24 in FITTKAU, E J, ILLIES, J, KLINGE, H, SCHABE, C H, SOLI, H (eds) Biogeography and Ecology in South America. Junk, The Hague. Vol 1 445 p.

SAUER, W 1965 Geologia del Ecuador. Min Education Quito, Ecuador, 384 p.

SAUER, W 1971 Geologie von Ecuador. Gebruder Borntraeger, Berlin 316 p [Vol 11 of Beitrage zur regionalen Geologie der Erde. H J Martini (ed)].

SCHUBERT, C 1974a Late Pleistocene Merida glaciation, Venezuelan Andes. Boreas 3 147–152.

SCHUBERT, C 1974b Late Pleistocene glaciation of Paramo de la Culata, north central Andes. Geol Rundsch 63 516–538.

SCHWERDTFEGER, W (ed) 1976 World Survey of Climatology Vol 12 Climates of Central and South America. Elsevier, Amsterdam 532 p.

SHAGAM, R 1975 The northern termination of the Andes pp 325–420 in NAIRN, A E M, STEHLI, F G (eds) The Ocean Basins and Margins, Vol 3 The Gulf of Mexico and the Caribbean. Plenum Press, N Y, 583 p.

SILLITOE, R H 1974 Tectonic segmentation of the Andes: Implications for magmatism and metallogeny. Nature 250 542–545.

SIMPSON, B B 1973 Contrasting modes of evolution in two groups of *Perezia* (Mutisieae Compositae) of southern South America. Taxon 22 525–536.

SIMPSON, B B 1975 Pleistocene changes in the flora of the high tropical Andes. Paleobiology 1 273–294.

SIMPSON, B B In press A revision of the genus *Polylepis* (Rosaceae Sanguisorbeae). Smithsonian Contrib Bot.

SIMPSON, B B, VERVOORST, F 1977 Physiographic settings of the study sites, pp 16–25 in ORIANS, G H, SOLBRIG, O T (eds) Convergent Evolution in Warm Deserts. Dowden, Hutchinson and Ross, Stroudsburg, Pa, 333 p.

SMITH, L B 1962 Origins of the flora of southern Brazil. Contrib U S Natl Herb 35 215–249.

SNELLING, N J 1963 Age of the Roraima Formation, British Guiana. Nature 198 1079–1080.

SNOW, J W 1976 The climate of northern South America, pp 295–404 in SCHWERDTFEGER, W (ed) Climates of Central and South America. Elsevier, Amsterdam 532 p [Vol 12 of World Survey of Climatology, H F Landsberg, ed in Chief].

STEINMANN, G 1930 Geologia del Peru. Carl Winters, Heidelberg 448 p.

TOSI, J A JR 1960 Zonas de vida natural en el Peru. Inst Interam Cienc Agric OEA (Organ Estados Unidos) Cent Trop Invest Ensenanza Grad Int Zona Andina Bol Tech 5 1–271.

TREWARTHA, C T 1961 The Earth's Problem Climates. Univ Wisconsin Press, Madison, 334 p.

TROLL, K 1927 Von Titikakasee zum Pooposee und zum Solar von Coipasa. Petermanns Mitt 73 218–222.

TROLL, K. 1959. Die tropischen Gibirge. Bonn Geogr. Abhandl. 25: 1-93.
TROLL, K. 1965. Seasonal climates of the earth, pp. 19-25 *in* RODENWALDT, F., JUSATZ, H. J. (eds.) 1965. World Maps of Climatology. Springer Verlag, New York. 2nd ed. 28 p.
TURNER, J. C. M. 1972. Cordillera Oriental, pp. 117-142 *in* LEANZA, A. F. (ed.) Geología Regional Argentina. Acad. Nac. Cien., Cordoba, 869 p.
VAN DER HAMMEN, T. 1974. The Pleistocene changes of vegetation and climate in tropical South America. J. Biogeogr. 1: 3-26.
VAN DER HAMMEN, T., WERNER, J. H., DOMMELEN, H. VAN. 1973. Palynological record of the upheaval of the northern Andes: a study of the Pliocene and lower Quaternary of the Colombian Eastern Cordillera and the early evolution of its high-Andean biota. Rev. Palaeobot. Palynol. 16: 1-122.
VUILLEUMIER, B. S. 1971. Pleistocene changes in the fauna and flora of South America. Science 173: 771-780.
WEBERBAUER, A. 1945. El Mundo Vegetal de los Andes Peruanos. Minist. Agric. Lima, Peru, 766 p.
YRIGOYEN, M. R. 1972. Cordillera Principal, pp. 345-364 *in* LEANZA, A. F. (ed.) Geología Regional Argentina. Acad. Nac. Cien., Cordoba, 869 p.

8. The Amphibians of the Lowland Tropical Forests

John D Lynch

*School of Life Sciences
University of Nebraska
Lincoln, Nebraska 68508
USA*

Prior to the separation of South America from Gondwanaland and through much of the Cretaceous, most of the continent supported a lowland tropical flora with a temperate flora to the extreme south (Savage, 1973) During the Cenozoic, tropical lowland floras were restricted because of the emergence of the Andean ranges and the expansion of arid and semiarid regions in western South America (Axelrod, 1960) The Andes separated lowland forests of extreme northwestern South America from those of central South America, and the developing arid zones separated those of central South America from those of the southeast

As used here "lowland tropical forests" refers to those forested environments from sea level to 1000 meters elevation Amphibians distributed within the savannas occurring in forests are not considered forest elements Thus, the tree frogs—*Hyla crepitans H pardalis*, and *H raniceps*—are ignored here, although each occasionally invades one or more of the major South American rainforests On the other hand, the marine toad *Bufo marinus* is relatively common in nonforested environments in Central America and northern South America and also is distributed through the northern forests penetrating even those aseasonal forests with very high annual precipitation (Chocó and Napo regions)

Although I have not always segregated the evergreen forests from those that are seasonally dry I have pointed out the subdivision within each major forest (The subdivisions usually are correlated with seasonal or aseasonal forests) Those forests that have pronounced and prolonged dry seasons are not included here As a general rule, such forests are inhabited by nearly the same suite of species found in adjacent nonforest environments (cerrado, llanos) The greatest difficulty (and least confidence) was to extract estimates of approximate altitudinal distributions for the many amphibians closely associated with the major mountain systems in South America (Andes Guiana Shield, Brasilian Shield, and coastal ranges) Published data are especially scant for the diverse fauna of southeastern Brasil

Several previous biogeographic essays (e g, Parker, 1935, Lutz, 1972 Lescure, 1975) on the Amazonian herpetofauna have dealt with members of both forested and nonforested assemblies in preliminary fashions The current effort suffers from some of the same limitations imposed on previous efforts, namely, incomplete distributional data (but probably not so incomplete as suggested by Heyer, 1976) and indefinite phylogenetic constructs

The South American rainforests exist as four or five disjunct elements (Fig 8 1) The most southern the Austral Forests, is temperate and very distinct faunistically, sharing only one genus (*Bufo*) and no species with the other forests The northern tropical forests are tenuously connected, chiefly by gallery forests and forest islands distributed through the nonforest areas separating them The Trans-Andean Forests are isolated from the vast Central Cis Andean Forests by the northern Andes but are connected weakly via the Northern Forests of Colombia and Venezuela, the latter are not entirely discrete (tenuous connections through the forests fringing the Merida Andes and Venezuelan llanos) The largest of the forests (approximately 80% of all tropical South American forests) is the Central Cis-Andean forest (Amazonian or *Hylaea*) drained by the Rio Amazonas and its tributaries The central forests become drier southeastwardly and grade into the cerrado on the northwestern face of the Brasilian Shield A less marked dry belt (Reinke's Corridor) is described by numerous, isolated and generally small savannas extending from

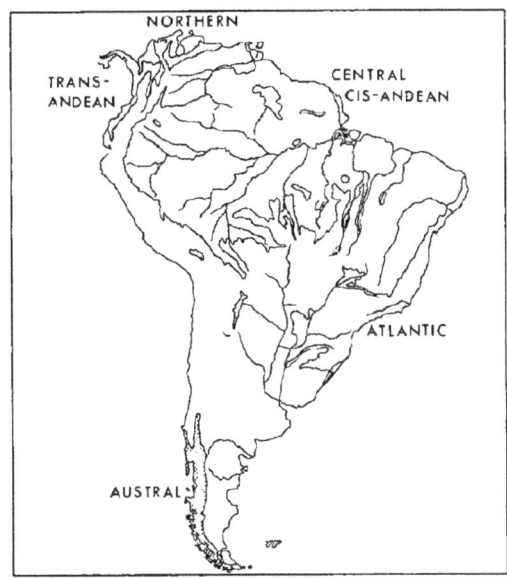

FIG 8 1 Rainforests of South America The fine-stippled forests are tropical lowland forests The coarse-stippled forest is temperate (afte Hueck 1966, and Schmithusen, 1968)

Pluviselvas sudamericanas El achurado fino muestra a las selvas tropicales de tierras bajas El achurado grueso a las selvas temperadas (de Hueck, 1966, y Schmithusen 1968)

Amazonian Venezuela southeastward to the mouth of the Rio Amazonas The central forests are tenuously connected to the Atlantic Forests of Brasil by gallery forests and forest islands in southern Brasil

The four tropical lowland forests (Trans-Andean, Northern, Central Cis-Andean, and Atlantic) harbor 530 species of forest Amphibia, 95 percent of which are restricted to one of the four forests (Fig 8 2) Only 26 species are shared by two or more forests and only five (all frogs)—*Bufo typhonius* (Bufonidae), *Hyla rubra* and *Phrynohyas venulosa* (Hylidae), *Leptodactylus wagneri* (Leptodactylidae), and *Rana palmipes* (Ranidae)—occur in all four forests Of the 126 species found in Trans-Andean Forests, 88 percent are endemic, 56 percent of the 39 species found in Northern Forests are endemic, 90 percent of the 225 species found in Central Cis-Andean Forests are endemic, and 92 percent of the 183 species of the Atlantic Forests are endemic

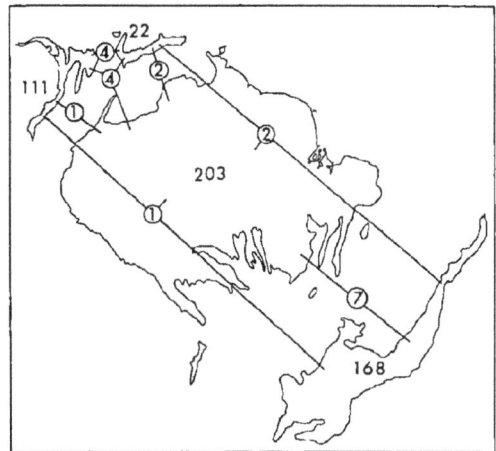

FIG 8 2 Numbers of endemic and shared amphibian species in the four tropical lowland forests of South America Five species are shared by all forests and not indicated on the figure The number of shared (noncosmopolitan) species is enclosed in the circle with lines pointing to the areas shared The geographic separation of the forests is exaggerated

Numero de especies de anfibios endemicos y compartidos en las cuatro regiones de selvas tropicales de tierras bajas de Sud America Cinco especies son compartidas por todas las regiones pero no se indican en la figura El numero de especies compartidas (nocosmopolitas) va en circulos con las lineas indicando las areas de pertenencia La separacion geografica de las selvas esta exagerada

The shared, noncosmopolitan amphibians include (Table 8 1) three caecilids (*Caecilia* and *Siphonops*), one toad (*Bufo*), one centrolenid frog (*Centrolenella*), one dendrobatid frog (*Phyllobates*), nine hylid frogs (*Hyla* and *Phyllomedusa*), five leptodactylid frogs (*Adenomera, Leptodactylus,* and *Physalaemus*), and one microhylid frog (*Relictivomer*) These and the cosmopolitan species well may prove to be South American '*Rana pipiens*' (Moore, 1944, 1975, Pace, 1974) once they are studied in detail Some evidence is accumulating to suggest this M S Hoogmoed has found no fewer than three species masquerading under the name *Bufo typhonius*" No fewer than two species presently are confused as *Hyla rubra* (M J Fouquette J Lescure pers comm) No fewer than three species make up *Leptodactylus pentadactylus* and no less than two make up *Leptodactylus wagneri*' (W R Heyer, pers comm) I am inclined to generalize

TABLE 8 1—Non-endemic Amphibians of South American Forests

	Trans-Andean	North	Central	Atlantic
Caecilians				
Caecilia subnigricans	+	+	−	−
Caecilia tentaculata	+	−	+	−
Siphonops annulatus	−	−	+	+
Anurans				
Adenomera hylaedactyla	−	+	+	+
Bufo marinus	+	+	+	−
Bufo typhonius	+	+	+	+
Centrolenella fleischmanni	+	+	+	−
Hyla albomarginata	−	+	+	+
Hyla boans	+	+	+	−
Hyla egleri	−	−	+	+
Hyla geographica	−	−	+	+
Hyla leucophyllata	−	−	+	+
Hyla luteocellata	−	+	+	−
Hyla minuta	−	−	+	+
Hyla rubra	+	+	+	+
Hyla senicula	−	−	+	+
Leptodactylus bolivianus	+	+	+	−
Leptodactylus pentadactylus	+	−	+	+
Leptodactylus pocilochilus	+	+	−	−
Leptodactylus wagneri	+	+	+	+
Phyllobates pictus	+	−	+	+
Phyllomedusa trinitatus	−	+	+	−
Phrynohyas venulosa	+	+	+	+
Physalaemus pustulosus	+	+	−	−
Rana palmipes	+	+	+	+
Relictivomer pearsei	+	+	−	−

these suggestions beyond these examples in part because I have participated in the recognition that 'Eleutherodactylus conspicillatus (or Hylodes gollmeri)" consisted of many species of frogs distributed through the forested habitats of lowland and montane South America (Lynch, 1975 Lynch and Hoogmoed, 1977, Rivero, 1961, Lynch and Myers, in prep) I predict that within a decade we will find that there exist very few 'widely distributed' species of forest amphibians, concomitantly, distinctions among different forest faunas will become greater

THE SOUTH AMERICAN AMPHIBIAN FAMILIES

Thirteen amphibian families occur in South American lowland forests (Table S 2) but only one (Brachycephalidae) is endemic The thirteen families differ in their relative appareneies in tropical lowland forests and in their global distributions

Primary distributional data are available in the taxonomically dated works of Cochran (1955), Cochran and Goin (1970), and Rivero (1961) treating southeastern Brasil Colombia and Venezuela respectively Lescure's (1976) account of the frogs of French Guiana is much more useful Lutz (1973) and the numerous and scattered works of Werner Bokermann are especially useful for Brasil

Taylor (1968) remains the most valuable source for caecilian data and Wake and Lynch (1976, and references therein) provided a recent summary for salamander distributions The largest group of amphibians (frogs and toads) is summarized the most poorly Duellman's (1977) account partially fills a void for centrolenid, hylid, and pseudid data but does not provide easy reference to primary distributional data

PLETHODONTIDAE
(Lungless Salamanders)

The family is primarily North American with one tribe radiating in the Neotropics (Wake, 1966) Bolitoglossa is well represented in montane environments in Colombia and Venezuela (Brame and Wake, 1963,

TABLE 8 2—Amphibian Complements of the Tropical Lowland Forests of South America
(Number of endemic species given in parenthesis)

Family	T-Andean	Northern	Central	Atlantic	Totals
Plethodontidae	9(9)	0	3(3)	0	12(12)
Caeciliidae	14(12)	2(1)	13(11)	8(7)	34(31)
Rhinatrematidae	2(2)	0	2(2)	0	4(4)
Typhlonectidae	1(1)	2(2)	5(5)	1(1)	9(9)
Brachycephalidae	0	0	0	2(2)	2(2)
Bufonidae	13(11)	4(2)	13(11)	8(7)	33(31)
Centrolenidae	5(4)	4(3)	9(8)	11(11)	27(26)
Dendrobatidae	19(19)	4(4)	24(23)	5(4)	51(50)
Hylidae	28(25)	11(5)	84(73)	69(61)	175(164)
Leptodactylidae	32(27)	10(5)	54(50)	67(64)	152(146)
Microhylidae	2(1)	1(0)	13(13)	10(10)	25(24)
Pipidae	0	0	4(4)	1(1)	5(5)
Ranidae	1(0)	1(0)	1(0)	1(0)	1(0)
	126(111)	39(22)	225(203)	183(168)	530(504)

1972) and *Oedipina* is a lowland Central American genus entering northwestern South America (Brame, 1968), also see Wake and Lynch (1976)

CAECILIIDAE
(Nontailed Caecilians)

The family occurs in the Neotropics, subsaharan Africa, the Seychelles, and peninsular India (Taylor, 1968) Of the eight genera found in lowland forests of South America one (*Dermophis*) is a central American genus (Savage and Wake, 1972), and two others (*Caecilia* and *Oscaecilia*) penetrate the forests of eastern Panamá

RHINATREMATIDAE
(Tailed Caecilians)

The family is autochthonous (Nussbaum, 1977) *Epicrionops* is best represented at moderate elevations in the northern Andes The monotypic *Rhinatrema* occurs in lowland forests in northeastern South America (Taylor, 1968)

TYPHLONECTIDAE
(Aquatic Caecilians)

The family is autochthonous (Taylor, 1968) *Chthonerpeton* is primarily a nonforest genus, whereas the other three genera are found in marshes and rivers of lowland forests (Taylor, 1968)

BRACHYCEPHALIDAE
(Brachycephalid Toads)

The family is known only from the lowland forests of southeastern Brasil (Izecksohn, 1971) Both genera are monotypic

BUFONIDAE
(True Toads)

The family and type-genus are nearly cosmopolitan (Blair, 1972) Eight bufonid genera occur in South America but only four occur in lowland forests (*Atelopus, Bufo, Dendrophryniscus,* and *Rhamphophryne*) *Atelopus* is primarily a montane genus in South America (McDiarmid, 1971, Peters, 1973) as is *Rhamphophryne* (Trueb, 1971) Some primary distributional data are available in Izecksohn (1976a) and Lescure (1973) The family is represented in lowland, nonforest environments (*Melanophryniscus*) as well as high nonforest environments (*Osornophryne*) *Bufo* ranges over most environments along altitudinal, latitudinal, and moisture dimensions (Cei, 1972)

CENTROLENIDAE
(Centrolenid Frogs)

This Neotropical family primarily is distributed at moderate altitudes in South America but several species of *Centrolenella* invade lowland forests (Duellman, 1977)

DENDROBATIDAE
(Poison dart Frogs)

Three genera are recognized (Savage, 1968), all of which occur in South American and lower Central America *Colostethus* is the most widely distributed (both geographically and altitudinally), whereas *Dendrobates* and

Phyllobates usually occur at elevations below 1000 m (Savage 1968, Silverstone, 1975 1976)

HYLIDAE
(Treetoads or Treefrogs)

Amphignathodontines, hylines, and phyllomedusines occur in a wide range of environments along both altitudinal and moisture dimensions, although only amphignathodontines could be viewed as successfully venturing onto the high Andes (Duellman 1977). Hemiphractines are lowland forest animals restricted to northwestern South America and Panamá (Trueb, 1974). Hylines are widely distributed outside of the Neotropics (Australo-Papuan, Holarctic, Oriental regions), the other three subfamilies are Neotropical. Some primary distributional data are available in Duellman (1971a, 1971b, 1972, 1973 1974), Duellman and Crump (1974) and Trueb and Duellman (1971).

LEPTODACTYLIDAE
(Leptodactylid Toads)

The family has invaded nearly every physiographic division of South America except the extremely xeric coast of Chile and Peru (Lynch 1971). Bufonids have only slightly narrower distributions (the two families are the most wide-ranging amphibian families in South America). Ceratophryines and leptodactylines are primarily lowland frogs ranging through xeric and mesic environments. Elosiines and telmatobiines primarily are found in mesic (low and high elevations) environments (*Odontophrynus* is a nonforest lowland genus). Primary distributional data for leptodactylid frogs are scattered widely Lynch (1971, and references therein) provided summaries of distributions for all genera. Other primary distributional data are available in Heyer (1970, 1973). Data for eleutherodactyline frogs represent summaries of unpublished data accumulated from museum study by the author.

MICROHYLIDAE
(Narrow-mouthed Frogs)

The family is pantropical but invades north temperate regions (Parker, 1934). All South American genera are endemic or occur in South America and lower Central America (Carvalho, 1954). The South American microhylids are primarily lowland forest animals but *Glossostoma aequatoriale* is Andean and *Dermatonotus* and *Elachistocleis* are nonforest genera (Dunn, 1949).

PIPIDAE
(Tongueless Frogs)

The pipinae is restricted to South America and adjacent Panamá (Savage, 1973). *Pipa parva* is a nonforest species but the other five pipines are lowland forest animals (Dunn, 1948 Izecksohn, 1976b).

PSEUDIDAE
(Pseudid Frogs)

The aquatic pseudids fringe the rainforests of tropical South America (Cochran and Goin, 1970, Gallardo, 1961, Savage, 1973) but do not invade the wet forests. Because their distribution is generally nonforest, I have not included them elsewhere in this account.

RANIDAE
(True Frogs)

This Holarctic, Ethiopian, and Oriental family barely penetrates Neotropical regions (Savage, 1973). A single species (*Rana palmipes*) is distributed widely over the northern half of lowland South America.

The two dominant families of amphibians in South America (Hylidae and Leptodactylidae) also are dominant in the lowland tropical forests (Table 8 3). In each of the four forests, these two families have the greatest numbers of species, accounting for 48 percent (Trans-Andean) 54 percent (Northern) 61 percent (Central Cis-Andean) and 84 percent (Atlantic) of the areal faunas. These families are the only South American amphibian families having more than one family-group (subfamilies, tribes) represented in the Neotropics. The two families account for 61 percent of the lowland tropical forest fauna of South America (327 of 530 species).

The family Hylidae currently is divided into four subfamilies (Duellman, 1970, 1977) three of which are Neotropical and essentially South American (Amphignathodonti-

TABLE 8 3—Hylid and Leptodactylid Complements of the Tropical Lowland Forests of South America (Numbers in parentheses are endemics)

Family-group	T-Andean	Northern	Central	Atlantic
Hylidae				
Amphignathodontinae	3(3)	2(2)	6(6)	7(7)
Hemiphractinae	1(1)	0	4(4)	0
Hylinae	18(15)	7(2)	66(56)	53(45)
Phyllomedusinae	6(6)	2(1)	8(7)	9(9)
Leptodactylidae				
Batrachylini	0	0	0	3(3)
Ceratophryinae	0	1(1)	1(1)	1(1)
Eleutherodactylini	21(24)	4(4)	33(33)	15(15)
Elosiinae	0	0	0	16(16)
Grypiscini	0	0	0	13(13)
Leptodactylinae	8(3)	5(0)	20(16)	14(11)
Odontophrynini	0	0	0	5(5)

nae, Hemiphractinae, and Phyllomedusinae) the fourth subfamily Hylinae, occurs in the Australo-Papuan Holarctic, Ethiopian (northern), and Oriental regions as well Hemiphractines occur only in Trans-Andean and Central Cis-Andean Forests (Trueb, 1974)

The family Leptodactylidae was considered to occur in the Nearctic, Neotropical Ethiopian and Australo-Papuan regions by Lynch (1971), but currently is considered to be restricted to the Nearctic and Neotropical regions (Heyer, 1975, Heyer and Liem, 1976, Lynch, 1973, Savage, 1973) Lynch (1971) divided the Neotropical leptodactylids into four subfamilies (Ceratophryinae, Elosiinae, Leptodactylinae and Telmatobiinae) Ceratophryines and elosiines are restricted to South America (Savage, 1973) The subfamily Telmatobiinae is divided into six tribes (Batrachylini, Calyptocephalellini, Eleutherodactylini, Grypiscini Odontophrynini, and Telmatobiini) by Lynch (1971, 1978) Two tribes (Calyptocephalellini and Telmatobiini) do not enter lowland tropical forests The Batrachylini occur in the temperate rainforests of Chile and Argentina and the tropical forests of southeastern Brasil (Atlantic Forests) Grypiscines and odontophrynines occur in Atlantic Forests but not in the other tropical forests, whereas eleutherodactylines occur in all four tropical forests

Thus, at the family-group level, the Atlantic Forests exhibit pronounced endemicity [Brachycephalidae, Batrachylini (shared with Austral Forests), Elosiinae Grypiscini and Odontophrynini (but shared with nonforest environments)] The most significant endemics at the family level are the Brachycephalidae, Elosiinae, and Grypiscini, because they are not found outside of the Atlantic Forests Although the four forests may be separated and linked in various combinations on the basis of family-group occurrences, generic and specific distributions provide more powerful tools to describe and differentiate amphibian faunas of the tropical forests

Eighty-three amphibian genera occur in the tropical lowland forests The salamander *Oedipina*, the caecilians *Dermophis* and *Parvicaecilia* and the anurans *Barycholos*, *Glossostoma*, and *Smilisca* occur only in Trans-Andean Forests *Glossostoma* also occurs in subparamo habitats in Andean Ecuador, and *Smilisca* is widespread in Central America in both forest and nonforest habitats

Seventeen genera (3 caecilians and 14 anurans) occur only in Central Cis Andean Forests All three caecilian genera (*Brasilotyphlus*, *Potomotyphlus*, and *Rhinatrema*) apparently are restricted to lowland forest habitats Of the 14 anurans the hylids—*Allophryne* and *Nyctimantis*, the leptodactylids—*Dischidodactylus*, *Hydrolaetare*, *Lithodytes*, and *Vanzolinius*, and the microhylids—*Ctenophryne Hamptophryne*, *Otophryne*, *Syncope*, and *Synapturanus*, are endemic forest genera *Pipa* also occurs as a nonforest element in northwestern South America and Panamá, *Edalorhina* (Leptodactylidae) and *Stefania* (Hylidae) have upland forest species

Twenty-one genera occur only in Atlantic forests The caecilian *Mimosiphonops* and the anurans *Arcovomer*, *Brachycephalus*, *Crossodactylodes*, *Crossodactylus*, *Cycloram-*

phus, *Dasypops*, *Fritziana*, *Hemipipa* *Hyophryne*, *Macrogenoglottus*, *Megaelosia* *Myersiella*, *Psyllophryne*, *Scythrophrys*, *Stereocyclops*, and *Thoropa* are lowland forest endemics. *Hylodes* and *Zachaenus* each have one upland species, *Proceratophrys* has at least one cerrado species, and *Chthonerpeton* (if actually represented in forested environments, see Taylor 1968) is primarily a nonforest genus of the Río Paraná drainage.

THE TRANS-ANDEAN FORESTS

The Trans-Andean Forests occupy the lowlands west of the Andes in Colombia and Ecuador (Chocó lowlands) and extend into Central America. Also, I have included the seasonally dry forests in the area of the Río Sinú and lower ríos Cauca and Magdalena, and the evergreen forests of the Río Magdalena. Haffer (1969) and Muller (1973, 1974) divided these Trans-Andean Forests into Chocoan and Nechí (Río Sinu and Río Cauca) units, and Muller (1973) separated the rainforests of the Río Magdalena as a distinct distributional center. Those divisions were accomplished largely on the basis of bird distributions and are not supported by amphibian distributions.

One hundred and twenty-six amphibians occur in the Trans-Andean Forests (Appendix S 1), including most of the salamanders known from lowland forests in South America. Endemism is pronounced—88 percent of the 126 species are restricted to Trans-Andean Forests. Of the 15 nonendemic amphibians, five are found in all tropical forests of South America (Table S 1), and four others occur in all but the Atlantic forests (Table S 1). Four species of frogs are shared by Trans-Andean and Northern forests; these species primarily are distributed within the Nechí subunit of the Trans-Andean Forests [*Leptodactylus bolivianus* (also Central), *L. poecilochilus*, *Physalaemus pustulosus*, and *Relictivomer pearsei*] and do not invade the wetter Chocó forests. *Bufo typhonius* (Bufonidae) and the caecilian *Caecilia subnigricans* occur in wetter areas, thereby forming a different pattern (Chocó and Río Magdalena).

No frogs are endemic to the Nechí or to the Magdalena forests, although a poison-dart frog *Dendrobates truncatus* is restricted to the pair of forests (Silverstone 1975) and only weakly differentiated from the Chocoan *D. auratus*. *Hyla phlebodes* (Hylidae), *Oedipina complex* (Plethodontidae), and *Smilisca sila* (Hylidae) occur in the Nechí forests but not in other Trans-Andean Forests in Colombia but are not endemic to the Nechí forests (Brame 1968, Duellman, 1977). Eighty-eight (70.4%) of the 126 Trans-Andean Forest amphibians are distributed in the Chocoan Forests of South America and Central America but not in the Nechí or Magdalenan forests. Fifty-six species (44.8% of the fauna) are endemic to the South American Chocó, and only eight of these range the length of the Chocó. The northern half of the Chocó and southern half (divided at approximately Buenaventura) contain 24 endemic species each (Fig 8.3). The most diverse Trans-Andean Forest fauna is that found in the Río San Juan Drainage where the northern and southern Chocoan faunas overlap. Some of the relatively widespread species (Table S 1) also occur in the Río San Juan Drainage, thereby heightening the diversity there, but these do not occur appreciably south of the drainage.

The relative poverty of the Nechí and Magdalena forests as well as those in southwestern Ecuador is marked. The most obvious factor that potentially reduces diversity in these areas is the seasonality of rainfall, although the low diversity associated with the Magdalena Forests may be a product of ecological insularity. Likewise, it could be argued that the southern forests of Ecuador are depauperate because of a peninsular effect; however those southern forests harbor some amphibians distributed in drier habitats and not extending up into the wetter forests (e.g. the leptodactylid frogs *Ceratophrys stolzmanni* *Leptodactylus labrosus*, and *Physalaemus pustulatus*.

Relatively few amphibians are distributed throughout the Trans-Andean Forests. *Bufo marinus*, *Phrynohyas venulosa* and *Smilisca phaeota* apparently occur in all subdivisions. *Eleutherodactylus raniformis* *Hyla boans*, *H. rubra*, and *Leptodactylus wagneri* occur in all except the southern Chocó (Fig 8.4) *Hemi-*

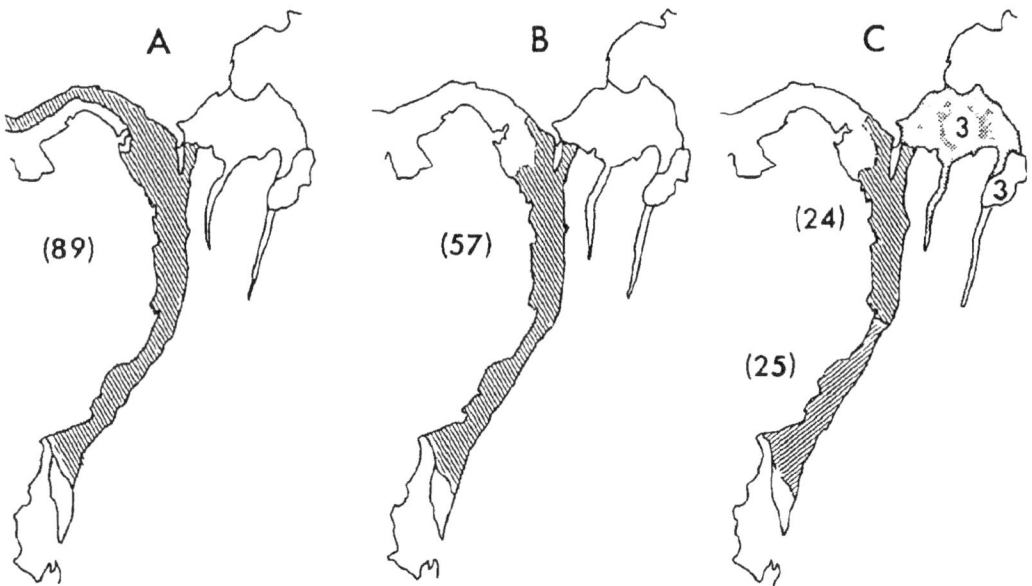

FIG 83 Endemism among Trans-Andean Forest amphibians A The distributions of 88 of the 126 Trans-Andean species are encompassed by the hatched area B 56 species are restricted to the South American Choco C Numbers of endemics in the northern and southern South American Choco (hatched), Nechi forests (stippled), and Magdalena forests (blank)

Endemismo de los anfibios transandinos A Las distribuciones de 88 de las 126 especies transandinas estan rodeadas por el area lineada B 56 especies estan restringidas al Choco sudamericano C Numero de endemismos en el norte y sur del Choco sudamerican (lineada), selvas de Nechi (achurada), y selvas de Magdalena (blanca)

phractus fasciatus occurs at lower elevations on the Andean slopes and appears to range throughout the forests where lower montane habitats exist *Bufo haematiticus, Caecilia thompsoni, Eleutherodactylus fitzingeri, E longirostris,* and *Leptodactylus pentadactylus* link the Chocó and the wet Magdalena Forests but do not occur in the drier Nechi Forests

THE NORTHERN FORESTS

The Northern Forests include those at the base of the Sierra Nevada de Santa Marta, the forest around the Maracaibo basin, those in the Falcón District of Venezuela, those associated with the coastal range of Venezuela, and those along the northwestern edge of the Venezuelan llanos The Northern Forests are bisected by the Sierra de Perija and the dry Península de Guana The assemblage was treated as three separate centers by Muller (1973) (Santa Marta, Catatumbo, and Venezuelan coastal forests centers), who considered the centers not well differentiated He separated them on the basis of vertebrates other than amphibians

This is the smallest and least diverse of the lowland forest units and has the lowest amount of endemism Only 39 species of amphibians are found in the Northern Forests (Appendix 8 2) Endemism is low (56 4%) compared to the other three forests, but comparable to that of the strictly Chocoan elements of the Trans-Andean Forests (44 8%) Some of the endemism (*Eleutherodactylus bicumulus, E rozei, E terraebolivans* Centrolenella sp , *Phyllomedusa medinae, Gastrotheca williamsoni, Flectonotus pygmaeus*) may reflect nothing more than montane slope species invading the lowland forests If that is the case for these 9 species the apparent endemism of the northern forests is markedly reduced to the point of being inconse-

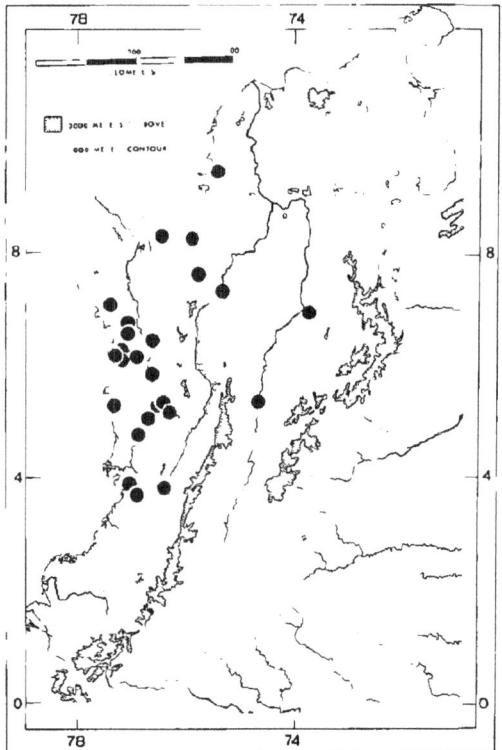

FIG 8 4 Distribution of *Eleutherodactylus raniformis* in Colombia
Distribución de Eleutherodactylus raniformis *en Colombia*

quential (*Atelopus cruciger*, *Bufo sternosignatus*, *Ceratophrys calcarata*, *Colostethus* of the *fuliginosus* group, *Eleutherodactylus maussi*, and the poorly known caecilians and hylids) The Northern Forests perhaps are best viewed as transitional forests between the two well-differentiated northern faunas (Trans-Andean and Central Cis-Andean)

THE CENTRAL CIS-ANDEAN FORESTS

Collectively, the Amazon Basin forests are termed the Central Cis-Andean forests This vast expanse of forest harbors 225 amphibian species (Appendix 8 3) of 12 families The most prominent families in order of decreasing richness, are Hylidae, Leptodactylidae, and Dendrobatidae, these three families account for 72 percent of the amphibian fauna

Although the largest unit of South American lowland forests, the Central Cis-Andean Forests are not subdivided by prominent physiographic features The terrain rises gently to the south onto the Brasilian Shield and becomes progressively more xeric with the forests giving way to the cerrado and caatinga To the north, the Central Cis-Andean Forests meet the Venezuelan and Colombian llanos

Rainfall is notably variable within the central forest (Haffer 1969, and this volume) with three areas of heavy rainfall (upper Amazon Basin in Ecuador and Perú, middle reaches of the Rio Madeira in Brasil, and along the Atlantic coast in the Guianas) A prominent moderately dry band (Reinke's Corridor) occurs inland of the Guianas and mouth of the Amazonas The belt is identified easily on vegetation maps as a chain of small to moderately large savannas Although rainfall is relatively high in the Rio Madeira region, it is seasonal as it is in much of southern and eastern *Hylaea* Those areas receiving less than 3000 mm annual precipitation experience seasonal rainfall

Muller (1973) recognized four dispersal centers (Guiana, Madeira, Napo, and Pará) based largely on endemism of birds Muller's dispersal centers generally are congruent with Haffer's (1974) forest refugia (also largely based on avian distributions) Although some amphibian examples appear to correspond well (Duellman 1972, Silverstone, 1975— *Hyla rostrata* group and *Dendrobates*, respectively), distribution patterns of amphibians in general are described poorly using these four or five centers and refugia

The whole of the Central Forests are linked by the following amphibians (asterisks indicate number of other forests where species occurs)

Adenomera andreae	*Hyla rubra*°°°
Adenomera hylaedactyla°°	*Leptodactylus pentadactylus*°°
Bufo marinus°	*Leptodactylus wagneri*°°°
Bufo typhonius°°°	
Ctenophryne geayi	*Osteocephalus taurinus*
Hydrolaetare schmidti	*Pipa pipa*
Hyla boans°°	*Phrynohyas venulosa*°°°
Hyla geographica°	*Phyllobates pictus*°
Hyla leucophyllata°	*Rana palmipes*°°°
Hyla minuta°	*Siphonops annulatus*°

In addition to these species, a pair of frog

species (*Hyla lanciformis* and *Hyla multifasciata*) link the eastern and western components of the Central Forests. The two species are closely related and possibly not distinct (Lutz, 1973).

Several species exhibit a distribution that I term "Amazonian Arc" (Fig 8 5). This distribution is most obvious in the frogs *Hamptophryne boliviana*, *Hyla fasciata*, *Lithodytes lineatus*, *Phyllomedusa bicolor*, and *Phyllomedusa vaillanti*, but also may characterize a series of species known essentially from that portion of the arc above the Rio Amazonas (*Atelopus pulcher*, *Dendrobates quinquevittatus*, *Dendrophryniscus minutus*, *Eleutherodactylus lacrimosus*, *Hyla brevifrons*, *Phrynohyas coriacea*, *Phyllobates femoralis*, and *Synapturanus mirandaribeiroi*). *Ceratophrys cornuta* is displaced somewhat from the arc, in that its northern distribution is associated with the Rio Amazonas. The distributions of all of the frogs cross Reinke's Corridor and avoid the Madeira and Tapajós drainages. The distributions of most Central Cis-Andean Forest species are more localized (Figs 8 6–8). The localization of distributions describes two areas of marked endemism. The most obvious is an area in the western portion of the Amazon Basin. The Napo-Ucayali Subunit (drainages of the Rios Huallago, Napo and Ucayali) contains 80 endemic species (2 salamanders, 5 caecilians and 73 anurans). It shares several other species with the Bolivian Unit and the extreme western supra-Amazon Unit (the Amazonian fringe species, e g, *Hyla rhodopepla*). The other area of marked endemism within Amazonian forests is the Guianan Area. Its species endemicity is reduced by sharing several species with the adjacent Venezuelan Guiana and Pará units. As is the case for the more generally distributed Amazonian amphibians, endemic amphibians are poorly represented in the Madeira-Tapajós Area. The species poverty (in terms of endemics) in the supra-Amazon Unit perhaps is explicable by the presence of the broad suite of species exhibiting Amazonian arc and northern Amazonian distributions. If we consider those more widely distributed species, the species densities of the Napo-Ucayali, Venezuelan Guiana, Guianan and Pará units also in-

Fig 8 5 Distribution of *Lithodytes lineatus*, an Amazonian arc distribution
Distribucíon de *Lithodytes lineatus*, un caso de distribución en arco Amazónico

crease accentuating the species poverty of the Madeira-Tapajos Unit

The Napo-Ucayali endemism is broad-based (Fig 8 8) rather than being a product of a radiation of a few amphibian groups. The dominant Amazonian families (Dendrobatidae, Hylidae, and Leptodactylidae) contribute substantially to the endemism of the area (2 amphignathodontine hylids, 3 bufonids, 4 centrolenids, 10 dendrobatids, 22 eleutherodactyline leptodactylids, 3 hemiphractine hylids, 18 hyline hylids, 2 leptodactyline leptodactylids, 5 microhylids, 1 pipid, 3 phyllomedusine hylids and 7 caecilians and salamanders)

THE ATLANTIC FORESTS

The Atlantic Forest amphibians are nearly as diverse (Appendix 8 4) as those of the Central Cis-Andean Forests but unlike the other South American tropical forests, the Atlantic Forests exhibit a greater dominance of hylid and leptodactylid frogs. Although dendrobatid frogs are a conspicuous element in the other forests, they are poorly represented in the Atlantic forests (5 species, 4 endemic). At the family-group level, the At-

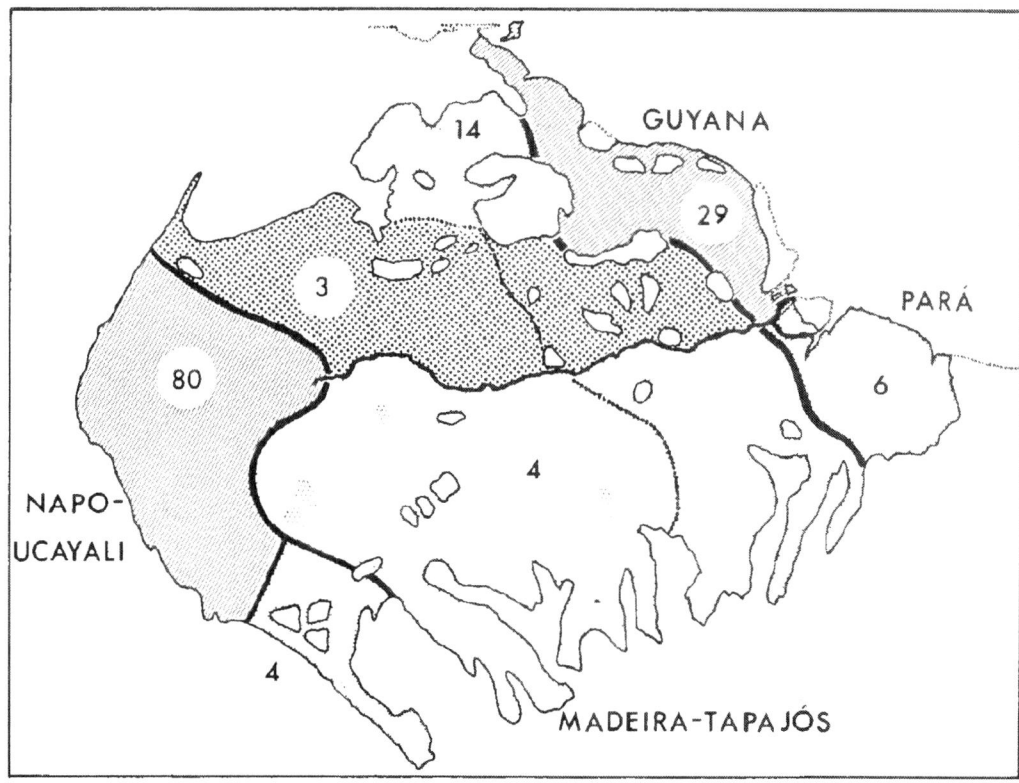

Fig. 8:6. Concentration of amphibian endemics within Central Cis-Andean Forests. Guyana, Madeira-Tapajós, Napo-Ucayali, and Pará subunits are labeled. The coarse-stippled zone (3 endemics) is supra-Amazon. The remaining subunits include the Bolivia (4 endemics) and Venezuelan Guyana (14 endemics) subunits.

Concentraciones de anfibios endémicos dentro de las selvas cisandinas centrales. Guayana, Madeira-Tapajós, Napo-Ucayali, y Pará están indicadas. El achurado grueso indica la zona supra-Amazónica (3 endemismos). Las restantes subunidades forestales incluyen a Bolivia (4 endemismos) y a la Guyana venezolana (14 endemismos) subunidades.

lantic forests are obviously unique in having batrachyline, elosiine, grypiscine, and odontophrynine leptodactylid frogs. Eleven families of amphibians and 183 species are known from the Atlantic forests. Of the 183 species, 168 (91.8%) are endemic to those forests.

Relatively few amphibians link all of the Atlantic Forests (*Bufo crucifer, Hyla faber, H. geographica, Leptodactylus mystacinus, L. pentadactylus,* and *Siphonops annulatus* appear to be distributed throughout the forests). These widespread species include two (*Hyla geographica* and *Siphonops annulatus*) also distributed over the whole of the Central Cis-Andean Forests and one (*Leptodactylus pentadactylus*) widely distributed in Central Cis-Andean and Trans-Andean forests. *Leptodactylus mystacinus* ranges through the forests as well as widely into nonforested environments (e.g., the Chaco; W. R. Heyer, pers. comm.). *Hyla faber* is the Atlantic forest replacement for *Hyla boans* (Lutz, 1973).

The frogs *Gastrotheca fissipes, Hyla leucophyllata, H. rubra, Leptodactylus mystaceus, L. troglodytes, L. wagneri, Phyllodytes luteolus,* and *Proceratophrys cristiceps* are broadly distributed through the northern portion of the Atlantic forests, and *Hyla fuscomarginata, H. senicula,* and *Siphonops paulensis* are widely distributed through the southern portions of the Atlantic Forests. West and south of Cabo Frio, one encounters a series of frogs distributed in the coastal band of the southern Atlantic Forests (*Crossodactylus*

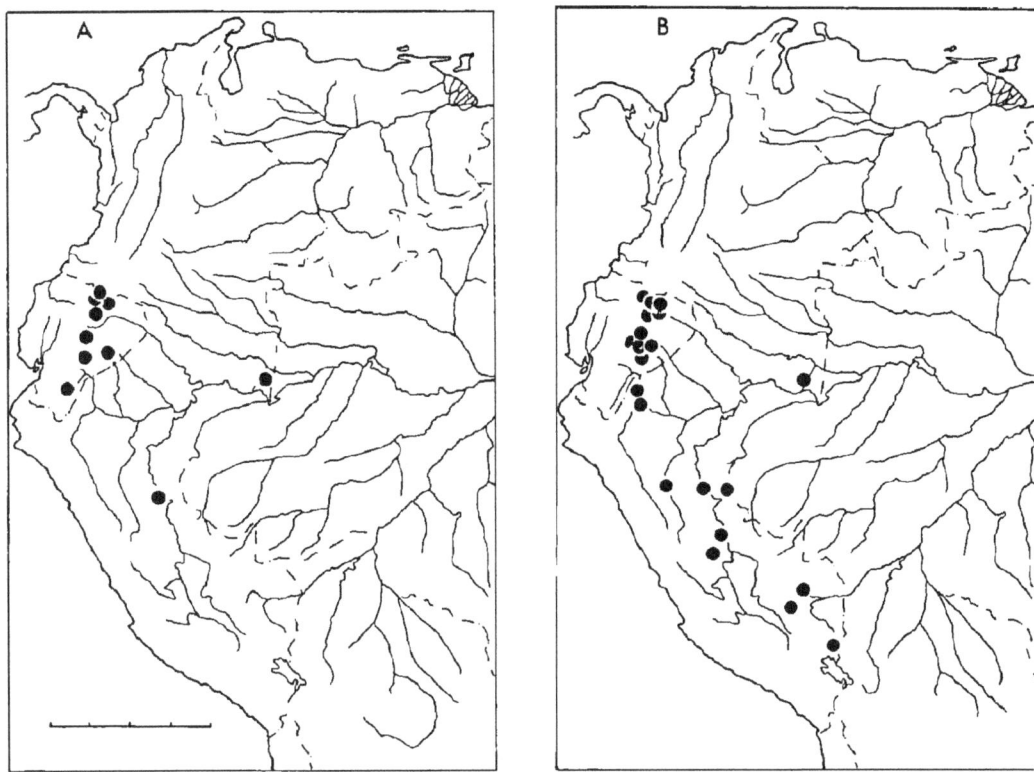

Fic 8 7 Napo-Ucayali distributions A *Eleutherodactylus acuminatus* B *E ockendeni* Both are eleutherodactyline leptodactylids
Distribuciones en el Napo-Ucayali A *Eleutherodactylus acuminatus* B *E ockendeni* Ambos son leptodactylidos eleutherodactylinos

dispar, *Cycloramphus asper, Flectonotus fissilis, Gastrotheca viridis, Hyla catharinae H hayii, Leptodactylus* sp N, *Phrynohyas imitatrix, Phyllomedusa fimbriata Proceratophrys appendiculata,* and *P boiei*)

Almost a dozen species of frogs link the northern and southern (chiefly coastal) portions of the Atlantic Forests These are *Bufo ictericus, B typhonius Eleutherodactylus binotatus, Hyla albomarginata, Hyla microps, Macrogenioglottus alipioi, Osteocephalus langsdorffii Phrynohyas mesophaea P venulosa* (from the west in the southern Atlantic Forests and from the north in the northern Atlantic Forests), *Thoropa miliaris,* and *Trachycephalus nigromaculatus*

The nonendemic species can be divided into two groups—those invading the Atlantic Forests from the north (*Adenomera hylae-* dactyla *Bufo typhonius, Hyla albomarginata, H eglem, H rubra, Leptodactylus wagneri Phrynohyas venulosa,* and *Rana palmipes*) and from the west (*Hyla geographica, H leucophyllata H semicula, Leptodactylus pentadactylus Phyllobates pictus,* and *Phrynohyas venulosa*)

Some of the distinctiveness of the Atlantic Forests is reduced if one views dendrobatids (abundant in Central Cis-Andean Forests) and closing leptodactylids (prominent in Atlantic Forests) as vicariants Such a view is consistent with current notions of the relationships of these two groups of frogs (Lynch 1971) Adding these to the other sets of vicariants of these two major forests (Table 8 4) tends to lessen the impression of nearly complete distinction of the two forests

Muller (1973) divided the Atlantic forests

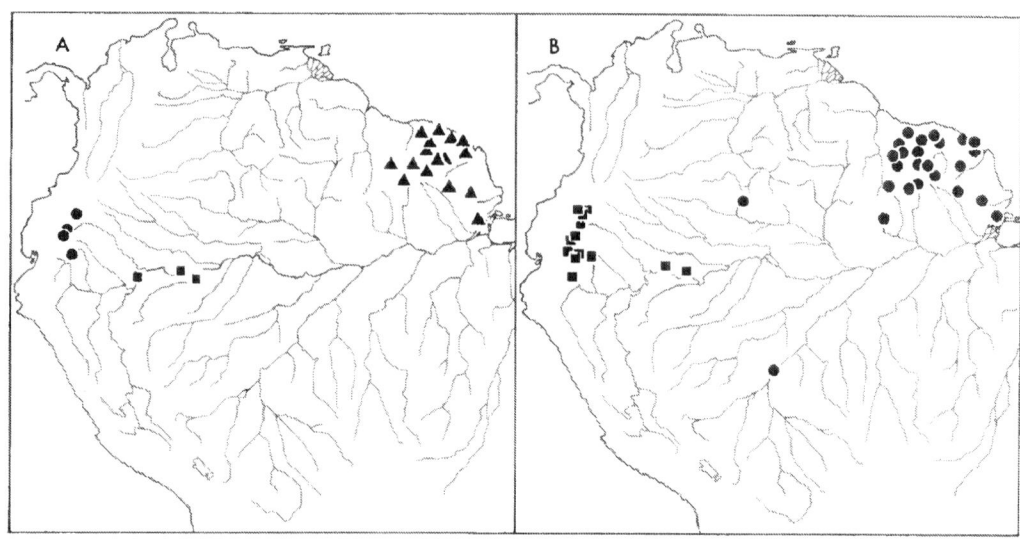

Fig. 8:8. Guianan and Napo-Ucayali distributions. A. Circles are *Syncope antenori*, squares represent both *Syncope carvalhoi* and *Euparkerella myrmecoides* (Microhylidae and eleutherodactyline leptodactylids, respectively), and triangles, *Eleutherodactylus chiastonotus*. B. Squares, *Eleutherodactylus nigrovittatus*; circles, *E. zeuctotylus*.

Distribuciones en Guyana y Napo-Ucayali. A. Los círculos representan a Syncope antenori, los cuadrados representan a Syncope carvalhoi y Euparkerella myrmecoides (Microhylidae y leptodactylido eleutherodactylino, respectivamente), y los triángulos representan a Eleutherodactylus chiastonotus. B. Cuadrados, Eleutherodactylus nigrovittatus; círculos, E. zeuctotylus.

into three subcenters (one north of Ilheus, one between Ilheus and Cabo Frio, and the third encompassing what I term southern—the Pernambuco, Bahia, and Paulista subcenters, respectively). I divided the Atlantic Forests into seven units and compiled species lists for each. Of the 183 species used, approximately one-third are endemic to the coastal forests between Cabo Frio and Paraná (Fig. 8:9). The other six areas exhibit low endemism, and all five coastal units are richer than the two inland areas (in endemics, as well as all amphibians). Recognizing Pernambuco and Bahia subcenters requires combining the Bahia and Espírito Santo units recognized here as the Bahia Unit. By so doing, the new Bahia Unit is second in endemicity only to the São Paulo Unit (11 Bahia + 13 Espírito Santo + 2 Bahia-Espírito Santo endemics = 26 endemics). Endemicity is lowest in those three subunits invaded by nonendemic taxa (Pernambuco, Minas Gerias, and Paraná units). Some of the endemics scored for the São Paulo Subunit may not occur below 1,000 m (*Centrolenella albotunica, C. divaricans, C. dubia, C. eurygnatha,* and *C. vanzolinii*);

Table 8:4.—Vicars of Central Cis-Andean and Atlantic Tropical Forests.

Central Cis-Andean	Atlantic	Source
Adenomera andreae	*Adenomera marmorata*	Heyer 1973
Adenomera hylaedactyla	*Adenomera bokermanni*	Heyer 1973
Dendrobatidae	Elosiinae	Noble 1931; Lynch 1971
Bufo marinus	*Bufo ictericus*	Cochran 1955; Gei 1972
Ceratophrys cornuta	*Ceratophrys aurita*	Cochran 1955
Eleutherodactylus (fitzingeri group)	*Eleutherodactylus* (binotatus group)	Lynch 1976
Hyla boans	*Hyla faber*	Lutz 1973
Hyla lanciformis-H. multifasciata	*Hyla albopunctata* (nonforest)	Lutz 1973
Osteocephalus taurinus	*Osteocephalus langsdorffi*	
Phrynohyas venulosa	*Phrynohyas mesophaea*	
Leptodactylus sp. "A"	*Leptodactylus mystaceus* + *Leptodactylus* sp. "N"	W. R. Heyer

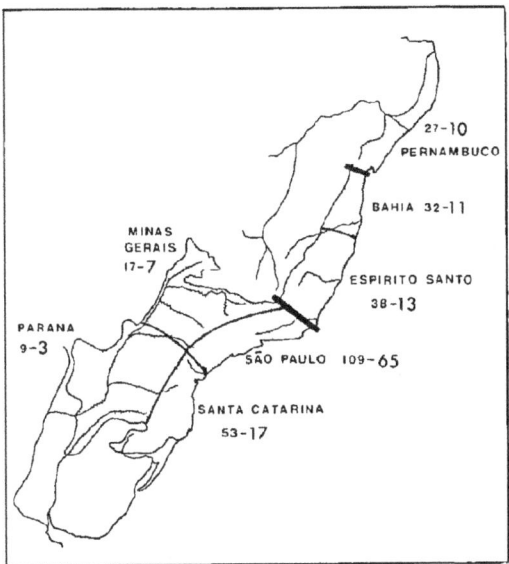

FIG 8 9 Amphibian species densities and endemicities in subunits of the Atlantic Forests The hyphenated numbers refer to Total amphibians—Endemic amphibians
Densidad de las especies anfibias y endemismos en las subunidades de las selvas atlanticas Los números equivalen a Anfibios total—Anfibios endemicos

even in the event that these five species are deleted, the endemism in the São Paulo and Atlantic forests remains at the same order of magnitude A large measure of the endemism of the São Paulo Unit can be ascribed to the distributions of the many montane rainforest species found on the several isolated serras of southeastern Brasil at elevations between 400 and 1200 m (Lutz, 1973) The contiguous lowland forest (below 400 m) acts as a barrier to broader distributions, and views occur on narrowly separated serras thus amplifying the faunistic distinction of the region (Lutz, 1973) Therefore, amphibians tend not to support Muller's (1973) subdivision of these forests into three subcenters

DISCUSSION

Perusal of the distributional data for the tropical lowland forest amphibians reveals a pattern by which allied species are allopatrically (or parapatrically) distributed The theme seems to be applicable to many, if not most, of the groups of forest amphibians (Fig 8 10) Such a pattern may be ecologically and/or historically mediated Haffer (1969, 1974, this volume) suggested that the pattern may be a function of repeated contraction of forests into forest islands during the cyclic climatic phases of the Pleistocene Duellman (1972), Duellman and Crump (1974), and Silverstone (1975) employed the model to explain distributional patterns in two groups of hylid frogs and some dendrobatid frogs, respectively

Clearly, Pleistocene variations in moisture patterns can be argued to have had dramatic effects on forest environments, and if those forest environments expand and contract alternatively, the forest amphibians will be subject to waves of dispersal and retreat with concomitant likelihoods of swamping and isolation The model can be employed readily to explain high species densities in some of the forests [operating in essentially the same fashion as Pianka's (1969) model for lizard diversities]

An Ecological Explanation

Rainforests require as little as 1 800 mm of annual precipitation if that precipitation is uniform over time (Richards, 1952), or, if some months are dry, more rainfall is required The so called aseasonal forests usually receive 3000 mm annual precipitation (or more) whereas rainforests existing within monsoon climates have pronounced dry seasons (one to three months with 0–60 mm rainfall) These extremes present dramatically different environments to forest-adapted amphibians

Amphibians exhibit an impressive array of reproductive modes in tropical South American forests (Table 8 5) Crump (1974) listed ten modes for frogs at Santa Cecilia in eastern Ecuador (Fig 8 11) These ten modes range from the most common (among amphibians as a whole Mode 1) wherein eggs are deposited in aquatic situations where the larvae undergo development, to the less common and more spectacular (Modes 8, 9, 10), in which development is direct (no tadpole) and the eggs terrestrial or carried about on specialized regions of the back of the adult

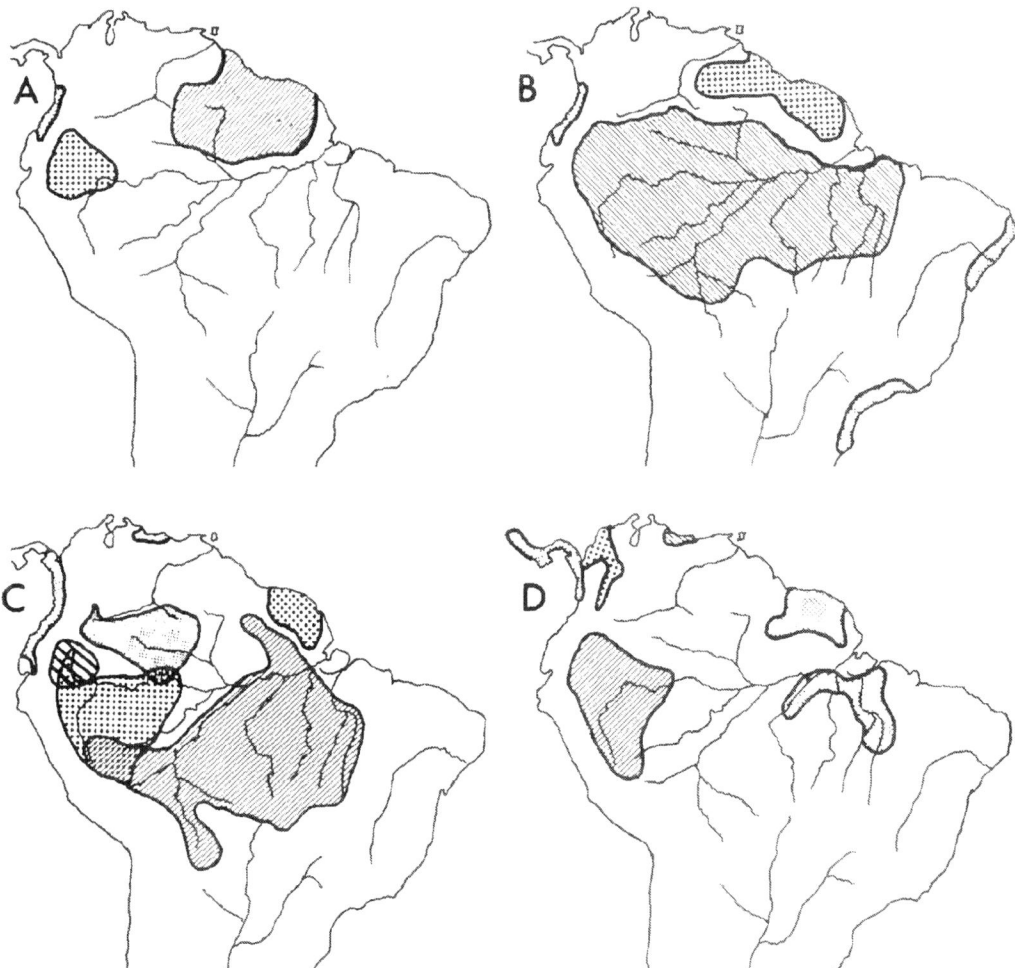

Fig. 8:10. Parapatric distribution patterns. A. *Bufo guttatus* group (3 species): Chocoan *B. blombergi*, Napoan *B. glaberrimus*, and Guianan *B. guttatus*. B. *Leptodactylus fuscus* group (5 species): Amazonian *L.* sp. "A," Guianan *L. longirostris*, Pernambucan *L. mystaceus*, Paulistan *L.* sp. "N," and Chocoan *L. ventrimaculatus*. C. *Eleutherodactylus fitzingeri* group (7 species): Chocoan *E. achatinus*, Guianan *E. chiastonotus*, Napoan *E. conspicillatus* (open hatching), Madeiran *E. fenestratus* (fine hatching), Ucayalian *E. peruvianus* (coarse stipple), Venezuelan *E. terraebolivaris* and supra-Amazonian *E. vilarsi* (fine stipple). D. Hatching (*Eleutherodactylus sulcatus* group, 2 species): Napo-Ucayalian *E. sulcatus*; Venezuelan *E. maussi*. Stipple (*Dendrobates tinctorius* group, 4 species): Chocoan *D. auratus*, Nechian *D. truncatus* (coarse stipple), Guianan *D. tinctorius*, and Paran *D. galactonotus*. Sources: A.) Cei (1972); B.) W. R. Heyer (pers. comm.); C.) Lynch (in prep.); D.) Lynch (1975), Silverstone (1975).

Patrones de distribución parapátricas. A. Grupo de *Bufo guttatus* (3 especies): *B. blombergi del Chocó*, *B. glaberrimus del Napo*, *B. guttatus guyanés*. B. Grupo de *Leptodactylus fuscus* (5 especies): *L.* sp. "A" del Amazonas, *L. longirostris* de Guyana, *L. mystaceus* de Pernambuco, *L.* sp. "N" Paulistano, y *L. ventrimaculatus* del Chocó. C. Grupo *Eleutherodactylus fitzingeri* (7 especies): *E. achatinus* del Chocó, *E. chiastonotus* de Guyana, *E. conspicillatus* de Napo (lineado amplio), *E. fenestratus* de Madeira (lineado fino), *E. peruvianus* del Ucayali (achurado grueso), *E. terraebolivaris* de Venezuela y *E. vilarsi* del Alto Amazonas (achurado fino). D. Lineado (Grupo de *Eleutherodactylus sulcatus*, 2 especies): Napo-Ucayali *E. sulcatus*; Venezuela, *E. maussi*. Achurado (Grupo de *Dendrobates tinctorius*, 4 especies): Chocó, *D. auratus*; Nechí, *D. truncatus* (achurado grueso), Guyana, *D. tinctorius*; y Pará, *D. galactonotus*. Fuentes: A.) Cei (1972); B.) W. R. Heyer (pers. comm.); C.) Lynch (en prep.); D) Lynch (1975), Silverstone (1975).

TABLE 8 5 —Distribution of Reproductive Modes Among Tropical Lowland Forest Amphibians

	Reproductive Mode									
	1	2	3	4	5	6	7	8	9	10
Plethodontidae	—	—	—	—	—	—	—	X	—	—
Brachycephalidae	—	X	—	—	—	—	—	—	—	—
Bufonidae	X	—	—	—	—	—	—	—	—	—
Centrolenidae	—	—	—	X	—	—	—	—	—	—
Dendrobatidae	—	—	—	—	—	X	—	—	—	—
Amphignathodontinae	—	—	—	—	—	—	—	—	—	X
Hemiphractinae	—	—	—	—	—	—	—	—	—	X
Hylinae	X	X	X	X	—	—	—	—	—	—
Phyllomedusinae	—	—	—	X	—	—	—	—	—	—
Batrachylini	X	—	—	—	—	—	—	—	—	—
Ceratophryinae	X	—	—	—	—	—	—	—	—	—
Eleutherodactylini	—	—	—	—	—	—	—	X	—	—
Elosiinae	X[1]	—	—	—	—	—	—	—	—	—
Grypiscini	—	—	—	—	—	—	—	X[2]	—	—
Leptodactylinae	—	—	—	—	X	—	X	—	—	—
Odontophrynini	X	—	—	—	—	—	—	—	—	—
Microhylidae	X	—	—	—	—	—	—	X	—	—
Pipidae	—	—	—	—	—	—	—	—	X	—
Ranidae	X	—	—	—	—	—	—	—	—	—

[1] On land or in water (Lutz, 1931)
[2] On land, live in decomposing jelly mass (Lutz, 1929)

(hemiphractine hylids and pipids) The modes are as follows (from Crump 1974 9-10) "(1) eggs deposited in ditches, puddles, swamps, ponds, lakes, and streams, with free-swimming aquatic larvae, (2) eggs deposited in tree cavity above ground, with free-swimming aquatic larvae, (3) eggs deposited in basin constructed on ground by male, with free-swimming aquatic larvae, (4) eggs deposited on vegetation above water, with free-swimming aquatic larvae (tadpoles hatch and fall into water), (5) eggs deposited in foam nest on or near water, with free-swimming aquatic larvae, (6) eggs deposited on land, with free-swimming aquatic larvae (tadpoles carried to water on dorsum of adult), (7) eggs deposited in foam nest on land and larvae develop within foam (8) eggs deposited out of water, with direct development, (9) eggs carried in depressions on dorsum of aquatic female, with direct development, (10) eggs carried in depressions on dorsum of terrestrial female, with direct development ' Seriation of the modes by Crump was along a dimension attempting to measure parental investment If the modes are reordered along a dimension attempting to describe dependence on forest-mediated environments, the order is as follows

least dependent → most dependent
(1, 2, 3, 9) (5) (4) (7) (6) (8, 10)

Those depositing eggs directly in water (with subsequent development occurring there as well) are less dependent on the high humidity provided by a forest than are those depositing eggs in terrestrial environments (where all needed water is extracted from the air) The truth and rationale of this generalization is supported by casual inspection of the range of forested and nonforested environments in which amphibians having various reproductive modes occur Amphibians of Mode 1 occur throughout the range of habitats occupied by amphibians (nonforests to aseasonal forests) Modes 2 and 3 are exhibited by so few amphibian species that no correlation can be advocated, I chose to treat each as minor variations of Mode 1 Likewise, Mode 9 is found in so few species as to challenge any generalization but, because these species occur in water, they might not be considered restricted to forest environments *per se* Frogs exhibiting Mode 5 are perhaps more characteristic of nonforested habitats than forested ones but range throughout the habitat profile Heyer (1969) examined some of the variations on the theme of Mode 5 Seem-

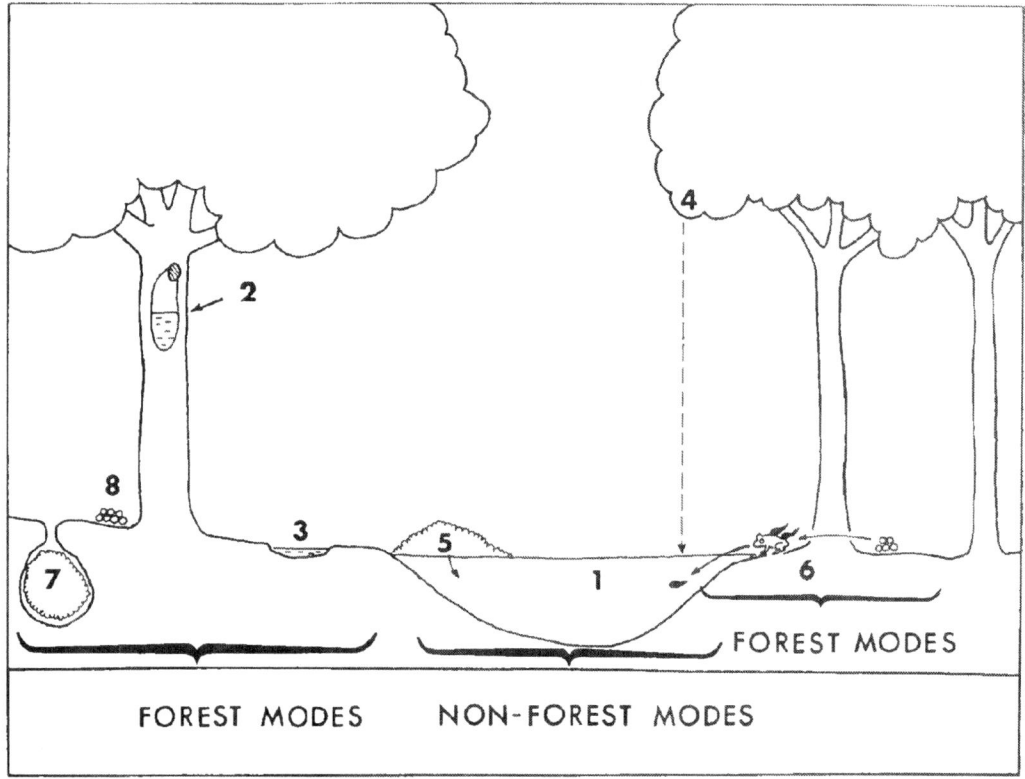

Fig. 8:11. Reproductive modes among rainforest anurans. Mode 9 *(Pipa* with direct development) and Mode 10 (amphignathodontine and hemiphractine hylids, direct development) not shown. Modes 5 and 7 involve foam nests; eggs are laid on vegetation in Mode 4 (after Crump, 1974).

Modos reproductivos de los anuros de la pluviselva. A los Modo 9 (Pipa con desarrollo directo) y 10 (hylidos amphignathodontinos y hemiphractinos, desarrollo directo) no se los muestra. Modos 5 y 7 tienen nidos de espuma; los huevos son puestos en la vegetación en el Modo 4 (de Crump, 1974).

ingly greater risks (and concomitantly, greater dependency) are taken by those amphibians depositing their eggs out of water (Modes 4–8, 10). The larvae of amphibians having Modes 5 and 7 presumably secure some protection from the foam. Those species employing Mode 4 (eggs on vegetation over water, larvae in water) have a more obvious association with wet environments (and therefore, more frequently forests) but also occur in nonforested habitats (llanos, scrub).

Anurans characterized by Modes 6, 7, 8, and 10 employ terrestrial eggs of various durations. Mode 10 constitutes a special case in that the embryos are carried about on the parent's back and moisture requirements may apply more to the adult than the embryos. Species with Mode 6 have terrestrial eggs which, upon hatching, yield tadpoles that pass some time on the parent's back but eventually are transported to bodies of water for "normal" development. Terrestrial eggs and embryos resulting in miniature replicas of the adult produced without submersion in water characterize Modes 7 and 8.

If the asserted sequence is correct, we should expect to discover different patterns of distribution (and patterns of endemism if Haffer's model is real) among different reproductive modes. Amphibians exhibiting Mode 1 should exhibit less endemism than those modes characterizing higher forest-fidelity (e.g., 6 and 8). Modes less dependent

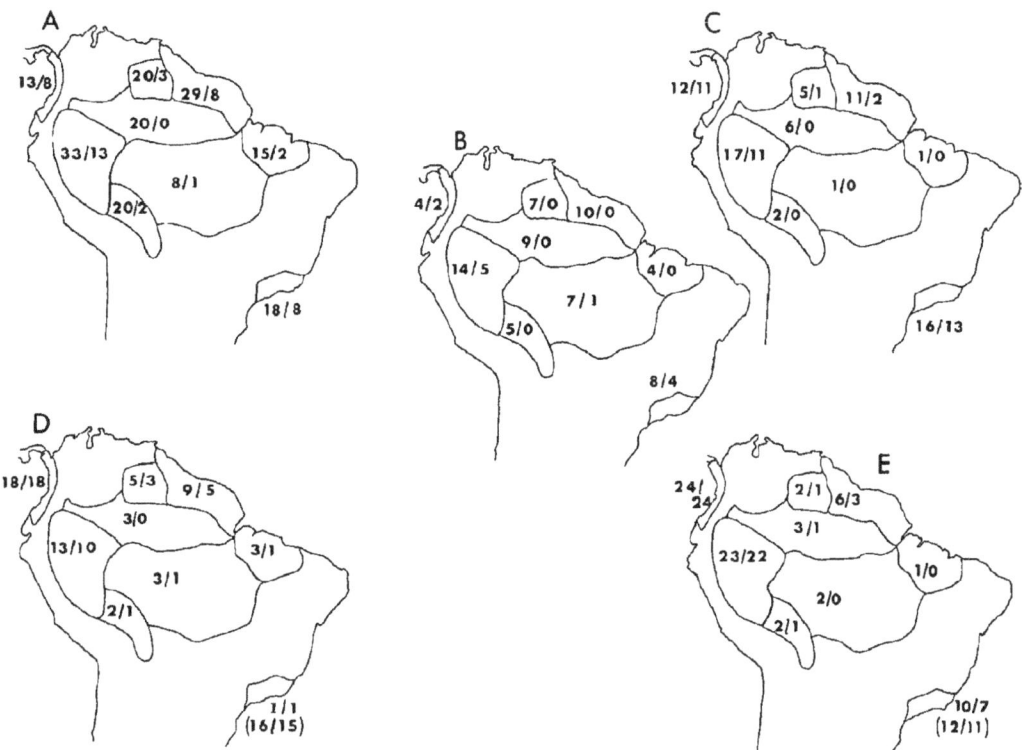

FIG 8 12 Species densities and endemicities of amphibians having various reproductive modes in South American rainforest units The first number is the number of species of the group in the area, the number following the solidus is the number of endemic species of the group in the area A Mode 1 Hylinae B Mode 5, Leptodactylidae (except *Adenomera*) C Mode 4 Centrolenidae, Hylinae, Phyllomedusinae D Mode 6 Dendrobatidae (the numbers in parentheses in southeastern Brasil refer to Elosinae) E Mode 8, Eleutherodactylini (the numbers in southeastern Brasil refer to Crypsicini)

Densidad de especies y endemismos de varios anfibios con diversos modos reproductivos en las selvas lluviosas de Sud America El primer numero es el numero de especies del grupo en el area, el numero siguiente a la línea diagonal representa el numero de especies endemicas del grupo en el área A Modo 1, Hylinae B Modo 5, Leptodactylidae (excepto Adenomera) C Modo 4, Centrolenidae, Hylinae, Phyllomedusinae D Modo 6 Dendrobatidae (los numeros entre paréntesis en el sudeste del Brasil refieren a Elosinae) E Modo 8, Eleutherodactylini (los numeros en parentesis en el sudeste del Brasil refieren a Grypsicini)

on special attributes of forest environments (high humidity) exhibit lower percentages of endemism than do forest-adapted modes over the same terrain (Fig 8 12)

Conversely, if the model is more realistic, we ought to expect the opposite pattern among the nonendemic taxa of amphibians found in South American lowland tropical forests (Table 8 1) We find departure from the expected numbers of species of each reproductive mode in that certain reproductive modes are "over-represented" or under represented" among the nonendemic taxa (Table 8 6) As might be predicted, modes with high-forest fidelity (6–8, 10) are collectively under-represented," whereas the modes of low-fidelity (1–5) are 'over-represented"

Such 'under-representation" and 'over representation' are also consistent with the notion that r-selected species tend to be better colonizers than K-selected species Crump's (1974) seriation of modes tends to describe one dimension of the r- and K-continuum, in general, frogs of lower numbered modes are more frequently r-selected species and those of high numbered modes K-selected species

TABLE 6.6—Frequencies of Frogs and Salamanders of Tropical Lowland Forests Exhibiting 10 Reproductive Modes Compared to Frequencies for Nonendemic Species

Mode	Number Species	Number of Nonendemic Species		
		Observed	Expected[a]	Deviation
1	184	12	9.2	+2.8
2	7	0	0.4	−0.4
3	3	1	0.2	+0.8
4	65	4	3.2	+0.8
5	30	5	1.5	+3.5
6	49 + 16[b]	1	3.2	−2.2
7	6	1	0.3	+0.7
8	91 + 13[c]	0	5.2	−5.2
9	5	0	0.2	−0.2
10	22	0	1.1	−1.1

[a] 5% of the 480 species are nonendemic. "Expected" values were computed by multiplying Number of species of a mode by 5%.
[b] Dendrobatids + elosiine leptodactylids. If elosiines are included in Mode 1 (see Table 5), the expected value for Mode 6 is 2.4 and the deviation −1.4, in that case the expected for Mode 1 would be 10.0 and the deviation +2.0
[c] Eleutherodactylines and plethodontids + grypiscine leptodactylids

(as judged from clutch size and/or egg size, Salthe and Duellman 1973)

Historical Explanations

The patterns of distribution and endemism among the South American, lowland forest amphibians seem explicable on an ecological basis. An historical component is implied by noting that the centers of endemism correspond well with the refugia postulated in Haffer's model. That species distributions correspond with a Pleistocene model does not require that the implied speciation be Pleistocene in age, only that at least part of the existing distribution pattern is a product of relatively recent perturbations.

Savage (1973) envisioned the late Mesozoic-Early Cenozoic amphibian fauna of South America as consisting of three tropical groups (caecilians, microhylid frogs, and pipid frogs) and two south temperate groups (ascaphid and leptodactyloid frogs). By the Paleocene, bufonid, hylid, and leptodactylid frogs had invaded the tropical zone (Estes and Reig, 1973, Savage, 1973). Subsequent to the Neogene emergence of the Panamanian Isthmus, bolitoglossine salamanders and ranid frogs invaded South America from the north.

The stem leptodactylids all radiate from southern South America (Lynch 1971, 1978, Savage, 1973), and most do not range appreciably north (Lynch, 1971, 1978). The roles of the old highland areas in the diversification of the amphibian fauna are obscure at best. The occurrence of a batrachyline leptodactylid frog (Thoropa), elosiine leptodactylid frogs, and grypiscine leptodactylid frogs associated with the Brasilian Highlands suggest the once important role of that highland mass in the Cenozoic radiation of leptodactylids on the continent. The advanced groups (dendrobatid and eleutherodactyline leptodactylid frogs) are not represented in southern South America and only poorly represented in the area of the Brasilian highlands, but they are dominant amphibian groups in the northern Andes and the adjacent lowland tropical forests.

The general absence of stem groups of amphibians associated with the Brasilian and/or the Guiana highlands and the youth of the Andes, compels most observers to conclude that the complex fauna was lowland in origin. Because the lowlands were once more equable than they are today, and because few groups persist in the temperate regions of southern South America, it may be concluded that most amphibian groups originated in the lowland rainforests.

The following apparently originated and/or diversified in the lowland rainforests of South America.

Caeciliidae	Hylinae
Rhinatrematidae°	Eleutherodactylini°
Typhlonectidae	Elosiinae
Brachycephalidae	Crypiscini
Dendrobatidae°	Microhylidae
Hemiphractinae	Pipinae

Those marked with an asterisk were greatly affected by the uplift of the northern Andes.

The following invaded the lowland tropical forests of South America from adjacent areas (Central America or nonforested environments).

Plethodontidae	Odontophrynini
Bufonidae	Ceratophryinae
Batrachylini	Ranidae
Leptodactylinae	

Amphignathodontinae and phyllomedusine hylids and centrolenid frogs (and possibly caeciliid and hylline stocks) do not fall into either pattern. Amphignathodontines and centrolenids are recent invaders of Central America (Savage, 1973) but are usually found in uplifted areas (discontinuous distributions). Phyllomedusines are much better represented in Central America (*Agalychnis* and *Pachymedusa*) and are essentially replaced in South America by *Phyllomedusa*, the replacement is suggestive of geographic separation of the two forest stocks during much of the Tertiary.

Some of these amphibian groups were isolated and radiating in Central America during much of the Tertiary. Savage (1973) cited bufonids, hylids (hylines and phyllomedusines), microhylids, and eleutherodactyline leptodactylids. Savage and Wake (1972) identified the Middle American caeciliids isolated in Central America during the same time period. Most of these isolates are recognizable in that the species groups or genera are essentially endemic to Central America and extend only into the Chocó in South America. Savage (1973) suggested that *Eleutherodactylus* and some derived genera underwent an Eocene-Miocene radiation in Middle America and subsequent to the uplift of the Panamanian Portal radiated into South America. My study of *Eleutherodactylus* does not confirm such a conviction. Ancestral relicts (*Hylactophryne* and *Ischnocnema*) persist at opposite ends of the center of *Eleutherodactylus* diversity and the wealth of species are distributed in the northern Andes. The species groups in eastern and southeastern Brasil are apparently primitive stocks, as is the *Eleutherodactylus discoidalis* group (distributed along the eastern edge of the Andes from northern Argentina to southern Colombia). The Middle American *Eleutherodactylus* include representatives of two groups, the endemic *alfredi* group in Mexico and Guatemala and the *fitzingeri* group, which is distributed nearly as widely as are mainland *Eleutherodactylus* (México to Bolivia and eastern Brasil), as well as South American groups in lower Central America (*biporcatus* and *unistrigatus* groups, Lynch, 1976). Some eleutherodactyline frogs certainly invaded Middle America prior to the Neogene uplift of the Panamanian Isthmus, but most of the radiation of the group occurred in the West Indies and in northern South America.

The development of biogeographic constructs (historical biogeography) without some defensible phylogenetic constructs is not science (see Rosen, 1975, for philosophy and methodology). Unfortunately, the sorts of phylogenetic input required to generate robust biogeographic constructs are not available for most lowland Amphibia. In spite of the impressive strides made in the past decade in tabulating systematic data for some of the larger amphibian groups in South America, our knowledge of the relationships within those groups remain regretfully nascent. This is less a critique of previous work than a statement of what remains to be done for most groups of tropical amphibians and reptiles. I do not believe that we have the systematic data necessary to generate formulations of how the tropical lowland forest amphibian groups developed in time and space.

ACKNOWLEDGMENTS

Most of the distributional data presented here represents summaries of unpublished data collected by colleagues. My thanks go to William E. Duellman, M. J. Fouquette Jr., W. Ronald Heyer, Marinus S. Hoogmoed, and Jean Lescure for sharing data. Gathering distributional data for eleutherodactyline frogs was facilitated by provision of working space by the curators at the American Museum of Natural History, British Museum (Natural History), National Museum of Natural History, The University of Kansas Museum of Natural History, and The University of Michigan Museum of Zoology, and financial support from The University of Nebraska Research Council.

I owe a major debt to several colleagues for serving as sources of stimulation and criticism, special thanks are extended to William E. Duellman, Linda Trueb, and Charles F. Walker. I defer to identify the many others to avoid failing to recall some.

RESUMEN

Las selvas tropicales de tierras bajas (pluviselvas, bajo 1000 m) de Sud América conforman cuatro unidades—1) Las selvas transandinas (Chocó, Nechí, y Magdalena), 2) Las selvas cisandinas centrales (Amazonía o Hylaea), 3) Las selvas nortinas (Santa Marta, Cuenca de Maracaibo, y la costa de Venezuela), y 4) Las selvas atlánticas (Este y sudeste del Brasil) Estas cuatro regiones forestales contienen 530 especies de anfibios pertenecientes a 13 familias (una de salamandras, tres de cecilios, y nueve de anuros)

El endemismo es pronunciado, solo 26 especies (4 9%) son compartidas por dos o mas regiones Las selvas nortinas son las más pobres en especies (39) y las menos distintas (56% de endemismo) Las selvas atlánticas contienen 183 especies (92% de endemismo), las selvas centrales 225 (90% de endemismo), y las selvas transandinas 126 (88% de endemismo)

Las ranas hylidas son dominantes en las cuatro regiones selváticas (atlántica, 38%, cisandina central 37%, nortina 26%, y transandina 25%) Los leptodactylidos de las selvas centrales, nortinas y transandinas son especialmente eleutherodactylinos y leptodactylinos mientras que los de las selvas atlánticas son primariamente elosinos, grypiscinos, leptodactylinos, y odontophryninos Ranas dendrobatidas son componentes prominentes de las selvas centrales, nortinas, y transandinas pero están sustancialmente ausentes en las selvas atlánticas

Cuatro áreas de un marcado endemismo se reconocen—1) Chocó sudamericano, 2) la cuenca del Amazonas superior (drenajes del Napo-Ucayali), 3) las Guayanas, y 4) la costa brasileira (área de Rio de Janeiro-São Paulo) Un cuarenta y cuatro por ciento (233) de todas las especies forestales de la fauna anfibia sudamericana están restringidas a estas cuatro regiones

Varios grupos de anfibios presentan un modelo distribucional congruente con la teoría de refugios forestales de Haffer Tal modelo consistente en oleadas de avance y retroceso de las selvas, puede ser utilizado para explicar la alta densidad de especies observada en algunos grupos Sin embargo, los anfibios están pobremente representados en algunos de los refugios propuestos Esta baja representación puede reflejar profundas diferencias entre selvas separadas por una estacionalidad en el regimen pluvial A diferencia de los amniotas o vertebrados acuáticos, la mayoría de los anfibios tratan de ser terrestrial sin tener los mecanismos adecuados para conservar agua La falta de estos mecanismos se hace mas notoria en las estrategias reproductivas de los anfibios

La alta densidad de especies (y endemismo) de los anfibios se correlaciona bien con las áreas de una alta y bien distribuida lluvia sin estacionalidad En regiones forestales, tales lluvias proveen con una serie de microhabitats de elevada humedad y de larga duración, ambas características necesarias para las mas frágiles modalidades reproductivas presentes en los anfibios (desarrollo directo, huevos y larvas terrestres) Tales ambientes no reducen necesariamente el exito de los mas comunes modos reproductivos como son los huevos y larvas desarrollandose en agua

La importancia de la modalidad reproductiva en sentido de proveer restricciones o aumentos de la capacidad de dispersión de los anfibios selváticos esta demonstrada por la observacion de que una mayor proporción de especies con modo 1 y modo 5 son no-endemicas que lo que pudiera predecirse y que una menor proporción de especies con modo 6 y modo 8 son no-endémicas que lo que pudiera predecirse si la ausencia de endemismo y el modo reproductivo no estuviesen relacionados Si la sensibilidad a la estacionalidad de las lluvias es un índice apropriado de fidelidad forestal, entones aquellos grupos que poseen los modos reproductivos más sensibles adquieren importancia para la inferencia de eventos climaticos y biogeograficos del pasado, estos incluyen a las salamandras bolitoglossinas, y ranas dendrobatidads y eleutherodactylinas

Las áreas de tierra altas han tenido sólo un limitado papel en el origen y dispersion de los anfibios de selvas tropicales de tierras bajas Las alturas del sudeste brasileño parecer haber servido como un islote de paso a la radiación de leptodactylidos fuera de la

Patagonia Los Andes del norte han contribuido a una fragmentación de ciertos grupos (ranas dendrobatidads y eleutherodactylinas y cecilios rhinatrematidos)

Los cecilios rhinatrematidos y typhlonectidos y los anuros amphignathodontinos brachycephalidos, centrolenidos, dendrobatidos, la mayoría de los eleutherodactylinos, elosiinos grypiscinos hemiphractinos y pipidos se originaron y diferenciaron al parecer en las selvas tropicales de tierras bajas de Sud America Ciertos otros grupos (cecilios caecilidos algunos bufónidos, hylinos, microhylidos, y phyllomedusinos y posiblemente algunos eleutherodactylinos) se originaron en estas selvas pero irradiación en Centro America también Las salamandras plethodontidos y los anuros ranidos son invasores recientes desde las selvas de Centro America, y los anuros batrachylinos, la mayoría de los bufónidos, ceratophryinos, leptodactylinos, y odontophryinos son invasores de ambientes sureños temperados y subtropicales

LITERATURE CITED

AXELROD, D I 1960 The evolution of flowering plants pp 227-305 *in* TAX, S (ed) Evolution after Darwin I Univ Chicago Press, 629 p

BLAIR, W F (ed) 1972 Evolution in the genus *Bufo* Univ Texas Press, Austin, 459 p

BRAME, A H, JR 1968 Systematics and evolution of the Mesoamerican salamander genus *Oedipina* J Herpetol 2 1-64

BRAME A H, JR WAKE, D B 1963 The salamanders of South America Nat Hist Mus Los Angeles Cty Contrib Sci (69) 1-72

BRAME, A H, JR, WAKE, D B 1972 New species of salamanders (genus *Bolitoglossa*) from Colombia, Ecuador, and Panama Ibid (219) 1-34

CARVALHO A L DE 1954 A preliminary synopsis of the genera of American microhylid frogs Occas Pap Mus Zool Univ Michigan (555) 1-20

CEI, J M 1972 *Bufo* of South America, pp 82-92 *in* BLAIR W F (ed) Evolution in the genus *Bufo* Univ Texas Press, Austin, 459 p

COCHRAN, D M 1955 Frogs of southeastern Brazil Bull U S Natl Mus (206) 1-423

COCHRAN, D M, COIN, C J 1970 Frogs of Colombia Ibid (288) 1-655

CRUMP M L 1974 Reproductive strategies in a tropical anuran community Univ Kansas Mus Nat Hist Misc Publ (61) 1-68

DUELLMAN, W E 1970 The hylid frogs of Middle America Univ Kansas Mus Nat Hist Monogr (1) 1-753

DUELLMAN W E 1971a A taxonomic review of South American hylid frogs, genus *Phrynohyas* Univ Kansas Mus Nat Hist Occas Pap (4) 1-21

DUELLMAN W E 1971b The identities of some Ecuadorian hylid frogs Herpetologica 27 212-227

DUELLMAN W E 1972 South American frogs of the *Hyla rostrata* group (Amphibia, Anura, Hylidae) Zool Meded Rijks Mus Nat Hist Leiden 47 177-192

DUELLMAN W E 1973 Frogs of the *Hyla geographica* group Copeia 1973 (3) 515-533

DUELLMAN, W E 1974 A reassessment of the taxonomic status of some Neotropical hylid frogs Univ Kansas Mus Nat Hist Occas Pap (27) 1-27

DUELLMAN, W F 1977 Liste der Rezenten Amphibien und Reptilien Hylidae Centrolenidae, Pseudidae Das Tierreich 95 1-225

DUELLMAN W E CRUMP M L 1974 Speciation in frogs of the *Hyla parviceps* group in the upper Amazon Basin Univ Kansas Mus Nat Hist Occas Pap (23) 1-40

DUNN, E R 1948 American frogs of the family Pipidae Amer Mus Novit (1384) 1-13

DUNN E R 1949 Notes on South American frogs of the family Microhylidae Ibid (1419) 1-21

ESTES R, REIG, O A 1973 The early fossil record of frogs A review of the evidence pp 11-63 *in* VIAL, J L (ed) Evolutionary biology of the anurans Contemporary research on major problems Univ Missouri Press, Columbia, 470 p

GALLARDO, J M 1961 On the species of Pseudidae (Amphibia Anura) Bull Mus Comp Zool Harvard Univ 125 111-134

HAFFER, J 1969 Speciation in Amazonian forest birds Science 165 131-137

HAFFER J 1974 Avian speciation in tropical South America with a systematic survey of the Toucans (Ramphastidae) and Jacamars (Galbulidae) Publ Nuttall Ornithol Club, Cambridge (14) 1-390

HEYER, W R 1969 The adaptive ecology of the species groups of the genus *Leptodactylus* (Amphibia Leptodactylidae) Evolution 23 421-428

HEYER, W R 1970 Studies on the frogs of the genus *Leptodactylus* (Amphibia Leptodactylidae) VI Biosystematics of the *melanonotus* group Nat Hist Mus Los Angeles Cty Contrib Sci (191) 1-48

HEYER W R 1973 Systematics of the *marmoratus* group of the frog genus *Leptodactylus* (Amphibia, Leptodactylidae) Ibid (251) 1-50

HEYER, W R 1975 A preliminary analysis of the intergeneric relationships of the frog family Leptodactylidae Smithsonian Contrib Zool (199) 1-55

HEYER, W R 1976 Notes on the frog fauna of the Amazon Basin Acta Amazonica 6 369-378

HEYER, W R, LIEM, D S 1976 Analysis of the intergeneric relationships of the Australian frog family Myobatrachidae Smithsonian Contrib Zool (233) 1–29

HUECK, K 1966 Die Wälder Südamerikas Fischer Verlag Stuttgart 422 p

IZECKSOHN, E 1971 Novo gênero e nova espécie de Brachycephalidae do Estado do Rio de Janeiro, Brasil Bol Mus Nac Rio de Janeiro Zool (280) 1–12

IZECKSOHN, E 1976a O status sistematico de Phrynyscus proboscideus Boulenger (Amphibia Anura Bufonidae) Rev Bras Biol 36 341–345

IZECKSOHN, E 1976b Uma nova espécie de Pipa, do estado do Amazonas, Brasil (Amphibia Anura Pipidae) Ibid 36 507–510

LESCURE, J 1973 Notes biogeographiques sur quelques Amphibiens du bassin supérior du Maroni C R Seances Soc Biogeogr (439) 58–63

LESCURE, J 1975 Biogeographie et ecologie des Amphibiens de Guyane Francaise Ibid (440) 68–82

LESCURE, J 1976 Contribution a l'étude des Amphibiens de Guyane francaise VI Liste preliminaire des Anoures Bull Mus Natl Hist Nat Zool Paris (265) 475–525

LUTZ, A 1929 Taxonomia e biologia do genero Cyclorhamphus Mem Inst Oswaldo Cruz 22(1) 1–25

LUTZ, A 1931 Observacoes sobre batrachios brasileiros Taxonomia e biologia des elosinas Ibid 24(4) 195–222

LUTZ, B 1972 Geographical and ecological notes on Cisandine to Platine frogs J Herpetol 6 83–100

LUTZ, B 1973 Brazilian species of Hyla Univ Texas Press, Austin, 265 p

LYNCH, J D 1971 Evolutionary relationships, osteology, and zoogeography of leptodactyloid frogs Univ Kansas Mus Nat Hist Misc Publ (53) 1–238

LYNCH, J D 1973 The transition from archaic to advanced frogs, pp 133–182 in VIAL J L (ed) Evolutionary biology of the anurans Contemporary research on major problems Univ Missouri Press Columbia, 470 p

LYNCH, J D 1975 The identity of the frog Eleutherodactylus conspicillatus (Gunther) with descriptions of two related species from northwestern South America Nat Hist Mus Los Angeles Cty Contrib Sci (272) 1–19

LYNCH, J D 1976 The species groups of the South American frogs of the genus Eleutherodactylus (Leptodactylidae) Univ Kansas Mus Nat Hist Occas Pap (61) 1–24

LYNCH, J D 1978 A reassessment of the telmatobiine leptodactylid frogs of Patagonia Ibid (72) 1–57

LYNCH, J D HOOGMOED, M S 1977 Two new species of Eleuthodactylus (Amphibia Leptodactylidae) from northeastern South America Proc Biol Soc Washington 90 424–439

LYNCH, J D, MYERS C W [in preparation] The frogs of the fitzingeri group of Eleutherodactylus in the Chocoan lowlands

McDIARMID R W 1971 Comparative morphology and evolution of frogs of the Neotropical genera Atelopus Dendrophryniscus Melanophryniscus, and Oreophrynella Nat Hist Mus Los Angeles Cty Sci Bull (12) 1–66

MOORE, J A 1944 Geographic variation in Rana pipiens Schreber of eastern North America Bull Amer Mus Nat Hist 82 345–370

MOORE J A 1975 Rana pipiens—the changing paradigm Amer Zool 15 837–849

MULLER, P 1973 Dispersal centres of terrestrial vertebrates in the Neotropical Realm Biogeographica 2, Junk The Hague, 244 p

MULLER P 1974 Aspects of zoogeography Junk The Hague, 208 p

NOBLE, G K 1931 The biology of the Amphibia McGraw-Hill Book Co, New York 577 p

NUSSBAUM R A 1977 Rhinatrematidae A new family of caecilians (Amphibia Gymnophiona) Occas Pap Mus Zool Univ Michigan (682) 1–30

PACE, A L 1974 Systematic and biological studies of the leopard frogs (Rana pipiens complex) of the United States Misc Publ Mus Zool Univ Michigan (148) 1–140

PARKER H W 1934 A monograph of the frogs of the family Microhylidae Brit Mus (Nat Hist), London, 208 p

PARKER H W 1935 The frogs, lizards and snakes of British Guiana Proc Zool Soc London 1935 (3) 505–530

PETERS, J A 1973 The frog genus Atelopus in Ecuador (Anura Bufonidae) Smithsonian Contrib Zool (145) 1–49

PIANKA E R 1969 Habitat specificity speciation, and species diversity in Australian desert lizards Ecology 50 498–502

RICHARDS P W 1952 The tropical rain forest Cambridge Univ Press, Cambridge, 450 p

RIVERO J A 1961 Salientia of Venezuela Bull Mus Comp Zool Harvard Univ 126 1–207

ROSEN D E 1975 A vicariance model of Caribbean biogeography Syst Zool 24 431–464

SALTHE, S N, DUELLMAN, W E 1973 Quantitative constraints associated with reproductive modes in anurans, pp 229–249 in VIAL, J L (ed) Evolutionary biology in the anurans Contemporary research on major problems Univ Missouri Press, Columbia, 470 p

SAVAGE, J M 1968 The dendrobatid frogs of Central America Copeia 1968(4) 745–776

SAVAGE, J M 1973 The geographical distribution of frogs Patterns and predictions, pp 351–445 in VIAL J L (ed) Evolutionary biology of the anurans Contemporary research on major problems Univ Missouri Press Columbia 470 p

SAVAGE, J M, WAKE, M 1972 Geographic variation and systematics of the Middle American caecilians, genera Dermophis and Gymnopis Copeia 1972(4) 680–695

SCHMITHUSEN, J 1968 Allgemeine Vegetationsgeographie Walter de Gruyter, Berlin, 436 p
SILVERSTONE, P A 1975 A revision of the poison-arrow frogs of the genus *Dendrobates* Wagler Nat Hist Mus Los Angeles Cty, Sci Bull (21) 1–55
SILVERSTONE, P A 1976 A revision of the poison arrow frogs of the genus *Phyllobates* Bibron in Sagra (family Dendrobatidae) Ibid (27) 1–53
TAYLOR, E H 1968 The caecilians of the world A taxonomic review Univ Kansas Press Lawrence, 848 p
TRUEB L 1971 Phylogenetic relationships of certain Neotropical toads with the description of a new genus (Anura Bufonidae) Nat Hist Mus Los Angeles Cty Contrib Sci (216) 1–40
TRUEB L 1974 Systematic relationships of Neotropical horned frogs, genus *Hemiphractus* (Anura Hylidae) Univ Kansas Mus Nat Hist Occas Pap (29) 1–60
TRUEB L, DUELLMAN W E 1971 A synopsis of Neotropical hylid frogs genus *Osteocephalus* Ibid (1) 1–47
WAKE D B 1966 Comparative osteology and evolution of the lungless salamanders, family Plethodontidae Mem South California Acad Sci 4 1–111
WAKE D B, LYNCH J F 1976 The distribution, ecology, and evolutionary history of plethodontid salamanders in tropical America Nat Hist Mus Los Angeles Cty Sci Bull (25) 1–65

APPENDICES

APPENDIX 8 1—Amphibians of the Trans-Andean Forests

Nonendemic taxa (i e, found in one or more other tropical lowland forests) are noted by an asterisk and letters denoting the lowland forests (T = Trans-Andean, N = Northern, C = Central Cis-Andean, A = Atlantic)

Salamanders
Oedipina complex
Oedipina parvipes
Bolitoglossa biseriata
Bolitoglossa chica
Bolitoglossa medemi
Bolitoglossa phalarosoma
Bolitoglossa silverstonei
Bolitoglossa sima
Bolitoglossa taylori (expected)

Caecilians
Epicrionops marmoratus
Epicrionops parkeri
Caecilia antioquiaensis
Caecilia caribea
Caecilia guntheri
Caecilia leucocephala
Caecilia nigricans
Caecilia perdita
Caecilia subnigricans °N
Caecilia tentaculata °C
Caecilia thompsoni
Dermophis parviceps
Oscaecilia ochrocephala
Oscaecilia polyzona
Parvicaecilia nicefori
Parvicaecilia pricei
Typhlonectes natans

Anurans
Atelopus bahos
Atelopus elegans
Atelopus glyphus
Atelopus longibrachius
Atelopus longirostris
Atelopus mindoensis
Atelopus spurrelli
Bufo blombergi
Bufo coniferus
Bufo haematiticus

Barchyolos pulcher
Leptodactylus bolivianus °NC
Leptodactylus melanonotus
Leptodactylus pentadactylus °AC
Leptodactylus poecilochilus °N
Leptodactylus ventrimaculatus
Leptodactylus wagneri °NCA
Physalaemus pustulosus °N
Eleutherodactylus sp "A"
Eleutherodactylus achatinus
Eleutherodactylus anomalus
Eleutherodactylus areolatus
Eleutherodactylus biporcatus
Eleutherodactylus bufoniformis
Eleutherodactylus caryophyllaceus
Eleutherodactylus capnfer
Eleutherodactylus cruentus
Eleutherodactylus diastema
Eleutherodactylus fitzingeri
Eleutherodactylus gaigeae
Eleutherodactylus gularis
Eleutherodactylus latidiscus
Eleutherodactylus longirostris
Eleutherodactylus moro
Eleutherodactylus ornatissimus
Eleutherodactylus raniformis
Eleutherodactylus ridens
Eleutherodactylus roseus
Eleutherodactylus subsigillatus
Eleutherodactylus taeniatus
Eleutherodactylus walkeri
Eleutherodactylus sp Z
Colostethus chocoensis
Colostethus imbricolus
Colostethus latinasus
Colostethus nubicola
Colostethus pratti
Colostethus talamancae
Dendrobates auratus
Dendrobates fulguritus
Dendrobates histrionicus

Dendrobates truncatus
Dendrobates viridis
Phyllobates anthonyi
Phyllobates aurotaenia
Phyllobates bicolor
Phyllobates boulengeri
Phyllobates espinosai
Agalychnis calcarifer
Agalychnis callidryas (expected)
Agalychnis litodryas
Agalychnis spurrelli
Phyllomedusa sp
Phyllomedusa venusta
Hemiphractus fasciatus
Gastrotheca angustifrons
Gastrotheca cornuta
Gastrotheca nicefori
Hyla boans °NC
Hyla boulengeri
Hyla ebraccata
Hyla gryllata
Hyla miliaria
Hyla pellucens
Hyla picturata
Hyla phlebodes
Hyla quinquefasciata
Hyla rosenbergi
Hyla rubra °NCA
Hyla rubracyla
Hyla subocularis
Hyla sugillata
Phrynohyas venulosa °NCA
Smilisca phaeota
Smilisca sila
Trachycephalus jordani
Centrolenella fleischmanni °NC
Centrolenella ilex
Centrolenella ocellifera
Centrolenella prosoblepon
Centrolenella spinosa
Glossostoma aterrimum

Bufo hypomelas
Bufo marinus °ᴺᶜ
Bufo typhonius °ᴺᶜᴬ

Dendrobates minutus
Dendrobates occultator

Relictivomer pearsei °ᴺ
Rana palmipes °ᴺᶜᴬ

APPENDIX 8.2—Amphibians of the Central Cis Andean Lowland Forests

Salamanders
Bolitoglossa altamazonica
Bolitoglossa equatoriana
Bolitoglossa peruviana

Caecilians
Epicrionops nigrus
Rhinatrema bicolor
Brasilotyphlus brazilensis
Caecilia bokermanni
Caecilia disossea
Caecilia dunni
Caecilia gracilis
Caecilia pressula
Caecilia tentaculata °ᵀ
Microcaecilia albiceps
Microcaecilia rabei
Microcaecilia unicolor
Oscaecilia bassleri
Oscaecilia zweifeli
Siphonops annulatus °ᴬ
Nectocaecilia ladigesi
Nectocaecilia petersi
Potomotyphlus kaupii
Typhlonectes compressicaudus
Typhlonectes obesus

Anurans
Pipa aspera
Pipa arrabali
Pipa snethlageae
Pipa pipa
Atelopus franciscus
Atelopus flavescens
Atelopus palmatus
Atelopus pulcher
Bufo ceratophrys
Bufo dapsilis
Bufo glaberrimus
Bufo guttatus
Bufo manicorensis
Bufo marinus °ᵀᴺ
Bufo typhonius °ᵀᴺᴬ
Dendrophryniscus minutus
Rhamphophryne festae
Ceratophrys cornuta
Adenomera andreae
Adenomera hylaedactyla °ᴺᴬ
Adenomera martinezi
Edalorhina perezi
Hydrolaetare schmidti
Leptodactylus sp.
Leptodactylus bolivianus °ᵀᴺ
Leptodactylus dantasi
Leptodactylus knudseni
Leptodactylus longirostris
Leptodactylus pentadactylus °ᵀᴬ

Eleutherodactylus gutturalis
Eleutherodactylus inguinalis
Eleutherodactylus lacrimosus
Eleutherodactylus lanthanites
Eleutherodactylus malkini
Eleutherodactylus marmoratus
Eleutherodactylus martiae
Eleutherodactylus nigrovittatus
Eleutherodactylus ockendeni
Eleutherodactylus orphnolaimus
Eleutherodactylus paululus
Eleutherodactylus peruvianus
Eleutherodactylus platydactylus
Eleutherodactylus pseudoacuminatus
Eleutherodactylus quaquaversus
Eleutherodactylus sulcatus
Eleutherodactylus trachyblepharis
Eleutherodactylus variabilis
Eleutherodactylus ventrimarmoratus
Eleutherodactylus vilarsi
Eleutherodactylus zeuctotylus
Euparkerella myrmecoides
Ischnocnema quixensis
Colostethus beebei
Colostethus brunneus
Colostethus degranvillei
Colostethus fuliginosus
Colostethus intermedius
Colostethus marchesianus
Colostethus sauli
Dendrobates azureus
Dendrobates galactonotus
Dendrobates leucomelas
Dendrobates quinquevittatus
Dendrobates steyermarki
Dendrobates tinctorius
Phyllobates bassleri
Phyllobates bolivianus
Phyllobates femoralis
Phyllobates ingeri
Phyllobates parvulus
Phyllobates pictus °ᴬ
Phyllobates pulchritectus
Phyllobates petersi
Phyllobates smaragdinus
Phyllobates trivittatus
Phyllobates zaparo
Agalychnis craspedopus
Phyllomedusa bicolor
Phyllomedusa buckleyi
Phyllomedusa palliata
Phyllomedusa tarsius
Phyllomedusa tomopterna
Phyllomedusa trinitatus °ᴺ
Phyllomedusa vaillanti
Hemiphractus bubalus
Hemiphractus johnsoni

Hyla cruentomma
Hyla dentei
Hyla egleri °ᴬ
Hyla epacrorhina
Hyla fasciata
Hyla favosa
Hyla fuentei
Hyla funerea
Hyla garbei
Hyla geographica °ᴬ
Hyla goinorum
Hyla grandisonae
Hyla granosa
Hyla haraldschultzi
Hyla helenae
Hyla hypselops
Hyla imitator
Hyla inframaculata
Hyla lanciformis
Hyla leucophyllata °ᴬ
Hyla luteocellata °ᴺ
Hyla marmorata
Hyla minima
Hyla minuta °ᴬ
Hyla multifasciata
Hyla ornatissima
Hyla parviceps
Hyla proboscidea
Hyla punctata
Hyla rhodopepla
Hyla riveroi
Hyla rossalleni
Hyla roeschmanni
Hyla rubra °ᵀᴺ
Hyla sarayacuensis
Hyla schubarti
Hyla semicula °ᴬ
Hyla steinbachi
Hyla surinamensis
Hyla tintinnabulum
Hyla triangulum
Hyla tuberculosa
Nyctimantis rugiceps
Osteocephalus buckleyi
Osteocephalus lepricum
Osteocephalus taurinus
Osteocephalus pearsoni
Osteocephalus verrucigerus
Phrynohyas coriacea
Phrynohyas venulosa °ᵀᴺᴬ
Phyllodytes auratus
Sphaenorhynchus carneus
Sphaenorhynchus dorisae
Sphaenorhynchus eurhostos
Centrolenella fleischmanni °ᵀᴺ
Centrolenella geijskesi
Centrolenella medemi

Leptodactylus rhodomystax
Leptodactylus rhodostigma
Leptodactylus rugosus
Leptodactylus stenodema
Leptodactylus ularsi
Leptodactylus wagneri °TNA
Lithodytes lineatus
Physalaemus petersi
Vanzolinius discodactylus
Dischidodactylus duidensis
Eleutherodactylus acuminatus
Eleutherodactylus altamazonicus
Eleutherodactylus carvalhoi
Eleutherodactylus chiastonotus
Eleutherodactylus conspicillatus
Eleutherodactylus croceoinguinis
Eleutherodactylus diadematus
Eleutherodactylus fenestratus
Eleutherodactylus granulosus

Hemiphractus proboscideus
Hemiphractus scutatus
Flectonotus fitzgeraldi
Gastrotheca longipes
Gastrotheca testudinea
Stefania evansi
Stefania goini
Stefania marahuaquensis
Allophryne ruthveni
Aparasphenodon venezolana
Hyla alboguttata
Hyla albomarginata °NA
Hyla baumgardneri
Hyla benitezi
Hyla bifurca
Hyla boesemani
Hyla bokermanni
Hyla boans °TN
Hyla brevifrons
Hyla calcarata

Centrolenella midas
Centrolenella munozorum
Centrolenella oyampiensis
Centrolenella pulido
Centrolenella ritae
Centrolenella taylori
Chiasmocleis atripes
Chiasmocleis bassleri
Chiasmocleis hudsoni
Chiasmocleis shudikarensis
Chiasmocleis ventrimaculata
Ctenophryne gayi
Hamptophryne boliviana
Otophryne robusta
Syncope antenori
Syncope carvalhoi
Synapturanus mirandaribeiroi
Synapturanus rabus
Synapturanus salseri
Rana palmipes °TNA

APPENDIX 8 3—Amphibians of the Northern Forests (Santa Marta Maracaibo Basin Falcon District Coastal Range, and Bases of Merida Andes)

Caecilians
Caecilia flavopunctata
Caecilia subnigricans °T
Nectocaecilia haydee
Typhlonectes venezuelense

Anurans
Atelopus cruciger
Bufo marinus °TC
Bufo sternosignatus
Bufo typhonius °TCA
Ceratophrys calcarata
Adenomera hylaedactyla °CA
Leptodactylus bolivianus °TC

Leptodactylus poecilochilus °T
Leptodactylus wagneri °TCA
Physalaemus pustulosus °T
Eleutherodactylus bicumulus
Eleutherodactylus maussi
Eleutherodactylus rozei
Eleutherodactylus terraebolivaris
Colostethus dunni
Colostethus herminae
Colostethus riveroi
Colostethus sp
Phyllomedusa medinae
Phyllomedusa trinitatus °C
Gastrotheca williamsoni

Flectonotus pygmaeus
Hyla albomarginata °CA
Hyla alemani
Hyla battersbyi
Hyla boans °TC
Hyla luteocellata °C
Hyla rubra °TCA
Phrynohyas venulosa °TCA
Centrolenella antisthenesi
Centrolenella fleischmanni °TC
Centrolenella orientalis
Centrolenella orocostalis
Relictivomer pearsei °T
Rana palmipes °TCA

APPENDIX 8 4—Amphibia of Atlantic Forests

Caecilians
Mimosiphonops vermiculatus
Oscaecilia hypereumeces
Siphonops annulatus °C
Siphonops confusionis
Siphonops hardyi
Siphonops insulanus
Siphonops leucoderus
Siphonops paulensis
Clathonerpeton braestrupi

Anurans
Hemipipa carvalhoi
Brachycephalus ephippium
Psyllophryne didactyla
Atelopus pernambucensis
Dendrophryniscus brevipollicatus
Dendrophryniscus leucomystax
Rhamphophryne proboscideus
Bufo crucifer
Bufo ictericus

Cycloramphus eleutherodactylus
Cycloramphus fuliginosus
Cycloramphus granulosus
Cycloramphus neglectus
Cycloramphus ohausi
Scythrophrys sawayae
Zachaenus parvulus
Zachaenus sanctaecatharinae
Proceratophrys appendiculatus
Proceratophrys boiei
Proceratophrys cristiceps
Proceratophrys fryi
Macrogenioglottus alipioi
Eleutherodactylus bilineatus
Eleutherodactylus binotatus
Eleutherodactylus gualteri
Eleutherodactylus guentheri
Eleutherodactylus henseli
Eleutherodactylus hoehnei
Eleutherodactylus nasutus
Eleutherodactylus octavioi

Hyla cuspidata
Hyla cymbalum
Hyla duartei
Hyla egleri °C
Hyla faber
Hyla flavoguttata
Hyla fuscomarginata
Hyla geographica °C
Hyla ayri
Hyla humilis
Hyla langei
Hyla leucophyllata °
Hyla limai
Hyla marginata
Hyla microps
Hyla minuta °C
Hyla nahdereri
Hyla oliverrai
Hyla pachychrus
Hyla prasina
Hyla rizibilis

Bufo typhonius °ᵀᴺᶜ
Bufo ocellatus
Ceratophrys aurita
Crossodactylus aeneus
Crossodactylus dispar
Crossodactylus gaudichaudii
Crossodactylus grandis
Crossodactylus schmidti
Crossodactylus trachystoma
Hylodes aspera
Hylodes glabrus
Hylodes lateristrigatus
Hylodes magalhaesi
Hylodes mertensi
Hylodes meridionalis
Hylodes nasus
Hylodes ornata
Hylodes perpliatus
Megaelosia goeldi
Adenomera bokermanni
Adenomera hylaedactyla °ᴺᶜ
Adenomera marmorata
Leptodactylus mystaceus
Leptodactylus mystacinus
Leptodactylus sp 'N
Leptodactylus pentadactylus °ᵀᶜ
Leptodactylus troglodytes
Leptodactylus wagneri °ᵀᴺᶜ
Physalaemus maculiventris
Physalaemus moreirae
Physalaemus nanus
Physalaemus olfersi
Physalaemus signiferus
Thoropa miliaris
Thoropa lutzi
Thoropa petropolitana
Crossodactylodes pintoi
Cycloramphus asper
Cycloramphus boulengeri
Cycloramphus diringshoefensi
Cycloramphus dubius

Eleutherodactylus paulodutrai
Eleutherodactylus parvus
Eleutherodactylus ramagii
Eleutherodactylus venancioi
Eleutherodactylus vinhai
Euparkerella brasiliensis
Ischnocnema verrucosa
Colostethus alagoanus
Colostethus capixaba
Colostethus carioca
Colostethus olfersioides
Phyllobates pictus °ᶜ
Phyllomedusa aspera
Phyllomedusa ayeaye
Phyllomedusa bahiana
Phyllomedusa centralis
Phyllomedusa distincta
Phyllomedusa fimbriata
Phyllomedusa guttata
Phyllomedusa marginata
Phyllomedusa rohdei
Flectonotus fissilis
Fritziana goeldii
Fritziana ohausi
Gastrotheca ernestoi
Gastrotheca fissipes
Gastrotheca microdisca
Gastrotheca viridis
Aparasphenodon brunoi
Hyla albicans
Hyla albofrenata
Hyla albolineata
Hyla albomarginata °ᴺᶜ
Hyla albosignata
Hyla astartea
Hyla aurata
Hyla ariadne
Hyla argyreornata
Hyla catharinae
Hyla claresignata
Hyla crospedospila

Hyla rubra °ᵀᴺᶜ
Hyla secedens
Hyla senicula °ᶜ
Hyla strigilata
Osteocephalus langsdorffii
Phyllodytes acuminatus
Phyllodytes luteolus
Phrynohyas imitatrix
Phrynohyas mesophaea
Phrynohyas venulosa °ᵀᴺᶜ
Sphaenorhynchus bromelicola
Sphaenorhynchus orophilus
Sphoenorhynchus palustris
Sphaenorhynchus pauloalvini
Sphaenorhynchus planicola
Sphaenorhynchus prasinus
Sphaenorhynchus surdus
Trachycephalus atlas
Trachycephalus nigromaculatus
Centrolenella albotunicata
Centrolenella bokermanni
Centrolenella divaricans
Centrolenella dubia
Centrolenella eurygnatha
Centrolenella lutzorum
Centrolenella parvula
Centrolenella petropolitana
Centrolenella surda
Centrolenella uranoscopa
Centrolenella vanzolinii
Arcovomer passarellii
Dasypops schirchi
Chiasmocleis albopunctata
Chiasmocleis bicegoi
Chiasmocleis centralis
Chiasmocleis schubarti
Chiasmocleis urbanae
Myersiella microps
Hyophryne histrio
Stereocyclops incrassatus
Rana palmipes °ᵀᴺᶜ

9. Origin and Distribution of Reptiles in Lowland Tropical Rainforests of South America

James R. Dixon

Department of Wildlife and Fisheries Sciences
Texas A&M University
College Station, Texas 77843
USA

The task of summarizing the distribution, natural history and evolution of approximately half of the known species of reptiles of South America is a nearly futile exercise because the taxonomy and distribution of many important groups are poorly known. Nevertheless, there are some redeeming values in any exercise—in this case a summary of the state of our knowledge of the distribution and ecology of the South American reptilian fauna.

As a matter of convenience throughout this paper, I refer to rainforest reptiles, rather than "tropical lowland rainforest reptiles." Rainforest reptiles include those genera and species that occur below 1000 m elevation and within the environs of rainforest (i.e., yearly temperature varying between 23° and 28°C, more or less continuous rainfall between 150 and 600 cm annually). In the context of this paper, any reptile that occurs within the conditions mentioned above qualifies as a rainforest species, although it may not be one ecologically. There are about 14 genera of savanna relicts within the confines of the rainforest environment, an additional 22 genera are aquatic, and about 30 genera are fossorial (Table 9.1). Several genera are wide ranging occupying many vegetation zones including rainforests. Therefore, the task of assigning a genus and/or its attendant species as rainforest endemics, frequently is difficult without some basic knowledge of their ecology.

There is a limited understanding of the evolution and distribution of rainforest reptiles in South America because only a few individuals (Vanzolini, 1972, 1974, 1976, Vanzolini and Rebouças-Spieker 1973, Duellman 1978, Fitch, 1970, Myers, 1974, Crump, 1971 Dixon and Soini 1975, 1977, Rand and Humphrey, 1968) have investigated these topics

Vanzolini (1967) discussed the problems of application of ecological principles to the Amazonian biota without having a firm understanding of the taxonomy and evolution of its constituent groups. Only through detailed taxonomic studies of various lowland tropical rainforest genera and species of reptiles (Uzzell, 1966, Oliver, 1948, Duellman 1958, Myers, 1974, Savage, 1960, Kluge, 1969, Peters, 1960, Gans, 1971, Dixon, 1973 1974a,b, Roze, 1967, Ruibal 1952) and geographic and/or ecological information (Rand and Humphrey, 1968, Crump, 1971 Beebe, 1944a-c, 1945, Vanzolini, 1968, 1972 1974, 1976, Vanzolini and Williams, 1970, Test, et al., 1966, Duellman, 1978) will the reptilian rainforest fauna ever be fully understood.

The following information obtained for forest associations and their included reptile species is only a rough estimate and, without doubt, will be subject to much future revision. We are raising questions that cannot be answered firmly without further studies on fossil histories, taxonomy, and ecology of particular reptile groups. Time is short, for the rainforests are rapidly being altered by man (Richards, 1973), and data concerning the reptile fauna soon may be impossible to obtain.

Without detailed natural history observations on the majority of the species, little can be accomplished concerning the relationships among rainforest reptiles. For example, the taxonomy and distribution of *Anolis* is so poorly known (Williams, 1976) that the large number of described South American taxa (80) is enough to confuse and mask the rela-

TABLE 9.1—Reptilian Genera that Contain A) Species that Are Savanna Relicts, B) Species that Are Aquatic or Semi-aquatic, C) Species that Are Semi-fossorial within Lowland Rainforest Situations

A			
Ameiva	Drymarchon	Leptodeira	Phimophis
Anolis	Gymnophthalmus	Mabuya	Tretioscincus
Cnemidophorus	Iguana	Mastigodryas	Tropidurus
Crotalus	Kentropyx	Pseudoboa	Tupinambis

B			
Caiman	Dracaena	Kinosternon	Podocnemis
Chelus	Eunectes	Melanosuchus	Pseudoeryx
Chelydra	Helicops	Neusticurus	Rhinoclemys
Chrysemys	Hydromedusa	Paleosuchus	Tretanorhinus
Crocodilurus	Hydrops	Phrynops	
Crocodylus	Hydrodynastes	Platemys	

C			
Amphisbaena	Diaphorolepis	Mesobaena	Stenorrhina
Amhus	Elapomorphus	Micrurus	Synophis
Anomalepis	Lnmochliophis	Ninia	Tantilla
Apostolepis	Enulius	Nothopsis	Typhlophis
Atractus	Geophis	Ophiodes	Typhlops
Aulura	Leposternon	Rhadinaea	
Bachia	Leptotyphlops	Saphenophis	
Broma	Liotyphlops	Sordellina	

tionships of other forest genera in any zoogeographical analyses. I estimated that there are 31+ species of anoles within the limits of the Chocoan rainforest (based upon all literature available, other than Williams, 1976). Williams' (1976) list of species groups reduces my list of Chocoan anoles to 18 species, while the number of species in the Amazon and Atlantic forests remain about the same 17(14) and 5(5), respectively. The disparity in the number of anole species recognized in the Chocoan forest represents a 1 percent error when comparing forest reptile species, 3 percent comparing only lizards, 9 percent comparing arboreal lizards, and 33 percent comparing species of *Anolis*.

Frequently a common and speciose genus of reptiles is also poorly understood (e.g. *Anolis*, *Gonatodes*, *Amphisbaena*, *Atractus*, *Bothrops*, *Oxyrhopus*, *Micrurus*, *Liophis*, *Leimadophis*). However some students of South American herpetology (e.g., Gans, 1962, Williams, 1976, Thomas, 1976, Wiest, in prep., Peters, 1960, Savage, 1960, Roze, 1966, Vanzolini, 1951, 1957, 1967, Vanzolini and Valencia, 1965, Oftedal, 1974) are making progress in systematic revisions of lowland rainforest reptile genera and species that eventually will lead to an improved understanding of the distribution of rainforest reptile species.

HISTORY OF THE TROPICAL RAINFORESTS AND THEIR REPTILIAN INHABITANTS

The Geological Evidence

There are many congruent facts that imply that the major uplift of the Andes occurred in the Late Cenozoic, thus beginning the formation of the modern Amazon Basin. The geologic evidence of Harrington (1962), Lohmann (1970), James (1971), Jenks (1956), Haffer (1974), Berry (1938), Herrero-Ducloux (1963), Rutland, et al. (1965) suggests that the older formations of the eastern basins were formed by the Andean uplift. Harrington (1962) suggested that part of the basin was covered by as much as 700 m of Tertiary deposits. The basins in eastern Perú and Ecuador accumulated fluvial sediments throughout much of the Tertiary and consist of both freshwater and brackish deposits. Several marine ingressions from the Pacific Ocean occurred through the middle of the Oligocene, followed by the union of the Ecuadorian and Peruvian Andes (at the Huancabamba Deflection), closing the last portal through the Andes to the Pacific (Harrington, 1962). Occasional marine ingressions of the Atlantic Ocean into the slowly rising Amazon Basin, via the portal between the Guiana and

Brasilian shields, the Orinoco (Llanos) Basin of Venezuela, or the Paraná Basin of Paraguay, is indicated by the presence of brackish and saltwater fossil deposits found in eastern Perú and Ecuador (Haffer, 1974).

It has been suggested that during the Late Cenozoic the upper Amazon Basin was a huge inland sea in which sediments were constantly being deposited through torrential rains upon the Andes. These runoffs created vast flood plains that were crossed by numerous meandering streams that now form the major river systems of the Amazon Basin. Although the narrow straits between the Guiana and Brasilian shields may have been blocked at times (with subsequent flow through the Orinoco or Paraná basins) an almost continuous connection with the Atlantic Ocean seems likely. Haffer's (1974) review of other studies indicates that Marajo Island, at the mouth of the Amazon, is underlain by over 4000 m of fossiliferous marine and brackish, Cretaceous and Tertiary sediments. The evidence suggests that continental fluvial sediments were transported both from east and west to the sub-Andean basin of the upper Amazon. Permanent, easterly directed flow of sediments probably followed the final major uplift of the Andes in late Pliocene and early Pleistocene.

Raven and Axelrod (1975) showed that the angiosperm flora of South America had a definite relationship to Africa through the Eocene, but as the plates (continents) drifted apart, each continent developed a unique flora. The process was enhanced by the Miocene orogenies in eastern Africa and western South America, changes in wind and temperature patterns associated with those orogenies, and the influence of angiosperms from tropical Asia that immigrated to the approaching African continent via sweepstakes dispersal. Much of the diversity of the tropical flora of Africa was diminished by the orogenies of the eastern plateau of Africa and associated wind, temperature, and hydrologic pattern shifts, but South America apparently maintained several centers of floral refugia (Haffer, 1974, Vanzolini, 1973, Muller, 1973, Vuilleumier, 1971) and thus retained a greater diversity of angiosperms. Historically, it seems that the rainforests were continuous geographically throughout much of the Early and Middle Cenozoic, subjected to disruption during the Miocene and Pliocene orogenies (Emiliani, 1956, Dorf, 1959, Tanner 1968), and severely restricted to relatively small refugia by wind, temperature, and rainfall patterns during and following the Pleistocene (Flint, 1971, Sioli, 1975, Simpson, 1975, Raven and Axelrod, 1975, Emiliani 1972, Haffer, 1974 Vuilleumier, 1971, Damuth and Fairbridge, 1970).

Most modern reptilian genera with wide distributions that also occur in rainforests lack fossil records in South America (*Amphisbaena, Ameiva, Iguana, Mabuya, Clelia, Epicrates, Erythrolamprus, Lachesis, Leptodeira, Leptophis, Mastigodryas, Spilotes, l'antilla Tripanurgos*). However their current distributions imply that they may have evolved concurrently with those widespread genera with recorded fossil histories in the Miocene and Pliocene (*Dracaena, Tupinambis, Teius, Diplolaemus* and *Crotalus*). Some of these genera are also xeric adapted, thus, it is impossible to postulate their origins without fossils or other evolutionary evidence. Estes and Price (1973) identified *Pristiguana* from the Upper Cretaceous in Brasil as the earliest known iguanid and suggested a Gondwanan origin of the family based on morphological paleontological, and zoogeographical considerations.

The Fossil Evidence

The fossil history of rainforest reptiles is relatively good for those groups with large skeletal features (e.g., turtles and crocodilians) but extremely poor for amphisbaenians, lizards, and snakes. The fossil record of amphibians and reptiles in South America has been documented by Báez and Gasparini (this volume). Only a few comments especially pertinent to rainforest groups are included here.

The presence of relatively modern gavials (Langston, 1965) in the Rio Magdalena of Colombia during the upper Oligocene and in the Pliocene in Argentina suggests that the lowland tropical vegetation was extensive throughout much of South America for long periods of time. This is further enhanced by the probable replacement of gavials as piscivorous carnivores by longirostrine crocodiles, first in northern South America and later in the south. Langston (1965) suggested that longirostrine crocodiles were more adaptive and were probably replacing the gavials (taking over the fish-eating niche) throughout the Cenozoic Era. Langston pointed out that the significance of the record is that longirostrine crocodiles were assuming this role, not alligatorids. However, the fossil record indicates that the alligatorids were evolving at the same time that longirostrine crocodiles presumably were competing with gavials. Climatic changes brought about by Mio-Pliocene orogenies may have severely limited the habitat and tolerances of longirostrine crocodiles and they, in turn, were competively excluded by alligatorids. The presence of modern crocodiles occupying parapatric geographic ranges in South America suggests that they (*C. acutus, C. intermedius*) are relicts of some ancient stock or populations that were excluded in earlier competition, were (or became) salt tolerant, survived in island refugia and are recent invaders.

The fossil history of South American turtles is even more confusing, perhaps owing to the conservative nature of the morphologies of the groups and the widespread distribution of the pleurodires in South America and the rest of the world. Many early fossils of pleurodires were misidentified and, only recently, have workers (Auffenberg, 1974, Wood, 1972, 1976, Wood and Gamero, 1971) attempted to unravel the myriad of names assigned to fossils discovered in the past two centuries. The presence of *Podocnemis* and *Chelus* in the Pliocene in Estado Falcón, Venezuela, *Chelus* in the Miocene in the upper Rio Magdalena Valley, Colombia, *Podocnemis* in the Late Cretaceous in Brasil and in the Eocene/Pliocene in Perú, suggests that turtles and crocodilians were occupying similar habitats during comparable periods of their evolution in South America.

The orogenies of the late Miocene and throughout much of the Pliocene disrupted the general distributions of many turtle and crocodile species and apparently caused the demise of four genera of turtles in South America (*Schwoeboemys, Parahydraspis, Stu-* *pendemys, Trionyx* and possibly *Taphrosphys*) and fourteen genera of crocodilians (*Gavialis, Sebecus, Charactosuchus, Rhamphostomopsis, Nettosuchus, Eocaiman, Brachygnathosuchus, Gryposuchus, Proalligator, Leptorrhamphus, Purussaurus, Ilchunaia, Notocaiman, Necrosuchus*). The majority of the species of those genera that survived the climatic, edaphic, and hydrologic shifts of Miocene/Pliocene eras (*Paleosuchus, Melanosuchus, Caiman, Crocodylus, Podocnemis, Chelus, Phrynops, Kinosternon, Rhinoclemmys, Chrysemys, Geochelone*) are those that exist today in Neotropical rainforests (Wood, 1976, Wood and Gamero, 1971, Wood and Patterson, 1973, Romer, 1956, Auffenberg, 1974, Langston 1965, Medina, 1976).

The presence of the lizard genera *Dracaena, Tupinambis*, and cf *Polychrus* (Estes, 1961) in the Miocene deposits of the upper Río Magdalena of Colombia strongly suggests that many contemporary lizard genera were widespread rainforest occupants. Although few fossil South American lizard and snake genera are currently known, many modern Cis-Andean and Trans-Andean genera were probably well differentiated prior to the orogeny of the Andes (Estes, 1961).

Although we have little evidence that tropical environments have remained, in part, from the Mesozoic to modern times, the fossil evidence of tropical reptiles in South America suggests persistent tropical environments in most areas of South America prior to the uplift of the Andes (Harrington, 1962).

Historical Relationships of Currently Disjunct Rainforests

The distribution of rainforest reptiles is dependent ultimately upon the history of environmental factors that have affected the habitat and the reptilian gene pool. The increased vagility of one group compared with another, the inherent, fixed attributes of a particular species versus those with highly variable attributes, the physical and ecological barriers between different and/or equal habitat areas through time, and diffuse competition from other organisms within the niche hypervolume all play major and/or minor roles in formulating the distribution of various groups of reptiles.

The relationship of the herpetofauna of the Chocoan Forest with those of other northern forests and the Amazon Forest is best understood by examining a series of geological events. Based upon present day distribution of rainforest reptiles, I suggest that there was a more or less continuous connection between rainforests prior to the major orogeny of the Andes. Simpson (1975) summarized several papers on the geology of the Andes that suggested the orogeny of the Andes maintained several centers of activity throughout the Cenozoic with the Venezuelan Andes rising in the Paleocene, the Colombian and Ecuadorian Andes in middle Eocene, followed by later Tertiary erosion. The Huancabamba Deflection remained open until the upper Pliocene, when the Cordillera of Perú and Chile was uplifted further. The Andean orogeny proceeded from east to west across the South American continent. First the rainforests of Venezuela were isolated from those in Colombia. Subsequently, the Colombian rainforests were isolated from the Amazonian rainforests, and finally, the Chocoan rainforests were separated from the Amazonian forests by the closure of the Huancabamba Deflection. Based on fossil and present distributions of some reptiles, there are indications that a lowland rainforest corridor may have existed between the Chocoan and Amazonian forests through the Huancabamba Deflection during the last major interglacial period. The fossil record reveals several genera that are geologically and genetically older than the Andes and that occur now, or occurred in the past, on both sides of the mountains. The ranges of several species of snakes belonging to three genera (*Chironius, Leimadophis, Leptophis*) seem to have been connected recently, probably through the Huancabamba Deflection.

The water gaps between Central America and South America may have been narrow enough to allow some interchange of faunas between the two continents during the Cenozoic (Hershkovitz, 1966; Savage, 1974). Land connections (not necessarily continuous) between those regions beginning in the Pliocene (Haffer, 1974) certainly allowed faunal interchange on a larger scale. Rainforest faunas probably were exchanged when local environmental conditions were appropriate after the closure of the Panamanian Portal.

The present reptilian fauna of the Chocoan forest seems to be influenced more by a Central American faunal element than by an Amazonian one. Perhaps this results from the proximity of, and continuous connection to, the Central American faunal element after closure of the Panamanian Portal (Table 9.2). This also suggests that there has been a longer period of faunal interchange between the Chocoan Forest and Central American rainforests than between those of Amazonia and the Chocó, especially following the orogeny of the Colombian and Ecuadorian Andes. This is not to deny that the Chocoan rainforest probably was isolated from the Central American and Amazonian rainforests (especially from the latter beginning in at least mid Pliocene) for periods of time sufficient to develop moderate amount of endemism.

Connection of the Amazonian and Atlantic rainforests seems to have occurred several times. Haffer (1974), Damuth and Fairbridge (1970), Vuilleumier (1971), Simpson (1975) and Raven and Axelrod (1975) have garnered evidence concerning the Quaternary history, especially that dealing with arid/humid (glacial/interglacial) phases from the Pleistocene to 2500 years ago. Most data place the end of the Wisconsin glaciation at 10,000 to 15,000 y b p, with two short arid cycles 4,000 and 2,500 y b p. These may have caused the present hiatus between the Amazon and Atlantic forests. Three to four glacial periods are postulated for the Andes and most other regions and there are five terrace levels along the Rio Amazonas resulting from cyclic erosion and aggradation (Haffer, 1974, this volume). I assume there was at least one preglacial period of long duration prior to the Pleistocene that was followed by four interglacial periods of various lengths of time after each of the four major glacial periods of the Pleistocene. Because the Amazonian forest is relatively young—800,000 to 1,800,000 years and has been affected variously by flooding and/or cool arid cycles I assume that the five recognized terrace levels are the result of preglacial and interglacial flooding. If we assume that each arid (glacial) phase created broad savanna regions and restricted the rain-

TABLE 9.2—A) North and Central American and/or Endemic Reptilian Genera that Contain Lowland Tropical Rainforest Species that Reach Their Southern Distributions in the Northern and Chocoan forests (° = Endemic to the Chocó Forest). B) South American Reptilian Genera that Contain Lowland Tropical Rainforest Species that Reach Their Northern Limits in the Northern and Choco forests († Indicates a Savanna Relict)

A			
Anomalepis	Crocodylus	Lampropeltis	Trachyboa°
Basiliscus	Diaphorolepis°	Masticophis	Tretanorhinus
Chelydra	Echinosaura°	Scaphiodontophis	Urganophis
Chrysemys	Emmochliophis°	Sibon	
Coniophanes	Enulius	Sphaerodactylus	
Corythophanes	Geophis	Stenorrhina	
B			
Alopoglossus	Helicops	Prionodactylus	Tropidophis
Amphisbaena	Liophis	Pseudoboa†	Tropidurus†
Atractus	Morunasaurus	Siphlophis	Tupinambis†
Enyalioides	Ophryoessoides	Tretioscincus	
Geochelone	Phimophis†	Tripanurgos	

forest to relatively small refugia (Fig 9.1), the union of the restricted Atlantic and Amazonian rainforests may have occurred an equal number of times during interglacials, probably along the northeastern part of Brasil. Paleobotanic and paleoedaphic evidence (Haffer 1974; Damuth and Fairbridge, 1974) suggests that the "Diagonal of Open Formations" (Vanzolini 1963, 1974) has been present from Late Tertiary to present with only minor alterations. Therefore, a belt of Amazonian forest may have reached the Atlantic forest as indicated above, or via the Rio Madeira-Rio Paraná Drainage around the west and south sides of the Brasilian Shield. A filter corridor through the Brasilian Shield along gallery forests also may have been possible, but these routes probably were restrictive. Many Amazonian reptiles have reached only the northern part of the Atlantic forest (e.g., *Anolis punctatus*, *A. ortoni*, *A. fuscoauratus*, *Kentropyx calcaratus*, *Bothrops bilineatus*, *Chironius carinatus*, *Coleodactylus meridionalis*, *Polychrus marmoratus*, *Tripanurgos compressus*, *Mastigodryas boddaerti*, *Dipsas indica*), thereby suggesting that the former route is the most plausible. Most Amazonian forest species that have reached the Atlantic forest show little or no geographic variation suggesting that a large number of species may have reached the Atlantic forest during the last Amazon-Atlantic connection (probably 3,000–5,000 y b p).

A speciation model.—From Wiest's (in prep.) work on the colubrid snake genus *Chironius*, it is feasible to postulate the number of times this genus extended its distribution into the Atlantic forest during interglacial periods with alternate glacial periods of speciation in both the Amazonian and Atlantic forests.

In the case of *Chironius*, there seems to be a progressive intrusion of recently-differentiated Amazonian stocks resulting from the repeated contraction of the forest into refugia during at least four glacial periods. Each interglacial expansion of the Amazonian forest that reached the Atlantic forest seemed to carry with it the more primitive members of each evolving gene pool. Without fossil evidence, the model is purely hypothetical, but Wiest (pers. comm.) constructed an independent model and we differ only on minor points. If we assume that the primitive stock of the gene pool is peripheral to the developing core and the set of characters defining the primitive conditions for *Chironius* are correct, the following sequence of events

Distribución propuesta para el Pleistoceno de los tipos de vegetación Suramericana durante los periodos de máxima glacial. D = Desierto, CI = Hielo Glacial, CL = Pastizales, M = Monte, NE = Bosque de Nothofagus, P = Paramo (Alpino), PS = Matorral semi-desértico de Patagonia, S = Sabana, TF/S = Matorral de bosque espinoso, TM = Bosque tropical montaño, TR = Bosque tropical lluvioso, TS-L/D = Bosque tropical semi-siempreverde/deciduo. La zona punteada y con líneas diagonales es en la cuenca amazónica puede haber sido un bosque húmedo tropical.

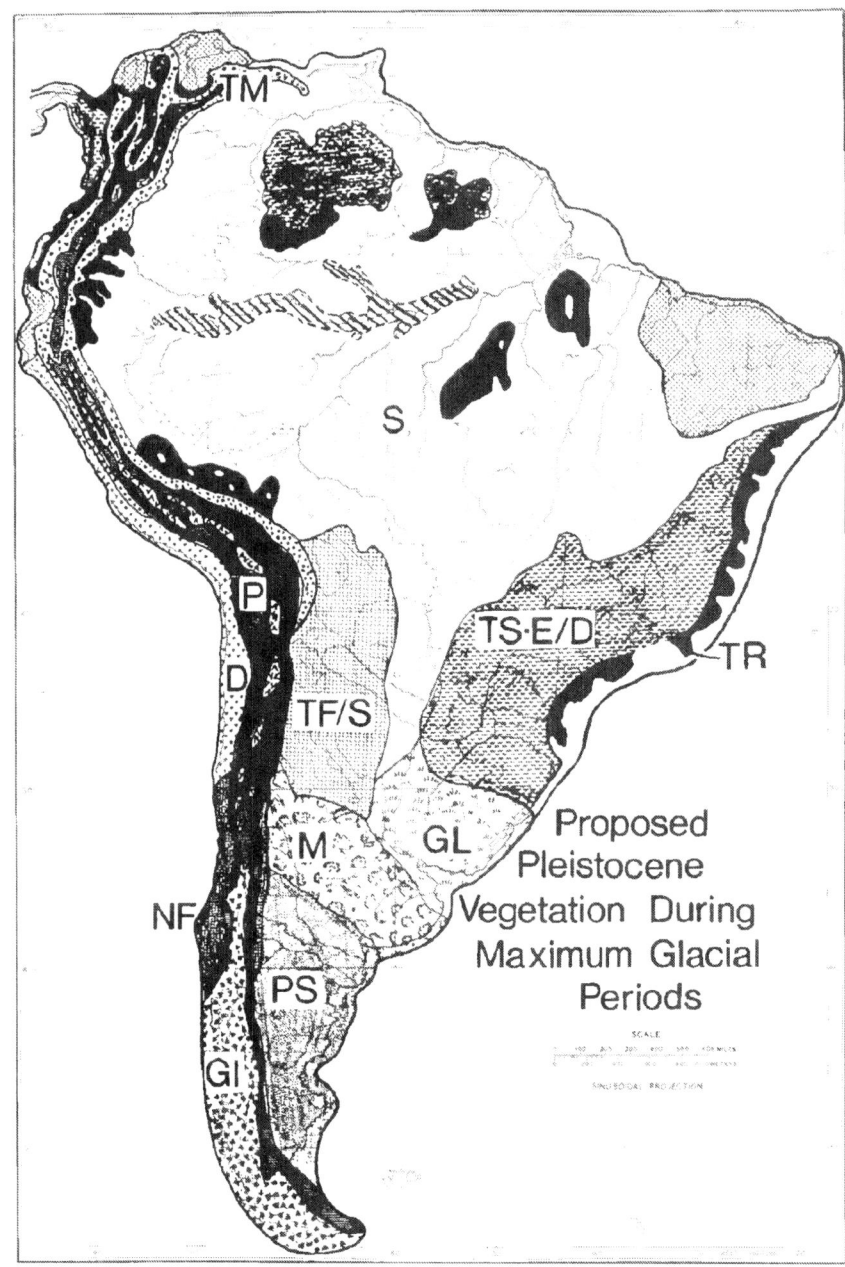

Fig. 9:1. Proposed Pleistocene distribution of South American vegetation types during maximum glacial periods. D = Desert; GI = Glacial Ice; GL = Grassland; M = Monte; NF = *Nothofagus* Forest; P = Páramo (Alpine); PS = Patagonian (Semi-desert Scrub); S = Savanna; TF/S = Thorn Forest/Scrub; TM = Tropical montane; TR = Tropical rainforest; TS-E/D = Tropical semi-evergreen/deciduous Forest. Dashed and diagonal lined area in Amazon Basin may have been an additional isolated tropical rainforest.

should represent the various invasions of *Chronius* stock (and possibly other reptiles) into the Atlantic forest

1. Proto-*Chronius* stock invaded the Atlantic forest during a pre-Pleistocene period when the two lowland tropical rainforests were connected along a coastal corridor, from the mouth of the Amazon eastward and southward along the northeastern part of Brasil
2. During the first major Pleistocene glacial period, the forests were discontinuous refugia with *C multiventris* and *C exoletus* as developing taxa in Amazonian refugia and *C bicarinatus* in Atlantic refugia Two additional species, *C quadricarinatus* and *flavolineatus*, were speciating in gallery forests within savannas (the Cerrado-Caatinga Diagonal" of Vanzolini, 1963, 1974) between the two rainforests
3. The first major Pleistocene interglacial period allowed expansion of the forest refugia and eventual reconnection of the Atlantic and Amazonian forests *Chronius quadricarinatus* and *C flavolineatus* evolved into full biological species and extended their ranges within the diagonal of open formations in Brasil where they have remained to the present time In Amazonia, *C multiventris* and *exoletus* had developed into biological species and now invaded the Atlantic forest coming into contact with *C bicarinatus*, a species with a different diet and probably not a competitor
4. The second, major glacial period again reduced the forests to discrete refugia The *C exoletus* stock remained in the Atlantic refugia with some contact with *C exoletus* populations in Amazonia along gallery forests while the Atlantic population of *C multiventris* became isolated and formed a vicariant biological species (*C foveatus*) *Chronius bicarinatus* remained undifferentiated in Atlantic refugia while *C multiventris* did likewise in the Amazonia refugia *Chronius scurrulus* developed into a biological species in one of the several Amazonian forest refuges
5. The second interglacial period allowed a reunion of the lowland rainforests *Chronius scurrulus* invaded the expanded Atlantic forest for the first time, while *C multiventris* and *exoletus* did so for the second time *Chronius foveatus* had developed in the Atlantic forest as an ecological equivalent of *C multiventris*, and the two species formed competitive populations *Chronius bicarinatus* did not differentiate Previously allopatric populations of *C exoletus* interbred along zones of contact
6. The third glacial period reduced the forests to discrete refugia *Chronius exoletus multiventris* and *scurrulus* remained undifferentiated populations in Amazonian refugia *Chronius carinatus* became a developing biological species from an isolated *C exoletus* stock in the Guianan Forest Refugium *Chronius bicarinatus* and *foveatus* remained relatively undifferentiated in Atlantic forest refugia, while the competing Atlantic populations of *C multiventris* became extinct The semi isolated Atlantic population of *C exoletus* differentiated subspecifically (*C e pyrrhopogon*) and an isolated Atlantic population of *C scurrulus* diverged into *C s laevicollis*
7. During the third interglacial period, a reunion of the two forests allowed for the reinvasion of *C exoletus, multiventris, scurrulus* and an initial invasion of *C carinatus* into the Atlantic Forest *Chronius bicarinatus* and *foveatus* remained intact, although the latter again became competitive with the invading *C multiventris* The once isolated populations of *C exoletus-scurrulus* formed intergrading complexes
8. The fourth glacial period reduced the forests into discrete refugia once more *Chronius exoletus, scurrulus, multiventris* and *carinatus* remained undifferentiated in Amazonian forest refugia, while an isolated population of Amazonian *C scurrulus* developed into a biological species (*C fuscus*) The isolated Atlantic Forest population of

C. multiventris was again outcompeted by *C. foveatus* and became extinct. The Atlantic populations of *C. exoletus* and *scurrulus* became isolated from their Amazonian parental stock and became increasingly isolated reproductively into *C. pyrrhopogon* and *laevicollis*, respectively. The Atlantic *C. bicarinatus* remained undifferentiated, and the Atlantic population of *C. carinatus* was restricted to small pockets of forest along the northeastern coast of Brasil owing to competition with *C. bicarinatus* and *foveatus*, and may have become extinct there at that time.

9. The fourth interglacial period (possibly the past 10,000 years) brings us to the current distribution of species of *Chironius* in the Amazonian and Atlantic forests. *Chironius exoletus, multiventris, scurrulus, carinatus,* and *fuscus* are sympatric and/or parapatric in Amazonia. The first four species may have briefly invaded the Atlantic forest during a connection of the two forests somewhere between 10,000 and 4,500 y.b.p., and the latter species invaded for the first time. Atlantic populations of *C. carinatus* and *fuscus* currently are undifferentiated from Amazonian populations. Atlantic populations of *C. scurrulus* have differentiated into an allopatric, recognizable race (*C. s. laevicollis*), whereas Atlantic populations of *C. exoletus* are weakly differentiated into a recognized subspecies, *C. e. pyrrhopogon*, that intergrades with the nominate race over a broad zone. *Chironius bicarinatus* and *foveatus* seem to be undifferentiated and distributed throughout the Atlantic Forest.

COMPOSITION OF THE HERPETOFAUNA

Faunal Similarity

At the rate taxonomists are describing new taxa of reptiles from the Neotropics (10–30 species per year), it will be a long time before we obtain sufficient knowledge to allow

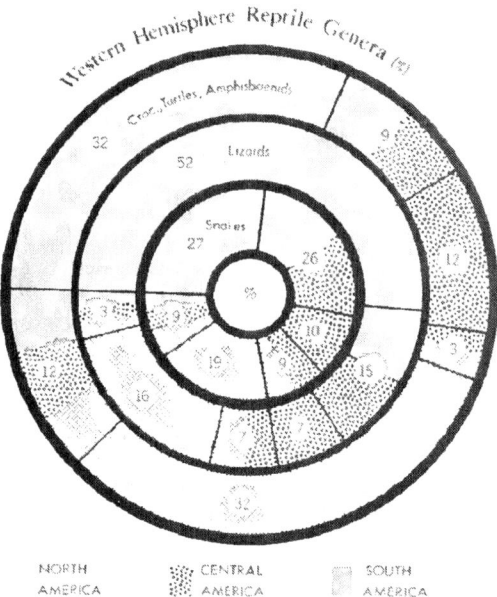

Fig. 9:2. The percentage of the 335 genera of reptiles in the Western Hemisphere that are endemic to, or shared with, each of the two major continents and the Central American corridor.

El porcentaje de los 335 géneros de reptiles en el Hemisferio Occidental que son endémicos para o compartidos con cada uno de los continentes mayores y con el corredor centroamericano.

us to comprehend the complex ecological structure of reptilian communities. Any number I mention is subject to immediate change, and should be accepted with a broad margin for error.

Of approximately 1,100 species and 203 genera of mainland South American reptiles, 550 species (149 genera) occur in the rainforests. This represents 73.4 percent of the total number of South American reptile genera and 49.5 percent of the species. It also represents 44.5 percent of all genera and 17.8 percent of the species in the Western Hemisphere (Fig. 9:2).

Of the 149 reptile genera, 21 (14.1%) are shared between the Chocó and the Amazon; 17 (10.7%) between the Atlantic and the Amazon; 3 (2.7%) between the Chocó and the Atlantic; 38 (25.5%) among all major Neotropical rainforests (Fig. 9:3, Table 9:3). Of the 550 species, 23 (4.3%) are shared between

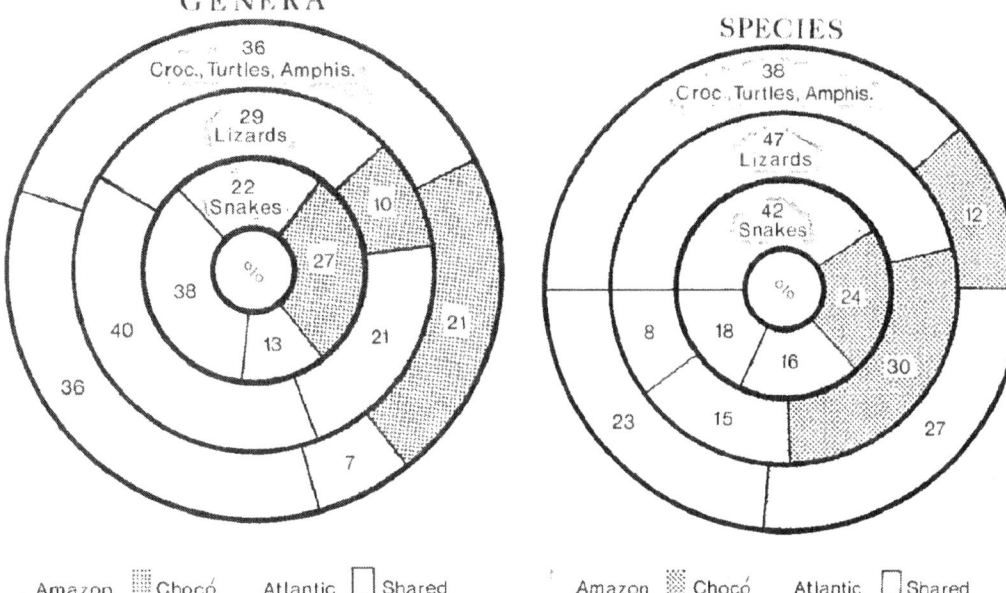

Fig. 9:3. Percentage of reptilian genera endemic to each of the major tropical rainforests and those shared between two or more of the forests.

El porcentaje de géneros de reptiles endémicos en cada uno de los bosques húmedos tropicales mayores y de aquellos comunes a dos o más bosques.

Fig. 9:4. Percentage of reptilian species endemic to each of the major tropical rainforests and those shared between two or more of the forests.

El porcentaje de especies de reptiles endémicas en cada uno de los bosques húmedos tropicales mayores y de aquellas comunes a dos o más bosques.

the Chocó and the Amazon; 43 (8.0%) between the Atlantic and Amazon; 1 (0.02%) between the Chocó and the Atlantic; 18 (3.1%) among all major Neotropical forests (Fig. 9:4, Appendix 9:1). The smaller trans-Andean forests (Magdalena, Sinu, Nechí, Santa Marta, Maracaibo, and coastal Venezuela) show little endemism (less than 4%) and those closest to the Chocó are essentially identical in their reptile faunas to the latter. Each of the more isolated of these forests (Santa Marta, Maracaibo, coastal Venezuela) contains one lowland rainforest endemic species. The coastal Venezuelan Forest shows closer affinities to the Amazon Forest, whereas the Maracaibo and Santa Marta forests contain a number of species that are broadly distributed in both Central and South America (see Appendix 9:1).

Of the 149 genera of rainforest reptiles, 72 (48.3%) are snakes, 63 (42.3%) are lizards [includes 5 (3.4%) amphisbaenids], 10 (6.7%) turtles and 4 (2.7%) crocodilians; of the species, 284 (51.4%) are snakes, 235 (43.0%) are lizards [includes 30 (5.5%) amphisbaenids], 24 (4.4%) turtles and 6 (1.1%) crocodilians. Of 95 lizard and 94 snake genera in South America, 63 (66.3%) and 72 (76.6%), respectively, occur in rainforests.

I agree with Burt (1958) and Udvardy (1969) that any formula chosen to obtain indices for similarities or differences between faunal elements depends upon the accuracy of the basic data set, the relative size and/or equivalent nature of each of the faunal areas and elements, and the taxonomic category chosen for the comparison (Fig. 9:5A).

Perhaps one of the best ways to compare faunal elements is to obtain subsets of data from equivalent areas within any given, major faunal region. The investigator thus gains an understanding of the variation within and between geographic subsets of data. It seems obvious that an increase in the number of species of any particular group from a given area will decrease the faunal similarity index

TABLE 9 3—Genera Shared among the Three Major Tropical Lowland Rainforests

Amazon/Atlantic	Amazon/Chocó	Amazon/Chocó/Atlantic	
Apostolepis	Alopoglossus	Ameiva	Mabuya
Cercosaura	Bachia	Amphisbaena	Mastigodryas
Coleodactylus	Boa	Anolis	Micrurus
Colobosaura	Cnemidophorus	Atractus	Oxyrhopus
Enyalius	Corallus	Bothrops	Polychrus
Hemidactylus	Dendrophidion	Caiman	Pseudoboa
Kentropyx	Drymarchon	Chironius	Pseustes
Leposternon	Drymobius	Clelia	Rhadinaea
Paleosuchus	Enyalioides	Dipsas	Spilotes
Pantodactylus	Gonatodes	Epicrates	Siphlophis
Philodryas	Gymnophthalmus	Erythrolamprus	Tantilla
Phrynops	Imantodes	Geochelone(?)	Tripanurgos
Platemys	Lepidoblepharis	Helicops	Tropidophis(?)
Podocnemis	Mobunasaurus	Iguana	Tupinambis
Thamnodynastes	Ninia	Kinosternon	Typhlops
Tropidurus	Oxybelis	Lachesis	Xenodon
Tupinambis	Phyllercus	Leimadophis	
Xenopholis	Prionodactylus	Leposoma	
Chocó/Atlantic	Ptychoglossus	Leptodeira	
Diploglossus	Rhinobothryum	Leptophis	
Liotyphlops	Sinophis	Leptotyphlops	
Lygophis	Thecadactylus	Lioplus	

(FSI) value proportionally (Fig 9 5B) It is also obvious that combination of different groups (e g, lizards snakes, turtles, crocodilians, or any other vertebrate groups) to arrive at a FSI value tends to mask the true relationship of each of the subsets (i e, lizards versus lizards) Each group (species, genus, family) has its own independent history, and only broad interpretations can be made when one major group (Reptilia) of one faunal area is compared to that of another (Fig 9 15c–e) Although the Amazonian and Atlantic forests tend to show a closer relationship to each other than to the Chocó Forest, there are 18 species and 38 genera that are common to all three forests When the common species are removed from consideration and attention is focused upon the probable origin of the species and/or genera a more meaningful relationship can be observed between various South American ecophysiographic regions (Fig 9 6)

South American rainforests have a high degree of endemism among reptiles However, when one considers the land area occupied by rainforests in South America (40%) and the proportion of South American reptiles that are endemic to rainforests (17%), it is apparent that there is high endemism elsewhere in South America and/or many widely distributed species

Area and Diversity

In order to appreciate the potential biotic diversity, one must first visualize the magnitude of the rainforests of South America (Fig 9 7) Those forests are the largest in the world, about 4 5 million sq km² before modern timber harvesting techniques were employed (Richards, 1973) as compared to those of Asia (approximately 2 8 million km²) or Africa (about 2 million km²)

The variation in size of independent rainforests does not seem to dictate the number of silvicolous lizards The predictors of diversity are the same for each forest—1) lowland tropical rainforest, 2) latitudes, 3) climate, 4) structural heterogeneity, and 5) degree of trophic specialization The only independent variable is total land area occupied by the rainforests Assuming that the predictors for each species in each forest are basically the same, the number of silvicolous-food-generalist species can be predicted for a given forest (e g, Chocó, 0 24, Amazon 4 0, Congo, 1 8, Thailand, 0 5 million km²) Thus, if lizards respond to a set of environmental parameters within the constraints of the physiognomy of the forest (e g, type of bark, roots, branching diameter, height, canopy, epiphytes), the number of species that are habitat specialists and food generalists should

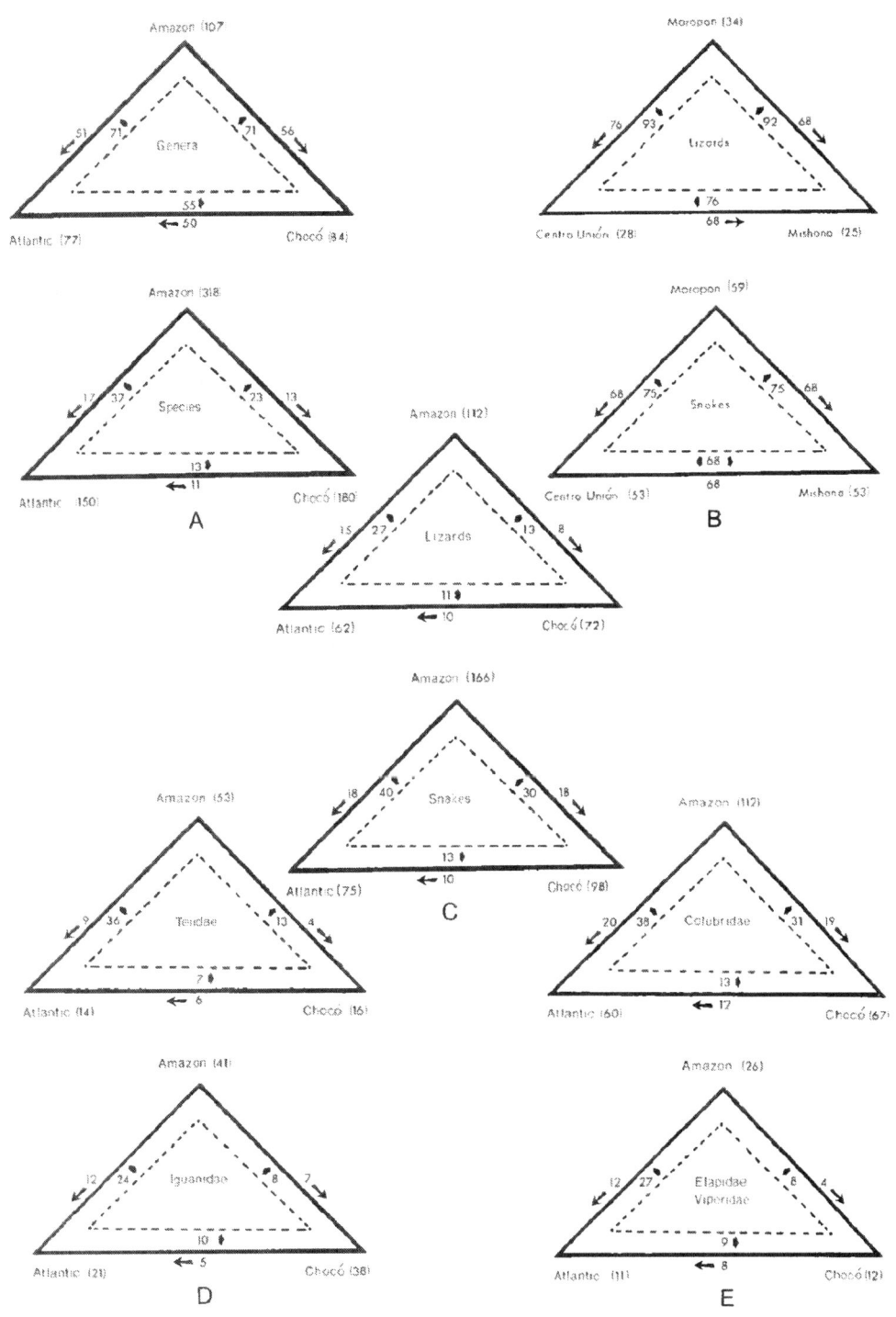

be relatively constant, providing that the age, evolution, and environmental conditions within the forests are similar. My knowledge of silvicolous lizards suggests that the Chocó contains about 38 species, Amazon 44, Congo 39 and Thailand 40. Thus, the predicted similarities in numbers of species between forests, regardless of size, apparently are realistic. Therefore, if we have knowledge of certain evolutionary and ecological parameters concerning the habitat and its attendant species, we should be able to predict the number of species that may occupy that habitat regardless of their generic or familial status or size of the forest. Iguanids and teiids basically fill the silvicolous-food-generalist role in the Chocó and Amazon forests, gekkonids and chamaeleonids in the Congo, and gekkonids and agamids in Thailand.

The constraints placed upon a terrestrial lizard are much more difficult to discern than those of a silvicolous arboreal one. Comparison of arboreal, eurytrophic lizards is possible between rainforests of similar latitudes, temperatures, and general physiognomy. However, comparison of terrestrial lizards is more difficult owing to the patchiness of the forest floor. Adequate knowledge of the habits of the animals in question is the only recourse for quality information on faunal relationships (Pianka 1974). For example, the numbers of lizards inhabiting the forest floor of the Chocó, Amazon, and Atlantic, and, in parentheses, those that are true leaf litter inhabitants of primary rainforest are 22(18) in the Chocó, 43(35) in the Amazon, and 19(18) in the Atlantic forest. These figures indicate that forest size may be important for terrestrial lizards; almost twice as many species of terrestrial lizards occur in the Amazon than in the other two forests. Among several possible explanations for the influence of forest size on the number of Amazonian lizards are the following: 1) Various segments of the Amazonian forest may have had different evolutionary histories owing to climatic alterations during the Quaternary, whereas the Chocó and Atlantic forests may have remained as single units (Fig 9.1). 2) Physical attributes of the forest floor (sand hills, lowland swamps, different soil properties, slope exposure, depth of leaf litter) may have affected speciation over time. 3) A longer ecotone between savanna and forest affected heterogeneity. I favor the first alternative because the distribution of reptiles coincides with postulated Quaternary refugia (Figs 9.8–9). Why such refugia would pro-

FIG 9.5 (A) The three tropical lowland rainforests of South America compared for reptilian faunal similarities based on genera and on species. Simpson's formula $(C/N_1) \times 100$ is used because it indicates the percentage of common taxa in the smaller of the two faunas, regardless of the size of the larger one. However, the larger fauna must also be compared to obtain similar data in the opposite direction. The solid lines of the triangle represent the percent of the common taxa in the larger of the two faunas (direction of arrow is from larger to smaller fauna) whereas the inner dashed line shows percentage of common taxa in the smaller of the two faunas (direction of arrow from smaller to larger fauna). Numbers in parentheses following names of forests represent number of taxa within that forest. (B) A Simpson formula $(C/N_1) \times 100$ comparison of species of lizards and snakes from three local rainforest sites within the Iquitos region, Peru. When faunas of equal size are compared (number of snakes between Centro Unión and Mishana) then Duellman's (1965) modified formula $(2C/N_1 + N_2) \times 100$ is used because the resulting Faunal Resemblance Factor compares Simpson's formula in both directions with a resultant average of the two percentages. (C, D, and E) Simpson's Formula $(C/N_1) \times 100$ comparing various reptilian species components in the three tropical lowland rainforests of South America.

(A) Comparación de los tres bosques tropicales de tierra baja de Sur America en base a similaridad de la fauna reptiliana en cuanto a generos y especies. Se uso la formula de Simpson $(C/N_1) \times 100$ porque indica el porcentaje de taxones comunes en la mas pequeña de las dos faunas, sin importar el tamaño de la mayor. Sin embargo la fauna mayor debe de ser también comparada para obtener datos similares en dirección opuesta. Las lineas solidas del triangulo representan el porcentaje de taxones comunes en la mas grande de las dos faunas (la dirección de la flecha va de la mayor a la menor fauna), mientras que la linea quebrada interior muestra el porcentaje de taxones comunes en la mas pequeña de las dos faunas (la dirección de la flecha va de la menor a la mayor fauna). (B) Comparacion de las especies de la lagartos y serpientes de tres localidades de bosque amazonico dentro de la region de Iquitos Peru usando la formula de taxa (como las de Centro Unión y Mishana), entonces, usamos la formula modificado por Duellman (1965) $(2C/N_1 + N_2) \times 100$ porque el factor de similaridad resultante compara en ambas direcciones con una resultante de la media de los dos porcentajes. (C D and E) Comparación de varias especies componentes de tres bosques tropicales de tierra baja en Sur America usando la formula de Simpson.

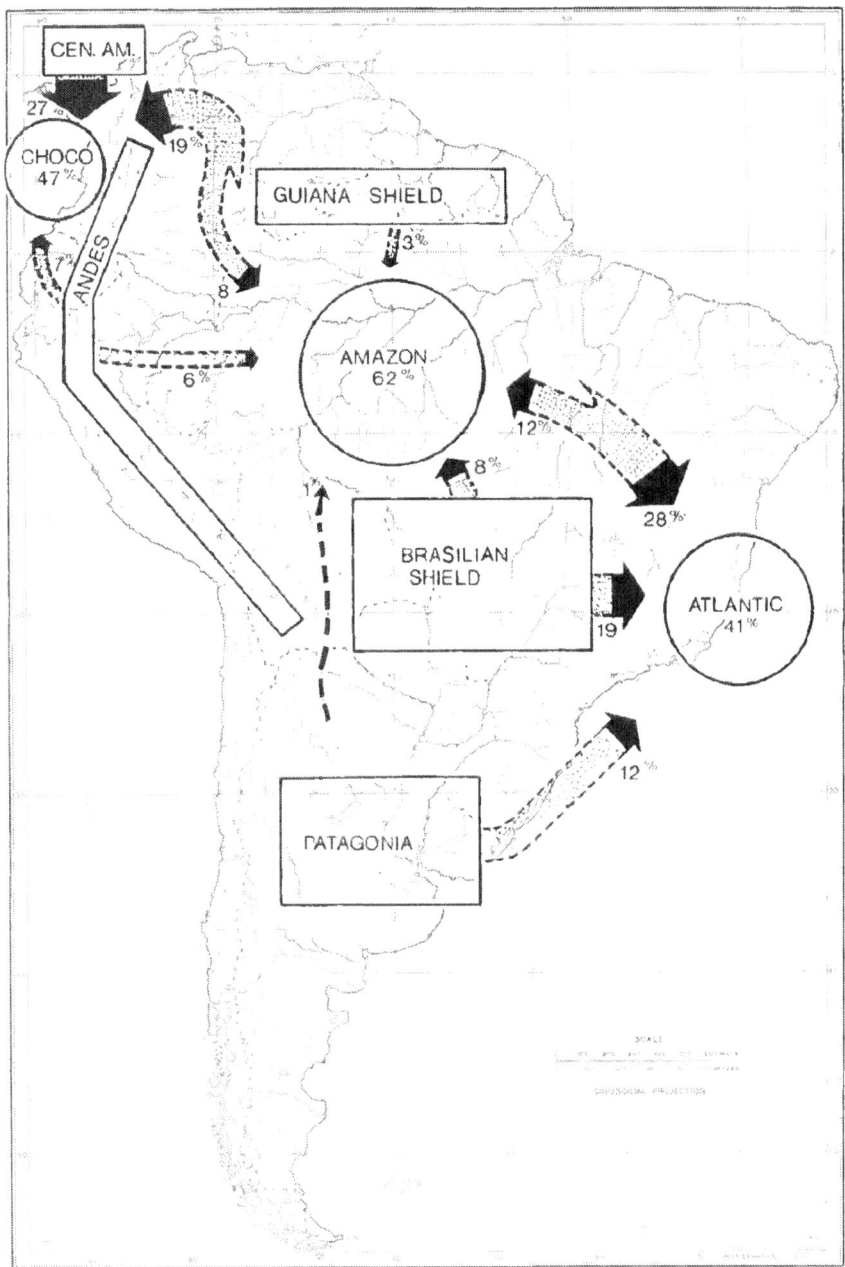

FIG. 9:6. Percentage contribution of nonendemic reptilian species to a particular rainforest. Number within a circle represents approximate percent of endemism of reptilian species for a particular forest.
 Contribución porcentual de especies no endémicas de reptiles a un bosque tropical particular. El número dentro del círculo representa el porcentaje aproximado de endemismo de especies de reptiles para un bosque en particular.

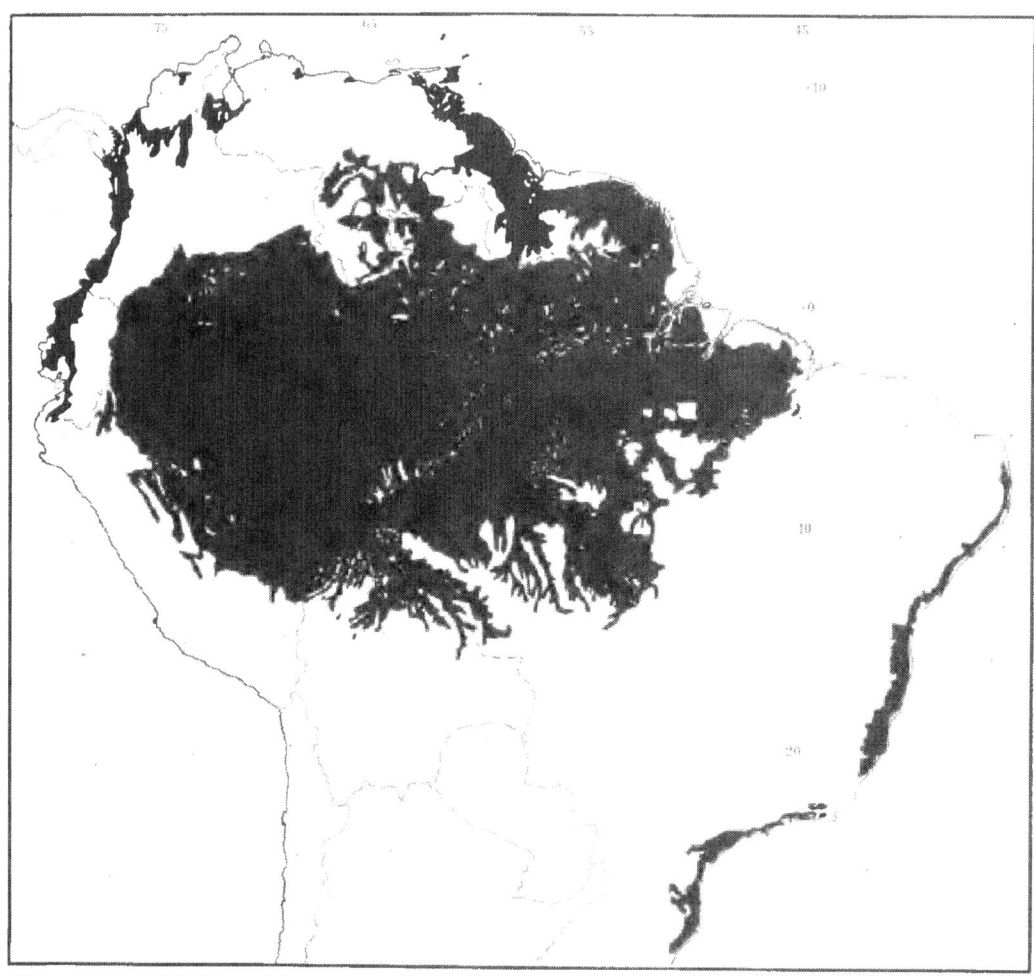

Fig. 9:7. Distribution of lowland tropical rainforests of South America (slightly modified from Hueck and Seibert, 1972).
Distribución de los bosques de tierra baja de Sur América (algo modificada de Hueck y Seibert, 1972).

duce more terrestrial species than arboreal species is difficult to answer, but I suggest that arboreal habitats may be more homogeneous than terrestrial ones. Otherwise, the number of species should be approximately equal in each region. If the postulated refugia of each forested region had similar physical and biological properties (e.g., topography, moisture, temperature, and habitat heterogeneity), the Chocó, western Amazon, eastern Amazon, and Atlantic forests should contain about the same number of terrestrial, rainforest lizard species. They do, with 18, 18, 17, and 18 species, respectively.

The most diverse group of lowland rainforest reptiles is the snakes (282+ species), but most species apparently have low population densities. Ecological data are lacking for many species (Dixon and Soini, 1977). Rainforest lizards seem to be habitat specialists and food generalists, whereas sympatric snakes seem to be habitat generalists and food specialists (Duellman, 1978). Shine (1977) found that six species of elapids in a

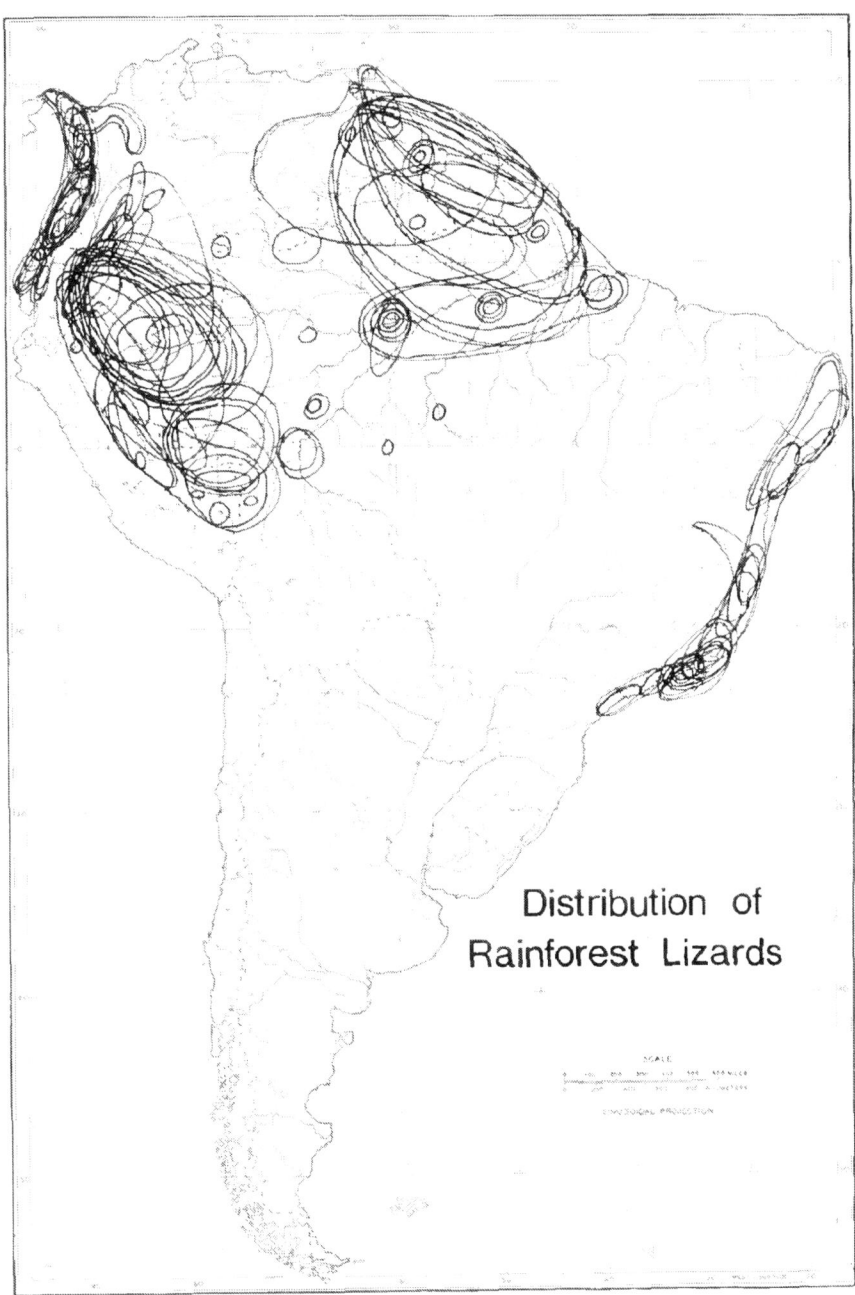

Fig. 9:8. Generalized ranges of rainforest lizards that show restricted distributions. In addition, there are 18 species of lizards that are distributed throughout the Amazonian forest.
    Distribuciones generalizadas de saurios de bosque que muestran distribuciones restringidas. Hay 18 especies adicionales distribuidas a lo largo del valle amazónico.

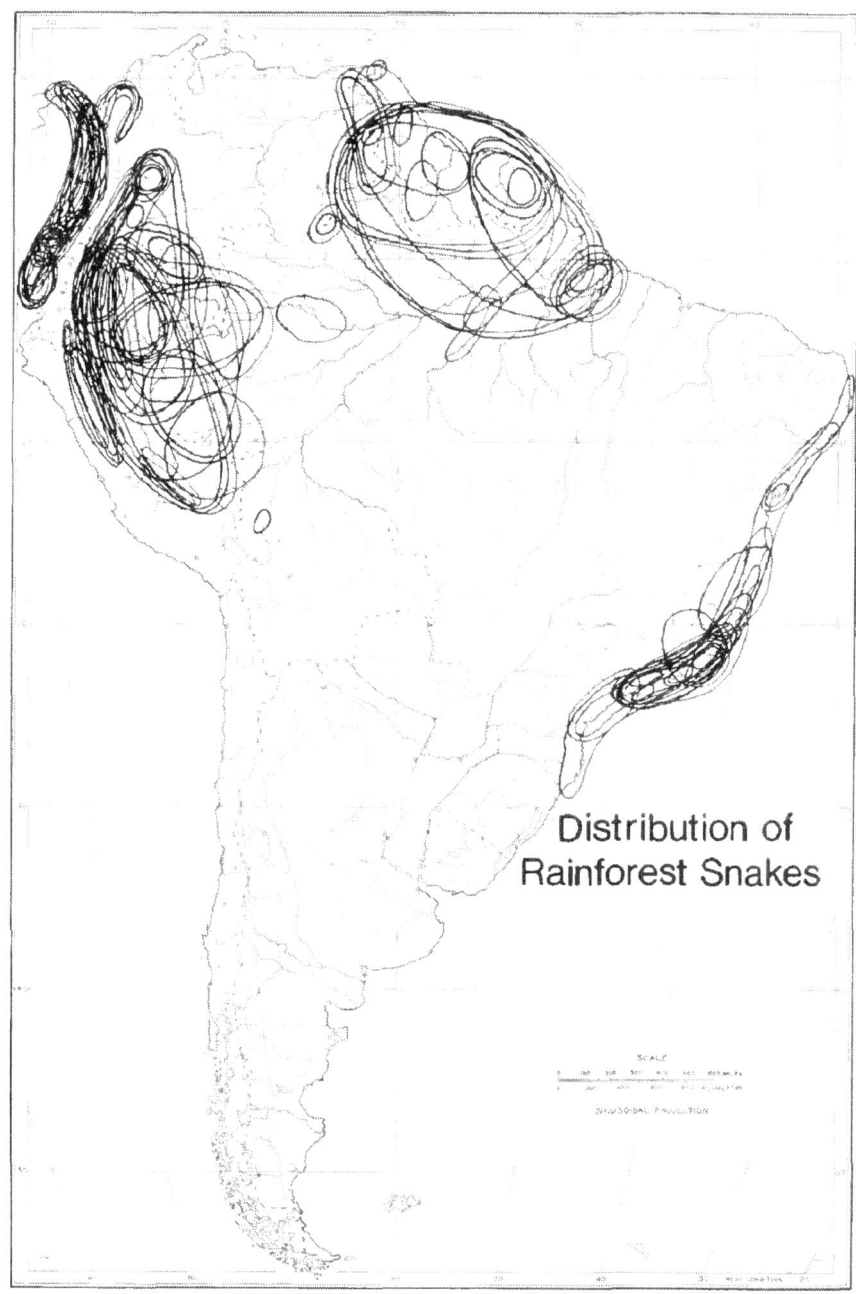

Fig. 9:9. Generalized ranges of rainforest snakes that show restricted distributions. In addition, there are 46 species of snakes that are distributed throughout the Amazon Basin.
Distribuciones generalizadas de serpientes de bosque que muestran distribuciones restringidas. Hay 46 especies adicionales distribuidas a lo largo del valle amazónico.

highland region of eastern Australia exhibited a habitat-specialist-food-generalist role. However, he also indicated that there was greater diversity of habitat than of food. My data suggest the opposite in South American rain forests, thus, greater diversity occurs among snakes than lizards. If both snakes and lizards assumed the role of specialists in habitat and food strata, they collectively would probably reach species densities similar to the 930 species of birds recorded from the Amazon by Haffer (1974). Birds are specialists in resource utilization (MacArthur et al. 1962, Diamond, 1973), and the number of species that utilize the diverse Amazonian forests is much greater than those of the reptiles. Some rainforest reptiles may be either food or habitat specialists or both (e.g. species of *Uracentron, Dracaena, Plica, Neusticurus, Dipsas, Typhlops*), but these represent relatively few species. There is also the possibility that organisms other than reptiles may be occupying roles seemingly well-suited for that group (Pianka, 1969).

CONCLUSIONS

We are not in a knowledgable position to answer many of the questions concerning biogeography and ecology of the reptile fauna of the rainforests, much less have a firm understanding of the systematics of the species of many common genera. Thus, a summary of facts into a compendium and then into a conclusion merely emphasizes the high points, producing only a small amount of light or slight sound in passing.

We have stirred only the surface of the water and perhaps before we reach the bottom, the facts will be lost to timber harvesting, vegetative monoculture, alteration of environments and death of stenotopic species. My paper pointedly demonstrates the absence of adequate knowledge of the geological, paleontological and ecological evidence to understand the evolutionary history of all but a few rainforest reptiles. While those whose bones are well preserved may offer some insight into their own histories, corollaries are inaccurate because of different histories of each independent lineage.

Therefore my opening statement of this paper is also my conclusion—we desperately need to solve the distributional and systematic problems of rainforest reptiles, knowledge basic to the understanding of their evolutionary histories.

ACKNOWLEDGMENTS

To Dr. Paulo E. Vanzolini, I feel that merely thanking him is an injustice for the help he has given me.

Colleagues have listened to my ideas about rainforest habitats and their attendant herpetofauna, and although some did not agree with my ideas, I salute them, one and all, for producing stimulating discussions. To Ron Heyer I owe a comradeship that goes beyond the boundaries of time. His advice will always be welcome. I graciously thank John Wiest and Robert Thomas for hours of philosophical discussion about snake evolution. Without their abilities to listen and express ideas, this paper never would have reached fruition. To all my graduate students, current and past, I owe a debt of gratitude.

RESUMEN

En la actualidad el orígen de los reptiles de las pluviselvas tropicales siempreverdes del Amazonas y Orinoco (*sensu stricto* Hueck and Seibert, 1972) se ubica en la antigua Gonwana Occidental. A principio y mediados del Cenozóico se desarrollo una fauna selvática sui géneris en el continente Sudamericano. A finales de dicha era, la conección con el nucleo Centroamericano tuvo lugar. Este hecho provocó el que la fauna suramericana influenciara y fuese influenciada por la fauna del núcleo Centroamericano.

De aproximadamente 1100 especies de reptiles de América del Sur, 550 (50%) se encuentran dentro de los limites de la pluviselva tropical siempreverde (entre 0 y 1000 m de elevación), que a su vez ocupa el 42% de la cobertura vegetal de América del Sur. De esas 500 especies, unas 300 (54%) son endémicas de la pluviselva, y el 74% de todos los generos de reptiles sudamericanos estan representados por una o más especies en esa formación.

Las pluviselvas tropicales siempreverdes de América del Sur han sufrido procesos de expansión y contracción durante los períodos glaciales e interglaciales, del Pleistoceno, y a menudo, se han conectado entre sí mediante corredores selváticos de variables dimensiones, permitiendo así repetidas migraciones de reptiles amazónicos hacia las selvas de la costa Atlántica del Brasil y en menor grado hacia las selvas del Chocó en Colombia. Las migraciones en sentido opuesto también parecen haber ocurrido, pero en menor intensidad. Las selvas del Atlántico y del Amazonas han estado en contacto con más frecuencia, mientras que la orogénesis andina ha obstaculizado y restringido la formación de corredores contínuos que favorecieran migraciones entre las selvas del Chocó y el Amazonas.

Antes de que la orogénesis andina ocurriese, deben de haber existido condiciones tropicales generalizados en todo el area, ya que la presencia de reptiles acuáticos y semi-acuáticos (cocodrilos, tortugas y algunos saurios) en ambas regiones así lo sugiere. Sin embargo, los cambios geológicos y climáticos posteriores causaron la extinción de muchas poblaciones y especies de reptiles acuáticos, evidenciándose este hecho en fosiles de especies selváticas localizadas en elevaciones considerables de 2000 y más metros.

Las estrategias de vida de los reptiles modernos de la pluviselva tropical son primariamente terrestres (43%), seguidos por los arborícolas (26%), semi-minadores y minadores (21%) y acuáticos (10%). Muchas de las formas terrestres ocupan zonas selváticas abiertas, semi-abiertas o modificadas. Algunas de las últimas son formas relictuales de las formaciones de savanas de los períodos glaciales. Algunas son antrópicas y el resto está formada por generalistas eurítípicos. Sólo unas pocas especies y géneros provenientes de los Andes y que han evolucionado aparentemente a lo largo del pié de monte han sido capaces de invadir con éxito las selvas de tierra baja. De allí que muchas de las especies de reptiles que están asociadas físicamente a situaciones selváticas (46%) no son asociados ecológicos.

Como puede esperarse los reptiles del Chocó están íntimamente asociados a la fauna Centroamericana, mientras que la fauna de reptiles del Atlántico muestra menor endemismo, menor número de especies, y una mayor afinidad con la de la pluviselva Amazónica.

Mientras que la teoría de refugios selváticos durante máximas glaciales puede explicar la ocurrencia de endemismos en varios segmentos de grandes porciones selváticas, el alto número de formas minadoras o semiminadoras endémicas puede haber evolucionado a través de cambios edáficos y climáticos independientes de la formación de refugios. Ciertamente, lo inverso parece ocurrir hoy día en el caso de la fauna relictual de savanas aisladas dentro de la pluviselva. La ausencia de refugios acuáticos de importancia durante las máximas glaciales puede ser la razón de la existencia de pocas especies endémicas de reptiles acuáticos en el área en la actualidad.

LITERATURE CITED

Auffenberg, W. 1974. Checklist of fossil land tortoises (Testudinidae). Bull. Florida State Mus. Biol. Ser. 18: 121-251.

Beebe, W. 1944a. Field notes on the lizards of Kartabo, British Guiana, and Caripito, Venezuela. Part 1. Gekkonidae. Zoologica 29: 145-160.

Beebe, W. 1944b. Field notes on the lizards of Kartabo, British Guiana, and Caripito, Venezuela. Part 2. Iguanidae. Ibid. 29: 195-216.

Beebe, W. 1944c. Field notes on the snakes of Kartabo, British Guiana, and Caripito, Venezuela. Ibid. 31: 11-52.

Beebe, W. 1945. Field notes on the lizards of Kartabo, British Guiana and Caripito, Venezuela. Part 3. Teiidae, Amphisbaenidae and Scincidae. Ibid. 30: 7-32.

Berry, E. W. 1938. Tertiary flora from the Rio Pichileufu, Argentina. Geol. Soc. Amer. Spec. Pap. (12): 1-149.

Burt, W. H. 1958. The history and affinities of the recent land mammals of western North America, pp. 131-154 in Hubbs, C. L. (ed.) Zoogeography. Publ. 51, Amer. Assoc. Adv. Sci., Washington, D. C. 509 p.

Crump, M. L. 1971. Quantitative analysis of the ecological distribution of a tropical herpetofauna. Univ. Kansas Mus. Nat. Hist. Occas. Pap. (3): 1-62.

Damuth, J. E., Fairbridge, R. W. 1970. Equatorial Atlantic deep-sea arkosic sands and ice-age aridity in tropical South America. Geol. Soc. Amer. Bull. 81: 189-206.

DIAMOND, J M 1973 Distributional ecology of New Guinea birds Science 179 767

DIXON, J R 1973 A systematic review of the teiid lizards, genus Bachia, with remarks on Heterodactylus and Anotosaura Univ Kansas Mus Nat Hist Misc Publ (57) 1–47

DIXON, J R 1974a Systematic review of the lizard genus Anotosaura (Teiidae) Herpetologica 30 13–18

DIXON, J R 1974b Systematic review of the microteiid genus Iphisa Ibid 30 133–139

DIXON, J R, SOINI, P 1975 The reptiles of the upper Amazon Basin, Iquitos Region, Peru I Lizards and amphisbaenians Milwaukee Publ Mus Contrib Biol Geol (4) 1–58

DIXON, J R, SOINI, P 1977 The reptiles of the upper Amazon Basin, Iquitos Region, Peru II Crocodilians, turtles and snakes Ibid (12) 1–91

DORF, E 1959 Climatic changes of the past and present Contrib Mus Paleontol Univ Michigan (13) 181–210

DUELLMAN, W E 1958 A monographic study of the colubrid snake genus Leptodeira Bull Amer Mus Nat Hist 114 1–152

DUELLMAN, W E 1965 A biogeographic account of the herpetofauna of Michoacan, Mexico Univ Kansas Mus Nat Hist Misc Publ 15 627–709

DUELLMAN, W E 1978 The biology of an equatorial herpetofauna in Amazonian Ecuador Univ Kansas Mus Nat Hist Misc Publ (65) 1–352

EMILIANI, C 1956 Oligocene and Miocene temperatures of the equatorial and subtropic Atlantic Ocean Geology 64 281–288

EMILIANI, C 1972 Quaternary paleotemperatures and the duration of the high temperature intervals Science 178 398–401

ESTES, R 1961 Miocene lizards from Colombia, South America Breviora (143) 1–11

ESTES R, PRICE, L I 1973 Iguanid lizard from the Upper Cretaceous of Brazil Science 180 748–751

FITCH H S 1970 Reproductive cycles in lizards and snakes Univ Kansas Mus Nat Hist Misc Publ (52) 1–247

FLINT R F 1971 Glacial and Quaternary Geology John Wiley and Sons, Inc New York 892 p

GANS, C 1962 Notes on amphisbaenids (Amphisbaenia Reptilia) 5 A redefinition and a bibliography of Amphisbaena alba Linne Amer Mus Novit (2105) 1–31

GANS, C 1971 Studies on amphisbaenians (Amphisbaenia, Reptilia) 4 A review of the amphisbaenid genus Leposternon Bull Amer Mus Nat Hist 144 381–464

HAFFER, J 1974 Avian speciation in tropical South America Publ Nuttall Ornitho Club, Cambridge (14) 1–390

HARRINGTON, H J 1962 Paleogeographic development of South America Bull Amer Assoc Pet Geol 46 1773–1814

HERRERO-DUCLOUX, A 1963 The Andes of western Argentina Mem Amer Assoc Pet Geol (2) 16–28

HERSHKOVITZ, P 1966 Mice, land bridges and Latin American faunal interchange, pp 725–751 in WENZEL, R L, TIPTON, V J (eds) Ectoparasites of Panama Field Museum of Natural History, Chicago, 861 p

HUECK, K, SEIBERT, P 1972 Vegetationskarte von Sudamerika Gustav Fischer Verlag, Stuttgart, 71 p

JAMES, D E 1971 Plate tectonic model for the evolution of the central Andes Geol Soc Amer Bull 82 3325–3346

JENKS W F 1956 Peru Geol Soc Amer Mem (65) 213–247

KLUGE, A G 1969 The evolution and geographical origin of the new world Hemidactylus mabouiabrookii complex (Gekkonidae, Sauria) Misc Publ Mus Zool Univ Michigan (138) 1–78

LANGSTON W, JR 1965 Fossil crocodilians from Colombia and the Cenozoic history of the Crocodilia in South America Univ Calif Publ Geol Sci (52) 1–157

LOHMANN, H H 1970 Outline of tectonic history of Bolivian Andes Bull Amer Assoc Pet Geol 54 735–757

MACARTHUR, R H, MACARTHUR, J W, PRELR, J 1962 On species diversity, II Prediction of bird census from habitat measurements Amer Nat 96 167–174

MEDINA, C J 1976 Crocodilians from Late Tertiary of northwestern Venezuela Melanosuchus fisheri, Sp Nov Breviora (438) 1–14

MULLER, P 1973 The dispersal centres of terrestrial vertebrates in the neotropical realm Biogeographica 2, W Junk, The Hague, 244 p

MYERS, C M 1974 The systematics of Rhadinaea (Colubridae), a genus of new world snakes Bull Amer Mus Nat Hist 153 1–262

OFTEDAL, O T 1974 A revision of the genus Anadia (Sauria, Teiidae) Arq Zool (Sao Paulo) 25 203–265

OLIVER, J A 1948 The relationships and zoogeography of the genus Thalerophis Oliver Bull Amer Mus Nat Hist, 92 161–280

PETERS, J A 1960 The snakes of the subfamily Dipsadinae Misc Publ Mus Zool Univ Michigan (114) 1–224

PIANKA, E R 1969 Habitat specificity, speciation, and species density in Australian desert lizards Ecology 50 498–502

PIANKA E R 1974 Niche overlap and diffuse competition Proc Natl Acad Sci 71 2141–2145

RAND A S, HUMPHREY, S S 1968 Interspecific competition among lizards at Belem, Pará Proc US Natl Mus 125 1–17

RAVEN, P H, AXELROD, D I 1975 History of the flora and fauna of Latin America Amer Sci 63 420–429

RICHARDS, P W 1973 The tropical rain forest Sci Amer 229 58–67

ROMER A S 1956 Osteology of the reptiles University of Chicago Press, Chicago, 772 p

ROZE, J A 1966 La taxonomia y zoogeografia de los ofidios en Venezuela Ed Biblioteca, Univ Central Venezuela, Caracas, 362 p

Roze, J. A. 1967 A check list of the new world venomous coral snakes (Elapidae), with descriptions of new forms. Amer. Mus. Novit. (2287) 1-60

Ruibal, R. 1952 Revisionary studies of some South American Teiidae. Bull. Mus. Comp. Zool. Harvard Univ. 106 477-529

Rutland, R. W. R., Guest, J. E., Grasty, R. L. 1965 Isotopic ages and Andean uplift. Nature 208 677-678

Savage, J. M. 1960 A revision of the Ecuadorian snakes of the colubrid genus *Atractus*. Misc. Publ. Mus. Zool. Univ. Michigan (112) 1-86

Savage, J. M. 1974 The Isthmian Link and the evolution of neotropical mammals. Nat. Hist. Mus. Los Angeles Cty. Contr. Sci. (260) 1-51

Shine, R. 1977 Habitats, diets, and sympatry in snakes: a study from Australia. Canadian J. Zool. 55 1118-1128

Simpson, B. B. 1975 Pleistocene changes in the flora of the high tropical Andes. Paleobiology 1 273-294

Sioli, H. 1975 Tropical rivers as expressions of their terrestrial environments, pp. 275-288 in Golley, F. B., Medina, E. (eds.) Tropical Ecological Systems: Trends in Terrestrial and Aquatic Research, Springer Verlag, New York-Berlin, 398 p

Tanner, W. F. 1968 Tertiary sea level symposium-introduction. Paleogeogr. Paleoclimatol. Paleoecol. 5 7-14

Test, F. H., Sexton, O. J., Heatwole, H. 1966 Reptiles of Rancho Grande and vicinity, Estado Aragua Venezuela. Misc. Publ. Mus. Zool. Univ. Michigan (128) 1-63

Thomas, R. A. 1976 A revision of the South American colubrid snake genus *Philodryas* Wagler 1830. PhD Dissert., Texas A&M University. 324 pp

Uvardy, M. D. F. 1969 Dynamic Zoogeography. D. Van Nostrand, Reinhold Co., New York, 445 p

Uzzell, T. M., Jr. 1966 Teiid lizards of the genus *Neusticurus* (Reptilia, Sauria). Bull. Amer. Mus. Nat. Hist. 132 279-327

Vanzolini, P. E. 1951 *Amphisbaena fuliginosa* Contribution to the knowledge of the Brasilian lizards of the family Amphisbaenidae Gray 1825. 6 On the differentiation of *Amphisbaena fuliginosa* Linne. Bull. Mus. Comp. Zool. Harvard Univ. 106 1-67

Vanzolini, P. E. 1957 O genero *Coleodactylus* (Sauria, Gekkonidae). Pap. Avul. Zool. (Sao Paulo) 13 1-17

Vanzolini, P. E. 1963 Problemas faunisticos de Cerrado, pp. 308-320 in Ed. da Univ. São Paulo, Simposio sobre o Cerrado, São Paulo, Brasil, 424 p

Vanzolini, P. E. 1967 Problems and programs in Amazonian zoology. Atas do Simposio sobre a Biota Amazonica 5 (Zool.) 85-95

Vanzolini, P. E. 1968 Geography of the South American Gekkonidae (Sauria). Arq. Zool. (Sao Paulo) 17 85-112

Vanzolini, P. E. 1972 Miscellaneous notes on the ecology of some Brasilian lizards (Sauria). Pap. Avul. Zool. (Sao Paulo) 26 83-115

Vanzolini, P. E. 1973 Paleoclimates, relief, and species multiplication in equatorial forests, pp. 255-258 in Meggers, B. J., Ayensu, E. S., Duckworth, E. D. (eds.) Tropical forest ecosystems in Africa and South America, a comparative review. Smithsonian Institution Press, Washington, D. C., 350 p

Vanzolini, P. E. 1974 Ecological and geographical distribution of lizards in Pernambuco, northeastern Brasil (Sauria). Pap. Avul. Zool. (Sao Paulo) 28 61-90

Vanzolini, P. E. 1976 On the lizards of a Cerrado-Caatinga contact. Evolutionary and zoogeographical implications (Sauria). Ibid 29 111-119

Vanzolini, P. E., Rebouças-Spieker, R. 1973 Notes on the ecology and limb proportions of Amazonian *Mabuya mabouya* (Sauria, Scincidae). Ibid 26 281-294

Vanzolini, P. E., Valencia, J. 1965 The genus *Dracaena*, with a brief consideration of macroteiid relationships (Sauria, Teiidae). Arq. Zool. (Sao Paulo) 13 7-35

Vanzolini, P. E., Williams, E. E. 1970 South American anoles. The geographic differentiation and evolution of the *Anolis chrysolepis* species group (Sauria, Iguanidae). Ibid 19 125-298

Vuilleumier, B. S. 1971 Pleistocene changes in the fauna and flora of South America. Science 173 771-780

Williams, E. E. 1976 South American anoles: the species groups. Pap. Avul. Zool. (Sao Paulo) 29 259-268

Wood, R. C. 1972 A fossil pelomedusid turtle from Puerto Rico. Breviora (392) 1-13

Wood, R. C. 1976 Two new species of *Chelus* (Testudines: Pleurodira) from the late Tertiary of northern South America. Ibid (435) 1-26

Wood, R. C., Gamero M., L. D. de 1971 *Podocnemis venezuelensis*, a new fossil pelomedusid (Testudines, Pleurodira) from the Pliocene of Venezuela and a review of the history of *Podocnemis* in South America. Ibid (376) 1-23

Wood, R. C., Patterson, B. 1973 A fossil trionychid turtle from South America. Ibid (405) 1-10

APPENDIX

APPENDIX 9 1—Distribution of reptilian genera and numbers of species associated with tropical rainforests of South America. An asterisk indicates the occurrence of a savanna relict within the forest area. A question mark indicates possible occurrence but distributional records are too general to establish exact habitat. The Amazonian forest reptilian fauna is divided into distributional tracts—Western Amazon (western third), Eastern Amazon (eastern third), Middle Amazon (middle third), and Widespread Amazon (those species that range throughout the Amazonian forest). The number in parentheses following the generic name is the number of species associated with rainforests, although some may not be ecological associates.

Genera	Eastern Amazon	Western Amazon	Middle Amazon	Widespread Amazon	Atlantic Forest	Chocó Forest	Northern Forests
Crocodilians							
Caiman (2)				1	1	1	1
Crocodylus (1)				—		1	1
Melanosuchus (1)				1			
Paleosuchus (2)				2	2?		
Turtles							
Chelydra (1)						1	
Chelus (1)				1			
Geochelone (2)			1*	1		1*	1*
Hydromedusa (2)				—	2?		
Kinosternon (3)				1	1	3	1
Phrynops (4)		1	1	2	2		
Platemys (3)			1	1	2		
Pseudemys (1)				—		1	1
Podocnemis (5)		1	1	3			
Rhinoclemys (2)			1			2	
Amphisbaenians							
Amphisbaena (30)	3	1	6	2	11	3	1
Aulura (1)			1				
Bronia (1)			1				
Leposternon (5)			2		5		
Mesobaena (1)		1					
Lizards							
Alopoglossus (6)	4			1		1	
Amapasaurus (1)			1				
Ameiva (5)				1	1	5	1
Anadia (2)						2	
Anisolepis (1)					1		
Anolis (33–46)	8		3	5	5	18	2
Arthrosaura (2)			1	1			
Bachia (13)	5		7			1	
Basiliscus (3)						3	1
Cnemidophorus (1)			1*			1*	1*
Corythophanes (1)						1	
Cercosaura (1)				1	1		
Colobodactylus (4)	1		2		1		
Colobosaura (1)			1				
Crocodilurus (1)			1				
Diploglossus (4)					2	2	
Dracaena (1)				1			
Ecpleopus (1)					1		
Enyalius (8)			1		7		
Enyalioides (7)	5					2	
Echinosaura (1)						1	
Euspondylus (2)	2						
Gymnodactylus (1)					1		
Gonatodes (7)	2		5	1		2	3
Hemidactylus (2)			1	1			
Heterodactylus (1)					1		
Iguana (1)				1	1	1	1
Iphisa (1)				1			
Kentropyx (6)	2	1	3		1		

APPENDIX 9.1 (continued)

Genera	Eastern Amazon	Western Amazon	Middle Amazon	Widespread Amazon	Atlantic Forest	Choco Forest	Northern Forests
Lepidoblepharis (7)				1		6	1
Leposoma (8)	1		2		2	3	1
Liolaemus (1)					1?		
Mabuya (7)	2		1	1	4	1	1
Morunasaurus (1)	1					1?	
Neusticurus (5)	3		2				
Ophiodes (1)					1		
Ophryoessoides (4)	3		1				1
Pantodactylus (2)	1				2		
Plica (2)				2			
Placosoma (2)					2		
Polychrus (4)	1			1	1	1	1
Prionodactylus (4)	3			1		1	
Pseudogonatodes (2)			1	1			
Ptychoglossus (4)	2			1		1	1
Sphaerodactylus (2)						2	
Stenocercus (2)	2						
Stenolepis (1)					1		
Strobilurus (1)					1°		
Thecadactylus (1)				1			1
Tretioscincus (2)			1°				1°
Tropidurus (4)			2°		2°		
Tupinambis (2)				1°	2°	1°	1°
Uracentron (3)	2		1				
Uranoscodon (1)			1				
Urostrophus (1)					1?		
Snakes							
Anilius (1)				1			
Anomalepis (1)						1	
Apostolepis (5)	2		2		1		
Atractus (25)	10		4	3	2	6	1
Boa (1)			1			1	1
Bothrops (21)	5		1	3	7	4	2
Chironius (12)	1		1	4	7	3	1
Clelia (3)	1			1	1	2	1
Corallus (3)				2		2	
Crotalus (1)			1°				
Dendrophidion (2)				1		2	
Dipsas (18)	6		4		5	5	1
Diaphorolepis (2)						2	
Drepanoides (1)	1						
Drymarchon (1)				1		1	1
Drymobius (2)				1		2	1
Drymoluber (1)				1			
Epicrates (1)				1	1	1	1
Elapomorphus (3)					3		
Emmochliophis (1)						1	
Erithus (2)						2	
Liythrolamprus (4)	2		1	1		3	2
Eunectes (3)			2	1			
Geophis (1)						1	
Helicops (11)	2	1	2	2	2	2	1
Helminthophis (1)							1
Hydrodynastes (1)			1				
Hydrops (2)				2			
Imantodes (3)				2		1	1
Lachesis (1)				1	1	1	
Lampropeltis (1)						1	1
Leimadophis (8)	2		1	2	1	2	1
Leptodeira (2)				1	1	2	1

APPENDIX 9 1 (concluded)

Genera	Eastern Amazon	Western Amazon	Middle Amazon	Widespread Amazon	Atlantic Forest	Choco Forest	Northern Forests
Leptophis (4)	2	.	.	1	1	3	1
Leptotyphlops (12)	5	.	7	.	2	3	2
Liotyphlops (5)	.	–	.	.	1	4	.
Liophis (9)	2	.	3	2	3	1	.
Lygophis (2)	–	–	.	.	1	1	.
Lystrophis (1)	.	–	.	.	1	.	–
Mastigodryas (3)	.	–	1	1	2	2	2
Micrurus (23)	5	1	2	5	3	7	3
Ninia (2)	1	.	1	.	.	1	1
Nothopsis (1)	.	.	–	.	.	1	.
Oxybelis (4)	.	.	.	3	.	2	1
Oxyrhopus (5)	.	.	1	4	2	1	1
Philodryas (4)	.	.	.	2	4	.	.
Plinoplus (1)	.	.	.	.	.	.	1°
Phocercus (1)	.	.	.	1	.	1	.
Pseudoboa (3)	.	.	1	1	1	1	.
Pseudoeryx (1)	.	.	.	1	.	.	.
Pseustes (4)	.	.	1	2	1	1	1
Ptychophis (1)	.	.	.	.	1?	.	.
Rhadinaea (10)	–	.	.	2	5	4	–
Rhinobothryum (2)	.	.	.	1	.	1	.
Saphenophis (1)	1	.	.	.	.	.	.
Scaphiodontophis (1)	.	.	.	.	.	1	.
Sibon (1)	.	.	–	.	.	1	1
Sibynomorphus (1)	.	.	.	.	1	.	.
Siphlophis (4)	.	.	1	1	2	.	.
Sordellina (1)	.	.	.	.	1	.	.
Spilotes (1)	.	.	.	1	1	1	1
Stenorrhina (1)	.	.	–	.	.	1	1
Synophis (2)	2	.	.	.	.	1	.
Tantilla (4)	.	.	.	1	1	4	2
Thamnodynastes (3)	.	.	1	1	1	.	.
Trachyboa (1)	.	.	–	.	.	1	.
Tretanorhinus (1)	.	.	.	.	.	1	.
Tripanurgos (1)	.	.	.	1	1	1	.
Tropidodryas (2)	.	.	.	.	2	.	.
Tropidophis (3)	2	.	.	.	1	1	.
Typhlophis (1)	.	.	1	.	.	.	.
Typhlops (4)	1	.	1	2	2	1	.
Ungaliophis (1)	.	.	.	.	.	1	.
Xenoboa (1)	.	.	.	.	1	.	.
Xenodon (6)	1	.	1	2	2	1	1
Xenopholis (1)	.	.	.	1	1	.	.

10. The Herpetofauna of the Guianan Region

Marinus S Hoogmoed

*Rijksmuseum van Natuurlijke Historie
Postbus 9517
2300 RA Leiden, The Netherlands*

Although this paper deals with a highland fauna, it is not limited to the reptiles and amphibians that occur at elevations of more than 1000 m. One of the main reasons for this is that 'highlands' above 1000 m in the Guiana area are few and occupy only a very small part of the total area of the Guiana Shield. Another reason is that our knowledge of the herpetofauna at higher elevations in Guiana is still very fragmentary. These facts prompted me to deal with the herpetofauna of the entire Guiana Shield.

The coast of the Guianas was discovered in 1499 by Alonso de Ojeda and Amerigo Vespucci. After the discovery of the so-called 'Spanish Main' or "Wild Coast" numerous expeditions tried to explore the interior in search of the fabulous El Dorado. Most famous of these adventurers was Sir Walter Raleigh, who undertook several expeditions into the interior of Guiana. Zoologically, these expeditions were of no importance whatsoever. From about the beginning of the 18th Century, zoological specimens, mainly from Surinam started to reach Europe, and an important percentage of the species of reptiles and amphibians described by Linnaeus in 1758 originated from the Guianas. One of the first scientific explorers of the interior was Von Humboldt, who in 1801 visited the Río Orinoco and the Cassiquiare Canal (Gleason, 1931). In 1835 Sir Robert Schomburgk started his explorations in Guyana and adjacent countries in order to settle the frontiers. During these explorations zoological collections were made that supplied a wealth of new data. Since Schomburgk's travels, an increasing number of scientific expeditions penetrated into the interior of lowland Guiana and it would lead us too far astray to try to deal with them here in any detail. I make an exception for the expeditions exploring the tepuis in Venezuela and Guyana several of which even at the present day remain unvisited. The most renowned of these tepuis is Roraima with an altitude of 2810 m, discovered in 1838 by Robert Schomburgk and climbed for the first time in 1884 by Im Thurn and Perkins.

The first zoological collection ever made near any tepui was assembled there in 1842 by Richard Schomburgk. Other collections were made at the foot in the 1880's. The first herpetological specimens from the summit were secured by Quelch and McConnell in 1894. In 1898 they made a second expedition to the summit plateau. The material of these expeditions contained several new species. Boulenger (1895, 1900) studied them and described the frogs *Oreophrynella quelchii, O. macconnelli, Otophryne robusta* and *Hylodes marmoratus*, and the lizards *Neusticurus rudis* and *Euspondylus leucostictus*. Of these species, only the first and the last came from the summit of the mountain, the other species were collected at the base. The next zoological expedition, on a much larger scale and under the auspices of the American Museum of Natural History, visited Roraima in 1927-28, spending two weeks on the summit and about two months at the base (Tate, 1928, 1930a,b 1932, 1939, Chapman 1931). Among the material collected were several reptiles and amphibians. In 1971, 1973 and 1974 Roraima was visited again, this time by parties with herpetologists as members (Warren, 1973). Their collections contained many novelties.

In 1928 Mount Duida, at the western end of the series of tepuis, was explored zoologically. The expedition was the first that succeeded in climbing the mountain and spent three months at the summit. Among the herpetological material collected were the types of the teiid lizards *Pantodactylus tyleri* and *Arthrosaura tatei*, of the hylid frog *Stef-*

ania goini, and of the leptodactylid frog *Elosia duidensis* In 1937-38 Auyantepui was zoologically explored From 1938 until the present, considerable exploration took place in the tepui region, mostly ornithological and botanical, but as a by-product many herpetological specimens were collected, some of which at the time being new to science were described by Roze (1958a,b, Auyantepui, Chimantátepui), Rivero (1961, 1965, 1966, 1967a,b, 1968a-d, 1970, 1971, Duida, Marahuaca, Chimantátepui, La Escalera region and other tepuis) and Lancini (1968, Cerro Jauá) The most recent biological exploration of some large tepuis were the expeditions to Cerro Jauá and Sarisariñama in 1974 and to Cerro Yapacana in 1978 These were some of the rare expeditions in which herpetologists participated (Nott 1975, Orejas-Miranda and Quesada, 1976) The herpetological results of these expeditions have not yet been published

DELIMITATION AND DESCRIPTION OF GUIANA

Guiana is the area bordered by the Río Orinoco, the Cassiquiare Canal (connecting the Orinoco and Amazon drainages), and the Río Negro in the west, by the Río Amazonas in the south and by the Atlantic Ocean in the north and the east The area comprises three political units in their entirety namely, Guyana, Surinam and French Guiana Of Venezuela it comprises the Estado Bolívar and the Territorio Federal Amazonas, known under the common denomer Guayana Of Brasil it comprises the Territorio do Amapá, the Territorio de Roraima and those parts of the states of Pará and Amazonas that are situated north of the Río Amazonas and Río Negro Recently Lescure (1977) and Descamps et al (1978) defined Guiana as the area bordered in the west by the Río Barama (Venezuela) and in the southeast by the Río Araguari (Brasil) The southern border would be formed by the watershed between rivers emptying directly into the Atlantic Ocean and rivers belonging to the Amazonian drainage In my opinion, this definition of Guiana is artificial and not in accordance with the biogeographical and geographical data (Fig 10 1) The Serra Acarai and the Tumuc Humac Mountains forming the divide between the French authors' Guiana and Amazonia apparently do form a geographical barrier for a number of endemic species (mainly frogs) but this is too small a proportion of the entire fauna to justify the definition of the Guiana area as they do Far more species are spread on both sides of the divide and occur both in the Orinoco and Amazon Basin (Haffer, 1974, Muller, 1973) In a discussion of the Guiana herpetofauna I think it is better to take into consideration biogeographical data of the majority of the (herpeto)fauna being studied, rather than rely only on those of some endemic frogs In that way the biogeographical definition of Guiana as accepted here, agrees closely with the geographical, geological and climatological data However, there are good grounds for considering the Guiana of the French authors as a subregion of the Guiana as here defined

Geologically, this area is a unit known as the Guiana Shield (Ganssei, 1954, Pittkau, 1974) of which small parts are situated west of the area as here delimited (Fig 10 2) Along the edges, notably in the north, the east and the south, there are belts of alluvial deposits, however, the core is made up of pre-Cambrian metamorphic and igneous rocks Together with the Brasilian Shield, it can be considered as part of the geological foundation of South America Since Paleozoic times these shields have not been submerged During the Mesozoic both shields were connected, for the Amazon was not yet present During the Late Cretaceous the area was slightly uplifted and the first signs of the present Amazon Basin became visible In the Tertiary there was a further uplift (Haffer, 1974) The higher, central parts of the Guiana Shield are covered with sandstone remnants of the Roraima Formation Deposition of this sandstone took place in Proterozoic time, 1600-1800 m y b p, as stream and delta deposits laid down in continental to epicontinental environments (Priem et al, 1973) After uplift, this formation covered the Guiana Shield as an extensive sandstone plateau or tableland, on which the early Guianan flora

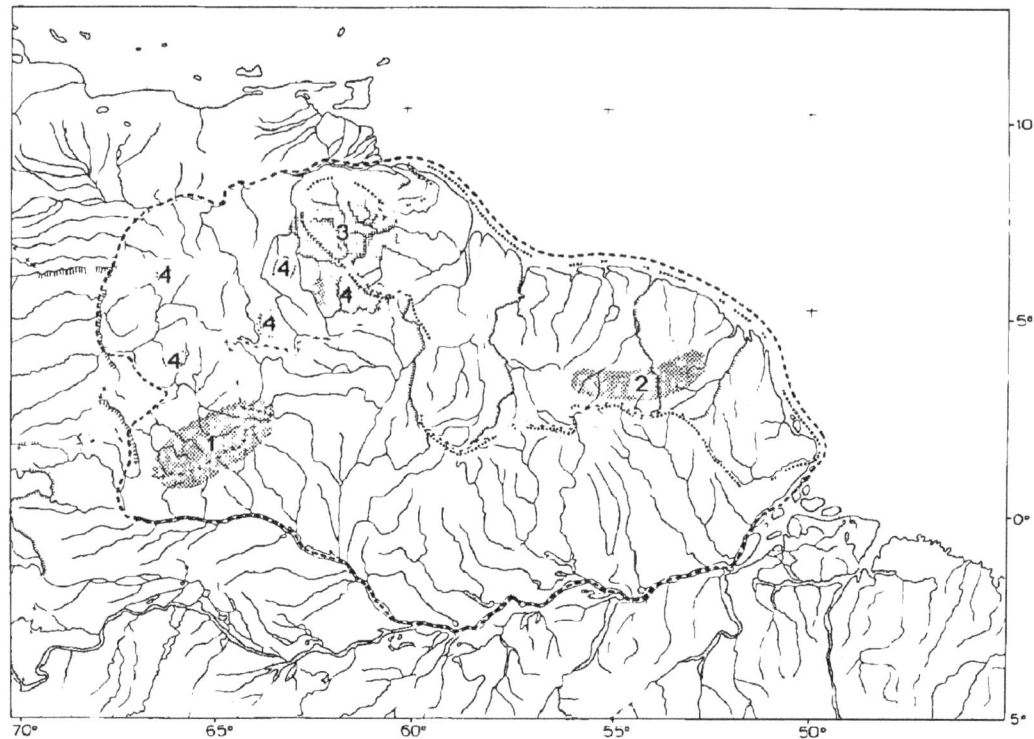

FIG 10 1 Map of Guiana showing the borders of the area as here defined (heavy broken line) and as defined by Descamps et al (1978) and by Lescure (1977) (heavy dotted line) Presumed forest refugia are gray and indicated by numbers 1 = Imeri Refuge, 2 = Guiana Refuge, 3 = Imataca Refuge, 4 = Tepui Refuges The line of fine dots (in this and the following maps of Guiana) represents the 200 m contour line

Mapa de la Guayana, mostrando los límites del territorio definido aquí (línea entrecortada gruesa) y el definido por Descamps et al (1978) y por Lescure (1977) (línea gruesa punteada) Supuestos refugios forestales en gris, indicados con números 1 = Refugio de Imeri, 2 = Refugio de Guayana, 3 = Refugio de Imataca, 4 = Refugios de Tepuyes La línea punteada fina (en este y los siguientes mapas) representa la línea de contorno de 200 m

developed (Maguire, 1970) During the Cretaceous and Tertiary uplift of the area, erosion shaped the present-day table mountains or tepuis These mountains consist of layered, unfossiliferous pink sandstones, with dolerite dikes and sills, reaching a maximum thickness of about 2400 m in Auyantepui in southeastern Venezuela and decreasing to 700 m in the Tafelberg in central Surinam (Haffer, 1974) At present, the Roraima Formation covers an area of about 450 000 km² and is spread over a total area of 1,200,000 km² in Venezuela, Guyana, Brasil and Surinam (Priem et al 1973) The greater part of the Roraima sandstone is concentrated in the Gran Sabana region of Venezuela and the adjacent parts of Brasil and Guyana, with many isolated remnants in the western part of the Estado Bolívar and in the Territorio Federal Amazonas and two outlying remnants in eastern Guyana and in central Surinam (Bisschops, 1969, Priem et al, 1973) (Fig 10 2) Some geologists (e g, Priem et al, 1973 1677) are of the opinion that "It is impossible to decide whether occurrences represent erosional remnants of a once-continuous cover of sediments deposited in a number of isolated basins" However, most geologists and biologists regard the present-day sandstone mountains as remnants of a once-continuous sandstone cover Also, one could imagine a combination of the possibilities, in which the western

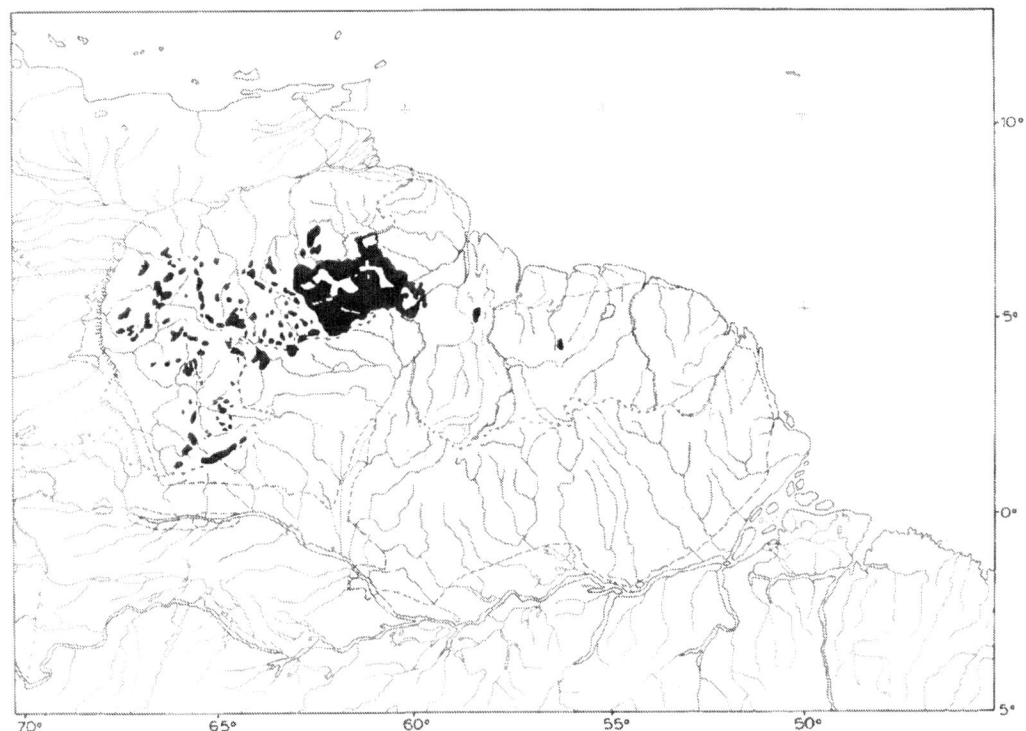

Fig. 10:2. Map of Guiana showing the extent of the Guiana Shield (gray area) and of the Roraima sandstone formation (black). The white areas in the sandstone represent gabbro (after Bisschops, 1969; Gansser, 1954; Priem et al., 1973).

Mapa de la Guayana mostrando la extensión del Escudo Guayani (gris) y de la formación Roraima (negro). Las areas blancas en el gres de Roraima representan gabbro (según Bisschops, 1969; Gansser, 1954; Priem et al., 1973).

Roraima Formation once formed a continuous cover and the two outlying areas in Demerara and Surinam could have been deposited in isolated basins. However, decisions on this subject should be reached by geologists, although perhaps biologists may contribute to the solution. In this paper I adhere to the view that the tepuis are remnants of a once-continuous formation. It seems useful to state that the arch of sandstone tepuis in southern Colombia, west of the Río Orinoco, and ending quite close to the Andes in the Sierra de Macarena, is not of the same as the Roraima Formation (Lescure, 1977). This sandstone is much younger and probably represents a deposition of erosional products of the Roraima Formation (Haffer, 1974; Paba-Silva and Van der Hammen, 1960). These tepuis probably arose by "Block fault-ing in conjunction with the Andean uplift toward the end of the Tertiary and at the beginning of the Pleistocene" (Haffer, 1974).

The Guiana Shield consists of an elevated portion in the west, rising from sea level to well over 1000 m in relatively extensive areas. This portion bears the sandstone tepuis of which the highest attain a height of 2810 m (Mount Roraima) and 3014 m (Serra de Neblina). These tepuis are mostly flattopped, with perpendicular cliffs several hundred meters high separating the plateau summits from the talus formed by the accumulation of erosional products at the base of the cliffs (Figs. 10:3–4).

The western part is separated from an eastern elevated part by a depression formed by the river systems of the Rio Branco and the Essequibo River, which may be connected

Fig. 10:3. The Tafelberg in Surinam, the easternmost remnant of the Roraima formation. Note the flat top, the steep, bare upper reaches of the flanks and the sloping talus covered with forest.

La Montaña Tafelberg en Surinam, el residuo más oriental de la formación Roraima. Obsérvase la cumbre aplanada, las flancos escarpados y rasos en su parte superior y el talud inclinado y cubierto de selva.

Fig. 10:4. View of several tepuis south of El Manteco, Estado Bolívar, Venezuela.
Vista de algunos tepuyes al sur de El Manteco, Estado Bolívar, Venezuela.

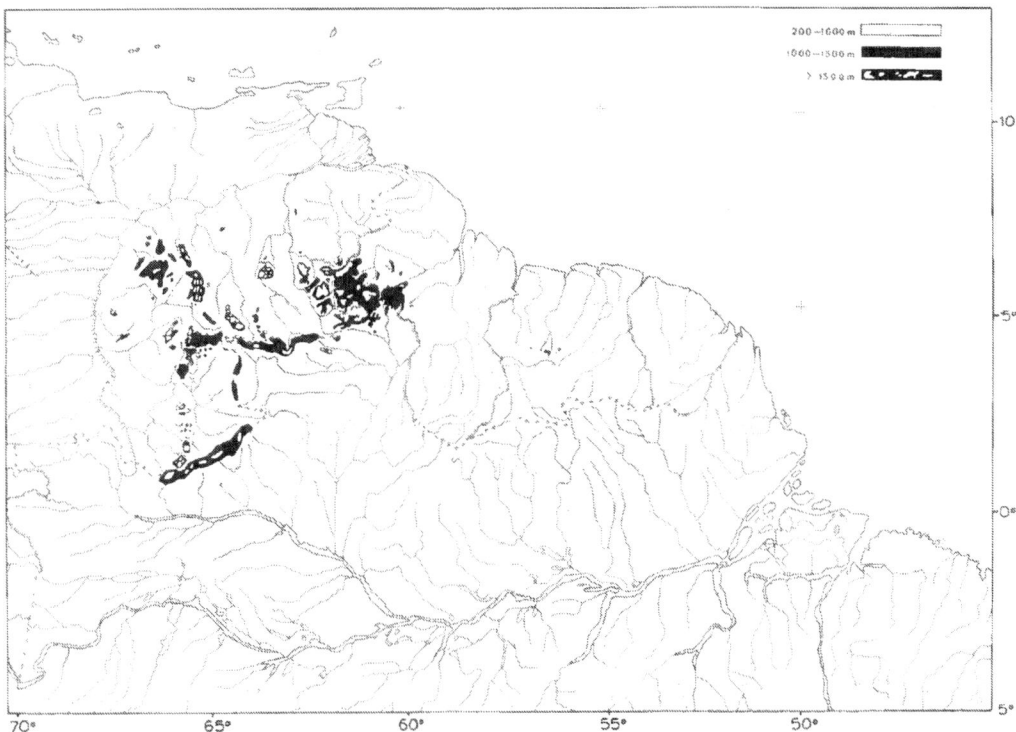

Fig. 10:5. Map of Guiana with the contour lines of 200, 1000 and 1500 m (after Mayr and Phelps, 1967).
Mapa de la Guayana con líneas de contorno de 200, 1000 y 1500 m (según Mayr y Phelps, 1967).

during the rainy season when large areas are inundated. The eastern part is much lower than the western one, reaching a maximum height of 1280 m (Julianatop) in central Surinam. From the divide between the Amazon Basin and rivers flowing north to the Atlantic Ocean (nowhere over 1000 m high), the country gradually slopes down to sea level. Thus, although the topography of eastern Guiana may be rather rugged, with many mountain ranges and valleys separating them, the area hardly ever exceeds 1000 m. In western Guiana, the topography is more or less the same, but on a higher level, with the consequence that more extensive areas are over 1000 m. However, superimposed on the Guiana Shield in this region are sandstone tepuis that may reach elevations of almost 3000 m (Fig. 10:5). The Guiana Highlands are also known as Pantepui.

The greater part of the area is covered by tropical rainforest, but savannas also play an important role. In the western and northwestern portion of the shield there are savannas more or less continuous with the llanos of central Venezuela. In the three Guianas there is a band of coastal savannas on white sand, reaching from Georgetown in the west to Cayenne in the east. East of Cayenne and in Amapá the white sand is absent and some extensive swamps in that region are dry savannas in the dry season. In Amapá this coastal belt is bordered on the west by a belt of cerrado—savanna with isolated trees. Isolated, extensive savanna complexes of the cerrado type are present (Hills, 1969) in southwestern Guyana (Rupununi), in southeastern Venezuela (Gran Sabana) and on the border between Surinam and Brasil (Sipaliwini/Paru savannas). Smaller, isolated savannas occur in Surinam and in Venezuela both on the Roraima sandstone and on other substrates (Fig. 10:6). On the higher points, starting at about 800 to 1000 m, cloud forest occurs with

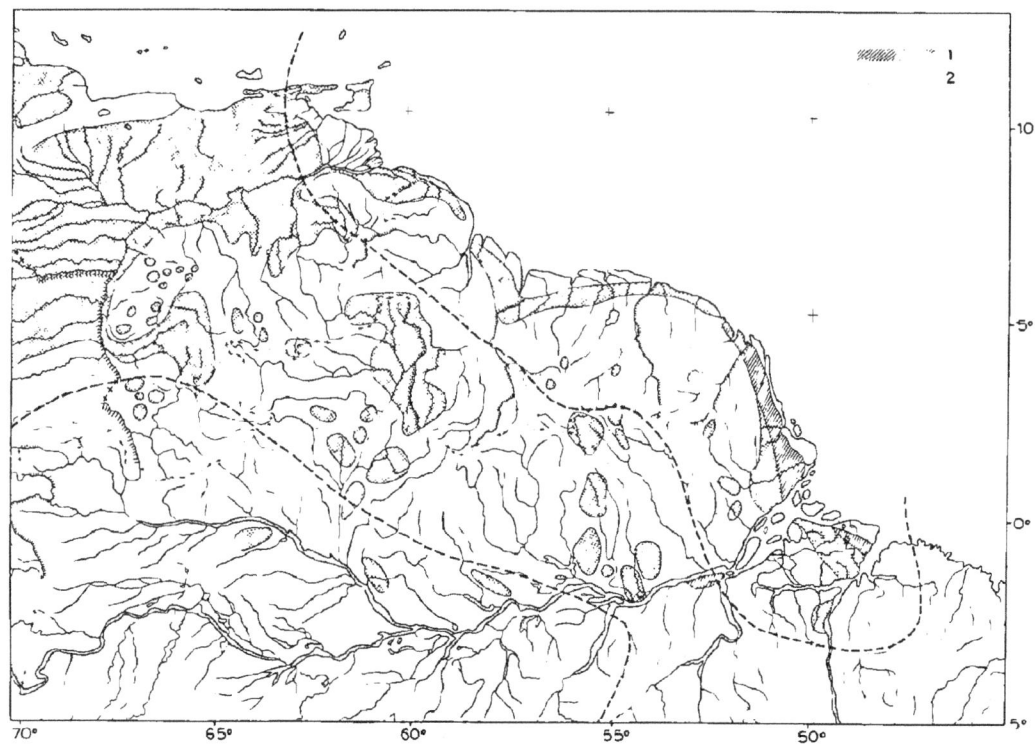

FIG 10 6 Map of Guiana showing the distribution of forest and savannas Forested areas white, savannas gray, inundated savannas hatched The zone with lower rainfall (cf Fig 10 7) has been indicated with heavy broken lines (after Hills, 1969, Muller, 1973, Oldenburger et al, 1973, Prance, 1973, Romariz, 1971 and personal field data)

Mapa de la Guayana mostrando la distribucion de selva y sabana Selva en blanco, cerrado en gris, campo rayado La zona menos lluviosa (cf Fig 10 7) se ha indicado con una linea entrecortada gruesa (segun Hills, 1969, Muller, 1973, Oldenburger et al, 1973, Prance, 1973, Romariz, 1974 y observaciones personales)

thick layers of mosses covering the trees, shrubs and the ground This is especially so on the talus of many of the tepuis The plateau summits of the smaller tepuis have only a shallow layer of soil, which is insufficient to support forest, thus, the vegetation is low, often savannalike The plateau summits of the larger (more extensive) tepuis is more diversified, and in some places a sufficiently deep layer of soil has accumulated to support moderately high forest, however, in other places there is only sparse vegetation (Chapman, 1931, Gleason, 1931, Maguire, 1945, 1955, 1970, Mayr and Phelps, 1967, Tate, 1928, 1930a,b 1932, 1938a,b, 1939, Tate and Hitchcock, 1930)

The climate of the region under discussion is characterized by two dry and two rainy seasons per year Their duration and the period of the year in which they fall are somewhat variable, and at higher elevations the distinction between dry and rainy seasons may be hardly evident, but in general this division holds true for the greater part of the area Within the area a wide zone with distinctly lower rainfall extends northwest-southeast connecting the llanos of Venezuela with the caatinga and cerrado region of central Brasil (Figs 10 6-7) Within this zone, which roughly covers the extreme southwestern part of Surinam, southern Guyana, southeastern Venezuela and the Guianan part of Pará, the annual rainfall is 2000 mm or less To the northeast and to the southwest the

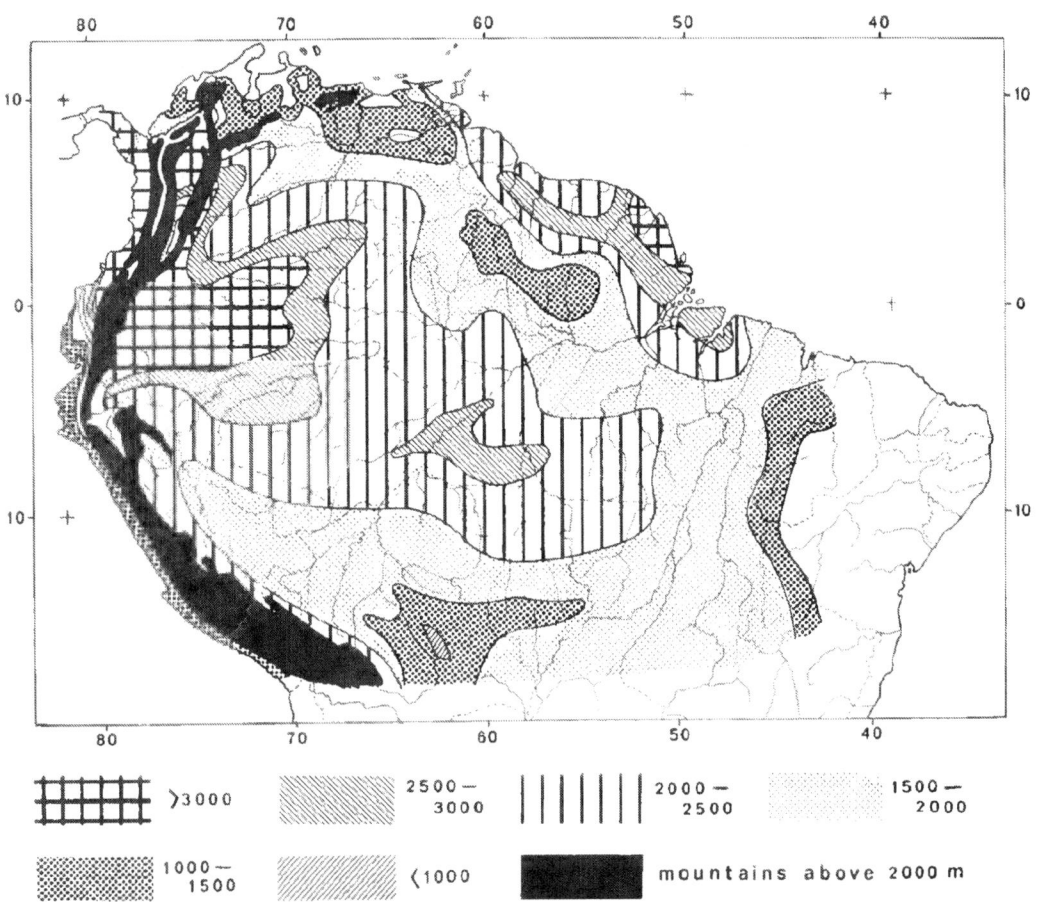

Fig. 10:7. Rainfall (mm) distribution in northern South America (after Prance, 1973; Reinke, 1962).
Distribución de la lluvia (mm) que cae anualmente en la parte norte de la América del Sur (según Prance, 1973, Reinke, 1962).

annual rainfall increases, reaching maxima of over 3000 mm in northeastern French Guiana and coastal Amapá and of some 2500 to 3000 mm in the upper Orinoco region (Reinke, 1962; Prance, 1973). Mean annual temperatures are between 24° and 27°C in the lowlands and decrease with increasing altitude.

During the last few years it has become increasingly clear that Pleistocene and Holocene climatic changes had a profound influence on the vegetation of northern South America, especially in Amazonia and adjacent regions. It is presumed that during dry climatic phases the rainforest disappeared from large stretches of the Amazon Basin and was restricted to refuges, mostly along its periphery (Brown et al., 1974; Haffer, 1969, 1974, this volume; Vanzolini, 1970a). Inversely, during the wet climatic phases the rainforest spread again from the refugia and the savanna vegetation and fauna retreated into refuges. Of importance in this connection are the Guiana, Tepui and Imerí forest refuges of Haffer (1969, 1974); the Guiana (forest), Pantepui (montane forest) and Roraima (savanna) centers of Müller (1973); and the Guiana, Imataca and Imerí refuges of Prance (1973), all of which are situated within the limits of the area considered here (Fig. 10:1). The aforementioned belt with a lower precipitation played an important role in the distribution of plants and animals during the different climatic periods. At present, the savanna complexes of interior Guiana are situated in this belt (Fig 10 6) However, during dry climatic phases probably much larger areas of it were covered with savanna, thereby providing a dispersal route for savanna inhabitants either to the north or to the south, and at the same time forming a barrier to east-west dispersal of forest inhabitants. On the other hand, both areas with higher rainfall adjacent to this dry belt, are thought to be the areas where forest refuges were situated during arid phases—to the northeast the Guiana refuge, to the southwest the Imerí refuge. During wet climatic phases, the forest spread from these refuges and invaded the savanna belt, fragmenting it into several isolated savanna complexes, as is the case today (Fig 10 6). The montane forests covering the slopes of the tepuis in southern Venezuela can be regarded as isolated occurrences of rainforest on places with favorable climatic conditions (high elevation, high rainfall) generally having unfavorable climatic and possibly edaphic conditions (Gran Sabana area). These forests, which are different from the tropical lowland rainforests, probably were only connected with the lowland forests during very wet climatic phases. Although Muller's concept of the Guiana center is much wider (and based on several different groups) than Haffer's, Prance's and others' Guiana refuge, I think we can synonymize the two without problems, the same is true for the Pantepui center and the Tepui refuge. There is no parallel in Muller's concepts of Haffer's and Prance's Imerí refuge. The Imataca refuge which was postulated by Prance (1973) for plants is only substantiated further by data from butterflies (Brown et al, 1974) (Fig 10 8)

HERPETOFAUNA

Although since 1894 quite a substantial number of reptiles and amphibians has been collected from the sandstone tepuis, only a small part of it was collected by herpetologists. This partly explains our scant and fragmentary knowledge of these groups. Thorough herpetological exploration of the tepui region starting with the now easily accessible La Escalera region in eastern Venezuela, probably will provide us with many interesting finds. Because our present knowledge is so fragmentary, it is often difficult to decide whether a certain species is really restricted to one tepui or not. The available data permit some zoogeographical conclusions, but those regarding the so-called endemics certainly have to be drawn with much reserve

Presently a total of 408 species of reptiles and amphibians is known to occur in the Guiana region (Table 10 1, Appendix 10 1). Seventy-six species are represented by 108 subspecies, which raises the number of species-group taxa for the region to 440. The herpetofauna of Guiana can be allocated to eight groups, which in turn can be partly subdivided

1 Endemic in Guiana region
  A Highland (over 1000 m)—18 amphibians, 9 reptiles
  B Lowland (below 1000 m)—74 amphibians, 50 reptiles
2 Amazonian
  A Peripheral along western and northern margin of basin—10 amphibians, 19 reptiles
  B With disjunct populations in upper Amazonia and near the mouth of the Amazon—2 amphibians, 1 reptile
  C Species of Amazon Basin occurring on southern edge of Guiana and along eastern margin, where they may reach French Guiana—3 amphibians, 11 reptiles
  D Widespread Amazonian, occurring throughout greater part of Guiana—39 amphibians, 62 reptiles
3 Widespread species (distribution extending from México or Central America over entire cis-Andean tropical South America)—12 amphibians, 35 reptiles
4 Species reaching their eastern distribution limit on the Guiana Shield, from Central America northwestern South America or upper Amazonia—11 amphibians, 17 reptiles

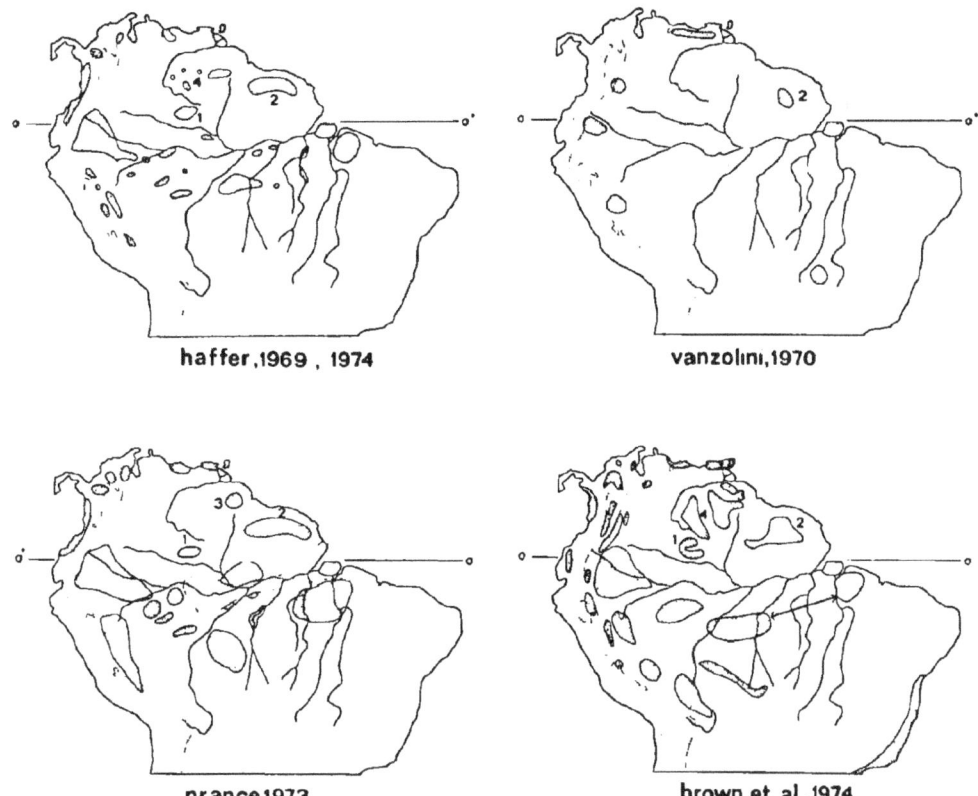

FIG 10 8 Location of forest refugia during arid periods according to several authors, numbers as in Fig 10 1

Situación de los refugios de selva durante los períodos secos según algunos autores, los números como en la Fig 10 1

5 Species from southeastern or central Brasil reaching Guiana, mostly not farther than French Guiana, some reaching Surinam or even Venezuela 8 amphibians, 13 reptiles

6 Cosmopolitan species 0 amphibians, 6 reptiles

7 Species imported from the Caribbean region 1 amphibian, 4 reptiles

8 Species with limited or uncertain distributions that may occur in the region 0 amphibians, 3 reptiles

The last three groups in the tabulation above are of no importance in the following considerations The five cosmopolitan species of sea turtles and one species of cosmopolitan gecko are of no importance here It is evident that the imported species do not need further attention Of the three species in the last group, it has not been established beyond doubt that they occur in the Guiana region Thus, there remain five important groups, totaling 177 amphibians and 217 reptiles, that reflect the complicated history of the Guiana herpetofauna and that are dealt with in detail later

Considerable differences exist between the percentages of reptiles and amphibians in five different groups and subgroups (Fig 10 9, Table 10 2) These groups are highland (1A) and lowland (1B) endemics, disjunct (2B) and widespread (2D) Amazonian, and wide-

TABLE 10:1.—Composition of the Guianan Herpetofauna. The columns contain the total numbers of species in a given family that inhabit the Guianas and the numbers of species that are endemic to the Guianas.

Family	Species Total	Species Endemic
Anurans		
Pipidae	2	1
Dendrobatidae	15	9
Ranidae	1	...
Leptodactylidae	38	12
Bufonidae	17	8
Hylidae	75	43
Pseudidae	2	...
Centrolenidae	7	6
Microhylidae	8	4
Total Anurans	165	83
Caecilians		
Rhinatrematidae	2	2
Typhlonectidae	2	1
Caeciliidae	9	6
Total Caecilians	13	9
Total Amphibians	178	92
Chelonians		
Cheloniidae	4	...
Dermochelyidae	1	...
Kinosternidae	1	...
Testudinae	2	...
Emydidae	1	...
Pelomedusidae	4	...
Chelidae	5	...
Total Chelonians	18	...
Crocodilians		
Crocodylidae	1	1
Alligatoridae	4	...
Total Crocodilians	5	1
Snakes		
Anomalepidae	2	1
Leptotyphlopidae	8	4
Typhlopidae	4	1
Aniliidae	1	...
Boidae	5	...
Dipsadidae	6	1
Colubridae	91	20
Elapidae	9	2
Crotalidae	6	...
Total Snakes	132	29
Lizards		
Gekkonidae	13	4
Iguanidae	18	3
Scincidae	1	...
Teiidae	33	16
Total Lizards	65	23
Amphisbaenians		
Amphisbaenidae	10	6
Total Amphisbaenians	10	6
Total Reptiles	230	59
Total Amphibians and Reptiles	408	151

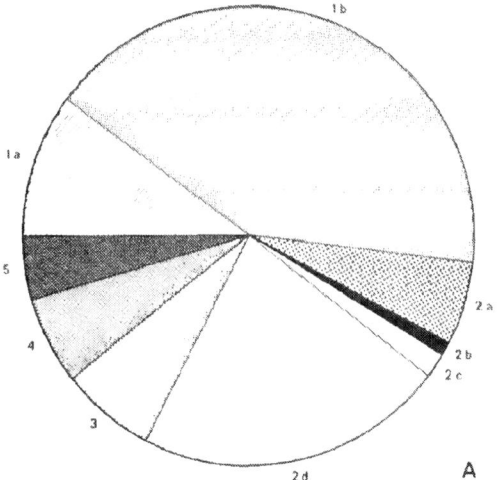

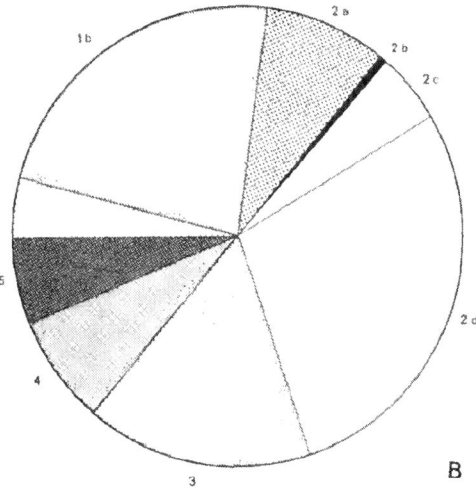

FIG. 10:9. Proportion of the total numbers of species accounted for by each group; numbers of groups as in Table 10.2. A = amphibians, B = reptiles.

Porcentaje que representa cada grupo del número total de especies; números de grupos como en la Tabla 10:2. A = anfibios, B = reptiles.

spread (3). Both in the widespread Amazonian and in the generally widespread species the percentage of reptiles is distinctly higher than that of amphibians; moreover, in the species reaching their eastern distribution limits in Guiana (4), and in the species com-

TABLE 10.2—Composition of the Guianan Herpetofauna
The columns contain the total number of species having a certain distribution and the percentage this group forms of the total number of species in the Guianan Region

Type of distribution	Species					
	Amphibians		Reptiles		Total	
	Number	Percentage	Number	Percentage	Number	Percentage
1 Endemics						
A Highland	18	10.17	9	4.15	27	6.85
B Lowland	74	41.81	50	23.04	124	31.47
		51.98		27.19		38.32
2 Amazonian						
A Periferal	10	5.64	19	8.75	29	7.36
B Disjunct	2	1.12	1	0.46	3	0.76
C Basin	3	1.69	11	5.06	14	3.55
D Widespread	39	22.03	62	28.57	101	25.63
		30.48		42.84		37.30
3 Widespread	12	6.77	35	16.12	47	11.92
4 Reaching eastern limit	11	6.21	17	7.83	28	7.10
5 From SE or C Brasil	8	4.51	13	5.99	21	5.32
Subtotal Guiana Region	177	99.95	217	99.97	394	99.96
6 Cosmopolitan			6		6	
7 Imported from Caribbean	1		4		5	
8 Uncertain distribution			3		3	
	178		230		408	

ing from the southeast (5), the percentage of reptiles is slightly higher than that of amphibians. In my opinion, this is the clue to the explanation of the differences observed. It is a reflection of the greater mobility of reptiles, as compared with the more sedentary habits of amphibians, which are restricted by their mode of reproduction. As there is a strict dependence on the kind of water (standing or running, large or small body of water), which for most species is very specific, this further restricts the possibilities for amphibian dispersal. Also species that have direct development on land are still dependent on water in the form of a high humidity. This explains the high endemism of this group in Guiana and also the higher percentage of disjunct Amazonian species of amphibians (Lynch, this volume). In all cases, the amphibians did not have the chance to expand their ranges far beyond the region of origin or from that of isolation during one of the climatic phases. Reptiles, given the same time and being independent of water for their reproduction, had a much greater rate of dispersal and either spread beyond the borders of Guiana (and thus ceased to be endemics of that region) or closed the gap between disjunct populations of one species.

I consider those species having distributions that do not, or hardly, exceed the borders of Guiana to be endemics. This is a fairly large area. Among the endemics several subdivisions can be recognized, the one between highland and lowland endemics will be discussed later. The other subdivision is between local and wide-ranging endemics, but this is partly artificial and mainly reflects our fragmentary knowledge of the species considered to be local.

Altitudinal Distribution

Of the indubitably native species only 55 (31% of total amphibians) species of frogs and 38 (18% of total reptiles) species of reptiles (lizards and snakes) (Appendix 10.1) occur at elevations of more than 1000 m. No caecilians, crocodilians, chelonians or amphisbaenians are known from above 1000 m. Of the species occurring over 1000 m, 37 frogs and 29 reptiles also occur below 1000 m, which leaves 18 frogs (10% of total) and 9 reptiles (4% of total) restricted to elevations of more than 1000 m. All of these are highland endemics, restricted to the western part of the Guiana Shield.

Highland endemics.—Most of these species have restricted distributions, usually consisting only of the summit or talus slopes of one or a few adjacent tepuis (Figs 10 10–11) As stated before, this either reflects our fragmentary knowledge of the herpetofauna of the Guiana Highlands, or these distributions are real and the comparable habitat on other tepuis is occupied by a related species However this has only been documented (and poorly so) for the endemic frog genus *Stefania*

The bufonid genus *Oreophrynella* from Roraima and Auyantepui is considered to be a specialized derivative from the general atelopodid stock and to have evolved in isolation since the Early Tertiary or the Cretaceous (McDiarmid, 1971) The same is true for the microhylid frog *Otophryne* (not an altitudinal endemic), composed only by *O robusta* with two subspecies—one restricted to high elevations on Chimantátepui, the other occurring in the greater part of interior Guiana at elevations of 200 to 1666 m Like *Oreophrynella*, *Otophryne* also shows a combination of primitive, derived and unique characters This is most easily explained by assuming that these frogs were subject to a long evolution in isolation on the sandstone formation, probably since the Cretaceous or Early Tertiary, the invasion of tropical lowland Guiana by *Otophryne* may be considered as secondary According to Lynch (pers comm), the leptodactylid frog *Hylodes duidensis* belongs to an undescribed genus of the tribe Eleutherodactylini Its relations are not clear, but it may have developed on the Guiana Shield as a highland derivative of the eleutherodactyline stock *Stefania* is an endemic, egg-brooding hylid frog genus clearly related to the northern Andean *Cryptobatrachus* According to Rivero (1970), these frogs can be divided into the *Stefania goini* group, with two species, and the *Stefania evansi* group with five species (and three undescribed ones) One member of the *goini* group occurs on Mount Duida in the west, the other on Chimantátepui in the east One member of the *evansi* group occurs on Cerro Marahuaca and the others on the eastern part of the Roraima Formation The distribution of the members of these species groups can be explained most easily by assuming that the genus *Stefania* arose from hylid stock in the Guiana Highlands, probably prior to the Oligocene Initially, the stock split into two groups, which during the most recent uplift of the area in Mio-Pliocene times became isolated on several tepuis and since differentiated into the several species now composing the two species groups The occurrence of *Stefania evansi* in lowland areas may be regarded, as in *Otophryne* as being secondarily, induced by the Pleistocene climatic changes, which lowered the general temperature of the area by about 3°C (Van der Hammen, 1974)

Species showing a slight degree of Andean relationships are members of the frog genera *Centrolenella* and *Eleutherodactylus*, and of the colubrid snake genus *Atractus*, all three genera probably evolved in or near the Andes, either in the foothills or in the lowlands, and subsequently spread to the east However, the endemic altitudinal species belonging to these genera have no direct relations with Andean species and probably are altitudinal forms derived from lowland species The matter is slightly different for the species of *Euspondylus*, a genus of teiid lizards of Andean origin, members of which live at medium to high altitudes in the Andes from Peru to Venezuela two species reached the higher altitudes of the Guiana Shield, possibly during a time of Pleistocene climatic depression The altitudinal endemics of the tree frog genus *Hyla* all apparently are related to lowland species groups

Riolama, a monotypic, endemic teiid lizard genus restricted to the summit of Mount Roraima, is known only from the type specimen Presumably it is related to *Leposoma* and its relatives, but its history is not clear It may have evolved from lowland microteiids by isolation on a sandstone tableland prior to the Oligocene, as was probably the case in *Stefania* The colubrid snakes *Liophis* and *Thamnodynastes* occur in lowland Amazonia and Guiana, but they seem to be of southern Brasilian origin and to have evolved into several altitudinal species in Guiana The nearest relative of the iguanid lizard, *Tropidurus bogerti*, is *T torquatus hispidus* (R Etheridge, pers comm), a member of a species or

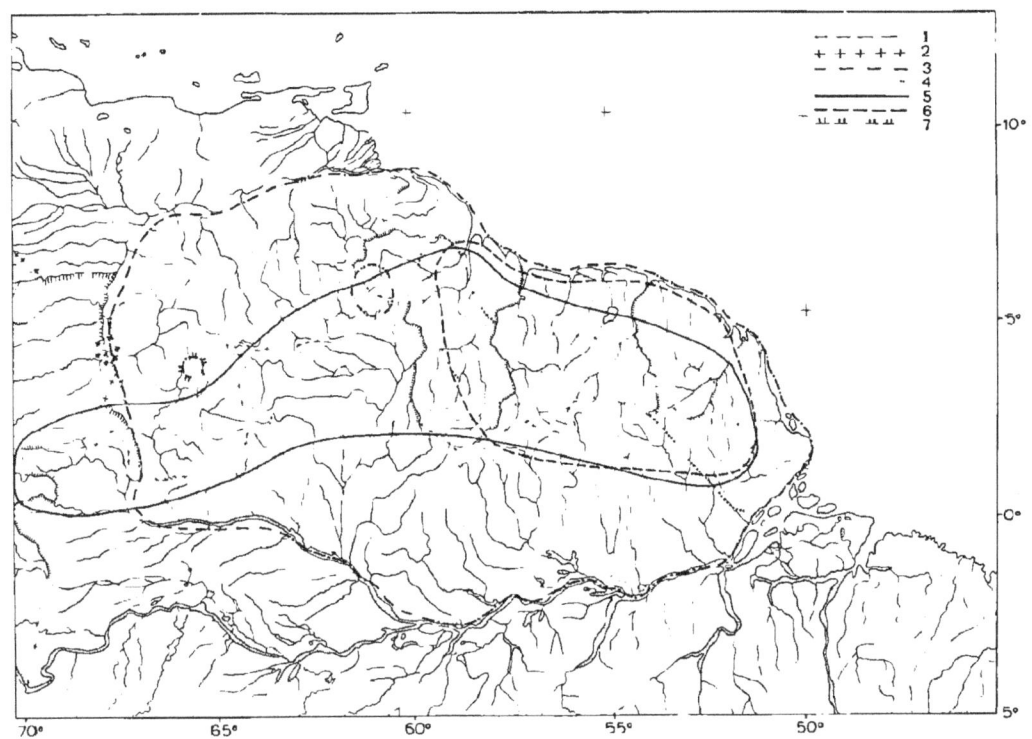

FIG 10 10 Distribution of some endemic species within Guiana
Distribución de algunas especies endémicas en la Guayana
1 = *Hyla multifasciata* 2 = *Aparasphenodon venezolanus* 3 = *Bufo nasicus, Hyla siblesz, Hyla lemai*
4 = *Hyla ornatissima* 5 = *Otophryne robusta* 6 = *Allophryne ruthveni* 7 = *Hyla ginesi Stefania goini
Stefania marahuaquensis, Hylodes" duidensis*

species complex, which may be of southeastern Brasilian origin The few altitudinal endemic subspecies all have evolved by isolation at higher altitudes from lowland relatives of different origins

Attempts to explain the origin of the fauna of Pantepui have been based on the distribution of birds (Chapman, 1931, Haffer, 1974, Mayr and Phelps, 1967) mammals (Tate, 1939), frogs (Rivero, 1965) and snails (Haas, 1957) Because of different dispersal abilities and different geological ages of the groups concerned, these studies came to different conclusions For instance, birds supposedly were able to reach Guiana from the Andes by (simply stated) flying from one mountain with suitable climate to the next This possibility doesn't exist for the other groups The distribution of the endemic Guianan herpetofauna can be explained with the aid of the following theories

1 The Mountain Bridge Theory as presented by several authors (Todd and Carriker, 1922, Haas, 1957) apparently is useless, because there is no geological evidence for a connection of southern Venezuela with the Andes As has been pointed out, the sandstone mountains (Sierra de Macarena) in southern Colombia are not the remnants of such a bridge

2 The Plateau Theory, starting from the assumption that "a more extensive tableland probably did exist on the Guayana shield during the Mesozoic and Tertiary, prior to an intensive erosional dissection" (Haffer, 1974 163) is useful to explain the presence of several

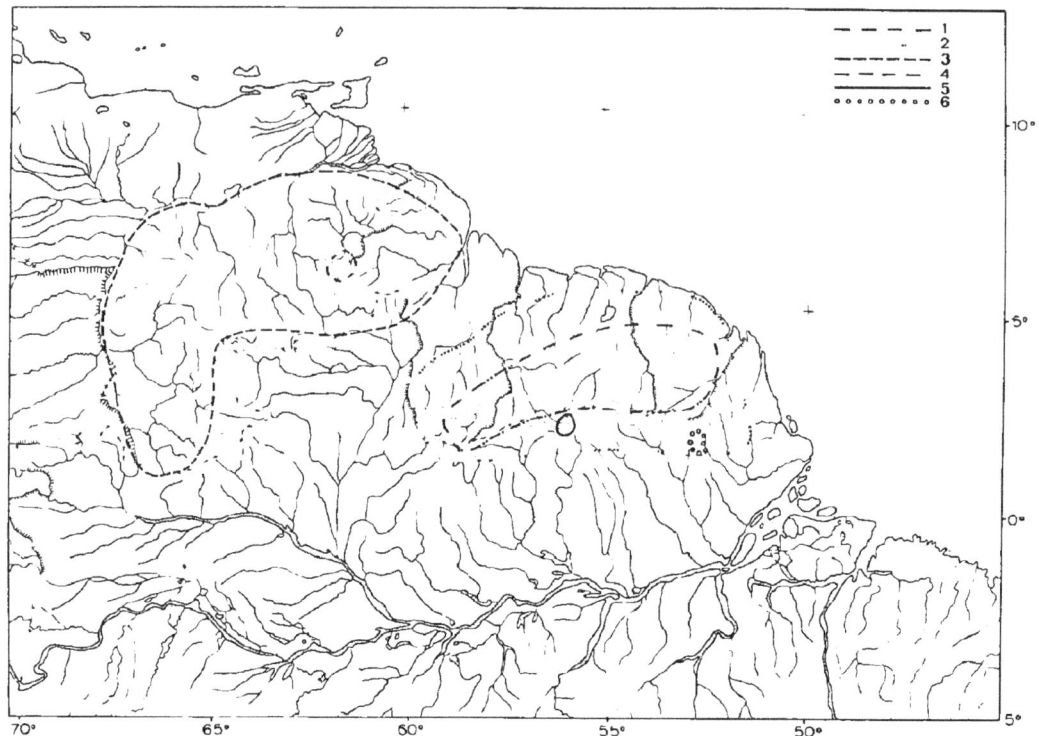

Fig. 10-11. Distribution of some endemic species within Guiana.
Distribución de algunas especies endémicas en la Guayana.
1 = *Hyla proboscidea*, 2 = *Dendrobates tinctorius*, 3 = *Dendrobates leucomelas*, 4 = *Hyla rodriguezi*, *Stefania scalae*, *Eleutherodactylus pulvinatus*, 5 = *Dendrobates azureus*, 6 = *Phyllobates pulchripectus*, *Amapasaurus tetradactylus*.

relicts, such as the frogs *Oreophrynella* and *Otophryne*. A slightly modified version, starting with the assumption that the Roraima Formation underwent orogenic movements that shaped it into a mountain range before erosion graded it into a plateau, which in turn was uplifted and eroded into its present shape, serves well to explain the distribution of the genus *Stefania* (Rivero, 1970).

3. The Modified Cool Climate Theory departs from the assumption that during the glacial periods of the Pleistocene, the lowlands between the Andes and Guiana, and within the Amazonian basin had a cooler climate. This indeed was true, the temperature of the lowlands having been about 3°C lower than at present (Van der Hammen, 1974), but this was not sufficient to make the lowlands subtropical instead of tropical, as had been assumed formerly (Chapman, 1931; Tate, 1939). However, it may have facilitated the dispersal of certain organisms because all life zones on mountains shifted to lower altitudes thus creating suitable habitats for subtropical organisms in places where they were formerly absent. These still widely-separated, subtropical habitats could have been of importance for birds. The distribution of amphibians and reptiles apparently related to Andean taxa could not have gone only via those "stepping stones" but most likely through the lowlands at times of cooler temperatures.

4. The Habitat Shift Theory assumes that part of the fauna of Pantepui was derived from tropical lowland elements that changed their habitat preference. It serves to explain the distribution and occurrence of the majority of the taxa living at higher elevations. They either differentiated in situ after invasion of the highlands by a lowland ancestor (most highland endemics) or are themselves widely distributed in the lowlands surrounding Pantepui and apparently have wide ecological amplitude.

5. The Distance Dispersal Theory, which assumes that the Guiana Highlands were colonized from distant sources by island hopping, is of no use in explaining the distribution of the herpetofauna although it seems to be useful for partly explaining the distribution of flying organisms (mainly vertebrates) (Mayr and Phelps, 1967).

Lowland endemics.—The lowland endemics are a rather mixed group, containing species restricted to elevations below 1000 m and species occurring from sea level to well above 1000 m. Several species occur from about sea level to a maximum of 2400 m. In a number of cases [*Neusticurus tatei*, *N. racenisi*, *N. rudis* (all three teiid lizards), *Stefania evansi* (hylid frog), *Otophryne robusta* (microhylid frog)] they clearly evolved on part of the sandstone plateau and secondarily invaded the tropical lowlands. Others, like *Dendrobates steyermarki* (poison-arrow frog), *Hyla ginesi*, *H. benitezi*, *H. kanaima*, *H. lemai*, *H. sibleszi*, *Stefania marahuaquensis*, *S. woodleyi* (hylid frogs) and *Euparkerella* sp. "A" (leptodactylid frog) have narrower elevational distributions, occurring only from about 600 to 1500 m. They also probably evolved at higher altitudes and secondarily invaded the adjacent lowlands, but apparently their ecological tolerance is not so great as that of the species in the first group. The remaining species occurring above 1000 m are actually lowland species, having arisen in tropical lowlands and from there extended their range by moving up onto the sandstone plateau, often to the base of the tepuis, sometimes even to the summit.

Dendrobates steyermarki known from an isolated sandstone mountain in western Venezuelan Guiana is most closely related to Andean species of the *Dendrobates minutus* group (Silverstone, 1975). This is the only Guianan lowland species showing such a link and probably this is a relict of a formerly more widespread group, which became isolated from the main body of the group when temperatures increased during one of the Pleistocene climatic phases.

Euparkerella, with recent representatives living at low to high elevations in areas periferal to the Amazon Basin (Roraima, Andes of Ecuador and Perú, southeastern Brasil), is represented by one endemic species. Its distribution may be explained by assuming that the presently known species are the survivors of a genus that once occupied a more extensive range covering the entire Amazon region and adjacent territories. When the range of the genus became discontinuous is not clear, but tentatively we may place that event in the early Pleistocene. It was probably caused by the evolution in the Amazon Basin of new groups of litter-adapted frogs.

There are five (monotypic) lowland endemic genera [*Allophryne* (hylid frog), *Rhinatrema* (caecilian), *Peltocephalus* (pelomedusid turtle), *Amapasaurus* (teiid lizard) and *Mesobaena* (amphisbaenian)], of which only *Allophryne*, *Rhinatrema* and *Peltocephalus* have more or less extensive ranges. *Amapasaurus* is restricted to a small area in eastern Guiana and *Mesobaena* to western Guiana. The ranges of the first four genera and of many endemic species coincide with that of the postulated Guiana Forest Refuge (Haffer, 1969, 1974; Lescure, 1975, 1977) or with parts of it (Figs. 10, 10–11). Therefore, it seems possible that these genera arose in this refuge during the early Pleistocene. The same holds true for most of the other lowland endemic species, but here we might date the specific diversification as late Pleistocene.

Endemic subspecies of species not endemic to Guiana probably arose during one of the more recent (late Pleistocene or Holocene) dry or wet climatic phases occurring in northern South America.

A few of the lowland endemics occurring in western Guiana, mainly around the headwaters of the Río Orinoco, seem to strengthen Haffer's view of an Imeri forest refuge. These endemics include one monotypic genus (*Mesobaena* amphisbaenian), eight species [*Aparasphenodon venezolanus* (tree frog), *Dendrobates leucomelas* and *D. steyermarki* (poison-arrow frogs), *Atractus insipidus*, *Helicops hogei*, *Liophis canaima* (all colubrid snakes), *Phyllodactylus dixoni* (gekkonid lizard), *Crocodylus intermedius* (crocodile)] and three subspecies [*Hydrops triangularis venezuelensis*, *Leptophis ahaetulla copei* (both colubrid snakes), *Micrurus surinamensis nattereri* (elapid snake)]. A similar situation is known in birds, with one endemic genus and nine endemic species (Haffer, 1974). Assuming a similar divergence rate for the organisms involved, this seems to point to at least three arid phases during which the forest fauna was isolated in this Imeri forest refuge.

Different patterns of distribution exist in Guiana. The endemic species are not evenly distributed throughout the area. As has been noted in the section on altitudinal distribution, all altitudinal endemics are restricted to the western part of the Guiana Shield, the area west of the Essequibo-Río Branco Depression. The ranges of most of the species that supposedly originated on the higher parts of the sandstone area do not extend far beyond, only a few reach the Essequibo River in the east. Exceptions, like the microhylid frog, *Otophryne robusta*, and the teiid lizard, *Neusticurus rudis*, extend their ranges beyond the Essequibo River. The Essequibo-Río Branco Depression seems to have been a barrier to the eastward distribution of a number of species, mainly Pantepui species. On the other hand, it was a barrier to the westward distribution of a number of species. The effect of this barrier is evident from the ranges of lowland endemics (Fig. 10.11). Of the 74 endemic species of lowland amphibians (Table 10.2, Appendix 10.1) 18 (24%) occur on both sides of the Essequibo-Río Branco Depression, 32 (43%) only occur east of the depression, and 24 (32%) only occur west of it. Of the 50 endemic species of lowland reptiles (Table 10.2, Appendix 10.1) 18 (36%) occur on both sides of the Essequibo-Río Branco Depression, 17 (34%) only occur east of the depression, and 15 (30%) only occur west of it. The picture changes distinctly when the altitudinal endemics also are considered. In that case the number of amphibians restricted to the western part of Guiana becomes 42 and the corresponding number of reptiles 24. The percentages change accordingly, for amphibians respectively 18 (22%), 32 (39%) and 42 (51%), for reptiles respectively 18 (31%), 17 (29%) and 24 (41%). Among the widespread endemics the proportion of reptiles is considerably higher than that of amphibians, in both the western and eastern endemics the proportion of amphibians is higher than that of reptiles, reflecting the greater mobility of reptiles. When only the lowland endemics are considered, the percentage of amphibian species restricted to the east is distinctly higher than that of species restricted to the west, in reptiles it is only slightly higher. This probably reflects the greater importance of the Guiana Refuge for amphibians, as compared to the importance of the Imeri Refuge. For reptiles, both refuges apparently were equally important. Why the Guiana Refuge was more important for amphibians than for reptiles remains a matter of conjecture. However, possibly it results from the greater dependence of amphibians on water and moist habitats. Thus isolation in different refuges was more severe for amphibians than for reptiles, reptiles restricted to different forest refuges probably came into contact earlier than the amphibians thus diminishing the possibilities of having attained reproductive incompatibility. Maybe it was simply a matter of size, the Guiana Refuge having been larger (and therefore possibly harboring more species) than the Imeri Refuge. Perhaps both factors played a role.

The Essequibo-Río Branco Depression also served as a route for lowland Amazonian species invading the northern part of Guiana.

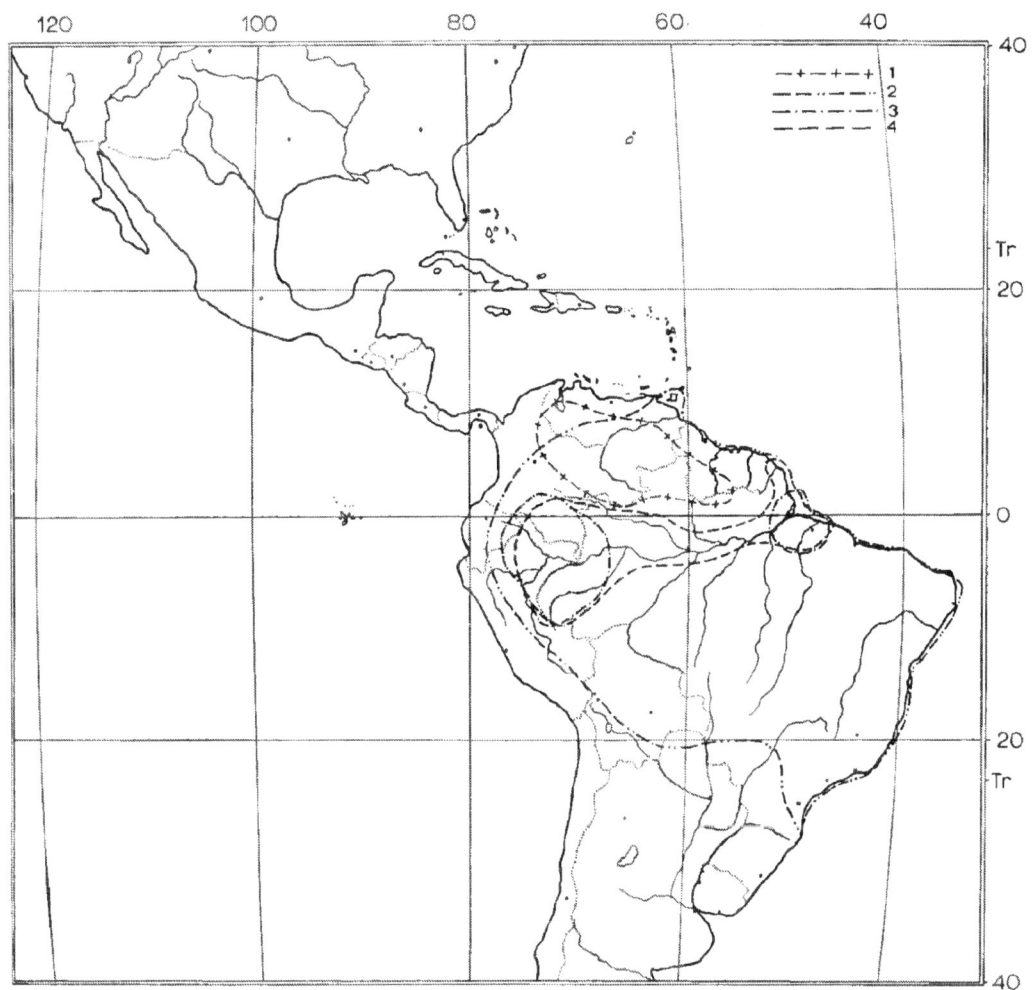

Fig. 10:12. Distribution of species belonging to the groups 2–5 (Table 10:2, Appendix 10:1).
Distribución de especies pertenecientas a los grupos 2–5 (Tabla 10:2, Apéndice 10:1).
1 = *Pseudopaludicola pusilla* (group 4). 2 = *Hyla geographica* (group 2d). 3 = *Lepidoblepharis festae* (group 2b). 4 = *Crocodilurus lacertinus* (group 2c).

Amazonian Species

I do not treat the other groups (Figs. 10:12–13) in the detail that I have done for the Guiana endemics, because they are dealt with by Dixon, Lynch, and Rivero-Blanco and Dixon (this volume).

A few species reach parts of Guiana because of certain hydrological features. The occurrence in Guyana of the aquatic Amazonian species *Melanosuchus niger* (the black caiman) and *Chelus fimbriatus* (the matamata) apparently is the result of the rainy season connection between the Río Branco and the Essequibo River via the flooded Rupununi Savanna. The occurrence of these species in eastern French Guiana can be explained in a similar way, because the extensive coastal swamps and inundated savannas in Amapá, during the rainy season form an unbroken connection between the Amazon and the Oyapoc, Approuague and Mahury basins. In

FIG. 10:13. Distribution of species belong to the groups 2–5 (Table 10:2, Appendix 10:1).
Distribución de especies pertenecientas a los grupos 2–5 (Tabla 10:2, Apéndice 10:1).
1 = *Lysapsus limellus* (group 5). 2 = *Lysapsus limellus laevis* (group 5). 3 = *Hyla senicula melanargyrea* (group 5). 4 = *Leptodactylus rhodomystax* (group 2a). 5 = *Phrynohyas venulosa* (group 3).

Surinam no such connections occur between the Corantijn or Marowijne river systems and the Amazon Basin; this explains the absence of these two species in that country.

Other species of the Amazon Valley apparently succeeded in reaching eastern French Guiana but did not penetrate farther west. The distribution of a few species with disjunct populations in upper Amazonia and near the mouth of the Río Amazonas (Table 10:2, Appendix 10:1, Fig. 10:12) is correlated with areas of high rainfall (over 2500 mm) (Fig. 10:7) and may have been caused by the most recent arid phase, which apparently ended 2000 years ago and caused a separation of the upper and lower Amazonian forests (and the animals living in them) (Haffer, 1974). A number of these species are distributed in an arciform area from Bolivia along the eastern foot of the Andes to the Guianas. This arc can be termed the Amazonian Arc. Lescure (1977) called the northern part of this arc (Serra do Navio to Loreto, Perú) the Roraima Arc, because he believed that all sandstone in this region belonged to the Roraima Formation. As pointed out before, this is not the case. However the existence of an arciform distribution pattern in several reptiles and amphibians seems to be real (Fig. 10.13). For at least one species, the toad *Bufo guttatus* this pattern apparently is caused by its being saxicolous. It is nearly always found associated with rocks, the geological nature of these rocks apparently is not important, as it may consist of either granite or sandstone. The absence of this species in central Amazonia is understandable, because in that area rocks are absent, only alluvial material is present. A number of Guianan endemics [*Otophryne robusta* (Fig. 10.10), *Leptodactylus rugosus*], which formerly were thought to be restricted to the northern part of the arc because of their close association with sandstone, now have been found associated with other types of rocks as well. For most of the species having the periferal or Amazonian Arc distribution it is not possible to explain simply their absence from central Amazonia. Possibly the presence of close relatives or other ecological competitors there is the most important reason.

Widespread Species

Most of the species in this group apparently had their origin in Amazonian South America, from there they dispersed into southern Central America (Fig. 10.13), a few are of Central American origin and dispersed into South America. One example of this last subgroup is the teiid lizard *Cnemidophorus l. lemniscatus*, occurring from Honduras to the mouth of the Amazon. This species occurs only along the coast in Guiana. The fact that this species is still extending its range along the lower Amazon (Vanzolini, 1970b) and that it does not occur in the far interior of the Guianas indicate that it is a recent immigrant from the northwest. The presence of forests in southern Surinam and French Guiana, was a barrier to the dispersal of *C. l. lemniscatus* (a savanna inhabitant) into the large inland edaphic savannas in the Sipaliwini/Paru area. Fluctuation of the size of the forests, thereby at times forming a barrier between the inland and coastal savannas, was responsible for the isolation of the inland savannas, lizards living there are distinctly different from the populations of the same species in savannas farther north (Hoogmoed 1973).

Species Reaching the Eastern Limit of Their Distributions on the Guiana Shield

Some of these species are of Central American origin, others of upper Amazonian, or coastal Venezuelan origin. A number of them are savanna inhabitants that just reach the western part of the Guiana Shield, where the llanos extend east of the Río Orinoco (the leptodactylid frog *Ceratophrys calcarata*). A few leptodactylid frogs (*Physalaemus pustulosus, Pleurodema brachyops*) reach the Rupununi Savanna, one leptodactylid frog (*Pseudopaludicola pusilla*) just reaches the Sipaliwini Savanna in Surinam (Fig. 10.12), and one tree frog (*Hyla rostrata*) so far has only been found in the vicinity of El Dorado (Venezuela) and possibly near Cayenne (French Guiana). All of these species have been dealt with in other sections.

Species From Southeastern or Central Brasil Reaching Guiana

Most of the species from southeastern or central Brasil reaching Guiana do not extend farther west than French Guiana or Surinam (Fig. 10.13), only seven [*Hyla x-signata* (tree frog), *Leptodactylus fuscus* (leptodactylid frog), *Pseudis paradoxus* (pseudid frog), *Phrynops geoffroanus* (chelid turtle), *Liophis miliaris* (colubrid snake), *Coleodactylus meridionalis* (gekkonid lizard), and *Tropidurus torquatus* (iguanid lizard)] reach Venezuela. The majority, if not all, of these species are inhabitants of savannas or open swamps, and their distributions are closely associated with those habitats. Apparently these species are recent immigrants from the southeast that either used the savanna corridor (central and northeastern Brasil to southeastern Venezuela) during the last arid phase (about 2000–3500 years ago), when the greater part of this area was covered with a cerradolike vegetation, or they used the open swampy coastal area of Amapá. Most of these species have not differentiated and when they have, the subspecies occurring in the Guianas is identical with the one in northeastern Brasil. The exceptions are the bufonid *Melanophryniscus moreirae*, and the pseudid frogs, *Pseudis paradoxus* and *Lysapsus limellus*, all of which have endemic subspecies in Guiana. The last two species may have reached Guiana during an earlier dry phase and probably along a different route (from Rio Tapajós via Rio Negro and Rio Branco to the north). Furthermore, *Pseudis paradoxus* reaches the western part of Guiana, whereas in Guiana *Lysapsus limellus* is only in the western part (Fig. 10.13).

ANALYSIS OF GEOGRAPHIC DISTRIBUTION

For three groups (frogs, lizards and snakes) data are sufficient to permit an attempt of comparison with localities outside the Guianan Region. However, data were scarce and comparisons for frogs only could be made with the Belém region (Crump, 1971), for lizards with Belém (Crump, 1971, Da Cunha, 1961) and Iquitos (Dixon and Soini, 1975), and for snakes only with Iquitos (Dixon and Soini, 1977). All data have been compiled in Tables 10.3–8. In these tables the total number of species in each locality is on the diagonal from upper left to lower right. The number of species common to each combination of regions is to the right and above the diagonal with the totals. To the left and below the diagonal are the Faunal Resemblance Factors (FRF) as computed for each combination of regions, using the formula (Duellman, 1965, 1966):

$$FRF = \frac{2C}{N_1 + N_2}$$

where N_1 and N_2 are the numbers of species occurring in any two given regions and C is the number of species common to the two regions compared. The computations were made both for forest- and savanna-inhabiting species.

The data for frogs (Tables 10.3–4) show that among forest inhabitants there is a distinctly higher resemblance between the anuran faunas of eastern Guiana (Guyana east of the Essequibo River, Surinam, French Guiana, and northern part of Amapá) and of the Brasilian part of Guiana (Guiana Region south of divide) than between both of

TABLE 10.3—Comparison of Rainforest Frog Faunas of Different Regions in Northeastern South America.

	Species in Common			
FRF	Western Guiana	Eastern Guiana	Brasilian part Guiana	Belém
Western Guiana	76	41	31	14
Eastern Guiana	0.51	83	42	22
Brasilian part Guiana	0.52	0.67	43	19
Belém	0.28	0.40	0.58	23

TABLE 10.4—Comparison of Savanna Frog Faunas of Different Regions in Northeastern South America.

	Species in Common			
FRF	Western Guiana	Eastern Guiana	Brasilian part Guiana	Belém
Western Guiana	36	23	20	13
Eastern Guiana	0.69	31	19	13
Brasilian part Guiana	0.69	0.72	22	12
Belém	0.51	0.46	0.65	15

TABLE 10.5—Comparison of Rainforest Snake Faunas of Different Regions in Northern South America.

	Species in Common			
FRF	Western Guiana	Eastern Guiana	Brasilian part Guiana	Iquitos
Western Guiana	80	65	53	51
Eastern Guiana	0.78	85	54	53
Brasilian part Guiana	0.75	0.74	60	46
Iquitos	0.65	0.62	0.63	84

TABLE 10.6—Comparison of Open Formation Snake Faunas of Different Regions in Northern South America.

	Species in Common			
FRF	Western Guiana	Eastern Guiana	Brasilian part Guiana	Iquitos
Western Guiana	19	14	11	4
Eastern Guiana	0.75	18	12	5
Brasilian part Guiana	0.68	0.77	13	4
Iquitos	0.33	0.43	0.44	5

TABLE 10 7—Comparison of Rainforest Lizard Faunas of Several Regions in Northern South America

F R F	Paramaribo	Cayenne	Lely Mountains	Alto Maraca	Iquitos	Bolivar	Belém	Brasilian part Guiana	Eastern Guiana	Western Guiana
Paramaribo	20	17	13	11	16	18	17	20	20	20
Cayenne	0 77	21	14	10	15	18	19	22	24	22
Lely Mountains	0 62	0 61	22	14	16	18	16	21	22	22
Alto Maraca	0 56	0 47	0 68	19	14	13	14	19	19	18
Iquitos	0 51	0 45	0 49	0 45	43	19	23	25	25	24
Bolivar	0 69	0 64	0 67	0 51	0 51	32	18	24	27	32
Belem	0 68	0 70	0 62	0 57	0 63	0 55	30	28	28	25
Brasilian part Guiana	0 66	0 68	0 67	0 64	0 60	0 66	0 80	40	34	35
Eastern Guiana	0 59	0 73	0 69	0 63	0 59	0 73	0 78	0 83	41	37
Western Guiana	0 59	0 61	0 63	0 54	0 53	0 81	0 64	0 80	0 84	47

TABLE 10 8—Comparison of Savanna Lizard Faunas of Several Regions in Northern South America

F R F	Paramaribo	Cayenne	Lely Mountains	Alto Maraca	Iquitos	Bolivar	Belem	Brasilian part Guiana	Eastern Guiana	Western Guiana
Paramaribo	3	3	0	0	0	3	2	3	3	3
Cayenne	1 0	3	0	0	0	3	2	3	3	3
Lely Mountains	0	0	0	0	0	0	0	0	0	0
Alto Maraca	0	0	0	0	0	0	0	0	0	0
Iquitos	0	0	0	0	0	0	0	0	0	0
Bolivar	0 35	0 35	0	0	0	14	2	4	6	14
Belem	0 80	0 80	0	0	0	0 25	2	2	2	2
Brasilian part Guiana	0 85	0 85	0	0	0	0 11	0 66	4	4	4
Eastern Guiana	0 66	0 66	0	0	0	0 60	0 50	0 80	6	6
Western Guiana	0 35	0 35	0	0	0	1 0	0 25	0 44	0 60	14

those areas and western Guiana (Guyana west of Essequibo River, Venezuelan Guayana) This could be explained by the barrier function of the Essequibo-Rio Branco Depression On the other hand, the resemblance between the forest anuran fauna of Belém as compared to the other regions, shows a steady decrease towards the west We see quite a different picture when comparing the savanna anuran faunas Here the resemblance between eastern Guiana and the Brasilian part of Guiana is only negligibly higher than that between both of those areas and western Guiana The resemblance between Belém and the Brasilian part of Guiana is in the same category as that between the three areas of the Guiana Region among themselves However, the resemblance between Belem and both eastern and western Guiana is distinctly lower Although 13 of the 15 species known from Belém occur throughout western and eastern Guiana, the resemblance factor is low because these species only are a fraction of the much larger savanna anuran fauna there, which contains a fairly high proportion of local endemics (which still may prove to be more widespread) and a number of species reaching their eastern distribution limits in Guiana Thus it can be concluded that for savanna-inhabiting frogs there are no barriers within Guiana and for that matter scarcely any barriers towards areas surrounding Gui ana. For forest-inhabiting frogs there is a distinct barrier within Guiana, formed by the Essequibo-Rio Branco Depression and also the forest anuran fauna is distinctly separated from that to the southeast. However, these conclusions are based only on data from four areas (three of which chosen with a certain bias) and therefore should be treated with much reserve, although they do confirm the picture that emerged from a first study of distribution maps. These findings for the anuran faunas can be most easily explained by assuming that the Essequibo-Rio Branco Depression not only served as a connection (and dispersal route for aquatic species) between Guiana and Amazonia, but also was the area that retained its savanna vegetation longest, as still indicated by the presence of large savanna areas in the border region of Guyana and Brasil and in the coastal area near the mouth of the Essequibo River. Thus, this area formed an efficient barrier to the dispersal of forest frogs, at the same time, it formed a dispersal route for savanna frogs. This situation apparently lasted until fairly recently, until under the influence of an increasingly wet climate the forests in the Guiana and Imerí refuges started to expand and met in the Essequibo-Rio Branco Depression. This explains why many forest species have their eastern or western distribution limits at the Essequibo-Rio Branco Depression. Several species that apparently were associated with one of the refuges in the region succeeded in crossing the depression, but this could have taken place only recently when the savanna vegetation was substituted by forest.

Comparison of the snake and lizard faunas of several localities gives quite a different picture. The data for forest-inhabiting snakes (Table 10.5) show that there is a great resemblance between different parts of the Guiana Region and that the resemblance with the forest snake fauna of Iquitos is fairly good, but distinctly lower than within Guiana. The data suggest a gradual transition within Guiana from west to east and also from Iquitos to Guiana, but owing to lack of data from intermediate localities this last hypothesis cannot be proved. Only five snakes inhabiting open formations are found in the Iquitos area, all of these are either associated with open aquatic or edge situations. Real savanna species are absent, because no suitable habitat is available in the region (Dixon and Soini, 1977). When comparing these snakes (Table 10.6) with the open formation species of Guiana, it is clear that the resemblance between Iquitos and the three parts of Guiana is small. Within Guiana there is a lower degree of resemblance between the snake faunas of western Guiana and the Brasilian part of Guiana but this is caused by the presence in western Guiana of several species reaching their eastern distribution limits there and in the Brasilian part of Guiana of species reaching their northern distribution limits there, and of species that are known only from the Amazon Basin. However, the data for snakes again are based only on four areas.

The lizards and amphisbaenians ("saurians") appeared to offer the best possibilities for a faunal analysis because there were several places from which representative samples seemed to be present (Tables 10.7–8). However, upon closer examination, it soon turned out that the data were not very reliable. This holds true for the forest lizards and amphisbaenians of Lely Mountains, Paramaribo, and Alto Maraca (Amapá). When compared with the entire region of which they are part, respectively eastern Guiana (twice) and the Brasilian part of Guiana they show resemblance factors of only 0.69, 0.59 and 0.64, respectively. These are hardly more, or even lower, than their respective resemblance factors with the lizard fauna of Belém (0.62, 0.68 and 0.57). For Cayenne the situation seems to be better, when compared with eastern Guiana it shows a resemblance factor of 0.73, but here we should keep in mind that the total number of species reported from this locality also contains old records that possibly refer to specimens that were shipped from Cayenne but actually did not occur there. From the remaining data it is clear that there is a diminishing resemblance westward between the rainforest lizard faunas of Belém and Guianan areas. Within Guiana the resemblance is high, and nowhere is a clear break apparent. The resemblance factor between Belém and Iquitos is slightly higher than that between Iquitos and the different parts of Guiana. Resemblance between Iquitos and western Guiana is smaller than that with the Brasilian part of Guiana. This apparent reversal of expected resemblances is the result of the influence of Amazonian species in the Brasilian part of Guiana and in eastern Guiana. Apparently there is a fairly well-developed barrier southwest of Guiana, separating the lizard faunas of Guiana and upper Amazonia. Again, our knowledge of areas intermediate between Iquitos and Guiana is poor, and the conclusions must be regarded as preliminary. When comparing the savanna lizard faunas of different regions (Table 10.8) we get a very different picture. There is no resemblance with Iquitos, where this category of lizards is completely absent. The agreement between Belem and the different Guianan areas diminishes westward, and there seems to be a break between western Guiana on the one hand and eastern Guiana and the Brasilian part of Guiana on the other. Upon closer examination, this apparent break is caused completely by the presence in western Guiana of a number of altitudinal endemics and of western species just reaching their eastern limits in Guiana. When these species (forming 60% of the savanna lizard fauna) are excluded, there are no breaks for the remaining general savanna lizards within Guiana, neither with Belém. The only break is between Iquitos and Guiana, and this can be completely explained by the absence of suitable savanna habitat in upper Amazonia. As for savanna-inhabiting frogs, the Essequibo-Rio Branco Depression formed no barrier to that part of the savanna inhabitants that had been in the area relatively long. For a number of local savanna endemics it seems to act as such, mainly because those endemics did not have the chance to expand their area of distribution.

On the basis of the data presented in Tables 10.3–8 it can be concluded that for forest inhabitants Guiana seems to be a real herpetogeographic entity well separated from surrounding areas to the southwest and the southeast. Within the area, the Essequibo-Rio Branco Depression forms a barrier for the distribution of a number of eastern forest species to the west and of western forest species to the east. No such function is present for savanna inhabitants that, with the exception of local endemics, are spread throughout the area. There is no separation to the southeast for savanna-inhabiting species which consequently show a great resemblance with the savanna fauna of northeastern Brasil.

The data do not present any evidence for the recognition of a Guiana Region as defined by Lescure (1977), distinct breaks between eastern Guiana and the Brasilian part of Guiana are nowhere evident.

CONCLUSIONS

The herpetofauna of Guiana, as it is known at present, is a composite fauna with a complex history. A number of endemic species belong to old genera (endemic or with disjunct, relict distributions) that apparently inhabited certain parts of the area since the Cretaceous. Other endemics probably originated in the region during periods of isolation in forest or savanna refuges, which are assumed to have existed during arid and wet phases in the Pleistocene–Holocene, respectively. The most important forest refuge was the Guiana Refuge on the northern slopes of the Tumuc-Humac and Acarai mountains. A less important role was played by the Imerí Refuge in the region of Serra Imerí and Serra da Neblina. The species restricted to higher altitudes survived the arid phases in disjunct forests on the higher slopes of the tepuis, collectively known as Tepui Refuges. During arid phases of the Pleistocene and Holocene the species isolated in the refuges underwent differentiation and depending on the time of their arrival in the area and also on their rates of evolution they differentiated into endemic genera, species, or subspecies.

Although some species show relationships to Andean species, these are not direct and only indicate that both Andean and Guianan species evolved from the same or related lowland species. The Guianan species of *Atractus* (colubrid snakes), *Eleutherodactylus* (leptodactylid frogs) and *Centrolenella* (glass frogs) are in this category. The presence of two species of the Andean teiid lizard genus *Euspondylus* in the Guiana Highlands is the only evidence for a direct link with the Andes. As these species are poorly known from only a few individuals each, their taxonomic position remains uncertain. Therefore, it would be premature to conclude on the basis of this meager evidence that there would have been any invasions of Guiana from the Andes.

A number of species invaded Guiana from the south via a wide belt of cerradolike vegetation, connecting central and northeastern Brasil with southeastern Venezuela, during the last arid phase. When the climate became more humid and the forests expanded, these species were left stranded on the isolated savannas of Guiana, most of them in the east. During this same period a number of savanna-inhabitants from northwestern South America invaded the western part of Guiana, where they exist today as representatives of the llanos fauna. Within Guiana there are differences between the western part, where sandstone tepuis are present, and the eastern part, which generally has a much lower elevation. A number of species (most of them endemic) are restricted to the sandstone region, others (mostly invaders from southern and central Brasil or from the Amazon Valley) occur only in the east. Apparently Guiana has been, and still is being, invaded from the northwest and from the southeast. Within Guiana the Essequibo-Rio Branco Depression seems to have acted as a barrier to the eastern dispersal of western elements and to a lesser extent for the dispersal of eastern elements to the west. The notable exceptions are some of the species from central and southeastern Brasil. Also this depression (and the low coastal area of Amapá) served as corridors into northern Guiana for a number of Amazonian species.

Endemism in the entire region is high in amphibians (52%) but much lower in reptiles (27%). At elevations above 1000 m, only frogs, lizards and snakes occur, endemism for frogs there is 33 percent, for reptiles 24 percent. Endemism for amphibians below 1000 m is 47 percent (frogs only 40%, caecilians only 69%), for reptiles 24 percent. From these data it is clear that although frogs have a high degree of endemism at higher elevations, the amount of endemism in the lowlands is even higher. However, part of this probably results from our still scanty knowledge of this group, of the 83 endemic frogs, 29 (35%) have yet to be named.

ACKNOWLEDGMENTS

Fieldwork in Surinam and Venezuela was supported by grants W956-2, W87-78 and WR87-131 from the Netherlands Foundation for the Advancement of Tropical Research (WOTRO), and by grants from the Royal Dutch Academy of Sciences (Melchior Treub Foundation) and the Treub Society. The photographs were made by Mr E. L. M. van Esch of the Rijksmuseum van Natuurlijke Historie, Leiden, from color slides taken by me. The drawings were made by Mr J. J. A. M. Wessendorp, also of the Rijksmuseum van Natuurlijke Historie. The Spanish text was checked by Dr F. Carrasquer of the Department of Spanish Language of the University of Leiden. Any mistakes are completely my responsibility.

RESUMEN

Limitado por el Orinoco, Brazo Cassiquiare, Rio Negro, el Amazonas y el Atlántico, la Guayana es geológicamente uno de los territorios más antiguos de América del Sur. Su mayor parte viene formado por el escudo guayaní precámbrico, cuya arenisca de Roraima cubre partes del sur de Venezuela y de la Guyana occidental, con restos aislados en la Guyana oriental y en el Surinam central. La altura media no pasa de los 1000 m, pero los restos areniscos pueden alcanzar hasta 3000 m. Debido a su posición aislada y a su elevación relativamente considerable, estas montañas (tepuyes) representan ser como islas subtropicales en un mar o llanura tropical. La exploración biológica de esta altiplanicie guayaní se emprendió a mediados del siglo pasado y se prosigue aún hoy, sin haber explorado más que una pequeña parte de los tepuyes y de una manera suficiente tan sólo su aspecto herpetológico. Dado este estado de cosas, por fuerza hemos de limitarnos a interpretar los datos obtenidos de la herpetofauna de la altiplanicie de la Guayana.

Actualmente se conocen en la Guayana 178 especies de anfibios y 230 reptiles, totalizando así las 408 especies herpetológicas. No se conoce las salamandras. En dicho número se comprenden cinco tortugas marinas, un chacón (Gekkonidae) cosmopolita, cinco especies importadas de las Antillas y tres cuya presencia en la Guayana es de orígen dudoso. El residuo puede clasificarse en cinco grandes grupos—endémicos (38%), amazónicos (37%), de vasta extensión (12%), llegando el límite oriental de su extensión hasta el escudo guayaní (7%) y a la Guayana del Brasil central y sudeste (5%). Si se consideran estos datos aisladamente, referidos a los reptiles y a los anfibios por separado, constatamos diferencias importantes. De los anfibios, el 52 porciento son endémicos, el 30 porciento son amazónicos y el 7 porciento de vasta extensión, mientras que para los reptiles tenemos los siguientes porcentajes—27, 42 y 16, respectivamente. Estas diferencias se explican por el hecho de que los anfibios necesitan para su reproducción agua y esta dependencia los hace más limitados que los reptiles en su capacidad de dispersión.

Noventa y dos especies de anfibios y 59 de reptiles son endémicos de la Guayana, con una pequeña porción fuera de los límites de la región que estamos describiendo. Las especies de los otros grupos pueden formar subespecies endémicas en este territorio (39 subespecies pertenecen a 29 especies). La mayor parte de las especies endémicas se concentran en la parte occidental de la Guayana y pueden clasificarse en endémicos de llanura y de altura, según se hallen por debajo o por encima de los 1000 m de altitud. Aproximadamente el 19 porciento de los anfibios endémicos y el 15 porciento de los reptiles endémicos son de altura, ateniéndonos sólo a la parte occidental. Géneros endémicos tales como *Otophryne* y *Oreophrynella* parecen representar reliquias del joven Terciario, *Stefania* parece representar una radiación reciente y la posición de *Riolama* no queda muy clara. Los géneros endémicos residuales (*Allophryne, Rhinatrema, Peltocephalus, Amapasaurus, Mesobaena*) son endémicos de llanura y su historial está probablemente asociado con el de los refugios de Guayana y de Imerí. Una especie endémica de *Euparkerella* apunta tener alguna relación con las montañas del sudeste brasileño. La "*Hylodes*" *duidensis* que hasta hace poco se creía estaba emparentada con formas del sudeste brasileño, resulta ser bastante diferente y más bien representa una derivación de los eleutherodactylini de llanura. La mayor parte de los endémicos de altura son derivaciones subtropicales de parientes de la llanura tropical. Los endémicos de altura tienen una extensión limitada a uno o varios tepuyes. El orígen de la mayor parte de los endémicos de llanura se explica probablemente por la formación en el pasado de refugios forestales a través de los cambios climáticos del período cuaternario. De esos supuestos refugios en la región es el de la Guayana el más importante, siendo de menor importancia el de Imerí. Estos refugios, separados por la sabana, han procurado en su día una especificación alopátrica en todo un territorio donde hasta hace poco se creía sin barreras ecológicas de importancia.

Las especies amazónicas las tratan otros autores en otros artículos. En todo caso se dividen en cuatro subgrupos. Algunas de estas especies llegan hasta la parte septentrional de la Guayana por la depresión del Essequibo-Río Branco, o siguiendo las formaciones abiertas del Amapá costero y de la Guayana francesa septentrional.

La mayor parte de las especies de vasta extensión son de orígen sudaméricano, y una especie de orígen centroamericano refuerza la hipótesis de los refugios forestales. Las especies que llegan al límite oriental del escudo guayaní son de orígen mixto y vienen tratadas en otros capítulos.

Las especies del Brasil central y sudeste que llegan a la Guayana están por lo general presente en la parte oriental y muchas de ellas asociadas a las vegetaciones abiertas. Su extensión es probablemente correlativa a la extensión de las vegetaciones abiertas del último período árido, como lo prueba su existencia en las sabanas actualmente aisladas de la Amazonia.

No parece que haya en la Guayana barreras geográficas de importancia, aunque la depresión del Essequibo-Río Branco ha debido de hacer de barrera a la extensión de ciertas especies de llanura y a no pocas formas de derivación de las de altura. La extensión característica en formas de llanura se debe probablemente, en la mayoría de los casos a la competición ecológica u a otras condiciones particulares del medio ambiente.

LITERATURE CITED

BISSCHOPS, J. H. 1969. The Roraima Formation in Surinam. Verh. K. Ned. Geol. Mijnbouwkd. Genoot. Geol. Ser. 27 109–117.

BOULENGER, G. A. 1895. Description of a new batrachian (Oreophryne Quelchii) discovered by Messrs J. J. Quelch and F. McConnell on the summit of Mt. Roraima. Ann. Mag. Nat. Hist. (6)15 521–522.

BOULENGER, G. A. 1900. Reptiles 53–54, Batrachians 55–56, in LANKESTER, E. R. 1900. Report on a collection made by Messrs F. V. McConnell and J. J. Quelch at Mount Roraima in British Guiana. Trans. Linn. Soc. London Zool. (2)8(2) 51–76.

BROWN, K. S., SHEPPARD, P. M., TURNER, J. R. G. 1974. Quaternary refugia in tropical America. Evidence from race formation in Heliconius butterflies. Proc. Roy. Soc. London B 187 369–378.

CHAPMAN, F. M. 1931. The upper zonal bird-life of Mts. Roraima and Duida. Bull. Amer. Mus. Nat. Hist. 63 1–135.

CRUMP, M. L. 1971. Quantitative analysis of the ecological distribution of a tropical herpetofauna. Univ. Kansas Mus. Nat. Hist. Occas. Pap. (3) 1–62.

CUNHA, O. R. DA 1961. II. Lacertílios da Amazônia. Os lagartos da Amazônia brasileira com especial referência aos representados na coleção do Museo Goeldi. Bol. Mus. Paraense Emílio Goeldi Nova Ser. Zool. (39) 1–189.

DESCAMPS, M., GASC, J. P., LESCURE, J., SASTRE, C. 1978. Étude des écosystèmes guyanais. II. Données biogéographiques sur la partie orientale des Guyanes. C. R. Séances Soc. Biogeogr. 467 55–82.

DIXON, J. R., SOINI, P. 1975. The reptiles of the upper Amazon Basin, Iquitos Region, Peru. I. Lizards and amphisbaenians. Contrib. Biol. Geol. Milwaukee Publ. Mus. (4) 1–58.

DIXON, J. R., SOINI, P. 1977. The reptiles of the upper Amazon Basin, Iquitos Region, Peru. II. Crocodilians, Turtles and snakes. Ibid. (12) 1–91.

DUELLMAN, W. E. 1965. A biogeographic account of the herpetofauna of Michoacan, México. Univ. Kansas Mus. Nat. Hist. Misc. Publ. 15 627–709.

DUELLMAN, W. E. 1966. The Central American herpetofauna. An ecological perspective. Copeia 1966(4) 700–719.

FITTKAU, E. J. 1974. Zur ökologischen Gliederung Amazoniens. I. Die erdgeschichtliche Entwicklung Amazoniens. Amazoniana 5 77–134.

GANSSER, A. 1954. The Guiana Shield (South America). Eclogae Geol. Helv. 47 77–117.

GLEASON, H. A. 1931. Botanical results of the Tyler-Duida Expedition. Bull. Torrey Bot. Club 58 277–506.

HAAS, F. 1957. Zur Tiergeographie von Amazonien und dem Guayana Schild. Mitt. Naturforsch. Ges. Bern 14 59–64.

HAFFER, J. 1969. Speciation in Amazonian forest birds. Science 165 131–137.

HAFFER, J. 1974. Avian speciation in tropical South America. With a systematic survey of the toucans (Rhamphastidae) and jacamars (Galbulidae). Publ. Nuttal Ornithol. Club, Cambridge (11) 1–390.

HILLS, T. L. 1969. The savanna landscapes of the Amazon Basin. Savanna Res. Ser. Dep. Geogr. McGill Univ. Montreal, (14) 1–38.

HOOGMOED, M. S. 1973. Notes on the herpetofauna of Surinam IV. The lizards and amphisbaenians of Surinam. Biogeographica 4 1–419.

LANCINI, A. R. 1968. El género Fuspondylus (Sauria, Teiidae) en Venezuela. Publ. Occas. Mus. Cienc. Nat. Zool. (12) 1–8.

LESCURE, J. 1975. Biogéographie et écologie des Amphibiens de Guyane Française. C. R. Séances Soc. Biogeogr. 440 68–82.

LESCURE, J. 1977. Diversité des origines biogéographiques chez les Amphibiens de la région guyanaise. Publ. Lab. Zool. École Normale Supér. 9 53–65.

MAGUIRE, B. 1945. Notes on the geology and geography of Tafelberg, Suriname. Geogr. Rev. 35 563–579.

MAGUIRE, B. 1955. Cerro de la Neblina, Amazonas, Venezuela. A newly discovered sandstone mountain. Ibid. 45 27–51.

MAGUIRE, B. 1970. On the flora of the Guayana highland. Biotropica 2 85–100.

MAYR, E., PHELPS, W. H., JR 1967. The origin of the bird fauna of the South Venezuelan Highlands. Bull. Amer. Mus. Nat. Hist. 136 269–328.

McDIARMID, R. W. 1971. Comparative morphology and evolution of frogs of the Neotropical genera Atelopus, Dendrophryniscus, Melanophryniscus, and Oreophrynella. Nat. Hist. Mus. Los Angeles Cty. Sci. Bull. (12) 1–66.

MULLER, P. 1973. The dispersal centres of terrestrial vertebrates in the Neotropical realm. A study in the evolution of the Neotropical biota and its native landscapes. Biogeographica 2 1–244.

NOTT, D. 1975. Into the lost world. A descent into prehistoric time. Prentice-Hall, Englewood Cliffs, N.J., 186 p.

OLDENBURGER, F H F, NOROL, R, RIEZEBOS, H T 1973 Ecological investigations on the vegetation of the Sipaliwini-savanna area (Southern Surinam) 1-51 (Mimeographed)

OREJAS MIRANDA, B, QUESADA, A 1976 Ecosistemas frágiles Ciencia Interamericana 17 9-15

PABA-SILVA, F VAN DER HAMMEN, T 1960 Sobre la geologia de la parte sur de la Macarena Bol Geol Bogotá 6 7-30

PRANCE, G T 1973 Phytogeographic support for the theory of Pleistocene forest refuges in the Amazon Basin, based on evidence from distribution patterns in Caryocaraceae, Chrysobalanaceae, Dichapetalaceae and Lecythidaceae Acta Amazonica 3 5-28

PRIEM, H N A, BOELRIJK, N, HEBEDA, E, VERDURMEN, L, VERSCHURE R 1973 Age of the Precambrian Roraima Formation in northeastern South America Evidence from isotopic dating of Roraima pyroclastic rocks in Surinam Geol Soc Amer Bull 84 1677-1684

REINKE, R 1962 Das Klima Amazoniens PhD Dissert Univ Tubingen, 101 p

RIVERO, J A 1961 Salientia of Venezuela Bull Mus Comp Zool Harvard Univ 126 1-207

RIVERO, J A 1965 (1964) The distribution of Venezuelan frogs V The Venezuelan Guayana Caribb J Sci 4 411-420

RIVERO, J A 1966 Notes on the genus *Cryptobatrachus* (Amphibia, Salientia) with the description of a new race and four new species of a new genus of hylid frogs Ibid 6 137-149

RIVERO, J A 1967a Anfibios coleccionados por la expedición Franco-Venezolana al Alto Orinoco 1951-1952 Ibid 7 145-154

RIVERO, J A 1967b A new race of *Otophryne robusta* Boulenger (Amphibia, Salientia) from the Chimanta-Tepui of Venezuela Ibid 7 155-158

RIVERO, J A 1968a A new species of *Llosia* (Amphibia, Salientia) from Mt Duida, Venezuela Amer Mus Novit (2334) 1-9

RIVERO, J A 1968b Los centrolénidos de Venezuela (Amphibia, Salientia) Mem Soc Cienc Nat La Salle 28 301-334

RIVERO, J A 1968c A new species of *Eleutherodactylus* (Amphibia, Salientia) from the Guyana region, Edo Bolívar, Venezuela Breviora (306) 1-11

RIVERO, J A 1968d A new species of *Hyla* (Amphibia, Salientia) from the Venezuelan Guayana Ibid (307) 1-5

RIVERO, J A 1970 On the origin, endemism and distribution of the genus *Stefania* Rivero (Amphibia, Salientia) with a description of a new species from southeastern Venezuela Bol Soc Venezolana Cienc Nat 28 456-481

RIVERO, J A 1971 Notas sobre los anfibios de Venezuela I Sobre los hílidos de la guayana venezolana Caribb J Sci 11 181-193

ROMARIZ, D A 1974 Aspectos da vegetação do Brasil Instituto Brasileiro de Geografia e Estatística, Diretoria técnica, Rio de Janeiro, 126 p

ROZE, J A 1958a Resultados zoologicos de la expedición de la Universidad Central de Venezuela a la región del Auyantepui en la Guayana venezolana Abril de 1956 5 Los reptiles del Auyantepui, Venezuela, basandose en las colecciones de las expediciones de Phelps-Tate, del American Museum of Natural History, 1937-1938, y de la Universidad Central de Venezuela, 1956 Acta Biol Venez 2 243-270

ROZE, J A 1958b Los reptiles del Chimantá tepui (Estado Bolívar, Venezuela) colectados por la expedición botánica del Chicago Natural History Museum Ibid 2 299-314

SILVERSTONE P A 1975 A revision of the poison-arrow frogs of the genus *Dendrobates* Wagler Nat Hist Mus Los Angeles Cty Sci Bull 21 1-55

TATE, G H H 1928 The Lost World of Mount Roraima The account of an expedition to a strange and little known flat-topped mountain in the heart of the South American jungle Nat Hist 28 318-328

TATE, G H H 1930a Notes on the Mount Roraima region Geogr Rev 20 53-68

TATE G H H 1930b Through Brazil to the summit of Mount Roraima Natl Geogr Mag 58 584-605

TATE, G H H 1932 Life zones at Mount Roraima Ecology 13 235-257

TATE, G H H 1938a Auyantepui Notes on the Phelps Venezuelan expedition Geogr Rev 28 452-474

TATE G H H 1938b A new "Lost World" Nat Hist 12 107-120, 153

TATE, G H H 1939 The mammals of the Guiana Region Bull Amer Mus Nat Hist 76 151-229

TATE, G H H, HITCHCOCK, C B 1930 The Cerro Duida Region of Venezuela Geogr Rev 20 31-52

TODD W E C, CARRIKER, M A, JR 1922 The birds of the Santa Marta region of Colombia A study in altitudinal distribution Ann Carnegie Mus 14 3-611

VAN DER HAMMEN, T 1974 The Pleistocene changes of vegetation and climate in tropical South America J Biogeogr 1 3-26

VANZOLINI, P E 1970a Zoologia sistematica, geografia e origem das especies Univ Sao Paulo, Inst Geografia Tese Monogr 3 1-56

VANZOLINI, P E 1970b Unisexual *Cnemidophorus lemniscatus* in the Amazonas valley a preliminary note (Sauria, Teiidae) Pap Avul Zool (Sao Paulo) 23 63-68

WARREN, A N 1973 Roraima Report of the 1971 British expedition to Mount Roraima in Guyana, South America Private publication, Oxford, 152 p

APPENDIX

APPENDIX 10 1—Altitudinal and geographical distribution of amphibians and reptiles in Guiana. Habitats: A = aquatic, D = dry forest, E = forest edge situations, M = marine, Mf = montane forest, P = peranthropic, R = rainforest, S = savanna and other open vegetation like swamps, Sa = saxicolous, X = unknown. Type of distribution: Ab = Amazon basin, Ad = Disjunct amazonian, Ae = Highland endemics, Am = Amazonian, Ap = Peripheral amazonian, Car = Caribbean, Cos = Cosmopolitan, Ea = Eastern hmt, Le = Lowland endemics, Sb = Southern Brasil, Unc = Uncertain, W = Widespread. Species noted by ° are endemic.

Species	Elevation (m)	Eastern Guiana	Western Guiana	Brasilian part of Guiana	Western and Central Venezuela	Amazonian Colombia	Amazonian Ecuador	Upper Amazonian Brasil	Amazonian Peru	Amazonian Bolivia	Type of distribution
Anurans											
Pipa aspera°	0-860	AR	AR	AR							Le
Pipa pipa	0-90	ARS	ARS			A	A	A	A	A	Am
Colostethus beebei°	0-490	R	R								Le
Colostethus brunneus	0-1524	R	R	R				R			Am
Colostethus degranvillei°	80-680										Le
Colostethus shrevei	457-1828		Mf				X	X			Ap
Colostethus sp 'A'°	701-2133		Mf			X					Lr
Colostethus sp 'B'°	1700		X								Ae
Dendrobates azureus°	315-430	R									Le
Dendrobates leucomelas°	50-800	R	DMf			X					Le
Dendrobates quinquevittatus	14-200	R		R		R	R	R	R		Ab
Dendrobates steyermarki°	600-1200		R								Lr
Dendrobates tinctorius°	0-610	R									Le
Phyllobates femoralis	14-610	R	R	R		R	R	R	R		Am
Phyllobates pictus	6-250	R	R	R		R	R	R	R	R	Am
Phyllobates pulchripectus°	120-310	R		R							Le
Phyllobates trivittatus	20-680	R	R			R		R	R		Am
Rana palmipes	0-457	R	R	R	R	R	R	R	R		W
Adenomera andreae	0-1234	R	R	R		R	R	R	R	R	Am
Adenomera hylaedactylus	0-500	R	R	R		R	R	R	R	R	Am
Adenomera lutzi°	± 450	R	X			X	X				Le
Ceratophrys calcarata	90		S			R		R	R		Ea
Ceratophrys cornuta	50-700	R	R	R		R					Am
Eleutherodactylus chiastonotus°	0-700	R	R	R							Le
Eleutherodactylus gutturalis°	30-310	R		R							Le
Eleutherodactylus marmoratus	180-700	R					R				Le
Eleutherodactylus lacrimosus	0-310	R		R			R	R			Ad
Eleutherodactylus marmoratus°	30-1463	R	RMf	R							Le
Eleutherodactylus pluvicanus°	1400		E		E						Ae
Fleutherodactylus terchi	0		E								Car
Lleutherodactylus vilarsi	1234		Mf			R			R		Fa
Eleutherodactylus zeuctotylus	0-700	R	R								Ap
Eleutherodactylus sp 'A'°	90-1463	R	R						R		Lr
Euparkerella sp "A"°	914		Mf								Le

APPENDIX 10.1—Altitudinal and geographical distribution of amphibians and reptiles in Guiana (continued)

Species	Elevation (m)	Eastern Guiana	Western Guiana	Brasilian part of Guiana	Western and Central Venezuela	Amazonian Colombia	Amazonian Ecuador	Upper Amazonian Brasil	Amazonian Peru	Amazonian Bolivia	Type of distribution
Hydrolaetare schmidti	0–80	A									Ab
'*Hylodes*' *duidensis*°	1402		R								Ae
Leptodactylus bolivianus	0–650	RES	RES	RES	RES	RES	RE	RE	RE	RE	W
Leptodactylus fuscus	0–1215	S	S	S	S	?		S		S	Sb
Leptodactylus longirostris	0–1340	S	S	S	S	S		S	?	?	Am
Leptodactylus macrosternum	240–305	S	R	S	S	R	R	S	R	S	Am
Leptodactylus mystaceus	0–700	R	RE	R	E	R	X	R	X	R	Am
Leptodactylus pentadactylus	0–500	RE	RE	R		R	R	R	X	X	W
Leptodactylus rhodomystax	0–650	R		R		R	R	R	R		Ap
Leptodactylus rugosus°	90–1368		Sa	Sa		Sa	RSa				Le
Leptodactylus stenodema	180–700	RSa		RSa		RSa	R				Am
Leptodactylus wagneri	0–1250	R	R	R	R	R	R	R	R	R	Am
Leptodactylus sp "A"°	100	Sa									Le
Leptodactylus sp "B"	0–620	R	?	?		?	?	?	?	?	Am
Leptodactylus sp "C"°	90		D								Le
Lithodytes lineatus	0–240	R	R	R		R	R	R	R		Am
Physalaemus ephippifer	75–300	SE	SE		S						Ea
Physalaemus ephippifer	30–240	R		R							Am
Physalaemus petersi	0–206	R		R		R	R		R		Ab
Physalaemus pustulosus	0–305		S		S						Ea
Pleurodema brachyops	0–305	S	S		S						Ea
Pseudopaludicola pusilla	50–240	R	S		S						Ea
Atelopus flavescens°	10–70	R									Le
Atelopus franciscus°	5	R									Le
Atelopus pulcher	80–600	R	R	R			R	R	R		Ap
Atelopus sp "A"°	0–206	R									Le
Bufo ceratophrys	?–1234		R			X	X		S		Ap
Bufo granulosus	0–1290	S	S	S	S	S		S	S		W
Bufo guttatus	30–900	RSa	RE	R		R	R	S	S	S	Ap
Bufo marinus	0–1290	SE	SE	SE	SE	SE	SE	SE	SE	SE	W
Bufo nasicus°	500–1350		R	R		R	R		R	R	Le
Bufo typhonius	0–1219	R	R	R	R	R	R	R	R	R	W
Bufo sp "A"°	0–206	R	R	R		R		R	R		Le
Bufo sp "B"°	0–300	R	R	R		R?	R	R	?		Am
Dendrophryniscus minutus	170	R	R	S							Am
Melanophryniscus moreirae	20		Mf								Sb
Oreophrynella macconnelli°	1067										Ae
Oreophrynella quelchii°	2590		S								Ae
Oreophrynella sp "A"°	2400		S								Ae
Allophryne ruthveni°	10–200	R	R								Le

APPENDIX 10 1—Altitudinal and geographical distribution of amphibians and reptiles in Guiana (continued)

Species	Elevation (m)	Eastern Guiana	Western Guiana	Brasilian part of Guiana	Western and Central Venezuela	Amazonian Colombia	Amazonian Ecuador	Upper Amazonian Brasil	Amazonian Peru	Amazonian Bolivia	Type of distribution
Aparasphenodon venezolanus	90		X								Le
Hyla baumgardneri	0–609		SD	S							Am
Hyla benitezi°	800–1700		SaMf								Le
Hyla boans	0–1216	R	R	R	R	R	R	R	R	R	W
Hyla boesemani°	0–650	S	S	S		R	R	R	R		Le
Hyla brevifrons	0–90	R		R		R	R	X	√		Ad
Hyla calcarata	0–200	R				R	R	X	R		Am
Hyla creptans	0–1420	S	S	S	S	S		R	R	R	W
Hyla egleri	0–240	SE	E	E							Am
Hyla fasciata	80–200	R					R	R	R	R	Am
Hyla fuentei°	20	S									Le
Hyla garbei	90–100	S				S	S	S	S		Ea
Hyla geographica	0–305	F	E	E	E	E	E	E	E	E	Am
Hyla gmesi°	610–1113		Mf								Le
Hyla grandisonae°	low		X								Lc
Hyla granosa	0–200	RE	RE	RE		RE	RL	RL	RE	RE	Am
Hyla helenae°	10	R	Mf								Le
Hyla kanaima°	700–1163		RMf								Le
Hyla lemai°	929–1400		Mf								Le
Hyla leucophyllata	20–650	RE	RE	RE		RE	RE	RE	RE	RE	Am
Hyla mamorata	0–600	F	E	E		E	E	E	E		Ap
Hyla microcephala	0–305		S		S	S					W
Hyla minuscula°	0–305	S	S	S	S						Le
Hyla minuta	0–1700	S	S	S	S						Am
Hyla multifasciata°	0–1290	SE	SE	SE							Lr
Hyla nana	0–20	S		S						S	Sb
Hyla ornatissima°	90–180	R	R	R							Le
Hyla proboscidea°	200–600										Le
Hyla punctata	0–20	S	S	S	S				S	S	Am
Hyla ranceps	0–10	S									Sb
Hyla rodriguezi°	1210–1400										Ae
Hyla rostrata	0–20	S	SMf			S					Ea
Hyla rubra	0–140	S	S	S	S				R		W
Hyla sencula	30	R	S								Sb
Hyla sibleszi°	900–1706		Mf								Lc
Hyla surinamensis°?	?										Le
Hyla x-signata	0–305	X		S							Le
Hyla sp "A"°	1102–1163	S	S								Sb
Hyla sp "B"°	1463		Mf								Ae
Hyla sp "C"°	130		Mf								Au
Hyla sp "D"°	0–240	R									Le
		S									Le

APPENDIX 10 1—Altitudinal and geographical distribution of amphibians and reptiles in Guiana (continued)

Species	Elevation (m)	Eastern Guiana	Western Guiana	Brasilian part of Guiana	Western and Central Venezuela	Amazonian Colombia	Amazonian Ecuador	Upper Amazonian Brasil	Amazonian Peru	Amazonian Bolivia	Type of distribution
Hyla sp E°	130	R									Le
Hyla sp "T"°	0	S									Le
Hyla sp C°	100–650	R									Le
Hyla sp "H"°	1210	S									Ae
Hyla sp I°	1700										Ae
Hyla sp J"°	?		S								Le
Hyla sp K°	240–305	S	X								Le
Hyla sp "L"°	0–240	L	S								Le
Hyla sp M°	110	E									Le
Hyla sp "N"°	140–210	E									Le
Hyla sp O°	1250–1290	SE	SE								Ae
Osteocephalus buckleyi	20–1102	R	R	R		R	R	R	R	R	Am
Osteocephalus leprieuri	0–2400	R	R			R	R	R	R		Ap
Osteocephalus taurinus	10–1250	RE	R	R		R	R	R	R	R	Am
Osteocephalus sp "A"°	200	R									Le
Phrynohyas coriacea	0	X						R	R		Ap
Phrynohyas resinifictrix°	10–90	R									Le
Phrynohyas venulosa	0–1231	SE	SE	R	SE	SE	SE	SF	SE	SE	W
Phyllomedusa bicolor	10–650	RES	RES	SE		RES	RES	RES	RES		Ap
Phyllomedusa hypocondrialis	0–650	ES	ES	RES		ES	ES	ES	ES	ES	Am
Phyllomedusa tomopterna	20–650	R		ES			R	R	R		Ea
Phyllomedusa trinitatis	0–200		RE								Am
Phyllomedusa vaillanti	0–650	R	R	R		R	R	R	R	R	Am
Sphaenorhynchus eurhostus	0–305	S	S	S		S		S			Am
Stefania evansi	10–1402		RMf								Le
Stefania ginesi°	2223		SSa								Ae
Stefania goini°	1402		X								Ae
Stefania marahuaquensis°	600–1200		Mf								Ae
Stefania scalae°	970–1200		Mf								Le
Stefania woodleyi°	700		RMf								Le
Stefana sp "A"°	1402		Mf								Ae
Stefana sp "B"°	1700		S								Ae
Stefana sp "C"°	2400		SSa								Ae
Lysapsus limellus	90–890	S	S	S					S	S	Sb
Pseudis paradoxus	0–550	R		S						S	Sb
Centrolenella fleischmanni	200	R			R	R					Ea
Centrolenella geyskesi°	200	R									Le
Centrolenella oyampiensis°	90										Le
Centrolenella pulidoi°	610		Mf								Le
Centrolenella taylori°	200–1320	R	RMf								Le

APPENDIX 10.1—Altitudinal and geographical distribution of amphibians and reptiles in Guiana (continued)

Species	Elevation (m)	Eastern Guiana	Western Guiana	Brasilian part of Guiana	Western and Central Venezuela	Amazonian Colombia	Amazonian Ecuador	Upper Amazonian Brasil	Amazonian Perú	Amazonian Bolivia	Type of distribution
Centrolenella sp "A"°	1234	X									Ae
Centrolenella sp B°	120–200	R									Le
Chasmocleis hudsoni°	200–240	R						R			Le
Ctenophryne geayi	0–300	R	R					R	R		Am
Elachistocleis ovalis	0–110	S	S	S	S	R		S	S	S	Am
Hamptophryne boliviana	0–1066	R	R			S	?	R	R	R	Am
Otophryne robusta°	0–240	SaR	SaMf	SaR							Le
Relictivomer pearsei	200–1981	S	S			X					EL
Synapturanus mirandaribeiroi°	20–1210	R	R	R		S		R			Le
Caecilians											
Epicrionops niger°	660										Le
Rhinatrema bivittatum°	20–300	R	R	R							Le
Potomotyphlus kaupii	0–50	A	A	A		A	A	A	A		Am
Typhlonectes compressicauda°	0–40	A	A	X							Le
Brasilotyphlus braziliensis°	40			R							Le
Caecilia gracilis	0–106	R	R								Am
Caecilia pressula°	250		V						X		Le
Caecilia tentaculata	0–250	R	R		R	R	R	R	R		W
Microcaecilia rabei°	100–400	R	R								Le
Microcaecilia unicolor°	0–690	R	R								Le
Microcaecilia sp "A"°	250										Le
Oscaecilia zweifeli°	50	A	A								Le
Siphonops annulatus	0–?	X	X	X	X	X	X	X	X	X	Am
Chelonians											
Caretta caretta	0	M	M								Cos
Chelonia mydas	0	M	M								Cos
Eretmochelys imbricata	0	M	M								Cos
Lepidochelys olivacea	0	M	M								Cos
Dermochelys coriacea	0	M	M								Cos
Kinosternon scorpioides	0–690	A	A	A	A	A	A	A	A	A	W
Testudo carbonaria	0–300	SR	SR	S	S	S		S	S	S	Am
Testudo denticulata	0–650	R	R	R	R	R		R	R	R	Am
Rhinoclemys punctularia	0–240	SAR	SAR	SAR	SAR	SAR	SAR				La
Peltocephalus tracaxus	0–100	SA	SA	SA				?			Ab
Podocnemis dumeriliana	0–100	A	A	?				A	A		Am
Podocnemis expansa	0–100	A	A	A		A		A	A		Am
Podocnemis erythrocephala	20–100			A		A		A			Am
Chelus fimbriatus	0–100	A	A	A		A	A	A	A	P	Ab
Phrynops geoffroanus	0–305			A		A	?		A	A	Sb
Phrynops gibbus	0–229	RA	A	A		SAR	A		RA		Ap

APPENDIX 10 1—Altitudinal and geographical distribution of amphibians and reptiles in Guiana (continued)

Species	Elevation (m)	Eastern Guiana	Western Guiana	Brazilian part of Guiana	Western and Central Venezuela	Amazonian Colombia	Amazonian Ecuador	Upper Amazonian Brasil	Amazonian Peru	Amazonian Bolivia	Type of distribution
Phrynops nasutus	10–80	A	A	A	-	A	A	A	A	A	Ap
Platemys platycephala	0–650	RA	RA	RA	-	A	A	A	A	?	Am
Crocodilians											
Crocodylus intermedius	0–100	A	A	A	A	A					Le
Caiman crocodilus	0–650	RAS	A	A	A	A	A	A	A	A	W
Paleosuchus palpebrosus	0–240	RAE	A	A		RA	A	A	A		Am
Paleosuchus trigonatus	100–300	RAE	A	A		RA	-	A	A	A	Am
Melanosuchus niger	0–200	A	A	A		A	A	A	A		Ab
Snakes											
Liotyphlops incertus	?	X			-	-					Le
Typhlophis squamosus	?	X	X	X	X						Am
Leptotyphlops amazonicus	90–160	R	S								Le
Leptotyphlops collaris	0–475										Le
Leptotyphlops cupinensis	650	R		R							Sb
Leptotyphlops dimidiatus	20	S	S	S							Le
Leptotyphlops macrolepis	0–200	R	X	X	X	X					Ea
Leptotyphlops septemstriatus	20–850	R	R	R					X		Le
Leptotyphlops tenella	0–496	R	X	R					?		Am
Leptotyphlops sp A	?		X	X			?	R	?		Am
Typhlops brongersmianus	0–500	R	R	R		R	R	R	R	R	Am
Typhlops lumbricalis	0										Car
Typhlops reticulatus	0–100	R	R	R	R	?	?	R	?	?	Am
Typhlops trinitatus	0	X	X								Le
Amlus scytale	0–2100	R	R	R		R	R	R	R	R	Am
Boa constructor	0–240	RES	RES	RES	RES	RES	RES	RES	RES	RES	W
Corallus caninus	0–100	R	R	R		R	R	R	R	R	Am
Corallus enydris	0–200	RES	RES	RES	RES	RES	RES	RES	RES	RES	W
Epicrates cenchria	0–1000	RES	RES	RES	RES	RES	RES	RES	RES	RES	W
Eunectes murinus	0–240	RAS	RAS	RAS	RAS	RAS	RAS	RAS	RAS	RAS	Am
Dipsas catesbyi	0–200	R	R	R		R	R	R	R	R	Am
Dipsas copei	0–200	X									Le
Dipsas indica	0–150	R	R	R		R	R	R	R	R	Am
Dipsas pavonina	0–200	R	R								Am
Dipsas variegata	0–100	X	R								Am
Sibon nebulata	0–890	RE	RE	RE		X	X		X		W
Apostolepis crucifer	0										Ea
Apostolepis quinquelineata	140–500	?									Unc
Atractus badius		R	R								Le
Atractus dudenensis	0–240	R	R			X	X	X	E	X	Am
Atractus elaps	2050–2133		X			X	X	X	R		At
	200		X			X	X	X	R		Ea

APPENDIX 10 1—Altitudinal and geographical distribution of amphibians and reptiles in Guiana (continued)

Species	Elevation (m)	Eastern Guiana	Western Guiana	Brasilian part of Guiana	Western and Central Venezuela	Amazonian Colombia	Amazonian Ecuador	Upper Amazonian Brasil	Amazonian Peru	Amazonian Bolivia	Type of distribution
Atractus favae°	0–20	X									Le
Atractus insipidus°	400		X								Le
Atractus latifrons	140	R	X			X	X	X	R		Ap
Atractus major	200					X	X	X	E		Ea
Atractus micheli°	0	X									Le
Atractus riveroi°	1000–2000	S	S								Ae
Atractus styrmaki	200–2160	X	X								Le
Atractus torquatus	0–240	R	R	X		X	X	X	?	X	Am
Atractus tulmcatus°	0	R	R								Le
Atractus sp "A"°	150–500	X									Le
Chironius bicarinatus	?	RE	RE	RE	RE	RE	RE	RE	RE		Sb
Chironius carinatus	0–1050	S	?	?						RE	W
Chironius cinnamomeus°	20	R	R	R							Le
Chironius cochranae°	0–240	RES	RES	RES	RES	RES	RES	RES	RES	RES	Lr
Chironius fuscus	0–2250	RES	RES	R	R	RES	R	R	R		W
Chironius scurulus	40	RS									Ab
Chironius sp "A"°	20–200	RES	RES	RES	X	X	X	X	ES	X	Le
Cleha cleha	0–500			S						S	W
Cyclagras gigas	0	R	R	R	R	R	R	R	R		Sb
Dendrophidion dendrophis	0–490	RE	RE	RE	R	R	R	R	RE	RE	W
Drepanoides anomalus	0–230	RE	RE	RE		RE	RE	RE	RE	RE	Ap
Drymarchon corais	0–240	R	R	R		R	R	R	R		W
Drymobius rhombifer	0–240	R	R	R		R	R	R	R		Ea
Dryocaluber dichrous	0–500	R									Ap
Elapomorphus quinquelineatus	0	Y									Sb
Erythrolamprus aesculapii	0–240	R	R	R	R	R	R	R	R	R	Am
Erythrolamprus bauperthusii	50				R						Ea
Helicops angulatus	0–100	A	A	A	A	A	A	A	A	A	Am
Helicops hagmanni	40										Ab
Helicops hogei°	?							?			Le
Helicops leopardinus	0		A	A		A	A	A	A	A	Am
Helicops polylepis	?	AS	A	A		A	?	A	RA	A	Ab
Helicops truttatus	?	AS	A	A	A	A	A	A	A	A	Ab
Hydrodynastes bicinctus	0–240	AS		AS		A	A	A	RA		Am
Hydrops martii	0–40	A	A	A		A	A	A	A		Ab
Hydrops triangularis	0–240	RA	A	A	A	A	A	A	RA	A	Am
Imantodes cenchoa	0–1050	R	R	R	R	R	R	R	R	R	W
Imantodes lentiferus	100	R				R	R	R	R		Ap
Leimadophis melanotus	0–890	ES	ES	E	ES	ES	E	E		E	F?
Leimadophis porcelogyrus	?	X									Sb

APPENDIX 10 1.—Altitudinal and geographical distribution of amphibians and reptiles in Guiana (continued)

Species	Elevation (m)	Eastern Guiana	Western Guiana	Brazilian part of Guiana	Western and Central Venezuela	Amazonian Colombia	Amazonian Ecuador	Upper Amazonian Brasil	Amazonian Peru	Amazonian Bolivia	Type of distribution
Leimadophis reginae	0–650	RES	MfRES	RES	RES	RES	RES	RES	RES	RES	W
Leimadophis typhlus	0–210	RE	RE	RE	RE	RE	RE	RE	RE	RE	Am
Leptodeira annulata	0–1250	RES	RES	RES	RES	RES	RES	RES	RES	RES	W
Leptophis ahaetulla	0–240	RES	RES	RES	RES	RES	RES	RES	RES	RES	W
Liophis breviceps	0–500	R				R	R	R	R		Ap
Liophis cananna°	500										Le
Liophis robella	0–40	AES	AES	AES		AES		AES	AES	AES	Am
Liophis nigeri°	1900										Ae
Liophis miliaris	30–1210	RAE	S	RAE						X	Sb
Liophis purpurans°	0–20	X	X								Le
Liophis trebbaui°	1020		Y								Ae
Liophis undulatus	0–20	Y									Ap
Lygophis lineatus	0–1250	S	S	S	S	S	X	X	S	S	W
Mastigodryas bifossatus	50–305	S	S	S	S	S	S	S	S	S	Am
Mastigodryas boddaerti	0–1800	RES	RFS	RES	RES	RES	RES	RES	RLS	RES	Am
Mastigodryas pleei	90–500	S	S		S	S					Ea
Ninia hudsoni	230	R					R				Ap
Oxybelis aeneus	0–500	RES	RES	RES	RES	RES	RES	RES	RES	RES	W
Oxybelis argenteus	0–500	R	R	R		X	X	R	R	R	Am
Oxybelis fulgidus	0–200	RE	R	R		X	X	X	E	X	W
Oxyrhopus petola	0–240	RE	RE	RE	RE	X	X	X	R	X	W
Oxyrhopus trigeminus	20			X							Sb
Oxyrhopus sp. A"°	200										Le
Philodryas olfersii	0–240	S	S	S		S		S	DS	DS	Am
Philodryas viridissimus	0–200	R	R	R		R	R	R	R	R	Am
Phimophis guerini	20	S									Sb
Phimophis guianensis	0–20	S	S		S						Ea
Pseudoboa coronata	0–100	R	R			R	R	R	RE	R	Ap
Pseudoboa neuwiedii	0–500	S	S		S	S		S			Ea
Pseudoeryx plicatilis	0	AS	A	A				A	RA	A	Am
Pseustes poecilonotus	30–490	RE	RE	RE	RE	RE	RE	RE	RE	RE	W
Pseustes sulphureus	0–240	RE	RE	RE		RE		RE	RE	RE	Am
Rhadinea brevirostris	30–210	R	R	R		R		R	R	R	Ab
Rhinobothryum lentiginosum	10–490	R	R					R	R	R	Am
Siphlophis cervinus	0–200	R	RE	R		R	RE	R	R	R	W
Spilotes pullatus	0–90	RE	RE	RE	RE	RE	RE	RE	RE	RL	W
Tantilla melanocephala	0–1200	RE	RES	RE	RE	RE	RE	RE	RE	RE	W
Thamnodynastes chunanta°	2200										Ae
Thamnodynastes pallidus	0–20	S	S		S	S		X	RE		Ap
Thamnodynastes strigilis	0–40	S	S					X			Am
Tripanurgos compressus	90	R	R	R		R	R	R	R	R	W

APPENDIX 10 1—Altitudinal and geographical distribution of amphibians and reptiles in Guiana (continued)

Species	Elevation (m)	Eastern Guiana	Western Guiana	Brasilian part of Guiana	Western and Central Venezuela	Amazonian Colombia	Amazonian Ecuador	Upper Amazonian Brasil	Amazonian Peru	Amazonian Bolivia	Type of distribution
Xenodon neuwiedii	?	X									Sb
Xenodon rabdocephalus	0–250	R	R			R	R	R	R	R	W
Xenodon severus	0–500	RES	RES	RES	RES	RES	RES	RES	RES	RES	Am
Xenodon werneri	80–200	R									Le
Xenopholis scalaris	230	R	R			R	R	R	R		Ap
Leptomicrurus collaris	150–850	R	R								Le
Micrurus averyi	609	R									Le
Micrurus hemprichi	500		R			R	R	R	R	R	Am
Micrurus ibiboboca	30	S									Sb
Micrurus isozonus	50				X	X					Fa
Micrurus lemniscatus	20–400	R	R	R		R	R	R	RS	R	Ap
Micrurus psyches	20–240	R	R			R	R	R			Ap
Micrurus spixii	80		R			R	R	R	R	R	Am
Micrurus surinamensis	30–90	SA	X	X		X	X	λ	A	X	Am
Bothrops atrox	0–1066	RES	RES	RES	RES	RES	RES	RES	RES	RES	Am
Bothrops bilineatus	200–475	R	R	R		R	R	R	R		Am
Bothrops brazili	20–822	R	R	R		R	R	R	R	R	Am
Bothrops castelnaudi	2000		S	S		R	R		R		Am
Crotalus durissus	0–2194	S	S	S	S						W
Lachesis muta	30–200	R	R	R		R	R	R	R	R	W
Lizards											
Coleodactylus amazonicus	0–690	R	R	R				R			Am
Coleodactylus meridionalis	200–800		R								Sb
Gonatodes annularis	100–929	R	R	R							Le
Gonatodes humeralis	0–700	RE	RED	RE		RE	RE	RE	RE	RE	Am
Gonatodes vittatus	?	λ			ES						Le
Hemidactylus mabouia	0–305	ES	ES		ES						Ea
Hemidactylus palaichthus	0–30	EP	EP	EP		EP	EP	EP	EP		Cos
Lepidoblepharis festae	50–550	λ	SSa	R		R	R	R	R		Le
Phyllodactylus dixoni	0–200										Ad
Pseudogonatodes guianensis	90	R	SSa								Le
Sphaerodactylus molei	50–240		RD		E				R		Ap
Thecadactylus rapicauda	0	E	E		E						Ea
	0–490	RE	RE	RE	RLS	RE	RE	RE	RE	RE	W
Anolis aeneus	0		P		S						Car
Anolis auratus	0–1700	S	S	S	S	S	S				W
Anolis chrysolepis	0–2100	R	RMf	R		R	R	R	R		Am
Anolis fuscoauratus	0–1066	RE	RE	RE	RE	RE	RE	RE	RE	RE	Ap
Anolis gibbiceps	?	X	X		λ						Ea
Anolis marmoratus	0–20	P									Car

APPENDIX 10 1.—Altitudinal and geographical distribution of amphibians and reptiles in Guiana (continued)

Species	Elevation (m)	Eastern Guiana	Western Guiana	Brasilian part of Guiana	Western and Central Venezuela	Amazonian Colombia	Amazonian Ecuador	Upper Amazonian Brasil	Amazonian Peru	Amazonian Bolivia	Type of distribution
Anolis ortoni	0–929	RE	RME	RE		RE	RE	RE	RE	RE	Am
Anolis punctatus	0–700	RE	RE	RE		RE	RE	RE	RE		Am
Anolis roquet	0		P		P						Car
Iguana iguana	0–305	REAS	REAS	REAS	REAS	REAS	REAS	REAS	REAS	REAS	W
Plica plica	0–970	R(Sa)	RE(Sa)	R		R	R	R	R	R	Am
Plica umbra	0–690	RE	R	R		R	R	R	R		Am
Polychrus marmoratus	0–1050	L	E	E	E	E	E	E	E	E	Am
Tropidurus bogerti°	1600–2400		SSa	S	S						At
Tropidurus torquatus	20–1020	SSa	SSa	S	S					S	Sb
Uracentron azureum°	0–500	R	R	R							Le
Uranoscodon superciliosa°	?		X		λ						Ea
Mabuya mabouya	0–250	RE	RE	RE							Le
Alopoglossus angulatus	0–490	RES	RES	RFS	RES	RES	RES	RES	RES	RES	W
Anapasaurus tetradactylus°	30–600	R	R	R			R	R	RE		Am
Ameiva ameiva	200										Le
Ameiva bifrontata	0–1150	RES	RES	RES	RES	RES	RES	RES	RES	RES	W
Arthrosaura kocki	50–305	S	S		S	S			S		Ea
Arthrosaura reticulata	0–690	R	R	R		R	R		R		Am
Bachia cophias°	40–2164	R	R	R					R		Ap
Bachia flavescens°	0–1100	R	R	R			R	R	R		Le
Bachia guianensis°	0–1100		R								Le
Bachia parkeri	90–300		RD								Le
Cercosaura ocellata	609	RE	S	RE							Ap
Cnemidophorus lemniscatus	0–305	S	S	S	S	S		R	R	R	Am
Crocodilurus lacertinus	0–90	RA	RA	RA				RA	RAE		Ab
Dracaena guianensis	0–40			RAE				RAE	RAE		Ab
Eusponditus phelpsi°	1700–1917		X								Ae
Eusponditus sp "A"	1450		X								Ae
Guiroplithalmus underwoodi°	0–500	RES	RES	RTS							Le
Iphisa elegans	0–650	R	R	R		R	R	R	R	R	Am
Kentropyx borchianus°	0	S	S								Le
Kentropyx calcaratus	0–1067	RE	RE	RE		RE	RL	RE	E	RE	Am
Kentropyx striatus	0–1420	S	S	S	S	S					Le
Kentropyx williamsoni°	10		λ	λ							Le
Leposoma guianense°	0–823	R	R	R							Le
Leposoma percarnatum°	0–450	RA	R	R							Le
Neusticurus bicarinatus	0–1000	RA	RA	RA				RA			Am
Neusticurus racenisi°	100–1215		X	λ							Le
Neusticurus rudis°	0–1800		RA								Le
Neusticurus tatei°	400–1100	RA	λ								Le

APPENDIX 10.1—Altitudinal and geographical distribution of amphibians and reptiles in Guiana (continued)

Species	Elevation (m)	Eastern Guiana	Western Guiana	Brasilian part of Guiana	Western and Central Venezuela	Amazonian Colombia	Amazonian Ecuador	Upper Amazonian Brasil	Amazonian Peru	Amazonian Bolivia	Type of distribution
Pronodactylus argulus	10–300	R	R	R		R	R	R	RE	R	Am
Ptychoglossus brevifrontalis	200	R					R		R		Ap
Riolama leucosticta°	2621		S	S	-						Ae
Tretioscincus agilis	0–700	R	RD	S			R				Am
Tupinambis nigropunctatus	0–540	RES	RES	RES	RES	RES		RES	RES		Am
Amphisbaenians											
Amphisbaena alba	0–305	RES	RES	RE	RES	RE	RE	RE	RE	RE	W
Amphisbaena fuliginosa	0–490	RES	RES	RES	RES	RES	RES	RES	ES	RES	W
Amphisbaena gracilis°	0			?							Le
Amphisbaena mitchelli	0		\								Unc
Amphisbaena rozei°	500–750		\	R							Le
Amphisbaena slevini°	40										Le
Amphisbaena stenocercer°	0	R									Le
Amphisbaena vanzolinii°	140–250	R		?							Le
Bronia brasiliana	?										Unc
Mesobaena huebneri°	100		\								Le
TOTAL AMPHIBIANS (178)		121	125	70							
TOTAL REPTILES (230)		172	186	135							
TOTAL SPECIES (408)		293	311	205							

11. Origin and Distribution of the Herpetofauna of the Dry Lowland Regions of Northern South America

Carlos Rivero-Blanco and James R. Dixon

Department of Wildlife and Fisheries Sciences
Texas A&M University
College Station, Texas 77843
USA

The lowland open formations of northeastern South America include the llanos of the Orinoco, and the Caribbean arid and semi-arid lowlands (Fig. 11.1). The dry lowlands of the Guianas, are discussed by Hoogmoed (this volume). The area of lowland open formations is large, the llanos of Venezuela alone occupy more than 180,000 km² (Ramia, 1967), and the Caribbean arid and semi-arid lowlands cover some 50,000 km² (Sarmiento, 1976).

These areas are geologically recent. The llanos of Colombia and Venezuela emerged during the Pleistocene and developed with the contribution of Andean sediments. The coastal desert areas were highly influenced by sea level oscillations during the same period, most of it is sedimentary in origin (Dirección de Geología, MMH, 1969). Although the topography of these areas varies, the dominant flat-land physiography is conspicuous throughout.

Climatic conditions vary considerably, but some general trends are noted. Annual rainfall maxima vary from 1000 to 2000 mm but the dry periods are usually six months or longer (Ewell and Madriz, 1968). Mean annual temperatures for the area are above 24°C (Ewell and Madriz, 1968).

Data pertaining to amphibian and reptile distributions were obtained from Cochran and Goin (1970), Dunn (1957), Medem (1968) and Ruthven (1922) for Colombia, Donoso-Barros (1968), Roze (1966), Rivero (1961), and Staton and Dixon (1977) for Venezuela. We utilized a number of publications denoting the ranges of individual species, but they are too numerous to mention here. Gorzula and Hoogmoed (pers. comm.) provided us with a list of amphibian and reptile species for the El Manteco region of the southeastern llanos of Venezuela.

VEGETATION

The llanos are extremely diverse and contain many habitat types: different forest associations, various types of savannas, and the ever-changing aquatic habitats along with subtle topographic features. This diversity makes it difficult to understand the llanos without collating the geologic, topographic, floristic, faunistic, edaphic, pyric, climatic and human intervention factors. In order to better understand such diversity and the characteristics of the reptilian and amphibian faunas one must refer to Beard's (1953) and Ramia's (1967) comprehensive works on the Neotropical savannas.

The herpetofauna of the llanos of the Orinoco and the Caribbean arid and semi-arid lowlands encounters a wide range of environments in the form of swift gradients. The rainfall patterns vary from almost six months of rain in the llanos to almost no rain in the coastal deserts. Vegetation provides abundant and (in some places) continuous shade in the llanos, but vegetation is sparse in the drier areas.

The following description of plant communities is based on Ramia (1967), Sarmiento (1976), and our own familiarity with the area. These habitat types fall within more generalized climatic types or life zones that have been proposed for by the area by Ewell and Madriz (1968) and Walter and Medina (1971).

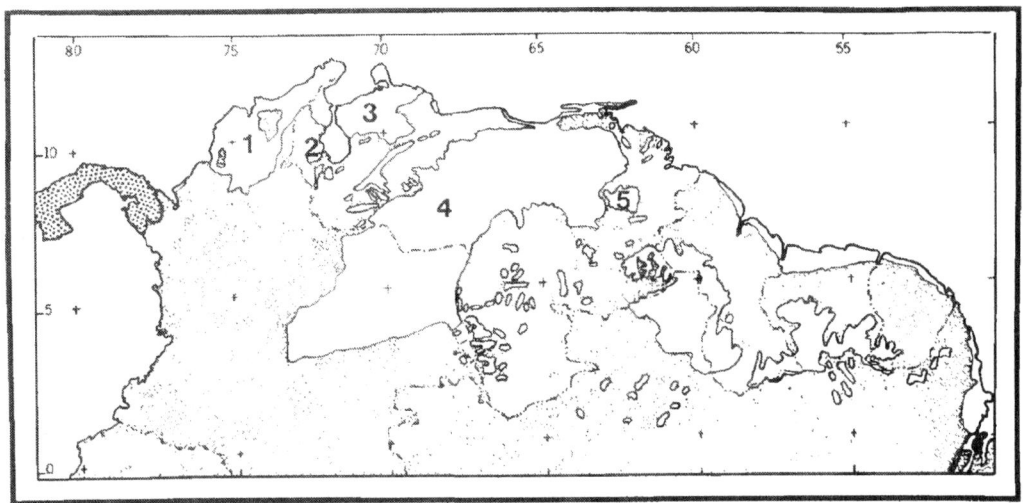

Fig. 11:1. The open savannas and hot, dry lowland regions of northern South America (after Hueck, 1966). Stippled areas are forests and mountains; heavily dotted area is part of Panamá excluded from the study. Numbers indicate locality zones in Appendix 11:1.

Sabanas abiertas y regiones de tierra baja seca y caliente del Norte de Sur América. Las Areas punteadas son bosques y montañas, y la zona con puntos gruesos es parte de Panamá, que no se incluye en el estudio. Los números indican zonas de localidad en el anexo 11:1.

Tropical Dry Forest

In northern Venezuela and Colombia this zone extends between sea level and 400 to 1000 m. The mean annual rainfall is 1000 to 1800 mm, and the mean temperature usually is above 24°C. The rainfall pattern is biseasonal with well-marked dry and wet seasons. Generally, the rainy season occurs between April and November.

Deciduous forest, matas and gallery forest.—These forests are characterized by two stories (Fig. 11:2-3). They have rather thick lower strata and an almost continuous canopy that covers about 66 percent of the surface area (Veillon, 1963). Three major types can be defined on the basis of physical characteristics: 1) continuous and extensive forest—of secondary origin in many areas owing to human intervention; 2) "Mata"—forested "islands" surrounded by savanna; and 3) gallery forests—associated with a variety of waterways, where the water content of the soil seems to be rather constant throughout the year.

Palmares.—The central llanos of Venezuela exhibit a unique physiognomy in the form of almost pure stands of the "Palma Llanera," *Copernicia tectorum* (Fig. 11:4). This plant forms associations with deciduous forests and the "espinal" (thorn thicket) or exists in pure, somewhat sparse stands in the savanna or as dense stands in flood savannas. The Estero de Camaguán in southern Estado Guarico is typical in that almost pure stands of the palm, *Copernicia*, can withstand both long and severe droughts and long floods with water levels up to depths of 1 m. In these savannas many grasses and other plants have growing seasons of only five or six months, but the palm apparently is adapted to extreme changes in water levels.

Morichales.—The dominant palm in this community is the Moriche palm, *Mauritia minor* (Fig. 11:5). The morichal community always is associated with soils of high, permanent water content in the eastern llanos of Venezuela and the southern llanos of Colombia. The term "morichal" commonly is used to describe the gallery forests of the eastern Venezuelan llanos, where this palm is the conspicuous species in the community.

Trachipogon savannas.—Several species of *Trachipogon* grasses (0.5–1 m high) domi-

FIG. 11:2. Gallery forest of a tributary of the Rio Apure, Estado Apure, Venezuela, during the late wet season.
Bosque de galería de un tributario del Río Apure, Estado Apure, Venezuela, en plena época de lluvias.

FIG. 11.3. Gallery forest of the Rio Apure, Estado Apure, Venezuela, during the late wet season.
Bosque de galería del Río Apure, Estado Apure, Venezuela, a finales de la época de lluvias.

Fig. 11:4. Pure stand of Palma Llanera, *Copernicia tectorum*, in the Estero de Camaguán, Estado Guárico, Venezuela, during the dry season.
Palmar de Copernicia tectorum en el Estero de Camaguán, Estado Guárico, Venezuela, durante la estación seca.

nate these sandy savannas (Fig. 11:6). In some areas there are no trees, whereas in others fire resistant trees (*Curatella, Bowdichia, Byrsonima* and *Roupala*) are common. These well-drained grasslands are rarely flooded and are burned annually so as to provide fresh food for cattle.

Paspalum savannas.—During the wet season these savannas normally are inundated, and apparently only one grass (*Paspalum fasciculatum*) is capable of living permanently in the area (Fig. 11:7). Normally, it attains a height of 2 m and forms dense, pure stands. These savannas are more common in the wettest areas of the western llanos of Venezuela.

Savannas of bancos, bajíos and esteros.— This type of savanna is more diverse in species of grasses than the former two savannas. It seems as though subtle topographic and structural variations of the soil and fluctuation of water level during the year increase plant diversity in these habitats. The Bancos are the higher ground, formed by the accumulation of sediment along the streams and never covered by water in the rainy season. Some bancos are pure savanna, whereas others are partly or completely forested (Fig. 11:4). Bajíos are covered with up to 20 cm of water during the wet season. Esteros are the lowest ground and may be covered by 1 m of water during the rainy season. The plant species composition in these savannas is constantly changing throughout the year. These changes probably result from the rather short periods when ideal conditions are available; a dynamic dry-wet cyclic succession occurs during a few months.

Medanales.—The driest sites in the llanos, lacking both trees and grass, are sand dunes in close association with *Trachipogon* savan-

Fig. 11:5. Pure stand of Moriche Palm, *Mauritia minor*, in the southern llanos of Estado Anzoátegui, Venezuela.

Palmar de *Mauritia minor* en los llanos del sur, Estado Anzoátegui, Venezuela.

nas and located mainly south of the Río Apure. Ramia (1967) described them as dynamic systems of sand dunes.

Aquatic habitats.—The rivers, caños, lagoons and temporary aquatic situations, such as esteros and bajíos, form an important habitat for many amphibians and reptiles of economic importance—turtles of the genus *Podocnemis* and crocodilians. This habitat is unique in the llanos and, although intrinsically different from the terrestrial habitats, it shares the dry-wet effects of the climate and oscillates in size (some disappear in the dry season). This results in brumation of many fish, reptiles, and amphibians.

Very Dry Tropical Forest

This type of forest occurs from sea level to 600 m where the mean annual temperatures are usually above 25°C; the mean annual rainfall is 500 to 1000 mm. The rainfall pattern is unimodal according to Ewell and Madriz (1968), but Walter and Medina (1971) used data from several coastal stations and concluded that there are two precipitation maxima—one between June and August and another at the end of the year. The trees are mostly deciduous (Fig. 11:8). Vellon (1963) observed that the "canopy species" provided only 25 percent of the cover. The ground usually is covered by dense thickets of *Bromelia humilis* (locally called "mayales"). Some cacti are abundant near the coast. These forests have been greatly disturbed by man. In some areas, human activity has left only bare soil and extremely eroded terrain.

There are two other vegetation communities within this forest; these were designated as Dry Evergreen, and Deciduous, bushlands by Sarmiento (1976). Dry Evergreen Bushland is distinguished by the presence of a closed canopy of low trees, shrubs 2 to 4 m high, sparse taller trees, and cacti up to 10 m high emerging occasionally. Two primary features are the absence of bare ground and predominance of evergreen bushes. Although Deciduous Bushland is similar in structure, deciduous bushes predominate.

Tropical Thorn Woodland

Sarmiento (1976) distinguished this vegetation type as lacking a continuous canopy and having large spaces of bare soil between sparse trees and shrubs (Fig. 11:9). The most common trees are those belonging to the genera *Capparis*, *Prosopis*, *Cercidium* and *Pithecolobium*. The Cactaceae is represented by *Mammallaria*, *Melocactus*, *Opuntia* and *Lemaireocerus*. The arid climate of this zone has an irregular precipitation pattern; however, there is a tendency for rains to increase towards the end of the year (Walter and Medina, 1971).

Dry formations common in certain inter-Andean valleys in Venezuela (usually around 1000 m or above) are typical rain shadows (Fig. 11:10). Ewell and Madriz (1968) classified the vegetation and climate of this life

Fig. 11.6. *Trachipogon* savannas in Estado Anzoátegui, Venezuela, with scattered Chaparro, *Curatella* sp.
Sabanas de Trachipogon *del estado Anzoátegui, Venezuela, con algunos Chaparros* Curatella *sp.*

Fig. 11.7. *Paspalum* savannas of the lower Río Apure, Estado Apure, Venezuela, with pure stands of *Paspalum fasciculatum*.
Sabanas de Paspalum fasciculatum *del Bajo Río Apure, Estado Apure, Venezuela.*

Fig. 11:8. Very dry tropical forest in early January, near the Laguna Unare, Estado Anzoátegui, Venezuela.

Bosque muy seco tropical a principios de enero, cerca de la Laguna de Unare, Estado Anzoátegui, Venezuela.

Fig. 11:9. Tropical thorn woodland community in Estado Lara, Venezuela.

Comunidad de matorral espinoso tropical en el Estado Lara, Venezuela.

zone as Premontane Thorn Woodland. The climate is very dry, and the temperatures (mean annual temperature less than 24°C) lower than those of the Tropical Thorn Woodland. Sarmiento (1976) suggested that these small areas were possible dispersal routes for plant communities at higher elevations between the Venezuelan Andes to the Atacama Desert.

Desert Scrub and Desert

The climatic regime of the desert scrub does not differ appreciably from that of the tropical thorn woodland. Floristically, it is an impoverished thorn woodland equivalent to the deserts of arid temperate areas (Sarmiento, 1976). The most arid areas are salt or sand deserts in the western Caribbean coast of Venezuela and Colombia (Fig. 11:11). Salt deserts are common along the coast with low shrubby Chenopodiaceae, while sand dunes are inhabited by *Acacia*, *Opuntia* and several geophytes (Sarmiento, 1976).

ORIGIN OF THE AMPHIBIAN AND REPTILE FAUNA

The geological and fossil evidence (see introduction and other sections of this symposium) suggests that there was a major alteration of climate in the late Quaternary in the lowlands of northern South America. Maritime wind shifts coupled with rain shadow effects associated with the rise of the Andes, provided the necessary physical traits to alter the climate from wet tropical to dry tropical, semiarid and/or arid desert regimes. The climatic and elevational shifts eliminated those less adaptive tropical species of the Magdalena and Maracaibo basins, while the Orinoco Embayment remained unchanged for a longer period of time. The latter region slowly filled with Andean and fluvial sediments from the north and west from Cretaceous to Recent times and is underlain by some 10,000 meters of deposits (Dirección de Geología, MMH, 1970). The extensive Colombian and Venezuelan llanos are prob-

Fig. 11:10. Premontane thorn woodland community of a rain shadow desert in the vicinity of Lagunillas, Estado Mérida, Venezuela (above 1000 m, mean temperature less than 24°C).
Comunidad de matorral espinoso premontano en el valle inter-andino de Lagunillas, Estado Mérida, Venezuela (Sobre 1000 m.s.n.m. y con una temperatura media anual por debajo de 24°C).

Fig. 11:11. Typical Médanos (sand dunes) in the desert scrub community of Estado Falcón, Venezuela.
Médanos (Dunas de Arena) en la comunidad de Maleza Desértica en el Estado Falcón, Venezuela.

ably less than one million years of age and formerly may have been more patchy than they are today. There is evidence that some areas of the llanos are maintained as a fire climax vegetation, while other parts are maintained by edaphic and climatic factors.

Studies of the cactus flora (Sarmiento, 1976) along the coastal zones of northeastern South America suggest that endemism is low and that phytogenetically, these zones are more closely allied with similar areas in Central America and the West Indies than that of northeastern Brasil. Sarmiento (1976) suggested that the origin of the flora is heterogeneous, with many plant species being contributed from nearby and less dry plant formations. In addition, the composition of the vegetation is strongly influenced by cosmopolitan or western hemisphere weeds which have greater numbers of species both north and south of the middle latitudes. The numbers of relictual, endemic taxa are relatively few, and are comprised of species typical of certain edaphic conditions or common forms of communities, such as tropical deciduous and dry tropical forests.

Although there is a series of arid vegetation islands along the Andes of Venezuela, Colombia and Perú, and many of these are only 200 to 300 km apart, the plant species show little relationship to those of the southern South American deserts. Most of the flora is more closely related to the arid floras of México, Central America and the western Caribbean. Furthermore, if we examine the plants and animals of the small, relictual, open formations within the present rainforests and those of the pantanal of western Brasil, we are left with the impression that both the flora and fauna once were connected across the Amazon Basin, probably during Pleistocene glacial maxima.

Herpetofaunal affinities of the northern lowland dry zones of South America are at variance with Sarmiento's (1976) conclusions concerning the flora. Some of the amphibians and reptiles occurring in the dry forests in northern South America are more common in lowland rainforests. At least 14 of 36 species of amphibians and 44 of 108 reptiles that occur in northern dry forests also inhabit Amazon forests. However, many of these species are fossorial, aquatic, or show wide tolerances for ecological situations, thus it is difficult to assign these species to a particular vegetation zone.

Some species and genera have affinities to Central America and to the dry zones of Brasil, whereas others are widely distributed north and south of the dry zones of northeastern South America. For example, the northern limit of *Leptodactylus bolivianus* is Costa Rica and *L. pentadactylus* Honduras, and both range southward to Bolivia. *Leptodactylus fragilis* and *L. poecilochilus* reach México and Costa Rica, respectively, but their southern limits border the Orinoco Basin. *Leptodactylus fuscus*, *macrosternum* and *wagneri* reach their southern limits in Brasil and Perú but their northern limits are the dry zones of northeastern South America and *L. rugosus* is restricted to the Guiana region. Thus, only one of the above species may be regarded as endemic to the dry zones of northern South America. The four endemic species of amphibians are those that belong to rather widespread genera that occur both north and south of the zone—e.g., *Hyla minuscula*, *H. wandae*, *Physalaemus enesefae*, and *Pipa parva*, one crocodilian, *Crocodylus intermedius*, one turtle, *Podocnemis vogli*, eleven lizards, *Anolis annectens*, *A. onca*, *Bachia bicolor*, *B. guianensis*, *B. talpa*, *Gonatodes vittatus*, *Hemidactylus palaichthus*, *Lepidoblepharis sanctaemartae*, *Ophryoessoides erythrogaster*, *Phyllodactylus dixoni*, *Tretioscincus bifasciatus*, nine snakes *Bothrops lansbergi*, *Crotalus vegrandis*, *Helicops danieli*, *H. scalaris*, *Leptotyphlops dimidiatus*, *Micrurus circinalis*, *M. dissoleucus*, *Phimophis guianensis*, and *Typhlops lehneri*.

Based upon present distribution patterns, a number of species of amphibians and reptiles may have evolved within the dry zones of northeastern South America and later spread north and south into similar habitats when favorable climates and corridors were available. Among these are the following: *Bufo granulosus*, *Hyla crepitans*, *Hyla rostrata*, *Leptodactylus bolivianus*, *Pseudis paradoxus*, *Geochelone carbonaria*, *Ameiva ameiva*, *A. bifrontata*, *Cnemidophorus lemniscatus*, *Gymnophthalmus speciosus*, *Tropidurus torquatus*, *Crotalus durissus*, *Mastigodryas pleei*, *Micrurus isozonus*, *Pseudoboa neuwiedi*, *Tantilla semicincta*, and *Thamnodynastes strigilis*.

Many wide ranging species occur in the northeastern South American dry zones, but some (*Bufo marinus*, *Hyla microcephala*, *H. rubra*, *Caiman crocodylus*, *Phrynohyas venulosa*, *Chrysemys scripta*, *Kinosternon scorpioides*, *Iguana iguana*, *Eunectes murinus*, *Heli-*

cops angulatus, Leptodeira annulata) are present because of the abundance of surface water six to eight months of the year or because of prey associated with abundant moisture

Other species (Ameiva ameiva, Thecadactylus rapicaudus, Tupinambis teguixin, Boa constrictor, Clelia clelia, Drymarchon corais, Epicrates cenchria, Imantodes cenchoa, Leptophis ahaetulla, Mastigodryas boddaerti, M bifossatus, Oxybelis aeneus, Spilotes pullatus, Sibon nebulata, Tantilla melanocephala) are adaptively plastic and survive in many harsh environments

In summary, herpetofauna of the lowland dry tropical zone of northern South America appears to be as heterogeneous as the flora Endemism is relatively low, probably owing to the relatively recent origin of the Orinoco Basin, its climate and vegetation

DIVERSITY OF AMPHIBIANS AND REPTILES

It is obvious that a diverse plant community affords a greater variety of resources than a less diverse one, and that more species of amphibians and reptiles are associated with plant communities that are structurally heterogeneous The structurally simple desert scrub community of coastal Venezuela appears to contain only one reptile (Cnemidophorus lemniscatus) and no amphibians As many as 48 species of amphibians and reptiles occur in a structurally heterogeneous dry forest zone near the center of the llanos and 75 species in a moderate heterogeneous dry forest zone in the Yuruari Savanna (Appendix 11 1)

Amphibians are more abundant where water or rainfall is more constant, the same is true for aquatic reptiles and to some extent arboreal species Amphibians are more numerous in gallery forests in llanos, matas and Paspalum savanna than in a palmares savanna In some areas reptile species are more numerous in broad contact zones between major llanos floral communities (heterogeneous nature of ecotone) than within one given vegetation type Table 11 1 indicates the relative diversity of species of amphibians and reptiles in particular floral communities within the llanos of Colombia and Venezuela

TABLE 11 1 —Distribution of the Herpetofauna of the Llanos (Exclusive of the Aquatic Species) in the Seven Basic Vegetation Communities Recognized by Venezuelan Botanists Ecologists and by Us

Species	Mata, Deciduous & Gallery Forests	Palmares	Monchales	Trachipogon Savanna	Medanales	Paspalum Savanna	Bancos, Bajios & Esteros Savannas
Anurans							
Bufo granulosus	—	+	—	—	—	+	+
Bufo guttatus	+	—	—	—	—	—	+
Bufo marinus	+	+	+	+	+	+	+
Dendrobates leucomelas	+	—	—	—	—	—	—
Llachistocleis ovalis	—	+	+	+	—	+	+
Hyla crepitans	+	+	+	—	—	+	+
Hyla microcephala	+	+	+	—	—	+	+
Hyla rostrata	+	—	—	—	—	—	—
Hyla rubra	+	+	+	—	—	+	+
Hyla wandae	+	—	—	—	—	—	—
Leptodactylus bolivianus	+	+	+	—	—	+	+
Leptodactylus fuscus	+	+	+	—	—	+	+
Leptodactylus macrosternon	+	+	+	—	—	+	+
Leptodactylus fragilis	+	+	+	—	—	+	+
Leptodactylus wagneri	+	+	+	—	—	+	+
Physalaemus enesefae	+	+	—	—	—	—	+
Physalaemus pustulosus	+	+	—	—	—	+	+
Phrynohyas venulosa	+	+	+	—	—	—	+
Phyllomedusa hypocondrialis	+	—	—	—	—	—	—
Pipa pipa	+	—	—	—	—	—	—
Pleurodema brachyops	+	+	+	—	—	+	+
Pseudis paradoxus	—	—	—	—	—	+	+

TABLE 11.1 (Continued)

Species	Mata Deciduous & Gallery Forests	Palmares	Trachypogon Morichales	Trachypogon Savanna	Trachypogon Medanales	Paspalum Savanna	Bancos, Bajos & Esteros Savannas
Amphisbaenians							
Amphisbaena alba	+	−	−	−	−	−	+
Amphisbaena fuliginosa	+	−	−	−	−	−	+
Lizards							
Anolis auratus	−	+	−	+	−	+	+
Cnemidophorus lemniscatus	+	+	+	+	+	+	+
Gymnophthalmus speciosus	−	+	−	−	−	+	+
Hemidactylus palaichthus	+	−	+	−	−	−	+
Iguana iguana	+	+	+	−	−	−	+
Kentropyx striatus	+	−	+	−	−	+	+
Phyllodactylus dixoni	−	−	−	+	−	−	−
Phyllodactylus ventralis	−	+	−	−	−	−	−
Tropidurus torquatus	+	+	+	−	−	−	+
Tupinambis teguixin	+	+	+	+	+	+	+
Snakes							
Boa constrictor	+	+	+	+	+	+	+
Chironius carinatus	−	+	+	−	−	−	+
Corallus enhydris	+	−	+	−	−	+	−
Crotalus durissus	+	+	+	+	−	−	+
Crotalus vegrandis	−	−	−	+	−	−	+
Drymarchon corais	+	+	+	−	−	−	+
Epicrates cenchria	+	+	+	−	−	+	+
Imantodes cenchoa	+	−	−	−	−	−	−
Leptodeira annulata	+	+	+	−	−	+	+
Leimadophis melanotus	+	+	+	−	−	+	+
Leimadophis reginae	+	−	−	−	−	−	−
Leimadophis typhlus	+	−	−	−	−	−	−
Leptophis ahaetulla	+	−	−	−	−	−	−
Lygophis lineatus	+	−	−	−	−	−	+
Masticophis mentovarius	−	−	−	+	−	−	−
Mastigodryas bifossatus	−	−	−	+	−	+	+
Micrurus isozonus	+	+	+	+	+	+	+
Oxybelis aeneus	+	+	+	−	−	−	+
Oxyrhopus petole	+	−	−	−	−	−	−
Phimophis guianensis	+	−	−	−	−	−	−
Pseudoboa neuwiedii	+	+	+	+	−	+	+
Spilotes pullatus	+	+	+	−	−	−	+
Thamnodynastes strigilis	+	+	+	−	−	+	+

Comparison of lizard faunas of the lowland dry forests of northern South America and the upper Amazon rainforest in Perú (Dixon and Soini 1975), reveals 34 and 38 species respectively. Duellman (1978) listed 29 species of lizards from an Amazonian site (Santa Cecilia, Ecuador), 26 of these occur at Iquitos, Perú. Owing to several physical and/or climatic barriers between various vegetation zones in the llanos and dry northern forests, local endemism is greater than in the upper Amazon Basin thereby resulting in a large total number of lizard species in the former region. As examples—*Pipa parva*, *Anolis annectens* are endemic to the Maracaibo Basin, *Ameiva ameiva* subsp., *Cnemidophorus lemniscatus* subsp., *Phyllodactylus dixoni*, *Crotalus vegrandis*, *Crocodylus intermedius*, *Podocnemis vogli* to the llanos, *Lepidoblepharis sanctaemartae*, *Ophryoessoides erythrogaster*, *Helicops danieli* to the Santa Marta Region, *Anolis onca* and *Tretioscincus bifasciatus* to the dry coastal areas of Venezuela.

The llanos and northern dry forests contain 56 species of snakes, whereas the upper Amazon region has 92 species (88 at Iquitos, 53 at Santa Cecilia). Santa Cecilia and the dry zones in northern South America share almost 30 percent of their species of snakes

Santa Cecilia shares 92 percent of its snake fauna with Iquitos whereas Apure Venezuela (llanos site), shares 43 percent of its snakes with Iquitos. At any one 10,000 km² site in the llanos region (total = 200,000 km²) only 14–17 species of snakes are present, a much lower number than at given sites in the upper Amazon Basin. Thus the structure of the land area, complexity of vegetation communities and climate, seem to be limiting factors for some, but not all species. Nearly equal numbers of species of lizards occur in highly varied habitats, but the number of snakes is highly variable (see Arnold, 1972, for further discussion). There should be about equal numbers of snakes species in each area if 1) lizards and amphibians can be considered as secondary consumers and snakes as tertiary consumers (predators on either one or both of the former) 2) the abiotic part of the environment is coarse grained (MacArthur and Levins, 1964) in terms of adaptations to the physical structure for both the llanos and the upper Amazon, and 3) the biotic part of the environment of these two areas is coarse grained in terms of food resources and cover. However the food resources and the climate of the llanos are coarse grained, whereas the food resources and climate in the upper Amazon are fine grained, therefore, we expect greater diversity of tertiary consumers in the Amazon than in the llanos. The availability of a variety of food resources during activity periods of a tertiary consumer in a relatively uniform environment would allow for more selection and greater speciation than where food resources may be equally available but with little or no variety and with greater fluctuations in climate (Arnold, 1972).

ACKNOWLEDGMENTS

We are especially grateful to Marinus S. Hoogmoed for amphibian data from Guianan savannas, Steve Gorzula for a current list of amphibians and reptiles from the Yuruari Savanna, and William Pyburn for information on anuran distribution in the Colombian llanos. We thank William Duellman for giving us the opportunity to present this paper on such short notice.

RESUMEN

En la presente contribución hemos tratado de examinar las relaciones zoogeográficas de la herpetofauna de las zonas bajas y secas de Sur América Nor-Occidental. En área abarca concretamente los Llanos del Orinoco y las zonas áridas y semi-áridas de las costas del Caribe, e incluye más de 300,000 km² de superficie que, en su mayor parte, está formada por sedimentos de origen pleistoceno (Fig. 1).

Unas 130 especies de anfibios y reptiles han sido señaladas para el área y se encuentran en una gran variedad de hábitats que van desde los bosques deciduos y de galería de los llanos del Orinoco hasta zonas áridas en las que predominan médanos arenosos, pasando por diversos grados de cobertura vegetal. Este gradiente de cobertura vegetal ejerce gran influencia en la distribución de las especies estudiadas, ya que los parámetros microclimáticos que se derivan de la disposición de la vegetación y, además, las características físicas que presentan las formaciones vegetales dan como resultado una gran diversidad de hábitats que pueden ser accesibles o no a los reptiles y anfibios que viven en la zona.

En el gradiente de cobertura vegetal se refleja la influencia de los Parámetros climáticos regionales. Los más conspícuos, como la precipitación y la temperatura aparentan ser de gran importancia.

En los Llanos, el régimen de lluvias parece regir en gran parte los fenómenos biológicos y favorece a aquellos organismos que están adaptados a vivir con abundancia de agua durante la mitad del año y carestía de agua durante la otra mitad. En las zonas extremadamente áridas del litoral la carestía de agua durante casi todo el año tiene gran influencia en la diversidad vegetal y en la composición florística de las comunidades vegetales. Este efecto se hace sentir también en la fauna y especialmente en los anfibios que están pobremente dotados para resistir la sequía prolongada.

Con el objeto de poner en claro las preferencias ecológicas de las especies de anfibios y reptiles de la zona en estudio, hemos tratado de hacer una clasificación de hábitats que está enmarcada dentro de tipos climáticos generales reconocidos para la región (Ewell y Madriz, 1968). Dentro de cada uno de los tipos climáticos presentamos una lista de los hábitats accesibles a la herpetofauna basándonos en experiencias personales y en conocidas clasificaciónes hechas por otros autores (Rama, 1967, Sarmiento, 1976).

La lista de hábitats es la siguiente. I— Bosque Seco Tropical. A) Bosques deciduos, Matas y Bosques de galería (Figs 11 2-11 3), B) Palmares (Fig 11 4), C) Morichales (Fig 11 5), D) Sabanas de *Trachipogon* (Fig 11 6), E) Sabanas de *Paspalum* (Fig 11 7), F) Sabanas de Bancos, Bajíos y Esteros (Fig 11 4), G) Medanales, y H) Ríos, caños y lagunas

II— Bosque muy Seco Tropical. Bosque muy seco (Fig 11 8), Monte seco siempreverde, Monte decíduo

III— Monte Espinoso Tropical (Fig 11 9)

IV— Maleza Desértica y Desierto (Fig 11 11)

Presentamos una lista de anfibios y reptiles en la que se señalan las preferencias ecológicas de las especies en relación con los hábitats terrestres que hemos identificado en el Bosque Seco Tropical (Tabla 11 1). El Apéndice 11 1 presenta la distribución conocida de las especies de anfibios y reptiles con respecto a las grandes zonas consideradas en el estudio

Sarmiento (1976), sugiere que el origen de la flora de las regiones secas de la costa del Caribe es heterogéneo. Algunas especies o grupos son cosmopolitas, otros endémicos, otros vienen del norte o del sur de América y la mayoría ha inmigrado a la zona en diferente época y por diferentes

Los Reptiles y Anfibios de esa región parecen confirmar las conclusiones de Sarmiento en lo que respecta al origen de la flora. La herpetofauna muestra afinidades con grupos de origen centro-americano y también con las zonas más secas de Brasil. Algunas especies son decididamente cosmopolitas mientras que unas pocas son endémicas a la región

Según nuestra lista de especies y su distribución, y la diversidad de hábitats accesibles en la zona en estudio se puede notar que el número de especies es mayor en aquellos hábitats de mayor diversidad física como los bosques o de mayor estabilidad microclimática, o donde las condiciones son más predecibles de año a año

Los ciclos estacionales de gran influencia ecológica como el del agua en la región llanera tienen influencia muy especial en la composición faunística, en el sentido de proporcionar un dinamismo único que presenta un reto para aquellas especies que no se pueden adaptar rápidamente a situaciones extremas de carestía o abundancia de agua. Muchas especies están activas sólo durante la parte favorable del año y esto hace que sea difícil de observar la totalidad de las especies en un determinado periodo del ciclo de lluvias

En ambientes más secos como los de las regiones xerófilas del litoral, las condiciones climáticas provocan, entre otros fenómenos, una sequía prolongada que sólo es soportada por un número escaso de reptiles y por muy pocos anfibios

La distribución de algunos grupos, como lagartos y serpientes, está sujeta a diferencias inherentes a dichos organismos en relación a su posición trófica y muy específicamente a sus requerimientos como consumidores, así como también a sus requerimientos específicos en cuanto a la estructura del hábitat

Las serpientes parecen no diferir de los lagartos en cuanto a su adaptabilidad hacia el medio físico y estructural del hábitat. En cambio las serpientes parecen ser consumidores terciarios que pueden explotar de manera más especializada el alimento disponible, mientras que los lagartos son más generalizados en sus dietas y por ello más propensos a competir por el recurso disponible. Debido a dichas características, creemos poder explicar la existencia de casi el doble de especies de serpientes en la zona estudiada

LITERATURE CITED

Arnold, S J 1972 Species densities of predators and their prey Amer Nat 106 220-236

BEARD, J S 1953 The savanna vegetation of northern tropical America Ecol Monogr 23 149-215
COCHRAN, D, GOIN, C J 1970 Frogs of Colombia Bull U S Natl Mus 288 1-655
DIRECCION DE GEOLOGIA, MMH, Venezuela 1970 Lexico Estratigrafico de Venezuela Bol Geol Publ Especial 4, 757 p
DIXON, J R, SOINI, P 1975 The reptiles of the upper Amazon basin, Iquitos region, Peru I Lizards and Amphisbaenians Milwaukee Publ Mus Contr Biol Geol (4) 1-58
DIXON, J R, SOINI, P 1977 The reptiles of the upper Amazon basin, Iquitos region Peru II Crocodilians, turtles and snakes Ibid (12) 1-91
DONOSO-BARROS, R 1968 The lizards of Venezuela (Check list and key) Caribb J Sci 8 105-122
DUELLMAN, W E 1978 The biology of an equatorial herpetofauna in Amazonian Ecuador Univ Kansas Mus Nat Hist Misc Publ 65 1-352
DUNN, E R 1957 Contributions to the herpetology of Colombia 1943-1946 Privately printed, 296 p
EWELL, J, MADRIZ, A 1968 Zonas de Vida de Venezuela, Memoria explicativa sobre el Mapa Ecologico MAC, Dir Invest, Caracas, 265 p
HOLDRIDGE, L R 1967 Life zone ecology tropical science center San Jose, Costa Rica, 206 p
HUECK, K 1966 Die Wälder Sudamerikas Gustav Fischer Verlag Stuttgart, 422 p
HUECK, K, SEIBERT, P 1972 Vegetationskarte von Südamerika Gustav Fischer Verlag, Stuttgart, 71 p, map
MACARTHUR, R H, LEVINS, R 1964 Competition habitat selection, and character displacement in a patchy environment Proc Natl Acad Sci 51 1207-1210
MEDEM, F 1968 El desarrollo de la herpetologia en Colombia Rev Acad Colombiana Cien Exactas Fis Nat 13 149-199
RAMIA, M 1967 Tipos de sabanas en los llanos de Venezuela Bol Soc Venezolana Cien Nat 112 264-287
RIVERO, J A 1961 Salientia of Venezuela Bull Mus Com Zool Harvard Univ (126) 1-207
ROZE, J A 1966 La taxonomia y zoogeografia de los ofidios de Venezuela Univ Central Venezuela Caracas, 362 p
RUTHVEN, A G 1922 The amphibians and reptiles of the Sierra Nevada de Santa Marta, Colombia Misc Publ Mus Zool Univ Michigan (8) 1-69
SARMIENTO, G 1976 Evolution of arid vegetation in tropical America pp 65-99 in GOODALL, D W (ed) Evolution of Desert Biota Univ Texas Press, Austin, 250 p
STATON, M A, DIXON, J R 1977 The herpetofauna of the central llanos of Venezuela noteworth records a tentative checklist and ecological notes J Herpetol 11 17-24
VEILLON, J P 1963 Relacion de ciertas caracteristicas de la masa forestal de unos bosques de las zoneas bajas de Venezuela con el factor climatico Humedad pluvial Acta Cient Venezolana 14 30-41
WALTER, H, MEDINA, E 1971 Caracterizacion climatica de Venezuela sobre la base de climadiagramas de estaciones particulares Bol Soc Venezolana Cien Nat 119/120 211-240

APPENDIX

APPENDIX 11 1—Species of amphibians and reptiles (150) recorded from savannas and dry forests of northern South America, exclusive of Ecuador and the northern Atacama Desert. Holdridge's (1967) vegetation zone system was utilized in determining vegetative communities. Numbers (1-5) of locality zones correspond to locations in figure 11 1.

Species	Vegetation Zone				Locality Zone				
	Bosque Seco Tropical (Dry Forest)	Bosque Muy Seco Tropical (Very Dry Forest)	Monte Espinoso Tropical (Thorn Woodland)	Maleza Desertica Tropical (Desert Scrub)	Santa Marta Region (1)	Maracaibo Basin (2)	Falcon Region and/or Coastal Desert (3)	Llanos (4)	Yuruari Savanna (5)
Anurans									
Bufo granulosus	+	+	−	−	+	+	+	+	+
Bufo guttatus	+	−	−	−	−	−	−	+	+
Bufo marinus	+	+	−	−	+	+	+	+	+
Ceratophrys calcarata	+	−	−	−	+	+	−	−	+
Dendrobates leucomelas	+	−	−	−	−	−	−	−	+
Elachistocleis ovalis	+	−	−	−	+	−	−	+	+
Hyla albomarginata	+	−	+	−	−	+	−	−	−
Hyla blairi	+	−	−	−	−	−	−	+	−
Hyla crepitans	+	−	−	−	+	−	−	+	+
Hyla egleri	+	−	−	−	−	−	−	+	+
Hyla geographica	+	−	−	−	−	−	−	−	+
Hyla kennedyi	+	−	−	−	−	−	−	+	−
Hyla leucophyllata	+	−	−	−	−	−	−	+	−
Hyla luteocellata	+	−	−	−	−	−	−	+	−
Hyla microcephala	+	−	−	−	+	−	−	+	+
Hyla minuscula	+	−	−	−	−	−	−	−	+
Hyla multifasciata	+	−	−	−	−	−	−	−	+
Hyla rostrata	+	−	−	−	−	−	−	+	−
Hyla rubra	+	−	−	−	−	−	−	+	+
Hyla wandae	+	−	−	−	−	−	−	+	−
Hyla x-signata	+	−	−	−	−	−	−	+	+
Leptodactylus bolivianus	+	−	−	−	+	−	−	+	+
Leptodactylus fragilis	+	−	−	−	+	−	−	+	+
Leptodactylus fuscus	+	−	−	−	+	−	−	+	+
Leptodactylus macrosternum	+	−	−	−	−	−	−	+	+
Leptodactylus pentadactylus	+	−	−	−	+	−	−	+	+
Leptodactylus poecilochilus	+	−	−	−	+	−	−	−	−
Leptodactylus rugosus	+	−	−	−	−	−	−	−	+
Leptodactylus wagneri	+	−	−	−	−	−	−	+	+
Phrynohyas venulosa	+	−	−	−	+	−	−	+	+
Physalaemus enesefae	+	−	−	−	−	−	−	+	+
Physalaemus pustulosus	+	−	−	−	+	−	−	+	+
Phyllomedusa hypocondrialis	+	−	−	−	−	−	−	−	−
Pipa parva	+	−	−	−	−	+	+	−	−
Pipa pipa	+	−	−	−	−	−	−	+	−
Pleurodema brachyops	+	−	−	−	+	−	−	+	+
Pseudis paradoxus	+	−	−	−	+	−	−	+	+
Pseudopaludicola pusilla	+	−	−	−	+	−	−	+	−
Pseudopaludicola sagittifer	+	−	−	−	+	−	−	−	−
Rana palmipes	+	−	−	−	−	−	−	−	−
Relictivomer pearsei	+	−	−	−	+	−	−	−	−
Sphaenorhynchus eurhostus	+	−	−	−	−	−	−	−	+
Crocodilians									
Caiman crocodilus	+	+	−	−	+	−	−	+	+
Crocodylus acutus	+	+	−	−	+	−	−	−	−

APPENDIX II 1 (Continued)

Species	Vegetation Zone				Locality Zone				
	Bosque Seco Tropical (Dry Forest)	Bosque Muy Seco Tropical (Very Dry Forest)	Monte Espinoso Tropical (Thorn Woodland)	Maleza Desertica Tropical (Desert Scrub)	Santa Marta Region (1)	Maracaibo Basin (2)	Falcon Region and/or Coastal Desert (3)	Llanos (4)	Yuruari Savanna (5)
Crocodylus intermedius	+	−	−	−	−	−	−	+	−
Paleosuchus palpebrosus	+	−	−	−	−	−	−	−	+
Turtles									
Chelus fimbriatus	+	+	−	−	−	−	−	−	−
Chrysemys scripta	+	+	−	−	+	−	−	−	−
Geochelone carbonaria	+	−	−	−	+	−	−	+	+
Kinosternon scorpioides	+	−	−	−	+	−	−	+	−
Phrynops geoffroanus	+	−	−	−	−	−	−	−	+
Podocnemis erytherocephala	+	−	−	−	−	−	−	+	−
Podocnemis expansa	+	−	−	−	−	−	−	+	−
Podocnemis unifilis	+	−	−	−	−	−	−	+	−
Podocnemis vogli	+	−	−	−	−	−	−	+	+
Rhinoclemys punctularia	+	−	−	−	−	−	−	+	−
Amphisbaenians									
Amphisbaena alba	+	−	−	−	−	−	−	+	+
Amphisbaena fuliginosa	+	−	−	−	−	−	−	+	+
Lizards									
Ameiva ameiva	+	−	−	−	+	+	−	+	+
Ameiva bifrontata	+	+	−	−	+	+	−	−	+
Anolis annectens	+	−	−	−	−	+	−	−	−
Anolis auratus	+	−	−	−	+	−	−	+	+
Anolis gaigei	+	−	−	−	+	−	−	−	−
Anolis onca	−	−	+	+	+	−	+	−	−
Bachia bicolor	+	−	−	−	+	−	−	−	−
Bachia guianensis	+	−	−	−	−	−	−	−	+
Bachia heteropa	+	+	+	−	−	+	+	−	−
Bachia talpa	+	−	−	−	+	−	−	−	−
Basiliscus basiliscus	+	−	−	−	+	+	−	−	−
Cercosaura ocellata	+	−	−	−	−	−	−	−	+
Cnemidophorus lemniscatus	+	+	+	+	+	+	+	+	+
Gonatodes albogularis	+	+	+	−	+	+	+	−	−
Gonatodes vittatus	+	+	+	−	+	+	+	−	+
Gymnophthalmus speciosus	+	+	−	−	+	−	+	+	−
Gymnophthalmus underwoodi	+	−	−	−	−	−	−	−	+
Hemidactylus brooki	−	+	−	−	+	−	−	−	−
Hemidactylus palaichthus	+	−	−	−	−	−	−	+	+
Iguana iguana	+	+	+	+	+	+	+	+	+
Kentropyx borkianus	+	−	−	−	−	−	−	+	+
Kentropyx striatus	+	−	−	−	−	−	−	+	+
Lepidoblepharis sanctaemartae	+	−	−	−	+	−	−	−	−
Leposoma rugiceps	+	−	−	−	+	−	−	−	+
Mabuya mabouya	+	−	−	−	−	−	−	−	−
Ophryoessoides erythrogaster	+	−	−	−	+	−	−	−	−
Phyllodactylus dixoni	+	−	−	−	−	−	−	+	−
Phyllodactylus ventralis	+	+	+	−	+	+	+	+	−
Polychrus marmoratus	+	−	−	−	+	−	−	−	+
Pseudogonatodes lunulatus	+	−	−	−	−	−	+	−	−
Sphaerodactylus molei	+	−	−	−	+	−	−	−	−
Thecadactylus rapicaudus	+	+	+	−	+	+	+	−	+

APPENDIX II.1 (Continued)

Species	Vegetation Zone				Locality Zone				
	Bosque Seco Tropical (Dry Forest)	Bosque Muy Seco Tropical (Very Dry Forest)	Monte Espinoso Tropical (Thorn Woodland)	Maleza Desertica Tropical (Desert Scrub)	Santa Marta Region (1)	Maracaibo Basin (2)	Falcon Region and/or Coastal Desert (3)	Llanos (4)	Yururi Savanna (5)
Tretioscincus bifasciatus	+	+	+	−	+	−	+	−	−
Tropidurus torquatus	+	−	−	−	−	−	−	+	+
Tupinambis teguixin	+	+	−	−	+	+	+	+	+
Snakes									
Boa constrictor	+	+	+	−	+	+	+	+	+
Bothrops lansbergi	+	−	−	−	+	−	−	−	−
Clelia clelia	+	−	−	−	+	−	−	−	+
Chironius carinatus	+	−	−	−	+	−	−	+	+
Corallus enhydris	+	−	−	−	+	−	−	+	−
Crotalus durissus	+	+	+	−	+	+	+	+	+
Crotalus vegrandis	+	−	−	−	−	−	−	−	−
Drymarchon corais	+	+	−	−	+	+	+	+	+
Drymobius margaritiferus	+	−	−	−	+	−	−	−	−
Enulius flavotorques	+	−	−	−	+	−	−	−	−
Epicrates cenchria	+	−	−	−	−	−	−	+	+
Eunectes murinus	+	−	−	−	−	−	−	+	+
Helicops angulatus	+	−	−	−	−	−	−	+	+
Helicops danieli	+	−	−	−	+	−	−	−	−
Helicops scalaris	+	−	−	−	+	−	−	−	−
Helminthopis flavoterminatus	−	−	−	−	−	+	−	−	−
Hydrops triangularis	−	−	−	−	−	−	−	+	+
Imantodes cenchoa	+	−	−	−	+	+	−	+	+
Leimadophis melanotus	+	−	−	−	+	+	−	+	+
Leimadophis reginae	+	−	−	−	−	−	−	+	+
Leimadophis typhlus	+	−	−	−	−	−	−	−	+
Leptodeira annulata	+	−	−	−	+	+	−	+	+
Leptodeira septentrionalis	+	−	−	−	+	−	−	−	−
Leptophis ahaetulla	+	−	−	−	−	−	−	+	+
Leptotyphlops macrolepis	+	−	−	−	+	−	−	−	−
Leptotyphlops dimidiatus	+	−	−	−	−	−	−	−	+
Liotyphlops albirostris	+	−	−	−	+	+	−	−	−
Lygophis lineatus	+	+	−	−	−	−	−	+	+
Masticophis mentovarius	+	+	+	−	−	−	+	+	+
Mastigodryas bifossatus	+	−	−	−	+	−	−	+	+
Mastigodryas boddaerti	+	−	−	−	+	−	−	−	+
Mastigodryas pleei	+	−	−	−	+	−	−	−	+
Micrurus caricicauda	+	−	−	−	+	−	−	−	−
Micrurus circinalis	+	+	−	−	−	−	+	−	−
Micrurus collaris	+	−	−	−	−	−	−	−	+
Micrurus dissoleucus	+	+	+	−	+	−	+	−	+
Micrurus isozonus	+	−	−	−	−	−	−	+	+
Micrurus lemniscatus	+	−	−	−	−	−	−	+	+
Micrurus psyches	+	−	−	−	−	−	−	+	+
Oxybelis aeneus	+	+	−	−	+	+	+	+	+
Oxybelis fulgidus	+	+	−	−	−	−	+	+	+
Oxyrhopus petola	+	+	−	−	−	−	−	+	+
Phimophis guianensis	+	+	+	+	+	+	+	+	+
Pseudoboa coronata	+	−	−	−	−	−	−	−	+
Pseudoboa neuwiedii	+	−	−	−	+	−	−	+	+

Appendix II 1 (Concluded)

Species	Locality Zone				Vegetation Zone				
	Bosque Seco Tropical (Dry Forest)	Bosque Muy Seco Tropical (Very Dry Forest)	Monte Espinoso Tropical (Thorn Woodland)	Maleza Desertica Tropical (Desert Scrub)	Santa Marta Region (1)	Maracaibo Basin (2)	Falcon Region and/or Coastal Desert (3)	Llanos (4)	Yurmari Savanna (5)
Pseustes poecilonotus	+	−	−	−	−	−	−	−	+
Rhinobothryum bovallii	+	−	−	−	+	−	−	−	−
Sibon nebulata	+	−	−	−	−	+	+	+	+
Spilotes pullatus	+	−	−	−	+	+	+	+	+
Tantilla melanocephala	+	+	−	−	+	−	+	−	+
Tantilla semicinctum	+	−	−	−	−	−	−	−	−
Thamnodynastes strigilis	+	+	+	−	−	+	−	+	+
Typhlops lehneri	+	−	−	−	−	−	+	−	−
Typhlops reticulatus	+	−	−	−	−	−	−	+	−
Xenodon rhabdocephalus	+	−	−	−	+	−	−	−	−
Xenodon severus	−	−	−	−	−	−	−	−	+

12 Composición, Distribución y Origen de la Herpetofauna Chaqueña

José M. Gallardo

Museo Argentino de Ciencias Naturales
Avenida Angel Gallardo 470
Buenos Aires, Argentina

Las primeras referencias sobre la herpetofauna chaqueña se tienen a través de los relatos y libros de los sacerdotes misioneros de la época colonial (Siglos XVII–XVIII). Los Padres Ruiz de Montoya, Lozano, Paucke, Juárez, Sánchez Labrador (véase referencias en Gallardo, 1961b) tienen descripciones y a veces grabados sobre diversas especies chaqueñas de ofidios, saurios, cocodrilos, y tortugas, con informaciones por observación directa y otras referencias de los indígenas del "Gran Chaco Gualamba." Algunos naturalistas viajeros como d'Orbigny (1847) también se refieren a algunos de los anfibios y reptiles de la región chaqueña. Como he indicado en un trabajo anterior (Gallardo, 1966c), años después Cope (1862) describe especies colectadas por la expedición del Capitán T. Page, luego sucesivamente Steindachner (1864), Boettger (1885), Boulenger (1889, 1894, 1898), Peracca (1895), Budgett (1899), Méhély (1904) se ocupan de la fauna chaqueña. Más recientemente deben mencionarse los trabajos de Muller y Hellmich (1936), Vellard (1948), Cei (1948, 1949, 1950, 1955), Barrio (1965), y Gallardo (1951, 1957, 1959, 1961a, 1962, 1964a–e, 1965a, 1966 a–c, 1968a,b, 1969a, 1971).

DESCRIPCIÓN DE LA REGIÓN CHAQUEÑA

La región chaqueña abarca una enorme área geográfica, que va desde el sur de San José de Chiquitos y las Serranías de Santiago en Bolivia hasta el norte de la Provincia de Córdoba en Argentina. Posee una longitud de norte al sur de 1280 km. Su ancho máximo en la Argentina, oscila entre 350–400 km, desde el este de Salta hasta la mitad de Formosa, o entre el este de Tucumán y la mitad de Chaco. Cubre los departamentos de Boquerón y Olimpo de Paraguay, al oeste del Río Paraguay. En la Argentina abarca toda la Provincia de Santiago del Estero y penetra en los valles del este de Jujuy, el este de Catamarca y de La Rioja y el norte de San Luis (Fig. 12.1). Presenta áreas ecotonales o de transición con otras faunas penetrando en el Paraguay hacia el este. En Brasil algunos elementos faunísticos del Chaco llegan al Mato Grosso, al sudeste y al nordeste a favor del Cerrado y la Caatinga, llegando aún hasta las Guayanas, y algunos elementos alcanzan el Uruguay. En la Argentina se superpone con otras formas—en el este de Formosa y Chaco, el oeste de Corrientes, el noroeste de Entre Ríos y el norte de Santa Fe. Ciertos elementos llegan a Mendoza, San Juan, La Pampa, y Río Negro.

La fauna chaqueña propiamente dicha se extiende por la llanura chaco-bonaerense en su parte norte la cual tiene una elevación entre 100 a 500 m. Por debajo de los 100 m existe la zona de transición faunística con la fauna litoral-mesopotámica, y por arriba de los 500 m con la fauna subandina. Algunos elementos chaqueños avanzan por las serranías bajas del oeste. Por la presencia o ausencia de ríos la fauna se distribuye de acuerdo a las limitaciones de su dispersión.

En la región chaqueña las lluvias máximas anuales se producen en verano (lo mismo que en la región subandina), en el área litoral-mesopotámica se producen en primavera y otoño, y en el área de transición faunística las épocas son intermedias. Los promedios anuales chaqueños van de 550 a 760 mm (en la Argentina), en el área de transición son prácticamente el doble, entre 1000 a 1460

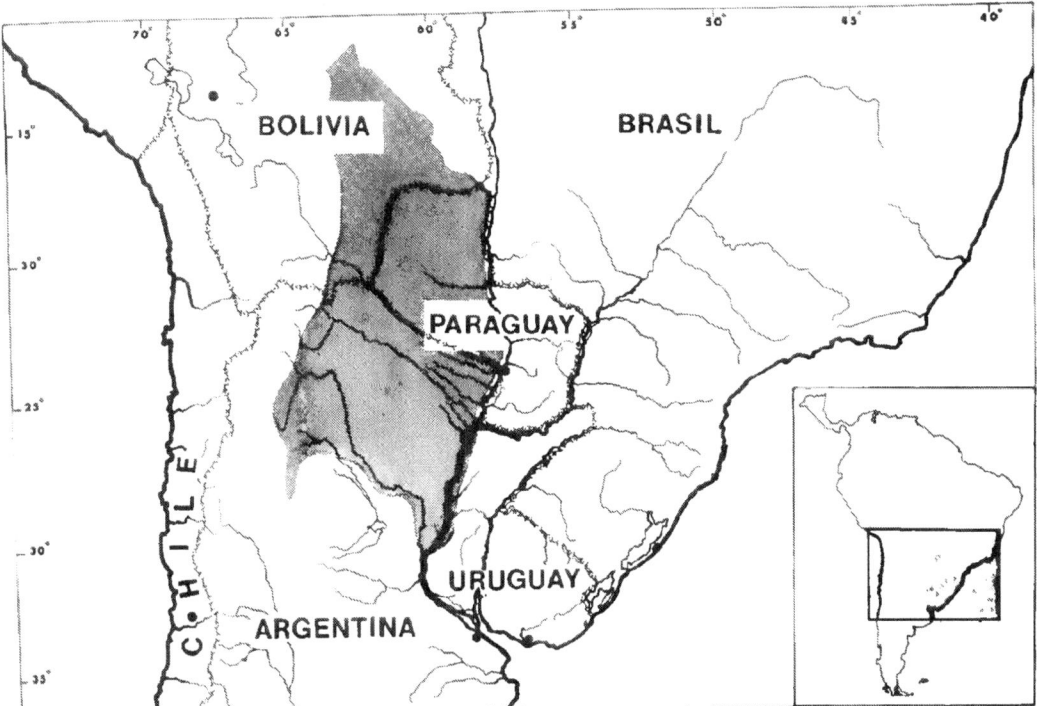

Fig. 12:1. En el mapa se ha indicado el área abarcada por la herpetofauna chaqueña y la zona de transición con la fauna litoral-mesopotámica. Se indican las ciudades capitales dentro del área y los ríos principales.
Map showing the area occupied by the Chacoan herpetofauna and the transition zone with the Litoral-Mesopotamian fauna. Capital cities and principal rivers are shown.

mm, y en el área subandina son menos de la mitad que en la chaqueña (160–325 mm). De modo que existe un escalón pluviométrico coincidente en general con el topográfico.

En cuanto a las temperaturas anuales hay diferencia entre el área ocupada por la fauna de transición y la ocupada por la litoral-mesopotámica, de la mitad de Santa Fe hacia el sur. Así en la primavera hay cinco meses de posibles temperaturas bajo cero (entre mayo y septiembre inclusive), con temperaturas mínimas de hasta −5° y −6°C. En la mitad sur de Santa Fe hay seis o siete meses de posibles temperaturas bajo cero (de abril o mayo a octubre inclusive), lo que amplía considerablemente el esquema anterior, además las mínimas pueden alcanzar los −10°C. Esto se halla ligado a un cambio faunístico, que coincide con la desaparación hacia el sur de la fauna herpetológica chaqueña.

En la región considerada domina el parque chaqueño, con bosques y árboles aislados (*Acacia, Prosopis, Schinopsis, Aspidosperma*) en pastizales de gramíneas (*Setaria, Digitaria, Trichloris*); a veces se trata de palmares (*Tritrinax, Copernicia*) o de matorrales espinosos (en especial, estos últimos, en áreas degradadas), otras son áreas de vegetación halófila o falta la vegetación casi totalmente en determinados espacios. Corresponde básicamente a la Provincia Chaqueña del Dominio Chaqueño (Cabrera, 1971), la herpetofauna chaqueña también puede extenderse por las provincias del Monte y del Espinal. No existe, en cambio, en ambientes puramente herbáceos como los del sur de Santa Fe y de Córdoba, y la Provincia de Buenos Aires, que corresponden a la llamada "Pampa húmeda." Es allí donde vemos que existe una componente climática y fitogeográfica que no favorece el avance de la herpetofauna chaqueña hacia el sur.

COMPOSICIÓN HERPETOFAUNÍSTICA

La herpetofauna chaqueña se compone con cinco familias de anfibios (14 géneros, 30 especies) y 13 familias de reptiles (35 géneros, 49 especies). Entre los anfibios hay una marcada abundancia de leptodactylidos (6 géneros, 16 especies) y en segundo término los hylidos (3 géneros, 7 especies). Los saurios tienen un marcado predominio de iguánidos (6 géneros, 7 especies) y en segundo término de teidos (5 géneros, 6 especies). De las 79 especies de anfibios y reptiles que habitan la región chaqueña, 40 especies (21 anfibios, 19 reptiles) son básicamente endémicas de esa región (Tabla 12.1).

ECOLOGÍA Y ADAPTACIONES

En las especies de anfibios y reptiles se notan interesantes adaptaciones a las condiciones ambientales.

Adaptaciones de los Anfibios

Las épocas de reproducción de los anfibios chaqueños se hallan en coincidencia con las épocas de lluvia, lo que resulta de vital importancia en un área relativamente seca. Pero dentro de ese contexto hay adaptaciones propias de algunas especies.

Construcción de nidos.—Hay varios tipos de nidos:

1. Nidos de espuma en cuevas en el suelo. Las ranas en épocas de lluvia hacen cuevas en el barro húmedo, es el macho que se encarga de esta construcción y el que asomado a la cueva canta llamando a la hembra. Esto es seguido por el amplexo, construcción del nido de espuma por la pareja, puesta y fecundación, la pareja luego abandona la cueva. El desarrollo embrionario y la primera parte de la vida larval ocurren dentro de la cueva. Una ulterior lluvia causa la inundación de la cueva y la salida de los renacuajos del nido, ellos completan rápidamente su desarrollo y metamorfosis. Este comportamiento se da en *Leptodactylus anceps*, *L. bufonius*, y *L. gualambensis*.

2. Nidos de espuma flotantes. No hay construcción de cuevas, por parte de las ranas los nidos son construidos por la pareja. Esto se da en las ranas *Leptodactylus chaquensis* y *L. laticeps*, y las especies de *Physalaemus* y *Pleurodema*.

3. Nidos en las hojas. Son construidos en hojas sobre ramas de árboles, sobre cuerpos de agua, adonde luego caen los renacuajos para completar su desarrollo larval. Tal sucede en las especies de *Phyllomedusa*, ranas arborícolas.

Desarrollo larval.—Varias estrategias son usadas por los renacuajos:

1. Desarrollo rápido de unas dos semanas de duración, se da en las ranas constructoras de cuevas en el suelo y nidos de espuma (véase las especies mencionadas anteriormente).

2. Desarrollo lento de una duración de uno o dos meses en los sapos del género *Bufo*, algunas ranas del género *Leptodactylus* y varios hylidos.

Adaptaciones contra el desecamiento.—En las épocas de receso reproductivo y de falta de lluvias, varias adaptaciones permiten la supervivencia en estos meses desfavorables:

1. Formas cavícolas. En particular las especies de *Ceratophrys*, *Lepidobatrachus*, *Odontophrynus*, y *Pleurodema* poseen tubérculos tarsales o metatarsales cavadores que facilitan su ocultamiento bajo tierra, donde permanecen hasta que se produzcan las lluvias.

2. Formas comensales. Algunas especies, como *Leptodactylus laticeps*, *L. chaquensis*, *L. bufonius*, y *Bufo arenarum*, se han adaptado a vivir en cuevas de roedores, especialmente de vizcacha (*Lagostomus maximus*), lo que les permite soportar largos períodos de sequías. Otros, como *Dermatonotus muelleri* y *Elachistocleis bicolor* habitan termiteros.

3. Acumulación de mudas de piel. Otra forma de defensa consiste en la accumulación de la muda, que se da en especial en las especies de *Ceratophrys* (Gallardo, 1953) y *Lepidobatrachus* (McClanahan, Shoemaker, y Ruibal,

Tabla 12 1 —Lista de los Anfibios y Reptiles Chaqueños y Sus Distribuciones en Regiones Ultrachaqueñas
(+ = presente − = ausente × = representado por otra subespecie ° = básicamente endémica de Chaco)

Especies	Litoral-Mesopotámica	Pampas	Patagonia	Región Subandina
Batracios				
Ceratophrys pierotti°	−	−	−	−
Ceratophrys sp °	−	−	−	−
Lepidobatrachus asper°	−	−	−	−
Lepidobatrachus llanensis°	−	−	−	+
Lepidobatrachus salinicola°	−	−	−	−
Leptodactylus anceps°	−	−	−	−
Leptodactylus buformus°	−	−	−	−
Leptodactylus chaquensis°	−	−	−	−
Leptodactylus gualambensis°	−	−	−	−
Leptodactylus laticeps°	−	−	−	−
Odontophrynus americanus	+	+	−	−
Physalaemus albonotatus°	−	−	−	−
Physalaemus biligonigerus	+	+	−	−
Pleurodema borellii°	−	−	−	−
Pleurodema guayapae	−	−	−	+
Pleurodema tucumana°	−	−	−	+
Bufo arenarum	×	×	−	+
Bufo granulosus	×	×	−	+
Bufo paracnemis	−	−	−	−
Melanophryniscus stelzneri	×	×	−	×
Pseudis paradoxus	×	×	−	−
Hyla acuminata°	−	−	−	−
Hyla fuscovaria°	−	−	−	−
Hyla raniceps	−	−	−	−
Hyla x-signata	−	−	−	−
Phrynohyas venulosa	−	−	−	−
Phyllomedusa hypocondrialis	−	−	−	−
Phyllomedusa sauvagii°	−	−	−	−
Elachistocleis bicolor	+	+	−	−
Dermatonotus mulleri°	−	−	−	−
Saurios				
Homonota horrida°	−	−	−	−
Phyllopezus pollicaris°	−	−	−	−
Leiosaurus paronae°	−	−	−	−
Liolaemus chacoensis°	−	−	−	−
Ophryoessoides caducus°	−	−	−	−
Pristidactylus cautieri°	−	−	−	−
Proctotretus dorllojuradoi°	−	−	−	−
Tropidurus spinulosus	−	−	−	−
Tropidurus sp °	−	−	−	−
Cnemidophorus leachi°	−	−	−	−
Gymnophthalmus rubricauda°	−	−	−	−
Kentropyx lagartija°	−	−	−	−
Kentropyx viridistriga°	−	−	−	−
Teius teyou	×	×	−	×
Tupinambis rufescens	−	−	−	−
Ophiodes intermedius	+	−	−	−
Mabuya frenata	+	−	−	−
Anfisbenios				
Amphisbaena camura°	−	−	−	−
Anops kingii	+	+	+	−
Leposternon microcephalum	+	+	−	−
Ofidios				
Leptotyphlops albipuncta°	−	−	−	+
Leptotyphlops unguirostris	−	−	−	−
Leptotyphlops weyrauchi°	−	−	−	+
Constrictor constrictor	+	+	−	+
Epicrates cenchria	+	−	−	−

Especies	Litoral Mesopotamica	Pampas	Patagonia	Region Subandina
Eunectes notaeus	+	–	–	–
Clelia clelia	+	–	–	–
Clelia occipitolutea	+	–	–	–
Elapomorphus tricolor	+	–	–	–
Leimadophis sagittifer	–	–	+	+
Lystrophis dorbignyi	+	+	–	–
Lystrophis semicinctus	+	+	–	+
Oxyrhopus rhombifer	+	+	–	+
Philodryas aestivus	+	+	–	–
Philodryas boroni	+	–	–	+
Philodryas patagoniensis	+	+	+	+
Philodryas psammophideus	–	–	–	+
Phimophis vittatus	–	–	–	+
Pseudotomodon trigonatus	–	–	+	+
Sibynomorphus turgidus	+	–	–	–
Waglerophis merremi	+	–	–	+
Micrurus frontalis	+	–	–	–
Bothrops alternatus	+	+	–	–
Bothrops neuwiedii	+	–	–	+
Crotalus durissus	+	+	–	+
Quelonios				
Kinosternon scorpioides	–	–	–	–
Geochelone petersi°	–	–	–	–
Cocodrilos				
Caiman latirostris	+	+	–	–

1976) Ademas los hylidos arborícolas *Phyllomedusa sauvagii* y *P. hypocondrialis* cubren el cuerpo entero con la secreción de lípidos de las glándulas cutáneas alveolares distribuída con las manos y los pies (Blaylock, Ruibal, y Platt-Aloia, 1976)

4. Refugios en huecos de árboles. El fondo de estos huecos es impermeabilizado por secreciones cutáneas, donde se protegen las ranas durante períodos de sequías. Este comportamiento es propio de un hylido, *Phrynohyas venulosa*

Otras Adaptaciones

Alimentación.—En los anfibios el consumo de presas es principalmente de artrópodos (insectos, arácnidos, y miriápodos), moluscos, y pequeños vertebrados. Los más grandes entre ellos (*Leptodactylus chaquensis, Bufo paracnemis, Ceratophrys*, y *Lepidobatrachus*) pueden capturar otros anfibios y roedores. En los saurios la dieta es principalmente de artrópodos, salvo los de gran tamaño, como *Tupinambis*, donde además de la dieta vegetal se agregan pequeños vertebrados y moluscos. En los ofidios se da la dieta de pequeños vertebrados, en especial anfibios y roedores a veces saurios, otros ofidios, o aves. En quelonios, *Geochelone* es básicamente vegetariana (cactos, frutos, y hojas), *Kinosternon* es animalívoro. En cocodrilos, *Caiman* varía la dieta con la edad, los juveniles se alimentan de insectos, moluscos, y anfibios, ya adultos capturan peces y vertebrados superiores.

Coloraciones en función defensiva.—En varios anfibios y reptiles se dan las coloraciones crípticas. Mientras que otros como *Leptodactylus laticeps* y *Micrurus* poseen coloraciones aposemáticas en relación con secreciones de acción tóxica o de veneno

Utilización del habitat.—Los anfibios salen de los refugios solamente en las épocas de lluvias. Varios saurios usan diferentes partes de su habitat estructural—bosques, pastizales, piedras, y el suelo (Fig 12 2)

Comportamiento territorial.—Se ha comprobado en algunos anfibios del género *Leptodactylus* y de *Phyllomedusa*, ademas de los saurios del género *Tropidurus*

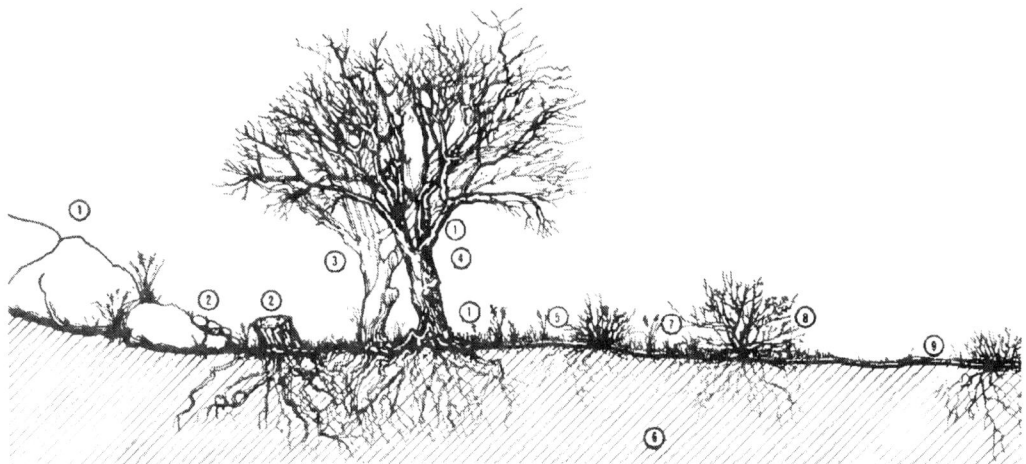

Fig. 12:2. Esquema de la utilización del habitat de algunos saurios y anfisbenios en la zona norte de Córdoba y sur de Santiago de Estero, Argentina.
Sketch of the habitat utilization by some lizards and amphisbaenians in the area north of Córdoba and south of Santiago del Estero, Argentina.
1. *Tropidurus spinulosus*, *Tropidurus* sp., 2. *Homonota horrida*, 3. *Leiosaurus paronae*, 4. *Pristidactylus cautieri*, 5. *Ophiodes intermedius*, 6. *Amphisbaena camura*, *Anops kingii*, 7. *Tupinambis rufescens*, *Teius teyou*, *Cnemidophorus leachi*, 8. *Proctotretus doellojuradoi*, 9. *Liolaemus chacoensis*.

ORIGEN Y RELACIONES DE LA HERPETOFAUNA

Con respecto a los anfibios y en grado menor a los saurios, se nota un paralelismo o aparente repetición de faunas con especies y subespecies vicariantes o cercanas entre sí, en las faunas chaqueña y litoral-mesopotámica (Tabla 12:2).

Parecería tratarse de dos faunas de un mismo origen guayano-brasileño, luego diferenciadas por aislamiento y nuevamente en contacto en algunos puntos o áreas más o menos amplias. Aquí cabe aplicar la teoría de los refugios, en períodos climáticos desfavorables, para luego producirse el repoblamiento en los períodos favorables.

En cuanto a los anfibios el papel de los sistemas hidrográficos ha sido fundamental para la distribución de las especies; esta acción continúa también en nuestros días. La teoría de los refugios y la de la fidelidad a los sistemas hidrográficos se complementan al explicar la subespeciación de *Bufo granulosus*

Tabla 12:2.—Especies y Subespecies Vicariantes o Cercanas Entre si en las Faunas Chaqueña y Litoral-Mesopotamia.

Chaqueña	Litoral-Mesopotamia
Ceratophrys sp.	*Ceratophrys ornata*
Leptodactylus anceps	*Leptodactylus prognathus*
Leptodactylus bufonius	*Leptodactylus mystacinus*
Leptodactylus chaquensis	*Leptodactylus ocellatus*
Leptodactylus gualambensis	*Leptodactylus gracilis*
Bufo arenarum chaguar	*Bufo arenarum platensis*
Bufo granulosus major	*Bufo granulosus fernandezae*
Pseudis paradoxus occidentalis	*Pseudis paradoxus platensis*
Liolaemus chacoensis	*Liolaemus wiegmannii*
Cnemidophorus leachi	*Cnemidophorus lacertoides*
Teius teyou cyanogaster	*Teius teyou teyou*
Tupinambis rufescens	*Tupinambis tequixin*

Fig. 12:3. *Mapa de las áreas ocupadas por las subespecies de* Bufo granulosus, *coincidentes con los llamados refugios (adaptado de Gallardo, 1965b).*

Map of the areas inhabited by the subspecies of *Bufo granulosus*, coinciding with the so-called refuges (adapted from Gallardo, 1965b).

1. *B. g. humboldti*, 2. *barbouri*, 3. *beebei*, 4. *merianae*, 5. *goeldi*, 6. *mini*, 7. *mirandaribeiroi*, 8. *lutzi*, 9. *granulosus*, 10. *major*, 11. *azarae*, 12. *fernandezae*, 13. *pygmaeus*, 14. *dorbignyi*.

y de *Pseudis paradoxus*. Así en dos trabajos anteriores (Gallardo, 1965b, 1969b) se describen 14 subespecies para *Bufo granulosus* (Fig. 12:3), correspondientes básicamente a los refugios que otros autores han asignado para diversas especies de animales (Haffer, 1969, 1974). Sin embargo, al mismo tiempo esas subespecies se extienden por los sistemas hidrográficos correspondientes; a la fauna chaqueña corresponde *Bufo granulosus major*. En otro trabajo sobre *Pseudis paradoxus* (Gallardo, 1961c) también se encuentra una coincidencia de este tipo, correspondiendo a la fauna chaqueña, *Pseudis paradoxus occidentalis*.

Los ofidios son de más amplia distribución y en general no responden tanto al modelo aplicable a los anfibios y saurios. Así de las 26 especies de ofidios citados para la fauna chaqueña, 8 también habitan la Provincia de Buenos Aires; mientras que los anfibios sólo dos a tres coinciden, sobre un total de 30 especies citadas para la fauna chaqueña. Entre los saurios chaqueños, *Leiosaurus paronae* tiene sus vicariantes en la fauna subandina y en la Patagonia—*L. catamarcensis* y *L. bellii*, respectivamente (Gallardo, 1961a). Otro tanto puede decirse con respecto a *Liolaemus chacoensis* y las especies subandinas y patagónicas del género *Liolaemus* y de *Homonota horrida* con respecto a sus vicariantes *H. borellii* y *H. darwinii*. Por lo que podemos suponer un parentesco andino-patagónico para algunos saurios chaqueños. Los cocodrilos se han distribuído a través de los ríos y han alcanzado localidades muy al oeste en la región; en esto coinciden con la distribución de los peces.

Hay constancias paleontológicas de un avance mucho más hacia el oeste de faunas similares a las del Río Paraná, lo que habría coincidido con un avance de una fauna originalmente de un ambiente más húmedo, que dió origen a la fauna herpetológica chaqueña, adaptada a condiciones climáticas más rigurosas. Así surge de los trabajos de Fernández (1976), quien señala el hallazgo de esta fauna acuática fósil, correspondiente al Eoceno (Formación Lumbreras), en la actual puna jujeña. Por otra parte el ambiente chaqueño se habría extendido muy hacia el sur, alcanzando el sudeste de la Provincia de Buenos Aires (Monte Hermoso), de acuerdo a los trabajos paleontológicos de Tonni (1974) y de Chani (1977), pues según dichos autores esto se debería a que habría habido fluctuaciones paleoecológicas de climas secos y climas húmedos entre el Plioceno superior y la actualidad. Véase Báez y Scillato Yane (este volumen) para una exposición completa de los paleoclimas de la región.

En general se nota actualmente un empobrecimiento faunístico hacia el sur, con respecto a la fauna de anfibios del sudeste de Brasil y la Provincia de Misiones, Argentina, en la fauna litoral-mesopotámica. Es así como en la Provincia de Buenos Aires de 22 especies existentes en el nordeste de la provincia quedan solamente seis en el sur. En zonas intermedias, como la Provincia de Corrientes, hay una duplicación de faunas al coexistir en parte de la provincia las faunas chaqueñas y litoral-mesopotámia (33 anfibios señalados para Corrientes).

SUMMARY

The Chacoan herpetofauna occupies the northern part of the Chaco-Bonariensian Plain having an elevation of 100 to 500 m. Below 100 m there is a transition to the Litoral-Mesopotamian fauna, above 500 m there is a transition to the subandean fauna. In the Chaco the rainfall gradient generally coincides with the topography. The vegetation principally is a Chacoan park type with monte and isolated trees interspersed in grassland, thorn bushes and halophytic vegetation are present locally. Rivers influence faunal distributions.

The herpetofauna is composed of five families of amphibians, five of lizards, one of amphisbaenians, five of snakes, two of turtles, and one of crocodilians. There is a total of 52 genera and 79 species (Table 12.1). The amphibians and to a lesser degree the lizards have a parallel origin with the Litoral-Mesopotamian fauna. Both apparently originated from the same Guiana-Brasilian stock, which differentiated later through isolation and reinvasion of some areas. This view fits the refugia theory for survival during unfavorable climatic periods with subsequent reinvasion of areas when favorable climates returned. River systems have been fundamental to the distribution of amphibians. Snakes have broader distributions and generally do not follow the patterns of amphibians and lizards. Turtles and crocodilians reach farthest west through the rivers, their distributions tend to coincide with those of the fish fauna. The Chacoan herpetofauna seems to have originated from the Paraná River fauna which in the past extended to the west, where it subsequently adapted to the more rigorous climatic conditions. Among the species of the Chacoan herpetofauna are several that show reproductive, dietary, and/or ethological adaptations denoting their adjustment to the conditions present on the Chaco-Bonariensian Plain.

BIBLIOGRAFIA

BARRIO, A. 1965. Afinidades del canto nupcial de la especies cavicolas del genero *Leptodactylus* (Anura Leptodactylidae). Physis 25:401–410.

BLAYLOCK, L. A., RUIBAL, R., PLATT-ALOIA, K. 1976. Skin structure and wiping behaviour of phyllomedusine frogs. Copeia 1976(2):283–295.

BOETTGER, O. 1885. Liste von Reptilien und Batrachiern aus Paraguay. Z. Naturforsch. 58:213–248.

BOULENGER, G. A. 1889. On a collection of batrachians made by Prof. Charles Spegazzini at Colonia Resistencia, South Chaco, Argentine Republic. Ann. Mus. Civ. Stor. Nat. Genova 7:246–249.

BOULENGER, G. A. 1894. List of reptiles and batrachians, collected by Dr. J. Bohls near Asunción Paraguay. Ann. Mag. Nat. Hist. (6)13:342–348.

BOULENGER, G. A. 1898. List of reptiles batrachians and fishes collected by Cav. Guido Boggiani in the northern Chaco. Ann. Mus. Civ. Stor. Nat. Genova (9)39:125–126.

BUDGETT, J. S. 1899. Notes on the batrachians of the Paraguayan Chaco, with observation upon their breeding habits and development especially with regard *Phyllomedusa hypochondrialis* Cope. Also description of new genus. Q. J. Microsc. Sci. 42:305–333.

CABRERA, A. L. 1971. Fitogeografia de la República Argentina. Bol. Soc. Argentina Bot. 14:1–42.

CEI, J. M. 1948. El ritmo estacional en los fenomenos ciclicos endocrinosexuales de la rana criolla (*Leptodactylus ocellatus* (L.)) del Norte Argentino. Acta Zool. Lilloana 6:283–331.

CEI, J. M. 1949. Generalidades sobre el ciclo sexual y el predominio de la espermitogenesis anual continua en varios batracios de la región chaqueña. Ibid 7:527–544.

CEI, J. M. 1950. *Leptodactylus chaquensis* n. sp. y el valor sistemático real de la especie linneana *Leptodactylus ocellatus* en la Argentina. Ibid 9:395–423.

CEI, J. M. 1955. Chacoan batrachian in central Argentina. Copeia 1955(4):291–293.

CHANI, J. M. 1977. Relaciones de un nuevo Teiidae (Lacertilia) fosil del Plioceno Superior de Argentina, *Callopistes bicuspidatus* n. sp. Rev. Inst. Miguel Lillo Publ. Espec. 133–153.

COPE, E. D. 1862. Catalogue of reptiles obtained during the exploration of the Paraná-Paraguay-Bermejo and Uruguay rivers by Cap. Thos. J. Page. Proc. Acad. Nat. Sci. Philadelphia 14:346–359.

D'ORBIGNY, A. 1847. Voyage dans l'Amerique Meridionale. Ière Partie Reptiles 5:5–12.

DUELLMAN, W. E., VELOSO, M. A. 1977. Phylogeny of *Pleurodema* (Anura, Leptodactylidae). A biogeographic model. Univ. Kansas Mus. Nat. Hist. Occas. Pap. (64):1–46.

FERNANDEZ, J 1976 Hallazgo de peces pulmonados fósiles en la puna jujeña Ann Soc Cient Argentina 201 13–18

GALLARDO J M 1951 Sobre un Teiidae (Reptilia Sauria) poco conocido para la fauna argentina Com Mus Argent Cienc Nat Bernardino Rivadavia Inst Nac Invest Cienc Nat Zool 2 1–8

GALLARDO J M 1953 El escuerzo como animal de terrano Ichthys 1 75–79

GALLARDO J M 1957 Las subespecies argentinas de *Bufo granulosus* Spix Rev Mus Argent Cienc Nat Bernardino Rivadavia Inst Nac Invest Cienc Nat Zool 3 337–374

GALLARDO, J M 1959 Sobre un Iguánidae del noroeste argentino, *Leiocephalus caducus* (Cope) Acta Zool Lilloana 17 485–497

GALLARDO, J M 1961a Estudio zoogeográfico del género *Leiosaurus* (Reptilia, Sauria) Physis 22 113–118

GALLARDO J M 1961b Panorama zoológico argentino Batracios y Reptiles Ibid 22 171–180

GALLARDO, J M 1961c On the species of Pseudidae (Amphibia, Anura) Bull Mus Comp Zool Harvard Univ 125 111–134

GALLARDO J M 1962 El género *Kentropyx* (Sauria, Teiidae) en la Republica Argentina Acta Zool Lilloana 18 243–250

GALLARDO, J M 1964a Los Anfibios de la Provincia de Entre Ríos, Argentina y algunas notas sobre su distribución geográfica y ecología Neotropica 10 23–28

GALLARDO, J M 1964b Consideraciones sobre *Leptodactylus ocellatus* (L) (Amphibia, Anura) y especies aisladas Physis 24 373–384

GALLARDO, J M 1964c *Leptodactylus gracilis* (D et B) y especies aisladas (Amphibia, Leptodactylidae) Rev Mus Argent Cienc Nat Bernardino Rivadavia Inst Nac Invest Cienc Nat Zool 9 37–57

GALLARDO, J M 1964d Una nueva forma de Pseudidae (Amphibia, Anura) y algunas consideraciones sobre las especies argentinas de esta familia Acta Zool Lilloana 20 193–209

GALLARDO, J M 1964e *Leptodactylus prognathus* Boul y *L mystacinus* (Burm) con sus respectivas especies aliadas (Amphibia Leptodactylidae del grupo Cavicola) Rev Mus Argent Cienc Nat Bernardino Rivadavia Inst Nac Invest Cienc Nat Zool 9 91–121

GALLARDO, J M 1965a Una nueva subespecie chaqueña *Bufo arenarum chaguar* (Amphibia, Bufonidae) Neotropica 11 84–88

GALLARDO, J M 1965b The species *Bufo granulosus* Spix (Salientia, Bufonidae) and its geographic variation Bull Mus Comp Zool Harvard Univ 134 107–138

GALLARDO, J M 1966a *Liolaemus lentus* nov sp (Iguanidae) de La Pampa y algunas observaciones sobre los saurios de dicha provincia argentina y del oeste de Buenos Aires Neotropica 12 13–29

GALLARDO J M 1966b Las especies argentinas del género *Ophiodes* Wagler Rev Mus Argent Cienc Nat Bernardino Rivadavia Inst Nac Invest Cienc Nat Zool 9 123–116

GALLARDO, J M 1966c Zoogeografía de los anfibios chaqueños Physis 26 67–81

GALLARDO J M 1968a Relaciones zoogeográficas de la fauna batracológica del oeste de la Provincia de Santa Fe (Argentina) Com Mus Argent Cienc Nat Bernardino Rivadavia Inst Nac Invest Cienc Nat Ecol 1 1–13

GALLARDO, J M 1968b Las especies argentinas del género *Mabuya* Fitzinger (Scincidae, Sauria) Rev Mus Argent Cienc Nats Bernardino Rivadavia Inst Nac Invest Cienc Nat Zool 9 177–196

GALLARDO J M 1968c Sobre la validez de algunas especies argentinas de *Pleurodema* (Anura Leptodactylidae) Physis 28 135–144

GALLARDO J M 1969a Especies de saurios (Reptilia) de la Provincia de Santa Fe, Argentina y consideraciones sobre su ecología y zoogeografía Neotropica 15 73–85

GALLARDO J M 1969b La distribución de las subespecies de *Bufo granulosus* Spix Su fidelidad a los sistemas hidrográficos Sudamericanos Cien Invest 25 406–416

GALLARDO, J M 1971 Composición faunística de los Saurios de la Provincia de La Pampa, República Argentina Neotropica 17 44–48

HAFFER, J 1969 Speciation in Amazonian forest birds Science 165 131–137

HAFFER J 1974 Avian speciation in tropical South America Publ Nuttall Ornithol Club, Cambridge 14 1–390

McCLANAHAN, L L JR SHOEMAKER, V H, RUIBAL, R 1976 Structure and Function of the Cocoon of a Ceratophryid Frog Copeia 1976 (1) 179–185

MEHELY L 1904 Investigations on Paraguayan batrachians Ann Mus Nat Hungary 2 207–231

MULLER L, HELLMICH, W 1936 Amphibien und Reptilien I Teil Amphibia, Cheloma, Loricata Wiss Ergeb Deutsch Gran Chaco-Expedition Stuttgart, 120 p

PERACCA, M G 1895 Viaggio del dott Alfredo Borelli nella Rep Argentina e nel Paraguay rettili ed anfibi Boll Mus Zool Torino 10(195) 1–32

STEINDACHNER, F 1864 Batrachologische Mitteilungen Verh Zool Bot Ges Wien 14 239–288

TONNI E P 1974 Un nuevo Cariámido (Aves, Gruiformes) del Plioceno Superior de la Provincia de Buenos Aires Ameghiniana 11 366–372

VELLARD J 1948 Batracios del Chaco Argentino Acta Zool Lilloana 5 137–174

13. The Patagonian Herpetofauna

José M Cei

Instituto de Biología Animal
Universidad Nacional de Cuyo
Casilla Correo 327
Mendoza, Argentina

The word Patagonia is derived from the term "Patagones," meaning big-legged men, applied to the tall Tehuelche Indians of southernmost South America by Ferdinand Magellan in 1520 Subsequently, this picturesque name came to be applied to a conspicuous continental region and to its biota

Biologically Patagonia can be defined as that region east of the Andes and extending southward to the Straits of Magellan and eastward to the Atlantic Ocean The northern boundary is not so clear cut Elements of the Pampean biota penetrate southward along the coast between the Rio Colorado and the Rio Negro (Fig 13 1) Also, in the west Patagonian landscapes and biota enter the volcanic regions of southern Mendoza, almost reaching the Río Atuel Basin The Patagonian region has a wide ecotonal zone with the Chacoan region (Gallardo this volume) The monte vegetation (Morello, 1958) with its several formations containing numerous subtropical elements extends south to the Península de Valdes, the monte enters the Río Chubut drainage and extends westward to the Río Neuquén, Río Agrio, and Río Limay valleys South of the Rio Negro, the monte associations exist in a system of saline lowlands (*bajos*) and reach irregular spurs of the Meseta de Somuncurá, a typical Patagonian environment (Cei, 1969a,b, Ruiz Leal, 1972) Nevertheless, there is a general, sometimes remarkable agreement between the phytogeographic boundaries of the Monte-Pampean and the Patagonian regions and the distribution patterns of their herpetofaunas Herein I emphasize the biota of the Cis-Andean steppe to the near exclusion of the Trans-Andean austral forest ecosystems treated by Formas (this volume)

Patagonia is a region of sedimentary rocks and soils, mostly tablelands subjected to prolonged erosion Scattered through the region are extensive areas of extrusive basaltic rocks The open landscape is dissected by transverse rivers descending from the snowy Andean cordillera, drainage is poor near the Atlantic coast Patagonia is subjected to severe seasonal drought with about five cold winter months and a cool dry summer infrequently interrupted by irregular rains and floods

HISTORY OF THE PATAGONIAN BIOTA

In contrast to the present, almost uniform steppe associations in Río Negro Chubut and Santa Cruz provinces, during Oligocene and Miocene times tropical and subtropical vegetation occurred along with xerophytic woodlands with luxuriant mesophytic gallery forests A comparison of the rich Miocene flora of Pichi Leufu, Río Negro (Berry, 1938) with analogous associations from Mirhoja, Chubut, Valcheta, Río Negro, and Río Chalia, Santa Cruz, shows a mixture of mesic tropical elements (*Ficus, Fagara, Nectandra, Tabebuia, Myristica, Sterculia,* tree ferns, *Erythroxylon, Oreopanax, Maytenus*), including climbers (*Buettneria, Banisteria, Bignonia, Cissus, Paullinia, Sapindus, Strychnos*), together with nontropical genera (*Araucaria, Azora, Berberis, Ginkgo, Laurelia, Embothrium, Fitzroya, Libocedrus, Podocarpus, Lomatia, Peumus Myrceugenia, Drimys*) Most of the latter are characteristic components of the present temperate Valdivian forest Nevertheless, xeric areas in the Middle Tertiary of Patagonia are suggested by certain paleofloras containing *Schinopsis, Schinus,* and *Cupania* The former is a significant genus of trees in the subtropical Chacoan region

Nothofagus forests were widespread in Patagonia in the Eocene and Oligocene, but

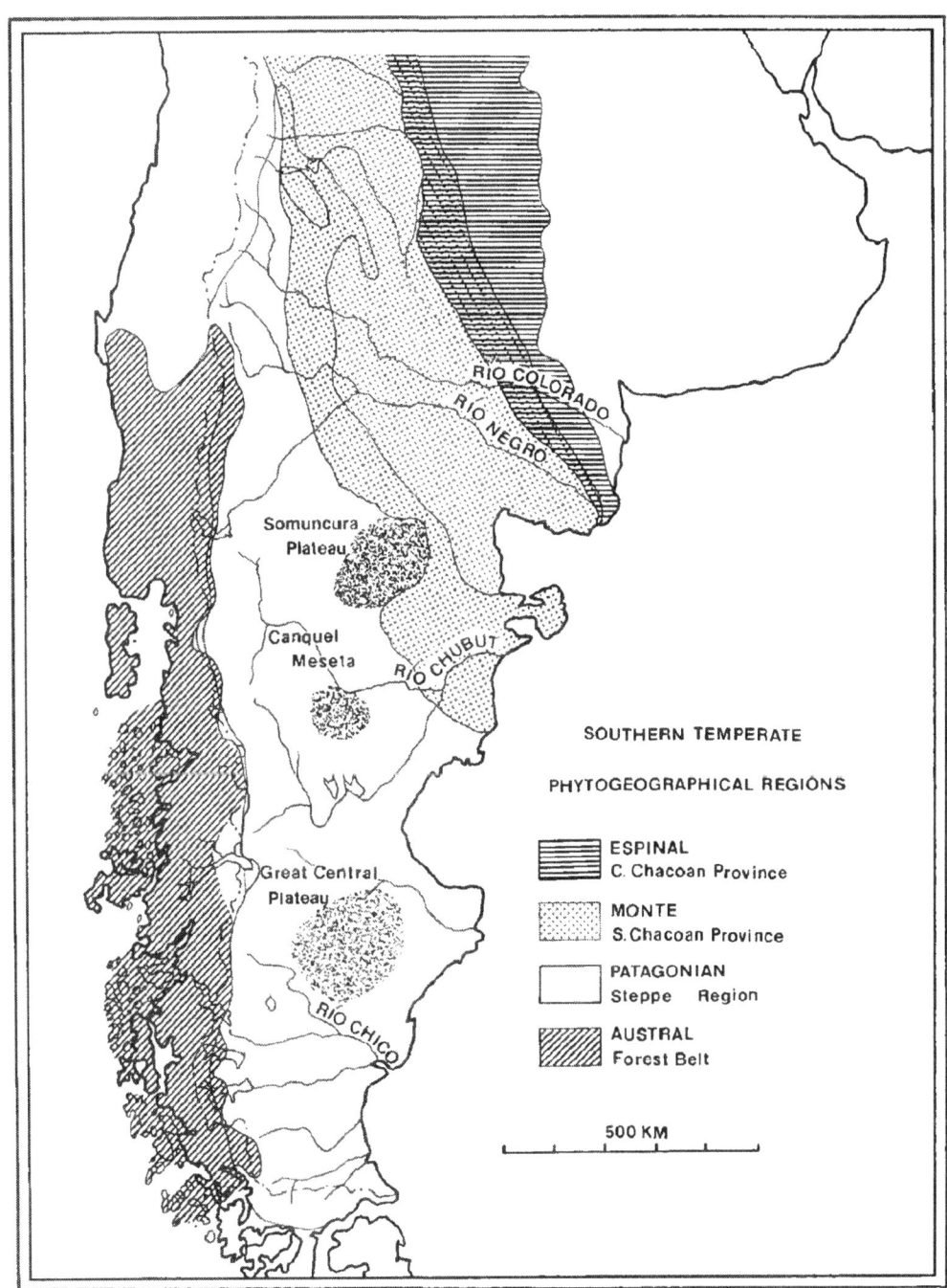

FIG. 13:1. Phytogeographic regions of austral South America.
Regiones fitogeográficas de Sud América austral.

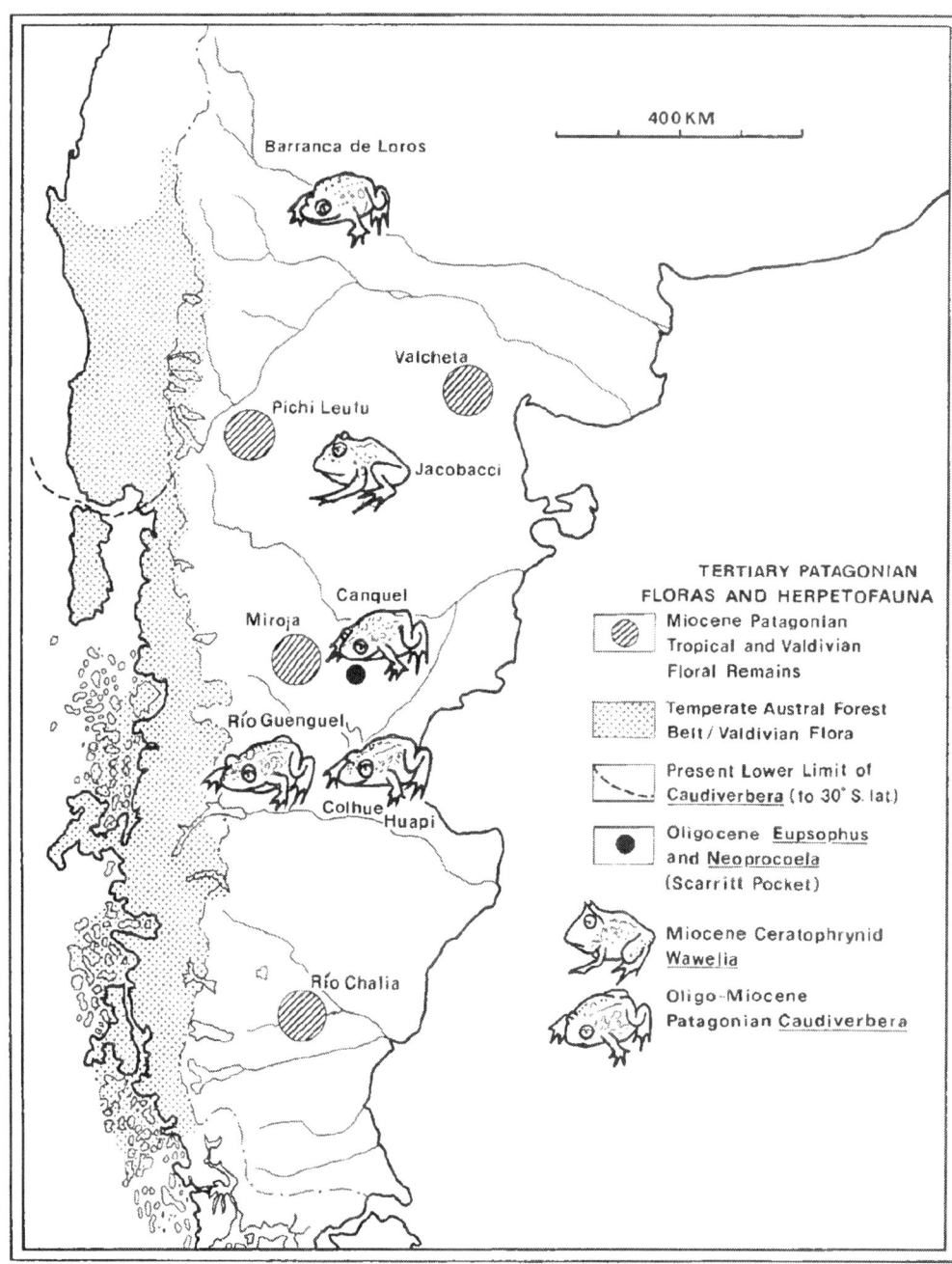

FIG. 13:2. Paleontological records of the lower Tertiary Patagonian flora and of leptodactylid frogs.
Hallazgos paleontológicos de flora patagónica del Terciario inferior y de anuros leptodactylidos.

these associations decreased and retreated southward and westward in the Middle and Late Tertiary. *Chusquea* bamboo groves occur in Cenozoic deposits at Laguna Hunco, Chubut. Further evidence of paleoclimatic conditions in Patagonia is derived from the extensive paleo-mammal faunas (Báez and Scillato Yané, this volume) and more limited paleo-herpetofaunas (Báez and Gasparini, this volume).

Primitive leptodactylid, ceratophrynine, and bufonid frogs have been recorded by Schaeffer (1949), Chaffee (1952), and Casamiquela (1963) from the Deseadan, early Oligocene Scarritt Pocket Formation (Canquel, Chubut) and from the upper Miocene of Río Negro (Fig 13.2). The living Chilean frog *Caudiverbera caudiverbera* is almost identical to the fossil frogs of the same genus. A fossil frog from the Oligocene of Chubut referred to *Eupsophus* by Schaeffer (1949) has been considered the same as living *E roseus*, a species characteristic of the *Nothofagus* forests of southern Chile (Bogart, 1970). These fossils clearly establish the presence of telmatobine frogs in Patagonia in the Oligocene and Miocene.

The Oligocene *Neoprocoela* was provisionally referred to a *Batrachophrynus* or *Telmatobius*-like leptodactylid stock by Schaeffer (1949). Tihen (1962) considered it to be a species of *Bufo* in the Palearctic *Bufo calamita* group. The fossil was again associated with the telmatobiine genera *Telmatobufo* and *Batrachophrynus* by Lynch (1971). New material from the same formation supports the inclusion of *Neoprocoela* in *Bufo* (Estes, pers comm). The placement of *Neoprocoela* in the *Bufo calamita* group has interesting biogeographical implications. Serological evidence (Cei, 1977) supports a relationship between the European *Bufo calamita* and the small *B variegatus* presently restricted to the austral *Nothofagus* forests of Argentina and Chile (Gallardo, 1962).

The presence of a ceratophrynne frog (*Wawela gerholdi*) in the Miocene provides herpetological evidence for the southward extent of tropical elements in the Middle Tertiary. Reptilian remains substantiate the long history of tropical elements in Patagonia. The fossil snake *Dinilysia patagonica* from the Upper Cretaceous of Neuquén is related to boids and aniliids that are widespread in tropical South America. Furthermore, boid snakes (*Madtsoia*), crocodilians (*Necrosuchus, Sebecus, Eocaiman*), and melanid and pelomedusid turtles from Paleocene-Eocene deposits in Chubut are indicative of tropical environments (Gasparini and Báez, 1975). Iguanid (*Erichosaurus debilis*) and teiid (*Diasemosaurus occidentalis*) lizards lived in southern Santa Cruz in the Miocene.

PATAGONIAN FAUNAL REGIONS

Two major faunal regions (habitats) can be defined in Patagonia. These are the northern or ancient region and the southern or Santa Cruz region; the border between these regions is approximately at the Río Chubut at 45°S (Fig 13.3). These habitats correspond to ancient physiographic areas: the Patagonian Massif and the Deseado Massif respectively (Figs 13.4–5). These massifs are ancient structural continental units known as nesocratons (Harrington, 1962). In spite of its less marked subpositive tendency in comparison with the Pampean Massif, the whole region of the Patagonian Massif has been a site of almost uninterrupted accumulation of continental deposits. More rarely it received shallow marine deposits peripherally at times of oceanic transgressions in the Eocene-early Oligocene, middle Oligocene, and middle Miocene. The smaller Deseado Massif had a subpositive tendency even less marked than the Patagonian Massif; accordingly, its relief was often depressed, and during prolonged subsidences it became a sedimentary area like the adjacent pericratonic basins (Harrington, 1962).

The northern or ancient Patagonian region extends through Neuquén, Río Negro, and Chubut provinces (Fig 13.6). The subcordilleran area in Neuquén is drained by the Río Agrio and Río Neuquén, which flow into the Río Limay, a tributary of the Río Negro. Extra-cordilleran mesetas include the large Meseta de Somuncurá (1000–1700 m eleva-

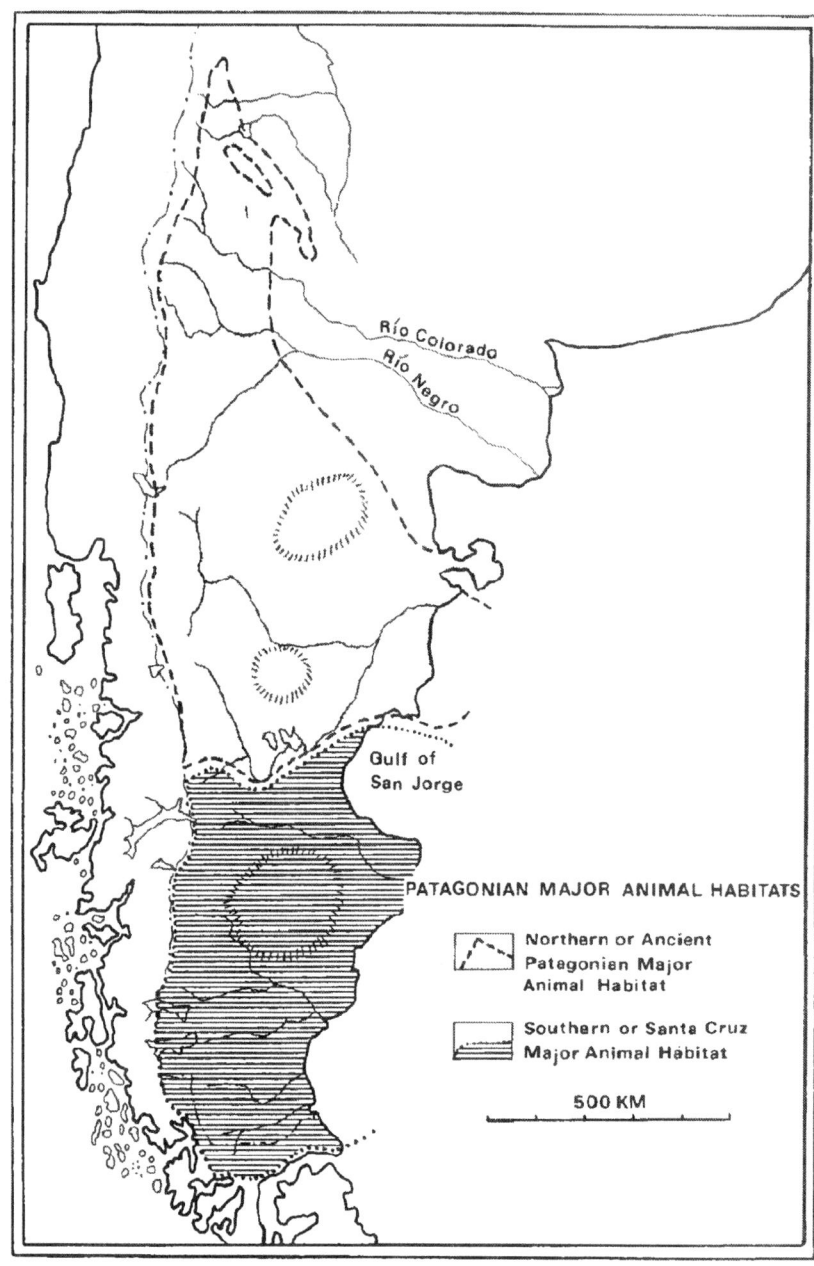

FIG. 13:3. Major herpetofaunal regions of Patagonia.
Regiones herpetofaunísticas fundamentales de Patagonia.

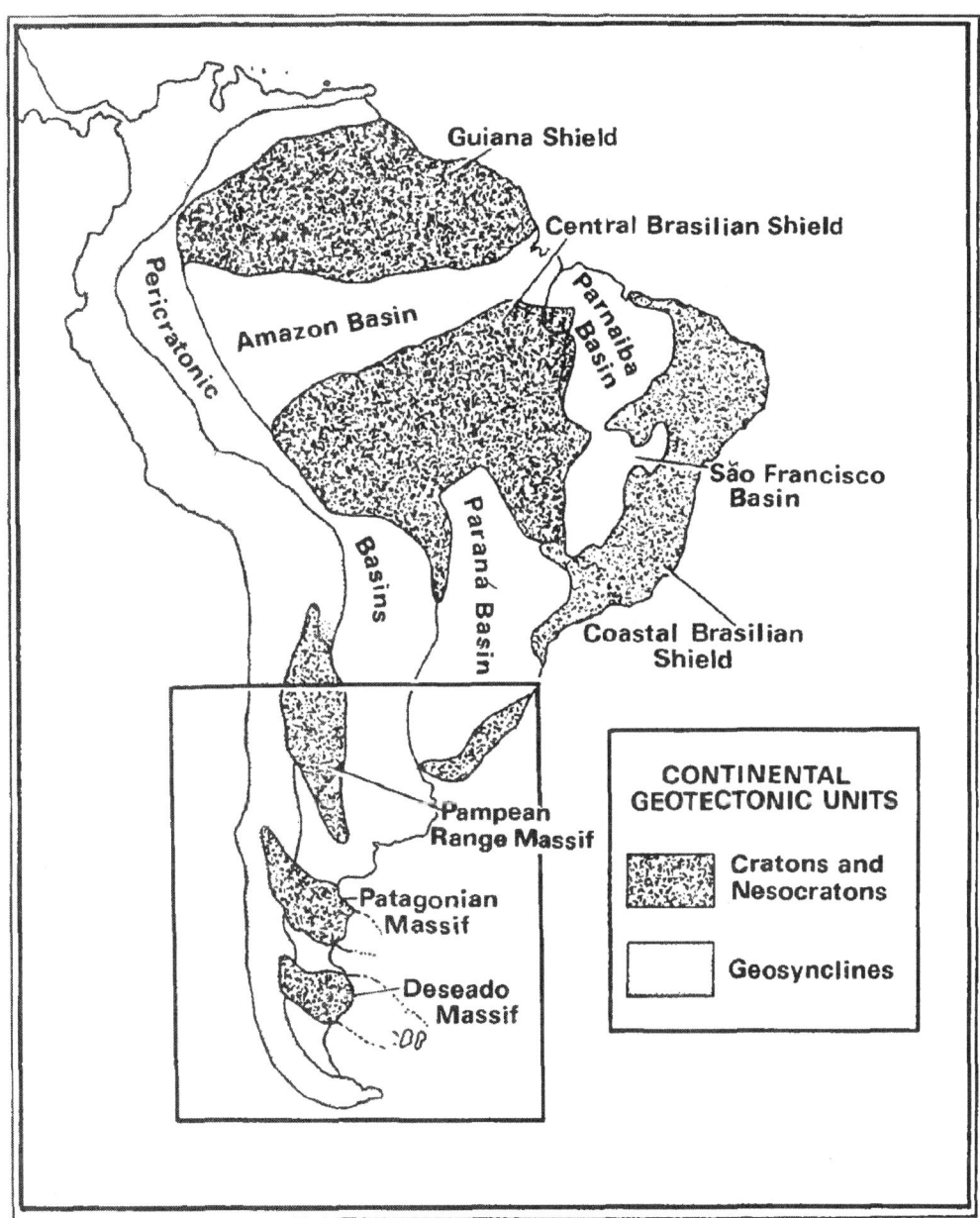

Fig. 13:4. General tectonic structure of South America (after Harrington, 1962). The area in the box is enlarged in figure 5.
Estructura geotectónica de Sud América (según Harrington, 1962). El área en el recorte aparece aumentada en la figura 5.

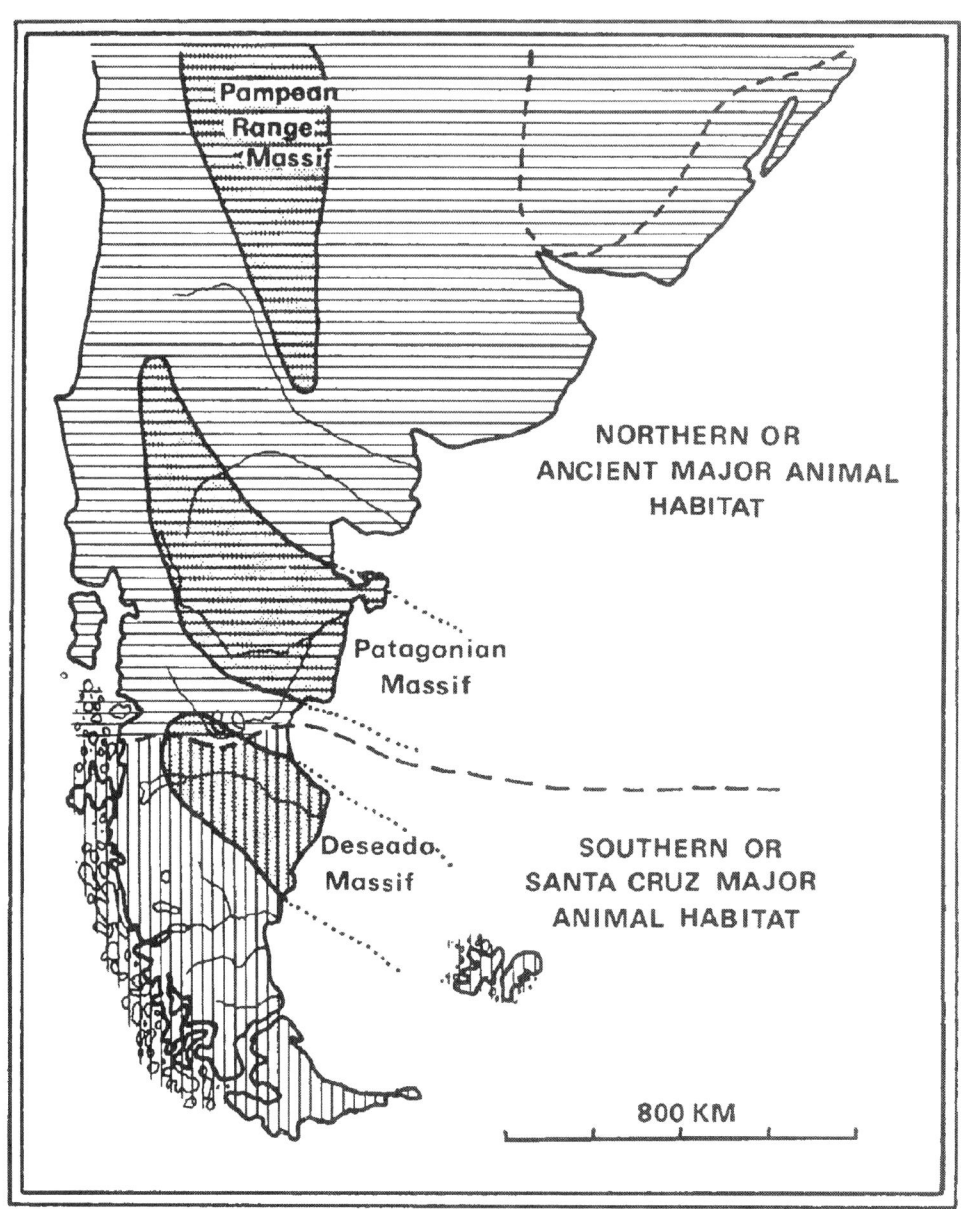

Fig. 13:5. Location of the southern massifs and their relation to the major Patagonian herpetofaunal regions.
Ubicación de los macizos australes y su relación con las regiones herpetofaunísticas fundamentales patagónicas.

tion) and the Meseta de Canquel, plus smaller mesetas of the same lower and middle Tertiary age along the Andean front, their small lakes are close to the last eastern patches of *Nothofagus* and *Araucaria* forests Along the base of the Andes there is an Austral-Patagonian ecotonal zone, however, it is much narrower than the Monte-Patagonian ecotone extending from the Río Colorado to Valcheta, onto the northern spurs of the Meseta de Somuncurá, and southward to near Bahía Camarones on the Atlantic coast (Cabrera, 1951)

Floristically, the ancient Patagonian region is characterized by a predominantly steppe vegetation with scattered green bushes (*Mulinum spinosum*), several grasses, low herbaceous plants, some spiny plants, and a variety of low bushes, additional kinds of plants are present in saline environments and riparian situations (Table 13 1) The most characteristic element of the monte formations is the creosote bush (*Larrea*), which is represented by five sympatric species in the ecotonal zone at Valcheta (Río Negro) In typical Patagonian landscapes only the low *Larrea ameghinoi* is present

The cool Patagonian steppes dominated by *Mulinum* and *Stipa*, with scattered creeping cushionlike plants, exist in western Neuquén, southwestern Río Negro, and in most of Chubut, provinces In these areas the steppes are commonly associated with basaltic landscapes resulting from the rampant Cenozoic volcanic activity The steppes are discontinuous in northern Neuquen and Rio Negro provinces, where they occur mostly at elevations of more than 900 to 1000 m

The southern or Santa Cruz Faunal Region extends from about 45°S to the Straits of Magellan (Fig 13 7) This region encompasses some distinct physiographic areas The arid valley of the Río Deseado borders the northern limits of the large Altiplanicie Central, a dead volcanic landscape with scattered clay basins and petrified early Cenozoic trees (*Araucarites*) South of the great plateau the drainage basins of the ríos Chalia, Santa Cruz, Coyle, and Gallegos provide more moist lowlands extending to the Straits of Magellan These rivers drain the glacial valleys of the

TABLE 13 1—Characteristic Types of Vegetation in the Ancient Patagonian Region

Herbs	Spiny or Sclerotic Plants
Stipa	*Chuquiraga*
Festuca	*Nassauvia*
Poa	*Ephedra*
Senecio filaginoides	*Styllingia*
Grindelia chiloensis	*Verbena*
Verbena ligustrina	*Pantacantha*
Acaena caespitosa	*Adesmia*
Shrubs	*Austrocactus*
Mulinum spinosum	Hydrophylic Plants
Colliguaja integerrima	*Juncus*
Berberis cuneata	*Carex*
Lycium tenuispinosum	*Ranunculus*
Anarthrophyllum rigidum	*Hypsela*
Anarthrophyllum desideratum	*Plagiobothrys*
Trevoa spinifer	*Acaena macrostemon*
Prosopis patagonica	*Caltha*
Larrea ameghinoi	*Cortaderia*
Halophylic Plants	*Azorella*
Atriplex	
Frankenia	
Spartina	

rugged southernmost Andean cordillera The Andes are commonly bordered by sharp-edged basaltic mesetas having elevations of 1000 to 1500 m

Phytogeographically, the Santa Cruz Faunal Region agrees with Cabrera's (1951) Patagonian districts—Patagonico Subandino, Patagonico Central, and Golfo de San Jorge The Patagonico Subandino includes the basaltic mesetas (e g Meseta Vizcachas, Meseta Asador, Meseta de la Muerte, and the Meseta de Lago del Sello) and the southern humid lowlands[1] In these areas open steppe associations of *Festuca monticola*, *Bromus macranthus*, *Hordeum comosum*, *Agropyron magellanicum*, *Poa* sp , and *Deschampsia* sp predominate, but some shrubs (*Berberis cuneata*, *Nassauvia aculeata*, or *Mulinum spinosum*) are present

Phytogeographic differences between the Sub-Andean district and the central and San Jorge districts are evident by the monotonous grasslands of *Stipa humilis* in the latter The grasses are interrupted by the broad circular bushes of the blackish 'mata negra' (*Verbena*

---

[1] Although the Sub-Andean District is considered to be a single physiographic unit (Fig 13 7) for purposes of herpetofaunal analysis I distinguish the Humid Southern Lowlands

TABLE 13.2—Comparison of the Herpetofaunas in Ten Districts in Patagonia
(Numbers of species in a given district are in boldface, numbers of species in common to two districts are in Roman, and the italics are Faunal Resemblance Factors [$N_1 + N_2 /2C$ (Duellman, 1966)])

	Monte	Monte-Patagonian Ecotone	Patagonian Steppe	Volcanic Highlands	Meseta de Somuncura	Altiplano Central	Coastal District	Humid Southern Lowlands	Sub-Andean Area	Meseta del Lago de Sello
Monte	**17**	17	2	3		1	1	-	-	-
Monte-Patagonian Ecotone	*0.69*	**32**	7	7	4	5	4	2	1	
Patagonian Steppe	*0.12*	*0.29*	**17**	12	7	8	7	3	3	
Volcanic Highlands	*0.14*	*0.25*	*0.57*	**25**	8	6	5	3	1	..
Meseta de Somuncura		*0.19*	*0.50*	*0.44*	**11**	5	4	2	1	..
Altiplano Central	*0.08*	*0.24*	*0.62*	*0.35*	*0.50*	**9**	8	3	4	-
Coastal District	*0.08*	*0.20*	*0.56*	*0.30*	*0.42*	*0.94*	**8**	2	4	
Humid Southern Lowlands	...	*0.11*	*0.26*	*0.19*	*0.24*	*0.40*	*0.29*	**6**	1	2
Sub-Andean Area	...	*0.06*	*0.29*	*0.07*	*0.13*	*0.62*	*0.67*	*0.20*	**4**	
Meseta del Lago de Sello	--							*0.44*		**3**

tridens). Where shrubby formations occur, dominant plants are *Prosopis patagonica*, *Lycium ameghinoi*, *Berberis cuneata*, *Chuquiraga aurea* and *avellanedae Brachycladus caespitosus*, *Acantholippia seriphioides*, *Pleurofora patagonica*, *Ameghinoa* sp., and *Euphorbia* sp. The small trees, *Trevoa patagonica*, around the Golfo de San Jorge and in the arid valley of the Río Deseado are the most conspicuous plants in the southern region.

COMPOSITION OF THE HERPETOFAUNA

The herpetofauna of the Patagonian steppe is composed of 60 species, six of which have two or more subspecies in Patagonia, the entire herpetofauna consists of 70 species and subspecies with a noticeable degree of endemism. The fauna is made up of 14 species of anurans (23.3%), one turtle (1.7%), 34 lizards (56.7%) and 11 snakes (18.3%). For purposes of discussion, the herpetofauna has been divided according to the two major faunal regions. Of the 60 Patagonian species, 56 occur in the northern or ancient Patagonian Region, and 13 occur in the southern or Santa Cruz Region, nine species are common to the two regions (Table 13.2, Appendix 13.1). Although lizards are dominant in both regions, they comprise a much higher percentage of the herpetofauna in the southern region (Fig. 13.8).

Northern Patagonian Herpetofauna

For purposes of analysis, the region has been divided into five ecophysiographic areas (Fig. 13.6)—1) Monte associations, 2) Monte-Patagonian ecotone 3) Patagonian steppe, 4) Volcanic highlands, and 5) Meseta de Somuncurá. The distributions of the species and subspecies of amphibians and reptiles in these five areas are tabulated in Appendix 13.1 The sole Patagonian turtle, *Geochelone donosobarrosi*, and all of the Patagonian anurans are in the northern region, although one species *Pleurodema bufonina*, is widely distributed in the southern region. Likewise the single amphisbaenian and all of the snakes are in the northern region, although *Bothrops ammodytoides* enters the southern region.

All of the 17 species occurring in the monte associations are among the 32 species in the Monte-Patagonian ecotone. Included in these areas are several species characteristic of, or related to species in, the more northern regions—Pampas and Chaco, this is true of

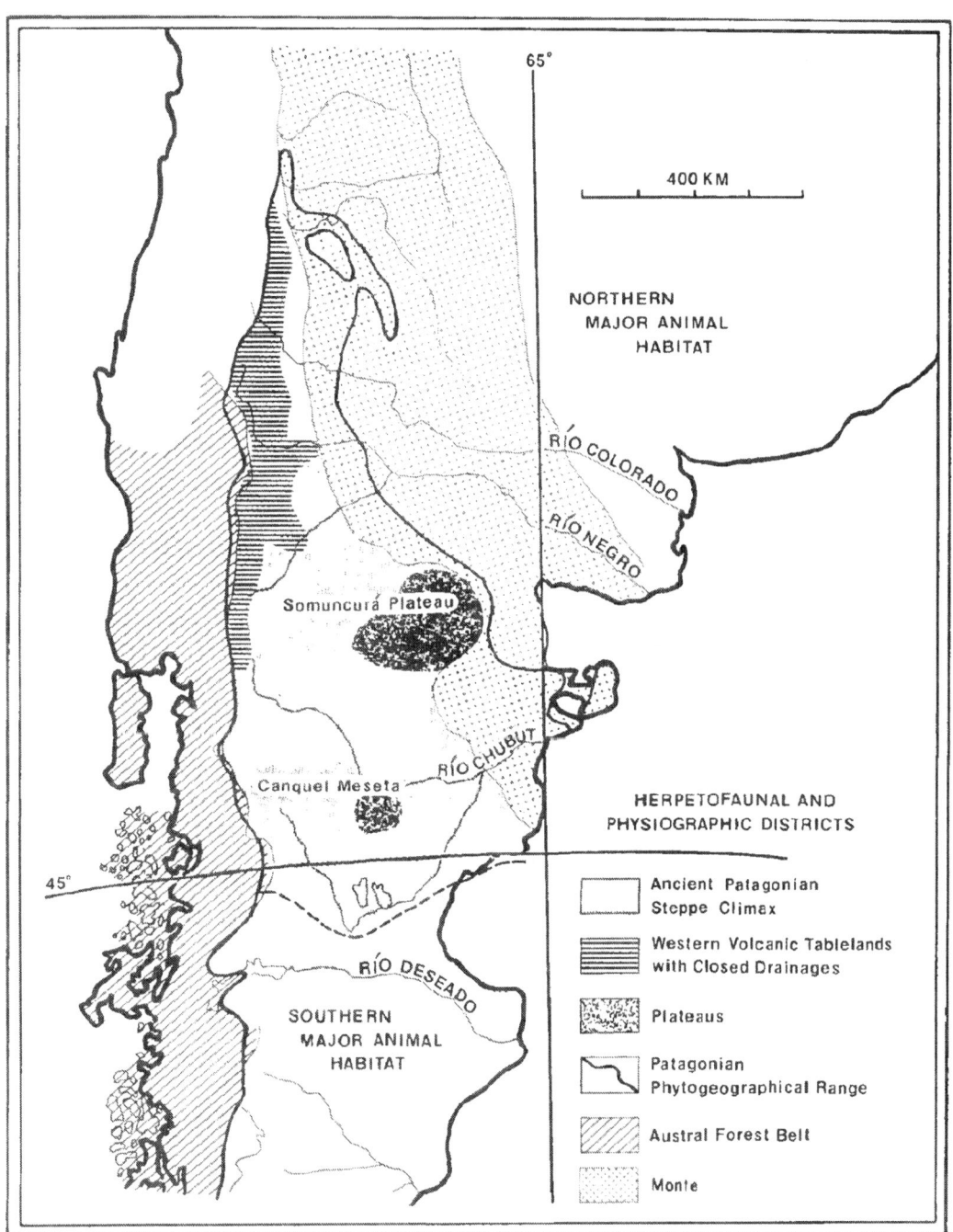

Fig. 13:6. Herpetofaunal and physiographic districts of the ancient Patagonian region.
Distritos herpetofaunísticos y fisiográficos de la región patagónica antigua.

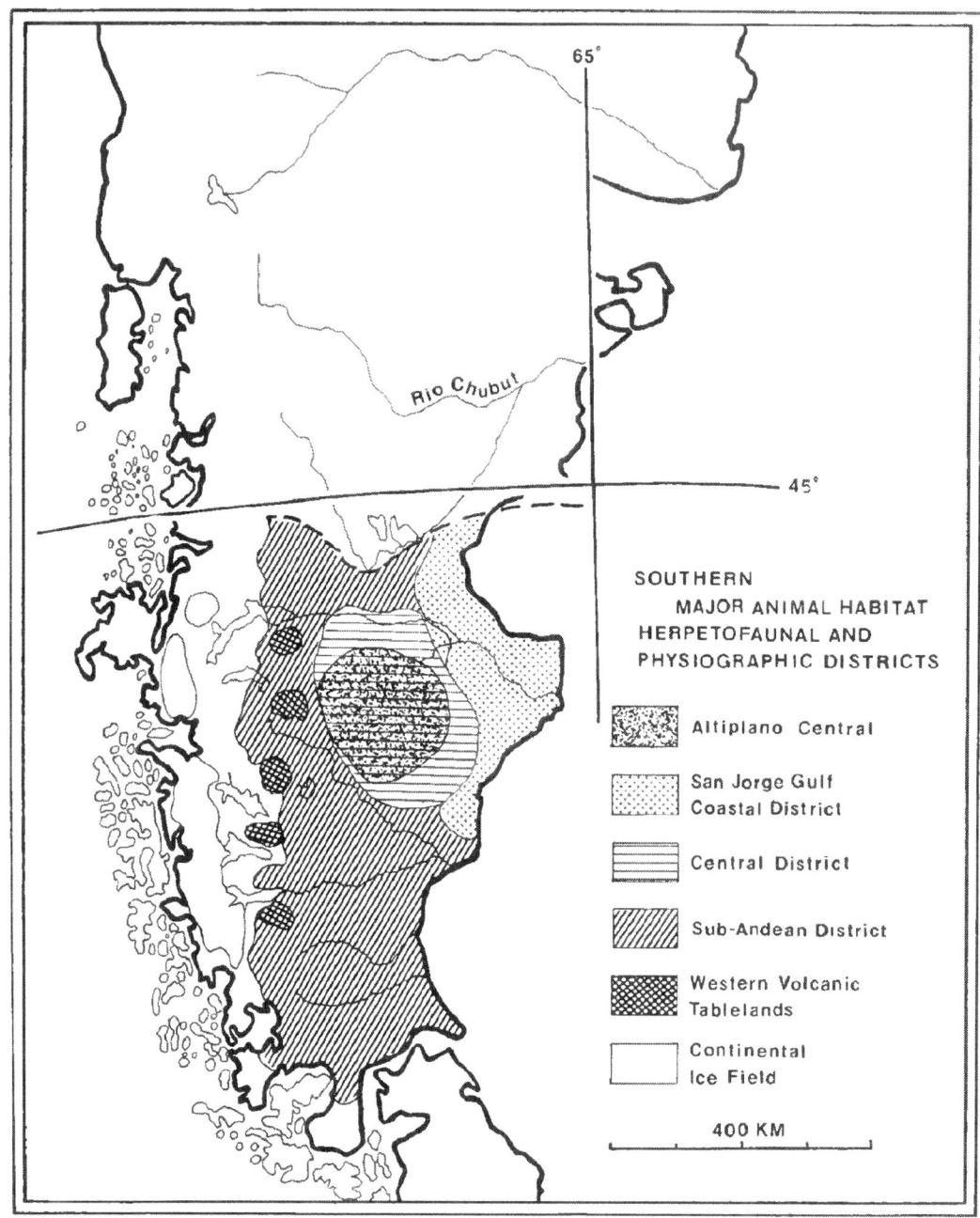

FIG. 13:7. Herpetofaunal and physiographic districts of the southern Patagonian region.
Distritos herpetofaunísticos y fisiográficos de la región sur-patagónica.

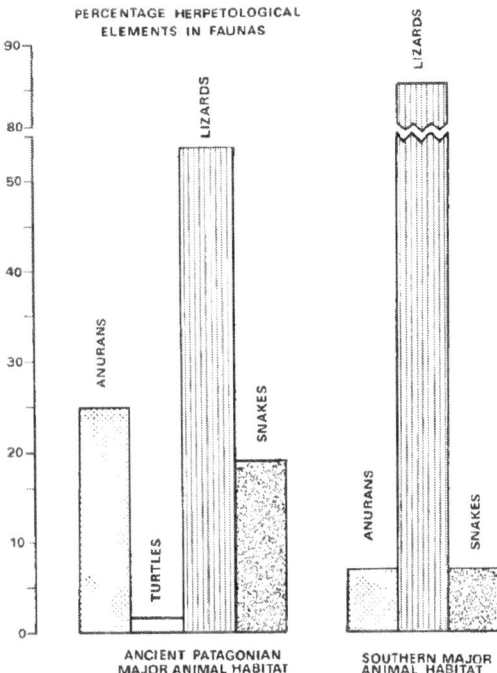

Fig. 13:8. Herpetofaunal composition of the Patagonian regions.
Composición herpetofaunística de las regiones patagónicas.

the anurans *Bufo arenarum* and *Leptodactylus ocellatus*, the lizard *Mabuya frenata*, and the snakes *Elapomorphus bilineatus*, *Lystrophis semicinctus*, and *Micrurus frontalis* (Fig. 13:9). The analysis of latitudinal distributions reveals that *Geochelone donosobarrosi* is a true member of the xerophytic scrub association south of the Río Colorado and only slightly penetrates the neighboring flats of the Pampean region. The distributions of the snake *Philodryas patagoniensis* and the lizard *Proctotretus pectinatus* extend eastward into the Pampean region (Figs. 13:10–11). On the contrary, the frog *Pleurodema bufonina* and the lizards *Homonota darwinii* and *Liolaemus bibronii* are characteristic Patagonian elements and only enter the monte peripherally; these species ascend the Andean slopes north of the Río Barrancas.

In the Patagonian steppes, extrusive basaltic rocks provide shelter for numerous lizards. *Liolaemus elongatus* is a conspicuous species in rocky areas, some of which also are inhabited by more cryptic lizards—*Liolaemus ceii* and *L. kriegi*. Isolated populations of *Phymaturus patagonicus* are subspecifically distinct—*P. p. patagonicus* in the valley of the Río Chubut and *P. p. indistinctus* in the Sierra de San Bernardo (Cei and Castro, 1973) (Fig. 13:12). *Liolaemus fitzingeri canqueli* inhabits the rocky slopes of the Meseta de Canquel and extends eastward through the salt flats to the coast, where it meets *L. f. fitzingeri*, the subspecies that is common in southern Chubut and Santa Cruz. *Diplolaemus bibronii*, more characteristic of the southern region, reaches the northern limits of its distribution at the edge of the Meseta de Somuncurá (Cei, 1971b).

Clay soils in the region hold water in the form of temporary ponds during the brief rainy season. These ponds and intermittent and permanent streams are the habitats and/or breeding sites for several species of anurans, especially leptodactylids (Barrio, 1973; Cei, 1969a,b, 1970b, 1972b; Cei and Roig, 1966, 1968; Gallardo, 1970). Some species have restricted ranges; for example, *Atelognathus solitarius* is known only from Arroyo Las Bayas, south of Pilcaniyeu, Río Negro.

Twenty-four species are known to inhabit the volcanic plateaus and extra-Andean highlands in western Neuquén and Río Negro provinces. Among them are four species of telmatobiine leptodactylid frogs (Fig. 13:3). The aquatic *Atelognathus patagonicus* is confined to the Laguna Blanca Basin. The semiterrestrial *Atelognathus praebasalticus* is composed of four geographically isolated subspecies—*A. p. praebasalticus* at Laguna Blanca, *A. p. agilis* at Laguna Casa de Piedra, *A. p. luisi* at Laguna Catan Lil, and *A. p. dobeslawi* at Barda de Santo Tomas (Cei, 1972b). *Atelognathus nitoi* and *Alsodes gargola gargola* have different distributional traits. In western Río Negro these frogs occur in small Andean lakes—Laguna Verde near Cerro Blanco at about 1450 m elevation (Barrio, 1973), and Laguna Tonchek and Laguna Schmoll at 1700 to 1750 m on the slopes of Cerro Catedral near Bariloche (Gallardo, 1970). Together with *Alsodes gargola*

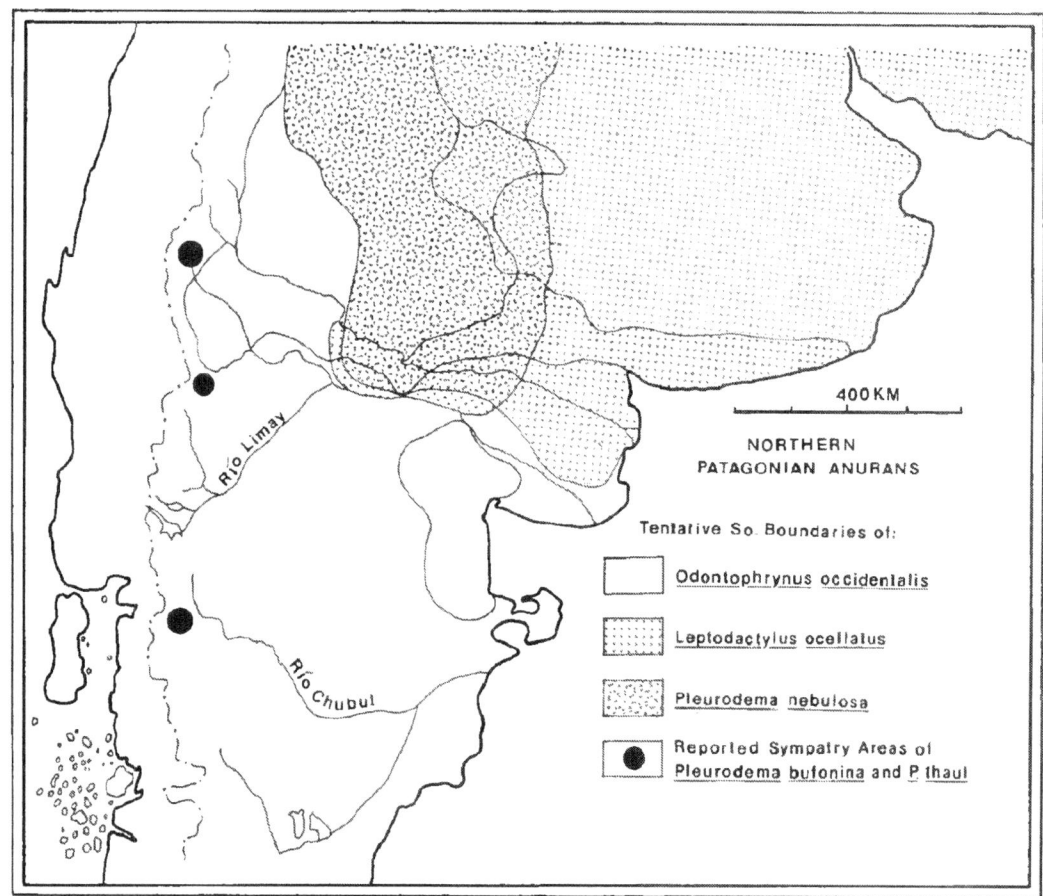

Fig. 13:9. Southern limits of distribution of taxa in the monte formation in northern Patagonia. Areas of sympatry of *Pleurodema bufonina* and *P. thaul* are indicated.

Límites meridionales de distribución de taxa en la formación del monte en el norte patagónico. Se indica las áreas de simpatría de Pleurodema bufonina *y* P. thaul.

neuquensis from the thermal brooks on the sandy Meseta Lonco Luan, 1500 m elevation in Neuquén (Cei, 1976), they belong to a transitional herpetofauna of the austral-Patagonian ecotone. Other transitional species are the frog *Pleurodema thaul* and two lizards, *Liolaemus tenuis* and *Diplolaemus leopardinus*, all characteristic inhabitants of *Araucaria* forests (Cei, 1970a, 1974b). On the xeric Meseta de Lonco Luán, dead patches of *Nothofagus* and *Chusquea* exist near the border of the *Araucaria* forests. *Liolaemus lineomaculatus* occurs on the Meseta de Lonco Luán. In other ecotonal and subandean areas of Neuquén, *Pleurodema thaul*, *Liolaemus chilensis*, and *L. buergeri* are found. The latter occurs sympatrically with the typical Patagonian lizards *Liolaemus elongatus* and *L. kriegi*. Likewise, the characteristic lizards of rocky Patagonian communities, *Phymaturus palluma* and *P. patagonicus zapalensis* occur on the basaltic plateaus. *Phymaturus palluma* extends northward in the Andes at elevations of 3000 to 3500 m to La Rioja and San Juan, and *P. patagonicus* has distinct populations (*P. p. payuniae* and *P. p. nevadoi*) to the

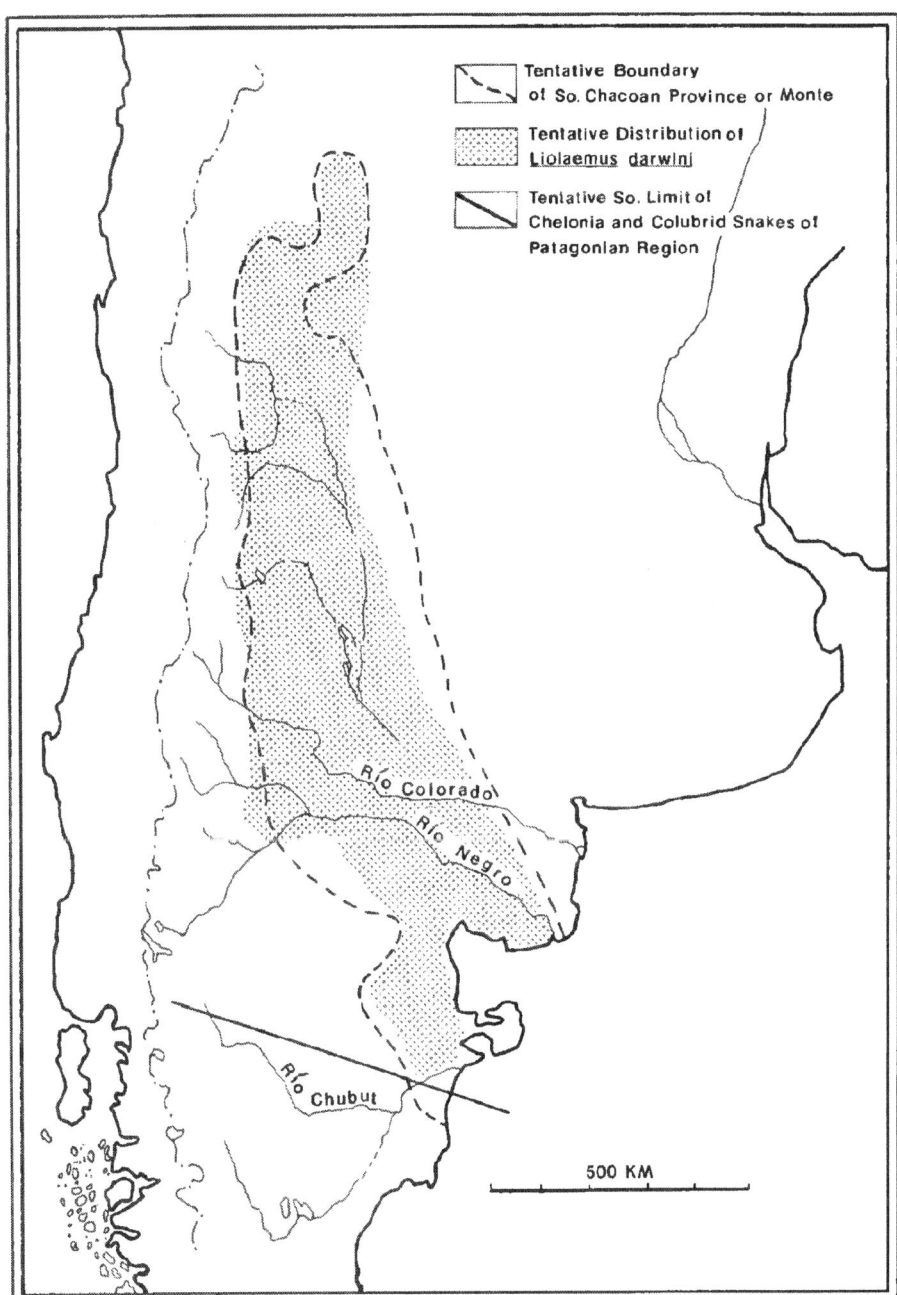

Fig. 13:10. Distribution of *Liolaemus darwinii*, a characteristic species of the monte formation. The southern edge of this formation is the southern limits of distribution of *Geochelone* and of colubrid snakes in northern Patagonia.

Distribución de Liolaemus darwinii, *especie característica de la formación del monte. El límite meridional de esta formación es el límite meridional de* Geochelone *y de los ofidios colúbridos en la Patagonia septentrional.*

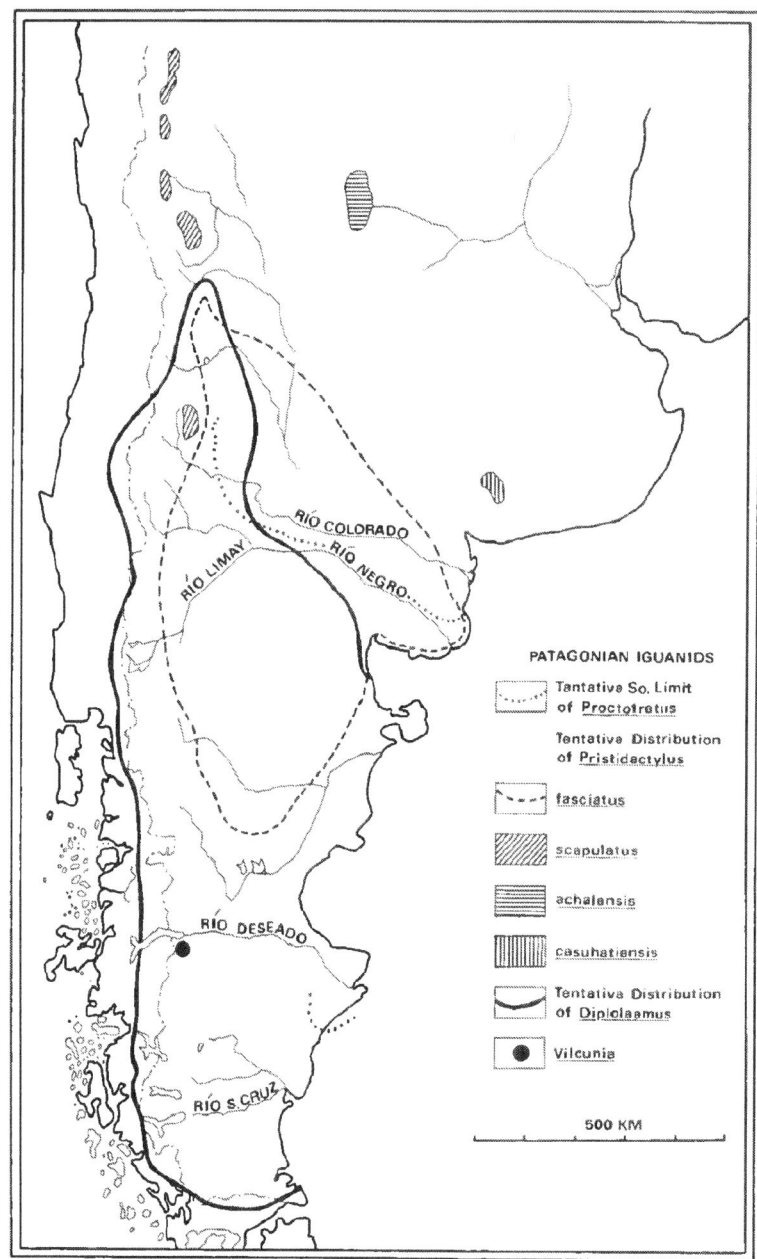

Fig. 13:11. Patterns of distribution of tropidurine iguanid lizards in Patagonia.
Distribución de los saurios iguánidos tropidurinos en Patagonia.

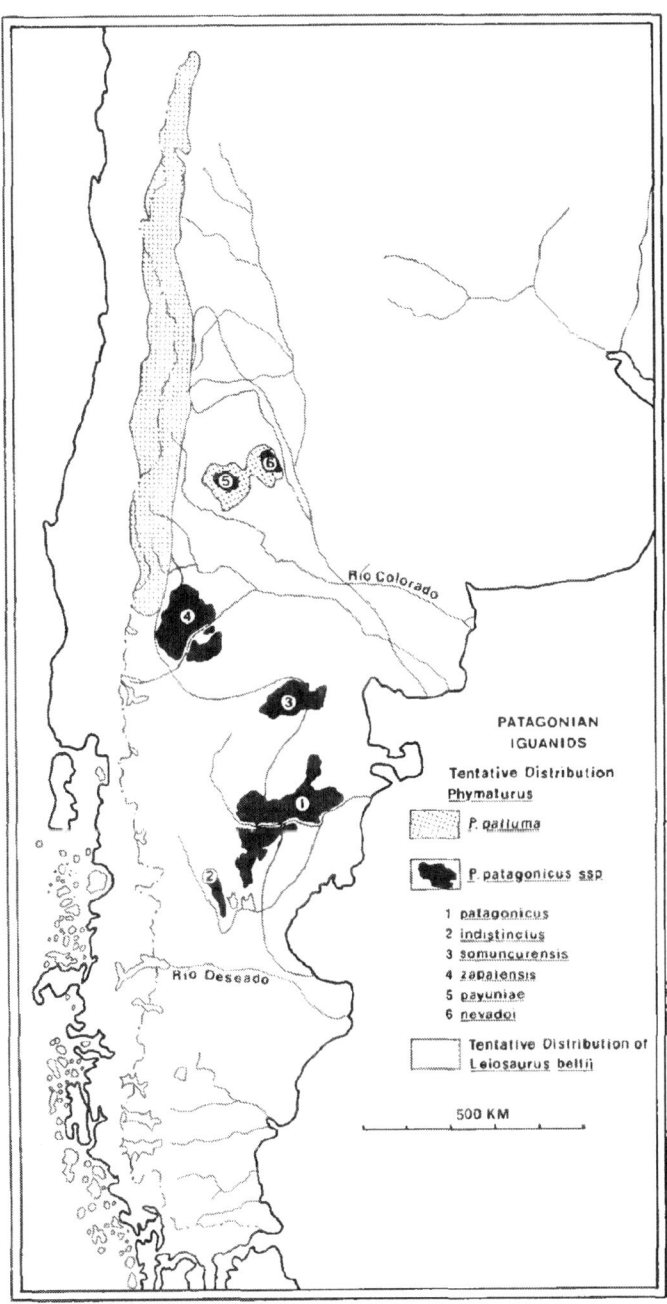

Fig. 13:12. Patterns of distribution of tropidurine iguanid lizards in Patagonia.
Distribución de los saurios iguánidos tropidurinos en Patagonia.

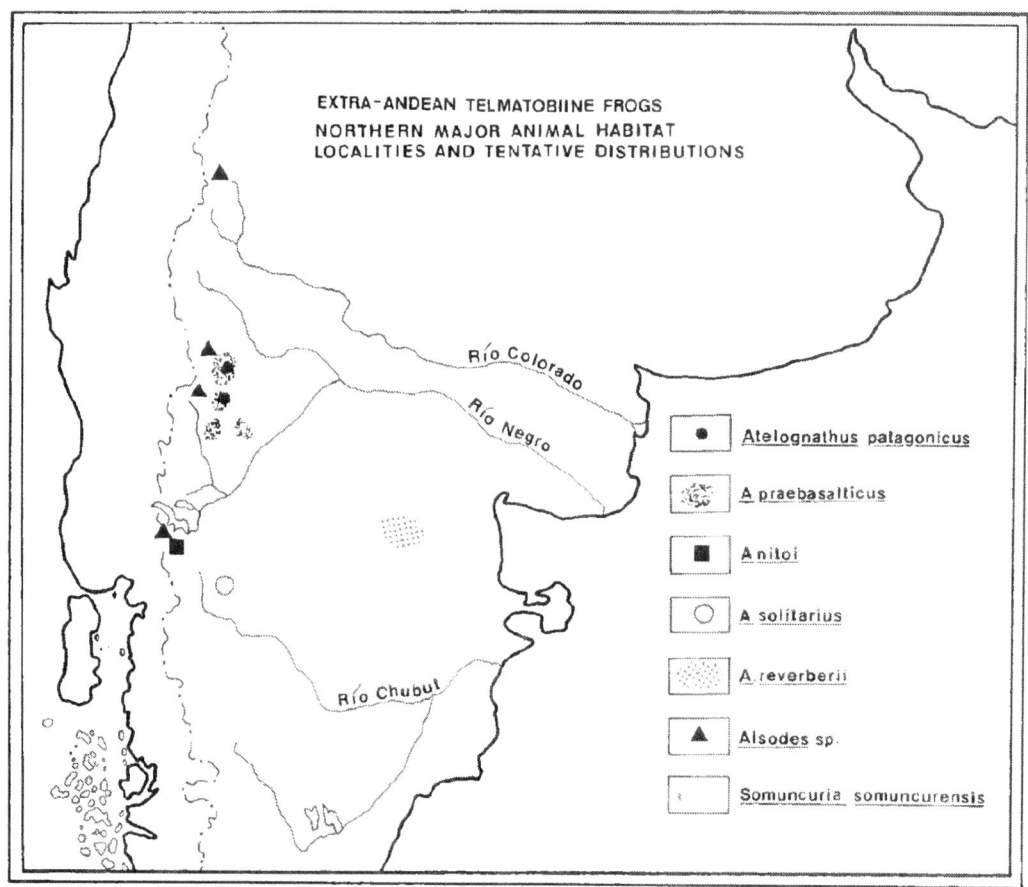

Fig. 13:13. Distribution of extra-Andean telmatobiine frogs in northern Patagonia.
Distribución de los anuros telmatobiinos extra-andinos en la Patagonia septentrional.

north in southern Mendoza Province (Cei and Castro, 1973; Cei and Roig, 1975) (Fig. 13:12).

The isolated Meseta de Somuncurá (150 × 80 km), with elevations to 1700 m, has some peculiar habitats. Between 800 and 1700 m, above the Monte-Patagonian ecotone, 11 species of amphibians and reptiles are known. Six of the species are widespread in Patagonia—*Pleurodema bufonina, Homonota darwinii, Diplolaemus darwinii, Liolaemus bibronii, L. boulengeri,* and *L. rothi.* Three other species and two subspecies are endemic —*Phymaturus patagonicus somuncurensis* and *Liolaemus elongatus petrophilus* are the endemic subspecies of lizards. The endemic *Liolaemus ruizleali* inhabits rocky summits of the meseta at 1200 to 1700 m. The two endemic, telmatobiine leptodactylid frogs have unique morphological and ecological traits. The monotypic *Somuncuria somuncurensis* lives in streams at 800 to 1000 m issuing from thermal springs on the northeastern slopes of the meseta. Inhabiting the same streams having a temperature of about 18°C is the endemic characid fish *Gymnocharacinus bergi.* Conversely, *Atelognathus reverberii,* a nearly fossorial frog, inhabits the arid plateau at elevations of more than 1000 m and breeds in small temporary pools.

Southern Patagonian Herpetofauna

The distributions of the 11 lizards, one snake, and one frog are examined with respect to five ecophysiographic areas (Fig 13 7)—1) Altiplano Central, 2) Coastal District, 3) Humid Southern Lowlands, 4) Sub-Andean Area, and 5) Meseta de Lago del Sello The distributions of the species and subspecies of amphibians and reptiles in these five areas are tabulated in Appendix 13 1, and the distributional relationships between the areas are analyzed in Table 13 2

Nine species occur in the Altiplano Central, all but the frog *Pleurodema bufonina* also occur in the coastal district Only six species occur in the humid southern lowlands, the southernmost frog *Pleurodema bufonina*, is rather rare there The lizard *Liolaemus magellanicus*, the only herpetofaunal species on Tierra del Fuego, is common on the southern end of the mainland Only four species (all lizards) occur in the sub-Andean region

The Meseta de Lago del Sello at 47°S is nearly 50 km in diameter On the top of the plateau, low grasses (*Festuca*, *Poa*, and *Stipa*) are dominant with thorny plants or cushion plants (*Benthamiella azorella*, *Verbena*, *Senecio*, *Nassauvia*), lichens are abundant in rocky areas Owing to the proximity of the great Patagonian Ice Field, cold winds whip the plateau, even in summer Only three iguanid lizards have been found on the plateau (1200–1600 m), the two species of *Liolaemus* are widespread in southern Patagonia whereas the monotypic *Vilcunia sylvanae* is endemic No amphibians have been found on the plateau, the widespread *Pleurodema bufonina* ascends the slopes to only 900 m

ORIGIN OF THE HERPETOFAUNA

The Patagonian herpetofauna is distinctive in the diversity of telmatobiine leptodactylid frogs and tropidurine iguanid lizards Most other species inhabiting Patagonia are members of groups that are mainly distributed to the north of Patagonia Thus, *Geochelone*, *Cnemidophorus*, *Mabuya*, *Homonota*, *Leptodactylus*, *Odontophrynus*, *Bufo arenarum*, and all of the genera of snakes are more northern groups

Bufo spinulosus and *Alsodes* are primarily Andean groups The former enters Patagonia in many disjunct valleys, the species does not occur on major basaltic mesetas In Patagonia *Alsodes* occurs only in the volcanic highlands adjacent to the Andes

Pleurodema is a primitive leptodactyline that may have originated in, and dispersed from, the austral forests (Duellman and Veloso 1977), the genus has dispersed northward in nonforested habitats to the Caribbean Two species are peripheral in Patagonia—*P thaul* in the austral forest—Patagonian steppe ecotone and *P nebulosa* in the monte *Pleurodema bufonina* is a widespread species endemic to Patagonian habitats Although *P thaul* and *bufonina* are distinctive in their morphology and behavior, populations intermediate between the species exist in high valleys in western Neuquen

Lynch (1978) provided an hypothesis for the evolution of lower telmatobiine frogs in Patagonia The peculiar monotypic *Somuncuria* is endemic to the Meseta de Somuncurá, whereas five species of *Atelognathus* occur in isolated basaltic areas in Patagonia The only extra-Patagonian *Atelognathus* is *A grandisonae* from Puerto Eden in extreme southern Chile

Among the iguanid lizards, the monotypic *Vilcunia* has characters of both *Proctotretus* and *Liolaemus* and is endemic to southern Patagonia (Donoso Barros and Cei 1971) *Diplolaemus* and *Phymaturus* are fundamentally austral genera (Figs 13 11–12) *Ctenoblepharis*, *Leiosaurus*, *Proctotretus*, and *Pristidactylus* are widely distributed to the north of Patagonia (Cei 1973c,d) Two species of *Proctotretus* are distributed in temperate areas in southern Brasil Uruguay, and central Argentina, *P pectinatus* occurs in the monte-Patagonian ecotone *Pristidactylus fasciatus* is primarily Patagonian but congeners occur in disjunct Andean areas (*P scapulatus*) and in isolated extra-Andean massifs of central Argentina—Sierra Grande de Córdoba (*P achalensis*) and Sierra de la Ventana (*P casuhatiensis*) (Gallardo, 1964, 1968, Cei and Castro, 1975)

Three major points relative to the origin and evolution of the Patagonian herpetofauna need to be emphasized

1. There has been a radiation of primitive leptodactylid frogs, remnants of Gondwanan elements Vuilleumier (1968) and Lynch (1971, 1978) noted the austral center of radiation of telmatobiine leptodactylids in Patagonia and the austral forests Formas (this volume) discussed the biogeography and ecology of the telmatobiines of the austral forests—*Alsodes Batrachyla, Caudiverbera, Eupsophus, Hylorina, Insuetophrynus*, and *Telmatobufo*, some of which also occur in Argentina (Cei 1978) The limited paleontological evidence supports the austral center of radiation (Schaeffer, 1949, Chaffee 1952, Casamiquela 1963, Estes and Reig, 1973)

2. An austral South American center of evolution and adaptive radiation of an ancestral stock of iguanid lizards is evident (Cei 1973c,d, 1975c, Cei and Castro, 1973) Fourteen genera are austral in Argentina and Chile, seven of these are Patagonian There are some 20 genera of iguanids in tropical South America and another ten genera in the Sonoran region of North America With the exception of *Anolis* and *Sceloporus*, no other iguanid genus displays such an impressive adaptive radiation as does *Liolaemus*, the dominant lizards in any Patagonian community In most of these same communities there exist representatives of the other Patagonian iguanid genera—*Diplolaemus, Leiosaurus, Phymaturus, Pristidactylus, Proctotretus*, and *Vilcunia*

3. An impressive post-Pleistocene adaptive radiation has taken place in four groups of Patagonian *Liolaemus* (see following section)

Thus, far from being a totally barren region biologically, irregularly colonized by elements from neighboring biotas, Patagonia has been, and apparently still is, a center of active speciation of several herpetofaunal elements The old radiations are supported by the scattered relicts unique witnesses to some of the most ancient steps in the history of continental vertebrates, whereas the Recent speciation of *Liolaemus* attests to the continued evolutionary activity in the region

Evolutionary Radiation of Patagonian Liolaemus

Lizards of the genus *Liolaemus* are widespread in temperate South America Three species range into southern Brasil, and several species occur in the Andes, two extending northward to central Perú (Duellman this volume) Twenty-six taxa are Patagonian or Andean-Patagonian

Four major evolutionary units can be recognized among the Patagonian *Liolaemus* as follows 1) *L fitzingeri* complex, 2) *L elongatus-kriegi* complex, 3) *L kingii-archeforus* complex, and 4) *L magellanicus-lineomaculatus* complex (Cei, 1971a 1972a, 1973a,b 1974a, 1975a,b, 1975d,e Cei and Scolaro, 1977, Scolaro and Cei 1977) The lizards that are not members of these groups are primarily peripheral to Patagonia and/or are ecotonal elements Some of these are members of transcordilleran groups—*Liolaemus altissimus chilensis cyanogaster, lemniscatus, pictus* and *tenuis L bibronii* is related to the Chilean *L fuscus Liolaemus boulengeri, darwinii*, and *gracilis* are members of the more northern monte fauna and are primarily peripheral in Patagonia (Fig 13 10)

Liolaemus fitzingeri complex —This group is characterized by 1) patch of enlarged scales on posterior surfaces of thighs, especially well developed in males (Fig 13 14), 2) high number (52–82) of blunt, slightly keeled scales around body, 3) high number (7–11) of preanal pores 4) stout body and relatively long tail, 1 5 times length of body, 5) tendency to have black venters and dark humeral collars, 6) predominate dorsal color patterns consisting of wide transverse dark blotches bordered posteriorly by white, but spotted erythristic, and melanistic variations not uncommon

Content *L fitzingeri canqueli, L fitzingeri fitzingeri, L fitzingeri melanops, L rothi, ?L ruizleali Liolaemus f fitzingeri* is the

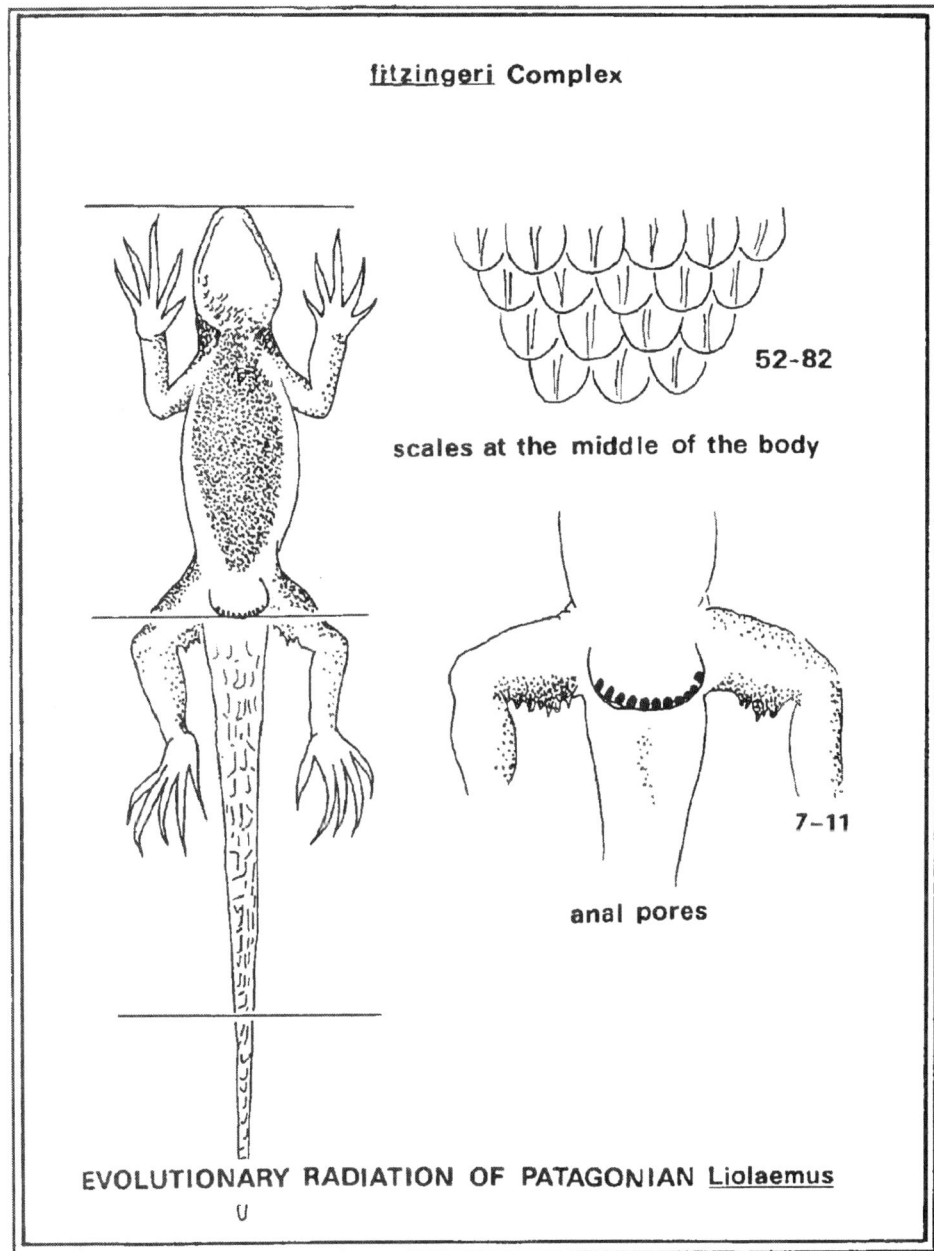

Fig. 13:14. Morphological traits of lizards of the *Liolaemus fitzingeri* complex.
Características morfológicas de los saurios del conjunto Liolaemus fitzingeri.

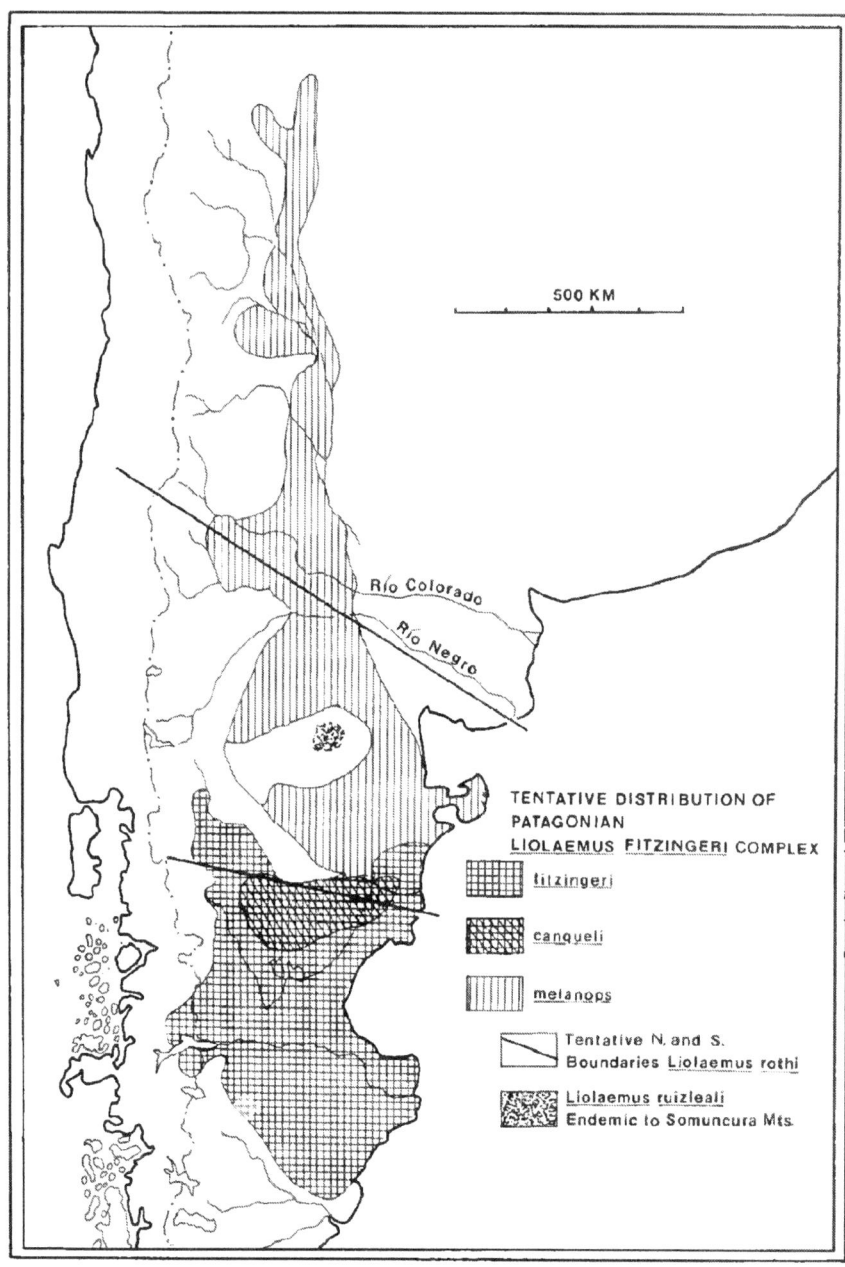

Fig. 13:15. Distribution of the *Liolaemus fitzingeri* complex in Patagonia.
Distribución del conjunto Liolaemus fitzingeri *en Patagonia.*

southernmost member of the group, inhabiting sandy Patagonian steppe in Santa Cruz and Chubut, it meets *L f canqueli* in the vicinity of Trelew and Dos Pozos on the coast of Chubut (Cei and Scolaro, 1977). The latter subspecies is characteristic of the arid volcanic massif of Canquel south of the Río Chubut. *Liolaemus f melanops* is distributed in coastal areas north of the Río Chubut to the Río Negro and thence inland through Mendoza to San Juan and La Rioja. *Liolaemus rothi* is endemic to northern Patagonia as is *L ruizleali*, known only from the Meseta de Somuncurá (Fig 13 15)

Members of the *Liolaemus fitzingeri* complex are mostly stout, polymorphic lizards that are psammophilous or fossorial. The polychromatism in these lizards has been a source of confusion. *Liolaemus melanops* was considered to be a color variety of *L fitzingeri* by Donoso-Barros (1966) and Peters and Donoso-Barros (1970), and as a northern subspecies of *L fitzingeri* by Cei (1975d). However, careful analyses of morphological and serological attributes may suggest that *L melanops* probably is a distinct species. Populations of *L f melanops* near Puerto Madryn are highly variable, some individuals are morphologically indistinguishable from *L goetschi* (Cei, 1975a), a monomorphic lizard extending from the Río Colorado north to San Juan and La Rioja. Serological analysis shows that populations formerly assigned to *L melanops* and *L goetschi* are conspecific, thus, only one taxon (*L melanops*) is recognized (Cei and Scolaro, 1977)

The serological distance between *L darwinii* and members of the *Liolaemus fitzingeri* complex suggests that *L darwinii* diverged early from the ancestral stock of that group. Although juveniles and females of *L darwinii* and *L boulengeri* are strikingly similar, a noticeable serological distance exists between the species, whereas *L boulengeri* is serologically closer to *L f melanops*

Liolaemus rothi has morphological characters that ally it with the *Liolaemus fitzingeri* group, but serologically it is not so distant from other Patagonian complexes of *Liolaemus* as are the other members of the *Liolaemus fitzingeri* group. *Liolaemus rothi* could be considered as a primitive, ecologically generalized species of the *Liolaemus fitzingeri* complex. The poorly known *L ruizleali* is morphologically close to *L rothi*, except that the postfemoral enlarged scales are absent in *L ruizleali*

Enlarged scales on the posterior surfaces of the thighs are characteristic of some other extra Patagonian *Liolaemus*. Such is the case in the Andean *L ornatus* and *L mocquardi* which morphologically are similar to *L darwinii*. The character also is present in *L wiegmanni* in southeastern Brasil, Uruguay, and the Argentine pampas, and in *L multimaculatus* from the Atlantic coast of Buenos Aires. Because of the many differences displayed by these two lizards from one another and from members of the *Liolaemus fitzingeri* complex, the enlarged postfemoral scales are considered to be independently evolved characters in these three lines

Liolaemus elongatus–kriegi complex —This group is characterized by 1) no patch of enlarged scales, but a row of projecting scales on posterior surface of thigh, 2) high number (72–120) of acuminate, keeled scales around body (Fig 13 16), 3) few (1–4) preanal pores, 4) slender body with very long tail, 5) absence of ventral melanism and dark nuchal collar, 6) dorsal pattern of blackish irregular stripes, not bordered by white, and confluent into vertebral and lateral bands

Content *L austromendocinus*, *L buergeri*, *L ceii*, *L elongatus elongatus*, *L elongatus petrophilus*, *L kriegi* *Liolaemus elongatus* is widespread in rocky habitats in Chubut, Río Negro, and Neuquen, and northward in the precordillera in Mendoza (Fig 13 17). It is a highly variable species and notable serological distances have been found among scattered, isolated populations (Cei, 1974a), only the population of the Meseta de Somuncurá has been recognized taxonomically—*L e petrophilus* *Liolaemus austromendocinus* occurs in arid habitats below 1500 m in volcanic regions in southern Mendoza and in the Río Neuquen and Río Colorado basins. *Liolaemus kriegi* occupies basaltic areas in Neuquen and Río Negro, where it occurs sympatrically with *L ceii*. *Liolaemus buergeri* occurs sympatrically with *L*

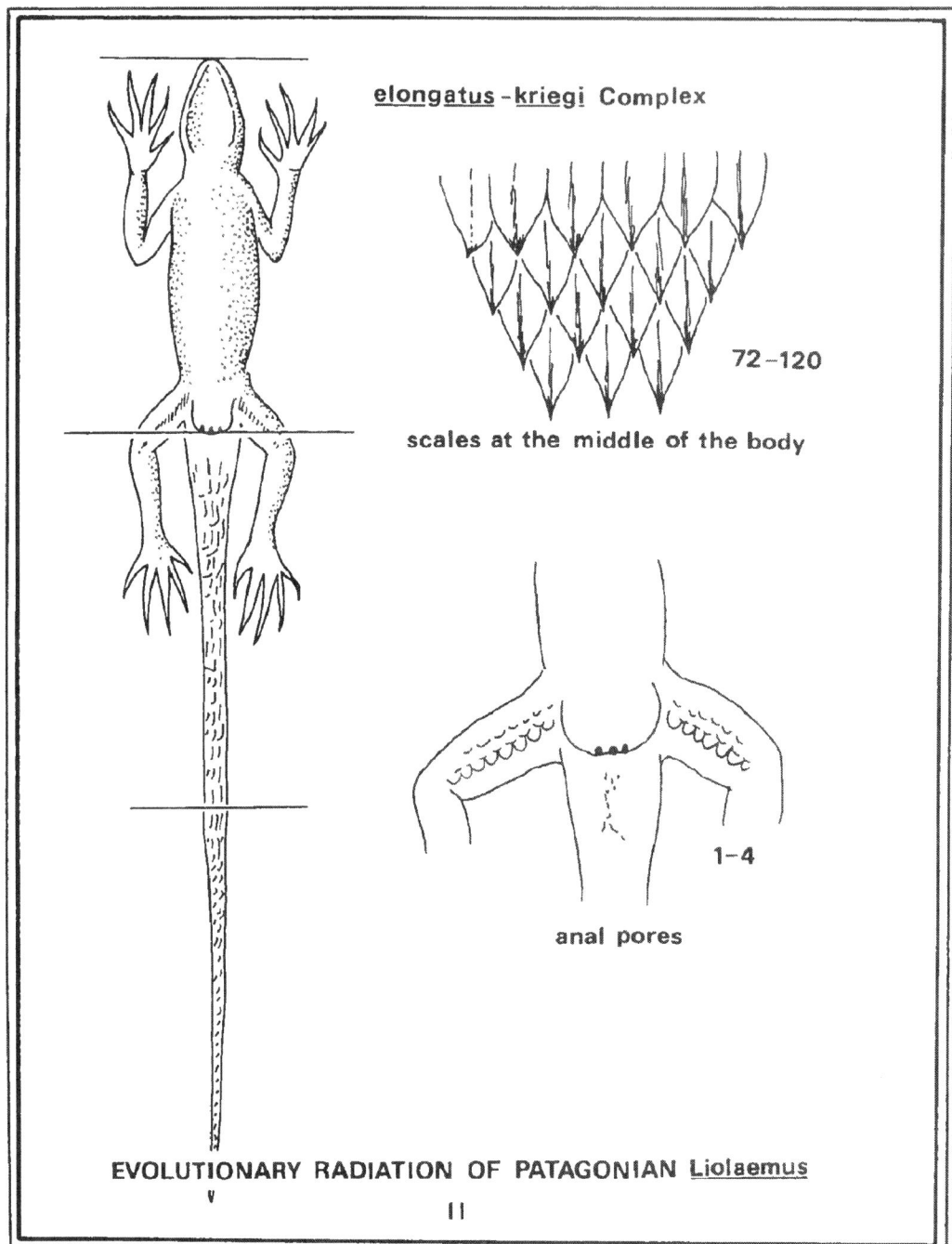

Fig. 13:16. Morphological traits of lizards of the *Liolaemus elongatus-kriegi* complex. Características morfológicas de los saurios del conjunto Liolaemus elongatus-kriegi.

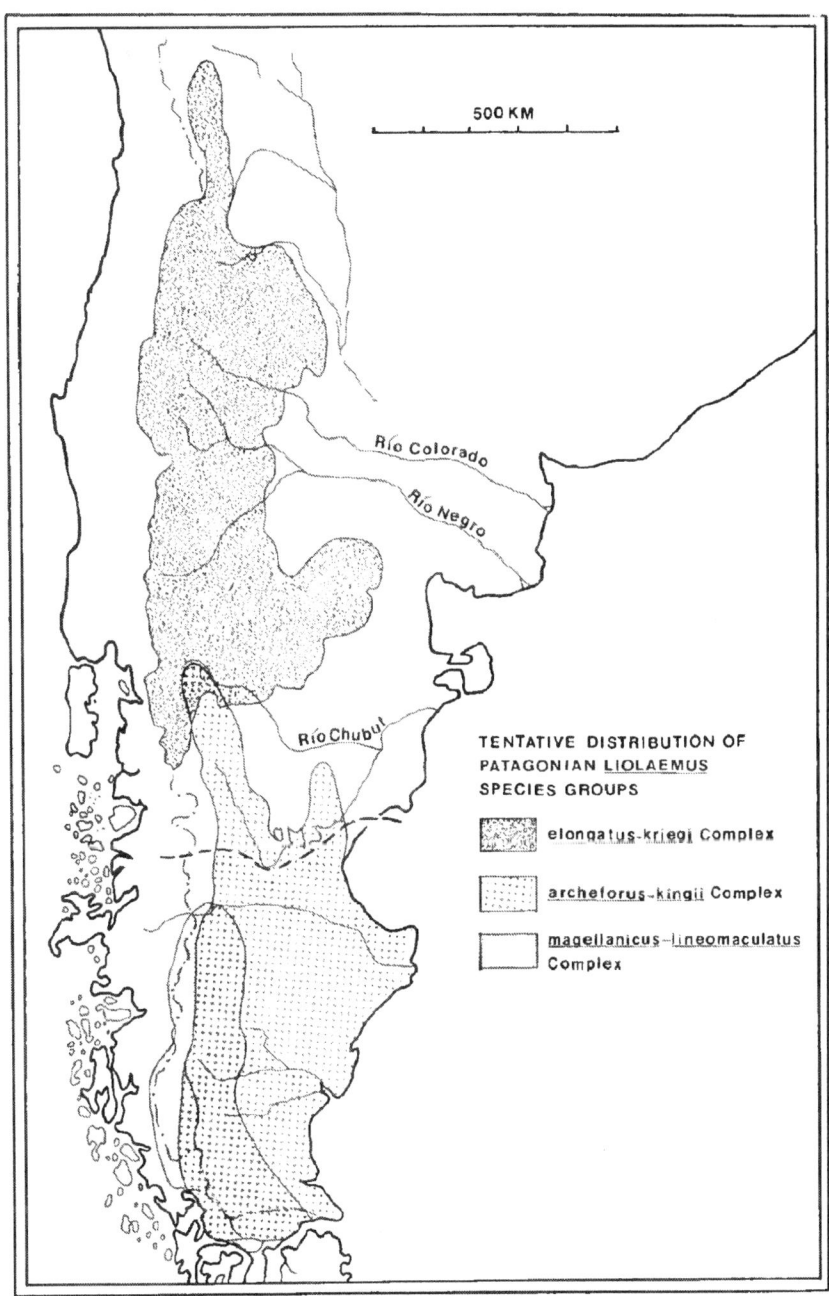

Fig. 13:17. Distributions of three *Liolaemus* species complexes in Patagonia. *Distribución de tres conjuntos específicos de* Liolaemus *en Patagonia.*

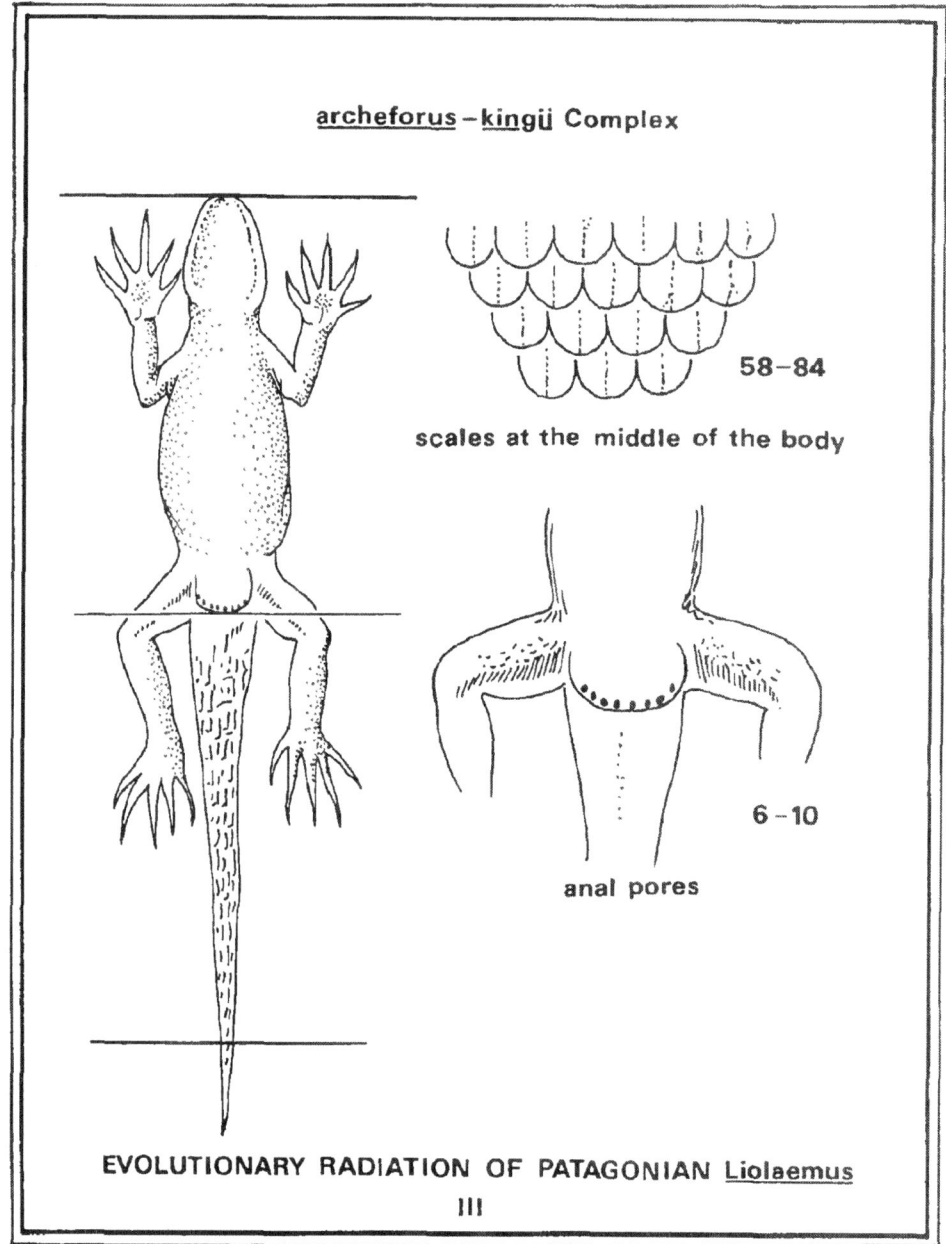

Fig. 13:18. Morphological traits of lizards of the *Liolaemus archeforus-kingii* complex. Características morfológicas de los saurios del conjunto Liolaemus archeforus-kingii.

elongatus or *austromendocinus* in Patagonian associations in southern Mendoza and with *L. elongatus* or *kriegi* in valleys in Neuquén. *Liolaemus buergeri* and *kriegi* occur in Patagonian habitats in Chile, presumably the transcordilleran migration was via Paso Pehuenche (2500 m, 36°S).

Several immunological cross-reactions among allopatric and sympatric populations of *L. austromendocinus* and *elongatus* show equally good specific levels of differentiation as among *L. elongatus*, *kriegi*, and *buergeri* (Cei, 1974a, 1975b).

Liolaemus kingii-archeforus complex — This group is characterized by 1) no patch of enlarged scales on the posterior surface of the thigh (Fig. 13.18), 2) moderately high number (58–84) of faintly keeled scales around body, 3) high number (6–10) of preanal pores, 4) short legs and relatively short tail, only slightly longer than body, 5) venter with dark spots, absence of dark nuchal collar, 6) a series of yellowish or whitish transverse bars on the dark dorsal ground color.

Contents *L. archeforus archeforus*, *L. archeforus sarmientoi*, *L. kingii*. This group is endemic to the southern faunal region (Fig. 13.17). *Liolaemus a. archeforus* occurs on the isolated Meseta de Lago del Sello, it is replaced by *L. a. sarmientoi* at lower elevations eastward in the Patagonian steppe between the Río Coyle and the Río Gallegos. *Liolaemus kingii*, which lies at a moderate serological distance from *L. archeforus*, is a rather stout, apparent ecological generalist inhabiting ravines and open bushy habitats in most of Santa Cruz. It reaches the Atlantic coast and in the western part of its range is broadly sympatric with *L. archeforus*.

Liolaemus magellanicus-lineomaculatus complex —This group is characterized by 1) no patch of enlarged scales on the posterior surface of thigh, 2) low number (40–70) of large, mucronate, acuminate (dorsally) scales around body, 3) moderate number (3–8) of preanal pores, 4) very short limbs and tail (Fig. 13.19), 5) absence of ventral melanism and dark nuchal collar, 6) dorsum irregularly spotted with black and having whitish longitudinal lines.

Content *L. lineomaculatus*, *L. magellanicus*. The latter occurs in the humid southern lowlands on the mainland and in isolated populations on Tierra del Fuego whereas *L. lineomaculatus* is found in the volcanic highlands in the ancient Patagonian region, where it inhabits open formations and *Araucaria* woodlands (Fig. 13.17). Occasional immaculate individuals of *L. lineomaculatus* are known (Cei, 1971a).

These last two complexes of *Liolaemus* are limited to austral Patagonia and are conservative in their diversity as compared to the *Liolaemus fitzingeri* and *elongatus-kriegi* complexes both of which apparently have undergone recent (post-Pleistocene) speciation. The results of these radiations are numerous morphologically similar species differing from one another biochemically and ecologically.

ACKNOWLEDGMENTS

I acknowledge the special interest and efforts of William E. Duellman in rewriting the original English draft of this manuscript and in his critical analysis of the distributional data. I also thank John D. Lynch for information about his research on the morphology and relationships of telmatobiine frogs in the Patagonian Region.

RESUMEN

Biologicamente, la Patagonia se define como la región al este de los Andes, extendiéndose hasta el Océano Atlántico, hacia el sur hasta el Estrecho de Magallanes, en el norte hay una zona de transición entre la biota patagónica y las del norte entre los ríos Negro y Colorado.

La Patagonia es una región de suelos de rocas sedimentarias y mesetas de rocas efusivas presentando severas sequías estacionales con cinco meses de invierno frío, veranos usualmente secos y clima fresco.

En contraste con las asociaciones de estepa uniformes que existen allí actualmente, una vegetación tropical y subtropical ocupó al mismo tiempo que bosques xerofíticos y bos-

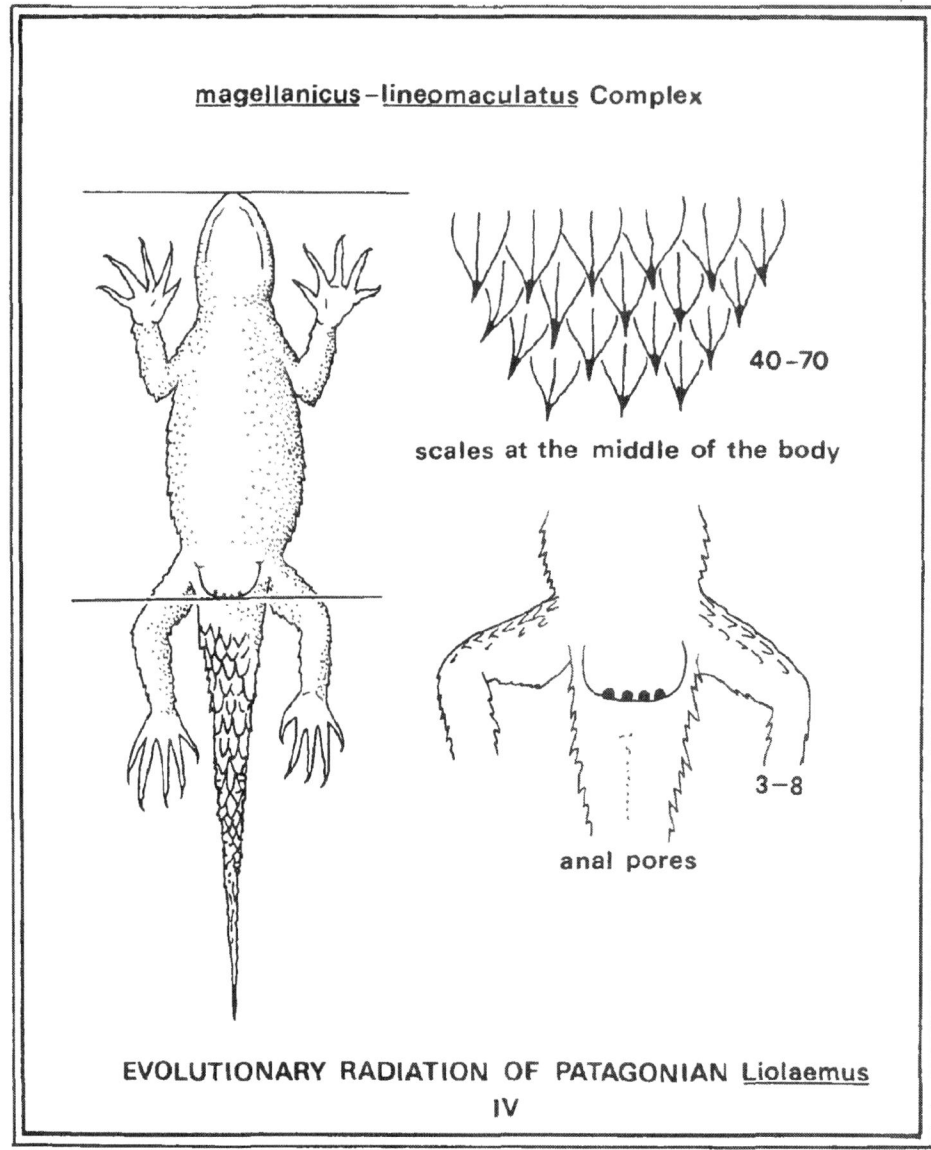

Fig. 13:19. Morphological traits of lizards of the *Liolaemus magellanicus–lineomaculatus* complex.
Características morfológicas de los saurios del conjunto Liolaemus magellanicus–lineomaculatus.

ques mesofíticos de galería durante el Oligoceno y el Mioceno. Bosques de *Nothofagus* existían durante el Eoceno y el Oligoceno. A mediados del Terciario los climas se volvieron más secos dando lugar a la expansión de la vegetación xerofítica.

En los depósitos del Oligoceno y del Mioceno telmatóbidos primitivos, ceratofrínidos, y bufónidos son conocidos, así como boideos primitivos, cocodrilos, y tortugas meiolanidas y pelomedúsidas están representados en los depósitos del Cretáceo superior y del Cenozoico inferior. Los fósiles existentes, la presente distribución y los patrones de especiación indican que la Patagonia ha sido una región importante para la evolución de la herpetofauna austral.

Dos regiones faunísticas se reconocen en la Patagonia—1) la región del norte, o Patagonia antigua, 2) la región del sur o de Santa Cruz. El límite entre estas dos regiones se encuentra aproximadamente en el Río Chubut 45°S (Fig 13.3).

La herpetofauna patagónica está compuesta de 60 especies: 14 anuros, 1 tortuga, 34 saurios, 11 ofidios. Hay un grado notable de endemismo. De las 60 especies, 56 ocurren el la región del norte, 13 especies en la región del sur, y nueve especies están representadas en ambas regiones. En la región del norte se encuentra la única tortuga y el único amphisbénido y todas las especies de ofidios y anuros, excepto una especie de rana (*Pleurodema bufonina*) y una especie de serpiente (*Bothrops ammodytoides*) que entran en la región del sur.

El grado de endemismo es alto, especialmente en los altiplanos volcánicos, en las estribaciones de los Andes y en las mesetas aisladas. Los géneros monotípicos *Somuncuria* y *Vilcunia* son endémicos de las mesetas así como las especies y/o subespecies de *Alsodes*, *Atelognathus*, *Liolaemus*, y *Phymaturus*.

En la Patagonia ha habido temprana expansión adaptativa de los telmatóbidos de la familia Leptodactylidae. La región también fue el centro de evolución de las diversas líneas de iguánidos, y actualmente es un centro de especiación de *Liolaemus*. Cuatro grupos de especies de *Liolaemus* tienen su centro de dispersión en la Patagonia. Estos han sufrido especiación post-pleistocénica y sucesiva dispersión en la región, con el resultado de muchas líneas de especies afines bioquímica y ecológicamente bien definidas.

LITERATURE CITED

BARRIO, A 1973 Una nueva especie de *Telmatobius* (Anura, Leptodactylidae) procedente del dominio austral cordillerano Argentino Physis 32C 207–213

BERRY, E W 1938 Tertiary flora from the Río Pichi Leufu, Argentina Geol Soc Amer Spec Pap (12) 1–149

BOGART, J P 1970 Systematic problems in the amphibians family Leptodactylidae (Anura) as indicated by karyotypic analysis Cytogenetics 9 369–383

CABRERA, A L 1951 Territorios fitogeográficos de la Republica Argentina Bol Soc Argentina Bot 4 21–65

CASAMIQUELA, R M 1963 Sobre un par de anuros del Mioceno de Río Negro (Patagonia) *Wawelia gerholdi* n gen et sp (Ceratophrydidae) y *Gigantobatrachus parodi* (Leptodactylidae) Ameghiniana 3 141–160

CEI, J M 1969a La meseta basáltica de Somuncurá, Río Negro Herpetofauna endémica y sus peculiares equilibrios biocenoticos Physis 28 257–271

CEI, J M 1969b The Patagonian telmatobiid fauna of the volcanic Somuncurá Plateau J Herpetol 3 1–18

CEI, J M 1970a Fluctuaciones biocenóticas y relictos herpetológicos de la planicie de Loncoluán (Neuquén) Acta Zool Lilloana 27 193–200

CEI, J M 1970b *Telmatobius solitarius* n sp, a new rare telmatobiid frog from the highland Patagonian territories (Río Negro Argentina) Herpetologica 26 18–23

CEI, J M 1971a Herpetología Patagónica—I *Liolaemus* del grupo *magellanicus* Caracteristicas taxonómicas y genéticas Physis 30 417–424

CEI, J M 1971b Herpetología Patagónica—II Notas sobre la distribución geográfica del genero *Diplolaemus* Ibid 30 471–474

CEI, J M 1972a Herpetología Patagónica—III Relaciones de afinidad seroproteínicas y filéticas en el genero *Liolaemus* Ibid 31 411–422

CEI, J M 1972b Herpetología Patagónica—V Las especies extracordilleranas alto-Patagónicas del genero *Telmatobius* Ibid 31 431–449

CEI, J M 1973a Herpetología Patagónica—VI Los *Liolaemus* del grupo *fitzingeri* en Santa Cruz y Chubut (Sauria, Iguanidae) Ibid 32C 447–458

CEI, J M 1973b Herpetología Patagónica—VII Notas ecológicas y morfológicas sobre *Liolaemus bibroni* y *L boulengeri* Ibid 32C 459–469

CEI, J M 1973c Comentarios sobre algunos generos de iguánidos *Diplolaemus*, *Leiosaurus*, *Aperopristis* y *Cupriguanus* Ibid 32C 269–276

CEI, J M 1973d Distribución geográfica y caracteres poblacionales de *Cupriguanus fasciatus* (D Orbigny) (Sauria, Iguanidae) Ibid 32C 255–262

CEI, J M 1974a Revision of the Patagonian lizards of the *Liolaemus elongatus* complex J Herpetol 8 219–229

CEI, J M 1974b Herpetología Patagónica—VIII La altiplanicie entre Primeros Pinos y Río Kilka, Neuquén Physis 33C 183–185

CEI, J M 1975a Herpetología Patagónica—IX *Liolaemus goetschi* y el conjunto *Liolaemus darwini-boulengeri* Ibid 34C 199–202

CEI, J M 1975b Herpetologia Patagónica—V El conjunto evolutivo de *Liolaemus elongatus* analisis serologico Ibid 34C 203–208

CEI, J M 1975c Herpetologia Patagonica—VI Diferenciacion serológica de *Diplolaemus darwini* y *Diplolaemus bibroni* en poblaciones alosimpátridas Ibid 34C 209–210

CEI, J M 1975d *Lialaemus melanops* Burmeister and the subspecific status of the *Liolaemus fitzingeri* group (Sauria-Iguanidae) J Herpetol 9 217–222

CEI, J M 1975e Southern Patagonian lizards of the *Liolaemus kingi* group Herpetologica 31 109–116

CEI, J M 1976 Remarks on some Neotropical amphibians of the genus *Alsodes* from southern Argentina (Anura, Leptodactylidae) Atti Soc Italia Sci Nat Mus Civ Stor Nat Milano 117 79–84

CEI, J M 1977 Serological relationships of the Patagonian toad *Bufo variegatus* (Gunther) Serol Mus Bull 52 2

CEI J M 1979 Amphibians of Argentina Monit Zool Italiano Monog Zool (in press)

CEI, J M, CASTRO, L P 1973 Taxonomic and serologic researches on the *Phymaturus patagonicus* complex J Herpetol 7 237–247

CEI, J M, CASTRO, L P 1975 A serological contribution to the taxonomic status of *Cupriguanus*, a South American genus of iguanid lizards Serol Mus Bull 51 5–6

CEI, J M, ROIG V G 1966 Caracteres biocenoticos de las lagunas basalticas del oeste de Neuquen Bol Est Geog Univ Nac Cuyo 13 182–201

CEI, J M, ROIG V G 1968 Telmatobiinos de las lagunas basalticas de Neuquen (Anura, Leptodactylidae) Physis 27 265–284

CEI, J M, ROIG, V G 1975 A new lizard from the Sierra del Nevado Mountains, central Argentina J Herpetol 9 256

CEI, J M, SCOLARO J A 1977 Herpetologia Patagonica—VIII La identidad de *Liolaemus goetschi* y de la forma *melanops* del grupo *Liolaemus fitzingeri* en Rio Negro y Chubut Physis 36C 225–226

CHAFFEE, R G 1952 The Deseadan vertebrate fauna of Scarritt Pocket, Patagonia Bull Amer Mus Nat Hist 98 509–562

DONOSO BARROS, R 1966 Reptiles de Chile Ed Univ Chile, Santiago, 458 p

DONOSO-BARROS, R, CEI, J M 1971 New lizards from Patagonian volcanic tablelands of Argentina J Herpetol 5 89–95

DUELLMAN, W E 1966 The Central American herpetofauna An ecological perspective Copeia 1966(4) 700–719

DUELLMAN W E, VELOSO M, A 1977 Phylogeny of *Pleurodema* (Anura Leptodactylidae) A biogeographic model Univ Kansas Mus Nat Hist Occas Pap (64) 1–46

ESTES, R, REIG, O A 1973 The early fossil record of frogs A review of the evidence, pp 11–63 in VIAL, J L (ed) Evolutionary biology of the anurans Contemporary research on major problems Univ Missouri Press, Columbia, 470 p

GALLARDO, J M 1962 A propósito de *Bufo variegatus* (Gunther) sapo del bosque humedo Antartandico, y las otras especies de *Bufo* neotropicales Physis 23 93–102

GALLARDO J M 1964 Los generos *Urostrophus* D & B y *Cupriguanus* gen n (Sauria Iguanidae) y sus especies Neotropica 10 125–136

GALLARDO J M 1968 Dos nuevas especies de Iguanidae (Sauria) de la Argentina Ibid 14 1–8

GALLARDO, J M 1970 A proposito de los Telmatobinae (Anura, Leptodactylidae) patagónicos Ibid 16 73–85

GASPARINI, Z B, BÁEZ A M 1975 Aportes al conocimiento de la herpetofauna terciaria de la Argentina Acta I Congr Argentino Paleontol Biostrat 2 377–413

HARRINGTON H J 1962 Paleogeographic development of South America Bull Amer Assoc Petrol Geol 46 1773–1814

LYNCH, J D 1971 Evolutionary relationships, osteology and zoogeography of leptodactyloid frogs Univ Kansas Mus Nat Hist Misc Publ (53) 1–238

LYNCH, J D 1978 A re-assessment of the telmatobiine leptodactylid frogs of Patagonia Univ Kansas Mus Nat Hist Occas Pap (72) 1–57

MORELLO, J 1958 La provincia fitogeográfica del monte Opera Lilloana 2 5–115

PETERS J A DONOSO-BARROS, R 1970 Catalogue of the Neotropical Squamata II Lizards and amphisbaenians Bull U S Natl Mus (297) 1–293

RUIZ LEAL, A 1972. Los confines boreal y austral de las provincias patagonicas y central respectivamente Bol Soc Argentina Bot 13 (Supplement) 89–118

SCHAEFFER, R 1949 Anurans from the early tertiary of Patagonia Bull Amer Mus Nat Hist 93 47–68

SCOLARO J A, CEI J M 1977 Herpetologia Patagonica—VII Los iguanidos del grupo *Liolaemus fitzingeri* en Chubut datos serologicos y posicion taxonomica Physis 36C 219–223

TIHEN, J A 1962 A review of the New World fossil bufonids Amer Midl Nat 68 1–50

VUILLEUMIER, F 1968 Origin of frogs of Patagonian forest Nature 219 87–90

APPENDIX

APPENDIX 13.1—Distribution of species and subspecies of amphibians and reptiles in ten districts of the two major faunal regions in Patagonia

Taxon	Northern Region					Southern Region				
	Monte	Monte-Patagonian Ecotone	Patagonian Steppe	Volcanic Highlands	Meseta de Somuncura	Altiplano Central	Coastal District	Humid Southern Lowlands	Sub-Andean Area	Meseta del Lago de Sello
Anurans										
Alsodes gargola gargola	−	−	−	+	−	−	−	−	−	−
Alsodes gargola neuquensis	−	−	−	+	−	−	−	−	−	−
Atelognathus nitoi	−	−	−	+	−	−	−	−	−	−
Atelognathus patagonicus	−	−	−	+	−	−	−	−	−	−
Atelognathus praebasalticus praebasalticus	−	−	−	+	−	−	−	−	−	−
Atelognathus praebasalticus agilis	−	−	−	+	−	−	−	−	−	−
Atelognathus praebasalticus dobeslawi	−	−	−	+	−	−	−	−	−	−
Atelognathus praebasalticus luisi	−	−	−	+	−	−	−	−	−	−
Atelognathus reverberii	−	−	−	−	+	−	−	−	−	−
Atelognathus solitarius	−	−	+	−	−	−	−	−	−	−
Leptodactylus ocellatus	−	+	−	−	−	−	−	−	−	−
Odontophrynus occidentalis	+	+	−	−	−	−	−	−	−	−
Pleurodema bufonina	−	+	+	+	+	−	+	+	+	−
Pleurodema nebulosa	+	+	−	−	−	−	−	−	−	−
Pleurodema thaul	−	−	−	+	−	−	−	−	−	−
Somuncuria somuncurensis	−	−	−	−	+	−	−	−	−	−
Bufo arenarum	+	+	−	−	−	−	−	−	−	−
Bufo spinulosus	−	−	+	+	−	−	−	−	−	−
Lizards										
Homonota darwinii	−	+	+	+	+	+	+	+	+	−
Homonota horrida	+	+	−	−	−	−	−	−	−	−
Ctenoblepharis donosobarrosi	+	+	−	−	−	−	−	−	−	−
Diplolaemus bibroni	−	+	−	−	−	+	+	+	+	−
Diplolaemus darwinii	−	−	+	+	+	+	+	−	−	−
Diplolaemus leopardinus	−	−	−	+	−	−	−	−	−	−
Leiosaurus belli	−	+	+	−	−	−	−	−	−	−
Liolaemus archeforus archeforus	−	−	−	−	−	−	−	−	−	+
Liolaemus archeforus sarmientoi	−	−	−	−	−	−	−	+	−	−
Liolaemus austromendocinus	−	+	−	−	−	−	−	−	−	−
Liolaemus bibronii	−	+	+	+	+	+	+	−	−	−
Liolaemus boulengeri	−	+	+	+	+	+	+	−	−	−
Liolaemus buergeri	−	−	−	+	−	−	−	−	−	−
Liolaemus ceii	−	−	+	+	−	−	−	−	−	−
Liolaemus chilensis	−	−	−	+	−	−	−	−	−	−
Liolaemus darwinii	+	+	−	−	−	−	−	−	−	−
Liolaemus elongatus elongatus	−	−	+	−	−	−	−	−	−	−
Liolaemus elongatus petrophilus	−	−	−	−	+	−	−	−	−	−
Liolaemus fitzingeri fitzingeri	−	−	−	−	−	+	+	−	+	−
Liolaemus fitzingeri canqueli	−	−	+	−	−	−	−	−	−	−
Liolaemus fitzingeri melanops	+	+	−	−	−	−	−	−	−	−
Liolaemus gracilis	+	+	−	−	−	−	−	−	−	−
Liolaemus kingii	−	−	−	−	−	+	+	−	+	−
Liolaemus kriegi	−	−	+	+	−	−	−	−	−	+
Liolaemus lineomaculatus	−	−	−	+	−	−	−	+	−	+
Liolaemus magellanicus	−	−	−	−	−	−	−	+	−	−
Liolaemus rothi	−	−	+	+	+	−	−	−	−	−

APPENDIX 13.1 (Concluded)

Taxon	Northern Region					Southern Region				
	Monte	Monte-Patagonian Ecotone	Patagonian Steppe	Volcanic Highlands	Meseta de Somuncura	Altiplano Central	Coastal District	Humid Southern Lowlands	Sub-Andean Area	Meseta del Lago de Sello
Liolaemus ruizleali	—	—	—	—	+	—	—	—	—	—
Liolaemus tenuis	—	—	—	+	—	—	—	—	—	—
Phymaturus palluma	—	—	—	+	—	—	—	—	—	—
Phymaturus patagonicus patagonicus	—	—	+	—	—	—	—	—	—	—
Phymaturus patagonicus indistinctus	—	—	+	—	—	—	—	—	—	—
Phymaturus patagonicus somuncurensis	—	—	—	—	+	—	—	—	—	—
Phymaturus patagonicus zapalensis	—	—	—	+	—	—	—	—	—	—
Pristidactylus fasciatus	+	+	+	+	—	—	—	—	—	—
Proctotretus pectinatus	—	+	—	—	—	—	—	—	—	—
Vilcunia sylvanae	—	—	—	—	—	—	—	—	—	+
Mabuya frenata	—	+	—	—	—	—	—	—	—	—
Cnemidophorus longicauda	+	+	—	—	—	—	—	—	—	—
Amphisbaenians										
Amphisbaena angustifrons	—	+	—	—	—	—	—	—	—	—
Snakes										
Leptotyphlops australis	+	+	—	—	—	—	—	—	—	—
Leptotyphlops borrichiana	+	+	—	—	—	—	—	—	—	—
Elapomorphus bilineatus	—	+	—	—	—	—	—	—	—	—
Leimadophis sagittifer	+	+	—	+	—	—	—	—	—	—
Lystrophis semicinctus	—	+	—	—	—	—	—	—	—	—
Philodryas burmeisteri	+	+	—	—	—	—	—	—	—	—
Philodryas patagoniensis	—	+	—	—	—	—	—	—	—	—
Philodryas psammophideus	+	+	—	—	—	—	—	—	—	—
Pseudotomodon trigonatus	+	+	—	—	—	—	—	—	—	—
Micrurus frontalis	—	+	—	—	—	—	—	—	—	—
Bothrops ammodytoides	+	+	+	+	—	+	+	—	—	—
Turtles										
Geochelone donosobarrosi	—	+	—	—	—	—	—	—	—	—
Total Taxa	17	32	18	29	11	9	8	6	4	3
Total Species	17	32	17	25	11	9	8	6	4	3

14. La Herpetofauna de los Bosques Temperados de Sudamérica

J. Ramón Formas

Instituto de Zoología
Universidad Austral de Chile
Casilla 567
Valdivia, Chile

Los bosques temperados de Sudamérica ubicados en el extremo sur de Chile y partes adyacentes de Argentina, se caracterizan por tener pocos taxa de anfibios (Vellard, 1957; Cei, 1962a; Darlington 1965; Vuilleumier, 1968) y reptiles (Hellmich, 1934, 1937; Donoso-Barros, 1960). Estos ambientes boscosos temperados, aislados en el norte por la estepa semiárida de *Acacia caven* y por este por la estepa fría patagónica, presentan once géneros de anuros, dos de saurios (*Liolaemus* y *Pristidactylus*) y dos de serpientes (*Alsophis* y *Tachymenis*). Entre los anuros se encuentran muchos endemismos (*Caudiverbera*, *Telmatobufo*, *Hylorina*, *Eupsophus*, *Batrachyla*, *Insuetophrynus* y *Rhinoderma*) y solamente *Alsodes*, *Atelognathus*, *Pleurodema* y *Bufo* exceden los límites del bosque. Existe aquí una familia monotípica (Rhinodermatidae) y tres géneros con una sola especie (*Caudiverbera*, *Hylorina* e *Insuetophrynus*). La mayoría de los géneros de anfibios poseen dos o tres especies (*Telmatobufo*, *Batrachyla*) y solamente los saurios del género *Liolaemus* son las que presentan la mayor diversificación (cinco especies) en el área.

Algunas de las especies existentes en el bosque temperado austral muestran notables adaptaciones a este biotopo las cuales se observan especialmente durante la reproducción y el desarrollo. Entre los anuros, destacan el cuidado parental de *Rhinoderma*, las posturas en terreno vegetal húmedo de las especies de *Batrachyla* y los renacuajos de los arroyos de montaña de *Telmatobufo australis*. La viviparidad aparece como la adaptación reproductiva más frecuente entre los reptiles (*Liolaemus cyanogaster*, *L. pictus* y *Tachymenis chilensis*).

Desde el punto de vista histórico, algunos anuros (*Caudiverbera* y *Eupsophus*) tienen una antigüedad que se remonta hasta el Terciario (Shaeffer, 1949).

Los endemismos, la pobreza de especies, la escasa diversificación de los géneros, las adaptaciones reproductivas y la antigüedad de algunos taxa, han sugerido diversas interpretaciones sobre el origen de los batracios en el bosque temperado sudamericano. Darlington (1965) considera a esta batracofauna como empobrecida y derivada de otras de amplia distribución en Sudamérica. Vellard (1957), Cei (1962a) y Vuilleumier (1968) proponen que la fauna de batracios australes está compuesta por géneros endémicos de probable origen Terciario y otros secundariamente emigrados a la región. Para los reptiles, Donoso-Barros (1966) postula géneros de origen septentrional (*Liolaemus*) y relictos de las selvas del Terciario (*Pristidactylus*).

En base a los antecedentes ecológicos e históricos de la región y de la sistemática, ecología y distribución de la herpetofauna se propone una hipótesis acerca del origen de los anfibios y reptiles que habitan los bosques temperados de Sudamérica.

CARACTERÍSTICAS DEL ÁREA

Los bosques temperados de Sudamérica se ubican especialmente al suroeste de la Cordillera de los Andes ocupando una franja de territorio chileno comprendida entre los 37° y 55°S de latitud sur (Cerceau-Larrival, 1968). Entre los paralelos 35 y 37, el bosque se desplaza levemente hacia el oriente penetrando en Argentina. Desde el punto de vista ecológico, estos biotopos boscosos están aislados del resto del continente sudamericano por estepas áridas o semiáridas. En el Valle Central chileno, al norte del paralelo 37, existe una estepa de marcadas condiciones xerofíticas en la cual predominan los matorrales de *Acacia caven* (Papilonaceae) (Mann, 1960). Este ambiente semiárido es una zona de transición entre los desiertos costeros de Sudamérica y los bosques temperados australes. Por el oriente, los biotopos boscosos limitan con la estepa fría de la Patagonia. Allí predominan las asociaciones de gramíneas (*Stipa, Poa*), compuestas (*Chuquiraga, Colliguaja*) y matorrales con plantas del género *Trevoa* (Rhamnaceae) (Solbrig, 1976). En la figura 14:1 se muestra la ubicación del bosque temperado en el continente sudamericano y los biotopos que lo circundan.

En el sur de Chile existen tres caracteres fisiográficos: la Cordillera de los Andes, la Cordillera de la Costa y el Valle Central. Estos dos últimos caracteres se aprecian marcadamente hasta el paralelo 41; desde allí al sur tienden a desaparecer siendo reemplazados por una intrincada geografía compuesta de islas, archipiélagos, penínsulas y fiordos (Región de los Canales). En la figura 14:2 se indican las características fisiográficas del área cubierta por los bosques australes temperados en el sur de Chile.

El factor más relevante de los Andes de esta región, es el vulcanismo extrusivo del Cuaternario (Brüggen, 1950) y las alturas aquí predominantes son los volcanes. Estos nunca bajan de los 2000 m y en algunos casos sobrepasan los 3000 m. Al sur del paralelo 37, límite norte de los bosques temperados, la altura de la Cordillera de los Andes decrece en relación con los sectores del centro y norte de Chile. Es así que en esas áreas, alcanza alturas promedios de 5000 m mientras que en el sur nunca sube de los 3000 m. Entre los paralelos 37 y 42 la actividad volcánica cuaternaria originó rocas ígneas tales como basaltos, andesitas y andesitas basálticas. También se pueden encontrar allí rocas sedimentarias correspondientes al Terciario y Cretácico continental, Jurásico Triásico y Paleozoico (Fuenzalida, 1965a; Muñoz Cristi, 1973). Al sur del paralelo 42 predominan

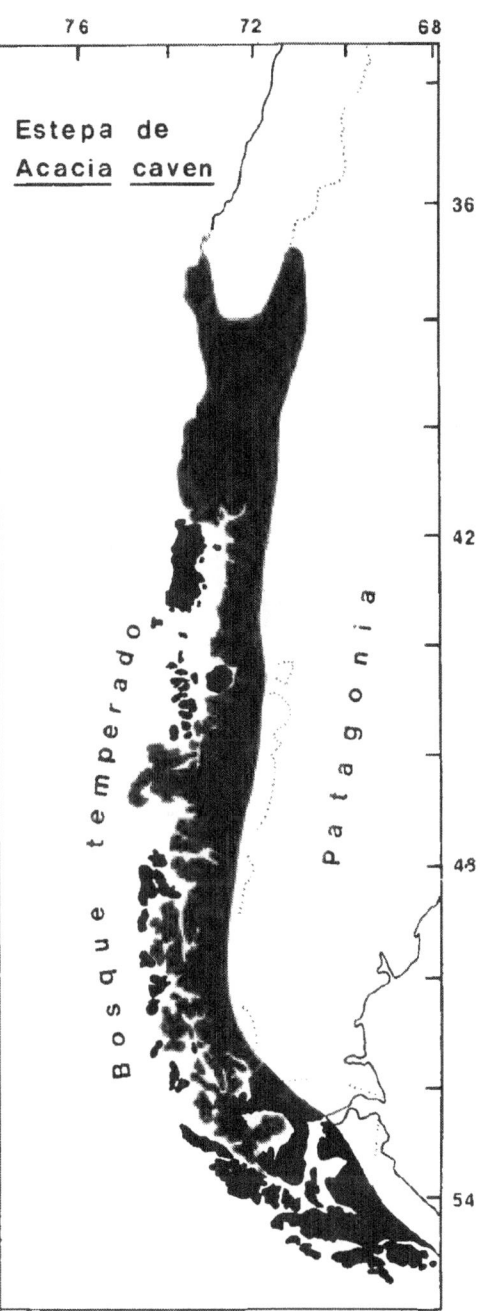

Fic. 14:1. *Ubicación del bosque temperado (negro) y biotopos que lo circundan.*
Map of the temperate austral forests (black) and neighboring biotopes.

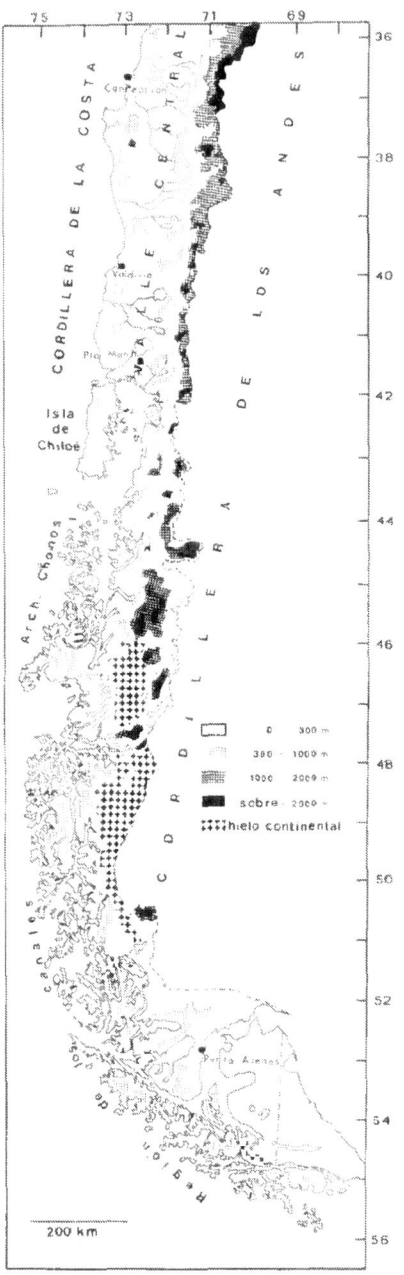

FIG. 14;2. *Caracteres fisiográficos del área cubierta por los bosques australes de Sudamérica.*
Physiography of the area covered by the austral forest of South America.

granitos, dioritas y granidioritas las cuales se originaron a través del vulcanismo intrusivo (Ruiz et al., 1965). La acción de los hielos ha sido un factor muy importante en el modelado del macizo andino de esta región. Hoy existen gran cantidad de glaciares, los cuales en la mayoría de los casos no salen de la Cordillera de los Andes, pero al sur de los 45°S algunos llegan hasta el nivel del mar (San Rafael; 46°40'S) (Lliboutry, 1956). Fuera de los glaciares existen dos grandes masas de hielo continental depositadas en la Cordillera de los Andes de las provincias de Aysén y Magallanes. La primera de ellas se ubica en los 47°S y la segunda de mayor longitud cubre una distancia comprendida entre los 48°10' y los 52°30'S (Lliboutry, 1956).

El Valle Central, ubicado entre la Cordillera de los Andes y la Cordillera de la Costa, es un rasgo fisiográfico del centro y sur de Chile. Esta larga depresión ubicada entre los 37° y 42°S tiene origen tectónico y se formó durante el Plioceno (Brüggen, 1950). La superficie de este gran valle longitudinal, que no alcanza más de 250 m de altura y 90 kms de ancho promedio, ha sido rellenada por depósitos de origen glaciar, fluvial y lacustre (Brüggen, 1950; Fuenzalida, 1965a). El Valle Central llega por el sur hasta el paralelo 41, allí se hunde en el mar para aparecer nuevamente en todo el sector occidental de la Isla de Chiloé. Hacia el sur de esta isla, desaparece definitivamente bajo el océano en la región del Archipiélago de los Chonos.

La Cordillera de la Costa es un carácter fisiográfico que se encuentra solamente en el territorio de Chile. En la región de los bosques temperados, este macizo costero tiende a presentarse fragmentado no alcanzando alturas superiores a los 1500 m (Cordillera de Nahuelbuta). Al sur de la ciudad de Valdivia (40°S) la cordillera costera se levanta sobre los 1000 m y constituye allí la llamada Cordillera Pelada que envía sus cordones hasta la ciudad de Maullín (41°30'S). Desde allí hacia el sur desaparece bajo el Canal de Chacao para reaparecer en la Isla de Chiloé. El macizo costero desaparece al sur de esta gran isla, pero sus últimos restos

Tabla 14 1.—Temperatura Media, Humedad Relativa y Precipitaciones de Diferentes Puntos del sur de Chile (según Hajek y Di Castri, 1975)

Lugar	Ubicación	Temperatura Media °C	Humedad Relativa %	Precipitaciones mm
Punta Lavapie	37°08'S–37°35'W	13 3	82	803 9
Contulmo	38°02'S–73°12'W	12 6	82	1896 0
Valdivia	39°48'S–73°14'W	11 9	83	2318 7
Pto Montt	41°28'S–72°57'W	11 2	85	2311 8
Castro	42°29'S–73°48'W	11 6	82	1598 5
Melinka	43°54'S–73°46'W	10 0	-	3137 7
Pto Aysen	45°24'S–72°42'W	9 0	86	2940 0
San Pedro	47°43'S–74°55'W	8 2	91	4266 3
Pto Eden	49°08'S–74°25'W	7 2	84	2313 1
San Isidro	53°47'S–70°58'W	5 9	81	848 5
Navarino	55°10'S–67°30'W	5 9	84	540 8

se aprecian con claridad en la península de Taitao (46°30'S) Las rocas metamórficas constituyen parte importante de la Cordillera de la Costa y es así que se encuentran micacitas, cuarcitas y filitas (Múnoz Cristi, 1973).

Toda la región de los bosques temperados está atravesada por ríos medianos de carácter exorreico, que se originan en el derretimiento de las nieves de los Andes (Bio-Bío, Toltén, Imperial) o tienen un régimen mixto (nieve y lluvia) Dentro de este último tipo se encuentran las hoyas de los ríos Valdivia Bueno y Maullín, que incluyen en su recorrido la entrada y salida por grandes sistemas lacustres (Fuenzalida, 1965b).

Fuera de los ríos, existe un gran sistema de lagos entre los paralelos 39 y 41 La mayoría de ellos son de tipo oligotrófico (Thomasson, 1963) y en muchos casos ocupan cuencas excavadas por los glaciares (Arenas, 1972) Este autor cita la presencia de morrenas terminales en los sectores occidentales de los lagos Calafquen Riñihue y Panguipulli Cinturones morrénicos han sido descritos para el lago Llanquihue (Bruggen 1950) y Ranco (Mercer y Laugenie, 1973) El mayor de los lagos de esta región es el Llanquihue (Provincia de Llanquihue) con 351 km² de superficie y uno de los menores es el Caburga (Provincia de Cautín) con 53 km² (ENDESA 1972) Algunos de estos cuerpos de agua son muy profundos y Arenas (1972) detectó 320 metros para el lago Riñihue (Provincia de Valdivia).

El clima de la región cubierta por los bosques temperados se caracteriza por ser frío y húmedo En la Tabla 14 1 se muestran las características climáticas de diferentes puntos del sur de Chile En general se observa un decremento de la temperatura en dirección al sur y un aumento de las precipitaciones en el mismo sentido La región de los bosques australes sudamericanos es azotada por fuertes tormentas las cuales son muy frecuentes en invierno Los vientos fríos y húmedos del oeste, originados en el anticiclón del Pacífico (35°S, 100°W), son los causantes de la lluvia y la humedad del sur de Chile (Fuenzalida 1965c) La influencia de algunos caracteres fisiográficos locales especialmente la Cordillera de la Costa determinan en el Valle Central algunas condiciones de mediterraneidad Por otro lado, no se debe olvidar que ningún lugar del sur de Chile se encuentra muy lejos del mar y que por lo tanto el océano tiene influencia en el clima Di Castri (1968) indica que el sur de Chile tiene un clima con influencia mediterránea y marítima Fuenzalida (1965c) usando el sistema de Koppen (1948) divide el sur de Chile en diferentes zonas climáticas templadas En el Valle Central se presenta un clima templado de verano seco y corta estación de sequía (Csb_), que se extiende entre los paralelos 35 y 39 Al sur de este punto, y en el mismo Valle Central, hay un clima templado húmedo de verano fresco y tendencia a seco (Ctsb) que se extiende hasta el paralelo 42 Toda la zona costera comprendida entre Concepción y la Isla de Chiloé se caracteriza por tener un clima templado húmedo de verano fresco (Cfb) Estas condiciones climáticas se extienden a Chiloé continental, archipiélago de los Chonos y Península de Taitao. Al sur del golfo de Penas (47°S) y en toda la región de los canales, hasta el paralelo 53, existe una zona de clima templado húmedo de verano fresco o frío (Cfc).

Los bosques temperados del sur de Chile, que cubren toda el área anteriormente descrita, se caracterizan por tener rasgos higromórficos. Estos se acentúan a partir del paralelo 38 y alcanzan un máximo desarrollo en los 45°S. Desde allí hacia el sur, hay una marcada tendencia al xeromorfismo debido a las bajas temperaturas y a los vientos predominantes del oeste. Los bosques australes son densos, siempre verdes y alcanzan alturas que superan los 40 m. En él hay varios estratos vegetacionales con un tupido sotobosque y un piso rico en vegetación. En este bosque es posible encontrar arbustos con hojas anchas, ya sea de tipo magnolia (*Drimys*) o laurel (*Laurelia*). Los troncos de los grandes árboles están cubiertos de enredaderas, musgos, helechos y líquenes. La abundancia de vegetación determina que la obscuridad sea un carácter predominante dentro del bosque.

La flora del bosque austral tiene varias especies endémicas entre las cuales destacan los árboles del género *Nothofagus* (Fagaceae). Es frecuente también encontrar taxa monotípicos, ya sea a nivel familiar o genérico. Entre los primeros destaca la familia Aextoxicaceae (*Aextoxicum punctatus*) y entre los segundos los géneros *Guevina* (Proteaceae), *Tepualia* (Mirtaceae), *Fitzroya* (Cupressaceae) y *Myzodendrum* (Myzodendraceae). Florísticamente los bosques temperados de Sudamérica tienen un origen doble austral y tropical (Reiche, 1937, Menéndez, 1969). Como típicos elementos australes destacan *Nothofagus*, *Fitzroya* y *Araucaria* y como componentes tropicales *Drimys*, *Fuchsia* y *Chusquea*.

A pesar que el bosque austral sudamericano muestra cierto grado de uniformidad, es posible encontrar ciertas variaciones locales. Entre ellas la más notable es el llamado "Bosque Valdiviano," el cual representa la región más característica de los bosques australes. Aquí se da una breve descripción de él en base a los trabajos de Reiche (1934), Pisano (1956), Oberdorfer (1960), Fuenzalida (1965d) y Quintanilla (1974).

El bosque valdiviano comienza en la Cordillera de los Andes a partir del paralelo 39, en la Cordillera de la Costa en el paralelo 40 y en el Valle Central en el paralelo 41. El límite sur no está claramente definido, pero se le puede situar entre los paralelos 43 y 44. En este bosque la humedad relativa es muy alta (84%) y la temperatura promedio anual es de 10.5°C. El verano es medianamente cálido y las lluvias tienen una distribución homogénea a través de todo el año. La pluviosidad anual fluctúa entre los 2000 y 2500 mm. La abundancia de precipitaciones, la existencia de suelos bien drenados con una capa freática profunda, la gran humedad y la alta temperatura en verano, permiten el desarrollo de un bosque rico en especies. Los troncos de los árboles están cubiertos por líquenes (*Usnea*), musgos epífitos, enredaderas (*Sarmienta* y *Luzuriaga*) y lianas (*Hydrangea* y *Cissus*). Aquí existe un sotobosque denso en el cual hay bambúes (*Chusquea quila*), arbustos (*Lomatia*, *Fuchsia*) y helechos (*Blechnum*, *Lophosoria*). El piso del bosque es rico en líquenes y helechos (*Dryopteris*, *Adiantum*). Tres son los árboles más característicos del bosque valdiviano: *Nothofagus dombeyi*, *Eucryphia cordifolia* y *Aextoxicum punctatus*. Otras especies importantes son aquí las coníferas, entre las cuales se pueden citar a *Fitzroya*, *Saxegotea*, *Podocarpus* y *Pilgerodendron*. *Fitzroya cupressoides* es el más alto de los árboles chilenos y alcanza alturas sobre los 55 m. Su diámetro puede alcanzar a los 5 m y se le han calculado edades sobre los 2000 años. Entre las especies secundarias se encuentran *Laurelia serrata*, *Drimys winteri*, *Weinmannia trichosperma* y *Persea lingue*.

Al norte del bosque valdiviano existe un bosque caducifolio en el cual destacan como especies más relevantes *Nothofagus obliqua* y *Guevina avellano*. En la cordillera de Nahuelbuta (Cordillera de la Costa) y en los Andes, entre los paralelos 37 y 40, se desarrollan bosques de *Araucaria araucana*. Estas formaciones boscosas, ubicadas entre los 1300 y 2000 m presentan también *Nothofagus pumilio* y *Nothofagus antarctica*.

Al sur del bosque valdiviano hay una selva

norpatagónica que se extiende hasta el paralelo 48 Allí destacan como árboles más importantes *Podocarpus salignus* y *Pilgerodendron uviferum* Al oeste de estas formaciones boscosas hay pantanos los cuales se ubican especialmente en las islas Aquí hay *Pernethya* (Ericaceae), *Gleichnia* (Pteridofita), pero también *Nothofagus betuloides* y *Nothofagus antarctica*

HISTORIA DEL ÁREA

El Terciario sudamericano se caracteriza especialmente por el levantamiento de la Cordillera de los Andes En el Cretácico Superior se hicieron sentir, en el oeste del continente, los primeros movimientos orogénicos del llamado ciclo Andino (Harrington, 1962) que originaron las diversas partes de la Cordillera de los Andes Durante el Eoceno, se aprecia un aceleramiento de los procesos orogenéticos que alcanzan gran desarrollo en el Mioceno, seguidos en el Plioceno de movimientos que dieron origen a la forma actual del macizo andino (Harrington, 1962, Haffer, 1970)

Al término del Terciario Inferior (Eoceno), y posiblemente en el Oligoceno, el territorio de Chile fue un área inestable Durante el Oligoceno se produjeron procesos de deformación y plegamiento en varias regiones del país, al final de las cuales el territorio adquirió las características de una región estable, en el que aparecieron sistemas de montañas de poco relieve (Fuenzalida 1965a) Durante el Mioceno hubo una gran transgresión marina que cubrió extensas areas del sur de Chile (Cecioni 1970) A fines del Plioceno o comienzos de la época siguiente Pleistoceno, el territorio chileno fue profundamente modificado por un fuerte tectonismo Este trajo como consecuencia el levantamiento de la Cordillera de los Andes de la Cordillera de la Costa y la formación del Valle Central (Bruggen, 1950, Fuenzalida, 1965a) Durante el Pleistoceno, ocurrieron en el extremo sur de Sudamérica fuertes procesos glaciares (Vuilleumier, 1971) La invasión de estas masas de hielo trajo como consecuencia fuertes modificaciones en el clima y en la fisiografía Las islas, archipiélagos y fiordos de la región de los canales, se formaron en gran medida por la acción del hielo glaciar (Bruggen, 1950, Fuenzalida, 1965a)

Los bosques australes sudamericanos, con sus elementos típicos (*Nothofagus*, *Araucaria* y *Laurelia*), han existido desde el Terciario (Jeannelle, 1967, Cerceau-Larrival, 1968) y se acepta que tuvieron una distribución gondwánica (Couper, 1960) En el extremo sur de Sudamérica alcanzaron un rango de extensión mucho más amplio que el que tienen hoy, llegando hasta la actual Patagonia (Menendez 1969) Durante el Eoceno muchos de los elementos de la flora tropical penetraron hacia el sur y aparecen en los estratos fosilíferos de Río Turbio, Argentina mezclados con elementos australes (Menéndez, 1969) Aquí las capas más inferiores muestran elementos típicamente sureños (*Nothofagus*) los cuales son reemplazados en los estratos superiores por elementos tropicales (*Persea*, *Psidun*) La coexistencia de una flora austral con una flora tropical se explica debido a que estos últimos elementos ocupaban las partes bajas (valles) y los australes las partes superiores de las montañas (Bruggen 1950, Menéndez 1969) Durante el Mioceno y Oligoceno la flora tropical retrocedió hacia el norte y simultáneamente se produjo un avance de la flora austral en la misma dirección, hasta los límites actuales del bosque temperado (Solbrig, 1976, Menéndez, 1969)

La extinción de los bosques australes en la actual Patagonia se debe, en gran medida al efecto que causó la Cordillera de los Andes al impedir la pasada de los vientos fríos y húmedos del oeste Durante el Paleoceno y el Eoceno el macizo andino estaba poco levantado y los vientos del Pacífico llegaban hasta los sectores orientales del extremo sudamericano Durante el Oligoceno la barrera de los Andes llegó a ser un obstáculo para ellos, los cuales se vieron definitivamente frenados en el Mioceno Al no haber lluvias ni humedad en el sector oriental del macizo andino, las formaciones boscosas desaparecieron, dando origen a la estepa semiárida patagónica (Solbrig, 1976) Fuera de los cambios del relieve y la vegetación ocurrieron variaciones simultáneas en las condiciones climáticas que afectaron el extremo austral de Sudamérica. Durante el Paleoceno el clima del continente fue más cálido que hoy (Solbrig, 1976) y después del Eoceno se aprecia un gradual enfriamiento y desecación (Axelrod y Bailey, 1969, Wolfe, 1971) el cual culmina en el Pleistoceno durante las etapas glaciares.

Fuera de los cambios anteriormente referidos es posible que la transgresión marina del Mioceno y las glaciaciones del Pleistoceno hayan afectado la distribución de la herpetofauna austral. La entrada miocénica del mar, afectó el sur de Chile entre los paralelos 37 y 41 (Bruggen 1950, Cecioni 1970 Illies, 1970, Auborn et al, 1973). Los estratos producidos por esta invasión del mar se encuentran en la región de Santiago (Navidad) y hacia el sur, en las áreas de Concepción (Ranquil), Temuco (Pilmahue), Osorno (Cheuqueno) y Chiloé. Según Bruggen (1950), en estos estratos hay areniscas arcillosas de grano fino y color gris claro que se distinguen por tener una abundancia de fósiles marinos. Illies (1970) indica que la transgresión marina tuvo baja profundidad y que como consecuencia de ella se produjeron una gran cantidad de islas y bahías que semejan los archipiélagos e islas de la costa del extremo sur occidental de Sudamérica.

Durante el Pleistoceno el hielo ocupó en el sur de Chile una amplia extensión cubriendo el área comprendida entre los 41° y 55°S (Vuilleumier, 1971). Sin embargo Bruggen (1948) para explicar la expansión del bosque de *Nothofagus* al sur de paralelo 41, en la época post-glacial propone que durante los períodos glaciales quedaron refugios boscosos en los faldeos de la costa del Pacífico sobre los glaciares. Condiciones parecidas a las supuestas por Bruggen se encuentran hoy en el glaciar de San Rafael. Aquí se sucedieron tres o cuatro glaciaciones (Bruggen, 1948, 1950, Auer, 1960, Vuilleumier, 1971, Simpson, este volumen) que penetraron en el Valle Central hasta la latitud de la ciudad de Santiago (Bruggen, 1950). Este autor ha descrito sistemas de morrenas terminales cerca del Río Maipo, al sur de Santiago (33°30'S), al norte de Curicó (35°S) y en la vecindad de Puerto Montt (40°30'S).

La presencia de morrenas en el Valle Central y en el sector oriental de la Cordillera de la Costa hacen presumir que las pendientes occidentales de este macizo costero no tuvieron influencia glaciar. Heusser (1966) e Illies (1970) indican que la Cordillera de la Costa permaneció fuera de la acción de estas masas de hielo.

COMPOSICIÓN DE LA HERPETOFAUNA

La herpetofauna de los bosques australes está compuesta de 28 especies, 20 de las cuales (71.4%) son anuros, seis son saurios (21.4%) y dos serpientes (7.1%). Los anuros (sapos y ranas) pertenecen a tres familias distintas Bufonidae, Leptodactylidae y Rhinodermatidae. Las serpientes pertenecen a la familia Colubridae y los saurios se ubican en la familia Iguanidae. En la Tabla 14.2 se muestra la composición herpetofaunística de los bosques temperados de Sudamérica.

DISTRIBUCIÓN DE LA HERPETOFAUNA

La herpetofauna de los bosques temperados sudamericanos presenta patrones de distribución característicos. Al norte del paralelo 44 existe la mayor concentración de géneros de anfibios y reptiles, los cuales a partir de esta latitud comienzan a disminuir gradualmente hacia el sur. La figura 14.3 muestra los patrones de distribución genérica de los anfibios y reptiles del bosque austral.

En la región costera del área comprendida entre los 39°30'S y los 40°20'S existe la mayor concentración de géneros de anuros. La zona con menor concentración de anfibios es la que se encuentra al sur del paralelo 50, llegando hasta allí solamente los anuros del género *Bufo*.

Algunos de las especies de anfibios presentes en el bosque tienen amplia distribución en él. Dentro de esta categoría se pueden incluir a *Rhinoderma darwinii*, *Batrachyla leptopus*, *Batrachyla taeniata*, *Eupsophus roseus*, *Eupsophus vittatus*, *Caudiverbera caudiverbera* y *Pleurodema thaul*. Otras especies ocupan rangos medianos (*Hylorina sylvatica*, *Alsodes monticola*, *Bufo variegatus*, *Bufo rubro-

TABLA 14 2.—Composicion de la Herpetofauna del Bosque Temperado de Sudamerica

Familia	Generos	Especie y Subespecie
Leptodactylidae	Alsodes	monticola
	Atelognathus	grandisonae
	Batrachyla	antartandica
		leptopus
		taeniata
	Caudiverbera	caudiverbera
	Eupsophus	roseus
		vanzolinii
		vittatus (= E. vertebralis)
		migueli
	Insuetophrynus	acarpicus
	Pleurodema	thaul
	Telmatobufo	australis
		venustus (= T. bullocki)
Rhinodermatidae	Rhinoderma	darwinii
		rufum
Bufonidae	Bufo	chilensis
		rubropunctatus
		variegatus
Iguanidae	Liolaemus	chilensis
		cyanogaster cyanogaster
		cyanogaster brattstroemi
		monticola villaricensis
		pictus pictus
		pictus chiloensis
		pictus major
		pictus talcanensis
		tenuis tenuis
		tenuis punctatissimus
	Pristidactylus	torquatus (= Cupriguanus)
Colubridae	Alsophis	chamissonis
	Tachymenis	chilensis (= T. peruviana)

punctatus, Batrachyla antartandica, Rhinoderma rufum y Bufo chilensis) y unas pocas están restringidas a ámbitos muy pequeños (Atelognathus grandisonae, Insuetophrynus acarpicus Telmatobufo australis, Telmatobufo venustus, Eupsophus vanzolinii y Eupsophus migueli) Las figuras 14 4–10 muestran los rangos de distribución de todas las especies de anuros presentes en el bosque temperado

Areas de simpatría han sido encontradas para algunas especies de batracios Rhinoderma darwinii y Rhinoderma rufum superponen su distribucion en Chiguayante (Provincia de Concepción) (Formas et al, 1975) Silva et al (1968) encontraron poblaciones simpátricas de Bufo variegatus y Bufo rubropunctatus en la Cordillera de los Andes de la Provincia de Llanquihue Batrachyla leptopus y Batrachyla antartandica tienen poblaciones que se superponen en el cerro Mirador (Cordillera Pelada, Provincia de Valdivia), Puerto Blest y Lago Frías (Nahuel Huapi, Argentina) y en El Correntoso (Puerto Montt, Chile) (Barrio, 1967a) Batrachyla taeniata y Batrachyla leptopus viven en condiciones de simpatría en los alrededores de la ciudad de Valdivia Eupsophus vittatus y Eupsophus roseus son simpátricas en un area muy amplia que cubre todo el rango de distribución de Eupsophus vittatus

Las figuras 14 11–15 muestran los rangos distribucionales de los reptiles del bosque temperado de Sudamerica Pristidactylus torquatus alcanza alturas que fluctúan entre los 50 m (Catamutún, Provincia de Valdivia) y los 1400 m (Cordillera de Nahuelbuta) Liolaemus monticola villaricensis tiene rangos de distribución altitudinal que fluctúa entre los 1000 m y los 1400 m (Hellmich 1950) Liolaemus chilensis ha sido colectada en alturas que varían entre los 100 m y 1200 m (Hellmich, 1950) Liolaemus pictus se ubica entre los 100 m y 800 m, mientras que Liolaemus cyanogaster lo hace entre los 10 m y

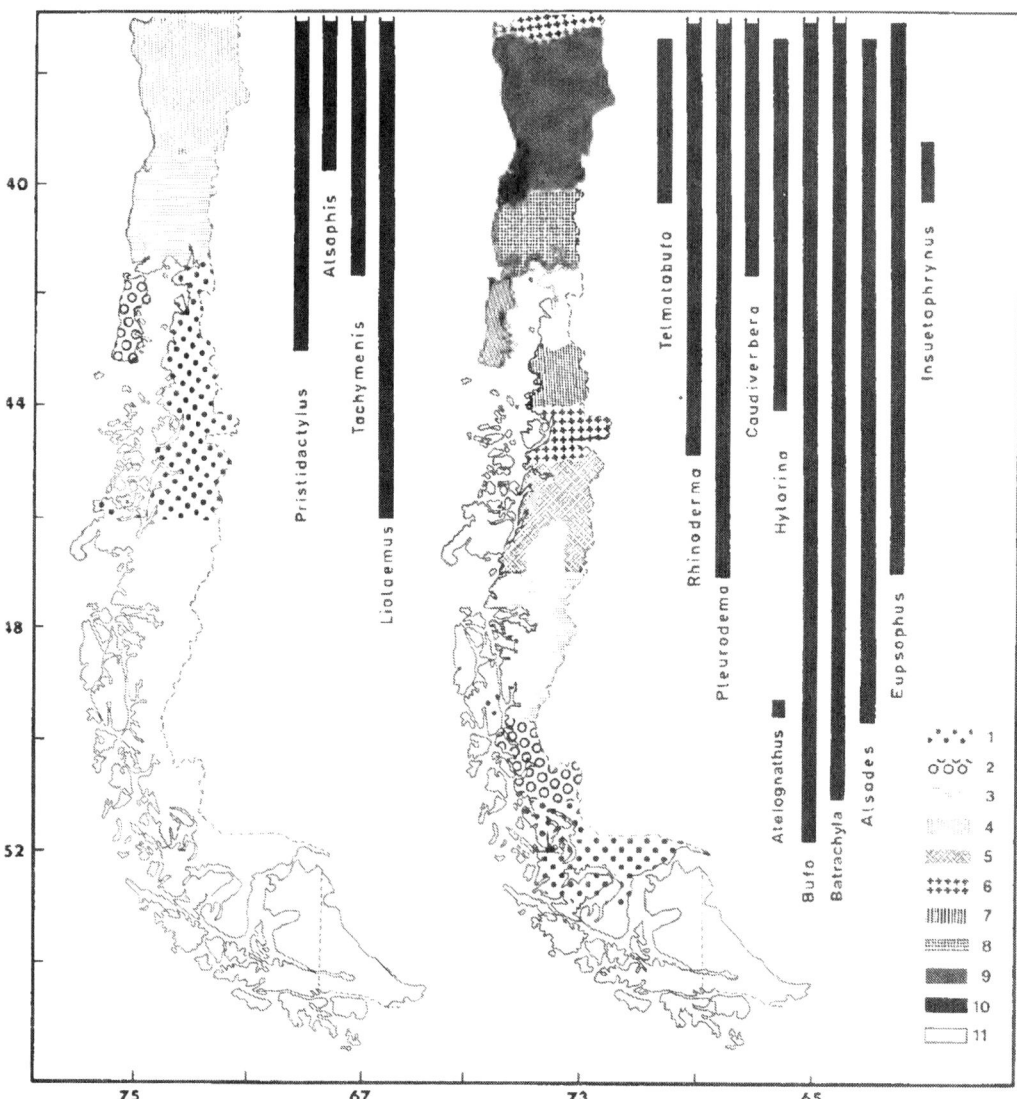

Fig. 14:3. *Patrones de distribución latitudinal de los géneros de anfibios y reptiles. Las áreas en blanco (11) corresponden a hielo continental o regiones carentes de anfibios o reptiles. Los números indican la densidad genérica.*

Latitudinal patterns of distribution of the genera of amphibians and reptiles. The white areas (11) represent ice-covered areas or areas free of amphibians or reptiles. The numbers indicate the generic density.

350 m. Ambas especies son simpátricas en una amplia área. *Liolaemus pictus* presenta tres subespecies (*L. p. chiloensis*, *L. p. major* y *L. p. talcanensis*) que se distribuyen en el archipiélago de Chiloé (Donoso-Barros, 1966; Urbina y Zúñiga, 1977). *Liolaemus cyanogaster* tiene una subespecie (*L. c. brattstroemi*) que se distribuye en la Isla Grande de Chiloé (Donoso-Barros, 1966). *Liolaemus tenuis* ocupa alturas que van desde el nivel del mar hasta los 1000 m y en la región costera es reemplazada por una subespecie, la

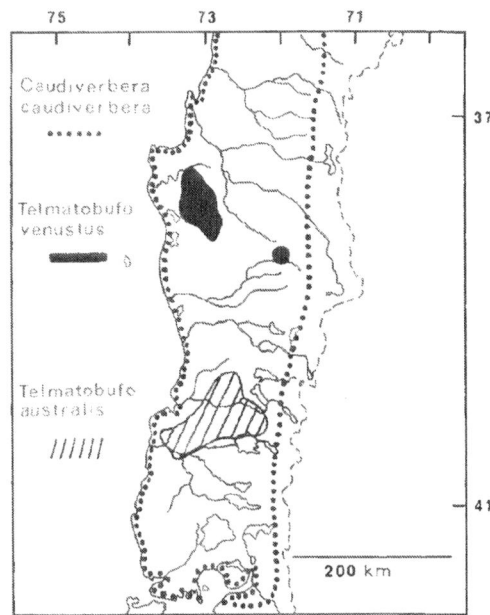

Fig. 14:4. *Patrón distribucional de las especies de* Telmatobufo *y* Caudiverbera caudiverbera *en el sur de Chile.*
Distribution pattern of *Telmatobufo* and *Caudiverbera caudiverbera* in southern Chile.

cual Donoso-Barros (1966) llama *Liolaemus tenuis punctatissimus.*

Tachymenis chilensis está desde el nivel del mar hasta los valles de la Cordillera de los Andes (Hellmich, 1937). *Alsophis chamissonis* ocupa el Valle Central y puede ascender en la Cordillera de los Andes hasta los 1500 m de altura.

Desde el comienzo del bosque temperado, en el paralelo 37, están presentes los cuatro géneros de reptiles existentes en el área, los cuales llegan juntos hasta el paralelo 40. Los saurios del género *Liolaemus* son las que alcanzan el límite más austral de distribución, ya que en esta área penetran hasta el paralelo 45. Es posible que la gradiente de disminución térmica que existe en dirección norte-sur, la cual se muestra en la Tabla 14:1, sea la responsable de este patrón distribucional que afecta tanto a anfibios como a reptiles.

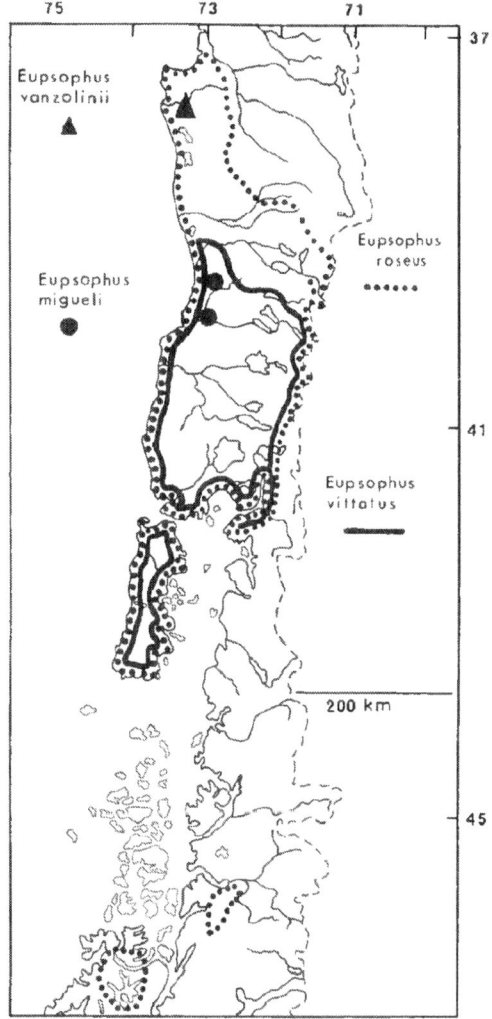

Fig. 14:5. *Patrón de distribución de las especies del género* Eupsophus *en el sur de Chile.*
Distribution pattern of the species of *Eupsophus* in southern Chile.

Altitudinalmente los anfibios llegan hasta los 1000 m; sin embargo *Pleurodema thaul, Bufo variegatus* y *Bufo chilensis* pueden alcanzar hasta los 2000 m. Es posible también que la temperatura sea un factor limitante en la distribución altitudinal de los anfibios. La figura 14:16 muestra el patrón de distribución altitudinal de los anfibios del bosque temperado.

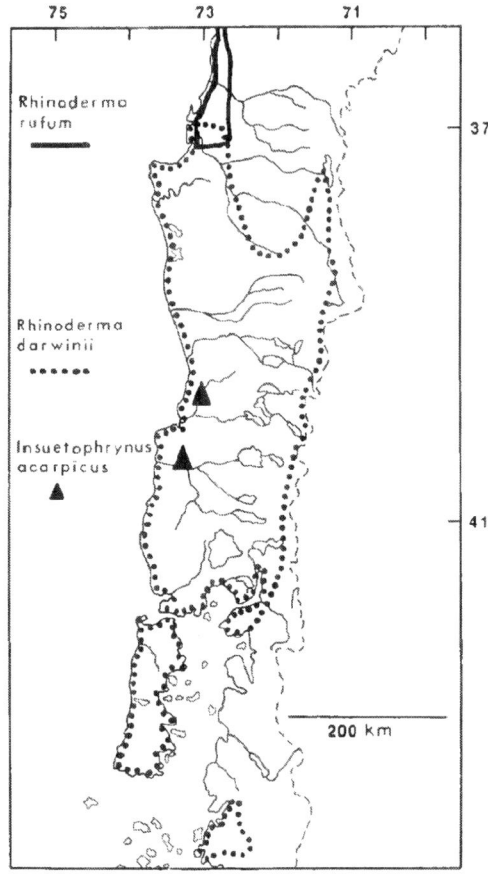

Fig. 14:6. *Patrones de distribución de las especies de los géneros* Rhinoderma *y* Insuetophrynus *en el sur de Chile.*
Distribution patterns of species of *Rhinoderma* and *Insuetophrynus* in southern Chile.

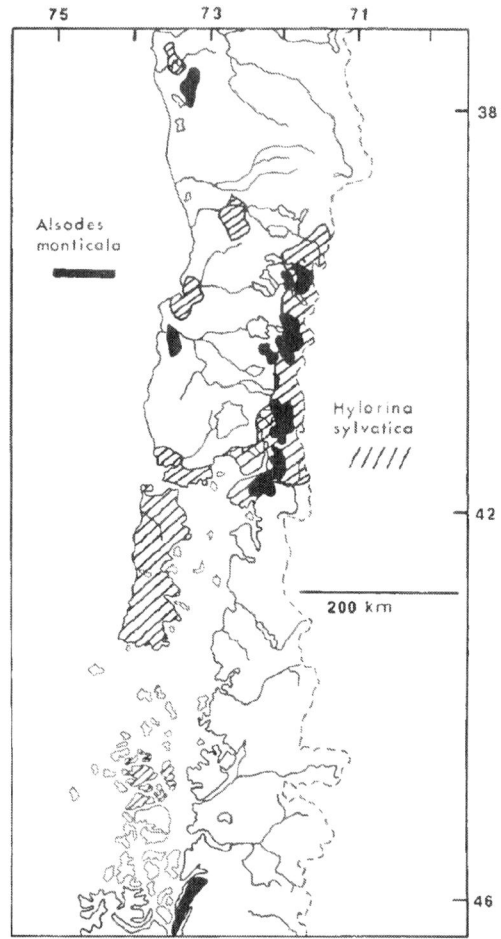

Fig. 14:7. *Patrones de distribución de* Hylorina sylvatica *y* Alsodes monticola *en el sur de Chile.*
Distribution patterns of *Hylorina sylvatica* and *Alsodes monticola* in southern Chile.

ECOLOGÍA DE LA HERPETOFAUNA

La mayoría de las especies de anuros vive en el piso del bosque, ya sea entre la vegetación (*Rhinoderma, Batrachyla*), la hojarasca (*Eupsophus*) y bajo troncos en descomposición o piedras (*Bufo, Alsodes*). *Telmatobufo* e *Insuetophrynus* está asociados a ambientes acuáticos de tipo lótico mientras *Caudiverbera* está en cuerpos de agua de tipo léntico. A pesar de la abundante vegetación que existe en el bosque austral no hay especies arbóreas; sin embargo en forma ocasional se han encontrado a algunos individuos de *Hylorina sylvatica* y *Batrachyla leptopus* (Busse, 1971) sobre ramas o troncos. *Pleurodema thaul* vive bajo troncos o piedras y también en lugares con fuerte intervención humana.

La mayoría de los saurios del género *Liolaemus* tiene hábitos trepadores y se encuentran especialmente en los arbustos del sotobosque (*Liolaemus pictus, Liolaemus cyanogaster, Liolaemus chilensis y Liolaemus tenuis*). *Liolaemus monticola villaricensis* vive preferentemente en las rocas y campos de lava de la Cordillera de los Andes (Hellmich, 1934). *Pristidactylus torquatus* es según

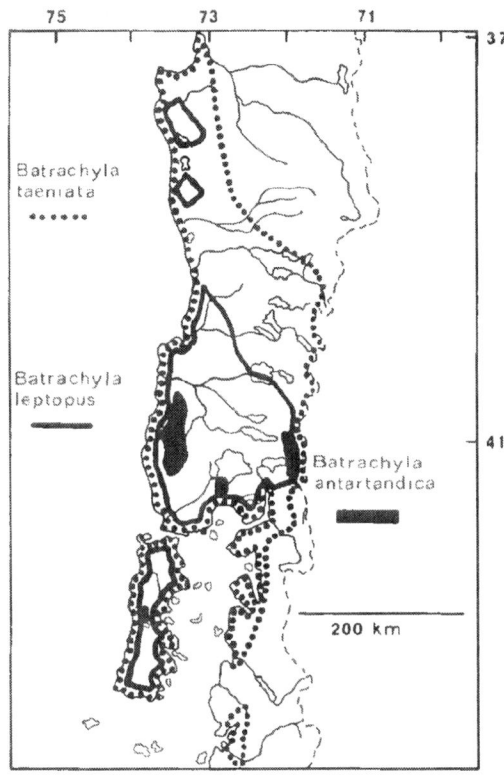

Fig. 14:8. *Patrones de distribución del género* Batrachyla *en el sur de Chile.*
Distribution patterns of *Batrachyla* in southern Chile.

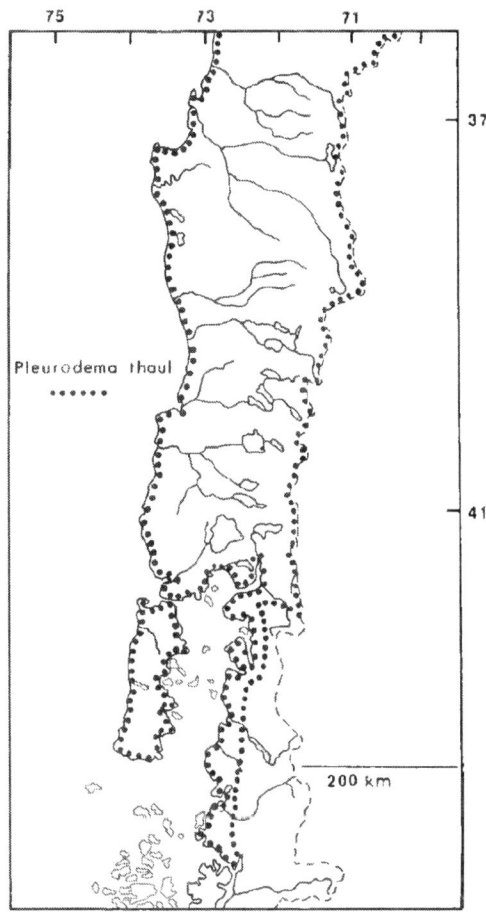

Fig. 14:9. *Rango de distribución de* Pleurodema thaul *en el sur de Chile.*
Range of distribution of *Pleurodema thaul* in southern Chile.

Donoso-Barros (1966) un lagarto que trepa en los troncos de los árboles del género *Nothofagus*. *Alsophis chamissonis* y *Tachymenis chilensis* son dos serpientes que viven en los lugares más secos del bosque; sin embargo la última especie puede también ser encontrada en lugares con mucha humedad.

No existen antecedentes suficientes para trazar un cuadro detallado sobre la alimentación de la herpetofauna del bosque austral. Los pocos datos disponibles permiten decir solamente que no hay animales altamente especializados en la alimentación.

Rhinoderma darwinii se alimenta de insectos (Schneider, 1930) lo mismo que *Telmatobufo venustus* (Schmidt, 1952). Rybertt y Daniel (1976) determinaron que *Eupsophus vittatus* y *Eupsophus roseus* se alimentan de insectos, larvas, ácaros, caracoles, escorpiones, pseudoescorpiones y oligoquetos. *Caudiverbera caudiverbera* come especialmente peces, batracios, larvas de insectos, crustáceos (*Aegla*) y hasta pájaros y pequeños mamíferos (Lira, 1946; Cei, 1962a).

La mayoría de los lagartos que habitan el bosque temperado tiene hábitos insectívoros, pero en *Liolaemus monticola villaricensis* se han detectado hábitos de herbivoría (Donoso-Barros, 1966). *Alsophis chamissonis* se alimenta especialmente de lagartijas de género *Liolaemus* y roedores (*Octodon degus* y *Mus*

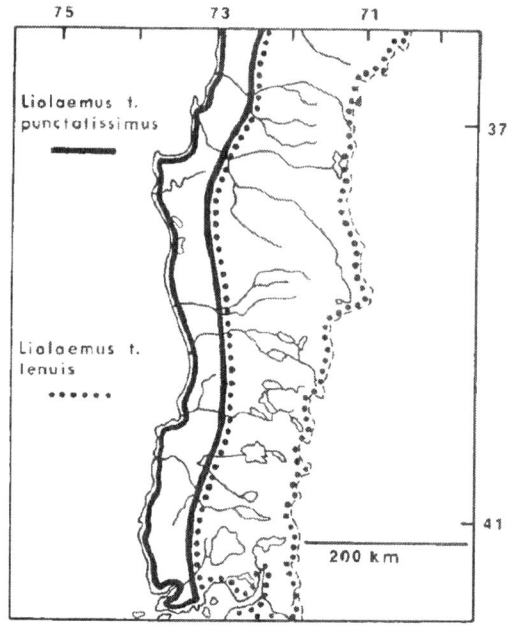

Fig. 14:11. *Patrón distribucional de* Liolaemus tenuis tenuis *y* L. t. punctatissimus *en el sur de Chile.*

Distribution pattern of *Liolaemus tenuis tenuis* and *L. t. punctatissimus* in southern Chile.

musculus) (Donoso-Barros, 1966). *Tachymenis chilensis* también consume grandes cantidades de saurios (*Liolaemus*).

La época de reproducción de anuros del bosque es relativamente conocida. En la Tabla 14:3 se indica la época del año en la cual los machos cantan y muestran callosidades sexuales. Los anfibios de estos biotopos ponen sus huevos ya sea en la tierra, en condiciones de semi-sumergimiento o directamente en el agua. En la Tabla 14:4 se muestra el lugar de ovipostura de cada especie, la forma del "cluster," el número de huevos y su diámetro.

En los últimos años ha habido un fuerte

Fig. 14:10. *Patrones distribucionales de las especies del género* Bufo *y* Atelognathus grandisonae *en el sur de Chile.*

Distribution patterns of the species of *Bufo* and *Atelognathus grandisonae* in southern Chile.
observación personal)
⁶ See footnote 4, p. 389.

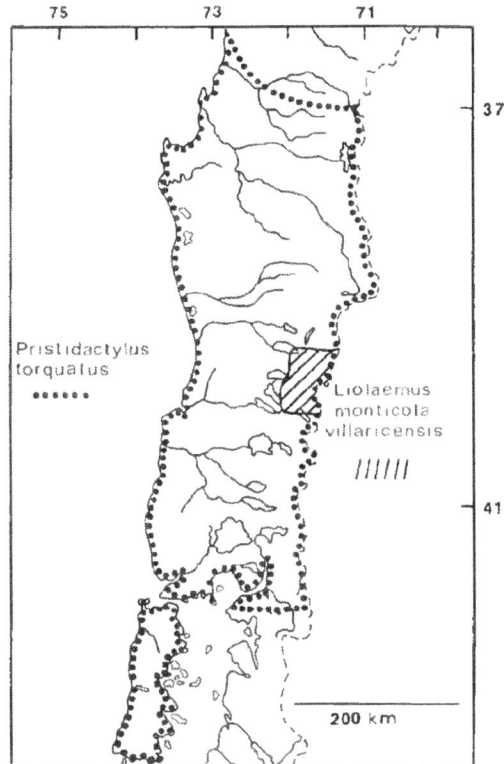

Fig. 14:12. Patrones de distribución de Pristidactylus torquatus y Liolaemus monticola villaricensis en el sur de Chile.
Distribution patterns of *Pristidactylus torquatus* and *Liolaemus monticola villaricensis* in southern Chile.

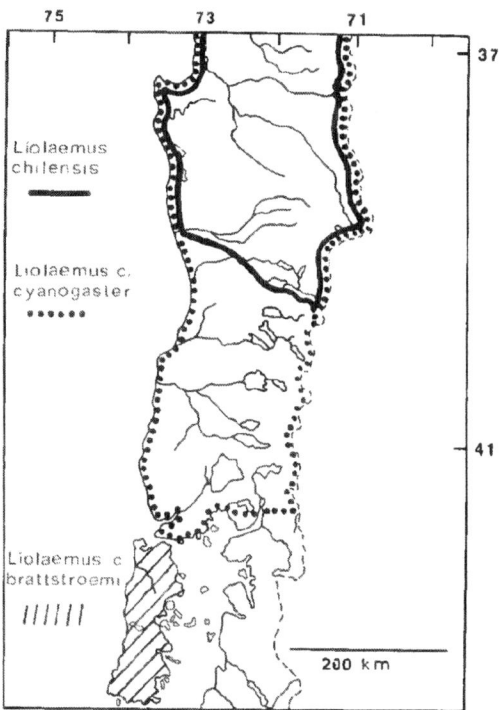

Fig. 14:13. Patrones de distribución de Liolaemus chilensis, L. cyanogaster cyanogaster y L. c. brattstroemi en el sur de Chile.
Distribution patterns of *Liolaemus chilensis, L. cyanogaster cyanogaster* and *L. c. brattstroemi* in southern Chile.

aumento en el conocimiento del desarrollo embrionario y larvario de sapos y ranas del bosque. En la Tabla 14:5 aparece la duración del período embrionario y larvario de algunos batracios del sur de Chile. La mayoría de las especies de anuros presentan larvas del tipo generalizado de Orton (1953); sin embargo existen también otros tipos larvarios adaptados a ambientes especiales. *Telmatobufo australis* posee un renacuajo adaptado a vivir en aguas frías y torrentosas, su boca tiene forma de ventosa y por medio de ella se adhiere a las piedras (Formas, 1972). La larva de *Caudiverbera caudiverbera* vive en grandes cuerpos de aguas abiertas y su cuerpo está adaptado a estos ambientes nectónicos. Su forma es redondeada, las aletas son altas y la punta de la cola es afilada. *Rhinoderma darwinii* muestra un patrón de desarrollo que tiene fuertes desviaciones del esquema corriente presentado por los anuros (Noble, 1931). Como consecuencia de ello la larva muestra reducciones en las aletas, forma del cuerpo y estructura de la boca (Jorquera, et al., 1972).

Las especies del género *Rhinoderma* (*darwinii* y *rufum*) muestran patrones de desarrollo únicos entre los anuros ya que algunas de las etapas del desarrollo transcurren en la bolsa gutural del macho. En la figura 14:17 se muestra comparativamente los ciclos de desarrollo de las especies de *Rhinoderma*. Los huevos de *R. darwinii* son depositados en terreno vegetal húmedo; posteriormente el macho toma con la boca los jóvenes embriones y los introduce en la bolsa bucal dentro de la cual se realiza el resto del desarrollo

TABLA 14 3—Meses del Año Durante los cuales los Machos de las Especies Listadas Cantan y Muestran Callosidades Sexuales (O = canto X = callosidades sexuales A = ambos)

Especies	E	F	M	A	M	J	J	A	S	O	N	D	Autores
Caudiverbera caudiverbera	X							A	A	A			(Cei, 1962a, Duellman, com pers)
Telmatobufo venustus							X						(Pefaur, 1971)
Eupsophus roseus								A	A				(Formas y Pugin, 1978)
Eupsophus vittatus										A	A		(Formas observacion personal)
Batrachyla leptopus	X	A	A	A									(Barrio, 1967a, Busse, 1971, Formas 1976, Duellman, com pers)
Batrachyla taeniata			A	A	A								(Busse, 1971, Formas, (observacion personal)
Batrachyla antartandica	A	A	O									O	(Barrio, 1967a Formas y Pugin, 1971, Formas, 1976)
Hylorina sylvatica	A												(Barrio 1967b)
Pleurodema thaul	X							A	A	A	A		(Cei 1962a Duellman, com pers)
Alsodes monticola	X	X											(Formas observacion personal)
Bufo chilensis							X	X	X				(Cei 1962a)
Bufo variegatus										X			(Formas y Pugin, 1978)
Insuetophrynus acarpicus	X	X	X										(Barrio, 1970)
Rhinoderma darwinii									O	O	O	O	(Cei, 1962a)
Rhinoderma rufum						O							(Formas et al 1975)

TABLA 14 4—Lugar de Ovipostura Forma del Cluster Numero y Diametro de los Huevos de los Anuros Listados

Especies	Lugar de ovipostura	Forma del cluster	Numero de huevos	Diametro de huevos (mm)	Autores
Caudiverbera caudiverbera	Aguas lenti	Globular	1000–10000	2 7–3 1	(Jorquera e Izquierdo, 1964, Cabrera 1977)
Batrachyla leptopus	Orilla del agua-en tierra	Racimo	93	3 0–8 3	(Formas, 1976)
Batrachyla taeniata	En tierra	Racimo	167–399	1 6–1 8	(Capurro, 1958 Formas, 1976)
Batrachyla antartandica	Musgo humedo-orilla agua	Racimo	28–56	3.0–4 0	(Formas y Pugin, 1971)
Hylorina sylvatica	Orilla del agua	Globular	480	2 0	(Barrio 1967b)
Pleurodema thaul	Vegetacion acuatica	Globular		1 4	(Cei, 1962a Izquierdo y Pereda, 1964)
Bufo chilensis	Orilla del agua	Acintada		2 0–2 5	(Cei 1962a)
Bufo variegatus	Orilla del agua	Acintada	350 450	2 1–2 5	(Formas y Pugin, 1978)
Rhinoderma darwinii	Vegetacion humeda	Racimo	30–40	1 0	(Wilhelm, 1927, 1932, Jorquera et al, 1972)
Rhinoderma rufum	Vegetacion	Racimo	12–24	2 5	(Formas et al 1975)

embrionario y todo el desarrollo larvario (Wilhelm, 1927, 1932) *Rhinoderma rufum* tambien deposita los huevos en terreno vegetal húmedo, el macho introduce los jóvenes embriones en la bolsa bucal dentro de la cual se hace el resto del período embrionario y las primeras etapas larvarias Posteriormente el macho expulsa al agua a los jóvenes renacuajos, los cuales se metamorfosean en este medio (Formas et al, 1975)

HISTORIA DE LA HERPETOFAUNA

La historia de la herpetofauna de los bosques australes de Sudamérica puede ser inferida a partir de algunos fósiles presentes en

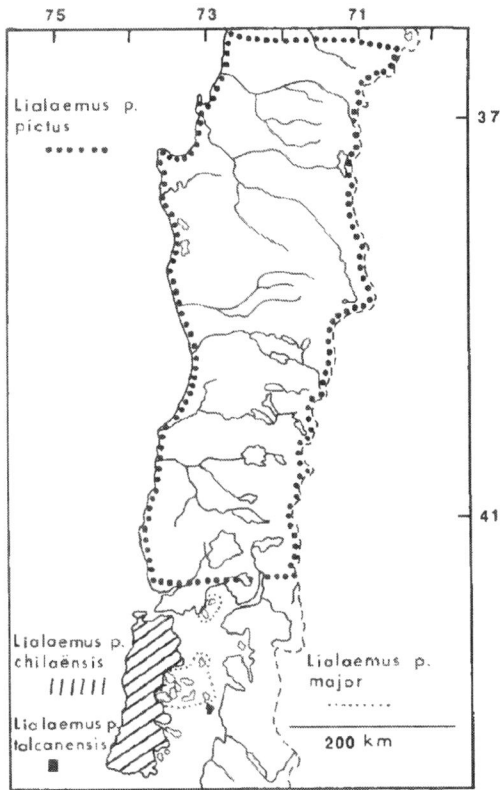

Fig. 14.14. *Patrones de distribución de* Liolaemus pictus pictus, L. p. chiloensis, L. p. major *y* L. p. talcanensis *en el sur de Chile.*

Distribution patterns of *Liolaemus pictus pictus, L. p. chiloensis, L. p. major* and *L. p. talcanensis* in southern Chile.

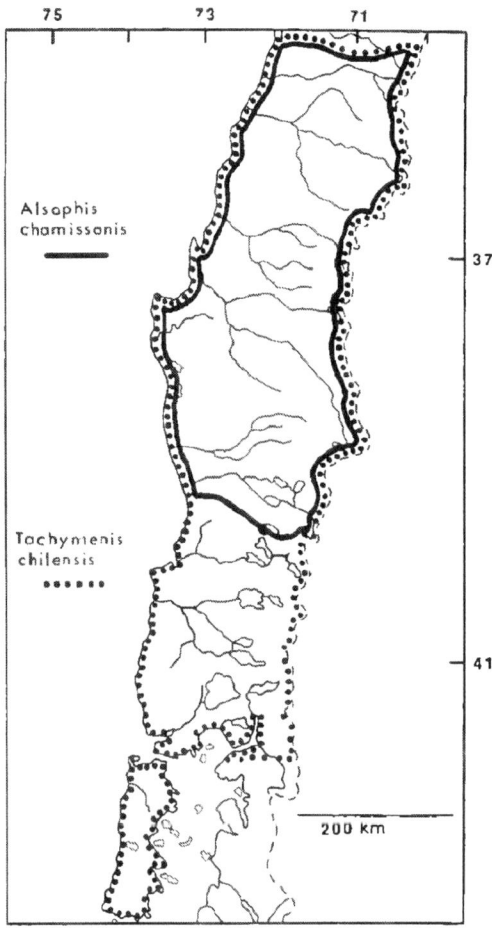

Fig. 14:15. *Rango de distribución de* Alsophis chamissonis *y* Tachymenis chilensis *en el sur de Chile.*

Range of distribution of *Alsophis chamissonis* and *Tachymenis chilensis* in southern Chile.

la Patagonia, de las relaciones de los diferentes taxa y de los patrones actuales de distribución.

Caudiverbera (Schaeffer, 1949) y algunas formas relacionadas, tales como *Gigantobatrachus* (Casamiquela, 1963) y *Eophractus* (Schaeffer, 1949) han sido reportadas en el Terciario Inferior de la Patagonia. Hecht (1963) indica que *Eophractus* (Eoceno inferior) y *Gigantobatrachus* (Mioceno superior) son parte de una simple línea filética del género *Caudiverbera*; sin embargo Lynch (1971) considera a *Eophractus* y *Gigantobatrachus* como sinónimos de *Caudiverbera*. Para este género el autor anteriormente citado reconoce dos especies: *Caudiverbera casa-* *mayorensis* (Eoceno) y *Caudiverbera caudiverbera* la cual se encuentra hoy en los bosques del sur de Chile y en los estratos del Oligoceno y Mioceno de la Patagonia.

Dentro de las ranas de la familia Leptodactylidae, *Caudiverbera* parece ser un género muy divergente y en base a sus caracteres osteológicos Reig (1960) propuso una nueva subfamilia (Calyptocephalellinae). Cei (1970) analiza desde el punto de vista serológico las relaciones de este género y propone una probable separación de él a par-

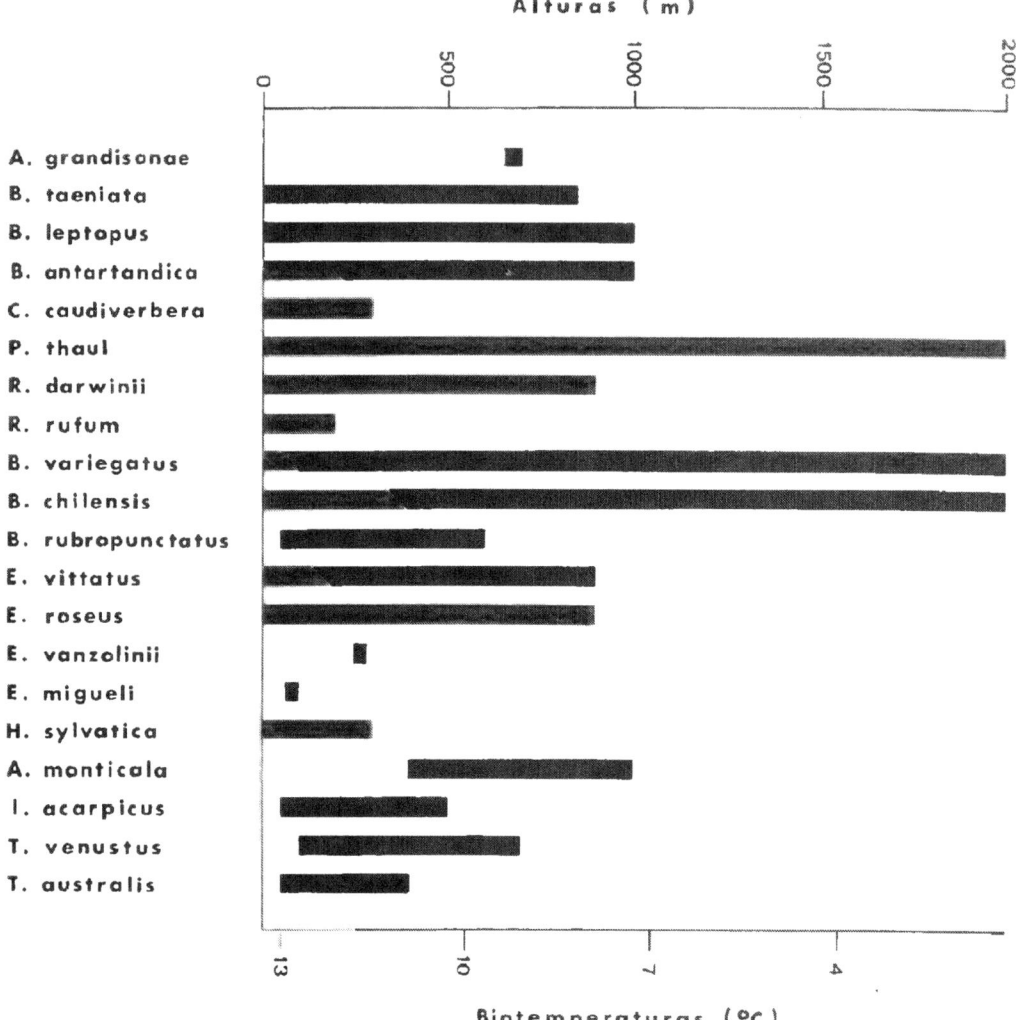

Fig. 14:16. *Distribución altitudinal de los anuros del bosque austral.*
Altitudinal distribution of anurans in the austral forest.

tir de un tronco prototelmatobino o protoleptodactilino. Por otra parte, este autor señala que *Caudiverbera* representa una línea evolutiva aparte y su rango de tribu monotípica parecería aceptable. Lynch (1978) crea la tribu Calyptocephalellini y en ella incluye a *Caudiverbera* y *Telmatobufo*. Heyer (1975) hace un análisis cladístico de los leptodactílidos basándose en caracteres derivados. En tres cladogramas presentados por este autor, *Caudiverbera* aparece más cerca de los escuerzos de la familia Ceratophrynidae que de los anuros de la subfamilia Telmatobiinae (Leptodactylidae). La ubicación de *Telmatobufo* y *Caudiverbera* en una tribu común se basa en gran medida en las afinidades que estos dos géneros presentan. Schmidt (1952) sugiere que *Telmatobufo* estaría muy relacionado con *Telmatobius*, un género con el cual este autor estaba muy familiarizado. Gallardo (1962a) considera que *Telmatobufo* y *Caudiverbera* estarían muy relacionados, pero no

TABLA 14 5—Duración del Periodo de Desarrollo Embrionario y Larvario de las Especies de Anuros Listadas

Especies	Desarrollo embrionario (días)	Temperatura °C	Autor	Periodo larvario (meses)	Temperatura °C	Autor
Caudiverbera caudiverbera	20	18	(Jorquera e Izquierdo, 1964)	24	Ambiente	(Cei, 1962a)
Eupsophus roseus				1	13-20	(Formas y Pugin, 1978)
Eupsophus vittatus		Ambiente		1	15	(Formas, observación personal)
Batrachyla leptopus	11	18-19	(Busse, 1971)	7	15-20	(Formas, 1976)
Batrachyla taeniata	20		(Cei, 1962a)	7	12-18	(Formas, 1976)
Batrachyla antartandica	10	18	(Formas y Pugin, 1971)	7	12-19	(Formas, 1976)
Hylorina sylvatica				12	12-18	(Formas, observación personal)
Pleurodema thaul	8	18	(Izquierdo y Poveda, 1964)	3	Ambiente	(Formas, observación personal)
Bufo chilensis	10.4	18	(Valencia in Cei 1962a)			
Rhinoderma darwini	20	18	(Jorquera et al, 1972)	1.4	Ambiente	(Jorquera et al, 1972)
Rhinoderma rufum	21	18	(Jorquera et al, 1974)	4	Ambiente	(Jorquera et al, 1974)

sustenta su opinión con datos Lynch (1971) comparte la opinión de Gallardo (1962a) e indica que ambos géneros tienen varios caracteres en común (acortamiento de los procesos transversos de las vértebras sacrales, la pupila vertical y la ausencia de tubérculo metatarsal interno) Desde el punto de vista cromosómico, Formas y Espinoza (1975) concluyeron que los cariotipos de *Caudiverbera* y *Telmatobufo* (*australis*) permiten establecer relaciones cariológicas entre ambos taxa Nuevos antecedentes cromosómicos aportados por Veneegas (1975) para *Telmatobufo venustus* confirman la similaridad cromosómica entre *Caudiverbera caudiverbera* y las especies de *Telmatobufo* Cei (1970) demostró desde un punto de vista serológico preliminar que *Telmatobufo* y *Telmatobius* eran indistinguibles genéricamente Lynch (1976, 1978) encontró una importante similitud entre la parte anterior del coxis de *Batrachophrynus* (*brachydactylus macrostomus*) y *Telmatobufo* (*venustus*) Las dos especies tienen la parte anterior de este hueso con forma vertebral La articulación sacrocoxígea es bicondilar y no hay precigoapófisis sobre el coxis, pero se presentan procesos trasversos y un gran foramen para el nervio espinal Según Lynch, estas estructuras son consistentes con una delección de la vértebra a través del sacro Si esto es cierto, entonces se podría postular que los ancestros de *Batrachophrynus* y *Telmatobufo* podrían haber tenido nueve vértebras presacrales, un carácter solamente presente hoy en los primitivos anuros de la familia Leiopelmatidae Este hallazgo nos parece de particular interés ya que podría ser un punto de apoyo para sostener la hipótesis de Savage (1973) quien plantea que las ranas de la familia Leptodactylidae se habrían originado en los bosques temperados de Sudamérica, a partir de un ancestro leiopelmato-leptodactiloideo en el Jurásico temprano La presencia de *Vieraella herbstii* en el Jurásico de Santa Cruz, Argentina y de *Notobatrachus degiustoi* en el Jurásico de la Patagonia Argentina, parecen también reforzar la hipótesis de Savage (1973) ya que ambas formas fósiles han sido relacionadas por Estes y Reig (1973) con las primitivas ranas de la familia Leiopelmatidae

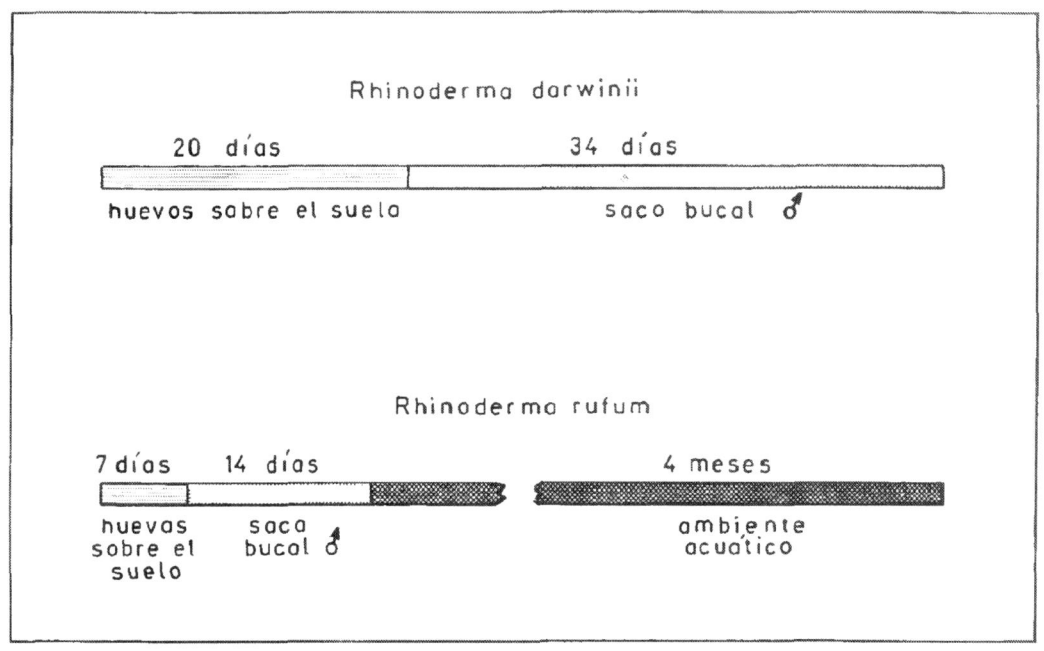

Fig. 14:17. *Modalidades de desarrollo de las dos especies del género* Rhinoderma. Modes of development in the two species of *Rhinoderma*.

La presencia de *Caudiverbera* en el Terciario de la Patagonia sugiere que estas ranas tuvieron una distribución pasada más amplia en el extremo sur del continente. Esta distribución fue probablemente restringida durante el Mioceno, cuando las condiciones que mantenían la existencia del bosque austral (vientos del oeste) desaparecieron en los sectores orientales de la Cordillera de los Andes (Solbrig, 1976). En Chile, la Ingresión Marina del Mioceno y las glaciaciones del Pleistoceno deben haber afectado profundamente la distribución de *Caudiverbera* y *Telmatobufo*. Estos cambios actuaron posiblemente de manera distinta sobre las especies de estos géneros ya que ambos ocupan ambientes acuáticos diferentes. La entrada del mar entre los paralelos 37 y 41 ocupó todos los ambientes lénticos y por lo tanto las poblaciones de *Caudiverbera* allí existentes desaparecieron. Sin embargo, más allá de los límites de la Ingresión Marina deben haber permanecido poblaciones aisladas de *Caudiverbera*, las cuales después de la retirada del mar reocuparon su distribución original. Illies (1970) postuló que durante el Mioceno hubo hacia el oeste gran cantidad de islas semejantes a las que existen hoy en la región de los canales. Estas masas de tierra, posiblemente de carácter montañoso, podrían haber albergado especies adaptadas a ambientes acuáticos de tipo lótico. Por lo tanto, las especies de *Telmatobufo* que muestran profundas adaptaciones a los arroyos de montaña podrían haber sido habitantes de estas islas.

Las glaciaciones del Pleistoceno cubrieron toda el área que está al sur del paralelo 41 (Vuilleumier, 1971) y el Valle Central hasta la latitud de Santiago (Brüggen, 1950). Sin embargo, al sur del paralelo 41, la expansión glaciar parece no haber cubierto totalmente la región como lo indica Vuilleumier (1971). Brüggen (1948) para explicar la expansión de los bosques en los períodos postglaciales de esta región, supone la existencia de refugios de *Nothofagus* sobre los glaciares del Pleistoceno. A partir de estos refugios boscosos, ubicados sobre la capa de hielo, se habría producido un repoblamiento del bosque original cuando el hielo desapareció. Si se supone que los glaciares subieron toda la región al sur del paralelo 41, como ha sido indicado por Vuilleumier es difícil entender entonces la presencia de anuros tales como *Hylorina sylvatica*, *Batrachyla antartandica* (Atalah y Sielfeld, 1976) y *Atelognathus grandisonae* (Lynch, 1975a) en las islas de la región de los canales e islas del sur de Chile. La presencia de anuros en las regiones anteriormente mencionadas, se podría explicar, si se considera que hubo refugios boscosos de *Nothofagus* que quedaron sobre los hielos glaciares. Por otro lado, si las regiones occidentales de la Cordillera de la Costa, al norte del paralelo 41 y hasta la latitud de Santiago, quedaron libres de la acción glaciar (Illies, 1970), es posible que los bosques ubicados en los faldeos occidentales de la Cordillera de la Costa, hayan sido también refugios costeros para las herpetofaunas que existían en esa área. En esta situación, es posible que la acción de los hielos haya desplazado hacia el norte los bosques haciéndolos llegar a una latitud mayor que la que actualmente ocupan. Reiche (1934) y Auer (1960) han dado ejemplos de plantas que indican que el bosque austral tuvo una expansión más norteña (30°S) que la que tienen actualmente. La presencia de *Batrachyla taeniata*, anuro típico del sur de Chile, en los bosques relictos de la provincia de Valparaíso (Quintero) (Capurro, 1958, Cei y Capurro, 1958) hace suponer también que algunas especies siguieron el avance hacia el norte del bosque austral durante los períodos glaciares.

Entre los más probables habitantes de los refugios occidentales de la Cordillera de la Costa, están las especies del género *Telmatobufo* las cuales muestran fuertes adaptaciones a los arroyos de montaña, sin embargo, *Caudiverbera* no pudo alcanzar estos refugios costeros debido a que es un género adaptado a ambientes lénticos y es muy posible que haya tenido que emigrar hacia el norte. Posteriormente al desaparecimiento de los glaciares, *Caudiverbera* reinvadió el Valle Central pero no logró penetrar en la Isla de Chiloé ya que la existencia del Canal de Chacao fue una barrera real para impedir la dispersión hacia el sur de esta especie.

La tribu Calyptocephalellini es endémica de los bosques australes de Sudamérica y sus géneros (*Caudiverbera* y *Telmatobufo*) presentan una diversidad específica muy baja. Hasta ahora se han descrito solamente dos especies de *Telmatobufo* (*venustus* y *australis*) y dos de *Caudiverbera*, una viviente (*C. caudiverbera*) que también se ha encontrado en el Terciario (Oligoceno y Mioceno) y *Caudiverbera casamayorensis* que aparece solamente en los estratos del Eoceno de la Patagonia.

Fuera de su antigüedad, *Caudiverbera* presenta 26 cromosomas, número que ha sido considerado primitivo para la familia Leptodactylidae (Reig, 1972). Por otro lado, Bogart (1973) y Morescalchi (1973) han propuesto también que un cariotipo con 26 cromosomas es primitivo para las familias no aicaicas de anuros. Las especies de *Telmatobufo* también son cariológicamente primitivas ($2n = 26$) y presentan en el coxis una dilatación en la parte anterior (*T. venustus*). La presencia de *Caudiverbera* y *Telmatobufo* en bosques que tienen una historia terciaria, la baja diversidad específica de los géneros (2 especies), la antigüedad de *Caudiverbera* (Terciario Inferior) y la presencia de caracteres primitivos (26 cromosomas y dilatación del coxis en *T. venustus*) en las especies de ambos géneros, nos hace suponer que *Telmatobufo* y *Caudiverbera* son miembros de una antigua radiación de leptodactílidos que alcanzó poca diversificación en el extremo sur de Sudamérica.

Schaeffer (1949) describió un *Eupsophus* sp en el Oligoceno de Chubut (sur de Argentina). En esta especie los nasales están en aparente contacto medio, condición que no se encuentra en las especies vivientes del género. Bogart (1970) señala que el fósil no es separable de *Eupsophus roseus*, forma viviente en el bosque templado. *Eupsophus* ha sido tradicionalmente un género muy confuso y mal definido, lo que ha traído como consecuencia falsas interpretaciones biogeográficas. Después de las revisiones de Cei (1960, 1962b), Grandison (1961) y Lynch (1972, 1975) se puede apreciar una cierta consistencia taxonómica para el género. *Eupsophus* está exclusivamente distribuido en el bosque temperado de Sudamérica Lynch (1978) ubica a *Eupsophus, Alsodes, Atelognathus, Batrachophrynus, Hylorina, Insuetophrynus Limnomedusa, Somuncuria* y *Telmatobius* en la tribu Telmatobiini de la subfamilia Telmatobiinae (Leptodactylidae) En el bosque austral solamente se encuentran los géneros *Alsodes Atelognathus, Eupsophus Hylorina* e *Insuetophrynus* La presencia de *Eupsophus* en el Oligoceno de la Patagonia nos hace suponer que el género tuvo en el Terciario una distribución más amplia que la actual y que su extinción allí fue debida a las mismas causas que restringieron los rangos distribucionales de *Caudiverbera* Lynch (1971) indica que *Eupsophus* está relacionado con *Hylorina* ya que ambos géneros comparten la misma forma de los cóndilos occipitales (Tipo II de Lynch)

Barrio (1970) basándose en caracteres morfológicos externos, especialmente las espinas nupciales, indica que *Alsodes* e *Insuetophrynus* están estrechamente relacionados Desde el punto de vista cromosómico, *Atelognathus, Hylorina, Alsodes* e *Insuetophrynus* (Bogart, 1970, Barrio y Rinaldi de Chieri, 1971, Barrio 1973), comparten una fórmula cromosómica primitiva de $2n = 26$ *Eupsophus, Hylorina* e *Insuetophrynus* están exclusivamente restringidos en su rango de distribución a los bosques del sur de Chile, sin embargo *Alsodes* sobrepasa por el norte el límite de este biotopo boscoso Es así que *A verrucosus, A gargola* y *A pehuenche* se encuentran en la Cordillera de los Andes mientras que *A nodosus* habita los bosques esclerófilos de Chile Central (Cei, 1962a,b) *Alsodes monticola* es la única especie restringida al bosque austral La presencia de especies sureñas con 26 cromosomas (*A monticola* y *A gargola*) (Barrio y Rinaldi de Chieri, 1971) hace suponer que a partir de ellas se hayan originado especies más derivadas con 22 cromosomas tal como se presenta en *Alsodes nodosus* (Brum Zorrilla y Saez, 1968, Kuramoto, 1972) El género *Atelognathus* posee una sola especie en el bosque temperado austral (*A grandisonae*) y cinco especies (*A nitoi, A patagonicus A praebasalticus* y *A solitarius*) en el centro-sur de Argentina Lynch (1978) indica que este género iradio desde el sur de Chile a la Patagonia Argentina

Si las especies de *Eupsophus* realizan sus posturas en las cercanías de los ambientes lóticos (Formas y Pugin 1978) y las larvas de *Alsodes monticola* muestran ciertas tendencias adaptativas a vivir en los arroyos de montaña (Formas, 1975) es posible que las especies de estos géneros hayan podido soportar las glaciaciones pleistocénicas en los refugios costeros de la Cordillera de la Costa anteriormente referidos

Batrachyla (Batrachylini) es un género exclusivo del bosque temperado, sin embargo *Batrachyla taeniata* es posible también encontrarla en bosques relictos de la zona central de Chile Las especies de *Batrachyla* presentan 26 cromosomas (Bogart, 1970, Barrio y Rinaldi de Chieri 1971) y dos especies (*B taeniata* y *B antartandica*) poseen un par acrocéntrico Fuera de los caracteres cariológicamente considerados primitivos (26 cromosomas) es posible encontrar en *Batrachyla leptopus* amplexus inguinal (Barrio 1967a, Formas, 1976) caracter etológico considerado primitivo para los anfibios anuros (Tihen, 1965) Durante las glaciaciones pleistocénicas, las especies de *Batrachyla* tuvieron dos alternativas emigrar hacia el norte junto con el bosque o refugiarse en los sectores libres de hielo en la Cordillera de la Costa, al norte del paralelo 41, o sobre los refugios boscosos de *Nothofagus* sobre los glaciares al sur del paralelo 41 La presencia de *Batrachyla taeniata* en los bosques relictos de la provincia de Valparaíso y los esclerófilos costeros de la Provincia de Aconcagua permiten confirmar la primera alternativa planteada y el encuentro de *Batrachyla antartandica* en la Isla Virtudes (51°31'S, 74°55'W) (Atalah y Sielfeld, 1976) confirmaría la segunda posibilidad

Los géneros de las tribus Telmatobiini (*Alsodes Eupsophus, Hylorina* e *Insuetophrynus*) y Batrachylini (*Batrachyla*) pertenecerían a una radiación que alcanzó su máxima diversificación en *Telmatobius* (30 especies) (Lynch 1978) y su mínima en *Insuetophrynus, Hylorina* y *Somuncuria* (una especie) Esta radiación parece ser antigua como lo plantea la presencia de *Eupsophus* en el Oligoceno de la Patagonia Además algunos de sus miembros poseen caracteres cromosomicos (2n = 26) y etológicos primitivos (amplexus inguinal en *Batrachyla leptopus*)

Pleurodema es el único género de la subfamilia Leptodactylinae presente en el bosque de *Nothofagus* del sur de Chile. La única especie existente aquí es *Pleurodema thaul*, sin embargo Lynch (1971) señala que esta especie podría tener un rango de superespecie. Duellman y Veloso (1977) indican que al menos dentro de los que se llama *Pleurodema thaul* existen tres especies las cuales se pueden diferenciar por su amplexus y cariotipo. El género *Pleurodema* tiene amplia distribución en Sudamérica, especialmente en los ambientes temperados y semi-áridos. Heyer (1975) considerando la presencia o ausencia de glándulas lumbares insinúa un probable origen difilético para el genero. Lynch (1971) basándose en la anatomía y configuración del renacuajo supone que *Pleurodema* es un miembro muy primitivo de la subfamilia Leptodactylinae y que el género presentaría relaciones con *Eupsophus*. Ambos se diferencian claramente en la morfología esternal y en la biología reproductiva. En la distribución cladística de Heyer (1975) basada en caracteres derivados, *Pleurodema* es agrupado con *Batrachyla*, *Batrachophrynus* y *Eupsophus*. Duellman y Veloso (1977) aportan datos que soportan la suposición de que *Pleurodema* podría ser considerado un leptodactilino primitivo, el cual estaría relacionado con *Eupsophus*. La existencia de *Eupsophus* fósiles en el Oligoceno de la Patagonia es muy sugestiva ya que si existió este género es posible que también haya estado *Pleurodema*. Si esto es cierto se puede suponer entonces que el género se haya originado en los bosques australes al menos en el Oligoceno y que secundariamente haya emigrado hacia el norte del continente (Duellman y Veloso, 1977).

Rhinoderma es un género de problemáticas relaciones filogenéticas dentro de la superfamilia Bufonoidea y del cual no existen evidencias fósiles. Este género, del cual solamente se han descrito dos especies (*Rhinoderma darwinii* y *R. rufum*) esta distribuido en los bosques temperados de *Nothofagus* del sur de Chile y en las regiones costeras de Chile Central (*R. rufum*) (Formas et al., 1975).

El género *Bufo* esta representado en el bosque austral por tres especies: *B. chilensis*, *B. rubropunctatus* y *B. variegatus*, siendo esta ultima un anuro de difícil ubicación taxonómica, ya que sus relaciones son oscuras y controvertidas. Cei y Espina (1957) lo consideran vinculado al grupo de *Bufo spinulosus*, sin embargo Capurro y Silva (1959) al hacer el estudio cromatográfico de la secreción de las parótidas hayan claras diferencias entre *Bufo spinulosus* (= *chilensis*) y *Bufo variegatus*. Gallardo (1962b) indica que *Bufo variegatus* no tiene ninguna relación con los *Bufo* sudamericanos del grupo *spinulosus* y que sus afinidades estarían con el grupo *calamita* de la región Holoártica. Martin (1972) coloca a *Bufo variegatus* en un grupo propio (grupo *variegatus*), sin embargo dice que es similar a los miembros del grupo *spinulosus* con los cuales probablemente estaría estrechamente relacionado. Cei (1977) demuestra, desde el punto de vista inmunológico, que *Bufo variegatus* presenta mayores relaciones con el grupo *calamita* que con las especies sudamericanas del grupo *spinulosus*. Además de las tres especies de *Bufo* anteriormente referidas, se ha citado en el área (Provincia de Llanquihue) la presencia de *Bufo spinulosus* (Silva et al., 1968), sin embargo estos datos necesitan ser confirmados.

Referente a la historia de los anfibios en los bosques australes de Sudamérica se han adelantado algunas hipótesis. Darlington (1965) indica que los anfibios de los bosques del sur de Chile son miembros de una fauna depauperada cuyos géneros poco diferenciados pertenecen a familias ampliamente distribuídas en Sudamérica.

Vellard (1957) refiere que los anuros de los bosques temperados del sur de Chile son relictos de faunas del Terciario, las cuales han podido vivir en el extremo sur de Sudamérica separadas del continente por fuertes barreras ecológicas. Vellard (1957) y Cei (1962a) llamaron la atención sobre la pobreza de taxa existente en el bosque temperado de Sudamérica, ya que muchas familias y géneros típicamente neotropicales están ausentes del bosque austral Vuilleumier (1968) señala que no se debe olvidar que los anuros del bosque del sur de Chile pertenecen a una zona temperada, las cuales contrastan en general con las áreas tropicales que son muy ricas en especies

Vuilleumier (1968) considera a la fauna de anuros del bosque temperado del sur de Chile como compuesta de cuatro elementos faunísticos 1) grupos de leptodactílidos autóctonos que no se han diversificado (Caudiverbera, Telmatobufo, Rhinoderma), 2) leptodactílidos autóctonos que secundariamente emigraron al norte de Sudamérica (Eupsophus), 3) leptodactílidos endémicos del bosque temperado, pero que han derivado de leptodactílidos tropicales (Batrachyla, Hylorina), 4) bufónidos y leptodactílidos que están ampliamente distribuidos en Sudamérica y que tienen más especies fuera del bosque austral que dentro de el (Pleurodema, Bufo)

De acuerdo a la discusión sobre el origen y las relaciones de los anuros del bosque austral, se proponen aquí tres grupos faunísticos para explicar la historia de los anfibios de este bosque

El primer elemento faunístico está compuesto de leptodactílidos (Caudiverbera, Telmatobufo, Hylorina, Batrachyla, Eupsophus, Insuetophrynus y Alsodes) y rhinodermátidos (Rhinoderma) originados en el extremo sur de Sudamérica Todos los géneros aquí indicados son endémicos del bosque austral, en algunos casos tienen una antigüedad que se remonta al Terciario Inferior y otros poseen características muy primitivas Es posible que los integrantes de este grupo faunístico se haya refugiado en los sectores occidentales de la Cordillera de la Costa durante las glaciaciones del Pleistoceno La inclusión de Rhinoderma género de enigmáticas relaciones filogenéticas se debe principalmente a la estrictez de su distribución dentro del bosque y sus adaptaciones reproductivas a este biotopo (cuidado de las crías en la bolsa del macho) La mayoría de los géneros de este grupo tiene muy pocas especies y Eupsophus y Alsodes parecen ser los más diversificados Esta primera agrupación faunística contiene la mayor cantidad de géneros del bosque austral, es endémico del área y rara vez sus especies sobrepasan sus límites

En el segundo grupo faunístico se incluye al género Pleurodema el cual tiene amplia distribución en Sudamérica, especialmente en los ambientes semiáridos Pleurodema es considerado un grupo originado en el extremo sur del continente y que posteriormente emigró al resto de Sudamérica en el cual adquirió gran diversificación (14 especies) (Duellman y Veloso, 1977) También en esta agrupación se incluye a Atelognathus el cual según Lynch (1978) irradio del sur de Chile hacia la Patagonia

El tercer grupo faunístico es poco definido pues está constituído por las especies del género Bufo cuyo origen en el bosque austral parece ser secundario Si Bufo variegatus está realmente relacionado con los sapos del grupo calamita, de la región Holoártica, es posible que su presencia en el bosque austral sea secundaria Según Cei (1971) Bufo chilensis y B rubropunctatus aparecen como un conjunto de antiguo abolengo filético, seguramente anterior al levantamiento andino Schaeffer (1949) describió Neoprocoela edentata en depósitos del Oligoceno inferior de Chubut (Argentina) Esta es una forma de problemática ubicación familiar ya que se ha considerado dentro de la familia Leptodactylidae (Schaeffer, 1949 Lynch, 1971) y Bufonidae (Tihen, 1962) Si Neoprocoela es un miembro del género Bufo como lo indica Tihen (1962) la presencia de los anuros de este género en el bosque austral parecería ser muy antigua

La batracofauna austral presenta once géneros de los cuales siete son endémicos de la región, otros (Pleurodema y Atelognathus) se han originado aquí, pero se diversificaron en Sudamérica y Bufo tiene un origen posiblemente secundario Por lo tanto se puede decir que la batracofauna de los bosques australes de Sudamérica es mayoritariamente endémica del área

Entre los reptiles existentes en los biotopos australes se encuentran saurios del género Liolaemus, el cual según Peters y Donoso-Barros (1970) incluye más de 54 especies Liolaemus se distribuye en el cono sur del continente sudamericano, ocupando regiones tales como Argentina, Bolivia, Brasil, Chile, Paraguay, Perú y Uruguay Las especies de este taxón tienen una gran versatilidad ecológica y se les encuentra a la orilla de la costa en los desiertos, en los bosques tropicales, estepas sabanas, grandes alturas de la Cordillera de los Andes y en las selvas australes. Donoso-Barros (1966) plantea que el género *Liolaemus* tiene su origen posiblemente en la región de Bolivia. Hellmich (1952) basado en la diversificación de las especies de *Liolaemus* tanto al este como al oeste del macizo andino, postula que la Cordillera de los Andes ha sido un elemento diferenciador de especies, a partir de un tronco preexistente antes del levantamiento de los Andes. Si *Liolaemus* se originó de un tronco preandino, cerca de la región de Bolivia, es posible que la presencia de las especies del género existente en el sur de Chile haya sido un fenómeno de emigración secundario. Parece ser que la invasión de *Liolaemus* en el bosque austral ha sido por la Cordillera de los Andes y por el Valle Central. A pesar de que la Patagonia es rica en reptiles, no existen especies compartidas entre los dos biotopos, sin embargo se observa una leve invasión de especies patagónicas, en el sur del bosque austral tales como *Liolaemus fitzingeri* y *L. bibronii* (Donoso-Barros, 1960), el saurio *Phymaturus patagonicus* (Cei y Castro, 1973) y el anuro *Pleurodema bufonina* (Cei, 1962a). La ingresión de especies patagónicas, en los límites del bosque templado, ha sido también referida por Cekalovic (1974). Las especies de *Liolaemus* que parecen haber ingresado por el Valle Central serían *Liolaemus tenuis*, *Liolaemus cyanogaster*, *Liolaemus pictus* y *Liolaemus chilensis*. *L. chilensis* ha sido incluida por Hellmich (1952) en su Grupo III, en el cual también está *L. gravenhorstii*. Todo este grupo de especies ocupan el Valle Central, especialmente la estepa de *Acacia caven*. La especie más sureña de este grupo (*Liolaemus chilensis*) es la que penetra en el límite norte del bosque austral. *Liolaemus pictus*, *L. cyanogaster* y *L. tenuis* han sido incluidas por Hellmich (1952) en su Grupo IV. De estas tres especies, *Liolaemus cyanogaster* y *L. pictus* están estrictamente restringidas al bosque de *Nothofagus*, pero *Liolaemus tenuis* alcanza por el norte hasta el paralelo 32. Finalmente *Liolaemus monticola* muestra una penetración en las partes altas del bosque, en la Cordillera de los Andes. Esta especie junto con *L. lorenzmulleri*, *L. schroderi*, *L. nigroviridis*, *L. leopardinus*, *L. altissimus* y *L. buergeri* representan un grupo alto andino (Hellmich, 1950) y la especie que ocupa los límites más bajos de los Andes es *L. monticola* la cual se desmembra hacia el sur en varias subespecies (*monticola chillanensis* y *monticola villaricensis*). De estas formas, solamente *Liolaemus monticola villaricensis* penetra al bosque austral.

Pristidactylus es otro género de iguánidos representado en el bosque por una sola especie, *Pristidactylus torquatus*. Existen dos especies más en Chile (*Pristidactylus alvaroi* y *P. valeriae*) (Donoso-Barros 1974) las cuales están en los bosques relictos del Cerro El Roble (Provincia de Valparaíso). En Argentina existen cuatro especies más *P. scapulatus*, *P. achalensis*, *P. casuhatiensis* y *P. fasciatus*. Las especies argentinas de *Pristidactylus* muestran una distribución discontínua (Cei, 1973). Este patrón sugiere que las especies del género se diferenciaron de un tronco primitivo posiblemente antes del levantamiento de los Andes.

Dos especies de serpientes llegan al bosque austral *Tachymenis chilensis* y *Alsophis chamissonis*. Esta última especie es ovípara y no penetra muy al sur llegando hasta Valdivia (Donoso-Barros, 1966). Maglio (1970) ha revisado las culebras del género *Alsophis*, el cual se distribuye especialmente en las islas del Caribe, noroeste de Sudamérica y extremo sur de América Central. Un pequeño grupo de especies *A. angustilineatus* del Perú y *A. chamissonis* se extienden hacia el sur por el oeste de Sudamérica. Maglio (1970) incluye a estas tres especies en el grupo *cantherigenus* e indica que *Alsophis chamissonis* muestra mucha similitud con *Alsophis cantherigenus* de Cuba. Según este autor es posible que las especies de las Indias Occidentales hayan derivado de un tronco ubicado en el oeste de Sudamérica en el cual se encuentran hoy *A. chamissonis*, *A. tachymenoides* y *A. angustilineatus*. Estas tres especies representarían un centro de especiación sobre las Galápagos y *Alsophis chamissonis* según Maglio, parece ser un relicto del tronco primitivo. La entrada de esta especie en el bosque austral sería por lo tanto secundaria pues su centro originario debe haber estado colocado al sur del Perú o norte de Chile.

El género *Tachymenis* posee seis especies (*T. affinis, T. peruviana, T. tarmensis, T. attenuata* y *T. surinamensis*) (Peters y Orejas-Miranda, 1970) las cuales están en Perú, Bolivia, Chile y Surinam. Al no existir registros fósiles ni estar claras las relaciones de estas especies es difícil tratar de establecer el origen de *Tachymenis chilensis* en el bosque de *Nothofagus*.

Muller (1973) establece que el sur de Chile es un centro de dispersión faunística en Sudamérica. Esta área, la cual el autor llama "The *Nothofagus* Center," está establecida en base a los anfibios y las aves endémicas. En relación con los anuros, el centro es definido por la distribución de *Telmatobufo, Batrachyla, Hylorina, Caudiverbera* y *Rhinoderma*. Aquí se estima que la base del "Centro de dispersión de *Nothofagus*" estaría constituído por los anuros endémicos del sur de Chile pertenecientes a los géneros *Caudiverbera, Hylorina, Telmatobufo, Batrachyla, Eupsophus, Insuetophrynus, Alsodes* y *Rhinoderma*. Esta modificación no altera el concepto de Muller, por el contrario, lo enriquece al agregar nuevos ejemplos que fortalecería su validez.

AGRADECIMIENTOS

Mi sincero reconocimiento a la ayuda prestada por Sonia Lacrampe, quien realizó todos los gráficos que ilustran este trabajo.

SUMMARY

The South American temperate forests are characterized by a low number of amphibians and reptiles—a total of 28 species. Among anurans, there are seven endemic genera (*Caudiverbera, Telmatobufo, Hylorina, Eupsophus, Batrachyla, Insuetophrynus,* and *Rhinoderma*), plus four that extend beyond the limits of the austral forests (*Alsodes, Atelognathus, Pleurodema,* and *Bufo*). Among reptiles represented by the genera *Liolaemus, Pristidactylus, Alsophis* and *Tachymenis* there are no endemics at the generic level. In general, the anurans have a low diversity, *Caudiverbera, Hylorina,* and *Insuetophrynus* are monotypic.

This small herpetofauna is mainly restricted to southern Chile between 37 and 55°S but also occurs in parts of adjacent Argentina. In southern Chile, three physiographic regions are evident—1) the Andean cordilleras, 2) the coastal cordillera, and 3) the central valley. Ecologically, the austral forests are isolated from the rest of the continent by arid and semiarid regions. North of 37°S in the central valley of Chile is a dry steppe characterized by *Acacia caven*. Eastward the austral forests are bordered by the cold Patagonian steppe.

The austral forest is floristically rich and contains several monotypic and endemic groups, such as *Eucryphia, Aextoxicum,* and *Fitzroya*. The Valdivian forest represents the maximum development of the austral forest. This is a dense, dark, evergreen forest composed of many bushes (*Lomatia, Fuchsia, Chusquea*), lianas (*Hydrangea, Cissus*), epiphytes (*Luzuriaga, Sarmentia*), ferns (*Lophosoria*) mosses and lichens (*Usnea*). Among the trees *Nothofagus Laurelia,* and *Podocarpus* are conspicuous. At elevations of more than 1000 m in the cordilleras there are conifers such as *Araucaria* and *Fitzroya*.

The climate of this region is temperate with Mediterranean and oceanic influences. The predominate winds come from the west, and they are responsible for the continuous rainy conditions of the austral forests.

During the Miocene the southern part of Chile suffered a marine introgression that isolated the western islands, which became refuges for the existing fauna of the area. The Pleistocene had three or four glacial periods. Glaciers covered nearly all of Chile south of 41°S, however, in that region some forested areas have been postulated as *Nothofagus* refuges. North of that latitude the central valley was strongly affected by glacial climates, however, all of the western slopes of the coastal cordillera remained ice-free. It is thought that these slopes were refuges for much of the herpetofauna that dwells today in southern Chile.

The highest concentration of the herpetofauna occurs in the northern part of the austral forest (37°S), whereas there is a gradual decrease in numbers towards the south. Only *Bufo* reaches 53°S. It is possible that the declining temperature gradient is the responsible factor for this distribution pattern. Altitudinally, most of the amphibians reach 1000 m, *Bufo* and *Pleurodema* exceed 2000 m.

Despite the denseness of the austral forests, no amphibians there have arboreal adaptations. The majority of anurans are restricted to the forest floor or to lotic or lentic aquatic environments. Occasionally *Hylorina sylvatica* and *Batrachyla leptopus* have been observed on branches and trunks of trees. Many lizards have arboreal tendencies.

Several anurans have adaptations in the embryonic and larval stages for the forest floor. One of the most notable occurs in *Rhinoderma*, in which the larvae develop in the vocal sac of the males. Other reproductive adaptations are related to egg-deposition sites. *Batrachyla taeniata* and *Rhinoderma* lay eggs in wet soil whereas *Eupsophus* lay eggs in water holes. Larvae of *Telmatobufo australis* are adapted to swift streams, whereas those of *Caudiverbera caudiverbera* are nectonic.

The most outstanding reproductive adaptation in the reptiles is vivipanty which is present in some *Liolaemus* (*cyanogaster* and *pictus*) and in the snake *Tachymenis chilensis*.

The history of the herpetofauna can be traced back to the Early Tertiary. *Caudiverbera* and *Eupsophus* have been found in strata in Patagonia where fossil plants associated with austral forests also were found, thereby indicating that the austral forests and at least some of its inhabitants were much more widespread than they are today.

Analyses of patterns of distribution of the different taxa, their phylogenetic relationships, and their age (inferred from the fossil data) provide the basis for the recognition of three herpetofaunal groups. The first, characterized by endemics primitive characters, and antiquity, includes *Caudiverbera*, *Telmatobufo*, *Hylorina*, *Batrachyla*, *Insuetophrynus*, *Alsodes*, *Rhinoderma*, and *Eupsophus*. This group of frogs probably originated in southern South America and dispersed northward in the austral forests.

The second faunal element contains *Pleurodema* and *Atelognathus*, which apparently originated in the austral forest and secondarily dispersed widely in South America. The third element contains the toads of the genus *Bufo*, which probably secondarily entered the austral forests. The reptiles had a different history; all of the groups seem to be secondary in the austral forests.

BIBLIOGRAFIA

ARENAS, J. N. 1972. Morfometria del Lago Riñihue (Prov. de Valdivia Chile). Mus. Nac. Hist. Nat. (Santiago de Chile) Publ. Ocas. 14: 3–15.

ATALAH, A., SIFFEDI, W. 1976. Presencia de *Batrachyla antartandica* Barrio en Magallanes. An. Inst. Pat. 7: 169–170.

AUBOUIN, J., BORELLO, A. V., CECIONI, G., CHARRIER, R. CHOTIN, P., FRUTOS, J., THIELE R. Y VICENTE, J. C. 1973. Esquisse paleogeographique et structurale des Andes Meridionales. Rev. Geog. Phys. Geol. Dynam. 15: 11–72.

AUER, V. 1960. The Quaternary history of Fuego-Patagonia. Proc. Roy. Soc. London 152: 507–516.

AXELROD, D. I., BAILEY, H. P. 1969. Paleotemperature analysis of Tertiary floras. Paleogeog. Paleoclimatol. Paleoecol. 6: 163–195.

BARRIO, A. 1967a. *Batrachyla antartandica* n. sp. (Anura Leptodactylidae). Descripcion y estudio comparativo con la especie genotipica, *B. leptopus* Bell. Physis 27: 101–109.

BARRIO, A. 1967b. Observaciones etoecologicas sobre *Hylorina sylvatica* Bell (Anura Leptodactylidae). Ibid 27: 153–157.

BARRIO, A. 1970. *Insuetophrynus acarpicus*, un nuevo leptodactilido finisternio sudamericano (Amphibia, Anura). Ibid 30: 331–341.

BARRIO, A. 1973. Una nueva especie de *Telmatobius* (Anura, Leptodactylidae) procedente del dominio austral cordillerano argentino. Physis 32: 207–213.

BARRIO, A., RINALDI DE CHIERI, P. 1971. Contribucion al esclarecimiento de la posicion taxofiletica de algunos batracios patagonicos de la familia Leptodactylidae mediante el analisis cariotipico. Ibid 30: 673–685.

BOGART, J. P. 1970. Systematic problems in the amphibian family Leptodactylidae (Anura) as indicated by karyotypic analysis. Cytogenetics 9: 369–383.

BOGART, J. P. 1973. Evolution of anuran karyotypes, pp. 337–339 in VIAL, J. L. (ed.) Evolutionary biology of the anurans. Contemporary research on major problems. Univ. Missouri Press Columbia, 470 p.

BRUGGEN, J 1948 La expansion del bosque en el sur de Chile en la epoca post-glacial Rev Univers 33 105-114

BRUGGEN, J 1950 Fundamentos de la geologia de Chile Inst Geogr Militar, Santiago 374 p

BRUM-ZORRILLA, N, SAEZ F A 1968 Chromosomes of Leptodactylidae (Amphibia, Anura) Experientia 24 969

BUSSE, K 1971 Desarrollo de *Batrachyla leptopus* Bell con observaciones sobre su ecologia y comportamiento (Amphibia, Leptodactylidae) Invest Zool Chil 15 5-63

CABRERA, J 1977 Adaptacion y cultivo de *Caudi verbera caudiverbera* (Linneus) en medios artificiales Gayana 5 111-112

CAPURRO L I 1955 Nota sobre la oviposturа y desarrollo de *Eupsophus taeniatus* (Giraid) Invest Zool Chil 4 208

CAPURRO, L F, SILVA, F C 1959 Valor taxonomico del estudio cromatogiáfico del veneno de las parotidas de *Bufo spinulosus* y *Bufo variegatus* Ibid 5 169-197

CASAMIQUELA, R M 1963 Sobre un par de anuros del Mioceno de Rio Negro (Patagonia) *Wawelia gerholdi* n gen et sp (Ceratophrydidae) y *Gigantobatrachus parodii* (Leptodactylidae) Ameghiniana 3 141-160

CECIONI, G 1970 Esquema de paleogeografia chilena Ed Univers, Santiago, 143 p

CEI J M 1960 A survey of the leptodactylid frogs, genus *Eupsophus* in Chile Breviora 118 1-13

CEI, J M 1962a Batracios de Chile Univ Chile, Santiago, 128 p

CEI J M 1962b El genero *Eupsophus* en Chile Invest Zool Chil 8 7-12

CEI J M 1970 La posicion filética de Telmatobiinae, su discusion reciente y significado critico de algunos inmunotests Act Zool Lilloana 27 181-192

CEI J M 1971 Analisis sero-inmunológico de diferentes niveles de especiacion en *Bufo* del grupo *spinulosus* Ibid 28 91-105

CEI, J M 1973 Comentarios sobre algunos generos de Iguanidos *Diplolaemus*, *Leiosaurus* *Aperopristis* y *Cupriguanus* Physis 32 269-276

CEI, J M 1977 Serological relationships of the patagonian toad *Bufo variegatus* (Gunther) Serolog Mus Bull 52 2

CEI J M CAPURRO L F 1958 Biologia y desarrollo de *Eupsophus taeniatus* (Girard) Invest Zool Chil 4 150-182

CEI J M, CASTRO, I P 1973 Taxonomic and serological researches on the *Phymaturus patagonicus* complex J Herpetol 7 237-247

CEI, J M ESPINA, S 1957 La vibracion sexual preventiva en poblaciones de *Bufo spinulosus* de Chile Invest Zool Chil 4 62-65

CEKALOVIC T 1974 Divisiones biogeograficas de la XII Region chilena (Magallanes) Bol Soc Biol Concepcion 48 297-314

CEROEAU-LARRIVAL T 1968 Contribution palynologique et biogeographique a l'etude biologique de l'Amerique australe pp 111-197 *in* DELAMERE DEBOUTTEVILLE, C RAPOPORT, E (eds) Biologie de l'Amerique australe, 4 C N R S Groupe Francais Argiles C R Reun Etud, Paris, 685 p

COUPER R A 1960 Southern Hemisphere Mesozoic and Tertiary Podocarpaceae and Fagaceae and their paleogeographic significance Proc Roy Soc London 152 491-500

DARLINGTON, P J 1965 Biogeography of the southern end of the world Harvard Press, Cambridge 236 p

DI CASTRI, F 1968 Esquisse Ecologique du Chili, pp 7-82 *in* DELAMERE DEBOUTTEVILLE, C, RAPOPORT E (eds) Biologie de l'Amerique australe 4 C N R S Groupe Francais Argiles C R Reun Etud Paris, 685 p

DONOSO-BARROS, R 1960 Ecologia de los reptiles chilenos Invest Zool Chil 6 65-72

DONOSO-BARROS, R 1966 Reptiles de Chile Univ Chile, Santiago 458 p

DONOSO-BARROS R 1974 Nuevos reptiles y anfibios de Chile Bol Soc Biol Concepcion 48 217-229

DUELLMAN W E VELOSO, A 1977 Phylogeny of *Pleurodema* (Anura Leptodactylidae) A biogeographic Model Univ Kansas Mus Nat Hist Occas Pap (64) 1-46

ENDESA 1972 Caudales medios mensuales retrospectivos Empresa Nacional de Electricidad, Santiago, 211 p

ESTES, R, REIG, O A 1973 The early fossil record of frogs A review of the evidence, pp 11-63 *in* VIAL, J L (ed) Evolutionary Biology of the anurans Contemporary research on major problems Univ Missouri Press, Columbia, 170 p

FORMAS, J R 1972 A second species of Chilean frog genus *Telmatobufo* (Anura Leptodactylidae) Ibid 6 1-13

FORMAS, J R 1975 Las larvas de las especies chilenas pertenecientes al genero *Eupsophus*, grupo *nodosus* (Anura Leptodactylidae) Bol Soc Biol Concepcion 49 231-237

FORMAS, J R 1976 Descriptions of *Batrachyla* (Amphibia, Anura Leptodactylidae) tadpoles J Herpetol 10 221-225

FORMAS J R ESPINOZA N D 1975 Karyological relationships of *Telmatobufo* (Anura, Leptodactylidae) Herpetologica 31 429-432

FORMAS, J R PUGIN, E 1971 Reproducción y desarrollo de *Batrachyla antartandica* Barrio (Anura Leptodactylidae) Mus Nac Hist Nat (Santiago de Chile) Bol 32 201-213

FORMAS, J R, PUGIN E 1978 Tadpoles of *Eupsophus roseus* and *Bufo variegatus* in Southern Chile J Herpetol 12 243-246

FORMAS, J R, PUGIN, L, JORQUERA, B 1975 La identidad del batracio chileno *Hemimectes rufus* Philippi, 1902 Physis 34 147-157

FUENZALIDA, H 1965a Orografia *In* GEOGRAFIA ECONOMICA DE CHILE CORFO, Santiago 7-33

FUENZALIDA, H 1965b Hidrografia *In* GEOGRAFIA ECONOMICA DE CHILE CORFO, Santiago 153-199

FUENZALIDA, H 1965c Clima In GEOGRAFIA ECONOMICA DE CHILE CORFO, Santiago 99–152
FUENZALIDA, H 1965d Biogeografía In GEOGRAFIA ECONOMICA DE CHILE CORFO, Santiago 228–267
GALLARDO, J M 1962a Los generos *Telmatobius* y *Batracophrynus* (Amphibia, Leptodactylidae) en la Argentina Neotropica 8 45–58
GALLARDO, J M 1962b A proposito de *Bufo variegatus* (Cunther), sapo del bosque humedo antartandico, y las otras especies de *Bufo* neotropicales Physis 64 93–102
GRANDISON, A G C 1961 Chilean species of the genus *Eupsophus* (Anura Leptodactylidae) Bull Br Mus (Nat Hist) Zool 8 111–149
HAFFER, J 1970 Geologic-climatic history and zoogeographic significance of the Uraba region northwestern Colombia Caldasia 10 603–636
HAJEK, E, DI CASTRI I 1975 Bioclimatografia de Chile Universidad Católica Santiago 107 p
HARRINGTON, H J 1962 Paleogeographic development of South America Bull Amer Assoc Petrol Geol 46 1773–1814
HECHT, M K 1963 Reevaluation of the early history of the frogs Part II Syst Zool 12 20–35
HELLMICH, W 1934 Die Eidechsen Chiles insbesonders die Gattung *Liolaemus* Abh Bayer Akad Wiss Math Naturwiss Kl 24 1–140
HELLMICH, W 1937 Anotaciones para el conocimiento de las culebras de Chile Rev Chilena Hist Nat 41 107–110
HELLMICH, W 1950 On ecotypic and autotypic characters, a contribution to the knowledge of the evolution of the genus *Liolaemus* (Iguanidae) Evolution 5 359–369
HELLMICH, W 1952 Contribucion al conocimiento de la sistemática y evolucion del genero *Liolaemus* Invest Zool Chil 8 7–15
HEUSSER C J 1966 Late-Pleistocene pollen diagrams from the Province of Llanquihue, Southern Chile Proc Amer Philos Soc 110 269–305
HEYER, W R 1975 A preliminary analysis of the intergeneric relationships of the frog family Leptodactylidae Smithsonian Contrib Zool 199 1–55
ILLIES, H 1970 Geologia de los alrededores de Valdivia Publ Ocas Univ Austral Chile Fac Cien Nat Mat, 50 p
IZQUIERDO, L, PERFOA, J 1964 Influencia de la temperatura ambiental sobre el desarrollo de *Pleurodema bibroni* Arch Biol Med Exper 1 141–151
JEANNEL, R 1967 Biogeographie de l'Amerique australe, pp 401–460 in DELAMERE DEBOUTTEVILLE C, RAPOPORT E (eds) Biologie de l'Amérique australe, 3 C N R S Groupe Francais Argiles C R Reun Etud Paris 834 p
JORQUERA, B, IZQUIERDO, L 1964 Tabla de desarrollo normal de *Calyptocephalella gayi* (Rana chilena) Biologica 36 43–53
JORQUERA, B, PUGIN E, GOICOECHEA, O 1972 Tabla de desarrollo normal de *Rhinoderma darwini* Arch Med Veter 4 1–15

JORQUERA B, PUGIN E, GOICOECHEA O 1974 Tabla de desarrollo normal de *Rhinoderma darwini* (Concepción) Bol Soc Biol Concepcion 48 127–146
KOPPIN W 1948 Climatologia Fondo Cult Econ Mexico, 340 p
KURAMOTO M 1972 Karyotypes of three leptodactylid frogs from Chile, with a discussion on the chromosomes numbers of the family Leptodactylidae Bull Fukuoka Univ Education 21 133–141
LIRA, E 1946 Limite de saciedad y sensacion de replecion en *Calyptocephalus gayi* Biologica 3 31–42
LYNCH, J D 1971 Evolutionary relationships, osteology, and zoogeography of leptodactyloid frogs Univ Kansas Mus Nat Hist Misc Publ (53) 1–238
LYNCH, J D 1972 Generic partitioning of the South American leptodactylid frog genus *Eupsophus* Fitzinger, 1843 (sensu lato) Bull South California Acad Sci 71 2–11
LYNCH, J D 1975a A new chilean frog of the extra-Andean assemblage of *Telmatobius* (Amphibia Leptodactylidae) Ibid 74 160–161
LYNCH, J D 1975b A review of the Andean leptodactylid frog genus *Phrynopus* Univ Kansas Mus Nat Hist Occas Pap (35) 1–51
LYNCH, J D 1976 The systematic significance of variation of the coccyx in some South American leptodactylid frogs Herpetol Rev 7 90 (Abstract)
LYNCH, J D 1978 A re-assessment of the telmatobiine leptodactylid frogs of Patagonia Univ Kansas Mus Nat Hist Occas Pap (72) 1–57
LLIBOUTRY L 1956 Nieves y glaciares de Chile Fd Univ Chile, Santiago, 471 p
MAGLIO V J 1970 West Indian xenodontine colubrid snakes Their probable origin, phylogeny, and zoogeography Bull Mus Comp Zool Harvard Univ 141 1–54
MANN G 1960 Regiones biogeograficas de Chile Invest Zool Chil 6 15–49
MARTIN, R F 1972 Evidence from osteology, pp 37–70 in BLAIR, W F (ed) Evolution in the genus *Bufo* Univ Texas Press, Austin, 459 p
MENENDEZ, C A 1969 Die fossilen floren Sudamerikas, pp 519–561 in FITTKAU, E J, ILLIES, J, KLINGE H, SCHAWE G, SIOLI, H (eds) Biogeography and ecology in South America, 2 W Junk, The Hague, 946 p
MERCER, J H, LAUGENIL, C 1973 Glacier in Chile ended a major readvancement about 36000 years ago some global comparisons Science 182 1017–1019
MORESCALCHI, A 1973 Amphibia, pp 233–238 in CHAIRELLI A B CAPANNA, F (eds) Cytotaxonomy and vertebrate evolution Acad Press London, New York, 783 p
MULLER, P 1973 The dispersal centres of terrestrial vertebrates in the Neotropical Realm A Junk, The Hague 224 p

MUÑOZ CRISTI, J. 1973. Geología de Chile. Ed. Andrés Bello, Santiago, 209 p.

NOBLE, C. K. 1931. The biology of the Amphibia. McGraw-Hill Book Co., New York, 577 p.

OBERDORFER, F. 1960. Pflanzensoziologische Studien in Chile, ein Vergleich mit Europa. Verlag J. Kramer, Weinheim, 208 p.

ORTON, G. L. 1953. The systematics of vertebrae larvae. Syst. Zool. 2: 63-75.

PEFAUR, J. 1971. Nota sobre *Telmatobufo bullocki* Schmidt (Anura, Leptodactylidae). Mus. Nac. Hist. Nat. (Santiago de Chile) Bol. 32: 215-225.

PETERS, J. A., DONOSO-BARROS, R. 1970. Catalogue of the Neotropical Squamata. Part II. Lizards and amphisbaenians. Bull. U. S. Natl. Mus. 297: 1-293.

PETERS, J., OREJAS-MIRANDA, B. 1970. Catalogue of the Neotropical Squamata. Part I. Snakes. Ibid. 1-347.

PISANO, E. 1956. Esquema de clasificación de las comunidades vegetales de Chile. Rev. Agron. Santiago 2: 30-33.

QUINTANILLA, V. 1974. La representación cartográfica preliminar de la vegetación chilena, un ensayo fitoecológico del sur de Chile. Ed. Univ. Valparaíso, 73 p.

REICHE, K. 1934. Geografía botánica de Chile. Imp. Univ. Santiago 1: 1-245.

REICHE, K. 1937. Geografía botánica de Chile. Imp. Univ. Santiago 2: 1-146.

REIG, O. A. 1960. Las relaciones genéricas del anuro chileno *Calyptocephaella gayi* (Dum. & Bibr.). Actas Trab. Cong. Sudamer. Zool. 4: 113-131.

REIG, O. A. 1972. *Macrogenioglotus* and the South American bufonid toads, pp. 14-36 *in* BLAIR, W. F. (ed.) Evolution in the genus *Bufo*. Univ. Texas Press, Austin, 459 p.

RUIZ, C., CORVALAN, J., AGUIRRE, L. 1965. Geología In GEOGRAFIA ECONOMICA DE CHILE. CORFO, Santiago 35-92.

RYBERTT, G., DANIEL, M. V. 1976. Rol de las poblaciones de anfibios en la subtrama trófica del suelo en el bosque San Martín, Valdivia-Chile. Tesis Univ. Austral Chile, 28 p.

SAVAGE, J. M. 1973. The geographic distribution of frogs. Patterns and predictions, pp. 351-455 *in* VIAL, J. L. (ed.) Evolutionary biology of the anurans. Contemporary research on major problems. Univ. Missouri Press, Columbia, 470 p.

SCHAEFFER, B. 1949. Anurans from the early Tertiary of Patagonia. Bull. Amer. Mus. Nat. Hist. 93: 47-68.

SCHMIDT, K. P. 1952. A new leptodactylid frog from Chile. Fieldiana Zool. 31: 11-15.

SCHNEIDER, C. O. 1930. Observaciones sobre batracios chilenos. Rev. Chil. Hist. Nat. 34: 220-223.

SILVA, F., VELOSO, A., SOLERVICENS, J., ORTIZ, J. C. 1968. Investigaciones Zoológicas en el Parque Nacional Vicente Pérez Rosales y Zona de Pargua. Mus. Nac. Hist. Nat. (Santiago de Chile) Bol. 148: 1-12.

SOLBRIG, O. T. 1976. The origin and floristic affinities of the South American temperate desert and semidesert regions, pp. 7-49 *in* GOODALL, D. W. (ed.) Evolution of desert biota. Univ. Texas Press, Austin, 244 p.

TIHEN, J. A. 1962. Osteological observations on New World *Bufo*. Amer. Midl. Nat. 67: 157-183.

TIHEN, J. A. 1965. Evolutionary trends in frogs. Amer. Zool. 5: 309-318.

THOMASSON, K. 1963. Araucanian lakes. Acta Phytogeogr. Suecia 47: 1-139.

URBINA, M., ZUÑIGA, O. 1977. *Liolaemus pictus talcanensis* nob. subsp. (Squamata-Iguanidae). Nuevo reptil para el Archipiélago de Chiloé. An. Mus. Hist. Nat. Valparaíso 10: 69-74.

VELLARD, J. 1957. Repartition des batracien dans les Andes au sud de l'Equateur. Trav. Inst. Français Etud. Andines, Lima, 5: 141-161.

VENEGAS, W. 1975. Los cromosomas de *Aruncus venustus* (Philippi) 1899 (= *Telmatobufo bullocki* Schmidt, 1952) Amphibia, Anura. Bol. Soc. Biol. Concepción 49: 71-77.

WILHELM, O. G. 1927. La *Rhinoderma darwinii* D. & B. Ibid. 1-2: 166-170.

WILHELM, O. G. 1932. Nuevas demostraciones acerca de la neomelia de la *Rhinoderma darwini*. Rev. Chilena Hist. Nat. 36: 166-170.

WOLFE, J. A. 1971. Tertiary climatic fluctuations and methods of analysis of Tertiary floras. Paleogeogr. Paleoclimatol. Paleoecol. 9: 27-57.

VUILLEUMIER, B. S. 1971. Pleistocene changes in the fauna and flora of South America. Science 173: 771-780.

VUILLEUMIER, F. 1968. Origin of frogs of Patagonian forests. Nature 219: 87-89.

15. The Herpetofauna of the Andes: Patterns of Distribution, Origin, Differentiation, and Present Communities

William E. Duellman

*Museum of Natural History and
Department of Systematics and Ecology
The University of Kansas
Lawrence, Kansas 66045
USA*

The Andes—the longest mountain chain in the world—extend nearly 8,000 km along the northern and western edges of South America. This young mountain chain contains many active volcanoes and innumerable dormant ones. More than a dozen peaks reach heights of more than 6,000 m; only the Himalayas and Pamirs in Asia have peaks that are higher. Frequent earthquakes attest to continuing tectonic activity. Spanning 66° of latitude through the tropics and southern temperate zone and reaching to within 1,300 km of the Antarctic Circle, the Andes are a major factor in the formation of climates in western South America. Blocking both easterly and westerly moisture-laden winds, the massive mountain range creates immense rain-shadows west of the Andes between 5° and 35°S and east of the Andes between 28° and 38°S. The eastern face of the Andes in the tropics and the western face north of the Equator and south of 37°S receive abundant rainfall. At high elevations daily temperatures vary as much as 20°C; in many areas freezing temperatures are a nightly occurrence.

Thus, the climates and environments of the Andes are highly diverse. At lower latitudes, the slopes receiving moisture-laden winds are covered with lush tropical forests, which give way at higher elevations to an elfin forest of stunted trees heavily laden with thick growths of mosses. Above tree line a variety of composites, including *frailejones* and cushion plants are dominant life forms in the páramos. In drier areas, vegetation may be nearly absent on the slopes and present only in valleys where bunch grasses form the puna vegetation. In the extreme south the austral forests extend nearly to snow line. Permanent snow and glaciers exist on the higher peaks throughout the Andes, and the Cordillera Real extending for about 300 km in Bolivia and the Cordillera Blanca about 400 km in length in Perú, are nearly continuous snow-covered ranges. The melting snow and glaciers provide water for countless Andean lakes, many of which are trapped in glacial cirques and reach gigantic proportions in Lago Titicaca (177 × 56 km, 3812 m) and myriads of small streams, some of which fed by heavy precipitation on the Andean slopes, grow and merge to form the giant tributaries of the Río Amazonas. For more general information on the Andes and excellent photographs, the reader is referred to the works by Morrison (1974, 1975); a real appreciation for early exploration in the Andes can be gained from Whymper (1892).

The complex topography and variety of environments resulting from tectonic events and climatic fluctuations in the Pleistocene and continuing to the present provide an array of habitats for a diverse Andean fauna that is far richer than one might expect. More than 700 species of amphibians and reptiles are known to inhabit the Andes. The purposes of this paper are to 1) describe the distributional patterns of the Andean herpetofauna, 2) determine the origin of the fauna, 3) hypothesize geological and climatic changes that influenced the differentiation and dispersal of the Andean herpetofauna, and 4) examine the existing herpetofaunal communities in the Andes.

METHODOLOGY

The Andean herpetofauna never has been reviewed or summarized in its entirety. Some faunistic studies contributed much basic data. Thus, Ruthven's (1922) report on the herpetofauna of the Sierra Nevada de Santa Marta, Rivero's (1961) account of the frogs of Venezuela, Cei (1962) study of Chilean amphibians, Rivero's (1963a) summary of the distribution of Venezuelan Andean frogs, Donoso-Barros (1966) account of the reptiles of Chile, Roze's (1966) summary of Venezuelan snakes, and Cochran and Goin's (1970) account of Colombian frogs have been useful sources of information, as have been the more limited papers on the Loja Basin in Ecuador by Parker (1932, 1934, 1938) and on the Titicaca Basin by Parker (1940). The catalogues of Neotropical squamates by Peters and Orejas Miranda (1970) and Peters and Donoso-Barros (1970) were a primary source for taxonomic literature on snakes and lizards, as were the checklists of leptodactylid frogs by Gorham (1966), *Eleutherodactylus* by Lynch (1976b), and hylid and centrolenid frogs by Duellman (1977).

Substantial distributional data are incorporated in numerous systematic studies, as follow: Brame and Wake (1963) on salamanders of the genus *Bolitoglossa*, Cei (1971, 1973, 1974a,b), and Cei and Castro (1973) on iguanid lizards, Cei (1972) on *Bufo*, Duellman (1972) on *Hyla*, Duellman (1974), and Duellman and Fritts (1972) on *Gastrotheca*, Duellman and Veloso (1977) on *Pleurodema*, Edwards (1974) on the frogs of the genus *Colostethus*, Fritts (1974) on lizards of the genus *Stenocercus*, Lynch (1975a–c, 1976b) on frogs of the genera *Eleutherodactylus* and *Phrynopus*, Montanucci (1973) on lizards of the genus *Pholidobolus*, Oftedal (1974) on lizards of the genus *Anadia*, Ruíz and Hernández (1976) on Colombian montane bufonids, Taylor (1968) on caecilians, Trueb (1971, 1974, 1979) on frogs of the genera *Rhamphophryne*, *Hemiphractus*, and *Telmatobius*, Uzzell (1970, 1973) on microteiid lizards, Vellard (1951–1960) on Peruvian frogs, and Veloso and Trueb (1976) on frogs of the genus *Telmatobius*.

Much of the distributional data used here has not been published previously. Some of the data were obtained from museum collections in the United States, Europe, and South America, but much of it is from the extensive Andean collections in the Museum of Natural History at The University of Kansas. Distributional data are provided for many unnamed species that are designated solely by letters.

The 727 species of amphibians and reptiles known to occur in the Andes were tabulated for 1) altitudinal ranges, 2) major habitats occupied, and 3) physiographic regions inhabited (Appendices 15.1–3). Only species occurring above 1,000 m are included. Many species primarily inhabiting lowlands, and only peripherally inhabiting Andean slopes, were excluded.

The 27 physiographic regions are classified and defined in six units, as follow. These units are arbitrary groupings and do not necessarily correspond to geomorphological regions.

A Venezuelan Andes

1. *Serranía de Paria*—Easternmost highlands on the Península de Paria
2. *Serranía de Turumiquire*—Isolated highland mass in northeastern Venezuela
3. *Cordillera de la Costa*—The coastal ranges of northern Venezuela
4. *Mérida Andes*—The eastern spur of the Andes in western Venezuela

B Sierra Nevada de Santa Marta

5. *Sierra Nevada de Santa Marta*—Isolated range in northern Colombia

C Northern Andes

6. *Cordillera Occidental in Colombia*—The Andes west of the Río Cauca Valley
7. *Cordillera Central in Colombia*—The Andean range between the Río Cauca and Río Magdalena valleys
8. *Cordillera Oriental in Colombia*—The Andes east of the Río Magdalena Valley
9. *Nudo de Pasto*—The highland mass in southern Colombia and extreme north-

ern Ecuador from which the Colombian and Ecuadorian cordilleras diverge

10. *Cordillera Occidental in Ecuador* — The western Andean range
11. *Cordillera Oriental in Ecuador* — The eastern Andean range
12. *Inter-Andean Basins in Ecuador* — The high valleys lying between the eastern and western ranges

D Huancabamba Depression

13. *Huancabamba Depression* — The low ranges and basins in northern Perú and southern Ecuador

E Central Andes

14. *Cordillera Central in Perú* — The Andean range in northern Perú between Río Marañón and Río Huallaga valleys
15. *Cordillera Oriental in northern Perú* — The eastern range of the Andes to the east of the Río Huallaga and Río Mantaro valleys
16. *Cordillera Oriental in southern Perú* — The eastern range of the Andes east and north of the Río Apurímac and the Altiplano
17. *Cordillera Occidental in northern Perú* — The western range of the Andes north of Lima
18. *Cordillera Occidental in southern Perú* — The western range of the Andes south of Lima
19. *Marañón Valley* — The upper valley of the Río Marañón between the Cordillera Occidental and Cordillera Central in northern Perú
20. *Huallaga Valley* — The upper valley of the Río Huallaga between the Cordillera Central and Cordillera Oriental in central Perú
21. *Mantaro-Apurímac Valleys* — The intermontane valleys of the Río Mantaro and Río Apurímac in central Perú
22. *Cordillera Oriental in Bolivia* — The Andes north and east of the Altiplano in Bolivia

F Southern Andes

23. *Altiplano* — The high Andean plateau in Bolivia, southern Perú, and northern Argentina
24. *Andes in northern Argentina* — The ranges east of the Altiplano to 27°S Lat
25. *Andes in northern Chile* — The ranges west of the Altiplano to 27°S Lat
26. *Andes in southern Chile* — The western slopes of the Andes south of 27°S Lat
27. *Andes in southern Argentina* — The eastern slopes of the Andes south of 27°S Lat

Many of the regions are definitive physiographically, whereas other divisions are ones of convenience for analyzing distributions. The Cordillera Central in Colombia is continuous with the Cordillera Oriental in Ecuador. The Cordillera Oriental in Perú is continuous with the Cordillera Oriental in Bolivia and the Andes in Argentina. The Cordillera Occidental in Perú is continuous with the Chilean Andes, the southern ranges of which are solely the western slopes of the Andes of southern Argentina.

The ten habitat types are defined, as follow (see Simpson, this volume, for more extensive descriptions and discussion of vegetation).

1. *Arid* — Sparse, xeric-adapted vegetation on the western cordilleras in Perú and northern and central Chile and on the eastern cordilleras in central Argentina characterized locally by legumes (*Acacia, Adesmia, Prosopis*), cactus, and terrestrial bromeliads (*Puya*) (Fig 15 1)
2. *Cloud forest* — The humid lush forests on the windward slopes from Venezuela to Bolivia are termed variously humid montane forest, upper montane forest, or *ceja* (Fig 15 2) The lower limits of this forest are usually no less than 1000 m, whereas the upper limit varies locally from 2600 to 3800 m Characterized by a diversity of woody plants, especially various species of *Podocarpus*, the cloud forest has many tree ferns and epiphytes
3. *Dry forest* — Xerophytic scrub forest

dominated by legumes principally *Acacia* and *Prosopis*, and a variety of cacti, is characteristic of the Andean slopes in southwestern Ecuador, the Huancabamba Depression, some interior valleys in Perú, Bolivia, and northern Argentina (Fig 15 3)

4 *Nothofagus forest*—This term applies to the austral cool temperate forests in southern Argentina and Chile dominated by various species of southern beech (*Nothofagus*) and conifers (*Araucaria, Cupressoides, Fitzroya*), see Formas (this volume) for a detailed discussion (Fig 15 4)

5 *Páramo*—The vegetation above tree line (2600–3800 m) in the northern Andes and Mérida Andes generally is composed of low (<1 m) herbaceous vegetation with some woody bushes (especially *Baccharis*), cushion plants (*Distichia*), grasses (especially *Festuca*) and in northern Ecuador, Colombia, and Venezuela the characteristic composites *Espeletia* (Fig 15 5)

6 *Patagonian scrub*—This cold-adapted, xerophilic vegetation formation characteristic of Patagonia ascends the eastern slopes of the Andes in central Argentina to elevations of about 3500 m and exists in local areas in Chile west of Andean passes (Fig 15 6) Bushes (*Mulinum Berberis*, and others) are mixed with grasses (*Festuca, Poa, Stipa*), herbs (*Senecio, Acaena* etc), and some low spiny sclerophylls (*Ephedra Adesmia*, etc)

7 *Puna*—The montane habitat above tree line that is drier than páramo and extends from southern Ecuador to northern Argentina is called puna The puna is dominated by bunch grasses (*Festuca, Poa*, and especially *Stipa*), in many extensive areas, grasses are the only evident vegetation (Fig 15 7) Composites, such as *Baccharis Lepidophyllum*, and *Senecio* are widespread, whereas low trees (*Polylepis*) and cushion plants (principally the umbellifer *Azorella*) are local in their distributions In many areas the puna grasses are grazed by domestic herds of sheep, llamas, and alpacas (Fig 15 8)

8 *Rainforest*—The lowland and lower montane (<1000 m) rainforests are not part of the Andean vegetation, notation of the occurrence of a species in this habitat indicates that it inhabits rainforest in addition to some Andean habitat, usually cloud forest

9 *Subpáramo*—A localized ecotone between cloud forest and páramo occurs sporadically at elevations of 2700 to 3500 m along the eastern Andean front from Colombia to Bolivia Usually the vegetation consists of stunted, closely packed trees (*Polylepis*) or bushes (*Baccharis*) heavily laden with mosses and in some areas supporting many bromeliads (Fig 15 9) The bamboo (*Chusquea*) usually is present

10 *Valley vegetation*—This term is applied to the vegetation of the high inter-Andean valleys, which for centuries have been modified by man so that remaining grasses have been grazed, and fields are devoted to crops, principally wheat and potatoes The numerous rock fences and irrigation ditches provide suitable habitats for many kinds of amphibians and reptiles (Fig 15 10)

The taxonomy of many Andean amphibians and reptiles is known inadequately Thorough taxonomic studies are needed for frogs of the genus *Telmatobius* (currently being studied by Linda Trueb), lizards of the genus *Proctoporus* (currently being studied by Thomas H Fritts) and snakes of the genus *Atractus* Taxonomic problems still remain in the large iguanid lizard genus *Liolaemus* and the hylid frog genus *Gastrotheca* Based on the recent rate of acquisition of new species of frogs of the genera *Centrolenella Colostethus*, and *Eleutherodactylus*, many more species remain to be discovered in unexplored and poorly collected ranges and valleys At the present time the Ecuadorian Andes, Mérida Andes, Cordillera de la Costa in Venezuela and southern Chilean Andes probably are the best-known regions, whereas the Cordillera Central in Perú, Cordillera Oriental

Fig. 15:1. Arid slopes on the west face of the Andes, 6 km E Lo Valdés, 2250 m, Provincia de Santiago, Chile.
Laderas áridas en el lado oeste de los Andes, 6 km E Lo Valdés, 2250 m, Provincia de Santiago, Chile.

Fig. 15:2. Cloud forest in Cordillera de la Costa, Rancho Grande, 1100 m, Estado de Aragua, Venezuela.
Selva de neblina en la Cordillera de la Costa, Rancho Grande, 1100 m, Estado de Aragua, Venezuela.

Fig. 15:3. Dry forest in an eastern valley, 15 km S Quiroga, 1750 m, Departamento de Cochabamba, Bolivia. *Selva seca en un valle del este, 15 km S Quiroga, 1750 m, Departamento de Cochabamba, Bolivia.*

Fig. 15:4. *Nothofagus* forest at Lago de Huechulafquen, 900 m, Provincia de Neuquén, Argentina. *Selvas de Nothofagus en el Lago de Huechulafquen, 900 m, Provincia de Neuquén, Argentina.*

Fig. 15:5. Páramo dominated by *Espeletia* in Páramo El Angel, 14 km SW Tulcán, 3340 m, Provincia de Carchi, Ecuador.
Paramo dominado por Espeletia *en el Páramo El Angel, 14 km SO Tulcán, 3340 m, Provincia de Carchi, Ecuador.*

Fig. 15:6. Patagonian scrub, with scattered *Adesmia*, on south slope of Paso El Choique, 1950 m, Provincia de Mendoza, Argentina.
Matorral patagónico, con Adesmia *dispersas, en la ladera sur del Paso El Choique, 1950 m, Provincia de Mendoza, Argentina.*

Fig. 15:7. Bunch grass puna, Pampas de Ramoscruz, 31 km W Orcos, 4120 m, Departamento de Ayacucho, Perú.
Puna con pasto en champas, Pampas de Ramoscruz, 31 km O Orcos, 4120 m, Departamento de Ayacucho, Perú.

Fig. 15:8. Rocky puna, Altiplano, 38 km W Challa, 4300 m, Departamento de Cochabamba, Bolivia.
Puna rocosa, Altiplano, 38 km O Challa, 4300 m, Departamento de Cochabamba, Bolivia.

Fig. 15:9. Subpáramo on Abra de Zamora, 2850 m, Provincia de Loja, Ecuador.
Subpáramo en Abra de Zamora, 2850 m, Provincia de Loja, Ecuador.

Fig. 15:10. Terraced valley at Puquina, 2900 m, Departamento de Moquegua, Perú.
Valle de andenes en Puquina, 2900 m, Departamento de Moquegua, Perú.

in northern Perú, Cordillera Oriental in Bolivia, and the Andes of northern Argentina probably are the poorest-known regions. Despite these limitations of the data and incomplete knowledge of the taxonomy, it is reasonable to determine broad distributional patterns and to interpret these patterns on the basis of generalized phylogenetic relationships and historical events in the Andes. Finally, an apology. I have written more about (and hopefully most accurately) the regions (northern Andes) and organisms (frogs) with which I am most familiar.

PATTERNS OF DISTRIBUTION

Each of the six major Andean units is discussed with respect to 1) historical geology, 2) physiography, 3) climate, and 4) herpetofauna. With the exception of the latter, the reader is referred to Simpson (this volume) for more complete discussions. The distributional data on the herpetofauna are summarized in Appendices 15.1–3.

Venezuelan Andes

The highest mountains in Venezuela are the Mérida, or Venezuelan, Andes. The complex ranges and intermontane valleys that comprise these mountains have a length of about 400 km and breadth of about 100 km (Oppenheim, 1937). The highest elevation is 5002 m on Pico Bolívar; snow line is between 4600 and 4700 m (Jahn, 1934). The Mérida Andes are separated from the Cordillera Oriental by elevations of less than 600 m in the Depresión de San Cristóbal or Cúcuta, at the Colombian-Venezuelan border. According to Liddle (1946), the Mérida Andes were distinct from the main chain of the Andes until the end of the Eocene; the last orogeny began in the Oligocene and continues to the present (Shagan, 1975). According to Schubert (1974), significantly high elevations were attained only late in the Pleistocene. Páramo habitats, which descend to 2400 m in some places, comprise only 3500 sq km of area in the Mérida Andes (Jahn, 1931).

The Cordillera de la Costa had a similar geological history of uplift as the Mérida Andes (Liddle, 1946), but the Cordillera de la Costa apparently was uplifted little or not at all in the Quaternary. Although some workers (e.g., Rivero, 1961) distinguish two major physiographic regions of the Cordillera de la Costa (Serranía del Litoral including the Serranía de Paria, and Serranía del Interior including the serranías incorporating Cerro Turumiquire and Cerro Periquito), I have recognized one major unit, the Cordillera de la Costa, and two isolated small ranges—the Serranía de Paria and Cerro Turumiquire. The Cordillera de la Costa is separated from the Mérida Andes by the low (±500 m), subhumid Depresión de Barquisimeto. The highest peak in the Cordillera de la Costa is Pico Naiguata at 2765 m (Aguerrevere and Zuloaga 1937); this and 13 other peaks more than 2000 m are in the littoral section of the cordillera, which rises abruptly from the Caribbean coast (Fig. 15.11). The interior section of the Cordillera de la Costa is broad and has few peaks exceeding 1000 m. Disjunct to the east is Cerro Turumiquire (2630 m). The Depresión de Unare separates the main part of the Cordillera de la Costa from the narrow ranges on the peninsulas of Araya and Paria, where only two peaks exceed heights of 800 m (Davey, 1949). The higher (>850 m) northern (seaward) slopes of the cordillera support luxuriant cloud forest which disintegrates into dry forest on most of the leeward slopes. Cloud forest occurs at elevations above 1500 m on Cerro Turumiquire and as low as 600 m in the Serranía de Paria.

In addition to the general references cited, distributional data for the Venezuelan highlands were obtained from Donoso Barros (1968), Rivero (1963a,b, 1964, 1968, 1972, 1974), Rivero and Mayorga (1973), Test, Sexton and Heatwole (1966), Williams (1974) and Williams, et al. (1970). Published data were supplemented by information provided by Scott J. Maness and by material collected by me in 1974.

Forty-eight amphibians and 32 reptiles occur principally at elevations of more than 1000 m in the Venezuelan highlands.[1] Of

---
[1] Rivero ("1976" [1978]) named three additional species of frogs (*Colostethus*) from the Mérida Andes.

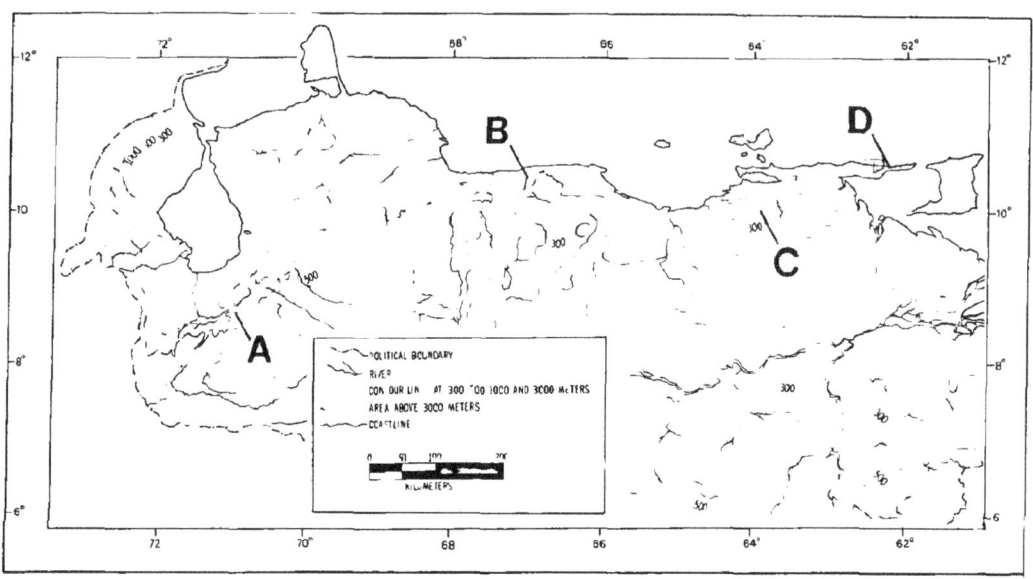

Fig 15 11 The Venezuelan Andes A Mérida Andes, B Cordillera de la Costa, C Cerro Turumiquire, D Serranía de Paria
Los Andes venezolanos A Los Andes de Mérida B Cordillera de la Costa C Cerro de Turumiquire D Serranía de Paria

these, only six are confined to elevations of more than 2500 m All six occur in the Mérida Andes and include four frogs (*Eleutherodactylus boconoensis, E ginesi, E lancinii, Atelopus mucubajiensis*) and two lizards (*Anadia bitaeniata, A brevirostris*) Only three other species exceed 2500 m—the salamander, *Bolitoglossa orestes*, and the frog, *Centrolenella buckleyi*, in the Mérida Andes, and the frog, *Colostethus mandelorum*, on Cerro Turumiquire

Only four species are known from the Serranía de Paria and seven from Cerro Turumiquire, each having three and five endemic species, respectively.[2] Of the 46 species in the Cordillera de la Costa, 34 are endemic Thus, in these three areas, specific endemism is 71–75 percent Only 18 (56%) of the 32 species in the Mérida Andes are endemic Despite the low (600 m) separation of the Mérida Andes from the Cordillera Oriental in Colombia, seven species occur in both cordilleras Two widespread frogs (*Hyla labialis* and *Centrolenella buckleyi*) inhabit subpáramo and páramo from 2000 to 2700 m in the Mérida Andes and similar habitats at 2400 to 3000 m (*Hyla*) and 2100 to 3400 m (*Centrolenella*) in Colombia The other species—*Gastrotheca nicefori* (1575 m), *Anolis nigropunctatus* (1200 m) *Chironius monticola* (1000–1600 m), *Leimadophis bimaculatus* (1400–2500 m), and *Micrurus mipartitus* (800–2000 m) inhabit cloud forest on both sides of the Depresión de San Cristóbal Other species in the Mérida Andes have affinities with species in the Colombian Andes *Atelopus oxyrhynchus* and *A mucubajiensis* are members of the *Atelopus ignescens* group, which is speciose in Colombia and Ecuador and occurs in the Sierra Nevada de Santa Marta (Rivero, 1963b) *Hyla platydactyla* is a member of the *Hyla bogotensis* group containing four species in the main Andean cordillera One salamander (*Bolitoglossa savagei*, 1000–2000 m) and one snake (*Micrurus mipartitus*, 1600–2000 m) occur in the Mérida Andes and the Sierra Nevada de Santa Marta in northern Colombia

---

[2] S J Gorzula (pers comm) collected six additional species of frogs (2 *Eleutherodactylus*, 3 *Centrolenella*, and *Flectonotus*) in the Serranía de Paria in 1978

The major faunal affinities between the Mérida Andes and Cordillera de la Costa are among six snakes—*Atractus badius, Chironius monticola, Dendrophidion percarinatus, Lampropeltis triangulum, Leimadophis zweifeli* and *Micrurus mipartitus*, all but two of which have lower distributional limits of less than 1000 m. No frogs or lizards are shared by the two cordilleras.

Two species of frogs (*Colostethus herminae* and *Eleutherodactylus urichi*) are shared between the Cordillera de la Costa and Cerro Turumiquire; the *Eleutherodactylus* also occurs in the Serranía de Paria and on Trinidad. According to John D. Lynch (pers. comm.), many of the *Eleutherodactylus* in the Cordillera de la Costa have affinities with West Indian species rather than with those in the Andes of Colombia and Ecuador. This faunal relationship also appears in the hylid frog *Flectonotus pygmaeus* that inhabits the Cordillera de la Costa and Isla Tobago north of Trinidad. Two other species are included in the genus—*F. fitzgeraldi* on Trinidad and *F. fissilis* in the highlands of southeastern Brasil.

Five inhabitants of cloud forest in the Venezuelan highlands (2 frogs—*Gastrotheca nicefori, Centrolenella fleischmanni,* 3 snakes —*Dendrophidion percarinatus, Lampropeltis triangulum, Micrurus mipartitus*) also occur in cloud forests in lower Central America. The hylid frog, *Phyllomedusa medinae*, belongs to a group having a species in lower Central America (*P. lemur*), one on the eastern slopes of the Andes in Ecuador (*P. buckleyi*) and an unnamed species on the Pacific slopes in Colombia (Duellman 1970).

Two monotypic genera of snakes (*Umbrivaga mertensi* and "*Urotheca*" *williamsi*) are endemic to the Cordillera de la Costa. No species are shared with the Guiana Highlands.

Thus each of the four regions of the Venezuelan highlands has endemic species of amphibians and reptiles; those of the two small highland areas (Cerro Turumiquire and Serranía de Paria) seem to have been derived from the Cordillera de la Costa, which shares few species with the Mérida Andes (Fig 15, 12). Thirty-two species occur in the Mérida Andes, as compared with 103 species in the Cordillera Oriental in Colombia, only seven species are in common. The most speciose genera in the Venezuelan highlands are *Eleutherodactylus, Colostethus, Centrolenella, Anolis, Anadia,* and *Atractus*, all of which are widespread and diverse in humid lowland and foothill habitats. Therefore it seems most likely that the species of these genera that are endemic to the highlands were derived from lowland ancestral stocks. A minor percentage of the fauna of the Mérida Andes apparently was derived from highland stocks in the Cordillera Oriental of Colombia. In the latter group are *Bolitoglossa orestes, B. savagei, Atelopus mucubajiensis, A. oxyrhynchus, Gastrotheca nicefori, Hyla labialis, Hyla platydactyla, Centrolenella buckleyi,* and *Anolis nigropunctatus*. Certainly in contrast to the Colombian and Ecuadorian ranges of the Andes, the fauna of the Mérida Andes is depauperate; this suggests that the Depresión de San Cristobal has been an effective barrier to the dispersal of most highland groups. Furthermore, the recency of elevation of the Mérida Andes, combined with late Pleistocene glaciation of the small areas now supporting páramo, may be partly responsible for the few high montane species of amphibians and reptiles.

Sierra Nevada de Santa Marta

An isolated volcanic range, the Sierra Nevada de Santa Marta, consists of an area of only about 16,000 sq km. The highest elevations, such as Pico Cristóbal Colón at 5775 m, are perpetually covered with snow. The sierra rises abruptly from the Caribbean coastal plain and is narrowly separated by arid lowlands at elevations of less than 500 m from the northern part of the Cordillera Oriental of the Andes; the northern part of the cordillera along the Colombian-Venezuelan border is the Sierra de Perijá which attains elevations of 3750 m. The first uplift of the Sierra Nevada de Santa Marta was in the Miocene, but the final uplift did not occur until the end of the Pleistocene (Gansser, 1955). According to Carriker (1922) cloud forest occurs at elevations of 1385 to 2200 m, but I have observed cloud forest on Cerro San Lorenzo (= Cerro Kennedy) at 2700 m.

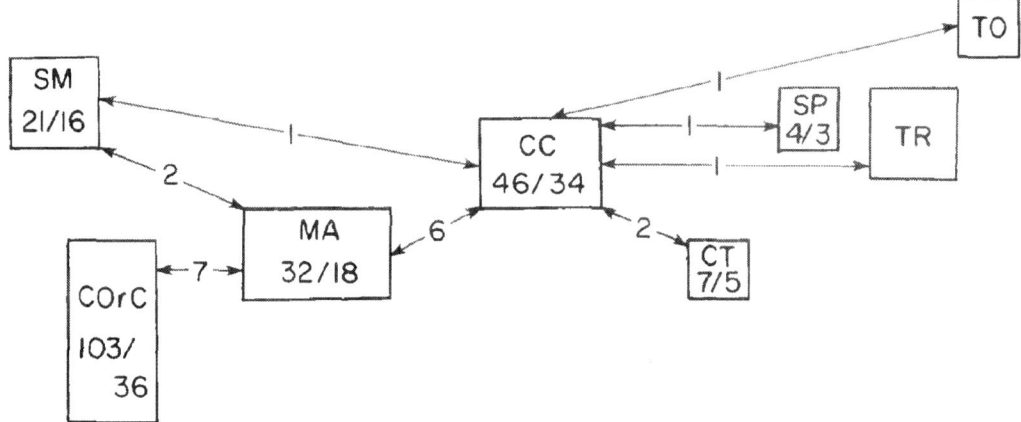

Fig. 15:12. Herpetofaunal comparisons of the regions of the Venezuelan Andes and adjacent areas. Numbers in blocks are number of species/number of endemic species; numbers of shared species are within arrows. CC = Cordillera de la Costa; COrC = Cordillera Oriental de Colombia; CT = Cerro Turumiquire; MA = Mérida Andes; SM = Sierra Nevada de Santa Marta; SP = Serranía de Paria; TO = Tobago; TR = Trinidad.
Comparaciones faunísticas de la herpetofauna de las regiones de los Andes venezolanos y áreas adyacentes. Números dentro de bloques representan número de especies/número de especies endémicas; número de especies en común están en las flechas.

Páramo exists above tree line to the lower limits of snow at about 4900 m (Carriker, 1922).

The basis for a discussion of the herpetofauna of the Sierra Nevada de Santa Marta is Ruthven's (1922) account, supplemented by my own field work in June 1974. Ruthven's taxonomy was modified by Brame and Wake (1963), Cochran and Goin (1970), Lynch (1975b, 1978a), Oftedal (1974), and Rivero (1963b).

Of the 21 species of amphibians and reptiles known from the páramo and cloud forest on the Sierra Nevada de Santa Marta, 16 are endemic. Four of the nonendemic species also occur in the Cordillera Oriental of the Andes. Of these, one frog, *Eleutherodactylus prolixodiscus*, and a teiid lizard, *Anadia pulchella*, occur at elevations of 2100 to 2700 m in the Cordillera Oriental. The frog *Amblyphrynus ingeri* inhabits cloud forests at 1720 to 1980 m in the Cordillera Oriental and the Cordillera Central. The snake *Micrurus mipartitus* occurs at elevations of less than 2000 m in the Colombian Andes, Sierra Nevada de Santa Marta, Mérida Andes, Cordillera de la Costa, and highlands in lower Central America. The salamander, *Bolitoglossa savagei*, inhabiting cloud forest at 1000 to 2100 m in the Sierra Nevada de Santa Marta also occurs at 2000 m in the Mérida Andes (Brame and Wake, 1963).

Of the 16 endemic species, three frogs (*Atelopus carrikeri*, *A. walkeri*, *Centrolenella* sp. "P") have relatives in the Cordillera Oriental and in the Mérida Andes. Two frogs (*Colostethus* sp. "A," *Cryptobatrachus boulengeri*) have relatives in the Colombian Andes. The relationships of the enigmatic frog *Geobatrachus walkeri* are unknown. The reptiles (*Pseudogonatodes*, *Anolis*, *Atractus*) and two frogs that are members of the *Eleutherodactylus fitzingeri* group (*E. carmelitae* and *E. insignitus*) have many congeners in the lowlands. The other species of *Eleutherodactylus* are members of the *Eleutherodactylus unistrigatus* group and have relationships with species in the Cordillera de la Costa in Venezuela (John D. Lynch, pers. comm.).

The apparent absence of tree frogs of the *Hyla bogotensis* group and *Gastrotheca* is noteworthy; both are represented by numerous species in the cloud forests in the Colombian Andes.

On the basis of the limited information available, it seems that some of the herpetofauna of the Sierra Nevada de Santa Marta might have been derived from the Cordillera

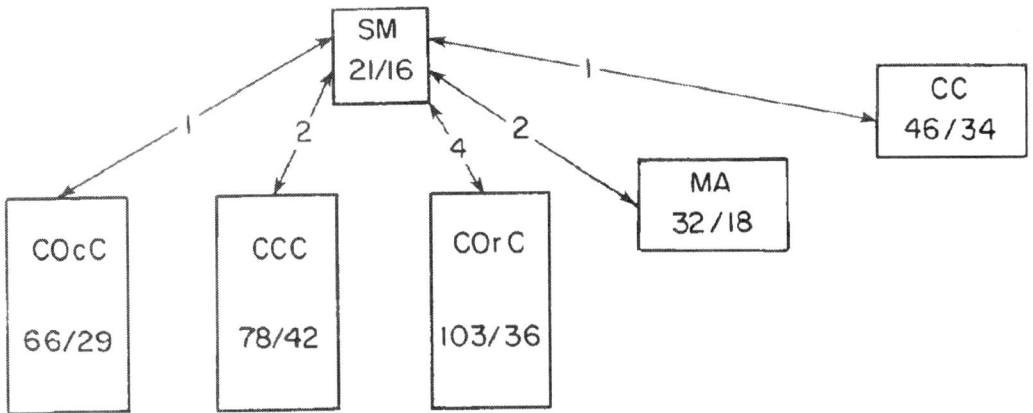

Fig. 15:13. Herpetofaunal comparisons of the Sierra Nevada de Santa Marta with other highlands. Numbers in blocks are number of species/number of endemic species; numbers of shared species are within arrows. CC = Cordillera de la Costa; CCC = Cordillera Central de Colombia; COcC = Cordillera Occidental de Colombia; COrC = Cordillera Oriental de Colombia; MA = Mérida Andes; SM = Sierra Nevada de Santa Marta.

Comparaciones faunísticas de la herpetofauna de la Sierra Nevada de Santa Marta con otras tierras de alturas. Números dentro de bloques representan número de especies/número de especies endémicas; número de especies en común están en las flechas.

de la Costa in Venezuela, some from the Mérida Andes, some from the Cordillera Oriental, and some from the surrounding lowlands (Fig. 15:13). With the exception of the widespread *Micrurus mipartitus*, no species are shared with the Central American highlands. Much exploration remains to be done in the Sierra Nevada de Santa Marta, a region that probably has many more species than known at present. Also, the geographically important but biologically unexplored Sierra de Perijá may hold the key to understanding the faunal relationships of the Sierra Nevada de Santa Marta.

Northern Andes

The northern Andes are comprised of five major north-south ranges diverging from the Nudo de Pasto and a series of high intermontane basins in Ecuador; the entire northern Andes extend for about 1800 km from the Caribbean lowlands at 10°50′N to the Huancabamba Depression at 4°30′S. Central to the physiography of the northern Andes is the high massif of the Nudo de Pasto in southern Colombia and northern Ecuador (Fig. 15:14). The Nudo de Pasto encompasses a north-south extent of about 110 km and a breadth of about 130 km. The nudo is bordered to the northwest by the Río Patía, to the northeast by the headwaters of the Río Caquetá, and to the south by the Río Chota. Much of the nudo is above 3000 m with two peaks, Volcán Chiles and Volcán Cumbal, reaching 4760 m.

The Andes north of the Nudo de Pasto form three distinct ranges. The western range, the Cordillera Occidental extends for about 650 km between the Pacific lowlands and the valley of the Río Cauca. The southern border is the Río Patía; the dry upper valley of the river at about 1200 m separates the Cordillera Occidental from the Nudo de Pasto. The Cordillera Occidental is narrow (<50 km) and lacks continuous high ridges; the two highest peaks are Cerro Tamaná (4200 m) and Pico Frontino (4080 m).

The Cordillera Central extends 750 km north from the Nudo de Pasto; this range about 100 km in width is bordered on the west by the valley of the Río Cauca and on the east by the valley of the Río Magdalena. Extensive areas are above 3000 m, and four peaks with permanent snow exceed 5000 m —Nevado del Huila (5760 m), Nevado del Quindío (5400 m), Nevado del Ruíz (5400 m), and Nevado del Tolima (5215 m).

The Cordillera Oriental is narrowly sep-

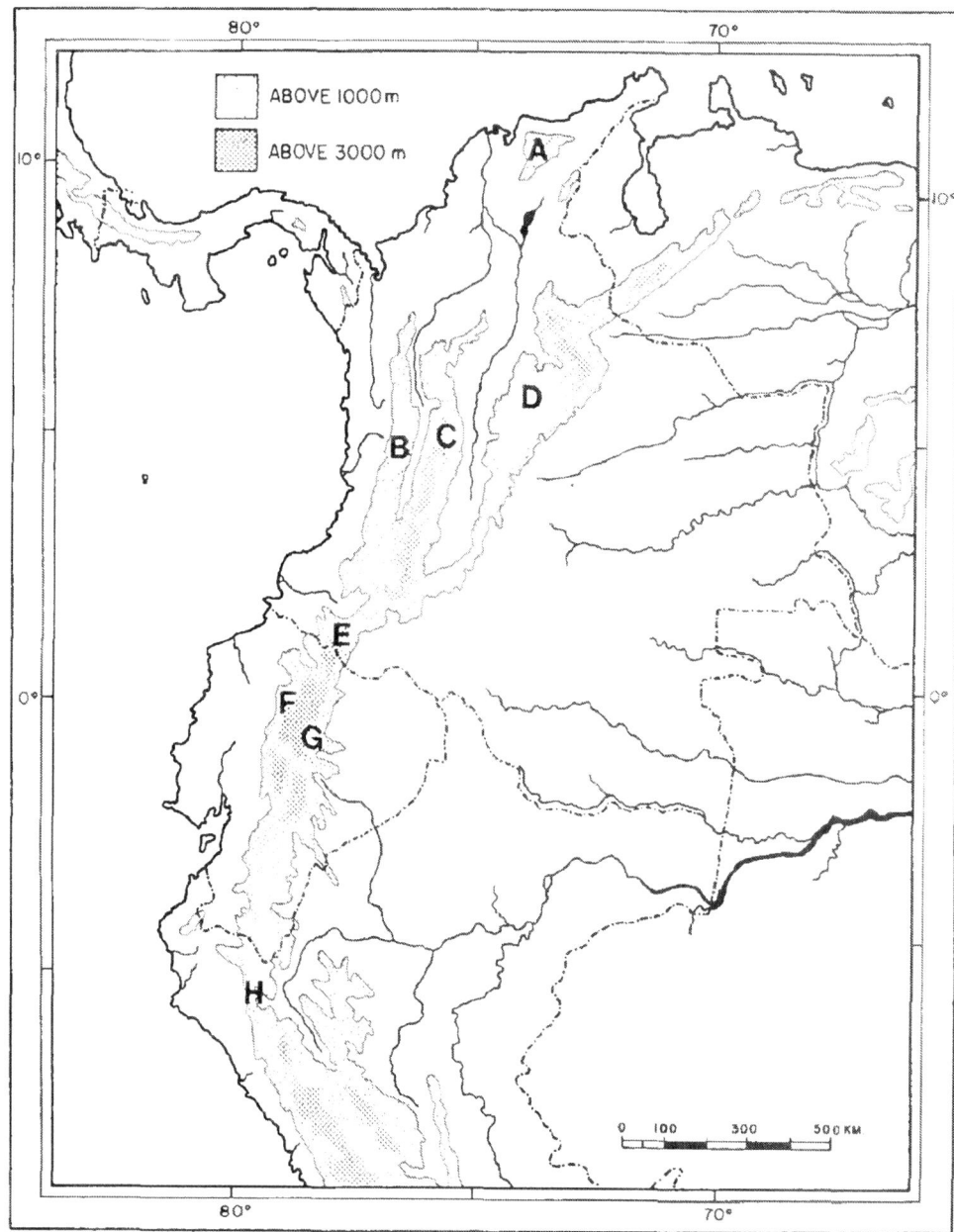

FIG. 15:14. The northern Andes. A. Sierra Nevada de Santa Marta; B. Cordillera Occidental de Colombia; C. Cordillera Central de Colombia; D. Cordillera Oriental de Colombia; E. Nudo de Pasto; F. Cordillera Occidental de Ecuador; G. Cordillera Oriental de Ecuador; H. Huancabamba Depression. The inter-Andean Basins lie between the Cordillera Occidental and the Cordillera Oriental in Ecuador.

Los Andes del norte. Las hoyas interandinas están entre la Cordillera Occidental y la Cordillera Oriental en Ecuador.

arated from the Nudo de Pasto by the upper Río Caquetá Valley at about 1200 m and extends about 1200 km north-northeastward to about 10°50′N, where the northern part of the cordillera closely approximates the disjunct Sierra Nevada de Santa Marta. The Cordillera Oriental reaches a width of 200 km where the topography is a complex array of ranges and basins. With the exception of the northern one-fourth of the cordillera, there are large areas at elevations above 3000 m; the highest peak is the Nevado del Cocuy (5493 m). Lying to the east of the Cordillera Oriental is the isolated Serranía de la Macarena which reaches elevations of more than 2000 m.

South of the Nudo de Pasto, the Cordillera Occidental of Ecuador extends southward for about 500 km. The Cordillera Occidental is limited in the north by the dry valley of the Río Chota at about 1500 m and in the south by the dry valley of the Río Jubones at about 900 m. The elevation of the entire southern two-thirds of the cordillera exceeds 3000 m. Many volcanoes in the cordillera exceed 4500 m; the highest is the majestic Volcán Chimborazo (6310 m), capped with snow and glaciers and the highest peak in the Andes north of Perú.

The Cordillera Oriental of Ecuador is continuous with the Nudo de Pasto and extends southward for about 620 km to the Huancabamba Depression. Unlike the western cordillera, the high elevations of the Cordillera Oriental are interrupted by the valleys of the Río Pastaza, Río Paute, and Río Zamora. The eastern cordillera has many volcanoes, the highest of which, Volcán Cayambe, reaches 5790 m; three volcanoes over 5000 m are active—Volcán Cotopaxi, Volcán Sangay, and Volcán Tungurahua. Whereas the Cordillera Occidental drops precipitously to the Pacific lowlands, the Cordillera Oriental slopes much more gradually into the Amazon Basin. Three disjunct highland areas rise from the foothills of the Cordillera Oriental—Cerro Sumaco (3900 m), Cordillera de Cutucú (2200 m), and Cordillera del Condor (2450 m).

Between the eastern and western cordilleras in Ecuador are 10 basins (*cuencas* or

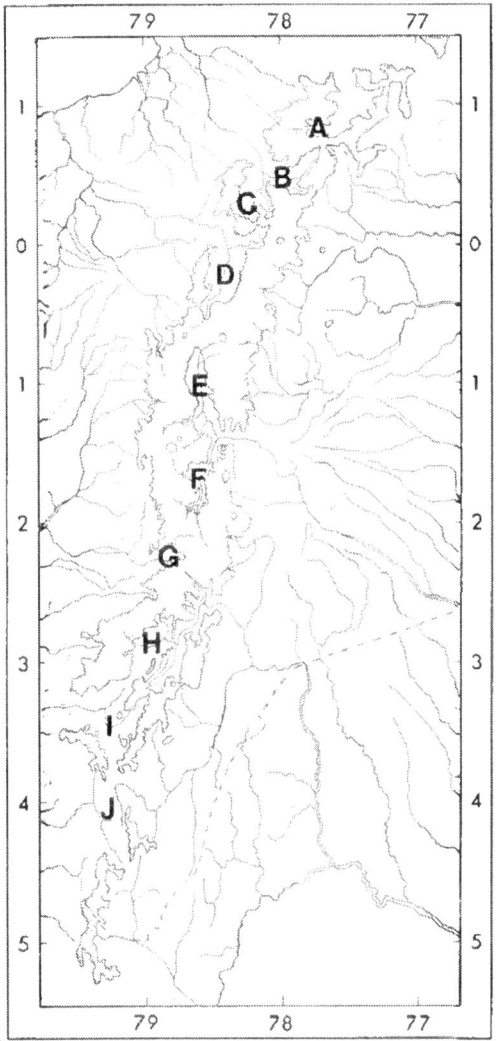

Fig. 15:15. The Inter-Andean Basins of Ecuador. A. Tulcán; B. Ibarra; C. Otavalo; D. Quito; E. Latacunga; F. Riobamba; G. Alausi; H. Cuenca; I. Saraguro; J. Loja. Area between 3000 and 5000 m is shaded.

Las hoyas interandinas de Ecuador. Las áreas entre 3000 y 5000 m están sombreadas.

hoyas) that are separated by transverse ridges (*nudos*) completely or partially separating the basins and in most cases connecting the eastern and western cordilleras. The basins have elevations ranging from 2000 to 3100 m (Fig. 15:15).

The northern Andes have received considerable geological study (Burgl, 1961; Herd and Naeser, 1974; Sauer, 1965, 1971; Shagam 1975) and intensive palynological investigation (van der Hammen, et al., 1973; van der Hammen, 1974). The conclusions of these workers and Simpson (this volume) indicate that the northern Andes probably had few areas over 1000 m above sea level at early Pliocene time. The major orogeny occurred at the end of the Pliocene with the uplift of the eastern cordilleras taking place before that of the western cordilleras. The absence of evidence of glaciation on some high peaks suggests that their final uplift occurred after the last major glaciation. Nonetheless most areas above 3700 m were glaciated; climatic depression was in the magnitude of 6-7°C with a downward shift of environments of about 1000 to 1200 m (van der Hammen 1974).

The extensive areas above tree line are humid and cool with annual precipitation of 1000 to 2000 mm and little seasonal fluctuation in temperature, but daily variation of 10°C or more (Cuatrecasas, 1968). These areas of páramo have grasses (*Festuca*), rosette herbs (*Espeletia* and *Senecio*) cushion plants (*Distichia*), and low bushes (*Baccharis*). The western slopes of the Cordillera Occidental and the eastern slopes of the Cordillera Oriental from the Depresión de San Cristóbal southward support luxuriant cloud forests. These humid montane forests also occur locally in the Cordillera Central, especially in the northern part. Subpáramo is common but localized in the eastern and western cordilleras. The inter-Andean basins in Ecuador possibly were subpáramo prior to human modification into cultivated fields and grazing of livestock.

In addition to the general publications already cited I have drawn information from the works on anurans by Duellman (1972 1973), Duellman and Altig (1978) Duellman and Simmons (1977) Lynch (1975a,b, 1976a 1979), Lynch and Duellman (1973 1979) Myers and Daly (1976a,b) and Peters (1973) The works Myers (1973, 1974) and Savage (1960) on colubrid snakes also were used. Much of the distributional data is based on the extensive collections in the Museum of Natural History at The University of Kansas and in the National Museum of Natural History.

Herpetologically, the northern Andes have the richest fauna in the continent; 415 (57%) of the 727 Andean species occur in this region. Of these, 345 species (83%) are endemic to the northern Andes. The taxonomic disposition of the 415 species (number of endemics in parentheses) is caecilians 15 (12), salamanders 11 (11), frogs 262 (225),[3] lizards 54 (40), snakes 73 (57). Seven genera (*Amphignathodon*, *Centrolene*, *Osornophryne*, *Phenacosaurus*, *Pholidobolus* *Saphenophis*, *Synophis*) are endemic to the northern Andes, and one (*Cryptobatrachus*) is endemic save for one species in the Sierra Nevada de Santa Marta.

Of the 70 species having ranges extending beyond the limits of the northern Andes, 43 also are present in the adjacent lowlands. Some of these also occur in the central Andes, especially species that inhabit rainforest and cloud forest. Thus 15 species are shared between the Cordillera Oriental in Ecuador and the Cordillera Central in Peru, and 20 are shared between the former and the Cordillera Oriental in Perú. Fourteen species on the Pacific slopes of the Cordillera Occidental in Colombia and Ecuador and/or the northern parts of the Colombian cordilleras are shared with the highlands in lower Central America; these include six frogs (*Gastrotheca micfori* *Hemiphractus fasciatus*, *Centrolenella fleischmanni*, *C. griffithsi*, *C. prosoblepon*, *C. valerioi*) five lizards (*Anolis antonii*, *A. chloris* *Basiliscus galeritus* *Polychrus gutturosus*, *Prionodactylus vertebralis*) and three snakes (*Dendrophidion percarinatus*, *Micrurus mipartitus*, *Bothrops schlegeli*) With the exception of *Gastrotheca nicefori* and *Centrolenella griffithsi* all of these species range well below 1000 m. As noted previously, four species are shared with the Sierra Nevada de

---

[3] Not included in these figures or in Appendix 15.2 are *Atelopus carauta* from 1300 m in the Cordillera Occidental of Colombia (Ruiz and Hernandez (1978) or *Colostethus abditaurantius* from 1450 m in the Cordillera Central of Colombia (Silverstone, 1975)

Santa Marta, and seven are shared with the Mérida Andes

If only those species that do not occur below 2500 m are considered, 72 of the 73 species are endemic to the northern Andes The exception is the boid snake *Tropidophis taczanowskyi*, which inhabits the Cordillera Oriental in Ecuador and the Cordillera Central in Perú

Within the northern Andes, only two species, *Centrolenella buckleyi* (2100–3400 m in subpáramo and páramo) and *Eleutherodactylus w-nigrum* (1230–2800 m in cloud forest and subpáramo) occur in all seven regions *Eleutherodactylus vertebralis* (2340–3500 m in subpáramo and páramo) occurs in the three Colombian cordilleras, the Nudo de Pasto, and the Cordillera Occidental in Ecuador Four species of frogs (*Eleutherodactylus buckleyi, E unistrigatus, Atelopus ignescens,* and *Gastrotheca riobambae*) distributed mostly above 2500 m occur in four regions, three snakes (*Chironius monticola, Rhadinaea laterostriga,* and *Micrurus mipartitus*) distributed below 2000 m also occur in four regions Of the remaining 405 species in the northern Andes, 155 species occur in two or three regions, and 250 are endemic to a given region, with the largest number of endemics in the Cordillera Oriental in Ecuador (74) and the Cordillera Occidental in Ecuador (65), but with the highest percent of endemism in the Cordillera Central in Colombia (54%)

The highest faunal similarities among the seven regions in the northern Andes are between the eastern cordilleras in Colombia and Ecuador (45 species in common) and the western cordilleras in Colombia and Ecuador (33 species in common) (Fig 15 16) The low number of species (23) and endemics (1 lizard, *Proctoporus laevis*) in the Nudo de Pasto reflects a bias in the analysis only high elevations (>2500 m) were assigned to the nudo The herpetofauna of the inter-Andean basins is composed mostly of species also inhabiting the adjacent cordilleras Only three species (2 lizards—*Pholidobolus montium, Proctoporus occulatus,* 1 snake—*Atractus lehmanni*) are restricted to the basins The southernmost basin (Loja) is considered to be part of the Huancabamba Depression

Only considering those 73 species that do not occur below 2500 m, a much different picture is evident (Fig 15 17) Endemism in each region ranges from 20 percent in the Nudo de Pasto to 100 percent in the Cordillera Occidental in Colombia Whereas the eastern cordilleras in Colombia and Ecuador and the western cordilleras in Colombia and Ecuador shared the greatest numbers of species when the entire fauna was considered, in an analysis of only the high montane species, they have no species in common

The greatest species richness and highest percentage of endemism in the northern Andes is amongst the frogs (especially *Colostethus, Eleutherodactylus,* and *Centrolenella*), which form 60 percent of the entire Andean herpetofauna, but 65 percent in the northern Andes and 71 percent in the Cordillera Oriental in Ecuador Although the entire fauna in the equatorial cordilleras is large, local communities are much smaller Altitudinal and latitudinal changes in community composition result in localized faunules in the cloud forest, subpáramo, and páramo with generally decreasing numbers of species at higher altitudes Equatorial transects in the Cordillera Occidental and Cordillera Oriental reveal the presence of 62 and 79 species, respectively (Fig 15 18) On the eastern slopes there is a diminution of species at about 2000 m, this is especially evident upon examining the altitudinal distribution of individual species (Fig 15 19) Analysis of broad latitudinal distributions of species on the eastern slopes of the Cordillera Oriental shows that even at lower elevations (1000–1500 m) more than one-third of the species have limited distributions, whereas this percentage nearly doubles at elevations above 2500 m (Table 15 1)

High species richness, especially for anurans, in the equatorial cordilleras can be ascribed to the equable conditions with moderate to cool temperatures and high humidity relatively constant throughout the year Local endemism especially in the Cordillera Oriental in Ecuador, most likely is due to the discontinuous highlands

Table 15 1—Latitudinal Distribution of 79 Species of Amphibians and Reptiles on the Andean Slopes of Ecuador

Elevation	N	Ecuador Only	Ecuador and Colombia	Ecuador and Peru	Colombia Ecuador Peru
1000–1500 m	44	17 (38 6%)	15 (34 1%)	6 (13 6%)	6 (13 6%)
1500–2500 m	43	25 (58 6%)	10 (22 7%)	6 (13 6%)	2 (04 5%)
>2500 m	17	11 (64 7%)	6 (35 3%)	0 (00 0%)	0 (00 0%)

Huancabamba Depression

Along the entire length of the main range of the Andes there is only one pass below tree line This is in the complex system of low ranges and basins collectively referred to as the Huancabamba Depression in northern Perú and extreme southern Ecuador Here, the northern extremity of the Cordillera Occidental of Peru is breached by the Abra de Porculla at 2145 m In the Huancabamba Depression, the major cordilleras either terminate or fragment into isolated ranges usually less than 3500 m high and separated by valleys mostly between 1000 and 2000 m above sea level (Fig 15 20) Several small rivers drain the Pacific slopes but east of the continental divide, all streams eventually flow into the Río Marañón The interior basins are dry and support dry forest dominated by legumes and cacti Except for the eastern front ranges, the east slopes are also dry, whereas the tops of ridges above 3000 m and the upper western slopes have a low cloud forest with many bromeliads

At the Huancabamba Depression there is a structural deflection of the Andean faults There were extensive marine transgressions through this area in the Cretaceous (Ham and Herrera, 1963) The northern Peruvian Andes were uplifted only moderately prior to the Pliocene, the present elevations and drainage patterns were probably attained in the Pleistocene (Steinmann, 1930, Harrington, 1956, Gansser, 1973)

Few papers have been published dealing with the fauna of the Huancabamba Depression, but information on the distribution of some of the taxa can be found in Barbour and Noble (1920b), Noble (1921), Vellard (1959), Duellman and Fritts (1972), Duellman (1974), Fritts (1974), Trueb and Duellman (1978), and Lynch (1979)

Forty-three species of amphibians and reptiles, exclusive of predominantly lowland taxa, are known from the Huancabamba Depression, 29 species including the monotypic genera *Polychroides* and *Macropholidus*, are endemic to the region [4] The endemics include 10 frogs, 10 snakes, and 9 lizards, six of the latter are members of the genus *Stenocercus*, most species of which occur southward in Perú Five of the frogs are *Eleutherodactylus* and two are aquatic *Telmatobius*

Six species occur in the depression and in the Andes to the north, and two species occur in the Andes to the south and in the depression Two species (1 frog—*Eleutherodactylus cajamarcensis*, 1 snake—*Philodryas simonsii*) occur in the depression and in the Andes to the north and south, 21 species occur on the Andean slopes to the north and south but not in the depression (Fig 15 21) Those species in the latter group are primarily inhabitants of cloud forests and rainforest on the eastern slopes of the Andes, 10 of the species are widely distributed at elevations below 1000 m, and only one snake (*Tropidophis taczanowskyi*) is not known from below 2000 m

Just as the Huancabamba Depression is a barrier to north-south dispersal of Andean species, it is a dispersal route between the arid Pacific lowlands and the Río Marañón Valley Several predominantly lowland taxa (*Phyllodactylus*, *Tropidurus*, *Leptodeira*) are so distributed

Central Andes

The Central Andes compose the most massive part of the Andean highlands (Fig 15 22) The Cordillera Occidental forms the backbone of the Andes south of the Huan-

---

[4] The recently described colubrid snake, *Sibynomorphus oneilli*, also is endemic (Rossman and Thomas, 1979)

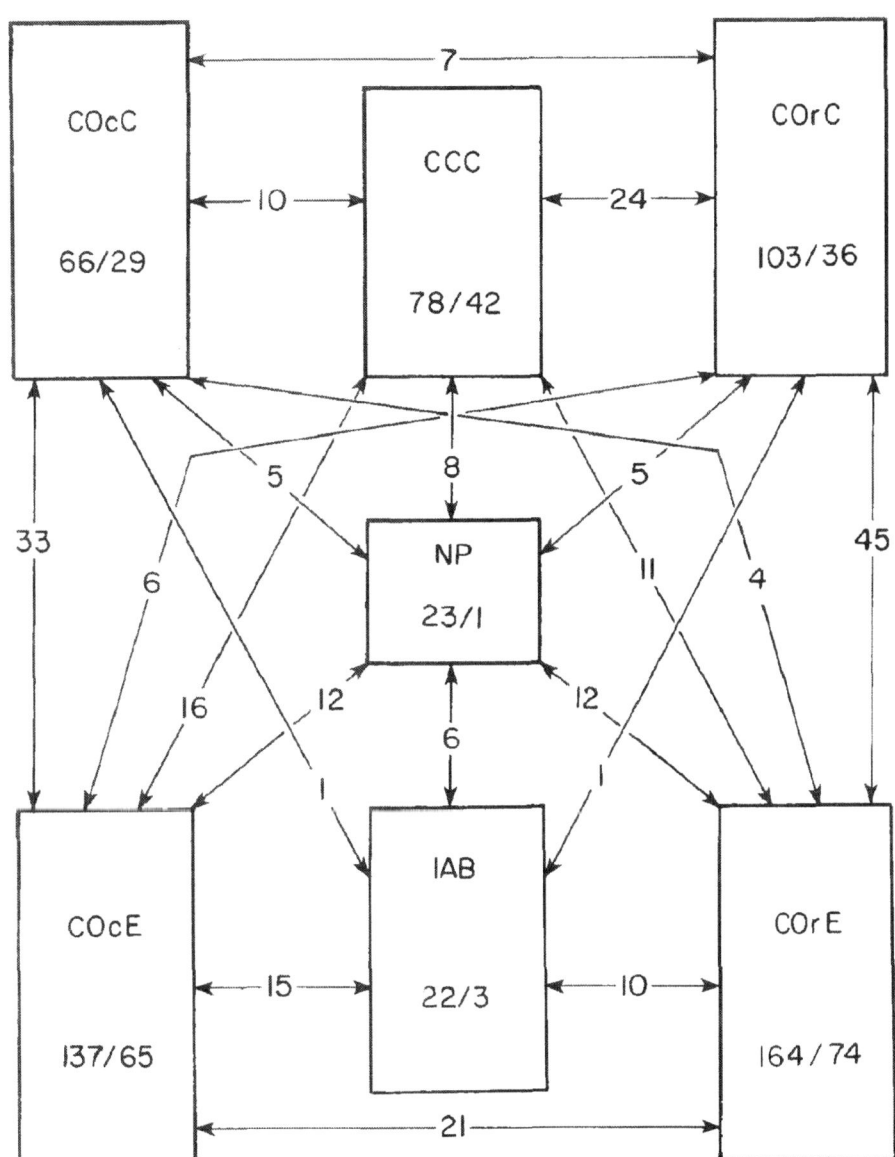

Fig. 15:16. Herpetofaunal comparisons of the regions of the northern Andes. Numbers in blocks are numbers of species/number of endemic species; numbers of shared species are within arrows. CCC = Cordillera Central de Colombia; COcC = Cordillera Occidental de Colombia; COcE = Cordillera Occidental de Ecuador; COrC = Cordillera Oriental de Colombia; COrE = Cordillera Oriental de Ecuador; IAB = Inter-Andean Basins; NP = Nudo de Pasto. One species is in common between CCC and IAB.

Comparaciones faunísticas de la herpetofauna de las regiones de los Andes del norte. Números dentro de bloques representan número de especies/número de especies endémicas; el número de especies en común están en las flechas. Una especies es compartida por CCC y IAB.

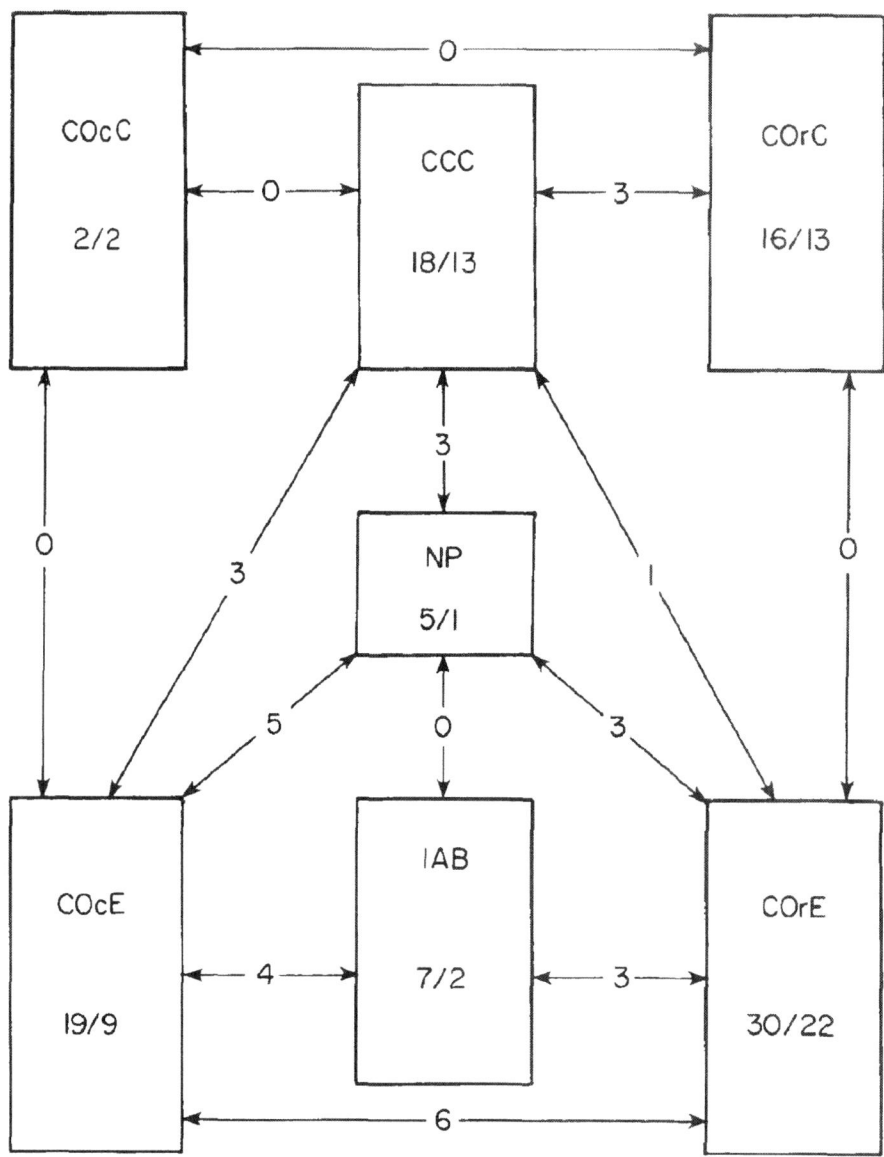

Fig. 15:17. Herpetofaunal comparisons of the regions of the northern Andes using only species that do not occur below 2500 m. Numbers and abbreviations are same as in figure 16.
Comparaciones faunísticas de la herpetofauna de las regiones de los Andes del norte, comprendiendo sólo aquellas especies que no bajan de los 2500 m. Números y abreviaciones igual que en la figura 16.

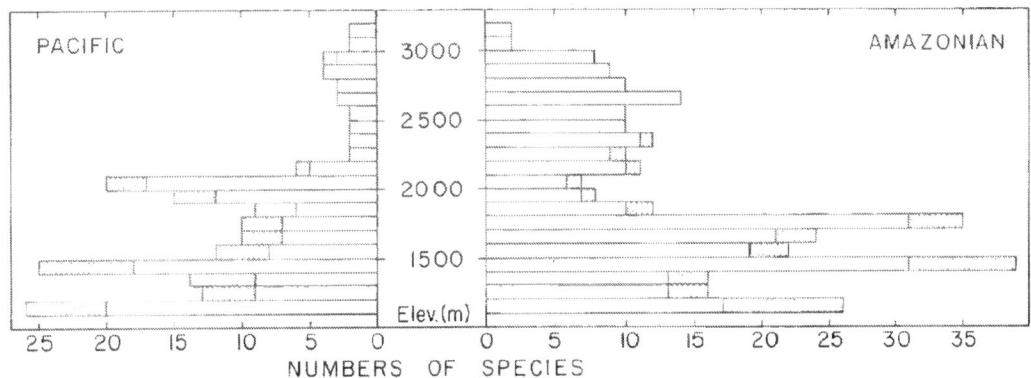

Fig. 15:18. Species abundance at different elevations along equatorial transects of the Andes in Ecuador; reptiles are shaded and amphibians are open symbols.
Abundancia de especies a diferentes alturas a lo largo de transects ecuatoriales en los Andes de Ecuador. Reptiles en símbolos sombreados y anfibios en símbolos claros.

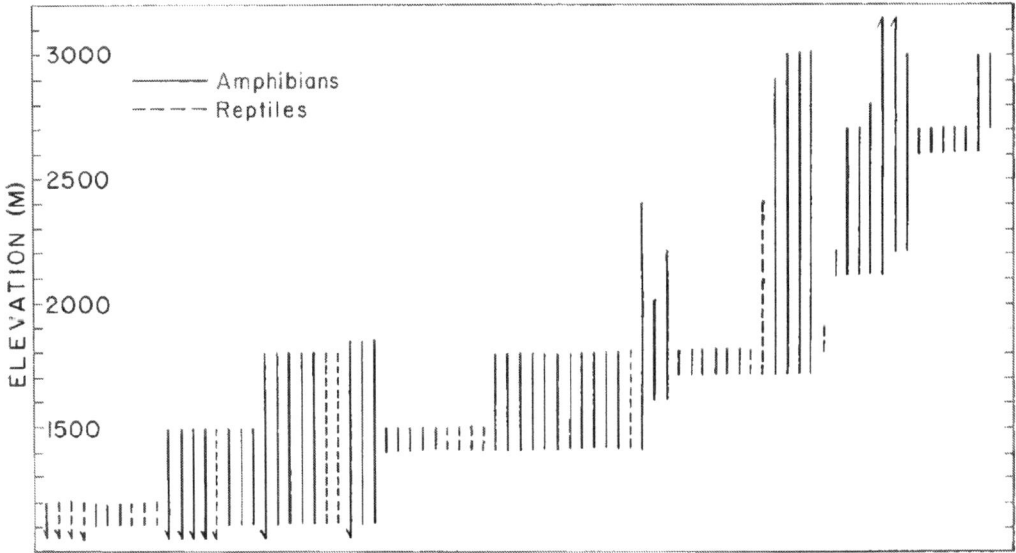

Fig. 15:19. Altitudinal distribution of amphibians (solid lines) and reptiles (broken lines) along an equatorial transect of the Cordillera Oriental in Ecuador.
Distribución altitudinal de anfibios (en líneas continuas) y reptiles (en líneas discontinuas) a lo largo de transect ecuatorial en la Cordillera Oriental en Ecuador.

cabamba Depression. Originating at about 6°S Lat., the western Cordillera reaches elevations in excess of 4000 m at 8°S Lat.; from that point only one pass exists below 4000 m for a distance of about 2800 km to 31°S Lat. The highest mountains in Perú are in the Cordillera Occidental; the Cordillera Blanca is nearly 400 km in length and is mostly above 5000 m. The highest peak is Nevado Huascarán (6745 m). Although the Cordillera Occidental is a continuous range, for the purposes of analysis, I have arbitrarily divided it into northern and southern sections in Perú; the point of division is at about the latitude of Lima, inland from which the high central Nudo de Pasco forms a high connection between the eastern and western cordilleras.

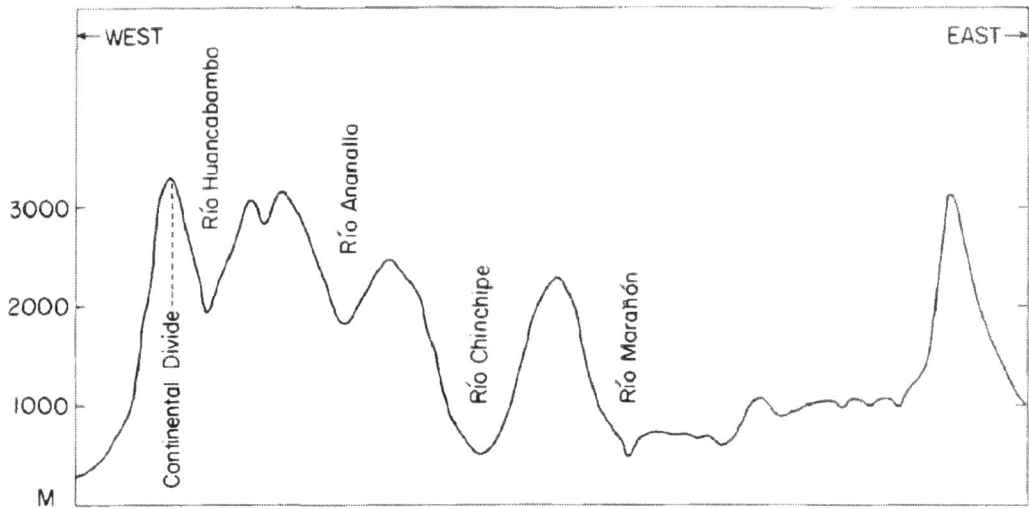

Fig. 15:20. Profile of the Huancabamba Depression at 5°15′S Lat.
Perfil de la Depresión de Huancabamba a 5°15′Lat. S.

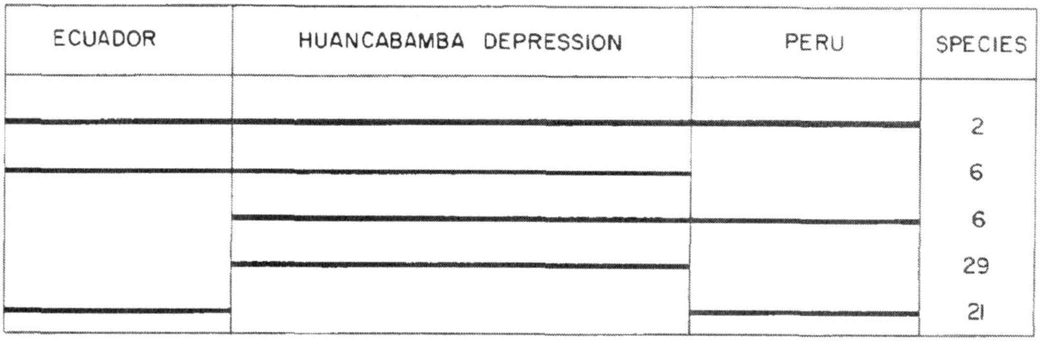

Fig. 15:21. Distribution patterns of Andean amphibians and reptiles in the Huancabamba Depression.
Patrones de distribución de anfibios y reptiles andinos en la Depresión de Huancabamba.

Whereas the western cordillera is a continuous highland range, the eastern cordilleras in Perú and Bolivia are made up of many high ranges separated by long north-south valleys, the major rivers of which break through the cordilleras and drop into the Amazon Basin. For purposes of analysis, I recognize the Cordillera Central in northern Perú (6°–10°S Lat.) bordered to the west by the Río Marañón Valley, the east by the Río Huallaga Valley, and to the south separated from the Nudo de Pasco by the Río Huertas. Although large areas of the Cordillera Central are over 4000 m, no peaks have permanent snow. The northern part of the Cordillera Oriental extending from 10°S to 12°S Lat. includes the Nudo de Pasco and cordilleras south to the Río Mantaro Valley, which also forms the eastern border of the region. In the northern part of the Cordillera Oriental, extensive areas are above 4000 m, and the Nevado Hueyta Pailana has permanent snow above 5000 m.

The southern part of the Cordillera Oriental in Perú begins at the Río Tambo Valley and is continuous with the eastern cordilleras of Bolivia. In Perú the eastern cordillera is bordered on the west by the Río Apurimac Valley and consists of many high ranges (Cordillera de Vilcabamba, Cordillera de Vilca-

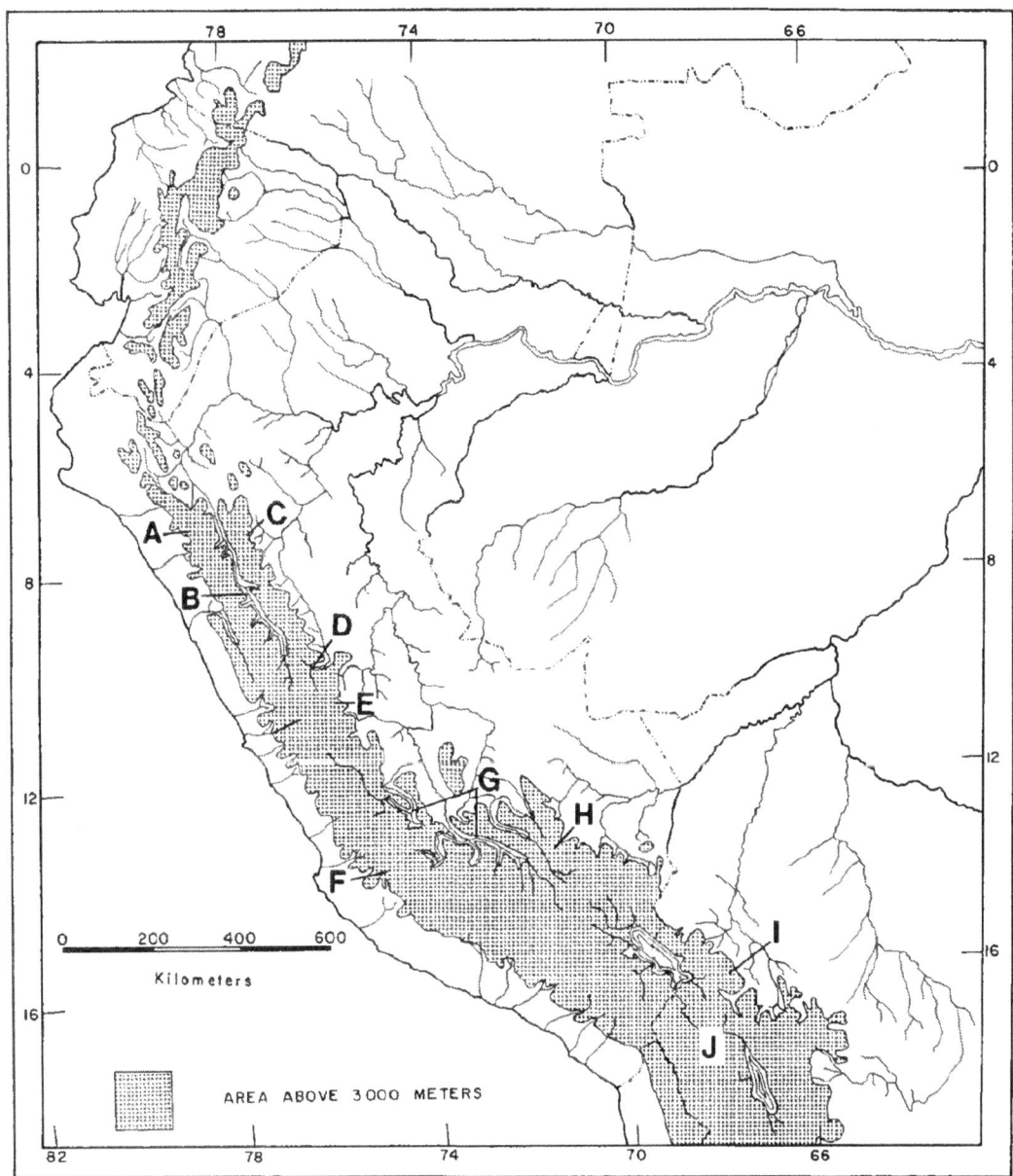

Fig. 15:22. The central Andes. A. Cordillera Occidental North; B. Upper Marañón Valley; C. Cordillera Central; D. Upper Huallaga Valley; E. Cordillera Oriental North; F. Cordillera Occidental South; G. Mantaro-Apurimac Valley; H. Cordillera Oriental South; I. Cordillera Oriental de Bolivia; J. Altiplano.
Los Andes centrales.

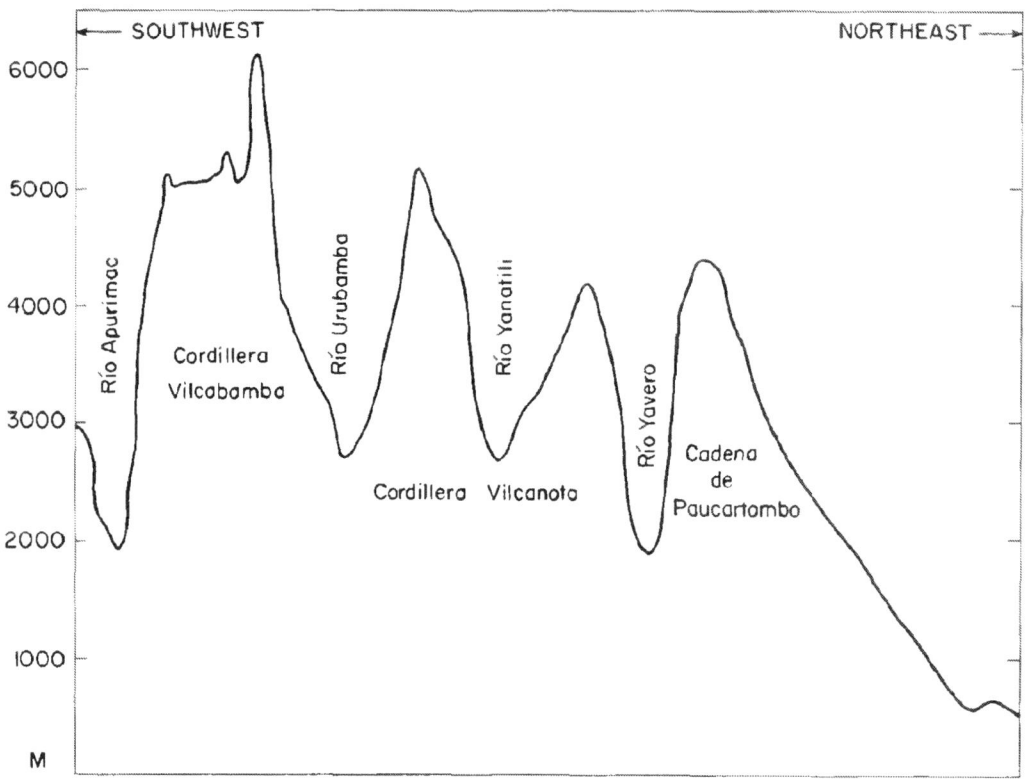

Fig. 15:23. Profile of the Cordillera Oriental in southern Perú.
Perfil de la Cordillera Oriental en el sur del Perú.

nota, and Cordillera de Carabaya) having many peaks with permanent snow, the highest of which is the Nevado Salcantaya (6271 m). Lower front ranges (Cadena de Paucartambo, Cadena de Pantiacolla) do not exceed 4500 m; the deep valleys separating the various ranges give a relief of 2000 to 3000 m to the cordillera (Fig. 15:23). The major rivers dissecting the mountains are the Río Apurimac, Río Urubamba, and Río Vilcanota.

In Bolivia the eastern cordillera consists of a single range, the Cordillera Real. In the northwest and to the southeast there are two ranges—the Cordillera Central separated by the Río Caipe from the outer range, the Cordillera Oriental. The highest peaks are in the snow-covered Cordillera Real, where four peaks exceed 6000 m, and the highest is Cerro Illimani (6460 m). The Cordillera Real drops precipitously into the Amazon Basin; the steep slopes dissected by deep ravines are known as the Yungas.

Rising from the lowlands of the upper Amazon Basin, several mountain ranges reaching above 2500 m are isolated from the main Andean cordillera. These ranges in Perú are, from north to south, Cerros de Otanahui, Cordillera Azul, Cerro de la Sal, and Serranía de Sira.

The major montane valleys separating the principal cordilleras are those of the Río Marañón, and Río Huallaga flowing northward in northern Perú, and the Río Mantaro flowing southeastward in central Perú, and the Río Apurimac flowing northwestward in southern Perú. The Mantaro and Apurimac converge to form the Río Ene; thus, these two valleys are placed together for the purposes of analysis.

The initial uplift of the central Andes was

in the Miocene (Harrington, 1962, Auboden, et al 1973) with final major uplift completed by the end of the Phocene and some additional elevation in the Pleistocene (Petersen, 1958, Dollfus, 1960, Rutland, et al, 1965, Ahlfeld 1970, James, 1971, 1973, Gansser, 1973) Considerable Pleistocene and Recent glaciation in the Peruvian cordilleras depressed snow lines as much as 1500 m during at least two glaciations (Hastenrath, 1967, Kinzl, 1968, Simpson this volume), the last major glaciation in the Cordillera de Vilcanota has been dated as 28,000 to 14,000 years b p (Mercer and Palacios, 1977)

The Cordillera Occidental is arid throughout its length with low xerophytic vegetation on the high Pacific slopes and puna on the high eastern slopes The eastern and northern slopes of the easternmost ranges of the eastern cordilleras support lush cloud forest, the crests of these outer ranges have subpáramo and/or wet puna habitats The western and southern slopes of the outer ranges are dry with puna and low xerophytic vegetation The high ridges of the interior ranges of the eastern cordilleras are drier than the outer ranges and have extensive areas of puna The deep valleys between the ranges are dry with low sclerophytic vegetation at higher elevations and dry scrub forest at lower elevations The high montane valleys are extensively cultivated and also support puna, much of which is grazed

The diverse herptofauna of the central Andes has never been summarized In addition to the general works cited previously, the following works are pertinent to the systematics and distribution of amphibians and reptiles of the central Andes Barbour and Noble (1920a) on southern Peruvian taxa, Dixon and Huey (1970) Dixon and Wright (1975) Fritts (1974) and Uzzell (1969, 1970) on lizards, Schmidt and Walker (1943) and Walker (1945) on snakes Duellman (1976, 1978a–c), Duellman and Fritts (1972), Duellman and Toft (1979), Gallardo (1961), Macedo (1960), Schmidt (1954), Silverstone (1975, 1976), and Vellard (1951–1960) on frogs

The herpetofauna of the central Andes, as presently known, consists of 159 species (75, or 48%, endemic to the regions)—5 caecilians (1), 89 frogs (52), 44 lizards (11), 21 snakes (11) One genus of frogs (*Batrachophrynus*) and one of lizards (*Opipeuter*) are endemic to the region Several genera are highly speciose in the central Andes—frogs of the genera *Phrynopus* (Lynch, 1975a), *Telmatobius* (Macedo 1960), and *Gastrotheca* (Duellman and Fritts, 1972), lizards of the genera *Euspondylus* (Uzzell, 1973) and *Stenocercus* (Fritts, 1974) Of the 84 species that occur in the central Andes and elsewhere, 13 also inhabit tropical forests east of the Andes, some of these and some others comprise the 23 species that also occur in humid montane habitats in the northern Andes Eight species also occur on the dry Pacific lowlands, and one of these inhabits dry forest in the northern Andes Eight species (including 2 of 23 noted above) occur in the central Andes and the Huancabamba Depression Only 12 species are shared between the central Andes and the southern Andes (including the Altiplano), one of these also ranges into the cis-Andean lowlands, two occur on the Pacific lowlands, and nine are restricted to high (>2500 m) elevations in the central Andes and at least in the northern parts of the southern Andes

No species of amphibian or reptile occurs in all nine of the regions within the central Andes The most widespread species are the frogs *Pleurodema marmorata*, *Telmatobius marmoratus*, *Bufo spinulosus*, the lizard *Liolaemus multiformis*, and the snake *Tachymenis peruviana* These are the only species that occur in eastern and western cordilleras and intermontane valleys The major similarities in the cordilleras are among the eastern ranges which individually share 9 to 14 species, with three species occurring in all four regions (Fig 15 24) Only three species are shared between the northern and southern parts of the Cordillera Occidental, and no more than five species are common to any part of the Cordillera Occidental and any range in the eastern cordilleras The similarities of the eastern ranges are principally in those species that inhabit the cloud forests between 1000 and 2000 m, the three species with distributions including all four regions of the eastern cordilleras are forest dwellers

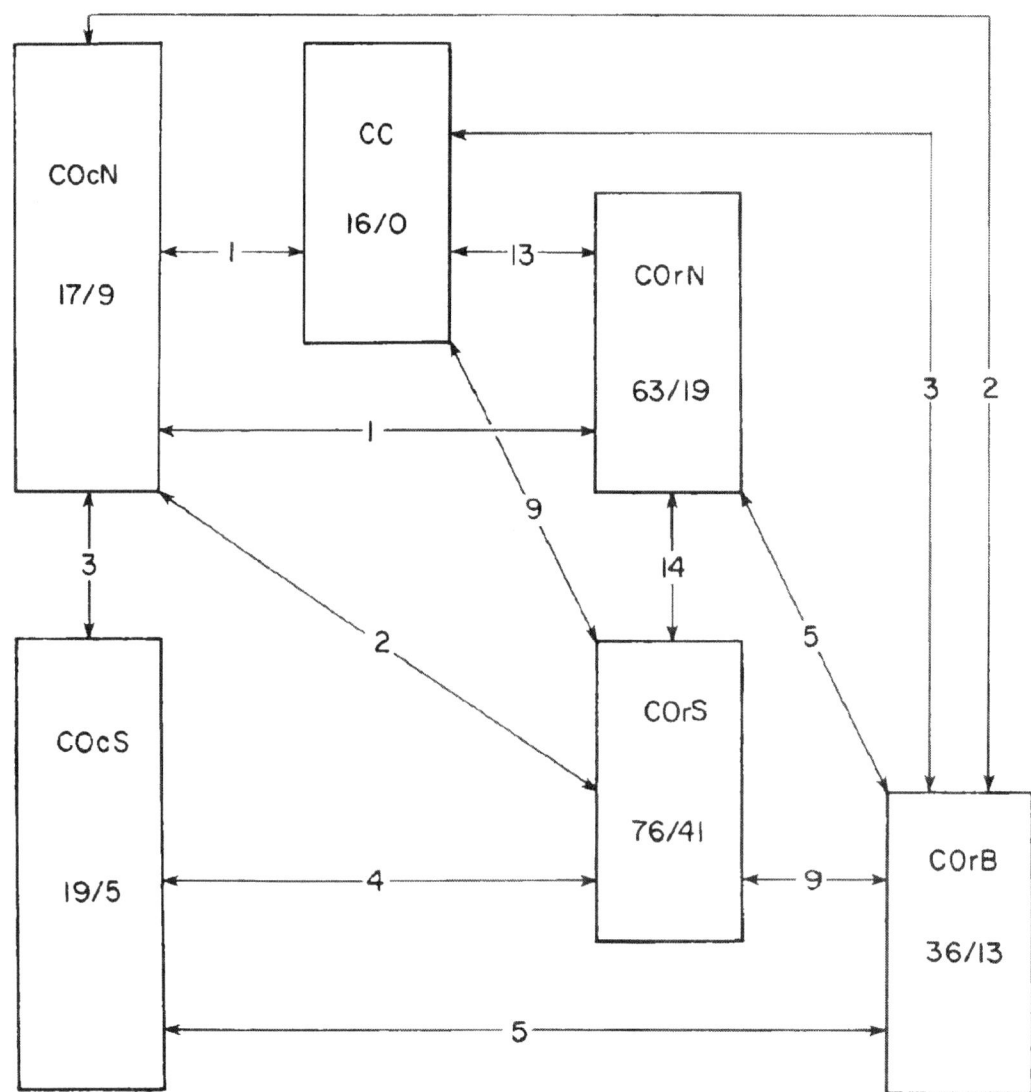

Fig. 15:24. Herpetofaunal comparisons of the Andean ranges in the central Andes. Numbers in blocks are number of species/number of endemic species; numbers of shared species are within arrows. CC = Cordillera Central; COcN = Cordillera Occidental North; COcS = Cordillera Occidental South; COrB = Cordillera Oriental de Bolivia; COrN = Cordillera Oriental North; COrS = Cordillera Oriental South.

Comparaciones faunísticas de la herpetofauna de las cordilleras andinas de los Andes centrales. Números dentro de bloques representan número de especies/número de especies endémicas; número de especies en común están en las flechas.

—two lizards (*Prionodactylus argulus* and *P. manicatus*) and one snake (*Chironius monticola*). The faunal list from the Cordillera Central is unrealistic; the area has not been studied adequately.

The species richness in the southern part of the Cordillera Oriental reflects the complex topography and diverse habitats in that region (Fig. 15:25). Elevational changes in one inter-Andean valley result in striking differ-

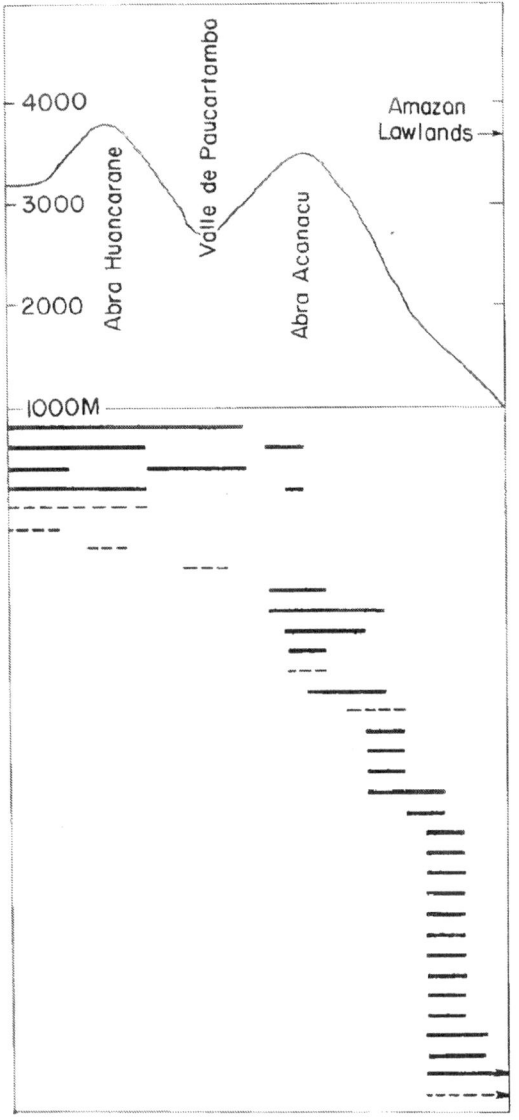

Fig. 15:25. Transect from the upper Río Vilcanota Valley across the Cordillera de Vilcanota (Abra Huancarane), Río Yavare Valley (Paucartambo), Cadena de Paucartambo (Abra Acanacu), and down the Río Cosñipata Valley to the Amazon lowlands. Each line is the distribution of one species; solid lines are amphibians and broken lines are reptiles.

Transect desde el valle del alto Río Vilcanota (Abra Huancarane), valle del Río Yavare (Paucartambo), Cadena de Paucartambo (Abra Acanacu), y hacia abajo del valle del Río Cosñipata hasta las tierras bajas del Amazonas. Cada línea representa la distribución de una especie; las líneas continuas representan a anfibios y las líneas discontinuas a reptiles.

ences in habitats and changes in species composition. For example, in the Río Urubamba Valley, three species of lizards of the genus *Proctoporus* replace one another along the length of the valley between the Cordillera de Vilcabamba and the Cordillera de Vilcanota. Likewise, in the same valley and Cordillera de Vilcanota, marsupial frogs have essentially parapatric distributions—*Gastrotheca marsupiata* is on the valley floor, *G. ochoai* inhabits bromeliads on the cliffs of the cordillera, and *G. excubitor* lives on the high parts of the cordillera (Duellman and Fritts, 1972).

The high montane valleys in Perú have a depauperate herpetofauna with a total of 20 species (7 endemic); otherwise, the species are shared with the neighboring cordilleras and to a lesser extent with the other valleys. The toad *Bufo trifolium* is the only species occurring in the Huallaga, Marañón, and Mantaro-Apurimac valleys, and the frog, *Gastrotheca peruana* occurs in the Huallaga and Marañón valleys. The most notable endemism is the monotypic frog genus *Batrachophrynus* restricted to Lago Junín and streams in the upper Río Mantaro Valley. Five species in the Mantaro-Apurimac Valley are shared with the Altiplano in southern Perú and Bolivia; all of these are widespread highland species.

Southern Andes

Included in the southern Andes are the cordilleras in Argentina and Chile and the Altiplano from southern Perú through Bolivia to Argentina. As noted previously, the Cordillera Occidental in Perú is continuous with the Andes of Chile and western Bolivia; the Cordillera Central in Bolivia is continuous with the Andes of northern Argentina. The Chilean and Argentinean ranges unite south of the Altiplano at about 27°S Lat. (Fig. 15:26).

The Altiplano, in its broadest sense, extends about 1400 km north–south; its greatest width is about 300 km in Bolivia. Elevations of this high plateau range from 3400 to 4000 m; drainage is centripetal, forming lakes or salt basins. Precipitation in the form of rain or snow is mostly in the summer and de-

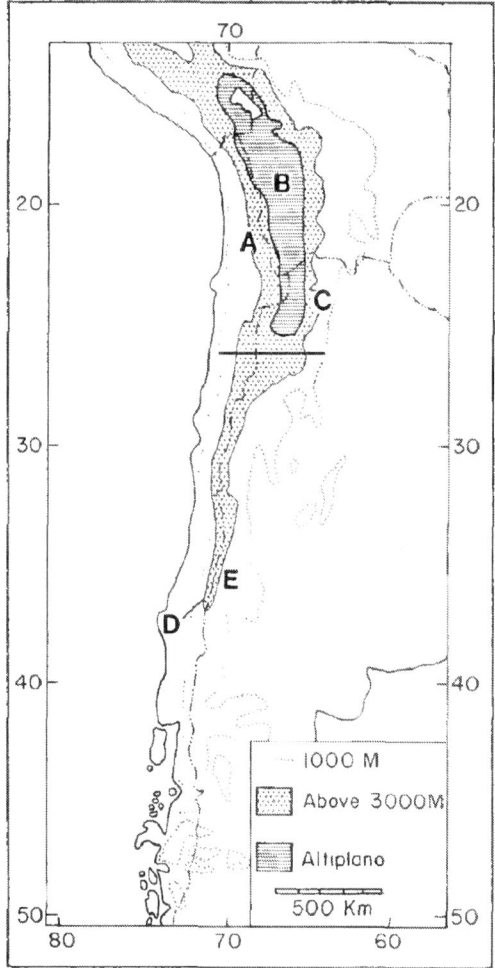

Fig. 15:26. The southern Andes. A. Northern Chile; B. Altiplano; C. Northern Argentina; D. Southern Chile; E. Southern Argentina.
Los Andes del sur.

creases from about 500 mm annually in the north to essentially zero in the south. The vegetation of the northern and eastern parts of the Altiplano is puna dominated by bunch grasses, principally *Festuca*, but also *Poa* and *Stipa*, low (<1 m) shrubs of *Adesmia* and *Parastrephia* (Troll, 1959; Cabrera, 1968). To the south and west even bunch grasses become sparse and eventually absent in extensive "salares."

The Andes of northern Argentina have extensive areas over 4500 m and some peaks exceeding 6000 m, the highest being Cerro Bonete (6872 m). North- and south-flowing rivers separate lower eastern front ranges from the higher major cordillera which descends westward to the Altiplano. The Andes in northern Chile from a high main cordillera with many snow-covered peaks exceeding 6000 m; the highest in the extreme north is Cerro Parinacota (6330 m), whereas farther south near the southern end of the Altiplano, Nevado Ojos del Salado reaches 6880 m. The Andean precordillera exceeds 4500 m in most areas and drops precipitously to the narrow, xeric coastal strip. South of 27°S Lat. the single Andean cordillera continues for 3000 km to the tip of the continent. Whereas many peaks in the northern part of the range exceed 6000 m, including Cerro Aconcagua at 6959 m (the highest mountain in the New World), to the south there are few peaks over 4000 m. Equally important biologically are the elevations of passes between the eastern and western slopes; north of 31°S Lat. there are no passes below 4000 m. Passes between 2000 and 3000 m exist between 35° and 37°S Lat., south of which are found the only passes below 2000 m. Of course, passes at higher latitudes are correspondingly higher biologically. Although the western slopes of the Andes descend rapidly to the Pacific coast or to the Valle Longitudinal separated from the Pacific by the Cordillera de la Costa, the eastern slopes are much more complex with numerous precordilleran ranges, some of which, such as the Sierra Grande and Sierra de San Luís, are completely separated from the principal cordillera. In the south, the Andes descend only to the Patagonian plateaus at 600 to 1300 m.

The Pacific slopes of the Andes in northern Chile (south to about 27°S Lat.) are extremely arid with little vegetation, which in some places consists of only scattered cacti; at elevations above 4000 m, puna grasses are present. In a transition area between the desert and the austral forests (30°–38°S Lat.) low, sparse matorral is present on the Pacific slopes (Simpson, this volume).

The Andes in northern Argentina have puna at high elevations and forest at lower elevations. From north to south (about 28°S Lat.) there is a change from cloud forest to evergreen forest and deciduous broadleaf forest. At about 26°S Lat to 38°S Lat, the eastern slopes of the Andes are arid with deciduous forest existing in river valleys and Patagonian scrub infiltrating the lower slopes to 2000 m (Roig, 1972); the Patagonian scrub crosses the continental divide at some low passes. South of 38°S Lat on the Pacific slopes and 36°S Lat on the eastern slopes are the austral forests characterized by a diversity of *Nothofagus* and in places dominated by *Araucaria* or *Fitzroya* (Formas, this volume). Within this area is the so-called lake region of the southern Andes where cold streams cascade down from glaciers.

The Andes in southern Chile and Argentina were uplifted nearly to their present heights by the end of the Miocene (Dott, et al., 1977). At that time, the initial uplift of the northern part of the Argentine, Chilean, and Bolivian Andes and the Altiplano took place (Petersen, 1958; Rutland, et al., 1965). The final, major orogeny of the Altiplano and the principal cordilleras in northern Argentina and Chile was completed by the end of the Pliocene (Turner, 1972; Yrigoyen, 1972; James, 1971, 1973), whereas at least some of the extra-cordilleran ranges in Argentina were elevated later (Simpson and Vervoorst, 1977), and the coastal cordillera of Chile was uplifted earlier (Okada, 1971). The southern Andes were extensively glaciated during the Pleistocene, with large montane glaciers persisting to the present; at the height of glaciation all of the Andes south of 30°S Lat were entirely glaciated (Patterson and Lanning, 1967; Heusser, 1974).

The herpetofauna of Chile has been reviewed thoroughly by Cei (1962) and Donoso-Barros (1966, 1970). Cei (1979) reviewed the amphibians of Argentina, but the reptiles have not been summarized. The only significant paper on the Altiplano is Parker's (1940). Important works dealing with frogs are, as follow: genus *Telmatobius*—Vellard (1946), Gallardo (1962), Laurent (1970, 1973, 1977), Veloso and Trueb (1976), and Cei (1977), genus *Gastrotheca*—Laurent (1967, 1969a,b, 1976), genus *Bufo*—Gallardo (1967), Cei (1968, 1972). Barrio (1965) discussed the *Hyla pulchella* complex, Duellman and Veloso (1977) reviewed *Pleurodema*, and Lynch (1978b) summarized data on *Alsodes*. The iguanid lizards have been studied by Cei (1971, 1973, 1974a,b), Cei and Castro (1973), and Donoso-Barros (1972).

The herpetofauna of the southern Andes consists of 64 species (30 frogs, 31 lizards, 3 snakes). No genera are endemic to the southern Andes, but austral endemics such as *Alsodes* are shared with the lowland forests, *Diplolaemus* and *Phymaturus* are shared with Patagonia and *Garthia* is shared with the Pacific coastal deserts. Of the 64 species, 36 are endemic. Of the 28 nonendemic species, 12 also occur in arid habitats east of the Andes, principally in Patagonia (e.g., the iguanid lizards *Diplolaemus leopardinus*, *Liolaemus bibronii*, *L. elongatus*). Six others occur in lowland *Nothofagus* forests (e.g., frogs such as *Alsodes nodosus* and *Bufo variegatus*), five occur on the arid Pacific lowlands (e.g., lizards such as *Phyllodactylus gerrhopygus* and *Tropidurus peruvianus*). The faunal similarities between the central and southern Andes have already been discussed.

Within the southern Andes, only two species, the toad *Bufo spinulosus* and the snake *Tachymenis peruviana*, occur in all five regions. Despite the high Andean divides, the southern Andes of Chile and those in Argentina share more species (10) than any other two regions (Fig. 15.27). Most of the endemics are frogs of the genera *Alsodes* and *Telmatobius* restricted to separate stream drainages and highland lizards of the genus *Liolaemus*.

The distribution of amphibians and reptiles on either side of the Andes in relation to passes through the high cordillera suggests that available structural habitat (or perhaps food) may limit their distributions instead of altitude and the associated climatic stresses. For example, at 33°S Lat the cordillera is breached by Puerto Bermejo at 3883 m. In the immediate vicinity of the pass two lizards *Liolaemus altissimus* and *L. fitzgeraldi*, reach elevations of 3500 m and 2800 m, respectively and occur on both sides of the Andes (Fig. 15.28). In the same area four other species of lizards occur only on the eastern slopes— *Liolaemus elongatus* (up to 2800 m), *L. rui-*

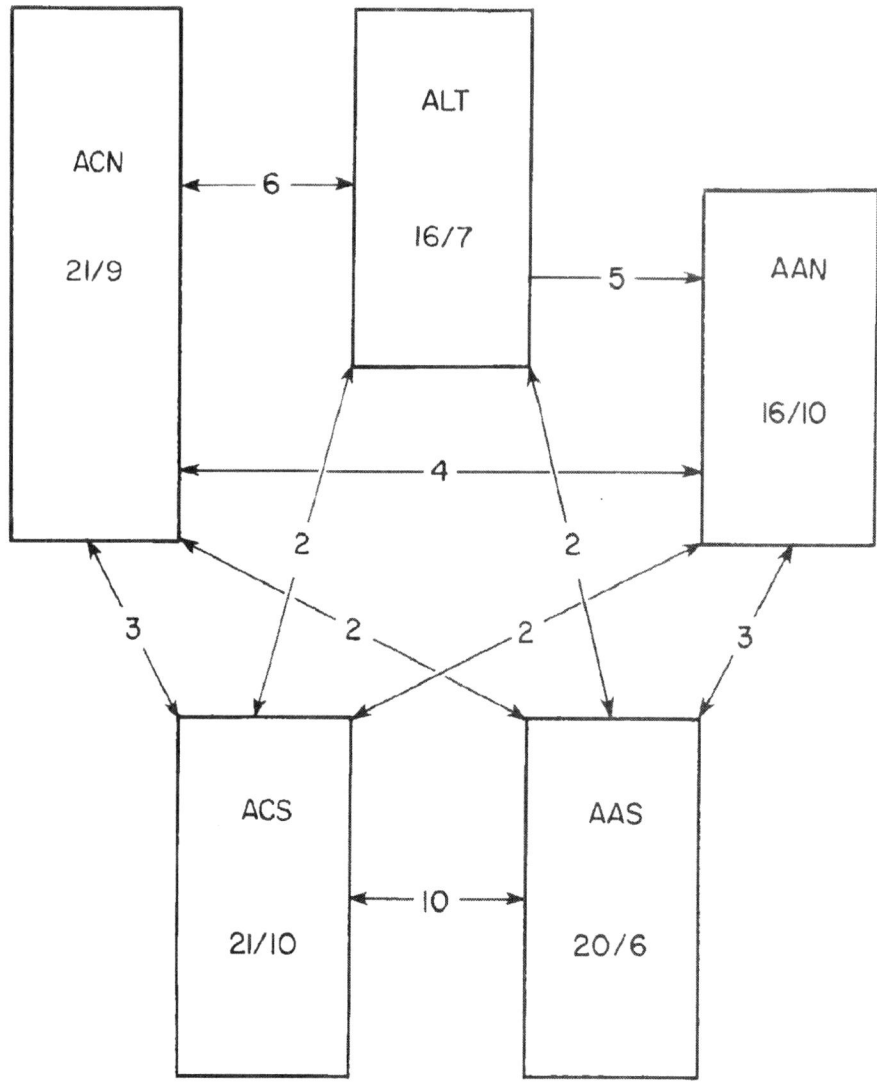

Fig. 15:27. Herpetofaunal comparisons of regions in the southern Andes. Numbers in blocks are numbers of species/number of endemic species; numbers of shared species are within arrows. AAN = Andes of Argentina north; AAS = Andes of Argentina south; ACN = Andes of Chile north; ACS = Andes of Chile south; ALT = Altiplano.

Comparaciones faunísticas de la herpetofauna de las regiones de los Andes del sur. Números dentro de bloques representan número de especies/número de especies endémicas; número de species en común están en las flechas.

bali (2900 m), *Phymaturus palluma* (3500 m), and *Pristidactylus scapulatus* (2900 m). Likewise, two species are restricted to the western slope—*Liolaemus leopardinus* (3000 m) and *L. nigroviridis* (3000 m). On the other hand, farther south there is continuity of habitat through much lower passes. For example, Patagonian scrub continues through Puerto de Buta Malin (37°30'S, 1800 m) onto the western side of the cordillera to Laguna

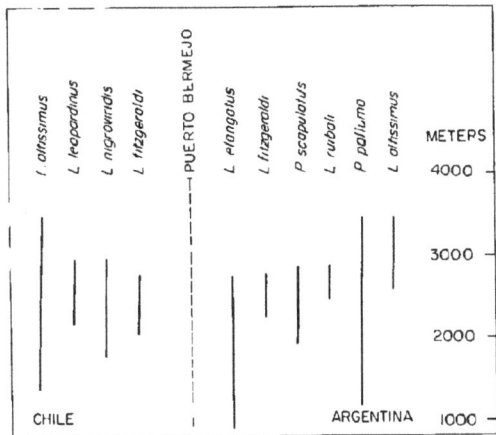

FIG 15 28 Distribution of iguanid lizards on eastern and western slopes of the Andes in the vicinity of Puerto Bermejo, 33°S Lat
Distribucion de saurios iguanidos en las laderas este y oeste de los Andes en la vecindad de Puerto Bermejo, 33°Lat S

de La Laja, where such typical Patagonian species as *Pleurodema bufonina Liolaemus kriegi*, and *Phymaturus palluma* occur

ANALYSIS OF DISTRIBUTION PATTERNS

Once the major patterns of distribution in the various physiographic regions of the Andes have been described and documented, it is desirable to analyze the total Andean herpetofauna The testing of the a priori division of the Andes into six major units shows that the faunal resemblance factors are all less than 0 1 except between the central Andes and the Southern Andes (Table 15 2) Thus, the recognition of the central and southern Andes as distinct major units is not so realistic as the distinction of the other units Although the Huancabamba Depression has some endemics, it shares eight species with the northern and eight with the central Andes

A cluster analysis of all 727 species in 27 regions emphasizes the close similarity between the Cordillera Occidental in southern Perú and in northern Chile (Fig 15 29) This analysis also shows the relatively close similarity of the eastern and western slopes of the Andes in southern Argentina and Chile, the similarity between the Altiplano and the Mantaro-Apurimac Valley and the similarity of the Cordillera Occidental in northern Perú with the upper Marañón and Huallaga valleys Likewise, the distinctness of the Venezuelan highlands Sierra Nevada de Santa Marta, and Huancabamba Depression are evident

A second analysis involved only those 147 species having distributions above 2500 m (Fig 15 30), this analysis eliminated four regions—Seriania de Paria, Cerro Turumiquire, Cordillera de la Costa and Sierra Nevada de Santa Marta The Mérida Andes and the Cordillera Occidental in Colombia are distinctive in sharing no taxa with any other region The other regions of the northern Andes cluster together and are weakly linked with the central and southern Andes and the Huancabamba Depression The Andes of southern Chile and southern Argentina each has two endemic species and no species shared with any other region, thus, each region is distinct from all of the others

These analyses and knowledge of the physiography and environments of the Andes allow a general interpretation of the kinds and effectiveness of barriers to herpetofaunal

TABLE 15 2—Faunal Resemblance of the Herpetofauna in Six Major Andean Regions
Numbers of species in a given region are in boldface, numbers of species in common to two regions are in Roman, and the faunal resemblance factors $[2C/(N_1 + N) = FRF]$ are in italics

	Venezuelan Andes	Sierra Nevada de Santa Marta	Northern Andes	Huancabamba Depression	Central Andes	Southern Andes
Venezuelan Andes	**80**	*0 040*	*0 028*	*0 000*	*0 008*	*0 000*
Sierra Nevada de Santa Marta	2	**21**	*0 018*	*0 000*	*0 000*	*0 000*
Northern Andes	7	4	**415**	*0 035*	*0 008*	*0 000*
Huancabamba Depression	0	0	8	**43**	*0 079*	*0 000*
Central Andes	1	0	23	8	**159**	*0 116*
Southern Andes	0	0	0	0	13	**64**

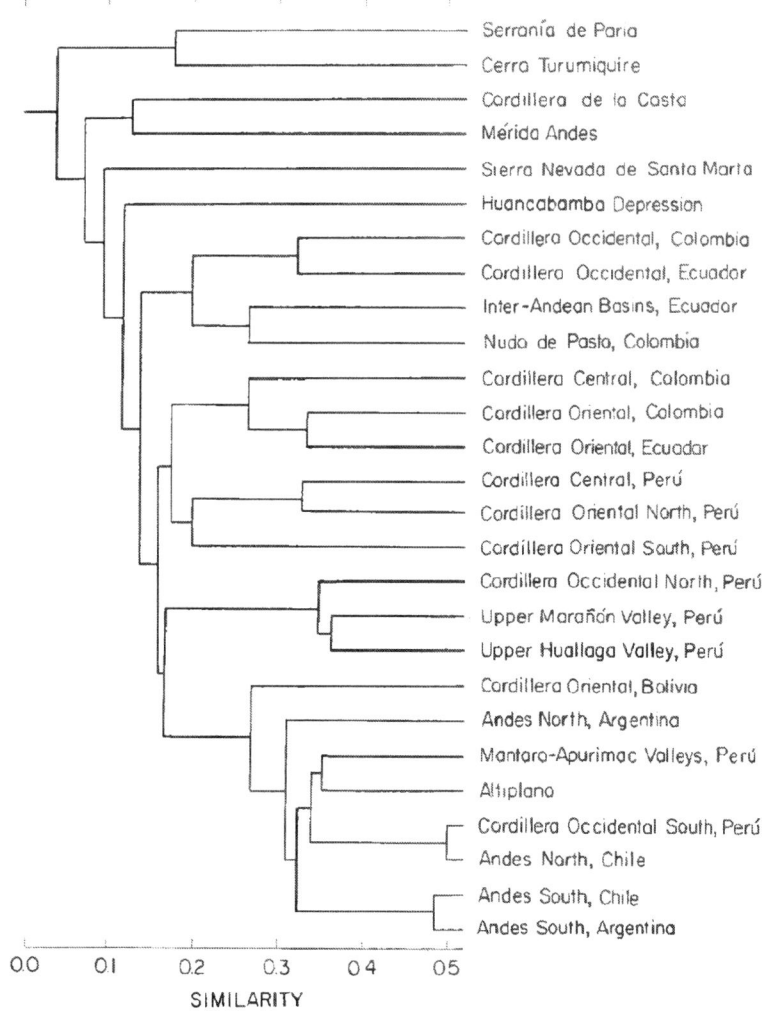

Fig. 15:29. Cluster analysis of 727 species of amphibians and reptiles in 27 physiographic regions of the Andes; analysis is by the unweighted pair-group method using arithmetic means.

Análisis de agrupación de 727 especies de anfibios y reptiles en 27 regiones fisiográficas de los Andes. El análisis usa el método de grupos de parejas no compensadas en sus promedios aritméticos.

dispersal in the Andes (Fig. 15:31). The physiographic barriers in the northern part of the Andes coincide with those demonstrated for birds by F. Vuilleumier (1977). The major physiographic barriers separate the major Andean regions—Mérida Andes, Sierra Nevada de Santa Marta, northern Andes and central Andes—from one another, whereas minor barriers are within major regions—between the Mérida Andes and the Cordillera de la Costa, and between the Cordillera Occidental in Colombia and the rest of the northern Andes. The major ecological barrier is the drastic change from cloud forest to relatively dry puna, which follows the upper reaches of the outer ranges of the eastern cor-

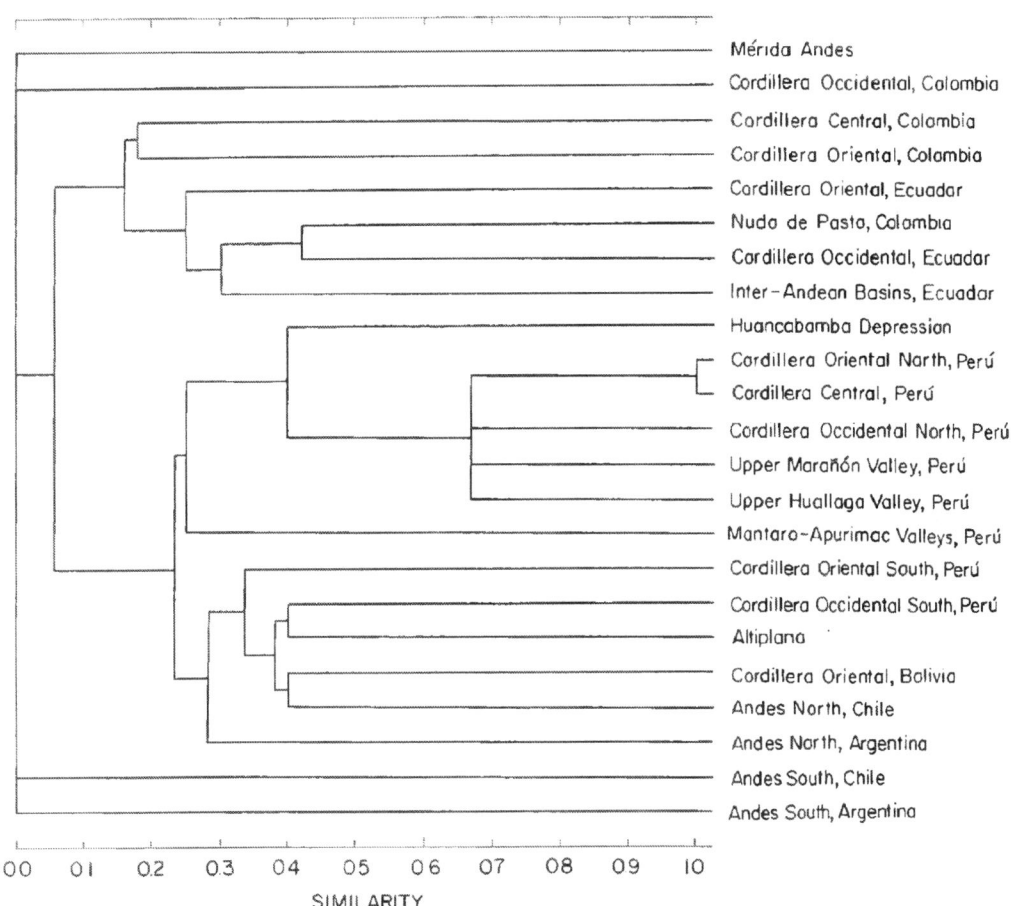

Fig. 15:30. Cluster analysis of 147 species of amphibians and reptiles occurring only above 2500 m in 23 physiographic regions of the Andes; analysis is by the unweighted pair-group method using arithmetic means.
Análisis de agrupación de 147 especies de anfibios y reptiles que habitan solamente por encima de los 2500 m en 23 regiones fisiográficas de los Andes. Método al igual que figura 29.

dillera in the central Andes. Comparatively broad latitudinal transition zones exist between the cloud forest and the deciduous forests on the eastern slopes in northern Argentina, and between the *Nothofagus* forests of the southern Andes and the arid slopes to the north. Faunal comparisons of these eight major ecogeographic regions in the Andes reveal that the regions separated by major geographical barriers or ecological differences have faunal resemblance factors of less than 0.1, whereas those separated by minor physiographic barriers have factors greater than 0.1 (Table 15:3).

It is obvious that species richness is highest in those tropical regions supporting both cloud forest and equable habitats above tree line—Cordillera Oriental in Ecuador (164 species), Cordillera Occidental in Ecuador (137 species), Cordillera Oriental in Colombia (103 species). Between the Equator and 24°S Lat. there is a dramatic decline in species richness, most notable in amphibians; farther south there is little change (Fig. 15:32).

Endemism is as high as 76 percent in the Sierra Nevada de Santa Marta, whereas the average percentage of endemic species in any

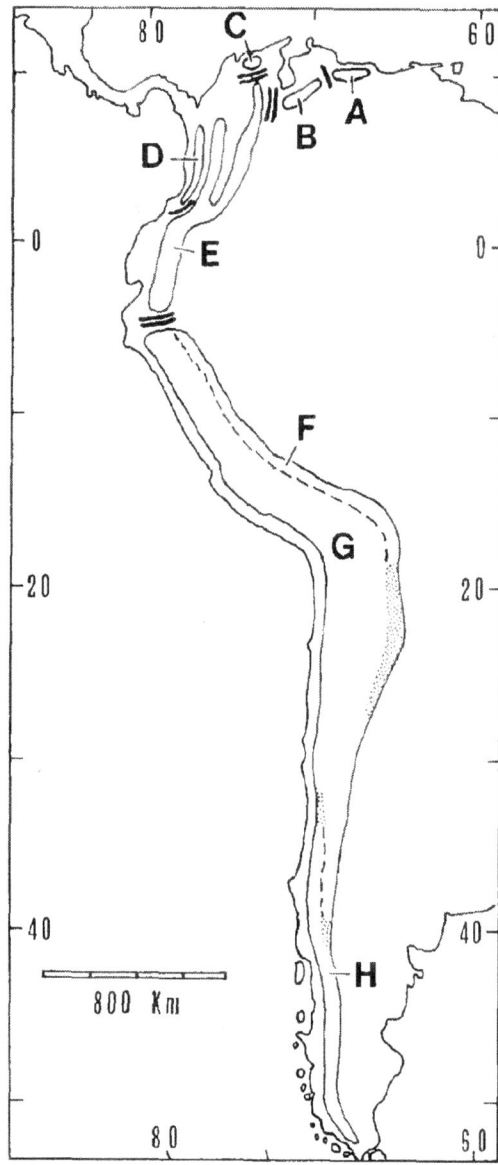

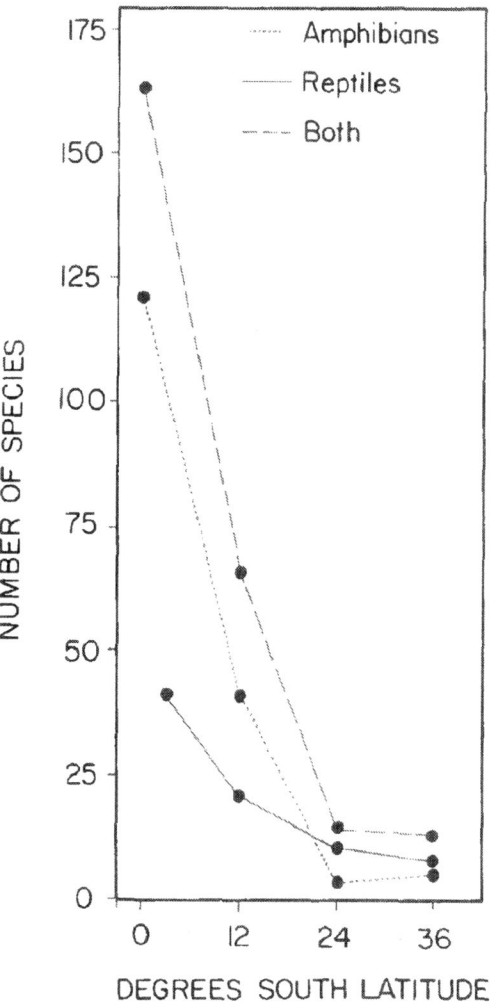

Fig. 15:31. Diagrammatic map of the Andes showing barriers to herpetofaunal dispersal. Two solid lines = major physiographic barriers; single solid lines = minor physiographic barriers; broken lines = major ecological barriers; shaded areas = transition zones between ecologically different regions. A. Cordillera de la Costa; B. Mérida Andes; C. Sierra Nevada de Santa Marta; D. Cordillera Occidental de Colombia; E. Northern Andes; F. Eastern slopes of central Andes; G. Nonforested central and southern Andes; H. Forested southern Andes.

Fig. 15:32. Herpetofaunal species richness at different latitudes in the Andes. Data were accumulated for species within one degree north and south of the latitude given; only species occurring above 1000 m are included.

Riqueza de especie de la herpetofauna a diferentes latitudes en los Andes. Información fue acumulada para las especies dentro de un grado al norte y al sur de la latitud dada; sólo las especies que ocurren por sobre los 1000 m están incluidas.

Mapa diagramático de los Andes mostrando barreras para la dispersión de la herpetofauna. Dos líneas continuas = barreras fisiográficas mayores; una línea continua = barrera fisiográfica menor; líneas discontinuas = barreras ecológicas mayores; áreas sombreadas = zonas de transición entre regiones diferentes ecológicamente.

TABLE 15.3—Faunal Resemblance of the Herpetofauna in Eight Major Zoo-geographic Regions of the Andes. Numbers of species in a given region are in boldface, numbers of species in common to two regions are in Roman, and the faunal resemblance factors $[2C/(N_1 + N_2) = FRF]$ are in italics.

	Cordillera de la Costa	Merida Andes	Sierra Nevada de Santa Marta	Cordillera Occidental, Colombia	Northern Andes	Eastern Front, Central Andes	Nonforested Cent. & S. Andes	Forested Southern Andes
Cordillera de la Costa	**46**	*0.129*	*0.030*	*0.054*	*0.008*	*0.013*	*0.000*	*0.000*
Merida Andes	5	**32**	*0.075*	*0.082*	*0.034*	*0.014*	*0.000*	*0.000*
Sierra Nevada de Santa Marta	1	2	**21**	*0.023*	*0.019*	*0.000*	*0.000*	*0.000*
Cordillera Occidental, Colombia	3	2	1	**66**	*0.163*	*0.011*	*0.000*	*0.000*
Northern Andes	2	7	4	37	**386**	*0.093*	*0.004*	*0.000*
Eastern Front, Central Andes	1	1	0	1	23	**107**	*0.049*	*0.000*
Nonforested Cent. & S. Andes	0	0	0	0	1	7	**78**	*0.055*
Forested Southern Andes	0	0	0	0	0	0	3	**31**

one of the 27 regions is 40.9 (Table 15.4). The apparent absence of endemics in the Cordillera Central of Perú probably is indicative of the poor sampling of the region, whereas the low values for the Nudo de Pasto, inter-Andean valleys in Ecuador, and the Marañón Valley in Perú are realistic in that most species in these regions are shared with adjacent regions. The presence of many species of a given genus in one region is indicative of local speciation and endemism. This is especially true of frogs of the genera *Eleutherodactylus*, *Colostethus*, and *Centrolenella* in the northern Andes, where the species per genus is 3.3 to 3.9 in the eastern cordilleras of Colombia and Ecuador and the Cordillera Occidental in Ecuador, this high number is approached only by the Cordillera Oriental in southern Perú (2.8), where there is also great differentiation of *Eleutherodactylus* and the Altiplano (2.7) where there are six species of *Liolaemus* (Table 15.4). However, there is no direct correlation between the total percentage of endemic species and the numbers of species per genus in that region. For example, the genus per species value is 1.6 in the Sierra Nevada de Santa Marta, where 76 percent of the species are endemic.

Substantial data on altitudinal differences in species richness and endemism are not available for most regions of the Andes. As already discussed in the account of the northern Andes, a distinct middle elevation fauna occurs in cloud forest and another element on the high ridges; species richness is much higher in the cloud forest, and endemism is likely to be high in both, certainly higher than in the adjacent lowlands (see especially Table 15.4 and Figs. 15.18–19).

EXTRA-ANDEAN FAUNAL RELATIONSHIPS

Once the Andean herpetofauna has been defined and circumscribed, it is necessary to ascertain the relationships of the faunas of the Andes before attempting to determine the origin of the Andean herpetofauna. Primarily this will be done at the generic level. Eighty-eight genera of amphibians and reptiles occur at elevations of more than 1000 m in the Andes. More than half (47) of these genera are not primarily Andean in their distribution. Some are represented in the Andes by lowland species that ascend the highlands to elevations of more than 1000 m (13 genera) and others (23 genera) have species restricted to Andean slopes, although most of the species occur elsewhere. The Andes are peripheral to

TABLE 15 4—Genera and Species of Amphibians and Reptiles in Each of 27 Regions of the Andes

Region	Genera	% Northern Genera	Species	% Northern Species	Endemic Species	% Species Endemic	Species per Genus
Serrania de Paria	3	100	4	100	3	75	1 3
Cerro Turumiquire	5	100	7	100	5	71	1 4
Cordillera de la Costa	26	100	46	100	34	74	1 8
Mérida Andes	16	100	32	100	18	56	2 0
Sierra Nevada de Santa Marta	13	100	21	100	16	76	1 6
Cordillera Occidental, Colombia	27	100	66	100	29	44	2 4
Cordillera Central, Colombia	31	100	78	100	42	54	2 3
Cordillera Central, Perú	12	100	16	100	0	0	1 3
Cordillera Oriental Colombia	30	97	103	99	36	35	3 4
Cordillera Oriental, Ecuador	42	95	164	98	74	45	3 9
Cordillera Occidental, Ecuador	41	93	137	95	65	47	3 3
Nudo de Pasto, Colombia	11	91	23	96	1	4	2 1
Cordillera Oriental North, Peru	30	90	63	92	19	30	2 1
Cordillera Oriental, Bolivia	21	86	36	89	13	36	1 7
Inter-Andean Basins, Ecuador	12	83	22	82	3	14	1 8
Huancabamba Depression	23	83	44	73	29	66	1 9
Cordillera Oriental South, Peru	28	79	76	84	41	55	2 8
Andes North, Argentina	9	33	16	25	10	63	1 8
Cordillera Occidental North, Peru	10	30	17	24	9	53	1 7
Mantaro-Apurimac Valleys Peru	8	25	12	17	4	33	1 5
Upper Marañon Valley, Peru	4	25	6	17	1	17	1 5
Upper Huallaga Valley, Peru	5	20	5	20	2	40	1 0
Altiplano	6	17	16	6	7	44	2 7
Cordillera Occidental South, Perú	9	0	19	0	5	26	2 1
Andes North, Chile	10	0	21	0	9	43	2 1
Andes South, Chile	9	0	21	0	10	48	2 3
Andes South, Argentina	9	0	20	0	6	30	2 2

the main distributions of 12 other genera, which do have representatives in the Andes (Table 15 5) Although these account for 55 percent of the Andean genera they include only 144 (20%) of the 727 species Only six of these 47 genera have more than five species in the Andes Caecilia (12), Anolis (18) Leptotyphlops (6), Dipsas (11), Leimadophis (6), and Bothrops (9)

Nineteen genera are endemic to the Andes, these contain 94 (13%) of the Andean species The other 22 genera containing 491 Andean species, are either widespread in the Neotropical Region or also occur in extra-Andean regions (Table 15 6) Two genera (Bufo and Hyla) are widespread and speciose in South America (and elsewhere), but are represented in the Andes by distinct groups (B spinulosus, H bogotensis, and H larinopygion groups), as well as lowland species on the slopes The speciose genus Eleutherodactylus is represented by 154 species in the Andes, but it occurs widely throughout the American tropics Four other genera of frogs —Atelopus (27 Andean species), Colostethus (39) Gastrotheca (33) and Centrolenella (45)—and one of snakes—Atractus (39)—are primarily Andean but are widespread in South America Likewise, two genera of iguanid lizards—Liolaemus (24 Andean species) and Stenocercus (26)—are speciose in the Andes, but the former is widespread in temperate South America, and the latter also occurs in the Amazon Basin Of the remaining genera, seven (Bolitoglossa, Rhamphophryne, Hemiphractus Anadia, Pronodactylus, Diaphorolepis, and Lygophis) also occur in the tropical lowlands and in Central America, whereas Euspondylus is extra-Andean only in the adjacent tropical lowlands Three genera (Alsodes, Ctenoblepharis, and Pachymenis) are extra-Andean only in temperate South America, along with Pleurodema, which also occurs widely in dry tropical regions

When viewing the distribution patterns of all 88 genera known from the Andes we find the greatest similarities with the Amazon

TABLE 15.5—Patterns of Andean Distributions of Genera that are Principally Extra-Andean

Lowland Species on Lower Slopes	Differentiated on Low-moderate Slopes	Peripheral to Range of Genus
Leptodactylus	Caecilia	Euparkerella
Phyllobates[1]	Epicrionops	Ischnocnema
Gonatodes	Dendrobates	Flectonotus
Polychrus	Osteocephalus	Phyllodactylus
Tropidurus	Phyllomedusa	Basiliscus
Alopoglossus	Glossostoma	Diplolaemus
Cercosaura	Gartha	Phymaturus
Neusticurus	Lepidoblepharis	Tropidophis
Ptychoglossus	Pseudogonatodes	Lampropeltis
Liotyphlops	Anolis	Liophis
Clelia	Enyalioides	Sibon
Leptophis	Pristidactylus	Sibynomorphus
Micrurus	Leptotyphlops	
	Chironius	
	Dendrophidion	
	Dipsas	
	Leimadophis	
	Mastigodryas	
	Oxyrhopus	
	Philodryas	
	Rhadinaea	
	Tantilla	
	Bothrops	

[1] Most of the species of *Phyllobates* recognized by Silverstone (1976) and listed in Appendix 15.2 have been placed in *Dendrobates* by Myers et al. (1978).

Basin and Central America, each having 47 and 46 genera, respectively, shared with the Andes, these are followed by 42 shared with the Chocó, 36 with southeastern Brasil and 35 with the Guiana Shield. Thirty-three genera are common to the Andes, Amazon Basin, Chocó, and Central America, whereas only 20 are shared by those four regions and the Guiana Shield and southeastern Brasil. The depauperate generic differentiation in temperate South America is reflected in the few number of genera shared by the Andes and Patagonia (11), the Atacama Desert (9), and the austral forests (6). Only four genera are common to all four regions, and only *Bufo* occurs in all of the regions delimited.

The occurrence of genera in the Andes and adjacent areas, such as the Amazon Basin and Patagonia is expected. More interesting are distributions that are disjunct. Six Andean genera also occur in southeastern Brasil but are either absent from the intervening area or have peculiarities about their distributions. The frogs (*Flectonotus*, *Euparkerella*, and *Ischnocnema*) each have one species in the Andes and one in southeastern Brasil; *Ischnocnema* also has one species in the upper Amazon Basin. Marsupial frogs (*Gastrotheca*) are represented by 33 species in the Andes and four in southeastern Brasil, but the genus is unknown in central South America. Two snakes also are represented in the two areas. *Sibynomorphus* has one species in the Andes, one in the Amazon Basin, two in the Chaco and two in southeastern Brasil.[2] *Tropidophis* has one species in the Andes, one in southeastern Brasil and 12 in the West Indies. Other genera that are represented in two or more of the highland regions (Andes, Brasilian highlands, Guiana highlands) also are widespread in the lowlands, although some genera, such as *Atractus*, are speciose in the highland regions and represented by few species in the intervening lowlands.

No strictly highland genus or species is shared by the Andes and the Guiana highlands. However, two closely related hylid frog genera are endemic to the regions—*Cryptobatrachus* (3 species) in the northern Andes and *Stefania* (6 species) in the Guiana highlands.

Thus, although the Andean herpetofauna is comprised of largely endemic species, only

[2] See footnote, p. 389.

19 genera are endemic to the Andes, the 93 species in these genera and 337 Andean species in eight other genera that are primarily Andean account for about 60 percent of the species in the Andes. The generic relationships of the Andean herpetofauna are primarily with the adjacent lowlands and Central America and not with the Brasilian and Guiana highlands.

ORIGIN OF THE ANDEAN HERPETOFAUNA

The poor fossil record of most Andean groups of amphibians and reptiles precludes any kind of accurate historical assessment of phylogenetic relationships and distribution patterns; see Báez and Gasparini (this volume) for a summary of the fossil evidence. Therefore, phylogenetic relationships must be hypothesized from systematic studies of extant taxa, and past distributions must be inferred from existing knowledge of past geological events and evidence concerning paleoclimates. Our knowledge of the geology of the Andes has been summarized by Simpson (this volume), who also synthesized the evidence for Late Cenozoic and Quaternary climatic changes; these phenomena also have been treated in detail for tropical South America by Haffer (this volume) and for temperate South America by Báez and Scillato Yané (this volume). Modern phylogenetic approaches using cladistics as the basis for vicariance or dispersal biogeography (Croizat, et al., 1974; Rosen, 1975; Platnick and Nelson, 1978) are ideal for analysis of faunal origins and subsequent differentiation, but in most groups of Andean amphibians and reptiles, the phylogenetic relationships have yet to be determined in any such refined manner.

Two current methods of determining centers of dispersal (and possibly of origin) involve generalized tracks (Croizat et al., 1974) and areas of congruence (Muller, 1973). The former is based on a cladistic approach and the latter simply on patterns of distribution. Because of the inadequate knowledge of the phylogenetic relationships of many components of the Andean herpetofauna, I have chosen to analyze the herpetofauna first by means of areas of congruence. Subsequent analysis of generalized tracks of those groups that are well known phylogenetically provides corroborating evidence. For purposes of analysis I have used 41 genera and species groups that are primarily Andean in their distribution or at least are highly speciose in the Andes. On the bases of their distributions and known (or presumed) phylogenetic relationships, they have been placed in either a northern assemblage or a southern assemblage (Table 15.7).

Southern Herpetofaunal Assemblage — Two major areas of congruence incorporate six of the nine groups in this assemblage: 1) Austral Forests—*Alsodes*, *Pleurodema*, *Bufo spinulosus* group, *Tachymenis*; 2) Patagonia—*Pleurodema*, *Ctenoblepharis*, *Liolaemus*. The other three genera (*Batrachophrynus*, *Telmatobius*, and *Stenocercus*) are derived from southern groups (Fig. 15.33).

Studies on iguanid lizards by Cei (1973, 1974a,b), Etheridge (1964, 1966, 1967), Paull et al. (1976), and Savage (1958) provide substantial evidence for the recognition of a temperate South American adaptive radiation of tropidurine iguanid lizards. Although the taxonomy of the large iguanid genus *Liolaemus* is still in an alpha state, it is evident that there is a major diversity of species groups in Patagonia and the adjacent Andean foothills and that by comparison with these regions, the *Liolaemus* diversity is less in the Austral forests, Atacama Desert, and the high Andes. Cei (1974a, pers. comm.) considers *Ctenoblepharis* to be derived from *Liolaemus*. *Stenocercus* seems to be a highland sister group of the lowland *Ophryoessoides* (Fritts, 1974); these genera apparently are derived from a tropidurine stock perhaps close to *Proctotretus* (Etheridge pers. comm.). *Tachymenis* is the only genus of snakes widespread in the cool temperate region and the high Andes; it seems to be related to *Philodryas*, which is most diverse in subtropical South America.

Lynch (1978b) provided a cladistic analysis of the genera of telmatobiine leptodactylid frogs; most of the genera are endemic to the

TABLE 15 6—Distribution of Andean Genera of Amphibians and Reptiles in Adjacent Extra-Andean Regions and Neotropical Highlands
(° = Endemic to Andes, numbers of species are Andean/Total)

Genus	Species	Central America	Choco	Amazon Basin	Guiana Highlands	South-eastern Brasil	Patagonia	Austral Forests	Atacama Desert
Caecilia	12/29	+	+	+	+	—	—	—	—
Epicrionops	4/9	—	+	+	+	—	—	—	—
Bolitoglossa	14/63	+	+	+	—	—	—	—	—
Alsodes	6/7	—	—	—	—	—	—	+	—
Amblyphrynus°	2/2	—	—	—	—	—	—	—	—
Batrachophrynus°	2/2	—	—	—	—	—	—	—	—
Eleutherodactylus	153/≅400	+	+	+	+	+	—	—	—
Euparkerella	1/2	—	—	—	—	+	—	—	—
Ischnocnema	1/3	—	—	+	—	+	—	—	—
Leptodactylus	2/32	+	+	+	+	+	—	—	—
Phrynopus°	14/14	—	—	—	—	—	—	—	—
Pleurodema	4/12	+	—	—	—	+	+	+	—
Telmatobius°	30/30	—	—	—	—	—	—	—	—
Geobatrachus°	1/1	—	—	—	—	—	—	—	—
Atelopus	27/39	+	+	+	+	—	—	—	—
Bufo	20/≅190	+	+	+	+	+	+	+	+
Osornophryne°	2/2	—	—	—	—	—	—	—	—
Rhamphophryne	3/6	+	—	+	—	+	—	—	—
Colostethus	39/64	+	+	+	+	+	—	—	—
Dendrobates	4/20	+	+	+	+	+	—	—	—
Phyllobates	3/20	+	+	+	+	—	—	—	—
Amphignathodon°	1/1	—	—	—	—	—	—	—	—
Cryptobatrachus°	3/3	—	—	—	—	—	—	—	—
Flectonotus	1/2	—	—	—	—	+	—	—	—
Gastrotheca	33/40	+	+	—	—	+	—	—	—
Hemiphractus	4/5	+	+	+	—	—	—	—	—
Hyla	21/≅275	+	+	+	+	+	—	—	—
Osteocephalus	2/6	—	—	+	+	+	—	—	—
Phyllomedusa	4/29	+	+	+	—	+	—	—	—
Centrolene°	1/1	—	—	—	—	—	—	—	—
Centrolenella	15/64	+	+	+	+	+	—	—	—
Glossostoma	1/2	+	+	—	—	—	—	—	—
Garthia	1/2	—	—	—	—	—	—	—	+
Gonatodes	3/17	+	+	+	+	+	—	—	—
Lepidoblepharis	1/8	+	+	—	—	—	—	—	—
Phyllodactylus	3/60	+	—	—	—	—	—	—	+
Pseudogonatodes	1/5	—	—	+	+	—	—	—	—
Anolis	18/≅200	+	+	+	+	+	—	—	—
Basiliscus	1/4	+	+	—	—	—	—	—	—
Ctenoblepharis	5/11	—	—	—	—	—	+	—	+
Diplolaemus	1/3	—	—	—	—	—	+	—	—
Enyalioides	2/8	+	+	+	—	—	—	—	—
Liolaemus	24/52	—	—	—	—	+	+	+	+
Phenacosaurus°	3/3	—	—	—	—	—	—	—	—
Phymaturus	1/2	—	—	—	—	—	+	—	—
Polychroides°	1/1	—	—	—	—	—	—	—	—
Polychrus	2/5	+	+	+	+	—	—	—	—
Pristidactylus	1/4	—	—	—	—	—	+	+	—
Stenocercus	26/29	—	—	+	—	—	—	—	—
Tropidurus	2/20	—	—	+	+	+	—	—	+
Alopoglossus	1/6	—	—	+	+	—	—	—	—
Anadia	7/11	+	+	—	—	—	—	—	—
Cercosaura	1/3	—	—	+	+	+	—	—	—
Euspondylus	5/9	—	+	—	—	—	—	—	—
Macropholidus°	1/1	—	—	—	—	—	—	—	—
Neusticurus	3/8	+	—	+	+	—	—	—	—
Opipeuter°	1/1	—	—	—	—	—	—	—	—
Pholidobolus°	5/5	—	—	—	—	—	—	—	—

TABLE 15 6 (Concluded)

Genus	Species	Central America	Chocó	Amazon Basin	Guiana Highlands	South-eastern Brasil	Patagonia	Austral Forests	Atacama Desert
Pnonodactylus	4/5	+	+	+	—	—	—	—	—
Proctoporus°	17/17	—	—	—	—	—	—	—	—
Ptychoglossus	2/6	+	+	+	—	—	—	—	—
Leptotyphlops	6/≅95	+	+	+	—	+	+	—	+
Liotyphlops	1/11	+	—	+	+	+	—	—	—
Tropidophis	1/15	—	—	—	+	—	—	—	—
Atractus	39/≅70	+	+	+	+	+	—	—	—
Chironius	1/16	+	+	+	+	+	—	—	—
Clelia	1/6	+	+	+	+	+	—	—	—
Dendrophidion	4/8	+	+	+	—	—	—	—	—
Diaphorolepis	1/2	+	—	—	—	—	—	—	—
Dipsas	11/31	+	+	+	+	+	—	—	—
Lampropeltis	1/12	+	+	—	—	—	—	—	—
Leimadophis	6/≅40	+	+	+	+	+	+	—	—
Leptophis	1/7	+	+	+	+	+	—	—	—
Liophis	1/25	—	—	+	+	+	—	—	—
Mastigodryas	1/11	+	+	+	+	+	—	—	—
Oxyrhopus	4/11	+	+	+	+	+	—	—	+
Philodryas	3/15	—	—	+	+	+	+	—	+
Rhadinaca	3/45	+	+	+	+	+	—	—	—
Saphenophis°	5/5	—	—	—	—	—	—	—	—
Sibon	1/9	+	+	—	—	—	—	—	—
Sibynomorphus	1/6	—	—	+	—	+	—	—	—
Synophis°	3/3	—	—	—	—	—	—	—	—
Tachymenis	4/6	—	—	—	—	—	—	+	—
Tantilla	3/50	+	+	+	—	—	—	—	—
Umbrivaga°	1/1	—	—	—	—	—	—	—	—
Urotheca°	1/1	—	—	—	—	—	—	—	—
Micrurus	5/46	+	+	+	+	+	—	—	—
Bothrops	9/59	+	+	+	+	+	+	—	—

TABLE 15 7—Hypothetical Centers of Origin of the Principal Genera and Species Groups of the Andean Herpetofauna
(Letters and numbers refer to fig 15 33)

A Southern Assemblage	B Northern Assemblage

1 From Austral Forests
  Alsodes
  Pleurodema (part)
  Bufo spinulosus group
  Tachymenis
2 From Patagonia
  Pleurodema (part)
  Ctenoblepharis
  Liolaemus
3 Derived from Southern Ancestors
  Batrachophrynus
  Telmatobius
  Stenocercus
	1 Derived from Tropical Lowland Ancestors
	  Amblyphrynus Centrolene
	  Phrynopus Phenacosaurus
	  Geobatrachus Polychroides
	  Atelopus ignescens group Anadia
	  Osornophryne Macropholidus
	  Rhamphophryne Opipeuter
	  Amphignathodon Pholidobolus
	  Cryptobatrachus Proctoporus
	  Gastrotheca (part) Diaphorolepis
	  Hemiphractus Saphenophis
	  Hyla bogotensis group Synophis
	  Hyla labialis group Umbrivaga
	  Hyla larinopygion group Urotheca
	2 From Tropical Lowlands
	  Eleutherodactylus unistrigatus group
	  Colostethus
	  Gastrotheca (part)
	  Centrolenella
	  Euspondylus
	  Prionodactylus
	  Atractus

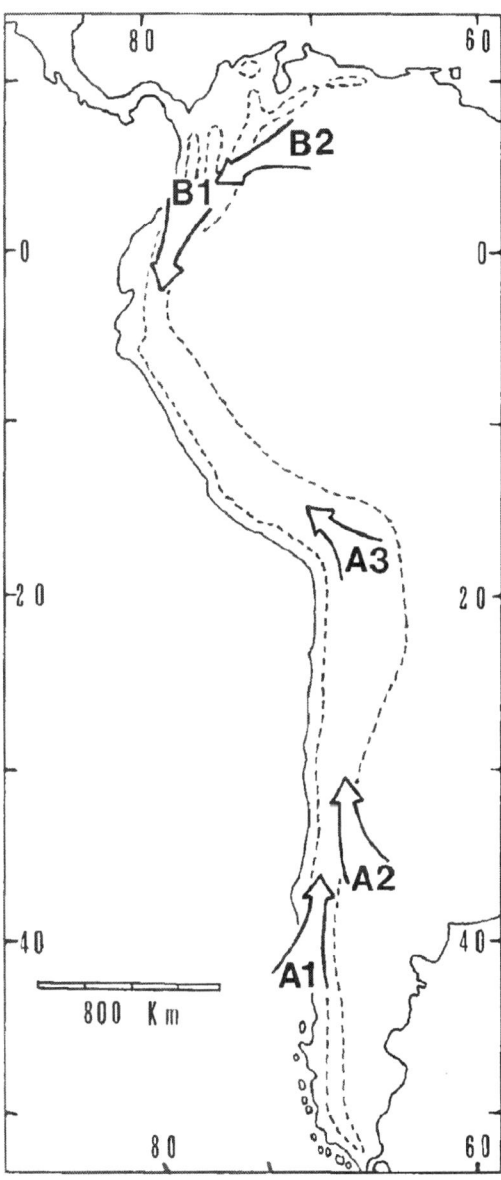

Fig. 15:33. Hypothesized origins and immigrations into Andean region of the historical components of the herpetofauna. Numbers and letters in arrows correspond to those in Table 7.

Orígenes e inmigraciones hipotéticos de los componentes históricos de la fauna dentro de la Región Andina. Los números y letras en las flechas corresponden a aquellos en la Tabla 7.

Austral forests. He showed that *Batrachophrynus* is a derivative of a sister group containing *Caudiverbera* and *Telmatobufo*, both of which are presently restricted to temperate southern Chile, but *Caudiverbera* has an extensive fossil record extending back to the lower Eocene of Patagonia. Lynch (1978b) also demonstrated that *Telmatobius* and *Alsodes* are sister groups and that these are most closely related to *Eupsophus*, a genus restricted to Austral forests. *Alsodes* also inhabits Austral forests as well as Andean slopes in central and southern Argentina and Chile, whereas *Telmatobius* is diverse in the high Andes from Argentina and Chile northward into Ecuador.

Pleurodema is a primitive leptodactyline (Lynch, 1971; Heyer, 1975). Duellman and Veloso (1977) summarized morphological and karyological evidence showing that *Pleurodema* can be derived from an *Eupsophus*-like stock of telmatobiines. Furthermore, Duellman and Veloso's (1977) cladistic analysis revealed two phyletic lines of *Pleurodema*, members of both of which occur in the Andes.

The *Bufo spinulosus* group with the apparently primitive *B. variegatus* confined to cool temperate South America, is primarily Andean, and extends northward into the Huancabamba Depression; some populations occur in the Atacama Desert and in Patagonia. Cei (1972) and Cei, et al. (1972) concluded that the *spinulosus* group is distinctive from other groups of *Bufo* in South America. On the evidence from biochemical analysis of parotoid gland secretions, Low (1972) concluded that the *spinulosus* group is most closely related to the *boreas* and *alvarius* groups in North America, and Blair (1972) suggested that the *spinulosus* group is related to the North American *boreas* group and the Eurasian *viridis* group. Estes and Reig (1973) reported *Bufo* from the late Paleocene of Brasil, and Blair (1972) concluded that the genus arose in South America, although Blair suggested that the *spinulosus* group arrived in South America from North America, a route that is entirely inconsistent with present knowledge of Central American geological history and the distribution of the toads in question.

Northern Herpetofaunal Assemblage.—Thirty-two genera and species groups comprise this assemblage. Some of these genera are disjunct from the major area of congruence in the Andes of southern Colombia and Ecuador, where 22 of the groups occur. The disjunct groups are in northern Colombia (*Cryptobatrachus, Phenacosaurus Euspondylus, Proctoporus*), Sierra Nevada de Santa Marta (*Geobatrachus*), Cordillera de la Costa (*Umbrivaga, "Urotheca"*), Huancabamba Depression (*Polychroides, Macropholidus*), and southern Perú and Bolivia (*Opipeuter*).

Within the northern herpetofaunal assemblage, two major groups are recognized—1) genera or species groups that evolved in the Andes and 2) genera that probably or possibly originated elsewhere and subsequently invaded the Andes (Table 15.7, Fig 15.33). For some genera (*Geobatrachus, Atractus, Diaphorolepis, Saphenophis, Synophis, Umbrivaga, "Urotheca"*) no meaningful statements can be made about their relationships, so they are omitted from the following discussion.

Among those groups that apparently evolved in the Andes, Lynch (1975a) provided a careful assessment of *Phrynopus* which he showed to be derived from an *Eleutherodactylus fitzingeri* group ancestor, frogs of that group are primarily lowland in distribution, although some species (notably *E w-nigrum*) inhabit the Andes. Lynch (1975b) analyzed the broad-headed eleutherodactyline frogs and showed that *Amblyphrynus* was most closely related to frogs of the *Eleutherodactylus sulcatus* group in the Amazon Basin, he suggested that *Amblyphrynus* might be an Andean eleutherodactyline prototype. Three bufonid genera occur in the northern Andes—*Atelopus* (*ignescens* group), *Osornophryne*, and *Rhamphophryne*. Although the genus *Atelopus* is widespread in the Neotropics, the thick-skinned, short-legged species of the *ignescens* group are confined to the northern part of the Andes, including the Sierra Nevada de Santa Marta and the Mérida Andes,

Atelopus apparently is most closely related to *Melanophryniscus* in subtropical South America (McDiarmid, 1971). Trueb (1971) offered various alternative hypotheses for the relationships of *Rhamphophryne*, the most plausible one geographically is that *Rhamphophryne* is related to, but not derived from, *Atelopus*. Ruiz and Hernandez (1976) demonstrated that *Osornophryne* is a specialized derivative of *Atelopus*.

Within the family Hylidae, *Hyla* is poorly represented in the Andes three groups of species are Andean—*labialis, larinopygion,* and *bogotensis* groups Only the latter is represented beyond the Andes (one species in the Chocó and one in Central America) There is no evidence to suggest that these groups are more closely related to one another than any is to various lowland groups. The other hylid genera in the Andes (*Amphignathodon, Gastrotheca Cryptobatrachus,* and *Hemiphractus*) are egg-brooders, a habit shared with *Stefania* in the Guiana Highlands and *Fritziana* and *Flectonotus* in southeastern Brasil the latter also occurs in the Cordillera de la Costa and Trinidad. These seven genera share specialized, umbrella-shaped gills in the developing embryos. *Hemiphractus* with its weird morphological modifications seems to be an early variant from the egg-brooding stock (Trueb, 1974) *Cryptobatrachus* is an obvious sister group to *Stefania* (Rivero, 1970) Although *Gastrotheca* also occurs in southeastern Brasil, the major center of differentiation is in the northern Andes *Amphignathodon* seems to be merely a *Gastrotheca* with mandibular teeth.

Although *Centrolenella* is diverse in Central America southeastern Brasil, and the Guiana Highlands, it is most speciose on the Andean slopes Members of all species groups of *Centrolenella* occur in the northern Andes, as does the only other genus in the family, the monotypic *Centrolene*

Only two iguanid genera are considered to be northern Andean. The Colombian *Phenacosaurus* is an apparent derivative of *Anolis* (Lazell, 1969 Gorman et al 1969) *Polychroides* is viewed as an upland derivative of *Polychrus*, although Gorman, et al (1969)

found no karyological differences and considered *Polychroides* to be indistinguishable from *Polychrus*. The other lizards are microteiids; the relationships of these have been partially analyzed by Presch (1978) who considered *Prionodactylus*, *Proctoporus*, and *Opipeuter* to belong to one lineage, *Euspondylus* and *Pholidobolus* to a second, and *Anadia* to a third that also includes the genera *Ecpleopus* and *Placosoma*, which are extra-Andean.

Of the remaining groups in the northern herpetofaunal assemblage, the microteiid lizard genera *Euspondylus* and *Prionodactylus* also occur in the lowlands and have related (perhaps derived) genera in the highlands—*Pholidobolus* and *Proctoporus*, respectively. The highly speciose dendrobatid genus *Colostethus* has some species in the lowlands, many species on the Andean slopes, and a few species in the high Andes; Edwards (1971) concluded from an analysis of *Colostethus* that most of the high Andean species were derived from groups on the lower slopes.

The most speciose group in the northern Andes is the *Eleutherodactylus unistrigatus* group. Lynch (1976b) identified the center of diversity of the group as the Andes of Colombia and Ecuador, but numerous species occur in the upper Amazon Basin, on the slopes of the Cordillera Oriental in Perú, in the Sierra Nevada de Santa Marta, and the Mérida Andes, and in the Cordillera de la Costa. The greatest species richness at any one site is in the cloud forests and in the upper Amazon Basin. Those species groups in the high Andes were derived from diverse ancestral stocks at lower elevations (Lynch, pers comm).

Extra-Andean Groups.—Many species inhabiting the Andes are members of groups that have their greatest diversity, and presumably their centers of origin, in extra-Andean regions. The outstanding example is the salamander genus *Bolitoglossa*, which is most speciose in Central America and probably did not enter South America until the late Pliocene. The Andean species are members of diverse groups of *Bolitoglossa* which also include some lowland and/or Central American species (Brame and Wake 1971). Other groups in this category are *Caecilia* and the *Bufo typhonius* group, both of which have species widely distributed in the lowlands of Central America, the Chocó, and the Amazon Basin, but which have species endemic to the Andean slopes.

In summary, the Andean herpetofauna evolved from ancestral stocks from the lowlands. These are readily assignable to two major Andean assemblages—northern and southern. The dispersal of the groups is reflected in their diminishing importance in the faunas of regions more remote from their centers of dispersal (Table 15.4) and the peripheral limits of their distributions (Figs 15.34–35). It is evident that the central Andes in Peru are a major area of transition between the northern and southern assemblages.

DISPERSAL AND DIFFERENTIATION

By comparison with the other highland regions in South America, the Andes are very young. Although some uplift occurred prior to the Miocene, the major tectonic events that resulted in the uplift of the Andes began only about 20 million years ago with major orogenies occurring toward the end of the Pliocene and through the Pleistocene—all within the last 2.5–4.5 million years. Climatic fluctuation during the Pleistocene is a final factor in the complex and geologically recent series of events that have molded the Andes and their environments into the features that we see today. Thus, the early evolution and dispersal of the herpetofauna must be viewed with respect to the mid-late Cenozoic events, whereas much of the dispersal and differentiation is intricately associated with Quaternary events.

In the early Tertiary southern South America was more equable than at present; the austral forests of *Araucaria*, *Laurelia*, and *Nothofagus* occurred northward at least to 30°S Lat in Chile and across Patagonia in the Oligocene (Jeannel 1967). Subsequent to the Eocene, there was gradual cooling and drying in southern South America. Associated with the rain shadows created by the rising Andes, a semideciduous xerophytic vegetation termed the Tertiary-Chaco Paleoflora by

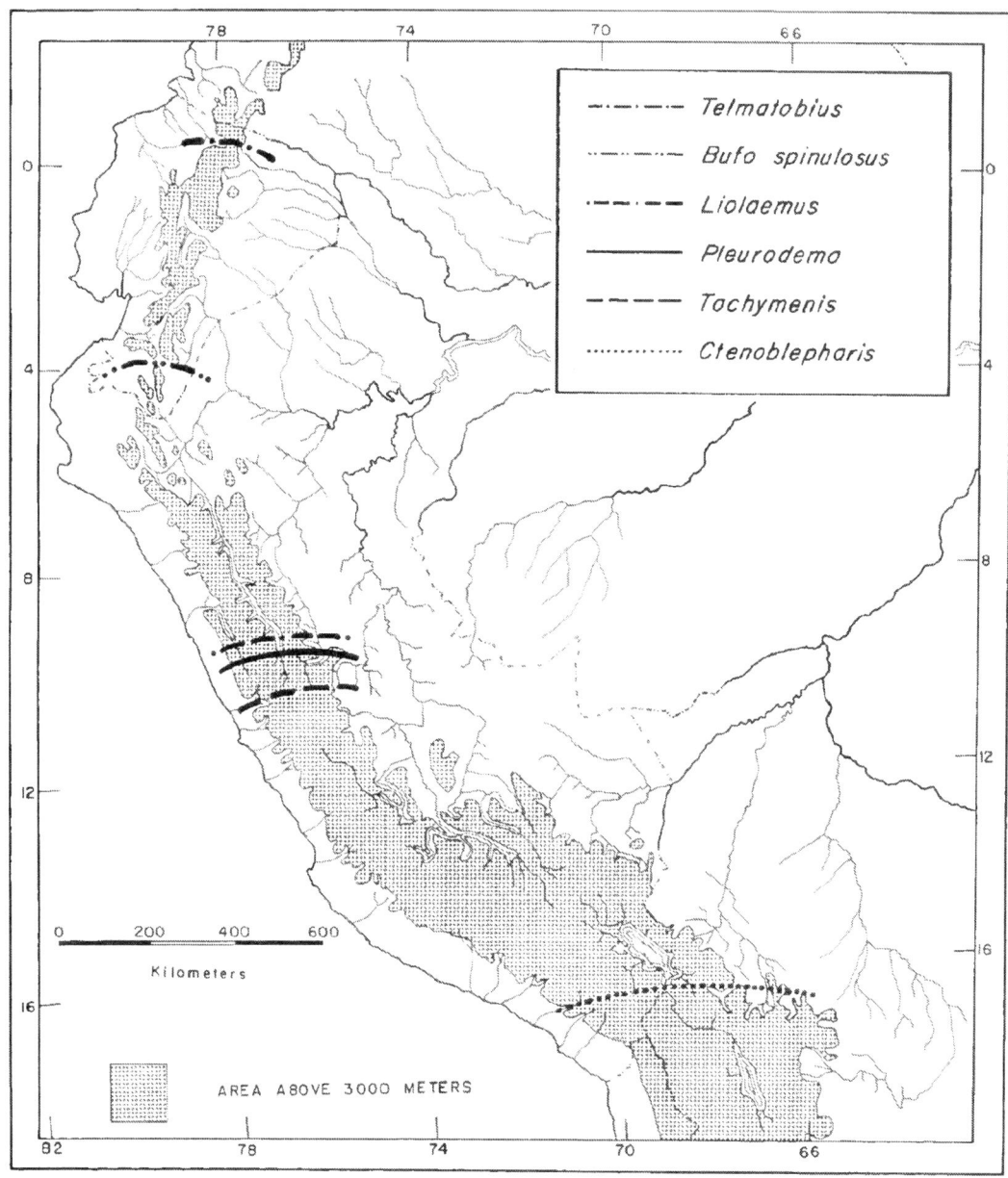

FIG. 15:34. Northern limits of distribution of genera of the southern herpetofaunal assemblage.
Límites de distribución norte de los géneros del conjunto herpetológico sureño.

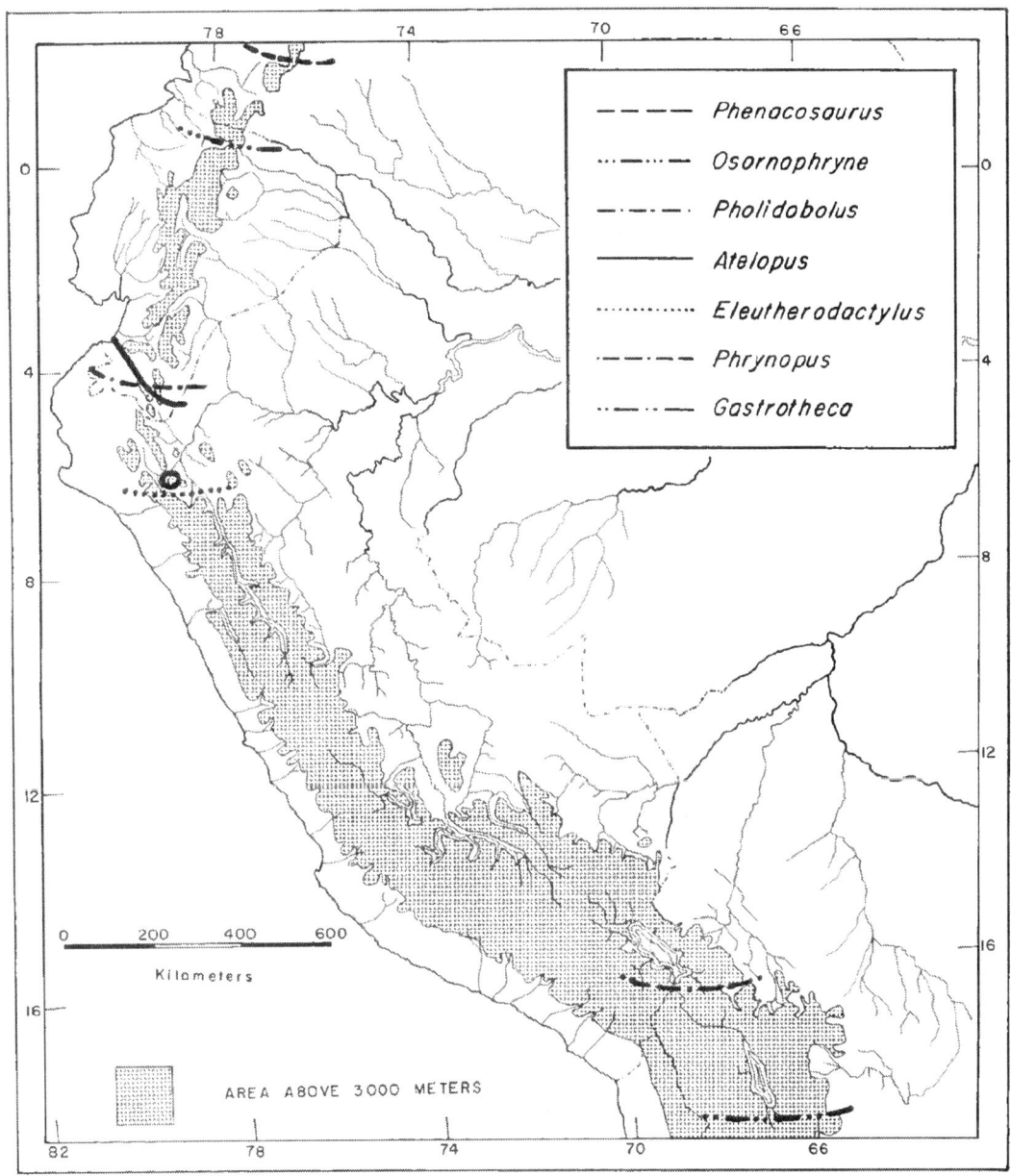

Fig. 15:35. Southern limits of distribution of genera of the northern herpetofaunal assemblage. Additional species of *Atelopus* and *Eleutherodactylus* have entered the eastern slopes of Perú and Bolivia from the Amazonian lowlands.

Límites de distribución sur de los géneros del conjunto herpetológico norteño. Especies adicionales de Atelopus y Eleutherodactylus han entrado a las laderas estes de Perú y Bolivia desde las tierras bajas del Amazonas.

Solbrig (1976), developed east and west of the Andes. Continued climatic desiccation along the Pacific coast resulted in the elimination or restriction of the Tertiary-Chaco Paleoflora, leaving disjunct distributions as far north as southern Ecuador (Jeannel, 1967). The development of the extreme xeric conditions of the Atacama Desert and the restriction of chaparral vegetation to central Chile occurred in the Pleistocene, when the Andean orogeny thrust the cordilleras to their present heights and the cold Humboldt Current assumed its present course. Prior to the present positioning of the Humboldt Current, more precipitation would have fallen on the western slopes of the Andes in Perú and northern Chile (Simpson, 1975a). Furthermore, climatic fluctuation during the Pleistocene provided at least intermittent, less xeric conditions along the coast (Campbell, 1976, 1979). The lacustrine deposits in the Altiplano probably are of Pleistocene age, when the area had an extensive lake system (Lohmann, 1970).

During the Middle and Late Tertiary, the northern Andes were being elevated. Different ranges had somewhat different histories with respect to uplift and volcanism, but the final uplift of all of the tropical ranges occurred in the late Pliocene and Pleistocene (Ahlfeld, 1970; Gansser, 1955; Sauer, 1971; van der Hammen, et al., 1973). Climatic change was principally a cooling effect with continued humid, but probably more equable, temperatures, with the exception of fluctuation of temperatures and precipitation correlated with glacial and interglacial stages (van der Hammen, et al., 1973). The structural depressions between some of the principal cordilleras (e.g. Cauca and Magdalena valleys and Huancabamba Depression) became more significant as the cordilleras were elevated (Simpson, 1975b).

Early workers, such as Chapman (1917) and Chardon (1938) attempting to explain the origin, speciation, and distribution of high Andean biotic components, were hampered by the then persistent ideas of the antiquity and immutability of the lowland forests and little or no knowledge of the Pleistocene climatic changes in the Andes. B. S. Vuilleumier (1971) summarized existing knowledge about Pleistocene climatic changes in South America and provided profound interpretations of the effects of these changes on the Andean flora and fauna. F. Vuilleumier (1970) examined the páramo avifauna of the northern Andes in light of the theory of island biogeography put forth by MacArthur and Wilson (1967); his results showed close correlations with predictions of numbers of species and endemics with island (= páramo) size and distance from the presumed source of immigration (see also Maunello and Roskaski 1974), but he did not consider Pleistocene climatic effects to be important to the avifauna. Haffer (1970, 1974) and van der Hammen (1972) emphasized that Pleistocene climatic fluctuations have been a primary factor in the expansion of ranges of the Andean biota. Simpson (1975b) performed an analysis of distribution of some groups of the páramo flora and found higher correlations between areas of glacial páramos, their distances from source areas, and the number of species than with the modern páramo parameters.

Few systematic and evolutionary studies on Andean amphibians and reptiles have attempted to explain patterns of speciation and distribution as the result of Pleistocene climatic changes (Duellman 1972, 1974; Fritts, 1974; Montanucci, 1973). It is constructive to examine selected groups of the herpetofauna in light of Late Tertiary and Quaternary tectonic events and climatic changes.

Northern Páramos.—The proposed depression of tree line by about 1000 m at glacial maxima would have resulted in extensive areas of páramo where now only relatively small páramo islands exist (Simpson, 1975b). F. Vuilleumier's (1970) and Simpson's (1975b) results on avian and floral distributions, respectively, suggest that herpetofaunal patterns should show positive correlations between the numbers of species and páramo-island size and distance from areas of emigration. One of the basic tenets of MacArthur and Wilson's (1967) theory of island biogeography is that there is dispersal from a source area and that the number of immigrants that become established on a given island is proportional to the size of the island and inversely proportional to its distance from the source area. An important consideration in this concept is the mode of dispersal—active (birds, bats, some reptiles, mammals, and insects), passive aerial (some plants and some insects), and passive wafting (everything else). With a few exceptions, amphibians and reptiles apparently reach oceanic islands by rafting. However, rafting is not a means of dispersal between montane islands. Therefore the presence of a species of frog or lizard on presently isolated páramo islands cannot be explained by direct dispersal, instead they must be considered as relictual isolates of former more widespread distributions. Brown (1971) reached the same conclusion with respect to North American montane mammals.

Climatic depression of as much as 1000 m would have united most of the present páramos in the Cordillera Oriental in Colombia into one extensive páramo; the same is true for those in the Cordillera Central of Colombia, the Nudo de Pasto, and the cordilleras in Ecuador (Fig. 15.36). There are groups of species that are endemic to the present páramos in the Cordillera Oriental of Colombia. For example, the *Eleutherodactylus elegans* complex of the *E. unistrigatus* group has three species (*affinis, bogotensis, elegans*) in the páramos in the vicinity of Bogotá, one species (*lynchi*) farther north in the Páramos de Guantiva, Rusia, and Vijajual and another (*mcefori*) still farther north in the Páramo de Almorzadero. Only two species occur in sympatry (*bogotensis* and *elegans* in Páramo de Choachí). All of the species currently live at elevations above 2800 m. Thus, the distribution of this species complex can be explained by 1) origin from one stock in the Cordillera Oriental, 2) widespread dispersal during time of climatic depression, 3) isolation and speciation during times of climatic elevation, 4) dispersal and secondary contact resulting in sympatry at subsequent time of climatic depression, and 5) present isolation on páramo islands.

Similar patterns are evident in the microteiid lizards of the genus *Pholidobolus*, five species of which inhabit the Andes from 1800 to 3960 m in Ecuador; with the exception of two cases of sympatry, their distributions are confined to particular combinations of cordilleras and/or inter-Andean valleys (Montanucci, 1973). Likewise, frogs of the *Eleutherodactylus curtipes* complex show allopatric distributions in the high cordilleras in southern Colombia and Ecuador, as do frogs of the genus *Phrynopus* in páramos and subparamos from Colombia to Perú (Lynch, 1975), and members of the *Gastrotheca marsupiata* group in Perú (Duellman and Fritts, 1972). The two species of high montane toads (*Osornophryne*) are now isolated in separate páramos in the Cordillera Central of Colombia and the Nudo de Pasto, but climatic depression of 1000 m would have united all of these páramos (Table 15.8).

Some phyletic lineages occur at high elevations in the Cordilleras in Colombia and Ecuador as well as in the Mérida Andes and/or the Sierra Nevada de Santa Marta. Thus, the 11 species in the *Atelopus ignescens* group are distributed principally above 2800 m in the cordilleras of Colombia and Ecuador (8 species), above 2350 m in the Sierra Nevada de Santa Marta (1 species) and above 2010 m in the Mérida Andes (2 species). Assuming that this group dispersed from the major northern Andean ranges, climatic depression would have had to have been more than 1000 m in order to allow them to disperse into the Sierra Nevada de Santa Marta and the Mérida Andes or at the time of dispersal the frogs were able to tolerate warmer condi-

TABLE 15.8—Genera and Species Groups Endemic, or Primarily Restricted to Regions of Major Pleistocene Paramo-Islands
(Letters refer to locations in fig. 36.)

Cordillera Oriental (A)	Cordillera Central (B)	Nudo de Pasto-Ecuador (C)
Eleutherodactylus bogotensis group	*Osornophryne*	*Eleutherodactylus curtipes* group
Bolitoglossa adspersa group	*Rhamphophryne*	*Eleutherodactylus unistrigatus* group
Phenacosaurus	*Gastrotheca aureomaculata* group	*Gastrotheca plumbea* group
		Pholidobolus

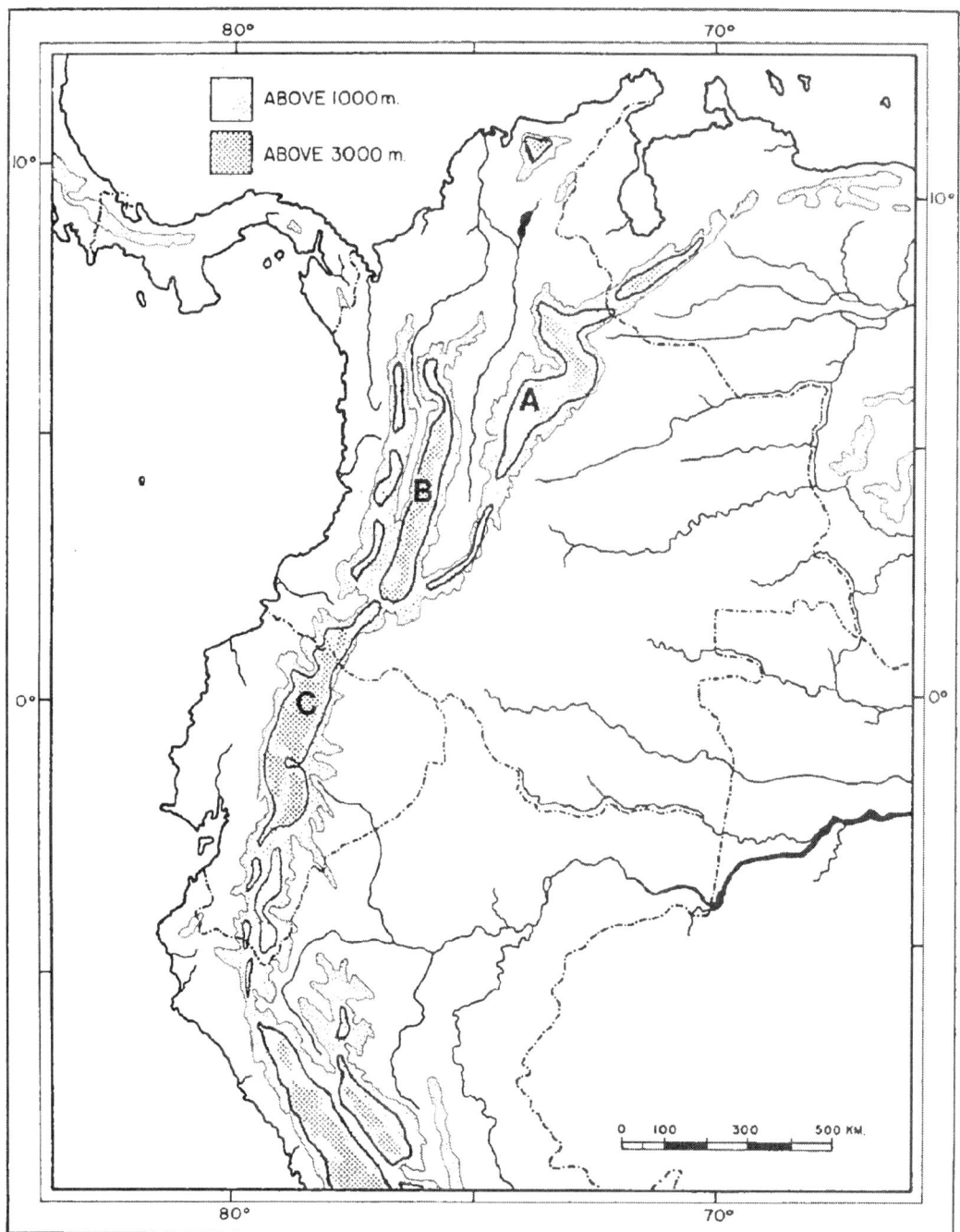

Fig. 15:36. The northern Andes showing approximate parameters of páramo islands (heavy lines) assuming a 1000 m climatic depression. Modified from Simpson (1975b). Letters refer to Table 8.

Los Andes del norte mostrando parametros aproximados de las islas de páramo (lineas gruesas), asumiendo una depresión climática de 1000 m. Modificada de Simpson (1975b). Las letras corresponden a la Tabla 8.

tions than they do now. The same is true for two other montane frogs—*Hyla labialis* (present range 2000–3000 m) and *Centrolenella buckleyi* (2000–3400 m).

Other groups of amphibians and reptiles in páramos and subpáramos have distributions that also extend down into cloud forests. Their presence as isolates in various ranges in the Andes can be explained by their formerly having wider distributions that included now uninhabitable lowlands. As the climates in the intervening lowlands became less equable, the animals became isolated in various montane habitats. Examples are frogs of the genus *Cryptobatrachus*, lizards of the genus *Anadia*, and salamanders of the genus *Bolitoglossa* (Fig. 15.37). The enigmatic frog *Geobatrachus* in the Sierra Nevada de Santa Marta presumably is a Pleistocene relict of some unknown lowland ancestor.

Cloud Forests—The montane rainforests or cloud forests are fragmented by low valleys and by high cordilleras. Presumably at times of depression of vegetation zones owing to climatic factors, cloud forest extended across some of the lower areas now supporting lowland tropical rainforest or dry forest. Thus, dispersal routes would have been available between the Sierra Nevada de Santa Marta, the Mérida Andes, the Cordillera de la Costa, and the Cordillera Oriental in Colombia, thereby permitting dispersal of some cloud forest groups such as *Bolitoglossa*, *Eleutherodactylus*, *Atelopus*, and *Centrolenella* in these areas. Likewise, dispersal between cloud forests in the Ecuadorian and Peruvian cordilleras would have been possible across the Huancabamba Depression, where cloud forests exists now only on isolated ridges. Climatic fluctuation apparently was important in the dispersal and speciation of stream inhabitants such as *Colostethus* and *Centrolenella*, many species of which are isolated in headwaters of confluent drainages but do not occur now in the areas of confluence.

Trans-Andean dispersal of cloud forest inhabitants must have occurred at times of climatic elevation or when the Andes were lower, with continuous cloud forest from the eastern to the western slopes. Numerous species of the genera *Eleutherodactylus*, *Atelopus*, *Rhamphophryne*, *Gastrotheca*, *Hemiphractus*, *Hyla*, and *Centrolenella* have close relatives on opposite sides of the Andes (Fig. 15.38). One member of the predominately lowland *Eleutherodactylus fitzingeri* group (*F. w-nigrum*) occurs at elevations of 1230–2800 m in cloud forests on both slopes of the three cordilleras in Colombia and on the Pacific and Amazonian slopes in Ecuador, and the snake *Chironius monticola* ranges through cloud forests from Venezuela to Bolivia (Fig. 15.39). Some of these groups also occur in the cloud forests in the highlands of Panamá. Each of the following groups—*Rhamphophryne*, *Gastrotheca*, *Hemiphractus* and the *Hyla bogotensis* group—has one representative there and many in the Andean cloud forests.

Central and Southern Andes—Although most taxonomic groups of the herpetofauna in the southern Andes are restricted to either the Patagonian or the Pacific slopes, some groups have related species on both sides—*Alsodes*, *Telmatobius*, and *Liolaemus*. In the far south some Patagonian species follow present continuous Patagonian scrub through low Andean passes, thus Patagonian species such as *Pleurodema bufonina*, *Diplolaemus leopardinus*, *Liolaemus kriegi*, and *Phymaturus palluma* occur on the Pacific slopes of Andean passes. Farther north, mostly different species occupy similar ecological niches on the two slopes, but *Liolaemus fitzingeri* has populations isolated on both slopes. This suggests that in the not too distant past, climatic conditions were elevated sufficiently that the lizards were able to disperse across the Andean divide.

The existing, continuous high montane habitats presently allow dispersal for such widespread species as *Pleurodema marmorata*, *Liolaemus multiformis*, *Tachymenis peruviana* and members of the *Bufo spinulosus* group; all are present on the Altiplano and in the cordilleras and high inter-Andean valleys northward at least to central Perú (Fig. 15.34). The extensive and more continuous high montane regions in the central Andes of Perú, Bolivia and northern Argentina and Chile seem to have afforded few opportunities for isolation and differentiation

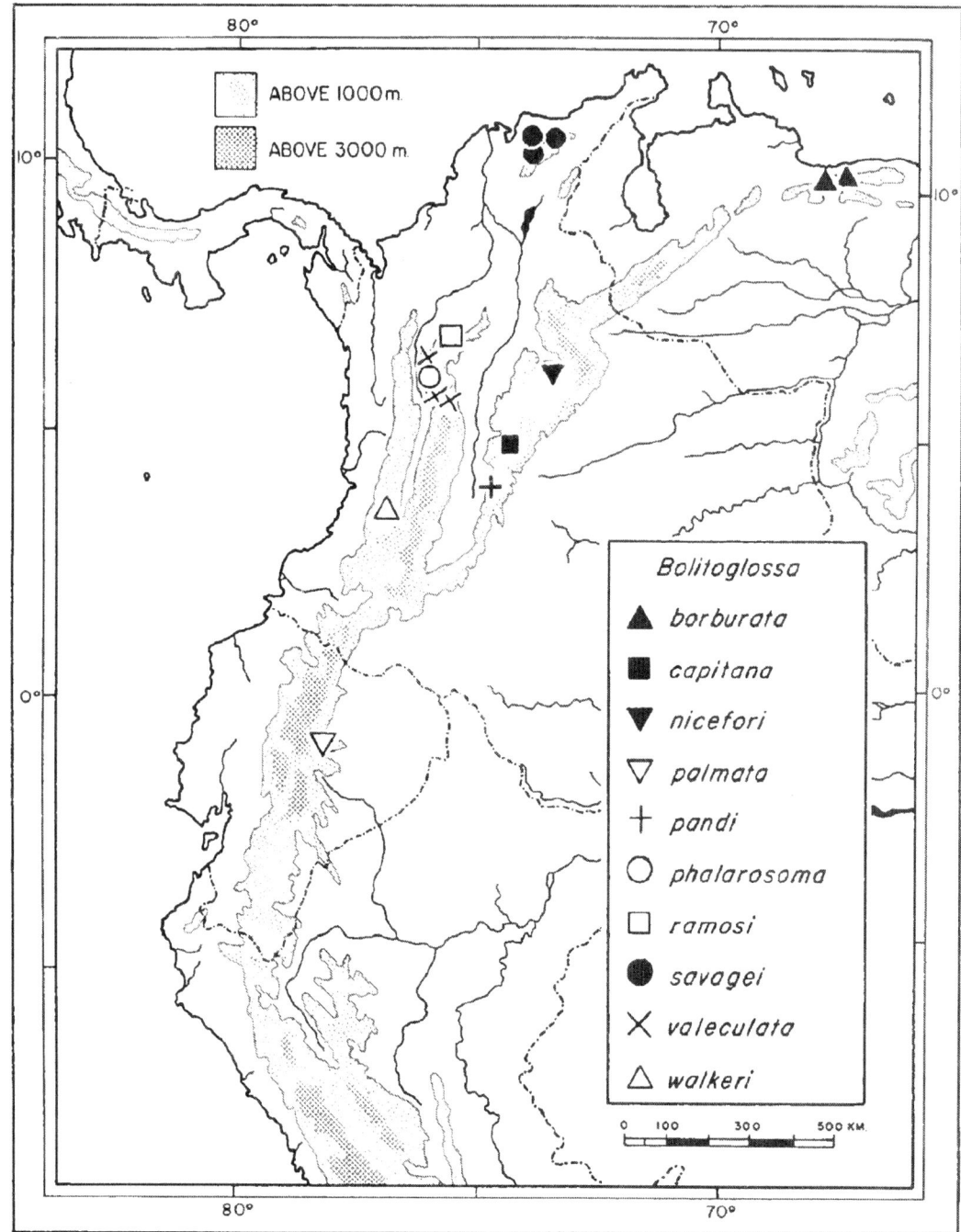

Fig. 15:37. Distribution of salamanders of the genus *Bolitoglossa* in the northern Andes.
Distribución de las salamandras del género Bolitoglossa *en los Andes del norte.*

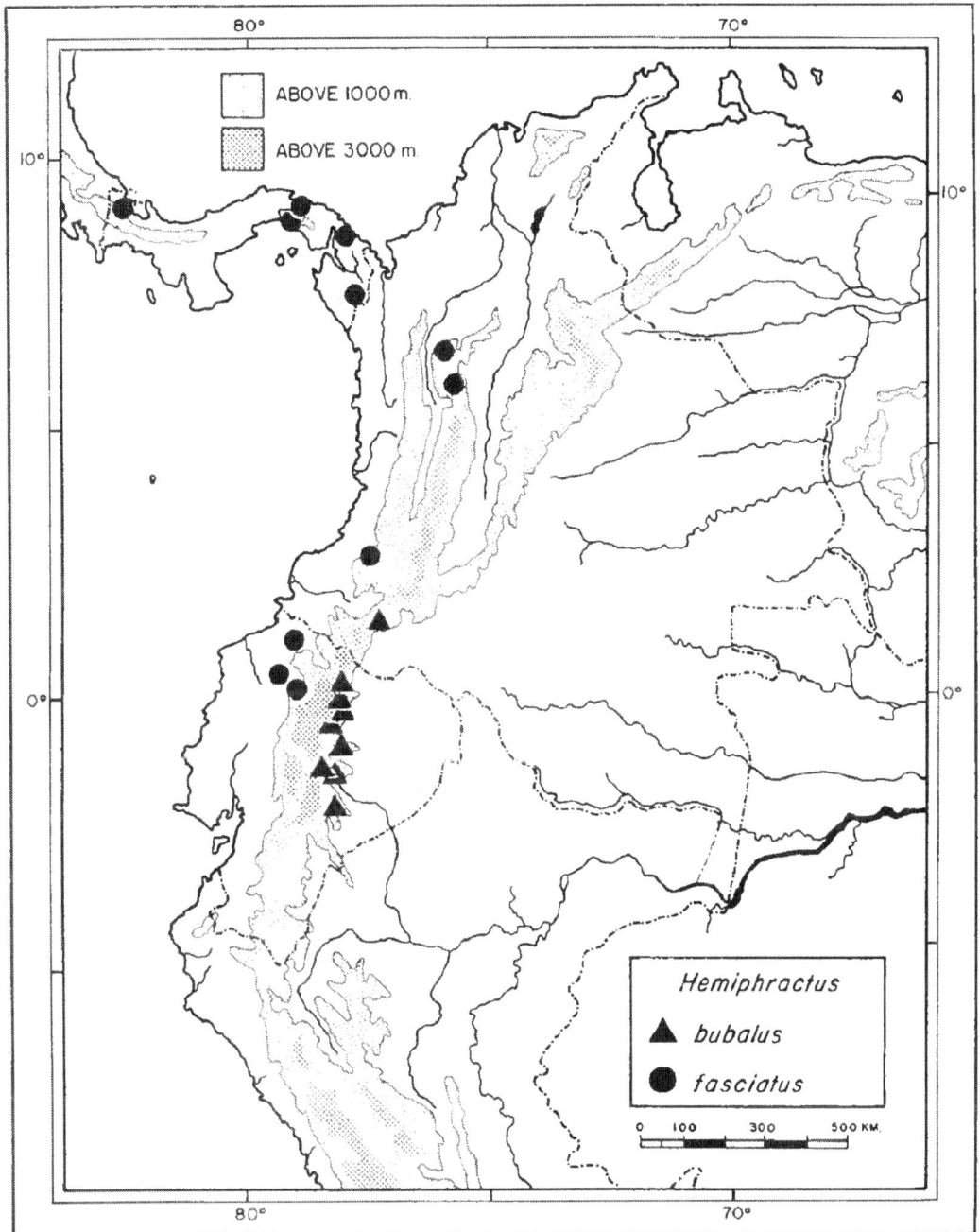

Fig. 15:38. Distribution of the two primarily Andean species of horned frogs, genus *Hemiphractus*. *Distribución de dos especies primariamente andinas de anuros cornudos, género* Hemiphractus.

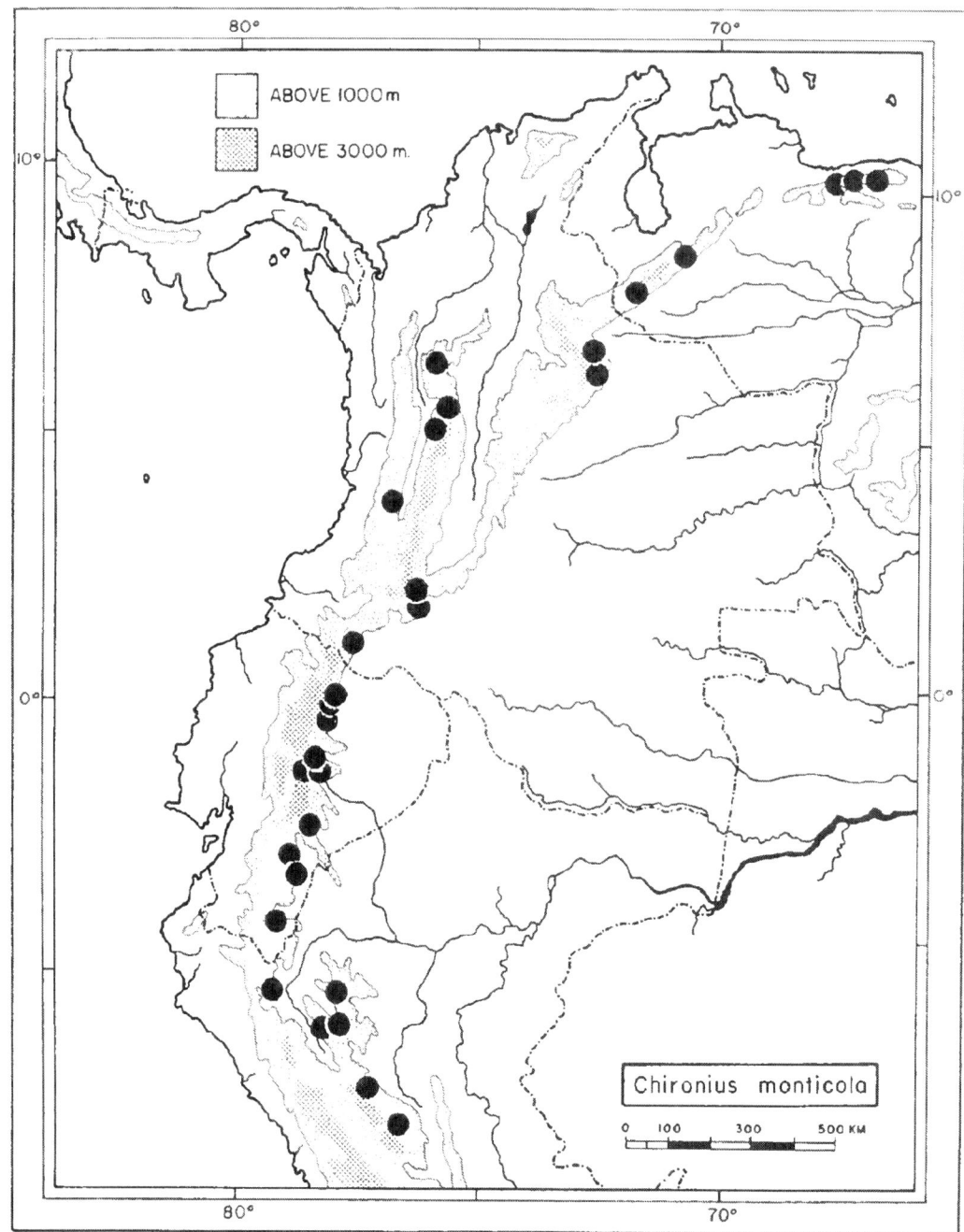

Fig. 15:39. Distribution of the snake *Chironius monticola*, an inhabitant of Andean cloud forests; the range extends southward into Bolivia.

Distribución de la culebra Chironius monticola, *un habitante de la selva de neblina; su rango se extiende hacia el sur hasta Bolivia.*

of high montane species during the Pleistocene. The notable exception is in the eastern front ranges of the Andes where páramo islands apparently persisted, expanded, and contracted resulting in isolated populations and speciation in frogs (*Phrynopus* and *Gastrotheca*) and lizards (*Proctoporus*).

Two genera are diverse in the central Andes and deserve individual consideration. Lizards of the genus *Stenocercus* primarily live in xeric habitats below 3500 m. Fritts (1974) analyzed the evolutionary relationships of the species and showed that three phyletic lines evolved in different parts of the central Andes; he considered that the complexities of the Andean orogenies in the Plio-Pleistocene and climatic fluctuation in the Pleistocene were the primary factors in speciation events in *Stenocercus*. The important thing here is that isolation was in valleys, not on mountain tops. At present, 23 species of the aquatic frogs *Telmatobius* are recognized in the central Andes, two others occur in the southern Andes and five others in the Huancabamba Depression and in Ecuador. On the Altiplano and in the Peruvian Andes most species occur at elevations in excess of 3000 m, where they live in cold streams; in many cases they are found most commonly in small rivulets near the crests of ridges at more than 4500 m. Most species are allopatric. It seems likely that the dispersal and subsequent isolation and speciation of these frogs was associated with climatic fluctuations and actual glaciation of the high central Andes in the Pleistocene. The systematic relationships of the species of *Telmatobius* presently are too poorly known to assess fully the historical biogeography of the group.

The other aquatic high Andean frog, *Batrachophrynus*, represented by two species in central Peru apparently is an ancient relict of a group having a widespread distribution southward prior to the uplift of the Andes.

In summary, the patterns of dispersal and differentiation of the high Andean herpetofauna are intimately associated with the elevation of the Andes in the late Pliocene and Pleistocene, glacial events during the Pleistocene, and climatic fluctuation during the Pleistocene. Likewise, these events influenced the dispersal and speciation of inhabitants of the Andean cloud forests. The greatest amount of isolation of high montane species took place in the dissected northern Andes and southward in the front ranges of the Cordillera Oriental in Peru. Hypothesized Pleistocene parameters of páramos commonly encompass the ranges of species or groups of closely related species now isolated on smaller páramo islands. Inability of high Andean species to disperse across unsuitable habitats between Pleistocene páramos resulted in major highland areas each having groups of species independently derived from lowland stocks, or at least separate centers of differentiation in these areas (Fig. 15.40). Thus, the results of F. Vuilleumier (1970) and Simpson (1975b) relating to avian and floral montane island biogeography differ from those dealing with the herpetofauna. Widespread distributions of some high montane species in the Altiplano and the central Andes are indicative of post-Pleistocene dispersal through existing suitable habitats. Tectonic and glacial events in the central Andes affected the dispersal and isolation of inhabitants of the presently xeric dry valleys and aquatic inhabitants of the high cordilleras, whereas in the southern Andes, these events resulted in the isolation of populations on eastern and western Andean slopes.

ANDEAN HERPETOFAUNAL COMMUNITIES

Community studies of the Andean herpetofauna are limited to a few papers. Péfaur and Duellman (1977) reported on community structure of the herpetofauna at 10 Andean sites; their analyses primarily were concerned with niche breadth and niche overlap with respect to structural habitat and food. Test, Sexton, and Heatwole (1966) reported on the reptiles from the Rancho Grande region in the Cordillera de la Costa in Venezuela; some inferences about the reptile community can be gained from their paper. Lynch (1976a, 1979) and Lynch and Duellman (1979) commented on eleutherodactyline frog communities in Ecuador.

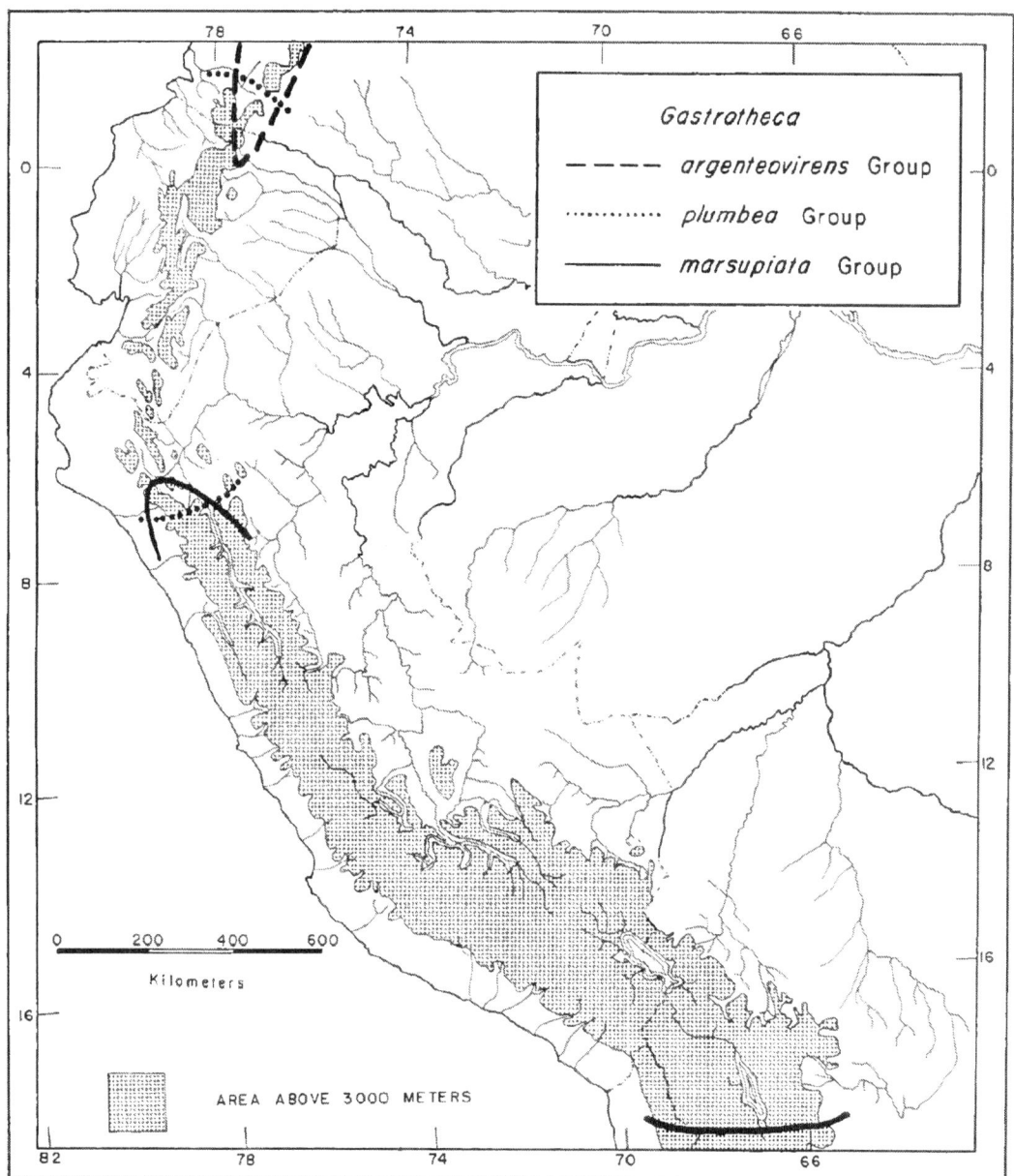

Fig. 15:40. Distributional limits of three species groups of montane marsupial frogs, genus *Gastrotheca*.
Límites distribucionales de tres grupos de especies de los anuros marsupiales de montaña, género *Gastrotheca*.

Communities may be defined in many ways. Here I am limiting a community to the herpetological components of a given site that are geographically sympatric but not necessarily syntopic. Thus, in a cloud forest community an arboreal *Gastrotheca* may be living some 20 m above a terrestrial *Bufo*, but they are considered to be members of the same community. The actual area encompassed at a given site is variable, but experience has shown that all members included in a given community can be expected to utilize at least some of the same resources at some stage in their life histories.

The following analysis of Andean herpetofaunal communities is based on data from 40 communities; most of the data were gathered by me and my field associates in 1974 and 1975, although some of the data from sites 14 and 16 were collected in 1971 and 1972. Sites 23 and 24 were studied in 1977, and data from sites 19–21 were collected by Thomas H. Fritts in 1970. The analysis is divided into three categories—cloud forest (CF), páramo and subpáramo in the northern Andes (P), and communities above tree line in the central and southern Andes (S). In the following list of sites, the category is given in parentheses, the numerical sequence refers to the location of the site in figure 15.41. Boldface words identify the sites in tables 15.9–14.

1. Páramo de **Guantiva**, 22 km SSW of Susacón, Norte de Santander, Colombia, 3000 m (P)
2. Páramo de la **Rusia**, Boyacá, Colombia, 3340 m (P)
3. Páramo de la **Vigajual**, Vado Hondo, Boyacá, Colombia, 2660 m (P)
4. Páramo de **Choachí**, Cundinamarca, Colombia, 3320 m (P)
5. Río **Calima**, Valle, Colombia, 1230 m (CF)
6. Páramo de las **Hermosas**, 7 km NE of Tenerife, Valle, Colombia, 2850 m (P)
7. Páramo de **Puracé**, Cauca, Colombia, 3300 m (P)
8. Nudo de **Pasto**, 8 km NE of Pasto, Nariño, Colombia, 3020 m (P)
9. Nudo de **Pisto**, 12 km E of Pasto, Nariño, Colombia, 3050 m (P)

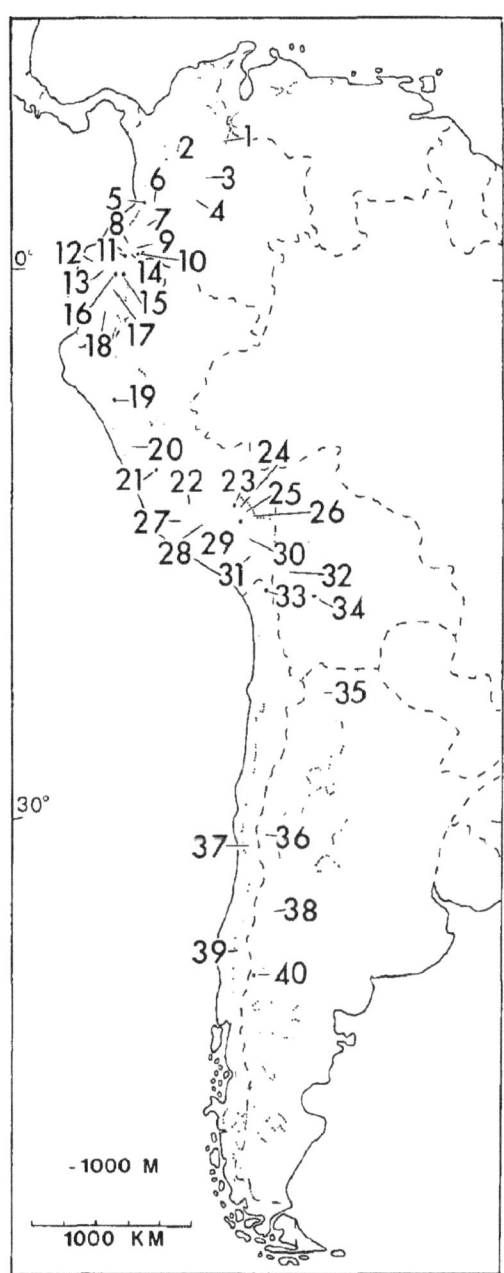

Fig. 15.41. Location of 40 herpetofaunal communities in the Andes. See text for sites designated by numbers.

Localidades para 40 comunidades herpetológicas de los Andes. Ver el texto para los sitios designados por número.

10 10 3 km W of El Pepino, Putumayo, Colombia, 1430 m (CF)
11 Páramo El Angel, 14 km SW of Tulcán, Carchi, Ecuador, 3350 m (P)
12 4 km NE of Dos Ríos, Pichincha, Ecuador, 1140 m (CF)
13 Quebrada Zapadores, 5 km ENE of Chiriboga, Pichincha, Ecuador, 2050 m (CF)
14 Río Azuela, Napo, Ecuador, 1740 m (CF)
15 Río Salado, Napo, Ecuador, 1410 m (CF)
16 Laguna de Papallacta, Napo, Ecuador 3330 m (P)
17 Mulaló, Cotopaxi, Ecuador, 2990 m (P)
18 Desierto de Palmira, 2 5 km S of Palmira, Ecuador 3110 m (P)
19 Huamachuco, La Libertad, Perú, 3350 m (S)
20 Huaraz, Ancash, Perú, 3250 m (S)
21 Comas, Junín, Peru 3220 m (S)
22 Abra Tapuna, Ayacucho, Perú, 3710 m (S)
23 Abra Malaga, Cuzco, Perú, 4080 m (S)
24 Abra Amparaes, Cuzco Perú, 3750 m (S)
25 Abra Acanacu Cuzco, Perú, 3520 m (S)
26 Río Cosñipata, Cuzco, Perú, 1700 m (CF)
27 Abra Toccloccasa, Ayacucho Perú, 3920 m (S)
28 Abra Soraccocha, Apurimac, Perú, 4080 m (S)
29 Abra Huancarane Cuzco, Perú, 3790 m (S)
30 Santa Rosa, Puno, Perú, 4010 m (S)
31 Puno, Puno, Perú, 3850 m (S)
32 13 km E of Tambillo, La Paz, Bolivia, 3880 m (S)
33 Portazuelo Chapiquiña, Tarapacá, Chile, 4080 m (S)
34 35 km W of Chala, Cochabamba Bolivia, 4380 m (S)
35 Río Grande, Jujuy Argentina 3520 m (S)
36 Quebrada del Toro, Sierra de Uspallata, Mendoza, Argentina, 2790 m (S)
37 Lo Valdés Santiago, Chile, 2250 m (S)
38 Paso, El Choique, Mendoza, Argentina, 2050 m (S)
39 Laguna La Laja, Bio-Bio, Chile, 1325 m (S)
40 Laguna Blanca, Neuquen Argentina, 1275 m (S)

In the following discussion of communities, emphasis is placed on the composition of the communities and the utilization of the structural habitat

CLOUD FOREST COMMUNITIES

Seven communities in cloud forests have a high preponderance of anurans (68–93, $\bar{x} = 83.3\%$) Frogs of the genera *Eleutherodactylus* (23–47, $\bar{x} = 32.1\%$) and *Centrolenella* (5–26, $\bar{x} = 17.1\%$) comprise about half of the species at any given site, although at some sites *Colostethus* make up 13 percent of the fauna, and at others bufonids comprise 15 percent of the fauna (Table 15 9)

Comparison of the species composition of the different communities in cloud forests reveals that even between closely approximated sites there are large differences in the component species (Table 15 10) For example, the highest coefficient (0 44) of community[6] is between the sites at the Río Azuela (1740 m) and the Río Salado on the eastern slopes of Ecuador, these sites are about 18 km (airline) apart El Pepino (1430 m) 165 km north of the Río Azuela has coefficients of 0 33 with the Río Azuela and 0 28 with the Río Salado Still lower coefficients exist among sites on the Pacific slopes and the lowest coefficients are between the Ecuadorian-Colombian sites and the Río Cosñipata, some 1750 km to the southeast These differences in species composition are to be expected because of the extremely limited latitudinal and altitudinal ranges of many

[6] Calculated by the formula $CC = 2C/(N_1 + N_2)$, where CC = coefficient of community, C = number of species in common N_1 = number of species in first community and N_2 = number of species in second community

TABLE 15.9—Herpetofaunal Composition of Seven Communities in Andean Cloud Forest

Group	Calima	Dos Rios	Zapadores	El Pepino	Azuela	Salado	Cosñipata
Eleutherodactylus	7	6	9	6	10	7	6
Other leptodactylids	–	–	–	1	–	–	2
Dendrobatids	–	2	–	–	4	2	1
Bufonids	–	2	1	–	2	2	4
Hyla	1	3	1	4	1	4	4
Other hylids	1	–	2	3	5	3	2
Centrolenids	5	4	4	1	6	4	4
Gekkonids	–	1	–	–	–	–	–
Iguanids	2	4	2	3	1	1	1
Microteiids	–	–	–	1	–	–	2
Snakes	3	3	–	–	1	1	–
TOTAL SPECIES	19	25	19	19	30	24	26

TABLE 15.10—Comparison of the Herpetofaunas in Seven Communities in Andean Cloud Forest (Numbers of species in a given community are in boldface, numbers of species in common to two communities are in Roman, and the Coefficients of Community are in italics.)

	Calima	Dos Rios	Zapadores	El Pepino	Azuela	Salado	Cosñipata
Calima	**19**	4	2	1	1	1	–
Dos Rios	*0.18*	**25**	3	–	–	–	–
Zapadores	*0.11*	*0.13*	**19**	1	1	1	–
El Pepino	*0.05*	–	*0.05*	**19**	8	6	1
Azuela	*0.04*	–	*0.04*	*0.33*	**30**	12	1
Salado	*0.04*	–	*0.04*	*0.28*	*0.44*	**24**	1
Cosñipata	–	–	–	*0.04*	*0.04*	*0.04*	**26**

species inhabiting the cloud forests (see Table 15.1 and Figs. 15.18–19). Thus, even though the structural habitat is essentially the same at sites separated by only 400–500 m elevation or 20–30 km distance (and one or more ridges and valleys) the species composition can be expected to be different by more than 50 percent.

Analysis of structural habitat utilization in cloud forest communities was restricted to the anurans, because they comprise the vast majority of the species in the communities. Four factors were analyzed—1) distance from water, 2) vertical distribution, 3) diel activity (noctural and diurnal), and 4) snout-vent length (largest adult male). Multivariate discriminant function analysis of the mean values of each species results in a three-dimensional plot of the component species each placed in a hypervolume of structural habitat utilization (Fig. 15.42). The illustration of the community at the Rio Azuela, used as an example, shows that the 28 species of frogs utilize the entire spectrum of the structural habitat. Most species segregate well on two or more axes, only one tight cluster exists (upper left). These are four species of *Centrolenella*, which differ from one another in mating call and calling site—two call from undersides of leaves and two from tops of leaves.

Páramo Communities

Herpetological communities in the páramos of the northern Andes have only 5–8 species, mostly (67–100, $\bar{x}$ = 86.9%) amphibians, with frogs of the genus *Eleutherodactylus* comprising 14–63 ($\bar{x}$ = 35.8) percent of the species in a given community. No more than three species of reptiles (all lizards) are found in any one community (Table 15.11).

In general, differences between communities are primarily a function of distance (also historical connection). As examples, the páramos of Guantiva, Rusia, and Vigajual are within 100 km of one another and differ in species composition only by the addition of one frog, *Atelopus ebenoides*, at Páramo de Vigajual. However, these three sites and Páramo de Chonchí, which has at least 50 percent of its species in common with the other three sites, are the only sites in the Cordillera Oriental in Colombia; these four sites have

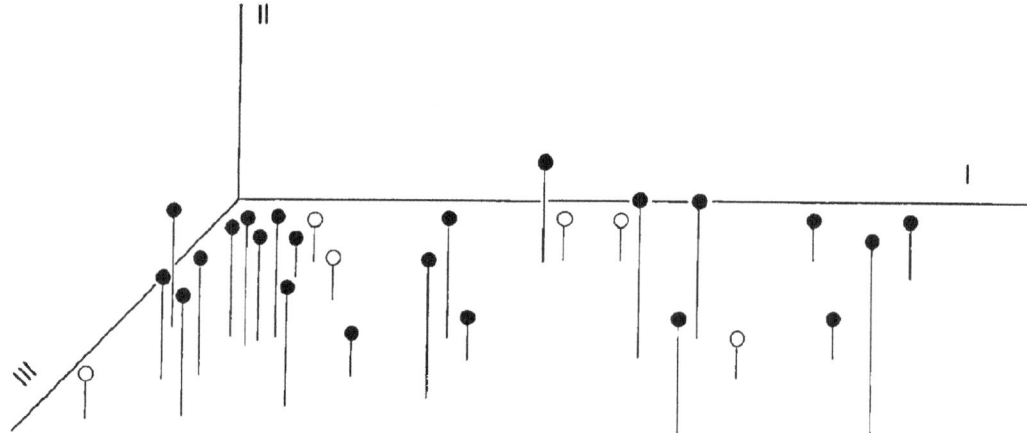

Fig 15 42 Three dimensional plot of the multivariate means of 28 species of frogs in a cloud forest community at the Río Azuela, Ecuador Axis I is size, increasing from left to right, Axis II is height above ground, increasing from bottom to top, Axis III is association with water, increasing from front to back Solid symbols are nocturnal species, open circles are diurnal ones

Distribucion tridimensional de los promedios multivariados de 28 especies de anuros en una comunidad de selva de neblina en el Río Azuela, Ecuador Eje I es tamaño incrementandose de izquierda a derecha, Eje II es altura sobre el suelo, incrementandose de abajo hacia arriba, Eje III es asociacion con agua incrementandose desde el frente hacia atras Simbolos llenos representan especies nocturnas, circulos claros representan especies diurnas

Table 15 11 — Herpetofaunal Composition of Twelve Communities in Northern Andean Paramos

Genus	Guantiva	Rusia	Vigajual	Choachi	Hermosas	Purace	NE Pasto	E Pasto	El Angel	Papallacta	Mulalo	Palmira
Bolitoglossa	1	1	1	1								
Eleutherodactylus	1	1	1	2	3	5	3	5	3	3	1	1
Phrynopus	1	1	1							1		
Telmatobius												1
Colostethus	1	1	1	1			1	1				
Atelopus			1		1	1	1	1	1	1	1	1
Osornophryne						1		1	1			
Gastrotheca					1				1	1	1	1
Hyla	1	1	1									
Centrolenella					1				1			
Stenocercus							1				1	1
Anadia	1	1	1	1	1							
Pholidobolus											2	1
Prionodactylus							1					
Proctoporus								1				
Total Species	6	6	7	5	7	7	8	8	7	6	6	6

no species in common with sites in the other cordilleras (Table 15 12)

In the relatively simple paramo communities, the differential utilization of resources was measured with respect to 1) distance from water, 2) utilization of rock cover, 3) diel activity, and 4) snout-vent length (largest adult male) The ratio of diurnal to nocturnal species varies from 1 3 to 5 3, all of the reptiles and frogs of the genera *Atelopus* and *Colostethus* are diurnal Using the Páramo de Vigajual as an example, it can be seen that the seven species in the community are distributed throughout the spectrum of

TABLE 15 12—Comparison of the Herpetofaunas in Twelve Communities in Northern Andean Paramos (Numbers of species in a given community are in boldface, numbers of species in common to two communities are in Roman, and the Coefficients of Community are in italics)

	Guantiva	Rusia	Vigajual	Choachi	Hermosas	Puracé	NE Pasto	E Pasto	El Angel	Papallacta	Mulalo	Palmira
Guantiva	**6**	6	6	3								
Rusia	*1 00*	**6**	6	3								
Vigajual	*0 92*	*0 92*	**7**	3	1	1						
Choachi	*0 55*	*0 55*	*0 50*	**5**								
Hermosas			*0 14*		**7**	3	1	1	2	1		
Puracé			*0 14*		*0 43*	**7**	1	4	3	1		
NE Pasto					*0 13*	*0 13*	**8**	3	3	1	1	1
E Pasto					*0 13*	*0 53*	*0 38*	**8**	4	2	1	1
El Angel					*0 29*	*0 43*	*0 40*	*0 53*	**7**	3	2	2
Papallacta					*0 15*	*0 15*	*0 14*	*0 29*	*0 46*	**6**	2	2
Mulalo							*0 14*	*0 14*	*0 31*	*0 33*	**6**	5
Palmira							*0 14*	*0 14*	*0 31*	*0 33*	*0 83*	**6**

resources, among the four small species of frogs (left side of Fig 15 43) two are nocturnal and two are diurnal

CENTRAL AND SOUTHERN ANDEAN COMMUNITIES

Herpetological communities in the high central and southern Andes have only 3–7 species, this number increases to 10 in communities at lower elevations in the Patagonian transition zone in the Andean foothills in southern Argentina Of the 21 communities analyzed (Table 15 13), four are on the eastern ridges of the Cordillera Oriental (Tapuna Málaga Amaparaes, Acanacu) and have 60–80 ($\bar{x} = 75\,5$) percent of the fauna composed of anurans Another 12 sites are in the drier central Andes, Cordillera Occidental, and Altiplano, where anurans comprise 33–75 ($\bar{x} = 57\,5$) percent of the fauna Five sites are on the arid slopes of the southern Andes, 0–50

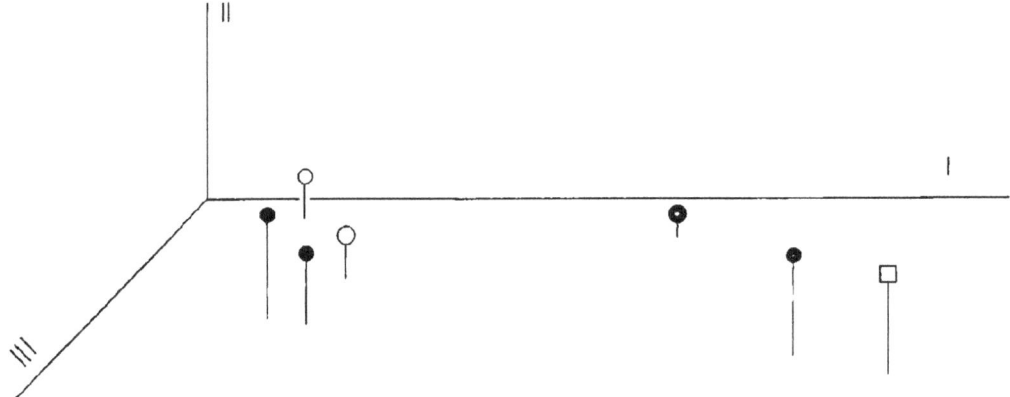

FIG 15 43 Three dimensional plot of the multivariate means of seven species in a páramo community at the Paramo de Vigajual, Colombia Axis I and III are the same as in figure 42, Axis II is association with rock, increasing from top to bottom Solid symbols are nocturnal species, open ones are diurnal, circles are amphibians squares are reptiles

Distribución tridimensional de los promedios multivariados de siete especies en una comunidad de páramo en el Paramo de Vigajual, Colombia Ejes I y III igual que en la figura 42, Eje II es asociación con rocas, incrementándose de abajo hacia arriba Los simbolos llenos representan especies nocturnas los simbolos claros diurnas, circulos son anfibios, cuadrados son reptiles

TABLE 15.13 – Herpetofaunal Composition of Twenty-one Communities in the Central and Southern Andes

Genus	Huamachuco	Huaráz	Comas	Tapuna	Málaga	Amparaes	Acanacu	Tocclocasa	Soraccocha	Huancarani	Santa Rosa	Puno	Tambillo	Chapiquiña	Chyla	Río Grande	Uspallata	Lo Valdes	El Chorque	La Laja	Blanca
Atelognathus	–	–	.	.	–	–	.	–	–	–	–	–	–	..	.	.	–	–	–	–	1
Phrynopus	–	–	–	1	1	.	2	–	–	–	–	–	–	–	–	.	–	–	–	–	–
Pleurodema	–	–	–	–	1	1	1	1	1	1	2	2	1	1	1	1	–	.	.	1	1
Telmatobius	1	–	1	–	1	2	2	1	1	–	1	1	.	1	–	1	.	–	–	–	–
Bufo	–	1	1	–	–	–	.	–	–	1	1	1	1	1	–	1	–	1	–	1	1
Gastrotheca	–	1	1	1	2	1	1	2	1	1	1	1	1	–	–	.	.	–	–	–	–
Homonota	–	–	–	–	–	–	–	.	–	–	.	–	–	–	–	.	–	–	1	–	1
Diplolaemus	–	–	–	–	–	–	–	–	–	–	–	–	–	–	–	–	–	.	1	–	1
Liolaemus	–	–	–	1	.	–	.	1	1	2	1	1	2	2	2	1	3	3	4	1	4
Phymaturus	–	–	–	–	–	.	–	–	–	–	–	–	–	–	.	–	1	–	–	1	1
Pristidactylus	–	–	–	–	–	–	–	–	–	–	–	–	–	–	–	–	1	1	–	–	–
Stenocercus	2	1	1	–	–	–	–	–	–	–	–	–	–	–	–	–	–	–	–	–	–
Proctoporus	–	–	–	1	1	1	1	1	1	1	–	–	–	–	–	–	–	–	–	–	–
Leptotyphlops	–	1	–	.	–	–	–	–	–	–	–	–	–	–	–	–	–	–	–	–	–
Philodryas	.	1	–	–	.	–	–	–	–	–	–	–	–	–	–	–	–	–	–	–	–
Tachymenis	–	–	–	–	–	–	–	–	–	–	1	1	–	–	–	–	–	–	–	–	–
TOTAL SPECIES	4	5	5	5	5	5	8	5	5	5	7	7	4	5	3	4	5	4	4	7	4	10

($\bar{x} = 21$) percent of the fauna is anurans. Lizards of the genus *Liolaemus* are conspicuous members of these communities except in northern Perú and on most of the humid eastern ridges in central and southern Perú. Elsewhere in the central and southern Andes, 1–4 species of *Liolaemus* are present and account for 14–75 ($\bar{x} = 37.8$) percent of the species within each community.

Within the central and southern Andes, comparative species composition of communities apparently is a function of habitat and distance of sites from one another (Table 15.14). Some species, such as the frogs *Phrynopus cophites* and *Gastrotheca excubitor* occur only in the more humid sites on the easternmost ridges of the Andes, whereas toads (*Bufo*) and lizards of the genus *Liolaemus* are absent at these sites. Farther south in Argentina and Chile, the high uninhabitable backbone of the Andes is an absolute barrier to amphibians and reptiles, thus, species compositions of sites at the same latitude but on opposite sides of the Andes are very different. However, in southern Argentina and Chile, where low passes exist in the Andes, species composition on the two sides of the Andes is more alike.

Resource utilization was analyzed in the same manner as in páramo communities; again, it is noteworthy that species utilize a broad spectrum of resources within a given community. For example, the community at Santa Rosa on the Altiplano has seven species—five frogs, one lizard, and one snake (Fig. 15.44). All of the amphibians are nocturnal and the reptiles are diurnal. Among the five frogs, *Telmatobius marmoratus* is aquatic, *Bufo spinulosus* and *Pleurodema marmorata* deposit eggs in shallow temporary pools whereas *Pleurodema cinerea* constructs a foam nest in ponds and *Gastrotheca marsupiata* broods its eggs in a pouch and subsequently releases its tadpoles into ponds.

At the southernmost site (Laguna Blanca) three species of amphibians are closely associated with the lake (Fig. 15.45). Of the seven lizards, *Homonota darwinii* is nocturnal. Two species of lizards (*Liolaemus bibronii* and *L. darwinii*) are associated with bunch grass, and the other four are associated with rocks. Of these, the herbivorous *Phymaturus patagonicus* seeks shelter in crevices in extrusive basaltic rocks. The other three species are similar in their size and habitat (clumped at right of Fig. 15.45). Of these, *Diplolaemus darwinii* is carnivorous, *Liolaemus elongatus* is primarily insectivorous, and *L. kriegi* is omnivorous, with more than 50 percent of its diet consisting of plants.

TABLE 15 14—Comparison of the Herpetofaunas in Twenty-one Communities in the Central and Southern Andes
(Numbers of species in a given community are in boldface, numbers of species in common to two communities are in Roman, and the Coefficients of Community are in italics)

	Huamachuco	Huaraz	Comas	Tapuna	Malaga	Amparaes	Acanacu	Toccloccasa	Soraccocha	Huancarane	Santa Rosa	Puno	Tambillo	Chapiquiña	Chala	Rio Grande	Uspallata	Lo Valdes	El Choique	La Laja	Blanca
Huamachuco	4																				
Huaraz	0 22	5																			
Comas			5	2	1	1	2	3	3		2	2									1
Tapuna			0 40	5	1	1	5	3	3		1	1									1
Malaga			0 20	0 20	5	4	5	3	3		1	1	1	1	1	1				1	1
Amparaes			0 20	0 20	0 80	5	4	3	3	1	1	1	1	1	1	1					1
Acanacu			0 20	0 31	0 77	0 62	8	4	4	2	2	2	1	1	1	1					1
Toccloccasa			0 31	0 60	0 60	0 60	0 62	5	5	2	2	2	1	1	1	1					1
Soraccocha			0 60	0 60	0 60	0 60	0 62	1 00	5	2	2	2	1	1	1	1					1
Huancarane			0 40	0 20	0 20	0 20	0 31	0 40	0 40	5	4	4	4	3	3	3		1		1	1
Santa Rosa			0 33	0 17	0 17	0 17	0 27	0 33	0 33	0 67	7	7	3	3	2	4		1		1	1
Puno			0 33	0 17	0 17	0 17	0 27	0 33	0 33	0 67	1 00	7	3	3	2	4		1		1	1
Tambillo			0 22		0 22	0 22	0 17	0 22	0 22	0 89	0 55	0 55	4	4	3	3		1		1	1
Chapiquiña			0 20		0 20	0 20	0 15	0 20	0 20	0 60	0 50	0 50	0 67	5	5	3		1		1	1
Chala					0 25	0 25	0 18	0 25	0 25	0 75	0 40	0 40	0 86	0 50	3	2				1	1
Rio Grande			0 22		0 22	0 22	0 17	0 22	0 22	0 67	0 73	0 73	0 75	0 75	0 57	4		1		1	1
Uspallata																	5		3		2
Lo Valdes			0 22							0 22	0 18	0 18	0 25	0 22		0 25	0 50	4		1	1
El Choique																			7	1	5
La Laja			0 22								0 18	0 18	0 25	0 22		0 25		0 25	0 18	4	3
Blanca			0 13							0 13	0 06	0 06	0 14	0 13		0 14	0 27	0 14	0 59	0 43	10

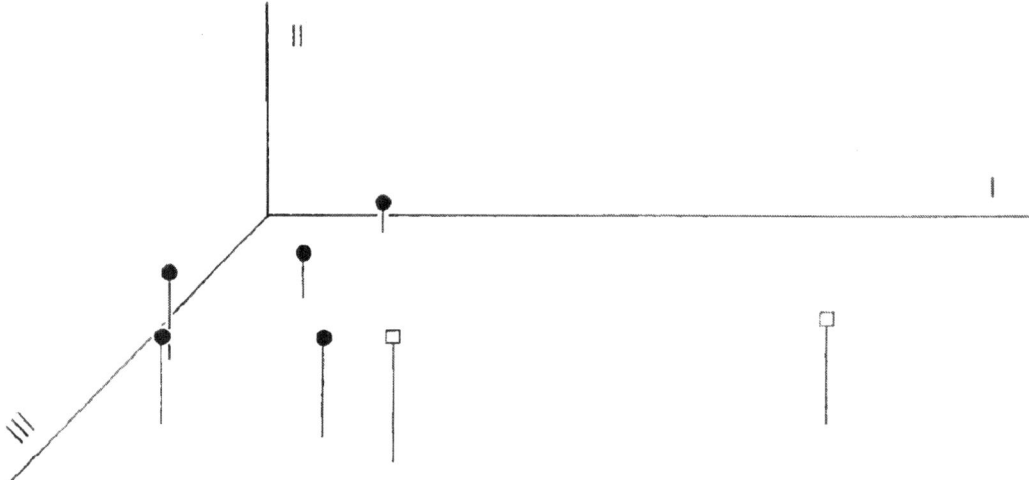

Fig. 15:44. Three dimensional plot of the multivariate means of seven species in a high Andean community at Santa Rosa, Perú. Axes and symbols are the same as in Figure 43.
Distribución tridimensional de los promedios multivariados de siete especies en una comunidad altoandina en Santa Rosa, Perú. Ejes y símbolos son los mismos que en la figura 43.

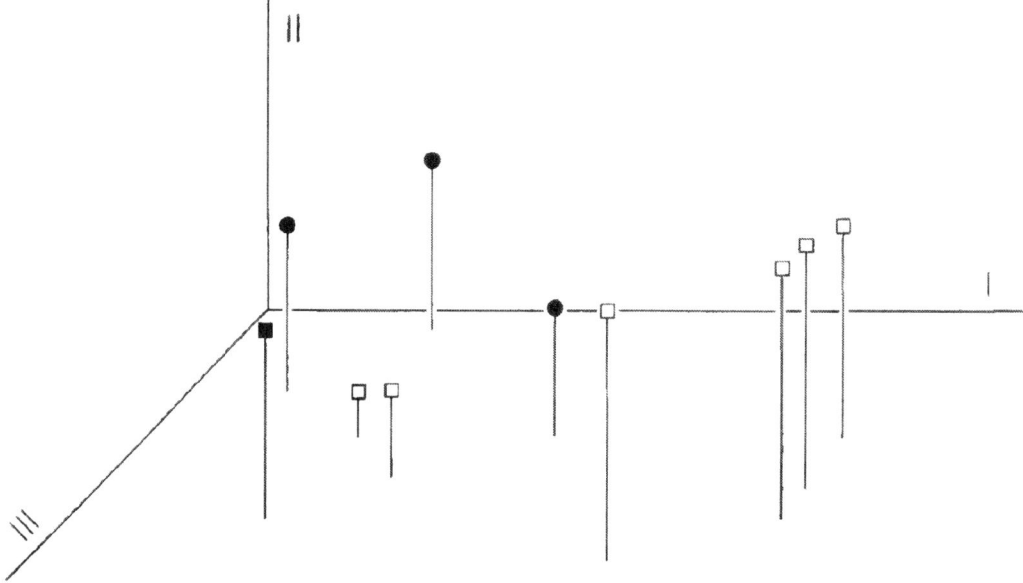

Fig. 15:45. Three dimensional plot of the multivariate means of ten species in a Patagonian-Andean community at Laguna Blanca, Argentina. Axes and symbols are the same as in figure 43.
Distribución tridimensional de los promedios multivariados de diez especies en una comunidad patagónico-andina en Laguna Blanca, Argentina. Ejes y símbolos son los mismos que en la figura 43.

INFLUENCE OF MAN

Human occupation of the Andes has existed for at least 10,000 years, and densely populated, heavily cultivated areas have been in continual, or nearly continual, use for about 8000 years (Engel, 1976). Although it is impossible to state with any degree of certainty that human activities have not caused the extirpation of any species of amphibian or reptile, it seems as though most human disturbance in the high Andes may be beneficial to most members of the herpetofauna. At least at the present time, man is a predator only on the large frogs *Telmatobius culeus* and *Batrachophrynus* in Andean lakes. On the other hand some agricultural practices are extremely beneficial to amphibians and reptiles. Irrigation systems, mostly small channels, provide sites for the development of tadpoles of *Gastrotheca, Bufo, Pleurodema, Centrolenella,* and *Telmatobius* as well as adults of the latter. The clearing of fields of rocks and placing these in piles or as fences creates seemingly ideal habitat for some frogs and especially some lizards of the genera *Liolaemus, Stenocercus, Pholidobolus,* and *Proctoporus.* Fence rows of planted *Agave* also provide excellent shelter for *Gastrotheca, Stenocercus,* and *Pholidobolus.* Perhaps the most detrimental human disturbance in the high Andes results from overgrazing by sheep. The indirect effect of overgrazing on populations of insects that are important food resources for frogs and lizards has yet to be measured.

Whereas human-herpetofaunal interactions in the high Andes do not seem to be highly detrimental to amphibians and reptiles, man's disturbance of the cloud forest has profound effects on the herpetofauna. The clearing of the forest for agriculture and grazing not only completely destroys the habitat of many species in a given area, but the consequent deleterious effects of erosion, silting and chemical changes influence streams below the destroyed areas. Although the clearing of cloud forests is detrimental or even devastating to most species, some frogs and lizards reach large populations in *cafetales* or in forest-edge habitats.

The high Andean herpetofauna seems to be reasonably safe from extirpation owing to human activities, because most of the species with restricted ranges occur in areas above normal human activity. Furthermore, some of these isolated páramos already have been set aside as national parks, especially in Colombia and Venezuela. Until the last decade most of the extensive areas of cloud forest were subject to little human disturbance. The steep Andean slopes mostly were accessible only on foot or with pack animals; settlements consisted only of small *ranchos* or *tambos* one day's travel apart. However, in recent years, many roads are being constructed from the highlands to the Amazonian and Chocoan lowlands; following the roads are colonists who quickly clear the forest. When the road from Papallacta to Lago Agrio, Ecuador, was opened in October 1971 it was possible to drive for many kilometers through pristine cloud forest. By April 1972 many of the areas of cloud forest already were gone. Certainly, if the unique and diverse biota of the cloud forests is to be preserved, several large reserves must be set aside in the very near future. Although steps have been taken in Perú with the Parque Manú and preliminary work in Ecuador with the Proyecto Cayambe-Coca, these are insufficient, because so many cloud forest inhabitants have restricted ranges.

ACKNOWLEDGMENTS

My field investigations on the Andean herpetofauna have spanned more than a decade; during that time many persons have aided me in innumerable ways, especially during a year-long sojourn in 1974–1975. Thus, I am grateful to Stephen Ayala, Jose M. Cei, the late Roberto Donoso-Barros, Pedro Durant, Ramon Fornas C., Jorge Hernández C., Raymond F. Laurent, Bruce MacBryde, Jaime E. Péfaur, and Alberto Veloso M. for logistic support and introduction to terrain new to me. Much information utilized herein was gathered by my field companions; for their efforts I thank David C. Cannatella, Dana K. Duellman, Thomas H. Fritts, Stephan Halloy, Oscar Ochoa M., and especially John E.

Simmons and Linda Trueb Field studies in the Andes were supported by grants from the National Geographic Society (1304) and the National Science Foundation (DEB 74-01998, DEB 76-09986)

John D Lynch and Jaime E Péfaur have been constant sources of information and ideas while I have been preparing this manuscript Furthermore, Péfaur has brought to my attention much pertinent literature and translated the Spanish resumé Lynch generously shared with me his first-hand knowledge of the Andes and his unequalled knowledge of *Eleutherodactylus* Linda Trueb and Stephen R Edwards attempted to answer my multitudinous questions about *Telmatobius* and *Colostethus*, respectively José M Cei, Richard E Etheridge, and Thomas H Fritts provided insights into problems related to the Andean iguanid lizards, and the latter tried to relieve my frustrations in dealing with the Andean microteiid lizards John A Wiest, Jr, generously provided data on *Chironius* and John W Wright shared with me his knowledge of the arid Peruvian slopes and the Huancabamba Depression The manuscript benefited from reviews by David C Cannatella Thomas H Fritts, John D Lynch, Jaime E Péfaur, John E Simmons, Beryl B Simpson, and Linda Trueb, but, of course, I assume responsibility for any and all errors of omission commission, and interpretation Debra K Bennett executed many of the illustrations My sincere thanks go to all of these colleagues for their contributions in my behalf

RESUMEN

Los Andes se prolongan por cerca de 8000 km cubriendo casi 66° de latitud desde el trópico hasta la región temperada del sur Por ende, los climas y ambientes en los Andes son extremadamente variados, incluyendo desde selvas de neblina hasta páramos, puna selvas secas, selvas australes y otros ambientes de montaña, donde la lluvia raramente cae Algunas áreas tienen clima estable, otras tienen fluctuaciones diarias de hasta 20°C, y todavía otras tienen períodos fríos y sequías

Las 727 especies de anfibios y reptiles que habitan a elevaciones mayores que 1000 m en los Andes fueron tabulados de acuerdo a sus distribuciones altitudinales y a los ambientes ocupados en 27 regiones fisiográficas de los Andes (Apéndices 15 1–3) Estas regiones fueron agrupadas en seis categorías mayores para propósitos de análisis de los patrones de distribución

Cada una de las cuatro regiones dentro de los Andes venezolanos tiene especies endémicas de anfibios y/o reptiles, aquellos de las dos pequeñas regiones de altura—Cerro Turumiquire y la Serranía de Paria—parecen haber derivado de la Cordillera de la Costa la cual comparte pocas especies con los Andes de Mérida De las 32 especies en los Andes de Mérida solo siete se encuentran el la Cordillera Oriental en Colombia En la aislada Sierra Nevada de Santa Marta 16 de las 21 especies en la selva nublada y páramo son endémicas Cuatro de las especies no-endémicas también ocurren en la Cordillera Oriental en Colombia y una es compartida con los Andes de Mérida

Los Andes del norte en Colombia y Ecuador, forman un complejo de montañas que irradian desde el Nudo de Pasto y se separan en Colombia por profundos ríos de orientación sur-norte, mientras que en Ecuador se separan por una serie de hoyas interandinas De las 415 especies en los Andes del norte 345 (88%) son endémicos, los sapos y ranas con 262 especies (225 endémicos) son el más diverso grupo Siete géneros de anfibios y reptiles (*Amphignathodon, Centrolene, Osornophryne, Phenacosaurus, Pholidobolus, Saphenophis,* y *Synophis*) son endémicos en los Andes del norte, y *Cryptobatrachus* es endémico—con la excepción de una especie en la Sierra Nevada de Santa Marta Varias (43) de las 70 especies no-endémicas se comparten con las tierras bajas adyacentes Sólo 23 especies son comunes con los Andes peruanos, y 14 especies con comunes con las tierras altas de Centroamérica, la mayoría de éstas son especies con distribución en baja elevaciones de las selvas de neblina o en las tierras bajas con selva tropical Si únicamente las 73 especies que no bajan de 2500 m se consideran, todas menos una son endémicas, la culebra *Tropidophis taczanowskyi* es común con los

Andes peruanos. Dentro de los Andes del norte, 250 especies con endémicas en una de las siete regiones fisiográficas, con el mayor número de endemismos en la Cordillera Oriental en Ecuador (74), y en la Cordillera Occidental en Ecuador (65), pero con el mayor porcentaje de endemismo (54%) en la Cordillera Central en Colombia. La mayor diversidad y el más alto porcentaje de endemismo en los Andes del norte ocurre en los sapos y ranas (especialmente *Colostethus*, *Eleutherodactylus*, y *Centrolenella*), quienes conforman al 65 por ciento de la herpetofauna del área. La herpetofauna de las hoyas interandinas parece haber derivado principalmente de las cordilleras adyacentes. La más alta similaridad faunística dentro de los Andes del norte ocurre entre las cordilleras del este en Colombia y Ecuador, pero cuando las especies de sobre 2500 m se consideran unicamente, estas regiones no tiene especies en común. En esta misma línea de análisis todas las especies altoandinas de la Cordillera Occidental en Colombia son endémicas.

La Depresión de Huancabamba es la mayor discontinuidad en la cadena principal de los Andes, el paso más bajo (Abra de Porculla) tiene 2145 m. Aparte de la predominante fauna de tierras bajas, 43 especies de anfibios y reptiles habitan la Depresión de Huancabamba, de ellos, 29 son endémicas a la región, incluyendo los géneros monotípicos *Polychroides* y *Macropholidus*. Seis especies ocurren en la depresión y en los Andes al norte, dos ocurren en la depresión y en los Andes al sur y dos son comunes a las tres regiones.

Los Andes centrales en Perú son divididos (para propósito de análisis) en cinco cadenas mayores y en tres valles intermontanos, mas la Cordillera Oriental en Bolivia. La herpetofauna consiste en 159 especies (76 endémicas). Dos géneros (*Batrachophrynus* y *Opipeuter*) son endémicos, y varios géneros tienen multiple número de especies—*Phrynopus*, *Telmatobius*, *Gastrotheca*, *Euspondylus*, *Proctoporus*, y *Stenocercus*. Sólo 12 especies son comunes con los Andes del sur (incluyendo el Altiplano), y 15 especies son comunes con las tierras bajas del este. Tres especies de anuros (*Pleurodema marmorata*, *Telmatobius marmoratus*, *Bufo spinulosus*), una de saurios (*Liolaemus multiformis*), y una culebra (*Tachymenis peruviana*) se distribuyen ampliamente y son las únicas especies que ocurren en las cordilleras del este y del oeste. La más alta tasa de endemismo en los Andes centrales ocurre en la parte sur de la Cordillera Oriental en Perú, donde 41 de las 76 especies son endémicas.

Los Andes del sur incluyen las cordilleras en Argentina y Chile y el Altiplano. Allí la herpetofauna consiste en 64 especies constituidas por 30 anuros, 31 saurios y tres culebras. Ningún género es endémico de los Andes del sur, pero ciertos endémicos australes como *Alsodes* se comparten con las selvas de tierras bajas, como *Diplolaemus* y *Phymaturus* con la Patagonia, y como *Garthia* con el desierto de la costa pacífica. De las 64 especies, 36 son endémicas, de las restantes 28, 12 son comunes con la Patagonia, seis con las selvas australes, cinco con las tierras bajas áridas del Pacífico, y 12 con los Andes centrales. La mayoría de los endémicos son anuros de los géneros *Alsodes* y *Telmatobius* restringidos a particulares sistemas de drenaje, y saurios de altura del género *Liolaemus*. Sólo *Bufo spinulosus* y *Tachymenis peruviana* se distribuyen a lo largo de los Andes del sur.

Un análisis distribucional de todas las 727 especies, y de las 147 especies distribuidas a alturas mayores de 2500 m (Figs. 15.29–30) proveé las bases para reconocer ocho regiones eeogeográficas mayores en los Andes (Fig. 15.31). Estas regiones están separadas por barreras fisiográficas o ecológicas.

De los 88 géneros de anfibios y reptiles que viven a alturas mayores de 1000 m en los Andes, 19 son endémicos a estas montañas, estos contienen sólo 94 (13%) de las especies andinas. Cuarenta y siete géneros son primariamente no-andinos, estos contienen 144 (20%) de las especies andinas. Los otros 22 generos contienen 491 (67%) de las especies andinas y son de distribución amplia en la región Neotropical o bien ocurren en regiones extrandinas también. Los Andes comparten 47 géneros con la selva amazónica, 46 con Centroamérica, 42 con el Chocó, 36 con el sureste brasileño, 35 con el Escudo Guayanés, 11 con la Patagonia, seis con las selvas australes, y nueve con el desierto de Atacama. Las relaciones genéricas de la herpetofauna andina se establecen primariamente con las tierras adyacentes y no con las tierras de alturas del Brasil o de las Guayanas.

La herpetofauna andina se originó por invasiones separadas desde las tierras bajas. Un conglomerado faunístico sureño está compuesto de grupos derivados de antiguos inmigrantes a la región andina y por inmigrantes tardíos de la Patagonia y selvas australes. El conglomerado faunístico norteño consiste en grupos derivados de antiguos y tardíos inmigrantes de tierras bajas tropicales. Los modelos de dispersión y especiación de la herpetofauna altoandina estan estrechamente asociados con los movimientos orogénicos del Plio-pleistoceno y con las fluctuaciones climáticas del Pleistoceno.

Un análisis de la composición específica de 40 comunidades andinas incluyó siete comunidades de selvas nublados, 12 comunidades de páramos, y 21 comunidades en los Andes centrales y del sur. Las comunidades de selvas nubladas contienen hasta 30 especies, la mitad de ellas aproximadamente pertenecen a *Eleutherodactylus* y *Centrolenella*. Los bajos coeficientes de comunidad reflejan un rango restringido de la mayoría de los habitantes de las selvas nubladas. En las comunidades de páramo, los anfibios conforman cerca 87 por ciento de 5–8 especies de cada comunidad (*Eleutherodactylus* conforma cerca del 36%). Las diferencias entre comunidades de páramos son una función de la distancia. Las comunidades en los altos Andes del centro y del sur tienen entre 3 y 7 especies, incrementándose hasta 10 en las comunidades de las laderas patagonicas de los Andes. Los reptiles, especialmente *Liolaemus*, son dominantes en las comunidades a excepción del frente este de los Andes peruanos, donde los anuros conforman hasta un 88 por ciento de las especies. La composición diferencial de las comunidades parece ser una función del ambiente y distancia entre sitios. Análisis multivariados de la utilización de la estructura del ambiente muestran que dentro de las comunidades las especies están utilizando un amplio espectro de recursos y que solo algunas especies quedan agrupadas en aquellos casos, características de comportamiento o reproducción tienden a separar a aquellas especies.

La actividad humana en los altos Andes aparentemente ha contribuido poco al detrimento de la herpetofauna por el contrario, la contrucción de canales de irrigación y el apilamiento de rocas y cercos ha provisto con importantes ambientes para varios anfibios y reptiles. El sobre pastoreo puede tener efectos negativos en los insectos que son importantes como alimento de la herpetofauna. La explotación de las selvas nublados en las laderas andinas ha tenido graves consecuencias sobre la herpetofauna, sólo algunas especies son capáces de sobrevivir en los claros resultantes. Se necesitan reservas naturales para preservar la peculiar fauna de las selvas de neblina, donde la mayoría de las especies endémicas altoandinas viven.

LITERATURE CITED

Aguerrevere, S. E., Zuloaga, C. 1937. Observaciones geologicas en la parte central de la Cordillera de la Costa. Bol. Geol. Min. 2–4 3–22

Ahlfeid, F. 1970. Zur Tektonic des Andien Bolivien. Geol. Rundsch. 59 1124–1140

Aubodin, J., Borrello, A. V., Cecioni, G., Charpier, R., Chotin, P., Frutos, J., Thiele, R., Vicente, J.-C. 1973. Esquisse paléogeographique et structurale des Andes Méridionales. Rev. Geogr. Phys. Geol. Dyn. 15 11–72

Barbour, T., Noble, G. K. 1920a. Amphibians and reptiles from southern Peru collected by the Peruvian expedition of 1914–1915 under the auspices of Yale University and the National Geographic Society. Proc. U.S. Natl. Mus. 58 609–620

Barbour, T., Noble, G. K. 1920b. Some amphibians from northwestern Peru with a revision of the genera Phyllobates and Telmatobius. Bull. Mus. Comp. Zool., Harvard Univ. 63 395–427

Barrio, A. 1965. Las subespecies de *Hyla pulchella* Dumeril y Bibron (Anura Hylidae). Physis 25 115–128

Blair, W. F. 1972. Summary pp. 329–343 in Blair, W. F. (ed.) Evolution in the genus *Bufo*. Univ. Texas Press, Austin, 459 p.

Brame, A. H. Jr., Wake, D. B. 1963. The salamanders of South America. Contrib. Sci. Los Angeles Cty. Mus. (69) 1–72

Brame, A. H., Jr., Wake, D. B. 1971. New species of salamanders (genus *Bolitoglossa*) from Colombia Ecuador and Panamá. Ibid (219) 1–34

BROWN, J H 1971 Mammals on mountaintops Nonequilibrium insular biogeography Amer Nat 105 467-478

BURGL, H 1961 Historia geológica de Colombia Rev Acad Colombiana Cien Exactas, Fis Nat 11 137-191

CABRERA, A L 1968 Ecologia vegetal de la puna, pp 91-116 in TROLL, C (ed) Geo-ecology of the mountainous regions of the tropical Americas Colloq Geog 9 1-223

CAMPBELL, K L, JR 1976 The late Pleistocene avifauna of La Carolina southwestern Ecuador, pp 155-168 in OLSON, S L (ed) Collected papers in avian paleontology honoring the 90th birthday of Alexander Wetmore Smithsonian Contrib Paleobiol (27) 1-211

CAMPBELL, K E, JR 1979 The Pleistocene avifauna of the Talara Tar Seeps northwestern Peru Roy Ontario Mus Life Sci Contrib (In press)

CARRIKER, M A, JR 1922 Description of the Santa Marta Region, pp 7-29 in RUTHVEN, A G The amphibians and reptiles of the Sierra Nevada de Santa Marta Colombia Misc Publ Mus Zool Univ Michigan (8) 1-69

CEI, J M 1962 Batracios de Chile Ed Univ Chile, Santiago, 128 + cvm p

CEI, J M 1968 Remarks on the geographical distribution and phyletic trends of South American toads Pearce-Sellards Ser Texas Mem Mus (13) 1-21

CEI, J M 1971 Consideraciones sobre las relaciones taxonomicas de *Phymaturus patagonicus* y *Phymaturus palluma* Acta Zool Lilloana 28 37-46

CEI, J M 1972 Bufo of South America, pp 82-92 in BLAIR, W F (ed) Evolution in the genus Bufo Univ Texas Press, Austin, 459 p

CEI J M 1973 Comentarios sobre algunos generos de iguanidos *Diplolaemus Leiosaurus Aperopristis* y *Cupriguanus* Physis 32 269-276

CEI, J M 1974a Two new species of *Ctenoblepharis* (Reptilia Iguanidae) from the arid environments of the Central Argentina (Mendoza Province) J Herpetol 8 71-75

CEI, J M 1974b Revision of the Patagonian iguanids of the *Liolaemus elongatus* complex Ibid 8 219-229

CEI J M 1977 A new species of *Telmatobius* (Amphibia, Anura, Leptodactylidae) from the northern mountains of San Juan Argentina Ibid 11 359-361

CEI J M 1979 Amphibians of Argentina Monit Zool Italiano Monog Zool (In press)

CEI J M, CASTRO L P 1973 Taxonomic and serological researches on the *Phymaturus patagonicus* complex J Herpetol 7 237-247

CEI J M, LESPAMER V, ROSEGHINI, M 1972 Biogenic amines pp 233-243 in BLAIR, W F (ed) Evolution in the genus Bufo Univ Texas Press Austin, 459 p

CHAPMAN F M 1917 The distribution of bird life in Colombia Bull Amer Mus Nat Hist 36 1-730

CHARDON C E 1938 Apuntaciones sobre el origen de la vida de los Andes Bol Soc Venezolana Cienc Nat 5 1-47

COCHRAN D M, GOIN C J 1970 Frogs of Colombia U S Natl Mus Bull (288) 1-655

CROIZAT L NELSON, G, ROSEN, D E 1974 Centers of origin and related concepts Syst Zool 23 265-287

CUATRECASAS J 1968 Paramo vegetation and its life forms pp 163-186 in TROLL C (ed) Geo-ecology of the mountainous regions of the tropical Americas Colloq Geog 9 1-223

DAVEY J C 1949 The Venezuelan Andes and the Coastal and Interior ranges Part 3 The eastern Coastal Range Min Mag 80(3) 137-144

DIXON, J R, HUEY R B 1970 Systematics of the lizards of the gekkonid genus *Phyllodactylus* of mainland South America Nat Hist Mus Los Angeles Cty Contrib Sci (192) 1-78

DIXON J R, WRIGHT, J W 1975 A review of the lizards of the iguanid genus *Tropidurus* in Peru Ibid (271) 1-39

DOLLFUS, O 1960 Presentation de la structure des Andes centrales peruviennes Trav Inst Francais Etud Andines 7 53-64

DONOSO-BARROS R 1966 Reptiles de Chile Ed Univ Chile Santiago, 458 p

DONOSO-BARROS R 1968 The lizards of Venezuela (checklist and key) Caribb J Sci 8 105-122

DONOSO-BARROS, R 1970 Catálogo herpetológico Chileno Mus Nac Hist Nat Bol (Santiago de Chile) 31 49-124

DONOSO-BARROS, R 1972 Contribución al conocimiento del genero *Ctenoblephans* Tschudi y *Phrynosaura* Werner (Sauria Iguanidae) Bol Soc Biol Concepcion 44 129-134

DOTT, R H, JR, WINN, R D JR, DEWIT, M L, BRUIIN, R L 1977 Tectonic and sedimentary significance of Cretaceous Tekenika Beds of Tierra del Fuego Nature 266 620-622

DUELLMAN, W E 1970 The hylid frogs of Middle America Univ Kansas Mus Nat Hist Monogr (1) 1-753

DUELLMAN, W F 1972 A review of the Neotropical frogs of the *Hyla bogotensis* group Univ Kansas Mus Nat Hist Occas Pap (11) 1-31

DUELLMAN, W E 1973 Descriptions of new hylid frogs from Colombia and Ecuador Herpetologica 29 219-227

DUELLMAN, W E 1974 A systematic review of the marsupial frogs (Hylidae *Gastrotheca*) of the Andes of Ecuador Univ Kansas Mus Nat Hist Occas Pap (22) 1-27

DUELLMAN, W E 1976 Centrolenid frogs from Peru Ibid (52) 1-11

DUELLMAN W E 1977 Liste der rezenten Amphibien und Reptilien Hylidae Centrolenidae, Pseudidae D is Tierreich (95) 1-225

DUELLMAN, W E 1978a Two new species of *Eleutherodactylus* (Anura Leptodactylidae) from the Peruvian Andes Trans Kansas Acad Sci 81 65-71

DUELLMAN, W E 1978b New species of leptodactylid frogs of the genus *Eleutherodactylus* from the Cosñipata Valley, Peru Proc Biol Soc Washington 91 418–430

DUELLMAN, W E 1978c Three new species of *Eleutherodactylus* from Amazonian Peru (Amphibia Anura Leptodactylidae) Herpetologica 34 264–270

DUELLMAN, W E, ALTIG, R 1978 New species of tree frogs (family Hylidae) from Colombia and Ecuador Ibid 34 177–185

DUELLMAN, W E, FRITTS, T H 1972 A taxonomic review of the southern Andean marsupial frogs (Hylidae *Gastrotheca*) Univ Kansas Mus Nat Hist Occas Pap (9) 1–37

DUELLMAN, W E, SIMMONS, J E 1977 A new species of *Eleutherodactylus* (Anura Leptodactylidae) from the Cordillera Oriental of Colombia Proc Biol Soc Washington 90 60–65

DUELLMAN, W E, TOFT, C A 1979 Anurans from Serrania de Sira, Amazonian Peru Taxonomy and biogeography Herpetologica 35 60–70

DUELLMAN, W E, VELOSO M, A 1977 Phylogeny of *Pleurodema* (Anura Leptodactylidae) A biogeographic model Univ Kansas Mus Nat Hist Occas Pap (64) 1–46

EDWARDS, S R 1974 A phenetic analysis of the genus *Colostethus* (Anura Dendrobatidae) Ph D Dissert Univ Kansas 419 p

EDWARDS, S R MS Systematics of the genus *Colostethus* (Anura Dendrobatidae)

ENGEL, F A 1976 An ancient world preserved Crown Publ, New York 314 p

ESTES, R, REIG, O A 1973 The early fossil record of frogs A review of the evidence, pp 11–63 *in* VIAL, J L (ed) Evolutionary biology of the anurans Contemporary research on major problems Univ Missouri Press Columbia, 470 p

ETHERIDGE, R 1964 Comparative osteology and systematic relationships of sceloporine lizards Copeia 1964(4) 610–631

ETHERIDGE, R 1966 The systematic relationships of West Indian and South American lizards referred to the iguanid genus *Leiocephalus* Ibid 1966 (1) 79–91

ETHERIDGE, R 1967 Lizard caudal vertebrae Ibid 1967(4) 699–744

FRITTS, T H 1974 A multivariate evolutionary analysis of the Andean iguanid lizards of the genus *Stenocercus* San Diego Soc Nat Hist Mem (7) 1–89

GALLARDO, J M 1961 Three new toads from South America *Bufo manicorensis*, *Bufo spinulosus altiperuvianus* and *Bufo quechua* Breviora (141) 1–8

GALLARDO, J M 1962 Los generos *Telmatobius* y *Batrachophrynus* (Amphibia Leptodactylidae) en la Argentina Neotropica 8 45–58

GALLARDO, J M 1967 *Bufo gnustae* sp nov del grupo de *B ockendeni* Boulenger, hallado en la Provincia de Jujuy, Argentina Ibid 13 54–56

GANSSER, A 1955 Ein Beitrage zur Geologie und Petrographie der Sierra Nevada de Santa Marta (Kolumbien, Sudamerika) Schweiz Mineral Petrogr Mitt 35 209–279

GANSSER, A 1973 Facts and theories on the Andes J Geol Soc London 129 93–131

GORHAM, S W 1966 Liste der rezenten Amphibien und Reptilien Ascaphidae, Leiopelmatidae, Pipidae, Discoglossidae, Pelobatidae, Leptodactylidae, Rhinophrynidae Das Tierreich (85) 1–222

GORMAN, G C, HUEY, R B, WILLIAMS, E E 1969 Cytotaxonomic studies on some unusual iguanid lizards assigned to the genera *Chamaeleolis*, *Polychrus*, *Polychroides*, and *Phenacosaurus*, with behavioral notes Breviora (316) 1–17

HAFFER, J 1970 Enstehung und Ausbreitung nord-Andiner Bergvogel Zool Jahrb Abt Syst Oekol Geogr Tiere 97 301–337

HAFFER, J 1974 Avian speciation in tropical South America Publ Nuttall Ornithol Club (14) 1–390

HAM, C K, HERRERA, L J, JR 1963 Role of subandean fault system in tectonics of eastern Peru and Ecuador, pp 47–61 *in* CHILDS, O E, BEEBE, B W (eds) Backbone of the Americas Mem Amer Assoc Pet Geol 2 1–320

HARRINGTON, H J 1956 Main morphostructural regions of South America, pp VII–XVIII *in* JENKS, W F (ed) Handbook of South American geology Geol Soc Amer Mem 65 1–378

HARRINGTON, H J 1962 Paleogeographic development of South America Bull Amer Assoc Pet Geol 46 1773–1814

HASTENRATH, S I 1967 Observations on the snow line in the Peruvian Andes J Glaciol 6 541–550

HERD, D C, NAESER, C W 1974 Radiometric evidence for pre-Wisconsin glaciation in the northern Andes Geology 2 603–604

HEUSSER, C J 1974 Vegetation and climate of the southern Chilean lake district during and since the last interglacial Quat Res (New York) 4 290–315

HEYER, W R 1975 A preliminary analysis of the intergeneric relationships of the frog family Leptodactylidae Smithsonian Contrib Zool (199) 1–55

JAHN, A 1931 Los paramos venezolanos, sus aspectos fisicos y su vegetacion Soc Venezolana Cienc Nat Bol 3 93–127

JAHN, A 1934 Las temperaturas medias y extremas de las zonas altitudinales de Venezuela Ibid 14 135–172

JAMES, D E 1971 Plate tectonic model for the evolution of the central Andes Geol Soc Amer Bull 82 3325–3346

JAMES, D E 1973 The evolution of the Andes Sci Amer 229(2) 60–70

JEANNEL, R 1967 Biogeographie de l Amerique australe, pp 401–460 *in* DELAMERE DEBOUTTEVILLE, C, RAPOPORT, E (eds) Biologie de l Amerique australe, 3 C N R S Groupe Francais Argiles C R Reun Etud, Paris, 834 p

KINZL, H. 1968. La glaciacion actual y pleistocenica en los Andes centrales, pp. 77-90 *in* TROLL, C. (ed.). Geoecology of the mountainous regions of the tropical Americas. Colloq. Geog. 9:1-223.

LAURENT, R. F. 1967. Descubrimiento del genero *Gastrotheca* Fitzinger en Argentina. Acta Zool. Lilloana 22:353-354.

LAURENT, R. F. 1969a. Estudio complementario de *Gastrotheca christiani* Laurent. Ibid. 25:123-136.

LAURENT, R. F. 1969b. Una segunda especie del genero *Gastrotheca* Fitzinger en Argentina. Ibid. 25:143-150.

LAURENT, R. F. 1970. Dos especies nuevas argentinas del género *Telmatobius* (Amphibia, Leptodactylidae). Ibid. 25:207-226.

LAURENT, R. F. 1973. Nuevos datos sobre el genero *Telmatobius* en el noroeste Argentino, con descripcion de una nueva especie de la Sierra del Manchao. Ibid. 30:163-187.

LAURENT, R. F. 1976. Nuevas notas sobre el genero *Gastrotheca* Fitzinger. Ibid. 32:31-64.

LAURENT, R. F. 1977. Contribucion al conocimiento del genero *Telmatobius* Wiegmann (4a Nota). Ibid. 32:189-206.

LAZELL, J. D. 1969. The genus *Phenacosaurus* (Sauria: Iguanidae). Breviora 325:1-24.

LIDDLE, R. A. 1946. The geology of Venezuela and Trinidad. 2nd ed. New York, 890 p.

LOHMANN, H. H. 1970. Outline of tectonic history of Bolivian Andes. Bull. Amer. Assoc. Pet. Geol. 54:735-757.

LOW, B. S. 1972. Evidence from parotoid-gland secretions, pp. 244-264 *in* BLAIR, W. F. (ed.). Evolution in the genus *Bufo*. Univ. Texas Press, Austin. 459 p.

LYNCH, J. D. 1971. Evolutionary relationships, osteology, and zoogeography of leptodactyloid frogs. Univ. Kansas Mus. Nat. Hist. Misc. Publ. (53):1-238.

LYNCH, J. D. 1975a. A review of the Andean leptodactylid frog genus *Phrynopus*. Univ. Kansas Mus. Nat. Hist. Occas. Pap. (35):1-51.

LYNCH, J. D. 1975b. A review of the broad-headed eleutherodactyline frogs of South America. Ibid. (38):1-46.

LYNCH, J. D. 1975c. The identity of the frog *Eleutherodactylus conspicillatus* (Gunther), with descriptions of two related species from northwestern South America (Amphibia: Leptodactylidae). Contrib. Sci. Los Angeles Cty. Mus. (272):1-19.

LYNCH, J. D. 1976a. New species of frogs (Leptodactylidae: *Eleutherodactylus*) from the Pacific versant of Ecuador. Univ. Kansas Mus. Nat. Hist. Occas. Pap. (55):1-33.

LYNCH, J. D. 1976b. The species groups of the South American frogs of the genus *Eleutherodactylus* (Leptodactylidae). Ibid. (61):1-24.

LYNCH, J. D. 1978a. A new eleutherodactyline frog from the Andes of northern Colombia (Leptodactylidae). Copeia 1978(1):17-21.

LYNCH, J. D. 1978b. A re-assessment of the telmatobiine leptodactylid frogs of Patagonia. Univ. Kansas Mus. Nat. Hist. Occas. Pap. (72):1-57.

LYNCH, J. D. 1979. Leptodactylid frogs of the genus *Eleutherodactylus* from the Andes of southern Ecuador. Univ. Kansas Mus. Nat. Hist. Misc. Publ. (66):1-62.

LYNCH, J. D., DUELLMAN, W. E. 1973. A review of the centrolenid frogs of Ecuador, with descriptions of new species. Univ. Kansas Mus. Nat. Hist. Occas. Pap. 10:1-66.

LYNCH, J. D., DUELLMAN, W. E. 1979. The *Eleutherodactylus* of the Amazonian slopes of the Ecuadorian Andes (Anura: Leptodactylidae). Univ. Kansas Mus. Nat. Hist. Misc. Publ. (In press).

MACARTHUR, R. A., WILSON, E. O. 1967. The theory of island biogeography. Monog. Pop. Biol. 1, Princeton Univ. Press, Princeton, New Jersey, 204 p.

MACEDO, H. DE. 1960. Vergleichende Untersuchungen an Arten der Gattung *Telmatobius* (Amphibia: Anura). Z. Wis. Zool. Abt. A 163:355-396.

MAURIELLO, D., ROSKOSKI, J. P. 1974. A re-analysis of Vuilleumier's data. Amer. Nat. 108:711-714.

McDIARMID, R. W. 1971. Comparative morphology and evolution of frogs of the Neotropical genera *Atelopus*, *Dendrophryniscus*, *Melanophryniscus*, and *Oreophrynella*. Nat. Hist. Mus. Los Angeles Cty. Sci. Bull. (12):1-66.

MERCER, J. H., PALACIOS M. O. 1977. Radiocarbon dating of the last glaciation in Peru. Geology 5:600-604.

MONTANUCCI, R. R. 1973. Systematics and evolution of the Andean lizard genus *Pholidobolus* (Sauria: Teiidae). Univ. Kansas Mus. Nat. Hist. Misc. Publ. (59):1-52.

MORRISON, T. 1974. Land above the clouds. Andre Deutsch Ltd., London. 223 p.

MORRISON, T. 1975. The Andes. Time-Life International. Amsterdam, 184 p.

MULLER, P. 1973. The dispersal centres of terrestrial vertebrates in the Neotropical Realm. Biogeographica 3. Junk. The Hague, 244 p.

MYERS, C. W. 1973. A new genus for Andean snakes related to *Lygophis boursieri* and a new species (Colubridae). Amer. Mus. Novit. (2522):1-37.

MYERS, C. W. 1974. The systematics of *Rhadinaea* (Colubridae) a genus of New World snakes. Bull. Amer. Mus. Nat. Hist. 153:1-262.

MYERS, C. W., DALY, J. W. 1976a. Preliminary evaluation of skin toxins and vocalizations in taxonomic and evolutionary studies of poison-dart frogs (Dendrobatidae). Ibid. 157:173-262.

MYERS, C. W., DALY, J. W. 1976b. A new species of poison frog (*Dendrobates*) from Andean Ecuador, including an analysis of its skin toxins. Univ. Kansas Mus. Nat. Hist. Occas. Pap. (59):1-12.

MYERS, C. W., DALY, J. W., MALKIN, B. 1978. A dangerously toxic new frog (*Phyllobates*) used by Embera Indians of western Colombia, with discussion of blowgun fabrication and dart poisoning. Bull. Amer. Mus. Nat. Hist. 161:307-366.

NOBLE, G. K. 1921. Some new lizards from northwestern Peru. Ann. N.Y. Acad. Sci. 29:133-139.

OFTEDAL, O T 1974 A revision of the genus Anadia (Sauria, Teiidae) Arq Zool (Sao Paulo) 25 203-265

OKADA, A 1971 On the neotectonics of the Atacama fault zone region—Preliminary notes on late Cenozoic faulting and geomorphic development of the coast range of northern Chile Bull Dep Geog Univ Tokyo 3 47-65

OPPENHEIM, V 1937 Contribution to the geology of the Venezuelan Andes Bol Inf Asoc Venezolana Geol Min Pet 1 25-45

PARKER, H W 1932 Some new or rare reptiles and amphibians from southern Ecuador Ann Mag Nat Hist (10)9 21-26

PARKER, H W 1934 Reptiles and amphibians from southern Ecuador Ibid (10)14 264-273

PARKER, H W 1938 The vertical distribution of some reptiles and amphibians in southern Ecuador Ibid (11)2 438-450

PARKER, H W 1940 The Percy Sladen Trust Expedition to Lake Titicaca in 1937 Amphibia Trans Linnean Soc London 1(2) 203-216

PATTERSON, T C LANNING, E P 1967 Los medios ambientes glacial tardio y postglacial de Sudamerica Bol Soc Geog Lima 86 1-19

PAULL, D, WILLIAMS, E E, HALL, W P 1976 Lizard karyotypes from the Galapagos Islands Chromosomes in phylogeny and evolution Breviora (441) 1-31

PÉFAUR, J E, DUELLMAN, W E 1977 Community structure in high Andean herpetofaunas Herpetol Rev 8(3) Suppl 6-7 (Abstract)

PETERS, J A 1973 The frog genus *Atelopus* in Ecuador Smithsonian Contrib Zool (145) 1-49

PETERS, J A, DONOSO-BARROS, R 1970 Catalogue of the Neotropical Squamata Part II Lizards and Amphisbaenians U S Natl Mus Bull (297) 1-293

PETERS, J A, OREJAS MIRANDA, B 1970 Catalogue of the Neotropical Squamata Part I Snakes Ibid (297) 1-347

PETERSEN, U 1958 Structure and uplift of the Andes of Peru, Bolivia, Chile, and adjacent Argentina Bol Soc Geol Peru 33 57-143

PRESCH, W 1978 Evolutionary relationships of microteiid lizards Joint Annual Meeting SSAR, ASIH, HL, Arizona State Univ, Tempe, Arizona, 31 May-7 June 1978 (Abstract of presented paper)

PLATNICK, N I, NELSON, G 1978 A method of analysis for historical biogeography Syst Zool 27 1-16

RIVERO, J A 1961 Salientia of Venezuela Bull Mus Comp Zool Harvard Univ (126) 1-207

RIVERO, J A 1963a The distribution of Venezuelan frogs II The Venezuelan Andes Caribb J Sci 3 87-102

RIVERO, J A 1963b Five new species of *Atelopus* from Colombia, with notes on other forms from Colombia and Ecuador Ibid 3 103-124

RIVERO, J A 1964 The distribution of Venezuelan frogs IV The coastal range Ibid 4 307-319

RIVERO, J A 1968 Los centrolénidos de Venezuela (Amphibia Salientia) Soc Cien Nat Salle Mem 28 301-334

RIVERO, J A 1970 On the origin endemism, and distribution of the genus *Stefania* Rivero (Amphibia Salientia) with a description of a new species from southeastern Venezuela Soc Venezolana Cienc Nat Bol 28 456-481

RIVERO, J A 1972 La ranita más elevada' de Venezuela Natura (Venezuela), Sept 1972 48-49

RIVERO, J A 1974 On *Atelopus oxyrhynchus* Boulenger (Amphibia, Salientia), with the description of a new race and a related new species from the Venezuelan paramos Soc Venezolana Cienc Nat Bol 29 600-612

RIVERO, J A 1976 [1978] Notas sobre los anfibios de Venezuela II Sobre los *Colostethus* de los Andes Venezolanos Soc Cien Nat Salle Mem 35 327-344

RIVERO, J A, MAYORGA, H 1973 Un nuevo *Eleutherodactylus* (Amphibia, Salientia) del Páramo de Guaramacal, Estado Trujillo, Venezuela Caribb J Sci 13 75-79

ROIG, F A 1972 Bosquejo fisionomico de la vegetacion de la Provincia de Mendoza Bol Soc Argentina Bot 13(supplement) 49-80

ROSEN, D F 1975 A vicariance model of Caribbean biogeography Syst Zool 24 431-464

ROSSMAN, D A, THOMAS, R 1979 A new dipsadine snake of the genus *Sibynomorphus* from Peru Louisiana St Univ Mus Zool Occas Pap (54) 1-6

ROZE, J 1966 La taxonomia y zoogeografía de los ofidios de Venezuela Univ Central Venezuela, Caracas, 362 p

RUIZ-C, P M, HERNANDEZ-C, J I 1976 Osornophryne, genero nuevo de anfibios bufónidos de Colombia y Ecuador Caldasia 11(54) 93-148

RUIZ-C, P M, HERNANDEZ-C, J I 1978 Una nueva especie Colombiana de Atelopus (Amphibia Bufonidae) Ibid 57 181-197

RUTHVEN, A G 1922 The amphibians and reptiles of the Sierra Nevada de Santa Marta, Colombia Misc Publ Mus Zool Univ Michigan (8) 1-69

RUTLAND, R W R, GUEST, J E, GRASTY, R L 1965 Isotopic ages and Andean uplift Nature 208 677-678

SAUER, W 1965 Geologia del Ecuador Min Educación, Quito, 384 p

SAUER, W 1971 Geologie von Ecuador Gebruder Bortraeger, Berlin, 316 p

SAVAGE, J M 1958 The iguanid lizard genera *Urosaurus* and *Uta* with remarks on related genera Zoologica 43(2) 41-54

SAVAGE, J M 1960 A revision of the Ecuadorian snakes of the colubrid genus *Atractus* Misc Publ Mus Zool Univ Michigan (112) 1-86

SCHMIDT, K P 1954 Notes on frogs of the genus *Telmatobius* with descriptions of two new Peruvian species Fieldiana Zool 34 277-287

SCHMIDT, K P WALKER W F, JR 1943 Three new snakes from the Peruvian Andes Field Mus Nat Hist Zool Ser 24 325-329

SCHUBERT, C 1974 Late Pleistocene Merida glaciation Venezuelan Andes Boreas 3 147–152

SHAGAM, R 1975 The northern termination of the Andes, pp 325–420 in NAIRN A L M, STEHLI F G (eds) The ocean basins and margins Vol 3 The Gulf of Mexico and the Caribbean Plenum Press, New York 706 p

SILVERSTONE, P A 1975a Two new species of *Colostethus* (Amphibia Anura Dendrobatidae) from Colombia Mus Nat Hist Los Angeles Cty Contrib Sci (268) 1–10

SILVERSTONE, P A 1975b A revision of the poison-arrow frogs of the genus *Dendrobates* Wagler Mus Nat Hist Los Angeles Cty Sci Bull (21) 1–55

SILVERSTONE, P A 1976 A revision of the poison-arrow frogs of the genus *Phyllobates* Bibron in Sagra (Family Dendrobatidae) Ibid (27) 1–53

SIMPSON, B B 1975a Glacial climates in the eastern tropical South Pacific Nature 253(5486) 34–36

SIMPSON, B B 1975b Pleistocene changes in the flora of the high tropical Andes Paleobiology 1 273–294

SIMPSON, B B, VERVOORST, F 1977 Physiographic settings of the study sites, pp 16–25 in ORIANS, G H, SOLBRIG O T (eds) Convergent evolution in warm deserts Dowden, Hutchinson and Ross Stroudsburg Pa, 333 p

SOLBRIG, O T 1976 The origin and floristic affinities of the South American temperate desert and semidesert regions, pp 7–49 in GOODALL, D W (ed) Evolution of desert biota Univ Texas Press, 250 p

STEINMANN, G 1930 Geologia del Peru Carl Winters, Heidelberg 448 p

TAYLOR, E H 1968 The caecilians of the world Univ Kansas Press, Lawrence, 848 p

TEST, F H, SEXTON, O J, HEATWOLE, H 1966 Reptiles of Rancho Grande and vicinity, Estado Aragua, Venezuela Misc Publ Mus Zool Univ Michigan (128) 1–63

TROLL, K 1959 Die tropischen Gebirge Bonner Geog Abhandl 25 1–93

TRUEB, L 1971 Phylogenetic relationships of certain Neotropical toads with the description of a new genus (Anura Bufonidae) Mus Nat Hist Los Angeles Cty Contrib Sci (216) 1–40

TRUEB L 1974 Systematic relationships of Neotropical horned frogs genus *Hemiphractus* (Anura Hylidae) Univ Kansas Mus Nat Hist Occas Pap (29) 1–60

TRUEB L 1979 Leptodactylid frogs of the genus *Telmatobius* in Ecuador with the description of a new species Copeia (4) (In press)

TRUEB L, DUELLMAN W E 1978 An extraordinary new marsupial frog from Peru (Hylidae Gastrotheca) Copeia 1978(3) 498–503

TURNER, J C M 1972 Cordillera Oriental, pp 117–142 in LEANZA A F (ed) Geologia regional Argentina Acad Nac Cien Cordoba, 869 p

UZZELL, T 1969 A new genus and species of teiid lizard from Bolivia Postilla (129) 1–15

UZZELL, T 1970 Teiid lizards of the genus *Proctoporus* from Bolivia and Peru Ibid (142) 1–39

UZZELL, T 1973 A revision of lizards of the genus *Prionodactylus*, with a new genus for *P leucostictus* and notes on the genus *Euspondylus* (Sauria Teiidae) Ibid (159) 1–67

VAN DER HAMMEN, T 1972 Historia de la vegetación y el medio ambiente del norte sudamericano Mem Symp I Congr Lat Amer Bot, Mexico, D F pp 119–134

VAN DER HAMMEN, T 1974 The Pleistocene changes of vegetation and climate in tropical South America J Biogeog 1 3–26

VAN DER HAMMEN, T, WERNER J H, DOMMELEN, H VAN 1973 Palynological record of the upheaval of the northern Andes A study of the Pliocene and Lower Quaternary of the Colombian eastern Cordillera and the early evolution of its high-Andean biota Rev Paleobot Palynol 16 1–122

VELLARD J 1946 El genero *Telmatobius* en la Republica Argentina Acta Zool Lilloana 3 313–326

VELLARD J 1951 Estudios sobre batracios andinos I—El grupo Telmatobius y formas afines Mem Mus Hist Nat Javier Prado (1) 1–89

VELLARD J 1953 Estudios sobre batracios andinos II—El grupo marmoratus y formas afines Ibid (2) 1–53

VELLARD, J 1955 Estudios sobre batracios andinos III—Los Telmatobius del grupo jelskii Ibid (4) 1–28

VELLARD J 1956 Repatition des batraciens dans les Andes au sud de l'Equateur Trav Inst Francais Etud Andines 5 141–162

VELLARD, J 1957 Estudios sobre batracios andinos IV—El genero Gastrotheca Mem Mus Hist Nat Javier Prado (5) 1–47

VELLARD J 1959 Estudios sobre batracios andinos V—El genero Bufo Ibid (8) 1–48

VELLARD J 1960a Estudios sobre batracios andinos VI—Notas complementarias sobre Telmatobius Ibid (10) 1–19

VELLARD, J 1960b Estudios sobre batracios andinos VII—El genero Pleurodema en los Andes Peruanos Ibid (10) 1–12

VELOSO M, A, TRUEB, L 1976 Description of a new species of telmatobiine frog, *Telmatobius* (Amphibia Leptodactylidae), from the Andes of northern Chile Univ Kansas Mus Nat Hist Occas Pap (62) 1–10

VUILLEUMIER, B S 1971 Pleistocene changes in the fauna and flora of South America Science 173 771–780

VUILLEUMIER, F 1970 Insular biogeography in continental regions I The northern Andes Amer Nat 104 373–388

VUILLEUMIER, F 1977 Barrieres ecogeographiques permettant la spéciation des oiseaux des hautes Andes, pp 29–52 in DESCIMON, H (ed) Biogéographie et evolution en Amérique tropicale Publ Lab Zool Ecole Normale Super (9) 1–344

WALKER W F, JR 1945 A study of the snake, *Pachynemis peruviana* Wiegmann and its allies Bull Mus Comp Zool Harvard Univ (96) 1–55

WHYMPER, E. 1892. Travels amongst the great Andes of the Equator. 2nd ed. John Murray, London, 456 p.

WILLIAMS, E. E. 1974. South American *Anolis*: Three new species related to *Anolis nigrolineatus* and *A. dissimilis*. Breviora (122):1-15.

WILLIAMS, E. E., RUIG, O. A., KIBLISKY, P., RIVERO-BLANCO, C. 1970. *Anolis jacare* Boulenger, a "solitary" anole from the Andes of Venezuela. Ibid. (353):1-15.

YRIGOYEN, M. R. 1972. Cordillera principal, pp 315-364 *in* LEANZA, A. F. (ed.) Geologia regional Argentina. Acad. Nac. Cien. Cordoba, 869 p.

APPENDICES

Appendices 1-3 include lists of the 727 species (462 amphibians and 265 reptiles) that formed the data base for the analysis of geographical distributions. For each species, the known altitudinal limits of distribution are given; the general habitat of each is coded as noted in the captions to the tables. The species are arranged sequentially in 1) ordinal categories (caecilians, salamanders, frogs, lizards, snakes), 2) phylogenetically by families, and 3) alphabetically by genus and species. Those species designated by letters have yet to be named. Only those species having primarily, or extensively, Andean distributions are included. Species that are widespread in the lowlands but ascend the Andean slopes to elevations of more than 1000 m have been excluded.

APPENDIX 15.1—Altitudinal and geographic distribution of amphibians and reptiles in the Andes and associated highlands of Venezuela. Habitats: C = cloud forest, P = páramo, R = rainforest, S = subparamo, X = unknown. Species noted by ° also occur in the Sierra Nevada de Santa Marta, °° also occur on Tobago or Trinidad, °°° also occur in Andes of Colombia, °°°° also occur in Andes of Colombia and Sierra Nevada de Santa Marta.

Species	Elevation	Mérida Andes	Cordillera de la Costa	Cerro Turumiquire	Serrania de Paria
Salamanders					
Bolitoglossa borburata	1000-1200		C		
Bolitoglossa orestes	2000-3500	SP			
Bolitoglossa savagei°	2000	S			
Frogs					
Eleutherodactylus anotis	950-1300		C		
Eleutherodactylus bimaculus	900-1200		C		
Eleutherodactylus boconoensis	2900	P			
Eleutherodactylus briceni	1620	C			
Eleutherodactylus ginesi	2800-4000	P			
Eleutherodactylus lancini	2800-3000	P			
Eleutherodactylus mausti	100-1150		RC		
Eleutherodactylus orocostalis	1900-2100		C		
Eleutherodactylus racenisi	1900-2100		C		
Eleutherodactylus reticulatus	1275		C		
Eleutherodactylus rozei	1000		C		
Eleutherodactylus stenodiscus	1275		C		
Eleutherodactylus terraebolivaris	650-1800		RC		
Eleutherodactylus turumiquirensis	1675			C	
Eleutherodactylus urichi°°	1000-2450		C	C	C
Eleutherodactylus williamsi	1900-2100		C		
Atelopus cruciger	200-1100		RC		
Atelopus mucubajiensis	2900-3100	P			
Atelopus oxyrhynchus	2010-3500	CP			
Bufo sternosignatus	200-1800		RC		
Colostethus alboguttatus	1600-2000	C			
Colostethus bromelicola	1200		C		
Colostethus collaris	1500-1600	C			
Colostethus dunni	370-1650		RC		
Colostethus herminae	150-1650		RC	C	
Colostethus mandelorum	2400-2630			C	
Colostethus meridensis	1600-1700	C			
Colostethus sp. 1ª	600				C

ª Species of *Colostethus* designated by numbers are being named in a manuscript by S. R. Edwards.

Species	Elevation	Merida Andes	Cordillera de la Costa	Cerro Turumuquire	Serrania de Paria
Colostethus riveroi	600	.	.	..	C
Flectonotus pygmaeus°°	1075–1200	.	C	.	.
Gastrotheca nicefori°°°	1575	C	.	.	.
Gastrotheca ovifera	1000–1800	..	C	.	.
Gastrotheca sp F"	650–1100	.	RC	.	.
Hyla battersbyi	1000	.	X	.	.
Hyla labialis°°°	2000	S	.	.	..
Hyla platydactyla	1600–2500	CP	.	.	..
Phyllomedusa medinae	1100	.	C	..	..
Centrolenella altitudinalis	2400	C	.	..	.
Centrolenella andina	840–1050	RC	..	.	.
Centrolenella antisthenesi	240–1100	.	RC	.	---
Centrolenella buckleyi°°°	2000–2700	SP	..	--	.
Centrolenella esteresi	1300–2400	C	--	.	.
Centrolenella fleischmanni°°°	1800	.	C	.	.
Centrolenella orientalis	1200	.	.	C	.
Centrolenella orocostalis	240–1200	.	RC	.	.
Lizards					
Gonatodes ceciliae	600	...	...	.	C
Gonatodes taniae	650–1100	.	RC	.	---
Anolis jacare	1500–1800	C	.	—	..
Anolis nigropunctatus	1200	C	.	..	.
Anolis squamulatus	200–1100	.	RC	.	---
Anolis tigrinus	1100	.	C	.	.
Anadia bitaeniata	2500–3050	P	.	.	.
Anadia blakei	1520–1830	.	.	C	.
Anadia brevifrontalis	2900–3600	P	.	.	.
Anadia marmorata	1100–2200	..	C	..	.
Euspondylus acutirostris	1100	.	C	..	.
Proctoporus achlyens	1100	.	C	.	..
Proctoporus luctuosus	1100	.	C	..	.
Snakes					
Liotyphlops caracasensis	800–1100	.	RC	.	.
Leptotyphlops affinis	1100–2000	CS	.	.	..
Leptotyphlops macrolepis	200–1800	RC	.	—	.
Atractus badius	400–2000	CS	RC	.	.
Atractus fuliginosus	±2000	.	.	C	---
Atractus lancinii	1700	.	C	—	..
Atractus univittatus	800–1100	.	RC	..	----
Atractus ventrimaculatus	1200–2000	CS	.	.	.
Atractus vittatus	800–1800	..	RC	—	..
Chironius monticola°°°	1100–1600	C	C	..	---
Dendrophidion percarinatus	600–1600	C	C	.	---
Lampropeltis triangulum	1300–1600	C	C	.	---
Leimadophis bimaculatus°°°	1400–2500	CS	.	.	..
Leimadophis zweifeli	600–1700	C	RC	.	.
Rhadinaea multilineata	800–2000	.	RC	.	--
Umbrivaga mertensi	1000–1200	.	C	.	.
Urotheca williamsi	1400–2000	.	C	.	.
Micrurus mipartatus°°°°	800–2000	CS	C	.	---
Bothrops medusa	1400–2000	.	C	.	.
TOTAL AMPHIBIANS (48)		18	25	5	3
TOTAL REPTILES (32)		14	21	2	1
TOTAL SPECIES (80)		32	46	7	4

APPENDIX 15 2—Altitudinal and geographic distribution of amphibians and reptiles in the Andes of Colombia and Ecuador, and the eastern cordilleras of Peru, Bolivia, and northern Argentina all highland species in the Huancabamba Depression are included Habitats C = cloud forest, D = dry forest, P = paramo or puna, R = rainforest S = subparamo, X = unknown Species noted by ° are those that are restricted to outlying ranges east of the Andes—Sierra de Macarena, Cordillera de Cutucu, Cordillera del Condor, Serranía de Sira Species noted by °° occur in the Cordillera Occidental in northern Peru

Species	Elevation	Sierra Nevada de Santa Marta	Cordillera Occidental, Ecuador	Cordillera Occidental, Colombia	Cordillera Central, Colombia	Nudo de Pasto, Colombia	Cordillera Oriental, Colombia	Cordillera Oriental, Ecuador	Cordillera Oriental, Peru	Cordillera Oriental, Bolivia	Cordillera Oriental, Argentina	Inter-Andean Basins, Ecuador	Huancabamba Depression
Caecilians													
Caecilia abitaguae	1100–1280							C					
Caecilia antioquiensis	1980				C								
Caecilia attenuata	1900							C	C				
Caecilia crassisquama	1400–1800							C					
Caecilia degenerata	1800–2200						C						
Caecilia occidentalis	1200–1700			C									
Caecilia orientalis	1660–1935							C					
Caecilia pachynema	1200–2000		C	C									
Caecilia parvipes	1650				C								
Caecilia subdermalis	± 2500				C								
Caecilia sp "A"	1860–2150		C										
Caecilia sp 'B'	2100		D										
Epicrionops bicolor	1200–1400		C						C				
Epicrionops peruvianus	1400								C				
Epicrionops petersi	1150–1900							C	C				
Epicrionops sp "A"	1980							C					
Salamanders													
Bolitoglossa adspersa	2500–3000						P						
Bolitoglossa capitana	1780						C						
Bolitoglossa hypacra	3610			P									
Bolitoglossa nicefori	1500				C								
Bolitoglossa palmata	2000							C					
Bolitoglossa pandi	1300						C						
Bolitoglossa phalarosoma	1500				C								
Bolitoglossa ramosi	1930				C								
Bolitoglossa savagei	1000–2100	C											
Bolitoglossa vallecula	2300–2700				S								
Bolitoglossa walkeri	1980–2050			C									
Bolitoglossa sp 'A'	2240			C									
Frogs													
Amblyphrynus helonotus	1200		C										
Amblyphrynus ingeri	1720–1980	C			C		C						
Eleutherodactylus sp '1 °'	2660								C				
Eleutherodactylus actites	2400		C										
Eleutherodactylus achatinus	140–1460		RC	RC									
Eleutherodactylus affinis	2800						P						
Eleutherodactylus appendiculatus	1960–2010		C										
Eleutherodactylus areolatus	130–2010		RC	RC									
Eleutherodactylus atratus	2200–1850								CS				
Eleutherodactylus bahonotus	2700–2800								S				

° Species of *Eleutherodactylus* designated by numbers are being named by Lynch and Duellman (1979)

APPENDIX 15.2 (Continued)

Species	Elevation	Sierra Nevada de Santa Marta	Cordillera Occidental, Ecuador	Cordillera Occidental, Colombia	Cordillera Central, Colombia	Nudo de Pasto, Colombia	Cordillera Oriental, Colombia	Cordillera Oriental, Ecuador	Cordillera Oriental Peru	Cordillera Oriental, Bolivia	Cordillera Oriental Argentina	Inter-Andean Basins, Ecuador	Huancabamba Depression
Eleutherodactylus barycnus	2200–3000							CS					
Eleutherodactylus bogotensis	2900–3250						P						
Eleutherodactylus bromeliaceus	1700–2620							C					
Eleutherodactylus buckleyi	3200–3700		P		P	P		P					
Eleutherodactylus cabrerai	2000				C								
Eleutherodactylus cajamercensis	1870–3000							S	S			S	D
Eleutherodactylus calcaratus	1000–2240			C									
Eleutherodactylus calcarulatus	1140–2240		C	C									
Eleutherodactylus carmelitae	1540–2530	C											
Eleutherodactylus celator	2530–2710		S					S					
Eleutherodactylus cerastes	500–1580		RC	RC									
Eleutherodactylus chloronotus	2280–3440						CS	CS					
Eleutherodactylus colodactylus	2195–3140							SP					
Eleutherodactylus sp "2"	1830							C					
Eleutherodactylus cornutus	500–2000						RC	RC					
Eleutherodactylus cosnipetae	1580–1700								C				
Eleutherodactylus sp "3"	1410–1700							C					
Eleutherodactylus cremnguis	1460–1540		C										
Eleutherodactylus crucifer	1540		C										
Eleutherodactylus cruentus	1540–2500	C											
Eleutherodactylus eruralis	?									X			
Eleutherodactylus cryophilus	2800–3100							S					
Eleutherodactylus cryptomelas	2470–3100							CS					
Eleutherodactylus curtipes	2900–4400		P			P		P					
Eleutherodactylus danae	1270–1700								C				
Eleutherodactylus delicatus	1390–2470	C											
Eleutherodactylus devillei	2200–3150						CS	CS					
Eleutherodactylus discoidalis	500–1150												D
Eleutherodactylus sp "4"	1100–1950						C	C					
Eleutherodactylus elassodiscus	1700–3200						CS	CS					
Eleutherodactylus elegans	2900–3300						P						
Eleutherodactylus sp "5"	2160–2600							C					
Eleutherodactylus erythropleurus	800–2130			RC									
Eleutherodactylus frater	1000–1050						RC						
Eleutherodactylus galdi	1000–1830							C					
Eleutherodactylus gladiator	2300–2900							C					
Eleutherodactylus glandulosus	2350–2890							C					
Eleutherodactylus gularis	1400				C								
Eleutherodactylus sp "6"	2160–2750							C					
Eleutherodactylus sp "7"	1270–1950				C		C	C					
Eleutherodactylus insignitus	1850–2160	C						C					
Eleutherodactylus sp "8"	1300–2160							C					
Eleutherodactylus lanthanites	300–1490						RC	RC					
Eleutherodactylus latidiscus	400–1230		RC	RC									
Eleutherodactylus leoni	1960–3100		CS			S		P				S	
Eleutherodactylus leucopus	2400–2700						C	C					
Eleutherodactylus lindae	1700								C				
Eleutherodactylus sp "9"	2135–2750							CS					
Eleutherodactylus luteolateralis	1140–1540		C										

APPENDIX 15.2 (Continued)

Species	Elevation	Sierra Nevada de Santa Marta	Cordillera Occidental, Ecuador	Cordillera Occidental, Colombia	Cordillera Central Colombia	Nudo de Pasto, Colombia	Cordillera Oriental, Colombia	Cordillera Oriental Ecuador	Cordillera Oriental, Peru	Cordillera Oriental, Bolivia	Cordillera Oriental Argentina	Inter-Andean Basins, Ecuador	Huancabamba Depression
Eleutherodactylus lymani	1000–2500												D
Eleutherodactylus lynchi	2460–3340						SP						
Eleutherodactylus megalops	1540–2470	C											
Eleutherodactylus mendax	200–2200								RC				
Eleutherodactylus myersi	2900–3600		P		P	P							
Eleutherodactylus necerus	700–1540		RC										
Eleutherodactylus nicefori	2850–3400						P						
Eleutherodactylus nigrogriseus	1150–2835							CS					
Eleutherodactylus nigrovittatus	300–1935						RC	RC					
Eleutherodactylus nyctophylax	1140–1540		C										
Eleutherodactylus oicesi	3160–3800							P					
Eleutherodactylus orestes	2720–2850							S					
Eleutherodactylus palmeri	800–1600			RC									
Eleutherodactylus parvillus	1460		C										
Eleutherodactylus pastazensis	1840							C					
Eleutherodactylus percultus	2800–2850							S					
Eleutherodactylus peruvianus	200–1910						C	C	RC				
Eleutherodactylus sp. 10	1100–1950				C		C	C					
Eleutherodactylus pharangobates	1870–2400								C				
Eleutherodactylus phoxocephalus	2000–2960		CS					S					
Eleutherodactylus platydactylus	1000–2600								C				
Eleutherodactylus sp. 11	1140–1490							C					
Eleutherodactylus prolixodiscus	2130–2485	C					C						
Eleutherodactylus proserpens	1700–2620							C					
Eleutherodactylus pugnax	1660–2540							C					
Eleutherodactylus pycnodermis	2600–3400							SP					
Eleutherodactylus pyrrhomerus	2150–2900		CS										
Eleutherodactylus quaquaversus	340–1830							RC					
Eleutherodactylus rhabdolaemus	300–2650								RC				
Eleutherodactylus riveti	2600–3400							SP					
Eleutherodactylus rubicundus	1000–1300							C					
Eleutherodactylus salapuitum	1700							C					
Eleutherodactylus sanctaemartae	1850–2870	CP											
Eleutherodactylus scutulus	2620							C					
Eleutherodactylus spinosus	1700–2830							CS					
Eleutherodactylus surdus	2500–3400		SP					SP					
Eleutherodactylus tamsitti	1400				C								
Eleutherodactylus thectopternus	1840–2540			C									
Eleutherodactylus thymelensis	3500–3860		P					P					
Eleutherodactylus thymelopsoides	2400–2460		C										
Eleutherodactylus trachyblepharis	400–1300							RC					
Eleutherodactylus trepidotus	3050–3650					P	P	P					
Eleutherodactylus unistrigatus	1900–3700		SP				P	SP				S	
Eleutherodactylus ventrimarmoratus	1100–1300							C					
Eleutherodactylus ventrivittatus	1100							X					
Eleutherodactylus versicolor	2650–3100							SP					
Eleutherodactylus vertebralis	2340–3500		P	S	SP	P	SP						
Eleutherodactylus viduus	2700–3100							SP					

APPENDIX 15 2 (Continued)

Species	Elevation	Sierra Nevada de Santa Marta	Cordillera Occidental, Ecuador	Cordillera Occidental, Colombia	Cordillera Central, Colombia	Nudo de Pasto, Colombia	Cordillera Oriental, Colombia	Cordillera Oriental, Ecuador	Cordillera Oriental, Peru	Cordillera Oriental, Bolivia	Cordillera Oriental, Argentina	Inter-Andean Basins, Ecuador	Huancabamba Depression
Eleutherodactylus viridicans	2170–2680				C								
Eleutherodactylus walkeri	220–1270	RC											
Eleutherodactylus w-nigrum	1230–2800		CS	CS	CS	S	CS	CS				S	
Eleutherodactylus sp "A"	1850–2160	C											
Eleutherodactylus sp "B"	2100–2750						C						
Eleutherodactylus sp "C"	3200				S								
Eleutherodactylus sp "D"	3750				P								
Eleutherodactylus sp "E"	2900–3000				S								
Eleutherodactylus sp "F"	3400				P								
Eleutherodactylus sp "G"	1230				C								
Eleutherodactylus sp "H"	1230–2010		C	C									
Eleutherodactylus sp "I"	1230			C									
Eleutherodactylus sp "J"	1540		C										
Eleutherodactylus sp "K"	1540		C										
Eleutherodactylus sp "L"	1960–2150		C										
Eleutherodactylus sp "M"	1540–2010		C										
Eleutherodactylus sp "N"	2400		C										
Eleutherodactylus sp "O"	2010–2700		C										
Eleutherodactylus sp "P"	2700		C										
Eleutherodactylus sp "Q"	2700		C										
Eleutherodactylus sp "R"	2700		C										
Eleutherodactylus sp "S"	1960–2700		C										
Eleutherodactylus sp "T"	2100		C										
Eleutherodactylus sp "U"	1160–1960		C										
Eleutherodactylus sp V	2120		C										
Eleutherodactylus sp "W"	2010–2580		C										
Eleutherodactylus sp X	1500–2580		C										
Eleutherodactylus sp "Y"	1740								C				
Eleutherodactylus sp Z	1740–2130												D
Eleutherodactylus sp "AA"	1740–2130												D
Eleutherodactylus sp "BB"	2130												D
Eleutherodactylus sp CC	1890												D
Euparkerella lochites°	1550						C						
Ischnocnema simmonsi°	1830						C						
Leptodactylus labrosus	1000–1700						C	CD					
Leptodactylus wagneri	200–1820						RC	RC	RC				
Phrynopus brunneus	3000–3200							S					
Phrynopus columbianus	1000–1300					C							
Phrynopus cophites	3400–4100								P				
Phrynopus flavomaculatus	2460–3100							CS					
Phrynopus laplacai	3400									S			
Phrynopus montium	3400								S				
Phrynopus nanus	2640–3400						P						
Phrynopus parkeri°°	2700–3100												
Phrynopus peraccae	3100–3350							SP					
Phrynopus pereger	2100–3700								SP				
Phrynopus peruanus	3600								P				
Phrynopus peruvianus	2400–3700								CP				

APPENDIX 15 2 (Continued)

Species	Elevation	Sierra Nevada de Santa Marta	Cordillera Occidental, Ecuador	Cordillera Occidental, Colombia	Cordillera Central, Colombia	Nudo de Pasto, Colombia	Cordillera Oriental, Colombia	Cordillera Oriental, Ecuador	Cordillera Oriental, Peru	Cordillera Oriental, Bolivia	Cordillera Oriental, Argentina	Inter-Andean Basins, Ecuador	Huancabamba Depression
Phrynopus simonsii°°	3050–3500												
Phrynopus wettsteini	2000								C				
Telmatobius ignavus	2000–2770												C
Telmatobius latirostris	2000												C
Telmatobius niger	2400–3500		SP					S				S	
Telmatobius vellardi	2760–3050							S				S	
Telmatobius sp "A"	2700–2850							S					
Geobatrachus walkeri	1550–2870	CP											
Atelopus arthuri	2800		S										
Atelopus bomolochus	2500–2800							CS					
Atelopus boulengeri	900–1830							C					
Atelopus carrikeri	2350–4400	P											
Atelopus ebenoides	2660–3600				SP		SP						
Atelopus elegans	300–1140		RC	RC									
Atelopus erythropus	1800–2500								C				
Atelopus halihelos	±1500							C					
Atelopus ignescens	2900–4500		P		P			P				S	
Atelopus longibrachius	800–1200		RC										
Atelopus longirostris	500–2500		RC	RC									
Atelopus mindoensis	900–2010		RC										
Atelopus nepiozomus	2000–3400							SP					
Atelopus nicefori	1800				C								
Atelopus pachydermus	2700–3100							S					
Atelopus palmatus	1150–1710							C					
Atelopus pedimarmoratus	2600–3100				S		S						
Atelopus planispinus°	±2000							C					
Atelopus rugulosus	2100–2500								C				
Atelopus tricolor	1700–2100								C				
Atelopus walkeri	1850–2160	C											
Atelopus sp "A"	1950						C						
Atelopus sp "B"	2800							S					
Atelopus sp "C"	2900								C				
Bufo chanchanensis	200–1460		RC										
Bufo fissipes	1800								C				
Bufo gnustae	±2000										D		
Bufo inca	1500–2000								C				
Bufo leptoscelis	1950								C				
Bufo limensis	100–2200												D
Bufo nesiotes°	1100–1280								C				
Bufo poeppigii	800–1670								RC				
Bufo quechua	2200–2600									C			
Bufo typhonius	100–1840						RC	RC	RC				
Bufo veraguensis	1300–1900								C	C			
Osornophryne bufoniformis	2700–3700		P		SP	P							
Osornophryne percrassa	3750				P								
Rhamphophryne macrorhina	1890–2130				C								
Rhamphophryne nicefori	2670				C								
Rhamphophryne rostrata	1890				C								

APPENDIX 13.2 (Continued)

Species	Elevation	Sierra Nevada de Santa Marta	Cordillera Occidental, Ecuador	Cordillera Occidental, Colombia	Cordillera Central, Colombia	Nudo de Pasto, Colombia	Cordillera Oriental, Colombia	Cordillera Oriental, Ecuador	Cordillera Oriental, Peru	Cordillera Oriental, Bolivia	Cordillera Oriental, Argentina	Inter-Andean Basins, Ecuador	Huancabamba Depression
Colostethus sp "2"	1100–2400						C						
Colostethus anthracinus	2500–3500						SP						
Colostethus sp "3"	1410–1740						C						
Colostethus sp 4	3700		P										
Colostethus bolivianus	800–1200									RC			
Colostethus sp 5	900–1190		RC										
Colostethus elachyhistus	800–2800		S						S			S	D
Colostethus sp 6	1800–2900				CS								
Colostethus fraterdanieli	1900				C								
Colostethus fuliginosus	180–1740				RC		C	C					
Colostethus sp 7	1900–2070									C			
Colostethus infraguttatus	340–1270		RC										
Colostethus kingsburyi	1150–1410							C					
Colostethus lehmanni	1900				C								
Colostethus mertensi	2170–2680			C									
Colostethus sp '8	1900–2350			C									
Colostethus sp 9'	2300–3500		SP										
Colostethus palmatus	900–2500						RC						
Colostethus sp 10'	1500–1700						C						
Colostethus sp 11°	1830						C						
Colostethus ramosi	1240				C								
Colostethus sp 12	1150–2790					S	C	C					
Colostethus sp 13'	2100–3500		S			P		S					
Colostethus subpunctatus	2100–3300						SP						
Colostethus sylvatica	1580–2970							C					D
Colostethus taeniatus	1740–2970						CS	CS					
Colostethus sp '14 °	1830							C					
Colostethus vertebralis	2500–3200		P					P				S	
Colostethus whymperi	1460–2120		C										
Colostethus sp "15 °°	1800												
Colostethus sp A"	670–2130	DC					C						
Dendrobates abditus	1650–1700						C						
Dendrobates lehmanni	850–1200			C									
Dendrobates opisthomelas	1160–2200			C	C								
Dendrobates viridis	200–1200			RC									
Phyllobates anthonyi	150–1690		DC										D
Phyllobates bicolor	25–1525			RC	RC								
Phyllobates bolivianus	800–1200									C			
Phyllobates tricolor	1250–1770		C										
Phyllobates sp A	1300–1600								C				
Amphignathodon guentheri	1200–2010				C			C					
Cryptobatrachus boulengeri	1230–1700	C											
Cryptobatrachus fuhrmanni	1600–2550				C		C						
Cryptobatrachus nicefori	1000–1200						C						
Gastrotheca andaquiensis	2000						C						
Gastrotheca argenteovirens	2850–3300				SP								
Gastrotheca aureomaculata	2300–2700				SP	SP							

[1] Species of *Colostethus* designated by numbers are being named in a manuscript by S. R. Edwards

Appendix 15 2 (Continued)

Species	Elevation	Sierra Nevada de Santa Marta	Cordillera Occidental, Ecuador	Cordillera Occidental, Colombia	Cordillera Central, Colombia	Nudo de Pasto, Colombia	Cordillera Oriental, Colombia	Cordillera Oriental, Ecuador	Cordillera Oriental, Peru	Cordillera Oriental, Bolivia	Cordillera Oriental, Argentina	Inter-Andean Basins, Ecuador	Huancabamba Depression
Gastrotheca cavia	2000–2890	S											
Gastrotheca christiani	2600										D		
Gastrotheca chrysosticta	1530										D		
Gastrotheca cornuta	200–1300		RC	RC									
Gastrotheca excubitor	3100–3550								P				
Gastrotheca galeata	1710–2130												D
Gastrotheca gracilis	1500–2000										D		
Gastrotheca griswoldi	3200–3800								P				
Gastrotheca helenae	3400						P						
Gastrotheca lojana	2100–2350												D
Gastrotheca marsupiata	2760–4360								SP	SP			
Gastrotheca medemi°	1140–1500						C						
Gastrotheca mertensi	2600–2900				S	S	S						
Gastrotheca monticola	1600–2500			S								S	D
Gastrotheca nicefori	800–2100				C		C						
Gastrotheca ochoai	2760–2800									D			
Gastrotheca peruana°°	2300–4600												
Gastrotheca plumbea	1300–2500		CS										
Gastrotheca psychrophila	2750–2850							S					
Gastrotheca riobambae	1800–4135		SP			SP		SP				S	
Gastrotheca testudinea	1100–1840								C	C			
Gastrotheca weinlandii	1100–1800				C		C	C	C				
Gastrotheca sp "A"	1750–2600				CS								
Gastrotheca sp "B"	2170–2540			C									
Gastrotheca sp C'	1100–1600						C	C					
Gastrotheca sp 'D'	2400									C			
Gastrotheca sp E	3500–3800								P				
Hemiphractus bubalus	300–1740						RC	RC					
Hemiphractus fasciatus	300–1600		RC	RC									
Hemiphractus johnsoni	300–1910				C		C	C	RC	C			
Hemiphractus scutatus	250–1800							RC	RC				
Hyla albopunctulata	300–1230			RC									
Hyla alytolylax	800–1540		C	C									
Hyla armata	1700–2400								C	C			
Hyla balzani	1200–1840									C			
Hyla bogotensis	2500–2900						SP	SP					
Hyla callipleura	500–1800								C	C			
Hyla carnifex	900–2010		C	C	C								
Hyla columbiana	1700–2000				C								
Hyla denticulenta	1400–2400				C								
Hyla labialis	2400–3000						SP						
Hyla larinopygion	1900–2660				C		C	C					
Hyla lascinia	1700–2850							SP					
Hyla lindae	2600–2660							C					
Hyla phyllognatha	610–1740						C	RC	RC				
Hyla pulchella	500–3300										DS	DS	
Hyla torrenticola	1400–1500							C	C				
Hyla sp 'A'	1750				C								

APPENDIX 15.2 (Continued)

Species	Elevation	Sierra Nevada de Santa Marta	Cordillera Occidental, Ecuador	Cordillera Occidental, Colombia	Cordillera Central, Colombia	Nudo de Pasto, Colombia	Cordillera Oriental, Colombia	Cordillera Oriental, Ecuador	Cordillera Oriental, Peru	Cordillera Oriental, Bolivia	Cordillera Oriental, Argentina	Inter-Andean Basins, Ecuador	Huancabamba Depression
Hyla sp "B"	1750				C								
Hyla sp "C"	2300		C										
Osteocephalus pearsoni	300–1620								RC	C			
Osteocephalus verrucigerus	500–1840						RC	RC	RC				
Phyllomedusa baltea°	1280								C				
Phyllomedusa boliviana	500–2000									D			
Phyllomedusa perinesos	1410–1490							C					
Centrolene geckoideum	1920–2150		C	C									
Centrolenella anomala	1740							C					
Centrolenella antioquiensis	1890–2475				C								
Centrolenella audax	1190–1700						C	C					
Centrolenella buckleyi	2100–3400		SP	SP	SP	SP	SP	SP				S	
Centrolenella cochranae	1100–1410							C					
Centrolenella flavopunctata	720–1800							C					
Centrolenella fleischmanni	200–1110		RC	RC									
Centrolenella grandisonae	1460–2000		C	C									
Centrolenella griffithsi	1200–2170		C	C									
Centrolenella johnelsi	2500				C								
Centrolenella mariae°	1550								C				
Centrolenella medemi	1100–1490						C	C					
Centrolenella megacheira	1490–1740						C	C					
Centrolenella ocellata	1200–1820							C					
Centrolenella ocellifera	700–2300		RC										
Centrolenella pellucida	1740							C					
Centrolenella peristicta	1410–1460		C										
Centrolenella pipilata	1700–1740							C					
Centrolenella prosoblepon	200–1410		RC	RC									
Centrolenella siren	1200–1950						C	C	C				
Centrolenella spiculata	1000–1700								C				
Centrolenella truebae	1700								C				
Centrolenella valeroi	200–1100		RC	RC									
Centrolenella sp A	1410–1490							C					
Centrolenella sp B'	2660							C					
Centrolenella sp C	1140–1540		C	C									
Centrolenella sp 'D'	1140		C										
Centrolenella sp E'	1540		C										
Centrolenella sp 'F'	1960–2150		C										
Centrolenella sp 'G'	1960–2010		C										
Centrolenella sp 'H'	1950						C						
Centrolenella sp 'I'	1230				C								
Centrolenella sp 'J'	1230				C								
Centrolenella sp 'K'	1230				C								
Centrolenella sp 'L'	1750					C							
Centrolenella sp 'M'	1750					C							
Centrolenella sp "N"	1750					C							
Centrolenella sp O	1050							C					
Centrolenella sp 'P'	1200–1850	C											
Glossostoma aequatoriale	2500–3615		SP									S	

APPENDIX 15.2 (Continued)

Species	Elevation	Sierra Nevada de Santa Marta	Cordillera Occidental, Ecuador	Cordillera Occidental, Colombia	Cordillera Central, Colombia	Nudo de Pasto, Colombia	Cordillera Oriental, Colombia	Cordillera Oriental, Ecuador	Cordillera Oriental, Peru	Cordillera Oriental, Bolivia	Cordillera Oriental, Argentina	Inter-Andean Basins, Ecuador	Huancabamba Depression
Lizards													
Gonatodes petersi	?						X						
Lepidoblepharis sp "A"	1150–1740							C					
Pseudogonatodes furvus	1500	C											
Anolis aequatorialis	1140–1510		C										
Anolis andianus	2060		C										
Anolis antonii	1960						C						
Anolis apollinaris	800–1250				RC		C						
Anolis boettgeri	1000–1100								C				
Anolis chloris	1200		C										
Anolis eulaemus	1100–1400			C									
Anolis fraseri	500–1600		RC	RC									
Anolis fuscoauratus	200–1450						RC	RC					
Anolis gemmosus	1140–1510		C										
Anolis proboscideus	1050–1500		C										
Anolis solitarius	1500–2000	C											
Anolis sp "A"	1150–1740						C	C					
Anolis sp B	1700–1820								C				
Basiliscus galeritus	300–1700		RC	RC									
Enyalioides oshaugnessyi	840–1150						C	C					
Enyalioides praestabilis	400–1830						RC	RC					
Phenacosaurus heterodermus	1800–3750				SP		SP						
Phenacosaurus nicefori	1900–2340						S						
Phenacosaurus orcesi	1750–3100							SP					
Polychroides peruvianus	1000–1750												D
Polychrus gutturosus	1500–1850		C	C									
Polychrus liogaster	900–1600									D	D		D
Stenocercus boettgeri	2900–3250									D			D
Stenocercus carrioni	1900												D
Stenocercus festae	2300–2900		D									S	
Stenocercus guentheri	2100–3890		P			P		P				S	
Stenocercus humeralis	2000–3000												D
Stenocercus ivitus	3100												C
Stenocercus nigromaculatus	1900–2300												D
Stenocercus nubicola	3100												C
Stenocercus ornatus	2065–2700												D
Stenocercus praeornatus	2150–3200									D			D
Stenocercus rhodomelas	1250–2100		D										
Stenocercus simonsii	2210–2500		D										
Stenocercus trachycephalus	1900–3200						S						
Stenocercus varius	1500–2010		C										
Alopoglossus buckleyi	1150–1830							C					
Anadia bogotensis	2000–3600				SP		SP						
Anadia pulchella	2100–2700	C					S						
Anadia rhombifer	500–1760		RC				C	C					
Cercosaura ocellata	1000–1600								C				
Euspondylus rahmi	2100–2500								C				
Euspondylus simonsii	1500–2980								C				

Appendix 15.2 (Continued)

Species	Elevation	Sierra Nevada de Santa Marta	Cordillera Occidental, Ecuador	Cordillera Occidental, Colombia	Cordillera Central, Colombia	Nudo de Pasto, Colombia	Cordillera Oriental, Colombia	Cordillera Oriental, Ecuador	Cordillera Oriental, Peru	Cordillera Oriental, Bolivia	Cordillera Oriental, Argentina	Inter-Andean Basins, Ecuador	Huancabamba Depression
Euspondylus spinalis	1200–2840								C				
Euspondylus stenolepis	2200				C								
Macropholidus ruthveni	3100												C
Neusticurus cochranae	1150–1300							C					
Neusticurus ecpleopus	200–1700						RC	RC	RC				
Neusticurus strangulatus	1100–1410							C	C				
Opipeuter xestus	1000–3000									C			
Pholidobolus affinis	1800–3050	P										S	
Pholidobolus annectens	2150–2335												D
Pholidobolus macbrydei	2315–3960	SP						SP					
Pholidobolus montium	2000–3190											S	
Pholidobolus prefrontalis	2295–2885	S										S	
Prionodactylus argus	100–1600						RC	RC	RC	RC			
Prionodactylus dicrus	600–1800							RC					
Prionodactylus manicatus	300–1750							RC	C	C			
Prionodactylus vertebralis	700–3020	RC	RC			S							C
Proctoporus bolivianus	3300–4080									P	P		
Proctoporus columbianus	2300–3000						CS	CS					
Proctoporus guentheri	1000–3200									CS	CS		
Proctoporus hypostictus	?		X										
Proctoporus laevis	3000					S							
Proctoporus meleagris	2200–3150	CS				S							
Proctoporus oculatus	2640–3300											S	
Proctoporus pachyurus	2900–3800									P			
Proctoporus simopterus	2500–3000	CS											
Proctoporus striatus	2200–2500						C						
Proctoporus unicolor	2800–3100		S									S	
Proctoporus ventrimaculatus	2200–2700									D			D
Proctoporus sp. 'A'	2300–2500							C					
Proctoporus sp. 'B'	2300–2500							C					
Proctoporus sp. 'C'	2400–3000									DC			
Ptychoglossus bicolor	1700				C								
Ptychoglossus brevifrontalis	200–1450						RC	RC					
Snakes													
Leptotyphlops anthracinus	1100–1850							C					
Leptotyphlops joshua	1700–1970				C		C						
Leptotyphlops nicefori	1750						C						
Leptotyphlops peruvianus	1400–1600								C				
Leptotyphlops teaguei	2350–2700												D
Tropidophis taczanowskyi	2500–2900								S	S			
Atractus boettgeri	?									X			
Atractus carrioni	2100–2275												D
Atractus crassicaudatus	1700–2800				C	S							
Atractus ecuadorensis	?							X					
Atractus emmeli	2400									C			
Atractus indistinctus	1200								C				
Atractus lasallei	2500			C									
Atractus lehmanni	2600											S	

APPENDIX 15.2 (Continued)

Species	Elevation	Sierra Nevada de Santa Marta	Cordillera Occidental, Ecuador	Cordillera Occidental, Colombia	Cordillera Central, Colombia	Nudo de Pasto, Colombia	Cordillera Oriental, Colombia	Cordillera Oriental, Ecuador	Cordillera Oriental, Peru	Cordillera Oriental, Bolivia	Cordillera Oriental, Argentina	Inter-Andean Basins, Ecuador	Huancabamba Depression
Atractus loveridgei	1970			C									
Atractus manizalesensis	1920			C									
Atractus melanogaster	1750–1900				C								
Atractus nicefori	1970			C									
Atractus nigricaudatus	3300							S					
Atractus nigriventris	3000						P						
Atractus obesus	2600–2700			S									
Atractus obtusirostris	1750–2100				C								
Atractus occidentalis	800–1200		RC										
Atractus oculotemporalis	1970			C									
Atractus pamplonensis	2280						S						
Atractus paucisicutatus	2900–3000							S					
Atractus resplendens	1100–1900							C					
Atractus roulei	1200–2785		C										
Atractus sanctaemartae	1200–2100	C											
Atractus trivittatus	3000						P						
Atractus variegatus	4000						P						
Atractus vertebralis	1800							C					
Atractus vertebrolineatus	1200						C						
Atractus wagleri	2600						S						
Atractus werneri	1800–2700						CS						
Atractus sp "A"	2620						S						
Atractus sp "B"	1830–1870							C					
Atractus sp "C"	1830							C					
Chironius monticola	1000–2800			C	C		C	C	C	C			
Clelia equatoriana	800–1460		RC										
Dendrophidion bivittatus	500–2300			RC		RC							
Dendrophidion brunneus	2100–2250												D
Dendrophidion percarinatus	1200–1600		C	C									
Diaphorolepis laevis	2150		C										
Dipsas ellipsifera	900–2150		RC										
Dipsas latifasciata	900–1200							RC	RC				
Dipsas latifrontalis	1600–1700						C	C					
Dipsas oreas	1100–1460		C										
Dipsas perijanensis	1700						C						
Dipsas peruana	2400									C			
Dipsas polylepis	1960												D
Dipsas pratti	1600–2400				C								
Dipsas sanctijoannis	1200–1800			C									
Dipsas schunkii	1000–1300									C			
Dipsas sp "A"	2075–2250												D
Leimadophis albiventris	1460–2120	C											
Leimadophis bimaculatus	1225–3250			C	CS		SP						
Leimadophis fraseri	2060–2700											S	D
Leimadophis pygmaeus	400–1860						RC	RC					
Leimadophis pseudocobella	1375–2500			C	C								
Leptophis riveti	200–1500		RC	RC									
Liophis subocularis	1200–2900		CS										

APPENDIX 15 2 (Concluded)

Species	Elevation	Sierra Nevada de Santa Marta	Cordillera Occidental, Ecuador	Cordillera Occidental, Colombia	Cordillera Central, Colombia	Nudo de Pasto, Colombia	Cordillera Oriental, Colombia	Cordillera Oriental, Ecuador	Cordillera Oriental, Peru	Cordillera Oriental, Bolivia	Cordillera Oriental, Argentina	Inter-Andean Basins, Ecuador	Huancabamba Depression
Mastigodryas danieli	1350–1400	-		C	-	-		-	-	-			-
Oxyrhopus doliatus	2400	-	- -		- - -	-	- - - -	-	C	-		- - -	-
Oxyrhopus fitzingeri	1500–2100	-										- -	D
Oxyrhopus leucomelas	1750–3000		- - -	-	CS	-	C	C				- - -	-
Oxyrhopus marcapatae	2000–2400		- -	-		- -		- -	C				-
Philodryas simonsii°°	1800–2700		D	-	- -		-	-	-	-		-	D
Rhadinaea decipiens	2740	- -	- -	-	C					-		-	- -
Rhadinaea laticristriga	800–2000		RC	RC		- -	C	C					- -
Saphenophis antioquiensis	2500				C	- -							
Saphenophis atahuallpae	2500		C						- -				
Saphenophis boursieri	300–1890	-	C	C	-	C							
Saphenophis sneiderni	1750			C									- -
Saphenophis tristriatus	3200	- -	-	-	S							- -	- -
Sibon dunni	2000	-	C					- -					
Sibynomorphus vagrans	1900						- -						D
Synophis bicolor	1100–1600	-			- -		C						
Synophis lasallei	450–2200						RC	RC	-				
Synophis miops	1050	- -	C						- -	- -			
Tantilla sp A	2600–2750	-	S	-						- -	- -		
Tantilla fraseri	1500–2400	- -	C						- -	- -			- -
Tantilla sp "B"	1200	- - -	D	-					- -	- -			- -
Micrurus annellatus	1600–2000					- - -		C	C	C		.	- -
Micrurus mipartitus	600–2000	RC	RC	RC	RC	-	RC	- -				- - -	-
Micrurus peruvianus	1200–1500	- - -			-	-	-	- -	- -			-	D
Micrurus psyches	1400–1660	-	-					C	- -				
Micrurus steindachneri	1000–1800	-	- - - -		-		C	- -				
Bothrops albocarinatus	500–1260					- - -		RC	-				-
Bothrops alticolus	2850							S	- - -				- - -
Bothrops andianus	2000–3300	-							CS	- -	-	-	-
Bothrops lojanus	2100–2250									- -			D
Bothrops oligolepis	2000–3300	- -						- - -	C	C	-	- - -	C
Bothrops pictus	1800					- - - -		- - - - -				- -	D
Bothrops schlegeli	100–1600		RC	RC	-	-		-	- - -			- -	
Bothrops xanthogrammus	2200		C	- - - -	- - - -	- - - -	- - - - -	-	-				- -
TOTAL AMPHIBIANS (374)		16	92	44	58	17	62	125	60	13	5	12	16
TOTAL REPTILES (176)		5	45	22	20	6	41	39	33	10	0	10	17
TOTAL SPECIES (550)		21	137	66	78	23	103	164	93	23	5	22	43

APPENDIX 15.3—Altitudinal and geographic distribution of amphibians and reptiles in the Andes of Peru, Bolivia, Argentina, and Chile. Habitats A = arid, C = cloud forest, N = *Nothofagus* forest, P = puna, S = Patagonian scrub, V = Valley vegetation

Species	Elevation	Cordillera Central, Peru	Cordillera Oriental North, Perú	Cordillera Oriental South, Peru	Cordillera Occidental North, Perú	Cordillera Occidental South, Perú	Marañón Valley, Perú	Huallaga Valley, Perú	Mantaro-Apurímac Valley, Perú	Altiplano	Cordillera Oriental, Bolivia	Northern Andes, Argentina	Southern Andes, Argentina	Southern Andes, Chile	Northern Andes, Chile
Frogs															
Alsodes gargola	1700–1750													N	
Alsodes illotus	?													A	
Alsodes laevis	2200												A		
Alsodes montanus	2200–2500												A		
Alsodes nodosus	0–1700													N	
Alsodes sp. "A"	2600												A		
Batrachophrynus brachydactylus	4000–4100								V						
Batrachophrynus microstomus	4000–4100								V						
Pleurodema borellii	400–3000										P	AP			
Pleurodema bufonina	0–2300													S	S
Pleurodema cinerea	2900–4100									P					
Pleurodema marmorata	3000–5000			P		P			V	P	P				P
Telmatobius albiventris	3800–3825									P					
Telmatobius arequipensis	2400–2600					AV									
Telmatobius atacamensis	3775										P				
Telmatobius brevipes	3000				A										
Telmatobius brevirostris	3000–3600								V						
Telmatobius ceiorum	1600–1800											A			
Telmatobius contrerasi	3050											A			
Telmatobius crawfordi	4100–4200				P										
Telmatobius culeus	2575–4150					VP				P					
Telmatobius halli	3000													A	
Telmatobius hauthali	2400–4000											A			
Telmatobius intermedius	3300				A										
Telmatobius jelskii	2700–4500			P		P			V						
Telmatobius juninensis	3650–3800			P											
Telmatobius marmoratus	2500–5000				P				V	P	P	P			P
Telmatobius oxycephalus	1600–3800											AP			
Telmatobius pefauri	3200														A
Telmatobius peruvianus	3000–3500				A										A
Telmatobius rimac	2300–3100				A										
Telmatobius sanborni	4000			P											
Telmatobius schreiteri	1200											A			
Telmatobius simonsi	2600–2800										A				
Telmatobius stephani	2000											A			
Telmatobius verrucosus	3800										P				
Telmatobius sp. "B"	3200–3500		P												
Bufo cophotis	2200–3500		A												
Bufo flavolineatus	4000–4600									VP					
Bufo rubropunctatus	100–1800													N	N
Bufo spinulosus	1000–5000			P		AV			V	P	AP	AP	A		AP
Bufo trifolium	2800–4600	P	P	P	A		V	V	V						
Bufo variegatus	300–1800													N	N
Bufo sp. "A"	3500–3750		P												
Bufo sp. "B"	2650											A			

APPENDIX 15 3 (Continued)

Species	Elevation	Cordillera Central, Perú	Cordillera Oriental North, Perú	Cordillera Oriental South, Perú	Cordillera Occidental North, Perú	Cordillera Occidental South, Perú	Marañon Valley, Perú	Huallaga Valley, Perú	Mantaro-Apurimac Valley, Perú	Altiplano	Cordillera Oriental, Bolivia	Northern Andes, Argentina	Southern Andes, Argentina	Southern Andes, Chile	Northern Andes, Chile
Lizards															
Garthia penai	1500–2400														A
Phyllodactylus gerrhopygus	0–2750					A									A
Phyllodactylus lepidopygus	0–1700				A	A									
Phyllodactylus reissi	0–2000				A		A								
Ctenoblepharis jamesi	3600–4600														A
Ctenoblepharis marmoratus	1200–1800										A				
Ctenoblepharis nigriceps	3000–3500														A
Ctenoblepharis schmidti	4000–4300														A
Ctenoblepharis stolzmanni	1000–3800					A									A
Diplolaemus leopardinus	1000–1600												S	S	
Liolaemus alticolor	2860–4800					AP				P	P				AP
Liolaemus altissimus	1400–3500												S	S	
Liolaemus bibroni	750–2800												SA		
Liolaemus boulengeri	1500–2500												SA		
Liolaemus constanzae	2000–2400														A
Liolaemus elongatus	960–2800												SA		
Liolaemus fitzgeraldi	2100–2800											A	A		
Liolaemus kriegi	1275–1950												S	S	
Liolaemus leopardinus	2200–3000													A	
Liolaemus lorenzmulleri	2300–3200														A
Liolaemus mocquardi	3800–4300										P				
Liolaemus monticola	1100–2000												A		
Liolaemus multiformis	3650–4880		P	A	AP					P	P	A			AP
Liolaemus nigroviridis	1800–3000												A	A	
Liolaemus nitidus	800–2300												A		
Liolaemus ornatus	3300–4300									P					
Liolaemus pantherinus	3500–4300									P					
Liolaemus paulinae	2700–3000														A
Liolaemus robertmertensi	1000–2600											A	A		
Liolaemus ruibali	2700–2900												A		
Liolaemus schroederi	1400–2200													A	
Liolaemus signifer	3600–4300									P					
Liolaemus tacnae	2400–3050					A									
Liolaemus walkeri	3400–4100	P							P						
Liolaemus sp "A"	4300			P											
Liolaemus sp "B"	4080														P
Liolaemus sp C	3820–4300									P					
Liolaemus sp D	2650									A					
Phymaturus palluma	1200–3500												SA	S	
Pristidactylus scapulatus	1950–2900												A		
Stenocercus apurimacus	1800–2700								A						
Stenocercus chrysopygus	2200–3500					A									
Stenocercus crassicaudatus	1000–2500		A								A				
Stenocercus cupreus	1900–2300							A							
Stenocercus empetrus	2650–3350				A	A									
Stenocercus formosus	1000–1600	C													

APPENDIX 15.3 (Concluded)

Species	Elevation	Cordillera Central, Peru	Cordillera Oriental North, Peru	Cordillera Oriental South, Peru	Cordillera Occidental North, Peru	Cordillera Occidental South, Peru	Marañon Valley, Peru	Huallaga Valley, Perú	Mantaro-Apurimac Valley, Perú	Altiplano	Cordillera Oriental, Bolivia	Northern Andes, Argentina	Southern Andes, Argentina	Southern Andes, Chile	Northern Andes, Chile
Stenocercus marmoratus	2750–3350										A				
Stenocercus melanopygus	2700–3250						A								
Stenocercus ochoai	2000–3000			A											
Stenocercus orientalis	2340						A								
Stenocercus ornatissimus	2000–3400				A										
Stenocercus variabilis	1200–3000			AV					V						
Tropidurus peruvianus	0–2600					A									A
Tropidurus tigris	0–2800				A	A									
Snakes															
Philodryas chamissonis	0–1800													NA	
Philodryas tachymenoides	0–3000					A									A
Tachymenis affinis	2200–2400			A					V						
Tachymenis attenuata	2500										?				
Tachymenis peruviana	70–1570		P	P		AP			P	P	P	A	N	N	AP
Tachymenis tarmensis	3000			P											
TOTAL AMPHIBIANS (45)		1	0	5	4	9	1	2	8	8	5	8	8	9	5
TOTAL REPTILES (60)		0	2	11	8	10	4	2	3	7	8	4	12	12	16
TOTAL SPECIES (105)		1	2	16	12	19	5	4	11	15	13	12	20	21	21

16. Refugia, Refuges and Minimum Critical Size: Problems in the Conservation of the Neotropical Herpetofauna

Thomas E. Lovejoy

World Wildlife Fund
1601 Connecticut Avenue, NW
Washington, D C 20009
USA

I divide my remarks into a consideration of the contributions biogeography can make to conservation of the South American herpetofauna and a discussion of what constitutes the minimum critical size of a reptile community such that it can maintain its structural integrity over reasonably long periods of time I also note that conservation contains questions of intrinsic scientific interest The term refuge is used in the sense of a wildlife refuge —a conservation area or unit, whereas refugia is used sensu Haffer (1969) to indicate remnant forest patches that persisted when rain forest was turned to a savanna-like environment during the drier portions of the Pleistocene

First, I raise the question as to whether the biogeography relevant for conservation purposes needs to include the traditional historical component? Isn't it enough just to know which species occur where?

If one ignores history and does not consider the refugia, then one could look at contours of endemism although both are defined by the same set of distributional data Yet one could also consider contours of species diversity Taking care not to leave out any species, one could choose the necessary number of areas of high species diversity so as to conserve the herpetofauna

Based on a very simple model of the refugia concept in which all species are in refugia, one could argue for the approach of contours of species diversity For if one chose the region where two refugia had come into contact one would end up with a reserve containing the species of both But as Haffer (this volume) showed, organisms seem to have varying abilities to disperse from refugia, and this results in a gradient of endemism that decreases away from the center of the refugium Clearly this complicates the task of getting all of the herpetofauna into reserves unless one follows contours of endemism as opposed to diversity In an extreme case one might have to draw reserve boundaries so large as to include the foci of both refugia

More importantly, we need to recognize that in refuges encompassing refugia and in those encompassing secondary contact areas, or what Remington (1968) termed suture zones, we are conserving two distinct kinds of biological communities To the extent we believe that the fundamental purposes of conservation include conserving future opportunities for biological research and maintaining evolutionary opportunities, it becomes important to conserve both

It is also important to note in setting up refuges of either sort we are in essence creating refugia to the extent we allow remaining areas to become highly modified by man, and man then becomes a force on evolution of a magnitude similar to Pleistocene climatic changes This really becomes a very serious question in terms of our own species managing its future without knowledge of the consequences, and argues more strongly than ever before for development of wise land use policies

We need to recognize, too that with all the best intentions and best design, reserves are not immune to influences originating outside the reserves Toxic substances immediately come to mind Moreover in an area such as the Amazon, massive conversion to pasture and agriculture (more than one-third of the primary forest has been cut) could have an important drying effect on climate,[1] an effect that climatological science seems unprepared or unable to predict. If Brasil's plan to protect five percent of the Amazon in conservation units is thus imperiled, it well could mean that man's environmental effect would be yet greater than the magnitude of the Pleistocene climatic changes.

The failure of paleoecologists to locate palynological evidence of the whereabouts of the deciduous forests of the northern United States during Pleistocene glaciations suggests that this forest may not be the highly co-evolved unit it was for so long thought to be. As a consequence we must exercise care not to leave government and nonscientific conservationists with the impression that because we talk of our centers of endemism as refugia they are indeed likely to be refugia in times of future climatic change. It should be forcefully pointed out that refugia, at least those not associated with features of geological relief, may well have been in different places in different periods, and that dry periods varied in duration and perhaps even in temperature. The deciduous forest of the northeast or the Amazonian hylaea did not necessarily move around as a unit. Yet with respect to the Amazon forests one wonders how so many one to one relationships and intricate systems like that of the oropendolas—giant cowbirds—*Philornis* flies (Smith 1969) could evolve if such were the case, or whether this then says something interesting about evolutionary rates in the tropics.

Having clearly indicated that the historical component of biogeography is important to conservation we now need to consider how to choose conservation areas when refugia for different groups do *not* coincide. In many cases this will be because the size of centers of endemism varies with the taxon. For instance, Brown (1977), in a recent analysis of Nymphalid butterflies, proposed 38 refugia plus an additional 20 subrefugia, whereas Vanzolini's (1973) reptilian refugia numbered about six. Such differences raise interesting questions about the size of the grain of the environment for different kinds of organisms, and says to the extent that non-overlap merely reflects the abundance of refugia of a particular taxon, the job is merely to create more refuges. But suppose a taxon with few but large refugia such as reptiles has a refugium which does not overlap with a refugium from a second taxon with numerous, smaller refugia. Given continued belief in the refugia hypothesis, the lack of coincidence of refugia most likely indicates our data base is inadequate, or may suggest interesting differences in speciation in the different groups.

The Brasilian government has taken the refugia approach in its recent document "Uma Analise de Prioridades em Conservacao da Natureza na Amazonia" (Wetterberg et al., 1977), choosing priority areas from overlays of refugia for heliconian butterflies, four plant families, birds and lizards, highest priority has been assigned to areas with the greatest coincidence of refugia. The document has been included in the national development plan, and further was adopted by the six (non-Guianan) Amazonian nations at their second technical meeting on conservation in Brasilia in July 1977. The Brasilian government is to be applauded for taking biogeography into account, but it is incumbent upon us to keep them aware of all refinements in our knowledge.

The problem of size of reserves has been considered recently by island biogeographers primarily using data dealing with birds. Their primary contribution to date has been to alert us to the problem that reserves can be too small to maintain their original species composition over time. We really know very little about the subject, even though it is involved very fundamentally with the structure and function of ecosystems.

Long before MacArthur and Wilson (1963, 1967) formally presented the theory of island biogeography it was known that the number of species increases with area, and this relationship alone tells us we can make a conservation area too small. That there is a minimum critical size of an ecosystem is per-

---

[1] Salati et al. (1978) and Villa Nova et al. (1976) estimated that slightly over half of the precipitation in the Amazon basin is forest-generated. Sufficient forest conversion presumably could initiate a drying trend.

haps not so apparent However, loss of species from too small an area obviously is inevitable if only because low density species will occur in numbers too low to reproduce or to withstand stochastic fluctuations Undoubtedly there are other processes involved in the decay process of an ecosystem with a species number too large for the area left intact by man, but to date they have not been explored An important question to test is one advanced by Lovejoy and Oren (1979), namely, whether this decay process leads to a predictable species composition of the impoverished community

There has been sharp controversy as to whether more species can be preserved by a series of small reserves rather than a large one (e g Diamond, 1975, Simberloff and Abele, 1976, Terborgh, 1976) Arguments that concentrate on simple numbers of species can be faulted for having tended to treat all species as equal but more importantly for ignoring that what we really want to preserve are functioning ecosystems, not some kind of glorified zoos [2] Ecosystem protection will require large areas or at least ones greater than the minimum critical size

Terborgh (1974) has estimated that for tropical rain forest birds, an area of about 1,000 square kilometers is needed in order to keep extinctions down to one percent of the original species complement per century This size is probably in the right order of magnitude but obviously minimum critical size will vary considerably with the taxon and ecosystem concerned

In designing reserves with ecosystem preservation in mind, the minimum critical size to be taken is that which is the largest of those of all the taxonomic components Yet there may be occasions when a reserve should be designed primarily for its herpetofaunal community Further, there are probably interesting things to be learned by consideration of factors relating to minimum critical size in different kinds of organisms

Almost all the work on minimum critical size of reptile communities has been carried out by Bruce Wilcox, who has kindly made his data available His studies are primarily concerned with the lizard faunas of islands in the Gulf of California (Wilcox, 1978) These land-bridge islands can be dated as to age of isolation on the basis of the depth of the water separating them from the mainland and a knowledge of rates of sea level rises at the end of the Pleistocene Consequently, these islands provide the first time sequence evidence of the decay process of supersaturated faunas of any sort

Wilcox also was able to estimate immigration and extinction rates for these lizard island communities and found the former so low as to be negligible in his calculations *Ameiva ameiva* and *Mabuya mabuya* notwithstanding this would seem to make sense because lizards probably do not have the dispersal facility of birds That the extinction rate is lower for lizards than birds may be reflective of a slower pulse to the dynamics of the poikilothermic system, or that poor dispersers may be good persisters (Oren pers comm)

If immigration rates are low and opportunities for dispersal to a conservation unit few, large areas are in order to maintain the original lizard biota However Wilcox (in preparation) suggests that the lower energy demands of poikilotherms should make higher biomass and densities possible, which, all other things being equal, would indicate that the area need not be as large as for a comparable avian community

I am not aware of data on minimum critical size for amphibian ecosystems although I would guess it to be yet smaller and frequently involving special features of the environment In any case this leaves plenty for herpetologists to do, as long as our species doesn't reduce the possible future directions in which biological knowledge can grow by doing away with Neotropical ecosystems in the name of supposed progress

ACKNOWLEDGMENTS

I acknowledge with gratitude the help of Jurgen Haffer, Philip S Humphrey, Ghillean

---

[2] This is not meant to denigrate in any fashion the important role zoos can play in education and captive propagation

T Prance, David C Oren, Bruce A Wilcox, and Richard O Bierregaard

RESUMEN

Gran parte de la herpetofauna así como otras biotas sudamericanas solo sobrevivirán en parques nacionales y reservas biológicas Las bases biogeográficas para el diseño de dichas áreas se nava en base a la teoría de los refugios Las reservas designadas para reptiles y anfibios podran ser más pequeñas que aquellas para aves

LITERATURE CITED

Brown, K S, Jr 1977 Centros de evolução, refugios quaternarios e conservação de patrimônios geneticos na região neotropical padroes de diferenciação em Ithomiinae (Lepidoptera Numphalidae) Acta Amazonica 7 75–137

Diamond, J M 1975 The island dilemma lessons for the design of natural reserves Biol Conser 7 129–146

Haffer, J 1969 Speciation in Amazonian forest birds Science 165 131–137

Lovejoy, T F, Oren, D C 1979 Minimum critical size of ecosystems, in Burgess, R L, Sharpe, D M (eds) Forest island dynamics in Man-dominated landscapes Springer-Verlag New York (In press)

MacArthur R H, Wilson, E O 1963 An equilibrium theory of insular biogeography Evol 17 373–387

MacArthur R H, Wilson, E O 1967 The Theory of Island Biogeography Princeton University Press Princeton, New Jersey 203 p

Remington, C L 1968 Suture-zones of hybrid interaction between recently joined biotas, pp 321–428 in Dobzhansky, T, Hecht, M K Steere W C (eds) Evolutionary Biology Vol 2 452 p

Salati E, Marques, J, Molion, L-C B 1978 Origem e distribução das chuvas na Amazonia Interciencia 3 200–205

Simberloff D S, Abele, L G 1976 Biogeography theory and conservation practice Science 191 285–286

Smith, N G 1969 The importance of being parasitized Nature 219 690–694

Terborgh, J 1974 Preservation of natural diversity The problem of extinction prone species Bioscience 24 715–722

Terborgh, J 1976 Island biogeography and conservation Strategy and limitations Science 193 1028–1029

Vanzolini, P E 1973 Paleoclimates, relief, and species multiplication in equatorial forests, pp 255–258 in Meggers, B J, Ayensu, E S, Duckworth, F D (eds) Tropical forest ecosystems in Africa and South America A comparative review Smithsonian Institution Press Washington, D C, 350 p

Villa Nova, N A, Salati F, Matsui, E 1976 Estimativa de evapotranspiração na bacia Amazonica Acta Amazonica 6 215–228

Wetterberg, G B, Jorge Padua, M J, Soares de Castro, C, Vasconcelos, J M C 1977 Uma analise de prioridades em conservação da natureza na Amazônia Projeto de Desenvolvimento e Pesquisa Florestal Instituto Brasileiro do Desenvolvimento Florestal, Ser Teen (8), PNUD/FAO/IBDF/BRA-545 Brasilia, 62 p

Wilcox B A 1978 Supersaturated island faunas A species-age relationship for lizards on post-Pleistocene land-bridge islands in the Gulf of California Science 199 996–998

Wilcox, B A In prep Comparative biogeography of vertebrates

SUBJECT INDEX

Roman numerals refer to text, italics to maps and photographs

Adaptive types
    arboreal colubrid snakes 64
    austral forest amphibians 361
    lowland amphibians 203, 301
    lowland reptiles 303
Africa
    faunal similarity with Australia 14
    faunal similarity with South America 14, 55, 57
    fossil record 57
    herpetofauna 57
    origin of herpetofauna 64
    separation from South America 29, 55, 219
    species/area 15
Altiplano 373, *378*, *398*, *399*
    climate 165
    herpetofauna 400
    tectonics 161, 400
    vegetation 170, 399
Altitudinal distribution
    Central Andes 398
    Guiana Highlands 252
    Northern Andes 388
    Southern Andes 350, 401
Andes 23, *158*, 371
    barriers to dispersal 165, *166*, 382, 389, 402, *405*
    Central Andes 373, *394*
    climate 158 164 387
    description 23, 157, 341, 371, 380, *381*, 385, 398, 399
    dispersal routes 412, 420
    displacement of vegetation zones 111, 172, 177
    distribution patterns 380 387 389, 396, 400, 402, 414, *415-416*, *421-423*, *425*, 443
    ecophysiographic regions 402, *405*
    endemism 381, 383, 387, 389, 404
    faunal similarities within 383, 388, 397, 401
    faunal similarities without 406
    geological history 157, 346, 387, 398
    glacial climates 173
    glaciation 151 172, 400
    habitats 373, *375-379*
    herpetofaunal communities 426
    human modifications 374, 431
    inter-Andean basins 373, 386
    origin of herpetofauna 409
    Quaternary history 172, 416
    species richness 387, 397, 401
    vegetation 169, 373
Areas of congruence 109
Arid Andean habitats 373, *375*, 399
Atacama Desert 22, 23, 117
Aunt Arctica 73
Austral forests 20, *310*, 341, *312*, 371, *376*
    climate 344
    distribution patterns 347, 349 354, 356
    endemism 363

    herpetofauna 347
    origin of herpetofauna 355
    physiography 342, *343*
    Quaternary history 178 343, 346
    vegetation 171, 309, 345
Australia 74
    connection with New Zealand 100
    endemism 98
    faunal similarity with Africa 14
    faunal similarity with South America 14 73, 100
    fossil record 88 97
    herpetofauna 73
    history of continent 74
    origin of herpetofauna 77 83, 91
    species/area 15
Australopapuan fauna
    distribution patterns 77, 80 84
    origins 90
Avifauna
    distribution patterns *122*, *124*, 129
    paramo islands 117

Barriers *166*
    Andean 165, 402, 405
    Austral forests 360
    Depresion de San Cristobal 382
    Essequibo-Rio Branco Depression 264
    Huancabamba Depression 389
    inter-Andean valleys 164
    Marañon Valley 167
Beringia 17
Biogeographical theories 55, 114, 254, 417
Brasilian Highlands
    age 163
    climate 167
    glaciation 180
    Quaternary history 180
    tectonics 163
    vegetation 171

Caatinga 22 299
Center of evolution 117
Centers of origin 70
Central America 16 383, 407
    connection with South America 16, 173
    faunal exchange with South America 17, 221, 414
    radiation of amphibians 208
Central Andes 373, *394*
    herpetofauna 389
    physiography 396
Cerrados 22, 299
Chaco 299, *300*
Chaco-Pampean Plain 141, *142*, 149
Chilean Archipelago 342
Chilean Lake District 344
Climate
    Altiplano 165

Andes 158, 164
Austral forests 341, 347
Australia 75
Brasilian Highlands 167
Chaco 299
Cretaceous 30
desiccation of 20, 75, 114, 143, 151, 347
Early Tertiary 30 41, 143
Guiana Highlands 168, 247
history of 182
Late Tertiary 20 143
Llanos 281
Patagonia 151
Pleistocene 20, 108, 113, 150, 172, 347, 417
Postglacial 114
Quaternary 113, 144
Tierra del Fuego 165
Cloud forest
   description 373, 375
   dispersal in 420
   distribution in Andes 373
Colonizers 66, 77, 181, 206
Communities 426
   Andean 428
   cloud forest 427
   Patagonian 431
   rainforest 227
Conservation 23, 134, 161
Cordillera de la Costa 372, 381
   herpetofauna 381
   physiography 380

Depresion de San Cristobal 380, 382
Depresión de Unare 380
Dispersal center 120
Dispersal model 70
Dispersal routes
   Andean 412
   Guianan 257
   Huancabamba Depression 221, 389
   lowland forests 202 221
   paramo 418
   trans-Andean 121, 420
Distribution center 117, 118 122
Distribution patterns
   Amazonian arc 198
   Andes 380, 387, 396, 400, 402, 414, *415-416*, *421-423*, *425*, 443
   Anolis 126
   Austral forests 347, *349-351*, *356*
   birds *127, 130*
   butterflies *126*
   Chaco 302
   continental 19, 21
   Dendrobates 126
   Guianan herpetofauna 249, *254-255*, *258-259*
   Huancabamba Depression 389
   languages *127*
   Llanos 290
   monkeys *127*
   Oriental Pacific 77, 80, *84*
   Patagonian 317, *321-325*, *329*, *332*, *338*
   plants 125, *127*
   rainforest amphibians *167-168*, *200-201* 203

   rainforest reptiles *230, 232 233*
   western Pacific islands 80, *82*
Dry Andean forests 373, 376

East Indies
   dispersal routes 80
   distribution patterns 77
Ecophysiographic regions 6
   Andean 402, *405*
   distribution of families in 5
Endemism
   Andes 381, 383, 387, 404
   Atlantic forest amphibians 201
   Austral forests 341, 362
   Australia 98
   Central cis-Andean amphibians 199
   Guianan region 249, 265
   Huancabamba Depression 389
   lowland tropical reptiles 225
   Napo-Ucayali amphibians 198
   Patagonia 325
   trans-Andean forest amphibians 196
   with respect to reproductive modes 206
Espinal 309, *310*
Essequibo-Rio Branco Depression 264
Evolutionary radiation
   leptodactylid frogs 207
   Liolaemus 327
   telmatobiine frogs 327
   tropidurine lizards 327
Evolutionary rates 20, 116, 131
Exploration of South America 1, 241
Extra-Andean mesetas 312, 326

Faunal exchange
   Africa with South America 56, 64
   Central America with South America 17
   West Indies with South America 18
Faunal origins
   Andes 409
   Australia 77
   Central America 17
   Chaco 301
   Guiana 254
   Holarctic 56
   India 56
   Laurasia 64
   lowland forest 207 221
   Oriental 77, 100
   Patagonia 326
   West Indies 19
Faunal similarity
   Africa 14, 55, 57
   Andes 407
   Atacama Desert 408
   Australia 14, 73 100
   Central America 14, 407
   Guiana 261
   highland regions 406
   Huancabamba Depression 389
   North America 16, 44
   Patagonia 317, 408
   Sierra Nevada de Santa Marta 384

within Andes 383, 388, 397, 401
within tropical forests 190, 221, 229, 291
Fossil record
    Africa 57, 61, 63
    amphisbaenians 62
    Australia 88, 89, 97
    birds 111
    caecilians 57
    crocodilians 61, 90
    Europe 62
    frogs 58, 89
    Laurasia 61
    mammals 114, 146, 148, 151
    salamanders 57
    snakes 63, 89
    South American amphibians 312, 356
    South American reptiles 219, 312
    South American taxa, list of 51
    turtles 61, 88, 97
Fossil sites 34, 34-38, 311

Galapagos Islands 17, 22, 364
Geological interpretations
    Amazon Basin 113, 287
Geomorphological interpretations 111, 183
Geomorphological units 160, 311-315
Glacial climatology, theory 181
Glacial phases
    ages 113, 173, 317
    climate 108, 113, 147, 150, 173, 179
    correlation with northern 146, 174, 178
    number 146, 173
Glaciers
    Andean 151, 172, 400
    Brasilian Highlands 180
    Chilean 178, 343, 347, 359
    Patagonian 146, 178
Gondwanaland
    breakup of 29, 55, 75, 219
    distributions in 14, 56, 65
    historical components of 16
Guiana Shield
    age 163
    climate 168, 247
    delimitation 242, 243-244, 246-248
    erosion 164
    geology 163, 242
    herpetofauna 249
    Quaternary history 180
    vegetation 172, 247

Habitats in Andes 373
Habitat utilization
    amphibians 351
    lizards 304
    reptiles 351
Herpetofauna, South American
    geographic origins of families 4
    fossil record 29, 51
    review of families 2
    taxonomic composition 3
Historical biogeographic analysis, method 118
Huallaga Valley 373, 393
Huancabamba Depression 22, 218, 221, 373, 389

Human modifications in Andes 374, 379, 434
Humboldt Current 20, 22, 99, 182, 417

Immunological distance and continental divergence 93
Immunological evidence of relationships
    hylid frogs 92
    phyllomedusine frogs 8
Inabresia 56, 58, 64
Insect distributions and speciation 123
Inter-Andean Basins 373, 386
    herpetofauna 388
    physiography 386
Interglacial phases
    climate 147, 150, 173, 179

Karyological evidence of relationships
    hylid frogs 91
    leptodactylid frogs 358, 360, 362
    microhylid frogs 60, 85, 87

Lago Titicaca 175, 371, 399
Lost Pacific continent 100
Lithostratigraphic units 144
Llanos 281, 282, 284-286

Mammal ages 144
Mammal distributions and speciation
    Amazon Basin 128
Mandibular musculature, frogs 81, 84, 86, 91
Mantaro-Apurimac Valley 373, 393
Marañon Valley 22, 373, 393
Megafaunal extinction 114, 145
Mérida Andes 372, 381
    herpetofauna 382
    physiography 380
Mesopotamia 141, 142, 148, 299
Montane rainforest 374
Monte 309, 310

Natural reserves 23, 434
    forest refugia 132
    size 462
New Guinea 74
    connection with Australia 76
    herpetofauna 81
New Zealand 74
    connection with Australia 100
    herpetofauna 99
Nonforests 22, 282
Northern Andes 372, 385
    herpetofauna 387
    physiography 384
Nudo de Pasto 372, 384

Oceanic dispersal 99

Paleofloras
    Maslin Bay 75
    Patagonian 311
    Tertiary-Chaco 19, 309, 414
    Valdivian 311
    West Gondwanan 19
Palynological interpretations 110, 163, 172

Pampas 309
Pampean Ranges 161
Panamanian Portal 173, 221
Pantepui 246
Paramo 377
    distribution 170 374
    floral composition 168
    fluctuation in size 418
Paramo islands 417, *419*
Paranense Sea 143, 149
Patagonia 141, *142*, 147 309
    distribution patterns 317, *321-325*, 329, 332
    faunal regions 312, *313* 315, *318-319*
    herpetofauna 317
    physiographic districts *318-319*
    steppe 20, *310*, 316, 374, 377
    vegetation 316
Plate tectonics
    Antarctica 29, 75
    Antarctic-Australian suture 75
    Australian-Oriental Plate collision 76, 89
    Caribbean Plate 18, 29
    Indian Plate 60, 70
    Nazca-South American Plate collision 161
    opening of South Atlantic 29, 55, 219
Pleistocene-Holocene boundary 144
Plio-Pleistocene boundary 144
Prehistoric man 128
Proto-Antilles 16
Puna 378, 399
    distribution 170, 374
    floral composition 170

Quaternary history
    Andes 172, 416
    Austral forests 178 346
    Brasilian Highlands 180
    Ethiopian Region 132
    Guiana Highlands 180, 248
    Neotropical Region 107, 219
    temperate lowlands 111, 146
    tropical lowlands 107 219

Radar images 108, 112
Rainfall patterns 109, *248*
Refuges 117, 120 461
Refugia
    forest 116, 123, *124*, 132 139 248, 359
    location during arid phases 129
    natural preserves 461
    nonforest 116
    speciation in 131, 202
Reinke's Corridor 189, 198, 260
Reproductive modes, amphibians 202, 206, 301, 353

Savanna
    gallery forest in 282, *283*
    grassland 108, 282, *282*, 286
    Guianan 246, *247*
    palm 282, *283*
    relicts in 218
    varsea campos 108
    woodland 108
Sea level changes, Pleistocene 110, 151

Secondary contact zones 118, *122*
Serological evidence of relationships, *Liolaemus* 330
Serra da Mantiqueira 161
Serro do Mar 161
Serranía de Paria 372, 381
Serranía de Turumiquire 372, 381
Sierra Nevada de Santa Marta 372, 382
    herpetofauna 383
    tectonics 157, 382
Southern Andes 372 399
    herpetofauna 400
    physiography 398
Speciation
    Andes 406, 424
    Chaco 304
    forest refugia 131, 202
    Patagonian lizards 327
Speciation model 222
Species/area
    Africa 15
    Australia 15
    South America 15
    tropical forest reptiles 227
Species richness
    Andes, southern Peru 397
    latitudinal gradient in Andes 404
    lowland rainforests 206, 231
    northern Andes 387
Sub-Andean region 111, *142* 148, 299
Subpáramo 379
    description 374
    distribution 374
    isolation of 420
Symposium participants *vii*

Taxonomic diversity
    Africa 15
    Australia 15
    South America 15
    West Indies 18
Tepuis 244, *245*
Tetrapods
    comparison of numbers between South
    America and world 3
Tierra del Fuego
    climate 165
    herpetofauna 326
    vegetation 171
Trans-Atlantic migration 56, 64
Trans-Pacific migration 11 99
Tropical dry forests 282 287-288, 300
Tropical rainforests 20, 22, 108, *109*, 189, *190*, 231,
    374, 408
    Amazonian 108, *227*
    amphibian faunas 190
    Atlantic 190, 198
    Central cis-Andean 189, 197
    Chocoan 327
    distribution of 22, 109 231
    Guianan 246
    northern 190, 196
    origin of fauna 207, 221
    reptilian faunas 217, 225
    trans-Andean 190, 195

Valle Central de Chile 342
Vegetation
    Andes 169, 374
    Austral forests 345
    Brasilian Highlands 171
    Chaco 300
    Guiana Highlands 172, 246, 247
    Llanos 281
    northern lowlands 281
    Patagonia 316
    Pleistocene 223
    vertical shifts in Andes 111, 172, 177

Vicariance model 18, 70, 117, 109

West Indies
    endemism 18
    origin of herpetofauna 19
    origin of islands 18
    taxonomic diversity 18
Western Pacific island faunas 99
    dispersal routes 80
    distribution patterns 82

TAXONOMIC INDEX

All scientific names of families and lower taxonomic levels are indexed, except those trivial names appearing in appendices. Roman numbers refer to text, italics refer to figures and boldface to appendices

Acacia 171, 287, 300, 373, 374
    caven 341, 342, 364
Acacioxylon 148
Acaena 173, 374
    caespitosa 316
    macrostemon 316
Acantholippia seriphioides 317
Achropogon 172
Acontinae 87
Acris 93
Acrochordidae 13, 88
Acrochordus 88
Adenomera 190, 206, 213, 214, 215, 269
    andreae 197, 201
    bokermanni 201
    hylaedactyla 191, 197, 200, 201
    marmorata 201
Adesmia 171, 316, 373, 374, 377, 399
    horrida 170
Adiantum 345
Aegla 352
Aextoxicum punctatus 345
Afrixalus 61
Agalychnis 8, 208, 212, 213
Agamidae 14, 15, 55, 57, 62, 65, 66, 71, 87
Agave 134
Agropyron magellanicum 316
Alligatoridae 31, 32, 33, 43, 44, 51, 52, 53, 54, 65, 220, 251
Allophryne 194, 214, 256, 270
    ruthveni 254
Alnus 163, 169, 173, 175
    jorullensis 169
Alopoglossus 222, 227, 238, 278, 408, 410, 453
Alouatta
    seniculus 128
    villosa 128
Alsodes 20, 325, 326, 327, 338, 341, 351, 361, 363, 365, 400, 407, 409, 410, 411, 412, 420, 457
    gargola 361
        gargola 320
        neuquensis 321
    monticola 347, 348, 351, 355, 361
    nodosus 361, 400
    pehuenche 361
    verrucosus 361
Alsophis 12, 19, 22, 341
    angustilineatus 364
    canthergerus 364
    chamissonis 348, 350, 352, 356, 364
    tachymenoides 364
Amapasaurus 238, 256, 278
    tetradactylus 255
Amblyphrynus 383, 410, 411, 413, 445
    ingeri 383
Amblyrhynchus 10, 17
Ameghinoa 317
Ameiva 18, 19, 123, 218, 219, 227, 238, 278, 296

ameiva 289, 290, 291, 463
    bifrontata 289
Amphibolurus 87
Amphichelydia 61
Amphignathodon 387, 410, 411, 413, 450
Amphignathodontinae 5, 8, 17, 61, 194, 204, 205, 208
Amphisbaena 11, 18, 218, 219, 222, 227, 238, 279, 296, 339
    alba 291
    camura 302, 304
    fuliginosa 291
Amphisbaenidae 3, 4, 5, 11, 14, 17, 32, 54, 56, 63, 65, 251
Anadia 238, 372, 382, 407, 410, 411, 414, 420, 429, 444, 453
    bitaeniata 381
    brevirostris 381
    pulchella 383
Anaea 125
Anarthrophyllum
    desideratum 316
    rigidum 316
Anemone 180
Anguidae 3, 4, 5, 11, 17, 32, 56, 65
Anilidae 3, 4, 5, 12, 32, 42, 51, 53, 251
Anilius 42, 218, 239, 274
Anisolepis 238
Anodontohyla 87
Anolis 2, 19, 22, 218, 227, 238, 277, 278, 296, 327, 382, 383, 407, 408, 410, 413, 444, 453
    annectens 289, 291
    antoni 387
    auratus 291
    chloris 387
    chrysolepis 123, 126
    chrysolepis group 123, 124
    fuscoruratus 222
    nigropunctatus 381, 382
    onca 289, 291
    ortoni 222
    punctatus 222
Anomalepidae 3, 4, 5, 11, 17, 18, 251
Anomalepis 11, 218, 222, 239
Anops kingi 302, 304
Aparasphenodon 214, 215, 271
    venezolanus 254, 257
Apodichelys lucianoi 51
Apodops 56, 57
    pricei 51
Aporophis 274
Apostolepis 13, 218, 227, 239, 274
Apuleia ferra 171
Araucaria 151, 171, 180, 309, 316, 321, 334, 345, 346, 374, 400, 414
    angustifolia 171
    araucana 345
Arcoromer 87, 194, 215

Arcophryne rotunda 95
Aristelliger 19
Arracacia 174
Arthrosaura 238, 278
    tatei 241
Ascaphus 3, 58, 100
Aspidites 89
Aspidosperma 300
Aster 169
Asterophryinae 79, 81, 82, 84
Asterophrys 87
Ateles
    fusciceps 128
    geoffroyi 128
Atelognathus 326, 338, 341, 361, 363, 431
    grandisonae 326, 348, 353, 360, 361
    nitoi 320, 325, 361
    patagonicus 320, 325, 361
    praebasalticus 320, 325, 361
        agilis 320
        doboslavi 320
        luisi 320
        praebasalticus 320
    reverberii 325
    solitarius 320, 325, 361
Atelopus 7, 192, 212, 213, 214, 270, 407, 410, 413, 416, 420, 429, 443, 449
    cercuta 387
    carrikeri 383
    cruciger 197
    ebenoides 428
    ignescens 388
    ignescens group 381, 411, 413, 418
    mucubajensis 381, 382
    oxyrhynchus 381, 382
    pulcher 198
    varius group 18
    walkeri 383
Atlapetes schistaceous 174
Atractus 18, 64, 218, 222, 227, 239, 253, 264, 274, 275, 374, 382, 383, 407, 408, 411, 413, **444**, 454, 455
    badius 382
    insipidus 257
    lehmanni 388
Atriplex 316
Aulura 218, 238
Auracantes 316
Australobatrachus 7
    ilius 89
Australocrinia 95
Austrocactus 316
Azara 180
Azemiops 64
Azora 309
Azorella 170, 173, 316, 374

Baccharis 169, 170, 175, 374, 387
Bachia 18, 218, 227, 238, 278, 296
    bicolor 289
    guianensis 289
    talpa 289
Balanerodus 43, 52
Banisteria 309

Bartsia 173
Barycholos 194, 212
Basiliscus 10, 222, 238, 296, 408, 410, 453
    galeritus 387
Batrachophrynus 312, 358, 361, 362, 396, 398, 409, 410, 411, 412, 424, 434, 457
    brachydactylus 358
    macrostomus 358
Batrachyla 20, 21, 96, 327, 341, 351, 352, 361, 362, 363, 365
    antartandica 348, 355, 358, 360, 361
    leptopus 347, 348, 351, 355, 358, 361, 362
    taeniata 347, 348, 355, 358, 360, 361
Batrachylini 194, 204, 207, 361
Berberis 173, 180, 309, 374
    cuneata 316, 317
Bignonia 309
Bipes 11
Blanus 11
Blechnum 345
Boa 18, 227, 239, 274, 297
    constrictor 290, 291
Bogertia 62
Boidae 3, 4, 5, 12, 14, 31, 32, 42, 51, 52, 53, 54, 63, 66, 88, 100, 251
Boiginae 64
Boiga 64
Boinae 55, 63
Boini 56, 63
Bolitoglossa 2, 22, 191, 212, 213, 372, 407, 410, 414, 420, 421, 429, 443, 445
    adspersa group 418
    orestes 381, 382
    savagei 381, 382, 383, 421
Bolitoglossini 56, 207
Boopis 180
Bothremydidae 61
Bothrops 13, 14, 18, 218, 227, 239, 277, 297, 339, 407, 408, 411, 444, 456
    alternatus 303
    ammodytoides 317
    bilineatus 222
    lansbergi 289
    neuwiedii 303
    schlegeli 387
Boulengerula 57
Bowdichia 284
Brachycephalidae 3, 4, 5, 7, 30, 60, 191, 192, 194, 204, 207
Brachycephalus 194, 214
Brachyclados caespitosus 317
Brachygnathosuchus 53, 220
Brachylophus 11, 98
    brevicephalus 98
    fasciatus 98
Brasilotyphlus 194, 213, 273
Breviceps 87
Briba 62
Brevicipitinae 60
Bromelia humilis 285
Bromus macranthus 316
Bromia 218, 238, 279
Brunellia 169
Buettneria 309

Bufo 4 7 39, 53 54 58, 189 190, 192 212, 213, 214, 215, 270, 295, 301, 338, 341, 351, 353 362, 363 400 407 410 412, 426, 431, 434, 443, 449, 457
    arenarum 59, 301, 302, 320, 326
        chaguar 304
        platensis 304
    blombergi 59, 203
    boreas group 412
    calamita 312
    calamita group 4 39, 312 362, 363
    chilensis 348, 350, 355, 358 362, 363
    coniferus 17
    crucifer 199
    glaberrimus 203
    granulosus 23, 289, 290, 302, 303, 305
        fernandezae 304 305
        major 304, 305
    guttatus 203, 260, 290
    guttatus group 203
    haematiticus 18, 196
    haematiticus group 59
    ictericus 200, 201
    marinus 4, 17, 33, 191, 195 197 201, 289, 290
    marinus group 39
    nasicus 254
    paracnemis 148, 302, 303
    regularis 59
    rubropunctatus 348 362, 363
    spinulosus 20, 326 362, 396, 400, 415, 431
    spinulosus group 7, 407, 409 411, 412, 420
    sternosignatus 197
    superciliaris 59
    trifolium 398
    typhonius 18, 190, 191, 195, 197, 200
    typhonius group 114
    valliceps group 17
    variegatus 312 347, 348, 350, 355, 362, 363 400 412
    viridis group 112
Bufonidae 3, 4 5, 14 15, 17 30 39, 44 51, 53 54, 56, 58, 59, 60, 65, 192 204, 207, 251
Byrsonima 284

Caecilia 9, 18, 57, 190, 192, 212, 213, 214, 273 407, 408 410 445
    thompsoni 196
    tentaculata 191
    subnigricans 191, 195
Caeciliidae 3, 4 5, 9, 17, 30 32 51, 56 57, 192, 207, 208
Caesalpinia echinata 171
Caiman 14, 33, 43, 52, 53, 218, 220, 227, 238 274, 295, 303
    crocodylus 289
    latirostris 33, 43 303
    yacare 43
Calamagrostis 169
Calamelaps 64
Callicebus
    moloch 128
    torquatus 128
Callicorini 125

Callopistes 22, 33, 41, 53
Callopsis 54
Calluella 81 82
Caltha 316
Calyptahyla 7, 18
Calyptocephalellinae 356
Calyptocephalellum 194, 357 360
Campylorhynchus griseus 130
Candoia 89
Capparis 285
Cardamine 171
Caretta 273
Carettochelyidae 88, 101
Carettochelys insculpta 88
Carex 316
Cariamidae 148
Caryocar 127
    amygdaliferum 127
    amygdaliforme 127
    dentatum 127
    edule 127
    gracile 127
    nuciferum 127
    pallidum 127
Caryocaraceae 125
Caudiverbera 20, 32 33 38, 52 53, 311, 327, 341, 351, 356, 357, 358, 359, 360 361, 363, 365, 412
    casamayorensis 52 356, 360
    caudiverbera 52, 53, 312, 347 348, 350 352, 354 355, 356 358
Cebidae 143
Cebus
    albifrons 128
    capucinus 128
    griseus 128
Cecropia 171
Centrolene 387, 410, 411, 413, 452
Centrolenella 2, 17, 21 190, 192 196, 212, 213, 214, 215 253, 264 272, 273, 374 381, 382, 383, 388, 406, 407 410, 411, 413, 420, 427, 428, 434 444, 452
    albotunica 201
    buckleyi 381, 382, 388, 420
    divaricans 201
    dubia 201
    eurygnatha 201
    fleischmanni 191, 382, 387
    griffithsi 387
    prosoblepon 387
    valerioi 387
    vanzolinii 201
Centrolenidae 3 4, 5 8 17, 22 30, 56, 60 192 204, 206, 208 251
Ceratophryinae 4, 5, 38, 96 193, 194 204, 207 357
Ceratophrys 38, 53, 54 213 214 215, 269, 295, 301, 302, 303, 304
    aurita 39, 201
    calcarata 197, 260
    cornuta 198 201
    ornata 38, 304
    pierotti 302
    stolzmanni 195
Cercidium 285

Cercosaura 227, 238, 278, 296, 408, 410, 453
Chaetophractus vellerosus 148
Chamaeleolis 19
Chamaeleontidae 55, 57, 62, 65, 66
Chamaelinorops 19
Changlosaurus 63
Chaperina 60
Characoidae 128
Charactosuchus 53, 220
    fieldsi 13
Chelidae 3, 4, 5, 9, 14, 31, 32, 44, **52**, 53, 97, 100, 251
Chelodina 97
Chelonia 273
Chelonidae 251
Chelonoides 40, 53
Chelus 40, 52, 53, 218, 220, 238, 273, 296
    colombianus 40
    fimbriatus 258
    lewisi 10
Chelycarapookidae 98
Chelycarapookus 98
    arcuatus 98, 100
Chelydra 9, 218, 222, 238
Chelydridae 3, 4, 5, 9, 17, 18, 31
Chersydrus 88
Chiasmocleis 60, 214, 215, 273
Chimantea 172
Chiromantis 60
Chironius 13, 18, 64, 220, 222, 227, 239, **275**, 297, 408, 411, 444, 455
    bicarinatus 224, 225
    carinatus 222, 225, 291
    exoletus 224, 225
        pyrrhopogon 225
    flavolineatus 224
    foveatus 224, 225
    fuscus 224, 225
    monticola 381, 382, 388, 397, 420, *423*
    multiventris 224, 225
    quadricarinatus 224
    scurrulus 224, 225
        laevicollis 224, 225
Chondropython 89
Chrysemys 9, 18, 218, 220, 222, 296
    scripta 289
Chrysobalanceae 125
Chthonerpeton 192, **194**, 214
Chuquiraga 170, 316, 342
    aurea 317
    avellanedae 317
Chusquea 312, 321, 345, 374
    penifolia 172
    quila 345
Cichlidae 128
Cissus 309, 345
Clelia 18, 219, 227, 239, **275**, 297, 408, 411, **455**
    clelia 290, 303
    occipitolutea 303
Clemantis 180
Clusia 169
Cnemidophorus 11, 18, 23, 218, 227, 238, 278, 296, 326, 339
    lacertoides 304
    leachi 302, *304*
    lemniscatus 289, 290, 291
        lemniscatus 260
Cocus 171
Coleodactylus 10, 227, 277
    meridionalis 222, 260
Colliguaja 342
    integerrima 316
Colobodactylus 238
Colobosaura 227, 238
Colombophis 53
    portai 42
Colostethus 2, 22, 192, 212, 213, 214, 215, 269, 372, 374, 380, 382, 383, 388, 406, 407, 410, 411, 414, 420, 427, 429, 443, 444, 450
    abditaurantius 387
    fuliginosus group 197
    herminae 382
    mandelorum 381
Colubridae 3, 1, 12, 14, 32, 33, 42, 53, 54, 63, 88, 228, 251
Colubrinae 5, 12, 13, 17, 18, 56
Columba
    corensis 130
    picazuro 130
Coniophanes 18, 222
Conolophus 10, 17
Constrictor constrictor 302
Copernicia 282, 300
    tectorum 282, *284*
Cophixalus 83, 84, 87
Cophylinae 60
Corallus 18, 227, 239, 274, 297
    enhydris 291
Cordicephalus 58
Cordylidae 14, 15, 57, 62, 66
Cornufer 78
Cortaderia
    modesta 172
Coryphospingus
    cucullatus 130
    pileatus 130
Corythophanes 222, 238
Cremolobus 175
Crepidophryne 7
Cricetinae 145
Cricosaura 19
Crinia 95
    haswelli 95
Crocodylidae 3, 4, 5, 14, 17, 31, 32, 33, 42, 43, 51, 53, 56, 61, 66, 100, 101, 251
Crocodilurus 218, 238, 278
    lacertinus 258
Crocodylus 14, 18, 43, 98, 218, 220, 222, 238, 274, 295, 296
    acutus 18, 220
    intermedius 220, 257, 289, 291
    johnsoni 98
    novaeguinae 98
    porosus 98
Crossochelys 52
Crossodactylodes 194, 215
Crossodactylus 194, 215
    dispar 199, 200

Crotalidae 251
Crotalinae 5, 17, 18, 42, 55, 56, 65, 66
Crotalus 14, 218 219, 239, 277, 297
    durissus 289, 291, 303
    tegrandis 289, 291
Crotaphopeltis 64
Crytobatrachus 23, 253, 387, 408, 411, 413, 420, 450
    boulengeri 383
Cryptodira 61
Crythiosaurus 63
Ctenoblepharis 326, 338, 407, 409, 410, 411, *415*, 458
Ctenophryne 194 214, 273
    geayi 197
Ctenosaura 18, 19
Cupania 309
Cupressoides 374
Cupriguanus 348
Curatella 284 286
Cyclagras 275
Cycloramphus 194, 214, 215
    asper 200
Cyclorana 7 91, 92, 93, 94, 95, 96
    alboguttatus 93, 94, 96
    australis 94
    brevipes 94
    dahlii 93
    inermis 93
Cycloraninae 95, 96
Cyclura 10, 19
Cylindrophis 42 88
Cynognathus 55 64

Dasypeltinae 57
Dasyphyllum 172
Dasypodidae 149
Dasypops 195 215
Dendrobates 126 192, 197, 212, 213, 269, 295, 408, 410, 450
    auratus 195, 203
    azureus 255
    galactonotus *126*, 203
    histrionicus 126
    leucomelas 126, 255, 257, 290
    minutus 250
    quinquevittatus 198
    steyermarki 256 257
    tinctorius 126, 203, 255
    tinctorius group 203
    trunctatus 195, 203
Dendrobatidae 3, 5, 7, 17, 22 30, 39, 56, 60, 192, 204, 206, 207, 251
Dendrophidion 13 227 239 275, 408, 411, 444, 455
    percarinatus 382, 387
Dendrophryniscus 7 192, 213, 214, 270
    minutus 198
Dermatonotus 60 87, 193
    mulleri 301, 302
Dermochelydae 251
Dermochelys 273
Dermophinae 56
Dermophis 9, 192, 194, 212
Deschampsia 316
Diaphorolepis 18 218, 222, 239, 407, 411, 413, 455

Diasemosaurus 52
    occidentalis 312
Dichapetalaceae 125
Dicrodon 41, 54
Didynamipus 60
Digitaria 300
Dinilysia 12, 42, 63
    patagonica 42, 312
Dinodon 88
Dipholostephium 170
Diplodactylidae 96
Diplodactylinae 97, 100
Diplodactylus vittatus 97
Diploglossus 11, 19, 227 238
Diplolaemus 219, 323, 326, 327, 338, 400, 408, 410, 431, 458
    bibronii 320
    darwinii 325, 431
    leopardinus 321 400, 420
Diplostephium 169, 171, 173
Dipsadoboa 64
Dipsadidae 251
Dipsas 227, 234, 239, 274, 407, 408, 411, 455
    indica 222
Dischidodactylus 194, 214
Discoglossidae 56 59
Discoglossus 59, 60
Dispholidinae 64
Disticha 374, 387
Doiuchotis 149, 150
Draba 173
Dracaena 33 41, 53 218, 219, 220, 234, 238, 278
Drapetes muscosa 178
Drepanoides 239, 275
Drimys 169, 171, 175, 176, 309, 345
    brasiliensis 171
    winteri 171, 345
Dromicus 12, 22
Drosophila 123
Drymarchon 13, 218, 227, 239, 275, 297
    corais 290, 291
Drymobius 13, 227, 239, 275, 297
Drymoluber 13, 239, 275
Dryopteris 345
Duidea 172
Dusycion australis 148
Dyrosauridae 61
Dyscophinae 60, 81
Dyscophus 60 87

Echimyidae 143, 148 149
Echinosaura 18, 222, 238
Leplcopus 238, 411
Edaloiluna 194, 213
Flachistocleis 18 60, 87 193, 273, 295
    bicolor 301, 302
    ovalis 290
Elapidae 11, 57, 66, 71, 88, 228, 251
Elapomorphus 13, 64, 218, 239, 275, 339
    bilineatus 320
    tricolor 303
Eleutherodactylini 4, 17, 194 204, 206, 207, 208
Lleutherodactylus 2, 17, 18 19, 22, 208, 212 213, 214, 215, 253, 264, 269, 372, 374, 382, 383,

388, 389, 406, 407, 410, 416 420, 427, 428,
    429 443, 445, 446, 447, 448
achatinus 203
acuminatus 200
affinis 418
alfredi group 208
biporcatus group 208
bicinnulus 196
binotatus 200
binotatus group 201
boconoensis 381
bogotensis 418
bogotensis group 418
buckleyi 388
cajamarcensis 389
carmelitae 383
chiastonotus 201, 203
conspicillatus 191, 203
curtipes complex 418
discoidalis 208
elegans 418
elegans complex 418
fenestratus 203
fitzingeri 196
fitzingeri group 201, 203, 208, 383, 413, 420
ginesi 381
inoptatus group 19
insignitus 383
lacrimosus 198
lancini 381
longirostris 196
lynchi 418
maussi 197, 203
nicefori 418
nigrovittatus 201
ockendeni 200
peruvianus 203
prohsodiscus 383
pulvinatus 255
raniformis 195, 197
rozei 196
sulcatus 203
sulcatus group 203, 413
terraebolivaris 196, 203
unistrigatus 208, 388
unistrigatus group 383, 411, 414, 418
urichi 382
vertebralis 388
vilarsi 203
w-nigrum 388, 420
zeuctotylus 201
Elosia duidensis 242, 253, 254
Elosiinae 4, 5 193, 194, 204, 206, 207
Elseya 97, 98
Embothrium 309
Emmochliophis 218, 222, 239
Emydidae 3, 4, 5, 9, 31, 44 53, 54, 61, 251
Emydura 97
    macquari 98
Engystomatidae 59
Enulius 218 222 239 297
Enyalioides 18, 22, 222, 227, 238 408, 410, 453
Enyalius 227, 238

Eocaiman 52, 53 220 312
    cavernensis 13
Eoxenopoides 58
Eophractus 356
Ephedra 143, 316 374
Epicrates 219, 227, 239, 274, 297
    cenchria 290, 291, 302
Epicrionops 9, 192, 212, 213, 273, 408 410, 445
Epilobium 171
Equus 175, 178
Erethizontidae 148
Eretmochelys 273
Erichosaurus debilis 312
Erycinae 63
Erymnochelys 61
Erythrolamprus 219, 227, 239 275
Erythroxylon 309
Escallonia 169, 172, 176 180
Espeletia 169 170 173, 374, 377, 387
Eublepharidae 96
Eublepharinae 62
Eucryphia cordifolia 345
Eugenia 169, 171
Eulychnia 171
Eumeces 11, 86, 87
Eunectes 33, 42, 53, 218 239, 274 297
    murinus 289
    notaeus 303
Euparkerella 213, 215 256 269, 408 410, 448
    myrmecoides 201
Euphorbia 317
Euphractus 148, 149, 150
Eupsophus 20, 33, 38, 52, 311 312, 327, 341 350,
    351, 360 361, 362, 363, 365, 412
    migueli 348
    roseus 312 347, 348, 352, 355, 358 360
    vanzolinii 348
    vertebralis 348
    vittatus 347, 348 352, 355, 358
Euspondylus 23, 238, 253, 265, 278 396, 407 410,
    411 413 414, 444 453, 454
    leucostictus 241
Eusuchia 31 33, 61
Euterpe 171

Fagara 309
Festuca 170, 316 326 374, 387, 399
    monticola 316
Feylininae 87
Ficus 309
Fitzroya 309, 345, 374, 400
    cupressoides 171, 345
Flectonotus 23 214 215 381, 408, 410, 413, 444
    fissilis 200, 382
    fitzgeraldi 382
    pygmaeus 196, 382
Fluvicola
    nengeta 130
    pica 130
Frankenia 316
Franseria 171
Fritziana 195, 215 413
Fuchsia 315

Galbula
    cyanescens 127
    galbula 127
    melanogenia 127
    pastazae 127
    ruficauda 127
        ruficauda 127
        rufoviridis 127
    tombacea 127
Gartlua 10, 22, 400, 408, 410, 458
Gastrophryne 8 60, 87
Gastrophrynoides 60
Gastrotheca 8, 18, 23, 212, 214, 215, 372, 374, 383, 396, 400 407, 408, 410, 411, 413, 416, 420, 424, 425, 426, 431, 434, 444, 450, 451
    argenteovirens group 425
    aureomaculata group 418
    excubitor 398, 431
    fissipes 199
    marsupiata 398, 431
    marsupiata group 418, 425
    nicefori 381, 382, 387
    ochoai 398
    peruana 398
    plumbea group 418, 425
    riobambae 388
    viridis 200
    williamsi 96
Gaultheria 169
Gavialidae 31 33, 43, 52, 53, 56, 61, 65
Gavialis 43, 52 220
Gekkonidae 3, 4, 10, 14, 15, 32, 41, 51, 56, 62, 65, 96, 99, 100 251
Gekkoninae 5, 17, 62, 96, 97
Gentiana 173
Genyophryne 79 81
Geobatrachus 8, 9, 410, 411, 413, 420, 449
    walkeri 383
Geochelone 9, 18, 33, 40, 41, 52 53, 54, 61, 220, 222, 227, 238 296, 303, 322, 326, 339
    carbonaria 33, 289
    chilensis 33
    denticulata 33
    donosobarrosi 317, 320
    gallardoi 40
    gringorum 40
    hesterna 33, 40
    petersi 303
Geocrinia laevis 90
Geoemyda 40, 54
Geonoma 171
Geophis 218, 222 239
Geotrypetes 56, 57
Geranium 169, 173
Gigantobatrachus 356
Ginkgo 309
Gletchnia 316
Glossarion 172
Glossostoma 18 60, 87 194, 212, 408, 410, 452
    aequatoriale 193
Gochnatia 170
Gonatodes 18, 218, 227, 238, 277, 296, 408, 410, 414, 453
    vittatus 289

Grindelia chiloensis 316
Grypiscini 4 194, 204, 206, 207
Gryposuchus 53, 220
Guei ma 345
    avellano 345
Gunnera 172, 176
Gymnochacinus bergi 325
Gymnodactylus 10, 238
Gymnophthalmus 18, 218, 227, 278, 296
    rubricauda 302
    speciosus 289 291
Gymnopis 9, 57
Gynograma 180
Gynoxys 169

Hamptophryne 87, 194, 214, 273
    boliviana 198
Hegetotheriidae 149
Heleioporus 95
Heleophryne 4, 96
Heleophryninae 56, 57, 96
Heliconius 123, 124, 125, 131
    erato 126
Helicops 64, 218, 222, 227, 239, 275, 297
    angulatus 290
    danieli 289, 291
    Logei 257
    scalaris 289
Helminthophis 11, 297
Hemidactylus 10, 18, 62, 227, 238, 277, 296
    brooki 62
    mabouia 62
    palaichthus 289, 291
Hemiphractinae 5, 8, 17, 193, 194, 204, 205, 207
Hemiphractus 8, 18, 212, 213, 214, 372, 407, 410, 411, 413, 420, 422, 451
    bubalus 421
    fasciatus 196, 387, 421
Hemipipa 195, 214
Herpelinae 56, 57
Heterodactylus 238
Homalopsinae 13
Homonota 62, 326, 338, 431
    borellii 305
    darwinii 305, 320, 325, 431
    horrida 302, 304, 305
Hoplophryninae 60
Hordeum comosum 316
Hydracthiops 64
Hydrangea 345
Hydrodynastes 218, 239, 275
Hydrolaetare 194, 213, 270
    schmidti 197
Hydromedusa 32, 40, 52 218, 238
Hydrops 218, 239, 275, 297
    triangularis 257
Hyla 7, 8, 18, 22, 39, 90, 92, 93, 190, 212, 213, 214, 215 253, 271, 272, 295, 372, 381, 407, 410, 444 451
    acuminata 302
    albomarginata 8 191, 200
    albopunctata 201
    benitezi 256
    boans 8, 191, 195 197, 201

bogotensis 8, 381
bogotensis group 383, 407, 111, 113, 120
brevifrons 198
catharinae 200
chinensis 91
crepitans 189, 289 290
ebraccata 17
egleri 191, 200
faber 199, 201
fasicata 198
fuscomarginata 199
fuscoraria 302
geographica 191, 197 199 200, 258
ginesi 254, 256
hayi 200
kanaima 256
labialis 381, 382 420
labialis group 411 413
lanciformis 198 201
larinopygion group 407, 411, 413
lemai 254, 256
leucophyllata 8, 191, 197, 199, 200
leucophyllata group 61
luteocellata 191
microcephala 17, 289, 290
microps 200
minuscula 289
minuta 191, 197
multifasciata 198, 201 251
ornatissima 254
pardalis 189
parviceps group 21
phlebodes 195
platydactyla 381, 382
proboscidea 255
pulchella complex 400
raniceps 189, 302
rhodopepla 198
rodriguezi 255
rostrata 260 289 290
rostrata group 197
rubra 8, 190, 191 195, 197, 200 289
senicula 199 200
melanargyrea 259
sibleszi 254, 256
wandae 289, 290
x-signata 260, 302
Hylactophryne 208
Hylidae 3, 1, 7, 14, 15, 30, 32, 39, 55, 56 60, 65, 73, 75, 89 90, 91 92 93, 100, 192, 193, 194, 207, 251
Hylinae 5, 17, 193 194 204 206, 207 208
Hylodes 195, 215, 270
duidensis 253, 254
gollmeri 191
mermoratus 241
Hylophorbus 81, 84
Hylorina 20 327 341 361, 363, 365
sylvatica 317, 351, 355 358, 360
Hymenochirus 58
Hyophryne 195, 215
Hypericum 169, 173
Hyperolidae 14, 55, 57, 60, 65
Hyperolius 61

Hypopachus 8 87
Hypothyris ninonia 126
Hypsela 316

Ichthyophiidae 57
Iguana 18, 41, 54, 218, 219, 227, 238, 278, 296
iguana 289, 291
Iguanidae 3, 4, 10, 15, 17 32 41 51, 52, 53, 54, 55, 56 57 62, 65, 99, 123, 228, 251
Iguaninae 5, 17
Ikanogatialis 53
Ilctunaia 52, 220
Ilex 169
paraguariensis 171
Imantodes 227, 239, 275, 297
cenchoa 290, 291
Indobatrachus 70
Insuetophrynus 327 341, 351, 361, 363, 365
acarpicus 348, 355
Iphisa 238, 278
Ischnocnema 208, 213 215, 408, 410, 448

Jamesonia 180
Juglans 169
australis 169
Juncus 316

Kalophrynus 60, 83
pleurostigma 83
Kaloula 60, 87
Kankanophryne 95
Kentropyx 18, 218, 227, 238, 278, 296
calcaratus 222
lagartija 302
striatus 291
viridistriga 302
Kinosternidae 3, 4 5, 9, 17, 18, 31, 40, 251
Kinosternon 9 218 220, 227, 238, 273, 296, 303
bauri 18
scorpioides 289
Kyarranus 96

Lacertidae 15, 55, 57, 62, 65, 66
Lachesis 219 227, 239, 277
muta 13
Lagostomus maximus 301
Lampropeltis 222 239, 108, 111, 444
triangulum 382
Laparrentophis 63
Larrea 316
ameghinoi 316
Laurelia 171, 309, 345, 346 414
serrata 345
Leguminosae 125
Leimadophis 12 218, 221 227, 239, 273, 276, 297 339, 407, 408, 411, 444 455
bimaculatus 381
melanotus 291
regina 291
sagittifer 303
typhlus 291
zweifeli 382
Leiocephalus 19
Leiopelma 3, 58, 100

archeyi 100
hamiltoni 100
hochstetteri 100
Leiopelmatidae 3, 4, 38 44, 57 58, 64
Leiosaurus 326, 327, 338
  belli 41, 305 324
  catamarcensis 305
  paronae 302, 304, 305
Lemaireocerus 285
Lepichina 180
Lepidobatrachus 301, 303
  asper 302
  llanensis 302
  salinicola 302
Lepidoblepharis 10 18, 227, 239 277, 296, 408, 410, 453
  festae 258
  sanctaemartae 289, 291
Lepidochelys 273
Lepidophyllum 170, 175, 374
Leposoma 227 239 253, 278, 296
Leposternon 54, 63, 218, 227, 238
  microcephalum 302
Leptodactylidae 3, 14, 15 22 30, 31, 38, 39, 44, 51, 52, 53 54, 55, 56, 60, 65, 73, 90, 91, 92 95, 96 101, 192, 193 194 198, 207 208, 251, 361
Leptodactylinae 4, 5 17, 193, 194, 204, 206, 207, 362
Leptodactylus 4 17 18 39 53 54, 190, 200, 201, 203, 212, 213, 214, 215, 270, 295, 301, 303, 326, 338, 408, 410, 448
  anceps 301, 302, 304
  bolivianus 191 195, 289, 290
  bufonius 301, 302 304
  chaquensis 301, 302, 303, 304
  fragilis 289, 290
  fuscus 60, 260, 289, 290
  fuscus group 203
  gracilis 304
  gualambensis 301, 302, 304
  labrosus 195
  laticeps 301, 302, 303
  longirostris 203
  macrosternum 289, 290
  mystaceus 199 201 203
  mystacinus 199, 301
  ocellatus 304 320
  pentadactylus 190, 191, 196, 197, 199, 200, 289
  poecilochilus 191, 195, 289
  prognathus 304
  rhodomystax 259
  rugosus 260, 289
  troglodytes 199
  ventrimaculatus 203
  wagneri 190, 191 195 197, 199, 200 289, 290
Leptodeira 64, 218 219 227, 239, 276, 297, 389
  annulata 290, 291
Leptomicrurus 13, 277
Leptophis 13, 64 219 221, 227, 240 276 297 408, 411 455
  ahaetulla 290, 291

copei 257
Leptorhamphus 220
Leptotyphlopidae 3, 4 5, 12, 14, 17, 56, 63, 65, 251
Leptotyphlops 19, 218, 227, 240, 274, 297, 339, 407, 408, 411, 431, 444, 454
  albipuncta 302
  dimidiatus 289
  unguirostris 302
  weyrauchi 302
Leucheria 171
Liasis 89
Libocedrus 309
Libycosuchidae 61
Llerasia 174
Limnodynastinae 96
Limnodynastes 89
  dumerili 90
  tasmaniensis 90
Limnomedusa 361
Limnophis 64
Liolaemus 19, 20, 21, 131, 239, 305 326, 327, 330, 338, 341, 350 351, 352, 353 363, 364, 374, 400, 406, 407, 409 410, 411 415, 420, 431, 434 458
  altissimus 327 364, 400
  archeforus complex 327 332, 333, 334
    archeforus 334
    sarmientoi 334
  austromendocinus 330, 334
  bibroni 320, 325, 327 364, 400, 431
  boulengeri 325, 327, 330
  buergeri 321, 330, 334, 364
  ceii 320 330
  chacoensis 302 304 305
  chilensis 321, 327 348, 351, 354, 364
  cyanogaster 327, 341, 348, 349, 351, 364
    brattstroemi 348, 349, 354
    cyanogaster 348 354
  darwini 322 327, 330, 431
  elongatus 320 321, 327, 330, 331, 332 334, 400, 431
    elongatus 330
    petrophilus 325, 330
  fitzgeraldi 400
  fitzingeri 330 331, 363, 420
    cauquel 320 327, 330
    fitzingeri 320, 327
    melanops 327 330
  fitzingeri complex 327 328, 329, 330
  fuscus 327
  goetschi 330
  gracilis 327
  gravenhorsti 364
  kingi 327 332, 333, 334
  kriegi 320, 321 330, 334, 402, 420, 431
  kriegi complex 327, 331, 332, 334
  lemniscatus 327
  leopardinus 364 401
  lineomaculatus 321 334
  lineomaculatus complex 327, 332 334 335
  lorenzmulleri 364
  magellanicus 326, 334
  magellanicus complex 327, 332, 334 335
  melanops 330

mocquardi 330
monticola 364
    chillanensis 361
    villaricensis 348, 351, 352, 354 364
multiformis 396, 420
multimaculatus 330
nigroviridis 361 101
ornatus 330
pictus 327, 344, 348, 349 351, 364
    pictus 348, 356
    chiloensis 348, 349 356
    major 348 349 356
    talcanensis 348, 349, 356
rothi 325, 327, 330
ruibali 401
ruizleali 325, 327 330
schroderi 364
tenuis 321 327, 349, 351, 364
    tenuis 348, 353
    punctatissimus 348, 350, 353
wiegmannii 304, 330
Liophis 218 222 227, 240 253, 276, 408 455
    canaima 257
    miliaris 260
Liotyphlops 11 218, 227, 240, 274, 297 408, 411, 444
Lithodytes 194 214 270
    lineatus 198
Litoria 7, 89, 90 91, 92 93, 94
    alboguttata 93, 94, 96
    amboinensis 91
    aurea 79 92, 94
    caerulea 75, 89, 92
    dahlii 93
    darlingtoni 91
    everetti 91
    ewingi 90
    freycineti 92
    inermis 93
    infrafrenata 91
    peroni 91
    peroni group 91
    raniformis 94
    rothi 91
    rubella 75
Livistona mariae 75
Lomatia 309 345
Lophosoria 345
Loricaria 169, 170, 173
Lovendgelaps 88
Lupinus 169 170
Luzuriaga 345
Lycium
    ameghinoi 317
    tenuispinosum 316
Lycodontinae 12, 57 64, 66
Lycophidion 64
Lycopodium 172
    fuegiana 178
Lygodactylus 10 62 65
Lygophis 12, 227 240, 276, 297, 407
    lineatus 291
Lygosominae 62, 87
Lyncodon 148, 150

Lysapsus 272
    limellus 259, 261
    laevis 259
Lysipomia 173
Lystrophis 240, 339
    dorbignyi 303
    semicinctus 303, 320

Mabuya 11, 18, 63, 65, 218, 219 227 239, 278, 296, 326, 339
    frenata 302, 320
    mabuya 163
Machaerium 171
Macrauchenia 175
Macrogenioglottus 194, 214
    alipioi 200
Macropholidus 389, 410, 411, 413, 454
Madtsoia 12, 42, 52, 63, 312
    bai 52, 89
    madagascariensis 89
Madtsoiinae 42, 100
Mammillaria 285
Mantipus 87
Masticophis 13, 222, 297
    mentovarius 291
Mastigodryas 13, 18, 218, 219, 227, 240, 276, 297, 408, 411, 456
    bifossatus 290, 291
    boddaerti 222, 290
    pleei 289
Mastodon 178
Mauritie minor 282, 285
Maytenus 309
Megaelosia 195, 215
Megalania 85
    prisca 85
Megalonychidae 143, 145, 149
Megatherioidae 143
Megatherium 175
Meiolaniidae 4 9, 31, 40 51, 52
Melanerpes candidus 130
Melanobatrachus 60
Melanophryniscus 7, 192, 270, 413
    moreirae 261
    stelzneri 302
Melanosuchus 14, 33, 43, 53, 218, 220, 238, 274
    niger 258
Melocactus 285
Memecyleae 125
Mesobaena 218 238, 256, 257, 279
Mesosuchia 43, 61
Mesotheriidae 149
Miconia 169, 172
Microcaecilia 213, 273
Microcavia 148, 150
Microhyla 60, 87
Microhylidae 3 4, 5 8, 14, 17 30, 56, 58, 59, 60, 65, 71, 79 83 84, 86, 101, 192, 193, 204, 207 208, 251
Microhylinae 60
Micruridae 3, 4 5, 13, 17, 18
Micrurinae 56 64, 66
Micruroides 13

Micrurus 13, 218 227 240, 277, 297, 303, 339, 408, 411, 444, 456
    circinalis 289
    dissoleucus 289
    frontalis 303, 320
    isozonus 289, 291
    mipartitus 381, 382, 383 384, 387, 388
    surinamensis nattereri 257
Mimosiphonops 194, 214
Mixophys 91
Morelia 89
Morpho 125
Morunasaurus 222, 227, 239
Mourasuchus 53
Mourin 125
Muehlenbergia 173
Mulinum 316, 374
    spinosum 316
Mus musculus 352
Mutisia 170 174, 175
Myersiella 195 215
Mylodon 146, 178
Mylodontidae 145
Myobatrachidae 56, 65, 70, 73, 94, 95, 96
Myobatrachinae 95, 96
Myobatrachus 95
Myrceugenella 171
Myrceugenia 176, 309
Myrica 172
Myristica 309
Myrmecophagidae 143, 148
Myzodendrum 345

Nassauvia 171, 316, 326
    aculeata 316
Natricinae 13
Natrix fasciata 18, 19
Neblina 172
Nectocaecilia 213 214
Necrosuchus 43 220, 312
    ionensis 42, 51
Nectandra 309
Nectophrynoides 59
Neobatrachus 95
Neochelys 61
Neoprocoela 4, 38, 39, 52, 311, 312, 363
    edentata 363
Nettosuchidae 31, 33, 43, 53
Nettosuchus 220
Neusticurus 218 234, 239, 278, 408, 410, 454
    racenisi 256
    rudis 241, 256, 257
    tatei 256
Nigerophis 63
Ninia 218 227 240 276
Niolamia patagonica 51
Niphogeton 174
Nordophyllum 170
Nothofagus 75, 170, 176, 178, 223, 309, 312, 316, 321, 345 346, 347, 352 359 360, 361, 362, 364, 365, 374, 376, 400, 404 414
    antarctica 171, 345 346
    betuloides 171, 346
    dombeyi 171, 345

    fusca 75
    menziesi 75
    obliqua 171, 345
    procera 171
    pumilio 171, 345
Nothopsis 218, 240
Nothrotheriinae 143, 149
Notobatrachus 3, 44, 58, 100
Notocaiman 220
    stromeri 43
Notosuchidae 61
Nyctimantis 194, 213
Nyctimystes 7, 90, 93
Nyctimystinae 90 93

Octodon degus 352
Octodontidae 149
Odatria 85
Odontophrynini 4, 194, 204, 207
Odontophrynus 193, 301, 326, 338
    americanus 302
Oedipina 2 192 194, 212
    complex 195
Ogmodon 88
Omoiotyphlops 63
Ophiodes 11, 218 239
    intermedius 302, 304
Ophryoessoides 222, 239, 296, 409
    caducus 302
    erythrogaster 289, 291
Opipeuter 396, 410, 411, 413 414, 454
Opuntia 285, 287
Oreopanax 169 309
Oreophryne 83, 84
Oreophrynella 7 253, 255, 270
    macconnelli 241
    quelchi 241
Oscaecilia 9, 18, 57, 192, 212 213 214, 273
Osornophryne 192, 387, 410, 411, 413, 416, 418, 429, 449
Osteocephalus 21, 22, 213 215, 272, 408, 410, 452
    langsdorffi 200, 201
    taurinus 197, 201
Osteopilus 7, 18
Otophryne 60 87, 194, 214 253, 255, 273
    robusta 241 253, 254, 256, 257, 260
Oxybelis 64, 227 240, 276 297
    aeneus 290, 291
Oxyrhopus 64 218, 227, 240, 276, 297, 408, 411, 456
    petola 291
    rhombifer 303

Pachymedusa 208
Palaeolama 151
Palaeophidae 63
Palaeobatrachidae 58
Palaeosuchus 14, 218, 220, 227, 238 274, 296
Palorchestes 98
    azael 98
Pantacantha 316
Pantodactylus 227, 239
    tyleri 241
Paracophyla 87
Paracrinia 95

Parahydraspis 220
Parastephia 170, 399
Parhoplophryne 60
Parides 125
Parkia pendula 171
Paruicaecilia 194, 212
Paspalum 284, 290
   fasciculatum 284, 286
Paullinia 309
Pelobatidae 56, 59
Pelochelys bibroni 88
Pelodryadidae 7, 65, 73, 90, 92, 93
Pelomedusidae 3, 4 5, 9, 14, 31 32, 39, 44, 51, 52, 53, 56, 61, 64, 65, 66, 251
Peltocephalus 256, 273
Perezia 171, 172, 175
Pernethya 346
Persea 346
   lingue 345
Peumus 309
Phenacosaurus 387, 410, 411, 413 416, 418 453
Philodryas 227, 240 276, 339, 408, 409, 411, 431, 456, 459
   aestivus 303
   baroni 303
   patagoniensis 303 320
   psammophideus 303
   simonsii 389
Philoria 96
Philornis 162
Philothamninae 64
Phimophis 218, 222, 240, 276, 297
   guianensis 23, 289, 291
   vittatus 303
Pholidobolus 372, 387, 410, 411, 413, 416 418, 429, 434, 454
   montium 388
Pholidosauridae 61
Phrynohyas 8, 212, 213, 215, 272, 295
   coriacea 198
   imitatrix 200
   mesophaea 200, 201
   venulosa 190, 191, 195, 197, 200, 201, 259, 289, 290, 302
Phrynomantis 87
   stictogaster 85, 87
Phrynomennae 60
Phrynomerus 60 87
Phrynops 218, 220, 227, 238, 273, 274, 296
   geoffroanus 260
Phrynopus 372, 396, 410, 411, 413, 416, 418, 424, 429, 431, 448, 449
   cophites 431
Phycoides 125
Phyllobates 190, 193, 212 213 215, 269, 408, 410, **450**
   femoralis 198
   pictus 191, 197, 200
   pulchripectus 255
Phyllodactylus 10, 18, 22, 23, 97, 277, 296, 389, 408, 410, 458
   dixoni 257, 289, 291
   gerrhopygus 400
   ventralis 291

Phyllodytes 213 215
   luteolus 199
Phyllomedusa 8, 190, 208, 212, 213, 214 215, 272, 290, 295, 301, 303, 408, 410, 444, 452
   bicolor 198
   buckleyi group 18
   fimbriata 200
   hypocondrialis 302, 303
   lemur 382
   medinae 196, 382
   sauvagii 302, 303
   trinitatis 191
   vaillanti 198
Phyllomedusinae 5, 8, 17, 90, 193, 194, 204, 206, 208
Phyllopezus 21
   pollicaris 302
Phymaturus 326, 327, 339, 400, 408, 410 431, 458
   palluma 321, 324, 401, 402, 420
   patagonicus 320, 321, 324, 364, 431
      indistinctus 320, 324
      nevadoi 321, 324
      patagonicus 320, 324
      payuniae 321, 324
      somuncurensis 324, 325
      zapalensis 321, 324
Physalaemus 4 17, 190, 212, 214, 215, 270, 295, 301
   albonotatus 302
   biligonigerus 60, 302
   enesefae 289, 290
   pustulatus 195
   pustulosus 191, 195, 260, 290
Pilgirodendrum 345
   uviferum 346
Pinguicula 171
Pipa 3, 18, 58, 194, 205, 213, 269, 295
   parva 3 193, 289, 291
   pipa 197, 290
Pipidae 3, 4, 5, 14 17, 30, 32, 38 39, 51, 52, 56, 58, 59, 60, 64, 65, 192, 193, 204, 207, 251
Pipinae 38, 207
Piptadenia peregrina 171
Pithecolobium 285
Placosoma 238, 414
Plagiobothrys 316
Planocrania datangensis 98
Platemys 98, 218, 227, 238
Platycheloides 61
Platychelys 61
Platemys 274
Platyhyla 87
Platymantis 77, 78, 79, 80
   batantae 77, 79
   cheesmanae 79
   gilliardi 77
   meyeri 77
   mimicus 77
   myersi 77
   papuensis 79, 81
   punctata 77, 79
   vitianus 98
   vitiensis 99
Platypelis 87
Platyplectron 95

Plethodontidae   2, 1 5, 17, 57, 191, 192, 201, 207
Plethodontohyla   87
Pleurodema   4 18, 20, 21, 23, 270, 295 301, 326,
   338, 341 362 363, 372, 400 407, 409, 410,
   411, 412, 415, 431, 434, 457
   borellii   302
   brachyops   21, 23, 260, 290
   bufonina   317, 320, 321, 325, 326, 364, 402,
      420
   cinerea   431
   guayapae   302
   marmorata   396 420
   nebulosa   326
   thaul   321, 326, 347 348 350, 351, 352, 355,
      358, 362
   tucumana   302
Pleurodira   52
Pleurofora patagonica   317
Plica   234, 239, 278
Phocercus   227 240
Poa   170, 316, 326, 342, 374, 399
   humilis   170
Podocarpus   75, 169, 171, 175, 178, 180, 309, 345,
   373
   andinus   178
   lambertii   171
   montanus   169
   nubigenus   169, 171
   oleifolius   169
   parleteoreu   169
   rospigliossii   169
   salignus   346
Podocnemidae   61, 65
Podocnemis   9 31 39, 41, 51, 53, 218, 220, 227, 238,
   273, 285, 296
   argentinensis   52
   hassleri   53
   brasiliensis   51
   elegans   39, 51
   expansa   33, 39
   vogli   289, 291
Polychroides   389, 410, 411, 413, 414, 453
Polychrus   220, 227, 239 278, 296, 408, 410, 413,
   414
   gutturosus   387
   marmoratus   222
Polylepis   163, 170, 173, 174, 175, 374
   australis   169
   cocuyensis   169
   sericea   169
Primula   171
Potomotyphlus   194, 213, 273
Prionodactylus   222, 227, 239, 279 407, 411, 414,
   429, 454
   argulus   397
   manicatus   397
   vertebralis   387
Pristidactylus   326, 327, 341, 364, 408 410, 431, 458
   achalensis   323, 326, 364
   alvaroi   364
   casuhatiensis   323, 326, 364
   fasciatus   323 326, 364
   pectinatus   326
   scapulatus   323, 326, 364, 401

   torquatus   348, 351, 354, 361
   valeriae   364
   vautieri   302, 304
Pristiguana   62, 219
   brasiliensis   51
Proalligator   220
Proceratophrys   195, 214
   boiei   200
   appendiculata   200
   cristiceps   199
Proctoporus   374, 398, 411, 413, 414 424, 429, 431,
   434, 444, 454
   laevis   388
   occulatus   388
Proctotretus   323 326, 327, 339 409
   doellojuradoi   302, 304
   pectinatus   320
Procyonidae   115
Proganochelydia   61
Prosopis   170, 171, 285, 300, 373, 374
   ferox   170
   patagonica   316, 317
Proterochersis   61
Proustia   171
Pseudemydura   97
Pseudemys   9 238
Pseudhymenochirus   58
Pseudidae   3, 1, 5, 7 30, 56, 60, 193, 251
Pseudis   272 295
   paradoxus   260, 261, 289, 290, 302, 305
      occidentalis   304, 305
      platensis   304
Pseudoboa   18 218, 222 227, 240, 276, 297
   neuwiedi   289, 291
Pseudoeryx   218 240 276
Pseudogonatodes   10, 238, 277, 296, 383, 408, 453
Pseudonaja   88
   nuchalis   88
Pseudopaludicola   270, 295
   pusilla   258 260
Pseudophryne   95
   occidentalis   95
Pseudotomodon   339
   trigonatus   303
Pseustes   227 240, 276, 298
Psidium   346
Psyllophryne   195, 214
Ptychadena   61
Ptychoglossus   227, 239, 279, 408, 411, 454
Ptychophis   240
Purussaurus   53, 220
Puya   170, 171, 173 373
Pycnophyllum   170
Pygopodidae   14, 98, 100
Python   89
Pythonini   55, 57, 63, 66, 71

Quelchia   172
Quercus   163, 173, 175

Ramanella   60, 87
Rana   79 82, 213 214, 215 269 295
   palmipes   8, 58, 190, 191, 193, 197, 200
   pipiens   190

Ranidae 3, 4, 5, 8, 14, 15, 17, 30, 39, 55 56, 58, 59, 60 65 77, 78 101, 192, 193, 204, 207, 251
Ranidella signifera 90
Ranunculus 171, 180, 316
Relictivomer 18, 190, 213, 214, 273, 295
    pearsei 191, 195
Rhacophoridae 90
Rhadinaea 218, 227, 240, 276, 408, 411, 444, 456
    laterestriga 388
Rhamnophis 64
Rhamphophryne 7, 18, 192, 213, 214, 372, 407 410, 411, 413, 418, 420 449
Rhamphostomopsis 33, 53, 220
Rheobatrachus 96
    silus 95
Rhinatrema 192, 194, 213, 256, 273
Rhinatrematidae 3, 4, 5, 9, 56, 57, 192, 207, 251
Rhineura 63
Rhinobothryum 227, 240, 276, 298
Rhinoclemys 9 218 220, 238, 273, 296
Rhinoderma 7, 311, 351 354 359 362, 363, 365
    darwinii 347, 348, 352, 354, 355, 358, 362
    rufum 348, 351, 355, 358, 362
Rhinodermatidae 3, 4, 5, 7, 30, 39, 60, 341
Rhinophrynidae 17
Rhizocephalum 173
Rhynchocephalia 99
Riolama 253, 279
Roupala 171, 284
Roxochelys 39
    vilavilensis 51
    wanderleyi 51
Rubiaceae 125

Saguinus 127, 128
    inustus 127, 128
    leucopus 127
    midas 127, 128
    oedipus
        geoffroyi 127, 128
        oedipus 127, 128
Salamandridae 56
Salomonelaps 88
Saltenia 58
    ibanezi 38, 51
Sambucus 169
    peruviana 169
Saphenophis 218, 240, 387, 411, 413, 456
Sapindus 309
Sarcosuchus 61
Sarmentia 315
Saxogotea 345
Scaphiodontophis 222, 240
Scaphiophryninae 59 60
Scelidotherium 175
Sceloporus 327
Schinopsis 300, 309
Schinus 309
Schweboemys 61, 220
Sciucella 11
Scincidae 3, 4, 5, 11, 14, 15, 17, 32, 56, 62, 66, 85, 101, 251
Scincinae 86, 87
Scincomorpha 62

Scolecomorphidae 14, 57
Scythrophrys 195, 214
Sebecidae 31, 32, 33, 43, 51, 52 53
Sebecosuchia 43
Sebecus 51 52 53, 220, 312
    icaeorhinus 98
Senecio 169, 170, 172, 175, 326, 374, 387
    filaginoides 316
Setaria 300
Shelania 58
Sibon 222 240 274, 298, 408, 411, 456
    nebulata 290
Sibynomorphus 240, 408, 411, 456
    oneilli 389
    turgidis 303
Siphlophis 222 227, 240, 276
Siphonops 190, 213, 214 273
    annulatus 191, 197, 199
    paulensis 199
Smilisca 8, 194, 212
    phaeota 195
    sila 195
Sminthillus 19
Somuncuria 326, 338, 361
    somuncurensis 325
Sordellina 218 240
Spartina 316
Sphaenorhynchus 213, 215, 272, 295
Sphaerodactylidae 96
Sphaerodactylinae 5, 17, 56
Sphaerodactylus 10, 19 222, 239, 277, 296
Sphenodon punctatus 98
Sphenophryne 83
Sphenophryninae 60 79, 81, 82 84
Spilotes 13, 219, 227, 240, 276, 298
    pullatus 290, 291
Stefania 23, 194, 214, 253, 255, 272, 408, 413
    evansi 256
    evansi group 253
    goini 242, 253
    goini group 253
    marahuaguensis 254, 256
    scalae 255
    woodleyi 256
Stegonotus 88
Stenocercus 239, 372, 389, 396, 407, 409, 410, 411, 424, 429, 431, 434, 453, 458, 459
Stenoglossa 59
Stenolepis 239
Stenopadus 172
Stenorrhina 218, 222, 240
Sterculia 309
Stereocyclops 87, 195, 215
Stipa 170, 316, 326, 342, 374, 399
    humilis 316
    ichu 170
Strobilurus 239
Strychnos 309
Stupendemys 53, 220
    geographicus 40
Styllingia 316
Swallenochloa 169
Synapturanus 194, 214, 273
    mirandaribeiroi 198

Syncope 194 **214**
    carvalhoi 201
    antenori 201
Synophis 218, 227, 240, 387, 411, 413, 456
Syrrhophus 19

Tabebuia 309
Tachymenis 341 365, 407, 409 411, *415*, 431, 459
    affinis 365
    attenuata 365
    chilensis 341 348 350, 352, 353, *356* 364, 365
    peruviana 20, 348, 365, 396, 400, 420
    surinamensis 365
    tarmensis 365
Tantilla 218, 219 227 240, 276, 298, 408, 411, 456
    melanocephala 290
    semicincta 289
Taphrosphys 40 52, 220
Tapirus
    bairdii 128
    terrestris 128
Tarentola 18 62
Taudactylus 95
Tecoma 171
Teiidae 44, 62, 65, 228, 251
Teius 219
    teyou 302, *304*
        cyanogaster 304
        teyou 304
Telmatobiinae 4 5 38, 60, 193, 194, 357, 361
Telmatobiini 4 194 361
Telmatobius 95, 312 357, 358, 361, 372 374, 389, 396, 400 409 410, 411, 412 *415*, 420, 424, 429 431 434 449, 457
    culeus 434
    marmoratus 396, 431
Telmatobufo 20, 312, 327, 341, 350, 351, 357 358 359 360 363 365, 442
    australis 341, 348, *354*, 358, 360
    bullocki 318
    venustus 348, 352, 355, 358, 360
Tepualia 345
Testudinidae 3, 4 5, 9, 14, 17, 31, 40, 44, 52, 54 56, 61, 251
Testudo 273
Thamnodynastes 227, **240**, 253, **276, 298**
    strigilis 289, 291
Thamnophis 13
Thecadactylus 10, 18 227, 239, 277, 296
    rapicaudus 290
Thelotornis 64
Thoracoliacus 58
Thoropa 195 207, 215
    miliaria 200
Thrasops 64
Tibouchina 172
Tillandsia 170
Todirostrum 123
Tomodactylus 19
Tomopterna delalandii 60
Trachipogon 282, 284
Trachyboa 12 18 222, 240
Trachycephalus 212, 215

    nigromaculatus 200
Tretanorhinus 18, 218, 222 240
Tretioscincus 218, 222 239, 279, 297
    bifasciatus 289 291
Trevoa 342
    patagonica 317
    spinifer 316
Trichloris 300
Trichocereus 171
    pascana 170
    terschecku 170
Trichocline 172
Trionychidae 4 10, 31, 40, 53, 61, 88
Trionyx 10, 220
    australiensis 97
Tripanurgos 219, 222, 227, 240, 276
    compressus 222
Tritrinax 300
Tropidodryas 240
Tropidophiidae 3, 4 5, 12, 17, 18
Tropidophis 12, 19, 222 227, 240, 408, 411, **454**
    taczanowskyi 388, 389
Tropidurinae 5
Tropidurus *21, 22, 23* 218, 222 227 239, 278, 297 302, 303 304, 389 408 410 **459**
    bogerti 253
    peruvianus 400
    spinulosus 302 304
    torquatus 260 289 291
        hispidus 253
Tupinambis 33 41, 52 53 54, 62, 85 218, 219, 220 222 227 239 279, 297 303
    rufescens 302 304
    teguixin 33, 290, 291 304
Typhlina 12, 88
Typhlonectes 212, 213, 214 273
Typhlonectidae 3 4, 5, 9, 56 57 192 207, 251
Typhlophis 218, 240
Typhlopidae 3, 4, 5 12, 14, 17, 56, 63, 65, 88, 101, 251
Typhlops 12, 19, 88, 218 227, 234, 240, 274, 298
    lehneri 289

Umbrivaga 411, 413 **444**
    mertensi 382
Ungoliophis 12 222, 240
Uperodon 60, 87
Uracentron 234, 239, 278
Uraeotyphlus 57
Uranoscodon 239, 278
Uropeltidae 70, 88
Urostrophus 239
Urotheca 411, 413 **444**
    williamsi 382
Usnea 345

Valeriana 173
Vanzolinius 194, 214
Varanidae 14 57, 62, 71, 85 101
Varanus 85
Verbena 316, 321 326
    ligustrina 316
    tridens 316
Vieraella 3 44, 58, 100

Vilcunia 323, 326, 327, 339
    sylvanae 326
Viperidae 3, 4, 13, 14, 32, 42, 54 64, 228
Viperinae 55, 57 65, 66

Wagleroplus merremii 303
Waweha 53, 311
    gerholdi 312
Weinmannia 169, 172
    fagaroides 169
    jahnii 169
    microphylla 169
Weismania trichosperma 315
Werneria 59, 170

Wetmorena 19
Wonambi 12, 89, 100
    naracoortensis 89

Xenoboa 240
Xenodon 227, 240, 277, 298
Xenodontinae 5, 12, 13, 17, 18, 56, 64, 66
Xenopholis 227, 240
Xenopus 3, 38, 58, 95
    pascuali 52
    romeri 51

Zachaenus 195, 214
Zuccagnia 170